MW00769852

Utah and the American Civil War

Utah and the American Civil War

THE WRITTEN RECORD

Edited by
Kenneth L. Alford

THE ARTHUR H. CLARK COMPANY
An imprint of the University of Oklahoma Press
Norman, Oklahoma
2017

This book is published with the generous assistance of the Brigham Young University Religious Studies Center, Provo, Utah.

Library of Congress Cataloging-in-Publication Data
Names: Alford, Kenneth L., 1955– editor.
Title: Utah and the American Civil War: The written record / edited by Kenneth L. Alford.
Description: Norman, Oklahoma : The Arthur H. Clark Company, an imprint of the University of Oklahoma Press, 2017. | Includes bibliographical references and index.
Identifiers: LCCN 2016051996 | ISBN 978-0-87062-441-4 (hardcover : alk. paper)
Subjects: LCSH: Utah—History—Civil War, 1861–1865—Sources. | United States—History—Civil War, 1861–1865—Sources.
Classification: LCC E532.95 .U83 2017 | DDC 979.2/02—dc23
LC record available at https://lccn.loc.gov/2016051996

The paper in this book meets the guidelines for permanence and durability of the Committee on Production Guidelines for Book Longevity of the Council on Library Resources, Inc. ∞

1 2 3 4 5 6 7 8 9 10

for
Sherilee
"MORE THAN YESTERDAY; LESS THAN TOMORROW."

Contents

List of Map and Tables . . . 9
Acknowledgments . . . 11

Introduction . . . 15
Timeline of United States and Utah Territory History . . . 19
1. Utah Territory and the Civil War: A Summary History . . . 35
2. History of the *War of the Rebellion Official Records* . . . 63
3. Records Overview . . . 67
4. Utah's Civil War Official Records . . . 77
5. Additional Records from Utah Territory . . . 577
Appendix A. Glossary and Abbreviations . . . 761
Appendix B. Chronological Records List . . . 779
Appendix C. Supplement to the *Official Records* . . . 791
Appendix D. *Official Records* Associated with Utah . . . 795
Appendix E. Utah's Territorial Borders . . . 801
Appendix F. Utah's Wartime Military Geography . . . 803
Appendix G. Military Units Serving in Utah Territory, 1861–1865 . . . 809
Appendix H. Records Listed by Senders and Receivers . . . 811
Bibliography . . . 819
Index . . . 829

Map and Tables

Map. Utah Territory's changing borders, 1861–1868 34

Table 3.1. Summary of Utah's Civil War records 68
Table 3.2. Utah Territory records in the *Official Records* 69
Table B.1. Utah Territory records by month 789–90

Acknowledgments

The Civil War has captured my interest and imagination for as long as I can remember. During the three decades I served on active duty as an officer in the United States Army, my family and I were stationed in northern Virginia three times. I never tired (much to the chagrin of my children) of visiting Gettysburg, Antietam, Manassas, Fredericksburg, Petersburg, Chancellorsville, and other Civil War battlefields near our home.

At the beginning of this project I (fortunately) did not have a clear understanding regarding how much work would be involved. I am grateful for the help from Richard E. Bennett, my department chair, in receiving the Brigham Young University Mentoring Environment Grant, which made this research possible, and I am appreciative of the many university donors who made those funds available.

During the years I let the idea for this volume percolate, I came across *Shoshonean Peoples and the Overland Trails: Frontiers of the Utah Superintendency of Indian Affairs, 1849–1869*, in which author Dale L. Morgan and editor Richard L. Saunders assembled Utah Territory Indian Superintendency reports. Their book provided an initial model for this volume.

Most of the searching, comparing, checking, deciphering, correcting, cataloging, and rechecking of the documents in this volume was completed by enthusiastic student research assistants from Brigham Young University. I am especially indebted to David Ostler and Brooklyn Parks. David was with me at the start as we worked to define the scope and our methodology for this project. With our shared computer-science backgrounds, we were able to figure out how to coax as much information as possible out of the existing digitized records. Brooklyn was the glue that kept the project on track and on schedule. I am also indebted to Talia Abbott, Clark Allen, Brooke Bons, Justin Childs, Camille Duncan, Jared Evans, Ingrid Gubler, Kayla McDonald, Meg Meiners, Elizabeth Nelson, Seth Nelson, Sarah Palmer, Patrick Phinney, Grant C. Price, Scott Williams, and Brendon Wolfe for their hard work, attention to detail, and good humor. I am obliged for additional transcription assistance from Beverly Yellowhorse, Patsy Peterson, and Larsen S. Boyer. I also appreciate the assistance of Ken Nelson, who willingly shared a host of useful historical insights and resources.

Help from cheerful archivists, librarians, and map specialists at Brigham Young University's L. Tom Perry Special Collections at the Harold B. Lee Library, the LDS Church History Library and Archives in Salt Lake City, the Utah State Historical Society, the National Archives, and the J. Willard Marriott Library at the University of Utah is most appreciated.

This volume was a collaborative effort between the University of Oklahoma Press and Brigham Young University's Religious Studies Center. I am grateful for the support, guidance, and assistance of Charles E. Rankin, Stephanie E. Evans, and Thomas W. Krause at the University of Oklahoma Press and Thomas Wayment and Brent Top at Brigham Young University. Additionally, I appreciate the time, talents, good ideas, and professionalism of the many reviewers, editors, and staff who contributed to this book, especially Ariane Smith and Galen Schroeder.

I am grateful for my parents, Ken and Dolores Alford, who have always supported me with their love and counsel. Special thanks and appreciation are due to my children (Suzanne, Marie, Christine, and Kenneth), their spouses (Kendall, David, Jeff, and Rachel), and our growing number of grandchildren, who make life wonderful, meaningful, and fun. My deepest appreciation and love is reserved, though, for my wife, Sherilee. She is my best friend, head cheerleader, therapist, co-conspirator, and confidant. I'm a better person because of you, Sherilee; I love you. Thank you for supporting me on this project in so many ways.

Utah and the American Civil War

Introduction

THE COMMON BELIEF THAT UTAH TERRITORY "SAT OUT" THE CIVIL War is incorrect. Although the territory was removed from the war's devastation and provided only one active-duty military unit (the Lot Smith Utah Cavalry Company in 1862),[1] the war deeply affected Utah and its inhabitants—from pioneers and Union soldiers stationed in Utah to the Native Americans they clashed with throughout the war.

Following the Civil War, the federal government authorized the collection, organization, and publication of official Union and Confederate records, including letters, orders, and reports. *The War of the Rebellion: A Compilation of the Official Records of the Union and Confederate Armies* (hereafter referred to as the *Official Records,* the *War of the Rebellion,* or the OR), a 128-volume series, was the result.[2] Publication of the *Official Records* was a monumental effort that spanned several decades in the late nineteenth and early twentieth centuries. The published records provide a wealth of primary source material for studying the Civil War. However, the *Official Records* are so large and complex that it is difficult to search for relevant records. The purpose of this volume is to help make war-related Civil War records pertaining to Utah Territory more accessible. (Documents pertaining to territorial government or statehood applications, for example, have not been included.)

In recent years, OR volumes have been digitized to improve access. The limits of optical character recognition software, though, mean that much of the OR remains obscure due to inaccurately digitized text. The small print and obsolete typefaces used make the word "Utah," for example, appear throughout the OR volumes as "Olab," "Utan," "0tah," "Utab," "Otan," "Otali," and many other permutations, a fact which leaves readers and researchers uncertain whether they have discovered all

1. Utah's contribution was similar to several other western states and territories. Dakota and Washington Territories each raised only one military unit. Oregon (which received statehood in 1859) and Nevada (which became a territory in March 1861 and a state in October 1864) mustered two units. Arizona, which became a separate territory in February 1863, contributed no military units. See Dyer, *A Compendium of the War of the Rebellion,* 1:39.
2. U.S. War Department, *The War of the Rebellion.*

of the relevant records. This challenge exists for all other search terms as well. The *OR*'s organization also compounds the difficulty of reviewing specific campaigns, time periods, and topics. As expected with such a large and extended publication effort, records that logically should be grouped together are sometimes spread across several volumes, making it a challenge to find and reassemble them.

The idea for this volume grew out of the frustration I experienced while researching and writing several chapters and appendices for the book *Civil War Saints.*[3] Records in the *War of the Rebellion* volumes were interesting and applicable, but they often proved difficult to find. After every bout with the *OR*, I had a nagging feeling that other relevant records might have been overlooked, and I frequently found myself wanting a better way to make this information more accessible. Eventually, I decided to create this single-volume reference work, the result of our research team carefully locating, proofing, and chronologically organizing Civil War records pertaining to Utah Territory. This effort marks the first time that records from the *OR* and additional Utah Territory Civil War records have been available together.

This volume begins with a timeline listing events (in parallel columns) that occurred in the States and Utah Territory. It includes a few prewar events and outlines the war years, 1861 through 1865, in greater detail. Chapter 1 provides an overview of Utah Territory during the Civil War. A brief history and explanation of the *OR* is found in chapter 2. Chapter 3 contains explanatory and summary information about Utah's Civil War records.

Chapter 4, "Utah's Civil War Official Records," contains *OR* records that directly relate to Utah Territory. Chapter 5, "Additional Records from Utah Territory," contains Utah-related Civil War records that did not find their way into the *Official Records* series. While not exhaustive, these records provide useful background for Utah's Civil War–related events. Each document has been assigned a unique record identifier—either "OR-#" (chapter 4) or "UT-#" (chapter 5). References to records within this volume use these identifiers. For example, "OR-214" refers to the June 24, 1863, dispatch from Brigadier General Patrick Edward Connor, U.S. Volunteers, commander, Headquarters District of Utah, to Lieutenant Colonel R. C. Drum, assistant adjutant-general, U.S. Army, San Francisco, California (published in the *War of the Rebellion Official Records,* Series 1, Volume 50, Part 2, pages 492–495).

Several appendices have been added to provide context and background for these records. The Utah Territory records contain many unfamiliar words, phrases, and abbreviations; appendix A is a glossary that defines them. Readers can learn, for example, that "aparejos" refers to "a packsaddle of stuffed leather or canvas" or that "Jno." was an accepted abbreviation for "John." Whenever possible, the definitions provided are from contemporary sources.

---

3. Alford, *Civil War Saints.*

Appendix B chronologically correlates the records appearing in chapters 4 and 5. In the 1990s Broadfoot Publishing Company of Wilmington, North Carolina, published an additional one hundred volumes of Civil War records that were not included in the *OR*.[4] Appendix C lists Utah-related references in the *Supplement* volumes. *OR* records associated with Utah Territory that do not include Utah-related keywords are listed in appendix D.

Congress reduced the borders of Utah Territory several times between the territory's creation in 1850 and statehood in 1896. Several of those changes occurred during the Civil War years, as outlined in appendix E. The many military departments and districts to which Utah was assigned during the war are explained in appendix F. Appendix G lists regiments that saw duty both in and closely associated with Utah Territory during the Civil War. In order to increase the accessibility of these wartime records, appendix H is a list of record originators and recipients organized alphabetically by record numbers. This volume concludes with a bibliography and an index.

Through this volume I hope to make records associated with Utah Territory's role during the Civil War more transparent, easier to access, and better known. While Utah made little impact on the numerous battlefields where blue- and gray-clad soldiers faced off against each other, Utah Territory was still very much involved and active during the Civil War, as this volume readily attests.

---

4. Hewitt, *Supplement to the Official Records*.

Timeline of United States and Utah Territory History

United States	Utah Territory
1846	
April 25: Mexican War begins	*July 1:* Captain James Allen, U.S. Army, requests the enlistment of five hundred Mormon volunteers
1847	
	July 22: Pioneer advance party enters the Salt Lake Valley *July 24:* Brigham Young and main body of pioneers enter the Salt Lake Valley
1848	
February 2: Treaty of Guadalupe Hidalgo ends the Mexican War	
1849	
June 1: Major Howard Stansbury leaves Fort Leavenworth on a two-year expedition to explore Utah's Salt Lake, Utah, and Cache Valleys	*March:* State of Deseret petition submitted to Congress *December 30:* First Mormon-Ute treaty signed
1850	
September 9: With the Compromise of 1850, California receives statehood and Utah Territory created	*June 15:* First issue of the *Deseret News* published

UNITED STATES	UTAH TERRITORY

1851

February 3: Brigham Young becomes governor of Utah Territory and superintendent of Indian Affairs

November 6: Stansbury Expedition returns to Fort Leavenworth

1852

August 28–29: Mormons publicly announce doctrine of plural marriage

1853

October 26: Lieutenant John W. Gunnison and seven men massacred by Indians in central Utah

1854

May 30: Kansas-Nebraska Act signed into law

August 31: Army expedition of Edward Steptoe arrives in Salt Lake City to investigate the Gunnison massacre

1857

March 4: President James Buchanan inaugurated

March 6: U.S. Supreme Court hands down decision in *Dred Scott v. Sanford*

United States	Utah Territory

1857 *(continued)*

United States

May 28: President Buchanan dispatches army expedition to suppress reported rebellion in Utah Territory, start of Utah War

July 11: President Buchanan appoints Alfred Cumming governor of Utah

Utah Territory

March 30: Associate Justice W. W. Drummond resigns seat on territorial supreme court, alleging criminal conduct by Mormon leaders

June/July: Brigham Young learns U.S. Army marching on Utah Territory

September 11: Mountain Meadows massacre

September 15: Brigham Young declares martial law; Utah militia deployed

1858

United States

April 21–October 15: Lincoln-Douglas debates

Utah Territory

February 25: Thomas L. Kane arrives in Salt Lake City to help mediate an end to the Utah War; Mormon mission and Nauvoo Legion outpost at Fort Limhi, Oregon Territory, attacked; U.S. senator Sam Houston delivers speech in defense of Mormons in U.S. Senate

June 26: U.S. Army marches through Salt Lake City, establishing garrison at Camp Floyd, essentially ending the Utah War

1859

United States

October 16–18: Abolitionist John Brown seizes Harper's Ferry (Virginia) armory, which is then recaptured by Marines and Colonel Robert E. Lee, USA

Utah Territory

July 13: Horace Greeley, *New York Tribune* editor, visits Salt Lake City, interviews Brigham Young

United States	Utah Territory

1860

United States

April 3: Pony Express begins
November 6: Abraham Lincoln elected president
December 20: South Carolina secedes from the Union

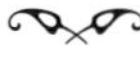

1861

United States

January 9: Mississippi secedes; *Star of the West* fired upon in Charleston Harbor (South Carolina)
January 10: Florida secedes
January 11: Alabama secedes
January 19: Georgia secedes
January 26: Louisiana secedes
January 29: Kansas gains statehood

February 4–8: Confederate States of America organized in Montgomery (Alabama)
February 18: Jefferson Davis inaugurated president of the Confederacy
February 23: Texas secedes
February 28: Colorado Territory formed, includes eastern portion of Utah Territory
March 2: Nevada Territory formed, includes western portion of Utah Territory; Nebraska Territory expanded out of northeastern Utah Territory
March 4: Abraham Lincoln inaugurated

Utah Territory

February: Joseph Morris, Morrisite leader, excommunicated from Mormon church
February 6: Camp Floyd renamed Fort Crittenden

United States	Utah Territory

1861 *(continued)*

United States

April 12: Fort Sumter (Charleston Harbor, South Carolina) bombarded by Confederate shore batteries
April 13: Fort Sumter surrenders
April 15: President Lincoln calls for seventy-five thousand militiamen to fight
April 17: Virginia secedes
May 6: Arkansas secedes
May 20: North Carolina secedes
June 8: Tennessee secedes
July 21: First Battle of Manassas (Virginia)
October 26: Pony Express ends
November 28: Missouri admitted to the Confederacy (but did not formally secede)

Utah Territory

April 6: Joseph Morris organizes new church in South Weber
May 17: Governor Cumming leaves Salt Lake City
August 9: Colonel Philip St. George Cooke's command marches east from Fort Bridger
October 18: Eastern telegraph reaches Salt Lake City; Brigham Young sends first message
October 24: Western telegraph reaches Salt Lake City
December 7: Governor John W. Dawson arrives in Salt Lake City
December 31: Governor Dawson flees Utah; territorial secretary Frank Fuller becomes acting governor

United States	Utah Territory

1862

Utah Territory

January 20: Statehood convention convenes in Salt Lake City
January 22: State constitution passed by convention
January 23: Utah territorial legislature and constitutional convention petition Congress for statehood

United States

April 6: Confederate general Albert Sidney Johnston killed at Battle of Shiloh
April 6–7: Costly Union victory at Battle of Shiloh
April 8: Morrill Anti-Bigamy Act introduced in House of Representatives

Utah Territory

April 14: General Assembly of the State of Deseret convenes

United States

April 25: Union captures New Orleans

Utah Territory

April 26: Nauvoo Legion militia troops, commanded by Colonel Robert T. Burton, depart Salt Lake City to protect mail routes
April 28: Brigham Young receives authorization to recruit a U.S. Army cavalry company to protect the Overland Trail
April 30: Utah Cavalry Company enlisted in Salt Lake City
May: Colonel Patrick Edward Connor and California Volunteers ordered to Utah
May 1: Utah Cavalry Company leaves Salt Lake City
May 24: Utah Territory's chief justice, John F. Kinney, issues a writ demanding Morrisites release any prisoners

United States

June 9–10: Constitution of State of Deseret introduced in Congress

Utah Territory

June 12: Robert T. Burton, deputy marshal, leads posse to capture Joseph Morris

1862 *(continued)*

United States

July 8: President Lincoln signs Morrill Anti-Bigamy Act

July 14: Congress adds western edge of Utah Territory to Nevada Territory

August 24: Edwin M. Stanton, secretary of war, authorizes re-enlistment of the Utah Cavalry

August 28–30: Second Battle of Manassas (Virginia)

September 17: Battle of Antietam (Maryland) ends

September 22: President Lincoln issues Emancipation Proclamation

December 13: Battle of Fredericksburg (Virginia)

Utah Territory

June 13: Two Morrisites and one posse member killed

June 15: Joseph Morris and other Morrisites killed in a skirmish; ninety Morrisites arrested

June 16: Morrisites brought to Salt Lake City to stand trial

July 7: Stephen S. Harding, Utah's new governor, arrives in Salt Lake City

July 12: Colonel Patrick Edward Connor and California Volunteers leave Stockton, California, bound for Utah

July 25: Private McNicol, a soldier in the Utah Cavalry Company, drowns in the Snake River

August 6: Colonel Connor takes command of the Military District of Utah

August 14: Utah Cavalry Company released from active duty

August 25: Utah governor Stephen S. Harding notifies General Henry W. Halleck that the Utah Cavalry will not re-enlist

October 17: Colonel Connor's troops arrive at Fort Crittenden

October 22: Colonel Connor's troops arrive at Salt Lake City and establish Camp Douglas

November 20–27: Expedition from Camp Douglas to Cache Valley

November 23: Indian skirmish at Cache Valley

United States	Utah Territory

1863	
January 1: Emancipation Proclamation takes effect	
	January 29: Bear River massacre
	March: Tensions rise between federal troops and Utahns; seven Morrisites convicted of second-degree murder, sixty-two convicted of resistance
March 3: Idaho Territory created	*March 3:* Mormons hold mass meeting in Salt Lake Tabernacle and petition removal of Governor Harding and two Utah territorial supreme court associate justices
	March 4: Governor Harding refuses to resign
	March 10: Brigham Young arrested for bigamy; not brought to trial
	March 29: Col. Connor promoted to brigadier general.
	March 31: Governor Harding pardons Morrisites
	April 1: Indian skirmish at Cedar, Utah
April 3: Indian attack Sweetwater Station on the Overland Trail	
	April 4–5: Indian skirmish at Spanish Fork Canyon
	April 12: Indian skirmish at Pleasant Grove
	April 15: Indian battle at Spanish Fork Canyon; one killed, four wounded
May 4: Battle of Chancellorsville (Virginia)	
	May 8: Indians raid Box Elder Valley
May 18: Siege of Vicksburg (Mississippi) begins	
	June 10: Indians attack stagecoach in Utah County, killing two
	June 11: Governor Harding leaves Utah
June 20: West Virginia joins the Union	

United States	Utah Territory

1863 *(continued)*

United States

July 1–3: Battle of Gettysburg (Pennsylvania)
July 4: Union captures Vicksburg (Mississippi)
July 13–15: Draft riots in New York City

September 19–20: Battle of Chickamauga (Georgia)

November 19: Lincoln delivers Gettysburg Address

December 3: President Lincoln issues his Ten-Percent Plan, beginning Reconstruction

Utah Territory

June 22: James D. Doty becomes governor of Utah
July 2: Peace treaty signed with Eastern Shoshone Indians

July 30: Peace treaty signed with Northwestern Shoshone Indians

October 12: Peace treaty signed with Goshute Indians
October 14: Peace treaty signed with Fort Hall Shoshone and Bannock Indians
November 20: First issue of *Union Vedette* published at Camp Douglas

1864

United States

March 7: Senate ratifies five Utah Territory Indian treaties

May 19: Congress passes a resolution authorizing printing of official war records
July 30: Battle of the Crater (Virginia)
September 2: Union captures Atlanta (Georgia)
October 31: Nevada gains statehood
November 8: Abraham Lincoln re-elected

Utah Territory

May 9–June 22: Expedition from Fort Crittenden to Fort Mojave, Arizona

United States	Utah Territory

1864 *(continued)*

United States

November 16: General William T. Sherman begins "march to the sea"

December 16: Battle of Nashville (Tennessee)

December 21: Union captures Savannah, Georgia

1865

United States

January 31: Thirteenth Amendment passed

March 4: Abraham Lincoln's second inauguration

April 2: Union captures Petersburg (Virginia)

April 3: Union captures Richmond (Virginia)

April 9: General Robert E. Lee surrenders the Army of Northern Virginia at Appomattox (Virginia)

April 12: Union captures Mobile (Alabama)

April 14: John Wilkes Booth shoots President Lincoln

April 15: Abraham Lincoln dies; Andrew Johnson inaugurated president

April 26: John Wilkes Booth killed by Union soldiers (Virginia); Confederate general Joseph E. Johnston surrenders

Utah Territory

April 9: Utah's Black Hawk Indian War begins (continues until October 1872)

United States	Utah Territory

1865 *(continued)*

United States

May 4: Confederate lieutenant general Richard Taylor surrenders Departments of Alabama, Mississippi, and East Louisiana

May 5: Confederate major general Dabney Maury surrenders the District of the Gulf

May 9: Confederate lieutenant general Nathan Bedford Forrest surrenders

May 10: Confederate president Jefferson Davis captured; Confederate major general Samuel Jones surrenders departments of Florida and South Georgia

May 12: Confederate brigadier general William T. Wofford surrenders forces of North Georgia

May 12–13: Battle of Palmito Ranch (Texas), the last battle of the Civil War

May 26: Confederate lieutenant general Simon B. Buckner surrenders; Indian skirmishes at Sweetwater Station

June 22: CSS *Shenandoah* fires upon Union whaling ships (last shots of the Civil War)

June 23: Confederate brigadier general Stand Watie surrenders at Doaksville (Indian Territory)

July 7: Lincoln conspirators hanged in Washington, D.C.

Utah Territory

June 11: Speaker of the House Schuyler Colfax visits Salt Lake City

June 13: Governor James D. Doty dies

July 15: Charles Durkee appointed governor

United States | Utah Territory

1865 *(continued)*

Utah Territory

July 18: Utah militia attacks Indian band, killing twelve
July 26: Indians attack Glenwood
September 21: Militia engages Indians near Fish Lake, killing seven
September 30: Governor Durkee arrives in Utah

United States

December 18: Thirteenth Amendment adopted

1866

United States

August 20: President Andrew Johnson signs Proclamation 157 proclaiming official end of the Civil War

1868

Utah Territory

January 29: Great Salt Lake City is renamed Salt Lake City

United States

February–May: President Andrew Johnson impeached
May 26: President Johnson acquitted by one vote
July 9: Fourteenth Amendment adopted

United States	Utah Territory

1869

United States	Utah Territory
March 4: Ulysses S. Grant inaugurated president	
	May 10: Transcontinental Railroad completed at Promontory Summit

1870

United States	Utah Territory
	February: Robert T. Burton tried and acquitted of the murder of Isabella Bowman, a Morrisite woman killed June 1862 at South Weber
March 30: Fifteenth Amendment adopted	

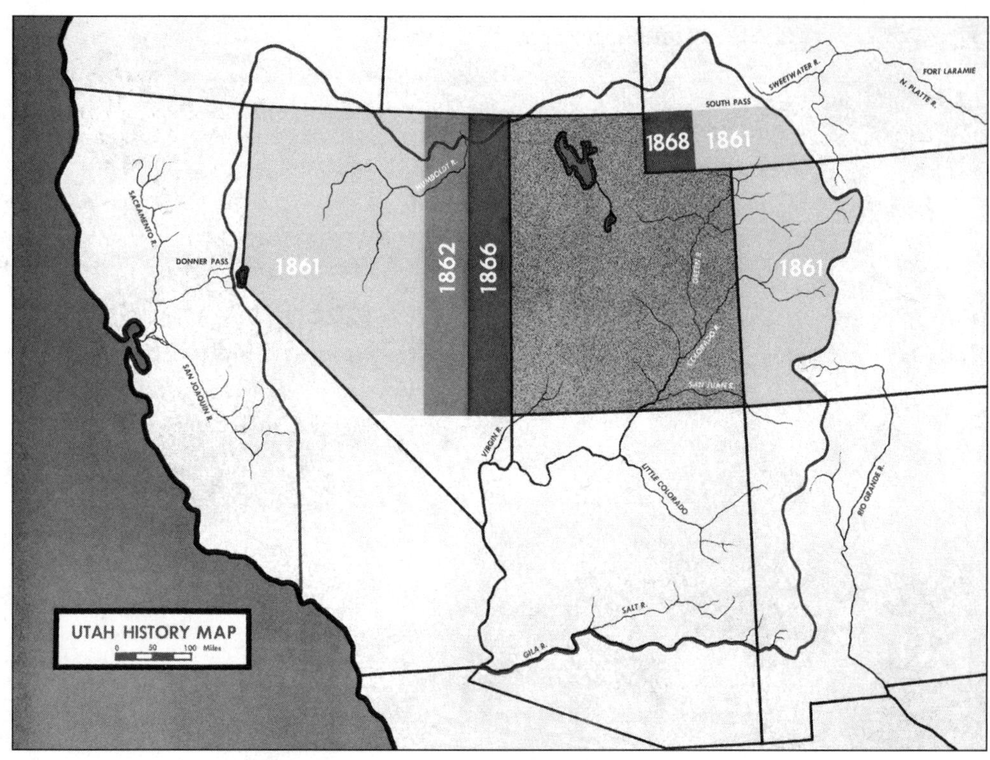

Utah Territory's changing borders, 1861–1868.
Courtesy of the Harold B. Lee Library, Brigham Young University.

CHAPTER I

Utah Territory and the Civil War: A Summary History

RUIN BY CIVIL WAR STARES
THIS WHOLE NATION IN THE FACE.
Deseret News
February 20, 1861[1]

THE CIVIL WAR CHANGED UTAH. WHILE NO BLUE AND GRAY BATTLES were fought within its changing territorial borders, the war significantly affected life in the territory and Utah's relationship with the nation.[2] Utah's role was "central to the American West during the Civil War . . . though it receives scant mention in Civil War histories and only a little more in volumes on the American West. Utah Territory would have been important because of its geographical position astride transportation and communications arteries even if it had not been an anomaly. And it was also unprecedented in this country, being both a civil and a religious entity of considerable size and influence," observed historian E. B. Long.[3]

The Civil War exerted an influence on Utah that was both subtle and blunt. This chapter provides background information and a year-by-year overview of

1. "Correspondence," *Deseret News,* February 20, 1861. This statement was included in a January 13, 1861, letter from Mormon elder William H. Miles of New York to a friend in Salt Lake City.
2. Few books have dealt exclusively with the subject of Utah and the Civil War. Here are four: Fisher, Lund, and Jensen, *Utah and the Civil War*; Long, *The Saints and the Union*; Alford, *Civil War Saints*; and Maxwell, *The Civil War Years in Utah*. Portions of this chapter expand research published by the author in Esplin and Alford, *Salt Lake City*; Alford, *Civil War Saints*; Rawson and Lyman, *The Mormon Wars*; and Esplin et al., *Far Away in the West.*
3. Long, *The Saints and the Union*, xi.

Utah Territory during the war in order to provide context for the records published together here.[4]

Prelude to War

Nothing is talked of but secession.

Deseret News

November 3, 1860[5]

Founded in 1830, the Church of Jesus Christ of Latter-day Saints (whose followers are commonly known as Mormons[6]) moved several times during the thirty years prior to the Civil War. Persecution, conflicts with neighbors, and revelations to leaders combined to relocate the largest concentration of members from New York to Ohio in 1831, to Missouri in 1838, to Illinois in 1839, to Nebraska in 1846, and finally to Utah. After reaching the Salt Lake Valley in July 1847 (which had been part of Mexico until February 1848[7]), Latter-day Saints longed for tranquility, but they received neither peace nor quiet. Indian conflicts, especially in the relatively fertile Utah Valley south of Salt Lake City, began soon after settlers arrived and continued throughout the Civil War and into the post-war years.[8] Utah's 1849 request for admission of the proposed state of Deseret was rejected, and Utah Territory was created as part of the Compromise of 1850, which began decades of conflict between federal officials and Utahns.

---

4. References to records in this volume use "OR-#" (chapter 4) and "UT-#" (chapter 5) identifiers. See chapter 3 for additional information. *OR* citations in this chapter include the record identifier, author, and date—for example: "OR-13 (L. Thomas to Brigadier-General Sumner, July 24, 1861)—but not the *OR* source citation (which lists the series, volume, and page numbers); that information is available at the end of each record in chapters 4 and 5.
5. "Telegraphic News by Pony Express," *Deseret News*, November 3, 1860.
6. "Mormon" is a nickname derived from church members' belief in *The Book of Mormon,* which claims to be the translated record of ancient American peoples. The formal name of the church is the Church of Jesus Christ of Latter-day Saints. Church members were also frequently referred to as Latter-day Saints (as in OR-417, for example) or Saints (as in OR-15).
7. The Mexican War, 1846–1848, ended near Mexico City with the signing of the Treaty of Guadalupe Hidalgo on February 2, 1848. The treaty transferred ownership of over half a million square miles to the United States, including most of present-day Utah. *Treaties,* 1:1107–1121.
8. While current usage favors "Native Americans" or "Native peoples," this volume will use the term "Indians" to conform to the common nineteenth-century usage that appears throughout these records. See, for example, William P. Dole to O. H. Irish, "Utah Superintendency," March 28, 1865, in *Report of the Commissioner of Indian Affairs*, 148–149.

During the popularly named Utah War (1857–1858), President James Buchanan sent a significant portion of the U.S. Army to quell a Mormon rebellion he incorrectly believed was occurring in Utah.[9] Immediately following the Utah War, almost one-fourth of the U.S. Army was deployed in Utah Territory—with a majority of the soldiers stationed at Camp Floyd, forty miles southwest of Salt Lake City.[10]

Public interest in Utah reached new heights during the Utah War. Mormons and the Utah War captured the popular imagination of the nation and were among the most frequent news stories—second only to articles about slavery and Kansas Territory.[11] The Utah War effectively ended on June 26, 1858, when Brevet Brigadier General Albert Sidney Johnston and his soldiers marched through Salt Lake City.

The nation's curiosity regarding Utah and Mormonism continued into and beyond the Civil War. The proximity of the Utah War to Southern secession meant Utah played a consequential role in the nation's military preparation for the Civil War: Utah was the army's last major deployment prior to the war and served, in hindsight, as a proving ground for tactics, training, weaponry, and logistics.[12]

Utah's unique relationship to the Civil War was influenced by both geography and politics. During the four years of war, 1861–1865, Utah's boundaries were reduced on three separate occasions. Utah's eastern border was adjusted in February 1861, when Colorado Territory was created. In March of that year, Nevada Territory was established, and Nebraska Territory was given the northeastern portion of Utah Territory (currently part of southern Wyoming). In July 1862, less than one week after President Abraham Lincoln signed the Morrill Anti-Bigamy Act (the first federal anti-polygamy legislation), all of Utah Territory west of the thirty-eighth degree of longitude was transferred to Nevada.[13] And Utah's internal political situation in the early 1860s was as volatile as her borders. During the course of the Civil War, Utah had four territorial governors and several acting governors, who served while the territory awaited the arrival of the next presidential appointee.

---

9. That interesting story is told elsewhere. See MacKinnon, *At Sword's Point, Part 1* and *Part 2*; Hafen, *Utah Expedition, 1857–1858*; Furniss, *The Mormon Conflict, 1850–1859*; and Bigler and Bagley, *The Mormon Rebellion*.

10. Salt Lake City was officially named Great Salt Lake City until 1868, but it will be referenced in this chapter as the more familiar Salt Lake City. Official Civil War records most frequently refer to "Salt Lake City" (OR-17, for example), but some references to "Great Salt Lake City" also appear (such as in OR-36).

11. During 1857–1858 there were over two thousand *New York Times* articles regarding Kansas or slavery and over a thousand articles about Utah or polygamy.

12. See MacKinnon, "Prelude to Civil War," 1–21.

13. Two additional boundary changes occurred in the years immediately following the Civil War. In May 1866 Nevada received additional land from Utah when it became a state. Utah's last boundary change took place in July 1868 when Wyoming Territory was created and Congress transferred Wyoming's southwest corner from Utah to Wyoming. See Neff, *History of Utah*, 691, 709.

While Latter-day Saints had never been popular in the American press, reporting took a noticeably negative turn following Mormon apostle Orson Pratt's public announcement defending the church's practice of polygamy in August 1852.[14] During the first Republican National Convention, which met in Philadelphia in June 1856, slavery and polygamy were jointly designated as "the twin relics of barbarism" and marked for extinction.[15] The Civil War provided the North with an opportunity to eliminate the "first relic"—slavery—but the "second relic"—polygamy—remained a topic of great interest, debate, and action throughout the war and increasingly in the decades that followed.

1860

ALL SIDES AND PARTIES AGREE THAT A DISSOLUTION IS INEVITABLE.
William H. Hooper,
Utah Territory's delegate to Congress[16]

Mormon resentment over President Buchanan's decision to send the army to Utah lingered for many years. According to Mormon apostle Orson Hyde, the federal government sent to Utah "[m]erchants, gamblers, whoremasters, thieves, murderers, false writers, drunkards, and to cap the climax, a drunken, debauched judiciary with plenty of bayonets to enforce their decrees. Some decent men came most likely; yet I know not one with whom I could safely trust the virtue of any female in their power."[17]

Beginning with South Carolina in December 1860, Southern secession caught almost no one by surprise. In the fall of 1860, the weekly Salt Lake *Deseret News* included numerous reports regarding the "impending crisis" that was "full of danger on every side."[18] The newspaper observed that since "the organization of the Government of the United States, there was never such a furor for political speechifying as now prevails from one end of the country to the other."[19] As citizens of a territory, Utahns could not vote in the 1860 presidential election, yet they followed the national political scene as closely as their circumstances allowed.

14. Orson Pratt in *Journal of Discourses*, 1:53.
15. "Polygamy and a New Rebellion," *New York Times,* June 19, 1862.
16. William H. Hooper to Charles C. Rich, December 29, 1860, quoted in Orton, "'We Will Admit You as a State,'" 214.
17. "Remarks by Elder Orson Hyde, Bowery, Oct. 7, 1860," *Deseret News,* October 24, 1860.
18. "The Secession Movement," *Deseret News,* December 29, 1860.
19. "News by Eastern Mail," *Deseret News,* October 24, 1860.

Mormons tended to see the hand of God in the overwhelming defeat of presidential candidate Stephen A. Douglas in November 1860. On May 18, 1843, during dinner with then-Judge Douglas, Joseph Smith, the church's founder and first president, reportedly told Douglas: "Judge, you will aspire to the presidency of the United States; and if ever you turn your hand against me or the Latter-day Saints, you will feel the weight of the hand of Almighty upon you; and you will live to see and know that I have testified the truth to you; for the conversation of this day will stick to you through life."[20] In June 1857, at the beginning of the Utah War, Douglas openly turned against the Mormons, stating that "it will become the duty of Congress to apply the knife and cut out this loathsome disgusting ulcer. No temporizing policy—no half-way measure will then answer."[21]

On December 20, 1860—coincidentally the same day that South Carolina seceded from the Union—Brigham Young wrote to William H. Hooper, Utah Territory's congressional delegate, regarding the precarious national situation: "By your letters and papers I perceive that the secession question was being violently agitated, but without much definite action. . . . But while the waves of commotion are [over] whelming nearly the whole country, Utah in her rock fortresses is biding her time to step in and rescue the constitution and aid all lovers of freedom in sustaining such laws as will secure justice and rights to all irrespective of creed or party."[22]

Any attempt to view the Civil War through the eyes of nineteenth-century Mormons must take into account Joseph Smith's revelation on war, which he recorded on Christmas Day 1832. Later added to the church's canon of scripture as Section 87 in the Doctrine and Covenants, this revelation states in part: "Verily, thus saith the Lord concerning the wars that will shortly come to pass, beginning at the rebellion of South Carolina, which will eventually terminate in the death and misery of many souls. . . . For behold, the Southern States shall be divided against the Northern States, and the Southern States will call on other nations, even the nation of Great Britain. . . . And it shall come to pass, after many days, slaves shall rise up against their masters, who shall be marshaled and disciplined for war."[23] Latter-day Saints saw in the Civil War a fulfillment of prophecy.

---

20. William Clayton, *Daily Journal,* as quoted in Roberts, *A Comprehensive History*, 5:393–394.

21. Douglas, "Kansas, Utah, and the Dred Scott Decision," address at State House, Springfield, Illinois, June 12, 1857. For a discussion of Douglas's speech, see Johannsen, *Stephen A. Douglas*, 566–575. See also "Comments Upon the Remarks of Hon. Stephen Arnold Douglas," *Deseret News*, September 2, 1857, for the Mormon response to Douglas's speech.

22. Brigham Young to William H. Hooper, December 20, 1860, Brigham Young Letters, Beinecke Library, quoted in Woodger, "Abraham Lincoln and the Mormons," 61–81.

23. Doctrine and Covenants (Salt Lake City: The Church of Jesus Christ of Latter-day Saints, 2013), 87:1, 3–4. While Joseph Smith's detractors might claim that his revelation reflected the Nullification Crisis that was threatening the nation in 1832, most Mormons consider it a prophetic utterance.

According to the eighth U.S. census (1860), there were 42,273 surveyed people in Utah Territory—22,224 white males, 19,990 white females, 13 free male colored and 17 female colored, and 29 slaves (18 male and 11 female).[24] Utah Territory was opened to slavery in 1850 under the concept of "popular sovereignty"—the same political doctrine often used by Mormons to support their nineteenth-century practice of polygamy.[25]

1861

UTAH HAS NOT SECEDED, BUT IS FIRM FOR THE CONSTITUTION AND LAWS OF OUR ONCE HAPPY COUNTRY.
Brigham Young[26]

From Utah's perspective, the issue was simple—Utah deserved statehood. Prior to the Civil War, Congress had ignored several such petitions from Utah. The most recent request was pending on Capitol Hill as Southern states began seceding. At the end of January, William Hooper was informed by the Committee on Territories that Congress was again denying Utah statehood.[27]

Brigham Young biographer John G. Turner concluded that "Young had no sympathy for either side in the Civil War."[28] Young saw himself and the Mormon church as firm supporters of "the Constitution of the United States and all righteous laws," but they were not, as Young declared in the Salt Lake Tabernacle on January 19, 1862, "by any means treasoners, secessionists, or abolitionists. We are neither negro-drivers

24. "The U.S. census for 1860 gives the number of colored persons in the Territory of Utah as 59, 30 free colored and 29 slaves. Of the slaves, Davis County had 10 and Salt Lake County 19." Beller, "Negro Slaves in Utah," 122–126. See also "1860 U.S. Census, Schedule 2—Slave Inhabitants, June 13, 1860," 629.

25. Orton, "'We Will Admit You as a State,'" 208–225. It is worth noting that three members of the 1847 vanguard pioneer company—Green Flake, Hark Lay, and Oscar Crosby—were slaves, and "[o]ddly enough, Utah was the only western territory in 1850 in which Negroes were held as slaves." See Lythgoe, "Negro Slavery in Utah," 40–54. Lythgoe suggests that "in the three years between the Mormon settlement of Salt Lake Valley in 1847 and the formal organization of Utah Territory in 1850, African American slavery was arguably illegal throughout the region as a result of Mexican law" and did not become legal until the Compromise of 1850 created Utah Territory. See Rich, "The True Policy for Utah" 1, 54–74; and Bringhurst, *Saints, Slaves, and Blacks.* Four years after Utah Territory was created, the popular sovereignty clause of the Kansas-Nebraska Act led to bloodshed as both proponents and opponents of slavery flooded into Kansas Territory in an effort to influence the vote.

26. UT-22. Brigham Young included this statement—the first telegram sent from Salt Lake City—to J. H. Wade, president of the Pacific Telegraph Company in Cleveland, Ohio. "The Completion of the Telegraph," *Deseret News,* October 23, 1861.

27. Hooper to Young, January 30, 1861. Quoted in Orton, "'We Will Admit You as a State,'" 219.

28. See Turner, *Brigham Young*, 317.

nor negro-worshippers."[29] In February Brigham Young commented that "There is no union in the North or in the South. The nation must crumble to nothing. They charged us with being rebels and rebels they will have in their Government. South Carolina has committed treason and if Prest. Buchanan had been a Smart man he would have hung up the first man who rebelled in South Carolina."[30]

When Confederate artillery, under the command of P. G. T. Beauregard, fired on Fort Sumter in Charleston Harbor during April 1861, America changed forever. Three weeks later, Apostle Heber C. Kimball asked: "Do any of you think this war is going to be over in a few days?" Answering his own question, he exclaimed, "If you do, you are greatly mistaken."[31] Initially, Utah Territory was as isolated from the war as anywhere on the continent could be—it seemed like a problem for the rest of the country, and tabernacle sermons and private journals alike thanked God for the removal of the church to the safety of the West. It did not take long, though, for the war to affect Utah.

Mormon loyalty was a national concern—not only during the Civil War but throughout the nineteenth century. During the Utah War, Latter-day Saints were portrayed as disloyal, and as the Civil War began there were lingering doubts among many Americans regarding the true loyalties of Utah. Mormons were generally portrayed in the press as being "openly inimical to the Government of the United States" while considering themselves "steadfast adherents to the Constitution."[32] Difficult relations between Utahns and federal officials, an important cause of the Utah War, continued during the Civil War, reinforcing previous perceptions.

Despite questions surrounding Mormon allegiance, the fact remained that Utah was important to the Union. Much of the territory's significance during the Civil War was a result of geography. For most of the war, there were continuing Confederate threats, both real and imagined, to transportation and communication routes that transited New Mexico Territory. When those routes became risky and uncertain, almost all wartime cross-country travel shifted into Utah.

A prioritized federal list for keeping the Overland Trail open would almost certainly have placed concerns regarding western secession (especially southern California and Oregon) first, communication second, transfer of western precious metals to

---

29. Brigham Young, January 19, 1862, in Van Wagoner, *The Complete Discourses of Brigham Young,* 1:1944. See also "Remarks by President Brigham Young," *Deseret News,* February 19, 1862.

30. *Brigham Young Office Journal,* February 2, 1861; *Complete Discourses,* 3:1742. This was a remarkable statement for Brigham Young to make, given his almost morbid fear of being summarily hung by the Buchanan administration's Utah Expedition during 1857–1858.

31. Heber C. Kimball, May 12, 1861, in *Journal of Discourses,* 9:134. See the timeline herein to compare wartime events with those in Utah Territory. There is an almost inexhaustible list of excellent resources regarding the Civil War; an excellent place to start is Shelby Foote's masterful trilogy *The Civil War: A Narrative.*

32. "From Washington (Telegraph to The Herald)," *The Boston Herald,* February 14, 1863.

help finance the war third, and, last but not least, continuing western emigration.[33] Utahns would have listed emigration first, followed closely by mail and telegraph communication.

By the beginning of May 1861, hostile actions on the trails—by both Indians and whites—caused Utah's departing governor, Alfred Cumming, to request that a detachment of soldiers from Fort Crittenden be sent to guard the Overland Trail "for the protection of the Mail, Express, and emigrants, and, if need be, for the chastisement of the Indians."[34] Soldiers were not sent but were instead ordered by the War Department to leave Utah and join the growing eastern fight. With the exception of seventeen soldiers left to garrison Fort Bridger, Colonel Philip St. George Cooke's entire Utah command of "ten companies of Infantry Artillery and Dragoons" marched east to join the growing conflict on August 9.[35] Indians roaming the Overland Trail became increasingly brazen in their stealing and pillaging—so much so that as the army departed, they "helped themselves to a goodly toll of Army cattle."[36] As the soldiers departed, they passed Mormon emigrants heading west.[37]

Brigham Young and church leaders were pleased with the army's departure. The church's removal to the West, which previously had been seen as a burden, was now viewed as a blessing. As Elder George A. Smith, a Mormon apostle, preached from the pulpit: "Now, brethren, are we not thankful that, at least, we can see the providence of the Almighty in suffering us to be driven into these valleys, where we can enjoy the sweets of true liberty—where none dare molest or make afraid?"[38] Brigham Young echoed that attitude: "Do we appreciate the blessings of this our mountain home, far removed from the war, blood, carnage and death that are laying low in the dust thousands of our fellow creatures in the very streets we have walked, and in the cities and towns where we have lived?"[39]

On July 24, Utah's Pioneer Day holiday, Brigadier General Lorenzo Thomas, the army's adjutant-general, notified Brigadier General Edwin V. Sumner, who was at

33. The Overland Trail refers broadly to any of the various trails from the Missouri River to the Pacific Ocean. In this volume it generally applies to the portion of those trails that crossed the Dakota and Utah Territories.

34. "Affairs in Utah," *New York Times,* June 2, 1861. "Affairs in Utah; Departure of Gov. Cumming for Georgia His Return Improbable Francis H. Wootten [*sic*] Governor pro tem. Whisky Licenses Trade, &c.," *New York Times,* June 17, 1861. Orson F. Whitney noted that "White men took part in these depredations," and Richard Vetterli suggested the whites involved may have been Southerners who sought to disrupt relations between Washington and the West. See Whitney, *The Making of the State*, 132; and Vetterli, *Mormonism, Americanism and Politics*, 519.

35. UT-16, P. St. Geo. Cooke to Bvt Br[i]g[adie]r Genl L. Thomas, August 9, 1861. Colonel Cooke first became associated with Mormons during the Mexican War.

36. "Affairs in Utah," *New York Times,* August 24, 1861, 5.

37. Hartley, "Latter-day Saint Emigration during the Civil War," 244.

38. George A. Smith, July 4, 1861, in *Journal of Discourses,* 8:360.

39. Brigham Young, January 26, 1862, in Journal History.

Department of the Pacific headquarters in San Francisco, that "One regiment of infantry and five companies of cavalry have been accepted from California to aid in protecting [the] Overland Mail Route via Salt Lake."[40] Although soldiers would not arrive in Salt Lake City for over a year, federal forces were beginning once again to move toward Utah.

Shortly before the army returned, a technological miracle occurred. On Friday, October 18, 1861, the eastern telegraph line from Omaha reached Salt Lake City. Utah could now communicate with the East in almost real time. The western telegraph line from Carson City arrived on October 24, and the nation found itself in possession of rapid coast-to-coast communication for the first time.[41]

Following the army's withdrawal from Utah, soldiers no longer patrolled the trails, maintained the telegraph stations, or ensured the safe and timely passage of the mails.[42] Indians quickly took advantage of the soldiers' absence. The *Deseret News* reported frequent attacks, and travel became increasingly dangerous.[43] Telegraph and mail stations were destroyed, stagecoaches and emigrants were attacked, and mail was scattered and burned by Ute, Shoshone, Kiowa, Bannock, and Cheyenne Indians.[44]

John W. Dawson arrived in Salt Lake City by mail stage on December 7 as the federally appointed, although not yet Senate-confirmed, territorial governor.[45] Dawson, President Lincoln's political appointee to replace Alfred Cumming as territorial governor, was a political chameleon, having been a member of the Whig, Democratic, Know-Nothing, American, and Republican parties prior to his appointment as Utah's territorial governor.[46] Just two days after his arrival in Salt Lake, Utah's territorial legislature passed an act "providing for an election on the 6th of Jan. of 65 Delegates to meet in Convention in this City [Salt Lake] on the 3d Monday in

---

40. OR-13, L. Thomas to Brigadier-General Sumner, July 24, 1861.

41. As was the case with the eastern telegraph, Brigham Young was given the honor of sending the first western-bound telegram message "to H. H. Carpentier President Overland Telegraph Company at ten minutes to 7 P.M. and at ten min. past 7 he received a reply from Mr. Carpentier dated 6 P.M. San Francisco, Cala." See Brigham Young Office Journal, October 24, 1861, CR 100 1, LDS Church History Library, Salt Lake City, Utah.

42. Between Colonel Philip St. George Cooke's departure in August 1861 and the arrival in Utah Territory (present-day western Nevada) of Colonel Patrick Edward Connor's California Volunteers in the summer of 1862, the U.S. Army did not have an organized presence between Fort Laramie and California. Fort Laramie, garrisoned in June 1849, provided security for the southeast portion of present-day Wyoming.

43. See Alford, "Indian Relations in Utah during the Civil War," in *Civil War Saints*, 203–25.

44. Blackhawk, *Violence over the Land*, 231; and Colton, *The Civil War in the Western Territories*, 166, 170. Those tribes tended to be equestrian. Nonequestrian tribes were generally less inclined to violence against soldiers and settlers.

45. "Affairs in Utah," *New York Times*, December 28, 1861. The *Times* reported that James Duane Doty, Utah's new superintendent of Indian Affairs, accompanied him. Doty would serve as Utah's governor from June 22, 1863, until his death on June 13, 1865.

46. Long, *The Saints and the Union*, 39.

January to form a Constitution, form a State Government, etc. preparatory to the admission of Utah [as a state]."[47]

Three days after his arrival, Dawson gave his first and only "Governor's Message to the Legislative Assembly of Utah," during which he issued several invitations for Utahns to join the national call to arms: "Men of Utah, are you ready to assist? . . . Here in this peaceful valley . . . far removed from the scenes of conflict, where your brethren and fellow citizens are ruthlessly shedding each other's blood, you can not but look with deep, earnest interest upon the struggle and its final result. . . . That the true interest of the people of Utah is with the Federal Union no rational man can doubt; and let no man urge a different course, for such will be a dangerous one."[48] Calling upon "the loyalty of this people," Dawson encouraged the territory to accept a $26,982 federal tax "levied on this Territory" in August 1861. (It was later paid.)[49]

Dawson served as governor for only three and a half weeks (December 7–31, 1861). On New Year's Eve, while "rumor upon rumor was in circulation," he fled the state after being accused "of making indecent proposals to Mormon women, one of whom drove him from her home with a fire shovel." The first night of his return trip east, he was robbed and severely beaten. Brigham Young reported to John Bernhisel in Washington, D.C., that "Several desperadoes asserted by some to have been hired by him as an escort . . . with the stage driver assaulted the Governor at the mail station between the Big and Little Mountains, and struck and kicked him quite severely. . . . The motives of the assailants for so brutal and cowardly an assault are unknown to me unless one of them was actuated by revenge for the Governors insult to Mrs. Williams, one of whose daughters it is said he is courting."[50] As historian E. B. Long noted, "The circumstances of the whole episode are cloudy and the stories vary."[51] Frank Fuller, Utah's territorial secretary, served as acting governor in Dawson's absence.[52]

---

47. Brigham Young to John Bernhisel, December 21, 1861, Brigham Young Letterpress Copybook.

48. John W. Dawson, December 10, 1861, "Governor's Message to the Legislative Assembly of Utah," accessed January 3, 2015, at https://archive.org/details/govemesslegislatooutahrich.

49. Ibid.

50. Brigham Young to John Bernhisel, January 4, 1862, Brigham Young Letterpress Copybook.

51. Long, *The Saints and the Union,* 46, 48. Ralph Y. McGinnis and Calvin N. Smith noted that when Dawson arrived in Washington, he learned that the U.S. Senate had refused to confirm his appointment as governor, and he would have been recalled from Utah even if he had not fled. McGinnis and Smith, *Abraham Lincoln and the Western Territories,* 100. According to a January 15, 1862, entry in the Brigham Young Office Journal, "Five of the scoundrels who robbed and beat the Governor [Dawson] are in custody." In *The Civil War Years in Utah* (95–115), Maxwell includes an engaging and extended, albeit speculative, reconstruction of events surrounding Governor John W. Dawson's panicked flight from Utah.

52. Frank Fuller, who was reportedly a close friend of Mark Twain, served as acting governor until Governor Stephen S. Harding arrived in July 1862. See "Frank Fuller Dead; Utah War Governor," *New York Times,* February 20, 1915.

1862

BY EXPRESS DIRECTION OF THE PRESIDENT . . .
YOU ARE HEREBY AUTHORIZED TO RAISE, ARM, AND EQUIP
ONE COMPANY OF CAVALRY FOR NINETY DAYS' SERVICE.
Brigadier General Lorenzo Thomas, U.S. Army adjutant-general, to Brigham Young[53]

A territory-wide election was held on January 6 to select delegates, and a state constitutional convention convened in Salt Lake City on January 15, 1862, with attendees "resolved that we would form a state government and live under it, whether admitted into the Union or not."[54] On January 20, convention delegates selected a committee to draft a constitution for the proposed state of Deseret.[55] The constitution was very much a product of its time—only "free white male citizen[s] of the United States" would be eligible to vote or serve in the state General Assembly, for example.[56] In short order, the convention appealed to the U.S. Congress for statehood.[57] The feeling in Utah was summed up in a letter to George Q. Cannon, a church apostle, from territorial delegate William H. Hooper. "We show our loyalty by trying to get in," he wrote, "while others are trying to get out."[58]

One northern reporter asked, "What is to be done with Utah? Shall she become one of the sisterhood of States, or shall she be kept out here in the cold a little longer?"[59] That question was answered in an earlier news report: "we shall have to tell Utah to wait."[60] E. B. Long concluded that "Had the Mormons abandoned polygamy it is possible and even probable that Utah would have been admitted" at that time.[61] But polygamy was not the only roadblock to Utah receiving statehood. Congress and the nation remained concerned about the unusual blend of church and state that existed in Utah, which became more obvious when the first territory-wide election unanimously chose Young as the first governor.

Through the opening months of 1862, snow, floods, and Indians combined to make

53. OR-54, L. Thomas to Mr. Brigham Young, April 28, 1862.
54. Brigham Young Office Journal, January 6, 1862.
55. "Deseret" is a *Book of Mormon* name defined as "honey bee" within that text. See Ether 2:3.
56. See "Constitution of the State of Deseret," *Deseret News*, January 29, 1862; also Brigham Young Office Journal, January 22 and 23, 1862. See also Morgan, *The State of Deseret*.
57. Roberts, *A Comprehensive History*, 5:3–7.
58. William H. Hooper to George Q. Cannon, December 16, 1860, in *Millennial Star* 23, no. 2 (January 12, 1861): 29–30. Hooper expressed a similar sentiment to Brigham Young in a December 4, 1860, letter (quoted in Orton, "'We Will Admit You as a State,'" 215).
59. "Affairs in Utah," *New York Times*, February 28, 1862.
60. "Utah Applying," *New York Times*, January 9, 1862.
61. Long, *The Saints and the Union*, 72.

mail and telegraphic communication on the Overland Trail increasingly sporadic. On April 11, acting governor Frank Fuller, along with John F. Kinney (chief justice of Utah Territory's Supreme Court), Edward R. Fox (Utah's surveyor general), officials from the Overland Mail Company, and the superintendent of the Pacific Telegraph Company, appealed to Secretary of War Edwin M. Stanton for assistance in controlling Indians on the trail. On April 14 Brigham Young notified John Bernhisel, then in Washington, D.C., that "the militia of Utah are ready and able as they ever have been, to take care of all the Indians within our borders, and are able and willing to protect the mail lines, if called upon to do so."[62]

On April 16 James H. Craig, brigadier general of volunteers headquartered at Fort Laramie, received orders making him responsible for protecting the entire Overland Trail, but he received too few soldiers to provide adequate security.[63] That same day an article in the *Deseret News* announced that "fifteen hundred troops from Gen. Halleck's department of the West have been ordered on the plains, from the Missouri river to the South Pass." The next sentence in the news report was not welcomed by Utah's residents: "The department of the Pacific has ordered for the immediate dispatch of an infantry regiment of California volunteers, supported by three companies of cavalry, on to the route from Fort Churchill [Nevada Territory] to South Pass via Salt Lake."[64]

Earlier that month, J. E. Eaton, the Overland Mail Company superintendent, requested assistance from Utah in securing the trail. On April 25 acting governor Frank Fuller issued a call to General Daniel H. Wells, commander of Utah's Nauvoo Legion militia, for "twenty mounted men duly officered and properly armed and equipped, carrying sufficient ammunition for thirty days' service in the field" to provide "military protection of mails, passengers, and the property of the mail company from the depredations of hostile Indians."[65] Colonel Robert T. Burton, the First Cavalry Regiment's commander and a Salt Lake County sheriff, together with twenty militiamen and four civilian teamsters, answered the call from General Wells.[66] They served on the trail from April to the end of May—contending with bad weather, rebuilding mail stations, gathering scattered mail, and repairing roads.[67]

---

62. Brigham Young to Hon. John M. Bernhisel, April 14, 1862, Brigham Young Letterpress Copybook.

63. See General Orders No. 6, Headquarters District of Kansas, April 16, 1862, *OR*, Series 1, Volume 13, page 362.

64. "Troops for the Plains," *Deseret News,* April 16, 1862.

65. UT-31, Frank Fuller to Gen. Daniel H. Wells, April 25, 1862. See Fisher, Lund, and Jensen, *Utah and the Civil War,* 112; and Brigham Young Office Journal, April 25, 1862.

66. Fisher, Lund, and Jensen, *Utah and the Civil War,* 113. An April 25, 1862, entry in the Brigham Young Journal History refers to Burton's unit as a posse. See Janet Burton Seegmiller's biography *Be Kind to the Poor: The Life Story of Robert Taylor Burton.*

67. "Eighty-Sixth Anniversary," *Deseret News,* July 2, 1862; "Annual Election—1862," *Deseret News,* July 30, 1862.

Ben Holladay, proprietor of the mail and stage lines from St. Joseph to San Francisco, worked behind the scenes with Secretary Stanton and others, including Senator Milton S. Latham of California, to convince President Lincoln to call for a Mormon military unit to provide trail security until "our own troops can reach the point where they are so much needed."[68] In a letter to Lincoln, Latham suggested that any such request be sent directly to Brigham Young.[69]

An April 24 army report signed by Adjutant General Thomas summarized military actions taken since November 1861 to secure the Overland Trail. He echoed the views of Senator Latham, encouraging the president to ask Brigham Young to provide soldiers—a strategy that offered "the most expeditious and economical remedy" for raising a military unit from Utah because of Young's "known influence over his own people, and over the [local] Indian tribes."[70] Lincoln authorized the War Department to contact Brigham Young (and not acting governor Fuller) on Monday, April 28. The telegram noted that "By express direction of the President of the United States you are hereby authorized to raise, arm, and equip one company of cavalry for ninety days' service."[71]

At 9:00 P.M., "within the hour" after receiving the War Department's telegram,[72] Brigham Young dictated a letter to his counselor, Daniel H. Wells, directing him to "forthwith muster said company into the service of the United States" so they could start "at once for the destination and service required."[73] Wells quickly penned Special Orders Number 3, directing that "Pursuant to instructions received this day from ex-Governor Brigham Young, and in compliance with a requisition from the President of the United States, Major [Lot] Smith of the Battalion of Life Guards is hereby directed to enlist by voluntary enrollment for the term of ninety days a company of mounted men."[74]

With prior service in the Mormon Battalion, Indian wars, the Utah War, and the Nauvoo Legion, Major Lot Smith was well respected within the territory. He served as a major in the Utah militia but accepted an active-duty army commission as a captain, the customary rank of a company commander in the U.S. Army's table of organization.[75] Utah's cavalry company was raised with local men and often

68. UT-34, A. Lincoln to Edwin M. Stanton, April 26, 1862.

69. Abraham Lincoln, endorsement, April 26, 1862, in Angle, *New Letters and Papers of Lincoln*, 291–292.

70. OR-52, L. Thomas, "Report on measures taken to make secure the Overland Mail Route to California," April 24, 1862.

71. OR-54, L. Thomas to Mr. Brigham Young, April 28, 1862.

72. Tullidge, *History of Salt Lake City*, 255.

73. UT-35, Brigham Young to Lieut. General Daniel H. Wells, April 28, 1862.

74. UT-38, Special Orders No. 3, Headquarters Nauvoo Legion, April 28, 1862.

75. Lot Smith had served as a major in the Nauvoo Legion since 1857. See Whitney, *Popular History of Utah*, 145.

borrowed animals. The company mustered at the Salt Lake Council House on April 30 to commission the officers and enlist the soldiers.[76] After the unit was formally organized, Brigham Young notified the War Department that the company would soon depart Salt Lake City.[77]

With just over one hundred soldiers and teamsters, together with nine wagons "for provisions and baggage," the Lot Smith Cavalry Company gathered at President Young's office in downtown Salt Lake City and departed during the afternoon of May 1.[78] Mountain snow made travel tedious, and Smith's command made little headway. The following day Brigham Young and Daniel H. Wells traveled up the canyon and spoke to the soldiers. Young counseled the men to remember that "although you are United States soldiers you are still members of the Church of Jesus Christ of Latter-day Saints, and while you have sworn allegiance to the constitution and government of our country, and we have vowed to preserve the Union, the best way to accomplish this high purpose is to shun all evil. . . . remember your prayers . . . establish peace with the Indians . . . always give ready obedience to the orders of your commanding officers." He promised the soldiers "as a servant of the Lord, that not one of you shall fall by the hand of an enemy.[79]

After a brief stop at Fort Bridger, the Utah cavalry set out for Independence Rock.[80] Improving the road as they traveled, they built three bridges in four days.[81] Finding that "many of the Mail stations were still smouldering when [they] came upon them. Wagon-loads of United States mail had been scattered and destroyed by the Indians" provided somber firsthand evidence why they had been called to protect the trail.[82] They rebuilt telegraph stations, recovered stolen horses and property, built and rebuilt bridges, and provided a military presence on the trail.

---

76. Brigham Young Office Journal, May 1, 1862. The three-month service provided by the Lot Smith Cavalry Company was not unique. Other short-term cavalry units in the West were formed, such as the "hundred-day men" who served with the Third Colorado Cavalry. See Colton, *The Civil War in the Western Territories,* 157.

77. UT-48, Brigham Young to Adj't Genl. L. Thomas, May 1, 1862. Some sources have listed an April 30, 1862, date for Young's telegram to Thomas. See, for example, Carter, *Utah during Civil War Years*, 389–390; and Young, "Lest We Forget: IV," 336.

78. Brigham Young Office Journal, May 1, 1862.

79. Fisher, Lund, and Jensen, *Utah and the Civil War,* 25–26. On July 25, 1862, Private (Daniel or Donald—records disagree on his first name) McNicol, a member of Lot Smith's company, drowned while crossing the Snake River; he was the unit's only fatality.

80. Independence Rock is a prominent rock formation and landmark located along the Sweetwater River, about five miles east of Devil's Gate and fifty-five miles southwest of present Casper, Wyoming, location 42° 29' 38.1" N 107° 07' 58.5" W. See Urbanek, *Wyoming Place Names*, 102. Independence Rock was so named because of the prevailing view of pioneer company captains that westbound groups who reached Independence Rock prior to July 4 would arrive safely at their destination on the Pacific Coast.

81. Harvey Coe Hullinger Journal, May 4–9, 1862, LDS Church History Library, Salt Lake City, Utah.

82. Fisher, Lund, and Jensen, *Utah and the Civil War,* 37.

According to army orders issued July 5, Patrick Edward Connor, a California militia officer, was to lead several companies of California Volunteers from Stockton, California, "to the vicinity of Salt Lake."[83] Connor's primary missions, as a newly commissioned colonel, were "to protect the Overland Mail Route"[84] and "the telegraph stations."[85] In one of his first reports to his superiors at San Francisco, Connor categorized Mormons as "a community of traitors, murderers, fanatics, and whores"[86]—an opinion he would retain throughout the war.

During late spring and early summer 1862, an internal insurrection in Utah reached a crisis point. A group of disaffected Mormons in South Weber known as Morrisites (followers of Joseph Morris, a British convert, who left Mormonism in 1861 and established their own church) fortified a stockade and formed their own militia.[87] Shortly after returning from patrolling the Overland Trail, Colonel Burton was summoned by the chief justice of Utah's supreme court, John F. Kinney, and charged with resolving the Morrisite stand-off.[88] Calling themselves a marshal's posse, Burton traveled to the Morrisite camp with over four hundred militiamen and two artillery pieces. Taking up a defensive position near the Morrisite stockade, Burton and Theodore McKean, a deputy marshal, demanded that they "peaceably and quietly surrender yourselves and the prisoners in your custody forthwith."[89] The multi-day standoff resulted in a Morrisite surrender, but only after shots were exchanged and warning artillery rounds killed two Morrisites. At least four Morrisites were killed, including Joseph Morris.

Elsewhere in the territory, the Lot Smith Cavalry Company returned to Fort Bridger in June.[90] Captain Smith notified Brigham Young on June 16 that General Craig was "much pleased with the promptness of our people attending to the call of the General Government . . . spoke in high terms of our people generally . . . [and] informed me that he had telegraphed President Lincoln to that effect." Craig, according to Smith, commented that the Utah Cavalry comprised "the most efficient troops he had for the present service" and recommended that the president "engage our Services for 3 Months longer."[91] In a subsequent report on June 27, Smith wrote

83. Born in County Kerry, Ireland, on St. Patrick's Day in 1820, Patrick Edward Connor fought in the Seminole War and was wounded during the Mexican War. At the beginning of the Civil War, Connor commanded the Stockton Blues, a California militia unit that was soon increased in size and designated as the Third Regiment of the California Volunteer Infantry. See Madsen, *Glory Hunter.*

84. OR-65, Special Orders No. 115, Hdqrs. Department of the Pacific, July 5, 1862.

85. OR-123, G. Wright to Brig. Gen. L. Thomas, December 15, 1862.

86. OR-87, P. Edw. Connor to Maj. R. C. Drum, September 14, 1862.

87. Morrisites are mentioned in OR-186 and OR-201.

88. Seegmiller, *Be Kind to the Poor,* 197, 217.

89. Bigler, *Forgotten Kingdom*, 212.

90. OR-66, Jas. Craig to General James G. Blunt, July 11, 1862.

91. UT-66, Lot Smith to President B. Young, June 16, 1862.

that Colonel William O. Collins, commander of the Ohio 11th Cavalry Regiment, "allow[s] we are best suited to guard this road, both men and horses; they are anxious to return, and if they have any influence . . . I imagine they will try to get [us] recalled and recommend [us] to Utah to furnish the necessary guard."[92]

By mid-August the soldiers in Utah's cavalry company had returned to Salt Lake City. Captain Smith told his men that they had "filled the bill and as far as he was concerned [they] were dismissed."[93] The Lot Smith Company was honorably discharged on August 14, 1862, after 107 days of military service.[94]

Shortly after the company was released, the War Department offered to extend their military service. Near the end of August, Secretary Stanton authorized General Craig to "raise 100 mounted men in the mountains and re-enlist the Utah troops for three months," but Brigham Young declined because Colonel Connor and his California Volunteers were marching toward Utah.[95] Young declared defiantly that "if the Government of the United States should now ask for a battalion of men to fight in the present battle-fields of the nation, while there is a camp of soldiers from abroad located within the corporate limits of this city, I would not ask one man to go; I would see them in hell first."[96] Utah's governor, Stephen S. Harding, informed the War Department that "things are not right."[97] A *New York Times* reporter suggested it was "much more likely that these Gentile Soldiers from California will create difficulties in Utah than that they will ever settle them. If the troops are designed to operate against the fragments of dying savages west of the Rocky Mountains, we are likely to have an Indian war on our hands this Summer, which, though barren enough of value, will be fertile enough of expenses."[98]

In the fall, Colonel Connor traveled in advance of his command to the Salt Lake Valley. He chose not to meet with either Governor Harding or Brigham Young. The site Connor selected for a new camp overlooked Salt Lake City "on an elevated spot which commands a full view of the city."[99] Established on October 26, 1862, and named

92. UT-67, Lot Smith to President Young, June 27, 1862.

93. Harvey Coe Hullinger Journal, August 10, 1862.

94. The original August 1862 muster-out roster is missing at the National Archives; it is unknown when it was removed. A handwritten copy made some time before 1929 still exists, though.

95. OR-80, Edwin M. Stanton to General James Craig, August 24, 1862. There is some confusion regarding the date that Secretary Stanton authorized re-enlisting the Utah cavalry. The telegraphic authorization from Stanton to Craig appears twice in the *OR* with two different dates—August 24 (OR-80) and August 27, 1862 (OR-82). See OR-79 for General Craig's request to Secretary Stanton for authority to re-enlist the Utah soldiers.

96. Brigham Young, *Journal of Discourses,* 10:107.

97. OR-81, Jas. Craig to Major-General Halleck, August 25, 1862.

98. "A Needless War in Prospect," *New York Times,* May 26, 1862, 4.

99. OR-108, P. Edw. Connor to Adjutant General, November 9, 1862.

after the late Senator Stephen A. Douglas, Camp Douglas (renamed Fort Douglas in 1878) headquartered the Union military presence in Utah Territory throughout the remainder of the Civil War and into the decades that followed. History does not record that Patrick Connor and Brigham Young ever met face to face, but it does note the continuing distrust they had for each other. Rising tensions between Camp Douglas personnel and the inhabitants of Salt Lake City began almost immediately.

In December Connor notified his superiors in San Francisco that "Indians are threatening the Overland Mail Route east and west of here. . . . and fears are entertained that they will attack some of the stations of the Overland Mail."[100] His attention became increasingly focused on what he perceived were the two biggest challenges to his and federal authority—Indians and Mormons.

1863

It is better to feed than fight the Indians
and that morality is an excellent policy,
even on the plains.
Deseret News
April 23, 1862[101]

The new year began on a note of frustration for Brigham Young. Congress had taken no serious action regarding Utah's statehood request during 1862, and there was little hope of a change. With soldiers settling into Camp Douglas, Connor turned his attention to "the marauding, thieving Indians." After Utah judges served "writs for the apprehension of several chiefs," the stage was set for a military confrontation.[102] On the bank of the Bear River in what is now southern Idaho (about 150 miles north of Camp Douglas, near the present town of Preston), a combined infantry and cavalry force of just over three hundred soldiers under the personal command of Colonel Connor attacked a large Indian camp on January 29, 1863. Mormon civilian guides, including Orrin Porter Rockwell, were also present.[103] Connor's goal was clearly stated in his battle report: "It was not my intention to take

100. OR-112, P. Edward Connor to Lieut. Col. R. C. Drum, December 2, 1862.

101. "The Troubles on the Eastern Route," *Deseret News,* April 23, 1862.

102. "The Battle of Bear River," *Deseret News,* February 11, 1863.

103. Orrin Porter Rockwell—a friend and bodyguard of Joseph Smith, founder of the Mormon church—was appointed as a deputy marshal of Salt Lake City in 1849, a position he held until his death in 1878. He was a folk hero among Mormons for his rough appearance, tough demeanor, and quick trigger. See Schindler, *Orrin Porter Rockwell.*

any prisoners."[104] As historian Harold Schindler summarized, "Bear River began as a battle, but it most certainly degenerated into a massacre"—one of the largest such atrocities in American history.[105] While only nineteen soldiers were killed in action, at least 250 Indian men, women, and children were slaughtered—the exact death toll is unknown.

The battle was hailed as a great victory. The *Deseret News* reported that "Col. Connor and the Volunteers who went north last week to look after the Indians on the Bear River have, in a very short space of time, done a larger amount of Indian killing than ever fell to the lot of any single expedition of which we have any knowledge."[106] General-in-chief of the Union Army Henry W. Halleck, who was widely known by his nickname "Old Brains," recommended to Secretary Stanton "that Colonel Connor be made a brigadier-general for the heroic conduct of himself and men in the battle of Bear River."[107] Promoted for his heavy-handed approach toward Indians,[108] Connor had within a year the reputation in some circles "of being the greatest Indian-fighter on the continent."[109]

Tensions between the army and the Mormons increased dramatically during the early months of 1863. It was not just the tenets of Mormonism that bothered Connor, who saw Mormons as "disloyal almost to a man" and felt that "treason, if not openly preached, [was] covertly encouraged."[110] He believed Brigham Young was "engaged in mounting cannon for the purpose of resisting the Government,"[111] reporting that the Mormons were "hard at work making cartridges" and that Young had placed a "guard of 300 men" at his home with which, from Connor's perspective, he could attempt to resist federal authority.[112] Connor's view was that "Mormonism as

104. OR-132, P. Edw. Connor to Lieut. Col R. C. Drum, February 6, 1863. Connor's blunt approach to Indian relations did not change throughout the war. In summer 1865, for example, General Connor directed Colonel N. Cole that "You will not receive overtures of peace or submission from Indians, but will attack and kill every male Indian over twelve years of age." Jno. Pope to Major-General Dodge, August 11, 1865, *OR*, Series 1, Volume 48, Part 1, page 356.

105. Schindler, "The Bear River Massacre," 302. See also Dickson, "Addendum," 234–35.

106. "The Fight with the Indians," *Deseret News,* February 4, 1863.

107. OR-140, G. Wright to Adjt. Gen. L. Thomas, February 20, 1863, first indorsement, H. W. Halleck to the Secretary of War, March 29, 1863. See also OR-164, OR-165, and OR-166. The army considered the battle at Bear River a legitimate military action, but Connor's biographer, Brigham D. Madsen, and many other historians, as well as tribal descendants, rightly label it as a massacre. See Barnes, "The Struggle to Control the Past," 81–104.

108. In August and September 1865 Connor commanded the Powder River Expedition against Sioux, Cheyenne, and Arapaho tribes in present-day Wyoming and Montana. Approximately one hundred Indian men, women, and children were killed during the expedition. See Hampton, "The Powder River Expedition 1865," 2–15.

109. Ware, *The Indian War of 1864*, 310.

110. OR-139, P. Edw. Connor to Lieut. Col. R. C. Drum, February 19, 1863.

111. OR-126, P. Edw. Connor to Lieut. Col. R. C. Drum, December 20, 1862.

112. OR-149, P. Edw. Connor to Lieut. Col. R. C. Drum, March 8, 1863.

preached and practiced in this Territory is not only subversive of morals, in conflict with the civilization of the present age, and oppressive on the people, but also deeply and boldly in contravention of the laws and best interests of the nation"; therefore, he sought "by every proper means in my power to arrest its progress and prevent its spread."[113] He believed there were but two ways to resolve the problem: "First, by dividing the Territory into four parts and adding the parts to the four adjoining Territories; second, by declaring martial law."[114]

Soon Connor came to see a third way to subvert Mormonism—by "inviting into the Territory large numbers of Gentiles to live among and dwell with the people." To accomplish this end, he "considered the discovery of gold, silver, and other valuable minerals in the Territory of the highest importance" and therefore "instructed commanders of posts and detachments to permit the men of their commands to prospect the country in the vicinity of their respective posts, whenever such course would not interfere with their military duties, and to furnish every proper facility for the discovery and opening of mines of gold, silver, and other minerals."[115] Knowing Brigham Young's well-known and public stance against mining,[116] Connor attempted to fill the void.

March 1863 was a particularly tense time between Mormons and the blue-panted soldiers. Governor Harding, together with Utah supreme court justices Charles B. Waite and Thomas I. Drake, sent reports to Washington that Mormon constitutional views were "dangerous and disloyal." They charged that Mormons were seeking to "stir up strife between the people of the Territory of Utah and the troops now in Camp Douglas."[117]

The cordial relations Harding enjoyed when he first arrived in Utah did not last long. On March 3, the anniversary of the first election in the self-proclaimed shadow state of Deseret, three thousand Mormons crowded into the Salt Lake City tabernacle to protest the perceived anti-Mormon policies of Governor Harding and Justices Drake and Waite. There was a "deep feeling of contempt manifest" toward Governor Harding.[118] From the tabernacle pulpit, Apostle John Taylor labeled Harding as "a most insidious foe" and "the most vindictive enemy that we have."[119]

113. OR-260, P. Edw. Connor to Lieut. Col. R. C. Drum, October 26, 1863.

114. OR-139, P. Edw. Connor to Lieut. Col. R. C. Drum, February 19, 1863. Connor's proposal for repealing Utah's Organic Act and redistributing its territory to neighboring states and territories echoed suggestions debated in Congress since the late 1850s. So too with the suggestion of martial law, which General William S. Harney, the Utah Expedition's initial commander, had sought unsuccessfully in June 1857.

115. OR-260, P. Edw. Connor to Lieut. Col. R. C. Drum, October 26, 1863.

116. See, for example, Van Wagoner, *The Complete Discourses of Brigham Young*, 325, 1824, 2131, 2162, and 2210.

117. Waite, *The Mormon Prophet and His Harem*, 104.

118. "Mass Meeting in the Tabernacle," *Deseret News*, March 4, 1863.

119. Waite, *The Mormon Prophet and His Harem*, 98–99. It should be noted that Waite's book, which is dedicated "To the suffering women of Utah" (5), is highly critical of Brigham Young and Mormonism.

Several Mormon elders visited Governor Harding and Justice Drake at the governor's residence the following day and "informed them that the people had sent them to request them to resign and leave the Territory." A similar request was left at the home of Justice Waite. Mormons placed a ten-man guard at the Church Historian's Office and fifty men at the Tithing Office and Tithing Barn. Cannons owned by the church were "all being put in a state of readiness."[120]

Army officers stationed at Camp Douglas entered the fray on March 8 by drafting a petition of their own to President Lincoln, supporting Harding, Waite, and Drake and asserting that Mormon charges were "a base and unqualified falsehood."[121] Rumors contributed to the growing tensions—chief among them was the persistent belief that the army planned to arrest Brigham Young.[122] Colonel Connor became alarmed on March 3 and again on March 4 when "Brigham caused to be removed from the Territorial arsenal to his residence all the ordnance and ordnance stores, and placed a large body of armed men in his yard, which is inclosed with a high stone wall."[123] Connor was uncertain whether Young's actions were offensive or defensive. A news report published in the *Daily Alta California* noted that "there is danger of a collision between the Mormons and our troops there."[124]

On March 8 Brigham Young addressed an audience in the Salt Lake Tabernacle about Latter-day Saint loyalty to the federal government. "We have proved our loyalty," said Young. "We have done everything that has been required of us."[125] Connor reported on March 9 that Young "raised the national flag over his residence for the first time I am told since his arrival in the Territory, but not, however, from motives of patriotism or for any loyal purpose, but as a signal to his people to assemble armed, which they immediately did, to the number of about 1,500."[126] The next day, Connor announced that Brigham Young and the Mormons "are determined to have trouble, and are trying to provoke me to bring it on, but they will fail."[127]

Tension throughout the city continued to increase, and Young was arrested on

---

120. March 4, 1863, in History of Brigham Young, Historian's Office History of the Church.

121. UT-94, P. Edward Connor et al. To His Excellency Abraham Lincoln, March 8, 1863.

122. See Stenhouse, *Rocky Mountain Saints*, and Varley, *Brigham and the Brigadier*, for information about "March Madness," as Varley titled it.

123. OR-158, P. Edw. Connor to Lieut. Col. R. C. Drum, March 15, 1863.

124. The *Daily Alta California* report is reprinted in "California Press on Utah Affairs," *Deseret News*, March 25, 1863.

125. Brigham Young, *Journal of Discourses*, 10:107, 109, 111.

126. OR-158, P. Edw. Connor to Lieut. Col. R. C. Drum, March 15, 1863. This may have been the first time Colonel Connor or his soldiers saw the national flag flying at Brigham Young's resident, but it was clearly not the first time a flag had been flown there. See, for example, "Affairs in Utah," *New York Times*, April 6, 1862, which reports that "The Stars and Stripes were flung to the breeze from Brigham's bee-hive mansion." See also "The Twenty-Fourth of July," *Deseret News*, July 30, 1862.

127. OR-152, P. Edw. Connor to Lieut. Col. R. C. Drum, March 10, 1863.

March 10 under the Morrill Anti-Bigamy Act of 1862.[128] He was quickly released on a two-thousand-dollar bond.[129] The flag at Brigham Young's residence was again raised on March 12—causing over one thousand Mormon militia members to assemble. As before, the territorial militia was dismissed, but Latter-day Saint guards patrolled the city at night. Connor recognized the friction that existed, but he took no responsibility for it. By the end of the month, General George Wright, understandably influenced by Connor's views, notified Washington that "the excitement at Salt Lake City, brought about by the treasonable acts of Brigham Young and his adherents, has somewhat subsided, yet I am fully satisfied that they only wait for a favorable opportunity to strike a blow against the Union."[130]

Following the Bear River massacre, a series of Indian treaties were negotiated and signed in rapid succession.[131] Indian attacks greatly subsided, and the trail became safer, for the time being. Brigham Young's approach that "Indians want feeding—not fighting" had lost out, and Patrick Connor's hardline approach had yielded the results he desired.[132]

The petition from Utah residents to President Lincoln resulted in Governor Harding's dismissal after serving just eleven months. His replacement, James Duane Doty, had earlier served as Utah's superintendent of Indian Affairs. Doty proved to be more sympathetic to Mormon views, noting in August 1863 that "Many of those difficulties arise from the mistaken notion that the interests of this people and those of the Government are at variance, I think they are not."[133] By all accounts an able politician, Doty was able to work effectively with both Young and Connor.

128. 37th Cong., Sess. 2, ch. 126, 12 Stat. 501 (1862). See Firmage and Mangrum, *Zion in the Courts,* 138–140.

129. Jensen, *Church Chronology*, 69. According to historian Dean C. Jessee, "The circumstances in the 1863 arrest of Brigham Young were as follows: Rumor of an impending arrest of President Young by a military force from Camp Douglas for an alleged infringement of the anti-bigamy law of 1862 threatened a confrontation between civilian and military forces in Salt Lake City. To avoid this, a 'friendly complaint' was preemptively filed against the Mormon leader [in a territorial, non-federal court], charging him with violation of the anti-bigamy law. The President was subsequently arrested and appeared in court, where his case was bound over for the next term. However, when the grand jury sat in 1864 it found no indictment against him and he was discharged." See Jessee, *Letters of Brigham Young to His Sons*, 88–89.

130. OR-167, G. Wright to Brig. Gen. L. Thomas, March 30, 1863. By July 1864 General Connor reported, "The policy pursued toward the Indians has had a most happy effect. That policy, as you are aware, involved certain and speedy punishment for past offenses, compelling them to sue for a suspension of hostilities, and on the resumption of peace, kindness and leniency toward the redskins. They fully understand that honesty and peace constitute their best and safest policy." See OR-308, P. Edw. Connor to Lieut. Col. R. C. Drum, July 1, 1864. Yet by February 1865 General Connor was again reporting that Indians "have again returned in increased force. The troops are insufficient to contend with them." See OR-383, P. E. Connor to Col. R. C. Drum, February 10, 1865.

131. See Alford, *Civil War Saints,* 218–220.

132. "Troops for the Plains," *Deseret News,* April 16, 1862.

133. OR-234, James Duane Doty to General [G. Wright], August 9, 1863.

1864

THE SAME SPYING, HOSTILE, HOUNDING SPIRIT IS STILL UPON OUR TRACK, THOUGH AT PRESENT IN ABEYANCE THROUGH HAVING MUCH TO ENGAGE ITS ATTENTION ELSEWHERE.
Deseret News
August 10, 1864[134]

The "longer Connor stayed in Utah, the more extreme became his language in describing the Mormons. But that was in part true on both sides, for the invective flew thick and the similes waxed more colorful," E. B. Long observed.[135] Inaction by Congress regarding Utah's repeated requests for statehood remained a thorn in Utah's side. John F. Kinney, Utah's recently selected congressional delegate, delivered a fiery speech before the House of Representatives on March 17, imploring Congress to take Utah's statehood request seriously. He observed that "the relation of the Territory to the parent Government may not inaptly be compared to that existing between the child and parent. You, sir, breathed us into existence; by your legislation were we created; [and] by your bestowments do we as an organization maintain our territorial government." During the course of his lengthy address, he painted an extended comparison between Utah's continuing territorial status and the relationship that once existed between the original thirteen colonies and Great Britain. In his view, Utah was subject to "taxation without representation and the appointment of officers to rule over the people without their consent," and Kinney concluded that "I leave it for the future historian to determine the respective merits of George III and Stephen S. Harding, late Governor of Utah." Utah's representative was particularly offended because Congress was preparing to "jump over Utah, and take in Nevada," which he called "but an offshoot of Utah" that "once belonged to her western boundary, has had a territorial existence of only about three years and has far less population than Utah."[136]

Kinney closed with a plea and a question: "We offer you our devotion, our industry, our enterprise, our wealth, our humble counsels in the affairs of the nation in this the darkest hour of our country's history. We present to you for a State your deserts reclaimed and fertilized by persevering industry and the sweat of uncomplaining toil. . . . Will you accept the offering?"[137] His speech was well received in Utah but had no effect on Congress. A few weeks later, the editor of the *Deseret News* lamented

134. "The Spirit of Trade," *Deseret News,* August 10, 1864.

135. Long, *The Saints and the Union,* 215.

136. "Utah Before Congress," *Deseret News,* April 27, 1864. Kinney's speech filled several pages of small typeset newsprint.

137. Ibid. Nevada was admitted as a state on October 31, 1864, in time for residents to cast their electoral votes for Abraham Lincoln in the 1864 presidential election. Congress increased Nevada's borders in became a state on March 1, 1867. Colorado was not admitted to the Union until August 1,

that it was "not very flattering to claims of justice to see younger Territories with a lesser population sliding easily into the Union, while Utah is left still at the door asking for admission."[138]

An important indicator of the Union Army's view of Utah's loyalty is found in an October 1864 letter from Major General Irvin McDowell—commander, Department of the Pacific—to Utah's Governor James Doty. In his letter signaling the possibility of a request for Utah troops, McDowell informed Doty that he had received "authority to raise, not to exceed four [military] companies from Utah in case they should be necessary."[139] While the rapid collapse of the Confederacy during the last six months of the war meant that McDowell never acted on this authorization, it is important to note that he and the "Governors of California and Oregon" were comfortable supporting the possibility that Utah could be asked to recruit hundreds of additional soldiers.

Utahns followed the 1864 presidential election closely, and most residents would have agreed with the *Deseret News*'s assessment that there "never was a time in the nation's history when the American people had a more solemn obligation to discharge than that which lies before them at the election in November."[140] Unlike 1860 when many Mormons were dissatisfied, the saints were pleased with Lincoln's reelection. The front page of the *Deseret News* observed, though, that "If we, in Utah, were permitted to enjoy the free exercise of the elective franchise we might feel a little more interested in these great National struggles for power."[141]

1865

In the Spring of 1861 South Carolina was more loyal to the Union than Utah is today.
New York Times
November 27, 1865[142]

Brigham Young had little patience for Patrick Connor or the soldiers stationed in the territory. He observed in a January 1865 address to the Utah territorial legislature

1876—a few weeks after Custer's June defeat at the Little Big Horn and the nation's July centennial celebration. Utah became the forty-fifth state on January 4, 1896.

138. "Our Affairs at Washington," *Deseret News,* April 27, 1864.

139. UT-139, Major General Irvin McDowell to His Excellency J. Duane Doty, October 3, 1864. See also UT-140, and UT-141. Confirming the sincerity of General McDowell's request, one week later, Captain John Green, assistant adjutant general of the San Francisco Volunteer Recruiting Service, sent Governor Doty the necessary forms and instructions to complete the unit enlistments. Utah's governor acknowledged receipt of both letters on October 21, 1864.

140. "Opening the Presidential Campaign," *Deseret News,* March 23, 1864.

141. "Eastern News," *Deseret News,* November 16, 1864.

142. "Affairs in Utah," *New York Times,* November 27, 1865.

that "I do not know the man [Connor]; as a citizen I have nothing against him, he wants to kill the truth, and sacrifice every virtue there is upon the earth that God has established, that is what makes me hate him."[143] The antipathy between Young and Connor was mutual, and they made no attempt to disguise their disgust for one another. Connor at one point informed his commanding officer, Major General G. M. Dodge, that "Brigham's power is evidently on the wane, the scepter is leaving his hands, and he is becoming desperate. I will attend to him . . . I have a peculiar way of managing him, and if you will trust to my judgment all will be well."[144] But as the war progressed, Young and Connor reached an accommodation. Each spoke disparagingly of the other, but they did not back their rhetoric with provocative acts.

While Congress paid little attention to the territory's petitions for statehood, the shadow government of the state of Deseret continued. Speaking on January 23 "in my capacity of Governor," Brigham Young declared that the "year which has just passed has been to our citizens a season of peace and prosperity."[145]

Lincoln's second inauguration on March 4, 1865, was widely anticipated and welcomed. Salt Lake City's celebration included concerts, speeches, and a mile-long parade. Soldiers from Camp Douglas and territorial militiamen lined the streets together "at the place appointed."[146] Soon after that, news of General Robert E. Lee's April 9 surrender at Appomattox had only recently reached Utah when "the horrifying intelligence that President Lincoln had been assassinated" was received. Throughout Salt Lake City, "business was generally suspended, flags were draped in mourning at halfmast, stores and other public buildings were closed and craped, . . . and a deep gloom palpably rested upon the minds of the citizens." The first Sunday after Lincoln's death, three Mormon apostles—Wilford Woodruff, Franklin D. Richards, and George Q. Cannon—delivered comments eulogizing the late president.[147]

Indian problems continued in Utah, but they escalated dramatically at the end of the war. The day General Lee surrendered was the beginning of Utah's Black Hawk Indian War (not to be confused with the earlier Black Hawk War of 1832), which continued intermittently for seven years in central and southern Utah. In 1866 "Indian attacks were so damaging and threats so ominous" that Mormon militia leaders vacated

143. George D. Watt's Report, Legislative Assembly, January 23, 1865, in Van Wagoner, *The Complete Discourses of Brigham Young*, 4:2260.

144. OR-428, P. Edw. Connor to Maj. Gen. G. M. Dodge, May 28, 1865. E. B. Long suggests that the initial mutual dislike evidenced during the Civil War may have softened in the years following the war: "Both during the war and afterwards, there seems to have grown up a certain mutual respect between Brigham Young and General Connor, both indisputably men of character and principles. In 1871 Brigham Young and others were arrested for 'lascivious cohabitation.' Connor is said to have offered to furnish $100,000 bond for the Mormon leader." Long, *The Saints and the Union*, 270.

145. "State of Deseret. Governor's Message," *Deseret News*, January 25, 1865.

146. "The Inaugural Celebration, *Union Vedette*, March 6, 1865.

147. "Our Nation's Mourning," *Deseret News*, April 19, 1865.

twenty-seven settlements in nine Utah counties.[148] Dozens of settlers and an indeterminate number of Indians were killed. The Black Hawk Indian War, prosecuted by Utah territorial troops with only limited federal involvement, was the last major challenge that Utah's Indians would mount against the encroaching American authority.

As the Civil War drew to a close, Utah experienced yet another change of governors when Governor Doty died in office on June 13.[149] Doty had "kept a middle course in the conflict between the Mormons and the federal presence in the Territory," and Utahns openly mourned his passing.[150] Flags flew at half-staff, Salt Lake City draped itself in black, and many businesses closed on the day of his funeral.[151]

Beginning in early summer, military forces in Utah were supplemented by several U.S. Volunteer infantry units called the Galvanized Yankees—former Confederate soldiers who were captured and later "accepted the blue uniform of the United States Army in exchange for freedom from prison."[152] Galvanized Yankees from the Sixth U.S. Volunteer Infantry Regiment arrived on the Wyoming plains in June. Historian Dee Brown wrote that "State Volunteers who had been guarding the Overland Mail and Pacific Telegraph lines were being mustered out in haste to avoid mass mutinies and desertions. In a matter of a few days, the 10 companies of the 6th [U.S. Volunteers] found themselves almost the sole guardians of 2,200 miles of telegraph lines and stage roads. From June [1865] until the spring of 1866, they marched and countermarched over considerable areas of Nebraska, Wyoming, Colorado, Kansas, and Utah."[153]

With the end of formal hostilities between the North and South, Utah once again returned to the pages of American newspapers. After reminding readers that "slavery and polygamy were the 'twin relics of barbarism,'" the *New York Sun,* for example, crowed in August that the "first part of this work has been accomplished. Slavery is an extinct institution, but its twin brother—polygamy—flourishes, spreads and multiplies. . . . Polygamy must follow slavery to its grave . . . let the Republican party now turn the vials of its wrath upon this sole remaining 'relic of barbarism.'"[154]

---

148. Culmsee, *Utah's Black Hawk War,* 12–13, 27. The nine counties were Summit, Wasatch, Sanpete, Sevier, Piute, Beaver, Iron, Kane, and Washington. Using Utah's current county map, the total would be ten counties—as Garfield County was then part of Kane County. Culmsee notes, "At times Sevier and Piute Counties and the Long Valley Northern portion of Kane [County] were completely abandoned. Major or extensive portions of the other six counties were abandoned" (13).

149. Governor Doty's death was just ten days before the last Confederate commander, Brigadier General Stand Watie, a Cherokee Indian, surrendered in present-day Oklahoma. See Colton, *The Civil War in the Western Territories,* 182–189; and W. P. Adair and James M. Bell to Brig. Gen. J. C. Veatch, 19 July 1865, *OR*, Series 1, Volume 58, Part 2, pages 1099–1101.

150. Long, *The Saints and the Union,* 268.

151. "Obituary," *Deseret News,* June 21, 1865.

152. Brown, *The Galvanized Yankees,* 1.

153. Ibid., 143.

154. "The New York *Sun* on the 'Mormons,'" *Deseret News,* September 6, 1865.

By September, the *Deseret News* was complaining that "the country is flooded with tales about the 'Mormons.'"[155] Physical and religious distance made it difficult, if not impossible, for Mormons to craft a favorable public image outside of Utah. A *New York Times* article demonstrated the width of the divide. Comparing Mormons in Utah to secessionists in the Confederacy, the paper suggested that "Utah was the first to go through with the solemn farce of declaring its little self independent of the United States. . . . [in] August, 1857 when Brigham Young . . . declared . . . that the umbilical cord that united this Territory with the United States was then and there cut. . . . The so-called State of Deseret . . . is in open rebellion against the United States; and the people, under the command of their leaders, are in open rebellion against the laws of the United States."[156] Even though the nation was weary from four years of the civil war that killed over a half million people, the reporter proffered that "There are folks who think the only thing to do is to fight the Saints, and reduce them to loyalty and monogamy at the point of the sword."[157] The November 1865 charge in the *New York Times* that "in the spring of 1861 South Carolina was more loyal to the Union than Utah is today" is staggering considering that by spring 1861 South Carolina had formally seceded, and Southern artillery had fired the opening rounds of the Civil War.[158]

Summary

Was there ever such a waste
of life and treasure since the world began?
Deseret News
August 10, 1864[159]

The Civil War changed Utah. By its end, the isolation of the territory was over, with the arrival of the telegraph in 1861 helping to integrate Utah into the life of the nation. Slowly throughout the course of the war, the fiery rhetoric from Mormon leaders regarding God's condemnation of the nation began to cool. As Salt Lake resident Martha Cragun Cox summarized, "The Saints in the valley were not greatly disturbed by the war, but were greatly interested in it."[160]

Utah's geographic location—a natural transit point for the trails, stage lines, mail

155. "The Way It Is Done," *Deseret News,* September 9, 1865.
156. "Affairs in Utah," *New York Times,* November 27, 1865.
157. "Affairs in Utah," *New York Times,* November 28, 1865.
158. "Affairs in Utah," *New York Times,* November 27, 1865.
159. "Startling Disclosures," *Deseret News,* August 10, 1864.
160. Martha Cragun Cox Journal, 67.

routes, and telegraph lines that traversed the nation—made it a vital link during the Civil War between the Northern states and the Pacific Coast. Approximately seventeen thousand Latter-day Saints reached Utah during the Civil War—about half the number who arrived between 1847 and 1860.[161] The assimilation accelerated after the war when the last spikes of the transcontinental railroad were driven at Promontory Summit on May 10, 1869.

The causes of the Utah War (1857–1858) were not resolved by 1861. Throughout the Civil War, the nation viewed Utah as disloyal—an attitude that baffled Utahns. Rumors about Mormon interest in joining the Confederacy have circulated for over 150 years; however, historians have searched in vain for evidence of serious Southern secessionist acts or attitudes among Utah's leadership. Even William Hooper, Utah's congressional delegate who as "a non-polygamous slaveholder and Southern sympathizer" was anything but a typical Mormon, stated "we can never side with her [the Confederate states] breaking up this our Fatherland, no Never—Never." [162] Brigham Young addressed this subject himself in March 1863, asking:

> What was the result a year ago, when our then Governor . . . called for men to go and guard the mail route? Were they promptly on hand? Yes, and when President Lincoln wrote to me requesting me to fit out one hundred men to guard the mail route, we at once enlisted the one hundred men for ninety days. . . . But all this does not prove any loyalty to political tyrants. . . .
>
> Now, as we are accused of secession, my counsel to this congregation is to secede, what from? From the Constitution of the United States? No. From the institutions of our country? No. Well then, what from? From sin and the practice thereof. That is my counsel to this congregation and to the whole world.[163]

Questions surrounding Mormon loyalty continued into the decades that followed. Americans remained skeptical of the power and influence Brigham Young wielded in Utah, but the Mormon practice of polygamy was a chief cause of the nation's negative view of Mormonism. While Mormons viewed polygamy as a sacred mandate from God, the nation generally identified it as an evil akin to slavery that must be eradicated. The legal and social conflict over polygamy that began during the Civil

---

161. Hartley, "Latter-day Saint Emigration during the Civil War," 261.

162. Orton, "'We Will Admit You as a State,'" 221. In *The Civil War Years in Utah*, historian John Gary Maxwell alleges that "the majority of Mormon leaders in Utah favored the South" (44). Similar assertions appear on pages 54, 57, 314, and 351–354, and the book's dust jacket declares that Maxwell found "indisputable evidence of Southern allegiance among Mormon leaders." While a limited number of statements regarding Southern sympathies in Utah do exist, to characterize them as demonstrating "Southern allegiance" overstates the available evidence, especially as it pertains to Mormon leadership. Utah Territory had no Southern allegiance and took no secessionist actions during the war. Instead, Utah went to extraordinary lengths in a concerted effort to receive statehood.

163. Brigham Young, *Journal of Discourses*, 10:107, 109, 111.

War with passage of the Morrill Anti-Bigamy Act in 1862 continued until the end of that century.

Utahns saw themselves as loyal Americans—fully qualified and worthy to be granted statehood. They remained dismayed as their numerous statehood petitions were rebuffed by Congress, especially as other territories received that honor ahead of them.[164] The shadow "State of Deseret" functioned side by side with the federal territorial government until 1870, when it was quietly and unceremoniously dismantled.[165] It was not until January 4, 1896, almost six years after Mormon church president Wilford Woodruff took the first steps toward ending polygamy, that Congress finally would grant Utah statehood.

The relationship between Utah and the rest of the nation is typified in the personality clash that played out during the war between Brigham Young and Patrick Connor. Both leaders held strong and conflicting views, yet neither reached out to their antagonist. Instead, they confronted each other with a war of words that almost resulted in a clash of arms in March 1863. But, as E. B. Long observed, "Both during the war and afterwards, there seems to have grown up a certain mutual respect between Brigham Young and General Connor, both indisputably men of character and principles."[166] Brigham Young served as Mormon church president until his death in August 1877. Surprisingly, General Connor, who had blustered so loudly and so often regarding the evils of Mormonism, chose to remain in Utah after he left the army in 1866. He died at Salt Lake City in 1891 and is buried at the Fort Douglas cemetery.

Utah played a unique role during the Civil War. It did not seek, yet it did not shirk, responsibility to serve. Asked to provide only one active duty military unit during the war, the service of the Lot Smith Cavalry Company provided Utah with an opportunity to demonstrate its loyalty to the Union. The Saints served well when called. The documents in this volume help to tell Utah's story during those momentous Civil War years.

---

164. Between 1849, when Utah first requested statehood, and 1896, when Utah was admitted as a state, Utahns watched Congress grant statehood to fourteen states: California (1850), Minnesota (1858), Oregon (1859), Kansas (1861), West Virginia (1863), Nevada (1864), Nebraska (1867), Colorado (1876), North Dakota (1889), South Dakota (1889), Montana (1889), Washington (1889), Idaho (1890), and Wyoming (1890).

165. Long, *The Saints and the Union,* 274.

166. Ibid., 270.

CHAPTER 2

History of the War of the Rebellion Official Records

Efforts to publish official Civil War records began even before the war ended. Henry Wager Halleck, general-in-chief of the Union Army, "in response to the difficulty he experienced writing his 1863 annual report advocated gathering and publishing Civil War official documents and reports."[1] Congress passed a resolution on May 19, 1864, authorizing a government-sponsored publication of official war records.[2] Originally envisioned as costing half a million dollars for the printing of ten thousand copies of approximately fifty volumes, the project continued to balloon in both cost (totaling almost three million dollars) and size (publishing 128 volumes). Volumes were published between 1880 and 1901.

Insight and information regarding the scope of the original *Official Records* publication effort can be gained from a brief history written by Confederate brigadier general Marcus J. Wright, who served as an agent of the United States War Department for the Collection of Military Records. He wrote:

> The war which was carried on in the United States in 1861–5, called "The War of the Rebellion," "The Civil War," "The War of Secession," and "The War Between the States," was one of the greatest conflicts of ancient or modern times. Official reports show that 2,865,028 men were mustered into the service of the United States. . . . The Confederate forces are estimated from 600,000 to 1,000,000 men. . . .
>
> The immensity and extent of our great Civil War are shown by the fact that there were fought 2,261 battles and engagements, which took place in the following named States: In New York, 1; Pennsylvania, 9; Maryland, 30; District of Columbia, 1; West Virginia, 80; Virginia, 519: North Carolina, 85; South Carolina, 60; Georgia, 108; Florida, 32; Alabama,

1. Aimone and Aimone, *A User's Guide to the Official Records of the American Civil War*, 1.
2. "A Resolution to Provide for the Printing of Official Reports of the Operations of the Armies of the United States," 38th Cong., Sess. 1, 13 Stat. 406 (1864).

78; Mississippi, 186; Louisiana, 118; Texas; 14: Arkansas, 167; Tennessee, 298; Kentucky, 138; Ohio, 3: Indiana, 4; Illinois, 1; Missouri, 244; Minnesota, 6; California, 6; Kansas, 7: Oregon, 4; Nevada, 2; Washington Territory, 1; Utah, 1;[3] New Mexico, 19; Nebraska, 2; Colorado, 4; Indian Territory, 17; Dakota, 11; Arizona, 4; and Idaho, 1.

It soon became evident that the official record of the War of 1861–5 must be compiled for the purposes of Government administration, as well as in the interest of history, and this work was projected near the close of the first administration of President Lincoln. It has continued during the tenure of succeeding Presidents, under the direction of the Secretaries of War, from Edwin M. Stanton, under whom it began, to Secretary Elihu Root, under whose direction it was completed. . . . The total number of volumes is 70; the total number of books, 128, many of the volumes containing several separate parts. The total cost of publication was $2,858,514.67.[4]

Three companion series were published by the Government Printing Office: a similar but smaller compilation for the Union and Confederate navies; an official atlas; and a photographic collection. Additional insights and details regarding the publication of the *War of the Rebellion Official Records* are available in the preface to the *Atlas to Accompany the Official Records of the Union and Confederate Armies.* George B. Davis, a U.S. Army major and judge advocate, together with Leslie J. Perry and Joseph W. Kirkley (identified as "civilian experts") wrote:

The work of preparing the records of the war for public use was begun under the resolution of Congress of May 19, 1864, by Adjt. Gen. E. D. Townsend, U. S. Army, who caused copies to be made of reports of battles on file in his office and steps to be taken to collect missing records. . . .

The first decisive step taken in this work was the act of June 23, 1874, providing the necessary means "to enable the Secretary of War to begin the publication of the Official Records of the War of the Rebellion, both of the Union and Confederate Armies," and directing him "to have copied for the Public Printer all reports, letters, telegrams, and general orders, not heretofore copied or printed, and properly arranged in chronological order." . . .

Subsequently, under meager appropriations, it was prosecuted in a somewhat desultory manner by various subordinates of the War Department until December 14, 1877, when the Secretary of War, perceiving that the undertaking needed the undivided attention of a single head, detailed Lieut. Col. Robert N. Scott, U. S. Army, to take charge of the bureau and devote himself exclusively to the work.

The act of June 23, 1874, greatly enlarged upon the first crude scheme of publication. On this more comprehensive basis it was determined that the volumes should include not only the battle reports, but also "all official documents that can be obtained by the compiler, and that appear to be of any historical value." Colonel Scott systematized the work and

3. The January 29, 1863, battle of Bear River was Utah's sole Civil War engagement. Dyer lists one engagement, seven skirmishes, and six expeditions for Utah Territory. See Dyer, *A Compendium of the War of the Rebellion,* 2:582, 594, 983–989.

4. Wright, "Records of the War Between the States," introduction.

the plan, and presented the records in the following order of arrangement, which has been adhered to by his successors:

The first series [embraces] the formal reports, both Union and Confederate, of the first seizures of United States property in the Southern States, and of all military operations in the field, with the correspondence, orders, and returns relating specially thereto, and, as proposed, is to be accompanied by an Atlas. . . .

The second series [contains] the correspondence, orders, reports, and returns, Union and Confederate, relating to prisoners of war, and (so far as the military authorities were concerned) to State or political prisoners.

The third series [contains] the correspondence, orders, reports, and returns of the Union authorities (embracing their correspondence with the Confederate officials) not relating specially to the subjects of the first and second series. It will set forth the annual and special reports of the Secretary of War, of the General-in-Chief, and of the chiefs of the several staff corps and departments; the calls for troops, and the correspondence between the National and the several State authorities.

The fourth series [exhibits] the correspondence, orders, reports, and returns of the Confederate authorities, similar to that indicated for the Union officials, as of the third series, but excluding the correspondence between the Union and Confederate authorities given in that series.

The first volume of the records was issued in the early fall of 1880. The act approved June 16, 1880, provided "for the printing and binding, under direction of the Secretary of War, of 10,000 copies of a compilation of the Official Records (Union and Confederate) of the War of the Rebellion, so far as the same may be ready for publication, during the fiscal year"; and that "of said number 7,000 copies shall be for the use of the House of Representatives, 2,000 copies for the use of the Senate, and 1,000 copies for the use of the Executive Departments." Under this act Colonel Scott proceeded to publish the first five volumes of the records.

Col. Robert N. Scott died March 5, 1887, before the completion of the work, which, during a ten years' service, he had come to love so dearly. At his death some twenty-six books only had been issued. . . .

The Secretary of War, May 7, 1887, assigned Lieut. Col. H. M. Lazelle, U.S. Army, to duty as the successor of Colonel Scott. He had continued in charge about two years, when, in the act approved March 2, 1889, it was provided—

That hereafter the preparation and publication of said records shall be conducted, under the Secretary of War, by a board of three persons, one of whom shall be an officer of the Army, and two civilian experts, to be appointed by the Secretary of War, the compensation of said civilian experts to be fixed by the Secretary of War.

The Secretary of War appointed Maj. George B. Davis, judge-advocate, U.S. Army, as the military member, and Leslie J. Perry, of Kansas, and Joseph W. Kirkley, of Maryland, as the civilian expert members of said board. The board assumed direction of the publication at the commencement of the fiscal year 1889, its first work beginning with Serial No. 36, of Vol. XXIV. . . .

Nothing is printed in these volumes except duly authenticated contemporaneous records of the war. The scope of the board's work is to decide upon and arrange the matter to be published; to correct and verify the orthography of the papers used, and occasionally to add a foot-note of explanation.[5]

As historians Alan and Barbara Aimone note, while the *Official Records* are of "unquestioned value," users "must recognize their limitations." They encouraged users of the *Official Records* to realize that:

> For all their usefulness, no study should rely on them exclusively. The very fact that the *Rebellion Records* were not edited for accuracy, is, not only an important asset, but also a significant liability. The researcher must balance the data from the *Rebellion Records* with material from other reference books or manuscripts to confirm facts, figures, dates, spellings and other details. Other than errors inherent in reproducing reports without editing the documents, researchers need to be mindful of unintentional errors or oversights made by the compilers. In addition, the OR can be criticized for "obscuring much of the war's social reality," notably the role of blacks as both soldiers and workers.[6]

The Aimones identify several limitations of the OR. First, some OR dates are inaccurate. Second, it is far from complete. Approximately one-third of Civil War operations are not documented in its pages. This is certainly true in the case of Utah's records; see chapter 5 for many of those missing records. Third, casualty and other statistics can be misleading or inaccurate. Fourth, some OR documents may be out of context. Fifth, while the OR editorial staff "allowed no change in facts or content," their style guidelines did allow for "correction of grammar and rewording for readability," which may have introduced "subtle differences in meaning and feeling." And, perhaps most importantly, it is essential to recognize that contemporary records reflect the bias, hubris, and emotions present when they were written—representing only "the intelligence available to leaders at that moment."[7]

Despite these recognized limitations, the "value of the *Rebellion Records* to the student of the Civil War cannot be overestimated. They historically have been and continue to be, by far, the most complete, accessible, unbiased documentation of the War of the Rebellion." They are truly "a gold mine of information" that, in the case of Utah Territory, is "yet to be fully unearthed, sifted, analyzed and refined."[8]

Historian Yael A. Sternhell observed that "the OR has served virtually every scholar working on the [Civil War]. . . . In many ways, it is the basis for what we know about the Civil War."[9] It can truly be said that "no research in that era can be complete without using the *Official Records*."[10] This volume significantly increases the availability and accessibility of Utah's official Civil War records.

---

5. Davis et al., *Atlas to Accompany the Official Records of the Union and Confederate Armies*, preface.
6. Aimone and Aimone, *A User's Guide to the Official Records of the American Civil War*, 42.
7. Ibid., 40, 42–45.
8. Ibid., 39.
9. Sternhell, "The Afterlives of a Confederate Archive," 1026.
10. Aimone and Aimone, *A User's Guide to the Official Records of the American Civil War*, 40.

CHAPTER 3

Records Overview

THIS CHAPTER PROVIDES AN OVERVIEW AND EXPLANATION OF UTAH'S Civil War records, which are drawn from the *War of the Rebellion Official Records* (chapter 4) and Utah Territorial records (chapter 5). They provide a unique first-person perspective of the war. As such, they have all the advantages and disadvantages of news reporting. While they may provide an incomplete view of the time, place, or circumstances, the importance of these records cannot be overstated. See table 3.1 for a summary of the record count.

HOW THE *OFFICIAL RECORDS* ARE ORGANIZED

A staggering number of records were published in the *OR*, and the simple truth is that there was no completely satisfactory way for the editors to organize those records. Publication based on chronology would fragment the results geographically; geographic boundaries can be arbitrary and changing—plus, the collection would then be fragmented chronologically. The *OR* editors attempted to separate the volumes geographically or by campaigns. Records within an individual *OR* volume were generally arranged chronologically.

The 128 *OR* volumes are organized into four series. Each series has multiple volumes; series 1 is the largest. Several volumes have multiple parts, published as separate volumes. A few parts were large enough to be published separately, with each part identified as a section. The exception to this organization is series 3, volume 4, which was published in section volumes but was not subdivided into parts. Utah-related records are found in series 1 (Military Operations, which includes formal reports and military field operations), series 2 (Prisoners, which includes correspondence, orders, and reports for Union and Confederate prisoners of war and political prisoners), and series 3 (Union Authorities, which includes correspondence, orders, and reports, as well as annual and special reports). We discovered no Utah-related records in series 4 (Confederate Authorities).

Each record in this volume includes the *OR* source citation. For example, OR-1 was published on pages 1–6 of series 1, volume 50, part 1. The records in chapter 4 are drawn from thirty *OR* volumes representing 23.4 percent of the *Official Record* series.

TABLE 3.1. SUMMARY OF UTAH'S CIVIL WAR RECORDS

Chapter	*Records Description*	*Record Identifier*	*Record Count*
4	*War of the Rebellion Official Records* (direct Utah Territory references)	OR-#	504
5	Additional Utah Territory Civil War records	UT-#	155
		TOTAL	659

The majority of Utah-related records occur in four volumes from series 1—volume 48 (parts 1 and 2) and volume 50 (parts 1 and 2). See table 3.2, which shows the dispersal of the Utah records across the whole publication. War Department General Orders 118, dated June 27, 1865, appears five times in five separate series 1 volumes within the *OR*, but appears only once in this compilation. In two instances (series 1, volume 47, part 3; and series 1, volume 49, part 2), it is the only Utah-related record in that volume (see OR-447 for details).

TYPES OF RECORDS

With over six hundred individual records, it is not surprising that many kinds of documents are included. The most common record types are correspondence, orders, reports, post returns, and command lists.

Correspondence

Correspondence (the most common record format) includes letters, dispatches, telegrams, newspaper articles, and news reports. A typical correspondence record layout is:

Record Identifier

SENDER'S MILITARY UNIT,
Sender's Location, Date Sent.

RECIPIENT:
Text of correspondence.
Salutation or authentication line:

SENDER,
Sender's Rank and/or Position.

ORIGINAL SOURCE

See OR-10, for example.

TABLE 3.2. UTAH TERRITORY RECORDS IN THE *OFFICIAL RECORDS*

Volume	*Ch. 4*
Series 1, Volume 1	2
Series 1, Volume 3	4
Series 1, Volume 4	1
Series 1, Volume 5	2
Series 1, Volume 8	1
Series 1, Volume 13	8
Series 1, Volume 15	1
Series 1, Volume 22, Part 2	7
Series 1, Volume 26, Part 1	1
Series 1, Volume 26, Part 2	1
Series 1, Volume 34, Part 3	2
Series 1, Volume 41, Part 1	3
Series 1, Volume 41, Part 2	2
Series 1, Volume 41, Part 3	5
Series 1, Volume 41, Part 4	5
Series 1, Volume 46, Part 3, Section 2 (*OR-447*)	1
Series 1, Volume 47, Part 3 (*OR-447*)	*
Series 1, Volume 48, Part 1	37
Series 1, Volume 48, Part 2	69
Series 1, Volume 49, Part 2 (*OR-447*)	*
Series 1, Volume 50, Part 1	67
Series 1, Volume 50, Part 2	262
Series 1, Volume 51, Part 2	1
Series 1, Volume 53	2
Series 2, Volume 2, Section 2	3
Series 2, Volume 7, Section 1	1
Series 3, Volume 1	7
Series 3, Volume 2	2
Series 3, Volume 3	2
Series 3, Volume 5	5
RECORD TOTALS	504
NUMBER OF *OR* VOLUMES	30

* See OR-447 "Editor's note" for clarification.

While the intended recipient of correspondence was generally listed after the sender's identifying information and date, some correspondence placed the intended recipient's name and position left justified at the bottom of the correspondence. Whenever possible, notes and commentary in the *OR* providing explanation or cross-referencing other correspondence have been included (see OR-487 and OR-488, for example).

When reading nineteenth-century correspondence, it is helpful to understand three terms that were popularly used to avoid misunderstanding calendar references:

- "Ultimo" (often abbreviated "ult.") refers to the previous month. For example, when the opening sentence of Major Patrick A. Gallagher's December 2, 1862, report (OR-113) states "on the afternoon of the 21st ultimo," he was referring to November 21, 1862.
- "Instant" (often abbreviated "inst.") refers to the current month. On November 28, 1862, when Major Edward McGarry notified 2nd Lieutenant Thomas S. Harris (OR-111) that he "left this camp on the night of the 20th instant and proceeded to Cache Valley," inclusion of the word "instant" clarified that he meant earlier that month.
- "Proximo" (often abbreviated "prox.") refers to the following month. For example, General George Wright's reference to "the 15th proximo" in his April 29, 1862 message to Brigadier General Lorenzo Thomas (OR-55) refers to May 15, 1862.

During the Civil War, salutations varied widely and became an art form in themselves. Several varied salutations are found in the opening records in chapter 4, for example: "By order"; "I am, sir, very respectfully, your obedient servant"; "I remain, yours, very truly"; "Yours, most respectfully"; "believe me to be, Governor, very truly, your friend"; "I remain your obedient servant"; "I have the honor to be, with high regard, your obedient servant"; "I am, general, &c."; "All of which is respectfully submitted"; "Yours"; "In haste, very respectfully"; and "Trusting that you will lend ear to my solicitation, I remain, dear sir, with much respect, your very obedient servant."

Orders

Orders were categorized as General Orders, Special Orders, and Orders. Each order was issued by or in the name of the commanding officer at an appropriately authorized headquarters. Orders usually follow this format:

Record Identifier

ORDER ISSUING HEADQUARTERS
Headquarters Location, Date Order Was Issued.

TYPE OF ORDER (GENERAL, SPECIAL, OTHER),
ORDER NUMBER
Text of order. Orders vary in length.
Authority by which this order was issued:

NAME OF ISSUING OFFICER
Position of Issuing Officer

ORIGINAL SOURCE

See OR-349, OR-384, and UT-79, for example.

Reports

There are two kinds of reports: expedition reports and administrative reports. Expedition reports were submitted following expeditions, battles, attacks, and skirmishes. A typical expedition report consisted of an overview followed by subordinate reports and eyewitness accounts (see OR-28, for example). Administrative reports generally focused on personnel and logistics (see OR-11, for example). Reports used numerous formats. Many of the reports included are quite lengthy and have been edited to remove non-relevant content. (Omissions are identified with an ellipsis: ". . .") Expedition report cover documents often follow this format:

Record Identifier

STARTING AND ENDING REPORT DATES.—
Brief report explanation and location.

Author of the Report.

ORDER ISSUING HEADQUARTERS
Headquarters Location, Date Order Was Issued.

ISSUING HEADQUARTERS,
Location, Date Issued.

REPORT RECIPIENT,
Position and/or location of recipient.
Report cover correspondence.
Salutation,

REPORT'S AUTHOR,
Author's position

[Editor's note: *Explanatory text or information regarding how to find report inclosures.*]

ORIGINAL SOURCE

See OR-105, for an example.

Expedition reports often include inclosures. Some inclosures were written for that report; others were earlier correspondence attached to that report. Relevant subordinate documents have been separated from cover correspondence in order to preserve the original order of the records, and an editor's note has been included referencing inclosures to their original published source (see OR-106, OR-107, and OR-109, for examples).

Post Returns

The Utah records (chapter 5) contain a few excerpts from Post Returns—standardized monthly reports detailing duty and personnel information (see UT-2 and UT-80, which include a portion of the information submitted). Subordinate units forwarded completed reports to their higher headquarters—companies to regiments, etc. Post and camp reports were received and retained by the War Department in Washington, D.C. Post Returns were generally completed by unit clerks and signed by unit commanders.

In 1864 August Valentine Kautz, a colonel in the Sixth U.S. Cavalry and Second Ohio Volunteer Cavalry, published a how-to book entitled *The Company Clerk.* Regarding the Post Return, Kautz explained: "The company monthly return is made out on printed blanks furnished by the Adjutant-General's Department, and is forwarded on the first day of the month to regimental head-quarters. . . . Great care and uniformity should be observed in order that the return may be copied *verbatim* on the regimental return." The Notes and Record of Events sections of Post Returns (see UT-1, UT-2, and UT-4, for example) included "*Actions* in which the company, or any portion of it, has been engaged; *scouts, marches, changes of stations, &c.; every thing of interest* relating to the *discipline, efficiency,* or *service* of the company, will be *minutely* and carefully noted, with *date, place, distances marched, c, &c.*"[1] Chapter 5 includes such records.

Command Lists

The *OR* contains several command lists (OR-129, OR-223, OR-268, OR-307, OR-393, and OR-419)—organizational snapshots of officers who served in leadership assignments on a specified date. The *OR* command lists provide an incomplete picture of military assignments during the war. The lists have been edited, with ellipsis added,

1. Kautz, *The Company Clerk,* 35–36. Italics in original. U.S. Army Post Return reports are on record at the National Archives in Record Group 94, Microform 617.

to remove departments, districts, and military units with no Utah connection. Command lists provide snapshots of command assignments affecting Utah and generally follow this format:

Record Identifier

Command listed, commander, effective date of the list.

GEOGRAPHICAL AREA

Location of camp, post, or station
RANK AND NAME OF COMMANDER
Unit(s) commanded

ORIGINAL SOURCE

How This Volume Is Organized

This volume includes source information for each record. A few stylistic comments will be helpful:

- Original formatting has been preserved as far as possible. The practice of formatting *OR* text in small caps (for originating headquarters and correspondence recipients, for example) has been duplicated. Sender names are usually printed in capital letters. Recipient units, locations, and sender duty positions and units are usually printed in italics. It should be noted that formatting was not consistently applied across all of the *OR* volumes.
- Records are listed chronologically in chapters 4 and 5.
- Rather than switching between "enclosure" and "inclosure," this volume will use the nineteenth-century spelling "inclosure."
- It was common practice for all types of records to quote other records, including orders and letters, etc. When this occurs, the quoted material is indented and typeset in smaller text. See OR-89, for example.
- A line of asterisks (* * * *) is a nineteenth-century version of an ellipsis—showing where the original editors of the *OR* redacted text. Additional text omissions, specific to this volume, are noted by a left-justified ellipsis: ". . ." Records that have been edited for this volume are also marked with "[*Extract*]" immediately after the record identifier. See OR-115 and OR-127 for examples.
- In order to save space and avoid duplication of records, the *OR* editors usually opted to include inclosures and other attachments with the cover correspondence

that referenced them. While that practice ensured correspondence would be published in context, it resulted in attached records being published out of chronological order. Inclosures and other attachments have been separated and restored to their original chronological ordering. An editor's note in both the cover document and the attachment informs readers of the relationships between those documents; see, for example, OR-18 and OR-19.

- Many records contain footnotes and comments from the *OR* editors. Relevant original notes have been included. Original notes that appear in the *OR* volumes are in plain text and marked by "*", "†", "‡", or "**"—annotations used within the *OR* (see OR-52, for an example). Editor clarifications that are tied to specific words or text are also marked by "*", "†", "‡", or "**", but appear in bracketed italics (as in OR-50, for example). Additional italicized "Editor's notes" (such as the note found at the end of OR-6) have been added throughout chapters 4 and 5 to provide appropriate explanatory information.

Table B.1 (in appendix B) is a chronologically ordered monthly record count from chapters 4 and 5. It should be noted that record UT-73, Lot Smith to Brigham Young, is undated. Based on the contents, Smith apparently sent it to Young during the spring or summer he commanded the cavalry company that bore his name (May–August 1862). For placement in chapter 5 and tabulation purposes, it has been tentatively dated August 1862.

Chapter 4: Utah's Civil War Official Records

OR records in chapter 4 directly reference Utah Territory. Each record contains one or more instances of at least one of these keywords connected to Utah Territory:

- Utah [Utah Territory]
- Salt Lake [Great Salt Lake, Great Salt Lake City, Salt Lake City]
- Fort Crittenden [Camp Crittenden]
- Fort Bridger
- Camp Floyd
- Camp Douglas
- Mormon [Mormons, Mormonism]
- Brigham Young

Each record has been assigned a unique record identifier (OR-1 through OR-504). Every record lists the *OR* volume where that record was published. Chapter 4 includes records from thirty *OR* volumes. Surprisingly, only three records in this volume appear to have been created by Confederates or Confederate sympathizers:

1. OR-4, M. Jeff Thompson, Colonel, Inspector of the Fourth Military District, Missouri Volunteer Militia, to "His Excellency Jefferson Davis, President of the Confederate States," dated Camp C. F. Jackson, near Saint Joseph, Missouri, May 6, 1861.
2. OR-34, an inclosure using redacted language with a coded signature addressed to "R. M. C., Esq.," written from North Branch [Lapeer County, Michigan], dated October 5, 1861.
3. OR-45, J. E. B. Stuart, Brigadier General Commanding, Headquarters Outposts Army of the Potomac, to Major Thomas A. Pratt, Assistant Adjutant General, dated December 23, 1861.

Chapter 5: Additional Records from Utah Territory

Documents published in the *Official Records* are not the only Utah-related documents produced during the Civil War. Chapter 5 contains additional Utah Territory records, none of which appear in the *OR*. The Military Records Division of the National Archives holds numerous documents relating to Civil War events in Utah Territory. Many of those documents have been included.

Records in chapter 5 were selected because they are similar in tone or content to *OR* records. General themes include security on the Overland Trail, Utah's relationship to the rest of the nation, military affairs at Camp Douglas or within the Department or District of Utah, and Indian relations. These records were assembled from many sources, including:

- The National Archives (most frequently Records Group 94)
- Utah State Historical Archives
- Salt Lake City's *Deseret News* newspaper
- Camp Douglas's *Union Vedette* newspaper
- Reports for the Commissioner of Indian Affairs
- Edward W. Tullidge's *The History of Salt Lake City* (1886)
- Seymour B. Young's "Lest We Forget" serial in the 1921–1922 *Improvement Era*
- *The Collected Works of Abraham Lincoln*

There are additional National Archive and other records regarding Utah Territory during the Civil War that have not been included. Many of those records are redundant or similar to included records. Several June 1861 documents pertain to charges of disloyalty alleged against Colonel Philip St. George Cooke, commander, Department of Utah, by fellow officers in spring 1861 (Records Group 94, Microcopy 619, Roll 65, File Number U21). See UT-2, UT-3, and UT-5 through UT-10. They provide a representative sample of the additional records available.

The chapter 5 records have been published together for the first time, and there are a few stylistic differences from the other record chapter that should be noted:

- Each document has a bolded title and date line preceding it.
- Previously published records generally retain their original published formatting.
- A few small stylistic changes have been made to make them more consistent with the *OR* record formats. For example, sender names have been capitalized, originating headquarters and recipients are listed in small caps, and heading dates are italicized.

Many records are holograph (handwritten document) transcriptions. To ensure that the transcriptions are as accurate as possible, each document has been checked at least three times by separate reviewers. These guidelines have been followed:

- Original spelling has been retained.
- Original paragraphing and spacing has usually been retained. Original line breaks and hyphenation have been removed.
- Illegible words or letters are identified by "[*illegible*]" in the text (see UT-27, for example).
- Dates are transcribed as originally written. In the nineteenth century, a double quotation mark sometimes followed the day of a month—for example, 19" June 1861. Dates could also be written: month day/two-digit year, for example: "Aug. 5/61" (see UT-13).
- Double quotation marks were also sometimes used with cardinal numbers, for example, 2" instead of 2nd or 2d (see UT-5).
- A single horizontal strikethrough bar has been used to indicate text that was crossed out in the original. For example, "went out, ~~of the Union~~ he would resign" (see UT-6).
- Text inserted or written above a line has been reproduced with superscription. For example, "to show the ^{entire} truth" (as in UT-9).
- All text underlined in chapter 5 was underlined in the original documents. For example, "required—to hear both sides a very essential" (see UT-7).
- Abbreviations appear frequently throughout these documents. In instances where an abbreviation may be misunderstood, missing text has been added in brackets. For example, "A.Q.M." appears as "A[ssistant].Q[uarter].M[as ter]" in UT-13.

CHAPTER 4

Utah's Civil War Official Records

THIS CHAPTER CONTAINS DOCUMENTS FROM THE *OFFICIAL RECORDS* that include one or more of the following keywords associated with Utah Territory: Utah [Utah Territory], Salt Lake [Great Salt Lake, Great Salt Lake City, Salt Lake City], Fort Crittenden [Camp Crittenden], Fort Bridger, Camp Floyd, Camp Douglas, Mormon [Mormons, Mormonism], and/or Brigham Young. Records are listed chronologically. See chapter 3 for additional details.

OR-1

[*Extract*]

OPERATIONS ON THE PACIFIC COAST.*

JANUARY 1, 1861–JUNE 30, 1865.

PART I.

SUMMARY OF THE PRINCIPAL EVENTS.†

August 8–9, 1861.—Attack on emigrant train, near the Great Salt Lake, Utah Ter.

August 6, 1862.—Col. P. Edward Connor, Third California Infantry, assumes command of the District of Utah.

September 30–Oct. 29, 1862.—Expedition from Fort Ruby, Nev. Ter., to Camp Douglas, Utah Ter., with affairs (Oct. 11 and 15) on the Humboldt River, Nev. Ter.

November 20–27, 1862.—Expedition from Camp Douglas to the Cache Valley, Utah Ter., with skirmish (23d) in Cache Valley.

January 29, 1863.—Engagement on the Bear River, Utah Ter.

March 26–Apr. 3, 1863.—Expedition from Camp Douglas to the Cedar Mountains, Utah Ter., with skirmish (April 1) at Cedar Fort.

April 2–6, 1863.—Expedition from Camp Douglas to the Spanish Fork, Utah Ter., with action (4th) at the Spanish Fork Cañon.

April 11–20, 1863.—Expedition from Camp Douglas to the Spanish Fork Cañon, Utah Ter., with skirmish (12th) at Pleasant Grove, and action (15th) at Spanish Fork Cañon.

May 5–30, 1863.—Expedition from Camp Douglas, Utah Ter., to Soda Springs, on the Bear River, Idaho Ter.

June 20, 1863.—Skirmish near Government Springs, Utah Ter.

August 20, 1863.—The District of Utah declared to include the Territory of Utah, Camp Ruby, Nev. Ter., and the new post at Soda Springs, Idaho Ter.

May 9–June 22, 1864.—Expedition from Fort Crittenden, Utah Ter., to Fort Mojave, Ariz. Ter.

February 17, 1865.—The Territory of Utah and that part of Nebraska Territory lying west of the twenty-seventh degree of longitude added to the Department of the Missouri.

* The operations reported in this volume were carried on in that portion of the territory of the United States lying west of the Rocky Mountains, including so much of the Territory of Utah as lay west of the one hundred and seventeenth meridian of west longitude and so much of the Territory of New Mexico as lay west of the one hundred and tenth meridian of west longitude. This area composed the Departments of California and Oregon. The Department of California was created by General Orders, No. 10, War Department, Adjutant-General's Office, of September 13, 1858, and included the territory west of the Rocky Mountains south of Oregon, except so much of Utah as lay east of the one hundred and seventeenth meridian of west longitude, and of New Mexico as lay east of the one hundred and tenth meridian of west longitude. . . .

† Of some of the minor conflicts noted in this summary no circumstantial reports are on file.

SOURCE: *OR*, SERIES 1, VOLUME 50, PART 1, PAGES 1–6

OR-2

[*Extract*]

Statement showing the distribution of the U.S. Army on the 1st day of January, 1861, with the changes between that date and the 15th of April, 1861.

[Compiled from the records of the Adjutant-General's Office.]

Department of the West

(Embracing the country west of the Mississippi River and east of the Rocky Mountains except the state of Texas and the Territory of Utah, and all of the New Mexico east of the one hundred and tenth degree of west longitude.)

. . .

DEPARTMENT OF CALIFORNIA.

(Comprising the country west of the Rocky Mountains south of Oregon and Washington Territory, excepting so much of Utah as lies east of the one hundred and seventeenth degree of west longitude and of New Mexico east of the one hundred and tenth degree of west longitude.)

. . .

Fort Churchill, Utah	A, 1st Dragoons	No change
	A and H, 6th Infantry	Do.*

Department of Utah

(Embracing so much of the Territory of Utah as lies east of the one hundred and seventeenth degree of west longitude.)

Camp Floyd **	B, E, and H, 2d Dragoons	No change
	A, B, and C, 4th Artillery	Do.
Fort Bridger	E and I, 10th Infantry	Do.
	B and G, 10th Infantry	Do.

* [Editor's note: *"Do." was an abbreviation for "ditto."*]
** Name changed to Fort Crittenden, February 6, 1861.

SOURCE: *OR*, SERIES 3, VOLUME 1, PAGES 23–26

OR-3

[*Extract*]

ALBANY, *May 1, 1861*

Hon. SIMON CAMERON,
Secretary of War:

DEAR SIR: I wish to call your attention to certain matters connected with the affairs of the State of Missouri, and particularly as regards the arsenal at Saint Louis.

1st. There seems but very little doubt at the present time, particularly in Illinois, as regards the secession of the State of Missouri from the Union. The secession movement in Northern Missouri and along the line of the Hannibal and Saint Joseph Railroad is scarcely stronger in any Southern State.

2d. Judging from what has been done elsewhere by the various seceding States, one of the first acts of secession by Missouri would be the seizure of the Hannibal and Saint Joseph Railroad, the interruption, if not the entire suppression, of Government and free State transportation and travel over it, and, if the contest continues, in the entire confiscation of the road and its property, as far as concerns Northern and Eastern interests.

3d. I also think that it is of vital importance to the Government that the Hannibal and Saint Joseph Railroad be preserved to its owners, and that its free and uninterrupted use be maintained at all times and at all hazards. It furnishes the only accessible and speedy route by which the Government can communicate with Kansas, Nebraska, and Utah, or with its military posts along the Western and Northwestern frontier to the foot of the Rocky Mountains, and, if allowed to fall into and remain in the hands of an enemy, it is easy to see how difficult and well-nigh impossible in such an emergency it would be for the Government to preserve its Western Territories and military posts, for the danger to which they would be exposed would indeed be serious, and they could only be supported at immense expense and loss both of time and of means.

4th. Quincy, in Illinois, which from the course of the Mississippi River projects into the Missouri at a distance of sixty-five miles west of Saint Louis, presents immense advantages as a military post, and as such should be occupied by the Government. By merely looking at the map you can see what an important position is Quincy. It is the key to Northern Missouri, Kansas, Utah, Nebraska, California, and Oregon. Missouri once against the Federal Government, the only present feasible and expeditious road by which troops, munitions, provisions, transportation, and general travel can pass is the Hannibal and Saint Joseph Railroad, over Northern Missouri, between those Western sections and the country east of the Mississippi River. The forces to be placed at Quincy should be placed there at once, to keep open the communication by way of the Hannibal and Saint Joseph Railroad.

. . .

I remain, yours, very truly,

ERASTUS CORNING

Source: *OR*, Series 1, Volume 1, pages 677–678

OR-4

Hdqrs. Fourth Mil. Dist., Missouri Vol. Militia,
Camp C. F. Jackson, near Saint Joseph, Mo.,
Monday, May 6, 1861

His Excellency Jefferson Davis,
President of the Confederate States, Montgomery, Ala.:

Sir: Your favor of the 25th ultimo has been received, and I am thankful for your courtesy. I hope, and have reasonable expectations now, that Missouri will soon wheel into line with her Southern sisters, in which case I and my men will be needed here at home. I believe that this portion of Missouri (north of the Missouri River) will be the principal battle-ground between the North and the South, as Saint Joseph, with its railroad connections, is the key to Kansas, New Mexico, Jefferson, [?] and Utah, and we have already been notified that the North has determined to hold this portion of the State, even though they lose all the rest of the slaveholding States, and they will either cover it over with dollars or blood, and the choice is for us to make. I have eight companies here in a camp of instruction, by order of our governor, and can assure you that they are all Blue Cockade boys, and if our leaders are disposed to sell this territory for money, our blood will remain at your service.

Yours, most respectfully,

M. JEFF. THOMPSON,
Colonel, Inspector of Fourth Military District

Source: *OR*, Series 1, Volume 1, page 690

OR-5

HEADQUARTERS OF THE ARMY,
Washington, D.C., May 17, 1861.

SPECIAL ORDERS,
No. 86½.

I. As soon as practicable after receiving this order the commanding officer of the Department of Utah will march to Fort Leavenworth with the ten companies under his command. Such public property as the means of transportation will not permit to be moved will be disposed of to the best possible advantage to the Government.

II. The Fifth and Seventh Regiments of Infantry and two companies of the Tenth Infantry, now in New Mexico, and two companies of the Tenth Infantry at Fort Wise will be put in march for Fort Leavenworth, via Forts Wise and Larned, with as little delay as practicable. Brevet Lieutenant-Colonel Canby will accompany the battalion of the Tenth Infantry. Colonel Loring will station the regiment of riflemen and four companies of dragoons, constituting the regular force to remain in the Department of New Mexico, at such points as in his judgment will best protect the interests of the United States. He will also assign to stations any volunteers who may be mustered into service and reported to him, under orders to be given by the War Department.

* * * *

By command of Lieutenant-General Scott:

E. D. TOWNSEND,
Assistant Adjutant-General.

SOURCE: *OR*, SERIES 1, VOLUME 53, PAGES 492–493

OR-6

[*Extract*]

BEAR RIVER CROSSING, *May 30, 1861.*

His Excellency Governor GILPIN,
Colorado Territory:

DEAR GOVERNOR: Knowing the deep interest you take in the welfare and advancement of this country, I wish to call your attention to the necessity which exists for keeping open the overland communication with California. From what I see and hear I am satisfied that this cannot be done if the military force is removed from the country. The present force is not adequate for all the necessities of the service, and if removed will lead to great disorders and losses on the part of the Government, as well as individuals. I am sorry to say that many of our men are deserting, and some of the officers are resigning, which gives an appearance of disaffection to the whole mass; but such is not the case, and they only need encouragement from the Government by being supplied with recruits and an assurance of support to meet every emergency that may arise.

. . .

Rest assured I shall do all in my power to advance the public interest, and I shall be glad to aid you at any time you may think I can do so.

Excuse this hasty note, and believe me to be, Governor, very truly, your friend,

A. PLEASONTON.

P. S.—I shall be glad to hear from you. My address will be Fort Crittenden, Utah.

A. P.

[Editor's note: *This document appears in the* Official Records *as an inclosure to correspondence from William Gilpin to the Hon. Simon Cameron, Secretary of War, June 6, 1861, 9:00 A.M. that is not included in this volume.*]

SOURCE: *OR*, SERIES 3, VOLUME 1, PAGES 257–258

OR-7

SAN BERNARDINO, *June 3, 1861.*

General E. V. SUMNER, U.S. Army,
Commander of the Pacific Division:

DEAR SIR: I beg to be excused for my presumption in addressing a letter to you when I am an utter stranger, yet feeling it to be my duty which I owe to my country, and believing that a fair, candid statement concerning the true position of all parties in this lower portion of the State may be useful to you, I thus lay them before you. There exists amongst us through all these southern counties a secret organization of secessionists, and in a settlement near Los Angeles there is an organized cavalry company which is ready at almost any moment to break out, holding an inveterate hatred toward the citizens of this place, and it is at this point they would make their first attack, and there are some in our midst who would receive them cheerfully and help them in their treacherous designs. I speak what I do know. I have only been here about seven weeks, and commenced the publication of a paper called the Weekly Patriot. I have received notice to stop the publication of strong Union sentiments, as it will be unsafe for me to continue them any longer, but I am not to [be] frightened at any intimidations or threats. I shall continue on in the way I have commenced, and keep a sharp lookout for any disturbance which may break out. We are, and have been, expecting a rising of the secessionists, notwithstanding the late Union demonstration at Los Angeles, and nothing but the presence of the U.S. troops prevents them from rising there. Secret meetings continue to be held all over this lower country, and secession and disunion is boldly avowed in our streets. Shooting continues to be the order of the day, and drunken desperadoes and Southern cutthroats damn the Stars and Stripes and endeavor to create disturbances all of the time. We have a singular population, composed of Mormons, Mormon apostates, who are even worse, gamblers, English Jews, and the devil's own population to boot, while we only have about a dozen good respectable families right in town, who are at the mercy of these desperadoes; and the secessionists of the Monte are only waiting the withdrawal of the troops from Los Angeles before they commence operations. If a company of dragoons could be stationed here it would give a feeling of security to every honest citizen and friend of the Union in this vicinity. Provisions are cheaper here than in any other part of the country, and it is the key to all the passes leading to Arizona and Salt Lake, and if a rebellion should arise the troops stationed here would form a nucleus around which every patriot can rally. For information as to who I am and my character I would refer you to Hon. N. Greene Curtis, grand master of the Grand Lodge of Masons, J. L. English, Hon. John G. Downey, Governor of this State, and of every prominent man in Sacramento, of which county I was formerly surveyor, and for myself I can inform you that I am a near relative of Major Sherman, of the flying artillery, U.S. Army, and I have seen service through the whole of the Mexican campaign.

With this information, hoping to receive an immediate reply, I remain your obedient servant,

EDWIN A. SHERMAN,
Editor of the Weekly Patriot.

P. S.—I will inform you from time to time whatever news I am able to gather, so that they may be of service to you.

Yours, truly,

E. A. S.

SOURCE: *OR*, SERIES 1, VOLUME 50, PART 1, PAGES 496–497

OR-8

Fort Walla Walla, Wash. Ter., *June 14, 1861.*

Col. L. Thomas,

Assistant Adjutant-General, Washington, D.C.:

Sir: I would beg leave very respectfully to submit for the consideration of the Honorable Secretary of War a few facts in relation to this Fort Benton wagon road and its influence upon military operations in this portion of the country. We have this summer, in addition to the disturbed state of the country at home, which has withdrawn a portion of the troops from Oregon, a mining excitement which is pouring all the restless and loose portion of the community into the Nez Percé country, and upon the very land which was promised them as their own exclusive soil, to be exempt from all encroachments of the whites. The Indians are naturally dissatisfied, and to keep peace troops will be needed in their very midst. This takes one company of dragoons from this post, who are now on the reservation, and there should be another out. There is a prospect also of a large emigration this summer via Fort Hall, and unless troops be on the road from this post to keep it clear of the Snakes there will be a repetition of last year's massacre at Salmon Falls, an occurrence too horrible almost to contemplate. It is also advisable to keep our posts sufficiently garrisoned for the protection of the public property. To meet all these requirements, with the drain upon us by Lieutenant Mullan's expedition for men and supplies, is too much. His escort of 100 men requires transportation and employés to be paid for out of the quartermaster's appropriation for this post to the amount of more than $100,000 a year, thereby embarrassing the regular and legitimate operations of the post—and to what purpose? His road has already cost $300,000, and now he can't travel the portion between this and the Bitter Root Mountains, a distance of 200 or 300 miles, but he is making a new road farther to the north, and when that is completed it will only be practicable a very few months in each year on account of the water, which renders the country a perfect lake. The road will never be a suitable emigrant or military road compared with the other, for the reasons which I have already given in my report to the Quartermaster-General, dated January 8, 1861. The distance from the usual starting point in the States, as can easily be seen by referring to the map, is 400 miles greater by this route, if he ever completes it, compared with the old road, and not half so good a road, and the danger will be more than double in the Sioux and Blackfoot country. These are plain facts. Now, if the object be to expend so large an amount of money for the benefit of this portion of the country, it can still be done, and some real benefit also derived by those who are nominally the objects of the enterprise by expending it on the old road in the manner recommended by me in my report referred to above. Mullan's escort and the $50,000 appropriated for this summer's emigration, if applied toward building a ferry or bridge at Fort Hall, to be protected by the Utah troops, and a ferry at Boisé under protection of this post, would be all that is necessary to make a splendid road from the Rocky Mountains to this country. Emigrants and troops could then reach this valley in three or four months from the States, and their animals not much the worse for the journey. They could cross Snake River at Fort Hall and travel on the north side of Boisé through plenty of grass, water, and all that is necessary for a good road. Mr. Craigie, an intelligent and trusty man, for many years in charge of the Hudson Bay Fort at Boisé, would be a very suitable person to take charge of the ferry at Boisé. He has a Snake wife and speaks the language perfectly, and if he were allowed a certain amount of beef cattle and provisions to give away occasionally to such Indians as come about him, it must have a very beneficial effect on reconciling them to the whites. Lieutenant Mullan's road can never be of any real benefit to any one, on account of the enormous expense in traveling up the Missouri by steam-boat, or the enormous distance and time required compared with the other, if they come by land all the way. The road by South Pass is the most direct, and the one cut out by nature for coming to this country, and you can never regard this Fort Benton scheme as anything else than a grand political humbug, and it is time it was stopped. I therefore most respectfully and earnestly suggest that the expedition be broken up before any more money is wasted on it. The troops will return to their legitimate duties and where their services are really needed, and Lieutenant Mullan ordered to his company.

I am, sir, very respectfully, your obedient servant,

E. STEEN,
Major, First Dragoons, Commanding.

SOURCE: *OR*, SERIES 1, VOLUME 50, PART 1, PAGES 515–517

OR-9

EXECUTIVE OFFICE,
Omaha, Nebr. Ter., June 24, 1861.

Hon. SIMON CAMERON,
Secretary of War:

SIR: I desire to call the attention of your Department to a few facts disclosed by a letter just received at our executive office from one of the most respected and reliable citizens of this Territory. I make the following quotations from the letter:

> Our Wisconsin friends opposite this portion of the Territory are quite excited and very anxious that the Nebraska regiment may be stationed in the southern part of the Territory near the Missouri border. In Holt and Andrew Counties, Mo., Union men are badly treated, and while they may be in the majority, having no arms they are overawed to a great extent.
>
> I have just learned this morning that "something is up" among the Otoe Indians. The Choctaws have been up among the Kaws, Sacs and Foxes, Otoes and Pawnees, and delegations have gone from all to the Choctaw Nation to hold a conference about something. The Otoes are sullen, and not at all disposed to be communicative. However, I think if the General Government can in any way hasten the back payments due to them we can manage the Otoes. I have believed for months past that we shall have difficulty with the Indians, and time only confirms me in that opinion.

I desire to state, in addition to the above, that in one county at least in the extreme southern part of this Territory there is believed to be an actual majority of secessionists.

I am also reliably informed that the Mormon emigrants, who are now crossing the Missouri River in great numbers at a point six miles above this city en route to Salt Lake, sympathize warmly with the secessionists. This emigration is much larger this year than usual, and comes mainly from England. I am satisfied, from what I have myself seen and heard, that, as a class, these people have little or no respect for our Government and institutions. They exercise a great influence over the Indian tribes located in this and the adjoining Territories, many of whom are at the present time dissatisfied with the Government. If they were disposed to make common cause with the secessionists in our own Territory and Missouri, the Indians also becoming their allies, they could easily exterminate the whole loyal population between the Missouri River and the Rocky Mountains before relief could be obtained from the Government.

In view of these facts, I would respectfully request that one or two regiments of troops, in addition to our own, now nearly full, may be so disposed in this Territory as to prevent the secessionists in Missouri and Southern Nebraska and the Mormons and Indians on our western borders from uniting for our destruction.

We have been obliged to put forth every energy to raise the regiment called from our Territory by the President; it will be a serious drain upon our sparse and limited population to furnish it. However, I am confident that it will be ready for service in ten days.

In addition to this regiment called into the three-years' service, the citizens of every settled precinct are organizing companies for home protection. In this connection I beg leave to state that the quotas of arms heretofore received by this Territory have been most shamefully squandered; so much so, in fact, that at the present time we have not a single stand of arms wherewith to arm our volunteer companies. We should have immediately 1,000 stand of arms to distribute among the companies already organized for home protection. This year's quota has not yet been received. Can it not be sent forward immediately? Will you advise me when and how I can draw for them?

I have the honor to be, sir, very respectfully, your obedient servant,

A. S. PADDOCK,
Secretary and Acting Governor.

SOURCE: *OR*, SERIES 3, VOLUME 1, PAGE 294

OR-10

ADJUTANT-GENERAL'S OFFICE,
Washington, June 27, 1861.

COMMANDING OFFICER U.S. ARMY IN UTAH TERRITORY:

Any subsistence stores in your department which have not already been disposed of you will keep for the use of troops that will be moved into Utah from California.

By order:

L. THOMAS,
Adjutant-General.

SOURCE: *OR*, SERIES 1, VOLUME 50, PART 1, PAGE 523

OR-II

[*Extract*]

Consolidated abstract from returns of the U.S. Army on or about June 30, 1861.

Command	Present for duty. Officers.	Present for duty. Men.	Aggregate present.	present and absent	Date of Return
Department of Annapolis (Banks).....................	......	......	......	......	No Returns.
Department of the East (Wool)........................	16	394	457	510	June 30, 1861.
Department of Florida (Brown).......................	65	1,594	1,939	2,088	June 30, 1861.
Department of Kentucky (Anderson).................	......	......	......	......	No Returns.
Department of New Mexico (Canby).................	54	1,464	1,941	2,466	June 30, 1861.
Department of Northeastern Virginia (McDowell)..	764	13,666	15,368	16,611	June 26, 1861.
Department of the Ohio* (McClellan)................	1,409	21,884	37,767	54,313	June 2, 1861.
Department of the Pacific (Sumner)..................	114	2,064	2,805	3,361	June 30, 1861.
Department of Pennsylvania (Patterson).............	747	15,865	16,694	17,188	June 30, 1861.
Department of Utah (Cooke)...........................	17	445	561	604	June 30, 1861.
Department of Virginia (Butler).......................	397	7,794	9,485	9,929	June 30, 1861.
Department of Washington (Mansfield).............	1,693	36,608	41,160	43,363	June 30, 1861.
Department of the West (Lyon).......................	58	1,328	1,717	1,921	June 26, 1861.
Total †..............	5,334	103,106	129,894	152,354	

War Department,
Washington, July 1, 1861.

The President of the United States:

Sir: I have the honor to submit the following report of the operations of this Department:

. . .

I cannot forbear to speak favorably of the volunteer system as a substitute for a cumbrous and dangerous standing army. It has heretofore by many been deemed unreliable and inefficient in a sudden emergency, but actual facts have proved the contrary. If it be urged that the enemies of order have gained some slight advantages at remote points by reason of the absence of a sufficient regular force, the unexampled rapidity of concentration of volunteers already witnessed is an ample refutation of the argument. A Government whose every citizen stands ready to march to its defense can never be overthrown, for none is so strong as that whose foundations rest immovably in the hearts of the people. The spectacle of more than a quarter of a million of citizens rushing to the field in defense of the Constitution must ever take rank among the most extraordinary facts of history. Its interest is vastly heightened by the lavish outpouring of States and individuals of voluntary contributions of money, reaching an aggregate thus far of more than ten millions of dollars.

But a few weeks since the men composing this great army were pursuing the avocations of peace. They gathered from the farm, from the workshop, from the factory, from the mine. The minister came from his pulpit, the merchant from his counting room, the professor and student from the college, the teacher and pupil from the common schools. Young men of fortune left luxurious homes for the tent and the camp. Native and foreign born alike came forward with a kindred enthusiasm. That a well-disciplined, homogeneous, and efficient force should be formed out of such a seemingly heterogeneous mass appears almost incredible. But what is the actual fact? Experienced men, who have had ample opportunity to familiarize themselves with the condition of European armies, concede that in point of personnel this patriot army is fully equal to the finest regular troops of the Old World. A more intelligent body of men, or one actuated by purer motives, was never before marshaled in the field.

The calling forth of this large and admirable force in vindication of the Constitution and the laws is in strict accordance with a wise prudence and economy, and at the same time in perfect harmony with the uniform practice of the Government. But three years ago, when the authority of the nation was contemptuously defied by the Mormons in Utah, the only safe policy consistent with the dignity of the Government was the prompt employment of such an overwhelming force for the suppression of the rebellion as removed all possibility of failure. It will hardly be credited, however, that the following language in relation to that period was penned by John B. Floyd, then Secretary of War, and now leading the rebel forces, who have even less to justify their action than the Mormons:

> When a small force was first sent to Utah, the Mormons attacked and destroyed their trains and made ready for a general attack upon the column. When a sufficient power was put on foot to put success beyond all doubt their bluster and bravado sank into whispers of terror and submission. This movement upon that Territory was demanded by the moral sentiment of the country, was due to a vindication of its laws and Constitution, and was essential to demonstrate the power of the Federal Government to chastise insubordination and quell rebellion, however formidable from numbers or position it might seem to be. Adequate preparations and a prompt advance of the Army was an act of mercy and humanity to those deluded people, for it prevented the effusion of blood.

I recommend the same vigorous and merciful policy now.

. . .

I have the honor to be, with high regard, your obedient servant,

SIMON CAMERON,
Secretary of War.

* Only a partial return on file.

† The consolidated abstracts published at intervals of six months in Series III and IV do not represent the full strength of either the Union or Confederate forces. Such classes as unattached officers and men, recruits in rendezvous, and organizations in process of formation are omitted. Only the numbers shown by army and department returns are given.

SOURCE: *OR*, SERIES 3, VOLUME 1, PAGES 301–310

OR-12

ADJUTANT-GENERAL'S OFFICE,
Washington, July 16, 1861.

Lieut. Gen. WINFIELD SCOTT,
Commanding the Army:

GENERAL: In consequence of the order removing the troops from the Oregon route, urgent applications have been made to the War Department to have a sufficient force stationed thereon to protect the overland mail. To aid in effecting this purpose, the Secretary of War desires, if it meet your approbation, that the paroled companies now stationed in New York Harbor be directed to take post in Utah.

I am, general, &c.,

L. THOMAS,
Adjutant-General.

SOURCE: *OR*, SERIES 1, VOLUME 50, PART 1, PAGE 537

OR-13

ADJUTANT-GENERAL'S OFFICE,
Washington, July 24, 1861.

Brigadier-General SUMNER,
Headquarters Department of the Pacific, San Francisco, Cal.:

One regiment of infantry and five companies of cavalry have been accepted from California to aid in protecting Overland Mail Route via Salt Lake. Please detail officers to muster these troops into service. Blanks will be sent by steamer.

By order:

L. THOMAS,
Adjutant-General.

SOURCE: *OR*, SERIES 1, VOLUME 50, PART 1, PAGE 543

OR-14

WAR DEPARTMENT, *July 24, 1861.*

GOVERNOR OF CALIFORNIA:

The War Department accepts for three years one regiment of infantry and five companies cavalry to guard the Overland Mail Route from Carson Valley to Salt Lake and Fort Lawrence. Colonel Waite will be put in command of department at Salt Lake City. General Sumner will detail mustering officer to muster in the men.

SIMON CAMERON,
Secretary of War.

SOURCE: *OR*, SERIES 1, VOLUME 50, PART 1, PAGE 543

OR-15

CONFIDENTIAL.
HEADQUARTERS CAMP FITZGERALD,
Near Los Angeles, Cal., July 31, 1861.

Maj. D. C. BUELL, U.S. Army,
Assistant Adjutant-General, San Francisco, Cal.:

MAJOR: I have the honor to acknowledge the receipt of your communication of the 18th instant. It seemed to have been delayed upon the road. I left for San Bernardino on the 24th, and returned thence this morning. I beg respectfully to report that I took many and various measures to learn the political sentiments of the people in that region, and also their sympathies with reference to this party or that, North and South. The population of San Bernardino is about 1,500 souls; 1,000 of these are Mormons. The rest may be made up of some few respectable Americans, of a good many Jew merchants, who control the business of the town, and go with any side that pays best for the time being; and then there follow adroit horse thieves and other unprincipled and desperate men, gathered into that point, as well from other parts of California as from Utah. There is a large sprinkling of this latter class. You can judge of a man whose character is such he could not be tolerated in Utah. Now, the Mormons, whatever their professions, hate us at heart. I append a paper in relation to this people which the general may regard as made up from reliable information. The Jews, as a rule, have no love for us. The outlaws hate, because they fear us. To these latter any change would be congenial which by hook or crook could be made profitable. All but the few respectable Americans would set us at defiance to-morrow if they dared to do so. The Americans seem to be the only ones there who really have principle enough to feel anything like patriotism. I believe the presence there of two or more companies of U.S. troops would encourage and sustain in their loyalty to the Union all those who yet have reverence for it, would bring back the wavering, and would exercise a wholesome restraint over the treasonable and vicious. A commander there would have to contend against Mormon influences. The county judge is a Mormon, the sheriff is a Mormon, the justice of the peace is a Mormon. In all ordinary trials the most of the jurymen would be Mormons. You can foresee that the administration of civil law by these officers would continue to be, as it doubtless is now, a farce. Following this idea you can figure at times difficulties between the men of a command and the citizens, and you can figure the results. If some plan could be devised by which these civil officers could be got to perform their duties in good faith, or resign and give place to others who would, or some plan by which the military could exercise more than a negative control, all that section of country might be counted on as for the Union, whatever betide our fortunes in this battle or that, and presupposing that no sane man doubts how the scales will finally preponderate. There is a place called Agua Mansa, six or seven miles from San Bernardino, it is settled mostly by Spanish people from New Mexico. It contains 600 souls. In the mines (in Holcomb and Bear Valleys), eight hours' ride from San Bernardino, there are 1,000 men. Of these 200 are said to be in favor of secession. The troops to be stationed at San Bernardino would doubtless exert a wholesome influence over all these. There is another thought in connection with this matter. Should it so happen that troops may be required to oppose enemies coming overland into California by the way of Arizona, those then stationed at San Bernardino would be already three marches from this point (the terminus of the telegraph) in that direction. Should they at any time be required to help fortify and to defend the harbor of San Diego (the most important on this coast after that of San Francisco, as the general well knows), they could in one day be set en route by telegraph and a dragoon express from here. Barley can be bought there at a cent a pound; beef for 5 cents, while all kinds of vegetables, fruit, poultry, &c., are cheap and abundant. The general did not wish persons to suspect the real purpose of my visit. I inclose the copy of a letter written by his Excellency Governor Downey to Mr. Sherman, at San Bernardino.* It arrived in that place before I did. Mr. Sherman may have had more reticence than most political men, for as a rule "to do good by stealth and blush to find it fame" is not their motto. What they do for the people they want the people to know, particularly when they seek the people's suffrage. I mention this to show how these matters go. I inclose a communication from Mr. Sherman in relation to the feeling of the people in that quarter.

All of which is respectfully submitted.

JAMES H. CARLETON,
Brevet Major, U.S. Army, Commanding.

[Inclosure No. 1.]

THE MORMONS AS A PEOPLE.

Nearly all Mormons are foreigners. Among these are Welsh, English, Norwegians, Swedes, some Germans, and a few French, They are evidently of the lowest and most ignorant grade of the people in the several countries from whence they have come. Mixed in with these are a few low, unprincipled Americans. The most intelligent and crafty of these, commencing with Brigham Young, are the directors and rulers of the whole mass. By a misapplication of the word, for amongst them nothing is sacred, their government is solely a hierarchy, and notwithstanding, in theory, they are assumed to be a population obedient to the laws of our common country, practically they scorn and deride, and set at defiance all laws that interfere with their safety or interest, save those promulgated by the grand council of the church. This council is composed of the twelve, Brigham Young being at present the great hierophant and president of that body. This council not only fixes and determines upon all important matters pertaining to the church, and the ecclesiastical measures growing out of them, but through bishops and elders, and minor councils, called councils of seventy, and through presidents of stakes (precincts), control even the temporal and domestic affairs of every family down to the last individual. When a person becomes a Mormon he has to be initiated by what are called degrees. While proceeding step by step through these the novice is obliged to take several terrible oaths. In these he swears to uphold the faith, and to yield perfect and unqualified obedience to the orders of the council and to the orders of those appointed over him. He swears, also, never to divulge the secret pass-words and grips and signs made known to him during this initiation. This ceremony is called the endowment. No man is a true and complete Mormon who has not been endowed, and every Mormon who has been thus endowed can, either by words, grips, or signs, recognize every other Mormon. Now these being the obligations under which these ignorant, deluded foreigners are bound, the most of them men who know nothing of our Government or its laws, it is easy to imagine what a sway, what a complete and absolute control the council and the prophet have over the minds and persons and possessions of every subordinate member of the church, both at home and abroad. There are not only the oaths to bind the conscience, but there is a real power, a hand raised to strike from existence those who show the least sign of disobedience or of recusancy. That hand is secret and invisible; it strikes at an unexpected moment, but it strikes none the less a mortal blow. It is the hand of the Danites or destroying angels. These Mormons, then, being mostly from foreign lands, with no knowledge of our Government or laws, no affection for or sympathy with our people, no reverence for our institutions, no love for our country, they follow blindly, ignorantly, but implicitly, the orders of council and of their prophet, impelled by their oaths and their faith on the one hand, and forced onward by their fears upon the other. They are taught, even from the pulpits, to abhor and contemn us as the slayers of the founder of their religion, as the persecutors of their people when the church was in its infancy. So their hands, like those of Ishmael against all other men, are always and instinctively raised against us. These are truths which not even the Mormons themselves deny. Now send the civil officers of the Government amongst them, and make even an attempt to administer the laws according to the forms of procedure established throughout the rest of the land, and they laugh at you to your face. Suppose a crime—say a murder—has been committed by a Mormon upon a Gentile. Who compose the jury to find the indictment? The brethren. Who are generally the witnesses before that jury? The brethren. Who are the officers and jailers who have custody of the prisoner before and after the trial? The brethren. Who are the members of the jury before whom the trial takes place? Still the brethren.

Who are the witnesses for the prosecution, and, more particularly, who are those for the defense? The brethren. Suppose the criminal should, after all this, be convicted and sentenced, there is still a pardoning power. Thus running a gauntlet all the way between the brethren (if they do not want him out of the way), what are not his chances for his life? Even though you have twenty armies there, has he any the less chances? It is preached from the pulpits that God sent the troops there as a blessing to the Saints. The troops scatter money broadcast throughout the land. All this in relation to Utah, but applicable to these Mormons. Such being the rulers, such the masses, such the oaths and obligations, and such the sentiments with which they regard our Government and people, what can you expect if the wholesome operation of our laws interferes with the absolute sway of the leaders, or with the interests or purposes or safety of the church, or with the liberty or life of a single member of the fraternity? What but the malignant hatred which battled villainy must feel while it is yet impotent to strike? What but crime, when assassin-like it can strike unseen? What but open sedition and treason among the whole people wherever it has gained strength?

JAMES H. CARLETON,
Brevet Major, U.S. Army.

* [Memorandum on back of letter in pencil:] Governor Downey's letter was not with the papers handed to Major Ketchum by General Sumner.

[Editor's note: *Inclosure No. 2 was removed for lack of relevance.*]

SOURCE: *OR*, SERIES 1, VOLUME 50, PART 1, PAGES 548–551

OR-16

SAN BERNARDINO, *August 5, 1861.*

Major CARLETON,
Commandant of U.S. Forces at Los Angeles:

SIR: For some time past I have desired to communicate to you certain facts respecting the secession sympathizers of this county important for you to know, but being a candidate for the office of senator, and busily engaged in traveling about the county, I have not had the time so to do. From certain events now known to me I feel it doubly my duty as a lover of the old flag and Constitution, and the peace and harmony of this section of the State, to make known to you what I know. On my visiting Bear and Holcomb Valleys, electioneering, or rather soon after while I was there, a man by the name of Brown, a large man, with whiskers, wearing a blue flannel coat, who a few days ago left for your city, and whom it would be well to watch, arrived in the mines from Sacramento. On the night after his arrival a meeting was called of men known as secessionists at the store of Samuel Kelsey. Major Rollins was sent for on the Mojave and attended the meeting as the leader and moving spirit, assisted by Samuel Kelsey. On the first night they mustered seventeen or twenty. Supposing it to be a meeting for political purposes, a friend of mine attended as a spy. All present were sworn to secrecy. This man Brown and Judge Campbell, candidate for senator on the secession ticket, addressed the meeting. The object of the meeting was to concentrate and ascertain the fighting strength of the seceders in the county, and enroll them as a force to act in connection with other forces throughout the State, having for their object the seizure of the public property here and in Utah, and to raise the standard of rebellion in California, and thus bring on civil war amongst us in this State. On the night subsequent another meeting was held, when more attended. Some of the leading secessionists (Major Rollins and Beall) have disposed of their effects in order to be at liberty to engage in the movement. The secessionists are not numerous, but active, energetic, and persevering and fighting men, while the Union men are the hard working and quiet citizens, unorganized and unsuspecting. Shortly after the second meeting I returned to this city. Brown and Kelsey came down on the same day, and two nights after a meeting was held in this city. Not being aware of the meeting, which was kept secret, being called until late in the evening, I could not find a friend to play secessionist and get invited. I since find, however, that a friend was there. The object of the meeting was the same as that of Holcomb. This man Kelsey is enterprising, cautious, and brave, and instills with the subtlety of the devil treason into the minds of the youth of the county who have the slightest sympathy with the South, and infuses into them his own ardor. I watch him close. Another enemy of no less formidable character is Mrs. Bettis; bold, determined, and unscrupulous, she combines all the qualities which make a woman one of the most dangerous of enemies and one of the best of friends. Her father, Mr. Rubottom, and brother and nephew, and brother and son, James M. Greenwade, at Temescal, all secessionists, she inspires with her own enthusiasm in the cause. John Rains, at Cucamonga, is another, but lacking all the qualities of the rest, and having but money and the reputation of being wealthy. Such is the state of the county at present. Disregard the reports you read in the Los Angeles Star about the Mormons and Whisky Point. They and the men who reside there are Union men, and in this matter are unjustly libeled by a secessionist paper and by a friend of Joseph Bridger, another of the secession candidates. It seems to me that if a company of soldiers were sent here as a nucleus for the Union men to rally around in case of difficulty, it would have a tendency to prevent, perhaps to keep subdued, the secession spirit, and infuse spirit into the Union men. In case of difficulty my life and fortune are for the cause, and I shall organize a company and place myself under your command. But God forbid the necessity.

I have the honor to remain, your obedient servant,

HENRY M. WILLIS.

[Editor's note: *This document is included as an inclosure to the correspondence from Captain John Davidson, First Dragoons, to Major D. C. Buell, August 10, 1861, that is not included in this volume.*]

SOURCE: *OR*, SERIES 1, VOLUME 50, PART 1, PAGES 564–565

OR-17

SAN BERNARDINO, CAL., *August 6, 1861.*

Major CARLETON:

DEAR SIR: I inclose to you a letter for General Sumner, which will give you an idea of the state of affairs here. I think two companies of troops are needed here. I think in a little while life will be unsafe here. I do not know anything more than I have written to General Sumner, but if troops do not come here this town will be in the hands of secessionists. I consulted with Judge Boren and Doctor Dickey. They agree with me. Please write at once. I am going to find out all their plans if possible, and will write to you soon,

I am, sir, very respectfully,

CLARENCE E. BENNETT.

I inclose a petition, with the request of Judge Boren to present it to Captain Hancock for his signature, and be so kind as to forward it and oblige us.*

Yours,

C. E. B.

[Inclosure.]

SAN BERNARDINO, CAL., *August 6, 1861.*

Brig. Gen. E. V. SUMNER, U.S. Army,

Commanding the Department of California:

DEAR SIR: I have not yet learned the name of the officer or posts of the soldiers referred to in my letter of July 29. Last night the secessionists received reports from all parts of the State, and they were considered very favorable, particularly in Sacramento and Tulare County, which is strong for secession. They are energetically at work all over this State. They now contemplate starting in two or three weeks a force of about 200 men to Utah and capture Fort Crittenden (Camp Floyd). There are many Mormons here, and they are enlisting all they can, and Mormons here have promised to raise from 300 to 500 in Utah, probably more, to join the party from here, rendezvous on the west side of Utah Lake, and go and take it in the night, take the mules, wagons, harness, and available plunder here, and then the transportation through via Texas to the Jeff. Davis Confederation, where they expect to get paid in cash (?). They are to go in squads, and when near there to travel in the night, so that the first intimation Colonel Cooke has of the attack will be his capture. As I was stationed there in Utah a long time, adjutant of the Tenth Infantry and post adjutant of Camp Floyd, have traveled from Salt Lake City here the southern route, I have had a good opportunity to ascertain the sentiments of the citizens of that Territory. As a general thing there is a deep and abiding hatred toward the Federal Government, and an expedition of this kind can confidently reckon on support in every town. Will you be kind enough to have an extract made of this and sent to Colonel Cooke? I am personally acquainted with him, and do not write to him, as there is a secession postmaster there, and I am watched now, and my letter might be opened. Last night in the secession meeting Dr. D. R. Dickey and myself were denounced in the most bitter terms, on account of our active Union operations, and we will be the first ones killed. My name must be kept secret. They are desperadoes, and are increasing daily, getting more confident of their ability. I today got their papers, except the paper that has the signatures of these traitors.

PREAMBLE.

Whereas, a crisis has arrived in our political affairs which demands the closest scrutiny and strictest vigilance of every true patriot as an American citizen; and whereas, we view with regret and heartfelt sorrow the existence of a civil war now waged by one portion of the American people against another; and whereas, also, we believe that this war has been called into requisition by the present Executive of the United States without the guarantee of the Constitution and without the assent of either branch of the American Congress in their legislative capacity; and believing this as an unjust, unholy, iniquitous, and unconstitutional war; therefore

Be it resolved, first, That we, as a portion of the citizens of the United States, will support the Constitution as it now stands, together with the amendments thereunto appended, and that we will strictly adhere to the decisions of the Supreme Court of the United States made under said Constitution where a collision or difference of opinion has heretofore or may hereafter occur between citizens of one State and those of another or between States and the Federal Government, foreign citizens, subjects, &c.

Second. Be it further resolved, That, in our opinion, the President has violated the most sacred palladium of American liberty by the suspension of the writ of habeas corpus, and thus depriving an American citizen of having the cause of his imprisonment inquired into by the proper tribunal.

Third. Be it further resolved, That we are in favor of sustaining the Southern States of the American Confederacy in all their constitutional rights; that we believe an unconstitutional war is now being waged against them to subject them to a taxation enormous and unequal and to deprive them in the end of their species of property called slaves.

Fourth. And be it lastly resolved, That we mutually pledge to each other our lives, our property, and our sacred honor to sustain our brethren of the Southern States in the just defense of all their constitutional rights, whether invaded by the present Executive or by a foreign foe.

OBLIGATION.

I (A. B.), here in the presence of these witnesses, before Almighty God, I promise and swear that I will not divulge or reveal any of the secrets of this institution to anyone except I know to be a brother (or to instruct candidates). I furthermore swear that I will obey the proper authorities when ordered to do so, and that I will assist a brother of this institution in his rights, individually or constitutionally, when required of me by him, if need be, with my life. All this I solemnly swear to obey, under the penalty of being shot.

J. J. Willis, H.C. Minor, W. W. Y. Gail, William Kilgore, J. S. Banks, J. S. Scale, Charles Seale, John Hambleton, W. Foreman, Hamilton Foreman, Samuel Kelsey, James H. Wilson, R. Gaines, C. Bogert (candidate for senator).

The list of names I did not see. These were at the bottom of the obligation, I think there are many who are participators who have not signed, and I am assured there is a long list of those who have. The painter, one of the gang, is now employed in making the flag. I copied this instrument of treason accurately. The headquarters of the traitors is in Holcomb Valley, and there is a strong organization. I think two companies of U.S. troops better be sent here at once. One of the members says he thinks in two weeks fighting will commence in this town if there are no U.S. troops here. The rumored defeat of the Federal troops has strengthened them considerably. The oath is administered while kneeling, with the left hand on the heart, the right hand upheld. Every Southerner has joined. Many, I think, join for plunder. There are additions every day. I think it best, as soon as the troops get here, to commence arresting and securing them. You see they have provided for that. As soon as one is arrested they are bound to release him. I will write soon if nothing happens to me.

In haste, very respectfully,

CLARENCE E. BENNETT.

P. S.—The grip: In taking hands pass your little finger between his little finger and third finger. Pass words: I say. Are you on it? You reply, I am on it, at the same time carry your right hand to your right side to the pistol butt, as if to draw your revolver. Then I say, What's your name? You say, R-A-B-E. Use the letters to spell bear—bear flag.

C. E. B.

* [Memorandum in pencil on back of letter:] Petition of Judge Boren not handed to Major Ketchum by General Sumner.

[Editor's note: *Clarence E. Bennett's correspondence is addressed to Brigadier General E. V. Sumner, "Commanding the Department of California." General Sumner actually commanded the Department of the Pacific, having replaced Brigadier General Albert Sidney Johnston earlier that year.*]

SOURCE: *OR*, SERIES 1, VOLUME 50, PART 1, PAGES 556–558

OR-18

LOS ANGELES, *August 9, 1861.*

Brig. Gen. E. V. SUMNER,

Commanding Department of the Pacific, San Francisco:

DEAR SIR: I am constrained by the aspect of political affairs in this quarter to bring the matter personally to your knowledge in the hope that you will deem it prudent to add to the United States command in this section at least two companies. You are probably aware that our community is composed largely of Californians and Mexicans, and among them some very dangerous characters, who are easily diverted from what is right and proper into any course which promises excitement and reward, either by theft or murder, or both. As there also exists in our community a class of persons who are endeavoring to work this element into shape for evil purposes, and as not very remote from here there is a Mormon settlement of about 1,000 persons, whose hostility to our Government is well known, and who at any time may join the secessionists in our midst, I am constrained to urge that you will kindly make further disposition of troops in this quarter and by their presence overrule any movement which may be made by disaffected persons to kindle the fire of domestic strife in this State. In thus addressing you I represent the sentiments of a large number of respectable residents, whose position and pursuits are of that character as would prevent their becoming active participants in case trouble should ensue.

Trusting that you will lend ear to my solicitation, I remain, dear sir, with much respect, your very obedient servant,

ABEL STEARNS.

[Editor's note: *This document appears in the* Official Records *as an inclosure to OR-19.*]

SOURCE: *OR*, SERIES 1, VOLUME 50, PART 1, PAGES 563–564

OR-19

[*Extract*]

HEADQUARTERS,
Camp Fitzgerald, Cal., August 10, 1861.

Maj. D. C. BUELL,
Assistant Adjutant-General, Department of the Pacific:

MAJOR: I have the honor to inclose the within communications just put in my hands by Major Carleton.

. . .

Should one or two companies be required to lend aid to those companies probably to be sent to San Bernardino, the home guard could be relied upon to take their places in event of difficulty.

I am, sir, your obedient servant,

JNO. W. DAVIDSON,
Captain, First Dragoons, Commanding.

[Inclosure No. 1.]

LOS ANGELES, *August 10, 1861,*

General E. V. SUMNER,
Commanding Pacific Division, San Francisco:

SIR: I feel it my duty as an old resident of this place to apprise you that all of us who are loyal and devoted to the Stars and Stripes, and that have something to lose in this section of the country, feel that we are in the greatest insecurity as to the public interest as well as to our own lives and property. No part of your command is composed of such discordant and menacing elements as it. Within we have open and avowed secessionists and Southern sympathizers, and I am sorry to say that they are chiefly composed of those who exercise most political influence with the native population, and already they have not failed to poison their minds against the Puritan fanatics of the North. We are threatened with rebellion across the plains by people of the Van Dorn stripe, if we are to credit the repeated reports of the Texan emigration, and in these disordered times it is not well to discredit them. Lower California, the asylum of cut throats and robbers, is on our immediate border. We are surrounded to a great extent by barbarous and hostile Indian tribes, that may at any moment be excited against us and the Government by rebels or marauding Mormons. I not only consider it necessary, but the part of prudence and timely vigilance, to station a lookout cavalry force at the Cajon Pass, or at some point close thereto. Please to receive my suggestions with indulgence, being made in a spirit to subserve public and private interests.

Your most obedient servant,

MATTHEW KELLER.

[Inclosure No. 2.]

[Editor's note: *See OR-18 for this inclosure.*]

SOURCE: *OR*, SERIES 1, VOLUME 50, PART 1, PAGES 562–563

OR-20

LOS ANGELES, *August 10, 1861.*

Brig. Gen. E. V. SUMNER,
Commanding Department of the Pacific, San Francisco:

DEAR SIR: Since addressing you under yesterday's date information has reached me of an organization among the secessionists at San Bernardino and the mines of Bear Valley (in the vicinity of this latter place) which has confirmed my belief, and increased my alarm with regard to our condition in this section of the State. It would appear from the information received that not only does a good understanding, but nearly complete organization, exist through all the southern counties from Stockton to the Mexico line, and the formation only awaits a head to develop the outrage in all its enormity. From the open condition of our country here running herds of animals are exposed to be turned into cavalry at any moment, and the option of Texas or Utah as the base of operations simply remains for determination among those who would carry the plan into effect. If upon the Northern side they can rely upon the Mormons, and if upon the Southern, then the Mexican element becomes powerful. In either event, there are always enough of this latter class to assist in procuring horses. Thus stands the case. The secessionists from the northern part of the State are continually arriving here in our midst. We have a disturbed and uncertain number of natives who are sympathizers, and to the east, the Mormons and vagabond miners, who are already enrolled to a great extent in opposition to the Government. These facts, combined with the lukewarm Union spirit of the place, give just cause for alarm. I sincerely trust, therefore, that you may deem it of sufficient importance to augment the number of troops suggested in mine of yesterday, firmly believing that a show of force, involving that respect for the laws which all good people should observe, is preferable to that extreme which invokes the necessity of its use, as is lamentably shown in the present condition of our country. I regret exceedingly the departure of Major Carleton and Captain Hancock, both of whom in these trying times have been equal to the emergency, and whose activity and energy have inspired the confidence of the community. In their absence I believe the command to fall upon Captain Davidson, whose long acquaintance with this country and the people I trust may be the means of retaining him amongst us in this position, apart from feelings of friendship for him based upon years of acquaintance.

Trusting that you will pardon this lengthy trespass upon your time, and incessant occupation, I remain, dear sir, with very much respect, your very obedient servant,

ABEL STEARNS.

SOURCE: *OR*, SERIES 1, VOLUME 50, PART 1, PAGES 565–566

OR-21

HEADQUARTERS,
Camp Fitzgerald, Cal., August 13, 1861.

Maj. D. C. BUELL,
Assistant Adjutant-General, U.S. Army:

MAJOR: After careful thought I have determined, as an officer intrusted with an important command here, to give my views with regard to the dispositions to be made to preserve good order and obedience to the laws in this section of the country. With due deference to older and wiser heads than mine, I believe the arrangement proposed would crush the egg of treason already laid in the counties of San Bernardino and Los Angeles, give the really good time to awake to their true interests and to listen to the promptings of that patriotism which, however it may be swayed by the passions of the hour, is yet deeply planted in every American heart. Therefore,

I. The depot of supplies for the troops to be at San Pedro, near the mouth of San Gabriel River; a company of infantry stationed there, with temporary work thrown up, and two or more pieces of artillery.

II. Two companies of infantry at Los Angeles, either in the town, or at least six miles from it. One month's subsistence always on hand.

III. Four companies, two of dragoons and two of infantry, at San Bernardino. I believe if any trouble arises it will begin there, because of the character of the surrounding population, and the fact that the outlets toward Utah by the Mojave, and toward Texas by the Colorado, invite and tempt by their facilities for escape. By all means keep this squadron of dragoons intact at one point. It is the only body of cavalry in the country and, with the drill Carleton and I have given it, is really efficient and can be relied on for 100 men in the saddle at need. An outpost from the San Bernardino command to be at Martin's ranch, in the Cajon Pass, to consist of an officer and, say, twelve men. Another at Temecula, on the route to Warner's ranch, same number. Both posts to report constantly to San Bernardino. The officer at San Bernardino to have district powers over Los Angeles troops, but not to touch San Pedro. A section of field pieces at Los Angeles and one at San Bernardino. An enterprising officer ought to be able to control at least open acts with these facilities placed at his command. If this arrangement cannot be made, then I respectfully ask authority to move this camp to San Pedro, and in the advantages of this step all my officers concur with me.

The men are being demoralized here, and I suspect are tampered with. The vitality they expend in debauch would be spent in fishing, hunting, boating, and manly exercises. From this point we could mainly control this section of country. There is a brass field piece here in town (6-pounder) belonging I am told to the State, now in the hands of the sheriff, Tomas Sanchez, a noted secessionist, which ought, I think, to be in my keeping. Can I get the order of the Governor to deliver it to me, through the general? The home guard about whom I wrote to the general of the date of August 10 have enrolled 100 members, under the accompanying pledge, and expect to have 100 more within a few days, when their returns come in. Can I have 150 stand of rifles or muskets sent me from the arsenal for issue to them? I will be responsible myself for their safe-keeping, and I think these people would be gratified by this mark of the general's confidence. Besides, they really need them. There are no arms worth mentioning in the hands of Union men. The fall election comes off September 5, at which time Dimmick, U.S. district attorney, and others fear an outbreak. It would be well if the San Bernardino command could be in position by then.

I am, sir, your most obedient servant,

JNO. W. DAVIDSON,
Captain, First Dragoons, Commanding.

If the general will grant my suggestion about the arms, it is important they should be here before the election comes off on the 5th September.

J. W. D.

[Editor's note: *An inclosure and indorsement were removed for lack of relevance.*]

SOURCE: *OR*, SERIES 1, VOLUME 50, PART 1, PAGES 567–569

OR-22

HEADQUARTERS,
Fort Bridger, Utah Ter., August 25, 1861.

Maj. J. H. CARLETON,
First Dragoons, U.S. Army, Commanding Volunteers:

MAJOR: Having learned that a number of volunteers under your command are about to leave California to take post along the Overland Mail Route, I consider it my duty to give you information with regard to the facilities afforded by this post for occupation by a portion of your command should it be desirable to occupy it. The post, as you may be aware, is pleasantly situated on Black's Fork of Green River, having several branches with fine running water through and near the post. Four companies could immediately find pleasant quarters and in a short time a number of other buildings sufficient to accommodate an equal number could be repaired. There are six sets of officers' quarters with four rooms each, two of them having kitchens detached. There is one stable fit for immediate use which will accommodate ninety horses, and another which will require considerable repairs before being fit for use. It would hold about fifty animals. The material for repairing could be obtained at the post. There are 200 head of commissary beef-cattle here. There are 400 bales and 300 boxes of clothing, camp, and garrison equipage, stationery and medical stores at the post. Most of this was removed from Fort Crittenden when that post was abandoned and stored here for the use of the volunteers. The subsistence stores here are quite limited in quantity. I have 6,000 pounds flour, 3,500 pounds bacon, 1,000 pounds sugar, 200 pounds coffee, 150 pounds rice, and 30 bushels beans, and but a small quantity of other stores. The post sutler here has a quantity of subsistence stores purchased at the late sale, which he has made me a written promise to retain until September 20, and sell at reasonable rates should it be necessary to purchase, provided the post should be garrisoned. He has 20,000 pounds States flour, 10,000 pounds bacon, 60 bushels beans, 10 barrels vinegar, 5 barrels molasses, 2,000 pounds sugar, 15 cases desiccated vegetables, 1,000 pounds tea, 400 gallons vinegar. Stock can be wintered near the post. There is a good sutler's store here, a post-office, and a telegraph station is expected to be established here by November.

I am, respectfully, your obedient servant,

J. C. CLARK,
Captain, Fourth Artillery, Commanding Post.

P. S.—The post sutler, Judge Carter, has contracted to furnish for the post, if needed, 3,000 bushels oats, 90 tons hay, 15 tons straw, and 1,000 cords wood, and states that he is willing to increase the amounts of the several articles to the requirements of the post. Will you please reply early for the information of the sutler?

J. C. C.

Source: *OR*, Series 1, Volume 50, Part 1, page 583

OR-23

Executive Department, Colorado Territory,
Denver, August 26, 1861.

Hon. Simon Cameron,
Secretary of War:

General: I send as special messenger, for the essential means of defense for this Territory and people, Benjamin R. Pegram, who is fully furnished with dispatches and instructions to represent the extreme dangers enveloping our position. This people are inclosed in a circle of hostile elements converging upon them, and are utterly destitute of arms, ammunition, or any weapons of self-preservation. The Indians are hostile, and pushed upon us by enemies and their emissaries from the outside.

New Mexico can only be regarded as likely to aid the advance of the enemy. A strong army corps, such as that lately withdrawn from Utah, will protect this people and reconquer New Mexico. I ask that this army corps may be stopped on its eastward march, and deflected down the foot of the mountains to this place. The greatest economy in time and military operations will be the result of such a policy. The population is 30,000, but so beleaguered and destitute of materials and provisions as to be helpless and without a place of retreat from the advancing enemy. The essential supplies are 10,000 muskets, rifles, and equipments; 2 field batteries and supplies of fixed ammunition for use in the field, and abundant reserve supplies.

The extreme desperation of our position, calmly appreciated, will, I know, secure your prompt action. Energy, loyalty, and bravery preeminently belong to the mountain people. To conquer their enemies appears to them more glorious than to perish. Essential military assistance is all they require to preserve themselves and assist their country's cause.

Very respectfully,

WILLIAM GILPIN,
Governor of Colorado.

[Editor's note: *This document appears in the* Official Records *as an inclosure to correspondence from Brigadier-General Samuel R. Curtis to Simon Cameron, Secretary of War, September 16, 1861, that is not included in this volume.*]

SOURCE: *OR*, SERIES 1, VOLUME 3, PAGE 496

OR-24

BOSTON, *August 27, 1861.*

Hon. SIMON CAMERON,
Secretary of War, Washington:

SIR: The State of Missouri is so important to the Union, that I suppose you will be glad of any information regarding it which comes from a reliable source. I hand you a few extracts from the late letters of Mr. Hayward, general agent of the Hannibal and Saint Joseph Railroad. Through the agencies of this line across the State he has great facility for obtaining information and judging of the progress of our cause in the northern portion of the State. His views with regard to the probable effect of measures which have been heretofore taken towards suppressing the rebellion in that vicinity have shown so clear a judgment as to give with us here much weight to his opinions.

With rebel camps forming undisturbed all along through that part of the State their early concentration into another formidable army may reasonably be looked for. All they seem to lack is a leader for a vigorous demonstration. It is the opinion of some of our best-informed citizens, obtained from their Southern correspondence, that the possession of Missouri is regarded of the utmost importance to the Southern cause. The possession of the lead mine of that State by the rebels will also be a most unfortunate thing for the country. Its position, lying between the rest of the free States and Kansas, Nebraska, Utah, and even California on the west, and controlling the banks of the Mississippi opposite Kentucky and half of Tennessee on the east, makes its early possession by the Government a vital matter connected with any movements in the Mississippi Valley. Surrounded as it is by free States, any delay in its subjugation will have a damaging effect upon the Government at home and a disastrous influence abroad. It is supposed that very great efforts will be made by the secessionists of that State to carry in their favor the election soon to be held for new State officers. Union voters near the borders are being driven out, and large numbers of others with their families put in such extreme peril that self-preservation is rapidly joining them to the forces of the enemy. While it may be true that the Union force can beat more than their number of rebels if it can get at them, the general character of the rebels in that State is such, that their subjugation by an equal number of Government soldiers will certainly be a very expensive and tedious process, if not a total failure. Large bodies of mounted guerrillas will require a large force and severe measures to bring them to terms, and it seems to me that every day's delay in pushing the most vigorous offensive measures in North Missouri is fraught with great peril and mischief that it will cost much blood and treasure to correct.

In view of the intense activity of the enemy—his rapidly gaining strength; his continued successes, with the choice of secession or Union soon to be voted on in the selection of State officers, and the larger part of the voters now in the control (by friendship or fear) of the rebels—seeing so much affecting not only that State, but the whole cause at stake there, I have felt it my duty to write you, upon whom rests so much of the responsibility in this matter.

Very respectfully, your obedient servant,

J. W. BROOKS.

[Editor's note: *Inclosures removed for lack of relevance.*]

SOURCE: *OR*, SERIES 1, VOLUME 3, PAGES 457–458

OR-25

EXECUTIVE DEPARTMENT,
Sacramento, Cal., September 2, 1861.

His Excellency ABRAHAM LINCOLN,
President of the United States:

SIR: The first requisition made upon this State for 1,500 volunteers has been filled and the command given to Colonel Carleton. It having been intimated by the War Department that it was your desire that this officer should have the command, I cheerfully complied, as I had every confidence in his experience, patriotism, and gallantry. I would now represent to your Excellency that the command of this expedition to Utah is a most important one, and will embrace a jurisdiction of some 1,500 miles. As colonel, he will have command of the First California Infantry and the First California Cavalry, being more than a colonel's command and less than that of a brigadier. I would respectfully ask, on behalf of the State, that this be created a separate department, and that Colonel Carleton be appointed brigadier-general of this brigade. I trust you will at once see the benefits that will result from this course.

As it is remote from headquarters on the Pacific, and being subject to have all communications cut off for four months in the year by snows, the officer in command of this department should be invested with ample power to act as circumstances might require. Besides, California has not yet been honored with a military appointment of this rank, and should your Excellency deem it advisable to accede to this request, I know of no man more deserving than Colonel Carleton, nor one who would reflect more credit upon the State, or give more satisfaction to the General Government.

I am, sir, very respectfully, your obedient servant,

JOHN G. DOWNEY.

SOURCE: *OR*, SERIES 1, VOLUME 50, PART 1, PAGES 600–601

OR-26

HEADQUARTERS,
Fort Churchill, Nev. Ter., September 7, 1861.

Capt. R. C. DRUM,
Asst. Adjt. Gen., Hdqrs. Dept. of the Pacific, San Francisco, Cal.:

SIR: I have the honor to report that information was telegraphed me yesterday from Virginia City that a party of seventy emigrants had been robbed by the Indians somewhere this side of Salt Lake and were left entirely destitute and starving. I immediately sent out a party of dragoons under the command of Lieutenant Baker, First Dragoons, with a supply of provisions to assist them and enable them to reach the settlements, and would respectfully ask the approval of the general commanding the department to the issues made them, as well as what more may be necessary for their immediate wants. A further report will be made on the return of Lieutenant Baker. I learn that the citizens of Virginia City have also sent out provisions and clothing, as they were expected to reach the sink of the Humboldt last evening.

I am, sir, very respectfully, your obedient servant,

GEO. A. H. BLAKE,
Lieutenant-Colonel First Dragoons, Commanding Post.

SOURCE: *OR*, SERIES 1, VOLUME 50, PART 1, PAGE 611

OR-27

Fort Churchill, Nev. Ter., *September 10, 1861.*

Sir: I have the honor to state that in compliance with orders dated headquarters Fort Churchill, September 6, 1861, I proceeded with a detachment, consisting of one noncommissioned officer and ten men, and a wagon containing provisions, for the purpose of assisting such emigrants as were absolutely in need of it. I found about thirty miles from this post (on the Carson River) a party of emigrants, about fifty in number, who had been attacked and robbed of everything (except what they had on their backs) about sixty-five miles northeast of Salt Lake. They stated that the party who attacked them were Indians, commanded by white men. They were attacked on the night of the 8th of August, and lost all their animals on the night of the 9th. They had since walked the whole distance to the Carson River, receiving such assistance from other trains as they were able to give them. I distributed 400 pounds of flour, 300 pounds of pork, 26 pounds of rice, 44 pounds sugar, 60 pounds coffee, and 1 quart of salt, which, with the assistance received from the citizens of Virginia and Carson Cities, will be sufficient to last them until they reach their destination. The women and children belonging to the party were brought to this post and have since gone on to Carson and Virginia.

I am, sir, very respectfully, your obedient servant,

E. M. BAKER,
Second Lieutenant, First Dragoons.

Lieut. Col. G. A. H. Blake.

[Editor's note: *This document is included as an inclosure to an Expedition Report covering August 8–9, 1861. See* OR-28.]

Source: *OR*, Series 1, Volume 50, Part 1, page 24

OR-28

AUGUST 8–9, 1861.—Attack on Emigrant Train near the Great Salt Lake, Utah, Ter.

Report of Lieut. Eugene M. Baker, First U.S. Dragoons.

HEADQUARTERS,
Fort Churchill, Nev. Ter., September 10, 1861.

Capt. R. C. DRUM,
Asst. Adjt. Gen., Hdqrs. Dept. of the Pacific, San Francisco, Cal.:

SIR: I have the honor to transmit herewith the report of Lieut. E. M. Baker, First Dragoons, who was detached from this post on the 6th of September, 1861, for the purpose of meeting and relieving a party of emigrants who were robbed by the Indians this side of Salt Lake. According to the statement of Mr. S. M. Harriman, in charge of the train, to me, the train consisted of 74 persons, 11 wagons, 89 head of work cattle, 5 horses, and 2 mules, which was the total number of the party when attacked. The total number brought into this post was 54, viz, 22 men, 13 women, and 19 children. The train was attacked on the night of the 8th of August, and abandoned on the morning of the 9th of August, 1861. Almost daily emigrant trains are passing in want of provisions, and I have issued such quantities necessary to carry them to the settlements, and for which I would ask the approval of the general commanding the department.

I am, sir, very respectfully, your obedient servant,

GEO. A. H. BLAKE,
Lieutenant-Colonel First Dragoons, Commanding Post.

[Editor's note: *OR-27 was attached to this document as an inclosure.*]

SOURCE: *OR*, SERIES 1, VOLUME 50, PART 1, PAGE 24

OR-29

[*Extract*]

Denver, Colo. Ter., *September 13, 1861.*

President of the United States:

Sir: Although assigned by you to a department which has no official cognizance of some of the matters herein communicated, the extraordinary perils which surround the judicial as well as the executive departments of this Territory seem to impose upon me as well as upon the Governor the duty to spread them before you.

This Territory, as you are aware, covers the natural fortresses as well as the parks and treasures of the Rocky Mountains between the thirty-seventh and forty-first parallels of latitude from which no enemy in possession would be easily dislodged without great cost and difficulty so long as it could derive support from either side of the ranges.

. . .

As it was known that Col. Philip St. George Cooke was at the time returning from Utah with his regiment and a full battery of artillery, it was resolved to send to him Mr. Bennett, our Delegate to Congress, in the hope of inducing him to turn down this way until we could procure orders from the Department for him to remain.

. . .

Now, although I am not advised of your reasons for recalling to the States the command of Colonel Cooke, I venture to submit to you the following requests:

. . .

Fourth. That if it should not be agreeable to the President to make the Governor a brigadier-general, that he send some other military officer here immediately, with suitable arms and munitions, to enable the Governor to hold this Territory, Utah, and New Mexico.

Fifth. That the parties connected with the Overland Mail and Express Route from Saint Joseph to California be required to desist from aiding and comforting disloyalists, or that their contract be taken from them by the Department. It is a notorious fact that the entire force of employés of that concern are malignant secessionists, who use their position to convey treasonable information to the enemy.

Sixth. That the Commissioner of Indian Affairs may be directed to act upon Governor Gilpin's communication of the 19th of June immediately, that these Indians may be placed under such arranged restraints as shall tend to bring them out of their present disorder.

Impressed as I am with the force of these suggestions, I have ventured, in a hurried manner, to spread them before you in this dispatch. We are holding this Territory by a thread. If that thread breaks before we get relief, God only knows when or how it will be regained.

I have the honor to be, sir, with profound esteem, your obedient servant,

BENJ. F. HALL,
Chief Justice of Colorado.

[First indorsement.]

October 2, 1861.

This communication ought to have been addressed to the Secretary of War, but it seems to have so much importance that I send it to you, and I suggest that after reading it you refer it to the Secretary of War and ask his attention to it.

WILLIAM H. SEWARD.

[Second indorsement.]

WAR DEPARTMENT,
October 15, 1861.

Respectfully referred to Lieutenant-General Scott.

THOMAS A. SCOTT,
Assistant Secretary.

[Third indorsement.]

HEADQUARTERS ARMY,
October 31, 1861.

Read and respectfully referred to the Adjutant-General.

By command of Major-General Scott:

E. D. TOWNSEND,
Assistant Adjutant-General.

SOURCE: *OR*, SERIES 3, VOLUME 1, PAGES 504–508

OR-30

SAN BERNARDINO, *September 14, 1861.*

Capt. JOHN W. DAVIDSON,
Commanding U.S. Dragoons, Camp Fitzgerald, Los Angeles:

SIR: We, the undersigned, members of the Union Club of San Bernardino, would most respectfully state that a company of cavalry has been organized by Mormons in this place under the name of the home guard; they pretend to be Union men while we have every reason to doubt their sincerity and loyalty. They are commanded by Mr. Clarence E. Bennett, late a lieutenant in the U.S. Army, stationed in Utah Territory, who resigned his commission and married the daughter of a Mormon high in that church of a damnable heresy and imposture, she being an actress on the stage. His sympathies being necessarily with that class of people who are sworn foes to the United States Government, and the present indications being of such a nature as lead us to believe that hostilities will break out between them and the Government ere long, we would most solemnly protest, as Union men who hold our country dearer than life, against any arms whatever being issued to these men. We believe it to be unsafe and injudicious, and we do [know] that some of these same men, when your command arrived here, insulted you by cheering for Jeff Davis in your presence.

Hoping that this protest of ours may have due weight with you, and that the contents of this letter may be made known to General Sumner and Governor Downey, we subscribe ourselves,

Your respectful and obedient servants,

EDWIN A. SHERMAN,
President of the Club.
JOS. H. PEREAU.
JAMES LEONARD.
Z. G. AYERS.
CHAS. MOGO.

[Editor's note: *This document appears in the* Official Records *as an inclosure to OR-31.*]

SOURCE: *OR*, SERIES 1, VOLUME 50, PART 1, PAGES 622–623

OR-31

HEADQUARTERS,
Camp Fitzgerald, Cal., September 16, 1861.

Capt. RICHARD C. DRUM,
Assistant Adjutant-General, San Francisco, Cal.:

CAPTAIN: The information given you in my letter of the 9th instant has received much corroboration within the last few days. Judge Terry is said to be at the head of the organization. Secret nightly meetings are reported to me to be held by armed men at the Monte (twelve miles from Los Angeles). With regard to the last I have sent out (and will continue to do so until something most positive is learned by me) nightly patrols of intelligent non-commissioned officers and one or two men, for the purpose of ascertaining where and by whom these meetings are held, and if possible their object. It is almost impossible to convey to the general the state of affairs down here. My ears are stuffed with all sorts of rumors and reports, and I have work to sift out what should be attended to and what not. You know I have not been an alarmist in my letters, nor have they ever stampeded me, but I think now that the depot of our supplies should be removed to a more secure position. At present it consists of a corral with a wooden fence, and the stores are placed in one large wooden shed and four hospital tents. It should be within brick or adobe walls, and in defensive buildings. I don't know, also, what the general's intentions are with regard to more troops at this particular point, but I think at least one company of infantry should be here. This would enable me to detach parts of the squadron through the country, never absent long, nor going far, which would tend to break up or discover these nests of disaffected and marauding parties. I inclose the within protest to the general. I am inclined to believe those who sign it to be correct. I thought while in San Bernardino that it had been the design of the Mormons there to cloak themselves as Union men for the purpose of splitting the Union vote. The insidious documents with regard to the income and other taxes circulated by the McConnell men among the Californians but a few days prior to the election, and the personal popularity of Tomas Sanchez were the influencing causes of the Spanish vote in this county. Rumor says that I am to go with the general. Will he pardon me for saying that, if so, I think this squadron should be filled up, even if it requires a company up north to be broken up, and the main object being to get one or more efficient officers with it.

I am, captain, your most obedient servant,

JNO. W. DAVIDSON,
Captain, First Cavalry, Commanding.

[Inclosure.]

[Editor's note: *See* OR-*30 for this inclosure.*]

SOURCE: *OR*, SERIES 1, VOLUME 50, PART 1, PAGES 621–622

OR-32

[*Extract*]

Fort Fauntleroy, N. Mex., *September 27, 1861.*

Hon. Simon Cameron:

Sir: As an old printer and soldier of the line in the grand Union Array, I exercise the privilege of addressing you this communication. Having resided sufficiently long in New Mexico and Arizona to become measurably acquainted with the wants and wishes of the people, of acquiring a practical knowledge of the geographical, physical, and moral condition of the country, and learning to a considerable extent the peculiarities of the inhabitants who are spread over this vast Territory, a region nearly four times as large as the State of Missouri, I feel that I can with some degree of safety and accuracy describe to you the present political condition and standing of the community.

. . .

The numerous Indian wars, the disregard of law and open defiance of courts and legislative enactments, the murders and robberies which are perpetrated with impunity all over the country, the demoralization of the U.S. Army, and the abandonment of their duty and of the Union in solemn contravention of their oath of officers high on the roll of military fame have all measurably proceeded from want of vigor and decisive action on the part of the executive head. Where there is no power to curb or restrain the populace, mob law and irresponsible rule will run riot over the land. Nothing is plainer and more certain. Sir, the frontier Territories, like Utah and New Mexico, Colorado and Nevada, &c., require men of brains and nerve to govern them. In the persons of Governor Nye and Governor Gilpin (of Nevada and Colorado) there are men appointed fit to be governors. Such has not been the case either in Utah or New Mexico. Hence polygamy and slavery and peonage, twin relics of barbarism and the offspring of an oligarchy, have had sway and are held up as an example of patriarchal observance for the guidance of the masses, instead of bringing them up to an enlightened standard of civilization, of progress, and improvement. It is about time that these institutions, relics of a dark age and of a deleterious tendency upon the customs and manners of the people, were swept out of existence. I thought this was part of the task to which the Republican party had pledged itself not to overlook. The duty to perform that which has been solemnly promised in full and open convention and ratified by the people in their primary capacity in the exercise of their constitutional privilege should not, in my humble judgment, be passed over for slight or transient causes.

. . .

Had a Republican governor been appointed for this Territory last May (instead of old Rencher, who is fit, perhaps, to govern Buncombe or Currituck Counties, in North Carolina) and sent to Santa Fé the robbing of Government trains, the burning and surrendering of military posts, and the disgraceful surrender of old Lynde, superannuated and unfit for service, of a U.S. force of 750 men to 350 Arizona cut-throats would never have occurred. It seems to me it was a great oversight in not sending to the Rio Grande from California three months ago some 10,000 or 12,000 troops, infantry and cavalry, to crush out the Texas and Arizona rebels. I fear it is too late now. I fear very much that the Confederate forces under the lead of General A. S. Johnston (formerly commanding officer in Utah and California), Col. John R. Baylor, Major Armistead, Major Waller, Colonel Ford, and Col. Thomas J. Mastin (a young, bold, chivalrous, and talented, but mistaken, Mississippian, the friend and pet of Jeff. Davis) will form a junction at La Mesilla before the arrival of troops from California and Kansas, capture Fort Craig (as they did Fillmore), Albuquerque, and Santa Fé, and thus get a permanent foothold in New Mexico, as they now have in Arizona. I very much fear this. Should such be the case, the Union cause will be terribly menaced, if not absolutely lost, on the Pacific side. Sir, in war there must be resolution, energy, will, iron will, and nerve to push things to their very utmost. Old fogy generals and governors have played the deuce with this region. They have permitted the demoralization of the army and the people, the spread of faro and monte banks, the reign of lynch law and filibusterism, vice and crime to run riot, and virtue, liberty, and intelligence to be overslaughed. There must be a change, a radical change, or the country is undone.

. . .

The times are big with the fate of "Caesar and of Rome," and without men at the head of affairs who can comprehend the epoch in which they live and have the nerve and resolution to carry them out, our system of government will inevitably be overthrown and a monarchy or despotism erected in its place. There is no escaping the dread alternative. I have written the foregoing at intervals snatched from military duty as a sentinel on the watch tower. I have no time to elaborate my ideas as fully as I could wish. These rough notes, however, may furnish you with a glimpse of the condition of public matters in this far-distant region of the Union, and give you a slight idea how affairs are conducted and progressing in New Mexico and Arizona. That is the object of this communication, "nothing extenuate or aught set down in malice." Yesterday was the day set apart by the President and Congress of the United States as a day of prayer, fasting, and humiliation for the success of the American arms and the return of peace. It was not observed at this post. If the trump of the archangel were sounded to-morrow and I was summoned to appear before the throne of the Great Jehovah to testify, I would aver that the facts set forth in the foregoing rough notes are true. I have nothing further to say.

Respectfully,

WM. NEED.

P. S.—There are a number of persons in this Territory holding office who are rank secessionists at heart, but pretend to loyalty to the Union to cloak their designs and to keep their places on account of the salary. They are here, as at Washington, mighty cunning, but won't do to be trusted. They require weeding out. I mark this letter Public Business (which you will excuse) in order to secure its safe transmission to Washington.

W. N.

SOURCE: *OR*, SERIES 1, VOLUME 50, PART 1, PAGES 635–641

OR-33

SAINT LOUIS, *October 3, 1861.*

Col. THOMAS A. SCOTT:

Dispatch just received.* Lane's victory over Parsons is important and complete. When Lane burned the town of Osceola every house exploded with concealed powder. Yesterday General Frémont ordered the Utah regulars to him. The commander replies that he has orders from McClellan to go to Washington. Think of that! This moment we have a rumor that Frémont is superseded. Is that so? All here is moving strong and well as an army can without money.

B. RUSH PLUMLY.

* Not found.

SOURCE: *OR*, SERIES 1, VOLUME 3, PAGES 516–517

OR-34

NORTH BRANCH, [LAPEER COUNTY, MICH.,] *October 5, 1861.*

R. M. C., Esq.

DEAR AND HONORED SIR: I write to inform you that C—s, the signature of the S— of S—, &c., attached with a number of skeleton P—ts, will be found at the house of R— L—, W. C. W., by the 9th instant.

The work, dear sir, goes bravely on; I have received replies from over sixty different localities and forwarded them to their proper destination, and I am happy to say thus far without a breath of suspicion or any accident. Our fellow-citizens are better prepared for the grand movement than even the most sanguine of our leaders dared to hope. The league is extending its ramifications in every direction and gaining new and valuable adherents daily. I feel greatly strengthened in the belief that when the hour comes to erect our glorious standard an overwhelming force will spring up at the first trumpet call. Many who are outwardly rabid in the tyrant's favor are with us heart and soul. I cannot, in common with C—s S—t, refrain from expressing my astonishment not to say delight at the unparalleled success and secrecy which has thus far attended the efforts of the brotherhood. God cannot help blessing a cause whose object is the restoration of a great nation to peace and unity by the overthrow of the blackest and most damnable despotism that ever usurped the liberties of a free people.

It is not difficult to convince an honest, intelligent man that the only way left to restore the Union and rescue the Constitution from beneath the feet of the tyrants where it is now lying is to insure by concerted action throughout the N— the success of the S—, until tired and disgusted the conservative element is strong enough to raise and unite if necessary with the A— of the S—, overrun the N— like a hurricane, sweeping the A— into eternity, or at least driving them into complete and unconditional submission. This is the only way in which our liberty and our country can be saved. Such a result would again unite the N. and S. in new bonds of amity and interest, restore the Union in all its former strength and beauty and the Constitution to the sacred niche from which it has been ruthlessly hurled by the despots. May the league prove the stepping-stone to such a result.

I have it from the best authority that the league is doing noble work in M—d, even among the F— S— at Ft. M—. If God continues to prosper our efforts the hour of a union between the N. and S. is not far distant. Prepared and united our force will prove irresistible and the accursed A— G— will be swept into the Atlantic.

President P— in his passage has drawn many brave and influential men to the league. P—y, of the L. C. D—t, sent a line to Dr. F— (by H., the Mormon elder), who as you perhaps know is just across the line from Port H—. The league is doing nobly in M., I. and Wis. He is cautious, but in common with others is gradually preparing the minds of the people for a great change. He expresses a fear that any attempt to draft men will produce a premature outbreak. I think his fear is well founded. A member of the league in Genesee who passed through the woods on his way with dispatches to Dr. F— told that any attempt to draft our friends there would bring on an open rupture. I think our leaders should look to this, as no doubt they will.

I am happy to say Dr. F— considers his mission accomplished and departs for R— by the 7th instant. Through us there is now an uninterrupted line of communication between the S— and Europe. He leaves Captain L—, a sure friend, in his place to receive correspondence, &c. Our obscurity is our greatest safeguard. The duties which devolve upon me could never be conducted in any place of note without attracting attention. I forwarded your request to the G— M— and am instructed to furnish you with the cipher and its key. I will send the same to Pt. H—, thence to W—.

I have much which I wish to communicate, but will wait until an opportunity offers to send it by a safe hand. I am obliged to send this by mail.

May God prosper the cause. The S— is doing gloriously. It wrings my very heart however to see our brave countrymen N. and S. sacrificed to carry out the hellish plans of our tyrant. May our project prove a second Sicilian Vespers, attended with all its success, but I fervently pray without its bloodshed.

Dear sir, excuse this confused and hurried letter, and allow me to sign myself,

Yours, in the cause,

∗ ⊐ < ∧ ǯ ‖ □

P. S.—Captain H. will give you instructions as to the disposition to be made of the C—s; the P—s are to be used as necessity requires.

[Editor's note: *This document appears in the* Official Records *as an inclosure to OR-42. The unusual signature characters appear in the original. See also OR-42 and OR-44.*]

SOURCE: *OR*, SERIES 2, VOLUME 2, SECTION 2, PAGES 1248–1249

OR-35

JEFFERSON CITY, MO., *October 11, 1861.*

GENERAL: In June, 1855, I left Saint Louis with seven steamboats, with stores and troops for the Upper Missouri River. I remained there on duty until 1857. I joined General Johnston and went to Utah. I returned from Utah last winter, on the first and only leave of absence I have had in twelve years. While on my way to Washington, in April, I stopped at Harrisburg; and, at the request of Governor Curtin, I remained there to assist in organizing the troops there assembling into camps and to put their commissariat into order. From there I was on duty constantly, day and night, at various posts—York, Cockeysville, Baltimore, Perryville, and Annapolis. Finally, about the 20th of July, I was ordered to report to General Frémont. I did so at New York. I was ordered on duty at Saint Louis, where I resumed similar labors to those I had been at in the East, and have been on my feet night and day since. A few days ago I received orders to report at this place for duty in the field.

I left all my public accounts open, in an incomplete and exposed condition, on my office table in Saint Louis, besides a vast deal of property not turned over. My health is so broken down that I am not able longer to stand up. I desire, as an act of simple justice to me, I be allowed to resume the leave of absence I surrendered in April (it would have expired 15th June), or else that I be ordered permanently to a post where I can get some rest, and be able to make up and forward to the Treasury Department my public accounts.

Your early reply to this is respectfully requested.

Respectfully,

P. T. TURNLEY,
Assistant Quartermaster.

General L. THOMAS, *Adjutant-General United States.*

Note.—My unsettled and unadjusted accounts will reach over one million and a half dollars.

[Editor's note: *This document appears in the* Official Records *as an attachment to Inclosure B to correspondence from Lorenzo Thomas to the Honorable Simon Cameron, October 21, 1861, that is not included in this volume.*]

SOURCE: *OR*, SERIES 1, VOLUME 3, PAGE 550

OR-36

WILLARD'S HOTEL, *October 19, 1861.*

THOMAS A. SCOTT:

DEAR SIR: While at Altoona last evening I received the following dispatch, which may be of interest:

> The Pacific telegraph line completed to Utah. A dispatch from Brigham Young dated Great Salt Lake City, October 18, to J. H. Wade, president of Pacific Telegraph Company, at Cleveland, Ohio, congratulates him and his associates upon the success of the enterprise, and expresses his devotion to the constitutional Government of the United States.

The line from San Francisco to Great Salt Lake City is nearly completed, and direct telegraphic communication between the Atlantic and the Pacific will no doubt be established by 1st of November.

Very respectfully,

ANSON STAGER.

SOURCE: *OR*, SERIES 1, VOLUME 50, PART 1, PAGE 666

OR-37

EXECUTIVE DEPARTMENT, COLORADO TERRITORY,
Denver, October 23, 1861.

Col. E. R. S. CANBY,
Commanding Department of New Mexico:

COLONEL: Accept my thanks for dispatches by express messenger (from Fort Garland), bearing date of the 7th and 11th instant.

I am greatly in your debt for a supply of blanks and books; an attention especially apropos at a point so utterly destitute of such essentials to public business. I will respond promptly to the request of Governor Connelly and yourself for medical men who can be found here.

I have further received notice from Capt. Elmer Otis, Fort Wise, of the arrival there of arms for four companies of volunteers. The strong and malignant element within this Territory, added to the destitution of arms and ammunition of any kind up to this time, has rendered absolutely necessary the delay to furnish a garrison for Fort Wise. The population of the Arkansas River is not numerous enough to furnish one company, and to send them from the mining region has been impossible, from want of arms, ammunition, food, clothing, transportation, or money to procure any of these essentials. I am incessantly occupied to comply with your requisitions at the earliest moment.

The malignant secession element of this Territory has numbered 7,500. It has been ably and secretly organized from November last, and requires extreme and extraordinary measures to meet and control its onslaught. The core of its strength has at present withdrawn to gather strength from Texas, Utah, Arkansas, and from the country of the Confederated Cherokee, Creek, and other Indians. They contemplate to return with overwhelming strength and precipitate the neighboring Indians upon us. To prepare for what may be accomplished by them is my duty. This country, everywhere open to the east, can only be defended by a sufficient force to meet the enemy in the field. It also enters into their plans to capture Forts Wise and Garland; to surround New Mexico and invade it from the north. The Indian populations west of Arkansas have united with the rebel war to the amount of 64,500, capable of furnishing an efficient army for operations upon these Territories, familiar with this country, and allied to the Georgians, who sympathize with secession, and form a large proportion of our mining population.

You will learn that a guerrilla party has been captured by Captain Otis near Fort Wise; the captain of this band, McKee, has been in jail for several weeks in this city.

Be well assured that I neglect no resource within my reach or attainable by energy to provide for the safety of this Territory, and produce a force capable of co-operating cordially in the operations in New Mexico, with which I am familiar.

Very respectfully,

WILLIAM GILPIN.

SOURCE: *OR*, SERIES 1, VOLUME 4, PAGE 73

OR-38

DENVER, COLO. TER., *October 30, 1861.*

Hon. WILLIAM H. SEWARD:

DEAR SIR: We make some progress. The train of the notorious A. B. Miller was captured in Kansas before it reached the Cherokee country, whither they were going. Captain Otis, at Fort Wise, has captured Captain McKee's party of sixty men with the horses and has turned them over to the marshal of this Territory, who has gone with a posse of cavalry to bring them in to me. Governor Gilpin has received a copy of the treaty of the Cherokees with the Confederates. We have apparently suppressed the rebellion here, but have well-grounded fears of an irruption upon us of the Cherokees unless they are diverted by movements east of them. New Mexico is reported fully awake, armed, and safe. This large addition to our stock of prisoners, and consequently to our responsibilities and to the public expense of keeping them, leads me to ask the advice of the Government as to what shall be done with them. We can imprison most of them in our prison here with the assistance of a military guard, and I will try, convict, and sentence them, if it is the pleasure of the Government. But I am inclined to doubt the propriety of trying and convicting any of them except the leaders until we are along further into the future.

I shall need instructions sooner than they can reach me by mail, and as the telegraph extends to Julesburg, ninety miles from here, a telegram will reach me in twenty-four hours. If it shall suit the President or yourself to afford me some indication of the wishes of the Government in respect to these prisoners by telegraph, I think it will come to me safely now, as the operator at and the messenger from the Julesburg office are loyal.

There is not much difference in effect here between malcontented office-seekers whom Governor Gilpin cannot appoint to office and the secessionists or open rebels. They seem to have no idea of loyalty either to the General or Territorial government. If one of them gets an order or contact for rations the rest turn in and fight him and the Governor. They number some 5,000 of the border ruffians of Kansas and the destroying angels of Brigham Young. I presume that they are the worst people on the face of the earth to govern.

* * * *

Very respectfully,

BENJ. F. HALL.

[Editor's note: *This document appears in the* Official Records *as an inclosure to correspondence from Secretary William H. Seward to Secretary Simon Cameron, November 13, 1861, that is not included in this volume.*]

Source: *OR*, Series 3, Volume 1, pages 636–637

OR-39

[*Extract*]

LATEST NEWS FROM WASHINGTON.

The latest from General Rosecrans—His army in fine condition.

Washington, *November 10.*—A dispatch to-day from Western Virginia states that General Rosecrans and his command are in fine condition and prepared to receive the enemy from any quarter they may approach, and the commander is confident of success.

Military appointments—Transportation of freight between Baltimore and Washington, &c.

Among the recently appointed brigadier-generals are Morgan, of Ohio, and Colonel Philip St. George Cooke, who recently brought hither his cavalry troops from Utah. He is a native of and appointed from Virginia. Much complaint is made that freight from the North is compelled to lie over at Baltimore to make room for the transportation to Washington of goods purchased in that city. The matter is now engaging the attention of Government officers. The German portion of the volunteers of the Army of the Potomac, principally belonging to Blenker's brigade, design having a torchlight procession in honor of General McClellan's succession to the command of the Armies of the United States. The Government has in contemplation the placing of trains of wagons between Washington and Baltimore for transportation of freight. The taking possession of the turnpike and putting the road and bridges in proper condition will probably become a public necessity. Messrs.

Gibbons & Co.'s express reports the fall of the bridge at Beltsville, thirteen miles from Washington.

[Editor's note: *This document appears in the* Official Records *as an indorsement to correspondence from G. T. Beauregard to General J. E. Johnston, November 15, 1861, that is not included in this volume.*]

SOURCE: *OR*, SERIES 1, VOLUME 51, PART 2, PAGES 379–380

OR-40

HEADQUARTERS DEPARTMENT OF THE PACIFIC,
San Francisco, November 20, 1861.

ASSISTANT ADJUTANT-GENERAL,
Headquarters of the Army, Washington, D.C.:

SIR: On the 16th instant I had the honor to acknowledge (by telegraph) the receipt of Major-General McClellan's dispatch of the 13th. I have recalled Colonel Carleton from his command in the southern district, and as soon as he arrives I shall organize his command of at least one regiment, for the protection of the Overland Mail Route. I have conferred with Mr. Louis McLane, the agent, as to the most suitable point to locate the troops, in order to afford the required protection. He suggests Simpson's Park, Ruby Valley, and Camp Floyd as the best positions to occupy. The first is 326 miles from Sacramento, Ruby Valley 98 miles from Simpson's, and Camp Floyd is 217 miles in advance of Ruby Valley. The weather for many days past has been tempestuous in the extreme, and the snow on the mountains is reported as very deep, and it may be next to an impossibility for the troops to cross over with their necessary supplies. Were it not for the starving condition of the Indians, no fears need be entertained of their committing any depredations. Twenty thousand dollars' worth of provisions, annually distributed to the friendly tribes along this section of the route, would save the Government vast sums of money. The contracts made last summer for the transportation of our supplies from this place to Ruby Valley were at the rate of about $400 per ton; and at this season it will cost much more. Everything is quiet on this coast; nothing of importance has transpired since my communication to the Adjutant-General of the Army, dated on the 16th instant, a copy of which was forwarded to the Headquarters of the Army. I have removed the Third Infantry California Volunteers from Stockton to Benicia Barracks. Four companies of this regiment are already at their stations; the remaining six have been organized, and are progressing favorably in recruiting. Clothing for all the troops in the department is being made here. Very soon the supply will be ample and of a superior quality, at a reasonable rate. On the 9th I inspected the troops at Fort Point, one company. Third Artillery, commanded by Brevet Major Austine, and on the 13th I inspected the troops at Alcatraz Island, two companies. Third Artillery, commanded by Major Burton. It affords me pleasure to report that I found the troops in high order. The armament of the fort, although incomplete, was found in handsome condition, and ready for any emergency.

Very respectfully, your obedient servant,

G. WRIGHT,
Brigadier-General, U.S. Army, Commanding.

Source: *OR*, Series 1, Volume 50, Part 1, pages 730–731

OR-41

Headquarters Department of the Pacific,
San Francisco, Cal., November 22, 1861.

His Excellency J. W. Nye,
Governor of Nevada Territory, Carson City:

Sir: I have received instructions from the Headquarters of the Army to send a regiment of troops, or more if I deem it necessary, to protect the Overland Mail Route. The command will be under Colonel Carleton, and will move as soon as the necessary arrangements can be made. I am informed that it is next to an impossibility for troops with their supplies to cross the mountains at this time, and my object in addressing Your Excellency is to obtain reliable data as to the practicability of the route, and particularly as to the condition of the Indians and the probability of their committing depredations on the stock of the mail company. As soon as practicable I design to establish troops at Simpson's Park, Ruby Valley, and Camp Floyd, and in the meantime is it within your power to issue such provisions to the starving Indians along the route as may be necessary for their existence? I have an extra supply of provisions at Fort Churchill, and although I am not authorized to issue to Indians, except in small quantities, yet I should not hesitate to sell it to the Indian Department, under existing circumstances, even if the Department should not be in funds, not doubting that such a course would be approved. I shall esteem it a favor to receive your views on the subject, with any suggestions you may deem pertinent. I have been assigned to the command of the department and remain on this coast. A service of more than nine years on the Pacific has familiarized me with the whole country and also with the character and temper of the inhabitants. The Union loving people of this coast are vastly in the ascendant, their fiat has gone forth, and no secession doctrine can flourish here. Nevertheless it behooves us to be watchful at all times. I shall not assume a threatening attitude, for the purpose of warning our enemies to refrain from unlawful acts, but pursuing the even tenor of my way, ever observant of impending events, and ready at all times to enforce a due respect and observance of the Constitution and laws of our country; and if it becomes my duty to act, I shall do so fearlessly, and without regard to personal consequences, feeling assured that I shall receive the cordial support of every true and loyal citizen on the Pacific Coast.

With great respect, I have the honor to be Your Excellency's obedient servant,

G. WRIGHT,

Brigadier-General, U.S. Army, Commanding Department.

SOURCE: *OR*, SERIES 1, VOLUME 50, PART 1, PAGE 735

OR-42

DETROIT, *November 26, 1861.*

Hon. W. H. SEWARD,

Secretary of State, Washington:

DEAR SIR: Inclosed please find the original letter from North Branch, Mich., addressed to a prominent citizen of this city whose name is withheld from me. It was thrown into the wrong box, and the person upon opening it discovering a conspiracy was on foot to overthrow the Government took it to a friend, and the friend to W. A. Howard, esq., postmaster, and after a delay of some three or four weeks it came into my hands, and I have permission to send it to you with this understanding on my part that it shall be returned when called for. My object in sending it now is that you may compare the writing and ink with that found on Dr. Guy S. Hopkins who is now confined in Fort Lafayette.

I will endeavor to give you the rendering of initials embraced in this mysterious letter according to our judgment, viz: R. M. C., Robert McClelland; C—s, circulars; S— of S—, Secretary of State; P—ts, prints; R— L—, W. C. W., R— L— (don't know), Windsor, Canada West; C—s S—t, Charles Stuart, colonel of Eleventh Regiment Michigan Volunteers, now filling up; N—, North; S—, South; A—, assistance; A—, abolitionists; M—d, Maryland: Ft. M—, Fort Monroe; Pres'nt P—, President Pierce; P—y, Purdey; L. C. D—t, League Club of Detroit; Doct.

[De] F— (don't know); H—, Mormon elder (don't know, am on his track); Port H—, Port Huron; Doct. [De] F— (supposed to be a Virginian who boarded at Port Sarnia about 1st of October last and registered his name as Jonathan Tripp, Virginia. Notes taken by my son, 7th of October); R—, Richmond; Capt. S— (don't know); G— M—, grand master or marshal; W—, Windsor (you will please note Sicilian Vespers); Capt. H— (don't know); p—s, passes. The signature you must figure out, for I cannot.

I have a number of names that I am on the lookout [for], and associate those sent forward and named in letter, viz: Capt. Walter P. Beach, N. H. Hart, lieutenant, and now filling up to go into Charles Stuart's regiment. David C. Wattles was to go as second lieutenant, but unfortunately he is on his way to Fort Lafayette. Others have been named, and if we are to believe those that come in daily contact with them they are rank secessionists and members of this League Club or Golden Circle. It is to be hoped that I may come across some more papers that will throw more light upon the subject. We have been to considerable expense in ferreting this matter out, having first to send a couple of detectives out to North Branch, and they employed the sheriff of Lapeer to assist them. They were gone about one week and returned with their report. I then waited until Dr. Guy S. Hopkins came in and arrested him, secured his papers and then sent out and arrested Butler and Wattles, all of which costs money. You will please advise me if I can embrace those expenses in my monthly account.

All of which is most respectfully submitted.

Your obedient servant,

W. H. BARSE.

P. S.—I will send Doctor Hopkins' other papers in by themselves as found in his possession.

BARSE.

[Inclosure.]

[Editor's note: *See* OR-34 *for this inclosure. Also see* OR-44 *for additional correspondence connected to this coded message.*]

Source: *OR*, Series 2, Volume 2, Section 2, pages 1247–1248

OR-43

HEADQUARTERS DEPARTMENT OF THE PACIFIC,
San Francisco, Cal., December 16, 1861.

LOUIS MCLANE, Esq.,
Agent Overland Mail Company, San Francisco, Cal.:

SIR: After my several interviews with you on the subject of the protection of the Overland Mail Route, and a careful consideration as to the most judicious course to pursue, I have reached the conclusion that the only feasible mode is to issue a moderate quantity of provisions to the Indians along the route, who are in a starving condition. It is next to impossible to send troops with their supplies over the mountains at this time; the expense would be enormous. The mail route must be protected, and I deem it my duty to act for the best interests of the Government and the country. Under these circumstances, in behalf of the Government I have to request that you issue in the course of the winter and spring to the Indians near your stations at and west of Camp Floyd, not to exceed 250 barrels of flour and 50,000 pounds of fresh beef, or equivalent in other articles of food. Feeling assured that the agents of the company will procure the provisions economically, and issue them judiciously, I cannot for a moment doubt that the Department will approve of my course, and that the company will be reimbursed by the United States Government.

Very respectfully, your obedient servant,

G. WRIGHT,
Brigadier-General, U.S. Army, Commanding Department.

SOURCE: *OR*, SERIES 1, VOLUME 50, PART 1, PAGE 766

OR-44

DEPARTMENT OF STATE, WASHINGTON, *December 20, 1861.*

FRANKLIN PIERCE, Esq.,
Concord, N. H.

SIR: I inclose an extract from a letter received at this Department from which it would appear that you were a member of a secret league the object of which is to overthrow the Government.

Any explanation upon the subject which you may offer would be acceptable.

I am, &c.,

WILLIAM H. SEWARD.

[Inclosure.]

North Branch, *October 5, 1861.*

* * * *

President P— in his passage has drawn many brave and influential men to the league. P—y, of the L. C. D—t, sent a line to Doctor F— (by H., the Mormon elder), who as you perhaps know is just across the line from Port H—. The league is doing nobly in M., I. and Wis. He is cautious, but in common with others is gradually preparing the minds of the people for a great change. He expresses a fear that any attempt to draft men will produce a premature outbreak. I think his fear is well founded. A member of the league in Genesee who passed through the woods on his way with dispatches to Doctor F— told that any attempt to draft our friends there would bring on an open rupture. I think our leaders should look to this, as no doubt they will.

* * * *

Yours, in the cause,

* ⊐ < ∧ ʒ || □

[Editor's note: *The dashes and coded signature, in the inclosure above, appear in the original* War of the Rebellion *record. The* Official Records *editors identified "North Branch" as North Branch, Michigan—see* OR-34 *and* OR-42. *It should also be noted that "North Branch, Chisago County, Minnesota," became a township in 1861 and may have also been the North Branch referenced.*]

Source: *OR*, Series 2, Volume 2, Section 2, page 1257

OR-45

[*Extract*]

Headquarters Outposts Army of the Potomac,
December 23, 1861.

Major: I have the honor to report that on the 20th instant I was placed in command of four regiments of infantry, 150 cavalry, and a battery of four pieces of artillery, viz. Eleventh Virginia Volunteers, Col. S. Garland, Jr.; Sixth South Carolina Volunteers, Lieutenant Colonel Secrest; Tenth Alabama Volunteers, Col. J. H. Forney, and First Kentucky Volunteers, Col. Thomas H. Taylor, making an aggregate force of 1,600 infantry; Sumter Flying Artillery (four pieces), Capt. A. S. Cutts; One hundredth [?] North Carolina Cavalry, Major Gordon, and Fifty-second [?] Virginia Cavalry, Captain Pitzer, for the purpose of covering an expedition of all the wagons of our army that could be spared (after hay) to the left of Dranesville.

I proceeded at once by the nearest route at daylight towards Dranesville, and the accompanying sketch* will show the route as well as the relative situation of other objects of interest in what I am about to narrate.

. . .

Our wounded, who were for the time prisoners, say that the enemy's loss was acknowledged by them to be very heavy, and among the officers killed or mortally wounded was Colonel Kane, of Utah notoriety; and citizens living below declared that they carried off twenty wagon loads of killed and wounded, besides many dead before them on their horses, and that as soon as their dead and wounded were removed they left the field precipitately, leaving behind much of the material which we left on the field, but which we recovered next day.

. . .

I have the honor to be, major, respectfully, your obedient servant,

J. E. B. STUART,
Brigadier-General, Commanding.

Maj. THOMAS A. PRATT, *Assistant Adjutant-General.*

* Not found.

SOURCE: *OR*, SERIES 1, VOLUME 5, PAGES 490–494

OR-46

HDQRS. FIRST CALIFORNIA VOLUNTEER INFANTRY,
Camp Latham, near Los Angeles, Cal., December 23, 1861.

All persons who have been arrested or who may be arrested in this State as secessionists or traitors to the country will be kept in confinement at Fort Yuma until final action is had on each case. The garrison of that fort will be at once increased to nine companies—one of artillery, six of infantry, and two of cavalry. Its defenses will be strengthened and some heavy guns mounted, and it will be well supplied with ammunition, provisions, and forage. It is reported that the Navajo Indians obstruct the route from Albuquerque to Los Angeles, now important as the only one on which the daily mail from the States can be carried, that of the north being blocked up with snow, that of the south being in possession of the rebels at its eastern end and on the Rio Grande. These Indians are therefore to be brought to terms. An expedition, consisting of seven companies, will move up the Colorado on Colonel Hoffman's trail. Three of these companies (infantry) will reoccupy Fort Navajo and re-establish the ferry. This force, as heretofore, will draw its supplies from Los Angeles. The other four—three of cavalry and one of infantry—will proceed on to Las Vegas, near the Potosi mines, on the Salt Lake road, and establish a post at the old Mormon fort. This is preliminary to the movement, already ordered, of troops next summer to Fort Crittenden, near Salt Lake. The new post at Las Vegas will be known as Fort Baker.

JAMES H. CARLETON,
Colonel First California Volunteers, Commanding.

Source: *OR*, Series 1, Volume 50, Part 1, page 782

OR-47

[*Extract*]

Patterson's Creek, *January 16, 1862.*

General McClellan:

General: I have the honor to reply to your inquiries.*

When by request, October 25, I gave my views to General Scott on the subject of protecting the Baltimore and Ohio Railroad, I recommended the occupation of Romney by Kelley, he to be immediately re-enforced, but beyond holding the point to break up guerrilla parties I did not propose a strong demonstration here.

. . .

If Colonel Grover, of Utah celebrity, were appointed brigadier-general he might relieve me.

Trusting that I have not exceeded the terms of your instructions, I am, respectfully,

F. W. LANDER,
Brigadier-General.

* Not found.

Source: *OR*, Series 1, Volume 5, pages 702–703

OR-48

[*Extract*]

WAR DEPARTMENT,
Washington City, D.C., February 25, 1862.

Hon. GALUSHA A. GROW,
Speaker of the House of Representatives:

SIR: I have the honor to transmit herewith the returns of the militia of the United States, and of their arms, accouterments, and ammunition for the year 1861, in conformity with the act of Congress of March 2, 1803, "to provide for the national defense by establishing an uniform militia," such returns to be laid before Congress by the first Monday in February.

Very respectfully, your obedient servant,

EDWIN M. STANTON,
Secretary of War.

Abstract of the general annual return of the militia of the United States by States and Territories, according to the act of March, 1863, for the year 1861.

[Inclosure No. 1]

	Washington Territory	Nebraska Territory	Kansas Territory	Territory of Utah	Territory of N. Mexico
Returns.					
For what year Recievd. [*sic*]	......	......	......	1853	......
Date	......	......	......	Oct. 28	......
Infantry.					
Commissioned officers including general, division, brigades, &c.	......	......	......	151	......
Non-commissioned officers, musicians, privates, &c.	......	......	......	1,593	......
Total	......	......	......	1,744	......

	Washington Territory	Nebraska Territory	Kansas Territory	Territory of Utah	Territory of N. Mexico
Cavalry					
Commissioned officers	......	......	......	127	......
Non-commissioned officers, musicians, privates, &c.	......	......	......	877	......
Total	......	......	......	1,044	......
Artillery					
Commissioned officers	......	......	......	7	......
Non-commissioned officers, musicians, privates, &c.	......	......	......	66	......
Total	......	......	......	73	......
Aggregate	......	......	......	2,821	......

L. THOMAS,
Adjutant-General.

[Inclosure No. 2]

ADJUTANT-GENERAL'S OFFICE,
Washington, February 3, 1862.

Abstract of annual returns of arms, accouterments, and ammunition of the militia of the United States for the year 1861.

	Washington Territory	Nebraska Territory	Kansas Territory	Territory of Utah	Territory of N. Mexico
Ordnance and ordnance stores.					
Brass Howitzers.	......	......	......	1	......
Iron Sponges and rammers.	......	......	......	2	......
Ammunition boxes.	......	......	......	2	......
Tumbrels or powder carts.	......	......	......	2	......
Sets of harness.	......	......	......	1	......

L. THOMAS,
Adjutant-General.

[Editor's note: *The columns and rows of both tables in this document have been edited to remove extraneous information.*]

SOURCE: *OR*, SERIES 3, VOLUME 1, PAGES 900–905

OR-49

SAN FRANCISCO, CAL., *March 26, 1862.*

Brig. Gen. L. THOMAS,
Adjutant-General U.S. Army, Washington City:

Your dispatch of 21st received. I had previously ordered Colonel Cornelius to prepare his regiment, six companies of Oregon cavalry, to move into the Walla Walla country, and thence to the mining districts; and as the season advances to move toward Fort Hall, to protect the emigrants. I conferred with Mr. Crawford on the subject. I can give protection to the Overland Mail Route as far as Salt Lake or Fort Bridger. I have two companies of cavalry now at Fort Churchill, and I have three companies of cavalry and six of volunteer infantry available and ready to move as soon as the roads are passable. I have an active and reliable colonel of volunteers, well suited for this service. Colonel Carleton is in Southern California, and moving as fast as the miry roads will permit toward Fort Yuma, with his expeditionary forces. He cannot be spared from that command.

G. WRIGHT,
Brigadier-General, U.S. Army, Commanding.

SOURCE: *OR*, SERIES 1, VOLUME 50, PART 1, PAGES 953–954

OR-50

HEADQUARTERS DEPARTMENT OF THE PACIFIC,
San Francisco, March 27, 1862.

Brig. Gen. L. THOMAS,
Adjutant-General U.S. Army, Washington, D.C.:

GENERAL: Inclosed herewith is a copy of a telegraphic dispatch which I had the honor to transmit to you yesterday in reply to yours of the 21st instant.* The propriety of my making arrangements for the protection of the emigrants as they approach my department had already received my careful consideration. The organization of the six companies of Oregon cavalry, under the command of Colonel Cornelius, it is expected, will be completed early in April. Two of those companies have been raised in the northern section of that State and four in the southern. The latter I have directed the colonel to order north as soon as the roads are passable, and then to prepare his whole command to march to Fort Walla Walla. The presence of troops in the mining districts of the Nez Percé and Salmon River countries will be absolutely necessary to preserve peace between our people and the Indians. The extravagant reports of the richness of those mines has created the wildest enthusiasm, and already a large number of men have gone from here to the Columbia River to be in readiness to move to the mines as soon as the route is practicable. As the emigrants approach this department it is certain that a large portion of them will be attracted to the mines in Oregon and Territory of Washington, and I propose, as the summer advances, to throw forward to the vicinity of Fort Hall, or farther, if necessary, a squadron or two of cavalry to afford them protection through the Snake River country. I have conferred with Mr. Crawford, the gentleman appointed to conduct the overland emigration. He is well acquainted with the route and fully understands the arrangements to be made for his safe passage through the Indian country. The protection of the Overland Mail Route will be provided for at the earliest moment practicable. At this moment neither troops nor supplies can cross the mountains without subjecting the Government to an enormous expense, which I do not deem it proper to incur unless an emergency should arise making it necessary. I have conferred with Mr. Louis McLane on this subject, and copy of a note he addressed me yesterday, and herewith inclosed,† will show you that no immediate danger is apprehended. The instructions of the Secretary of War will be carried out as soon as practicable. I believe that ample protection can be given to the overland mail as far east as Salt Lake by the force I have reported as available at once for that purpose, viz, five companies of cavalry and six of infantry; should it, however, be found insufficient, it can be increased. In the present aspect of our foreign relations, prudential considerations require that a strong force should be kept at or near this city. I have now three companies of artillery and one of the Ninth Infantry in the two permanent forts, I have seven companies of the Ninth Infantry at the Presidio, but they are very much reduced, one of them having just returned from the East, with only its non-commissioned officers, and 100 of our best men being on the escort of Lieutenant Mullan's wagon-road expedition. The three companies of cavalry near this city and the six companies of the Third Infantry California Volunteers, now at Benicia Barracks, I design for the overland mail protection. I have the headquarters and five companies of the Fourth Infantry California Volunteers, encamped at Sacramento. I shall soon move them down to Benicia or in the neighborhood of this city, according to circumstances. In the southern district Colonel Carleton is advancing on Fort Yuma with his own regiment (First Infantry) and First Cavalry (five companies), and the Light Battery Company A, Third Artillery. The roads are still in a bad condition, and loaded wagons cannot move. I have also now in the southern district the Fifth Infantry California Volunteers, Colonel Bowie, and four companies of the Second Cavalry. Colonel Bowie will be left in command of that district after the advance of Carleton.

Very respectfully, your obedient servant,

G. WRIGHT,
Brigadier-General, U.S. Army, Commanding.

* [*Refers to* OR-49.]

† [*Refers to Louis McLane to General Wright, March 26, 1862.* OR, *Series 1, Volume 50, Part 1, page 954.*]

SOURCE: *OR*, SERIES 1, VOLUME 50, PART 1, PAGES 956–957

OR-51

SAINT LOUIS, *April 10, 1862.*
From Fort Leavenworth, April 8, 1862.

Maj. Gen. H. W. HALLECK:

From the best information obtainable at least 2,000 Indians can be armed. Arms for that number are now going forward to Humboldt. Taking out troops for New Mexico will leave three regiments of infantry, four of cavalry, and two batteries in this State.

General Curtis seems not to have received your order returning Kansas troops.

Texans reported leaving New Mexico. If true, might not one mounted regiment be left on the plains.

Snake Indians, Bannocks, and Mormons reported committing depredations about South Pass.

J. W. DENVER,
Brigadier-General, Commanding.

SOURCE: *OR*, SERIES 1, VOLUME 8, PAGES 679–680

OR-52

Report on measures taken to make secure the Overland Mail Route to California.

Adjutant-General's Office,
Washington, April 24, 1862.

First. November 13, 1861, Major-General McClellan directed Brigadier-General Wright to order the necessary force, two or three regiments—if possible, under Colonel Carleton—to protect the Overland Mail Route, and to confer with Louis McLane, esq., about the location of the troops.

Second. General Wright's reply, marked A,* shows the season to be too late to send troops and supplies, reports he has agreed with the Governor of Nevada to issue provisions from Fort Churchill (Carson's Valley) to the Indians, and the Governor and himself feel sure that measure will keep the Indians quiet and the route secure until spring. The Governor's letter is inclosed in General Wright's.

Third. December 10, 1861, General Wright reports the Overland Mail Route cannot be depended on because of storms of rain and snow, and suggests sending letters by sea through express (marked B.†)

Fourth. January 9, 1862, General Wright alludes to apprehensions of Indian hostilities on the overland route, but says quiet has thus far been preserved, and the issue of provisions has had a good effect (marked C‡).

Fifth. March 21, 1862, orders were sent from the Secretary of War to Brigadier-General Wright to make necessary preparations and disposition of his troops to protect emigrants and the Overland Mail Route from Indian hostilities and depredations, a report called for of what he could do, and whether Colonel Carleton could have the immediate direction.

Sixth. General Wright's reply, marked D,** received this day by mail, reports five companies of cavalry (of which two are at Fort Churchill) and six of infantry ready to move on the overland route as soon as the season will permit, and says he can protect the route as far as Salt Lake or Fort Bridger. Mr. McLane's note inclosed says the Overland Company expect that troops will be permanently stationed on the mail route for the protection of the mails and treasure. This ends the report as far as the Department of the Pacific is concerned.

Seventh. February 26, 1862, the commander of Fort Kearny was ordered to "give protection to the stock and property of the Overland Mail Company and not allow any interference in carrying the U.S. mails, under color of any civil authority or pretense whatever." Copy of this was sent to General Hunter, commanding Department of Kansas.

Eighth. April 2, 1862, the following dispatch was sent to Col. E. B. Alexander, Tenth U.S. Infantry, at Fort Laramie:

> Complaints are made that you have neglected to furnish men and arms for protection to the Overland Mail Route. The Secretary of War now peremptorily directs that you afford every necessary protection in men and means, also report why this has not been previously done.

Ninth. Colonel Alexander's reply (marked E) does not believe in reports of Indian hostilities near his post. Will not trust employés of the mail company because many are secessionists. Refers to report of March 2 (which should be 22d) for reasons why he did not send men and arms.

Tenth. Colonel Alexander's report of March 22 (marked F.)

Eleventh. April 10, 1862, the following dispatch was sent to General Denver, commanding at Fort Leavenworth:

> The Secretary of War directs that you afford every necessary protection to the Overland Mail Route against Indians and other depredations.

Twelfth. And the following was sent to the same officer April 11, 1862:

> Send daily a stage load of soldiers from Leavenworth or Atchison, or any nearer point, until each station in the Indian country where depredations are committed shall have ample protection. Let rations be furnished from Laramie and Kearny or until other arrangements can be made by the Overland Company, with whom the Government can settle afterwards. The Secretary desires everything in your power to be done to give the fullest protection to the Overland Mail Route.

There are no mounted troops in the vicinity and considerable time would elapse before they could be placed in position to guard the part of the mail route said to be subject to molestation, which is nearer Salt Lake than Fort Laramie. The suggestion of the acting Governor and other civil functionaries of Utah that a regiment of mounted men be raised is that Territory is not concurred in because it is not supposed so large a force is necessary. The proposition of Senator Latham, deemed by him most expedient and reasonable, is that Brigham Young be authorized to raise, arm, and equip a company of 100 mounted men for not less than three months, to protect the mail and route, and the telegraph line west of Salt Lake near Independence Rock, from Indian depredations and to recover the stock and property of the mail company which has been stolen. From the personal interest Brigham Young is said to have in the telegraphic communication with Salt Lake and from his known influence over his own people, and over the Indian tribes around, this plan is supposed to offer the most expeditious and economical remedy to the obstructions to the mail route. The objection to this plan is that Brigham Young is not a functionary recognized by the United States Government, and a requisition for volunteers from Utah should be made upon the Governor of the Territory. There are two companies of the Third

Regular Cavalry, paroled men, now at Detroit. These might be mounted and sent to the point where troops are required, but a considerable time would elapse before they could reach there.

Respectfully submitted.

L. THOMAS,
Adjutant-General.

* [*Refers to Wright to Thomas, December 9, 1861.* OR, *Series 1, Volume 50, Part 1, pages 753–754.*]
† [*Refers to Wright to Thomas, December 10, 1861.* OR, *Series 1, Volume 50, Part 1, page 757.*]
‡ [*Refers to Wright to Thomas, January 9, 1862.* OR, *Series 1, Volume 50, Part 1, pages 798–799.*]
** [*Refers to Wright to Thomas, March 26, 1862.* OR, *Series 1, Volume 50, Part 1, pages 953–954.*]

SOURCE: *OR*, SERIES 1, VOLUME 50, PART 1, PAGES 1022–1024

OR-53

HEADQUARTERS DEPARTMENT OF THE MISSISSIPPI,
Saint Louis, April 27, 1862.

Major-General HALLECK,
Pittsburg, Tenn.:

On the 19th instant two companies cavalry sent from Camp Wild by Captain Backus to Fort Union, at request of Governor of New Mexico and Major Paul, commanding Fort Union. On 23d instant Colonel Alexander, commanding Fort Laramie, reports Indians took stages and Flowers' party at Ice Springs, wounding 6 out of 9. Stock taken from Green River and herder killed. Two men killed on Harris' Fork. Stock run off from Three Crossings of Sweet Water. Indians say "Mormons good men; all others bad men."

By orders from Washington detachment of soldiers are to be sent in the stages. Colonel Alexander sent first detachment on 23d instant. General Sturgis ordered this to be continued until mail stations shall be secured.

W. SCOTT KETCHUM,
Brigadier-General, Acting Inspector-General.

SOURCE: *OR*, SERIES 1, VOLUME 13, PAGE 366

OR-54

ADJUTANT-GENERAL'S OFFICE,
Washington, April 28, 1862.

Mr. BRIGHAM YOUNG,
Salt Lake City, Utah:

By express direction of the President of the United States you are hereby authorized to raise, arm, and equip one company of cavalry for ninety days' service. This company will be organized as follows:

One captain, 1 first lieutenant, 1 second lieutenant, 1 first sergeant, 1 quartermaster-sergeant, 4 sergeants, 8 corporals, 2 musicians, 2 farriers, 1 saddler, 1 wagoner, and from 56 to 72 privates. The company will be employed to protect the property of the telegraph and overland mail companies in or about Independence Rock, where depredations have been committed, and will be continued in service only till the U.S. troops can reach the point where they are so much needed. It may therefore be disbanded previous to the expiration of the ninety days. It will not be employed for any offensive operations other than may grow out of the duty hereinbefore assigned to it. The officers of the company will be mustered into the U.S. service by any civil officer of the United States Government at Salt Lake City competent to administer the oath. The men will then be enlisted by the company officers. The men employed in the service above named will be entitled to receive no other than the allowances authorized by law to soldiers in the service of the United States. Until the proper staff officer for subsisting these men arrive you will please furnish subsistence for them yourself, keeping an accurate account thereof for future settlement with the United States Government.

By order of the Secretary of War:

L. THOMAS,
Adjutant-General.

SOURCE: *OR*, SERIES 3, VOLUME 2, PAGE 27

OR-55

HEADQUARTERS DEPARTMENT OF THE PACIFIC,
San Francisco, April 29, 1862.

Brig. Gen. L. THOMAS,
Adjutant General U.S. Army, Washington, D.C.:

GENERAL: The route of the overland mail will not be practicable for wagons before the end of May; in the meantime we are preparing the outfit for the troops designated for that line. The southern expedition under Colonel Carleton has drawn off all our extra means of transportation, and we shall be compelled to purchase wagons, mules, &c., here. The wagons are now being manufactured in this city. We are still embarrassed for want of funds; the credit of the Government, however, is good, but we must necessarily pay more than we should have to do if we had the cash in hand. The mail route at this moment, as far as the limits of this department, can be traveled in perfect safety; had it been otherwise, I would have forced a passage over the mountains and thrown troops on the line at any cost. I presume it is the design of the department to have troops distributed along the line to afford permanent protection for the mails and treasure. With the treasure, of course the escort would have to be continued all the way, and mounted troops would be required for this service monthly or semi-monthly. The distance from Sacramento to Fort Bridger is about 800 miles, and it will be important to have a careful examination of the whole route made and suitable points selected for posts. Ruby Valley is well spoken of; it is about midway between Fort Churchill and Camp Floyd. On the 15th proximo I shall advance Colonel Connor's command toward the mountains and have it prepared to cross as soon as possible. A year's supply of clothing, subsistence, &c., will be sent over as soon as the roads are in good order.

Very respectfully, your obedient servant,

G. WRIGHT,
Brigadier-General, U.S. Army, Commanding.

SOURCE: *OR*, SERIES 1, VOLUME 50, PART 1, PAGE 1039

OR-56

CAMP LATHAM, SOUTHERN DISTRICT OF CALIFORNIA,
May 3, 1862.

Lieut. Col. GEORGE S. EVANS,
Second Cavalry California Volunteers, Commanding Camp:

COLONEL: I have the honor to make the following report of my trip to the Mojave:

In pursuance of the annexed written instructions* I left Camp Drum on the 6th day of April, A.D. 1862, and arrived at Camp Cady on the 14th day of April, A.D. 1862, seeing and hearing of nothing unusual on the route, except at Lane's Crossing of the Mojave, where I was informed by Mr. Lane that a wagon loaded with powder had crossed there a few days previous, said to be going to Salt Lake. I remained at Camp Cady until the 24th of April, seeing and hearing of nothing unusual, and meeting no parties that I could suspect of treasonable intentions toward the Government. On the 24th I left Camp Cady for Camp Latham, and on arriving at Lane's Crossing, some seventy miles above Camp Cady, I was informed by Mr. Lane that during my absence at Camp Cady another wagon loaded with powder, said to be for Salt Lake, had passed. I was informed by the parties keeping the toll-gate at Cajon Pass that armed men in small parties had been passing through all the winter and spring.

All of which is most respectfully submitted.

N. P. PIERCE,
Second Lieut. Co. G, 2d California Cav. Vols., Comdg. Detachment.

* [*Refers to Pierce from Cutler, April 5, 1862.* OR, *Series 1, Volume 50, Part 1, pages 985–986.*]

SOURCE: *OR*, SERIES 1, VOLUME 50, PART 1, PAGES 1049–1050

OR-57

HEADQUARTERS DEPARTMENT OF THE PACIFIC,
San Francisco, May 13, 1862.

Brig. Gen. L. THOMAS,
Adjutant-General U.S. Army, Washington, D.C.:

GENERAL: I have just heard from Major Drum. He was at Fort Yuma on the last day of April; had completed his inspection, and would leave the same day on his return to these headquarters, inspecting the troops near Los Angeles and San Pedro on his way. Colonel Carleton was at Fort Yuma, pushing his troops forward into Arizona. The major, after inspecting the troops, says: "The troops are all in fine spirits, and anxious for the movement eastward;" and further, "It has fallen to the lot of few men to take into the field so well instructed a body of volunteer troops as compose Carleton's command." With such men and officers, I look for a speedy re-establishment of our authority over Arizona and New Mexico. In Arizona it will be necessary to hold the country under a military governor until such time as the civil authorities can be reorganized. To-day I received a telegraphic dispatch from Governor Nye, at Carson City, Nev. Ter. The Indian disturbances at Honey Lake and that region of country have been quelled, and everything is quiet. Colonel Steinberger, First Infantry Washington Territory Volunteers, has reached Fort Vancouver with four full companies of his regiment, and assumed command of the District of Oregon. Colonel Lippitt, Second Infantry California Volunteers, commanding the District of Humboldt, is at work energetically, bringing those Indians under subjection. The country is a difficult one to operate in, and it will take time to collect all those Indians and place them on reservations. A large assemblage of Indians at the Owen's Lake country, some 300 miles southeast from here, rendered it necessary to send a force of three companies of cavalry from Los Angeles to protect our people and their property and chastise the Indians. The country generally is quiet and prosperous. The sympathizers with the rebels are careful to keep within the pale of the law. The season is more than a month later than usual. The snow on the Sierra Nevada Mountains is very deep, and certainly not before the middle of June will it be possible for Colonel Connor, with his troops and supplies, to cross over toward Salt Lake.

Very respectfully, your most obedient servant,

G. WRIGHT,
Brigadier-General, U.S. Army, Commanding.

SOURCE: *OR*, SERIES 1, VOLUME 50, PART 1, PAGE 1069

OR-58

HEADQUARTERS DEPARTMENT OF THE PACIFIC,
San Francisco, May 30, 1862.

Brig. Gen. L. THOMAS,
Adjutant-General U.S. Army, Washington, D.C.:

GENERAL: Since I received instructions from your office to prepare a command for the protection of the Overland Mail Route, I have received no instructions as to how far east it was intended that I should send my troops. Col. P. E. Connor, Third

Infantry California Volunteers, whom I appointed to command all the troops on the mail route, has advanced with seven companies of his regiment and is now encamped near Stockton. Supplies are being collected and transportation preparing for crossing the Sierra Nevada, as soon as the roads are practicable for wagons, probably about the 20th of June. I have two companies of cavalry at Fort Churchill, and one company temporarily near Pyramid Lake, which, with the two companies of the same regiment, Second Cavalry California Volunteers, now near this city, will constitute the mounted force I designed for Colonel Connor's command. Three companies of the Third Infantry California Volunteers are now serving in the District of Humboldt. I propose, as soon as their services can be spared, to order them to join Colonel Connor. At present there seems to be no danger apprehended on the mail route between here and Salt Lake. Unless otherwise instructed, I shall advance Colonel Connor to the neighborhood of Salt Lake, establishing one, possibly two, intermediate stations between Fort Churchill and Utah. Colonel Connor has with him two field pieces and three mountain howitzers, with equipments and ammunition.

With great respect, your most obedient servant,

G. WRIGHT,
Brigadier-General, U.S. Army, Commanding.

SOURCE: *OR*, SERIES 1, VOLUME 50, PART 1, PAGES 1109–1110

OR-59

HEADQUARTERS DEPARTMENT OF THE PACIFIC,
San Francisco, Cal., June 6, 1862.

Capt. JULIAN MCALLISTER,
Ordnance Corps, Commanding Benicia Arsenal, Benicia, Cal.:

SIR: In reply to your letter of yesterday I am directed by the general commanding the department to inform you that when the three companies of Connor's regiment now in the Humboldt District join their regiment there will probably be about 800 infantry on the line and at Salt Lake.

Very respectfully, your obedient servant,

RICHD. C. DRUM,
Assistant Adjutant-General.

SOURCE: *OR*, SERIES 1, VOLUME 50, PART 1, PAGE 1121

OR-60

Headquarters Department of the Pacific,
San Francisco, June 12, 1862.

Brig. Gen. L. Thomas,
Adjutant-General U.S. Army, Washington, D.C.:

General: I have nothing later from Brigadier-General Carleton's command than was reported in my communication of yesterday. I have this morning received reports from Colonel Lippitt, commanding the District of Humboldt. The colonel has ten companies of infantry and one of cavalry actively engaged in subduing the Indians in his district. Nearly 300 Indians have been collected and brought into Fort Humboldt preparatory to their removal to the reservation; still there is a strong band of Indians, well armed, who are constantly attacking small parties and isolated settlements. This band must be subdued and captured before we can have peace throughout that region. The country presents almost insurmountable obstacles to the movements of the troops. The dense forests, with obscure trails, with which the Indians are well acquainted, afford them every advantage. Nevertheless, Colonel Lippitt and the troops under his command have exhibited a zeal, energy, and perseverance which must ultimately result in success. Colonel Connor, Third Infantry California Volunteers, is, with his regiment, encamped near Stockton. Transportation and supplies are being collected for a movement on the Overland Mail Route as soon as the mountain road is passable for wagons. The department quartermaster general, Lieutenant-Colonel Babbitt, is now closing his contracts for the transportation of supplies to Ruby Valley, and also to Salt Lake. From the District of Oregon I have nothing special to report. Colonel Steinberger having relieved Lieutenant-Colonel Cady in command of the District of Oregon, I have authorized the latter officer to remain at Fort Vancouver for the present, he being in ill health and receiving medical treatment by the surgeon at that post. Most of the volunteer regiments of California require a considerable number of recruits to till them up. Owing to the pressing wants of the service, companies were organized at the minimum number and hastily thrown out to remote posts to relieve the regular troops ordered East. Those companies have received no accessions to their numbers since that time, and have been, in fact, materially reduced by the casualties of the service. Under these circumstances I would respectfully ask that authority be granted to fill the volunteer regiments in this department by reopening the recruiting stations.

Very respectfully, your obedient servant,

G. WRIGHT,
Brigadier-General, U.S. Army, Commanding.

Source: *OR*, Series 1, Volume 50, Part 1, pages 1133–1134

OR-61

HEADQUARTERS DEPARTMENT OF THE PACIFIC,
San Francisco, June 21, 1862.

Brig. Gen. L. THOMAS,
Adjutant-General U.S. Army, Washington, D.C.:

GENERAL: My latest dispatches from Brigadier-General Carleton were received this morning, dated June 1. The general was then at Fort Barrett, Pima Villages, Ariz. Ter. The general says that the crossing "the Gila desert was terrible." Lieutenant Shinn, commanding the light artillery battery, reached Fort Barrett on the 31st of May, and was to march for Tucson on the 1st of June; his horses in good working order, but a little thin. Thus far the expedition has been successively prosecuted. Arizona is securely occupied notwithstanding the predictions of traitors that we should be compelled to abandon everything in the midst of the desert. General Carleton dispatched a messenger with a communication to General Canby, but he was unable to go up the Salinas on account of the high water in that river. The general would again make an effort to communicate with Canby from Tucson. From the District of Oregon my latest date, June 10, represents everything as quiet. Colonel Cornelius, with two companies of Oregon cavalry, had reached Fort Walla Walla, and three more companies of the same regiment had reached the Willamette Valley en route for Walla Walla. Colonel Connor, Third Infantry California Volunteers, with his regiment, is still encamped near Stockton, in readiness to cross the mountains at an early day. Colonel Sims, Second Cavalry California Volunteers, now at Camp Alert, near this City, has been ordered to hold himself in readiness to move with his headquarters and two companies to join the command of Colonel Connor for the protection of the Overland Mail Route. I have not yet designated the positions to be occupied along the mail route, but in the absence of any special instructions from the War Department I have assumed it as important that a strong post should be established in the vicinity of Salt Lake, and contracts have been made for the transportation to that place of a year's supply for 800 men. An intermediate station, probably at Ruby Valley, will also be established for 300 men. Under instructions from your office, Brigadier-General Alvord has reported to me for temporary duty. I have received no orders as to the wishes of the Department as to the disposition of General Alvord, and I shall assign him to the command of the District of Oregon.

Very respectfully, your obedient servant,

G. WRIGHT,
Brigadier-General, U.S. Army, Commanding.

SOURCE: *OR*, SERIES 1, VOLUME 50, PART 1, PAGE 1151

OR-62

FORT LARAMIE, *June 26, 1862.*

Brig. Gen. JAMES G. BLUNT:

Indians committing depredations almost daily between Green River and Salt Lake. This is outside your department. I am using the company of Utah troops in that region, but they are not sufficient. My other troops are now distributed on 300 miles of line, and it would be dangerous to send any of them away, if I had the authority to go beyond your department. What shall I do? The California troops cannot reach the disputed district for some weeks to come.

JAS. CRAIG,
Brigadier-General.

SOURCE: *OR*, SERIES 1, VOLUME 13, PAGE 451

OR-63

HEADQUARTERS DEPARTMENT OF THE PACIFIC,
San Francisco, June 28, 1862.

Brig. Gen. L. THOMAS,
Adjutant-General U.S. Army, Washington, D.C.:

GENERAL: On the 26th instant I reviewed and inspected the Third Infantry California Volunteers, commanded by Col. P. E. Connor, encamped near Stockton. The regiment made a very fine appearance; the arms, clothing, and equipments were in high order. The industry and untiring zeal and energy of Colonel Connor is manifest throughout. He has a regiment that the State may well be proud of. Colonel Connor has a field battery of four guns in fine order which he will take with him on his march to Salt Lake. The colonel will march on the 5th proximo. I am preparing the headquarters and two companies of the Second Cavalry, under Colonel Sims, now encamped at Camp Alert, near this city, to follow the movement of Colonel Connor, in connection with forces destined for the protection of the Overland Mail Route.

Very respectfully, your obedient servant,

G. WRIGHT,
Brigadier-General, U.S. Army, Commanding.

SOURCE: *OR*, SERIES 1, VOLUME 50, PART 1, PAGES 1164–1165

OR-64

FORT LARAMIE, *July 1, 1862.*

General BLUNT:

One hundred and sixty head of animals taken from emigrants at Ice Springs night before last. I must again urge the commanding general to send me more troops. I cannot cover 500 miles of road with the small force now here. The Indians do and can get in between my detachment. I have taken measures to get the Colorado troops, if there are any mounted men there. I am now of opinion that the Snakes, Crows, Cheyennes, and one band of Sioux have taken part in the depredations. The road is in danger daily from Platte Bridge to Salt Lake Valley. Two men were murdered on the 21st at Rocky Ridge. My troops will be in pursuit as soon as an express rider can reach them.

The telegraph wire is down west of this post.

JAS. CRAIG,
Brigadier-General.

SOURCE: *OR*, SERIES 1, VOLUME 13, PAGE 459

OR-65

HDQRS. DEPARTMENT OF THE PACIFIC,
San Francisco, Cal., July 5, 1862.

SPECIAL ORDERS,
No. 115.

1. Under instructions from the War Department to protect the Overland Mail Route within this department, the Third Infantry California Volunteers and the headquarters, with five companies of the Second Cavalry California Volunteers, are designated for that purpose.

2. Col. P. Edward Connor, Third Infantry California Volunteers, the senior officer of the column, will move, with his headquarters and seven companies of his regiment, now encamped near Stockton, as soon as practicable, crossing the Sierra Nevada Mountains and advancing on the Territory of Utah.

3. Col. Columbus Sims, Second Cavalry California Volunteers, will move from his camp near this city at an early day, with his headquarters and two companies of his regiment, by water to Sacramento, and thence by land along the mail route.

4. After crossing the Sierra Nevada Mountains, Colonel Sims will report to Colonel Connor, by whose orders he will be governed in his further movements.

5. Colonel Connor will establish a post at Ruby Valley, with the headquarters of the Second Cavalry and Companies H and K of the same regiment, and then advance to the vicinity of Salt Lake with his seven companies of infantry, Price's company of the Second Cavalry, and his field battery, and select a suitable position for a post.

6. The different staff departments will furnish the necessary transportation and supplies to insure a prompt movement.

By order of Brigadier-General Wright:

RICHD. C. DRUM,
Assistant Adjutant-General.

SOURCE: *OR*, SERIES 1, VOLUME 50, PART 2, PAGES 5–6

OR-66

HEADQUARTERS,
Fort Laramie, July 11, 1862.

General JAMES G. BLUNT,
Fort Leavenworth:

GENERAL: I am in receipt to-day of a dispatch informing me that the Postmaster-General has ordered the Overland Mail Company to abandon the North Platte and Sweet Water portion of the route and remove their stages and stock to a route south of this running through Bridger Pass. As I feel uncertain as to my duty, and as the stages and stock are now being concentrated preparatory to removal, I have thought proper to send Lieutenant Wilcox, Fourth U.S. Cavalry, to you with this letter. My instructions require me to protect the overland mail along the telegraph line, and the emigration not being mentioned, I have up to this time directed my attention to the safety of all these. My recollection of the act of Congress is that the mail company are not confined to any particular pass or route, but are to run from the Missouri River to a point in California daily, supplying Denver City and Salt Lake City twice a week. On the application of agents I have to-day ordered two small escorts, one of 25, the other of 30, men, to accompany the stages and protect them to the new route, and until I receive your orders I will retain upon the present route the larger portion of the troops to protect the telegraph line and the emigration, at least until the emigration, which consists principally of family trains, has passed through my district. I do this because the Indians evince a disposition to rob the trains and destroy the wires. Indeed I am satisfied that unless the Government is ready to abandon this route both for mails and emigrants an Indian war is inevitable. All the tribes in these mountains, except perhaps one of the Lenox bands, are in bad humor; charge the Government with bad faith and breaches of promise in failing to send them an agent and presents. They have come in by hundreds from the Upper Missouri, attacked and robbed emigrant trains and mail stations, and in one instance last week they robbed a mail station within two hours after a detachment of Colonel Collins' troops had passed, and carried the herdsman away with them to prevent him from notifying the troops for successful pursuit. That renegade white men are with them I have no doubt. I have a white man in the guard-house, who was found in possession of pocket-book, money, and papers of an emigrant, who is missing and believed to have been murdered. I am satisfied that the mail company and the Government would both be benefited by the change of routes at a proper time, and so wrote the Postmaster-General some weeks since. Then everything was quiet. Since that time the Indians have made hostile demonstrations, and I fear if the mail and all the troops leave this route the Indians will suppose they were frightened away, and will destroy the telegraph line and probably rob and murder such small parties as are not able to defend themselves. I have directed all the officers on the line to urge upon the emigrants the necessity of forming strong companies and exercising vigilance. In obedience to your order and the urgent calls of the mail company I sent the Utah troops to Bridger to guard the line from that post to Salt Lake, which leaves me only Colonel Collins' Sixth Ohio Cavalry, about 300 strong, and two skeleton companies of Fourth Regiment Cavalry, about 60 men, mounted upon horses purchased seven years ago, to protect the 400 miles intervening between this post and Fort Bridger. I need not say that this force cannot protect a line of such length unless the Indians are willing to behave well. I think I am doing all that can be done with so small a force mounted as they are and without any grain forage. My scouts inform me that a portion of the stolen property is now in an Indian village on Beaver Creek but little more than 100 miles south of this post. It consists of 1,000 lodges, say 3,000 fighting men. I suppose I could whip these Indians if I could concentrate my command and go against them; but in the first place my troops are distributed along a line of 500 miles, and in the second place if I take the troops all away from the line the mail stock, telegraph line, and emigrants would be almost certain to suffer. I am therefore compelled to await re-enforcements, or at least until the emigration is out of danger. If a regiment of mounted troops could be sent by boat to Fort Pierre, which is only 300 miles north of this post, a joint campaign could be made against those tribes, which I think would result in giving peace to this region for years to come. Presuming it to be the intention of the Government to keep the troops somewhere in this region during the coming winter, I beg to urge the necessity of sending authority to procure hay for the animals, and also to send grain, or authority to purchase it, in Colorado. Unless the hay contract is let soon it will be difficult to procure it within reasonable distance. Parties here are anxious to furnish it at less figures than it cost last year. I omitted to say above that under your telegraphic order I have kept at this post the escort furnished by you to the Governor of Utah. I also sent to Denver City to inquire the number and description of troops in that vicinity, and received for answer that there were 4 officers and 6 privates all told. The troops ordered from California on this line have probably not started. They have not got as far east as Carson Valley.

This letter is already too long. I leave Lieutenant Wilcox to explain anything I have omitted.

I am, general, respectfully, your obedient servant,

JAS. CRAIG.

SOURCE: *OR*, SERIES 1, VOLUME 13, PAGES 468–469

OR-67

HDQRS. THIRD CALIFORNIA VOLUNTEER INFANTRY,
Stockton, July 12, 1862.

Maj. R. C. DRUM,
Asst. Adjt. Gen., Department of the Pacific, San Francisco:

MAJOR: I have the honor to report that my command started from Camp Halleck this morning at 9 o'clock en route for Salt Lake City. I will march to-day to Camp No. 1, seven miles north of Stockton, where we will remain until Monday morning. Any communication from department headquarters can be forwarded to this city until Thursday next, and subsequently to Placerville. My train is heavily laden and I was compelled to take the ten teams which I intended to leave for the other companies of my regiment with me, but will send them back in four or five days, but I fear I will not be able to get along without five of them at least, and respectfully ask that I may be permitted to take them if I find I cannot get along without. The forty-five teams of my command are now loaded with 3,000 [pounds] each, and the other ten are also loaded with the same weight. To be sure the wagons will be getting lighter every day, but when starting from Fort Churchill and Ruby Valley we will have the same weight, and at a time when the mules will be considerably reduced in strength and flesh. The men are carrying their knapsacks. I have detailed Second Lieutenant Gilman, of Company K, to remain in charge of wagons, mules, and property left for the other companies.

Very respectfully, your obedient servant,

P. EWD. CONNOR,
Colonel Third California Volunteer Infantry.

[First indorsement.]

Respectfully referred to Lieutenant-Colonel Babbitt for his information.
By order:

R. C. DRUM,
Assistant Adjutant-General.

[Second indorsement.]

[Editor's note: *See* OR, *Series 1, Volume 50, Part 2, pages 19–20 for this inclosure.*]

SOURCE: *OR*, SERIES 1, VOLUME 50, PART 2, PAGE 19

OR-68

HEADQUARTERS DEPARTMENT OF THE PACIFIC,
San Francisco, July 25, 1862.

Brig. Gen. L. THOMAS,
Adjutant-General U.S. Army, Washington, D.C.:

GENERAL: Colonel Connor, Third Infantry California Volunteers, with his regiment, has passed the Sierra and is probably now in the vicinity of Carson City, Nev. Ter. Colonel Sims, with headquarters and two companies Second Cavalry California Volunteers, left this city on the 21st instant, and are now advancing on the Overland Mail Route and will join Colonel Connor beyond the mountains. This force, with the addition of one company of cavalry from Fort Churchill, will move forward and establish a post at Ruby Valley and another in the vicinity of Salt Lake, the latter to be the headquarters of Colonel Connor. Supplies for a year are being thrown forward for all the troops on the mail route, including Fort Churchill. In the District of Oregon all is quiet. The headquarters of the First Infantry Washington Territory Volunteers, Colonel Steinberger commanding, have been established at Fort Walla Walla. The Oregon cavalry company at Walla Walla were ordered to move on the 15th of July, on the emigrant road, to meet the approaching emigration and afford them protection through the Indian country. In the District of Humboldt Indian difficulties still continue. The troops have been zealous and indefatigable in their exertions, and more than 400 Indians have been captured and brought into Fort Humboldt and await the action of the superintendent of Indian affairs for their removal to some reservation. The Indian difficulties on Owen's Lake and River and Mono Lake, on the eastern border of this State, have nearly terminated, and it is expected that a permanent peace may be soon established.

Very respectfully, your obedient servant,

G. WRIGHT,
Brigadier-General, U.S. Army, Commanding.

SOURCE: *OR*, SERIES 1, VOLUME 50, PART 2, PAGES 39–40

OR-69

HDQRS. THIRD INFANTRY CALIFORNIA VOLUNTEERS,
Camp 16, Fort Churchill, Nev. Ter., August 3, 1862.

Maj. R. C. DRUM, U.S. Army,
Asst. Adjt. Gen., Department of the Pacific, San Francisco:

MAJOR: I have the honor to report my arrival at this post with my command. The men are in excellent health and spirits and have stood the trip remarkably well. The animals are all in good order, as I made it my particular duty to attend to their being well taken care of, and embraced every opportunity that was afforded to obtain good forage. The roads were, with little exception, in good order, and I am myself much pleased with the result so far. I find since entering this Territory that there are many sympathizers with the Southern rebels along our entire route; but while they are loud-mouthed brawlers before our arrival, are very careful in the expressions of such sentiments during our stay at any point. Still, they are known and can be identified as open and avowed secessionists. I have not as yet taken any steps to check them by arrest and punishment, but await further instructions from headquarters. I desire and shall remain here only sufficient time to overhaul and repair the wagons and harness and allow the animals to recruit, when, unless I receive orders to the contrary, shall take my departure for Salt Lake City or its vicinity. From the information I have received there is an immense immigration on the route this season, and I fear I will find grass rather scarce, consequently I contemplate dividing my command at this point, to reunite at Ruby Valley. Colonel Sims has not yet arrived, nor have I heard from him. I find that matters at this post are being conducted with care and economy, for which Major McDermit deserves favorable mention.

Very respectfully, your obedient servant,

P. EDW. CONNOR,
Colonel Third Infantry California Volunteers.

SOURCE: *OR*, SERIES 1, VOLUME 50, PART 2, PAGES 48–49

OR-70

HEADQUARTERS DISTRICT OF UTAH,
Fort Churchill, August 6, 1862.

ORDERS,
No. 1.

The undersigned, pursuant to orders from department headquarters, hereby assumes command of the Military District of Utah, comprising the Territories of Utah and Nevada. In assuming command of the district I especially enjoin on all disbursing officers the necessity of being particularly attentive, careful, and economical in the disbursement of the public funds, and that they in no instance purchase from persons who have at any time, by word or act, manifested disloyalty to the Federal Government. Being credibly informed that there are in this district persons who, while claiming and receiving protection to life and property, are endeavoring to destroy and defame the principles and institutions of a Government under whose benign influence they have been so long protected, it is therefore most rigidly enjoined upon all commanders of posts, camps, and detachments to cause to be promptly arrested and closely confined until they have taken the oath of allegiance to the United States, all persons who from this date shall be guilty of uttering treasonable sentiments against the Government, and upon a repetition of the offense to be again arrested and confined until the fact shall be communicated to these headquarters. Traitors shall not utter treasonable sentiments in this district with impunity, but must seek a more genial soil, or receive the punishment they so richly merit.

By order of P. Edward Connor, colonel Third Infantry California Volunteers, commanding District of Utah:

JAS. W. STILLMAN,
Acting Assistant Adjutant-General.

SOURCE: *OR*, SERIES 1, VOLUME 50, PART 2, PAGE 55

OR-71

Headquarters District of Utah,
Fort Churchill, August 11, 1862.

Maj. R. C. Drum,
Asst. Adjt. Gen., Department of the Pacific, San Francisco:

Major: I have the honor to report the arrival of Colonel Sims' command at this post to-day with Captain Smith under guard, and the men and the majority of the officers in a state of insubordination. The command lost thirty men by desertion on the route, and I am informed by Major McGarry and other officers that if the companies designated for that purpose are left at Ruby Valley with Colonel Sims in command there will not be thirty of them left in sixty days. On the route the officers threatened to leave the colonel and march their companies to this post without him. Last night the command encamped in the vicinity of Virginia City, and the colonel dispatched an officer to me for a force to suppress a contemplated mutiny among the men. He also feared a demonstration by the citizens of Virginia City to release Captain Smith from confinement. I conjectured that his fears were groundless and did not send a force, but telegraphed to him to make a forced march to this post to-day, which he did. Matters are all right now, and will remain so while they are under my immediate command. A majority of the officers and the men beg that I will not leave them at Ruby Valley with their colonel, but to take them with me to Salt Lake. I certainly fear that so leaving them will not be beneficial to the interests of the Government, nor to the discipline of the command. Under the circumstances I would respectfully recommend that I be permitted to take the command to Salt Lake, and defer garrisoning Ruby Valley until spring, by which time I will guarantee they will be a credit to the service. From information gleaned since my arrival in this Territory I understand that Ruby Valley is a bleak, inhospitable place no forage, nor timber to build with, and, as far as the Indians are concerned, entirely unnecessary to keep troops there. Cavalry can be subsisted for one-fourth less at Salt Lake than at Ruby. I take pleasure in announcing the good health and high state of discipline of my own regiment. On Wednesday next I review and inspect the troops at this post, and on Thursday I again take up the line of march. I have been necessarily delayed in repairing my wagons and putting them in a thoroughly serviceable condition. I understand from Major McDermit, that the presence of Captain Rowe's company at Adobe Meadows is unnecessary, and that the expense of foraging and subsisting the company there is very high. From the manner in which affairs were managed while he commanded this post last winter, I am of the opinion that a little wholesome discipline would be greatly beneficial to him as well as the Government. I am much pleased with the care and economy practiced by Major McDermit at this post, and shall leave him in command.

Very respectfully, your obedient servant,

P. EDW. CONNOR,
Colonel Third Infantry California Volunteers, Comdg. District.

SOURCE: *OR*, SERIES 1, VOLUME 50, PART 2, PAGES 60–61

OR-72

HDQRS. DEPARTMENT OF THE PACIFIC,
San Francisco, Cal., August 14, 1862.

SPECIAL ORDERS,
No. 140.

* * * *

5. Companies A, B, and D, Third Infantry, will, on their arrival in this city from the District of Humboldt, proceed to Stockton, Cal., where they will go into camp preparatory to taking up the line of march for Salt Lake. Companies A and C, Fourth Infantry, will, on their arrival from Oregon, proceed to and take post at Benicia Barracks. The assistant quartermaster will provide the necessary transportation.

By order of Brigadier-General Wright:

RICHD. C. DRUM,
Assistant Adjutant-General.

SOURCE: *OR*, SERIES 1, VOLUME 50, PART 2, PAGES 64–65

OR-73

SAN FRANCISCO, *August 15, 1862.*

COL. P. E. CONNOR,
Fort Churchill:
(Care Major McDermit.)

Two companies of infantry under Pollock will be stationed at Ruby Valley. Sims and his command, also Rowe's company, will go to Salt Lake with you. Give orders necessary for the movement.

R. C. DRUM,
Assistant Adjutant-General.

SOURCE: *OR*, SERIES 1, VOLUME 50, PART 2, PAGE 67

OR-74

Headquarters District of Utah,
Fort Churchill, August 15, 1862.

Orders,
No. 6.

1. Captain Rowe's company, Second Cavalry California Volunteers, is relieved from duty at Adobe Meadows, and will immediately report to Colonel Sims at this post.

* * * *

3. Colonel Sims with his headquarters and Captain McCleave's company of his regiment will remain at this post until the arrival of Captain Rowe's company, and will then proceed with the two companies named to Salt Lake City and report to the colonel commanding.

4. Major McGarry, with Captain Smith's company, Second Cavalry, will take up the line of march to-morrow and join the advance column without delay.

* * * *

P. EDW. CONNOR,
Colonel Third Infantry California Volunteers, Comdg. District.

Source: *OR*, Series 1, Volume 50, Part 2, page 67

OR-75

San Francisco, *August 19, 1862.*

Col. P. E. Connor,
Third Infantry California Volunteers, Comdg. District of Utah:
(Via Fort Churchill, Nev. Ter.)

Direct Colonel Sims to turn over his command to Major McGarry. Colonel Sims will await further orders at Fort Churchill, but will not relieve McDermit in command.

By order:

R. C. DRUM,
Assistant Adjutant-General.

Source: *OR*, Series 1, Volume 50, Part 2, page 82

OR-76

HEADQUARTERS DEPARTMENT OF THE PACIFIC,
San Francisco, Cal., August 19, 1862.

Col. P. EDWARD CONNOR,
Third Infantry California Volunteers, Comdg. District of Utah:
(Via Fort Churchill, Nev. Ter.)

SIR: Inclosed I have the honor to transmit, by direction of the general commanding the department, an article* taken from the Territorial Enterprise, published in Virginia City, Nev. Ter. The general desires you to make a full and minute investigation into the matter complained of and report the result to this office. You will also report specifically as to Colonel Sims behavior as an officer and gentleman since leaving this city with his command.

Very respectfully, your obedient servant,

R. C. DRUM,
Assistant Adjutant-General.

* Not found as an inclosure.

SOURCE: *OR*, SERIES 1, VOLUME 50, PART 2, PAGE 82

OR-77

HEADQUARTERS DISTRICT OF UTAH,
Camp No. 21, Cold Springs, Nev. Ter., August 20, 1862.

ORDERS,
No. 7.

I. In pursuance of instructions from department headquarters Col. Columbus Sims, Second Cavalry California Volunteers, is hereby directed to turn over his command to Major McGarry, of same regiment.

II. Colonel Sims will remain at Fort Churchill and await further orders, but will not relieve Major McDermit in command at that post.

By order of P. Edw. Connor, colonel Third Infantry California Volunteers, commanding district:

JAS. W. STILLMAN,
Acting Assistant Adjutant-General.

[Editor's note: *This order is referenced in OR-78.*]

SOURCE: *OR*, SERIES 1, VOLUME 50, PART 2, PAGE 84

OR-78

HEADQUARTERS DISTRICT OF UTAH,
Camp No. 21, Cold Springs, August 21, 1862.

Maj. R. C. DRUM,
Assistant Adjutant-General, San Francisco:

MAJOR: I have the honor to inclose to you a copy of District Orders, No. 7.* I desire also to suggest that it would not be advisable, or even safe, to send Captain Moore's battalion on this route with less than twenty wagons. I take pleasure in acknowledging the receipt of your dispatch in relation to Doctors Williamson and Furley. You will please have all letters for myself and command directed to Fort Churchill until I arrive at Salt Lake, as I send a mail bag to Carson City every other day. I desire that you will communicate with me as to whether I shall leave Assistant Surgeon Kirkpatrick with Lieutenant-Colonel Pollock at Ruby Valley. I am also pleased to add that the command is in good health and spirits.

Very respectfully, your obedient servant,

P. EDW. CONNOR,
Colonel, Commanding District.

[First indorsement.]

Respectfully referred to Lieutenant-Colonel Babbitt for his information and opinion.

By order:

R. C. DRUM,
Assistant Adjutant-General.

[Second indorsement.]

September 4, 1862.

I can furnish the command under Captain Moore with seventeen wagons, an ambulance, and a traveling forge. I think that number of wagons will prove sufficient, as they have no mounted force for which to transport forage over any part of the route.

Respectfully, &c.,

E. B. BABBITT,
Deputy Quartermaster-General.

* [*Refers to* OR-77.]

SOURCE: *OR*, SERIES 1, VOLUME 50, PART 2, PAGE 85

OR-79

FORT LARAMIE, *August 23, 1862—2.15 P.M.*

Hon. E. M. STANTON:

My department commander is in the field, and I cannot communicate with him. Indians, from Minnesota to Pike's Peak, and from Salt Lake to near Fort Kearny, committing many depredations. I have only about 500 troops, scattered on the telegraph and overland mail lines. Horses worn by patrolling both roads. If I concentrate my force to go against Indians, mail line, telegraph, and public property will be destroyed. If you cannot send re-enforcements from States, will you give me authority to raise 100 mounted men in the mountains and re-enlist the Utah troops for a limited time? The troops furnish their own horses. Answer by telegraph. We have no mails at this post. I am building new post on new mail route near Medicine Bow Mountain. Will you name it either Stanton, Halleck, Baker, or Lincoln?

JAS. CRAIG.

SOURCE: *OR*, SERIES 1, VOLUME 13, PAGE 592

OR-80

WAR DEPARTMENT,
Washington City, D.C., August 24, 1862.

General JAMES CRAIG,
Fort Laramie:

You are authorized to raise 100 mounted men in the mountains and re-enlist the Utah troops for three months as requested in your telegram received to-day. It is impossible to send you re-enforcements. You will hereafter report to Major-General Halleck, General-in-Chief, for instructions when required from Washington.

EDWIN M. STANTON,
Secretary of War.

SOURCE: *OR*, SERIES 3, VOLUME 2, PAGE 453

OR-81

FORT LARAMIE, WYO., *August 25, 1862—5.10 P.M.*

Major-General HALLECK:

Governor Harding, of Utah, in dispatch of to-day in relation to reenlistment of Mormon troops, after saying he had interview with Brigham Young, closed dispatch as follows: "You need not expect anything for the present. Things are not right."

I am satisfied rebel agents have been at work among the Indians. Many emigrants who passed through to Salmon River mines were from border slave States, and some had left home because it was too hot. I will try to raise company of mounted men, as authorized by Secretary of War.

JAS. CRAIG,
Brigadier-General.

SOURCE: *OR*, SERIES 1, VOLUME 13, PAGE 596

OR-82

WASHINGTON, *August 27, 1862.*

Brig. Gen. JAMES CRAIG,
Fort Laramie:

You are authorized to raise 100 mounted men in the mountains and re-enlist the Utah troops for three months, as requested in your telegram received *to-day*. It is impossible to send you re-enforcements. You will hereafter report to Major-General Halleck, general-in-chief, for instructions when required from Washington.

EDWIN M. STANTON.

SOURCE: *OR*, SERIES 1, VOLUME 13, PAGE 600

OR-83

HEADQUARTERS,
Fort Laramie, August 30, 1862.

General JAMES G. BLUNT:

SIR: I inclose a copy of a dispatch sent by me to the Secretary of War; also a copy of his reply. Your absence from department headquarters was my reason for corresponding directly with the Secretary. Having failed to re-enlist the Mormon troops, and finding the mountain men hereabouts very reluctant to go into the service, and having information this morning, upon which I can rely, that several thousand Indians from the Upper Missouri are now approaching this post with the avowed intention of making war, I have determined to send Mr. F. Ewing to Denver to confer with the Acting Governor of Colorado, and to department headquarters with such information for you as I deem it unsafe to transmit by telegraph. I am impelled to this course also because we have had no mail here for eight weeks except when I sent 160 miles for it.

You are aware that my small force is employed in protecting the telegraph line from this post to western boundary of your department, over 300 miles, and also protecting the new mail route from South Platte to Bridger's Pass, more than 200 miles, and garrisoning this post. This duty, together with escorting subsistence trains to the different detachments scattered along both routes, has disabled many of the horses and given the troops active duty. I have stationed at each of five telegraph stations west of this post a detachment of from 25 to 30 men, and have contracted for 30 tons of hay to be delivered at four of these stations. At the remaining station no hay can be had without hauling from 40 to 50 miles, and I will be obliged to either furnish no protection at that place or station infantry there. The detachments are poorly supplied with transportation, but I expect to subsist them by sending portion of the contractor's trains forward as they arrive at this post. I am sadly in want of ammunition, but suppose a supply to be on the way now. My information from vicinity of Fort Hall and beyond to Salmon River is that the Indians have murdered many emigrants.

I also learn that Washakie, the former chief of the Snakes, but deposed by his tribe through the influence of the Mormon authorities, is of opinion that the Snakes and Blackfeet are preparing to come against these scattered detachments on the telegraph line. Now the alternative is presented to me of standing on the defensive and trying to save the public property here and the telegraph line or of concentrating my troops, less than 500 mounted men, and marching against the Indians with less than 10 rounds of ammunition to the man, and in my judgment the telegraph line would be destroyed within three days, probably the mail line too, and my forces have at least a fair chance to be thrashed. To all this may be added that there are only 20 mounted troops at Denver, and the people there frightened at recent raids of the Ute Indians into their frontier settlements.

Now, general, if you cannot do better send me the Maryville company on foot and without arms. I can manage to arm them here and use them to garrison some post or station. Send me more ammunition as soon as you can; give me authority to raise two companies in Colorado instead of the mountain men and the Mormons. The Mormons will not come and mountain men are scarce and reluctant, and in my opinion both are to some extent disloyal. I am convinced that nearly all the French in these mountains are unfriendly to the Government. They are wary and prudent; but that some vicious influence is at work among the Indians is proved by the fact that there never was a time in the history of the country when so many tribes distant from and hostile to each other were exhibiting hostility to the whites.

I am 160 miles from mail route. In replying I hope you will use the wires. Mr. Ewing, who is intelligent and loyal, will be able to inform you of my prospects in Colorado, as he will go to Leavenworth via Denver. In the mean time I will call in the mountain men near this post and arm them. I feed such as I am sure are loyal and will confine the others in the guard-house until I hear from you and the Governor of Colorado.

I will only add that I will carefully avoid doing anything that would inaugurate a war with the Indians, knowing that such prudence would invite criticism, but I pursued this course because I believe the first blow I struck would insure the destruction of the emigrants, the telegraph and mail lines, and that I had not troops enough to prevent.

Respectfully, your obedient servant,

JAS. CRAIG,
Brigadier-General.

SOURCE: *OR*, SERIES 1, VOLUME 13, PAGES 607–608

OR-84

HEADQUARTERS DEPARTMENT OF THE PACIFIC,
San Francisco, September 1, 1862.

Brig. Gen. L. THOMAS,
Adjutant-General U.S. Army, Washington, D.C.:

GENERAL: Colonel Connor, with seven companies of Third Infantry California Volunteers and three companies Second Cavalry, will reach Ruby Valley to-day en route for Salt Lake. The command is in good health, and under the admirable discipline established by Colonel Connor is perfectly reliable for any service required of it. From Brigadier General Carleton I have no late official reports. He has a fine body of troops, probably now on the Rio Grande; I shall continue to throw forward supplies to meet all his wants. From the District of Oregon I have nothing special to report; all is quiet in the Indian country, and a strong cavalry force is on the road to protect the approaching overland emigration. In the District of Humboldt the Indian disturbances still continue; the troops under Colonel Lippitt, Second Infantry California Volunteers, are vigorously prosecuting Hostilities; many Indians have been killed, and we have now some 800 at the different military stations who have either been captured or who have voluntarily surrendered. The superintendent of Indian affairs has made arrangements to have all these Indians placed on a reservation on Smith's River, in the northwest section of the State of California. The steamer which leaves here on the 5th instant will transport the Indians to Crescent City, near which point I have a battalion of the Second Infantry California Volunteers to take charge of them. I have brought down from Oregon the residue of the Second Infantry California Volunteers, and sent them to serve in the District of Humboldt. I have also brought down from Humboldt the three companies of the Third Infantry California Volunteers (Connor's regiment), preparatory to their movement in the direction of Salt Lake. The Washington Territory regiment, Colonel Steinberger, is doing well. Six full companies have been raised here; five of them are now in the District of Oregon, and the sixth will go up on the next steamer. I have never received any special instructions as to the disposition of the forces I designated for the protection of the Overland Mail Route, but I have assumed it as a matter of course that the route between this and Salt Lake City came under my special supervision, and have acted accordingly.

Very respectfully, your obedient servant,

G. WRIGHT,

Brigadier-General, U.S. Army., Commanding.

SOURCE: *OR*, SERIES 1, VOLUME 50, PART 2, PAGES 95–96

OR-85

Headquarters Third Regiment,
Ruby Valley, September 2, 1862. (Received 10 A.M. 4th.)

Maj. R. C. Drum:

Arrived yesterday. Shall leave for Salt Lake in stage in three days. Command will not move until I return, if then. No supplies here or ahead. Major McGarry left Fort Churchill yesterday.

P. E. CONNOR,
Colonel Third Infantry California Volunteers.

Source: *OR*, Series 1, Volume 50, Part 2, page 97

OR-86

Fort Crittenden, *September 11, 1862—9 P.M.*

Maj. R. C. Drum:

I leave for Ruby to-night. Will arrive there Saturday night. Will write from there.

P. E. CONNOR,
Colonel Third Infantry California Volunteers.

Source: *OR*, Series 1, Volume 50, Part 2, page 113

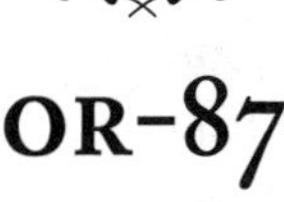

OR-87

Headquarters District of Utah,
Fort Ruby, September 14, 1862.

Maj. R. C. Drum,
Assistant Adjutant-General, San Francisco, Cal.:

Major: I have the honor to report my return to this post from Salt Lake last evening. I am glad I made the journey, as it will be the means of saving my command much suffering for want of water. The country between this point and Salt Lake is an alkali desert, scarce of wood and water, but I have made such arrangements as will enable me to take my command over with comparative comfort. It will be impossible for me to describe what I saw and heard in Salt Lake, so as to make you realize the enormity of Mormonism; suffice it, that I found them a community of traitors, murderers, fanatics, and whores. The people publicly rejoice at reverses to our arms, and thank God that the American Government is gone, as they term it, while their prophet and bishops preach treason from the pulpit. The Federal officers are entirely powerless, and talk in whispers for fear of being overheard by Brigham's spies. Brigham Young rules with despotic sway, and death by assassination is the penalty of disobedience to his commands. I have a difficult and dangerous task before me, and will endeavor to act with prudence and firmness.

I examined the country in the vicinity of the city to find a suitable location for a post. Fort Crittenden (Camp Floyd) is in ruins, except the few buildings, of which I send you a description, and for which the owner asks $15,000.* There are also some buildings purchased by and belonging to the Overland Mail Company, and now occupied by them, but which are not for sale. Of the remaining buildings there is nothing left but the adobes, except two or three buildings owned by former sutlers, which are in tolerable repair, and could be purchased cheap. If it were designed to establish a permanent post, most of the buildings would have to be torn down and removed, as many of them are half a mile from the officers' quarters, or what was known as headquarters. The latter buildings are the only ones in tolerable repair; the others require doors, windows, and considerable work to place them in habitable order. The land is considered a Government reserve, but the post is badly located, being on the edge of the reserve and adjoining a small village, inhabited by a class of persons of questionable character. There is good grazing on the reserve, which is the only redeeming quality, in my opinion, it has. There are sufficient adobes on the ground to erect such additional buildings as I may require, but good timber is scarce, and the saw-mills are sixty miles distant.

I found another location, which I like better for various reasons, which I shall explain. It is on a plateau about three miles from Salt Lake City; in the vicinity of good timber and saw-mills, and at a point where hay, grain, and other produce can be purchased cheaper than at Fort Crittenden. It is also a point which commands the city, and where 1,000 troops would be more efficient than 3,000 on the other side of the Jordan. If the general decides that I shall locate there, I intend to quietly intrench my position, and then say to the Saints of Utah, enough of your treason; but if it is intended that I shall merely protect the overland mail and permit the Mormons to act and utter treason, then I had as well locate at Crittenden. The Federal officers desire and beg that I will locate near the city. The Governor especially is very urgent in the matter. It is certainly rather late in the season to build quarters, but I believe I could make my command comfortable before very cold weather sets in. It is raining here now, and snowing on the surrounding mountains. It is important that I should know the general's decision as soon as possible, as winter is fast approaching.

Communication by mail or telegraph will, until my arrival at Salt Lake, reach me earlier by being directed to Ruby Valley than to any other point.

I have the honor to remain, your obedient servant.

P. EDW. CONNOR,
Colonel Third Infty. California Vols., Comdg. District of Utah.

* Description omitted.

SOURCE: *OR*, SERIES 1, VOLUME 50, PART 2, PAGES 119–120

[Editor's note: *This document is referenced in OR-90.*]

OR-88

EXECUTIVE DEPARTMENT,
Carson City, September 15, 1862.

Brigadier-General WRIGHT, U.S. Army,
Commanding Pacific Department:

SIR: I have seen an order issued from the Department at Washington in relation to the treatment of prisoners who speak disrespectfully of the Government. I see likewise that you are about to appoint a military commission to act upon and decide the several cases arising in this department. How are we to bring such cases before said commission? Is there power; if so, where does it exist, to transport them across the mountains? Can we have a commission appointed for this Territory? Treason is very openly spoken here now since Colonel Connor's proclamation. The trouble lies here in the fact that there is only one company stationed at the fort, and they can raise a force any day more than sufficient to overpower them. To obviate this difficulty I can furnish you with two or three companies, or have them at hand subject to call if you can furnish them with arms. The arms that we had are now pretty much distributed to such companies as have and are now forming. I have taken pains to so distribute these companies as to secure the greatest efficiency in case of trouble. I am quite apprehensive that there is a band of guerrillas forming in this Territory to burn, rob, and plunder all of the loyal citizens they can reach. They formed under the pretense of going east to join the rebel army, and received material aid from the rebel sympathizers here to help them across. They now think they are lurking about the country, and threaten to destroy it. I am quite certain that these Indian difficulties on the plains are brought about by the interference of the secessionists. I am of the opinion that there will be a necessity for stationing troops from the Humboldt to Ruby Valley. There has been some bloody work there within a few days.

I think a portion of the command destined for Salt Lake should halt in the neighborhood of Gravelly Ford until the emigration has passed. The depredations appear to be committed north of the line of march of Colonel Connor's command; the troops keep the mail road and the emigration north. It seems too bad that so many should be killed so near their journey's end. You will know much better than I do what to do. I will inclose a copy of a letter from my Indian agent from Humboldt, showing the state of things there, and I have to-day heard of much more bloody butchery. If I can procure arms I can put a thousand good men in a condition to render good and efficient aid in any emergency. Can I do it? I see a troublesome winter before us and am anxious to be prepared for it. How to be prepared and what to do are the points upon which I desire your counsel and advice. I hear the mutterings and desire to prepare for the storm. At the bottom of all these troubles are the cursed rebels. If we could send them all to Alcatraz the troubles would end. The sooner the work is commenced and consummated the better. If we could have those in our midst removed the exciting cause would be gone. If you will advise me in relation to, first, what is the best to be done with the traitors and how it is to be done; second, what can be done with the Indian troubles; third, in relation to arms, &c., I will be much obliged to you.

I have the honor to be, your humble servant,

JAMES W. NYE,
Governor of Nevada Territory.

SOURCE: *OR*, SERIES 1, VOLUME 50, PART 2, PAGES 123–124

OR-89

HDQRS. DEPARTMENT OF THE PACIFIC,
San Francisco, Cal., September 17, 1862.

GENERAL ORDERS,
No. 34.

In pursuance of an act of the Congress of the United States entitled "An act to suppress insurrection, to punish treason and rebellion, to seize and confiscate the property of rebels, and for other purposes," approved July 17, 1862, the attention of all persons in this military department (embracing the States of California and Oregon, and the Territories of Washington, Utah, Nevada, and that portion of New Mexico known as Arizona) is called to the following provisions of said act:

SECTION 5. *And be it further enacted*, That to insure the speedy termination of the present rebellion it shall be the duty of the President of the United States to cause the seizure of all the estate and property, money, stocks, credits, and the effects of the persons hereinafter named in this section, and to apply and use the same and the proceeds thereof for the support of the Army of the United States; that is to say:

* * * *

Sixthly. Of any person who, owning property in any loyal State or Territory of the United States, or in the District of Columbia, shall hereafter assist and give aid and comfort to such rebellion; and all sales, transfers, or conveyances of any such property shall be null and void; and it shall be sufficient bar to any suit brought by such person for the possession or the use of such property, or any of it, to allege and prove that he is one of the persons described in this section.

By order of Brigadier-General Wright:

R. C. DRUM,
Assistant Adjutant-General.

SOURCE: *OR*, SERIES 1, VOLUME 50, PART 2, PAGES 125–126

OR-90

HEADQUARTERS DEPARTMENT OF THE PACIFIC,
San Francisco, September 22, 1862.

Brig. Gen. L. THOMAS,
Adjutant-General U.S. Army, Washington, D.C.:

GENERAL: I have the honor to inclose herewith a copy of a communication from Col. P. E. Connor, Third Infantry California Volunteers, commanding the District of Utah, dated at Fort Ruby, Ruby Valley, September 14, 1862.* Colonel Connor is now on his march to Salt Lake, and I have instructed him to take up his position at the place he suggests, three miles from the city, as that appears to be the best location for the accomplishment of the object in view, viz, the protection of the Overland Mail Route and the due execution of the laws of the United States. The energy of Colonel Connor, coupled with his sound judgment and decision of character, point him out as eminently fitted for the command with which I have intrusted him.

Very respectfully, your obedient servant,

G. WRIGHT,
Brigadier-General, U.S. Army, Commanding.

* [*Refers to OR-87.*]

SOURCE: *OR*, SERIES 1, VOLUME 50, PART 2, PAGE 130

OR-91

RUBY VALLEY, NEV. TER., *September 24, 1862.*

Major-General HALLECK,

Washington, D.C.:

The Third Infantry California Volunteers has been in service one year and marched 600 miles; it is well officered and thoroughly drilled; it is of no service on the Overland Mail Route, as there is cavalry sufficient for its protection in Utah District. The regiment will authorize the paymaster to withhold $30,000 of pay now due if the Government will order it east, and it pledges General Halleck never to disgrace the flag, himself, or California. The men enlisted to fight traitors, and can do so more effectually than raw recruits, and ask that they may at least be placed on the same footing in regard to transportation east. If the above sum is insufficient we will pay our own passage from San Francisco to Panama.

By order of the regiment:

P. EDW. CONNOR,
Colonel, Commanding.

SOURCE: *OR*, SERIES 1, VOLUME 50, PART 2, PAGE 133

OR-92

HEADQUARTERS DISTRICT OF UTAH,
Fort Ruby, September 29, 1862.

Maj. EDWARD MCGARRY,

Second Cavalry California Volunteers, Fort Ruby:

MAJOR: You will proceed hence to-morrow morning with Company H, of your regiment, to the confluence of the South Fork with the main Humboldt River, and there await until joined by Captain Smith's company (K), of your regiment. On the route thence you will examine every valley or place where you have reason to believe guerrillas or hostile Indians are congregated, whom you will capture; but if they resist you will destroy them. In no instance will you molest women or children. If on the route to Humboldt friendly Indians deliver to you Indians who were concerned in the late murder of emigrants, you will (being satisfied of their guilt) immediately hang them, and leave their bodies thus exposed as an example of what evil-doers may expect while I command in this district. When you are joined by Captain Smith's company you will proceed by the northern overland route via City of Rocks to a point about ten miles north of Salt Lake City, where you will leave your command and report to me in person if I am in the vicinity of the city. If not, await further orders at the point designated. On the route from South Fork of Humboldt to Bear River you will spare no pains to discover the whereabouts of a band of traitors or guerrillas reported to be encamped in the vicinity of Humboldt, and who are believed to be the instigators, if not the participants, in the late Indian murders. If you should discover such a band you will take them prisoners and convey them to headquarters near Salt Lake, but if they should resist you will destroy them without mercy. You will also destroy every male Indian whom you may encounter in the vicinity of the late massacres. This course may seem harsh and severe, but I desire that the order may be rigidly enforced, as I am satisfied that in the end it will prove the most merciful.

Very respectfully, your obedient servant,

P. EDW. CONNOR,
Colonel Third Infantry California Volunteers, Comdg. District.

[Editor's note: *This document appears in the* Official Records *as an inclosure to OR-93.*]

SOURCE: *OR*, SERIES 1, VOLUME 50, PART 2, PAGE 144

OR-93

HEADQUARTERS DISTRICT OF UTAH,
Fort Ruby, October 1, 1862.

[Maj. R. C. DRUM,
Assistant Adjutant-General, Department of the Pacific:]

MAJOR: I have the honor to report that in consequence of the non-arrival of supplies I have been unable to advance from this post to my destination. Some supplies have arrived, sufficient to warrant me to leave to-morrow. I would respectfully ask for instructions as to the kind of quarters I am to erect, whether temporary cantonments, or to erect with a view to permanency. Captain Rowe desires to withdraw his resignation. He presented it under excitement on account of Captain McLean's ranking him. I approved it, as I have made it a rule to so do under all circumstances. The captain has proven himself an efficient and intelligent officer since joining my command, although I do not approve of his course at Fort Churchill last winter. As a military necessity I would respectfully recommend that the order accepting his resignation be rescinded, as the two companies of cavalry now with me are commanded by second lieutenants of little experience. Captain Price is on sick leave, and

Captains Smith and McLean have gone with Major McGarry. The inclosed letter of instructions explains itself. Captain Smith's company left day before yesterday for Gravelly Ford, with instructions to scour the country in that vicinity well before joining the major. Inclosed I have the honor to forward a regimental order made by Major McGarry, changing his adjutant. Since my arrival at this post I have had sufficient timber cut and hauled to erect winter quarters, store-house, &c., for the command to remain here, viz, Companies C and F, of my regiment. The labor has all been done and several buildings partly erected by a few extra-duty men, the police, and teams of the command. It is necessary and important that I should have money to pay for such supplies as I am compelled to purchase of the Mormons, viz, forage, beef, &c. Otherwise Brigham may seize the want of it as a pretext to prevent his people from supplying me. The people of Utah are under the impression that I am to winter at Fort Crittenden, and I am credibly informed by letter this morning that the flag-staff at Fort Crittenden was cut down since my visit and hauled away by Brigham's order. The staff belonged to the reservation, and was not sold by the Government at the time of the sale of the other property. Inclosed I have the honor to transmit a communication from Captain Rowe, and charges against Private Cox, of Company M, Second Cavalry. I have now in confinement three general prisoners, and would respectfully ask that a general court-martial be convened at as early a day as practicable. A reply to the application of Captain Rowe by telegraph is respectfully requested.

P. EDW. CONNOR,
Colonel Third Infantry California Volunteers, Comdg. District.

[Inclosure.]

[Editor's note: *See OR-92 for this inclosure.*]

SOURCE: *OR*, SERIES 1, VOLUME 50, PART 2, PAGES 143–144

OR-94

FORT CHURCHILL, NEV. TER., *October 3, 1862.*

Col. R. C. DRUM,
Assistant Adjutant-General, Department of the Pacific:

COLONEL: I had a talk with Governor Nye several days ago. He was very positive that the secessionists are moving in this Territory, and thought there was a band of guerrillas out near Ruby Valley, &c. His information was gained from a man at Gold Hill who is a secessionist and very rich, but being afraid of having his property confiscated, the Governor says, is giving him information which I think is all gammon. Probably one-third of the population of this Territory are secession sympathizers. None have as yet refused to take the oath of allegiance. There is considerable excitement at Carson, Gold Hill, and Virginia Cities about reported secession movements. I think it is helped along from the fact that there are a number of persons whose interest it would be to have a large number of troops at these places, and also those who sympathize with the rebels are always starting and helping along reports. There were a number of rebel bummers at these places without any visible means of support, who have gone off somewhere, probably some had means given them to go east. One party of secessionists of fifteen persons going east were attacked by the Indians on the Humboldt, and all but one supposed to be killed. I do not think from the information I could gain from the emigrants who came that route that secessionists have anything to do with the Indian difficulties there. There are Mormons keeping ferries in the neighborhood of the Indian troubles who sell ammunition and arms to them, and if there are any trains worth robbing the Indians are sure to be informed of it by these scoundrels, and probably a few white men who are rebels to all governments. The Indians have good arms, and on the approach of the troops retreat into the mountains, where they are inaccessible to an immediate attack. They ought to be completely wiped out, which could only be done by establishing a post there well provisioned and clothed and armed in the winter time. The winters are very cold, but it is the best time to hunt them.

Very respectfully, yours,

A. BROWN.

SOURCE: *OR*, SERIES 1, VOLUME 50, PART 2, PAGES 148–149

OR-95

HEADQUARTERS DEPARTMENT OF THE PACIFIC,
San Francisco, October 4, 1862.

Brig. Gen. L. THOMAS,
Adjutant-General U.S. Army, Washington, D.C.:

GENERAL: I am still without late advices from Brigadier-General Carleton. I have received dispatches from Maj. D. Fergusson, First Cavalry, commanding in Arizona, dated at Tucson, 18th of September. He had heard nothing from General Carleton since the 4th of August. General Carleton's force is deemed ample, in co-operation with that previously in New Mexico, to hold securely that country; or even, should it be deemed advisable, to advance into Texas and create a diversion in our favor, should it be the design of Government to re-establish our authority in that State at once, by landing a force on its southern borders. I learn (unofficially) that Brigadier-General Canby has been withdrawn from New Mexico; if so, I presume that General Carleton is now in command of all the troops in that country. Colonel Connor, Third Infantry, having established a post at Ruby Valley, is now on his march to Salt Lake, and on his arrival there will establish himself near the city, as I have already advised you. Affairs in the District of Oregon, under the management of Brigadier-General Alvord, are quiet. In the District of Humboldt the Indian difficulties still continue. However, nearly 1,000 Indians have been captured or induced to surrender to the military authorities and have been transferred to the reservations. Arrangements have been made to so dispose of the troops as to afford the greatest possible security to the settlements. I am happy to say that quiet prevails generally throughout the department; yet we must not disguise the fact that there is a large element of opposition on this coast, and that it is only by watchfulness, prudence, and prompt action in case of emergency that we can expect to preserve the peace. I telegraphed to you a few days since asking that 20,000 stand of small-arms and equipments might be sent here by the first steamer. I hope they will be sent; occasion might arise rendering it necessary to use them. I would most respectfully request that authority be given for raising another volunteer regiment of infantry in California for service here, as I do not think it would be prudent to send beyond the limits of the department any more troops raised on this coast. I have deemed it proper to prohibit the transmission through the United States mails and post-offices, and express, of several newspapers published in California and Oregon. They were violent in their denunciations of the Administration, of its policy, and the war, thereby discouraging enlistments in the army. You can rest assured that I shall take no measures to disturb the quiet of this country unnecessarily; but if it becomes necessary to strike, I shall be prepared to do so effectively.

Very respectfully, your obedient servant,

G. WRIGHT,
Brigadier-General, U.S. Army, Commanding.

SOURCE: *OR*, SERIES 1, VOLUME 50, PART 2, PAGES 149–150

OR-96

[*Extract*]

HEADQUARTERS DISTRICT OF OREGON,
Fort Vancouver, Wash. Ter., October 14, 1862.

ASSISTANT ADJUTANT-GENERAL,
Headquarters Department of the Pacific, San Francisco, Cal.:

SIR: I am satisfied that a post ought to be established at or in the vicinity of Fort Boisé next summer, and it is the object of this communication to recommend that authority be obtained from the War Department to establish it.

. . .

Colonel Maury was not able to get possession of any of the guilty authors of the massacre of September, 1860. My instructions to him of the 12th of July contemplated his doing so if possible. But so far no opportunity has occurred. Those Indians deserve to be well punished for all their offenses, and an efficient campaign against them next summer should be prosecuted. The establishment of a military post in their country would check them more effectually and permanently than any other step. But, until they should get a good whipping, that post would be harassed by the thieves. Gorged with plunder and steeped in blood, the appetite for robbing and marauding has been sharpened and cherished by their success and impunity. The dispatch of General Wright of two years since (above referred to) contemplated an active campaign against them; and no doubt but for the secession movement the proposition would have been carried into effect. A large share of the attacks on the emigrants and other travelers occurred between the South Pass and Fort Hall. The dispatch above mentioned recommended that early notice should be given in the newspapers when a column would leave Utah for the protection of the emigrants, so that they might avail themselves of the escort. As this department now embraces Utah, I recommend that orders be given that a command shall leave Fort Crittenden, Utah Ter., about the 15th of June next, proceed to some eligible point near the South Pass to intercept the emigrants, and, having gathered together sufficient to render it proper to move for their protection, to repair on the emigrant road to Salmon Falls, on Snake River, there to meet a command from this district about the end of August.

. . .

I have the honor to be, very respectfully, your obedient servant,

BENJAMIN ALVORD,
Brigadier-General, U.S. Vols., Commanding District.

SOURCE: *OR*, SERIES 1, VOLUME 50, PART 2, PAGES 172–174

OR-97

FORT CRITTENDEN, *October 17, 1862—9.13 P.M.*

Maj. R. C. DRUM:

Have just arrived. Will cross the Jordan to-morrow.

P. E. CONNOR.

SOURCE: *OR*, SERIES 1, VOLUME 50, PART 2, PAGE 180

OR-98

HEADQUARTERS DEPARTMENT OF NEW MEXICO
Santa Fé, N. Mex., October 18, 1862.

Hon. MONTGOMERY BLAIR,
Postmaster-General, Washington, D.C.:

SIR: Last winter General George Wright, commanding the Department of the Pacific, submitted to the General-in-Chief a proposition to have the Southern Overland Mail Route opened by volunteers from California, and to have certain forts in New Mexico then held by the rebels reoccupied by our troops. General McClellan acceded to this, and I was directed to organize and conduct a military expedition from California across the great desert to the Rio Grande, to give practicable effect to the proposition. This duty has been done. Our troops now occupy Mesilla and Tucson, Ariz. Ter. Besides, I have established a post at Apache Pass, and have now in successful operation a chain of vedettes from Tucson to Los Angeles, in California. One great purpose had in view by this movement was to give your department an opportunity to remove the overland mail from its present route, where, in the Sierra Nevada and eastward from the range of mountains to Salt Lake, for months in the year the mail is obstructed by snows. Tons of mail matter it is said the company was obliged to leave along the road on this account last winter. The Bannock and Shoshone Indians west of Salt Lake, and the Sioux Indians between Salt Lake and Kansas, are more hostile and offer greater risks to the safe transit of the mails by that route than are offered by any Indians on the southern mail route. If the mail should run from Independence, Mo., or Fort Leavenworth, Kans., via Santa Fé, N. Mex., thence down the Rio Grande to Mesilla, and thence over the Southern Overland Mail Route to Los Angeles, Cal., it would have little or no obstructions by Indians;

would absorb the present mail to New Mexico; would afford to this Territory a daily mail; would absorb the present mail from Los Angeles to San Francisco, Cal., and afford that portion of California with a daily mail. It would run through a country where in winter there are no obstructions by snows, and over which it ran in other years almost invariably inside of schedule time. On the southern route from Mesilla to Los Angeles the road is good; the stations are nearly all built, and many are yet in tolerable repair; the wells are dug, &c., and I have been informed by the agent of the company in San Francisco, Mr. Louis McLane, that if the southern mail route should again be opened the road could be restocked and the mail set running in sixty days from the time the order to that effect should be given. Time has proved and will always prove that the Northern Overland Mail Route in winter is not a sure, safe, practicable route. No sophistries can stop the snow from blocking the road west of Salt Lake and through the Sierra Nevada, and none can prove that the southern mail route is not now entirely practicable. Should the people on the Pacific Coast be granted a daily overland mail by your Department, your Department will be sure to find that it must be by the southern route.

This being a matter of great moment to them, as well as of official interest to yourself, I have felt constrained to write to you this letter, and have the honor to be, very respectfully, your obedient servant,

JAMES H. CARLETON.
Brigadier-General, Commanding.

SOURCE: *OR*, SERIES 1, VOLUME 50, PART 2, PAGES 181–182

OR-99

SALT LAKE, *October 20, 1862—9.30 P.M.*

Maj. R. C. DRUM:

Just arrived. Encamped on site of new post. Command in good health and discipline.

P. E. CONNOR,
Colonel Third Infantry California Volunteers.

SOURCE: *OR*, SERIES 1, VOLUME 50, PART 2, PAGE 187

OR-100

HEADQUARTERS DEPARTMENT OF THE PACIFIC,
San Francisco, October 20, 1862.

Brig. Gen. L. THOMAS,
Adjutant-General U.S. Army, Washington, D.C.:

GENERAL: Colonel Connor, commanding expedition for the protection of Overland Mail Route, telegraphs me from Fort Crittenden October 17: "Have just arrived; will cross the Jordan to-morrow."

Very respectfully, your obedient servant,

G. WRIGHT,
Brigadier-General, U.S. Army, Commanding.

SOURCE: *OR*, SERIES 1, VOLUME 50, PART 2, PAGE 187

OR-101

HEADQUARTERS DEPARTMENT OF THE PACIFIC,
San Francisco, October 23, 1862.

Brig. Gen. L. THOMAS,
Adjutant-General U.S. Army, Washington, D.C.:

GENERAL: I am advised by Colonel Connor of his arrival with his command at Salt Lake City on the 20th instant, and occupation of the site for a new post. The colonel reports his command in good health and discipline. I also inclose a copy of a communication received from Maj. D. Fergusson, First Cavalry California Volunteers, dated at Tucson, Ariz. Ter., October 4, with two inclosures, all relating to the occupation of Arizona by the rebel troops previous to the arrival of the Column from California.

Very respectfully, your most obedient servant,

G. WRIGHT,
Brigadier-General, U.S. Army, Commanding.

SOURCE: *OR*, SERIES 1, VOLUME 50, PART 2, PAGE 191

OR-102

[*Extract*]

Talk of Brig. Gen. Benjamin Alvord to the chiefs of the Nez Percé Indians, assembled at the Lapwai Agency, Wash. Ter., on the 24th of October, 1862.

I left Fort Vancouver to visit you before I had heard of the murders in your country. . . .

When encamped near The Dalles in May, 1853, your men were seen to kneel on the ground and say their prayers and worship in truth and sincerity the great God of Heaven. You won in that way my respect and regard. Could I have had my will, I would have raised a wall as high as the heavens around you to keep out intruders. It is very sad to find that the discovery of gold and the consequent rush of miners to this country should have brought such a mass of the very worst white men in contact with you, and thus impeded your improvement. Better if all the gold found there were sunk in the ocean than that such injustice should be done you. In this unfortunate and unlooked-for state of affairs the best the Government can do for you is to provide, as it has, for the making of a new treaty, so as to compensate you so far as possible for the unauthorized occupation of the gold mines by our people. It is true that no amount of money can compensate you for your injured feelings. But the making of this treaty is not given to me. It is in other hands.

It will be my duty after a new treaty is made to aid the Indian agent in enforcing it. . . .

When the Pacific railroad is built, which the present Congress has provided for commencing, we can communicate so quickly with Washington that such delays will be at an end. Some of you and some of your sons will yet visit the Great Father at Washington on that railroad. Believe not the deceitful words of the cunning and slanderous men who say that this great Government has lost its power. The very reverse is true. Never was the Government so mighty and terrible in its power. Never did it have so many rifles or so many soldiers. It has a million of brave and gallant warriors in the field. In the very midst of such a war it makes a beginning, as I have already said, of a Pacific railroad. Owing to the delays interposed by the Southern States, that measure was never before started. The Northern people have all the country from here to Texas, including California, Utah, New Mexico, Nebraska, and Kansas—nearly all to the Mississippi River. You are under a great, a proud, a rich, and a generous Government, and never did we have more noble, patient, and faithful allies than the Nez Percés. It takes fire to temper steel. Temptation is the test and trial of virtue. If a Nez Percé's lodge will stand rain and storm and hail and hurricane, it is then well pitched; it is then firmly secured to the earth. The sun may shine, but fair weather and sunshine are no test for it. It required all this severe and harassing treatment by the gold diggers to show how true and honest and straightforward a Nez Percé can be. Such fidelity shall always have my praise. We wish in return for it not only to be fair, not only to be just, but to be also as kind and as generous as possible toward you.

BENJ. ALVORD,

Brigadier-General, Commanding District.

(Copy for Maj. J. S. Rinearson, First Oregon Cavalry.)

SOURCE: *OR*, SERIES 1, VOLUME 50, PART 2, PAGES 192–193

OR-103

HEADQUARTERS DEPARTMENT OF THE PACIFIC,

San Francisco, October 25, 1862.

Brig. Gen. L. THOMAS,

Adjutant-General U.S. Army, Washington, D.C.:

GENERAL: A few days since I had an interview with His Excellency J. W. Nye, Governor of Nevada Territory. It is well known that many persons in the Territory of Nevada sympathize strongly with the rebellion, and the character of many of the emigrants recently arrived in that country has only added to the disloyal element previously there. The Governor, anxious for the welfare of the Territory, came to consult with me as to the best means to be adopted to crush any attempt of the disaffected to raise the standard of rebellion. The Governor had already organized and armed four companies of loyal men at different points in the Territory, and he proposed to organize two more of infantry and one of cavalry, composed of good men and true, who would be always ready to meet any emergency which might arise. To enable the Governor to carry out his patriotic views I have placed at his disposal 100 stand of small-arms and equipments, also such arms and equipments for a company of cavalry as could be spared from our limited supply. For the same purposes I some time since placed at the disposal of His Excellency Governor Stanford, of the State of California, 500 stand of small-arms, to enable him to organize and arm companies of good Union men at certain points in the State. The Governors are particularly careful that none but men of undoubted loyalty shall enter the companies, and the very fact of having such organizations of men well armed and ready to act will go far to prevent any demonstrations of disloyalty. I have placed these arms at the disposal of the Governors without any special authority from the General-in-Chief or the War Department, not doubting that my acts would be approved, having for their object the maintenance of the peace and quiet of the country. I beg here to renew my former request that 20,000 stand of small-arms and equipments may be sent to this coast at an early day; they may be needed, and remote as we are from the source of our supplies, prudential considerations demand that in an emergency we should be able to call out and arm 30,000 men at once. I would also respectfully recommend that another regiment of infantry be raised in this State, and that the First Cavalry Regiment of California Volunteers be increased to twelve companies. It will be recollected that this regiment, now consisting of only five companies, commanded by a lieutenant-colonel, was originally organized for special service with the command designated to protect the Overland Mail Route; subsequently its destination was changed to Southern California; it is now in Arizona and New Mexico, having formed a part of the Column from California under Brigadier-General Carleton. Owing to the vast extent of this department, and the detaching of large forces to New Mexico and Utah, the increase herein recommended is deemed absolutely necessary. I am compelled in the present state of our affairs to post troops at a great number of points, and it is highly important that they should be sufficiently strong to command respect for the Government of the United States.

Very respectfully, your most obedient servant,

G. WRIGHT,
Brigadier-General, U.S. Army, Commanding.

Source: *OR*, Series 1, Volume 50, Part 2, pages 193–194

OR-104

Headquarters District of Utah,
Camp No. 49, near Salt Lake City, October 26, 1862.

Orders,
No. 14.

Pursuant to orders from department headquarters a military post is hereby established at this camp, to be called Camp Douglas. The following is declared to constitute the military reserve pertaining to this post. Commencing at a post due north one mile distant from the garrison flag staff, and running thence west one mile, thence south two miles, thence east two miles, thence north two miles, and thence west one mile, to the place of beginning, containing 2,560 acres more or less.

By order of:

P. EDW. CONNOR,
Colonel Third Infantry California Volunteers, Comdg. District.

SOURCE: *OR*, SERIES 1, VOLUME 50, PART 2, PAGE 195

OR-105

[*Extract*]

JUNE 16–OCTOBER 30, 1862.—Emigrant road expedition from Omaha, Nebr. Ter., to Portland, Oreg.

Report of Capt. Medorem Crawford, U.S. Army, Assistant Quartermaster.

PORTLAND, OREG., *October 30, 1862.*

SIR: The duty of conducting an escort for the protection of emigrants to Oregon, &c., having been assigned me by the Secretary of War, and having performed that service, I deem it my duty, as it is certainly my pleasure, to comply with your request by reporting to you the principal incidents of my trip.

Having organized my company, procured my transportation and provisions, I left Omaha, Nebr. Ter., on the 16th of June. My company consisted of fifty mounted men, armed with rifles and revolvers, who were instructed in the duties of sentinels and drilled in the simpler evolutions of cavalry tactics. Our route lay on the north side of and immediately along the Platte River, up the Sweetwater, over the Lander road to near Fort Hall, and from thence on the south side of Snake River to Walla Walla. The movement westward was very large. Emigrants to Oregon, Washington Territory, California, Salt Lake, and Denver were on this road. Some had started in April, and were consequently several hundred miles in advance of the rear portion of the emigration. Feeling it to be my duty to protect the rear, I did not hasten on the first part of the trip, but urged upon the emigrants whom I fell in with as I proceeded the necessity of husbanding the strength of their teams so as to be able to perform the journey over the barren deserts of Snake River, the necessity for which my last year's experience had taught me. I soon found that a large proportion of the emigrants had started for the Salmon River mines under the very erroneous impression as to the locality of them. A guide of the route had been published and extensively circulated on the frontier, representing those mines as being within 180 miles of Fort Hall, not giving the locality of the road, but saying—good grass and plenty of water all the way. Under this impression many emigrants had overloaded their wagons and taxed their teams beyond their strength, and so positive were they that they could reach the mines without going down Snake River that many of them disregarded my counsel to dispense with comparatively useless articles with which they were encumbered. The result was that as soon as we left the Platte Valley and encountered the heavy sand and hills their teams and wagons began to fail. They then found it necessary to do what I had advised long before, dispense with heavy and useless articles, but unfortunately it was too late to save many of their teams. From this point to Powder River article after article of furniture and wagon after wagon were left along, and scarcely a camp was left without some evidence of property abandoned. The large number of teams which were ahead of us had cut up the road to such an extent that the dust was very deep and its alkaline properties fatal to cattle. There were over forty head of dead cattle between the Owyhee and Malheur Rivers, a distance of sixteen miles, and we found the proportion nearly as great at other points along Snake River. The first evidence of Indian depredations we saw was a grave at the crossing of New Fork of Green River.

. . .

The recent discoveries of gold on Boisé River will doubtless attract large parties from the States next season, and a road on the north side will be very necessary. Should such be the case, and large numbers of emigrants with families flock to that country, I fear that unless some protection is furnished by the Government the Indians will make an indiscriminate slaughter,

I have the honor to be, very respectfully, your obedient servant,

MEDOREM CRAWFORD,
Captain and Assistant Quartermaster.

Brigadier-General Alvord,
U.S. Army.

Source: *OR*, Series 1, Volume 50, Part 1, pages 153–155

OR-106

Hdqrs. Second Cavalry California Volunteers,
Camp Douglas, Utah, October 31, 1862.

Colonel: Agreeably to your orders, dated Fort Ruby, Nev. Ter., September 29, to proceed thence on the next day (the 30th) with Company H, Second Cavalry California Volunteers, on the northern Overland Route, via the "City of Rocks," in quest of guerrillas or hostile Indians supposed to have congregated there, I have the honor to report that, having left Fort Ruby on the day specified, I overtook, on the second day's march, Capt. S. P. Smith, of the Second Cavalry, who preceded me with his company the day before, and who was encamped in Pine Valley. Here I remained awaiting the return of the Indians who accompanied Captain Smith, and who had been sent out by him to bring in hostile Indians. Having been informed that fires were seen near our camp, I dispatched Captain Smith with a portion of his company, at night, to learn of them. He returned next morning and reported, "No trace of Indians." On the morning of the 4th we took up the line of march, on the route designated, and arrived at Gravelly Ford on the 5th without having discovered any Indians. Here on the 7th I sent Captain Smith and Lieut. Darwin Chase with a party of men down the river, and Lieut. George D. Conrad up the south side of the Humboldt, with instructions to scour the country for hostile Indians or guerrillas, and to report to me, at a place designated, on the north side of the Humboldt, where I encamped on the 9th with the balance of the command. This evening (the 9th) some of the command enticed into the camp three Indians; two of them were armed with rifles and the other with bow and arrows. I immediately ordered their arms taken from them, and placed them under a guard, intending to retain them until the arrival of my interpreter, who was with the detachment under Lieutenant Conrad. A short time after their arrest the Indians made an attempt to obtain their arms, and, having succeeded, they resisted the guard and broke and ran a short distance; they were fired upon by the guard and crippled. Fearing that they would escape, and not wishing to hazard the lives of my men in recapturing them alive, I ordered the guard to fire and they were killed on the spot. Here on the 10th Captain Smith joined the command, and reported that he had received no information nor had he seen any signs of guerrillas or hostile Indians.

On the 11th I proceeded on the march, having sent out the officers of the command with instructions that if Indians were found to bring them into camp. Captain Smith, having been sent in advance, had not proceeded more than ten or twelve miles when he came upon a party of about fourteen or fifteen Indians, who were armed with rifles and bows and arrows. He surrounded them and took from them their arms. Immediately after, the Indians attempted to escape by jumping in the river. They were fired upon and nine of them killed. On the same day Lieutenant Conrad and party brought into camp three Indians and an Indian child. Captain Smith returned in the evening with two squaws. Next day (the 12th) Captain McLean returned, bringing in one Indian and a squaw. Same day Lieutenant Clark returned with one Indian; another Indian was captured during the evening. The next day (the 13th) I told two of the Indians, through the interpreter, that if they would go and bring in Indians who were engaged in the massacre of emigrants I would release them, but that if they did not return that night I would kill all the Indians I held as prisoners in camp. The next morning (the 14th), hearing nothing from the Indians I had sent out the day previous, I put to death four of those remaining, and released the squaws and child, telling them that we were sent there to punish Indians who were engaged in the massacre of emigrants, and instructed them to tell all the Indians that if they did not desist from killing emigrants that I would return there next summer and destroy them. On the next day (the 15th) I sent Lieutenants Chase and Conrad with a detachment on the south side of the Humboldt with instructions as before. They came upon a party of Indians encamped in the mountains, armed with rifles and bows and arrows. They were surrounded and their arms taken from them. The Indians, attempting to escape, were fired upon, when eight of their number were killed. The balance of the route no traces of Indians were seen. On the 28th I arrived at the place designated by you; the next day, at about 3 o'clock P.M., arrived at this camp. The route is a good one, with an abundance of grass and water. In conclusion, it affords me great pleasure to report the efficiency of the officers and the good conduct of the men of the command, without the loss of any.

I have the honor to be, very respectfully, your obedient servant,

EDWARD McGARRY,
Major, Second Cavalry California Volunteers.

Col. P. EDWARD CONNOR,
Third Infantry California Volunteers,
Commanding District of Utah, Camp Douglas, Utah.

[Editor's note: *This document appears in the* Official Records *as an inclosure to OR-107.*]

SOURCE: *OR*, SERIES 1, VOLUME 50, PART 1, PAGES 178–179

OR-107

HEADQUARTERS DISTRICT OF UTAH,
Camp Douglas, Utah, November 6, 1862.

Lieut. Col. R. C. DRUM,
Asst. Adjt. Gen., Dept. of the Pacific, San Francisco, Cal.:

COLONEL: I have the honor to transmit herewith a copy of the report of Major McGarry, Second Cavalry California Volunteers, detailing the result of his expedition to capture guerrillas and punish Indians engaged in the late massacres on the Humboldt River, for the information of the general commanding the department. I am satisfied from verbal information received from officers of the expedition that the Indians who have been punished were a part of those who had committed the late murders, and that the punishment was well merited. I hope and believe that the lesson taught them will have a salutary effect in checking future massacres on that route.

Very respectfully, your obedient servant.

P. EDWARD CONNOR,
Colonel Third Infantry California Volunteers, Comdg. District.

[Editor's note: *This document is included as an inclosure to an Expedition Report covering September 30–October 29, 1862. See* OR-109. *Attached report is* OR-106.]

SOURCE: *OR*, SERIES 1, VOLUME 50, PART 1, PAGES 177–178

OR-108

HEADQUARTERS DISTRICT OF UTAH,
Camp Douglas, Utah Ter., November 9, 1862.

ADJUTANT-GENERAL,
Washington, D.C.:

GENERAL: I have the honor to inform you that pursuant to orders from headquarters Department of the Pacific on the 26th day of October, 1862, I established a military post in Utah Territory, and which I have named Camp Douglas. It is situated at a distance of three miles east of Great Salt Lake City, at which place there is a post-office and telegraph office, with good facilities for communication both east and west daily. It is situated at the foot and on the west side of a range of mountains which form the divide between Weber River and the Great Salt Lake Valley. It is on an elevated spot which commands a full view of the city and the Great Salt Lake and Valley, with a plentiful supply of wood and water in its vicinity, and in the neighborhood of numerous quarries of stone adapted to building barracks. If it is contemplated to establish a permanent post in this Territory I know of no spot so desirable as this. Besides the above advantages, it is the center from which diverge three roads to California, two to Oregon, and the great Overland Mail Route to the east. The low price of forage for animals is an additional advantage which it possesses, and the health of the soldiers has also materially improved since their arrival here.

I am, very respectfully, your obedient servant,

P. EDW. CONNOR,
Colonel Third Infantry California Volunteers, Comdg. District.

SOURCE: *OR*, SERIES 1, VOLUME 50, PART 2, PAGE 218

OR-109

SEPTEMBER 30–OCTOBER 29, 1862.—Expedition from Fort Ruby, Nev., Ter., to Camp Douglas, Utah Ter., with affairs (October 11 and 15) on the Humboldt River, Nev. Ter.

Report of Maj. Edward McGarry, Second California Cavalry.

HEADQUARTERS DEPARTMENT OF THE PACIFIC,
San Francisco, November 18, 1862.

Brig. Gen. L. THOMAS,
Adjutant-General U.S. Army, Washington, D.C.:

GENERAL: I have the honor to inclose herewith a copy of a letter from Col. P. E. Connor, Third Infantry California Volunteers, commanding the District of Utah, dated November 6, 1862, also a copy of the report of Maj. E. McGarry, Second Cavalry California Volunteers, detailing the result of his expedition to capture guerrillas and punish Indians engaged in the late massacres on the Humboldt River. The swift retributive punishment which has been meted out to those Indians will doubtless have the effect of preventing a repetition of their barbarities. It is the only way to deal with those savages.

Very respectfully, your obedient servant,

G. WRIGHT,
Brigadier-General, U.S. Army, Commanding.

[Inclosure.]

[Editor's note: *See OR-107 for this inclosure; see also OR-106.*]

SOURCE: *OR*, SERIES 1, VOLUME 50, PART 1, PAGE 177

OR-110

HEADQUARTERS DISTRICT OF UTAH,
Camp Douglas, Utah Ter., November 20, 1862.

Maj. E. McGARRY,
Second Cavalry California Volunteers:

MAJOR: You will proceed this P.M. with a detachment of sixty men of your command to Cache Valley, at which point are encamped Bear Hunter's tribe of Snake and Bannock Indians, who, I am credibly informed, have in their possession an emigrant boy about ten years of age, whose parents were murdered last summer by Indians. The boy's uncle is at present at Cache Valley and will guide you to where the boy is. You will march by night and by a trail which will be shown you by a guide who will accompany your command. Surround the Indians, if possible, before they become aware of your presence, and hold them prisoners while you send a part of your men to a valley about two miles from the Indian camp, where, I am told, there is a large number of stock stolen from murdered emigrants, which, if you have reason to believe that my information is correct, you will drive to this post. You will search the Indian camp thoroughly for the emigrant boy, and if you should not find him you will demand him of the Indians, and if not given up you will bring three of their principal men to this post as hostages. You will also investigate as to their complicity in the massacres of last summer, and if you have reason to believe any of them are guilty you will bring all such to this post for trial. You will not fire upon the Indians unless you find it necessary to the proper execution of your instructions.

P. EDWARD CONNOR,
Colonel Third Infantry California Volunteers, Comdg. District.

SOURCE: *OR*, SERIES 1, VOLUME 50, PART 2, PAGES 228–229

OR-111

HDQRS. SECOND CALVARY CALIFORNIA VOLUNTEERS,
Camp Douglas, Utah, November 28, 1862.

LIEUTENANT: I have the honor to report that, agreeable to instructions of the colonel commanding the district, I left this camp on the night of the 20th instant and proceeded to Cache Valley, where I arrived about 11 P.M. on the 22d, a distance of 100 miles, where I was met by Mr. Van Orman, the uncle of the emigrant boy you ordered me to rescue from the Indians; he informed me that Chief Bear Hunter was encamped with thirty or forty of his tribe, Shoshones, Snakes, and Bannocks, about two miles distant. I left the horses in the settlement culled Providence in charge of a guard, and started about 1 o'clock for the Indian camp; the night was dark and cold, and we did not find the camp until the morning of the 23d. I then divided my command into three parties under Captain Smith, Lieutenant Conrad, and myself, with instructions to surround the camp and close in upon them at daybreak. I found in a tent two squaws; the Indians had all left that night, as I perceived that the fires in their huts were not extinguished. I then returned to where I had left the horses, at which place I arrived about 7 A.M. Captain Smith brought in one Indian, caught in trying to escape; I made a prisoner of him. About 8 o'clock a party of mounted Indians, I should think thirty or forty, armed with rifles, bows and arrows, made their appearance from a cañon on a bench between the settlement and hills, about a mile from the settlement, and made a warlike display, such as shouting, riding in a circle, and all sorts of antics known only to their race. I immediately ordered my men to mount, divided them as before, sent Captain Smith to the right, Lieutenant Conrad to the left, and I took the center, driving the Indians into the cañon; when I arrived at the mouth of the cañon I halted for the purpose of reconnoitering; just at that time the Indians opened fire upon Lieutenant Conrad; I then ordered my men to commence firing and to kill every Indian they could see; by this time the Indians had possession of the cañon and hills on both sides. I found it would be impossible to enter the cañon without exposing my men greatly. I therefore re-enforced Lieutenant Conrad on the left of the cañon, with orders to take the hill on the left of the cañon at all hazards. About the time the re-enforcements reported to him Chief Bear Hunter made his appearance on a hilltop on the right, with a flag of truce (as I was informed afterward); I at the time took it to be a warlike demonstration; a citizen who heard his halloing came up to me and told me that the chief said they did not want to fight any more. I then ordered my men to cease firing, and told him to say to the chief if they would surrender and come in I would not kill them, which terms they acceded to. Chief Bear Hunter, with twenty or more of his warriors, then came in. I took them into the settlement, took Bear Hunter and four others that I thought to be prominent Indians and examined them (through an interpreter) as to the whereabouts of the white boy, and ascertained that he had been sent away some days before. I told Bear Hunter to send some of his tribe and bring the boy to me; that I should hold the five as hostages until they delivered him to me. He dispatched three of his men, and they returned the next day about noon with the boy. I then released Bear Hunter and the four others. I killed 3 and wounded 1 Indian in the fight. I was told by Bear Hunter that an Indian known as Woeber Tom, alias Utah Tom, communicated the information of our approach. In relation to the emigrant stock I was ordered to examine into and bring into camp, I could not find any such, and from the information I could gather I am of the opinion all or nearly all of the stock taken by the Indians last summer is now in the Humboldt country. I left Cache Valley on the morning of the 25th, and arrived at this camp on the afternoon of the 27th, without the loss or scratch of man or horse. It affords me great pleasure to report to the colonel commanding the good conduct of the command, and during the fight, which lasted about two hours, the officers and men behaved handsomely.

Very respectfully, your obedient servant,

EDWARD McGARRY,
Major, Second Cavalry California Volunteers.

Second Lieut. THOMAS S. HARRIS,
Second Cavalry California Volunteers,
Acting Assistant Adjutant-General, District of Utah.

[Editor's note: *This document appears in the* Official Records *as an inclosure to OR-112.*]

SOURCE: *OR*, SERIES 1, VOLUME 50, PART 1, PAGES 182–183

OR-112

HEADQUARTERS DISTRICT OF UTAH,
Camp Douglas, Utah, December 2, 1862.

Lieut. Col. R. C. DRUM,
Asst. Adjt. Gen., Dept. of the Pacific, San Francisco, Cal.:

COLONEL: I have the honor to inclose a letter of instruction to Major McGarry and his report of the expedition upon which he was sent. The uncle of the boy, who is now at this post, is a resident of Oregon, and, as he informs me, has been in search of the boy for two years. Three sisters of his, who were captured at the same time, are dead, he also informs me that three expeditions had previously been sent out from Oregon for the recovery of the children, one of which was under command of Captain Dent, of the Ninth Infantry. The Indians are threatening the Overland Mail Route east and west of here. I have no fears of the western end, as the lessons I have been teaching them and the messages I send them make them fear me. About a week since I sent ten men to protect the telegraph station at Big Sandy, which was threatened by Indians. On Saturday last they stole 100 horses from Fort Bridger Reserve, belonging to some mountaineers, who are wintering there, and fears are entertained that they will attack some of the stations of the Overland Mail. I have therefore ordered Company I, Captain Lewis, of my regiment, to garrison Fort Bridger this winter. I shall order detachments of his company to the different stations in this district east of here, if I find it will be necessary. Pacific Springs Station, lately attacked by Indians, is just east of the line dividing this district and the Department of the West, and has been garrisoned by troops from that department. The telegraph station at Big Sandy is in the District of Oregon. I shall leave the ten men now there at that point until I am satisfied there is no further danger from Indians, unless otherwise ordered.

I have the honor to remain, very respectfully, your obedient servant,

P. EDWARD CONNOR,
Colonel Third Infantry California Volunteers, Comdg. District.

[Editor's note: *This document is included as an inclosure to an Expedition Report covering November 20–27, 1862. See OR-123. Attached letter is OR-111.*]

SOURCE: *OR*, SERIES 1, VOLUME 50, PART 1, PAGES 181–182

OR-113

NOVEMBER 22–27, 1862.—Expedition from Fort Ruby, Nev. Ter., to the Sierra Nevada Mountains.

Report of Maj. Patrick A. Gallagher, Third California Infantry.

FORT RUBY, NEV. TER., *December 2, 1862.*

LIEUTENANT: I have the honor to report that on the afternoon of the 21st ultimo one of the herders belonging to this post, who was some thirty-five miles down the valley, came in and reported that 10 horses, 1 mule, and 1 head of beef had been stolen by the Indians the night before. I immediately telegraphed the fact to you. On the morning of the 22d I started with a party, consisting of Captain Potts and forty-two men of Company F, Third Infantry California Volunteers, with six days' rations, for the purpose of recovering the stock and punishing the guilty parties. We left this post at 10 on the morning of the 22d, and after marching thirty miles encamped at 9 P.M. On the morning of the 23d we started at sunrise, and after marching thirty miles over a rough, swampy road, where we had to make bridges, &c., for our wagon, we encamped for the night about sundown. On the morning of the 24th, finding it impossible to proceed farther with the wagon, Captain Potts and myself, with three men (mounted), went ahead, leaving the command under Sergeant Buxton to follow on as fast as possible, leaving eight men as a guard to the wagon. I made a reconnaissance of the whole valley north to the mountains, and finding no pass through the mountains, nor signs of either stock or Indians, returned and met the command about twenty-five miles from our morning camp. The men suffering very much from fatigue and cold, and our rations being nearly exhausted, I deemed it advisable to return to the fort, where we arrived on the afternoon of the 27th. From my personal observations I am satisfied that there are no Indians in this valley north of this fort, and those that stole the stock came from Thousand Spring Valley, or that vicinity, probably belonging to the Bannock tribe. In conclusion, I would say that the men who were with me have done nobly, having marched a distance of 170 miles in less than five days (myself and Captain Potts and the three men with us some thirty miles farther), with weather intensely cold, and they thinly clad, without a murmur. I must say I am proud of them.

Very respectfully, your obedient servant,

P. A. GALLAGHER,
Major Third Infantry California Volunteers, Commanding Post,

Lieut. THOMAS S. HARRIS,
Acting Assistant Adjutant-General, District of Utah.

SOURCE: *OR*, SERIES 1, VOLUME 50, PART 1, PAGES 183–184

OR-114

WASHINGTON, D.C., *December 6, 1862.*

Maj. Gen. GEORGE WRIGHT,
San Francisco, Cal.:

Your attention is called to the propriety of garrisoning Fort Bridger with a part of the California regiment.

H. W. HALLECK,
General-in-Chief.

SOURCE: *OR*, SERIES 1, VOLUME 50, PART 2, PAGE 241

OR-115

HDQRS. DEPARTMENT OF THE PACIFIC,
San Francisco, Cal., December 6, 1862.

SPECIAL ORDERS,
No. 220.

* * * *

7. Lieut. Col. George S. Evans, Second Cavalry California Volunteers, will proceed without delay to Camp Douglas, near Salt Lake City, and assume command of his regiment.

8. Company F, Second Cavalry California Volunteers, will on Thursday next proceed to and take post at Camp Union, near Sacramento. The enlisted men, except Sergeant Manning, belonging to this company, on duty at the provost-marshal's office, will be relieved from duty thereat and sent to their company. A number of men equal to that now on duty at the provost office will be selected from the Second Cavalry recruits at the Presidio to replace those of Company F, relieved. The Second Cavalry recruits at the Presidio not required for duty as provost guard will remain at that post under the command of Lieutenant Starr, Second Cavalry California Volunteers.

* * * *

By order of Brigadier-General Wright:

RICHD. C. DRUM,
Assistant Adjutant-General.

SOURCE: *OR*, SERIES 1, VOLUME 50, PART 2, PAGE 241

OR-116

WASHINGTON, D.C., *December 9, 1862.*

Brigadier-General WRIGHT,
San Francisco, Cal.:

All communications received at the War Department from Overland Mail Company, Post-Office Department, and Department of the Interior urge the removal of Colonel Connor's command to Fort Bridger and Ham's Fork, as a check upon the Indians.

H. W. HALLECK,
General-in-Chief.

SOURCE: *OR*, SERIES 1, VOLUME 50, PART 2, PAGE 244

OR-117

HEADQUARTERS DEPARTMENT OF THE PACIFIC,
San Francisco, December 9, 1862.

Brig. Gen. L. THOMAS,
Adjutant-General U.S. Army, Washington, D.C.:

GENERAL: I have the honor to acknowledge the receipt of Major-General Halleck's telegraphic dispatch of the 6th instant, calling my attention to the propriety of garrisoning Fort Bridger. My latest accounts from Fort Bridger, obtained from an officer who passed there, represented everything as quiet in that neighborhood, and I have received no intimation from Colonel Connor, the commandant of that district, as to the necessity of posting troops at Fort Bridger. However, as it is an important station of the Overland Mail Company, and good quarters already built, I have directed Colonel Connor to detach one or two companies from his command and occupy Bridger. I have two companies of Third Infantry California Volunteers (Connor's), now at Sacramento, and one company of the same regiment at Fort Churchill. In the early spring, or as soon as the roads are passable, I shall send them forward to Salt Lake. From the best information I can obtain, I am fully satisfied that we should have a force in the Salt Lake Valley of at least 2,000 men; commanded by a firm and discreet officer. Without entering into details I am well convinced that prudential considerations demand the presence of a force in that country strong enough to look down any opposition.

Very respectfully, your obedient servant,

G. WRIGHT,
Brigadier-General, U.S. Army, Commanding.

SOURCE: *OR*, SERIES 1, VOLUME 50, PART 2, PAGES 244–245

OR-118

San Francisco, *December 11, 1862.*

Adjt. Gen. L. Thomas,
Washington, D.C.:

Your dispatch of 2d instant received. Please notify Governor Stanford by telegraph. Your dispatch of 6th instant received. Fort Bridger ordered to be garrisoned.

G. WRIGHT,
Brigadier-General, U.S. Army, Commanding.

Source: *OR*, Series 1, Volume 50, Part 2, page 249

OR-119

San Francisco, Cal., *December 12, 1862.*

Adjt. Gen. Lorenzo Thomas,
Washington, D.C.:

Major-General Halleck's dispatch of 9th received. Occupation of Bridger previously ordered. Colonel Connor directed to occupy other points if necessary.

G. WRIGHT,
Brigadier-General, U.S. Army, Commanding.

Source: *OR*, Series 1, Volume 50, Part 2, page 249

OR-120

Headquarters Department of the Pacific,
San Francisco, December 12, 1862.

Brig. Gen. L. Thomas,
Adjutant-General U.S. Army, Washington, D.C.:

General: I have this day acknowledged by telegraph the receipt of Major-General Halleck's dispatch of the 9th instant, in reference to the occupation of Fort Bridger and Ham's Fork by the troops of Colonel Connor. I had already ordered the reoccupation of Fort Bridger, and I have now sent instructions to Colonel Connor to occupy such other points as he may deem necessary to guard against Indian disturbances on the Overland Mail Route. I would not recommend the entire abandonment of the position now occupied by Colonel Connor, in close proximity to Salt Lake City, where he is erecting temporary shelter for his men.

Very respectfully, your obedient servant,

G. WRIGHT,
Brigadier-General, U.S. Army, Commanding.

SOURCE: *OR*, SERIES 1, VOLUME 50, PART 2, PAGE 249

OR-121

HEADQUARTERS DEPARTMENT OF THE PACIFIC,
San Francisco, Cal., December 12, 1862.

Col. P. EDWARD CONNOR,
Third Infantry California Volunteers,
Comdg. District of Utah, Salt Lake City, Utah Ter.:

SIR: Inclosed you will receive a copy of a telegram from the General-in-Chief to the department commander.* In addition to the garrison sent to Bridger, the general commanding desires you to occupy such other points on or near the overland route as you may deem essential for its proper protection, retaining, however, your present position.

Very respectfully, your obedient servant,

R. C. DRUM,
Assistant Adjutant-General.

* [*Refers to OR-114. This document is referenced in OR-126.*]

SOURCE: *OR*, SERIES 1, VOLUME 50, PART 2, PAGE 251

OR-122

EXECUTIVE OFFICE,
Santa Fé, N. Mex., December 13, 1862.

Hon. W. H. SEWARD,
Secretary, State Department, Washington City:

SIR: I have the honor to inclose herewith a copy of my message to the Legislature of this Territory,* and I would most respectfully invite your attention to page 15,† and again urge the importance of additional troops for this Territory.

I am reliably informed that some 5,000 rebel troops from Texas are preparing to invade New Mexico, with the intention of obtaining possession of this Territory and Colorado, and then, with Utah under Brigham Young, to establish a number of slave States.

The present war originated in consequence of the desire of the South to establish slavery in the Territories, and I am fully satisfied that they have not given up their intention, but will take advantage of any opportunity to accomplish it. And I believe that when our troops have taken possession of the coast of Texas and proceeded into the interior that the rebels will retreat into this and Colorado Territory, and to save this country from falling into the hands of the enemy and laid waste we should be fully able to meet and repulse them. I have therefore, with the concurrence of Brigadier-General Carleton, commanding this department, asked the Secretary of War to authorize the raising of two regiments of volunteers, with authority to recruit them either in this Territory or Colorado. As I have not heard from that Department, you will aid us and probably save our country by calling the attention of the President and honorable Secretary of War to this subject and obtaining for us the order desired.

I have the honor to be, very respectfully, your obedient servant,

W. F. M. ARNY,
Secretary and Acting Governor New Mexico.

* Not found.
† The message to the legislature was not attached.

[Editor's note: *This document appears in the* Official Records *as an inclosure to correspondence from Secretary William H. Seward to the Hon. E. M. Stanton, secretary of war, January 7, 1863, that is not included in this volume.*]

SOURCE: *OR*, SERIES 1, VOLUME 15, PAGES 641–642

OR-123

NOVEMBER 20–27, 1862.—Expedition from Camp Douglas to the Cache Valley, Utah Ter., with skirmish (23d) in the Cache Valley.

Report of Maj. Edward McGarry, Second California Cavalry.

HEADQUARTERS DEPARTMENT OF THE PACIFIC,
San Francisco, December 15, 1862.

Brig. Gen. L. THOMAS,
Adjutant-General U.S. Army, Washington, D.C.:

GENERAL: I have the honor to inclose herewith a communication addressed to my headquarters by Col. P. E. Connor, commanding the District of Utah, dated at Camp Douglas, December 2, 1862, with a copy of his instructions to Maj. E. McGarry, Second Cavalry California Volunteers, and a report from the latter officer of the execution of his orders. In Colonel Connor's communication, it will be observed that he is taking every precaution to guard effectively the Overland Mail Route, and also the telegraph stations; and to his energy and sound judgment may safely be confided that important duty.

Very respectfully, your most obedient servant,

G. WRIGHT,
Brigadier-General, U.S. Army, Commanding.

[Editor's note: *See OR-112 and OR-111 for the correspondence included with this report.*]

SOURCE: *OR*, SERIES 1, VOLUME 50, PART 1, PAGE 181

OR-124

HEADQUARTERS DEPARTMENT OF THE PACIFIC,
San Francisco, Cal., December 15, 1862.

His Excellency WILLIAM PICKERING,
Governor of Washington Territory, Olympia, Wash. Ter.:

GOVERNOR: I have the honor to acknowledge the receipt of Your Excellency's communication of the 21st ultimo. I think that with the force I shall have during the coming year at or in the vicinity of Salt Lake, and the re-enforcements which I propose to send to the Walla Walla District, ample protection will be afforded for all emigrants approaching this country, provided they themselves exercise ordinary precautions, and will avail themselves of the offered escorts; but if they on entering the Indian country scatter in every direction, I cannot be responsible for their safety. I have already recommended the establishment of a strong military post on the Snake River, which with the movable column to be sent out during the summer and fall mouths will, it is believed, effectually prevent a recurrence of those scenes of murder and pillage which have been enacted for so many years past.

With great respect, I have the honor to be, Your Excellency's obedient servant,

G. WRIGHT,
Brigadier-General, U.S. Army, Commanding.

Source: *OR*, Series 1, Volume 50, Part 2, page 252

OR-125

Headquarters Department of the Pacific,
San Francisco, Cal., December 16, 1862.

Col. P. Edward Connor,
Third Infty. California Vols., Comdg. Dist. of Utah,
Camp Douglas, Salt Lake City, Utah Ter.:

Sir: Your letter transmitting Maj. Edward McGarry's report of an expedition to recover a white boy held by the Indians has been submitted to the department commander, and by him forwarded for the information of the War Department. The general commends your activity and promptness, as well as the good conduct of Major McGarry and the officers and men under his command. All that you have done and propose to do is approved by the general, who feels that he can safely rely upon your sound judgment for conducting to a favorable issue the delicate duty assigned you.

Very respectfully, your obedient servant,

R. C. DRUM,
Assistant Adjutant-General.

Source: *OR*, Series 1, Volume 50, Part 2, pages 253–254

OR-126

HEADQUARTERS DISTRICT OF UTAH,
Camp Douglas, December 20, 1862.

Lieut. Col. R. C. DRUM,
Asst. Adjt. Gen., Dept. of the Pacific, San Francisco, Cal.:

SIR: Your communication of date December 12, 1862,* inclosing telegram from General-in-Chief to department commander, is just received. In reply I have the honor to inform you that since my arrival here I have been aware that efforts were being made to dissever my command. The real Governor of this Territory, Brigham Young, and his satellites on the one hand, and agents and contractors on the other, have since my arrival here constantly worked to separate this command, the former, with his usual sagacity, for the attainment of his own purposes and without the least doubt of his success (high authority states that he has openly boasted, in fact, that he would drive me away from here before spring), and the latter from a desire to make money out of the Government. Judge Carter, agent of the Overland Mail Company east of here and sutler of Fort Bridger, with other interested persons within this district, have not so much the interests of the Government or the Overland Mail Company at heart as a desire to speculate upon the necessities of this command by selling to it supplies, of which Judge Carter has large quantities on hand. As an evidence of this fact that gentleman has been the only one of a great many among those interested largely in the Overland Mail Company who has desired the establishment of more posts on the line; and I am now satisfied that the rumor started by him previous to my garrisoning Fort Bridger of 100 head of stock being stolen by Indians from the reservation was false, and circulated for the purpose of having troops ordered to that post. I am reliably informed that the so-called President Young is making active preparations indicating a determination on his part to oppose the Government of the United States in the spring, provided Utah is not admitted into the Union as a State, or in case of a foreign war or serious reverse to our arms. It is constantly asserted by him and his agents that this command should be moved and scattered along the line of the Overland Mail Company as a "check against Indians," who they say are ready to attack the property at any moment; and many willing converts to this fear are found among Brigham's hosts. But no one having the interest of the Government or the company in view can be found here credulous enough to be blind to the real motives which actuate their desires. Brigham Young is now engaged in mounting cannon for the purpose of resisting the Government, and has reports circulated, which have reached the ears of those highest in authority, in order to mature his plans, gain time, and prepare his cannon. Desirable as this would be to him I hope to defeat his intentions. From a careful scrutiny of the state of affairs here and a thorough knowledge of the country, I am satisfied I occupy every necessary position. The entire line from Ruby Valley to

Ham's Fork is completely under my control, and while, in my opinion, there exists no necessity for troops at Fort Bridger, to quiet the apprehensions of the Overland Mail Company, if they have any (which I doubt), and to obey the orders of the general commanding, I shall continue to garrison Fort Bridger, and will immediately send a sufficient force to occupy Ham's Fork, although I am of the opinion there is no real necessity for it. My present position was selected for its availability, and commanding as it does not only all the avenues to but even the town itself, it is an important one, and I am not surprised that Brigham Young considers its occupancy dangerous to his interests. The presence of this command here, which the informants of the General-in-Chief desire so much to have removed, indicates that my information regarding the real intentions of these people is correct, and events will prove that in selecting my position and carrying out my own views the interest of the Government and of the Overland Mail Company has been anticipated. I am truly glad that the department commander has given me discretionary powers in the premises. I am credibly informed and believe that Mormons have instigated the late attack by Indians on the telegraph station at Pacific Springs in order to draw my forces to that point. Mormons also, in the northern part of this valley, encourage depredations by the Humboldt Indians by purchasing of them property of which massacred immigrants have been despoiled by giving them in exchange therefor powder, lead, and produce. I have heretofore refrained from submitting a report of these transactions to the general commanding for the reason that I desired to be previously well informed.

Very respectfully, your obedient servant,

P. EDW. CONNOR,
Colonel Third Infantry California Volunteers, Comdg. District.

* [*Refers to OR-121.*]

SOURCE: *OR*, SERIES 1, VOLUME 50, PART 2, PAGES 256–257

OR-127

[*Extract*]

HEADQUARTERS DEPARTMENT OF THE PACIFIC,
San Francisco, December 23, 1862.

Brig. Gen. L. THOMAS,
Adjutant-General U.S. Army, Washington, D.C.:

GENERAL: I have already forwarded estimates and asked for authority to establish a military post at or near Fort Boisé, on the Snake River. The great necessity for a strong garrison in that quarter is daily becoming more apparent. In the very heart of the mining districts of the north, and on the route by which the vast emigration from the East approaches that country, a strong military force can afford protection to all against those wandering bands of Indians which infest that section, and maintain peace between the races. In accordance with the authority of the Secretary of War, communicated to me through your office, I suspended the further organization of the regiment of Oregon cavalry on the completion of the sixth company. It is now deemed important that the regiment should be completed, and I have directed Brigadier-General Alvord to call out six more companies and organize the regiment in accordance with General Orders, No. 126, current series. Inclosed herewith is a slip from a paper published at Lewiston, Wash. Ter., relative to the navigation of Snake River, and the probability that steamers will be able to ascend as far as Boisé or Salmon Falls.

Hoping that my action in completing the Oregon regiment may be approved, and that the establishment of a post at Fort Boisé may be authorized, I have the honor to be, your most obedient servant,

G. WRIGHT,
Brigadier-General, U.S. Army, Commanding.

[Inclosure.]

NAVIGATION OF SNAKE RIVER.—STEAMERS TO THE BOISÉ MINES.

Our readers will remember that in our issue of October 24 we alluded to the navigation of Snake River, and furnished the outlines of the explorers who were sent up to Boisé to examine the river.

. . .

The examination of the river has resulted in establishing the fact that Snake is navigable for steamers, and will be much safer to travel than the river is from Lewiston to the mouth of Snake. This is equally as gratifying to the projector of the scheme as it is to the citizens of Lewiston and the country at large. A new route will now be opened for steam, the results of which cannot now be foretold. We shall penetrate Nevada and Utah Territories by steam, as it is well known that it is only ninety miles from Fort Boisé to Salmon Falls, on Snake River. Salmon Falls is within 250 miles of Salt Lake City. A new avenue of trade will then be opened, and those who have risked their fortune and periled their lives are justly entitled to the gratitude of the people, and a rich reward shall be their portion. But a few more suns will rise and set before the shrill whistle of the steamer will reverberate along the banks of this noble river, and its echo will be heard for ages yet to come through the ravines, gorges, cañons, and on the mountain tops in our golden land, as a symbol of ambition, perseverance, and goaheadativeness. More anon.

Source: *OR*, Series 1, Volume 50, Part 2, pages 259–261

OR-128

[*Extract*]

EXECUTIVE OFFICE,
Olympia, Wash. Ter., December 29, 1862.

General GEORGE WRIGHT, U.S. Army,
Comdg. Military Department of the Pacific, San Francisco:

DEAR SIR: I feel deeply and earnestly the importance of the present Congress providing for a line of military posts along the emigrant route across this Territory. From this view I have considered it my duty to recommend our Territorial Legislature, now in session, to memorialize Congress in behalf of suitable appropriations to secure the construction of those necessary military establishments at the earliest day practicable as the only efficacious plan by which the lives and property of all future emigrants can be securely protected. Also for a memorial for the extinction of the Indian title to all lands over which the said emigrant road passes, for the purpose of more effectually commanding and preserving the peace and quiet of all overland travelers from the South Pass to the Columbia River. By securing the whole length of the road upon lands belonging exclusively to the United States will give us a more certain hope of being better able to preserve travelers from Indian molestation than we can possibly expect to accomplish so long as the road passes over lands yet belonging to the Indians. Also for a memorial for such additional mail routes as the Legislature knows the increasing population needs. Both houses of the Legislature have unanimously passed suitable memorials for all these purposes, one of which prays for establishing a mail route from South Pass or from Salt Lake along the said emigrant road down Snake River Valley to Walla Walla.

. . .

I am, with great respect, your obedient servant,

WILLIAM PICKERING,
Governor of Washington Territory.

SOURCE: *OR*, SERIES 1, VOLUME 50, PART 2, PAGES 268–269

OR-129

[*Extract*]

Organization of troops in the Department of the Pacific, Brig. Gen. George Wright, U.S. Army, commanding, December 31, 1862.

. . .

DISTRICT OF UTAH.
Col. P. EDWARD CONNOR.

Camp Douglas, Utah Ter.
Col. P. EDWARD CONNOR.
3d California (four companies),
2d California Cavalry (four companies).

Fort Bridger, Utah Ter.
Capt. MICAJAH G. LEWIS.
3d California, Company I.

Fort Ruby, Nev. Ter.
Maj. PATRICK A. GALLAGHER.
3d California, Companies C and F.

Fort Churchill, Nev. Ter.
Maj. CHARLES MCDERMIT.
3d California, Company A,
2d California Cavalry, Company L.

SOURCE: *OR*, SERIES 1, VOLUME 50, PART 2, PAGE 273

OR-130

HEADQUARTERS DEPARTMENT OF THE PACIFIC,
San Francisco, January 3, 1863.

Brig. Gen. L. THOMAS,
Adjutant-General U.S. Army, Washington, D.C.:

GENERAL: For the information of the General-in-Chief and War Department I have the honor to inclose herewith a communication, dated on the 20th ultimo, from Col. P. E. Connor, Third Infantry California Volunteers, commanding the District of Utah.* Colonel Connor is a man of observation, undaunted firmness, and self-possession under all circumstances, and his views of the state of affairs in Utah can be relied on. I have written to Colonel Connor fully in relation to the policy I desire him to pursue in Utah. With the small force now in that Territory the greatest prudence is required, and in the early spring I propose to throw forward to Salt Lake such a re-enforcement as will insure respect to our flag and a due observance of the laws of the United States.

Very respectfully, your most obedient servant,

G. WRIGHT,
Brigadier-General, U.S. Army, Commanding.

* [*Refers to* OR-126.]

SOURCE: *OR*, SERIES 1, VOLUME 50, PART 2, PAGE 275

OR-131

SUBSISTENCE OFFICE,
San Francisco, Cal., January 31, 1863.

Col. J. P. TAYLOR,
Commissary-General of Subsistence, Washington, D.C.:

COLONEL: For the supply of subsistence stores for the troops stationed in the vicinity of Salt Lake City, Utah Ter., for the year commencing November 1, 1863, I am directed by the department commander to cause to be purchased in that Territory such stores as may be obtained there at a less cost to the United States than their cost here added to the expense of transportation to Salt Lake. The supply required will be 400,000 rations. Under the directions above named the greater portion of these stores (except coffee, sugar, rice, and soap) will be obtained in Utah Territory. This will largely increase the expense of the subsistence for the coming year of the troops in this department, and in connection with this subject I have the honor to request your attention to the matter of my letter to you dated May 7, 1862, to which I have received no reply. For the transportation of stores from here to Salt Lake last summer the quartermaster paid 20 cents per pound. From the best information I have I judge that the price of freight will not be less (will not be less than 35 to 40 cents in anything but coin) than that amount next summer. In view of this, I have to submit to your consideration the question whether it be advisable to ship from Saint Louis the 400,000 rations of coffee, sugar, rice, and soap, or to send these articles from San Francisco. I have respect fully to request instructions on the subject.

Very respectfully, your obedient servant,

JNO. KELLOGG,
Captain and Commissary of Subsistence.

[Indorsement]

SAN FRANCISCO, CAL., *February 16, 1863.*

Respectfully submitted to the department commander with my letter of this date, to be forwarded (at his discretion) with my letter to Washington.

Your obedient servant,

E. B. BABBITT,
Deputy Quartermaster-General.

[Editor's note: *These documents appear in the* Official Records *as an inclosure to OR-135.*]

SOURCE: *OR*, SERIES 1, VOLUME 50, PART 2, PAGES 313–314

OR-132

HEADQUARTERS DISTRICT OF UTAH,
Camp Douglas, Utah Ter., February 6, 1863.

COLONEL: I have the honor to report that from information received from various sources of the encampment of a large body of Indians on Bear River, in Utah Territory, 140 miles north of this point, who had murdered several miners during the winter, passing to and from the settlements in this valley to the Beaver Head mines, east of the Rocky Mountains, and being satisfied that they were a part of the same band who had been murdering emigrants on the Overland Mail Route for the last fifteen years, and the principal actors and leaders in the horrid massacres of the past summer, I determined, although the season was unfavorable to an expedition in consequence of the cold weather and deep snow, to chastise them if possible. Feeling assured that secrecy was the surest way to success, I determined to deceive the Indians by sending a small force in advance, judging, and rightly, they would not fear a small number. On the 22d ultimo I ordered Company K, Third Infantry California Volunteers, Captain Hoyt, two howitzers, under command of Lieutenant Honeyman, and twelve men of the Second Cavalry California Volunteers, with a train of fifteen wagons, carrying twenty days' supplies, to proceed in that direction. On the 24th ultimo I proceeded with detachments from Companies A, H, K, and M, Second Cavalry California Volunteers, numbering 220 men, accompanied by Major McGarry, Second Cavalry California Volunteers; Surgeon Reid, Third Infantry California Volunteers; Captains McLean and Price and Lieutenants Chase, Clark, Quinn, and Conrad, Second Cavalry California Volunteers; Major Gallagher, Third Infantry California Volunteers, and Captain Berry, Second Cavalry California Volunteers, who were present at this post attending general court-martial, as volunteers. I marched the first night to Brigham City, sixty-eight miles distant. The second night's march from Camp Douglas I overtook the infantry and artillery at the town of Mendon and ordered them to march again that night. I resumed my march with the cavalry and overtook the infantry at Franklin, Utah Ter., about twelve miles from the Indian encampment. I ordered Captain Hoyt, with the infantry, howitzers, and train, to move at 1 o'clock the next morning, intending to start with the cavalry about two hours thereafter, in order to reach the Indian encampment at the same time and surround it before daylight, but in consequence of the difficulty in procuring a guide to the ford of the river, Captain Hoyt did not move until after 3 A.M. I moved the cavalry in about one hour afterward, passing the infantry, artillery, and wagons about four miles from the Indian encampment. As daylight was approaching I was apprehensive that the Indians would discover the strength of my force and make their escape. I therefore made a rapid march with the cavalry and reached the bank of the river shortly after daylight in full view of the Indian encampment, and about one mile distant. I immediately ordered Major McGarry to advance with the cavalry and surround before attacking them, while I remained a few minutes in the rear to give orders to the infantry and artillery. On my arrival on the field I found that Major McGarry had dismounted the cavalry and was engaged with the Indians, who had sallied out of their hiding places on foot and horseback, and with fiendish malignity waved the scalps of white women and challenged the troops to battle, at the same time attacking them. Finding it impossible to surround them, in consequence of the nature of the ground, he accepted their challenge. The position of the Indians was one of strong natural defenses, and almost inaccessible to the troops, being in a deep, dry ravine from six to twelve feet deep and from thirty to forty feet wide, with very abrupt banks and running across level table-land, along which they had constructed steps from which they could deliver their fire without being themselves exposed. Under the embankments they had constructed artificial covers of willows thickly woven together, from behind which they could fire without being observed. After being engaged about twenty minutes I found it was impossible to dislodge them without great sacrifice of life. I accordingly ordered Major McGarry with twenty men to turn their left flank, which was in the ravine where it entered the mountains. Shortly afterward Captain Hoyt reached the ford three-quarters of a mile distant, but found it impossible to cross footmen. Some of them tried it, however, rushing into the river, but, finding it deep and rapid, retired. I immediately ordered a detachment of cavalry with led horses to cross the infantry, which was done accordingly, and upon their arrival upon the field I ordered them to the support of Major McGarry's flanking party, who shortly afterward succeeded in turning the enemy's flank. Up to this time, in consequence of being exposed on a level and open plain while the Indians were under cover, they had every advantage of us, fighting with the ferocity of demons. My men fell fast and thick around me, but after flanking them we had the advantage and made good use of it. I ordered the flanking party to advance down the ravine on either side, which gave us the advantage of an enfilading fire and caused some of the Indians to give way and run toward the north of the ravine. At this point I had a company stationed, who shot them as they ran out. I also ordered a detachment of cavalry across the ravine to cut off the retreat of any fugitives who might escape the company at the mouth of the ravine. But few tried to escape, however, but continued fighting with unyielding obstinacy, frequently engaging hand to hand with the troops until killed in their hiding places. The most of those who did escape from the ravine were afterward shot in attempting to swim the river, or killed while desperately fighting under cover of the dense willow thicket which lined the river-banks. To give you an idea of the desperate character of the fight, you are respectfully referred to the list of killed and wounded transmitted herewith. The fight commenced about 6 o'clock in the morning and continued until 10. At the commencement of the battle the hands of some of the men were so benumbed with cold that it was with difficulty they could load their pieces. Their suffering during the march was awful beyond description, but they steadily continued on without regard to hunger, cold, or thirst, not a murmur escaping them to indicate their sensibilities to pain or fatigue. Their uncomplaining endurance during their four nights' march from Camp Douglas to the battle-field is worthy of the highest praise. The weather was intensely cold, and not less than seventy-five had their feet frozen, and some of them I fear will be crippled for life. I should mention here that in my march from this post no assistance was rendered by the Mormons, who seemed indisposed to divulge any information regarding the Indians and charged enormous prices for every article furnished my command. I have also to report to the general commanding that previous to my departure Chief Justice Kinney, of Great Salt Lake City, made a requisition for troops for the purpose of arresting the Indian chiefs Bear Hunter, San Pitch, and Sagwich. I informed the marshal that my arrangements for our expedition against the Indians were made, and that it was not my intention to take any prisoners, but that he could accompany me. Marshal Gibbs accordingly accompanied me and rendered efficient aid in caring for the wounded. I take great pleasure in awarding to Major McGarry, Second Calvary California Volunteers; Major Gallagher and Surg. R. K. Reid, Third Infantry California Volunteers, the highest praise for their skill, gallantry, and bravery throughout the engagement, and to the company officers the highest praise is due without invidious distinction for their bravery, courage, and determination evidenced throughout the engagement. Their obedience to orders, attention, kindness, and care for the wounded is no less worthy of notice. Of the good conduct and bravery of both officers and men California has reason to be proud. We found 224 bodies on the field, among which were those of the chiefs Bear Hunter, Sagwich, and Leight. How many more were killed than stated I am unable to say, as the condition of the wounded rendered their immediate removal a necessity. I was unable to examine the field. I captured 175 horses, some arms, destroyed over seventy lodges, a large quantity of wheat and other provisions, which had been furnished them by the Mormons; left a small quantity of wheat for the sustenance of 160 captive squaws and children, whom I left on the field. The chiefs Pocatello and San Pitch, with their bands of murderers, are still at large. I hope to be able to kill or capture them before spring. If I succeed, the Overland Route west of the Rocky Mountains will be rid of the bedouins who have harassed and murdered emigrants on that route for a series of years. In consequence of the number of men left on the route with frozen feet and those with the train and howitzers and guarding the cavalry horses, I did not have to exceed 200 men engaged. The enemy had about 300 warriors, mostly well armed with rifles and having plenty of ammunition, which rumor says they received from inhabitants of this Territory in exchange for the property of massacred emigrants. The position of the Indians was one of great natural strength, and had I not succeeded in flanking them the mortality in my command would have been terrible. In consequence of the deep snow, the howitzers did not reach the field in time to be used in the action.

I have the honor to remain, very respectfully, your obedient servant,

P. EDW. CONNOR,

Colonel Third Infantry California Volunteers, Comdg. District.

Lieut. Col. R. C. Drum, U.S. Army,

Assistant Adjutant-General, Department of the Pacific.

ADDENDA.

[Editor's note: *This document is included as an inclosure to an Expedition Report covering January 29, 1863. See OR-140. The addenda referenced here appears as OR-164.*]

SOURCE: *OR*, SERIES 1, VOLUME 50, PART 1, PAGES 185–187

OR-133

[*Extract*]

HEADQUARTERS DISTRICT OF OREGON,
Fort Vancouver, Wash. Ter., February 10, 1863.

ASSISTANT ADJUTANT-GENERAL,
Headquarters Department of the Pacific, San Francisco, Cal.:

COLONEL: I have the honor to submit, for the information of the general commanding the department, a report on the subject of the establishment of a post at Fort Boisé and an expedition against the Snake Indians agreeably to your instructions of the 16th ultimo. Those instructions say that I am authorized to make arrangements for the establishment of that post if I deem it necessary. My views, as set forth in full in my dispatch of the 14th of October, as to the importance of such a post, remain unchanged. Everything I predicted as to the rush of miners to the gold fields in that quarter has been more than fulfilled.

. . .

It is expected Capt. Medorem Crawford, assistant quartermaster, will be ordered to return east to bring out another escort to emigrants. If so, I would arrange for him to come over that road. I should also hope (as I said in my letter of the 14th of October) that you will instruct the commanding officer at Camp Douglas, near Salt Lake City, to send an expedition to a point beyond the South Pass to protect the emigrants as far at least as Fort Hall, or until it meets the command from Fort Boisé. The troops I send out against the Snakes, after finishing that undertaking, for which they will have time before the emigration reaches them, should remain on the emigrant road until the other troops shall meet them.

. . .

Very respectfully, your obedient servant,

BENJ. ALVORD,
Brigadier-General, U.S. Volunteers, Commanding District.

SOURCE: *OR*, SERIES 1, VOLUME 50, PART 2, PAGES 308–310

OR-134

[*Extract*]

Department of the Interior, Census Office,
Washington, February 11, 1863.

Hon. J. P. Usher,
Secretary of the Interior:

Sir: Respecting the number of free colored persons in the United States of the arms-bearing age, I have the honor to submit tabular statements, herewith accompanying, which show the number of such persons of eighteen and under forty-five, and hypothetically the proportion in the free States which may be supposed available from this population upon the data furnished by the number of white persons who have entered the military service from the various States and Territories.

. . .

Be the reasons what they may, the fact is evident that the colored population in the Northern and Western States holds an inferior place physically to the whites, and could hardly be relied upon to supply proportionate numbers of able-bodied men. From the tables presented it appears that the whole number of free colored men in the United States of the arms-bearing age amounts to less than 91,000, and that they are nearly equally divided between the free and slave-holding States. If, however, we concede the probability of this class of persons enlisting for military duty in numbers proportionate to the white population, they would in all the States and Territories supply 18 regiments of 1,000 men each, while the non-slaveholding States and the District of Columbia would supply nearly 10 regiments. The State of Maine would furnish 50 men. New Hampshire 20, Massachusetts 400, Rhode Island 160, Vermont 30, New York and Pennsylvania could supply 4,000, while in any other State but Ohio it would be impossible to raise a full regiment. I send you also a table giving the number of slaves in the United States of the arms-bearing age, which reaches nearly the figure of 750,000, the condition and circumstances of whom preclude all calculations as to what proportion could be made available as men at arms.

I have the honor to be, very respectfully, your obedient servant,

JOS. C. G. KENNEDY,
Superintendent.

[Inclosure No. 1]

States	White males between the ages 18 and 45.	Free colored males between the ages 18 and 45.	Slave males between the ages 18 and 45.
Alabama	99,987	391	83,945
Arkansas	65,231	22	23,088
California	169,973	1,918	....
Connecticut	94,411	1,760	....
Delaware	18,273	3,597	289
Florida	15,739	131	12,028
Georgia	111,005	583	83,819
Illinois	375,026	1,622	....
Indiana	265,295	2,219	....
Iowa	139,316	249	....
Kansas	27,976	126	....
Kentucky	180,589	1,650	40,285
Louisiana	83,456	3,205	75,548
Maine	122,238	272	....
Maryland	102,715	15,149	16,108
Massachusetts	258,419	1,973	....
Michigan	164,007	1,622	....
Minnesota	41,226	61	....
Mississippi	70,295	130	85,777
Missouri	232,781	701	20,466
New Hampshire	63,610	103	....
New Jersey	132,219	4,866	....
New York	796,881	10,208	....
North Carolina	115,369	5,150	55,020
Ohio	459,534	7,161	....
Oregon	15,781	38	....
Pennsylvania	555,172	10,844	....
Rhode Island	35,502	809	....
South Carolina	55,046	1,522	70,798
Tennessee	159,353	1,162	50,047
Texas	92,145	62	36,140
Vermont	60,580	140	....
Virginia	196,587	9,309	92,119
Wisconsin	159,335	292	....
Colorado	29,377	5	....
Dakota	835	5	....
District of Columbia	12,797	1,823	....
Nebraska	8,920	15	....
Nevada	5,344	27	....
New Mexico	19,003	16	....

Utah	6,830	5	....
Washington	5,905	17	....
Total	5,624,065	90,955	745,477

[Inclosure No. 2]

Non-slave-holding States—Free colored males between 18 and 45.

States	Males	Number available in the ratio wherewith the whites have been supplied.*
California	1,918	383
Connecticut	1,760	352
Illinois	1,622	324
Indiana	2,219	444
Iowa	249	49
Kansas	126	25
Maine	272	54
Massachusetts	1,973	394
Michigan	1,622	324
Minnesota	61	12
New Hampshire	103	20
New Jersey	4,866	973
New York	10,208	2,041
Ohio	7,161	1,432
Oregon	38	7
Pennsylvania	10,844	2,169
Rhode Island	809	162
Vermont	140	28
Wisconsin	292	58
Colorado	5	1
Dakota	5	1
Nebraska	15	3
Nevada	27	5
New Mexico	16	3
Utah	5	1
Washington	17	3
District of Columbia	1,823	364
Total	48,191	9,631

* The War Department declines giving the figures to enable me to fill this column officially, but the Figures in the column will prove very near true.

J.C.G.K.

Source: *OR*, Series 3, Volume 3, pages 43–45

OR-135

DEPUTY QUARTERMASTER-GENERAL'S OFFICE,
San Francisco, Cal., February 16, 1863.

Brig. Gen. GEORGE WRIGHT,
Commanding Department, Sacramento, Cal.:

GENERAL: I have been examining into the subject of comparative cost of transportation of army supplies for the troops in Utah from the Pacific Coast on one hand and the Missouri frontier on the other. I respectfully submit the following facts as the result, which I respectfully suggest are of sufficient importance to justify an early reference of the question to the Adjutant-General or the Quartermaster-General U.S. Army: Merchants at Salt Lake paid last year 12 cents per pound for transportation of their goods from the Missouri border. We paid here, with the benefit of strong competition, 20 cents to same point. There is little probability that the same service can be had in the ensuing spring for less than 35 cents per pound in Treasury notes, while it may cost 40 cents. I think there can be no question as to the course pointed out by true economy. The original cost of supplies, especially of subsistence, will not be as great at the East as on this coast, while a large freight for supplies from the East is paid firstly, for its transportation to San Francisco, and, secondly, still more for its transportation 600 miles inland. Captain Kellogg, commissary of subsistence here, addressed the Commissary-General upon the subject about fifteen days since. This is respectfully submitted for your consideration, and, if you deem it proper, to be then forwarded to the Adjutant-General or the Quartermaster-General.

Your obedient servant,

E. B. BABBITT,
Deputy Quartermaster-General.

[Inclosure.]

[Editor's note: *See* OR-131 *for this inclosure; an additional indorsement to this correspondence was removed for lack of relevance. This document is referenced in* OR-138.]

SOURCE: *OR*, SERIES 1, VOLUME 50, PART 2, PAGE 313

OR-136

EXECUTIVE DEPARTMENT, UTAH TERRITORY,
Great Salt Lake City, February 16, 1863.

General G. WRIGHT:

(Through Col. R. C. Drum, Assistant Adjutant-General, Department of the Pacific, San Francisco, Cal.)

SIR: I hope that you will not deem me too officious in addressing this communication to you. For a few days past there has been a rumor (perhaps it is nothing else) that Col. P. Edward Connor, whose command is stationed near this city, is to be called elsewhere with the troops. I cannot believe that such an order would be given if the true condition of things here was understood. Indeed, in my opinion, the withdrawal of his force at this time would make his advent into this Territory a great misfortune to those who have evinced a kindness to him and loyalty to the General Government, for I am not mistaken as to what will follow upon such an act. It would not be safe for those persons to remain in this city. They, at least, will have subjected themselves to insult and contumely, if nothing worse. The recent brilliant victory over the hostile Indians north of here, on Bear River, instead of becoming a cause for future safety to emigrants would only have a tendency to enrage those still banded together for the purpose of murder and plunder, inasmuch as the dread of punishment would be thereby removed from their minds, and the fact that so terrible a chastisement had been administered by U.S. troops, and not by Mormons, would become a subtle and plausible argument in the mouth of the powers here to induce them to form a still closer alliance with that power for common mischief in keeping out in future all troops whose presence was not desired. It is already understood that Mormons were daily in the habit of visiting the camps of the band recently annihilated by Colonel Connor's command, and were enabled to pass through their country with safety where a Gentile would have been robbed and murdered without mercy. These things are well understood here, and the reasons clearly known. Secret agents of the church are employed to form a league for a common safety and a common purpose. This is not mere conjecture. I have not a doubt but that it will be the last time that U.S. soldiers will have the privilege of entering this Territory peaceably if Colonel Connor is now ordered away. I do not say that Mormons would meet our troops openly in such an attempt, although there are strong reasons for believing that they would, yet I have no doubt but the Indians would be encouraged to do so, and all possible succor would be given them by the powers here. If it is determined on by the General Government to have these troops withdrawn it would be but justice to the Federal officers here to order them home also, for there would not remain a shadow of its authority in their hands. In advising you in regard to these facts I desire to say that I do not wish to create any unnecessary alarm or apprehensions not well grounded. The facts, unpleasant as they are, still remain, and I know of no divided opinions with Federal officers here on that subject. The opinion with them I believe is universal. If I were allowed to make a suggestion further I would say that the command here under Colonel Connor should be increased with at least two additional regiments as soon as possible. The base of operations should be here, which would enable him to send out parties sufficiently strong to invite success. In this suggestion, however, I would interpose nothing against the opinions of the brave and accomplished commander, in whom we all have so much confidence. I will only add that in the withdrawal of the troops the General Government virtually abandons her sovereignty over this Territory.

I have the honor to remain, your obedient servant,

S. S. HARDING,
Governor of Utah Territory.

SOURCE: *OR*, SERIES 1, VOLUME 50, PART 2, PAGES 314–315

OR-137

HDQRS. DEPARTMENT OF THE PACIFIC,
San Francisco, Cal., February 19, 1863.

GENERAL ORDERS,
No. 6.

The general commanding the department has the gratification of announcing a signal victory gained by the California Volunteers under the command of Col. P. Edward Connor, on the 29th of January, 1863, over a large body of hostile Indians, strongly posted on Bear River, Utah Ter., about 150 miles north of Salt Lake City. The force engaged consisted of Companies A, H, K, and M, Second Cavalry, under the immediate command of Maj. Edward McGarry, Second Cavalry, and Company K, Third Infantry. The battle lasted four hours, and its severity is well attested by the loss of the combatants, 224 Indians being left on the field, while the loss of the troops was 15 men killed and 4 officers and 40 men wounded, out of a force not exceeding 200 actually engaged. One officer (Lieutenant Chase, Second Cavalry) and 5 enlisted men have since died of their wounds. Colonel Connor awards the highest praise to Major McGarry, Second Cavalry, and Major Gallagher and Surgeon Reid, Third Infantry, for their coolness, gallantry, and skill, and bears testimony to the perseverance and gallantry of company officers throughout the action, and closes his report by saying: "Of the good conduct and bravery of both officers and men California has reason to be proud."

By order of Brigadier-General Wright:

R. C. DRUM,
Assistant Adjutant-General.

SOURCE: *OR*, SERIES 1, VOLUME 50, PART 2, PAGE 318

OR-138

HEADQUARTERS DEPARTMENT OF THE PACIFIC,
San Francisco, Cal., February 19, 1863.

Brig. Gen. L. THOMAS,
Adjutant-General U.S. Army, Washington, D.C.:

GENERAL: After a careful investigation of the subject and procuring the most reliable information as to the cost of transportation of army supplies to the troops in the Territory of Utah, I feel warranted in recommending that all supplies for that district be sent from Missouri. Inclosed herewith is a communication addressed to me by Lieut. Col. E. B. Babbitt, deputy quartermaster-general, together with copy of a letter from Capt. John Kellogg, my chief commissary.* Should it be determined to send the supplies from the Missouri frontier, I beg that I may be notified by telegraph, as the season is fast approaching when arrangements must be made for purchasing and transporting.

Very respectfully, your obedient servant,

G. WRIGHT,
Brigadier-General, U.S. Army, Commanding.

* [*Refers to OR-135.*]

SOURCE: *OR*, SERIES 1, VOLUME 50, PART 2, PAGE 318

OR-139

HEADQUARTERS DISTRICT OF UTAH,
Camp Douglas, Utah Ter., February 19, 1863.

Lieut. Col. R. C. DRUM, U.S. Army,
Asst. Adjt. Gen., Department of the Pacific, San Francisco:

COLONEL: I desire respectfully to call the attention of the general commanding to the state of affairs existing in this Territory, and to matters which, in my opinion, should receive the immediate attention of the Government. I can only allude briefly to the frequent and flagrant violations of the law and the audacious interference with its operations. The law for the prohibition of polygamy is daily violated under the very eyes of the Federal courts by citizens and members of the Mormon Church, who are composed chiefly of the very lowest class of foreigners and aliens. Naturally opposed to our laws, they do not hesitate at violating them, and are willing tools in the hands of their leaders, hesitating at the commission of no crime. Political machinations, plundering expeditions, Indian barterings, and intrigues are things of daily occurrence and are constantly brought to my notice. Not the least respect is paid to the marriage relation; instances of incestuous connections and the crime of bigamy are not only tolerated but encouraged by the Mormon creed, which is inimical to the U.S. laws, winks at murder, pillage, and rapine, and is the very embodiment of hypocrisy; mocks at God and insults the nation. Civil law is a perfectly dead letter in the statute books; they have the right of trial by jury, and under their rule it becomes the instrument of oppression to those who are so independent as to be without the pale of the church and so unfortunate as to need its aid. The people, from Brigham down to the very lowest, are disloyal almost to a man, and treason, if not openly preached, is covertly encouraged and willful and infamous misrepresentations as to the intention of the Government toward this people constantly made under the specious guise of heavenly revelations. Under the same convenient cloak Brigham has been engaged in mounting cannon, ostensibly for protection against Indian depredations, and by this means has placed himself in a position of formidable importance as an enemy. He has fifteen cannon, 9, 12, and 24 pounders, ready for use, and workmen have been engaged for a long time past in manufacturing fixed ammunition of every description, and I truly believe only awaits a serious reverse to our arms, or a foreign war, to break out into open rebellion, and if I understand the signification of his preparations they mean rebellion and nothing else. From the time of my arrival in this district until the present Brigham has shown unmistakable evidences of hatred and disloyalty to the Government, and a disposition to embarrass my command by charging enormous prices for such articles as he knew

I would require, and forbidding their sale at a less price than that fixed by himself or his bishops. As an evidence of this fact your attention is respectfully called to the inclosed list* of prices prescribed by one Bishop Miller at his instigation. I have been a careful observer of affairs, and have known many of his plans and transactions without the facts being known to him, and if the crimes and designs of this people were known and understood by the people of the United States as I understand and know them, it would cause such a burst of indignation as would result in the utter annihilation of this whole people, and if the present rebellion is a punishment for any national sin, I believe it is for permitting this unholy, blasphemous, and unnatural institution to exist almost in the heart of the nation, ignoring its horrid crimes and allowing it to extend its ramifications into every grade of society in defiance of laws human and divine. To relate the revolting crimes and the numerous outrages which are daily perpetrated by Brigham and his church were superfluous. Suffice it to say, then, if the social and political attitude of this people is such as I believe it is, the sooner we are rid of the evil, and the nation of the stigma, the better it will be for us. To accomplish this I would respectfully suggest that there are but two ways, according to my views, by which the laws can be enforced and rendered effectual. First, by dividing the Territory into four parts and adding the parts to the four adjoining Territories; second, by declaring martial law, when if my force should be increased to 3,000 men, a light battery, and three pieces of heavy ordnance, I will guarantee to take such measures as will give Brigham no alternative but to obey the law, and then put a brief end to the institution of polygamy. I learn from reliable authority that the satellites and agents of Brigham are making strenuous efforts in Washington to have my command removed from this Territory, and unless my force is increased as above I would respectfully recommend the same myself; and at the same time I do not hesitate to predict, in case of the removal of the troops from this district, that it will cost the Government a treasure of money and blood before it could regain the position and advantages we now possess. Individually I would prefer to serve in another field. At the same time there is much to do here, and it would give me great pleasure to contribute my humble services to blot out this stigma on our national honor.

Very respectfully, your obedient servant,

P. EDW. CONNOR,
Colonel Third Infantry California Volunteers, Commanding.

* Omitted.

[Editor's note: *This document is referenced in OR-148.*]

Source: *OR*, Series 1, Volume 50, Part 2, pages 318–320

OR-140

JANUARY 29, 1863.—Engagement on the Bear River, Utah Ter.

Report of Col. P. Edward Connor, Third California Infantry, commanding District of Utah.

HEADQUARTERS DEPARTMENT OF THE PACIFIC,
San Francisco, February 20, 1863.

Adjt. Gen. L. THOMAS, U.S. Army,
Washington, D.C.:

SIR: I have the honor to inclose herewith the report of Col. P. E. Connor, Third Infantry California Volunteers, of the battle fought on the 29th of January, on Bear River, Utah Ter., between U.S. troops and hostile Indians. Our victory was complete; 224 of the enemy left dead on the field. Colonel Connor's loss was heavy. Out of 200 men engaged 14 were killed on the field and 4 officers and 49 men wounded; 1 officer and 5 of the men wounded have since died. Colonel Connor's report of the suffering of his troops on the march and the gallant and heroic conduct of both officers and men in that terrible combat will commend the Column from California and its brave commander to the favorable notice of the General-in-Chief and War Department.

Very respectfully, your obedient servant,

G. WRIGHT,
Brigadier-General, U.S. Army, Commanding.

[First indorsement.]

March 29, 1863.

Respectfully referred to the Secretary of War, with the recommendation that Colonel Connor be made a brigadier-general for the heroic conduct of himself and men in the battle of Bear River.

H. W. HALLECK,
General-in-Chief.

[Second indorsement.]

Approved and appointment ordered.

EDWIN M. STANTON.

[Editor's note: *See OR-132 for the attached inclosure to the Second Indorsement. This document is referenced in OR-165.*]

SOURCE: *OR*, SERIES 1, VOLUME 50, PART 1, PAGES 184–185

OR-141

HEADQUARTERS DEPARTMENT OF THE PACIFIC,
San Francisco, Cal., February 20, 1863.

Capt. JULIAN MCALLISTER,
Ordnance Department, Comdg. Benicia Arsenal, Benicia, Cal.:

SIR: The battalion of the Third Infantry California Volunteers, at present encamped at Sacramento, will be ordered to proceed early in the spring to Camp Douglas, near Salt Lake City. The general commanding desires you to have the ordnance stores required for the troops in the district prepared, so as to forward them with Lieutenant-Colonel Pollock's command at the time specified above.

Very respectfully, your obedient servant,

R. C. DRUM,
Assistant Adjutant-General.

SOURCE: *OR*, SERIES 1, VOLUME 50, PART 2, PAGE 320

OR-142

HEADQUARTERS,
Camp Douglas, Utah Ter., February 26, 1863.

Lieut. Col. R. C. DRUM,
Asst. Adjt. Gen., U.S. Army, Dept. of the Pacific, San Francisco:

COLONEL: I have the honor to submit the following inspection report of the troops, public property, and buildings at this post, as required by Special Orders, No. 15, Department of the Pacific, January 17, 1863. In compliance with the above, I have carefully inspected and examined into each department. This post is garrisoned by the headquarters and Companies A, H, K, and M, Second Cavalry California Volunteers, and the headquarters and Companies E, G, H, and K, Third Infantry California Volunteers, both of which regiments have conformed to the organization prescribed in General Orders, No. 126, War Department.

The discipline of the troops is excellent, but their instruction in military exercises is not as good as I would like, which is, however, attributable to the time consumed in the march from California to this post, the time consumed in the construction of cantonments and on detached service, and the inclemency of the season, which has allowed of but few drills in the last eight months. They are, however, well instructed in their other duties. The clothing, arms, equipments, and accouterments of the infantry are in good condition, kept clean and in good order; their clothing is well preserved, is kept very neat, and is warm and comfortable, though the supply of some articles nearly exhausted. The kitchen, mess furniture, &c., of the companies in good order, cleanly, and carefully kept, the food well cooked, wholesome, and plentiful in quantity. The books, papers, and files neatly kept, and the company fund properly and judiciously expended in the purchase of necessaries for the men.

The quarters or cantonments are thirty-two in number, and are temporary shelters of tents placed over excavations four feet deep, with good stone and adobe fireplace. They are warm and comfortable, capable of accommodating twelve men each, are all dry, well ventilated, and convenient to good water. They are kept clean and in good order.

The quarters occupied by the cavalry companies are constructed in the same mariner, and are equal in every respect to the infantry in comfort and conveniences. The mess, kitchen, and company furniture is also well preserved; is in good order; the company books, papers, files, &c., kept with system, and the funds fairly and judiciously expended in the purchase of such articles as are needed by the men. Their clothing is, however, scanty, old, and badly out of repair, much of it quite worn out, having been worn a long time. Many of the men are quite ragged, and before a new supply of clothing can be had will be quite destitute. Their arms, accouterments, and equipments of all kinds need repairs, and some of them are totally unfit for service. Their belts are much worn and are nearly worthless; many of the carbines broken and unfit for service and others useless and wanting repairs. Two companies are armed with Whitney rifles, a very unwieldy arm and quite unsuited to cavalry service, being difficult to load or carry on horseback. Many of these are also out of repair, and some of them unfit for use by reason of long service. A large number of the pistols used are also out of repair, and some totally unserviceable, never having been repaired since they have been in use. I also find quite a large number of the carbine cartridges are too short for those pieces and some entirely useless. The horse equipments, excepting the saddles, are also in very bad order, having been worn a long time and badly wanting repairs, particularly the bridles and bits; the latter are made of cold iron, are very narrow, chafe the horse's mouth, and are easily broken. The horses are in very good condition as to appearance and keeping, but are generally light and rather small for efficient field service. A few of them are worn out and unfit for use.

The officers' quarters consist of thirteen small buildings constructed of logs and adobes over ground excavations of from three to four feet deep and covered with boards, straw, and earth. They have good fire places, and average four rooms each. The building occupied by the commanding officer is above ground, constructed of adobes, contains five rooms, two of which are occupied as adjutants' offices. The above are all temporary structures and only adapted to shelter this winter. The guard house contains three rooms and a cell; the bake house, one room and a large oven. These are also above ground and are built of stone and adobes; they are substantial structures and well adapted to the wants of the command. The commissary's and quartermaster's offices and stores are all under one cover, constructed of paulins stretched over a substantial frame 200 feet long. The hospital consists of a small log structure and three hospital tents, rendered warm and comfortable by boards and earth; is in excellent condition and well arranged for the comfort and convenience of the sick this winter; has good fireplaces, and it is well supplied with all the medical stores necessary. The sick and wounded receive every attention and all the luxuries the country affords. But little sickness has prevailed at the post.

At this date, owing to wounds and injuries received on the march to and at the battle of Bear River, the morning report shows seventy sick in quarters and twenty-two in hospital; one officer and six men have died of their wounds, all being shot in a vital part; four men have had their toes amputated, and two have lost a finger each. The inmates of the hospital are now doing well and, with one exception, will all probably recover. There are four cavalry stables, two quartermaster's stables, and one blacksmith's shop, all of which are constructed of willows bound together by uprights and well lined and covered with straw and earth. The stables are very warm, well drained, and convenient to good water. The buildings combine comfort with economy, and the materials used in their construction will answer every purpose in the erection of more permanent quarters. The post treasurer's books are well and neatly kept. The fund is divided among the companies at the post. The capacity of the officers conducting the administrative and staff departments, good. Their books and papers are in good order, and their respective duties discharged with fidelity and economy to the Government and credit to themselves. There is $403.25 in U.S. Treasury notes on hand in the quartermaster's department. The condition of all the public property, with the exception of a few wagons (which need repair), is good, having been well taken care of and carefully used. There is no post school, but several moral and religious societies exercise a healthful influence in the command. Divine service is well attended. There are but two desertions to record during the last two months. Courts-martial are rare, have been seldom for grave offenses, and very few offenders requiring punishment. The officers of the post are, with two exceptions, gentlemen of sound health, good moral character, and temperate habits, and attentive and efficient in the discharge of their duties. Inclosed herewith I have the honor to transmit rolls of officers and men who have been mustered into the service since the organization of the companies and regiments.

Very respectfully, your obedient servant,

P. EDW. CONNOR,
Colonel Third Infantry California Volunteers, Inspecting Officer.

[Editor's note: *This document is referenced in OR-181.*]

SOURCE: *OR*, SERIES 1, VOLUME 50, PART 2, PAGES 325–327

OR-143

HEADQUARTERS DEPARTMENT OF THE PACIFIC,
San Francisco, Cal., February 28, 1863.

His Excellency Governor HARDING,
Great Salt Lake City, Utah Ter.:

GOVERNOR: I have the honor to acknowledge the receipt of Your Excellency's communication of the 16th instant. I have to assure Your Excellency that so far from there being any design on my part to remove the troops or any portion of them from Utah I am now making preparations to send re-enforcements to Colonel Connor early in the spring. The views which Your Excellency takes of the affairs of Utah are precisely such as I have already communicated to my Government. Some time since I informed the War Department of my design to re-enforce Colonel Connor, setting forth fully the necessity of our maintaining a respectable force in that country.

With great respect, I have the honor to be, Your Excellency's obedient servant,

G. WRIGHT,
Brigadier-General, U.S. Army, Commanding.

SOURCE: *OR*, SERIES 1, VOLUME 50, PART 2, PAGES 330–331

OR-144

CAMP DOUGLAS, SALT LAKE, *March 3, 1863.*

Lieut. Col. R. C. DRUM,
Assistant Adjutant-General:

Excited meeting of Mormons held to-day in Tabernacle; appointed committee; asked Governor Harding and Federal Judges Waite and Drake, the only Federal officers here who dare to do their duty, to resign. Have no fears for me.

P. EDW. CONNOR,
Colonel Third California Volunteer Infantry.

SOURCE: *OR*, SERIES 1, VOLUME 50, PART 2, PAGE 334

OR-145

Remarks of Brigham Young, March 3, 1863, not published in Deseret News *of March 4, 1863.*

Of the Governor he said:

"Let him go back to his (Governor Harding's) friends if he has any. He has none, either in heaven or hell or anywhere else. This man, who is sent here to govern the Territory—man, did I say? Thing, I mean; a nigger worshiper. A black-hearted abolitionist is what he is and what he represents and these two things I do utterly despise. He wants to have the telegraph torn down and the mail stopped and turned by the way of Panama," and to the people he said, "Do you acknowledge this man Harding as your Governor?" (Voices: No; you are our Governor.") "Yes," said he (Brigham), "I am your Governor. Will you allow such a man to remain in the Territory?" (Voices: "No; put him out.") "Yes," replied Brigham, "put him out. Harding and Drake and Waite must leave the Territory. If they will not resign, and if the President will not remove them, the people must attend to it. I will let him (Harding) know who is Governor. I am Governor. If he attempts to interfere with my affairs, woe! woe! unto him."

Of the judges he said:

Judges Drake and Waite are perfect fools and tools for the Governor. If they could get the power, as they want to do, to have the marshal choose juries of cut throats, blacklegs, soldiers, and desperadoes of California, and if we are to be tried by such men, what would become of us?

Reply of His Excellency Governor Harding to the Mormon committee who waited upon him, presented the resolutions passed by the mass meeting held on the 3d instant, and requested him to resign and leave the Territory.

Having stated the object of this visit, the Governor replied to them in substance as follows:

Gentlemen, I believe that I understand this matter perfectly. You may go back and tell your constituents that I will not resign my office of Governor, and that I will not leave this Territory until it shall please the President to send me away. I came here a messenger of peace and good will to your people, but I confess that my opinions about many things have changed. But I came also, sirs, to discharge my duties honestly and faithfully to my Government, and I will do it to the last. It is in your power to do me personal violence, to shed my blood, but this will not deter me from my purpose. If the President can be made to believe that I have acted wrongfully, that I have been unfaithful to the trust that he has confided to me, he will doubtless remove me. Then I shall be glad to return to my family and home in the States, and will do so carrying with me no unjust resentments toward you or anybody else, but I will not be driven away. I will not cowardly desert my post. I may be in danger by staying, but my mind is fixed. I desire to have no trouble. I am anxious to live and again meet my family, but if necessary an administrator can settle my affairs. Let me now say to you, sirs, in conclusion, and as this is said to be a band of prophets, I, too, will prophesy if one drop of my blood is shed by your ministers of vengeance while I am in the discharge of my duty, it will be avenged, and not one stone or adobe in your city will remain upon another. Your allegations in this paper are false, without the shadow of truth. You condemn my message as an insult to you, and yet you dare not publish it for fear that your judgment will not be sustained by the people themselves. That I have done you wrong in representing you to the Government as disloyal is simply preposterous. Your people, public teachers, and bishops have time and time again admitted the fact. I am now done, sirs, and you understand me.

Reply of His Honor Judge Drake on the same occasion. He said:

The communications you have made are of some importance. As they are intended to affect me, I desire to say something before you go. It is no small thing to request a citizen to leave a country. Are you aware of the magnitude of the business you have undertaken? I deny that you have any cause for such conduct toward me. I am an American citizen; have a right to go to any part of the Republic. I have a right to petition or ask this Government to amend the laws or to pass laws. You, Taylor and Pratt, are men of experience, and reputed to be men of learning, and ought to know better than to insult a man by such means; that it is mean and contemptible. That on your part, Taylor, a foreigner, it is impudence unequaled; and Pratt, a citizen, ought to know better than to trample on the rights of a citizen by performing such a dirty enterprise.

Judge Drake continued:

Your resolutions are false, and the man that drafted them knew it to be so; and I further understand that Brigham Young, in the meeting at the Tabernacle, called me a fool and the tool of the Governor.

Here Taylor admitted that Young did say so.

The judge then said:

Go back to Brigham Young, your master, that embodiment of sin and shame and disgust, and tell him that I neither fear him, nor love him, nor hate him, but that I utterly despise; tell him, whose tools and tricksters you are, that I did not come here by his permission, and that I will not go away at his desire or by his directions ; I have given no cause of offense to any one; I have not entered a Mormon house since I came here; your wives and daughters have not been disturbed by me, and I have not even looked upon your concubines or lewd women. I am no skulk from the punishment of crimes; I tell you if you, or this man you so faithfully serve, attempt to interfere with my lawful business, you will meet with trouble of a character you do not expect; a horse-thief or a murderer has, when arrested, a right to speak in court, and unless in such capacity and such circumstances, don't you ever dare to speak to me again.

Reply of Judge Waite to the committee on the same occasion:

> To comply with your wishes, gentlemen, under such circumstances, would be to admit impliedly, at least, one of two things: either that I was sensible of having done something wrong, or that I was afraid to remain at my post and perform my duty. I am not conscious either of guilt or fear. I am therefore obliged respectfully to decline acceding to your request.

[Editor's note: *This document appears in the* Official Records *as an inclosure to OR-167.*]

SOURCE: *OR*, SERIES 1, VOLUME 50, PART 2, PAGES 372–374

OR-146

HEADQUARTERS,
Camp Douglas, Salt Lake, March 5, 1863—9.45 P.M.

Lieut. Col. R. C. DRUM:

Brigham removed ordnance and ordnance stores from Territorial arsenal and had guard of fifty men around his residence last night; do not propose to trouble him; he fears I will.

P. EDW. CONNOR,
Colonel Third California Volunteer Infantry.

SOURCE: *OR*, SERIES 1, VOLUME 50, PART 2, PAGE 340

OR-147

HEADQUARTERS DISTRICT OF OREGON,
Fort Vancouver, Wash. Ter., March 6, 1863.

His Excellency A. C. GIBBS,
Governor of Oregon, Portland, Oreg.:

SIR: I have the honor to acknowledge the reception of your letter of the 5th instant inclosing to me the letter of A. D. Barnard, esq., on the part of certain citizens of Corvallis, urging that Fort Hoskins shall not be abandoned. It has been decided that a detachment of twenty or thirty men will be left at that post. If the company of Oregon volunteers now being raised by Lieutenant Small at Eugene City can be completed, I think I am justified in saying it will be stationed at Fort Hoskins. The companies stationed at Forts Yamhill and Hoskins since the autumn of 1861 were raised in California. Oregon has furnished seven companies, California seven regiments, since the war began. The population of California is not ten times that of Oregon. I know well the patriotic sentiments of Your Excellency and of the masses of the people of Oregon. I know that in former wars the people of Oregon have promptly and gallantly rallied for the defense of the frontier, and that they would now come forward if they were thoroughly convinced of the necessity. California has sent troops to Arizona, New Mexico, Utah, and Oregon, and her volunteers have recently achieved a brilliant victory over the Indians on the soil of Washington Territory the same Snake Indians against whom troops from this quarter will operate.

I have the honor to be, very respectfully, your obedient servant,

BENJ. ALVORD,
Brigadier-General, U.S. Volunteers, Commanding District.

SOURCE: *OR*, SERIES 1, VOLUME 50, PART 2, PAGES 340–341

OR-148

HEADQUARTERS DEPARTMENT OF THE PACIFIC,
San Francisco, Cal., March 7, 1863.

Brig. Gen. L. THOMAS,
Adjutant-General U.S. Army, Washington, D.C.:

GENERAL: For the information of the General-in-Chief and War Department I have the honor to transmit herewith a communication from Col. P. Edward Connor, Third Infantry California Volunteers, commanding District of Utah, dated at Camp Douglas, Utah Ter., February 19, 1863.* As soon as the roads are practicable I shall push forward to Salt Lake the balance of Colonel Connor's regiment, four companies, and if possible one or two companies of the Second Cavalry California Volunteers.

Very respectfully, your obedient servant,

G. WRIGHT,
Brigadier-General, U.S. Army, Commanding.

* [*Refers to OR-139.*]

SOURCE: *OR*, SERIES 1, VOLUME 50, PART 2, PAGE 341

OR-149

Camp Douglas, *March 8, 1863.*
(Received 2 P.M.)

Lieut. Col. R. C. Drum:

Mormons hard at work making cartridges; guard of 300 men at Brigham's nightly; don't understand what he is about; suppose he fears I will arrest him. I am quite safe.

P. EDW. CONNOR,
Colonel Third California Volunteer Infantry.

Source: *OR*, Series 1, Volume 50, Part 2, page 342

OR-150

Camp Douglas, *March 9, 1863—4 P.M.*

Lieut. Col. R. C. Drum:

Brigham just raised national colors on his house and called his people to arms. They are responding, and rushing to his house. He is trying to frighten somebody or is frightened himself.

P. EDW. CONNOR,
Colonel Third California Volunteer Infantry.

Source: *OR*, Series 1, Volume 50, Part 2, page 342

OR-151

[*Extract*]

War Dept., Adjt. General's Office,
Washington, March 10, 1863.

General Orders,
No. 58.

I. The following is the twenty-sixth section of the act "For enrolling and calling out the national forces, and for other purposes, approved March 3, 1863:

Sec. 26. *And be it further enacted.* That immediately after the passage of this act the President shall issue his proclamation declaring that all soldiers now absent from their regiments without leave may return, within a time specified, to such place or places as he may indicate in his proclamation, and be restored to their respective regiments without punishment, except the forfeiture of their pay and allowances during their absence; and all deserters who shall not return within the time so specified by the President, shall, upon being arrested, be punished as the law provides.

II. The following places are designated as rendezvous to which soldiers absent without leave may report themselves to the officers named on or before the 1st day of April next under the proclamation of the President of this date:

At Augusta, Me., to Maj. F. N. Clarke, U.S. Army.

. . .

At Salt Lake City, Utah Ter., to the commanding officer.

III. Commanding officers at the above-named places of rendezvous, or, in the absence of commanding officers, superintendents of recruiting service, recruiting officers, and mustering and disbursing officers, win take charge of all soldiers presenting themselves as above directed and cause their names to be enrolled, and copy of said roll will, on or before the 10th day of April, be sent to the Adjutant-General of the Army.

The soldiers so reporting themselves will be sent without delay to their several regiments, a list of those sent being furnished to the commanding officer of the regiment, and a duplicate to the Adjutant-General of the Army. The commanding officer of the regiment will immediately report to the Adjutant-General of the Army the receipt of any soldiers so sent to him.

By order of the Secretary of War:

L. THOMAS,
Adjutant-General.

Source: *OR*, Series 3, Volume 3, pages 61–62

OR-152

Camp Douglas, *March 10, 1863—1 p.m.*

Lieut. Col. R. C. Drum:

Flag yesterday was first raised by Brigham in this Territory. Was a signal to his people, who assembled armed to number of 1,500; two pieces of cannon. They are determined to have trouble, and are trying to provoke me to bring it on, but they will fail. They swear I shall not be re-enforced, and if attempted will cut them off in detail and attack me. I am not giving any cause of offense. Rosse turns out to be an impostor. He had several private interviews with Brigham. I thought him a Southern emissary. Found no papers to convict, and released him.

P. EDW. CONNOR,
Colonel Third California Volunteer Infantry.

Source: *OR*, Series 1, Volume 50, Part 2, page 344

OR-153

San Francisco, *March 11, 1863.*

Adjt. Gen. L. Thomas,
Washington, D.C.:

Excitement at Salt Lake. Brigham Young raised national colors on his house and called his people to arms. Colonel Connor and troops cool and waiting events. He will telegraph direct to you if anything important takes place.

G. WRIGHT,
Brigadier-General, U.S. Army, Commanding.

Source: *OR*, Series 1, Volume 50, Part 2, page 345

OR-154

Sacramento, *March 11, 1863.*

Col. P. E. Connor,
Salt Lake:

Be prudent and cautious. Hold your troops well in hand. A day of retribution will come. Telegraph direct to Adjutant-General Thomas any important events.

G. WRIGHT,
Brigadier-General, U.S. Army, Commanding.

Source: *OR*, Series 1, Volume 50, Part 2, page 347

OR-155

SALT LAKE, *March 12, 1863—9 P.M.*

Lieut. Col. R. C. DRUM:

Brigham hoisted signal flag this afternoon; 1,500 armed men assembled; subsequently dismissed Mormon guards; patrols on duty nightly.

P. E. CONNOR,
Colonel Third California Volunteer Infantry.

SOURCE: *OR*, SERIES 1, VOLUME 50, PART 2, PAGE 348

OR-156

[*Extract*]

HEADQUARTERS DEPARTMENT OF THE PACIFIC,
San Francisco, March 14, 1863.

Brig. Gen. L. THOMAS,
Adjutant-General U.S. Army, Washington, D.C.:

GENERAL: Within the last ten days affairs in Utah have assumed a threatening aspect. My latest dispatch from Colonel Connor, dated on the 12th, says that Brigham Young hoisted a signal flag that day and assembled 1,500 armed men. They were subsequently dismissed, but Mormon guards patrol the city nightly. Colonel Connor is impressed with the belief that they are courting an attack by his forces; that they do not wish to take the initiative, but will do all in their power to provoke a combat. I have telegraphed to Connor to be prudent and cautious. He has a commanding position, with ample supplies. As soon as the roads are passable I will throw forward the residue of Connor's regiment and such other troops as can be spared. I have directed Colonel Connor to telegraph direct to you anything very important. We are raising the additional regiment of infantry and the seven companies of cavalry, but the recruiting is slow; the greatest embarrassment is the want of funds. We cannot possibly get along on this coast without specie; with Treasury notes fluctuating in value, frequently at a discount of 50 per cent., it is impossible to make contracts, and when purchases are made we pay nearly double price.

. . .

With great respect, your obedient servant,

G. WRIGHT,
Brigadier-General, U.S. Army, Commanding.

SOURCE: *OR*, SERIES 1, VOLUME 50, PART 2, PAGES 350–351

OR-157

HEADQUARTERS DISTRICT OF OREGON,
Fort Vancouver, Wash. Ter., March 14, 1863.

ROWLAND CHAMBERS, J. H. CALDWELL, J. FIELD, ISAAC KING, and other inhabitants of King's Valley, Benton County, Oreg.:

GENTLEMEN: Your petition to the Governor of Oregon in reference to the abandonment of Fort Hoskins has been referred to me. In reply I have to say that it has been decided not to abandon it, but twenty or thirty men will be left there. In the meantime if the public-spirited and patriotic citizens of your county and those adjoining will fill up the volunteer company now being raised by Lieut. H. C. Small at Eugene City, I can safely promise you that so far as I am concerned it shall be stationed at Fort Hoskins. Oregon has not raised her share of troops. California has sent nearly nine regiments, and Oregon but seven companies, into the field. California has her volunteers in New Mexico, Utah, and Washington Territories, as well as in Oregon guarding your Willamette Valley. I know that the masses of your people are gallant and patriotic, and will freely offer their services when there is a necessity. Troops are now needed to serve on your own soil and on your own frontier. A post should be established at Fort Boisé and an expedition made against the Snake Indians, all requiring more troops.

I have the honor to be, with high respect, your obedient servant,

BENJ. ALVORD,
Brigadier-General, U.S. Volunteers, Commanding District.

SOURCE: *OR*, SERIES 1, VOLUME 50, PART 2, PAGE 351

OR-158

HEADQUARTERS,
Camp Douglas, Utah Ter., March 15, 1863.

Lieut. Col. R. C. DRUM,
Assistant Adjutant-General, U.S. Army,
Department of the Pacific, San Francisco, Cal.:

COLONEL: I have the honor to communicate for the information of the general commanding the following facts in relation to the extraordinary proceedings of the people of the Territory during the last twelve days. On Tuesday, the 3d instant, an excited meeting was held in the Mormon tabernacle in Salt Lake City, at which resolutions were passed asking His Excellency Governor Harding, and Associate Justices Drake and Waite, to resign and leave the Territory. The reason they give for this action is that those gentlemen caused a bill to be presented before Congress which they say is inimical to their interests; but I have reason to believe that such is not their real cause of grievance, and that because those gentlemen do not choose to become the tools and creatures of Brigham Young, and follow in the footsteps of ex-Governor Cumming, the present Chief Justice Kinney, and the present Secretary of State, Frank Fuller, is the real cause of this action against them. The latter officers, Messrs. Kinney and Fuller, disgrace their commissions and the Government they represent, and I unhesitatingly assert that while the former, Chief Justice Kinney, holds his office no conviction can be had before his court against a Mormon unless Brigham Young would sanction such conviction. This appears strong language, but the assertions are susceptible of proof and manifest to every resident and loyal citizen of the Territory. On Tuesday, the 3d, and between the hours of 10 P.M. and 3 A.M. of the 4th instant Brigham caused to be removed from the Territorial arsenal to his residence all the ordnance and ordnance stores, and placed a large body of armed men in his yard, which is inclosed with a high stone wall. On Monday, the 9th, he raised the national flag over his residence for the first time I am told since his arrival in the Territory, but not, however, from motives of patriotism or for any loyal purpose, but as a signal to his people to assemble armed, which they immediately did, to the number of about 1,500. The same farce was performed again on the 12th instant, and the only excuse his adherents give for this extraordinary proceeding is that he feared I would arrest him for uttering treasonable language, but in my opinion that is not the true cause, as there has been nothing in my conduct or language which could be construed so as to induce that belief further than what I said when I first entered the Territory, to the effect that "any person, whosoever he might be, who was guilty of using treasonable language would be arrested and sent to Alcatraz

Island." Since my arrival the people of the Territory have been treated kindly and courteously by both my officers and men, who have never given one of them cause for complaint, which the people freely acknowledge. But notwithstanding this, the courtesy we have given is returned with abuse. They rail at us in their sermons in which we are also classed with cut throats and gamblers, our Government cursed and vilified in their public speeches and meetings, and those of their people who supply this camp with vegetables, eggs, butter, and produce are proscribed and shamefully abused for extending such favors. The late armed display was a mere ruse to frighten the proscribed Federal officers from the Territory; or else they desire to have a conflict with the Government, and are endeavoring to provoke me into inaugurating it. The latter I believe to be the real motive, however Brigham Young may try to disguise the fact. As evidence to substantiate the latter belief, he made use of the following language in a speech delivered at the Tabernacle on Monday [Tuesday], the 3d instant:

> Joseph Smith, told me thirty years ago that these prophecies were bound to come true. He hoped they would. He would like to live in heaven with the Government of the United States, but he had no desire to live with a people who had brought ruin and disgrace upon their own heads, he would not live with or have anything to do with the United States. He would have a free and independent government to himself, where he could enjoy his civil and religious liberties. That Smith had told him that the South would rise against the North, and the North against the South, and that they would fight until both parties were destroyed, and for my part I give it godspeed, for they shed the blood of the Prophet.

And on Sunday, the 8th instant, he said:

> Is there anything we would not do to show our loyalty to the Government? Yes. If the present Administration should ask us for 1,000 men, or even 500, to go down there (meaning to fight the rebels), I would see them damned first, and then they could not have them while those soldiers are in our vicinity.

And at the same place and on the same day Heber Kimball, second president of the Mormon Church, said: "We can defy the whole Federal Government." To which the congregation responded: "That's so! We can." The people are by order of Brigham Young busily engaged in preparing ammunition and cannon, and their foundry for some weeks past has been used for casting cannon balls; they also loudly assert that I shall not be re-enforced, and that if the attempt is made they will cut off the re-enforcements in detail and attack me. The law against polygamy is a dead letter on the statute books. Brigham has lately violated it, and boasts that he will have as many wives as he desires, and advises his people to pursue the same course. American citizens (who are not Mormons) can not hold real estate in the Territory, and those who undertake to do so are abused and threatened, their property stolen or confiscated by the Mormon courts upon a charge manufactured for the occasion.

I have applications daily from people of the Mormon faith who desire to leave the Territory, and who say they cannot do so without protection from me, as they fear they would be arrested, their property taken from them on some trumped-up charge, and probably their lives taken. They have ample grounds for their fears, for such has been the fate of many a poor wretch who dared to apostatize and leave the Mormon Church. Yesterday morning Brigham Young started to the northern settlements, with a guard of 150 mounted men. Previous to starting they were drawn up in front of his residence, and as the Governor's son, who is also his private secretary, was passing, some of them shouted "three cheers for Ex-Governor Harding [Cumming?], and long life to Jeff. Davis." Companies are drilled daily and exercised in target practice. I had contemplated and have all preparations made for another expedition against the Indians, this being the best and most favorable season for that service, for the reason that in the summer the Indians scatter so in the mountains that it is impossible to make a successful campaign against them. But in consequence of the hostile attitude of the Mormons I will be compelled to forego such duty for the season.

Such is a plain and brief statement of the facts as they exist here, and unless re-enforced, as I have requested in a former communication, I would respectfully recommend that my command be withdrawn from the Territory and the Mormons be left to further preparation of their infamous conduct until such time as the Government can spare the number of troops required to forever put a stop to their outrageous, unnatural, and treasonable institutions. My command is in no immediate danger, but if the present preparations of the Mormons should continue I will be compelled for the preservation of my command to strike at the heads of the church, which I can do with safety, for they being once in my power their followers will not dare touch me; but if I remain in my present position (although a strong one) for them to attack me, I am lost, as they have about 5,000 men capable of bearing arms and cannon of heavier caliber than mine. In any event the general commanding can rest assured that I will do nothing rashly or hastily, and my intercourse with them will be, as heretofore, courteous and firm. I herewith inclose the replies of His Excellency Governor Harding and Judges Waite and Drake to the Mormon committee who waited on them the day after the meeting of the 3d instant.

I have the honor to be, very respectfully, your obedient servant,

P. EDW. CONNOR,

Colonel Third Infantry California Volunteers, Commanding Post.

[Editor's note: *This document appears in the* Official Records *as an inclosure to OR-167.*]

SOURCE: *OR*, SERIES 1, VOLUME 50, PART 2, PAGES 370–372

OR-159

War Department,
Washington, March 19, 1863—1.35 P.M.

Col. P. E. Connor,
Camp Douglas, Salt Lake City, Utah:

All arms and military munitions intended for use against the authority of the United States are liable to seizure. You will exercise your discretion in regard to making such seizures. You will be cautious and prudent, but when you act do so with firmness and decision.

H. W. HALLECK,
General-in-Chief.

Source: *OR*, Series 1, Volume 50, Part 2, page 358

OR-160

Cleveland, Ohio, *March 20, 1863.*

Colonel Stager, or
T. T. Eckert:

A collision at Salt Lake seems almost sure, which, we think, from the knowledge we have and the best information we can get, has been brought on by misrepresentation as to the loyalty of the Mormons. Could the Government be induced to suspend proceedings until testimony can be produced to show the facts? If desired one or both of us will come to Washington and explain personally such facts as we have been able to gather from our acquaintance with the people of that country for the last two years, all of which you are familiar with and can explain.

J. H. WADE.
E. CREIGHTON.

Source: *OR*, Series 1, Volume 50, Part 2, page 359

OR-161

SAN FRANCISCO, CAL.,
March 23, 1863—1 P.M.

Adjt. Gen. L. THOMAS:

Orders of Major-General Halleck, dated 19th instant, received. Affairs at Great Salt Lake have somewhat subsided. Re-enforcements will advance. Some infantry and cavalry regiments (volunteers) are being raised. This country quiet, except Indian disturbances.

G. WRIGHT,
Brigadier-General.

SOURCE: *OR*, SERIES 1, VOLUME 50, PART 2, PAGE 360

OR-162

SALT LAKE, *March 23, 1863.*

Lieut. Col. R. C. DRUM:

Overland mail attacked by Humboldt Indians 100 miles east of Ruby. Driver and two station keepers killed. Am taking measures to prevent recurrence.

P. EDW. CONNOR,
Colonel Third California Volunteer Infantry.

SOURCE: *OR*, SERIES 1, VOLUME 50, PART 2, PAGE 363

OR-163

HEADQUARTERS DEPARTMENT OF THE PACIFIC,
San Francisco, Cal., March 24, 1863.

Col. P. E. CONNOR,
Third Infantry California Volunteers, Salt Lake City:

McGarry will return to your command, taking good news.

R. C. DRUM,
Assistant Adjutant-General.

SOURCE: *OR*, SERIES 1, VOLUME 50, PART 2, PAGE 364

OR-164

WASHINGTON, D.C., *March 29, 1863.*

Brig. Gen. P. E. CONNOR,
Camp Douglas, near Salt Lake City, Utah:

I congratulate you and your command on their heroic conduct and brilliant victory on Bear River. You are this day appointed a brigadier-general.

H. W. HALLECK,
General-in-Chief.

[Editor's note: *This document appears in the* Official Records *as an inclosure to OR-132.*]

SOURCE: *OR*, SERIES 1, VOLUME 50, PART 1, PAGE 187

OR-165

WASHINGTON, D.C., *March 29, 1863.*

Brig. Gen. G. WRIGHT,
Commanding Department of the Pacific, San Francisco, Cal.:

GENERAL: I have this day received your letter of February 20,* inclosing Col. P. E. Connor's report of his severe battle and splendid victory on Bear River, Utah Ter. After a forced march of 140 miles in mid-winter, and through deep snows, in which seventy-six of his men were disabled by frozen feet, he and his gallant band of only 200 attacked 300 Indian warriors in their stronghold, and after a hard-fought battle of four hours destroyed the entire band, leaving 224 dead upon the field. Our loss in the battle was 14 killed and 49 wounded. Colonel Connor and the brave Third California Infantry deserve the highest praise for their gallant and heroic conduct.

Very respectfully your obedient servant,

H. W. HALLECK,
General-in-Chief.

* [*Refers to* OR-*140*.]

SOURCE: *OR*, SERIES 1, VOLUME 50, PART 2, PAGES 368–369

OR-166

CAMP DOUGLAS, *March 29, 1863.*

Col. R. C. DRUM:

I received the following dispatch to-day:

I congratulate you and your command on their heroic conduct and brilliant victory on Bear River. You are this day appointed a brigadier-general.

H. W. HALLECK.
General-in-Chief.

P. EDW. CONNOR.

SOURCE: *OR*, SERIES 1, VOLUME 50, PART 2, PAGE 369

OR-167

HEADQUARTERS DEPARTMENT OF THE PACIFIC,
San Francisco, March 30, 1863.

Brig. Gen. L. THOMAS,
Adjutant-General U.S. Army, Washington, D.C.:

GENERAL: I have the honor to transmit herewith, for the consideration of the General-in-Chief and War Department, a communication dated on the 15th instant and addressed to my headquarters by Col. P. E. Connor, Third Infantry California Volunteers, commanding at Camp Douglas, Utah Ter., together with the remarks of Brigham Young on the 3d of March, and the replies of Governor Harding and Judges Drake and Waite to the Mormon committee who waited upon those gentlemen and presented the resolutions passed by the mass meeting held on the 3d instant requesting them to resign and leave the Territory. The astounding developments exhibited in these documents demand serious consideration and prompt action to enforce obedience to our laws and to sustain and support the officers of the General Government in the proper discharge of their duties. Although the excitement at Great Salt Lake City, brought about by the treasonable acts of Brigham Young and his adherents, has somewhat subsided, yet I am fully satisfied that they only wait for a favorable opportunity to strike a blow against the Union. When Colonel Connor approached Salt Lake City he submitted to me the question as to the location of his camp. Brigham Young was exceedingly anxious that the troops should reoccupy Camp Crittenden or some point remote from the city, but after mature consideration I came to the conclusion that the site of the present camp was the most eligible for the accomplishment of the objects in view. It is a commanding position, looking down on the city, and hence has been dreaded by the Mormon chief. The good order and strict discipline enforced by Colonel Connor have left the people of the city without any cause of complaint on account of the proximity of the troops, but they have doubtless great apprehensions that their odious institutions, so repugnant to civilized society, may receive a check by the presence of a large body of loyal men sworn to maintain the laws and authority of the United States.

Colonel Connor has a strong position and is in no immediate danger, and I shall throw forward re-enforcements as soon as they can be procured. As they advance toward Salt Lake the command will be increased by the addition of such troops as can be spared from the posts east of the Sierra Nevada. By late telegraphic dispatches I am advised of attacks on two or three of the overland mail stations by Indians beyond Ruby Valley. Detachments of cavalry from Salt Lake and Fort Churchill have been ordered along the line to punish the offenders and protect the mail. The cavalry company from Fort Churchill will then unite with other troops en route for Salt Lake. Captain Selfridge, commandant of the navy-yard at Mare Island, having received information that an organization existed in Solano County, composed of rebel sympathizers, with the purpose of seizing the yard and destroying the public property, recalled the U.S. steamer Saginaw, then lying in the harbor of San Francisco and on the eve of departure on a cruise south, as I reported some days since. A feverish anxiety exists in the public mind that organizations inimical to the Government are prepared and will strike when an opportunity offers a fair prospect of success. I shall take care that no such opportunity is presented.

Very respectfully, your obedient servant,

G. WRIGHT,

Brigadier-General, U.S. Army, Commanding.

[Inclosure 1.]

[Editor's note: *See* OR-*158 for this inclosure.*]

[Inclosure 2.]

[Editor's note: *See* OR-*145 for this inclosure.*]

Source: *OR*, Series 1, Volume 50, Part 2, pages 369–370

OR-168

Headquarters Department of the Pacific,
San Francisco, Cal., March 30, 1863.

Maj. Edward McGarry,
Second Cavalry California Volunteers, San Francisco, Cal.:

Sir: The department commander has this day ordered that you will proceed to Ruby Valley and assume command of all the troops pertaining to that camp as well as others sent forward as a re-enforcement. You are especially assigned to this duty to operate against the bands of Indians now depredating on the overland route west of Salt Lake City. On your arrival (or before, if you think it necessary) at Ruby Valley you will report by telegraph to Colonel Connor for additional instructions, for the purpose of co-operating with any movements thought necessary from Camp Douglas. The general desires you to give such directions regarding supplies, both of subsistence and forage, as you may desire for the best interests of the service. The reduction of the present garrison at Fort Churchill will leave a large surplus of subsistence and possibly of forage at that post. You will therefore inquire into the possibility of having this surplusage thrown forward at such points as you or Colonel Connor may deem necessary to occupy at reasonable cost. I will forward a copy of this letter to Colonel Connor by to-day's mail.

Very respectfully, your obedient servant,

R. C. DRUM,
Assistant Adjutant-General.

Source: *OR*, Series 1, Volume 50, Part 2, page 374

OR-169

[*Extract*]

HEADQUARTERS DEPARTMENT OF THE PACIFIC,
San Francisco, Cal., March 31, 1863.

Brig. Gen. L. THOMAS,
Adjutant-General U.S. Army, Washington, D.C.:

GENERAL: For some time past I have been throwing forward the balance of the Fourth Infantry California Volunteers from Benicia to the southern section of this State.

. . .

The cavalry force authorized to be raised in this State will be prepared for service as soon as possible. The General-in-Chief has already approved my plan of sending the additional companies to complete the First Cavalry California Volunteers by the southern route to New Mexico, but when ready to move it may possibly be deemed expedient to move them to New Mexico, via Great Salt Lake City.

. . .

I should be glad to organize at least two light artillery batteries at once. I have a cavalry company (Second California Volunteers) of excellent material, both officers and men, and with horses very well suited for a battery. I can convert this company into light artillery without any expense.

. . .

Very respectfully, your most obedient servant,

G. WRIGHT,
Brigadier-General, U.S. Army, Commanding.

SOURCE: *OR*, SERIES 1, VOLUME 50, PART 2, PAGES 375–376

OR-170

HDQRS. DEPARTMENT OF THE PACIFIC,
San Francisco, Cal., March 31, 1863.

SPECIAL ORDERS,
No. 85.

* * * *

2. The Third Infantry Battalion, at Camp Union, Cal., will, under the command of Lieut. Col. R. Pollock, take up its line of march for Camp Douglas, Utah Ter., as soon after the 5th proximo as possible, taking the field piece and caisson now at Camp Union. The quartermaster's department will furnish the necessary transportation for the movement above directed, as well as animals for hauling the field piece and caisson.

By order of Brigadier-General Wright:

RICHD. C. DRUM,
Assistant Adjutant-General.

SOURCE: *OR*, SERIES 1, VOLUME 50, PART 2, PAGE 376

OR-171

FORT CRITTENDEN, UTAH TER., *April 1, 1863.*

Brigadier-General CONNOR,
Camp Douglas:

I do hereby certify to the statement* as being correct, and as regards the Mormons on horseback riding up to the Indians. I think there is treachery on their part.

WM. S. WALLACE,
Agent Overland Mail Company.

* [*Refers to* OR-175.]

[Editor's note: *This document is included as an inclosure to an Expedition Report covering March 26–April 3, 1863. See* OR-178.]

SOURCE: *OR*, SERIES 1, VOLUME 50, PART 1, PAGE 199

OR-172

Headquarters Department of the Pacific,
San Francisco, Cal., April 2, 1863.

His Excellency O. Clemens,
Governor of Nevada Territory, Carson City, Nev.:

Sir: I have been authorized by the War Department to raise volunteer companies in Nevada Territory for the purpose of moving east on the Overland Mail Route in the direction of Great Salt Lake City. If it is possible to raise three or four companies in the Territory for this service, I have to request Your Excellency may be pleased to have them organized. I should be glad to get two companies of cavalry and two of infantry; the mounted troops to furnish their own horses and equipments. Arms, ammunition, &c., will be furnished by the United States. Should Your Excellency consider it probable that this volunteer force can be raised, even one company will be accepted. I will send you a plan of organization and an officer with the necessary instructions for mustering them into the service.

With great respect, I have the honor to be, your obedient servant,

G. WRIGHT,
Brigadier-General, U.S. Army, Commanding.

Source: *OR*, Series 1, Volume 50, Part 2, page 379

OR-173

Fort Ruby, Nev. Ter., *April 2, 1863.*

Lieut. W. L. Ustick,
Acting Assistant Adjutant-General, District of Utah:

Lieutenant: On my arrival here I found that there was a large band of Indians encamped at the station who had been there a period of some two months. I was informed by Captain May that they were at feud with the Indians who are now infesting the road; that they claimed protection and professed friendship, and so far as my information extends have done nothing to militate against their professions. I have telegraphed to-day to the general commanding the district in relation to sending me an interpreter, whom, under the present state of affairs, I cannot well do without. The only one here who can talk with them is a man by the name of

Hawes, whose character is such that I cannot place any dependence on him. I find, by traveling over the line, that a great deal of unnecessary excitement is caused by the drivers themselves, who imagine danger when there is none. I have disposed of every man who can possibly be spared from this post in such a manner along the road that I apprehend no further trouble, and shall continue to use every means in my power to keep the road open and safe. I sent instructions to Lieutenant Quinn to stop two or three days in the vicinity of Deep Creek and Spring Valley (as I learned there that there was a band of Indians at Pleasant Valley, distant about twenty-five or thirty miles from the latter place) and reconnoiter the ground thereabouts and see what truth there was in the report. I have information from a very good source that ammunition has been sold to Indians along the road this winter past. As soon as I feel able to investigate the matter thoroughly I will report. I have heard nothing yet from Captain Smith, and probably will not until he arrives, as I have no means of communication in that direction. Since I commenced writing this have received a dispatch from Mr. Cook, dated "Middle Gate, April 2, 5 P.M.," which states that everything west is quiet. Captain May left to-day for California, having turned over all company property to Lieutenant Allen.

Very respectfully, your obedient servant,

P. A. GALLAGHER,
Major Third Infantry California Volunteers, Comdg. Post.

SOURCE: *OR*, SERIES 1, VOLUME 50, PART 2, PAGE 379

OR-174

HEADQUARTERS DEPARTMENT OF THE PACIFIC,
San Francisco, Cal., April 3, 1863.

Capt. JOHN KELLOGG,
Commissary of Subsistence, San Francisco, Cal.:

SIR: I am instructed to inform you, in reply to your letter of the 1st instant, that it is the design of the department commander to increase the force at Salt Lake to 1,500 men. The general desires you to have stores for the above named number placed at the depot in that district.

Very respectfully, your obedient servant,

R. C. DRUM,
Assistant Adjutant-General.

SOURCE: *OR*, SERIES 1, VOLUME 50, PART 2, PAGE 380

OR-175

No. 2.

Report of Lieut. Anthony Ethier, Second California Cavalry.

Camp Douglas, Utah Ter., *April 6, 1863.*

Sir: I have the honor to report to the colonel commanding that in pursuance of orders of the 26th of March I started with twenty-five men of Company A, Second California Volunteer Cavalry, at 6 p.m. from this camp en route for Skull Valley and surrounding [country]. After traveling thirty miles, encamped that night at the mills on the borders of Great Salt Lake. Next morning, the 27th, raised camp at 7 o'clock and arrived at Knowlton's ranch, Skull Valley, at 6.30 p.m. Distance of fifty-five miles from the mills. Next morning, the 28th, at 7 o'clock started across Skull Valley to Hastings' Springs, accompanied by Mr. Knowlton and five of his men. Finding no sign of Indians, crossed the Cedar Mountains and traveled ten miles due west on a desert. Finding no sign of Indians returned to west side of Cedar Mountains and camped at 8 p.m., without water. Distance traveled, thirty-five miles. On the morning of the 29th raised camp about daylight; traveled six or eight miles southward on the western side of Cedar Mountains, examining all the ravines for Indian signs; finding none, recrossed Cedar Mountains nearly opposite the Beckwith Springs, then returned to Knowlton's ranch; distance traveled, thirty-five miles. Next morning, the 30th, raised camp at 6 o'clock; traveled southward down Skull Valley toward the mail route, and arrived at Simpson's Springs at 9 o'clock that night. Distance traveled, sixty miles. Men and horses very tired. Horses very sore-footed by reason of traveling through a rocky and uneven country. Next morning, the 31st, raised camp at 10 o'clock and traveled to Point Lookout. Distance, eighteen miles.

Started from camp at 3 a.m. the 1st instant, and proceeded to Rush Valley and took breakfast there. Here I received General Connor's dispatch to return to Camp Douglas immediately. Started again at 8 o'clock for Camp Crittenden. Arrived there at 2.30 p.m. At 3 p.m., while looking through a spy-glass, saw some Indians coming out of Trough Cañon, traveling on the eastern side of the western hills. My horses being very much jaded and sore footed, I required the mail agent, Mr. Wallace, to furnish me with a coach. Myself with thirteen men in the coach and eight mounted on the best horses proceeded to overtake the Indians, which we did at Cedar Fort, they having taken a position for battle previous to my arriving there. The natural defenses of the position were very strong, which you will see by the diagram* accompanying this report. The Mormons, through treachery, I suppose, and wishing to see my party destroyed, gave me false report as to the position of the Indians and also in regard to their numbers, there being at the time but two Indians in sight, chiefs on horseback riding the war circle. In examining the ground I saw what I thought was their actual position. I acted on my own judgment, not on the information received, which I firmly believe saved my party from destruction After forming my line of battle, as you will see by the diagram, my men advanced gallantly to the attack, but receiving a withering fire from a quarter we least expected, we were forced to give way. Returning again to the attack, had the pleasure of seeing one of the chiefs fall mortally wounded. There being no more Indians in sight, and continuing to receive a severe fire from an unseen foe, I concluded to withdraw my men, when Mr. Wallace, who was present on the field, came and informed me that my horses were in danger of capture. Although the Mormons were at the spot where my horses were at the time, not farther than 100 yards from the Indians, not a shot was fired at them. On arriving at the place where my horses were and repulsing the Indians I concluded to return to Camp Crittenden, but before going offered to leave a guard of twelve men at Cedar Fort, which they refused; but after consulting among themselves they asked me to leave a guard of eight men, which I promised to do, at the same time having no idea of fulfilling my promise for fear of treachery, of which I was convinced immediately afterward by seeing, while I was not more than 100 yards from the fort, a Mormon riding off to Indians, and meeting several of them on the trail, proceeded to the hills with them, where they held conversation in plain sight of me. I then being satisfied that there was treachery, returned to Camp Crittenden, from which place I reported the facts to General Connor. On the 2d instant I found out from the wife of Mr. Savage, the Mormon who went up on the hills to speak to the Indians, that after returning from the Indian camp he held a council with the Mormons at the fort, and then left for Salt Lake City to inform Brigham Young of my doings there. This man Savage is the same who reported to General Connor of his wagons being robbed last winter on Bear River. I have since learned that those Indians were called Old Soldier's Band, of San Pete Valley, and numbered 150 warriors, of which two-thirds were present at the battle. The 3d instant, according to orders, I reported to Captain Price at Cedar Fort at 9 A.M.

All of which is respectfully submitted.

I have the honor to be, very respectfully, your obedient servant,

ANTHONY ETHIER,

Second Lieutenant Company A, Second California Vol. Cavalry.

* Not found.

[Editor's note: *This document is included as a Report No. 2 to an Expedition Report covering March 26–April 3, 1863. See OR-178.*]

SOURCE: *OR*, SERIES 1, VOLUME 50, PART 1, PAGES 200–201

OR-176

APRIL 2–6, 1863.—Expedition from Camp Douglas to the Spanish Fork, Utah Ter., with action (4th) at the Spanish Fork Cañon.

Report of Capt. George F. Price, Second California Cavalry, commanding expedition.

CAMP DOUGLAS, UTAH TER., *April 6, 1863.*

LIEUTENANT: I have the honor to report that pursuant to instruction received from Brigadier-General Connor, commanding District of Utah, I left this camp at 1 A.M. of the 2d instant with Lieutenant Conrad and fifty-one men of Company M, Second Cavalry California Volunteers; crossed the Jordan River seven miles south of Great Salt Lake City, and moved up the west side of the river, traveling until 8.30 A.M., when I arrived in Cedar Valley, thirty miles south of the camp. Examined the valley thoroughly without discovering any fresh Indian signs; arrived at Cedar Fort, in upper western portion of the valley, at 11.15 A.M., where Lieutenant Ethier with twenty-six men of Company A, Second Cavalry California Volunteers, reported to me for duty per verbal order of general commanding the district. With this force proceeded to and arrived at Fort Crittenden at 12.15 P.M.; distance traveled, forty-five miles; horses and men greatly fatigued. On the following morning left Crittenden. Learning that the band of Indians with whom Lieutenant Ethier had a skirmish near Cedar Fort on the afternoon of the 1st instant had moved in a southeasterly direction from Cedar Valley, I determined to pursue them. Resuming the march, the command traveled to the head of Cedar Valley; from thence crossed into Utah Valley, and arrived at the southeastern extremity of Lake Utah at 10.30 A.M.; from thence proceeded to Goshen, the most southern settlement of the valley, where I arrived at 2 P.M.; compelled to halt on account of forage; several of the horses almost unserviceable. The surrounding country was thoroughly examined without discovering any Indian sign; direct distance traveled, twenty-six miles. At sunset I sent Sergeant Gordon with four men well armed on a scout into Juab Valley. They traveled twenty miles south of Goshen, making a night ride of forty miles, returning to camp at 4 A.M. of the 4th instant without making any discoveries further than the fact that a body of Indians were encamped on Salt Creek, still farther to the south of his ride some forty miles. At 6 A.M. of the same day, being satisfied that I was south and west of the Indians, started across the valley searching the hills and bottoms surrounding Utah Lake. Arrived at the town of Spanish Fork at 3 P.M., being everywhere assured that no Indians had been seen for ten days. I had not been encamped three hours when two Indians were discovered on the point of the hill, we on the southeast portion of the town. A scouting party was immediately sent out, who soon returned with intelligence that the Indians already mentioned had entered Spanish Fork Cañon. At this time the sun was scarcely an hour high, but I did not feel like losing even this small chance if there were any Indians in the cañon. "Boots and saddles" and "to horse" were immediately sounded, taking the men away from supper, and in less than five minutes such was the eagerness of the men that the entire detachment, excepting the guard (six), was in the saddle and en route for the cañon, four miles from the camp. Arriving there I found the Indians in considerable force, numbering in sight between forty and fifty, being posted on both sides of the cañon, a large stream of water (Spanish Fork) separating us from the south side. Lieutenant Conrad with fifteen men was ordered to make movement to the right and gain the south side of the cañon. Immediately after Lieutenant Ethier with twenty-five men was ordered to move to the left and gain the north bank of the cañon, while the center, under my own command, moved directly to the front, and as the center approached the mouth of the cañon within rifle-shot the Indians opened a brisk fire upon us, rather annoying, but without accomplishing any injury. The flanking parties having gained their position, a forward movement was made at the same moment. The Indians retreated before us, until finally they broke into a run under fire up the cañon, the detachment following them eagerly, but well under restraint. The Indians were driven until they reached a point in the cañon where it would have been extreme folly and a useless sacrifice of life for us to follow. It being by this time quite dark, and not having yet discovered the strength of the enemy (the cañon being a very bad one—in fact, I have rarely seen a better one for a fight), the assembly was sounded and the detachments commenced returning to camp, being then about three-quarters of a mile up the cañon. During the march back, under cover of the night, the Indians hovered on our rear, discharging their pieces at us. A lively skirmish then ensued, and various expedients were resorted to in order to trap the Indians, but without avail. During this skirmish the horses were never out of a walk unless when they were dashing back upon the enemy. It is impossible for me to state the number of Indians killed or wounded during this brief action and subsequently driving them up the cañon. It is known positively, however, that 1 Indian and 1 pony were killed, and several acted as though they were wounded. The Indians fired the first shot. The flank movements made by Lieutenants Conrad and Ethier were finely executed, and reflect credit upon these young officers, while the men behaved with their usual gallantry. Pickets were thrown out during the night, but without any result further than knowing that the Indians did not leave the cañon.

On the following morning (5th) a scouting party was sent in advance of the detachments without discovering any Indians. Not desiring to be caught in a trap, I ordered another flanking movement as on the evening previous, and then proceeded up the cañon until we arrived at the point gained on the previous evening without discovering any signs. Then with a portion of the command moved up the cañon three miles from that point, it growing worse and more dangerous in its character. Caught an

Indian and killed him. Found several signs which satisfied me that the enemy was in full retreat through the cañon, running for San Pete Valley. Shortly after killing the Indian saw fires on the highest point on the north side entirely beyond our reach. They fired a few random shots at us. As the cañon is twenty-five miles long, and gradually closes in until very narrow, presenting on each side an almost impassable barrier of rocks, it was deemed proper to give up the pursuit, as it could result in no good and might cost life. Added to this the horses were severely jaded and the men about out of rations. The appearance of this cañon as seen by daylight fully confirms the opinion formed of it the evening before. Having offered them battle twice and driven them twice, it was useless to attempt more. The assembly was sounded, and we left the cañon without molestation and proceeded to Provo, where we camped. Citizens after the skirmish said there were 200 of the enemy, but I don't credit the story, for we offered battle with only thirty men and gave every chance, so that if there had been that number they would certainly have accepted. It is doubtful whether the band will return into Utah Valley for some time to come. At 2 A.M. of the 6th instant left Provo and returned to camp at 3 P.M. same day, reporting to Captain Black, commanding post. The direct distance traveled, exclusive of scouts, &c., was 165 miles, an average of thirty-three miles each day. Horses and men are much fatigued. My officers and men conducted themselves fully in keeping with previous reputation.

Very respectfully, your obedient servant,

GEO. F. PRICE,

Captain, Second Cavalry California Vols., Comdg. Expedition.

Lieut. T. S. HARRIS,

Adjutant Second Cavalry California Volunteers.

SOURCE: *OR*, SERIES 1, VOLUME 50, PART 1, PAGES 201–203

OR-177

FORT RUBY, NEV. TER., *April 8, 1863.*

Lieut. W. L. USTICK,

Acting Assistant Adjutant-General, District of Utah:

LIEUTENANT: I have the honor to inform the general commanding that Lieutenant Quinn, with his detachment, arrived this noon, having seen no Indians on his route, although he left the road in several places and scoured the country for a distance of twenty to thirty miles. As soon as his horses are rested I shall send him in another direction. I am very much in need of a blacksmith, as there is none at the post, and some ten or twelve of the cavalry horses need shoeing very badly, and it is impossible to procure one in this vicinity. Inclosed I send a copy of Special Orders, No. 87, Department of the Pacific, received this day.*

Very respectfully, your obedient servant,

P. A. GALLAGHER,
Major Third Infantry California Volunteers, Commanding Post.

* [*Refers to Drum's Special Order No. 87, April 2, 1863.* OR, *Series 1, Volume 50, Part 2, page 378.*]

SOURCE: *OR*, SERIES 1, VOLUME 50, PART 2, PAGE 385

OR-178

MARCH 26–APRIL 3, 1863.—Expedition from Camp Douglas to the Cedar Mountains, Utah Ter., with skirmish (April 1) at Cedar Fort.

REPORTS.

No. 1.—Brig. Gen. P. Edward Connor, U.S. Army, commanding District of Utah.
No. 2.—Lieut. Anthony Ethier, Second California Cavalry.

No. 1.

Report of Brig. Gen. P. Edward Connor, U.S. Army, commanding District of Utah.

HEADQUARTERS DISTRICT OF UTAH,
Camp Douglas, Utah Ter., April 9, 1863.

COLONEL: I have the honor to inform you that at present all is quiet in this district. The Indians who committed the late depredations on the Overland Mail Route west of here, I have reason to believe, were Goshutes, who have lived in the Mormon settlements of Tooele Valley this winter, and were encouraged and instigated to the raid by Mormons. The Indians, finding that I had the line well protected and cavalry scouring the country in every direction in pursuit of them, made their way back to Cedar Valley near Fort Crittenden on their way south. At that point they were encountered by Lieutenant Ethier, of the Second California Volunteer Cavalry, with twenty three men. I herewith inclose Lieutenant Ethier's report, by which you will perceive that the Mormons instead of assisting to punish Indians for bad conduct actually encouraged them. I also inclose a telegram from William S. Wallace, agent of the Overland Mail Company at Fort Crittenden, verifying the statements made by Lieutenant Ethier as to the conduct of the Mormons, &c. From the evidence before me I am well satisfied that the Mormons are the real instigators of the late raid. Brigham Young has sent commissioners to Washington for the purpose, I am told, of proposing to the Government to take charge of the overland mail and emigrant route in this Territory for half the amount it costs at present, provided the troops are withdrawn. And also to use their influence with the President to have the Governor and Judges Waite and Drake removed. Until the return of the commissioners I have no fears of any further trouble, but upon their return, and if their mission prove unsuccessful, then I have every reason to fear there will be trouble, as they are determined that the laws shall not be executed, and the three officers named are as equally determined that the laws shall be enforced. If the troops should be withdrawn the Mormons are well aware that the Governor and judges would be compelled to leave with them, as their lives would not be safe one hour after the withdrawal of the troops if they remained. The object of Brigham in encouraging Indian raids at present is, undoubtedly, to induce the Government to withdraw the troops from this post and have them stationed at different points on the mail line. They also wish to impress upon the Government the idea that his people can protect the line better than troops can, and there is no doubt but he can, as the Indians are completely under his control and do just as he tells them. I have taken all necessary steps to protect the mail line from further depredations, and am sanguine of being able to punish the perpetrators of the late outrages. I would most earnestly urge the necessity of sending with the re-enforcements two cannon of large caliber, say 24 or 32 pounders, and two 12-pounder field guns with caissons, battery wagons, &c., which, with the two 6-pounder field guns at this post, will make a light battery of four guns. I would also recommend that one 12-pounder mountain howitzer be sent for the post at Fort Bridger. With the above guns and a force of at least 3,000 men I can be of service to the Government, and in all probability prevent a civil war; otherwise the result is doubtful. I again respectfully call the attention of the general commanding to the fact that this people are at heart disloyal, and are only waiting a favorable opportunity to demonstrate that fact, consequently I would recommend that unless strongly re-enforced, my command be withdrawn. I consider that I would be derelict in my duty to my country and to my command, whose lives are in my hands, did I not urgently represent the dangers menacing them, or if I asked for a smaller body of men than the number called for in this and previous communications. The danger, in my opinion, is not immediate, and perhaps may not be until the season shall have so far advanced that re-enforcements cannot be sent here.

Very respectfully, your obedient servant,

P. EDW. CONNOR,

Brigadier-General, U.S. Volunteers, Commanding District of Utah.

Lieut. Col. R. C. DRUM,

Assistant Adjutant-General, U.S. Army.

[Inclosure.]

[Editor's note: *See OR-171 for this inclosure.*]

[No. 2]

[Editor's note: *See* OR*-175 for this inclosure.*]

SOURCE: *OR*, SERIES 1, VOLUME 50, PART 1, PAGES 198–199

OR-179

HEADQUARTERS CAMP DOUGLASS [*sic*],
Utah, April 13, 1863.

Maj. Gen. H. W. HALLECK,
General-in-Chief:

Unless immediately re-enforced with cavalry, the Indians, urged on by Mormons, will break up the overland mail and make the emigrant route impassable.

P. EDWD. CONNOR,
Brigadier-General.

SOURCE: *OR*, SERIES 1, VOLUME 22, PART 2, PAGE 215

OR-180

HEADQUARTERS DISTRICT OF UTAH,
Camp Douglas, April 13, 1863. (Received 3 P.M.)

Lieut. Col. R. C. DRUM,
Assistant Adjutant-General:

Unless speedily re-enforced with cavalry the overland mail will be broken up and the emigrant route will be impassable. The Indians, urged on by the Mormons, are congregating for that purpose. Five of my men had a fight with 100 Indians yesterday in a Mormon town, and not a Mormon would help them. I lost 12 mules, 5 of which, with 3 Indians, were killed by a shot from a howitzer my men had with them. The men were in advance of an expedition under Colonel Evans.

P. EDW. CONNOR,
Brigadier-General, U.S. Army, Commanding District.

SOURCE: *OR*, SERIES 1, VOLUME 50, PART 2, PAGE 391

OR-181

HEADQUARTERS DEPARTMENT OF THE PACIFIC,
San Francisco, April 14, 1863.

Brig. Gen. L. THOMAS,
Adjutant-General U.S. Army, Washington, D.C.:

GENERAL: I have the honor to inclose herewith the report of Col. P. E. Connor, Third Infantry California Volunteers, of his inspection of the troops, buildings, and property at Camp Douglas, near Great Salt Lake City, Utah Territory.*

Very respectfully, your obedient servant,

G. WRIGHT,
Brigadier-General, U.S. Army, Commanding.

* [*Refers to* OR-*142.*]

SOURCE: *OR*, SERIES 1, VOLUME 50, PART 2, PAGE 392

OR-182

WASHINGTON, *April 15, 1863—3.15 P.M.*

Brig. Gen. GEORGE WRIGHT:

The Secretary of War authorizes you to raise additional regiments in California and Nevada to re-enforce General Connor and protect the overland route. Cannot companies be raised in Nevada and pushed forward immediately? General Connor may be able to raise some companies in Utah or out of emigrant trains.

H. W. HALLECK,
General-in-Chief.

SOURCE: *OR*, SERIES 1, VOLUME 50, PART 2, PAGE 398

OR-183

HEADQUARTERS DISTRICT OF UTAH,
April 16, 1863. (Received 10 A.M. 17th.)

Lieut. Col. R. C. DRUM:

Detachment cavalry under Colonel Evans had fight with Indians yesterday at Spanish Fork Cañon, seventy miles south. Lieutenant Peel killed, 2 sergeants wounded; 30 Indians killed and their horses captured. The command will arrive to-morrow.

P. EDW. CONNOR,
Brigadier-General.

SOURCE: *OR*, SERIES 1, VOLUME 50, PART 2, PAGE 404

OR-184

[*Extract*]

HEADQUARTERS DEPARTMENT OF THE PACIFIC,
San Francisco, April 20, 1863.

Brig. Gen. L. THOMAS,
Adjutant-General U.S. Army, Washington, D.C.:

GENERAL: I have received Major-General Halleck's dispatch of the 15th instant. I had previously called upon the acting Governor of Nevada Territory for troops to operate on the Overland Mail Route, in the direction of Salt Lake, and from his reply I think we can raise in that Territory 200 mounted men, and possibly two companies of infantry. I have urged upon the Governor the necessity of promptly enrolling the companies. Although the line is comparatively quiet just now, yet it is liable to interruption at any moment by predatory bands of Indians. The two companies of the Third Infantry California Volunteers, now at Camp Union, Sacramento, will be put on the march for Utah as soon as practicable; at this moment it is impossible to forage our animals east of Carson City. The cavalry company stationed at Fort Churchill was under orders to move along the mail line, but I was compelled to send it first to aid in quelling the Indian disturbances in Owen's River Valley; when this is accomplished the company will be advanced promptly toward Salt Lake. We have had many affairs with the Indians lately in the District of Humboldt, in the Owen's River Valley, on the overland mail line, and south of Camp Douglas, in all of which our troops have been victorious; a large number of Indians have been killed and their property, with their women and children, captured. The California troops have behaved most gallantly, and deserve the highest credit.

. . .

With great respect, your most obedient servant,

G. WRIGHT,
Brigadier-General, U.S. Army, Commanding.

SOURCE: *OR*, SERIES 1, VOLUME 50, PART 2, PAGE 407

OR-185

HEADQUARTERS DEPARTMENT OF THE PACIFIC,
San Francisco, Cal., April 22, 1863.

Capt. M. A. MCLAUGHLIN,
Second Cavalry California Volunteers,
Commanding Forces in Owen's River Valley:
(Through Lieutenant-Colonel Jones, commanding Camp Babbitt, Cal.)

SIR: Whenever in your judgment the services of Captain Brown's company of cavalry are no longer essential in quelling the Indian disturbances in the Owen's River country, the general commanding directs that you will order it to proceed to Fort Churchill, Nev. Ter., where the captain will make immediate preparation for proceeding to join General Connor at or near Salt Lake City.

Very respectfully, your obedient servant,

R. C. DRUM,
Assistant Adjutant-General.

Colonel will forward this by express if practicable.

SOURCE: *OR*, SERIES 1, VOLUME 50, PART 2, PAGE 410

OR-186

HEADQUARTERS DISTRICT OF UTAH,
Camp Douglas, Utah Ter., April 22, 1863.

Lieut. Col. R. C. DRUM, U.S. Army,
Assistant Adjutant-General, Department of the Pacific:

COLONEL: I received on the 15th instant a copy of the dispatch from the General-in-Chief to the general commanding the department, which says I may be able to raise companies in Utah or out of emigrant trains. The latter would be impossible, as the emigrants coming this way are afflicted with the gold fever, and the Mormons are too disloyal to be trusted with arms, even if they would enlist, which I doubt. There is, however, a class of people here known as Morrisites, who have left the Mormon Church, and are persecuted by the Mormons to such an extent that they are actually suffering for the necessaries of life. A company could be raised from among them to garrison a post which I contemplate establishing on the overland emigrant route about 150 miles north of this post, in Idaho Territory, and about 40 miles from where the road from this place to Beaverhead Mines intersects the road from the east to California, Oregon, and the above mines, and in the vicinity of the summer resort of hostile Indians. It is an important point and should be occupied immediately by troops for the protection of the overland emigration. Although not in my district, I contemplate sending a company of infantry there next week. Another object I have in view is to form the nucleus of an anti-Mormon settlement, and a refuge for all who desire to leave the Mormon Church, and have not the means to emigrate farther. Large numbers of them will accompany the expedition and settle in the vicinity of the post. I consider the policy of establishing such a settlement of loyal people in close proximity to the Mormons of great benefit and importance to the Government for many reasons. I only fear that the poor people who may settle there will suffer for the necessaries of life, as most of them have families; therefore I would respectfully recommend that I be permitted to enlist a company from among them for twelve months, with the understanding that they are to garrison that post, and meanwhile they could make use of their time when off duty in cultivating the soil and laying the foundation of their future homes. The Mormons have stripped them of almost everything they possessed, and they are consequently very poor, but they are industrious. They propose that if they cannot be enlisted on the above terms they will do necessary post duty, provided I issue them arms and rations. In either case their services would save me a company of infantry for other duty. I respectfully ask the early consideration and orders of the general commanding on the above propositions, and would respectfully recommend the latter one as being in my opinion the most favorable to the Government, as with one of my present officers and six men to conduct matters and see to the care and preservation of arms, &c., I am satisfied the Government would be greatly benefited in many respects by adopting the proposition. I understand by telegraph to-day that there are 1,200 cavalry at Denver. If the attention of the General-in-Chief were called to the fact he would probably send some of them here, and I need them very much.

Very respectfully, your obedient servant,

P. EDW. CONNOR,
Brigadier-General, U.S. Volunteers, Commanding District.

SOURCE: *OR*, SERIES 1, VOLUME 50, PART 2, PAGES 410–411

OR-187

HEADQUARTERS DISTRICT OF UTAH,
Camp Douglas, Utah Ter., April 28, 1863.

Col. R. C. DRUM.
Asst. Adjt. Gen., U.S. Army, Department of the Pacific:

COLONEL: I regret that circumstances again compel me to urge upon the general commanding the necessity of sending re-enforcements to this district. The Indians are congregating in large force in the vicinity of the Mormon settlements south of this post, with a view of depredating on the overland mail and emigrant routes, and are incited and encouraged in their hellish work by Brigham Young, by whose direction they are also supplied with food, and by his people with ammunition, which I have no means of preventing, nor can I strike at them before they get stronger, as in order to reach them I have to pass through Mormon settlements, and the Mormons notify the Indians of my approach, when they scatter to their inaccessible mountain retreats, and thus avoid me. I understand the agents of the Overland Mail Company are opposed to having more troops sent here. Why, I am unable to say. I can only surmise, but cannot prove anything, as nothing can be proved here against a Mormon, or one of their Gentile favorites. I deem it a duty I owe to my command to notify the Government through the general commanding of the danger to which they are exposed from the treachery, fanaticism, and disloyalty of this people in case of a serious reverse to our arms in the East. I have also serious fears in consequence of my small command being necessarily scattered over a large extent of territory, of being overpowered in detail by the hordes of Indians now congregating under Mormon auspices, and who my spies inform me are to be joined by Mormons disguised as Indians. Brigham Young has complete control of the Indians of the Territory, and could, if he chose, prevent the horrors that will soon be enacted on the overland route, and which with the force at my command I am powerless to prevent. If the exigencies of the service will not admit of my being adequately re-enforced, I would again respectfully recommend that Brigham Young's offer to protect the overland mail and emigrant route for a certain sum be accepted, and my command withdrawn, in which case the obnoxious Federal officers would of course have to leave.

Very respectfully, your obedient servant,

P. EDW. CONNOR,
Brigadier-General, U.S. Volunteers, Commanding District.

[Editor's note: *This document is referenced in OR-194.*]

SOURCE: *OR*, SERIES 1, VOLUME 50, PART 2, PAGE 415

OR-188

HEADQUARTERS DEPARTMENT OF THE PACIFIC,
San Francisco, April 30, 1863.

Brig. Gen. L. THOMAS,
Adjutant-General U.S. Army, Washington, D.C.:

GENERAL: I have the honor to acknowledge the receipt of two communications from Major-General Halleck, dated respectively on the 29th and 31st of March. A copy of the first has been sent to Brigadier-General Connor, commanding the District of Utah. The information conveyed in the second letter of the General-in-Chief that an iron-clad vessel is already on its way to this coast will produce the most happy effect in allaying the apprehensions which have for some time past existed in the public mind in regard to the defenses of San Francisco. At this moment everything is quiet on the Overland Mail Route and also in the Territory of Utah; but I shall not be lulled into a false security, but use every effort to throw forward re-enforcements as soon as possible. We are, however, laboring in this country under the greatest difficulties and embarrassments, both in the procurement of men and means. One cause is the high price of labor and the wonderful developments constantly being made in the mining districts in this State and in the adjoining Territory of Nevada; and a still greater and controlling cause is the depreciation of our currency. Gold being the basis of our circulation, coin only is used in all business transactions, and Treasury notes can only be used at a discount of at least 35 cents on the dollar. This operates with peculiar hardship on all persons in the service of the Government whose compensation is fixed by law. My latest advices from Brigadier-General Alvord represent every thing as quiet in the District of Oregon. A council will be held early in May with the Nez Percé Indians, whither General Alvord had ordered Colonel Steinberger and Major Lugenbeel with a suitable force; and then the expedition to chastise the Snake Indians will be pressed forward, in connection with the establishment of Fort Boisé. I have directed General Alvord to send Maj. P. Lugenbeel as commander, and Capt. W. B. Hughes as quartermaster, to build the new post at Boisé. Major Lugenbeel and Captain Hughes are very industrious, active, and economical, with much experience in planning and building, and peculiarly adapted to this duty. It is quite probable that Major Lugenbeel has been already promoted; should such be the case, I hope you will authorize me to keep both him and Captain Hughes for this important duty.

Very respectfully, your obedient servant,

G. WRIGHT,
Brigadier-General U.S. Army, Commanding.

SOURCE: *OR*, SERIES 1, VOLUME 50, PART 2, PAGES 416–417

OR-189

Fort Ruby, Nev. Ter., *May 2, 1863.*

Lieut. W. L. Ustick,

Acting Assistant Adjutant-General, District of Utah:

Lieutenant: I have the honor to acknowledge the receipt of your letter dated 28th ultimo this morning. Previous to receiving it I had sent Captain Potts to Spring Valley and vicinity to join Captain Smith with the infantry in an expedition against Indians, whom I have good reason to believe are encamped at the base of a mountain about forty or fifty miles from Spring Valley Station, in a northerly direction. My information is derived from friendly Indians who live in this valley, four of whom accompany Captain Smith as guides and are held as hostages. They report that the Indians have in their possession quite a large band of horses and mules, and their strength is supposed to be from 100 to 150. I feel confident that the expedition will be successful. I am making all arrangements for the departure of the company (F) and as soon as Captain Potts returns will order him to leave immediately. The instructions of the general commanding in relation to the cavalry have been anticipated by me, and they have not at any time been kept at this post longer than was absolutely necessary to rest and shoe their horses. They have twenty days' rations with them at this time, and as their depot will be either at Spring Valley or Skull Creek, it will be an easy matter for me to send them more if wanted. My whole aim has been the detection and punishment of the Indians who have been committing depredations on the Overland Mail Line, and to that end I am disposing of the forces at my command in such a manner that I think the time is not far distant when they will receive a chastisement that will not soon be forgotten.

Very respectfully, your obedient servant,

P. A. GALLAGHER,

Major-Third Infantry California Volunteers, Commanding Post.

Source: *OR*, Series 1, Volume 50, Part 2, page 420

OR-190

APRIL 11–20, 1863.—Expedition from Camp Douglas to the Spanish Fork Cañon, Utah Ter., with skirmish (12th) at Pleasant Grove, and action (15th) at Spanish Fork Cañon.

Report of Col. George S. Evans, Second California Cavalry, commanding expedition.

HEADQUARTERS DEPARTMENT OF THE PACIFIC,
San Francisco, May 4, 1863.

Brig. Gen. L. THOMAS,
Adjutant-General U.S. Army, Washington, D.C.:

GENERAL: I have the honor to transmit herewith the report of Col. George S. Evans, Second Cavalry California Volunteers, of an expedition against Indians at Spanish Fork, Utah Ter. This adds another to the highly commendatory and successful expeditions which have been sent out from Camp Douglas within the present year. I beg leave to ask your attention to the statements of Colonel Evans in relation to the conduct of the Mormons. It was only a continuation of their perfidious acts which commenced when our troops arrived in Utah. But I trust that the day is fast approaching when retributive justice will be meted out to these worse than open traitors to their country.

Very respectfully, your obedient servant,

G. WRIGHT,
Brigadier-General, U.S. Army, Commanding.

CAMP DOUGLAS, UTAH TER., *April 17, 1863.*

SIR: I have the honor to report that in pursuance of special instructions from General P. Edward Connor, commanding District of Utah, I ordered Lieutenant Honeyman, of the Third California Volunteer Infantry, with five gunners and one howitzer, with ammunition (covered up in an ambulance as a blind), to start from this post on the morning of April 11 and proceed to the town of Pleasant Grove, situated in a southeasterly direction and distant forty miles from this camp, and there await my coming or further orders. That on Sunday evening, April 12, at 6 o'clock, in pursuance of the same instructions, I started for the same town with forty-seven men of Company A, commanded by Second Lieut. A. Ethier, and forty-nine men of Company H, Second California Volunteer Cavalry, commanded by First Lieut. C. D. Clark and Second Lieut. James Bradley, for the purpose of making that town the base of operations against a band of hostile Indians, the same who committed the late depredations upon the overland stages between Salt Lake City and Ruby Valley, and who were reported to be in Spanish Fork Cañon, thirty-five miles in a southerly direction from Pleasant Grove; that I reached the town of Pleasant Grove at 3 A.M. April 13 and found that Lieutenant Honeyman had arrived there on the previous morning, and had put his animals up in a corral of one of the Mormon settlers to await my arrival or further orders; that at 6 P.M. of the same day a band of some 100 Indians came rushing down upon the town, and dismounting on the outskirts deployed into the town skulking behind adobe fences, hay-stacks, &c., until they completely surrounded the building in which Lieutenant Honeyman and his five men were, when they commenced firing upon him. The lieutenant when he first discovered the approach of the Indians—they being yet some miles from the house in which he was—immediately set his men to work uncovering, getting out of the ambulance, and putting together for action his howitzer, which being done he loaded with shell with a 600-yards fuse, and ran his piece up to the cross street, at the end of which the Indians had dismounted, with the intention of using it against them as they started into the town, but they deploying as above stated rendered it impossible for him to use his gun to any advantage, and finding that the Indians were surrounding him he very prudently retired to the house where his ambulance and mules were. By this time the Indians were within some thirty or forty yards of him, and he, seeing that unless something was done promptly he and his little party would be massacred, very wisely took possession of the house (a small adobe) and prepared to defend himself as best he could. After firing two shots from the house with the howitzer the walls of the building became so much cracked that he was compelled to cease firing for fear of the building falling. The Indians in the meantime from the adobe wall-fence and haystacks in the vicinity were pouring an incessant shower of balls into the house, which they kept up from about sundown until 8 o'clock at night, literally riddling the door and windows, but fortunately without killing or wounding anyone in the building, although the stovepipe, pans, plates, and almost everything in the house except the men received a shot. At 8 o'clock the Indians ceased firing and left the town, taking with them the provisions, blankets, &c., of the lieutenant and his five men, as also the Government animals that were left alive, seven in number, five having been killed during the engagement. I enter into details in mentioning these seemingly unimportant facts, not because I deem them of any importance in themselves, but that they may be taken and considered in connection with the strange but stubborn fact that all this occurred in the town of Pleasant Grove in the face and eyes of a population of several hundred people calling themselves civilized and American citizens—God save the mark! Eight in the heart of a Mormon town, where there were perhaps not less than 100 or 150 white men (Mormons), in the broad daylight 75 or 100 savages attack and attempt to murder six American citizens and do carry off mules, harness, and other Government property, and not a hand is lifted to assist or protect them or to prevent the stealing of the Government property; but on the contrary they stand around the street corners and on top of their houses and hay-stacks complacently looking on, apparently well pleased at the prospect of six Gentiles (soldiers) being murdered. They actually assisted the Indians in catching the Government mules that had effected their escape from the corral, and from their natural fear of the redskins were endeavoring to keep beyond their reach. The foregoing facts speak for themselves. Comment is unnecessary further than to say that Lieutenant Honeyman believes and thinks that he has prima facie evidence of the fact upon which to found his belief that the savages were informed by the Mormons of his presence in the town with only five men, and, as they supposed, a wagon load of provisions, bound for Fort Bridger, and that it was a contrived and partnership arrangement between some of the Mormons and the Indians to murder his little party, take the property, and divide the spoils.

In the morning (April 13) as soon as light I started out scouts in different directions to find the course that the Indians had taken, and at the same time sent an express to the general commanding, notifying him what had occurred, and the position I was in as to transportation for my howitzer and ammunition, as well as to the want of animals for the gunners to ride, &c., and received that evening in reply notice from the general that he had ordered Captain Price with his company to join me, and that he had sent with them mules for the howitzer and gunners in place of those stolen by the Indians. Captain Price arrived with his company, numbering sixty men, about 11 o'clock at night, bringing with him the animals for the howitzer, &c. In the meantime my scouts had returned with the information that they could get no trace of the Indians, excepting that eight of them had passed through the town of Provo, some ten miles to the south of Pleasant Grove with the stolen animals, on their way and in the direction of Spanish Fork. The Mormons, however, insisted upon it that the body of the Indians had scattered, and by different routes, had concentrated in what is known as Dry Cañon, where they had a considerable encampment, and their women and children, and as Lieutenant Honeyman seemed also to think that the Indians who attacked him had come out of this Dry Cañon, and as I could find no evidence of a large body of Indians traveling farther south, I concluded to make a drive on Dry Cañon and satisfy myself as to the fact whether they were there or not. I accordingly started in the morning at 7 o'clock with the howitzer and fifty men up what is known as Provo Cañon, and sent Lieutenants Clark and Bradley with the same number of men up Dry Cañon, the two cañons connecting, or at least there being an outlet at the head of Dry Cañon leading over and into Provo Cañon. In this way with the force in Provo Cañon I was certain to head and cut off the enemy from retreat, provided he was, as represented, encamped in Dry Cañon. I, however, found from actual examination after scouring every nook and corner of the two cañons, over almost impassable ledges, the men walking and leading their horses and climbing for six hours (and losing one horse which fell down a precipice, breaking his neck), that there were no Indians in that section, nor had there been for weeks; that the statements of the Mormons in regard to the Indians were premeditated lies, gotten up for the purpose of misleading me, and giving the latter time either to get away or prepare for battle. In coming out of Provo Cañon I went across some points of mountains to the southward, discovering the Indian trail at last where they had concentrated and traveled in force toward the celebrated impregnable (so-called) Spanish Fork. I immediately proceeded to and through the town of Provo, it being in the direction and the best road to Spanish Fork, intending to pursue the enemy rapidly; but at this town, fifteen miles from Spanish Fork, I received reliable information by means of a soldier dressed as a citizen and passing himself off as a Mormon, that one Potter, a Mormon, had gone into the cañon to notify the Indians of my approach, of the number of men I had, &c., and that there were other Mormons watching around to give the Indians notice of my every movement. Under the circumstances I found that it was necessary for me to practice a little deception on the Mormons if I expected to accomplish anything in the way of catching and particularly of surprising the Indians. So I encamped on the south side of the town of Provo, far enough away from the town to be able to slip off in the night without their knowledge, and giving out the impression that I should stay all night and in the morning send scouts up to Spanish Fork to ascertain whether the Indians were really there and what their number was, &c.; and to completely allay any suspicions regarding my moving during the night I made verbal arrangements and contracts to have hay and grain delivered for the command in the morning, and in fact the men themselves believed they were to remain until morning. But at midnight I had them awakened noiselessly, without the sound of a bugle note, saddled up and slipped off with the intention of reaching the mouth of the cañon before daylight, and making my arrangements to advance up the cañon as soon as it was light enough for the men to see to walk and climb the mountains.

I reached the mouth of the cañon just as day was breaking on the 15th of April; had my one wagon with provisions and the ambulance driven up parallel to each other and thirty paces apart, and, taking the lariat ropes off the horses' necks, tied them together, making a picket rope, and stretched it from one vehicle to the other. I then dismounted Captain Price's company (sixty men), and twenty men of Company H, leaving Lieutenant Finnerty with twenty men to guard the eighty horses, which were tied up to the picket rope; directed Captain Price to take Lieutenant Weed and forty men across the river to deploy as flankers and skirmishers on the south side of the cañon, and Lieutenant Clark to take Lieutenant Bradley and forty men to deploy as flankers and skirmishers on the left, or north, side of the cañon, myself taking Lieutenant Ethier, Adjutant Harris, and Lieutenant Peel, with about fifty men, and Lieutenant Honeyman, with the howitzer and accompanying gunners, up the center of the cañon. By the time these preliminaries were arranged it had reached the hour of 4.30 A.M. and would have been quite light but for the heavy rain that was falling. After moving up in this order, my flankers having almost insurmountable mountain spurs to cross that were running down into the Spanish Fork, necessarily making their movements very slow, at 5 A.M., and after getting into the cañon about a mile, the enemy, from his chosen positions on the right, left, and front, opened fire The howitzer having been run up on the spur of a mountain, Lieutenant Honeyman, in charge of it, could easily see where the enemy's fire was the heaviest, and with great coolness and skill he dropped his shell among them, the center in the meantime moving steadily up until they came right onto the brink of a deep side ravine in which the enemy had his main force, and opened on him with the revolvers. This was too much for him; he could not stand such close quarters. When it came to meeting the cool but piercing eye of the white men in deadly conflict, face to face, the redskins quailed, and they began to give way. Then the "forward" and "charge" were sounded and the fight became a running one, the Indians taking advantage of every little outlet from the main cañon, as they retreated up it, to make their escape. At 11 A.M., after chasing the enemy with cavalry fourteen miles up the cañon, scattering him like quails, and finding that my horses were giving out, and knowing that I had a long road to retrace through a dangerous cañon, I ordered the "recall" and "assembly" sounded.

The result of the expedition and battle is that although the Indians were in possession and expecting us later in the day we surprised them as to the time of our coming. We killed about 30 warriors, their chief among the number, and wounded many more who made their escape for the time, but who will undoubtedly die; recaptured 3 [mules] and 1 horse, with saddles, bridles, &c., that had been stolen from Lieutenant Honeyman, and 18 horses, saddles, bridles, quite a number of good rifles, and other plunder of the Indians; losing on our side 1 killed—Lieut. F. A. Peel, regimental quartermaster, Second California Volunteer Cavalry—and 2 wounded—Regimental Quartermaster Sergeant Brown and Sergeant Booth, of Company M, Second California Volunteer Cavalry. By the accompanying rough draft* of the cañon, and taking into consideration the fact that it is twenty-five miles long, you will see that it is an exceedingly strong hold, and will not be surprised at its being called by the Mormons and heretofore believed by the Indians to be the impenetrable and impregnable cañon; one such as none but California troops could drive a superior or even an equal number of Indians from. The enemy's force, from the best information I can get, was about 200 warriors. To Lieutenant Honeyman, and his coolness and skill in using his howitzer, is in a great measure due the credit of the battle being won with so slight a loss on our side. As for the Second Cavalry, both officers and men behaved as soldiers should, and it would be unfair to make any invidious distinctions. Suffice it to say that they sustained their well-earned fame as the "Fighting Second."

All of which is respectfully submitted.

GEO. S. EVANS,

Colonel Second California Vol. Cav., Commanding Expedition.

Lieut. W. L. Ustick,

Acting Assistant Adjutant-General, District of Utah,

* Not found.

Source: *OR*, Series 1, Volume 50, Part 1, pages 204–208

OR-191

Headquarters Department of the Pacific,
San Francisco, Cal., May 6, 1863.

Brig. Gen. P. E. Connor, U.S. Volunteers,
Commanding District of Utah, Salt Lake City, Utah Ter.:

Sir: In reply to your letter of the 22d ultimo, relative to raising troops from emigrants, &c., the department commander directs that if the people living in Utah from whom you expect to raise one or more companies will enlist for three years or during the war, you can proceed to their organization into a company of infantry, furnishing the necessary rolls, &c., to Lieutenant-Colonel Ringgold, commissary of musters.

Very respectfully, your obedient servant,

R. C. DRUM,
Assistant Adjutant-General.

Source: *OR*, Series 1, Volume 50, Part 2, page 427

OR-192

Headquarters District of Oregon,
Fort Vancouver, Wash. Ter., May 9, 1863.

Brig. Gen. P. Edward Connor, U.S. Volunteers,
Commanding District of Utah, near Salt Lake City, Utah:

General: It will be proper for you to know what movements of troops are contemplated by me in the Snake country the coming summer. I shall at all events establish a post at Fort Boisé. Col. R. F. Maury, First Oregon Cavalry, with three companies of that regiment, is now encamped at Fort Lapwai, on the Nez Percé Reservation. That reservation having for the past two years been overrun by the gold diggers, in contempt of the treaty securing to the Nez Percé said reservation, a council has been invited to assemble there to make a new treaty and indemnify that tribe (which has always heretofore been so friendly to the whites) for its losses. But there is a disaffected party in the tribe. The movements of Col. R. F. Maury depend on events in that quarter. If matters work favorably (as I trust they will) Colonel Maury in June will proceed to Fort Boisé, and two companies of infantry being added to his command, he will proceed eastward from that post and endeavor to meet the head of the emigration from the States at the crossing of the Snake River above Fort Hall. Captain Crawford with an emigrant escort party of 100 men from Omaha, Nebr., promised to bring the head of the emigration there from the 10th to the 20th of August. I expect by that movement Colonel Maury will be able to strike an efficient blow at the Snakes, and protect the emigration which should return on his trail by the road north of Snake River. Private letters say that parties from Denver, Pike's Peak, and Salt Lake are going across to Boisé now in early spring. I fear they will have to fight their way. If you are able to protect the emigrants or others who take the road south of Snake River by an escort to proceed as far as Salmon Falls, it will be a very desirable thing. As the main emigration and Colonel Maury will take the north road above described, which crosses Snake River above Fort Hall, small parties on the old road on the south side of Snake River will stand in greater danger than ever. All these facts I bring to your attention for your information. I know nothing of your orders or plans. I appreciate highly the signal blow your gallant troops gave last winter to the Indians on Bear River, in Washington Territory, and know that to the extent of your force you will take good care of the Snakes in your vicinity.

I have the honor to be, your obedient servant,

BENJ. ALVORD,
Brigadier-General, U.S. Volunteers, Commanding District.

SOURCE: *OR*, SERIES 1, VOLUME 50, PART 2, PAGES 428–429

OR-193

SACRAMENTO, CAL., *May 11, 1863—11 A.M.*

General L. THOMAS,
Adjutant-General U.S. Army:

Volunteer troops from California cannot cross the mountains and reach Salt Lake before the latter part of July. In the meantime, if practicable, I would recommend that re-enforcements be thrown forward immediately from the Missouri frontier.

G. WRIGHT,
Brigadier-General.

SOURCE: *OR*, SERIES 1, VOLUME 50, PART 2, PAGE 429

OR-194

HEADQUARTERS DEPARTMENT OF THE PACIFIC,
San Francisco, Cal., May 11, 1863.

Brig. Gen. L. THOMAS,
Adjutant-General U.S. Army, Washington, D.C.:

GENERAL: I have the honor to transmit herewith a communication addressed to my headquarters by Brig. Gen. P. Edward Connor, commanding the District of Utah, dated on the 28th ultimo.* I am doing all that is in my power to re enforce General Connor. The battalion of the Third Infantry will march from Sacramento in a few days, and I am advised by the acting Governor of Nevada Territory that he is using the most strenuous exertions to comply with my requisition on him for two companies of cavalry and two of infantry. I think that with prudence and good management we need apprehend no immediate disturbance in Utah, but we should have there a military force strong enough to look down all opposition and maintain the supremacy of our laws and institutions. I telegraphed you to-day recommending, if it were possible, that re-enforcements for Connor be sent at once from the adjoining department east of him. Under no circumstances could I for a moment entertain the idea of recommending the withdrawal of our troops from Utah. At whatever cost, the great highway connecting the Eastern States with the Pacific must be kept open and under the control of the United States.

G. WRIGHT,
Brigadier-General, U.S. Army, Commanding.

* [*Refers to* OR-*187.*]

SOURCE: *OR*, SERIES 1, VOLUME 50, PART 2, PAGE 430

OR-195

HEADQUARTERS DEPARTMENT OF THE PACIFIC,
San Francisco, Cal., May 11, 1863.

His Excellency S. S. HARDING,
Governor of Utah Territory, Great Salt Lake City, Utah Ter.:

SIR: I have the honor to acknowledge the receipt of Your Excellency's communication of the 27th ultimo, for which I have to thank you. The condition of affairs in Utah has for a long time past received my most serious consideration. I have been kept fully informed on all the topics embraced in Your Excellency's letter by Brigadier-General Connor, and I am now straining every nerve to throw forward re-enforcements. A battalion of the Third Infantry, now at Sacramento, will march in a few days, taking with it two 6-pounder brass guns, one 12 pounder field howitzer, and one 12-pounder mountain howitzer, with an ample supply of ammunition. The company of Second Cavalry which was at Fort Churchill is temporarily engaged in the Owen's Valley district. It will be thrown forward toward Utah at an early day. The acting Governor of Nevada Territory is making strenuous exertions to comply with my requisition for two companies of cavalry and two of infantry, with a fair prospect of success. When raised it is designed to move them promptly to Salt Lake. I have telegraphed to the Adjutant-General of the Army requesting, if it is possible to do so, that re-enforcements for General Connor be promptly advanced from the military department east of you. I can assure you, Governor, that I am fully sensible to the importance of maintaining the supremacy of our laws and institutions in the Territory of Utah, and can only regret that the force at my disposal is so inadequate to meet the emergency.

With great respect, I have the honor to be, Your Excellency's obedient servant,

G. WRIGHT,

Brigadier-General, U.S. Army, Commanding.

SOURCE: *OR*, SERIES 1, VOLUME 50, PART 2, PAGE 430

OR-196

HEADQUARTERS DEPARTMENT OF THE PACIFIC,

San Francisco, Cal., May 20, 1863.

Capt. M. A. MCLAUGHLIN,

Second Cavalry California Volunteers,

Comdg. Camp Independence, Owen's River Valley, Cal.:

SIR: It is desirable that Captain Brown's company of cavalry should commence its march to Salt Lake at the earliest day possible. In consideration, however, of the reasons set forth in your letter of the 6th instant, the general commanding instructs me to say that its movement in the direction indicated above will be delayed for the present. This delay should not extend beyond the 20th of June next.

Very respectfully, your obedient servant,

R. C. DRUM,

Assistant Adjutant-General.

SOURCE: *OR*, SERIES 1, VOLUME 50, PART 2, PAGES 448–449

OR-197

[*Extract*]

WASHINGTON, D.C., *May 22, 1863*.

Maj. Gen. JOHN M. SCHOFIELD,
Saint Louis, Mo.:

GENERAL: You have been ordered, by the direction of the President, to relieve Maj. Gen. S. R. Curtis from the command of the Department of the Missouri. This is one of the most important military departments in the United States, and the command will require the exercise of military talent as well as administrative ability, and the utmost vigilance. Your acquaintance with the country and the leading men of your department will be of great value to you in the performance of the arduous and important duties of your command.

It is not intended to embarrass you with minute and detailed instructions.

. . .

There has been no hostile force in Kansas since the beginning of this war, nor has there been, so far as I could learn, any danger of an invasion of that State, or of an insurrection of its inhabitants against the Government and authority of the United States; and yet a very large force has been kept and supported there, at an enormous expense to the National Treasury, and to the annoyance and injury of the inhabitants of the bordering territory. Both while in command of that department and since, I have endeavored to bring these forces into the field, where they could be made useful to the Government; but in these efforts I have been overruled, and, for reasons which I could never fully understand, these enormously expensive troops have been left in Kansas, where they were of no possible use, or sent into Missouri, where they were very much worse than useless. In my opinion, they should be either sent to Salt Lake, to guard the emigrant trains, or moved south to fight the rebels. In whatever use you may determine to make of these troops, you will have all the support which the War Department and these headquarters can give you. A regiment of Nebraska cavalry, on report of General Curtis that it could be spared from his department, was ordered some time ago to report for duty to General Pope, at Sioux City, for operations against the Indians. The authorities of Nebraska afterward protested against this order, and General Curtis asked that it be rescinded. This was refused. Nevertheless, General Pope reports that the order has never been complied with, and I cannot ascertain from General Curtis how the matter now really stands. You will immediately examine into this matter, and either carry out the original order to General Curtis, or use these troops to escort emigrant trains to Salt Lake, as under existing circumstances you may deem best. You will, as soon as you ascertain the real facts of the case, advise General Pope, and give him all possible assistance in his contemplated Indian campaign. At this distance, and acting under very imperfect information, I cannot give you on these subjects very positive or minute instructions. Much must be left to your discretion and more enlightened judgment; but we will leave for the present, active military operations in the field, and direct our attention for a moment to administrative matter, which will constitute the most annoying, arduous, perplexing, and responsible duties of your command.

. . .

I can only advise you, in regard to such matters, to consult the best authorities, and to act with deliberation and [coolness?] upon each separate question as it arises. A hasty and inconsiderate decision often leads to serious difficulties and embarrassment. On such matters I will give you all the assistance which time and opportunity will permit. In referring these questions to these headquarters, you will take into consideration that I have very little time to devote to a single military department, and more particularly to an individual case.

In conclusion, general, I desire to assure you that in the high and responsible position and duties to which you are assigned you will have all the support, assistance, and co-operation which can be given you from these headquarters. You owe your present appointment entirely to the choice of the President himself. I have not, directly or indirectly, interfered in the matter; but I fully concur in the choice, and will give you all possible support and assistance in the performance of the arduous duties imposed upon you.

. . .

If you can raise any troops in Northern Missouri, Kansas, Nebraska, or Colorado to guard emigrant trains, report by telegraph.

Very respectfully, your obedient servant,

H. W. HALLECK,
General-in-Chief.

SOURCE: *OR*, SERIES 1, VOLUME 22, PART 2, PAGES 290–292

OR-198

HDQRS. DEPARTMENT OF THE PACIFIC,
San Francisco, Cal., May 25, 1863.

SPECIAL ORDERS,
No. 126.

1. Maj. John M. O'Neill, Second Cavalry California Volunteers, will without delay proceed to Camp Douglas, near Salt Lake, and report for duty to the commanding

officer thereof. The quartermaster's department will furnish Major O'Neill transportation in kind from this city to Salt Lake.

. . .

* * * *

By order of Brigadier-General Wright:

RICHD. C. DRUM,
Assistant Adjutant-General.

SOURCE: *OR*, SERIES 1, VOLUME 50, PART 2, PAGE 453

OR-199

[*Extract*]

HEADQUARTERS DISTRICT OF OREGON,
Fort Vancouver, Wash. Ter., May 29, 1863.

Col. R. F. MAURY,
First Oregon Cavalry, Commanding Expedition against the Snake Indians, Fort Lapwai, Idaho Ter.:

COLONEL: You have received Special Orders, No. 56, from these headquarters, and will proceed by such route as you may select to the vicinity of the point likely to be chosen as the site of new Fort Boisé.

. . .

The vicinity of Camas Prairie north of Salmon Falls is supposed to be the stronghold of the Snakes. On your return I advise that you should encamp at some suitable point in that region best calculated to keep the Indians in check, and from which you can throw out small parties for the protection of the rear of the emigration. Of course great vigilance in guarding your animals will at all times be necessary, not only from Indians, but also from white thieves and robbers who may infest your path. I have suggested to General Connor, at Salt Lake City, the propriety of his sending, if he has them to spare, some troops on the road south of Snake River, at least as far as Salmon Falls.

Very respectfully, your obedient servant,

BENJ. ALVORD,
Brigadier-General, U.S. Volunteers, Commanding District.

SOURCE: *OR*, SERIES 1, VOLUME 50, PART 2, PAGES 464–465

OR-200

CAMP DOUGLAS, *May 31, 1863.*
(Received 8.10 P.M.)

Lieut. Col. R. C. DRUM:
I arrived last evening from the north. All quiet.

P. E. CONNOR,
Brigadier-General.

SOURCE: *OR*, SERIES 1, VOLUME 50, PART 2, PAGE 468

OR-201

MAY 5–30, 1863.—Expedition from Camp Douglas, Utah Ter., to Soda Springs, on the Bear River, Idaho Ter.

Report of Brig. Gen. P. Edward Connor, U.S. Army, commanding District of Utah.

HEADQUARTERS DISTRICT OF UTAH,
Camp Douglas, Utah Ter., June 2, 1863.

COLONEL: I have the honor to report to the general commanding the department that on the 5th of May ultimo Company H, Third Infantry California Volunteers, Captain Black left this post, pursuant to my orders, en route, via Box Elder. Bear River, Cache and Marsh Valleys, for a point at or near the great bend of Bear River known as Soda Springs, Idaho Ter., for the purpose of establishing a new post in that region for the protection of the overland emigration to Oregon, California, and the Bannock City mines. Accompanying this expedition and under its protection were a large number of persons heretofore resident of this Territory, seceders (under the name of Morrisites) from the Mormon Church. Many, if not all, of these having been reduced by the long-continued persecutions of the Mormons to the most abject poverty, have for some months past claimed and received the protection and assistance of the forces under my command. Prudential reasons, applying as well to this command as to the Morrisites themselves, rendered it advisable that they should be removed from the vicinity of this camp and beyond the evil influences and powers of the Mormon hierarchy. Regarding the expedition to Soda Springs, Idaho Ter., as presenting a favorable opportunity for this purpose, I ordered transportation to be provided for the most indigent and the distribution of provisions to the destitute, both en route and after arrival at the new post, until such time as by industry and well-directed effort these impoverished and persecuted people should be able to support themselves. Some of them were able to furnish their own teams and wagons. Most of them gathered up their household goods and provided themselves with a scanty supply of provisions for their sustenance. They numbered in all 100 souls, comprised of 53 families, 7 single men, and 4 widows. On the next day, May 6, I followed with Company H, Second Cavalry California Volunteers, Lieutenant Clark commanding, and overtook the main train and infantry twenty-five miles north of this city. Proceeding thence by easy marches of from fifteen to eighteen miles per day along the eastern shore of Great Salt Lake, the entire command arrived at Brigham City (or Box Elder), sixty miles north. May 8. Here leaving the infantry and train to proceed by the old beaten road through Cache and Marsh Valleys and across the mountains, via Sublett's Cut-Off, I took the cavalry by a less frequented road, crossing Bear River at the lower ferry; thence up the plateau lying between the Malade and Bear Rivers, over the mountains dividing the waters of the Great Basin from those of Snake and Columbia Rivers; thence down the westerly side of Marsh Valley, crossing the Port Neuf River north of Sublett's Cut-Off, and down the east and right bank of that river to Snake River Ferry, a distance of 200 miles from this post, arriving at that point May 13. Our general course to the ferry was a little east of due north, passing through a series of valleys well watered and with light timber along the streams and on the mountain sides. The luxuriant vegetation at this early season of the year furnishing good grass for the animals, as well as the evidences of last year's growth, bespoke the fertility of the soil and its adaptation to agriculture. This remark more especially applies to Marsh Valley, lying due north of and adjoining Cache Valley, the latter being already thickly settled by Mormons, whose most northerly settlements extend within fifteen or twenty miles of the first-mentioned valley, the Bear River and a low ridge dividing the two valleys. After leaving Brigham City the command performed two night marches, the first of twelve and the second of thirty-five miles, as I had reason to believe that wandering bands of hostile savages, remnants of the Shoshones, engaged or connected with [those] who took part in the battle of Bear River (29th of January last), were in the neighborhood and might be surprised and punished for repeated and recent outrages on emigrants and settlers. In this expectation, however, I was disappointed, few, if any, traces of Indians being found, and thenceforward the command proceeded by daily marches. In Port Neuf Valley we came upon two lodges of Indians (Shoshones), who came unhesitatingly into camp with their squaws, satisfactorily answered all questions propounded, and gave evidence of friendly disposition toward the whites. Giving them to understand the determination of the Government to punish summarily all bad Indians, and receiving assurances of future good conduct on their part, I passed on without molesting these Indians. At Snake River Ferry were several large trains of emigrants bound north to the mines, and here recruiting their animals. Here also was an encampment of seventeen lodges of Shoshone (or Snake) Indians, numbering in all, including those who came in the next day, 250 or 300. They were well mounted and had grazing in the vicinity a considerable number of stock. These Indians were reliably represented to me as friendly and peaceable, and have been living at the ferry during the past winter. Being accompanied by Judge Doty, superintendent of Indian affairs for Utah, a conference was held with the Indians on the night of our arrival attended by the chiefs, old and young men, and squaws. Through an interpreter many questions were asked as to the locality of hostile chiefs and their bands, and the power of the Government duly impressed upon them. They were informed that the troops had been sent to this region to protect good Indians and whites, and equally to punish bad Indians and bad white men; that it was my determination to visit the most summary punishment, even to extermination, on Indians who committed depredations upon the lives and property of emigrants or settlers. They were also assured that if bad whites trespassed upon their rights the report of the facts to me or my officers would be followed by punishment on the malefactors and a prompt remedy of all grievances to the extent of my power. After the customary smoking with the chiefs and a grand dance by men and squaws, I ordered the distribution among them of a small quantity of bacon, flour, and sugar. The conference was satisfactory, and the exhibition of the force at my command in that far-off region, as well as our rapid march through a country rarely traversed by whites, evidently had a good effect. I learned from them that Pocatello, the great chief of the hostile Shoshones, had gone a long distance off on the Lower Snake, probably in the vicinity of the Humboldt; that Saquache [Sagwich?], one of the leaders, who escaped wounded from the battle of Bear River, was somewhere in the south near the Mormon settlements of Cache Valley, and San Pitch still farther east. The region immediately about the Snake River at this ferry, which is about ten miles east of old Fort Hall, is a dry, barren sand plain, the road to the ferry being exceedingly heavy and difficult to traverse. Grass of tolerable quality and quantity is to be found several miles to the eastward on the Blackfoot Creek, which here empties into the Snake after running for perhaps thirty miles parallel with and not far from the river. The Snake here is a rapid stream 250 yards in width, and at this season 20 feet in depth, and is seldom or never fordable at this point. Beyond and to the northward the plain of sage brush and grease wood extends some fifty miles to a high range of mountains, three high buttes in the midst of the plain forming a prominent landmark. The distance from Soda Springs to this ferry, via the Bridger and Fort Hall emigrant road, is upward of seventy miles, pursuing a northwesterly course. Emigrants from the East via this road for the new mines, leaving the ferry travel up the Snake River in nearly an easterly direction about seventy miles to a point nearly due north of Soda Springs, thus following from Soda Springs along two sides of a triangle, either of which is seventy miles long, a distance of 140 miles. With the design of finding a practicable route for a wagon road through some pass in the mountains whereby a move direct course could be made, I sent Lieutenant Clark with a detachment of twenty-five men with five days' rations and orders to cross the Blackfoot near its source at the base of the foothills, and, proceeding up the Snake sixty or seventy-five miles, turn to the south, seek out such pass, and join the command at Soda Springs. This expedition was eminently successful, finding a good pass for a road along the base of the triangle mentioned above, striking Snake River seventy miles above and east of the present ferry. At this point a ferry has been established, and in a short time a good boat will be in running order. With the main body of the cavalry, train, &c., I left the Blackfoot about fifteen miles east of the ferry, and pursuing a southeasterly course across the divide by a good natural road, arrived at Soda Springs on the 17th of May, passing through large and fertile valleys lying along Ross Fork of Snake River and the North Branch of the Port Neuf. The infantry with the settlers not having yet arrived, detachments under Lieutenants Bradley and Ustick were dispatched north and south to explore the country and find a route for a direct and practicable wagon road to the settlements in Cache Valley and to report on the character of country explored.

On the 20th Company H, Third Infantry, arrived, after a long and tedious trip, accompanied by their charge, the settlers for the new town. A suitable and eligible location was selected on the north bank of Bear River, near the great bend, and four miles east of where the Soda Springs Valley opens into Old Crater Valley, the latter some fifty miles in length and twenty in width. The sight was surveyed immediately east of the springs, as was also one mile square for a military reservation, adjoining on the east the town site, in latitude about 42½ north and longitude 111½ west. The water is good and abundant as well from the river as from the numerous mountain streams easily diverted for purposes of irrigation. Back of the town and north wood for fuel is abundant, while on the opposite side of the river timber of large growth suitable for building purposes is found at a distance of less than two miles. The soil, judging from the growth of the native grasses and the appearance of the ground, is susceptible of cultivation and the raising of valuable crops, the shortness of the season and the altitude of the place alone rendering this at all doubtful. The settlers were allotted building lots of fair size, and proceeded immediately to the erection of shelters for themselves and families. After remaining at this post for six days, establishing the infantry at the new post and looking to the present and immediate future wants of the settlers, on the 30th of May I returned to this post via the Mormon settlements in Cache Valley. The explorations above referred to satisfied me of the fertility of the country surrounding Soda Springs and of the entire practicability of making at small expense of labor a good wagon road from the northern settlements of Cache Valley, crossing Bear River at or near the battleground through a gap in the mountains, and thence northerly along the western bank of Bear River to Soda Springs. This road will be much more direct than the old road traversed by the infantry company, and the distance can be reduced from

200 miles, as at present, to about 150 or 160 miles. This road, connecting with the new road explored by Lieutenant Clark north from Soda Springs to Bannock City, will render the distance from the latter place to this point not more than 350 miles. The new road north from Soda Springs to Snake River will shorten the route of emigrants from the East via Fort Bridger not less than seventy miles, as well as present a route well watered and furnishing good feed for animals, with abundance of game. The expedition has traveled in a direct line about 500 miles, and has carefully explored a region of country over 1,000 miles in extent heretofore little known, and concerning which only the most vague and crude ideas were held. Before leaving Soda Springs I sent a detachment of twenty men over the mountains to pass through Bear Lake Valley in hopes of finding the band of Sagwich, supposed to be roaming in that section. The detachment was unsuccessful in its object, and it joined the command a few days after at Franklin, the most northerly settlement in Cache Valley, having thoroughly searched the region through which it passed. In this connection I may add that having occasion to send an empty train to Carson for quartermaster's stores, I furnished to 150 Morrisites transportation to that point, and they have already safely arrived at their destination.

Very respectfully, your obedient servant,

P. EDW. CONNOR,
Brigadier-General, U.S. Volunteers, Commanding District.

Lieut. Col. R. C. DRUM,
Assistant Adjutant-General, U.S. Army, Department of the Pacific, San Francisco, Cal.

SOURCE: *OR*, SERIES 1, VOLUME 50, PART 1, PAGES 226–229

OR-202

CAMP DOUGLAS, *June 2, 1863.*

Lieut. Col. R. C. DRUM:

Indians are suing for peace. I leave for Bridger to-day to meet 500 of them. My policy will win.

P. E. CONNOR,
Brigadier-General, U.S. Army.

SOURCE: *OR*, SERIES 1, VOLUME 50, PART 2, PAGE 470

OR-203

CAMP DOUGLAS, *June 7, 1863—8 P.M.*

Lieut. Col. R. C. DRUM:

Just returned from Bridger. Made treaty with 650 Snake Indians. They delivered 150 stolen horses to me.

P. E. CONNOR,
Brigadier-General.

SOURCE: *OR*, SERIES 1, VOLUME 50, PART 2, PAGE 474

OR-204

HEADQUARTERS DEPARTMENT OF THE PACIFIC,
San Francisco, June 9, 1863.

Brig. Gen. L. THOMAS,
Adjutant-General U.S. Army, Washington, D.C.:

GENERAL: The active and energetic campaigns which have been made against the Indians in the Owen's River Valley, Cal., and in the District of Utah during the past winter and spring have had the most happy results in bringing those Indians to sue for peace. A very large number of Indians have been killed, and the great mass of the survivors have laid down their arms and met the commanders in those districts in council. General Connor returned to Camp Douglas, Salt Lake, on the 7th instant, from Fort Bridger, where he had made a treaty with 650 Snake Indians, who delivered to him 150 stolen horses.

Very respectfully, your obedient servant,

G. WRIGHT,
Brigadier-General, U.S. Army, Commanding.

SOURCE: *OR*, SERIES 1, VOLUME 50, PART 2, PAGE 478

OR-205

HEADQUARTERS DISTRICT OF UTAH,
Salt Lake City, Utah Ter., June 10, 1863.

Brig. Gen. BENJAMIN ALVORD, U.S. Volunteers,
Comdg. District of Oregon, Fort Vancouver, Wash. Ter.:

GENERAL: Your communication of the 8th ultimo was duly received while en route to Snake River. I acted upon your suggestion and posted a company of infantry at Soda Springs, Big Bend of Bear River, in Idaho Territory, and a detachment of ten men on Snake River at a new ferry lately established, about sixty miles above Fort Hall. While at the lower ferry, in the vicinity of Fort Hall, I met about 200 Snake Indians, with whom I had a talk. They are friendly, and will remain so. Those also in the vicinity of and on the road to Bannock City are friendly. I had a talk with 700 Snake Indians at Fort Bridger last week. They say they are tired of fighting and want to be at peace. They gave me up 150 horses and mules which they had stolen. The fight of last winter is telling on them. There are two small bands at large yet, who are hostile. They number about 100 men. Troops are now in pursuit of them, and I hope soon to destroy them. I have no fears for the safety of the emigration to the Bannock Mines. How it will be to the Boisé Mines I am unable to say. I will, as you have suggested, take care of the emigration on the south side of Snake River as far west as longitude 114. The Ute Indians, with whom Colonel Evans had a fight at Spanish Fork this spring, have sent word that they desire to make peace with me. On the whole, I consider the Indian troubles in my district very near at an end.

I have the honor to remain, very respectfully, your obedient servant,

P. EDW. CONNOR,
Brigadier-General, U.S. Volunteers, Commanding District.

SOURCE: *OR*, SERIES 1, VOLUME 50, PART 2, PAGE 479

OR-206

San Francisco, *June 11, 1863.*

Maj. Charles McDermit,
Fort Churchill:

Brown's company will move to the support of General Connor as soon after its arrival as possible. Report its departure by telegraph to Connor. Hold Company A in readiness to leave for Salt Lake.

R. C. DRUM,
Assistant Adjutant-General.

Source: *OR*, Series 1, Volume 50, Part 2, page 480

OR-207

Headquarters District of Utah,
Camp Douglas, June 11, 1863—2.15 P.M.

Lieut. Col. R. C. Drum,
Assistant Adjutant-General:

A powerful tribe (the Southern Utes) have commenced hostilities; killed driver and employé of mail company twenty-five miles west of here yesterday. Rumor says 1,600 of them in Mormon settlements south on way to attack me and destroy overland mail. The Snake Indians, with the exception of two small bands, are peaceable and have given up stolen property. Goshutes still troublesome. My force much scattered; should be doubled at once. I am surrounded by enemies, white and red.

P. EDW. CONNOR,
Brigadier-General, U.S. Army, Commanding District.

Source: *OR*, Series 1, Volume 50, Part 2, page 481

OR-208

HEADQUARTERS DEPARTMENT OF THE PACIFIC,
San Francisco, Cal., June 12, 1863.

Maj. JOHN M. O'NEILL,
Second Cavalry California Volunteers, San Francisco, Cal.:

SIR: The general commanding the department directs that you will at once proceed to join General Connor's command at or in the vicinity of Salt Lake City. As there may be some difficulty in proceeding alone over the overland route, you will join and take command of the troops under Captain Brown, Second Cavalry, which will probably leave Fort Churchill to-day.

Very respectfully, your obedient servant,

R. C. DRUM,
Assistant Adjutant-General.

SOURCE: *OR*, SERIES 1, VOLUME 50, PART 2, PAGE 481

OR-209

HEADQUARTERS DEPARTMENT OF UTAH,
Camp Douglas, Salt Lake, June 12, 1863.

Maj. Gen. H. W. HALLECK,
General-in-Chief:

A powerful tribe, the Southern Utes, are threatening the overland stage, east and west. My forces are inadequate to its protection. Have received no re-enforcements from California. Could a regiment of cavalry be sent from Denver?

P. EDWARD CONNOR,
Brigadier-General, Commanding.

SOURCE: *OR*, SERIES 1, VOLUME 50, PART 2, PAGE 481

OR-210

[*Extract*]

HEADQUARTERS DEPARTMENT OF THE PACIFIC,
San Francisco, June 14, 1863.

Brig. Gen. L. THOMAS,
Adjutant-General U.S. Army, Washington, D.C.:

GENERAL: I have to report the departure from Camp Union, Sacramento, on the 10th instant, of two companies of Third Infantry California Volunteers and a detachment of the Second Cavalry California Volunteers for Salt Lake, Utah, the whole under command of Lieut. Col. J. B. Moore, Third Infantry. I sent with this command two brass 6-pounder guns, one 12-pounder howitzer, and one 12-pounder mountain howitzer. I inspected the command previous to its marching and found it in admirable order and well prepared to move rapidly along the overland mail line to its destination

. . .

The company of the Second Cavalry lately with the troops in Owen's River Valley has returned to Fort Churchill, and will immediately be put on the march for Salt Lake. One of the companies called for from Nevada Territory is ready to be mustered in, and will be promptly advanced on the mail line.

. . .

Very respectfully, your obedient servant,

G. WRIGHT,
Brigadier-General, U.S. Army, Commanding.

SOURCE: *OR*, SERIES 1, VOLUME 50, PART 2, PAGE 484

OR-211

DENVER CITY, MO., *June 18, 1863.*

Major-General SCHOFIELD:

A war council of Sioux, Cheyennes, and Arapahoes to be held between here and Fort Laramie soon. That part of Idaho Territory taken from Nebraska should be in this district, to enable us to protect ourselves and the overland route from here to Salt Lake. Please telegraph order if made to Colonel Chivington.

JOHN EVANS,
Governor of Colorado Territory.

SOURCE: *OR*, SERIES 1, VOLUME 22, PART 2, PAGE 325

OR-212

FORT CRITTENDEN, *June 19, 1863.*

DEAR DAVE: I have just received a note from you. It was very short, but still it was better than none. Well, I have been to Salt Creek on a visit, and I enjoyed myself the best kind. I got back last night, with Mr. Shell. They behaved very kind to me and treated me well. While I was gone the Indians captured another stage and killed two men. It happened about two miles this side the ford of the River Jordan. They brought the scalps of the poor men they killed down to Salt Creek, and I saw them, and a great many other things belonging to the stage. You had better believe it made me feel mad. I got dreadfully excited. The bishop down there treated the Indians with tobacco and ordered the people to feed them, and it made me so mad that I pitched into them and told them what I thought of them, and then I felt better.

* * * *

PHEBE WESTWOOD.

[Editor's note: *This document appears in the* Official Records *as a sub-inclosure to OR-219.*]

SOURCE: *OR*, SERIES 1, VOLUME 50, PART 2, PAGE 500

OR-213

JUNE 20, 1863.—Skirmish near Government Springs, Utah Ter.

Report of Brig. Gen. P. Edward Connor, U.S. Army, commanding District of Utah.

SALT LAKE CITY, *June 22, 1863.*

Expedition from Bridger under Captain Lewis captured fifty of San Pitch's band. Captain Smith killed ten Indians Saturday last near Government Springs. Utes collecting in settlements south in large numbers, and threatening destruction to soldiers and overland mail. Have only sixty men for duty at Camp Douglas.

P. E. CONNOR,
Brigadier-General, Commanding District.

Lieut. Col. R. C. Drum,
Assistant Adjutant-General.

Source: *OR*, Series 1, Volume 50, Part 1, page 229

OR-214

Headquarters District of Utah,
Great Salt Lake City, Utah Ter., June 24, 1863.

Lieut. Col. R. C. Drum,
Assistant Adjutant-General, U.S. Army, San Francisco, Cal.:

Colonel: In view of the isolated condition of this district and the tardiness with which re-enforcements reach me, considering the advance already made in the season during which it is possible for troops to reach these headquarters, I deem it my duty no longer to delay presenting most respectfully the following statements for the information of the President of the United States, through the commanding general, relative to affairs in this Territory. In former communications the construction of Utah society and its peculiar polity, partaking of all the characteristics of the old patriarchal governments and the worst features of a fanatical and unlimited despotism, have perhaps been sufficiently set forth. I may be permitted, however, to add that the authority of the Church is here recognized as supreme above and beyond constitutions, laws, or regulations of the civil authorities. Not merely is the Church government here, as compared with the civil, a wheel within a wheel, subordinate to the right powers of the President and Congress, but in its practical workings is superior to and transcends all authority emanating from whatever source. The world has never seen a despotism so complete, so limitless, so transcendent, controlling not alone the outward and internal civil polity of the Territory, but entering into all the details of everyday life and the minutiæ of the domestic economy of each individual, as is exhibited in the construction of the Mormon Church. Of that church Brigham Young is the acknowledged head and recognized despot. Upon his will alone depend as well the acts of public officials as the course, temper, and feeling of the humblest member of his flock. Fanaticism can go no further than it has in this case, and from one end of the Territory to the other the will of Brigham Young is supreme, made known and manifested through his apostles, bishops, and subordinates resident in towns, villages, wards, and hamlets. Whether in all instances this tremendous authority is upheld by a species of devout religious fanaticism or enforced by fear in many the majority of cases upon those who would otherwise break from their thraldom, it is unnecessary now to express an opinion, but that it exists cannot be doubted and is not denied. The consequence is that the rightful authority of the United States is exercised only by sufferance, and peace and a doubtful quiet maintained only upon the slender thread of one man's will or whim. I cannot but recognize the glaring fact that in dealing with this people in the most trivial, as in the most momentous matters, I am but dealing with their supreme monarch; that it is in his power at any time to lay an embargo upon his entire people against the sale of any article of sustenance or use to my command; that no act, word, or deed of any Gentile escapes his ear, through the medium of an extended and truckling system of espionage; that no secret military movement against hostile Indians can be undertaken without the latter becoming possessed of the number, time of starting, direction, equipments, &c. Such a state of affairs would be dangerous even were the head of this system actuated by kindly feelings and a humane disposition, but it becomes intolerable when on every hand are found striking and undutiable evidences of hatred to the Government, disloyalty to the Union, and affiliation and sympathy with treason in the East and savage massacre and plunder all around and about us.

It is difficult to restrain indignation when the harangues of the prophet and his aspostles [*sic*] each Sabbath fill the crowded synagogue with flippant expressions of disloyalty and vulgar threats against the Union and those brave hearts yielding up their lives upon the battle-field; when each reverse to our arms is, with mock tears and sneering lamentations, pointed at as evidence of the truth of Joe Smith's prophecies and Brigham's weekly threats, and each demonstration of traitors, tortured into magnificent victories, is held up to the admiration of the gaping throng as abundant proof of the impotence of Government and the sure destruction of the Constitution and Union. Yet all this must be endured by those who visit the tabernacle of the Saints on almost every Sabbath of the year. Were the exhibitions of hatred to the Government and its ministers, civil and military, confined to these vapid word discharges of long-cultivated spleen, it might be endured in silence, but such is not the case. The whole people are being thus educated (if indeed the term education may be applied in any sense to a community so plunged in the depth of ignorance and fanaticism). The whole people are being educated into the most complete hatred of the Government and the institutions under which we live, the two cardinal points in Mormon religion being contempt and hatred to the Union and faith in and subservience to the head of the Church. With no regard for the South, and in fact probably a repugnance to slavery and Southern institutions, the rebel cause appeals to and receives their hearty sympathy merely because it is regarded as the appointed means of destroying the Government. How far the ramifications of the Mormon Church as a religion extend among the Indian tribes within and adjoining this Territory I am unable to say, but that Brigham Young has an immense influence over the savages and maintains frequent and intimate relations with them is past a doubt. I have the strongest reasons, based on many proofs, for believing that the recent raid on the Overland Mail Line, the massacre of drivers, and the stealing of stock were incited by white Mormons, and not improbably under the direct orders of the head of the Church. But whether this be strictly the fact or not, it is beyond the possibility of doubt that the Indians met with aid, food, and encouragement from nearly the whole Mormon people.

It is in proof before me that the savages have been collecting for weeks in and near the southern Mormon settlements; that they passed through a dozen towns in small parties and large bands coming north ward, avowing their purpose to slaughter and steal, to kill soldiers and break up the Overland Mail Line; that they were fed from place to place by the people and drew supplies from the public granaries; that in some instances they sent their couriers ahead to the next town to notify the bishop that they were coming, and to have prepared a beef for them, and that their demands were complied with and no intimation sent to these headquarters of the impending slaughter. Not only did they boast that they would kill emigrants and break up the overland mail, but that they were gathering in sufficient force to attack Camp Douglas and drive the military from the country. I have reason also to believe that Brigham Young himself received frequent couriers as well from his bishops as from the Indian chiefs, asking for advice and orders. What these latter were of course I am unable to judge, save from his character and the results which followed. It is in proof before me from reliable witnesses that the Indians, after the recent massacre on the overland road, retired through the Mormon towns rehearsing their exploits and exhibiting the reeking scalps they had taken from their murdered victims. It is likewise significant of Mormon complicity that the savages seldom or never molest the Mormons or steal their stock, but pass through their settlements and by their defenseless ranches content with the aid the Mormons volunteer to give them. It cannot be said in explanation of allowing the Indians to proceed on their bloody mission that the latter were too powerful to be attacked or resisted, for it is notorious that the hostile savages passed along in bands of a dozen or twenty through settlements of 500 or 600 inhabitants. The only explanation of this course on their part ever given is that the policy of the Mormons is and ever has been to feed rather than fight the Indians, and that to interfere with them when bound on their raids north would provoke massacre and pillage on the defenseless heads of isolated Mormon ranchmen and wood choppers in the canons. But even this furnishes no excuse, however flimsy, why no intimation was ever sent to these headquarters of Indian designs openly avowed and notorious in their several communities. In other communities where free will and independent action are at all tolerated on the part of individuals these facts might not be so significant, but might be laid at the door of a few evil-disposed and bad-hearted men; but here, where not only the actions, but the very thoughts, feelings, sentiments, and words of the entire people are under the supreme control and absolute dictation of the head of the Church, it is hard to resist the conclusion that he is responsible for the acts of his ignorant and deluded followers.

As in some degree explanatory of this insidious and damnable course on the part of Brigham Young, I may state that it is understood here that he has offered to protect the Overland Mail Line against the Indians for a given sum of money, on condition that the military shall be withdrawn; and to the end that the impotence of the latter may be made manifest, these brutal raids are incited along unprotected parts of the line, and at times when danger is not expected. That the presence of the military in this Territory is unwelcome to the hierarchy of Brigham Young cannot be doubted. It has to a great extent abridged his powers, limited his dictation, and secured protection to those whose persecutions cried aloud to Heaven. It has released from deepest bond age and from pillage, torture, and organized robbery hundreds of poor deluded men and women enticed hither by promises and allurements, and in many ways has tended to ameliorate the condition of his serfs, and to that extent has shorn the chief of his power. Hence his desire, by propositions such as that referred to, to have my command withdrawn. I may say that I have little doubt that Brigham Young could cause the Indians to desist from attacks on the Overland Mail Line, and were the protection of that institution the only or the main object of Government in establishing troops in this Territory, it might be well to accede to his wishes. But I cannot forget that unsuspecting emigrants with their wives and little ones, and all their earthly goods, seeking a peaceful home in the far West, would be entirely at the mercy of this man and his savage and plundering red allies. What that mercy was before the troops lined the emigrant road the sad record of the past too plainly tells, and the solitary graves and bleaching bones from the Rocky Mountains to the Carson and Humboldt partially reveal. The tales of horror, of bloodshed, and plunder one can hear, and the evidence of which he can see throughout all this desolate region awaken him to the fact that the great overland mail, important as it is to the East and to the West, cannot be regarded as the only care of the Government, or its protection and security the only demand on humanity.

In view of the foregoing facts, presented without conscious prejudice or other than just feeling against glaring iniquity, I beg leave most respectfully and earnestly to impress upon the commanding general that the force under my command is entirely inadequate to the protection of the overland mail and telegraph lines and the several emigrant roads passing through the regions of hostile Indians within this district; much less is it able in addition to cope with forcible resistance to the laws or the outbreak of armed treason liable to occur on any serious reverse to our arms in the East, or at any attempt on the part of the authorities to enforce laws conflicting with the tenets of the Mormon Church or inimical to any of their practices. The season will soon have passed when it will be practicable for re-enforcements to reach me, and with the winter will come increased activity on the part of the Indians, and it may be more open and rebellious conduct on the part of the Mormons. I have purposely refrained from any expression of opinion on the tenets of the religion of this most singular people, or their open and flagrant violations of the civil law for the suppression of polygamy, leaving these matters where they properly belong, with civil departments of Government.

Very respectfully, your obedient servant,

P. EDW. CONNOR,
Brigadier-General, U.S. Volunteers, Commanding District.

[Editor's note: *This document is referenced in* OR-225.]

SOURCE: *OR*, SERIES 1, VOLUME 50, PART 2, PAGES 492–495

OR-215

FORT RUBY, NEV. TER., *June 25, 1863.*

Capt. C. H. HEMPSTEAD,
Acting Assistant Adjutant-General, District of Utah:

CAPTAIN: I have the honor to inform the general commanding that I was told a day or two since of a letter written by a lady at Fort Crittenden to her husband, who is a blacksmith in the employ of the Overland Mail Company, from which some important information might be obtained. Last night I succeeded in finding the husband, and made the inclosed extract from the letter. I am informed that she is a woman of good character, perfectly reliable, and well known at Fort Crittenden and vicinity. Her husband, who is at the station at work, informs me that she will be happy to give you all the information she is possessed of, but desires that you will protect her. I have this day stopped a train of emigrants, mostly rebels, and a great many of them formerly soldiers in Price's army. They number 60 men, with 300 head of mules. As soon as I have investigated the matter I will report by letter.

Very respectfully, your obedient servant,

P. A. GALLAGHER,
Major Third California Volunteer Infantry, Commanding Post.

[Sub-Inclosure.]

[Editor's note: *This document appears in the* Official Records *as an inclosure to* OR-219. *The sub-inclosure is* OR-212.]

SOURCE: *OR*, SERIES 1, VOLUME 50, PART 2, PAGE 500

OR-216

FORT RUBY, NEV. TER., *June 26, 1863.*

Capt. C. H. HEMPSTEAD,

Acting Assistant Adjutant-General, District of Utah:

CAPTAIN: I have the honor to inform the* general commanding that on yesterday morning I stopped a train of emigrants passing through this valley, comprising sixty men, the most of whom, I was informed, were secessionists. After a close and thorough investigation I found that but eleven of them had been in Price's army in Missouri, and the balance very lukewarm toward the Government, the majority of whom were leaving the Eastern States to avoid the conscription. I learned enough of their action toward our men at Big Sandy and other places to have made it a very serious matter for them could I have fastened it upon them or any one of them, but I could not get the proof. The only one upon whom I could prove anything serious was a young man named John Dimmitt, from Ralls County, Mo., who while traveling along the Platte River pulled up a small American flag which had been planted on the bank of the river by some other emigrants, threw it under his feet, and trampled on it. This was sworn to by two men in the train, whose depositions I have. I have him in close confinement, and await the orders of the district commander as to what disposition shall be made of him. I found that all those who had been in the rebel army had either been exchanged or paroled, and had taken the oath of allegiance, and some had given bonds. Before releasing them I had them all drawn up in line beneath our flag and administered the oath to them in presence of the whole command. They were all badly frightened, evidently thinking that they had got themselves into a bad situation, and I think it will be a lesson to them that they will not soon forget.

Very respectfully, your obedient servant,

P. A. GALLAGHER,

Major Third Infantry California Volunteers, Commanding Post.

* Handwritten note in original text clarifying this is Connor.

SOURCE: *OR*, SERIES 1, VOLUME 50, PART 2, PAGES 495–496

OR-217

Headquarters Department of the Pacific,
San Francisco, June 27, 1863.

Brig. Gen. L. Thomas,
Adjutant-General U. S Army, Washington, D.C.:

General: The command of infantry and cavalry under Lieutenant-Colonel Moore, reported in my communication to you under date of 14th instant, reached Fort Churchill on the 25th, and after a brief halt will advance toward Salt Lake. The cavalry company recently stationed at Fort Churchill will be thrown in advance of Moore's command to Salt Lake, affording protection to the overland mail. One full company of Nevada Territory cavalry has been mustered into service at Fort Churchill, and another company will complete its organization at an early day. Brigadier-General Connor went to Fort Bridger in the early part of this month and was met by a large band of Shoshone Indians, with whom he made a treaty of peace and friendship; they surrendered a large number of horses and other property stolen or captured from white people. Notwithstanding the oft-repeated attacks on the overland stages by the Indians, yet it is believed that no serious interruption can take place. It requires great vigilance and activity to afford protection on a line of 600 or 800 miles in length, but it must be done, and the mail shall pass safely, even if I have to send a cavalry escort with every stage.

My advices from Brigadier-General Alvord are as late as the 14th instant; everything was progressing well in the District of Oregon. A satisfactory treaty has been made with the great Nez Percé tribe of Indians, and the troops under Colonel Maury, of the Oregon cavalry, had left Fort Lapwai for the summer campaign on the Upper Snake River to afford protection to the emigrants. The command under Major Lugenbeel left Fort Walla Walla on the 8th instant for Fort Boisé to establish a permanent post in that quarter. Inclosed here with is the report of Brigadier-General Connor of his expedition to Soda Springs, Idaho Ter., and the establishment of a post for the protection of emigrants and mail.* The report contains much valuable information as to the character and resources of the country traversed.

Very respectfully, your obedient servant,

G. WRIGHT,
Brigadier-General, U.S. Army, Commanding.

* [*Refers to* OR-201.]

Source: *OR*, Series 1, Volume 50, Part 2, pages 496–497

OR-218

JUNE 23, 1863.—Affair at Cañon Station, Nev. Ter.

Report of Maj. Patrick A. Gallagher, Third California Infantry.

FORT RUBY, NEV. TER., *June 28, 1863.*

CAPTAIN: Inclosed I have the honor to transmit corrected proceedings of garrison court. I would also inform the general commanding that on yesterday Assistant Surgeon Kirkpatrick returned to this post from Cañon Station with Private Abbot, of Company E, who was sounded at that place on the 23d instant. I learn from Abbott that on the morning of the 23d Corporal Hervey and himself left the station as a guard to the water cart. After they had left Privates Burgher and Elliott also left to go hunting, leaving the station unprotected, something which has not been done since the troops have been guarding the road. Between 11 and 12 A.M. as the water cart was returning they were fired upon by Indians, who had made a screen of sage bushes, and Corporal Hervey was shot dead. Private Abbott, although wounded by a ball through his neck, jumped out of the wagon and seized Hervey's gun and pistol, and returned the fire, as also did the driver of the water cart. He is confident that they hit three or four of them. This happened within about 500 yards of the station. They immediately drove there, thinking if the balance of the guard was there they might get some of the Indians, but found them gone. Soon after they saw two or three Indians going up the mountain south of the station, one of whom had a bright gun. Although they were upward of 1,200 yards off they fired at them, and from their actions immediately after think that one of them was hit. An express was immediately sent to Deep Creek, and eight of the cavalry left for the scene at once. On their arrival they found the body of Elliott with thirty-five ball holes in it, horribly mutilated, but not scalped. Soon after they found the body of Burgher with four ball holes in it, and in about the same condition as Elliott's. The bodies of all three were taken to Deep Creek and there buried under the supervision of Lieutenant Hosmer, who left his post immediately on the receipt of the news. The Indians succeeded in getting Burgher's musket and fifty rounds of ammunition; also a double-barreled shotgun and a small quantity of powder and shot from Elliott. I have ordered Lieutenant Quinn to scout in that vicinity, and if possible discover their place of concealment. I have also increased the infantry force along the road, sending every man that can be spared from the garrison. I feel perfectly satisfied that if Burgher and Elliott had not disobeyed orders and left the station they would not have been killed, but on the contrary would have had an opportunity of rendering a good account of some of the Indians, as they were within range of their pieces, and there were seventeen counted.

Very respectfully, your obedient servant,

P. A. GALLAGHER,
Major Third Infantry California Volunteers, Commanding Post.

Capt. C. H. HEMPSTEAD,
Acting Assistant Adjutant-General, District of Utah.

SOURCE: *OR*, SERIES 1, VOLUME 50, PART 1, PAGE 230

OR-219

HEADQUARTERS DISTRICT OF UTAH,
Great Salt Lake City, Utah Ter., June 28, 1863.

Lieut. Col. R. C. DRUM, U.S. Army,
Assistant Adjutant-General, San Francisco, Cal.:

COLONEL: I have the honor to inclose copies of letters this day received from Major Gallagher and Mrs. Phebe Westwood, relative to the conduct of the Indians who committed the recent raid on the Overland Mail Line, and of the reception of the latter by the authorities and people of the Mormon settlements at Salt Creek. I beg leave to invite the attention of the commanding general to the facts set forth, and ask that the papers inclosed be filed with my letter of 25th instant as bearing directly on the subjects therein discussed. The letter of Mrs. Westwood, I may add, is but corroborative of testimony reaching me from various sources, but as it comes in an authentic and concise shape it is forwarded for the information of the commanding general.

Very respectfully, your obedient servant,

P. EDW. CONNOR,
Brigadier-General, U.S. Volunteers, Commanding District.

[Inclosure.]

[Editor's note: *See* OR-215 *for this inclosure.*]

[Sub-Inclosure.]

[Editor's note: *See* OR-212 *for this sub-inclosure.*]

SOURCE: *OR*, SERIES 1, VOLUME 50, PART 2, PAGES 499–500

OR-220

HEADQUARTERS DISTRICT OF UTAH,
Great Salt Lake City, Utah Ter., June 29, 1863.

Lieut. Col. R. C. DRUM, U.S. Army,
Assistant Adjutant-General, San Francisco, Cal.:

COLONEL: I have the honor herewith to inclose copy of Special Orders, No. 1, dated Camp Connor, Idaho Ter., May 23, 1863, establishing that post.* As the commanding officer has omitted to comply entirely with paragraph III, General Orders, No. 18, current series, headquarters Department of the Pacific, I beg leave to inform the department commander that Camp Connor adjoins Soda Springs, Idaho Ter.; that the nearest post-office is Logan, Cache Valley, Utah Ter., distant about seventy miles, and the best route of communication is via Great Salt Lake City, through Cache Valley to Franklin, and thence crossing Bear River at Blair's Ferry, along the new military road, as set forth in my communication of the 2d instant.

I have the honor to remain, very respectfully, your obedient servant,

P. EDW. CONNOR,
Brigadier-General, U.S. Volunteers, Commanding District.

* [*Refers to Black's Special Orders No. 1, May 23, 1863.* OR, *Series 1, Volume 50, Part 2, page 453.*]

SOURCE: *OR*, SERIES 1, VOLUME 50, PART 2, PAGES 501–502

OR-221

HEADQUARTERS DISTRICT OF COLORADO,
Denver, Colo., June 30, 1863.

Maj. E. W. WYNKOOP,
Comdg. Indian Expedition on Overland Mail Route, Colorado:

SIR: In addition to the orders you have heretofore received, the colonel commanding directs me to say that he desires you to prohibit all persons whomsoever from accompanying your command except your officers, non-commissioned officers, and privates, who have been regularly detached as your command, the servants of officers, persons regularly employed in the quartermaster's and commissary departments, your guide, and such officers of other corps and personal friends as you may desire to accompany you; and it is particularly enjoined that no camp followers, except the regular sutler, be allowed to traffic with teamsters or soldiers, and no wagon-master, in the employ of the quartermaster's or commissary departments, will be allowed to trade with ranches, Indians, or soldiers, nor will wagon masters or others, in such employ, be allowed to take and keep with your command any animals of any kind whatever. And you will cause all persons accompanying your command, and in the employ of the quartermaster's and commissary departments, and your guides to take and subscribe to the accompanying oath of allegiance to the Government of the United States (marked A)* and you will promptly discharge all who hesitate in the least about taking said oath, taking their names and description, noting the fact that they would not willingly and cheerfully take the oath, and they will not hereafter be employed in any of the departments of this district.

You will proceed to Camp Collins, where you will be joined by Companies B and M, First Colorado Cavalry, and your command will be joined by Company I, First Colorado Cavalry, as soon as it can be fitted out for the field. With your command thus constituted, you will proceed west, on the Overland Stage Route, as far as Fort Bridger, and chastise any Indians who may have committed depredations on either the ranches or emigrants. You will not report your command for duty to General Connor, but will co-operate with him in any way that may be for the good of the service and the safety of settlers and travelers on the overland line, and especially for the security of the mail line to and from the Pacific States. You will report all to these headquarters.

The other interests of the district permitting, the colonel will join your command in about ten days, and in the mean time (and whether the colonel joins your command or not) he has full confidence that you will manage the expedition for the best interests of the service and the reputation, honor, and glory of the First Colorado Cavalry.

You will make a small detail in charge of a trusty non-commissioned officer, and leave them in charge of the Government property at Camp Collins.

With sentiments of the highest respect, your obedient servant,

S. S. SOULE,

First Lieut. First Colorado Cavalry, and Actg. Asst. Adjt. Gen.

P. S.—The administering the oath had better be delayed until you reach Camp Collins, for the reason that your train is now so scattered.

* Not found.

SOURCE: *OR*, SERIES 1, VOLUME 22, PART 2, PAGES 368–369

OR-222

Abstract from return of the Department of the Pacific, Brig. Gen. George Wright, U.S. Army, commanding, for June 30, 1863.

Command	Present for duty. Officers	Present for duty. Men	Aggregate present	Aggregate present and absent	Pieces of Artillery. Heavy	Pieces of Artillery. Field
General headquarters......	17	1	19	20	....	....
California*......	77	1,549	2,110	2,335	174	10
District of Oregon (Alvord)......	64	709	1,044	1,172	4	20
District of Humboldt (Whipple)......	27	262	416	545	....	1
District of Utah (Connor)......	42	920	1,195	1,037	....	9
District of Southern California (Curtis)	42	591	863	999	....	1
Total	259	4,032	5,647	6,378	178	41

* Including San Francisco, the Presidio, Fort Point, Alcatraz Island, Benicia Barracks and Arsenal, Fort Crook, Camp Union, and Camp Baker, Oreg.

Source: *OR*, Series 1, Volume 50, Part 2, page 505

OR-223

[*Extract*]

Organization of troops in the Department of the Pacific, Brig. Gen. George Wright, U.S. Army, commanding, June 30, 1863.

. . .

DISTRICT OF UTAH.
Brig. Gen. P. Edward Connor.

Camp Douglas, Utah Ter.
Col. Robert Pollock.
2d California Cavalry, Companies A and H,
3d California (four companies).

Fort Bridger, Utah Ter.
Capt. George F. Price.
2d California Cavalry, Company M,
3d California, Company I.

Fort Churchill, Nev. Ter.
Maj. Charles McDermit.
2d California Cavalry, Company L,
3d California, Company A,
1st Battalion Nevada Cavalry, Company B.

Camp Connor, Idaho Ter.
Capt. David Black.
3d California, Company H.

En Route.
3d California, Companies B and D,* Lieut. Col. Jeremiah B. Moore,
3d California, Company K,† Capt. John F. Staples.

* En route from Camp Union, Cal., to Camp Douglas, Utah Ter.
† En route from Camp Douglas to Fort Crittenden, Utah Ter.

Source: *OR*, Series 1, Volume 50, Part 2, page 507

OR-224

Fort Halleck, Idaho, *July 10, 1863*.

Colonel Chivington,
Commanding District of Colorado:

Sir: On the 24th of last month a band of Ute Indians, numbering 60, came near this post and sent a squad in to beg provisions, saying that they wanted to be friendly with the whites. They got provisions and left. On the 2d of this month they stole fourteen head of horses and mules from the mail company at Elk Mountain Station. I sent a party after them, but they could not be overtaken. On the 6th they took three horses from Cooper's Creek from the mail company. I started 70 men from this post, with Lieutenants [Henry] Brandley and [Hugh H.] Williams, at 1 o'clock on the morning of the 7th, to go in pursuit of a large party of Ute Indians who were reported about 30 miles from this place with the mail stock. After a hard ride of 30 miles, they came up with the Indians a short time after daylight. The Indians had got wind of them, and had run the stock through the pass and into the mountains, and when the troops came up they (the Indians) commenced firing upon them from the brush and timber, as they had made arrangements for a regular battle, having piled up stones on the side hill for breastworks. The troops answered the fire promptly, dismounted, and charged up the steep hill-side through the brush and timber, driving the Indians before them, who steadily fell back, contesting every foot of the ground until they were finally driven over the hill, when they broke and scattered through the mountains. The Indians poured down a perfect storm of bullets upon the troops, but their aim was too high, as they invariably shot over, a common fault in shooting down hill; had they not shot over they would have annihilated the troops, for there were nearly 300 Indians, and the fight lasted two hours. We had 5 men wounded. Sergeant [S. N.] Waugh has since died; was shot through the body. One of the others is badly wounded. We have got information from what is considered a reliable source that the Indians lost over 60 killed and wounded; over 20 killed on the field. When the Indians broke and scattered, the troops were firing their last round of cartridges, and, not having any ammunition, were obliged to return to the post, after eating breakfast on the battle-field.

There is supposed to be about 1,000 of these Salt Lake Utes in this vicinity, and they are making great threats of revenging the loss of their braves killed on the 7th, and every night some depredation is committed on the mail stations. On the 8th, four head of mules were taken from the mail station at Rock Creek, and one horse killed had three arrows in him. On the 9th, two mules were taken from Medicine Bow Station and the station plundered. It is absolutely necessary that more troops be stationed in this vicinity to protect the mail line. I can get none at Fort Laramie. There should be another company at this post, and one company west of here, say at the Platte, also one at Cooper's Creek or Laramie River. If you could send troops for a short time they would do much good. Colonel Collins is on the road with 600 troops for this part of the country.

I am, very respectfully, your obedient servant,

A. ALLEN,
Captain Ninth Kansas Volunteer Cavalry.

P. S.—Both officers and men deserve great credit for the bravery shown in the fight.

SOURCE: *OR*, SERIES 1, VOLUME 22, PART 2, PAGES 362–363

OR-225

HEADQUARTERS DEPARTMENT OF THE PACIFIC,
San Francisco, Cal., July 10, 1863.

Brig. Gen. L. THOMAS,
Adjutant-General U.S. Army, Washington, D.C.:

GENERAL: For the information of the General-in-Chief and War Department, I have the honor to inclose herewith a communication addressed to my headquarters by Brig. Gen. P. E. Connor, commanding the District of Utah, dated at Great Salt Lake City, June 24, 1863.* The condition of affairs in Utah and the civil polity which prevails under the supreme authority of Brigham Young, the head of the Mormon Church, is clearly set forth in the report of General Connor. At the request of the general I forward this report to general headquarters, although the facts are doubtless well known at the War Department. In connection with the request for re-enforcements, I have to report that the command which marched from Sacramento, as reported in my letter to you dated on the 14th of June, is already in advance of Fort Churchill, on its way to Salt Lake. The company of the Second Cavalry and the company of the Third Infantry, lately stationed at Churchill, have also been ordered to proceed at once to Salt Lake. The acting Governor of Nevada Territory informs me that he finds it impossible to raise infantry companies in that mining region, but feels confident of being able to raise two more companies of cavalry, if I would accept them. I have answered in the affirmative, that I would accept them on the same conditions as the others; that is, they are to furnish their own horses and equipments.

Very respectfully, your obedient servant,

G. WRIGHT,
Brigadier-General, U.S. Army, Commanding.

* [*Refers to* OR-214.]

SOURCE: *OR*, SERIES 1, VOLUME 50, PART 2, PAGE 516

OR-226

HEADQUARTERS DEPARTMENT OF THE PACIFIC,
San Francisco, Cal., July 11, 1863.

Brig. Gen. P. EDWARD CONNOR, U.S. Volunteers,
Commanding District of Utah, Salt Lake City, Utah Ter.:

GENERAL: I am instructed by the general commanding the department that your order relating to the disloyal element coming to this department is approved. The condition of affairs on this coast, and the immense effort now being made by the enemies of our Government to detach us therefrom, require the greatest watchfulness on the part of officers. The general is exceedingly gratified at your prompt action in this matter.

Very respectfully, your obedient servant,

R. C. DRUM,
Assistant Adjutant-General.

SOURCE: *OR*, SERIES 1, VOLUME 50, PART 2, PAGE 519

OR-227

HEADQUARTERS DISTRICT OF UTAH,
Great Salt Lake City, Utah Ter., July 18, 1863.

Lieut. Col. R. C. DRUM, U.S. Army,
Assistant Adjutant-General, San Francisco, Cal.:

COLONEL: I have the honor to inform the general commanding the department that a short time since I received overtures from the several chiefs of the tribe of Indians known as the Southern Utes, recently hostile, asking a suspension of hostilities and desiring peace. The inadequacy of my command rendered it impracticable to administer to them more severe punishment than had already been inflicted, and for this reason, as well as from motives of prudence and humanity, I responded favorably to the overtures and appointed Tuesday, the 14th of July, and Spanish Fork Reservation as the time and place of conference with all who chose to avail themselves of the opportunity offered. Banners were dispatched in various directions, as well by the Indians as by me, and the several bands of the hostile tribe notified of the time, place, and object of meeting. I may here remark that some weeks previously I had in like manner induced the band of Utes under the lead of the chief Little Soldier to come in and hold a conference with me, and that a satisfactory understanding was arrived at between us. Little Soldier delivered up all the Government stock in his hands, and received from me the Indian ponies, thirteen in number, captured at Spanish Fork last April. After consultation with Governor Doty, acting superintendent of Indian affairs, this band was located in the valley of the West Mountain, about twenty-five miles west of this city, and proper measures taken by the superintendent to provide for their immediate wants. The kindly treatment bestowed on Little Soldier and his band on the first indication of a desire for peace on their part unquestionably had a good effect on the remainder of the tribe, who had been repeatedly assured by the Mormons that I intended to entice them in and wage a war of extermination upon them, whether they wished for peace or not.

One of the results of the treaty with Little Soldier was the overtures of the balance of the chiefs above referred to. Accordingly, on the 10th instant, accompanied by Governor Doty, my staff, and an escort of twenty men of Company A, Second California Volunteer Cavalry, I left this city for Spanish Fork Reservation, distant about sixty miles south in Utah Valley. Halting at Springville, a few miles north of the old reservation, I ascertained that between 600 and 700 Indians, under their several chiefs, were encamped not far off in Spanish Fork Cañon. They were much alarmed at the display of cavalry, so great has become their dread of the soldiers and so persistent the efforts of bad white men to convince them that I was acting treacherously with them. Prompt assurances of good faith on my part moderated their fears, and the following morning, Tuesday, the 14th, we proceeded to the farm house on the old reservation. In due time the chiefs, accompanied by their warriors, well armed and mounted, made their appearance and cautiously approached. Everything consistent with propriety and dignity was done to allay their fears and suspicions, and after some time the effort succeeded. The chiefs, surrounded by their warriors, assembled in front of the house, and there I briefly addressed them, through an interpreter. The chiefs present comprised the leading men of the tribe and representatives from every band of the Utes heretofore hostile. Of the chiefs of separate bands who took part in the conference I may mention Antero, Tabby, Canosh, Ute-Pete, Au-ke-wah-kus, and Black Hawk. My address was brief, assuring them that as they desired peace I was there to grant it on proper terms; that the Government wished to protect all good Indians, and was equally determined and able to severely punish all bad ones. I sought to disabuse their minds of the idea so industriously circulated among them that I wanted to exterminate or fight them, at the same time giving them to understand my entire readiness and ability to punish every hostile act. At the conclusion of my speech Governor Doty addressed the tribe, reiterated what I had said, and told them it was his duty and pleasure to provide for their immediate wants. He distributed presents among them, including tobacco, ten beef-cattle, and fifty sacks of flour. The chiefs then, one after the other, responded, expressing regret for past bad acts and their hearty desire for peace. To this they pledged themselves and their several bands. The conference and treaty closed most satisfactorily, and the Indians departed for their encampment well pleased with the result. I am satisfied that the happiest results will follow; that the Utes are heartily tired of war, and will be the last to break the peace and again inaugurate the troubles recently visited upon them by our troops. Every leading chief of the tribe, except San Pitch, was present. The latter is very sick and unable to travel, but sent word that he would abide by the treaty and desired peace.

The range of this tribe is from Deep Creek, on the west, to Fort Bridger, on the east, and mainly south of and along the stage line, so that this treaty effectually relieves any apprehension along the line between the points named. To the north is the Snake or Shoshone tribe. With these I formed a treaty at Bridger on the 5th of June, as stated in my communication of the 15th ultimo. The several bands have been once more united under the chieftainship of the peaceful Wa-shakee, and are living in quiet contentment near Bridger, under the charge and guardianship of the Indian Department. Since the date of the Snake treaty I have received a message from Pocatello, the celebrated Snake chief, begging for peace and asking for a conference. He says he is tired of war, and has been effectually driven from the Territory with a small remnant of his once powerful band. He now sues for peace, and having responded favorably to his request I will meet him at an early day, and will conclude with him what I have no doubt will prove a lasting peace. Thus at last I have the pleasure to report peace with the Indian on all hands, save only a few hostile Goshutes west and north of Deep Creek. These cannot number more than 100 braves, and I have dispatched two companies of the Second Cavalry under Capt. S. P. Smith, who will scour the entire surrounding country and kill or drive off the last remaining hostile band. I have little doubt that on hearing of the treaty made with the Utes the Goshutes, at least those who escape Captain Smith, will sue for peace. I may therefore confidently report the end of Indian difficulties on the Overland Stage Line and within this district, from the Snake River, on the north, to Arizona, on the south, and from Green River to Carson Valley.

Having thus concluded the main, if not the only special, duty assigned me and the brave, hardy troops under my command, under circumstances far from propitious, and difficulties impossible to be fully under stood at a distance, I beg leave at this, an appropriate time, respectfully to lay my views before the general commanding as to future operations. As heretofore frequently represented, the forces under my command are too meager in numbers to accomplish much more than guard the stage road from hostile Indians, and even for this purpose they are scarcely adequate when there is a general uprising of the savages along its entire length, as was recently the case. This trouble, however, I am well satisfied is now at an end. The punishment administered to the Indians and the hardships endured by them in consequence of our war upon them during the winter and spring have made them heartily and sincerely desirous of continued peace. Without the most criminal conduct on the part of bad white men no apprehension need be entertained of future trouble with either the Snake or Ute tribe. For any other purpose than suppressing Indian difficulties the force at my command is manifestly and ridiculously inadequate, and its presence here, no matter how circumspect and prudent we may be, is necessarily but a source of irritation to a people who regard us as trespassers and enemies no less than as armed representatives of a Government they have always hated, and which I fear they are now learning to despise. If it be the intention of the Government to take hold of the Mormon question with a strong hand, suppress the evil deeds of this peculiar people, and enforce the laws of the land upon an unwilling and hostile community, it can only be done by promptly and materially re-enforcing the command now in this district; but I am constrained to believe that for reasons which I have no doubt properly commend themselves to the authorities at Washington, such is not the present intention of the Government. This being the case, and in view of the peaceful condition of Indian affairs in this Territory, I beg leave respectfully to suggest the propriety and advisability of withdrawing the California Volunteers from this district to California, where I cannot but believe, their services may be required, and where they certainly can be more useful to Government than to remain in garrison here. I am sure that under existing circumstances our presence in this Territory is a source of annoyance to the people, of constant complaint and alarm, of jealousy and apprehension, which are liable at any moment to break out in open hostility and unfortunate collision, beyond the control of human power. Unable as we are effectually to overawe or suppress continued exhibitions of enmity and hatred, and violation of law, our feebleness to cope successfully with the Mormons being as well known to them as to ourselves, the presence of our small force here but tends to irritate and provoke those difficulties which it is certainly desirable to avoid until the Government shall be prepared to assume other relations toward the people of this Territory and the autocrat of the Church. I have already had the honor to inform the commanding general of the fact that there are now crossing the plains an immense emigration, four-fifths of whom are loudly and notoriously disloyal to the Government and bent on the destruction of the Union, if their voices or deeds can accomplish it. I am convinced that not less than 15,000 or 20,000 traitors will this year cross the continent and become incorporated in the population of California and Oregon. The measures taken by me to meet the exigencies have also been reported, but it is apparent that administering the oath of allegiance has but little restraining effect, being but lightly regarded by men who have so fallen from their high estate as American citizens as to lose all respect for the Government of their fathers and regard for the institutions of their country.

In the language of your favor of the 11th instant, this day received, I am satisfied that the condition of affairs on this (Pacific) coast, and the immense effort now being made by the enemies of our Government to detach us therefrom, requires the greatest watchfulness on the part of officers, and when I see each day so many disloyal men seeking the West to add their strength to the already emboldened body of traitors in California, I not only appreciate the impolicy of sending re-enforcements hither, but rather the propriety of recalling the California quota in this district, where now they are not needed. It is unnecessary for me to refer to what is manifestly each day transpiring in California the increasing boldness and defiant attitude of disloyal men assembled under cover of party names, or the manifold evidences of treason able sentiments all around you, for the commanding general must be better possessed of such knowledge than I possibly can be; but in the present state of affairs there and here I have esteemed it my duty to set forth the facts of the case in this district and tender the suggestion herein contained. Should it meet the approval of the general I would also suggest that the four companies of Nevada cavalry now being raised would be ample to guard the stage and telegraph lines in this district and protect public property within the Territory, while at the same time they would not be a source of alarm and irritation to the strange people of Utah. In connection with the foregoing I may say that the California column in this Territory can safely take up its line of march as late as the 15th of September and reach California in fifty days. Their experience, soldierly bearing, and excellent quality, eminently fit them for service either in California or wherever the country needs patriotic hearts, and willing stalwart arms. While writing this letter another message from Pocatello has reached me suing for peace, offering to treat on my own terms, and proposing to meet me at Brigham City, sixty-eight miles north of here, on the 30th instant. He also says that the Bannocks, with whom he and his band have lately been ranging, and who frequent Snake River and the sources of the Humboldt, are also desirous of making a treaty, and some of their chiefs will accompany him.

I have the honor to remain, very respectfully, your obedient servant,

P. EDW. CONNOR,

Brigadier-General, U.S. Volunteers, Commanding District.

[Editor's note: *This document is referenced in OR-230.*]

SOURCE: *OR*, SERIES 1, VOLUME 50, PART 2, PAGES 527–531

OR-228

[*Extract*]

HEADQUARTERS NAVAJO EXPEDITION,
Camp at Pueblo Colorado, N. Mex., July 24, 1863.

SIR: I have the honor to report that in obedience to General Orders, No. 15, current series, Headquarters Department of New Mexico, I left camp near Los Lunas, N. Mex., July 7, 1863, en route to Pueblo Colorado, N. Mex., with Companies D, K, L, and M, First New Mexico Volunteers, the only companies of the expedition which had arrived at the place of rendezvous up to that time.

. . .

I arrived with my command at Fort Defiance on the 20th instant, where I found a large quantity of wheat, say 100,000 pounds, which was also fed to the public animals. The Utah Indians had preceded us on this day's march; killed 1 man (Navajo), and captured 20 sheep.

Shortly after encamping, I was joined by 19 Ute warriors, who had been operating against the Navajoes on their own account. They report having met a party of Utes returning to their country, having 11 captives, women and children; and that there are two other parties now in this country; they themselves saw no Navajoes. I have hired 5 of this party as spies. I remained at Fort Defiance on the 21st. On the 22d I left for this place with the board appointed to select a site for Fort Canby, taking with me the field and staff, and 70 men of the command, and the Ute Indians. About one-third the distance from Defiance, I left the command and pushed on with the Utes. When about 9 miles from this point, and on the Kio de Pueblo Colorado, we came on a small party of Navajoes, and killed 3 men. From a Pah-Ute woman captured, I ascertained that a strong party of Navajoes, with a large herd of sheep, cattle, and horses, were at a pond of water about 35 miles west of here, and would remain there all night. I immediately determined to pursue them with the command as soon as possible after its arrival.

It reached here about 5 P.M., and at 7.30 P.M. I started. At 5 o'clock next morning, 23d, I arrived at the water only to find that the Navajoes with their stock had left the previous evening. I followed their trail for two hours, and until many of the horses had given out, and only returned on my own conviction, supported by the superior knowledge of Kan-a-at-sa, that it would be impossible to overtake them without having to travel some 90 miles without water, and this my horses could not do.

On my return route, the Ute Indians killed 8 Navajoes, making a total of 12 killed since my arrival in this country.

I arrived at this place with the party yesterday evening at 5 o'clock, having been nearly thirty-six hours continuously in the saddle. The remainder of the command left behind at Fort Defiance arrived here yesterday at 4 o'clock in the afternoon, also Captain Carey and Lieutenant Cook.

I would respectfully call the attention of the general commanding the department to the valuable services rendered by the Ute Indians, and earnestly request that I may be authorized to send an officer to their country to employ at least 30 more Utes as spies for the expedition.

I am, sir, very respectfully, your obedient servant,

C. CARSON,

Colonel First New Mexico Vols., Comdg. Navajo Expedition.

ASSISTANT ADJUTANT-GENERAL,

Headquarters Department of New Mexico, Santa Fé, N. Mex.

[Editor's note: *This document appears in the* Official Records *as an inclosure to correspondence from Brigadier-General James H. Carleton to Brigadier-General Lorenzo Thomas, September 5, 1863, that is not included in this volume.*]

SOURCE: *OR*, SERIES 1, VOLUME 26, PART 1, PAGES 233–234

OR-229

BOX ELDER, UTAH TER., *July 30, 1863*

OFFICER COMDG. THE TROOPS OF THE UNITED STATES
AT FORT BOISÉ AND IN THE SNAKE RIVER COUNTRY:

A treaty of peace was this day concluded at this place by General Connor and myself with the bands of the Shoshones, of which Pocatello, San Pitch, and Sagwich are the principal chiefs. This information is given that these Shoshones may not be injured when met by the troops, if they are at the time behaving themselves well. A treaty of peace has also been entered into at Fort Bridger with other bands of the Shoshones, and it is understood that all of that nation are at peace with the United States and are under a pledge to remain friendly.

JAMES DUANE DOTY,

Commander and Governor of Utah Territory.

[Editor's note: *This document appears in the* Official Records *as an inclosure to OR-235.*]

SOURCE: *OR*, SERIES 1, VOLUME 50, PART 1, PAGES 219–220

OR-230

HEADQUARTERS DEPARTMENT OF THE PACIFIC,
San Francisco, July 31, 1863.

ADJUTANT-GENERAL U.S. ARMY,
Washington, D.C.:

SIR: I have the honor to inclose herewith, for the consideration of the General-in-Chief and War Department, a communication addressed to my headquarters by Brig. Gen. P. E. Connor, commanding the District of Utah, dated at Great Salt Lake City, July 18, 1863.* The different tribes of Indians living within the District of Utah appear anxious for peace. Most of them have already made treaties of peace with General Connor, and I am sure that with the re-enforcements I have sent forward the Overland Mail Route will be perfectly safe. I have been for some time considering as to the propriety of removing the troops from the immediate vicinity of Great Salt Lake City to the old position at Camp Floyd. Supplies are more easily obtained at the latter place, and it would obviate the irritations and complaints which are constantly arising between the soldiers and citizens. I have written to Governor Doty and General Connor on this subject, and should I decide to remove the troops to Camp Floyd I propose to establish the headquarters of the district in Great Salt Lake City. I shall not withdraw the troops from Utah. The presence of the force now there is indispensable for the protection of the Overland Mail Route and the general safety of the country. I have troops enough in California for present wants. Should it become necessary to use force to preserve the peace and quiet of this State we have plenty of loyal Union-loving men and arms in abundance to meet the crisis.

With great respect, your most obedient servant,

G. WRIGHT,
Brigadier-General, U.S. Army, Commanding.

* [*Refers to* OR-227.]

SOURCE: *OR*, SERIES 1, VOLUME 50, PART 2, PAGES 545–546

OR-231

SALT LAKE, *July 31, 1863—7:35 P.M.*

Col. R. C. DRUM:

Made treaty with remaining bands of Snake Indians yesterday. Muster-rolls have already been forwarded.

P. E. CONNOR,
Brigadier-General.

SOURCE: *OR*, SERIES 1, VOLUME 50, PART 2, PAGE 547

OR-232

HEADQUARTERS DEPARTMENT OF THE PACIFIC,
San Francisco, Cal., July 31, 1863.

Brig. Gen. P. E. CONNOR, U.S. Volunteers,
Commanding District of Utah, Salt Lake City, Utah Ter.:

GENERAL: The department commander has it in contemplation to reoccupy Fort or Camp Crittenden as the principal military post in the District of Utah. Several considerations have induced the general to believe that that is the most eligible position for the mass of the troops, both for the protection of the overland route, which is the principal object of the Government in sending a force into Utah, and giving general security to persons and property therein. The general desires you to make immediate preparations to this end, ascertaining through disinterested parties at what the buildings, &c., could possibly be obtained and when possession could be given. Should the terms be reasonable and no objection existing, Lieutenant-Colonel Moore's command will halt at Camp Crittenden and retain possession. The change of camp will not affect the district headquarters, which will still remain in Salt Lake City, should you so desire it. You will advise the general by telegraph, if you think necessary, at what price the property can be obtained and when the command at Camp Douglas can be moved to Camp Crittenden.

Very respectfully, your obedient servant,

R. C. DRUM,
Assistant Adjutant-General.

SOURCE: *OR*, SERIES 1, VOLUME 50, PART 2, PAGES 547–548

OR-233

[*Extract*]

HDQRS. EXPEDITION AGAINST THE SNAKE INDIANS,
Camp No. 33, Camas Prairie, Idaho Ter., August 4, 1863.

His Excellency Governor GIBBS,
Portland, Oreg.:

GOVERNOR:

. . .

The emigrants say the Indians (there being from 700 to 900 collected at Fort Hall) are very much frightened, and those going east are doing so for the ostensible purpose of effecting a treaty with General Connor. I would judge that from 1,000 to 2,000 have been in the habit of living in this valley, with a good, large quantity of stock. If Connor treats and keeps them in Utah it will be a good thing for Idaho. If he treats and they return here without military to look after them it will be merely a postponement of difficulties. They appear to have been well advised of our movements and objects, deserting the valley and vicinity entirely some three or four weeks previous to our arrival. I have had scouting parties out in every direction for thirty or forty miles without finding a single Indian.

. . .

The emigration of last season passed this camp about the last of July, and this season, from the mildness of last winter, was much earlier than last. They are generally in good health and well supplied.

Very respectfully, your obedient servant,

R. F. MAURY,
Colonel First Oregon Cavalry, Commanding.

SOURCE: *OR*, SERIES 1, VOLUME 50, PART 2, PAGE 555

OR-234

GREAT SALT LAKE CITY, *August 9, 1863.*

GENERAL: I have the pleasure to acknowledge your letter dated July 31, which came here while I was on a visit to some of the Goshute tribe in Tooele Valley, who are suing for peace protest that they are friendly to the whites and are afraid the soldiers will kill them. This is the condition in which I desire to see all the tribes in this Territory. They now realize the fact that the Americans are the masters of this country, and it is my purpose to make them continue to feel and to acknowledge it. Without this there can be no permanent peace here and no security upon the routes of travel. This has been mainly accomplished by the vigor and bravery of the troops under your command. The continued occupation of the posts at Soda Springs, Fort Bridger, and Ruby I deem indispensable, and that frequent excursions be made by the cavalry along the roads east and west of these points and north and south of this place. Your troops have displaced the Mormon power over these Indians, and it is of great importance to Government at this moment that it be kept where it is for a year or two at least. This city is the seat of all power in this country, and the only point from which the authority of the Government over the Indians or people can be, I think, successfully maintained. But it is only in case of hostilities by the Indians or open resistance to the laws and the judiciary that the soldiery can be usefully employed here. At present there appears to be no danger of a collision between the troops at Camp Douglas and the inhabitants of this town. Several of our most respected citizens were apprehensive at one time that seizures of citizens would be attempted without due authority, but it is now believed their fears were groundless, or if not, that the crisis has passed, and the inhabitants and troops are now associating together upon the most friendly terms. There are reasons which cannot now be given why it is supposed Brigham Young does not desire the presence of troops either here or at any place in the Territory; but I think it would be a detriment to the public service if this post should be abandoned at present, and until there shall appear a manifest occasion for it. If a collision occurs between the civil officers of the United States and the Mormons this is the place where it must occur, and where those officers will require instant protection and assistance. I presume you are aware that a military organization exists among these people in this city and in every settlement, which, it is understood, is provided expressly to be used to maintain the Mormon authority whenever it shall conflict with that of the United States. While I do not think such a conflict is likely now to occur, yet prudence and duty require that we should be prepared for it at the right point. The sword is not the weapon, as I conceive, with which to correct errors of either morals or religion, and I am sure, general, that you no more than myself would wish to see it so employed; but it may well be used to resist the attacks of fanatics upon the constituted authorities of our country engaged in the performance of their duty. This, like all other governments in the United States, is a government of the people, and should be administered for their benefit. This is no more than is required by the people of every State. I have perhaps written in reply to your request with greater freedom on this subject than you desire, but it is one of much importance to this people and to the Government of the United States. Whilst I would most earnestly recommend additional troops at Soda Springs, Fort Bridger, and a new post in Uintah Valley, where the Ute Indians are to be collected and settled, I do not think the force at this point should be increased or diminished at this time. The favorable sentiments you express in regard to myself are very gratifying and much esteemed. I was fully aware of the difficulties of the position by the fate of my predecessors and the knowledge acquired during my residence here. Many of those difficulties arise from the mistaken notion that the interests of this people and those of the Government are at variance. I think they are not, and that they may possibly become reconciled by one who seeks for peace, which is, as heretofore, my mission.

I remain, with great regard, general, your obedient servant,

JAMES DUANE DOTY.

[Editor's note: *This document appears in the* Official Records *as an inclosure to OR-239.*]

SOURCE: *OR*, SERIES 1, VOLUME 50, PART 2, PAGES 583–584

OR-235

HEADQUARTERS EXPEDITION AGAINST SNAKE INDIANS,
Camp No. 39, on Lost River, Idaho Ter., August 15, 1863.

SIR: I have the honor to transmit herewith copy of a letter this day received from Governor Doty, of Utah Territory. My command will be at the ferry above Fort Hall day after to-morrow. The distance from here is said to be fifty-two miles, forty of which is entirely destitute of water. I have received no tidings of Captain Crawford's command.

Very respectfully, your obedient servant,

R. F. MAURY,
Colonel First Cavalry Oregon Volunteers, Commanding.

ACTING ASSISTANT ADJUTANT-GENERAL,
Headquarters District of Oregon, Fort Vancouver, Wash. Ter.

[Inclosure.]

[Editor's note: *See OR-229 for this inclosure.*]

SOURCE: *OR*, SERIES 1, VOLUME 50, PART 1, PAGE 219

OR-236

Hdqrs. Department of the Pacific,
San Francisco, Cal., August 18, 1863.

Special Orders,
No. 193.

3. Maj. Edward McGarry, Second Cavalry California Volunteers, will proceed without delay to Camp Douglas, near Salt Lake City. The quartermaster's department will furnish the necessary transportation.

By order of Brigadier-General Wright:

RICHD. C. DRUM,
Assistant Adjutant-General.

Source: *OR*, Series 1, Volume 50, Part 2, page 578

OR-237

[*Extract*]

Headquarters District of Oregon,
Fort Vancouver, Wash. Ter., August 18, 1863.

Assistant Adjutant-General,
Hdqrs. Department of the Pacific, San Francisco, Cal.:

Colonel: I have the honor to report, for the information of the general commanding the department, that Maj. P. Lugenbeel, Nineteenth U.S. Infantry, commanding expedition to Boisé, has located the new military post of Fort Boisé. The site selected is on a small creek one mile and a quarter from Boisé River, on the north side, forty-three miles from its confluence with the Snake River, and 250 miles from Fort Walla Walla. Many of the roads through that country run near it; those from the eastern States, Salt Lake, and Washington Territory in sight. Some difficulty is experienced in building the post in consequence of the low rates of legal-tender notes. In that country they bear merely a nominal value. The depreciation of the Government currency not only embarrasses the quartermaster's department, but also tends greatly to disaffect the men. The difference between their pay and the promises held out by the richest mines perhaps on the coast (the proximity of which makes them all the more tempting) is so great that many desertions occur.

. . .

I am, very respectfully, your obedient servant,

BENJ. ALVORD,
Brigadier-General, U.S. Volunteers, Commanding District.

SOURCE: *OR*, SERIES 1, VOLUME 50, PART 2, PAGES 579–580

OR-238

HEADQUARTERS DEPARTMENT OF THE PACIFIC,
San Francisco, Cal., August 19, 1863.

Brig. Gen. P. E. CONNOR, U.S. Volunteers,
Commanding District of Utah, Salt Lake City, Utah Ter.:

GENERAL: The instructions from these headquarters relative to changing the position occupied by your command from Camp Douglas to Camp Crittenden, and directing the movement of Lieutenant-Colonel Moore's command, are modified by the general commanding to the extent that if, in your judgment, the withdrawal of the troops from Camp Douglas would produce an impression on the minds of the Mormons that the removal was in consequence of disapprobation of your course while in command, or in any manner injurious to the interests of the Government, you will retain Camp Douglas as your principal station. Believing that it would be well to reoccupy Camp Crittenden now or at some future day, the general desires you to ascertain at what price it can be purchased, and if the sum asked is small you can purchase and use it for such purposes as may be deemed necessary.

Respectfully, your obedient servant,

R. C. DRUM,
Assistant Adjutant-General.

SOURCE: *OR*, SERIES 1, VOLUME 50, PART 2, PAGE 581

OR-239

HEADQUARTERS DEPARTMENT OF THE PACIFIC,
San Francisco, August 20, 1863.

ADJUTANT-GENERAL U.S. ARMY,
Washington, D.C.:

SIR: I have the honor to inclose herewith a communication addressed to me by His Excellency James D. Doty, Governor of the Territory of Utah. It will doubtless be gratifying to the General-in-Chief and War Department to learn that the Indian difficulties in the Territory have been brought at last to a happy termination, and that a good feeling exists between the troops and inhabitants, promising peace and quiet in the country. In my communication addressed to you on the 31st of July I advised you that I had under consideration the propriety of removing the troops from the immediate vicinity of Great Salt Lake City to the old position of Fort Crittenden, but previous to the receipt of the Governor's letter I had determined to maintain our present station at Camp Douglas. Two full companies of Nevada Territory cavalry now at Fort Churchill will move in a few days toward Salt Lake. The condition of affairs in California remains unchanged. The near approach of the general election for State and Federal officers creates some excitement in the public mind, but no apprehensions of any serious disturbances are entertained. The election is a very important one, as it fixes the status of the State for the next four years. I have no doubt the Union party will carry the State by an overwhelming majority. The superintendent of Indian affairs for the Southern District of California having removed all the Indians (1,000 in number) from Owen's River Valley to the reservation near Fort Tejon, I have reoccupied that post with a squadron of cavalry. I have also sent three companies of the Second Infantry California Volunteers, with the headquarters of the regiment, to reoccupy Fort Miller, in Fresno County. In Fresno, as well as in the adjoining county of Tulare, there is a large element of disloyalty, and the presence of troops in that quarter is indispensably necessary, at least until after the election. Some Indian difficulties in Butte County, east of the Sacramento River, made it necessary to send a force there. Lieutenant-Colonel Hooker, Sixth Infantry California Volunteers, with two companies of infantry and a detachment of cavalry, has been ordered up to remove the Indians, as well as to look after certain of the disaffected whites. I have nothing special to report of Southern California. With my troops at San Pedro, Los Angeles, San Bernardino, Yuma, and San Diego, peace, quiet, and respect for the laws will be maintained. In the District of Oregon quiet prevails. The new post on the Boisé River is being built as rapidly as circumstances will permit. The cavalry under Colonel Maury, Oregon volunteers, now on the emigrant road, will fall back late in the fall, and owing to the scarcity of forage at Boisé will winter at Fort Walla Walla.

Very respectfully, your obedient servant,

G. WRIGHT,
Brigadier-General, U.S. Army, Commanding.

[Inclosure.]

[Editor's note: *See* OR-*234 for this inclosure.*]

SOURCE: *OR*, SERIES 1, VOLUME 50, PART 2, PAGES 582–583

OR-240

[*Extract*]

HDQRS. DEPARTMENT OF THE PACIFIC,
San Francisco, Cal., August 20, 1863

SPECIAL ORDERS,
No. 195.

* * * *

5. The District of Utah will include the Territory of Utah, Camp Ruby, Nev. Ter., and the new post established at Soda Springs, in the Territory of Idaho.

By order of Brigadier-General Wright:

RICHD. C. DRUM,
Assistant Adjutant-General.

SOURCE: *OR*, SERIES 1, VOLUME 50, PART 2, PAGES 584–585

OR-241

HDQRS. EXPEDITION AGAINST THE SNAKE INDIANS,
Camp on Port Neuf River, August 23, 1863.

Brig. Gen. P. EDWARD CONNOR,
Commanding District of Utah, Great Salt Lake City, Utah Ter.:

GENERAL: I have the honor to acknowledge the receipt of yours dated August 1. I had received one of same date and tenor from Governor Doty while en route to this camp. There are no Indians on the north side of Snake River between this and Fort Boisé. The emigration thus far has gone through without trouble or interruption from any source. The Bannock Indians referred to by you I find encamped near old Fort Hall. They express great desire to be at peace. I have no authority to treat with them, but have adopted your suggestions with regard to them. Most all the Indians that live northwest of Salt Lake visit the country known as the camas grounds, and remain in that vicinity till the salmon or fishing season commences, and I fear unless they are collected and settled, and a supervisory control exercised, that difficulties will recur on their periodical visits for the purpose of gathering roots, as mining parties are scattered through the country generally, and frequently offering great temptation for them to steal, and not unfrequently committing aggressions, which induce retaliation and war. I hope to find on the south side of Snake River on my return to Fort Walla Walla the remaining portions of what are known as the Shoshone or Snake Indians, and to be able to inflict such punishment as their crimes deserve. They are, I think, on the headwaters of the streams which enter Snake River below the Salmon Falls. I will remain in this camp for several days, awaiting the arrival (if there is any more) of the rear of emigration for Oregon and Washington.

Very respectfully, your obedient servant,

R. F. MAURY,
Colonel First Oregon Cavalry, Commanding.

SOURCE: *OR*, SERIES 1, VOLUME 50, PART 2, PAGE 588

OR-242

HDQRS. EXPEDITION AGAINST THE SNAKE INDIANS,
Camp No. 42, Near Fort Hall, Idaho Ter., August 24, 1863.

GENERAL: I have the honor to inform you that my command arrived at this camp in good health and condition on the 18th instant, having marched a distance of 170 miles from our depot in Camas Prairie, which we left on the 9th instant. Our present camp is on the Port Neuf River, about four miles from Fort Hall and about eighteen miles below the ferry across Snake River, at the mouth of Blackfoot Creek. After leaving Camas Prairie and the adjacent valleys, many of which are of good size and present every appearance of fertility, there is no country offering any inducement for settlement or affording supplies of any kind for the Indians, the streams all sinking at the line of an immense lava field, which approaches the base of the mountains so closely in many places for miles that there is barely a passage for wagons. Water and grass, however, is sufficient, with exception of about sixty miles at this end of the march. The road is generally level and good, with exception of having occasionally to pass over points of the lava fields. I arrived at and crossed Snake River on the 17th, when I met Captain Crawford, of the overland escort, both reaching the ferry in the same hour. He had left his camp on Ross Fork, where the routes for the north and south sides of Snake River separate, and was undetermined as to which he would take. After consultation he concluded, on account of the forty-mile drive on the north side, and the report that one train of forty wagons had preceded him on the south side, to follow the latter route. He reports that there has been no difficulty or trouble of any nature with the emigration this season up to this point. There has been none from this west. He thinks he has the rear of the emigration, consisting of seventy or eighty wagons with him, having telegraphed from the last station to the rear some 200 miles, and getting information that none had passed that point since his party, and that none had been heard of in rear of that. With the exception of his party, and an occasional team transporting goods or produce from Salt Lake to Bannock City, in the Beaver Head country none have passed our camp or been heard of. Captain Crawford and party were in good health and generally well supplied, and stock in good condition. The emigrants have had good teams and are well supplied, though the emigration, as compared with that of last season is very small. About 250 wagons have passed over the route on the north side of the river, and probably 110, including Captain Crawford's party, on the south side. I will wait in this camp some days yet when I will return to Camas Prairie; from thence, as indicated heretofore I will cross the river with the cavalry at or near Salmon Falls and visit the headwaters of the streams entering from the south, meeting my supplies for return to Walla Walla at Owyhee or Malheur, the infantry returning by the same route we came to Fort Boisé. At the falls and on these streams I am in hopes I may be able to satisfy the desire of my command and the ends of justice by inflicting punishment upon such Indians as have not been embraced in the treaties made by General Connor and Governor Doty. Our relations with all the Indians in this section are explained by the letter of Governor Doty, copy of which was transmitted heretofore, and the copy of one received from General Connor on my arrival at the ferry near my present camp, which goes forward by this express. The only Indians I have found are those alluded to by the latter, who appear very friendly and say that General Connor has promised to visit and treat with them. A good many of the leading men of the tribes treated with, now living farther east, have visited my camp, generally having letters of recommendation from Governor Doty. I have no doubt that from the rapid succession of settlements in and bordering upon all the country of which they have been heretofore almost the sole occupants, their desire for peace and disposition to behave themselves is sincere, but all experience shows that unless collected and settled in some named district, and some control exercised over them, robberies, &c., will be of annual recurrence. Small parties of our people, and, no doubt, sometimes aggravations and aggressions by these parties traveling in every direction, searching every stream and mountain for gold, offer temptations, sharpened by the curtailment of hunting and fishing privileges (which our settlements naturally cause), which are not easy to be resisted. The south side of Camas Prairie would afford an excellent settlement for them. Camas abounds [with] an abundance of small fish in the streams, plenty of grass, and being adjacent to Snake River, affords opportunities of fishing below the great falls, above which salmon cannot pass. This would not interfere with settlements on the north side, which embraces the largest extent of good lands. All the Indians living northwest of Salt Lake visit the grounds in the spring and summer, putting up their winter supply of camas, and after the root season is over, resort to the falls and other points on the Snake to put up fish. All that were in the valley were collected by messengers east of Fort Hall three or four weeks in advance of our arrival. Necessity will beyond doubt compel them to keep up their visits to the camas grounds, and there is good reason to believe that, if permitted, the usual thefts and outrages would be the consequence, unless settled in the presence of some controlling power. The effect of failure to commit the usual robberies is easily detected among those here by the destitution of which they complain, and scarcity of powder, lead, &c. The great outrages committed heretofore by the frequenters of the country between Boisé and Fort Hall causes some regret that accounts should be canceled so easily, but no doubt the punishment inflicted by General Connor, and the disposition of citizens with whom they have come in contact, have satisfied them that any other policy than their present would lead to extermination.

Very respectfully, your obedient servant,

R. F. MAURY,

Colonel First Cavalry Oregon Volunteers, Commanding.

Brig. Gen. B. ALVORD,

Commanding District of Oregon, Fort Vancouver, Wash. Ter.

SOURCE: *OR*, SERIES 1, VOLUME 50, PART 1, PAGES 220–221

OR-243

WASHINGTON, D.C., *September 5, 1863.*

Major-General SCHOFIELD,
Fort Leavenworth, Kans.:

Delegate from Colorado Territory represents that a Colorado regiment can very well be spared to re-enforce General Connor in Utah. If so, it should be sent immediately.

H. W. HALLECK,
General-in-Chief.

SOURCE: *OR*, SERIES 1, VOLUME 22, PART 2, PAGE 512

OR-244

[*Extract*]

HDQRS. EXPEDITION AGAINST THE SNAKE INDIANS,
Camp No. 51, Camas Prairie, Idaho Ter., September 10, 1863.

SIR: I have the honor to report the arrival of my command at this camp on the evening of the 5th instant in good health.

. . .

Of the prospects of the expedition to the south side of Snake River anything said at present can only be conjecture. The same may be said as to the permanency of the peace or treaties made with the Snake or Shoshone Indians. It is evident, however, to my mind, that it cannot last when these Indians are allowed the privilege of their old resorts or of scattering generally over the country. We found on the waters of McArthur's River the body of an Indian killed about the 20th August, as we inferred from the date of papers found near the body. Such acts will certainly lead to retaliation, and most likely unsuspecting parties be the sufferers. I learn also that a good many of Pocatello's people crossed over from Snake River to the waters of Lost River the day after the command crossed what is known as the desert. These will undoubtedly scatter over the country, as heretofore, according to interest or inclination, and cannot fail to come into communication with more or less of our people who are ignorant of existing treaties, or of the tribe to which they may belong. In fact, such knowledge by many is of little importance, and makes but little difference in their disposition to them. Pocatello was at our camp on the Port Neuf the day before we left. In acknowledging the receipt of General Connor's letter (copy of which has been forwarded) I remarked, "I hope to find on the south side of Snake River on my return to Fort Walla Walla the remaining portions of what are known as the Shoshone or Snake Indians, and to be able to inflict such punishment as their crimes deserve." Since my return to this camp I learn (unofficially) that an Indian agent, with military escort from Utah, had gone down on the south side of Snake River and returned to Utah by the same route. I know nothing of the object of his visit, but taking into consideration the fact that a number of white people are intimately associated with these Indians, and their facilities for getting information, I doubt whether I succeed in finding any body of Indians of sufficient force to warrant me in attacking them; and in the case of the small parties that I may be able to capture, or that may come to my camp, I cannot possibly obtain such evidence as would warrant me in hanging them. I will move early in the morning, and shall endeavor to keep you advised of my future movements and acts as often as possible.

Very respectfully, your obedient servant,

R. F. MAURY,
Colonel First Cavalry Oregon Volunteers, Commanding.

ACTING ASSISTANT ADJUTANT-GENERAL,
Headquarters District of Oregon, Fort Vancouver, Wash. Ter.

SOURCE: *OR*, SERIES 1, VOLUME 50, PART 1, PAGES 221–222

OR-245

HEADQUARTERS DISTRICT OF COLORADO,
Denver, Colo., September 12, 1863.

Maj. Gen. JOHN M. SCHOFIELD,
Commanding Department of the Missouri:

SIR: I have the honor to acknowledge the receipt of your telegram, dated Kansas City, Mo., September 7, and referring to the "representation that a regiment could now be spared from my district, and that it is needed in Utah." I answered by telegraph yesterday morning, and now reply more at length.

There is no point in the district that, in my judgment, would be safe with a less number of troops than now stationed at it, except at Camp Weld, near this city. There is now stationed at this place Companies A, G, and I, First Colorado Cavalry; one section of First Colorado Battery, or Captain McLain's company Colorado Volunteers (true relation hardly known), and half of Company G, Third Colorado Volunteers. I have kept more troops here than was demanded for immediate protection, first, because it is central, and I could from time to time, as necessity seemed to require, re-enforce the places that were threatened; second, because I have had to do a great deal of escort duty from this place, by direction of the War Department and Department of the Missouri, and under the circumstances I think this has all been necessary.

The Overland Stage Company has applied to me for additional protection between where their line enters the mountains and Fort Bridger, a distance of between 300 and 400 miles. On this route Fort Halleck is located, where Company B, Ninth Kansas Cavalry, has been stationed, but it is now relieved and ordered to Leavenworth, Kans.

I have directed Lieutenant-Colonel Collins, at your suggestion, to divide his command between the Overland Stage Line and the line of the Pacific Telegraph Company, which would afford them each ample protection, but no more than ample, in my opinion.

I have had to send another company to Fort Lyon, in consequence of the threatening attitude of the Kiowa and Comanche Indians, below that post on the Arkansas River, the Santa Fé route.

The civil officers of Conejos and Costilla Counties have all resigned, and there is only the United States commissioner and deputy United States marshal to carry on the affairs of Government there.

The commissioner has urged me to proclaim martial law in those counties, but, deeming this not best, I have assured him that he should have all needful protection and aid in the enforcement of the laws of the United States, and have instructed Lieut. Col. S. F. Tappan, commanding at Fort Garland, accordingly.

The Indians who committed the theft and robbery in the neighborhoods of Laramie and Halleck are now in camp at the Conejos agency, 50 miles from Fort Garland. I have thought it best not to irritate them, as they are the same who were represented at Washington last winter, and Governor Evans and Dr. Steck (Superintendents, respectively, of Indian Affairs in Colorado and New Mexico), and Indian Agents Whiteley and Head are to have a council and make a treaty with them on the 1st of October next; but if they refuse to indemnify the stage company and Mr. Richard, then, of course, we shall try to make them; otherwise they will steal and rob the country over, and so interfere with the stage company's stock that they could not run, and the mails would cease.

Whoever represented that a regiment could be spared from this district could not have known whereof he represented, or did not care about the safety of Colorado; perhaps wanted the job of transporting the troops to Utah.

Colorado, in my judgment, is not of second importance to any State or Territory to the General Government. If protected and kept quiet, she will yield twenty millions of gold this year, and double yearly for years to come, and, in view of the national debt, I think this important, very!

I hope the major-general commanding will not think that I have any sinister design in keeping troops here that ought to be elsewhere. If a special inspector (an officer on the commanding general's staff) could be sent out here (one who would agree to endure the fatigue of travel and privation of fare) to travel over this district, and see its wants and importance, I should be very glad to have him represent to the commanding general the state of things in this district. Light makes manifest.

I am, sir, with much respect, your obedient servant,

J. M. CHIVINGTON,
Colonel First Colorado Cavalry, Comdg. District of Colorado.

SOURCE: *OR*, SERIES 1, VOLUME 22, PART 2, PAGES 527–529

OR-246

SALT LAKE, *September 17, 1863.*

Col. R. C. DRUM:

Major Gallagher's command arrived this morning in fine order; 241 votes cast in the command; every one for the Union ticket.

P. E. CONNOR,
Brigadier-General.

SOURCE: *OR*, SERIES 1, VOLUME 50, PART 2, PAGE 620

OR-247

QUARTERMASTER'S OFFICE,
Fort Leavenworth, September 21, 1863.

General M. C. MEIGS,
Quartermaster-General, U.S. Army, Washington, D.C.:

GENERAL: In obedience to instructions contained in your General Orders, No. 13, of July 22, 1863, I have the honor to report that during the year ending 30th of June, 1863, I was stationed at this place, attending to the various duties pertaining to the quartermaster s department at this depot.*

During the year I have promptly furnished the necessary transportation for all the troops, subsistence, quartermaster's, ordnance, and medical stores required for all the troops serving in Utah, New Mexico, Colorado, Nebraska, Kansas, the Indian country west of the State of Arkansas as far south as the Arkansas River, the two western tiers of counties of the State of Missouri north of the thirty-eighth parallel and south of the Missouri River, and the western tier of counties of the States of Missouri and Arkansas south of the thirty-eighth parallel and to the Arkansas River. I have provided all the quarter masters supplies, clothing, &c., for all this vast extent of country, except Utah and New Mexico, and for the latter Territory I supplied 600 cavalry horses and 100 wagons and teams complete. With rail roads and water communications the supply of the section of country referred to would be but a small undertaking, but the magnitude and labor of the duties I have performed can be better understood when you recollect that the troops scattered over this vast extent of country have been supplied by the common road wagon over unimproved roads, obstructed by high water in summer and by ice in winter, and the most of them passing through a perfect wilderness, where there is no forage or other supplies except grass. I say this is no small undertaking when you take the above circumstances into consideration, together with the distances of the points to be supplied from this depot. That you may understand this, I will give you some of the principal points to which I have had to send large quantities of supplies and their distances from this depot, with the weight of stores sent to each, viz:

Post or station.	Number of miles from Fort Leavenworth.	Stores transported (pounds).
Salt Lake City, Utah Ter.	1,837	662,720
Fort Union, N. Mex.	735	6,364,263
Fort Laramie, Nebr.	600	832,134
Fort Lyon, Colo.	500	440,900
Fort Larned, Kans.	266	811,956
Fort Kearny, Nebr.	275	592,206
Fort Scott, Kans.	125	8,106,501
Fort Gibson, Cherokee Nation.	300	
To other posts and stations.	.....	1,801,664

A much larger business has been done by other officers at other points, but the facilities for doing business and the number of officers to perform the labor and divide the responsibility have been in the same proportion to the magnitude of the business. I do not say it with any spirit of fault-finding or complaint, but all the duties of this depot, comprising every description of business transacted by the quarter master s department, have been performed by myself, with no officer to share the labor and responsibility except one military store-keeper in charge of clothing. There was shod at this depot during the year 11,101 mules and 5,058 horses; 2,500 wagons and ambulances have been repaired in the shops under my charge. In addition to my other duties I have conducted two very large Government farms, on which was cultivated and secured for the use of your department 2,200,000 pounds of timothy hay, 749 bushels of corn, 650 bushels of oats, besides furnishing pasturage for a large number of public animals. The repair of tents, wagon covers, harness, tent poles, &c., I have no account of, but they have been large. Transportation has been furnished for the supplies and equipage of a large number of troops moving from one point to another. Means furnished was Government wagons, which returned to this depot, and I have no account of the number of troops so transported. The troops in the section of country I have had control over have all been promptly supplied, and no troops have ever been better supplied, so far as the quantity and quality of the supplies are concerned. Their means of transportation, clothing, equipage, &c., have been excellent and the character of their artillery and cavalry horses superior. I have worked hard, have accomplished a great deal under the circumstances, every branch of my business, to its minutest particular, having been conducted under my own immediate personal superintendence, and I hope at least to obtain credit for industry, attention to duty, and at all times having the best interest of the service in view and laboring constantly to that end.

Very respectfully, your obedient servant,

L. C. EASTON,
Major and Quartermaster, U.S. Army.

* Some unimportant details here omitted.

SOURCE: *OR*, SERIES 1, VOLUME 53, PAGES 570–571

OR-248

[*Extract*]

HDQRS. EXPEDITION AGAINST THE SNAKE INDIANS,
Camp No. 56, Salmon Falls, Idaho Ter., September 22, 1863.

His Excellency Governor A. C. GIBBS,
Portland, Oreg.:

GOVERNOR: Under proper circumstances I would be glad to send you accounts of battles fought and won by the First Oregon Volunteer Cavalry, but, as in bargains, it takes two parties to make a fight. We have searched thus far in vain, and I am well satisfied that so far as the country at present examined, and we have examined thoroughly all within the scope of our route and instructions, that there are, if any, very few Indians except the few we find at our present camp. They are destitute and beg permission to live at the falls, feeling, I am satisfied, their utter helplessness as well as dependence upon our charity. There are in some points of the country evidences of periodical visits by considerable numbers of Indians, especially in Camas Prairie, but I think it is generally in the spring and composed entirely of the Indians treated with by the Governor of Utah. I will continue my examination of the country as far as Malheur River on the west side of Snake River. If I find no Indians I will at least be able to form a tolerably correct opinion as to the numbers and tribes who inhabit or visit the country. I am now of the opinion, taking into consideration those treated with, that the number occupying this section of country has been largely overestimated; that they are generally poor and destitute almost to starvation, and have depended in a great measure for winter food upon the charities of the emigration and such stock as was abandoned or could be stolen from them, eating during the winter all stock stolen or picked up. The emigration has been very small; in fact, of men, I think the emigration for the East has been the largest. Parties are constantly passing even as late as this in most instances, I think, of men who have families on the other side, and the largest number of them of last year's emigration. Trade appears to increase to Salt Lake, and a daily line of stages from Salt Lake to the Boisé Mines is talked of for next season. I think the next summer will witness a continuous line of settlements from Boisé River to Salt Lake.

. . .

The command continues in excellent health, and with the exception of a few men lost while waiting on Boisé River for supplies, maintain their usual good reputation for soldierly bearing and patriotism, though of course a little restive under the disappointment of not having had as yet an opportunity of trying their mettle in actual conflict with the enemies of their country's flag.

. . .

Very respectfully, your obedient servant,

R. F. MAURY,

Colonel First Oregon Cavalry, Commanding.

Source: *OR*, Series 1, Volume 50, Part 2, pages 624–625

OR-249

[*Extract*]

HDQRS. EXPEDITION AGAINST THE SNAKE INDIANS,
Camp No. 56, Salmon Falls Creek, Idaho Ter., September 23, 1863.

SIR: Since my last of September 10 nothing of any importance has occurred. I arrived with the command at the Salmon Falls on the 15th and crossed to the south side on the 16th, establishing the present camp. All in good health. The few Indians we find here are miserably poor and almost destitute. Represent themselves as very friendly and ask permission to live undisturbed in the vicinity. I have represented to them that as long as they remained here without molesting in any manner our people who may travel through the country they might expect to live in peace, but on the contrary they could expect nothing but extermination; that I did not come out to make them presents or to buy a peace, but to make them feel and understand that they must not only behave themselves, but that in the event of bad faith or conduct they would be pursued and punished. There are about thirty or forty of them living within eight miles above and below the falls. Most of them were here last September while I was camped in the neighborhood. They are of course like all other Indians, and have probably been guilty of acts of violence and robbery, but neither during the last nor this season have I heard of any complaints against them.

. . .

The travel from the mines to Salt Lake and the east continues in small parties without the least difficulty. I am inclined to the opinion that more men have gone east than came west by the Snake River roads.

Very respectfully, your obedient servant,

R. F. MAURY,
Colonel First Cavalry Oregon Volunteers, Commanding.

ACTING ASSISTANT ADJUTANT-GENERAL,
Headquarters District of Oregon, Fort Vancouver, Wash. Ter.

SOURCE: *OR*, SERIES 1, VOLUME 50, PART 1, PAGES 222–223

OR-250

Salt Lake, *September 27, 1863.*

Col. R. C. Drum:

I leave this morning for Soda Springs to hold treaty with Bannock Indians. Will be gone about three weeks. Communications will reach me.

P. E. CONNOR,
Brigadier-General.

Source: *OR*, Series 1, Volume 50, Part 2, page 629

OR-251

Headquarters Department of the Pacific,
San Francisco, September 28, 1863.

Col. E. D. Townsend,
Asst. Adjt. Gen., Hdqrs. of the Army, Washington, D.C.:

Colonel: I have been highly gratified with the condition of affairs in the eastern part of this State as well as in the Territory of Nevada. I was absent about three weeks, and, traveling on horseback, I had an excellent opportunity for making an examination of the country and the character of the inhabitants. On the road over the mountains I found the way thronged with wagons of the largest size transporting goods to Washoe and Reese River. The almost fabulous reports of the richness of the Reese River mines have drawn to that place a large number of people from this side, as well as arrested the tide of emigration from the East, and it is probable that the population of that district in the course of the next year will rival that of Virginia City and its surroundings. The truly loyal and intense love for the Union which pervades the great masses of the people in the Territory of Nevada has been made manifest in their late election; from the highest to the lowest every office has been filled by the election of sound Union men. I visited Carson City, the seat of government of Nevada, as well as Silver City, Gold Hill, and Virginia City, located in the rich mining districts, and everywhere I found a prosperous and happy people. From Virginia City I proceeded to Fort Churchill, situated on the Carson River. The post is commanded by Maj. Charles McDermit, of the Second Cavalry California Volunteers, an officer of great merit, irreproachable in his habits, industrious, and careful of the interests of the Government.

At Fort Churchill I found three companies of cavalry, Nevada Territory volunteers, also a detachment of a fourth company in process of organization. A finer body of men I never saw; orderly, well-behaved, and undergoing a thorough course of instruction and discipline. Two of these companies are under orders for the District of Utah, and will march early in the next month. The post of Fort Churchill I found in admirable order. I critically inspected all the departments and found the Government property well taken care of and economically used, and the officers zealous and attentive to their duties. After my inspection at Fort Churchill I hastended back to my headquarters, finding everything quiet in this quarter. I am greatly pained at an accident which happened to Maj. R. W. Kirkham, quartermaster, who accompanied me on my tour. At Carson City he unfortunately walked out of an open doorway at the end of a hall where there was no balcony, and falling some fourteen feet bruised himself much and fractured his thigh bone. I brought him back with me, but he will probably be laid up eight or ten weeks.

Very respectfully, your obedient servant,

G. WRIGHT,
Brigadier-General, U.S. Army, Commanding.

SOURCE: *OR*, SERIES 1, VOLUME 50, PART 2, PAGE 630

OR-252

HDQRS. DEPARTMENT OF THE PACIFIC,
San Francisco, Cal., September 29, 1863.

SPECIAL ORDERS,
No. 223.

* * * *

2. Companies A and B, Nevada Cavalry, will, as soon as their equipment is completed, take up their march for Camp Douglas, District of Utah. The quartermaster's department will furnish the necessary transportation for the movement above directed.

By order of Brigadier-General Wright:

RICHD. C. DRUM,
Assistant Adjutant-General.

SOURCE: *OR*, SERIES 1, VOLUME 50, PART 2, PAGE 631

OR-253

San Francisco, *September 29, 1863.*

Maj. Charles McDermit,
Fort Churchill, Nev. Ter.:

The two cavalry companies will commence the march to Salt Lake as soon as they are fully equipped. Order for the movement published to-day.

R. C. DRUM,
Assistant Adjutant-General.

Source: *OR*, Series 1, Volume 50, Part 2, page 631

OR-254

[*Extract*]

No. 7.

Report of Surg. James M. McNulty, U.S. Army, Acting Medical Inspector.

Santa Fé, N. Mex., *October—, 1863.*

Brig. Gen. W. A. Hammond,
Surgeon-General U.S. Army, Washington, D.C.:

General: Agreeably to the wish conveyed in your letter of July 27, 1863, I send you the following history of that portion of the California Volunteers known as the Column from California. The march of this column from the Pacific Ocean to the Rio Grande is somewhat remarkable, from the fact that almost the entire distance is a desert waste, with great scarcity of water and that of the worst quality. Men marching day after day through the burning sands and nearly suffocated with alkali dust required to be made of stern stuff—of such were the men composing this column. Men inured to mountain life in California, pioneers and miners; men self-reliant and enduring; men equal to any emergency, if guided by a firm hand and clear head. That they were equal to a great emergency is evinced by the fact that they conquered vast deserts, and accomplished a march not equaled in modern times, traversing a distance of nearly a thousand miles and almost the entire route over a sterile waste.

I am, sir, very respectfully, your obedient servant,

JAMES M. McNULTY,
Surgeon, U.S. Volunteers, Acting Medical Inspector.

On the 22d of July, 1861, the President of the United States approved "An act to authorize the employment of volunteers to aid in enforcing the laws and protecting public property." Under this act was raised in California one regiment of infantry and five companies of cavalry. These were called respectively the First Infantry and First Cavalry California Volunteers. The troops were raised for the protection of the Overland Mail Route between California and the Eastern States, by way of Salt Lake City. The force was placed under the command of Bvt. Maj. James H. Carleton, First U.S. Cavalry, with the rank of colonel. The regiments rendezvoused at Oakland, opposite San Francisco, Cal. During the latter part of August and the month of September they had acquired nearly their full complement of men. Active preparations were making to put the command in the best condition for active field service, and by the 1st of October everything was in readiness for the movement of the troops. About this time the spirit of rebellion became manifest in California. "Treason stalked abroad." In the southern part of the State an open rupture was apprehended. In consequence of this condition of affairs the command of Colonel Carleton was diverted from its original destination by General Sumner department commander, and moved to the infected district. About the 1st of October the troops moved down the coast and formed a camp near Los Angeles, called Camp Latham.

. . .

On the 12th of January Colonel Carleton was summoned to San Francisco, to consult with Colonel Wright in reference to the movement of troops into Utah. About this time rumors reached California, that Van Dorn, of the rebel service, was fitting out an expedition for the invasion of California by way of Arizona. The fact was well established that Arizona and a portion of New Mexico were occupied by Confederate troops, and it was apparent to all that California was more accessible through Arizona by way of Fort Yuma than any other point. Fort Yuma, located on the Colorado River, on the southeastern line of the State, is our extreme outpost. Surrounded as it is by a vast desert, if once in the possession of an enemy the key to the State was lost.

In view of all these threatened dangers to the State and coast, General Wright suggested to the War Department that perhaps the Government would be better served by throwing the California troops into Arizona and driving the rebels from that Territory. A double object would thus be gained; first, an effectual guard would be kept against any invasion of the Pacific coast from that quarter; second, the California troops would fall in the rear of the Confederate forces then in New Mexico and assist the Federal forces in expelling them from that Territory.

. . .

Very respectfully,

J. M. McNULTY,
Surgeon, U.S. Volunteers.

[Editor's note: *This document is included as an inclosure to an Expedition Report covering April 13–September 20, 1862. See* OR, *Series 1, Volume 50, Part 1, page 88. It should also be noted that the editors of the* War of the Rebellion *included this expedition report in two separate volumes: Series 1, Volume 9 (pages 553–603), and Series 1, Volume 50, Part 1. While the same report appears in both volumes, the report components are organized differently. The Volume 9 version lists only three numbered reports with numerous inclosures and subinclosures; the Volume 50, Part 1, Expedition Report lists seven numbered reports.*]

SOURCE: *OR*, SERIES 1, VOLUME 50, PART 1, PAGES 136–145

OR-255

HEADQUARTERS DEPARTMENT OF THE PACIFIC,
San Francisco, October 2, 1863.

Col. E. D. TOWNSEND,
Asst. Adjt. Gen., Hdqrs. of the Army, Washington, D.C.:

COLONEL: For the information of the General-in-Chief and War Department, I have the honor to report that, independent of occasional Indian disturbances, quiet prevails throughout this department. The late elections indicate, unmistakably, the feeling of a vast majority of the people on this coast, assuring the Government the hearty support of a loyal people to crush a rebellion which aims at the dissolution of the Union. The people on this coast, although far removed from the scenes of war, and really experiencing none of its hardships, yet have a deep-rooted affection for the Union, and will nobly stand by the Administration in the prosecution of the war until our flag shall wave in triumph over the whole country. I have but few Indian disturbances to speak of. In the State of Oregon, as well as in the Territories of Washington, Idaho, Nevada, and Utah, we have peace and quiet between the races. In the northeastern portion of California the condition of our Indian affairs has not materially changed. Constant depredations by small bands involves the necessity of keeping our troops on the move. I cannot promise peace between the whites and Indians in the District of Humboldt without the removal of the latter to some reservation in the southern portion of the State where they cannot get back to their old haunts. This has been the difficulty experienced during the last few years. Our military forces have gathered up a large number of Indians and transferred them to the superintendent of Indian affairs, by whom they have been placed on the different reservations within the district, but it has been found impossible to keep them there. They escape, return to their old familiar grounds, and frequently engage again in depredations upon the settlements. I have just been asked by Lieutenant-Colonel Whipple as to the disposition to be made of his Indian prisoners; that is, the active young warriors, who can only be kept in that district by being held constantly under a guard, fed and clothed by the Government without rendering any service. After consideration I have determined to bring twenty of these able-bodied Indians down here and make them work on the fortifications now being erected on Angel Island and other points around the city. If the plan succeeds, and these Indians are found to be of service, I will bring more of them here, where they can at least render a return for the food and clothing necessary for them.

Very respectfully, your obedient servant,

G. WRIGHT,
Brigadier-General, U.S. Army, Commanding.

SOURCE: *OR*, SERIES 1, VOLUME 50, PART 2, PAGE 637

OR-256

FORT RUBY, NEV. TER., *October 3, 1863.*

Capt. M. G. LEWIS,
Asst. Adjt. Gen., Dist. of Utah, Salt Lake City, Utah Ter.:

SIR: I have the honor to inform the general commanding the District of Utah that his communication of September 23 was duly received. I have ordered in some of the men now on the mail route. Those that are to remain are at stations between Deep Creek and Fish Springs. I do not think they will be long required to remain out. The Indians are quite desirous to meet and make peace; still the station keepers pretend fear, while in fact I believe they only want the soldiers with them for companions and assistants. I shall order them all in as soon as the treaty is made. The train from Salt Lake in charge of Wagonmaster Riley arrived here last night. I started two teams to Reese River this morning for the Fort Churchill freight I am informed by telegram that it started from Fort Churchill on Monday last. I expect my teams to return by the 10th instant, and I shall start Captain Smith's company the very moment my teams arrive. The general's instructions in regard to prospecting for gold and silver are so ambiguous that I am at a loss to determine what he really desired. I could not think that he intended that an exploring expedition should be sent from this post, or that large parties of soldiers should be sent out to gobble up all the mining and water privileges, thereby shutting up and preventing them being worked by others. The general is well aware that I have not the facilities for an exploring party. I have but six horses and sixteen mules here beside Captain Smith's command, and his horses should not be worn out before they commence their march for Camp Douglas, and I require all the post teams to do the work required here. I have to keep them busy all the time; therefore, to satisfy and allay the excitement that exists with the men (without in my opinion any just cause), I have decided to grant seven days' leave to two-tenths of the men, and already nearly all the number allowed have gone out prospecting. Governors Doty, of Utah Territory, and Nye, of Nevada Territory, have been here and made a treaty with the Shoshones. I do not think there will be any trouble with them hereafter. Lieut. S. E. Jocelyn, Third Infantry California Volunteers, arrived at this post with a communication from the commanding general directing me to furnish facilities for the accomplishment of the object of his mission. In the absence of any written instructions from the general, or any order from any member of his staff, I could not properly take official notice of the lieutenant other than simply recognizing him as an officer of the U.S. service, and presume him to be on duty. It is very mortifying to me, and I deeply regret that the general should have found it necessary to have dispatched a lieutenant from near his headquarters to have executed a mission at or near this post that could not have been intrusted to its commander to execute. I have endeavored faithfully to perform my duty to my Government and to those under whom I serve, and I am much annoyed at the want of confidence that the commanding general has in this case manifested toward me; therefore, I respectfully ask the general to at an early day relieve me from the command of this post.

I am, very respectfully, your humble servant,

J. B. MOORE,
Lieutenant-Colonel Third Infantry California Volunteers.

SOURCE: *OR*, SERIES 1, VOLUME 50, PART 2, PAGES 638–639

OR-257

[*Extract*]

HDQRS. EXPEDITION AGAINST THE SNAKE INDIANS,
Camp No. 61, on Bruneau or Goose Creek, Idaho Ter., October 5, 1863.

SIR: As indicated in my letter of 23d ultimo, the command moved from Salmon Falls Creek on the 25th and reached this camp on the 29th, halting one day at the Three Islands, thirty miles below Salmon Falls. The road from the falls does not follow the river. I sent out parties while en route to the Three Islands to collect in all the Indians on either side of the river, or to attack in case of finding any considerable force of them. These were the Indians whom I mentioned in my last as intending to visit. About forty were collected. They live a family in a place, on either side of the river for a distance of thirty or forty miles; have no arms, and a very small number of Indian ponies; not an average of one to each family. As in the case of those at the falls they expressed great desire for peace and a willingness to do anything or go anywhere they might be directed. I had no evidence of guilt or of complaints and endeavored to impress the importance to them of not only not molesting our people themselves, but of giving, in the event of any being molested in their vicinity, such information as would lead to the punishment of the guilty. There are from 80 to 100 of this party, all Shoshones, and, aware of the treaties made at Salt Lake, scattered along the river from the great falls to the mouth of this stream, a distance of 100 miles. Something should be done with them, for if disposed to behave themselves they are liable to be punished for the depredations of the roaming and more enterprising bands that occupy the country to the south and west.

. . .

Very respectfully, your obedient servant,

R. F. MAURY,
Colonel First Cavalry Oregon Volunteers.

ACTING ASSISTANT ADJUTANT-GENERAL,
Headquarters District of Oregon, Fort Vancouver, Wash. Ter.

SOURCE: *OR*, SERIES 1, VOLUME 50, PART 1, PAGES 223–225

OR-258

[*Extract*]

JULY 7, 1862–OCTOBER 6, 1863.—Operations in the District of Oregon.

Report of Brig. Gen. Benjamin Alvord, U.S. Army, commanding the District of Oregon.

. . .

HEADQUARTERS DISTRICT OF OREGON,
Fort Vancouver, Wash. Ter., October 6, 1863.

GENERAL: I have the honor to report for the information of the War Department the operations of the troops in the District of Oregon since I assumed command on the 7th of July, 1862. The boundaries of the district are the same known on military maps as those of the old Department of Oregon, including all of the former Territory of Oregon as organized in 1848, excepting the valleys of the Umpqua and Rogue Rivers. It now includes part of the State of Oregon, all of Washington Territory, and the portion of Idaho Territory west of the Rocky Mountains.

. . .

All those Indian tribes have remained at peace with whom the Indian wars of 1855, 1856, and 1858 were carried on, and the only Indians who have committed assaults upon the frontier have been the Snakes. The Snakes speak the Comanche language, have the same habits, and are in fact a branch of the Comanche tribes of the region east of the Rocky Mountains.

. . .

Colonel Maury, with three companies of First Oregon Cavalry and two of infantry, was ordered to proceed in July last from Fort Boisé to a point on Snake River above Fort Hall for the protection of the emigration. He has at last dates successfully carried out the plan, and on the 17th of August, 1863, met Capt. M. Crawford, assistant quartermaster, in charge of the emigrant escort, at the ferry on Snake River, as had been arranged by me early in the spring when Captain Crawford left here for Washington City. Owing to the pacification effected by General Connor and Governor Doty, of Utah, the Snake Indians upon that route have been very quiet this summer.

. . .

I am, with high respect, your obedient servant,

BENJ. ALVORD,
Brigadier-General, U.S. Volunteers, Commanding District.

ADJUTANT-GENERAL U.S. ARMY,
Washington, D.C.

SOURCE: *OR*, SERIES 1, VOLUME 50, PART 1, PAGES 156–158

OR-259

HEADQUARTERS DEPARTMENT OF THE PACIFIC,
San Francisco, October 19, 1863.

Col. E. D. TOWNSEND,
Asst. Adjt. Gen., Hdqrs. of the Army, Washington, D.C.:

COLONEL: By my direction two companies of cavalry, Nevada Territory volunteers, marched from Fort Churchill on the 10th instant for Salt Lake. This is the last command I propose to send on that line this fall. Everything is perfectly quiet on the route, Indians peaceable, and no indications of any disturbance on the mail route. I have two more companies of Nevada cavalry organizing at Fort Churchill (one already filled), which will constitute the garrison of that post, detaching a command of twenty-five men and one officer as an outpost at Smoke Creek, about 100 miles to the north. The troops in the department are healthy, and, independent of occasional Indian raids on the white settlements, everything is quiet.

Very respectfully, your obedient servant,

G. WRIGHT,
Brigadier-General, U.S. Army, Commanding.

SOURCE: *OR*, SERIES 1, VOLUME 50, PART 2, PAGE 652

OR-260

HEADQUARTERS DISTRICT OF UTAH,
Great Salt Lake City, Utah Ter., October 26, 1863.

Lieut. Col. R. C. DRUM, U.S. Army,
Assistant Adjutant-General, San Francisco, Cal.:

COLONEL: In former communications I have had the honor fully to set forth my views to the department commander relative to the condition of the Mormon people and the sentiments of their leaders, and have endeavored to present my opinions as to the settlement of the Mormon question, so far as it has necessarily thrust itself upon me in the performance of strictly military duties. I need hardly repeat that it has been my constant endeavor to maintain amicable relations with the people, and avoid conflict so far as was compatible with the strict and proper fulfillment of the obligations resting upon me, fully understanding that it was no part of my business to interfere with the religious tenets or even the illegal practices of this peculiar people except when called upon by the civil authorities. The open declarations of hostility to the Government on the part of their public men, and their bold, continued, and unceasing teachings of disloyalty have time and again tended to produce excitements leading to collision, which have only been avoided by the most temperate and moderate course of the officers and men of my command. Until such time, therefore, as the Government, in the interest of humanity and the vindication of its offended dignity and laws, shall deem it advisable to inaugurate by force an observance of its recorded laws, and come to the relief of a people oppressed and downtrodden by a most galling church tyranny, my own course has been plainly marked by the dictates of policy and the manifest necessity of the case. Entertaining the opinion that Mormonism as preached and practiced in this Territory is not only subversive of morals, in conflict with the civilization of the present age, and oppressive on the people, but also deeply and boldly in contravention of the laws and best interests of the nation, I have sought by every proper means in my power to arrest its progress and prevent its spread. As a question for the civilian, I can conceive of but two ways of striking at its root and annihilating its baneful influence: The one by an adequate military force, acting under martial law and punishing with a strong hand every infraction of law or loyalty; the other by inviting into the Territory large numbers of Gentiles to live among and dwell with the people. The former I am aware is at the present time impracticable, even though it were deemed advisable. The latter, if practicable, is perhaps in any event the wiser course. With these remarks I desire to inform the department commander that I have considered the discovery of gold, silver, and other valuable minerals in the Territory of the highest importance, and as presenting the only prospect of bringing hither such a population as is desirable or possible. The discovery of such mines would unquestionably induce an immigration to the Territory of a hardy, industrious, and enterprising population as could not but result in the happiest effects, and in my opinion presents the only sure means of settling peaceably the Mormon question. Their presence and intercourse with the people already here would greatly tend to disabuse the minds of the latter of the false, frivolous, yet dangerous and constant, teachings of the leaders, that the Government is their enemy and persecutor for opinion's sake. As I have said, these doctrines are continually being preached to them until the mass of the people believe that the Government instead of desiring their welfare seeks their destruction. To the end, then, that the inducements to come hither may be presented to the teeming populations of the East and West, seeking new fields of exploration and prosperity, I have looked upon the discovery of mines in the Territory as in the highest degree important first to this people and secondly to the Government, for the reasons stated. Having reason to believe that the Territory is full of mineral wealth, I have instructed commanders of posts and detachments to permit the men of their commands to prospect the country in the vicinity of their respective posts, whenever such course would not interfere with their military duties, and to furnish every proper facility for the discovery and opening of mines of gold, silver, and other minerals. The results so far have exceeded my most sanguine expectations. Already reliable reports reach me of the discovery of rich gold, silver, and copper mines in almost every direction, and that by spring one of the largest and most hopeful fields of mining operations will be opened to the hardy and adventurous of our people. Both gold quartz and silver leads have been discovered at Egan Cañon, about 200 miles west of this place; also in Ruby Valley, and at points along the mail route. The Goose Creek Mountains, 150 miles northwest of this city, are believed to contain rich mines of precious metals. The mountains in the immediate vicinity of this place are being explored and prospected, and I have reason to believe with successful results.

Already, within a distance of from twenty-five to fifty miles of this city, in the East and West mountains, mines have been discovered yielding, with imperfect tests, rich indications of silver, and largely charged with lead and cop per ores. The work is still going on, and I have little doubt that rich veins of silver, and probably gold, will be discovered in almost every direction, and still nearer to Great Salt Lake City. I may also mention that near Camp Connor, 150 miles north of this place, large deposits of salt, sulphur, and extensive beds of coal have been found, while the springs adjoining the camp yield immense deposits of the carbonate of soda, which will one day, I have no doubt, be of very considerable commercial value. If I be not mistaken in these anticipations, I have no reason to doubt that the Mormon question will at an early day be finally settled by peaceable means, without the increased expenditure of a dollar by Government, or, still more important, without the loss of a single soldier in conflict. I have every confidence, therefore, in being able to accomplish this desirable result without the aid of another soldier in addition to those already under my command, notwithstanding the obstacles sought to be thrown in my way by the Mormon leaders, who see in the present policy the sure downfall of their most odious church system of tyranny. I have no fear for the future and believe the dawn is breaking upon this deluded people, even though their elders, and bishops, and chief priests may escape the personal punishment their sins against law and crimes against humanity and the Government so richly merit.

I have the honor to remain, very respectfully, your obedient servant,

P. EDW. CONNOR,

Brigadier-General, U.S. Volunteers, Commanding District.

[Editor's note: *This document is referenced in* OR-265.]

SOURCE: *OR*, SERIES 1, VOLUME 50, PART 2, PAGES 655–657

OR-261

HEADQUARTERS DISTRICT OF UTAH,
Great Salt Lake City, October 27, 1863.

Lieut. Col. R. C. DRUM,
Assistant Adjutant-General, U.S. Army, San Francisco, Cal.:

COLONEL: I have the honor to inform the department commander that I have just returned from Camp Connor, Idaho, where, in connection with Governor Doty, acting superintendent of Indian affairs, a final treaty of peace was concluded with the last remaining band of Shoshone Indians, and that on the 12th instant another treaty was made in Tooele Valley by the deputy superintendent and an officer of my staff, acting for Governor Doty and myself, with some 250 of the Goshute tribe, lately hostile. With the satisfactory conclusion of these treaties I have the honor to report the settlement of terms of peace with all the Indians within this military district from the Snake River on the north to the lower settlements of Utah, and from the Rocky Mountains on the east to Reese River on the west, a region heretofore constantly infested by roving bands of savages, and desolated by their horrid barbarities on passing emigrants for a long series of years. For the first time in the history of the country it may now be truly announced that the great emigrant roads through the Territory may be safely traversed by single persons without danger to life or property or fear of molestation by Indians.

In my recent trip to the north, I met single persons traveling to and from the Bannock and Boisé mines through a region of country never before traversed except in strong parties of from fifteen to twenty-five well armed, and in constant danger of massacre. I have the pleasure, therefore, to report that through the indomitable bravery, activity, and willingly endured hardships of the California column under my command, the Indian country within this district is freed from hostile savages, and travel through it by unarmed persons, emigrants, miners, or others is perfectly safe and exempt from the dangers heretofore besetting them on every hand. That this happy state of affairs will continue I have every reason to believe, as the Indians, one and all, with whom I have come in contact, are evidently seriously inclined to peace in the future, and, after the severe experiences of last winter, spring, and summer, will hesitate long ere they again provoke hostilities.

I have the honor to remain, very respectfully, your obedient servant,

P. EDWARD CONNOR,
Brigadier-General, Commanding District.

[Editor's note: *This document is referenced in* OR-264.]

SOURCE: *OR*, SERIES 1, VOLUME 50, PART 2, PAGES 658–659

OR-262

WAR DEPARTMENT,
Washington City, October 30, 1863—1.55 P.M.

Governor NYE,
Carson City, Nev. Ter.:

The Government will accept volunteers to go to Salt Lake, but there does not seem to be any propriety in raising them in Nevada to send them to New York.

EDWIN M. STANTON,
Secretary of War.

SOURCE: *OR*, SERIES 1, VOLUME 50, PART 2, PAGE 662

OR-263

HDQRS. DEPARTMENT OF THE PACIFIC,
San Francisco, Cal., November 6, 1863.

SPECIAL ORDERS,
NO. 251.

Lieut. Col. William Jones, Second Cavalry California Volunteers, will on receipt of this order turn over the command of the troops at Camp Babbitt, Visalia, to the officer next in rank, and proceed to Camp Douglas, near Salt Lake City, Utah Ter., and report to Brig. Gen. P. Edward Connor for duty. He will report first at San Francisco, to be mustered in as colonel. The quartermaster's department will furnish the necessary transportation.

By order of Brigadier-General Wright:

E. SPARROW PURDY,
Assistant Adjutant-General.

SOURCE: *OR*, SERIES 1, VOLUME 50, PART 2, PAGE 663

OR-264

Headquarters Department of the Pacific,
San Francisco, November 9, 1863.

Col. E. D. Townsend,
Asst. Adjt. Gen., Hdqrs. of the Army, Washington, D.C.:

Colonel: I have the honor to inclose herewith a copy of a communication addressed to my headquarters by Brig. Gen. P. E. Connor, commanding the District of Utah, dated October 27, 1863, conveying the pleasant intelligence that treaties of peace have finally been concluded with all the different bands of Indians within that district.* Hoping that this happy state of affairs in the District of Utah, brought about by the distinguished bravery and good conduct of the California column, may continue without interruption, I have the honor to be, your most obedient servant,

G. WRIGHT,
Brigadier-General, U.S. Army, Commanding.

* [*Refers to* OR-261.]

Source: *OR*, Series 1, Volume 50, Part 2, page 668

OR-265

Headquarters Department of the Pacific,
San Francisco, November 10, 1863.

Col. E. D. Townsend,
Asst. Adjt. Gen., Hdqrs. of the Army, Washington, D.C.:

Colonel: For the information of the General-in-Chief and honorable Secretary of War, I have the honor to submit the inclosed communication, addressed to my headquarters by Brig. Gen. P. E. Connor, commanding the District of Utah.* When I sent General Connor to establish posts in Utah and take command of that district I impressed upon him the necessity of pursuing a conservative policy with those people, and on several occasions subsequently it has only been with forbearance and sound judgment that a collision has been avoided. The late discovery of valuable mines in the Territory will, it is believed, draw thither a large population in the course of a year or two, and if so, it will exercise a powerful influence to wipe out that damning stain upon the Christian morality of the American people.

Very respectfully, your obedient servant,

G. WRIGHT,
Brigadier-General, U.S. Army, Commanding.

* [*Refers to* OR-260.]

SOURCE: *OR*, SERIES 1, VOLUME 50, PART 2, PAGE 669

OR-266

HEADQUARTERS DEPARTMENT OF THE PACIFIC,
San Francisco, November 20, 1863.

Col. E. D. TOWNSEND,
Asst. Adjt. Gen., Hdqrs. of the Army, Washington, D.C.:

COLONEL: I have the honor to inclose herewith a copy of my General Orders, No. 40, current series.* I have heretofore frequently reported to the Department the difficulties and embarrassments we labored under in this department in raising and organizing volunteers. In consequence of the sparse population over a vast extent of country, it was found impracticable for the Governors of States and Territories to conduct the recruiting service without the aid of the military authorities. Anxious as I have been for some time past to make the experiment of relying solely upon the Governor, I have prepared and issued the order above referred to. In recruiting for the new organizations, under the superintendency of the commissary of musters, the greatest economy has been enjoined and enforced, and I feel sure that the best interests of the Government have been subserved. My letter addressed to Adjutant-General Thomas on the 8th of June last I beg leave to call your attention to, as well as your answer to that communication, dated on the 7th of July, in which you say that the General-in-Chief approves the course pursued by me.

To you, who served so long in this department, I need not recapitulate the delays and difficulties I have encountered in my efforts to comply with the orders and regulations from the War Department. One thing is certain, the peace and quiet of a country extending from the British possessions on the north to the Republic of Mexico on the south, and from the Pacific Ocean on the west to the farthest limits of the Territory of Utah in the east, have been preserved; and besides that, the troops which I organized and sent forth from California reconquered the Territories of Arizona and New Mexico, at one time overrun by the rebel forces, and have held undisturbed possession of that country since the summer of 1862. I can also speak with pride of the gallant conduct of the troops I organized and sent forth from this State for the protection of the Overland Mail Route and occupation of the Territory of Utah.

In the execution of all the varied duties and responsibilities in this remote department it has frequently been necessary for me to act promptly and assume responsibilities which, in time of peace, I should have deferred for the decision of the General-in-Chief and War Department. I am not aware that during my command of this department a single charge has ever been made against me of malfeasance in office, or of a disregard of the best interests of the Government, and I have no apprehension that any charges of that kind will be made. I have done, and shall do, what seems to be my duty, acknowledging my responsibility to the General-in-Chief, the Secretary of War, and to the President of the United States, under the concluding paragraph of his letter to the Missouri delegation of 5th of October. I beg leave most respectfully to ask of the Secretary of War an approval of all I have done in the matter of raising, organizing, and appointing officers for volunteer organizations in this department. I ask for this because we may experience some objections by the accounting officers, in cases where the regulations of the Department have not been strictly followed.

Very respectfully, your obedient servant,

G. WRIGHT,
Brigadier-General, U.S. Army, Commanding.

*[Editor's note: *Refers to General Orders No. 40, November 14, 1863. See* OR, *Series 1, Volume 50, Part 2, pages 673–674.*]

SOURCE: *OR*, SERIES 1, VOLUME 50, PART 2, PAGES 676–677

OR-267

[*Extract*]

HEADQUARTERS CAVALRY OF THE WEST,
San Antonio, December 27, 1863.

[Capt. EDMUND P. TURNER,
Assistant Adjutant-General:]

CAPTAIN: I have the honor to acknowledge receipt of communication dated December 19, 1863;* also of December 22, both having reached me to-day.

. . .

The instructions of the major-general commanding will be promptly executed. I shall send a courier to Colonel [J. E.] McCord, and through him ask Governor Murrah for as many companies as can be spared from the Frontier Regiment. Colonel McCord is anxious to accompany me, and I have no doubt but that I shall obtain at least four of his companies. I have already addressed a communication to Colonel Benavides, and I shall again write him at length. I propose moving in the direction of Goliad, thence across country to old Fort Merrit, thence to the ranch of San Diego, thence to or near the Great Salt Lake.

. . .

The question of subsistence will be of primary importance. Beef abounds upon the whole line, and can be driven from above on foot; breadstuffs will be scarce. I understand there are 500,000 pounds of flour at Fort McIntosh (Laredo). I shall direct Colonel Benavides to have it transported upon Mexican carts, if he can procure them, to Salt Lake or some point on the line of march.

. . .

I shall use every effort to keep the object of the expedition entirely secret, and shall get the editor of the Herald to intimate that it is intended for Indianola. I would respectfully request the major-general commanding to allow Lieutenant-Colonel Dickinson to co-operate with me. I shall have no one else near me whom I feel has the confidence, and would, in the same degree, represent the views and wishes of the major-general commanding. Entertaining these ideas, I respectfully suggest that his presence would add materially to the chances of success.

I have the honor to be, your obedient servant,

[JOHN S. FORD.]

* Authorizing him to organize "as many companies for special service for three months in the west" as he might be able to raise.

SOURCE: *OR*, SERIES 1, VOLUME 26, PART 2, PAGES 543–544

OR-268

[*Extract*]

Abstract from the return of the Department of the Pacific, Brig. Gen. George Wright, U.S. Army, commanding, for the December 31, 1863.

Command	Present for duty. Officers	Present for duty. Men	Aggregate present	Aggregate present and absent	Pieces of Artillery. Heavy	Pieces of Artillery. Field
General headquarters......	17	1	19	20	....	....
District of California (Wright)......	77	1,549	2,110	2,335	174	10
District of Oregon (Alvord)......	64	709	1,044	1,172	4	20
District of Humboldt (Whipple)......	27	262	416	545	....	1
District of Utah (Connor)......	42	920	1,195	1,037	....	9
District of Southern California (Curtis)	42	591	863	999	....	1
Total	259	4,032	5,647	6,378	178	41

Organization of troops in the Department of the Pacific, Brig. Gen. George Wright, U.S. Army, commanding, December 31, 1863.

. . .

DISTRICT OF UTAH.
Brig. Gen. P. EDWARD CONNOR.

Camp Douglas, Utah Ter.
Col. ROBERT POLLOCK.
3d California (six companies),
2d California Cavalry (four companies),
1st Nevada Cavalry, Companies A and B.

Fort Bridger, Utah Ter.
Maj. PATRICK A. GALLAGHER.
2d California Cavalry, Company M.
3d California, Company I.

Fort Ruby, Nev. Ter.
Lieut. Col. JEREMIAH B. MOORE.
3d California, Companies B and E.

Camp Connor, Idaho Ter.
Capt. DAVID BLACK.
3d California, Company H.

SOURCE: *OR*, SERIES 1, VOLUME 50, PART 2, PAGES 711–713

OR-269

HOUSE OF REPRESENTATIVES,
Washington City, D.C., January 4, 1864.

Maj. Gen. H. W. HALLECK:

SIR: Permit me to call your attention, and through you the attention of the honorable Secretary of War, to the fact that Camp Douglas, in Utah Territory, is located within the corporate limits of Great Salt Lake City, much to the inconvenience of the people. The California volunteers, commanded by General P. Edward Connor, were stationed in Utah, as understood, for the purpose of protecting emigration, the overland mail, and telegraph from Indian depredations. Without pausing to inquire why General Connor should have located his camp within the limits of a peaceful and loyal city rather than in the Indian country or along the road requiring protection, or, if he desired to establish his headquarters near the settlements, why he did not occupy Camp Crittenden or some place outside the limits of the capital city I repeat, without inquiry or comment concerning the wisdom of the location to facilitate the object of the expedition, the necessity for the troops in Utah does not now exist. We are informed by the message of the Governor delivered to the Utah Legislature, now in session, that peace with the Indians prevails. Gentlemen now in this city just in from Salt Lake corroborate this statement and affirm that travel through Utah and to and from the mines is perfectly safe. This being the case, I cannot but believe that the object of the expedition has been fully accomplished, and as the Delegate from Utah I hope I may be excused for respectfully suggesting that the removal of the command under General Connor would very much accommodate the people I have the honor to represent. While there the command has been and will probably continue to be supplied from the products of the soil. The crop last year, in consequence of a general scarcity of water, was very short, and serious fears are now entertained that the wheat crop of last season will scarcely be sufficient to supply the wants of the people until the next harvest. Camp Douglas is located upon the east branch of the city, about three miles from Main street and near the occupied portion of the east part of the city. The inhabitants of the city are entirely dependent for water upon the streams which flow from the mountain east and northeast of the city, and a large number of families are supplied exclusively from the small stream which flows through Camp Douglas. This stream by passing through Camp Douglas and its large corrals becomes very filthy and unfit for the domestic use of the families below. Again, a large number of the citizens depend upon range for their stock on the branch contiguous to and where Camp Douglas is located. You will learn by the inclosed order of General Connor that this stock, which has heretofore grazed upon this branch undisturbed, is now to suffer the penalty of death if found on its accustomed pasture grounds. This is also a great hardship to a people who have at the risk of their lives settled a great interior desert and who by their enterprise and industry have located and built up a flourishing colony midway the oceans, indispensable to the Government in its interoceanic communications, and greatly to the comfort and convenience of the emigrants and miners in developing the mineral wealth of the Pacific Slope. General Connor frequently, in conversation with me last summer, expressed an anxious desire to be transferred with his brave officers and men to the Potomac, where they could participate in the great struggle to maintain the authority of the Government in its well-directed efforts to subdue this wicked rebellion. I am confident no greater favor could be conferred upon the gallant general than by permitting him to take part in the active scenes of war. As the late chief justice of Utah, having been honored with the office under three successive administrations (my duties only terminating last August), having held many courts in Utah, and familiar with the sentiments of the people for nine years, I consider it my duty to your department to say that I know that the people of Utah are loyal to the Constitution and Government of the United States. As chief justice I have administered the new oath to the members of the Legislature prescribed by Congress for officers of the Government, and none have ever hesitated to take it, and although jurors are not included within the law, yet it was my custom to qualify them by this oath, and not in a single instance did a juror ever decline to be qualified by it. The direct tax was at once assumed by the Legislature, and memorials have been passed full of noble sentiments of patriotism. I am aware that converse opinions impugning the loyalty of the people have been freely expressed and circulated, but such opinions are only entertained by corrupt, weak, or mistaken, or ignorant minds. In conclusion, treaties having been formed with the Indians, peace with them and the emigrants restored, transit and travel now entirely safe and secure, the people loyal, may I not, as the representative of Utah, ask that General Connor with his soldiers be removed from the Territory and the people restored to their former rights of water and pasturage and permitted to enjoy undisturbed the blessings which God and nature have given them as the pioneer settlers of the distant valleys of the Rocky Mountains? Will you please honor me with a copy of such decision as the honorable Secretary of War may make in the premises?

I have the honor to be, with sentiments of respect, your obedient servant,

JOHN F. KINNEY.

[Indorsement.]

Respectfully referred to Brigadier-General Connor for report.

H. W. HALLECK,
General-in-Chief.

[Editor's note: *This document is referenced in* OR-273 *and* OR-274.]

SOURCE: *OR*, SERIES 1, VOLUME 50, PART 2, PAGES 715–717

OR-270

[*Extract*]

HEADQUARTERS DEPARTMENT OF THE PACIFIC,
San Francisco, February 3, 1864.

Col. E. D. TOWNSEND,
Assistant Adjutant-General, Washington City, D.C.:

COLONEL: I have the honor to acknowledge the receipt of your telegram of the 28th of January.

. . .

I have purchased a very large number of wagons and mules within the last two years. For General Carleton's expedition I had to buy 200 wagons and more than 1,200 mules, and a very large number of wagons and mules for General Connor's expedition to Salt Lake and the re-enforcements since sent to the same place. Thus it will be seen that the heavy expenditures for the means of transportation in this department have been rendered necessary in preparing commands for the Department of New Mexico and other remote districts. I have also to acknowledge the receipt of a telegram from Major Williams, assistant adjutant-general, dated January 28, inviting my attention to the expediency of granting furloughs to soldiers of the Regular Army who may re-enlist before the 1st of March. The necessary instructions have been given.

Very respectfully, your obedient servant,

G. WRIGHT,
Brigadier-General, U.S. Army, Commanding.

SOURCE: *OR*, SERIES 1, VOLUME 50, PART 2, PAGES 739–740

OR-271

Franklin, Utah Ter., *February 5, 1864.*

Brigadier-General Connor,

Commanding Camp Douglas.

Dear Sir: In view of the following matters we have thought it necessary to acquaint you with the actions of the citizens here. It is a constant stream of burlesque against the Government and you and your soldiers—such as "Thank God the buzzards are picking the bones of the U.S. Army," and that you and your army are "a set of vagabond hirelings," and that "the day was not far distant when you and your army would have to leave this country," and various other expressions of like import too numerous to mention. There is one other item we think necessary to mention. A few of the citizens here have boasted that they took $16,000 worth of Government stock in 1857. There are men here who make that boast, and can be pointed out any day. They preach to their minute men to look well to their guns, and to lay in powder and keep their horses fat. They preach at Logan for the minute men there to be in readiness to be here in two hours. We have behaved ourselves as well as any set of men ever did, and still they make these threats and abuse us and our country every time they preach. Some of the boys expect to prospect west of Box Elder as soon as spring opens, and they (the Mormons) make their brags that we shan't prospect for gold in the country. We leave these lines to your kind consideration. They are written at the request of all the miners.

Nothing more at present, but remain your friends,

M. MONCHARD,
M. LEBEAU,
PETE LUFFING,
[AND 23 OTHERS.]

[Editor's note: *This document appears in the* Official Records *as an inclosure to* OR-273.]

Source: *OR*, Series 1, Volume 50, Part 2, pages 751–752

OR-272

[*Extract*]

Headquarters District of Oregon,
Fort Vancouver, Wash. Ter., February 10, 1864.

His Excellency A. C. Gibbs,
Governor of Oregon, Portland, Oreg.:

Governor: A letter from a recruiting officer in Oregon to Col. R. F. Maury, of the First Oregon Cavalry, says that the idea prevails that there is "no necessity for more troops; indeed, that to keep troops in this district is a useless expense," &c. Every person acquainted with the wants of the frontier understands how idle such remarks are. But I desire to say distinctly that more troops are necessary, and that we have next spring and summer important work for the Oregon cavalry to perform.

. . .

Thus you will perceive that it is hoped that the troops will be able to assist the mining population in prospecting, occupying, and exploring that portion of Oregon east of the Cascade Mountains, which is now a center of great attraction to the public on this coast. It contains no doubt immensely valuable mineral deposits. It is doubtless the intention of the brave and hardy miners to explore it; in any event it is my earnest wish to give them all the assistance and protection in my power. To aid in such an interesting development should be the aim and policy of the Government. Besides the ordinary wants of the Indian frontier we shall require troops for the fortifications now building at the mouth of the river. I am just advised from department headquarters that a small expedition will probably be sent from Lapwai next summer to explore the route from Lemhi (the Mormon fort) to the mouth of the Big Horn on the Yellowstone. Until the 1st of March next large bounties are given for recruits—$302 for those who enlist and $402 to those who re-enlist. This is by recent legislation of Congress, of the 12th ultimo. Thus now is the time for adventurous spirits to join the First Oregon Cavalry. Except from the Snakes no Indian troubles are now anticipated. Those who may lightly say that troops are not wanted are little aware how much the profound peace and security which now reigns on our whole Indian frontier is due to the movements of the troops, and especially of the Oregon cavalry, during the last two summers.

. . .

I am happy to say that thus the most efficient protection has been given to the incoming emigrations of 1862 and 1863. The gallant spirits of the First Oregon Cavalry, who have borne like good soldiers the hardships of the campaigns, are entitled to my thanks for the efficient and cheerful manner in which they have discharged the duty, although they had not the good fortune to meet an enemy. Well do I know that the ardent desire of many of them would be to join in the war in the East, where it would rejoice them to battle in the glorious cause of unity, freedom, and nationality for which the armies of the Republic are now contending.

I have the honor to be, very respectfully, your obedient servant,

BENJ. ALVORD,
Brigadier-General, U.S. Volunteers, Commanding District.

SOURCE: *OR*, SERIES 1, VOLUME 50, PART 2, PAGES 744–746

OR-273

HEADQUARTERS DISTRICT OF UTAH,
Camp Douglas, Utah Ter., February 15, 1864.

General HENRY W. HALLECK,
General-in-Chief, Washington, D.C.:

GENERAL: I have the honor to acknowledge the receipt of a certified copy of a communication addressed, through the General-in Chief, to the honorable Secretary of War by Hon. J. F. Kinney,* Delegate from the Territory of Utah, transmitted to me for report, and to submit the following as my views on the several subjects contained in the communication referred to: In regard to the first point made by Mr. Kinney, relating to the location of Camp Douglas, I am not apprised whether the camp is within the limits of Great Salt Lake City, as the authorities may have chosen to prescribe in a charter or describe in an ordinance. For aught I know to the contrary, the Territorial or city authorities may have extended their city jurisdiction on paper over the whole tract of country from the mountains to the Jordan. It was and is a question which has occasioned me neither to make careful inquiry nor to exercise much consideration. I recognized the supreme authority of the United States as existing here, however little it may be respected by the leaders or masses of the people, and established my camp on what is unquestionably public domain, never reduced to adverse possession by cities, towns, or private persons, so far as I am aware. I did not recognize the right now claimed by the Legislature or city to embrace a vast region of country for city or any other purposes antagonistic to the interests of the Government when that Government desired or required any part of such domain. Mr. Kinney is at a loss to understand why General Connor should locate his camp within the limits of a peaceful and loyal city, and why he did not occupy Camp

Crittenden. In reply I have to say that Camp Douglas is on the public domain at least two miles distant from the nearest house in the city. It was selected on account of its salubrious and convenient site and abundance of water. The alleged annoyance to the citizens from the fact that one of the several streams running through or near the city is rendered filthy by the presence of the troops is greatly exaggerated, and is in my opinion an excuse for rather than a well-founded cause of complaint. My reasons for locating the camp were at the time of location, and are still, regarded as good and sufficient. First. It was and is desirable that the camp should be at some central point in the district, where supplies of forage could be most advantageously procured and whence roads diverge in all directions north, south, east, and west. These advantages could best be secured at its present location. Second. I deemed it not only prudent but absolutely necessary to the respect due to and the dignity of the Government that the camp should be located and maintained in the immediate vicinity of the headquarters of Brigham Young and his attendant nest of traitors. Previous to my arrival I was not only informed, but it was bruited about in every direction among the people, that the forces under my command, soldiers marching to the relief and for the protection of the Territory, would not be permitted to cross the Jordan on the west. This threat, publicly given out, I subsequently found to have been intended as an intimidation, with a view to stopping the command at Fort Crittenden. How much the desire of speculators to sell to Government the buildings at the latter point at exorbitant rates had to do with the origin of the threat I deem it unnecessary here to argue. Mr. Kinney over states the fact very considerably when he dwells on the loyalty and peacefulness of the people of Utah. They are bound down by a system of church tyranny more complete than that which held the bondmen of ancient Rome in early days or now enthralls Afric's sons on the cotton fields of the South. The world has never seen a system of bondage, abject slavery, espionage, and constant, unremitting tyranny in the most trivial relations of life more galling than that which Brigham Young oppresses the people in the name of religion. His teachings and those of his elders all tend to impress disloyalty upon the minds of his subjects and antagonism toward the Government, in which he recognizes neither authority over him nor goodness in itself. Until my arrival and location in his immediate presence his pulpit harangues were but iterated and reiterated denunciations of the Union and outbursts of bold-faced treason. Even now he and his chosen apostles, the minions of himself and the teachers of the people, can hardly conceal their inborn treason or repress the traitorous words which fill their hearts and break upon the ear in ill-concealed sneers and covert insinuations against the Government which fosters and protects them in their iniquities. As a specimen of the loyalty and peacefulness of the man from whom this people receive their ideas, as well of religion as of morality and the Government of the United States, I quote a brief paragraph from one of the so-called sermons of Brigham Young, delivered in presence of the assembled multitude on the 6th of October, 1863, at the Bowery, in Salt Lake City, to the semi-annual conference then in session, viz:

> As for those who Abraham Lincoln has sent here, if they meddle with our domestic affairs I will send them to hell across lots, and as for those apostates running around here, they will probably fall down and their bowels will gush out, or they will bleed somewhere else.

A sermon as remarkable for its innate treason, villainous hatred of the Government, and extreme vulgarity as it is for its grammatical construction. Were it not that these words as used by the chief priest of the church are susceptible of the most complete and overwhelming proof, it would pass credence that they were ever used by any man, however debased, in any pulpit in the land. Taught, led, governed, tyrannized over by such men, by means of the most perfect system extending throughout the whole people and down into the deepest recesses of everyday private and domestic life, covered by the thin gauze of a superstition called religion, unparalleled in the history of the world and a disgrace at once to the civilization of the nineteenth century and the free institutions of the land, it is not to be wondered at that the people, ignorant and deluded, should have attained a state of feeling not merely inimical to the Government, but bordering on treason, only suppressed for the time by the presence of the troops or the personal fears of the wily, traitorous, and treacherous leaders. When, therefore, Mr. Delegate Kinney affects patriotism himself, and with persecuted air and earnest professions characterizes the people of Utah as either loyal or peaceful, he but excites a smile upon the lips of even the casual passer-through of this land of polygamy, treason, and kindred crimes. I beg to assure the Department that the presence of the troops both in the Territory and on the present Government reservation at Camp Douglas has done much to prevent treasonable out bursts and conflict with this peculiar people and is doing much in a quiet way to lead the community back to allegiance and proper respect and regard for the Government. Brigham Young has impiously sworn and prophesied that the troops should either be destroyed or removed from Camp Douglas; and should the department intervene to remove the troops, not only would it not commend the Government to the mass of the people, but it would serve to strengthen his power and fulfill his prophecies. Not only would such a course be injurious to the Government itself, but the transfer of the troops would be regarded by thousands of the citizens, suffering under a worse than Egyptian bondage, as the withdrawal of the last ray of hope and an abandonment of them to their hard fate. That their condition has been much ameliorated since the arrival of the troops I have the strongest and best reasons for believing, and many look forward eagerly and hopefully to the time when the power of the Government shall be felt or the incoming of a new population may relieve them from a galling despotism and restore them to their long-lost rights as American citizens. I have had recent evidence of the boasted loyalty of these people in the return of an expedition sent to the south for the protection of miners. The officer in charge, Lieut. John Quinn, Second California Volunteer Cavalry, in his official report states that in many places not only could he not obtain forage for his animals at any price, the people asseverating that they would not sell a grain to Uncle Sam's minions, but he was absolutely prohibited from entering their farm-houses or seeking shelter from the winter storms in barns, sheds, and outhouses. I have also learned from credible witnesses that in cases, not few or exceptional, Gentile merchants and traders visiting the southern settlements to purchase flour and grain are invariably asked if they are buying for the troops, with the declaration of the farmers that if so grain and flour would not be sold at any price. The mere suspicion of being an agent of the Government in search of supplies is sufficient to violate any contract previously made and debar the purchaser from obtaining a bushel of wheat or a sack of flour or other produce. I inclose for the information of the Department a certified copy of a communication just received by me from miners, citizens of the United States, wintering in the neighboring town of Franklin, near the northern border of the Territory. I need hardly say that the utmost protection will be afforded them should it be required, but it is surely an anomalous position of affairs that citizens of the United States, peacefully seeking the settlement of a Territory of their common country, and that Territory professing through its Delegate loyalty and peacefulness, merely asking the hospitality accorded to humanity, should be compelled to look for protection from the armed troops of the Union. The hypocrisy of claiming either loyalty or peacefulness for such a people is too palpable to require further comment.

In reference to the special order directing stray cattle found on the reserve to be shot, which is complained of by Mr. Kinney as emanating from me, the Department is respectfully informed that the same was issued by Colonel Pollock, commanding Camp Douglas, and immediately on coming to my knowledge it was revoked by me and has not in a single instance been executed. The Department is informed that Mr. Kinney is mistaken in the assertion that this command is subsisted to any considerable extent from the "products of the soil of the Territory." Our subsistence supplies are entirely drawn from the East, except only flour, beef, and vegetables, for which articles we are now paying exorbitant rates, induced and purposely made so by the edict of Brigham Young to his people not to sell to the troops. In this manner have the contractors (Gentiles) been broken up and forced out of the field of supplying, and Brigham himself, or his chosen bishops, derive the profits from the enormous and unreasonable prices demanded and necessarily paid. For the same reasons the wood and hay contractors have been unable to fulfill their contracts, and the troops were compelled to go into the mountains twenty miles distant in the dead of winter to cut and transport timber for fuel, while the animals, from sheer necessity, had all been turned out to exist upon the light herbage to be found upon snow-clad hills and wintry plains. In consequence of this, not only have the troops at times suffered for want of fuel, but the cavalry has necessarily been dismounted, and many of our animals have perished for lack of food, when it is a conceded and well known fact that there is an abundance of forage in the Territory, for which the contractors have in vain offered the most exorbitant rates. After this statement of facts bearing on the subject I deem it my duty to the Government and the country to add that I would regard it as extremely injudicious and impolitic in every sense for the Department to comply with the request of Mr. Delegate Kinney, and it would only do so under the most decided and earnest, yet respectful, protest on my part. In conclusion I may be permitted to add that while an order transferring either myself or my command to the active scenes of the East would but be responsive to my own and the universal heartfelt desire of the troops under me, I must beg leave, respectfully, to suggest that neither they nor I have constituted Mr. Kinney our spokesman, and with a proper appreciation of his unasked-for interposition to that end and a due respect for the position he holds, would prefer communicating our wishes on proper occasions through some other and, probably, more congenial channel.

I have the honor to remain, very respectfully, your obedient servant,

P. EDW. CONNOR,
Brigadier-General, U.S. Volunteers, Commanding District.

* [*Refers to* OR-*269.*]

[Inclosure.]

[Editor's note: *See* OR-*271 for this inclosure.*]

SOURCE: *OR*, SERIES 1, VOLUME 50, PART 2, PAGES 748–751

OR-274

HEADQUARTERS DISTRICT OF UTAH,
Camp Douglas, Utah Ter., February 23, 1864.

Lieut. Col. R. C. DRUM, U.S. Army,
Assistant Adjutant-General, San Francisco, Cal.:

COLONEL: Inclosed herewith I have the honor to transmit, for the information of the general commanding the department, a certified copy of a petition from the Hon. John F. Kinney, Delegate to Congress from Utah Territory, to the General-in-Chief, and through him to the honorable Secretary of War, urging the removal of myself and command from Camp Douglas, which petition was respectfully referred by the General-in-Chief to myself for report.* I also inclose copy of such report, forwarded to the General-in-Chief, and a communication from miners residing at Franklin, Utah Ter., in relation to the disloyalty of the people in that place and vicinity.

Very respectfully, your obedient servant,

P. EDW. CONNOR,
Brigadier-General, Commanding.

* [*Refers to* OR-269.]

SOURCE: *OR*, SERIES 1, VOLUME 50, PART 2, PAGE 768

OR-275

[*Extract*]

HEADQUARTERS DISTRICT OF OREGON,
Fort Vancouver, Wash. Ter., February 25, 1864.

ASSISTANT ADJUTANT-GENERAL,
Hdqrs. Department of the Pacific, San Francisco, Cal.:

COLONEL: I have the honor to acknowledge the reception of your letter of the 28th ultimo, which says, speaking of the exploration proposed by General Totten from Lemhi (a Mormon settlement) to the Three Forks of the Upper Missouri, "General Wright desires me to say that the exploration referred to should, if possible, be made during the coming summer. You will, therefore, make the necessary arrangements for carrying out the wishes of the Government as indicated in the last para graph of General Totten's letter." As indicated in my letter of the 20th instant, I recommend that this matter be postponed to another season for the following reasons: I have just had a long interview with Judge Tufts, Speaker of the House of Representatives of Idaho Territory. He is from Virginia City, in what is called the Beaver Head country, about forty miles this side of the Three Forks, and gives me interesting statistics of the rapid settlement of that country. Within a year and a half a mining population of 12,000 souls has settled within a district of 100 miles east and west by forty north and south. The chief towns are Virginia City, East Bannock, Nevada City, Bivan's Gulch, and Gallatin, the latter at the Three Forks, the former higher up to the very headwaters of the Missouri, at the base of the Rocky Mountains on the eastern slope. Lemhi is just opposite East Bannock at the base of the Rocky

Mountains, on their western slope. They cannot be more than seventy miles apart. I respectfully represent that the whites are so rapidly exploring that country that by waiting another year any exploration will be vastly expedited. I am sure there is no good pass in the Rocky Mountains between Lemhi and East Bannock. From the statements of Judge Tufts I am satisfied that the best route for a road from new Fort Boisé to Virginia City, on the Three Forks, is to go by the emigrant road via the Three Buttes until you get on the wagon road from Salt Lake via Fort Hall to East Bannock. This crosses the Rocky Mountains near High Bank Creek. (See military map of the Department of Oregon, 1859.) This is now a well-traveled road in some parts. What the people of that country want now is military protection. That must come from the Northwestern States. I saw the Hon. W. H. Wallace, late Governor, but now Delegate from Idaho Territory, as he passed here. (By the way, I was much gratified when Idaho Territory elected a Union candidate.) I wrote him a letter, which I authorized him to show to the Secretary of War, recommending that a force should be sent to that country near the Three Forks from the Northwestern States.

. . .

The Crow Indians on the Yellowstone threaten the whites and object to the explorations of the miners. The Sioux are fast approaching the Crows. A military force is needed there, and I respectfully recommend to the general commanding the department that he make such representations to the Secretary of War as will materially aid Governor Wallace in getting the troops referred to. It is beyond my district and the Department of the Pacific, but as the seat of government of Idaho Territory is at Lewiston, on this side of the mountains, they naturally look to us for assistance. Since writing you on the 20th instant I have ordered twenty-five cavalry, under Lieutenant Waymire, from Fort Dalles to the South Fork of John Day's River, on the road to Canyon City, for the protection of the whites, some depredations having been committed by the Indians. This detachment will join Captain Drake after he starts, two months later.

I am, very respectfully, your obedient servant,

BENJ. ALVORD,
Brigadier-General, U.S. Volunteers, Commanding District.

SOURCE: *OR*, SERIES 1, VOLUME 50, PART 2, PAGES 769–771

OR-276

HEADQUARTERS DISTRICT OF UTAH,
Camp Douglas, Utah Ter., March 1, 1864.

CIRCULAR.

The undersigned has received numerous letters of complaint and inquiry from parties within and without the district, the former alleging that certain residents of Utah Territory indulge in threats and menaces against miners and others desirous of prospecting for precious metals, and the latter asking what, if any, protection will be accorded to those coming hither to develop the mineral resources of the country. Without giving undue importance to the thoughtless or reckless words of misguided prejudices, or bad-hearted men who may be guilty of such threats as those referred to, and indulging the hope that they are but individual expressions rather than menaces issued by any presumed or presumptuous authority whatever, the undersigned takes occasion to repeat what no loyal citizen will gainsay, that this Territory is the public property of the nation, whose wish and interest it is that it be developed at the earliest possible day in all its rich resources—mineral as well as agricultural, pastoral, and mechanical. To this end citizens of the United States, and all desirous of becoming such, are freely invited by public law and national policy to come hither to enrich themselves and advance the general welfare from out the public store, which a bountiful Providence has scattered through these richly laden mountains and fertile plains. The mines are thrown open to the hardy and industrious, and it is announced that they will receive the amplest protection in life, property, and rights against aggression from whatever source, Indian or white.

The undersigned has abundant reason to know that the mountains of Utah, north, south, east, and west, are prolific in mineral wealth. Gold, silver, iron, copper, lead, and coal are found in almost every direction, in quantities which promise the richest results to the adventurous explorer and the industrious miner.

In giving assurance of entire protection to all who may come hither to prospect for mines, the undersigned wishes at this time most earnestly, and yet firmly, to warn all, whether permanent residents or not of the Territory, that should violence be offered or attempted to be offered to miners in the pursuit of their lawful occupation, the offender or offenders, one or many, will be tried as public enemies, and punished to the utmost extent of martial law.

The undersigned does not desire to indulge in useless threats, but wishes most fully and explicitly to apprise all of their rights, and warn misguided men of the inevitable result should they seek to obstruct citizens in those rights, or throw obstacles in the way of the development of the public domain. While miners will be thus protected, they must understand that no interference with the vested rights of the people of the Territory will be tolerated, and they are expected to conform in all things to the laws of the land, which recognize in their fullest extent the claims of the bona fide settlers on public lands. While the troops have been sent to this district to protect from a savage foe the homes and premises of the settler and the public interests of the nation, they are also here to preserve the public peace, secure to all the inestimable blessings of liberty, and preserve intact the honor, dignity, and rights of the citizen vested by a free Constitution, and which belong to the humblest equally with the highest in the land. This, their mission, it is the duty of the undersigned to see fulfilled by kindly and warning words, if possible, but if not, still to be enforced at every hazard and at any cost. He cannot permit the public peace and the welfare of all to be jeoparded by the foolish threats or wicked actions of a few.

P. EDW. CONNOR,
Brigadier-General, U.S. Volunteers, Commanding District.

SOURCE: *OR*, SERIES 1, VOLUME 50, PART 2, PAGES 774–775

OR-277

[*Extract*]

HEADQUARTERS DISTRICT OF OREGON,
Fort Vancouver, Wash. Ter., March 3, 1864.

Maj. Gen. SAMUEL R. CURTIS,
Comdg. Department of Kansas, Fort Leavenworth, Kans.:

GENERAL: I perceive that you are placed in command of the Department of Kansas extending to the Rocky Mountains. My district extends to those mountains, embracing the boundaries of old Oregon Territory. I write to invite your attention to the defense needed for the settlements in Idaho Territory at the base of those mountains on the headwaters of the Missouri. Within 100 miles westerly of the Three Forks of the Missouri (where the Jefferson, the Madison, and the Gallatin unite) there are now 12,000 miners. Virginia City has 5,000 souls. The other towns are East Bannock, Bivan's Gulch, Nevada City, and Gallatin. It is a very rich mineral district, and large numbers of whites will emigrate thither this coming season. Idaho Territory extends from Fort Boisé to beyond Fort Laramie. The authorities of that Territory have been in contact with me and have applied for troops, as also the settlements in the Bitter Root country, at the base of the Rocky Mountains on their western slope. The latter as well as the former should be protected by troops from the Northwestern States. We have but a few troops in this district, and they by the tempting attractions of this coast are fast dwindling away by desertion; few will re-enlist and their time expires next winter. I therefore respectfully submit to you that a force should be sent by you to take possession of that country. I should, in reference to this side the mountains, only ask that two mounted companies should be sent to the Bitter Root country (to the Indian agency), the post to belong of course to your department and excepted from my district. That region will be supplied from Saint Louis and the Lower Missouri, and the troops should come thence. Mr. Chouteau, of Saint Louis, confidently expects that steamers can go up the Yellowstone to the mouth of Clark's Fork, or perhaps to Big Elbow. It will no doubt be tried next summer. A few companies of infantry should go by steamer to the head of navigation on the Yellowstone, where probably some eligible site for a large post can be found. Nearly a regiment of mounted troops should be sent thither by land I suppose over the emigrant road via Fort Laramie. I am not sufficiently acquainted with the route via Fort Randall to know whether troops could reach the Yellowstone better by that route. I do know that a wagon road to Virginia City, Idaho Ter., by way of Fort Laramie, does exist, viz, by continuing upon the old emigrant road via the South Pass until the troops shall get on the well-traveled wagon road from Salt Lake City to Virginia City. Doubtless an exploration from the Three Forks to Fort Laramie would subsequently find a good road across.

. . .

Seeing by the papers that you are assigned to the command, I have resolved to lay the matter before you. It is eminently wise policy to encourage emigration to the Territories and the establishment of a chain of settlements from the Mississippi to the Pacific.

I have the honor to be, very respectfully, your obedient servant,

BENJ. ALVORD,

Brigadier-General, U.S. Volunteers, Commanding District.

SOURCE: *OR*, SERIES 1, VOLUME 50, PART 2, PAGES 776–777

OR-278

HEADQUARTERS DISTRICT OF OREGON,
Fort Vancouver, Wash. Ter., March 4, 1864.

Capt. F. SEIDENSTRIKER, or
Commanding Officer at Fort Boisé, Idaho Ter.:

CAPTAIN: Your letters of the 7th and 11th ultimo have been received. Your course in supplying with rations the destitute Indians near your post, and in ordering the quartermaster's department to hire an interpreter, is approved by the general commanding the district. The general commanding does not approve of your sending for all the Indians at Salmon Falls if it is for the purpose of subsisting them. It will stagger the quartermaster's department to transport subsistence for the troops at Fort Boisé and the expeditions to start from there next summer. It is allowable to issue rations in cases of extreme destitution, but the Indians must be taught to rely on their own efforts for subsistence. If the Indians from Salmon Falls come in you will inform them, as Colonel Maury did, of our friendly disposition toward peaceable and quiet Indians, and that our punishments are confined to those who steal from and murder the whites. Treaties were made last summer by Governor Doty, of Utah, with large bands of the Snakes, and it will be well for all those Indians to understand that if they behave themselves they will not be disturbed by the troops. But for subsistence tell them they must rely, as heretofore, on digging their roots and fishing. They will not be disturbed in fishing at Salmon Falls. In reference to the subsistence of Indians see paragraph V, of General Orders, No. 2, of the 5th of January, 1864, from headquarters Department of the Pacific.

By order of General Alvord:

I am, sir, very respectfully, your obedient servant,

J. W. HOPKINS,
First Lieutenant, First Oregon Cavalry, Actg. Asst. Adjt. Gen.

SOURCE: *OR*, SERIES 1, VOLUME 50, PART 2, PAGES 777–778

OR-279

HEADQUARTERS DEPARTMENT OF THE PACIFIC,
San Francisco, March 5, 1864.

ADJUTANT-GENERAL U.S. ARMY,
Washington, D.C.:

SIR: Brig. Gen. P. E. Connor, commanding the District of Utah, has submitted to me a copy of a communication addressed to Major-General Halleck on the 4th of January last by the Hon. J. F. Kinney, Delegate to Congress from Utah, together with his (Connor's) reply to General Halleck. During the last year the removal of the troops from Camp Douglas was maturely and carefully considered, and I was fully persuaded that the present location at Camp Douglas was the proper position. I have but little faith in the loyalty of the Mormons. They threatened last year to destroy any re-enforcements from California approaching Camp Douglas, but I sent them and they reached there in safety. I would most earnestly recommend not only that Camp Douglas be maintained, but that it be strongly re-enforced.

Very respectfully, your obedient servant.

G. WRIGHT,
Brigadier-General, U.S. Army, Commanding.

SOURCE: *OR*, SERIES 1, VOLUME 50, PART 2, PAGE 778

OR-280

HEADQUARTERS,
Fort Walla Walla, Wash. Ter., March 6, 1864.

ACTING ASSISTANT ADJUTANT-GENERAL,
Hdqrs. District of Oregon, Fort Vancouver, Wash. Ter.:

SIR: Your communication of the 26th ultimo, advising me of the contemplated movement of troops from this post, reached me on the evening of the 3d instant. Everything will be done here that it is practicable to accomplish to put Captain Currey's command properly in the field. The means of transportation on hand is, however, so limited that what we can spare beyond the requirements of the post will not suffice for the expedition. I inclose herewith a tabular statement of the whole available means of transportation, furnished me by Lieutenant Cabanis.*

The condition of the articles is also represented, and the number of each that we shall require for the use of the post. We can furnish ninety-nine pack animals but have so little pack furniture that it is scarcely worth taking into account. I have examined the wagons and aparejos to-day carefully, and find that a number of the former reported as unserviceable can be put in good repair. The aparejos are those that have been on hand at this post ever since Major Kirkham had charge of the quartermaster's department. The whole lot was reported unserviceable last year, but for fear the new ones ordered for Colonel Maury's expedition would not arrive in time, about 136 of them were put in some sort of condition, and were used by him, and turned in on his return in the fall. They have been repaired over and over again, and have seen such hard service that they are not now worth the expense and labor of any further repairs. The leather is rotten and will not hold when sewed, and the under surface that should be soft, smooth, and even is hard and wrinkled. There are probably twenty or twenty-five that can be put in tolerable order, but certainly not more, and even these will prove costly. The new aparejos (100) alluded to above did arrive too late for Colonel Maury's expedition, and are, I am informed, stored at Fort Lapwai. These, however, may be wanted at that post, if as is reported a command will be fitted out there to explore the country in the direction of the old Mormon Fort Lemhi. There are plenty of pack-saddles in good condition here, but as there has never been any use for them, Lieutenant Cabanis had them put on an inspection report. The trees are of the old-fashioned pattern, and are almost worthless in packing. The lash ropes, &c., belonging to the aparejos are in pretty good order. The pack train of ninety-nine animals that we can supply here will I think be large enough to meet all the requirements of the expedition that it is intended to meet; for besides being able to carry all the camp equipage, ammunition, &c., that the command will need, and after furnishing riding animals for packers, herders, &c., there will still be left enough to transport subsistence stores for forty-five or fifty days. There will then remain some 50,000 pounds of subsistence stores to be transported in wagons. If it is the intention of the general to direct the establishment of a supply depot at which Captain Currey can replenish his packs when exhausted, and which will be permanent during the expedition, ten or twelve wagons will suffice for the purpose. This train can make several trips during the summer from Fort Boisé and carry stores in sufficient quantity to keep the command well supplied. As the force under Captain Currey will be too small to warrant him in leaving any portion of it, to establish and guard his depot, I would recommend that a detachment of at least two commissioned officers and fifty infantry soldiers be sent with him to be assigned to this duty. I should also think a mounted escort requisite to insure the safety of the wagon train while en route. It does not seem to me necessary that Captain Currey should be required to go all the way to Fort Boisé preparatory to making a start. He has to return over very nearly the same road from Boisé to the mouth of the Owyhee that he will take in going up, and I would suggest the propriety of his camping in that vicinity until joined by the infantry and Lieutenant Hobart's detachment. They can be directed to meet him at that point on a certain date; or should he be obliged to await their arrival, he can in the meantime examine the country and determine the most practicable route upon which to direct the wagon train, and thus save much valuable time. His horses and pack animals would also have a good opportunity to improve during the interval. I also inclose a statement* of the subsistence stores on hand at this post, what will be required for the use of the present garrison until May 1, what will be required from that date until August 1, and what will be available for the use of the expedition. It is believed that the new stores will commence to arrive prior to August 1, so that the troops left in garrison will have an abundance of stores on hand. Should I be mistaken in this, please advise me. I will have everything here prepared and at the disposal of the general as many days prior to May 1 as possible.

Very respectfully, your obedient servant,

T. C. ENGLISH,
Lieutenant-Colonel First Washington Territory Infantry, Comdg.

* Omitted.

SOURCE: *OR*, SERIES 1, VOLUME 50, PART 2, PAGES 781–782

OR-281

HEADQUARTERS DEPARTMENT OF THE PACIFIC,
San Francisco, Cal., March 12, 1864.

Brig. Gen. P. E. CONNOR, U.S. Volunteers,
Commanding District of Utah:

GENERAL: The general commanding the department, having read with care your circular of March 1, desires me to say that he approves the position taken for protection of all loyal American citizens who may seek a home in the Territory of Utah. The laws of Congress for the protection of citizens must be enforced.

Very respectfully, your obedient servant,

R. C. DRUM,
Assistant Adjutant-General.

SOURCE: *OR*, SERIES 1, VOLUME 50, PART 2, PAGE 787

OR-282

Headquarters District of Utah,
Camp Douglas, Utah Ter., March 18, 1864.

Special Orders,
No. 24.

Lieut. Col. William Jones and Capt. Samuel P. Smith, Second Cavalry California Volunteers, will proceed west of Salt Lake to select a cavalry camp.

By command of Brigadier-General Connor:

M. G. LEWIS,
Assistant Adjutant-General.

Source: *OR*, Series 1, Volume 50, Part 2, page 795

OR-283

Camp Douglas, Utah Ter.,
March 30, 1864.

Lieut. Col. R. C. Drum,
San Francisco, Cal.:

My Dear Colonel: The more I think and inquire about the Colorado route the more convinced I am of the necessity and importance of opening the route. Communication at all seasons of the year with navigable waters will be of the utmost importance to the speedy development of this Territory. Consequently I have concluded to make a military road from this place to Fort Mojave, and shall start a force for that purpose as soon as the grass has grown sufficiently to sustain the animals. Will you answer, if possible, the following questions? Are there commissary stores at Fort Mojave, so that the command I will send can draw there for the return trip? How many months in the year can the river be navigated to Fort Mojave? I can make a new road to the fort in a distance of about 500 miles, which can be traveled at all seasons of the year. In fact, winter would be the most preferable time on account of the heat in the summer. If our supplies can be sent by steam to the mouth of the Colorado, and thence shipped to Mojave as speedily as possible, I recommend they be sent that way. Otherwise a few articles most needed could be sent the Placerville route and the balance be sent by sailing vessel to the mouth of the river. All quiet in Jerusalem.

Sincerely, your friend,

P. EDW. CONNOR.

[Editor's note: *Indorsement removed for lack of relevance.*]

SOURCE: *OR*, SERIES 1, VOLUME 50, PART 2, PAGES 802–803

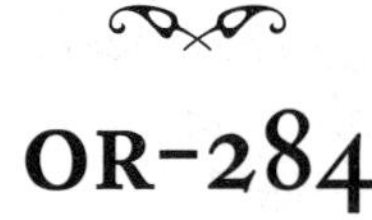

OR-284

HDQRS. DEPT. OF THE MISSOURI,
Saint Louis, Mo., April 2, 1864.

GENERAL ORDERS,
No. 50.

I. General Orders, No. 32, current series, from these headquarters, is amended as follows: First. Provost-marshals of sub-districts are authorized and required to issue the permits therein provided for, upon the approval of district provost-marshals and district commanders. They will keep the same record books required of district provost-marshals in paragraph IV of the order. Second. The order will not be so construed as to prevent the issue of permits to purchase arms and ammunition to loyal men desiring to cross the plains, and who can produce evidence that they are not attempting to evade the conscription act or the enrollment of militia in the State of Missouri.

II. All restrictions imposed in General Orders, No. 32, affecting the legitimate, bona-fide trade with New Mexico, Utah, and other loyal sections of the country west of Missouri, are hereby removed, as far as purchasers from those sections are concerned. Sellers of arms and ammunition will be held to a rigid compliance with the terms of the order affecting them; but all traders pursuing a legitimate trade with the sections above indicated will be permitted to purchase at Kansas City, Westport, Saint Joseph, and Saint Louis, with the same freedom as before the war.

By command of Major-General Rosecrans:

O.D. GREENE,
Assistant Adjutant-General.

SOURCE: *OR*, SERIES 1, VOLUME 34, PART 3, PAGES 21–22

OR-285

HEADQUARTERS DEPARTMENT OF THE PACIFIC,
San Francisco, April 9, 1864.

ADJUTANT-GENERAL U.S. ARMY,
Washington, D.C.:

SIR: The condition of affairs in this department is unchanged. In the District of Oregon Brigadier-General Alvord is organizing small commands to move over the country toward Snake River for the protection of settlers and emigrants approaching from the east. In the District of Humboldt, Colonel Black, Sixth Infantry California Volunteers, is prosecuting vigorously the war against the hostile Indians, and if a reservation is set apart remote from that country I hope at an early day to send those Indians to it. In the District of Southern California quiet prevails. The seventh and last company of the First Cavalry California Volunteers has marched for Arizona. In the District of Utah there is no change to report. General Connor recommends that the volunteers raised in California and now serving in Utah be discharged there at the expiration of their service. I have ordered it so done unless instructions to the contrary shall be received from the War Department. Recruiting for a regiment of infantry in Nevada Territory is progressing favorably well. If we can raise a regiment I propose to send it to Utah in the course of the summer.

Very respectfully, your obedient servant,

G. WRIGHT,
Brigadier-General, U.S. Army, Commanding.

SOURCE: *OR*, SERIES 1, VOLUME 50, PART 2, PAGE 809

OR-286

HEADQUARTERS DISTRICT OF OREGON,
Fort Vancouver, Wash. Ter., April 9, 1864.

Col. R. F. MAURY,
First Oregon Cavalry, Commanding Fort Dalles, Oreg.:

COLONEL: The general commanding the district directs me to acknowledge the reception of your letter of the 6th instant stating that "it is perfectly practicable and desirable to the Government and Indians to collect and settle all these roving tribes. * * * Considerations of humanity and economy prompt immediate steps to remedy both evils—extermination and the cost of fitting out expeditions every summer." The general concurs fully with you in these views. The only question is the way of practically effecting the object. He expects soon to get a copy of the treaty made with the Snakes in Utah, and will send you a copy of it. Any feasible and practicable scheme of getting the Snakes under our control will command instant attention from these headquarters. They are a roving, nomadic race. They speak the Comanche language, and are Comanches—a tribe hard to tame, not accustomed to a fixed place of abode; have no homes and no country; cannot by treaty surrender any lands, for they claim none. Such is supposed to be their condition. If placed on a reservation it is doubtful whether they would stay there. As the commanding officer at Fort Boisé, the general will desire from you your views in full from time to time. Several questions would occur: Where can a reservation be found? If near Goose Lake, could it be found north of the California line? No reservation would avail if there were not troops near to look after the Indians. The general has already had a conversation on this subject with J. W. P. Huntington, esq., superintendent of Indian affairs for Oregon. He will continue to confer with him on that subject, and recommend that he seek from Congress an appropriation for the subsistence of the Indians who may come in and submit. At Fort Boisé the general desires you to avail yourself of every opportunity to impress upon the Indians the importance of their submission to the authorities and preserving the peace. Captain Currey will be instructed to be governed by any views you may submit to him on this subject during the coming summer. After a good whipping they would perhaps be more ready for a treaty than now. If Captain Drake shall at any time find himself in position to talk with them, he may embrace it to inculcate upon those Indians the importance of their giving up their roving and marauding habits. He may sound them as to their willingness to go on some fixed reservation, and particularly ascertain whether they have any head chiefs with whom we could treat. Information of this nature will be important for the Indian Department to receive, and the general wishes to be able to give it to Mr. Huntington, whether received from yourself, Captain Currey, or Captain Drake. The great want will be sufficient troops, especially if a new military post near Goose Lake should become a necessity. Please show this letter to Captain Drake and furnish him with a copy of the same.

I have the honor to be, very respectfully, your obedient servant.

J. W. HOPKINS,
First Lieutenant, First Oregon Cavalry, Actg. Asst. Adjt. Gen.

SOURCE: *OR*, SERIES 1, VOLUME 50, PART 2, PAGES 810–811

OR-287

[*Extract*]

HEADQUARTERS DEPARTMENT OF THE PACIFIC,
San Francisco, April 11, 1864.

His Excellency JAMES W. NYE,
Governor of Nevada Territory, Carson City:

SIR: I have the honor to acknowledge the receipt of Your Excellency's communication of the 5th instant in relation to the disposition of troops during the coming summer, in order to afford protection to the mining population as well as to the emigrants approaching from the eastern States.*

. . .

Expeditions have been prepared at Camp Douglas, near Great Salt Lake City, for the purpose of affording protection to all loyal citizens coming to this country. It is intended, as far as our limited means may allow, to give protection over all the routes leading into this country, and that leading by the "City of Rocks" and the country north of the Humboldt will not be overlooked. I am most happy to reply to Your Excellency's communication, as it is only in that way I can learn the wants of the people in remote and sparsely settled districts which troops have rarely traversed.

With great respect, Your Excellency's obedient servant,

G. WRIGHT,
Brigadier-General, U.S. Army, Commanding.

* [*Refers to Carleton to Wright, March 7, 1864.* OR, *Series 1, Volume 50, Part 2, pages 783–784.*]

SOURCE: *OR*, SERIES 1, VOLUME 50, PART 2, PAGES 812–813

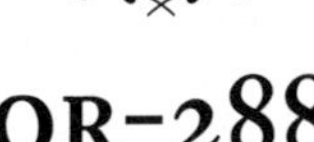

OR-288

WAR DEPARTMENT, ADJUTANT-GENERAL'S OFFICE,
Washington, April 13, 1864.

Brig. Gen. GEORGE WRIGHT, U.S. Volunteers,
Commanding Department of the Pacific, San Francisco, Cal.:

SIR: I have the honor to acknowledge the receipt of your communication of the 5th ultimo in which you inclose a communication from Brigadier-General Alvord, commanding the District of Oregon, and recommend the views therein expressed by General Alvord to the favorable consideration of the General-in-Chief and the War Department. General Alvord's communication relates to the exploration of the country from Lemhi (a Mormon settlement) to the Three Forks of the Upper Missouri, which was proposed by Brigadier-General Totten in November, 1863, for the present season. General Alvord recommends, for the reasons stated in his communication, that the exploration be postponed to another season. I am directed to notify you that the Secretary of War approves the views of Brigadier-General Alvord, and that the exploration will be accordingly postponed.

I am, sir, very respectfully, your obedient servant,

E. D. TOWNSEND,
Assistant Adjutant-General.

SOURCE: *OR*, SERIES 1, VOLUME 50, PART 2, PAGE 818

OR-289

HEADQUARTERS DISTRICT OF UTAH,
Camp Douglas, Utah Ter., April 13, 1864.

SPECIAL ORDERS,
No. 32.

I. Lieut. Col. William Jones, Second Cavalry California Volunteers, will, on receipt of this order, turn over the command of the troops at the Rush Valley Reservation to Maj. John M. O'Neill, of the same regiment.

II. Lieutenant-Colonel Jones, upon being relieved, will repair immediately to Camp Babbitt, Visalia, Cal. Captain Stover, assistant quartermaster, will furnish the necessary transportation to Sacramento, Cal.

By command of Brigadier-General Connor:

M. G. LEWIS,
Assistant Adjutant-General.

SOURCE: *OR*, SERIES 1, VOLUME 50, PART 2, PAGE 818

OR-290

HDQRS. DEPARTMENT OF THE PACIFIC,
San Francisco, Cal., April 14, 1864.

SPECIAL ORDERS,
No. 80.

1. Lieut. Col. A. A. C. Williams, Nevada Territory cavalry, will proceed to Camp Douglas and report to Brig. Gen. P. Edward Connor, commanding District of Utah, to command the battalion of Nevada Territory cavalry.

* * * *

By order of Brigadier-General Wright:

RICHD. C. DRUM,
Assistant Adjutant-General.

SOURCE: *OR*, SERIES 1, VOLUME 50, PART 2, PAGE 820

OR-291

HEADQUARTERS DISTRICT OF UTAH,
Camp Douglas, Utah Ter., April 23, 1864.

SPECIAL ORDERS,
No. 36.

Captain Price's company (M), Second Cavalry California Volunteers, now at Fort Bridger, will take up the line of march for Camp Douglas, Utah Ter., on Monday, May 2, 1864, and on arrival at the latter post Captain Price will report to the commanding officer for duty.

By command of Brigadier-General Connor:

M. G. LEWIS,
Assistant Adjutant-General.

SOURCE: *OR*, SERIES 1, VOLUME 50, PART 2, PAGE 825

OR-292

[*Extract*]

Headquarters Department of Kansas,
Fort Leavenworth, April 25, 1864.

Col. E. D. Townsend,
Assistant Adjutant-General:

I telegraphed you on the 16th instant, calling your attention to erroneous impressions created by a report from your office as published in Senate Ex. Doc. 32, which stated my force at about 16,000. Your dispatch of the 17th, turning over the Indian Territory to the Department of Arkansas, was duly received and my officers and troops are duly informed. I now call your attention to my trimonthly report of the 20th, which was forwarded on the 22d instant, which shows all my forces present for duty only 4,350.

. . .

Knowing the desire to mass forces on special and desirable movements, I fear this department will be again subject to devastation such as transpired at Shawnee, Olathe, Humboldt, Baxter Springs, and Lawrence, because of the absence of the people of Kansas who have joined our remote and more advanced columns of volunteer forces. In consequence of past disasters I am obliged to place guards at many important towns to prevent a general departure of terrified inhabitants; and the little force I have is therefore all employed guarding the overland mail route, the Santa Fé route, and the posts and stores of my command. The posts are so widely separated, and some of them so remote, extending to Idaho and nearly to Salt Lake, I cannot concentrate, as you will perceive, any considerable number to resist a raid if one be made into Southern Kansas.

I hope, therefore, you will present to the honorable the Secretary of War the necessity of immediately strengthening in some way my available force to resist assaults from rebels approaching through the Indian Territory on the line of Quantrill's last movement, which was about the meridian of 96 or 97 degrees.

I have the honor to be, colonel, your obedient servant,

S. R. CURTIS,
Major-General.

Source: *OR*, Series 1, Volume 34, Part 3, pages 288–289

OR-293

HEADQUARTERS DEPARTMENT OF THE PACIFIC,
San Francisco, April 30, 1864.

ADJUTANT-GENERAL U.S. ARMY,
Washington, D.C.:

SIR: I have six companies of cavalry, Nevada Territory volunteers, mustered into service. Two of these companies I sent to Camp Douglas, Utah Ter., last October; the remaining four are at Fort Churchill. Only one of the companies at Churchill have been mounted. My design was to send all the Nevada cavalry to Utah, but the threatening aspect of our foreign relations, indicating the propriety of my holding all my available force well in hand and prepared for concentration on the Pacific Coast, has caused me to hesitate until the policy of my Government is known. In consequence of the enormous cost of forage at Fort Churchill, I have suspended the purchase of horses for mounting the three cavalry companies now there until their destination is determined on. Under the call I made on the Governor of Nevada Territory for a regiment of infantry, 200 men have been enrolled; they are at Fort Churchill. The Governor is quite confident of his ability to complete the organization of the regiment. During the quiet and peaceful times on this coast we cannot expect to raise many volunteers, but if we should have a foreign war there will be no lack of men.

Very respectfully, your obedient servant,

G. WRIGHT,
Brigadier-General, U.S. Army, Commanding.

SOURCE: *OR*, SERIES 1, VOLUME 50, PART 2, PAGE 833

OR-294

HEADQUARTERS DISTRICT OF UTAH,
Camp Douglas, Utah Ter., April 30, 1864.

SPECIAL ORDERS,
No. 40.

I. Captain Smith's company (K), Second Cavalry California Volunteers, will proceed on Tuesday next, the 3d proximo, via Camp Douglas, to scour the country in the vicinity of Raft River, City of Rocks, the Port Neuf River, and Fort Hall, in

Idaho Territory, in search of five lodges of hostile Shoshone Indians, who failed to attend the treaties of last year, and who have lately been committing depredations on emigrants en route to Idaho, and if found they will be punished. The peaceable Indians in the northern settlements and in the vicinity of the ferries on Snake River, east of Fort Hall, will not be molested. The company will take three months rations and will return and report to these headquarters on or about the 31st day of July next, unless otherwise ordered.

II. Captain Baldwin's company (B), Nevada Territory cavalry, will proceed on Tuesday next, via Camp Douglas, to Uintah Valley in this Territory, for the protection of miners and exploration of the resources of the valley. The company will take three months rations and proceed to and report to the commanding officer of Fort Bridger for duty on or about the 31st day of July next, unless otherwise ordered.

III. Captain Berry's company (A), Second Cavalry California Volunteers, will proceed on Saturday next south to what is known as the Beaver and Reese River road, and will scour the country between Cedar Swamp and the newly discovered silver mines in Washington County, Utah Ter., for the protection of miners and exploration of the resources of the country. The company will take ninety days rations and report on or about the 31st day of July next to the commanding officer Second Cavalry California Volunteers, unless otherwise ordered.

IV. More specific instructions will be issued to company commanders from these headquarters. The quartermaster's department will furnish the necessary teams for transportation.

By command of Brigadier-General Connor:

M. G. LEWIS,
Assistant Adjutant-General.

SOURCE: *OR*, SERIES 1, VOLUME 50, PART 2, PAGE 834

OR-295

OFFICE OF SUPERINTENDENT OF INDIAN AFFAIRS,
Salem, Oreg., May 2, 1864.

Brig. Gen. B. ALVORD,
Commanding District of Oregon, Vancouver, Wash. Ter.:

SIR: The copy of your letter to Col. R. F. Maury (dated 8th ultimo) which you were kind enough to furnish for the information of this office reached me after some delay. I intended when at Portland last week to have gone over to Vancouver for the purpose of calling upon you and conferring with reference to Indian affairs, not only east of the Cascade Mountains, but at other points. I do not think at this late day, and at a time when the demands upon the Treasury are so great, that it will be of any use to attempt to obtain an appropriation for the support of Indians who are now and have long been hostile to the whites, and in a condition of actual war. It is uncertain when they can be brought under control, if indeed the process of taming them does not result in their extermination. If, however, they are persuaded or whipped into a willingness to submit to the authority of the United States, and, ceasing their savage hostility, will collect on a reservation, I do not know of a location more adapted to their wants or less objectionable, when the interests of whites are considered, than the tract reserved for those purposes in the Klamath Lake country. A copy of the notice of this reservation is herewith inclosed, which will acquaint you with its boundaries. The new post, Fort Klamath, is near the northwest corner of the tract. Some provisions could probably be made for their support (should they remove there this summer) until Congress at its session next December could make an appropriation for the purpose. You are probably aware that Congress has at its present session appropriated $20,000 for the purpose of treating with the tribes of Southeastern Oregon, purchasing their lands, &c., and I hope that the operations of the military department will meet with such success that it will be practicable to include the roving bands of Snakes as well as the Klamath and Modoc tribes. The information now in possession of this office in regard to these tribes (which, I may remark, is meager and unsatisfactory) does not correspond with the opinion expressed in your letter to Colonel Maury, "that they have no homes and no country, and cannot by treaty surrender their lands, for they claim none;" but on the contrary indicate that they do claim all the land embraced in Southeastern Oregon together with parts of Idaho, Utah, and perhaps Nevada. The copy of my letter of June 1* last to the Commissioner of Indian Affairs contains the facts now attainable and my opinion of what should be done, and I take the liberty to inclose it herewith for your information. If you obtain from Colonel Maury or any other source information of value to this office in relation to these Indians I request that it be communicated.

I am, general, very respectfully, your obedient servant,

J. W. PERIT HUNTINGTON,
Superintendent of Indian Affairs in Oregon.

* [*Refers to Huntington to Dole, June 1, 1863.* OR, *Series 1, Volume 50, Part 2, pages 468–470.*]

[Inclosure.]

[Editor's note: *Inclosure removed for lack of relevance.*]

SOURCE: *OR*, SERIES 1, VOLUME 50, PART 2, PAGES 836–837

OR-296

[*Extract*]

HEADQUARTERS DEPARTMENT OF THE PACIFIC,
San Francisco, May 2, 1864.

ADJUTANT-GENERAL U.S. ARMY,
Washington, D.C.:

SIR: The general condition of affairs in this department remains unchanged. Recruiting progresses as favorably as could be expected; the troops are in good health and judiciously posted for the preservation of the peace and quiet of the land. The programme for the movable columns during the summer for the protection of immigrants from the eastern States is as follows: Troops from the District of Oregon to move from Forts Dalles and Walla Walla, to be advanced southeasterly to the upper waters of the Snake River. Troops from the District of Utah will afford protection along the great thoroughfares through that Territory and Southern Idaho. A command from Fort Klamath will move in an easterly direction over Southern Oregon to the Owyhee River and the southern portion of Idaho Territory; and a command from Fort Churchill will move northward and scout in the vicinity of Lakes Pyramid, Humboldt, and Honey, affording protection along the Humboldt route. This arrangement will afford ample protection to the settlements within our borders as well as to the immigrants approaching from the east.

. . .

Very respectfully, your obedient servant,

G. WRIGHT,
Brigadier-General, U.S. Army, Commanding.

SOURCE: *OR*, SERIES 1, VOLUME 50, PART 2, PAGES 837–838

OR-297

HEADQUARTERS DISTRICT OF UTAH,
Camp Douglas, Utah Ter., May 9, 1864.

Capt. SAMUEL P. SMITH,
Co. K, Second California Vol. Cavalry, Comdg. Expedition:

CAPTAIN: You will proceed by easy marches to Raft River, Idaho Ter., or vicinity, where you will establish a depot for your supplies, and then return four of your wagons (driven by citizens) to this post. After establishing your camp you will take steps to capture or kill the male adults of live lodges of Snake Indians who have for years infested the roads in that vicinity, and who have of late been stealing from and attacking emigrants to Idaho. You will be particular that friendly Indians are not molested, but treated kindly by your command. The lady of the honorable Judge Waite and a woman fleeing from Mormon persecution will accompany you. You will give them transportation and protection as far as Fort Boisé, sending a small escort from Raft River to Boisé for their protection. You will render ample protection to emigrants south of Snake River and between City of Rocks and the Port Neuf River, and at the same time thoroughly prospect the country for precious metals, particularly placer gold, and report from time to time the result to this office. You will be particular that your horses are taken good care of and kept in good order, and you will return to this post, unless otherwise instructed, on or about the 1st day of August next.

By command of Brigadier-General Connor:

M. G. LEWIS,
Assistant Adjutant-General.

[Editor's note: *This document appears in the* Official Records *as an inclosure to OR-300.*]

SOURCE: *OR*, SERIES 1, VOLUME 50, PART 2, PAGE 845

OR-298

HEADQUARTERS DISTRICT OF UTAH,
Camp Douglas, Utah Ter., May 11, 1864.

Capt. N. BALDWIN,
First Nevada Territory Vol. Cavalry, Comdg. Expedition:

CAPTAIN: You will proceed with your company to-morrow by way of Parley's Park to Uintah Valley, in this Territory, and at some central point establish a temporary depot for your supplies, after which you will return to this post the four teams with your command, driven by citizens. You will afford ample protection to prospectors and miners, and the Indians in that valley being all friendly, they will be treated with kindness by your command. You will cause the valley and vicinity to be thoroughly prospected by your men, and will report from time to time the result to this office. The discovery of placer mines is of especial importance. You will therefore devote the most of your attention to their discovery. You will proceed to Fort Bridger, Utah

Ter., by the way of Brown's Hole, on Green River, and report to the commanding officer of that post for duty on or about the 1st day of August next.

By command of Brigadier-General Connor:

M. G. LEWIS,
Assistant Adjutant-General.

[Editor's note: *This document appears in the* Official Records *as an inclosure to* OR-*300*.]

SOURCE: *OR*, SERIES 1, VOLUME 50, PART 2, PAGE 846

OR-299

HEADQUARTERS DISTRICT OF UTAH,
Camp Douglas, Utah Ter., May 13, 1864.

Capt. DAVID J. BERRY,
Co. A, Second California Vol. Cavalry, Comdg. Expedition:

CAPTAIN: You will proceed with your company from your present camp in a southerly direction to Tintic Valley, and from thence south by the most practicable route to the Meadow Valley mining district, situated about 100 miles west of Cedar City, in this Territory. You will select a camp about midway between Cedar Swamp and Meadow Valley, where you will leave a part of your company with the bulk of your supplies, and then return four of your teams to Camp Relief. You will then, during the period designed for you to remain detached, scout the country between Cedar Swamp and Meadow Valley, and afford protection to miners from Mormons and Indians, and watch the Parowan Indians, who again threaten to attack the overland mail coaches. You will thoroughly explore and prospect the country over which you travel, and if successful in finding placer diggings, you will at once report the fact to these headquarters. You will report with your command at your regimental headquarters on or about the 1st day of August next, unless otherwise ordered.

By command of Brigadier-General Connor:

M. G. LEWIS,
Assistant Adjutant-General.

[Editor's note: *This document appears in the* Official Records *as an inclosure to* OR-*300*.]

SOURCE: *OR*, SERIES 1, VOLUME 50, PART 2, PAGE 845

OR-300

HEADQUARTERS DISTRICT OF UTAH,
Camp Douglas, Utah Ter., May 15, 1864.

Lieut. Col. R. C. DRUM,
Asst. Adjt. Gen., Dept. of the Pacific, San Francisco, Cal.:

COLONEL: Inclosed herewith I have the honor to forward, for the information of the general commanding, copies of instructions to company commanders in this district who are now absent with their companies on detached service.

Very respectfully, your obedient servant,

P. EDW. CONNOR,
Brigadier-General, U.S. Volunteers, Commanding Post.

[Inclosure No. 1.]

[Editor's note: *See OR-297 for this inclosure.*]

[Inclosure No. 2.]

[Editor's note: *See OR-299 for this inclosure.*]

[Inclosure No. 3.]

[Editor's note: *See OR-298 for this inclosure.*]

SOURCE: *OR*, SERIES 1, VOLUME 50, PART 2, PAGE 844

OR-301

HEADQUARTERS MILITARY DIVISION OF THE MISSOURI,
Saint Louis, May 24, 1865. (Received 6 P.M.)

Lieutenant-General GRANT:

The following dispatch from General Dodge just received. We have not at present troops enough to furnish escorts to all these parties, but hope soon to clear the region of Indians. We will certainly do so as soon as I can get the brigade of cavalry now here mounted:

FORT LEAVENWORTH, *May 24, 1865.*

Major-General POPE:

I find on arrival here some five surveying parties under general contract, two Indian agents, one wagon-road company, and others, all asking for escorts. The country they operate in is entirely unsafe, and it will take at least two regiments, part infantry and part cavalry, to supply the demand. This is getting to be a serious question and I would like your advice. If I give escorts I will have to bring the troops here to do it. The parties seem to have proper claims on the Government. The freight contractors to Utah and New Mexico have to be guarded, and the number of trains leaving on Government account will use up a small army. The Indian agents have goods, but Colonel Livingston got after their Indians and used them up. I think all the band that was engaged in robberies this side of Kearny were killed.

G. M. DODGE,
Major-General

JNO. POPE,
Major-General.

SOURCE: *OR*, SERIES 1, VOLUME 48, PART 2, PAGE 583

OR-302

[*Extract*]

HEADQUARTERS DISTRICT OF OREGON,
Fort Vancouver, Wash. Ter., May 31, 1864.

Maj. Gen. SAMUEL R. CURTIS, U.S. Volunteers,
Comdg. Department of Kansas, Fort Leavenworth, Kans.:

GENERAL: I have to acknowledge the reception of your letter of the 19th ultimo. It has gratified me to receive your cordial response and expression of interest in the policy of encouraging settlements and the protection of the residents in Eastern Idaho. I suppose Congress by this time has passed the law making a separate Territory of that portion of Idaho Territory east of the Rocky Mountains under the name of Montana Territory.

. . .

To-day the land route to the Beaver Head country, as it is styled by the people (meaning the country around East Bannock and Virginia City), is via the South Pass until they get near Fort Hall on the well-traveled wagon road from Salt Lake to Beaver Head, recrossing the Rocky Mountains at a low pass near High Bank

Creek. This avoids all those Indians now being pursued by General Sully. It is the route for troops to go, at least for the first season; afterward, as I said in my letter of the 3d of March, the troops could ascertain and explore a more direct road to Fort Laramie. Troops now sent there must probably go expecting to be subsisted independently of any depot on the Yellowstone, unless it is already accomplished; for it is ere this reaches you too late doubtless to take advantage of this spring's rise of water, but a command could obtain flour and beef from Salt Lake for the first year. We have rumors of troubles from the Indians on the Upper Yellowstone, but I am not fully advised on the subject. It is not too late for troops to leave for Eastern Idaho after the reception of this letter. I shall, as you invite, freely communicate to you all the facts which I think may interest you concerning that country.

I have the honor to be, very respectfully, your obedient servant,

BENJ. ALVORD,
Brigadier-General, U.S. Volunteers, Commanding District.

SOURCE: *OR*, SERIES 1, VOLUME 50, PART 2, PAGES 858–859

OR-303

FORT RUBY, NEV. TER., *June 7, 1864.*

Captain LEWIS,
Assistant Adjutant-General, Camp Douglas, Utah Ter.:

CAPTAIN: I have the honor to acknowledge the receipt of commanding General's telegram of yesterday. I visited Deep Creek Station on the 26th ultimo, and was so well satisfied that no men were needed there that I ordered the detachment in. Since the reported trouble in Major Egan's lodging camp and the letter received from Sergeant Jones, which I forwarded you, I have strengthened the command at Eight-Mile Station (Fort Trinity), and have directed Sergeant Jones to send men on the stage when the convenience of the mail and passengers will allow them to ride, stopping over a trip or two at Antelope, Deep Creek, and Cañon Station. That will keep men on the road and at the stations all the time. I have four teams sent to Fort Churchill, one on the road with the supplies for the men, and only four mules at the post for service. If I venture the road team with men and supplies for new stations at Deep Creek and Cañon Station I shall have to postpone the prospecting trip mentioned in my letter of the 5th instant. I intended to use the mules with the road team to pack rations for Lieutenant Hosmer's party. Will not the general revoke the order sending men to Cañon and Deep Creek Stations? Please answer by telegraph. I really do not think any more soldiers are needed on the road than there are now. I cannot answer for Company B just now. Nearly one-half of the company is absent on various duties. Those just relieved on the road will be in in a few days. I will then get their wishes and answer by telegraph.

I am, very respectfully, your humble servant,

J. B. MOORE,
Lieutenant-Colonel Third Infantry California Vols., Comdg. Post.

SOURCE: *OR*, SERIES 1, VOLUME 50, PART 2, PAGES 861–862

OR-304

HEADQUARTERS,
Fort Boisé, Idaho Ter., June 7, 1864.

ACTING ASSISTANT ADJUTANT-GENERAL,
Hdqrs. District of Oregon, Fort Vancouver, Wash. Ter.:

SIR: I believe that Captain Currey has established his depot on the Owyhee, at the mouth of Jordan Creek, about fifty miles west of the Owyhee mines. This will obviate the necessity of any detachment in that vicinity as indicated in your letter of April 28. The route to the captain's depot is through Boonville, the principal place in the Owyhee mines. I will, however, send in a short time a detachment to remain out until fall, consisting mostly of the cavalry, to visit Camas Prairie, the Three Islands, Salmon Falls, Rock Creek, &c. I have not yet learned what route the mail from Salt Lake will travel. The immigration will no doubt adopt the same route. The presence of the detachment on it will add to the safety of both and demonstrate the necessity on the part of the Indians and lawless white men of honest pursuits, and may determine whether any considerable number of Indians go east from the section of country to be traversed by Captains Drake and Currey. I learn unofficially that General Connor has established a camp of one company of cavalry at the mouth of Raft River. From it they will be able to detect any traveling or roaming parties who escape through the Goose Creek and Humboldt Mountains, and will be generally of much benefit to the security and peace of the immigration to Oregon and California.

Very respectfully, your obedient servant,

R. F. MAURY,
Colonel First Oregon Cavalry, Commanding.

SOURCE: *OR*, SERIES 1, VOLUME 50, PART 2, PAGE 862

OR-305

Fort Bridger, Wash. Ter., *June 20, 1864.*

Capt. M. G. Lewis,
Assistant Adjutant-General, District of Utah:

Sir: I have the honor to report to the general commanding that one of Washakee's Indians, named Wo-an-gant, brought to this post yesterday nineteen horses which had been stolen and delivered them into my charge, making the following statement: He says that being out hunting in the Wind River Mountains he came to four lodges of Indians, and that they are a branch of the Snake tribe called by the Shoshones, Sheepeaters. They informed him that they had stolen twenty-three horses from white men who were mining or prospecting some two months before near Beaver Head. This Indian says he told them that a treaty had been made with the whites last summer, which was the first information they had of it. They delivered up to him twenty horses (three having got away from them) to be brought by him to Fort Bridger. One of the horses was kept by one of Washakee's Indians, which I think I can get. Nineteen of the horses are here, which I shall keep until I know the wishes of the general in regard to them.

Very respectfully, your obedient servant,

P. A. GALLAGHER,
Major Third California Volunteer Infantry, Commanding Post.

[Editor's note: *This document appears in the* Official Records *as an inclosure to OR-308.*]

Source: *OR*, Series 1, Volume 50, Part 2, page 888

OR-306

MAY 9–JUNE 22, 1864.—Expedition from Fort Crittenden, Utah Ter., to Fort Mojave, Ariz. Ter.

Report of Capt. George F. Price, Second California Cavalry, commanding expedition.

SALT LAKE AND FORT MOJAVE WAGON ROAD EXPEDITION,
Camp 31, Fort Mojave, Ariz. Ter., Wednesday, June 22, 1864.

SIR: I have the honor to submit herewith preliminary report of this expedition to this camp. A full and complete map of my route, together with complete history of the expedition, will be furnished as soon as practicable after my arrival at Camp Douglas. It is intended to furnish in this preliminary report sufficient information to enable the general commanding District of Utah to determine how far the expedition was successful, to what extent it succeeded in accomplishing his wishes, and whether a route from the Colorado River to Salt Lake City can be made superior to the present route from Carson City to Salt Lake, or equal to it. In obedience to letter of instructions of May 7, 1864, from headquarters District of Utah, I left Camp Douglas on morning of 9th of May, 1864, with Lieutenant Conrad and sixty-one non-commissioned officers and men, four six-mule teams, and sixty-four Government horses. I arrived at Fort Crittenden on the 11th of May, from which point I was instructed to commence my operations. I here determined to move the column and teams by the San Bernardino road, sending out small parties to the west to explore the country. Upon arrival at Muddy Creek the wisdom of this measure was apparent, for had I attempted to haul my teams on any one of the routes run by my side scouts, would have been destitute of horses and means of transportation long before arrival at Mountain Meadow. I moved the column by easy marches to Mountain Meadow, a distance of 302½ miles, in sixteen days, having good water and grass along the route, with as fine a road as I ever traveled over. To this point six of my horses had become unserviceable and were run in the herd. Two of my teams gave evidence of failing, and I commenced feeding them from my private grain. At this point I also erected a monument in memory of the victims of the Mountain Meadow massacre, which fact was at that time communicated to you in an official letter. From Mountain Meadow to Muddy Creek my stock failed rapidly. I employed every means in my power to keep it up, making short drives, working at the teams whenever a pull was required, and keeping a working party ahead to improve the road. The distance was ninety-eight miles, and I occupied nine days in traveling it, besides resting at Mountain Meadow two days, and then did not get two of the teams into camp at Muddy [Creek] until three days after making the camp; was compelled to pack the loads in and give the mules empty wagons, which then they could scarcely haul. Leaving the Rio Virgin for Muddy, had to rise a large hill, a mile long. At that point was compelled to pack outfit on horses; then place all mules to wagons, and sixty men with ropes in addition to get them on top of the hill. It was not so much the condition of the route which broke down my means of transportation as it was the fact of having old and worn-out mules, who commenced failing on a road which was equal to a turnpike.

I made Camp 24, on Muddy, June 3, 1864, having succeeded in getting all my stock in, excepting one mule and one horse died and one horse strayed. Total distance from Camp Douglas, 396 miles 6 furlongs and 21 rods. My side scouts from Fort Crittenden to Muddy are as follows: One from Fort Crittenden to Hound Valley, via Tintic Valley, Oak Creek, and Sevier River, 101 miles; one from Radford's to Cedar City, via Deseret Settlement, Sevier River, Sevier Lake, Sink of Beaver, and Black Rock Springs; distance, 156 miles. No wagons accompanied either of these scouts. Neither could wagons have accompanied them, the routes being across heavy sand, rank growth of sage brush, no grass, and but little water on routes, and it at long intervals. The third and most important side scout started from Corn Creek, south of Fillmore, taking with it one six mule team, the best one I had, with twenty days' rations. This scout, after almost superhuman exertions, succeeded in making New Mines, west of Beaver City, and passing down to Black Mountains were forced to come in my route to San Bernardino road at Mountain Meadow. Distance traveled, 350 miles. All of these scouts reported barren, desolate country, and no chance to run a natural wagon road where there could be found wood, water, and grass. A carefully prepared map of each of these side scouts has been made, together with complete daily journal, which will be submitted with final report. By means of these scouts I was possessed with much valuable information, and succeeded in running a complete line from Fort Crittenden to Clover and Meadow Valleys, to within a distance of seventy miles of Muddy Creek, and at one point on the side scout being 115 miles west of Beaver City. The last-named scout joined me at Muddy on 5th June, having occupied twenty days, with team and horses much jaded. It thus became evident to me that I could not continue the expedition with all of my teams and horses, and accordingly left Sergeant Gass with fifteen men at Muddy, having in charge two wagons, nineteen horses, and eleven mules, together with all of outfit not absolute necessary for me to have, and by reducing rations of those who were to accompany me was enabled to leave him rations for thirty days. He was instructed to run line from Muddy to Clover Valley as soon as horses were rested enough to do so, and to await at that point (Muddy) orders from me. None of the horses or mules left behind were in condition to cross to the Vegas; in fact, could not have driven them across the desert loose.

I left Muddy on Tuesday evening, June 7, 1864, with forty-five men, forty-seven horses, and ten teams, having only provisions and water barrels on them. The men were reduced to one blanket and their saddle-bags, each containing one shirt, one pair drawers, and one pair of socks, Mr. Conrad and self doing the same, leaving all our mess kit, bedding, &c., at Muddy. Succeeded in crossing the desert without much trouble, and found at Vegas plenty of excellent water and grass. Had to leave at that place two horses which could not proceed any farther. After resting there until evening of 9th June resumed march from Las Vegas for El Dorado Cañon; distance, forty-four miles. Traveled to Mesquite Springs that night, when halted until daybreak, using the spring water, which was very bad. Next day (10th) resumed march. After traveling up grade eighteen miles halted at grass; mules and horses much exhausted: gave horses three quarts of water each, and men had one quart each issued to them. Wagons and troops then separated, former taking road, latter taking trail. We made water in mountains which stood in pot holes in the rocks, and was only rain water. About dark horses were crazy for water, and had the men been compelled to travel five miles farther some of them would have gone crazy. On this route four horses gave out and had to be shot. Next morning went down into El Dorado Cañon and made Camp 27. Water enough standing in cañon for stock, but no grass. Teams came in some two or three hours afterward; mules scarcely able to stand in the harness. I remained in cañon until next day in the afternoon, when resumed march for Mojave. Arrived at Lewis' Spring with many of the horses exhausted, men nearly all walking. Upon arrival at spring could not obtain water enough for the stock. Horses arrived there about reveille; team mules did not get in until middle of afternoon, and then only brought in one wagon. It became evident to me that I would be compelled to leave them. Had taken precaution to send party from El Dorado Cañon to Mojave by river trail, and knew that fresh mules would come out in few days. Left Sergeant Gordon and nine men at Lewis' Spring with the teams; also left with them about all the provisions I had; also left with him ten horses who could not travel any farther. Six additional horses were shot or left en route from El Dorado Cañon to Lewis' Spring, making a total of twelve horses shot or left at water and grass since leaving Muddy. I then started from Lewis' Spring for Rock Springs with twenty-five horses all told, and upon arrival there found no water for stock. Drove them out to Government Hole, where they obtained enough to quench thirst. Found a stray cow and shot her for meat. Next day resumed march for Piute Creek, and from Piute Creek arrived here on the 16th instant completely worn out and exhausted, half the men barefooted, horses scarcely able to walk, not because they were poor in flesh, but because the route from Vegas here affords but little grass and water, and where the grass is there is no water, and where water is found there is no grass. I was very thankful that I had succeeded in getting here. At Piute Creek met six fresh mules going out to meet my wagons, taking also some provisions to the men. From Fillmore to Cedar City the route makes a circle into the east, and I ran three observation lines as follows: One from Corn Creek to Beaver City; one from Corn Creek to Parowan, and one from Corn Creek to Cedar City, None of these are practicable, for want of water and grass. The streams starting out from the mountains do not run down more than from one to six miles, excepting Beaver Creek. I found the maps extant of the country through which I traveled very incorrect. No reliance whatever can be placed upon the maps for any portion of the country south of Fillmore. I ran the distance from Camp Douglas to El Dorado Cañon, 488 miles, and from Camp Douglas to Fort Mojave, 585 miles four furlongs and nineteen rods. The route can be shortened from El Dorado Cañon probably twenty-five or thirty miles, and from Fort Mojave at least sixty miles, which will be done on return trip. On Tuesday (21st) dispatched an express for Muddy, with orders to Sergeant Gass to resume line of march for Camp Douglas. I cannot obtain any fresh teams or horses at this post. There are but few animals here, and they are in but little better condition than my own. The condition of my stock may be stated as follows:

Left at Muddy June 7, 1864, 19 horses and 11 mules, worn out and unserviceable; left at Las Vegas, June 9, 2 horses, unserviceable; shot en route to Rock Springs, 10 horses; left at Rock Springs, 2 horses; left at Lewis' Spring, 12 mules and 10 horses. Total rendered unserviceable en route, including mule and horse died before reaching Muddy and 1 horse strayed, 24 mules and 45 horses. My team mules were driven in yesterday. The stock I have here will not be in condition to resume travel for at least one month, and I doubt my ability to return much of it to Camp Douglas. Plenty of provisions can be obtained here, but I do not purpose taking full supply when starting, only enough to supply to Mountain Meadow, intending that teams will meet me from Camp Douglas at or near that point. You will be advised fully of my plan of operation in time to meet me at Mountain Meadow, should I so adopt. I repeat that the condition of my stock is not caused so much by the character of the road as it is from the fact that the team mules were old, worn out, and almost unserviceable at the start for a march of such magnitude. The delay of the teams also delayed the troops, keeping it in poor range much longer than it would have been had the teams been serviceable. You will remember that at Camp Douglas I remarked that not less than fifteen of my horses were totally unfit for this expedition. I made the same remark to the general commanding, and was told that he could not do better for me. This I believe, and am satisfied I had as good an outfit as could be at that time furnished. Yet the fact cannot be denied that the outfit was entirely inadequate to the wants of the expedition. As a natural result the route proved severe upon both men and animals, and both frequently suffered intensely from want of water, and also from fatigue incident to misfortune of getting through with' broken down teams. As soon as the teams commenced failing I issued private grain belonging to Mr. Conrad and self amounting to 800 pounds. As regards the route I have fully made up my mind as follows: While I will not yet say that road cannot be opened west of present traveled route until learn result of line run from Muddy to Clover Valley, am decided that no nearer, better or more practicable route can be run than the present one from Camp Douglas to Las Vegas; and having traveled from Carson City to Salt

Lake over the mail road, state without any hesitation that the route I have traveled to mouth of El Dorado Cañon is superior in every respect to it, and that the total length of route need not exceed 450 miles. There is no occasion to run the southern terminus of road below El Dorado Cañon. Steam-boats can navigate the river as easily to the cañon or to a point eight miles above it, as they can and do to La Paz, 200 miles south of Mojave. I will locate the southern terminus of road either at mouth of El Dorado Cañon or at a landing eight miles above, running from thence to Las Vegas to Muddy, Virgin River, Clara River, Mountain Meadow, Cedar, Beaver, Fillmore, west side of Utah Lake to Salt Lake City. Nature of road as follows: From El Dorado Cañon forty-four miles desert to Las Vegas, where find most excellent water and grass; from Las Vegas to Muddy forty-seven miles desert, where find good water and abundance of grass; from Muddy to Virgin, twenty miles, good road; on Virgin to Beaver down thirty-two miles sandy road, heavy hauling; from Beaver down to Clara River, good road; from Clara River to Mountain Meadow, heavy road; from Mountain Meadow to Salt Lake City, 302½ miles, a turnpike road, supplied with wood, water, and grass; longest drive on it without water is twenty-seven miles. Best time to start freight trains from El Dorado Cañon on or about 20th April, as follows: A train of 100 Government wagons, divided into five parts, each part two days in advance of rear, each twenty wagons to have two grain and water wagons along, and every wagon to have water barrel holding twenty-five gallons. Feed grain to Mountain Meadow anyhow, haul water to Muddy Creek: from these two points load grain and water wagons from other teams, and the through trip can be made in twenty-six to twenty-eight days, easy. So well satisfied am I of this fact would be willing to take charge of such a train and stake my commission on bringing it through without loss of an animal, except from natural causes, provided that at the start the outfit was of a No. 1 quality. To start out any other kind of stock would simply result in delays and losses, and also injure the reputation of the route. It is useless to run a road from the cañon to Fort Mojave. It would make nearly 100 miles additional land carriage over a country poorly supplied with water and grass. The Colorado River can be navigated to El Dorado Cañon with greater ease than the Sacramento River can be navigated from Knight's Landing to Red Bluff, using the same kind of boats as are employed on the Upper Sacramento River. There are no obstructions in the Colorado River excepting the occasional shifting of sandbars, which is peculiar to the Missouri, Mississippi, and Sacramento Rivers. No apportions [*sic*] of public money are necessary to improve the navigation of the river. Rich mines are located along it from a point seventy miles south of La Paz to the mouth of the Virgin; the country is rapidly filling up with an energetic people, and private enterprises can easily do all that is required and receive handsome profit from any outlay thus made. The so-termed Colorado Steam Navigation Company runs one heavy, good-for-nothing boat to La Paz, which town property is mostly owned by that arrangement. Instead of placing good boats on the river, the company acts as though it wished to retard the opening of the country, and it is my decided opinion that this company is seeking to obtain from the Government a large appropriation for the ostensible purpose of improving the navigation. Steam-boat brought a load of freight to this post on 20th May last and said would return immediately. Mr. Hardy has over 300 tons of freight lying at La Paz awaiting transportation from this model company, and when it is a notorious fact that the river is as easily navigated from La Paz to El Dorado Cañon as it is from Fort Yuma to La Paz, no reasonable excuse can be offered for such conduct on the part of a company professing a great desire to open the river and supply the wants of a region rapidly developing in great mineral wealth. All the steamers they could place on the river could run down every trip loaded to utmost capacity with rock from the many ledges and receive four cents per pound for freighting it. A steam company could make fortune upon fortune at the business of freighting rock down the river. It is scarcely a year since the mines were discovered in this section of Arizona, and now there are over 100,000 persons interested in them. Many of these ledges rival in richness the Comstock and Gould and Curry, of Nevada Territory, and it is my belief that ledges will be discovered all the way from here to Salt Lake City in the mountains of the Colorado, the Virgin, and the Sevier Rivers. The importance of opening the navigation of the Colorado River and establishing good wagon-road communication from head of navigation to Salt Lake City cannot be urged too strongly or impressed too firmly upon the minds of those in authority who have the power within their hands of prosecuting such a work to a successful termination. I passed through numerous bands of Indians from Mountain Meadow to this point, and had no trouble with them. On the contrary, found them the most inveterate beggars I ever met. In conversation with Indians at Muddy they charged the Mormons with the Mountain Meadow massacre, naming John D. Lee and Jacob Hamblin as two of the principal leaders in that affair. I have now communicated about all that I deem worthy of note at present time. The daily journal of the expedition will when finished embody every detail occurring from day to day, which, together with the map of routes, will affor[d] complete information, and will I trust meet the approval of the general commanding, and I desire you to assure him that no effort has been spared on my part to make the expedition successful and to accomplish his wishes in regard to it. Whatever of hardships and suffering the expedition may have endured amounts to nothing if success, in his judgment, has not been accomplished by it. The health of the command is excellent.

Very respectfully, your obedient servant,

GEO. F. PRICE,

Captain, Second California Cavalry, Commanding Expedition.

Capt. M. G. Lewis,

Assistant Adjutant-General, District of Utah.

Source: *OR*, Series 1, Volume 50, Part 1, pages 355–360

OR-307

[*Extract*]

Organization of troops in the Department of the Pacific, Brig. Gen. George Wright, U.S. Army, commanding, June 30, 1864.

. . .

DISTRICT OF UTAH.
Brig. Gen. P. Edward Connor.

Camp Douglas, Utah Ter.
Col. Robert Pollock.
2d California Cavalry, Company M.
3d California (six companies).

Fort Bridger, Utah Ter.
Maj. Patrick A. Gallagher.
3d California, Company I.

Fort Ruby, Nev. Ter.
Lieut. Col. Jeremiah B. Moore.
3d California, Companies B and E.

Camp Connor, Idaho Ter.
Capt. David Black.
3d California, Company H.

Camp Conness, Utah Ter.
Maj. John M. O'Neil.
2d California Cavalry (four companies),
1st Nevada Cavalry, Companies A and B.

Source: *OR*, Series 1, Volume 50, Part 2, page 885

OR-308

HEADQUARTERS DISTRICT OF UTAH,
Camp Douglas, Utah Ter., near Great Salt Lake City, July 1, 1864.

Lieut. Col. R. C. DRUM, U.S. Army,
Assistant Adjutant-General, San Francisco, Cal.:

COLONEL: I have the honor and the pleasure to report for the information of the department commander that affairs in this district have assumed and still maintain a most peaceful and propitious aspect. The policy pursued toward the Indians has had a most happy effect. That policy, as you are aware, involved certain and speedy punishment for past offenses, compelling them to sue for a suspension of hostilities, and on the resumption of peace, kindness and leniency toward the redskins. They fully understand that honesty and peace constitute their best and safest policy. In consequence every chief of any importance in the district has given in his adhesion with profuse promises of future good conduct. Throughout the length and breadth of the Territory peace exists with all the wandering and heretofore savage and marauding bands. During the past winter and spring at various times the several chiefs and petty leaders have visited Camp Douglas, where they have been kindly received and hospitably treated by the command. In default of ability on the part of the Indian Department to provide fully for their wants, and also in pursuance of what was esteemed sound policy, I have from time to time distributed among them small quantities of provisions, such as flour, sugar, &c., to meet their immediate necessities, and in testimony of the good will of the military authorities toward them as long as they behave themselves and manifest a peaceful disposition. As a marked instance of the beneficial results and effects of the policy pursued I beg leave to invite your attention to the inclosed official report of Major Gallagher, commanding Fort Bridger, relative to the restoration of nineteen head of horses stolen last year from miners near Beaver Head by a wandering band of Shoshones. Measures have been taken to enable the owners of the stock to prove property and reclaim it. So far, then, as Indian matters are concerned I have to report peace throughout the Territory, and except the continued and frequent violation of the anti-polygamic law of Congress by the Mormons, and a covert and deep-rooted hostility to the Government by the leaders, affairs in this Territory may be said to be wearing a cheerful aspect beyond any former period. Instances of outrages upon unsuspecting and innocent emigrants by Indians and whites which so long disgraced this Territory are of very rare occurrence, if indeed they have not ceased entirely. This peaceful and happy condition of affairs has enabled me to pursue most vigorously the policy heretofore indicated of settling the Mormon question by peaceful means in the early development of the undoubtedly rich mineral wealth of the Territory. Wherever it could be done without interference with military duties, commanders of companies and posts have been directed to allow parties of soldiers to prospect the country and open its mines. Such disposition of the force under my command as would insure protection to citizens (miners) throughout the Territory against threatened interference by the Mormons has been made, and the country already feels the beneficial influences resulting from such a course. Miners and others, Gentiles, are flocking hither in considerable numbers, and the day is not far distant when a loyal Gentile population, acting in concert with the now oppressed but dissatisfied saints, will peacefully revolutionize the odious system of church domination which has so long bound down a deluded and ignorant community and threatened the peace and welfare of the people and country. You will permit me, however, to add that the present state of affairs and future prospects are predicated upon the presence and continuance of an ample force of military in this district. If from any cause the quota, of troops in this Territory should be withdrawn or permitted to fall much below the number now here the result would be disastrous indeed. The Indians incited by bad white men could not be relied on to maintain peace toward the emigration, the old system of church despotism would revive in tenfold vigor, the working of mines by Gentiles or disenthralled Mormons would be checked, if not entirely stopped, and the Territory would lapse again into its normal condition of disloyalty and abject subserviency to a traitorous church organization and open and avowed treason to the national Government. I have also the pleasure to report that the crops of the Territory are in a most prosperous condition, and a bountiful harvest beyond any former precedent is confidently anticipated. It is an axiom of political economy that a people raised above poverty and want with pecuniary independence opened cannot long remain in ignorance and the abject tools of despotism.

I have the honor to remain, colonel, very respectfully, your obedient servant,

P. EDW. CONNOR,
Brigadier-General, Commanding.

[Inclosure.]

[Editor's note: *See* OR-*305 for this inclosure.*]

Source: *OR*, Series 1, Volume 50, Part 2, pages 887–888

OR-309

HEADQUARTERS DISTRICT OF UTAH,
Camp Douglas, Utah, near Great Salt Lake City, July 2, 1864.

[Lieut. Col. R. C. DRUM:]

COLONEL: I have the honor to inform the department commander that I have recently become cognizant of a persistent effort on the part of a few merchants and traders doing business in Great Salt Lake City to institute a forced change in the currency of the Territory, viz, from national Treasury notes to gold coin. Without knowing whether the movement had its origin in a desire to depreciate the national currency, and to this extent weaken the arm of Government, or in the selfish greed for gain, or, as is most probable, both combined, my first impulse was to arrest the originators on the first overt act to that end, and crush out at once and forever so unpatriotic and suicidal a policy. I have, however, on reflection, deemed it proper to submit the facts to the department commander, and ask for specific instructions on the subject should the attempt be actually made. You are respectfully informed that up to this time the only currency of the Territory has been that established by the Government—legal-tender notes—and notwithstanding the product of northern mines, in dust, there is not sufficient gold and silver coin in the Territory to suffice for one day's need in commerce, trade, and barter.

The only effect of the forcible measures threatened to be inaugurated by the merchants would therefore be to depreciate to an enormous extent the current value of the national currency, and disseminate among a suspicious people the opinion that the Government was fast going to pieces, and its pledged securities little better than blank paper. The efforts of bad men among them to sneer at the impotence of the Government and depreciate it in any manner would be furthered, and our great nation become a byword and reproach among a deluded community, already deeply inoculated with enmity and disloyalty toward it. In almost every other community the inevitable laws of trade would check and prevent the inauguration of so suicidal a policy as that indicated under the circumstances existing in this Territory, but it is greatly to be feared that unless some stringent measures are authorized, a very few disloyal and greedy merchants, owing and neither feeling any allegiance to nor regard for the nation, may consummate a most disastrous stroke in the forcible change of the currency. The whole matter is respectfully submitted to the department commander for early instructions, by telegraph, if deemed advisable.

I remain, colonel, very respectfully, your obedient servant,

P. EDWARD CONNOR,
Brigadier-General, Commanding.

SOURCE: *OR*, SERIES 1, VOLUME 50, PART 2, PAGES 889–890

OR-310

[*Extract*]

HEADQUARTERS,
Fort Boisé, Idaho Ter., July 3, 1864.

First Lieut. JOHN W. HOPKINS,
Actg. Asst. Adjt. Gen., Headquarters District of Oregon:

SIR: I have had no intelligence direct from Captain Currey's expedition since about the 15th of June. They were then all well and quiet, not having found any Indians.

. . .

There are no Indians at Salmon Falls or on Snake River below that point, and but few in Camas Prairie or vicinity, and those mostly the Indians who were at this post during winter and spring. They are engaged in fishing on South Boisé River and digging roots in Camas Prairie by consent of miners and occupants of the country. Captain Smith, of the California volunteers, from District of Utah, is actively engaged in patrolling Snake River from his depot on Raft River to Salmon Falls. I do not look for any difficulty between this place and Fort Hall. Emigrants from the States are beginning to arrive.

Very respectfully, your obedient servant,

R. F. MAURY,
Colonel First Oregon Volunteers, Commanding.

SOURCE: *OR*, SERIES 1, VOLUME 50, PART 2, PAGES 890–891

OR-311

HEADQUARTERS DISTRICT OF UTAH,
Camp Douglas, Utah Ter., near Great Salt Lake City, July 9, 1864.

Lieut. Col. R. C. DRUM,
Assistant Adjutant-General, U.S. Army,
Department of the Pacific, San Francisco, Cal.:

COLONEL: Referring to the letter I had the honor of addressing you on the 2d instant relative to the attempt to depreciate the national currency by inaugurating in Utah a gold and silver currency, I beg leave to state that I have had reason since that date for modifying my opinion in relation thereto and the statements therein made. I then entertained and expressed the opinion that this unpatriotic movement had no other or deeper origin than the greed or disloyalty of certain merchants in Great Salt Lake City. It has since been rendered patent to all the world that the real origin of the movement was Brigham Young, the traitor head of the Mormon Church and people. On last Sabbath in the tabernacle one of the twelve apostles, the supple tool of Brigham Young, announced to the congregation the new policy, and counseled (which is here equivalent to an order) a gold currency in contradiction to that provided by the nation. It was announced that $12 per hundred would be charged for flour, and that a convention would be called early in August to establish prices under the new policy. The next day the one article of flour rose in our markets from $15 to $23 per hundred, and it is still rising in price. If other evidence were necessary of the deep complicity of Brigham Young in this as in all other unpatriotic movements designed to cripple the Government and lead his dupes to the very verge of treason, the following single extract from the leading editorial article in the last issue of the Deseret News, July 7, the quasi organ of the church, which draws its whole inspiration from Brigham himself, would be sufficient. The whole article is replete with economic solecism and the crudest fallacies concerning currency, and is leveled directly at the integrity of national Treasury notes. A single paragraph will suffice:

> Mechanics, laborers, producers, and all concerned will understand at a glance that we deem greenbacks the most uncertain in value of all the commodities in their possession, and we trust will govern themselves accordingly, lest, though retiring at night with pockets overflowing with currency, they awake bankrupt.

In addition to this a daily paper has recently been started in the city, nominally under the control of T. B. H. Stenhouse, the nation's Mormon postmaster in Great Salt Lake City, but really an offshoot of the church organ. This paper, called the Telegraph, under the guise of commercial articles, as well as in its leading editorials, is daily engaged in puffing up the movement, insidiously bearing the national currency and advocating gold as the basis of trade, barter, and commerce. The word has gone forth to the people from the tabernacle, from the church organ, and its little coadjutor, while the high priest of iniquity and hypocrisy is perambulating the Territory, instilling the poison into the popular ear and striking a most fatal blow at the vital interests of the Territory, as well as at the currency of the nation. The convention will assemble early in August proximo, to more fully carry out the behests and traitorous designs of Brigham Young, a man hardly second in disloyalty and evil intent to Jeff. Davis himself. Without dwelling on the details of the effects of this unpatriotic movement, I beg leave again to ask for instructions from the department commander as to the course to be pursued, and for authority to check this most villainous undertaking of rank and deeply dyed traitors.

I have the honor to remain, very respectfully, your obedient servant,

P. EDW. CONNOR,
Brigadier-General, Commanding.

SOURCE: *OR*, SERIES 1, VOLUME 50, PART 2, PAGES 893–894

OR-312

HEADQUARTERS DISTRICT OF UTAH,
Camp Douglas, Utah Ter., near Great Salt Lake City, July 12, 1864.

Lieut. Col. R. C. DRUM,
Assistant Adjutant-General, U.S. Army, San Francisco, Cal.:

COLONEL: For the information of the general commanding the department I have the honor to inform you that I have deemed it advisable to establish a provost guard in Great Salt Lake City, and for that purpose issued the necessary orders on the 9th instant, a copy of which has been duly forwarded to department headquarters. The main motives which at this time impelled this course are briefly as follows: The people of this Territory, under the implicit guidance of Brigham Young, are steeped in disloyalty and omit no opportunity of making display of it and injuring the Government by every means in their power. The recent gold currency movement (more fully adverted to in previous communications) has its origin in the disloyalty of the church authorities and their determination to depreciate the national currency. Wherever the arch traitor Brigham Young has been recently among the settlements instilling his poison in the minds of the people, Treasury notes are depreciated to a mere tithe of their value, and in not a few instances refused and repudiated altogether. I am in hopes that the establishment of a provost guard in the city, under the command of discreet officers, may be beneficial in its effect of checking, if not defeating altogether, the machinations of those bold, bad men. In addition to this, it has long been apparent that there was necessity for such guard to take care of soldiers visiting the city, and to prevent noisy demonstrations of disloyalty by emigrants passing through to California and Nevada.

I have the honor to remain, very respectfully, your obedient servant,

P. EDW. CONNOR,
Brigadier-General, U.S. Volunteers, Commanding District.

SOURCE: *OR*, SERIES 1, VOLUME 50, PART 2, PAGES 899–900

OR-313

Camp Douglas, *July 13, 1864.*

Lieut. Col. R. C. Drum,

Assistant Adjutant-General:

Encouraged by the unfavorable news from the East, the Mormons are assuming a very hostile attitude. They have about 1,000 men under arms and are still assembling, and threaten to drive my provost guard from the city; alleged excuse for armed demonstration, the presence of the provost guard in the city. My command is much scattered, having only 300 men at this camp. If conflict takes place, which I will endeavor to avoid, can hold my position until re-enforced from neighboring Territories.

P. EDW. CONNOR,

Brigadier-General, Commanding.

Source: *OR*, Series 1, Volume 50, Part 2, pages 901–902

OR-314

Camp Douglas, *July 15, 1864.*

Lieut. Col. R. C. Drum,

Assistant Adjutant-General:

Finding that I am prepared to resist any attack, and knowing that the city is at the mercy of my guns and will be surely destroyed if my troops are attacked, the Mormons seem to be quieting down somewhat, although armed forces are assembling inside of Brigham's yard, and having nightly drills with artillery and infantry. My impression is that there is no immediate probability of conflict. The excitement is dying away among the masses of the people; still in many parts of the Territory the national currency is openly repudiated under the dictation of the church. The leaders are buying up from the emigrants and others all the arms and ammunition possible.

P. EDW. CONNOR,

Brigadier-General, Commanding.

Source: *OR*, Series 1, Volume 50, Part 2, page 904

OR-315

San Francisco, *July 15, 1864.*

Brig. Gen. P. E. Connor,
Salt Lake City:

The major general commanding the department approves of your determination to avoid a conflict with the Mormons. Do so by all means. Is there not some other cause than the mere presence of the guard in the city? Examine closely. Remove the guards and troops sooner than their presence should cause a war.

RICHD. C. DRUM,
Assistant Adjutant-General.

Source: *OR*, Series 1, Volume 50, Part 2, page 904

OR-316

Hdqrs. Department of the Pacific,
San Francisco, Cal., July 16, 1864.

Special Orders,
No. 155.

* * * *

5. Maj. Edward McGarry, Second Cavalry California Volunteers, will proceed to Camp Douglas, near Salt Lake City, and report to Brig. Gen. P. Edward Connor, commanding District of Utah, for duty. The major will assume command of the Second Regiment of Cavalry California Volunteers. The quartermasters department will advance to Major McGarry sufficient funds to enable him to reach his destination without delay.

By command of Major-General McDowell:

RICHD. C. DRUM,
Assistant Adjutant-General.

Source: *OR*, Series 1, Volume 50, Part 2, pages 906–907

OR-317

HEADQUARTERS DEPARTMENT OF THE PACIFIC,
San Francisco, July 16, 1864.

Brig. Gen. P. E. CONNOR,
Commanding District of Utah:

GENERAL: I have the honor to acknowledge the receipt of your letter of July 1, reporting the peaceable state of affairs in your district, and of July 2, reporting the determination of a few Salt Lake merchants to initiate a forced change in the currency of the Territory, and requesting the instruction of the department commander in relation to the course you shall take in the matter, it having been your first impulse to crush out at once and forever so unpatriotic and suicidal a policy. Soon after the receipt of these letters came your telegrams of the 13th, received last night, and of the 15th, received to-day, reporting a threatened insurrection on the part of the Mormons, on the alleged pretext of the presence of the provost guard in Salt Lake City. Last night I telegraphed you in answer to yours of the 13th as follows: "The major-general commanding the department approves of your determination to avoid a conflict with the Mormons. Do so by all means. Is there not some other cause than the mere presence of the guard in the city? Examine closely. Remove the guard and troops rather than their presence should cost a war." The major-general commanding directs me to say that he has every confidence in your discretion and good judgment, as he has in your zeal and ability, and is certain he will not have to appeal to these high qualities in vain. The condition of affairs at Salt Lake as reported by you is very critical, not only as regards your own command, but as regards this department and the whole country. The question is, are we at this time, and as we are now situated, in a condition to undertake to carry on a war against the Mormons—for any cause whatever—if it can possibly be avoided; not whether there are not matters that require to be changed, bad government and worse morals to be corrected, and the authority of the National Government to be more thoroughly enforced; but can we not pass all these by for the present, at least, and thus avoid weakening the General Government, now taxed to its utmost and struggling for its very existence. Your forces are very few and scattered—so the general finds those in the other districts—so undoubtedly will be found those in the Territories adjoining you. To send you the forces necessary to resist the Mormons, much more to assail them, would require more means and men than could be gathered together and sent to you from this coast; to send away those which could be had would leave it in the hands of secessionists, and that at a time the inhabitants are looking with anxiety to the troubled and critical state of foreign affairs.

A war with the Mormons would be the opportunity which our domestic enemies would not fail to improve, and it is not too much to say that at this time such a war would prove fatal to the Union cause in this department. Under these circumstances, the major-general considers that it is the course of true patriotism for you not to embark in any hostilities, nor suffer yourself to be drawn into any course which will lead to hostilities. It is infinitely better that you should, under the present circumstances, avoid contact with them. The object of troops being at this time in Utah is to protect the overland route and not to endeavor to correct the evil conduct, manifest as it is, of the inhabitants of that Territory. This undoubtedly will tax your forbearance and your prudence to the utmost, but the general trusts it will not do so in vain. At this distance the general is unable to give you specific instructions as to the particular things to be done or to be avoided, and must necessarily leave the details in your hands.

To insure this dispatch reaching you it is sent by the hands of that excellent officer Major McGarry, whom you will retain, if you require him, at the headquarters of his regiment. He is informed of the contents of this dispatch, so that he may communicate them in case he has to destroy it. It would be well, however, it they were kept by you in strict confidence. A telegraphic cipher is also sent.

Very respectfully, your most obedient servant,

R. C. DRUM,
Assistant Adjutant-General.

SOURCE: *OR*, SERIES 1, VOLUME 50, PART 2, PAGES 909–910

OR-318

SALT LAKE CITY, *July 16, 1864.*

Col. R. C. DRUM,
Assistant Adjutant-General:

The excitement is fast abating; any indication of weakness or vacillation on my part would precipitate trouble. The presence of the provost guard was simply the excuse for the development of the innate and persistent disloyalty of the church leaders, who seek to force me into some position which will secure my removal and a consequent over throw of my policy in Utah. The removal of the provost guard under the circumstances would be disastrous in the extreme. My opinion is decided that a firm front presented to their armed demonstrations will alone secure peace and counteract the machinations of the traitor leaders of this fanatical and deluded people.

P. EDW. CONNOR,
Brigadier-General, Commanding.

SOURCE: *OR*, SERIES 1, VOLUME 50, PART 2, PAGE 910

OR-319

HDQRS. DEPARTMENT OF THE PACIFIC,
San Francisco, Cal., July 19, 1864.

SPECIAL ORDERS,
No. 156.

1. Col. Francis J. Lippitt, Second Infantry California Volunteers, will repair to Fort Miller and assume command of his regiment, headquarters Fort Miller. The quartermaster's department will furnish the necessary transportation.

2. Lieut. Col. William Jones, Second Cavalry California Volunteers, will proceed to Camp Douglas, near Salt Lake City, and report to Brig. Gen. P. Edward Connor, commanding District of Utah. The quartermaster's department will furnish the necessary transportation.

By command of Major-General McDowell:

RICHD. C. DRUM,
Assistant Adjutant-General.

SOURCE: *OR*, SERIES 1, VOLUME 50, PART 2, PAGE 912

OR-320

HEADQUARTERS DEPARTMENT OF THE PACIFIC,
San Francisco, July 19, 1864.

Brig. Gen. P. E. CONNOR, U.S. Volunteers,
Commanding District of Utah:

GENERAL: I have the honor to acknowledge the receipt of a copy of Special Orders, No. 53, from your headquarters, appointing a provost-marshal and detailing a company as a provost guard to be quartered in the city of Salt Lake. The necessity for posting a guard in the city is not apparent to the commanding general, while on the other hand much dissatisfaction may result from such a movement. If the object was to keep soldiers out of the city and return stragglers or loungers to their companies it might have been accomplished by sending a patrol from Camp Douglas daily. The order above referred to will be revoked and the guard withdrawn.

Very respectfully, your obedient servant,

RICHD. C. DRUM,
Assistant Adjutant-General.

SOURCE: *OR*, SERIES 1, VOLUME 50, PART 2, PAGE 913

OR-321

SAN FRANCISCO, *July 20, 1864.*

Brig. Gen. P. E. CONNOR,
Salt Lake City:

In answer to your letter of the 9th and telegram of 13th instant, the major-general commanding directs me to say that he does not at this day deem it expedient to interfere by military force to regulate the currency in the District of Utah.

RICHD. C. DRUM,
Assistant Adjutant-General.

SOURCE: *OR*, SERIES 1, VOLUME 50, PART 2, PAGE 914

OR-322

HEADQUARTERS DISTRICT OF UTAH,
Camp Douglas, Utah Ter., near Great Salt Lake City, July 24, 1864.

Lieut. Col. R. C. DRUM,
Assistant Adjutant-General, U.S. Army,
Department of the Pacific, San Francisco, Cal.:

COLONEL: I have the honor to acknowledge the receipt at the hands of Major McGarry, Second Cavalry California Volunteers, of your dispatch of the 16th instant, communicating to me the views of the major-general commanding the department in reference to present and future Mormon complications in Utah, and also your favor of same date inclosing a telegraphic cipher.

Last night I telegraphed you as follows:

> McGarry has arrived; all quiet. The wishes of the commanding general will be strictly complied with.

With the addition of three or four companies from Fort Churchill I will be responsible for the protection of the overland mail and the peaceable solution of the Mormon question. I am aware how difficult it must be, even after the fullest exposition in writing, for one at a distance to fully comprehend the state of affairs existing in this Territory, and I feel sensible of the high honor done me by the commanding general in his expressions of reliance on my judgment and discretion. At the same time I am thankful for the very full exposition you have given me of the views of the commanding general, and take this occasion to repeat that they shall be implicitly observed by me, with the confident hope that nothing shall occur in my power to prevent which will cause him to feel that his reliance in me has been misplaced. For manifest reasons some of the acts performed by me or things done may at a distance appear a deviation from the peaceful policy which is at once my own aim and the desire of the general commanding, but I beg leave respectfully to assure you that those acts have been at times absolutely necessary to insure peace, and certainly always, in my judgment, calculated to promote it. The commanding general by this time, I presume, fully understands that in case of a foreign war the overland mail would stand in far more danger from the Mormons than from Indians or other foes, and to protect that route it is necessary that the former should understand most fully that there is not only the intention but there is also the power to hold them in check. The presence of the troops here, while giving no just cause of offense, and without infringing in the least upon the rights of any citizen, is potent to prevent difficulties and obstructions which would assuredly result in war. The exhibition of firmness and determination, accompanied by a display of force, will, I am confident, secure peace and prevent complications. Such addition to my present command as has been asked for, and which I hope is in the power of the general commanding to give, I am confident will enable me to do all that is necessary, and I have no hesitation in pledging myself to the maintenance of peace in Utah without compromising the dignity of my Government or pandering in the least to the threats or expostulations of the treasonable organization which holds so great a sway in this Territory. So long as my guns command the city as they do, and the force under my command is not too much reduced, I have no fear and will be responsible for the result. Brigham Young will not commence hostilities, I think, and I need hardly say that I will not inaugurate them so long as peace is possible without dishonor. I trust that I fully appreciate the anxiety with which the commanding general, in view of the circumstances surrounding him, regards the possibility of conflict in this Territory, and so appreciating, I need hardly add that nothing will be done by me tending to complicate the undoubtedly bad state of affairs existing here.

I have the honor to remain, very respectfully, your obedient servant,

P. EDW. CONNOR,
Brigadier-General, Commanding.

SOURCE: *OR*, SERIES 1, VOLUME 50, PART 2, PAGES 916–917

OR-323

HEADQUARTERS DISTRICT OF UTAH,
Camp Douglas, Utah Ter.,
Near Great Salt Lake City, July 26, 1864.

SPECIAL ORDERS,
No. 59.

Maj. Edward McGarry, Second Cavalry California Volunteers, will proceed to Camp Connor, Utah Ter., and assume command of the Second Cavalry California Volunteers.

By command of Brigadier-General Connor:

M. G. LEWIS,
Assistant Adjutant-General, U.S. Volunteers.

SOURCE: *OR*, SERIES 1, VOLUME 50, PART 2, PAGE 921

OR-324

SAN FRANCISCO, *July 27, 1864.*

Brig. Gen. P. E. CONNOR,
Commanding District of Utah, Salt Lake City:

The general is willing a small police guard (less than a company) shall be kept in the city of Great Salt Lake for police purposes, connected with the troops, to prevent them committing any disorders or being absent without authority, but let it have nothing to do with the Mormon question. The companies of Third Infantry at Ruby will be relieved by a company from Fort Churchill, and you can draw them in as soon as relieved. The four companies of cavalry now at Fort Churchill will be sent to replace the troops at Camp Douglas who are mustered out. Two of these companies will come to you dismounted and will be mounted and equipped by you from the horses and equipments of the men of Second Cavalry as they are mustered out.

RICHD. C. DRUM,
Assistant Adjutant-General.

SOURCE: *OR*, SERIES 1, VOLUME 50, PART 2, PAGE 923

OR-325

HDQRS. DEPARTMENT OF THE PACIFIC
San Francisco, Cal., July 28, 1864.

GENERAL ORDERS,
No. 39.

As soon as the necessary transportation can be procured the following movements of troops will be carried into effect in the order in which they are numbered:

1. Company A, Nevada Territory infantry, will proceed to the Smoke Creek country and relieve the company of cavalry now operating there. When relieved the latter will return to Fort Churchill, preparatory to marching to Camp Douglas, Utah Ter.

2. Company B, Nevada Territory infantry, will proceed to and take post at Camp Ruby. As soon after its arrival as practicable Lieutenant-Colonel Moore, Third Infantry California Volunteers, with the two companies (B and E) of his regiment, will take up the line of march for Camp Douglas.

3. Companies C, D, E, and F, Nevada Territory Cavalry, will proceed by squadron to Camp Douglas, the dismounted companies marching first and some days in advance of the mounted squadron. The dismounted companies will be mounted and equipped in Utah from the horses and equipments of the Second Cavalry California Volunteers as the men of the latter regiment are mustered out of the service.

By command of Major-General McDowell:

R. C. DRUM,
Assistant Adjutant-General.

SOURCE: *OR*, SERIES 1, VOLUME 50, PART 2, PAGES 923–924

OR-326

SAN FRANCISCO, *August 1, 1864.*

Maj. CHARLES MCDERMIT,

Second California Volunteer Cavalry, Comdg. Fort Churchill:

The four companies of Nevada cavalry are ordered to Salt Lake. One company of Nevada infantry relieves the cavalry company in Smoke Creek region, and one company goes to Camp Ruby; the other remains at Fort Churchill.

RICHD. C. DRUM,
Assistant Adjutant-General.

SOURCE: *OR*, SERIES 1, VOLUME 50, PART 2, PAGE 926

OR-327

SAN FRANCISCO, *August 5, 1864.*

Brig. Gen. P. E. CONNOR,

Salt Lake City:

Have the Indian troubles east of Salt Lake been settled?

RICHD. C. DRUM,
Assistant Adjutant-General.

SOURCE: *OR*, SERIES 1, VOLUME 50, PART 2, PAGE 932

OR-328

Camp Douglas, *August 5, 1864.*
(Received 9.30 P.M. 6th)

Col. R. C. Drum,
Assistant Adjutant-General:

All settled before I left Bridger last Saturday. Do not apprehend any further trouble from Indians.

P. E. CONNOR,
Brigadier-General, Commanding.

Source: *OR*, Series 1, Volume 50, Part 2, page 932

OR-329

[*Extract*]

Headquarters,
Fort Boisé, Idaho Ter., August 8, 1864.

Acting Assistant Adjutant-General,
Hdqrs. District of Oregon, Fort Vancouver, Wash. Ter.:

Sir: Although nothing of sufficient importance has occurred at this post or information received from the scene of operations of the several expeditions in the field since the departure of Colonel Maury with his command to form the subject of a special communication, yet, knowing the interest which will be felt by the general commanding the district and his desire to be in receipt of frequent advices, whether of great moment or otherwise, I have deemed it proper to address this communication, however unimportant it may appear, giving a brief statement of events which have transpired, of rumors circulated, and such other information as has come to my knowledge.

. . .

Nothing further has been heard relative to the reported outrages in the vicinity of Salmon Falls, and the Indians on Camas Prairie appear to be quiet. I am informed, however, by the agent of the stage company that from some indications on the part of Indians south and east of Snake River, they are apprehensive of having difficulty between the river and Salt Lake, and are fearful of losing their stock. The company evidently relies upon military protection to secure them an uninterrupted line of communication.

. . .

Should anything important occur at the post or any news reach here from the field of operations in the Indian country the general commanding can rely upon being promptly advised.

Very respectfully, your obedient servant,

F. SEIDENSTRIKER,
Captain, First Washington Territory Infantry, Commanding.

P. S. Since writing the above I have become satisfied that I misunderstood Sergeant Mallinsbery (the expressman from Camp Alvord) in his statement with regard to the expressman who left here for Captain Currey's command on the 20th of July. He had arrived at Camp Alvord en route for Captain Currey's headquarters, but had not yet returned, and hence the cause of their unnecessary anxiety at that camp and the original misunderstanding and apparent mystery involved in the case.

F. S.

SOURCE: *OR*, SERIES 1, VOLUME 50, PART 2, PAGES 933–936

OR-330

HEADQUARTERS DEPARTMENT OF THE PACIFIC,
San Francisco, August 9, 1864.

Brig. Gen. P. E. CONNOR, U.S. Volunteers,
Commanding District of Utah:

GENERAL: I am instructed to inform you that since the general orders directing the movements of troops from Fort Churchill have been issued, the commanding general has directed the chief quartermaster at these headquarters to mount the two companies of Nevada cavalry previous to the commencement of the march.

Very respectfully, your obedient servant,

RICHD. C. DRUM,
Assistant Adjutant-General.

SOURCE: *OR*, SERIES 1, VOLUME 50, PART 2, PAGE 936

OR-331

NEBRASKA CITY, *August 15, 1864.*

Major-General CURTIS:

Mr. Lewis, a freighter of this place, who loaded at Atchison, reports that he left the Atchison and Fort Kearny road near Big Sandy a few days since, brought his train to Beatrice and corralled. The Indians attacked a mule train above Sandy and were driven off. They then attacked an ox train loaded with machinery in charge of Comstock, and stampeded all his stock and killed 2 men. They attacked two trains of about twenty-five wagons each and drove off all their stock. The mule train first mentioned was loaded with merchandise for Salt Lake, which they threw out of their wagons, took the men in that belonged to the ox train, and left for Atchison in haste. No troops have left Brownville 10 P.M.

O. P. MASON.

SOURCE: *OR*, SERIES 1, VOLUME 41, PART 2, PAGES 721–722

OR-332

[*Extract*]

HEADQUARTERS DEPARTMENT OF THE PACIFIC,
San Francisco, August 17, 1864.

ADJUTANT-GENERAL OF THE ARMY,
War Department, Washington, D.C.:

SIR: I have to report as follows concerning the state of the department for the month of July: In the District of Oregon there have been some small parties of troops sent out to guard emigrant routes, and there is a difficulty existing with the Quilliute tribe of Indians, who refuse to surrender the murderers of Cook. The district commander proposes to send an expedition to force them to do so. In the District of Humboldt Indian difficulties are now quieted, and the superintendent of Indian affairs has gone up to make arrangements for establishing an Indian reservation on the Trinity River at Fort Gaston. It was the intention of my predecessor to remove the Indians in this section to Catalina Island, and he had for this purpose taken possession of the island. But the Indian Department has refused to have the Indians removed, and requires them to be kept in the section in which they now live. In the expeditions made after hostile Indians many are taken as prisoners, and as in the case in the Humboldt District, sometimes several hundred have to be fed from the military supplies. The Commissary Department at Washington refuses to allow their officers to issue subsistence to Indians, save in small quantities when visiting military posts, and refuses to permit any regular daily or periodical issues. This they urge is the duty of the Indian Department. On the other hand the Indian Department decide that they cannot feed Indians who are prisoners in the hands of the military; that the military have always fed their own prisoners; that they cannot refund money disbursed by officers over whom they have no control; that if Indians are turned over to them at their reservations they will be provided for, &c. These clashing routine decisions of these departments tend [to em] barrass the service, which requires a course not provided for by the Regulations. We have now several hundred Indians in our custody. Some were brought in; some came in and surrendered. Their country has been scoured by our military parties and their food destroyed and no Indian agent present. We have been obliged to feed them till the Indian Department receives them. To refuse to do so would drive them to the necessity of committing fresh depredations, and thus reopen the war. Having fed refugees from slavery and prisoners of war in the East, I am at a loss to see any reason for not doing the same to the red man in the West in cases where we have taken him from his country and destroyed his means of subsisting and there is no agent at hand with food to keep him from starving, or from fighting that he may not starve. The officer of the commissary department at this station and the Indian superintendent here are doing all they can to soften these impracticable rules and save the frontier from the fresh outbreak which a compliance with them would unquestionably produce.

In the District of Utah matters have been in a very delicate state with the Mormons. On the 1st of July Brigadier-General Connor, who is stationed near Great Salt Lake City, telegraphed me that the Mormons were arming to drive him out of the city; that they had 1,000 men under arms, and were still gathering; that he could hold his position till re-enforced from neighboring Territories. I transmit herewith (marked A, B, C, D, E, F) the correspondence had with him in the matter.* General Connor bears the reputation of being a good soldier, and his last letter shows he deserves the reputation.

. . .

In the District of Southern California, the secession element is reported to be greater in proportion than elsewhere, and it is in that quarter that principally an outbreak is looked for. No open hostile movements have as yet been made.

. . .

Very respectfully, your obedient servant,

IRVIN McDOWELL,
Major-General, Commanding Department.

* [*Refers to* OR-*300*, OR-*280*, OR-*283*, OR-*284*, *and* OR-*288*.]

SOURCE: *OR*, SERIES 1, VOLUME 50, PART 2, PAGES 947–949

OR-333

[*Extract*]

HEADQUARTERS DEPARTMENT OF THE MISSOURI,
OFFICE OF PROVOST-MARSHAL-GENERAL,
Saint Louis, Mo., August 20, 1864.

[General W. S. ROSECRANS:]

GENERAL: I have the honor to forward you herewith additional testimony relating to the existence, objects, and purposes of the secret association known as "The Order of the American Knights," which removes all possible doubt, if any yet remained, of the existence of such an order, and of its disloyal objects and treasonable character. Document marked A is a brief statement, made under oath by Charles L. Hunt, at his own instance and of his own free will and accord. It will be perceived, by reference to it, that he freely and frankly admits that the statement made by him under oath at the time of his arrest was untrue. In that statement he denied all knowledge of the existence of such an order, and also that he was a member of it. In the last statement, which is forwarded herewith, he says he knows that there is such a secret association as the O. A. K.; that he is a member of the same, having joined it over a year-since; has been the grand commander of the order for the State of Missouri, but resigned the grand commandership and withdrew from the order just previous to his arrest. He also now so far qualifies his former statement under oath as to admit that all those whom be met at Vallandigham's headquarters at Canada in April last were members of the order.

Document B is the sworn examination of Charles B. Dunn, who, it will be seen, not only acknowledges the existence of the order, but admits himself to be the deputy grand commander of it for the State of Missouri, and virtually sustains the truth of all the representations made of it in my former report.

. . .

Messrs. Hunt, Dunn, and Smith, having thus voluntarily unbosomed their secret, confessed their connection with the order, expressed their anxiety to sever themselves from it and renounce all its obligations, have, on their own special application, been released from imprisonment by taking the oath of allegiance and giving bond with surety for their loyal behavior hereafter, and that they will appear for trial for their past conduct when called for, the first named giving bond in $10,000 and the latter each in $5,000.

J. P. SANDERSON,
Provost-Marshal-General.

. . .

B.

Charles E. Dunn, of lawful age, being duly sworn, deposes and says, that he was born in Maryland and raised in Illinois and Missouri, living in this State about fifteen years, and engaged as superintendent of gaslights for the Saint Louis Gaslight Company.

Question. Have you ever taken the oath of allegiance to the Federal Government?

Answer. I have, having voted at all local elections for the time I have lived in Saint Louis.

Question. Are you now and have you been during the existing rebellion an unconditional Union man?

Answer. I am a peace man, opposed to secession.

Question. Are you in favor of arming the negroes?

Answer. If they are to be free, yes; if not, and this war is to be carried on under the Constitution, I think arming them will do more injury than good.

Question. Have you during the existing rebellion given an earnest support to the Federal Government in efforts to suppress said rebellion?

Answer. I do not know anything to the contrary.

Question. What is your age?

Answer. I am forty years old.

Question. Have you ever been in military service?

Answer. I was a lieutenant in the Mormon war in 1845.

Question. What were your relations with the "Minute Men" in this city at the commencement of this rebellion?

Answer. Had nothing to do with them.

Question. Have you during the present rebellion given aid in any manner to those engaged in it?

Answer. Not to my knowledge.

Question. Have you within the last three years, directly or indirectly been the recipient of written or verbal communications from any one, and particularly Sterling Price, of the so-called Confederate Army?

Answer. No, sir.

Question. Are you not regarded by your relatives and correspondents as a rebel sympathizer?

Answer. I do not know.

* * * *

[Editor's note: *Testimony from additional witnesses has been removed for lack of relevance.*]

Source: *OR*, Series 2, Volume 7, Section 1, pages 626–628

OR-334

FORT LEAVENWORTH, *August 27, 1864.*

Brig. Gen. C. B. FISK,
Saint Joseph, Mo.:

The safest way to Kearny is by Omaha. General Curtis is still at Fort Kearny, and I presume will arrange to protect overland mail before he returns. I think there is no unusual difficulty with Indians between Fort Bridger and Montana, but that road never has been very safe.

S. S. CURTIS,
Major and Aide-de-Camp.

SOURCE: *OR*, SERIES 1, VOLUME 41, PART 2, PAGE 893

OR-335

HEADQUARTERS DISTRICT OF UTAH,
Camp Douglas, Utah Ter.,
Near Great Salt Lake City, August 27, 1864.

SPECIAL ORDERS,
No. 65.

Captain Price's company (M), Second Cavalry California Volunteers, will proceed on Monday next to Camp Connor, Utah Ter., and report to the commanding officer of that post for duty.

By command of Brigadier-General Connor:

M. G. LEWIS,
Assistant Adjutant-General.

SOURCE: *OR*, SERIES 1, VOLUME 50, PART 2, PAGE 958

OR-336

HDQRS. DEPARTMENT OF THE PACIFIC,
San Francisco, Cal., August 30, 1864

SPECIAL ORDERS,
No. 189.

* * * *

3. Maj. Milo George, Nevada cavalry, will proceed with the last company of his regiment leaving Fort Churchill to Camp Douglas, Utah Ter.

* * * *

By command of Major-General McDowell:

R. C. DRUM,
Assistant Adjutant-General.

SOURCE: *OR*, SERIES 1, VOLUME 50, PART 2, PAGE 960

OR-337

VANCOUVER, WASH. TER., *August 31, 1864.*

Maj. Gen. H. W. HALLECK,
Chief of Staff:

I beg to ask for the same authority for continuing, consolidating, mustering in, and mustering out volunteer regiments or companies in the State of Oregon and the Territories in the Department of the Pacific, as has been given in your telegram of August 18 for California. The troops, old and new, for Oregon and Nevada not to exceed in all for each a regiment of cavalry and a regiment of infantry. The troops for Washington Territory not to exceed a regiment of infantry. Those for Idaho and Utah not to exceed four companies of cavalry or infantry in each, as the state of the service from time to time may require.

I. McDOWELL,
Major-General, Commanding Department.

I concur in the above.

ADDISON C. GIBBS,
Governor of Oregon.

SOURCE: *OR*, SERIES 1, VOLUME 50, PART 2, PAGE 961

OR-338

MARKLEEVILLE, *August 31, 1864.*

Major-General McDOWELL:

DEAR SIR: We, the undersigned citizens of Alpine County, desire to communicate to you as the commanding officer of the Department of the Pacific a few facts which we are sure should be in your possession, and which will before long affect our State and Nation seriously. We will be as brief as possible, knowing that your time must be to some extent taken up with communications from the interior. You must be aware ere this of a secret organization, ramified throughout the State, which has for its object a system of guerrilla warfare and wholesale plundering. All this (learned through a detective whom we have had at work and through Governor Nye, of Nevada Territory,) is to be ushered in by a general uprising of the secesh forces. We have had our eyes upon that branch of that organization here in our place, and have taken such precautionary measures that they have become alarmed and they are now stealing away by ones and twos to the place of rendezvous, which we learn is in the neighborhood of San Fernando Mission, Lower California, and from what we glean from detective source, we are satisfied that there they are now congregating, ostensibly to mine but really to raid, and have a good supply of arms and ammunition and provisions. We are no alarmists and we confide to you, as our commanding officer, what we believe to be true from the evidence before us. The programme is to rendezvous there, and when the time of rising comes to sound the tocsin of war on our coast, aided by the French in Mexico, the Mormons and Indians on our east, and the secesh among us, by a bold stroke take the State out of the Union and erect a Pacific republic. We learn that on the 7th of September a steamer will leave San Francisco for Lower California, and we write this to-day so that you may be able to take advantage of that steamer to send a spy there to ascertain the correctness of this statement. We have written Governor Low before of this organization; also to Governor Nye, but these matters have so impressed us here that we felt it our duty to lay them before you. There is military company here, but at present unarmed, which company hereby, through its commanding officer, tenders its services to move at once when ordered. That a great day is coming upon the people of this coast we feel satisfied and we may as well realize it first as last; for our part we expect it and we are ready. These forces are organizing and drop off for the rendezvous in small squads, the hard times favoring this emigration movement. One Stepfield, who we feel sure has a commission from Jeff. Davis, is the grand sanhedrim here, and he has a man by the name of Edwards with him in the capacity of a spy. They have gone and the men are following one at a time. We have abundant testimony here obtained from men who belonged to the organization, but drew out when they found out the real object. This testimony we do not like to commit to paper, but you can have it when you deem it necessary. We will not trust more to paper now. Should you at any time need our services either here or elsewhere, command us.

Very respectfully, your obedient servants,

D.C. MITCHELL,
Captain Alpine Rifles.
O. F. THORNTON,
of Mount Bullion.
G. W. MAULL.
W. I. JOHNSTON,
County Treasurer.

P. S.—This was written for General McDowell, but since it was written we learn that you are in command in San Francisco and we direct to you.

Respectfully,

D.C. MITCHELL.

[Editor's note: *Indorsement removed for lack of relevance.*]

SOURCE: *OR*, SERIES 1, VOLUME 50, PART 2, PAGES 961–963

OR-339

CAMP DOUGLAS, *September 1, 1864.*
(Received 10 A.M. 2d.)

Col. R. C. DRUM:

All quiet. I assumed command of Camp Douglas to-day. The furnaces in Rush Valley are a decided success. Much rejoicing among miners. Brigham left for a six weeks' trip to the southern settlements this morning to subdue the growing spirit of resistance to his authority. The tocsin of his downfall is sounding.

P. EDWARD CONNOR.

SOURCE: *OR*, SERIES 1, VOLUME 50, PART 2, PAGE 966

OR-340

Camp on Dry Creek, *September 6, 1864.*

Maj. S. S. Curtis:

Trains are passing through from Leavenworth from Kearny to Denver and Salt Lake. Escorts are not needed. Have explored up Beaver and Republican to a point on Cottonwood. No buffalo about here, and very few Indians. Am moving eastward.

S. R. CURTIS,
Major-General.

Source: *OR*, Series 1, Volume 41, Part 3, page 112

OR-341

Headquarters District of Indiana,
Indianapolis, September 15, 1864.

Major-General Rosecrans,
Commanding, &c.:

I herewith send you a copy of the article which led to the apprehension of Hart, alias Burgess, alias Quantrill. Several men of undoubted character have visited him and say that he is Quantrill. There is a strange delusion if he is not the man. All the evidence so far is very strong against him, and would convict him before any jury in the country.

I have the honor to be, your obedient servant,

ALVIN P. HOVEY,
Brevet Major-General, Commanding.

[Inclosure.]

WHO IS QUANTRILL?

Last Sunday two men were arrested at the Bates House as rebel spies. One goes by the name of Johnson, the other gave his name as Hart, but afterward acknowledged it to be Burgess. Some time last spring a communication was widely published, giving a history of Quantrill, which communication we give below. Without leading questions or any suspicion of the article, Burgess, in giving an account of himself, names nearly all the circumstances therein mentioned down to the killing of the

Mexican. Doctor Burgess, surgeon of the Seventeenth Kentucky Infantry, states that he had a brother who left home a number of years since, from whom they had no direct communication, but that from what he had learned by various sources he believed him to be the man known as Quantrill. This man arrested on Sunday, knowing nothing of this, says he is a brother of Doctor Burgess, of the Seventeenth Kentucky. These circumstances are so clear as to warrant the use of all necessary means to establish the identity of the prisoner; and it is hoped that all persons who know anything of Quantrill will communicate with the authorities here. General Hovey is making diligent inquiry in regard to the matter. It will be borne in mind that Quantrill appears to have been out of active service for some time, and it is not unlikely that he has been acting as a spy. The following is the article referred to:

> Having seen so many different stories about the murderer Quantrill, whose recent atrocities at Lawrence have thrilled the country, I deem it my duty to show the public, through your columns, who he is and something of his history. His name is really Henry Volney Burgess, and he was born in Todd County, Ky.
>
> At one time he was a resident of Hopkinsville, in that State, and during the excitement of 1846 concerning the Davis murder, for which E. A. Pennington was executed, and he not having a very good reputation, he went to Memphis and there associated himself with Fisher and Worthington, two gamblers, until the spring of 1850, when he removed to Texas, and was partner with a company of sports, such as Dean Mountain Jack, Old Horn, and others. He was very successful for a while, and changed his name to Hart.
>
> He made the acquaintance of a very fine girl who lived on the banks of the Rio Honda, twenty-eight miles from Castorville, Tex., and by representing himself as a land speculator, and having considerable money and fine mules attached to his ambulance, won and married the girl on the 21st of May; and about the 5th of June started with his bride for California, but meeting with ill luck at Fort Davis and El Paso, lost all his outfit and money, and was compelled to remain there some time, living with a man named Ben Bowell, in Franklin, Tex.
>
> During this time Charles Giddings, owner of the stage line from El Paso to San Antonio, saw his father-in-law and told him who Hart was and what he was doing. The old man came up with me to El Paso for his daughter, and would have killed her husband, but he crossed the river and could not be found. Hart came to me and represented himself broke, and wishing to come to California to make money by honest toil to support his wife and heir in expectancy, and as my company was small and the Indians bad, I consented. On our arrival at Mazatlin, Mex., he killed a Mexican robber named Miguel, and was tried before the alcalde and acquitted.
>
> When we arrived at Los Angelos he left me, and I never saw him till the fall of 1856. I started home by way of Arizona Territory, and found Hart and Harrison at Taos, N. Mex., on their way to Utah. Captain Marcy was purchasing mules for the Utah army and I sold mine, but had to go to Fort Bridger for pay, and Hart again accompanied me, but this time with plenty of means. I remained in Utah for one year. During that time he won some $80,000, including 100 head of cattle from different parties. But the fast living of the chief, as he was called, soon relieved him of his money, and he left for parts unknown. On my arrival at Denver City he was there, and shot and killed a man named Jack O'Neil on the race course.

I again lost sight of him for some time, but after the rebellion broke out he made his way from Mexico to Arkansas, and was there joined by a few of his old associates, and proceeded to Missouri and commenced his career of murder. There was a man who came with me from Santa Fé, N. Mex., this spring who saw him, and he (Quantrill) sent a message to me by him, stating that he was in all his glory now.

SOURCE: *OR*, SERIES 1, VOLUME 41, PART 3, PAGES 202–203

OR-342

AUSTIN, *September 17, 1864.*

Brig. Gen. P. E. CONNOR:

DEAR SIR: The undersigned, loyal citizens of this Government, believing in the supremacy of Federal laws, the perpetuity of the Union, and the defeat of traitors and the suppression of the rebellion both in words and acts, beg leave to represent the necessity of having a proper military force in this place. Copperheadism and secession are rampant in this city, and as it is the first place of any consequence reached by the emigrants, the numerical force of those opposed to our Government promises to be in the ascendant, which element will be kept in subjection by the presence of Federal soldiers. The approaching election increases the necessity, and as forage and accommodations here are abundant and as cavalry troops are soon expected in our midst we earnestly request that you will take such measures to give us a sufficient force (military) until the November election as will protect Union interests, humble rebels, and defend the true interests of the Government. This step we deem necessary for the cause of our country and the success of our political canvass, and without your aid we may be defeated in spite of our patriotic efforts and purposes. There is no time to be lost, and by your immediate attention and compliance with our request you will accomplish much good to a cause to which our lives are devoted.

Very truly, your Union fellow-citizens,

T. A. WATTERSON.
RICHARD BROWN.
I. W. MORGAN.
S. B. MOORE.
THOMAS WREN.
H. G. WORTHINGTON.
D. R. ASHLEY.
MULF. NICKERSON.
THOS. J. TESSNANT.
MORZ MILLER.

[First indorsement.]

AUSTIN, NEV. TER., *September 18, 1864.*

Brig. Gen. P. E. CONNOR:

GENERAL: Although but a comparative stranger in Austin, having just arrived here with my company on the march to Fort Ruby, I fully indorse the foregoing statement and believe it to be entirely correct, and am satisfied that Austin and the Reese River country not only require an armed force till after the November election, but permanently.

Most respectfully, your obedient servant,

GEORGE A. THURSTON,
Captain Company B, First Infantry Nevada Territory Vols.

[Second indorsement.]

HEADQUARTERS DISTRICT OF UTAH,
Camp Douglas, Utah Ter., September 22, 1864.

Respectfully referred to the department commander, with the recommendation that if practicable a detachment of cavalry from Fort Churchill be stationed at or near Austin until after the November election. From my knowledge of the people of Austin and the emigration this year from the East, as well as from the character of the petitioners, I have no doubt that the interests of loyal citizens and of the Government would be subserved by such military protection as is asked for. I have at present under my command no available troops for that purpose.

Very respectfully, your obedient servant,

P. EDW. CONNOR,
Brigadier-General, Commanding.

[Editor's note: *This document, with two indorsements, has been left intact to provide context for the second indorsement (which is the only portion that mentions "Utah").*]

SOURCE: *OR*, SERIES 1, VOLUME 50, PART 2, PAGES 979–980

OR-343

[*Extract*]

AUGUST 27–OCTOBER 5, 1864.—Expedition from Fort Boisé to Salmon Falls, Idaho Ter., with skirmishes.

REPORTS.

No. 1.—Col. Reuben F. Maury, First Oregon Cavalry.

. . .

No. 1.

Reports of Col. Reuben F. Maury, First Oregon Cavalry.

HEADQUARTERS,
Fort Boisé, Idaho Ter., September 17, 1864.

SIR: Letters to the 14th have been received from Lieutenant Hobart. He was then with the cavalry of his command at Three Islands, about thirty miles below Salmon Falls, and was hastening by night marches to the Upper Bruneau, where he had been informed, through a prisoner captured on the 13th, of a camp of fifteen or twenty lodges with considerable stock. On the 13th the lieutenant found and attacked a considerable camp above the Three Islands, killing five men and wounding others. They were a party that had lately stolen some flour, &c, at the crossing of the Malade River. The flour was found in their camp. I have heretofore neglected to mention that Lieutenant Hobart while en route to Salmon Falls met Mr. Z. Van Orman, the uncle of the Van Orman children, with one of the children—supposed to be—(he obtained it, I think, through the Indian agent. Salt Lake, last winter), and employed him as guide and interpreter. His familiarity with their language, as well as personal knowledge of many Indians, makes him of great service. The Indian killed was from the Owyhee.

. . .

Very respectfully, your obedient servant,

R. F. MAURY,
Colonel First Oregon Cavalry, Commanding.

First Lieut. JOHN W. HOPKINS,
First Oregon Cavalry, Actg. Asst. Adjt. Gen.,
Fort Vancouver, Wash. Ter.

SOURCE: *OR*, SERIES 1, VOLUME 50, PART 1, PAGE 386

OR-344

HEADQUARTERS DISTRICT OF UTAH,
Camp Douglas, Utah Ter.,
Near Great Salt Lake City, September 19, 1864.

SPECIAL ORDERS,
No. 69.

I. Maj. Edward McGarry, Second Cavalry California Volunteers, with the headquarters and companies of his regiment stationed at Camp Connor, Utah Ter., will march for this post at as early a day as practicable, and will report to the post commander for duty.

* * * *

By command of Brigadier-General Connor:

M. G. LEWIS,
Assistant Adjutant-General.

SOURCE: *OR*, SERIES 1, VOLUME 50, PART 2, PAGE 981

OR-345

SAN FRANCISCO, *September 21, 1864.*

Maj. CHARLES MCDERMIT,
Fort Churchill, Nev. Ter.:

Stop all movement of troops from Fort Churchill to Salt Lake until further orders.

By order:

R. C. DRUM,
Assistant Adjutant-General.

SOURCE: *OR*, SERIES 1, VOLUME 50, PART 2, PAGE 982

OR-346

HEADQUARTERS,
Fort Boisé, Idaho Ter., September 21, 1864.

Lieut. J. W. HOPKINS,
Actg. Asst. Adjt. Gen., Dist. of Oregon, Fort Vancouver, Wash. Ter.:

SIR: Information from Lieutenant West, First Washington Territory Infantry, who constitutes part of Lieutenant Hobart's command, has been received. He was then on Rock Creek, fifty miles above Salmon Falls, and was in pursuit of a party of Indians that had stolen sixteen head of work cattle from one of the mail stations in that vicinity. Small parties of Indians on the south and west of Snake River appear to be very active in stealing. The Overland Mail Company represent the necessity of troops at Fort Hall. This is an important point, where the travel from Salt Lake to the East Bannock or Beaver Head country and the east to Oregon and Washington Territory and the Boisé country intersect. No complaints of Indians are made, but road agents have been depredating, and it is feared that, from the general spirit of lawlessness pervading a certain class, that the danger from this source may increase. It is my opinion that this point should have, as soon as can be, at least a temporary camp of considerable strength.

Very respectfully, your obedient servant,

R. F. MAURY,
Colonel First Oregon Cavalry, Commanding.

SOURCE: *OR*, SERIES 1, VOLUME 50, PART 2, PAGE 983

OR-347

STATE OF CALIFORNIA, EXECUTIVE DEPARTMENT,
Sacramento, September 26, 1864.

Maj. Gen. IRVIN MCDOWELL,
Commanding Department of the Pacific:

GENERAL: I am informed that the troops at Fort Ruby (a portion of Third Infantry California Volunteers) have not moved as yet toward Salt Lake. If such be the case, the correctness of which you can ascertain by telegraph, I would suggest and urge that, instead of those men being marched 250 miles away from home in order to reach headquarters to be discharged, that you give instructions to the post commander at Fort Ruby to retain them at that point until their time expires, which will be in a few days, and let them be discharged and mustered out at that post in order that they may be able to return home before winter sets in.

Very respectfully, your obedient servant,

F. F. LOW,
Governor.

SOURCE: *OR*, SERIES 1, VOLUME 50, PART 2, PAGES 990–991

OR-348

SAN FRANCISCO, *September 26, 1864.*

General P. E. CONNOR,
Salt Lake City:

Order Major McGarry with headquarters of Second Cavalry to take post at Camp Union, Sacramento.

By order:

R. C. DRUM,
Assistant Adjutant-General.

SOURCE: *OR*, SERIES 1, VOLUME 50, PART 2, PAGE 992

OR-349

HEADQUARTERS DISTRICT OF UTAH,
Camp Douglas, Utah Ter.,
Near Great Salt Lake City, September 27, 1864.

SPECIAL ORDERS,
No. 74.

I. Pursuant to orders from department headquarters, Maj. Edward McGarry, Second Cavalry California Volunteers, with the headquarters of his regiment will proceed to Camp Union, Sacramento, Cal., and report to Brigadier-General Wright, commanding District of California, for duty.

* * * *

By command of Brigadier-General Connor:

CHAS. H. HEMPSTEAD,
Captain and Commissary of Subsistence, U.S. Volunteers,
Acting Assistant Adjutant-General.

Source: *OR*, Series 1, Volume 50, Part 2, pages 994–995

OR-350

Hdqrs. Department of the Pacific,
San Francisco, Cal., September 29, 1864.

Special Orders,
No. 210.

* * * *

7. As fast as the companies of the Third California Volunteer Infantry at Utah shall be diminished by the expiration of the terms of service of the enlisted men, so as to call for it, they will be consolidated under such special instructions as shall be given by Brigadier-General Connor into such number of companies of the maximum organization as will contain all the men of that regiment who remain in service. General Connor will select the officers to command these consolidated companies, and those not so retained will be mustered out of service. The field and staff of the regiment will also be mustered out of service as it is reduced; the colonel, major, and assistant surgeon and regimental staff when the regiment is below five companies, and the lieutenant-colonel and surgeon when the number falls below three full companies.

8. No infantry recruits will be sent from California to Utah till further orders. Those now at Camp Union will be retained there.

* * * *

By command of Major-General McDowell:

RICHD. C. DRUM,
Assistant Adjutant-General.

Source: *OR*, Series 1, Volume 50, Part 2, page 995

OR-351

HEADQUARTERS DEPARTMENT OF THE PACIFIC,
San Francisco, October 1, 1864.

His Excellency, F. F. Low,
Governor of California, Sacramento:

SIR: I have the honor to acknowledge the receipt of your three letters of the 26th ultimo. Immediate steps were taken in the matter of the troops at Fort Ruby, as you will have seen from the copy of the order in the case which was sent you. It had been represented to me that many of the men of the Third Regiment there had acquired interests in Utah, and it was asked they might be mustered out there, and they were ordered to Great Salt Lake City, as there only could the Pay Department place a paymaster to pay them off, and then, only in Utah, was there a mustering officer.

I have promised in the best practicable way I could command to meet your views, and those of others interested in the question, and now every man of the regiment at Fort Ruby has his choice as to the place of his discharge—Utah or California.

The copy of our telegram to the Secretary of War has been sent to you, and I have given orders to the commanding officer at Benicia Arsenal to furnish the amunition you require in the way you designate.

I have the honor to be, very respectfully, your most obedient servant.

IRVIN McDOWELL,
Major-General, Commanding Department.

SOURCE: *OR*, SERIES 1, VOLUME 50, PART 2, PAGES 996–997

OR-352

HEADQUARTERS DEPARTMENT OF THE PACIFIC,
San Francisco, October 3, 1864.

His Excellency J. DUANE DOTY,
Governor of Utah, Great Salt Lake City:

SIR: I telegraphed for and have received authority to raise, to the extent the circumstances of the service may require, certain forces in the several States and Territories of this department. The Governors of California and Oregon joined with me in the application for the quota arbitrarily established for their respective States, but you were too far off to be consulted at the time, and I therefore asked in advance of doing so for authority to raise not to exceed four companies from Utah, in case they should be necessary. I have supposed it might become expedient and that it might be possible to raise that number in addition to the recruits the forces now there might be able to make in the Territory among its loyal inhabitants. Under the authority, therefore, given to that effect from the War Department, I have the honor to request that you will, in connection with the provost-marshal-general's department, raise by voluntary enlistment for the service of the United States four companies of infantry, to be mustered into service at Great Salt Lake City, or such other points as may be determined upon and shall be most convenient. As the U.S. forces in Utah are simply for the protection of the overland communications and the keeping the peace between the whites and Indians and maintaining the authority of the United States, and have no special reference to the Mormons, I have supposed the raising of these companies, if practicable to do so, would meet with no opposition from that community. Will you please write me fully on this question? If the companies can be raised I need hardly say it is of great importance that the officers to command them and the battalion should be men not only of character and education and judgment, but of unquestionable loyalty to the United States. The acting assistant provost-marshal, Brigadier-General Mason, will confer with you concerning the details of this duty, and Brigadier-General Connor, commanding District of Utah, will aid you in every way within his power to get these companies into the service at the earliest day practicable, so as to meet in part the deficiencies arising from the muster out of the principal part of the forces under his command.

I have the honor to be, very respectfully, your obedient servant,

IRVIN McDOWELL,
Major-General, Commanding Department.

[Editor's note: *This document appears in the* Official Records *as an inclosure to OR-353.*]

SOURCE: *OR*, SERIES 1, VOLUME 50, PART 2, PAGE 1000

OR-353

HEADQUARTERS DEPARTMENT OF THE PACIFIC,
San Francisco, October 3, 1864.

Brig. Gen. P. E. CONNOR, U.S. Volunteers,
Commanding District of Utah:

GENERAL: I have the honor to transmit herewith inclosed, by direction of the major-general commanding, a copy of his letter to the Governor of Utah Territory relative to raising for service on the overland route four companies of infantry in that Territory. The general desires you to afford all facilities in your power to raise these companies in Utah, as it may be difficult to send you forces from this part of the department. The general is gratified at the announcement made in your letter of the 22d ultimo that the condition of affairs in your district is such as not to require additional forces from this side, where it is probable they may be required.

I am, general, very respectfully, your obedient servant,

R. C. DRUM,
Assistant Adjutant-General.

[Inclosure.]

[Editor's note: *See* OR-352 *for this inclosure.*]

SOURCE: *OR*, SERIES 1, VOLUME 50, PART 2, PAGE 999

OR-354

ATCHISON, KANS., *October 10, 1864.*

Maj. Gen. S. R. CURTIS:

DEAR SIR: R. P. West, messenger from Salt Lake City to this place on the Overland Stage Line, has just reached this place. He reports that on the 7th instant Lieutenant Bremer of Nebraska cavalry, while on a scout on Elk Creek (a branch of Little Blue), having only two men with him at the time, was killed by Indians concealed in brush. His men brought off his body and Mr. West saw it at Pawnee Ranch and conversed with one of the men. From all I can learn I am perfectly satisfied that we can expect no peace with these Indians until the Government carries war into their camps and inflicts heavy damage upon them. The patrolling the road and a merely defensive policy, it seems to me, will do nothing. The Indians can assail trains and coaches as soon as they are out of view of military stations, and continue their murder and pillage in small parties as long as they please. We must open war in its most serious form with them, follow them to their fastnesses, and slay without sparing all who can fight. A winter campaign well devised would utterly break their power and learn them to fear if not respect our Government.

With the kindest wishes, general, for your health and welfare, I am, truly, your friend,

B. M. HUGHES,
Attorney for Overland Stage Line.

Mr. Holliday has reached Salt Lake safely after a narrow escape from Indians.

SOURCE: *OR*, SERIES 1, VOLUME 41, PART 3, PAGE 768

OR-355

HEADQUARTERS DISTRICT OF UTAH,
Camp Douglas, Utah Ter.,
Near Great Salt Lake City, October 11, 1864.

SPECIAL ORDERS,
No. 79.

I. Maj. John M. O'Neill, Second Cavalry California Volunteers, will proceed without delay to Fort Bridger, Utah Ter., and relieve Lieutenant-Colonel Williams, First Battalion Nevada Cavalry, in the command of that post.

II. Lieutenant-Colonel Williams will, upon being relieved, proceed to Camp Douglas, Utah Ter., and report to the commanding officer for duty. The quartermaster's department will furnish the necessary transportation.

By command of Brigadier-General Connor:

M. G. LEWIS,
Assistant Adjutant-General.

SOURCE: *OR*, SERIES 1, VOLUME 50, PART 2, PAGE 1009

OR-356

HEADQUARTERS DISTRICT OF COLORADO,
Denver, October 14, 1864.

BEN. HOLLIDAY,
Salt Lake City:

Line will be protected between here and Julesburg. Am ready to extend my lines farther. Had fight and killed 12 near Valley Station. Our boys are awake.

J. M. CHIVINGTON,
Colonel, Commanding District.

SOURCE: *OR*, SERIES 1, VOLUME 41, PART 3, PAGE 877

OR-357

HEADQUARTERS DISTRICT OF UTAH,
Camp Douglas, Utah, near Great Salt Lake City, October 14, 1864.

Brig. Gen. L. THOMAS,
Adjutant-General U.S. Army, Washington, D.C.:
(Through Maj. Gen. Irvin McDowell, commanding Department of the Pacific, San Francisco, Cal.)

GENERAL: I have the honor to ask from the honorable Secretary of War leave of absence from my district for sixty days in order to enable me to visit New York City on important private business. In preferring this request at this time I beg leave respectfully to represent that I have since my manhood been nine years in the military service of the United States, for the last two years stationed in this district, and during all that time have not received a leave of absence from my post of duty. I deem it proper also to add that the policy inaugurated by me in the conduct of affairs in this district has worked so beneficially and its results are now so apparent, that I am satisfied that the granting of this request at this time would not be detrimental to the public service. Since my advent to this Territory it is the first time when I could reconcile my convictions of duty with a prolonged absence from the district. But I now feel assured that for the time mentioned as the period of my absence no danger can reasonably be apprehended from the hostility of Indians or the machinations of the foes of the government of Utah. Hence the foregoing request is preferred with the hope that it may be granted.

I have the honor to remain, very respectfully, your obedient servant,

P. EDW. CONNOR,
Brigadier-General, U.S. Volunteers, Comdg. District of Utah.

SOURCE: *OR*, SERIES 1, VOLUME 50, PART 2, PAGE 1011

OR-358

SALT LAKE, *October 15, 1864.*

Hon. E. M. STANTON:

Indians are attacking mail-coaches every few days forty to sixty miles west of Fort Kearny. Unless immediate measures are taken to stop depredations the great overland mails must again be stopped. I most respectfully urge that General Connor be assigned to this duty at once. His familiarity with Indian warfare, prompt and efficient protection to the Western line, and wholesome dread of the savages of his name, point to him above all others as the man for the work of punishing these marauders. The winter is approaching, when Indians can alone be tracked, pursued, and severely punished. It is the right time for the work, and Connor can do it. I but express the firm conviction of all who have witnessed his prompt operations, and now see the result in Utah. Everything is quiet here, and Connor can well be spared for the necessary time to accomplish the work speedily and effectually with the means at his command.

BEN. HOLLIDAY,
Overland Mail Contractor, of New York.

SOURCE: *OR*, SERIES 1, VOLUME 41, PART 3, PAGE 903

OR-359

WAR DEPARTMENT,
Washington, October 16, 1864.

Brig. Gen. P. E. CONNOR,
Salt Lake City, Utah:

Give all the protection in your power to the overland route between you and Fort Kearny, without regard to department lines. General Curtis' forces have been diverted by rebel raids from Arkansas.

H. W. HALLECK,
Major-General and Chief of Staff.

[Editor's note: *This document is referenced in OR-361.*]

SOURCE: *OR*, SERIES 1, VOLUME 41, PART 4, PAGE 24

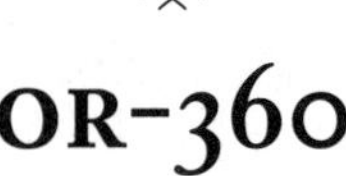

OR-360

SALT LAKE, UTAH TER., *October 17, 1864.*

Major-General HALLECK,
Chief of Staff:

To render efficient the protection required the troops between Salt Lake and Kearny, inclusive, should be subject to my orders irrespective of department lines.

Do I understand your telegram to mean that? I will take from here two cavalry companies, but may require others now on the eastern road.

P. E. CONNOR,
Brigadier-General.

SOURCE: *OR*, SERIES 1, VOLUME 41, PART 4, PAGE 63

OR-361

CAMP DOUGLAS, UTAH TER., *October 17, 1864.*

Col. R. C. DRUM,
Assistant Adjutant-General:

Have just received the following telegram from Washington:*

With the general commanding's permission I will send two companies Second Cavalry down the road. Only 200 men of Second Cavalry in this district. Would recommend that they be consolidated into two companies, and the officers of H and K sent to California, and of it to Salt Lake to recruit; or K could be recruited in Montana.

P. EDWARD CONNOR,
Brigadier-General, Commanding District.

* [*Refers to OR-359.*]

SOURCE: *OR*, SERIES 1, VOLUME 50, PART 2, PAGE 1014

OR-362

WASHINGTON, D.C., *October 18, 1864.*

Brig. Gen. P. E. CONNOR,
Salt Lake City, Utah:

Order not intended to transfer troops or change commanders, except where parts of different commands act together, when ranking officer takes general command temporarily, as provided in Army Regulations.

H. W. HALLECK,
Major-General and Chief of Staff.

SOURCE: *OR*, SERIES 1, VOLUME 41, PART 4, PAGE 101

OR-363

HEADQUARTERS DISTRICT OF COLORADO,
Denver, Colo. Ter., October 26, 1864.

Maj. C. S. CHARLOT,
Asst. Adjt. Gen., Dept. of Kansas, Fort Leavenworth:

Received following telegram from Salt Lake, 22d:

> I am ordered by Secretary of War to give all protection in my power to overland stage between here and Fort Kearny. I contemplate going down with two companies of my cavalry. Can we get a fight out of Indians this winter? Can you send grain out on road to meet my command? How many troops can you spare for a campaign? Answer.
>
> P. E. CONNOR,
> *Brigadier-General, U.S. Army.*

Have department lines been changed? If not, will I allow him to give direction to matters in this district? Line perfectly protected to Julesburg. The line this side Julesburg ought to be in this district, as my troops are taking care of it.

J. M. CHIVINGTON,
Colonel, Commanding District.

SOURCE: *OR*, SERIES 1, VOLUME 41, PART 4, PAGE 259

OR-364

HEADQUARTERS DISTRICT OF UTAH,
Camp Douglas, Utah Ter., near Great Salt Lake City,
October 30, 1864.

Lieutenant-Colonel DRUM, U.S. Army,
Asst. Adjt. Gen., Dept. of the Pacific, San Francisco, Cal.:

COLONEL: On the 17th instant I had the honor to transmit to you a telegram, dated 16th instant, from Major-General Halleck, instructing me to render all the protection in my power to the overland route between this point and Fort Kearny. Regarding that dispatch as looking to my going down the road in person and assuming control of the troops between the points named, I deemed it proper to address General Halleck a telegram, informing him of my intention to send eastward two companies of cavalry and proceed myself in person, and also asking further instructions in the premises. In response the following telegram was received, viz:

WASHINGTON, *October 18, 1864.*

Brigadier-General CONNOR:

Order not intended to transfer troops or change commands, except where parts of different commands act together, when ranking officer takes general command temporarily, as provided in Army Regulations.

H. W. HALLECK.

In response to a telegram from me to Governor John Evans, of Colorado Territory, I have received the following dispatch, viz:

DENVER, *October 24, 1864.*

Brigadier-General CONNOR:

I am glad that yon are coming. I have no doubt the Indians may be chastened during the winter, which they very much need. Bring all the force you can, then pursue, kill, and destroy them; until which we will have no permanent peace on the plains.

JOHN EVANS,
Governor of Colorado.

In pursuance of the foregoing and the telegram which I had the honor to transmit to you on the 17th instant I propose to start two full companies of the Second California Volunteer Cavalry, viz, Companies L and M, on or about the 4th proximo. The necessary arrangements for forage on the route between here and Denver have been made, at which last-named place the troops will arrive in about twenty-five days. In the meantime I design proceeding hence to Denver by stage next week, where I hope to be able to gather the necessary information, after examining the field, to guide the future movements of my troops. Should I find it practicable and advisable to make a winter's campaign, with a fair probability of severely punishing the savages, of which I now entertain little doubt, I will make such arrangements and disposition of the troops as may be necessary, and immediately return to this post by stage. As soon thereafter as everything necessary for a vigorous campaign can be prepared I propose to return and assume personal command of the expedition, making Denver the base of operations. As my absence from the district (with which I will be in constant communication) will be but temporary, not exceeding, perhaps, a fortnight, I will retain command, leaving a competent officer here to attend to details. Should my confident expectations regarding the possibility of a winter campaign against the Sioux, Arapahoes, and Cheyennes not be realized after personal examination I purpose to make immediately, my troops will go into suitable winter quarters ready for such service as may be required by the exigencies of either district. There is no doubt that until the savages eastward of Denver shall have been thoroughly defeated and severely punished no permanent peace can be hoped for; nor can their frequent raids upon the overland route be prevented by any number of troops at the disposal of the Government. I am equally clear in the opinion that the winter or early spring is the only time when Indians can be successfully pursued, punished, and brought to terms. If this be possible, as I now think it is, I need hardly add that the most vigorous measures will be taken at the earliest possible day. Tour instructions in the premises have been most carefully noted and will be strictly obeyed. I trust that the movements above set forth will meet with the approbation and concurrence of the general commanding the department, to whom I will report from time to time regarding my future actions.

Very respectfully, your obedient servant,

P. EDW. CONNOR,
Brigadier-General, U.S. Volunteers, Comdg. District of Utah.

SOURCE: *OR*, SERIES 1, VOLUME 50, PART 2, PAGES 1036–1037

OR-365

[*Extract*]

SEPTEMBER 29–NOVEMBER 30, 1864.—Operations against Indians in Nebraska and Colorado.

NO. 1.

Reports of Col. Robert R. Livingston, First Nebraska Cavalry, commanding Eastern Sub-District of Nebraska.

HEADQUARTERS EASTERN SUB-DISTRICT OF NEBRASKA.
Fort Kearny, Nebr. Ter., November 1, 1864.

SIR: I have the honor respectfully to submit the following report of military operations in this sub-district since I assumed command on the 29th September last, in obedience to Special Field Orders, No. 2, dated at Fort Kearny, Nebr. Ter., September 29, 1864:

On the 26th day of September I arrived at this post with the command, which moved from here with me on the 28th August, 1864, under orders of Maj. Gen. S. R. Curtis, after marching 800 miles in search of hostile Indians along the waters of the Republican and Solomon Rivers. On the 29th September, 1864, I was ordered to assume command of the Eastern Sub-District of Nebraska, comprising a territory of 400 miles of country from the Missouri River to and including Julesburg, Colo. Ter., through which the several roads from Leavenworth, Atchison, Nebraska City, Plattsmouth, and Omaha, converging at and a little east of this post, continue west, forming the Great Overland Mail Route to Salt Lake, Colorado, Idaho, Nevada, and California. The troops placed at my disposal consisted of one battalion Seventh Iowa Cavalry Volunteers, one battalion Nebraska Veteran Cavalry, the veteran portion of my own regiment, and four companies of Nebraska militia, together with thirteen pieces of artillery, giving an aggregate of 971 men and thirteen pieces of artillery.

. . .

I have the honor to be, general, very respectfully, your most obedient servant,

R. R. LIVINGSTON,

Colonel First Regt. Nebraska Cav. Veteran Vols., Commanding. Eastern Sub-District of Nebraska.

[Editor's note: *Reports No. 2–7 have been removed for lack of relevance.*]

SOURCE: *OR*, SERIES 1, VOLUME 41, PART 1, PAGES 824–832

OR-366

NOVEMBER 5–14, 1864.—Operations in Colorado Territory.

Report of Brig. Gen. P. Edward Connor, U.S. Army, commanding District of Utah.

DENVER, COLO. TER., *November 21, 1864*

GENERAL: I have the honor to report that in pursuance of the determination, of which you were apprised by telegraph, I left Camp Douglas on the 5th instant and arrived here on the night of the 14th. The winter season has set in unusually early and with great severity on both sides of the Rocky Mountain range, and heavy storms and deep snows have prevailed during almost the entire current month. The roads in many places between Fort Bridger and this point are blocked and impassable for loaded trains, and destitute of forage. In view of these facts, and the additional one that [if] my cavalry could get through at all, the horses would be useless for active service after arrival in this vicinity, while the men would necessarily suffer much from the intense cold, I have deemed it prudent to halt at Fort Bridger, Wyo. Ter., the two companies of cavalry which left Camp Douglas on the 6th instant. Since my arrival here I find the Indian country intersected and cut up by several military districts, the commanders of which appear to be of opinion that they can spare no troops for a winter campaign against the Indians. Possessing no authority to move any of these troops, which, in my judgment, could be spared for such purpose, and it being impossible to transport hither my own men, I am unable to even attempt an expedition against the savages, who, I am credibly informed, are now in winter quarters on the Republican Fork and the Arkansas River. Any expedition against the Indians which would not probably result in their signal chastisement, would be productive of harm rather than good, and until suitable arrangements to that end shall have been made, I do not deem it wise or prudent either to undertake or advise a campaign against them. I hope to be able to transport my two companies of cavalry hither early in the spring, before the savages break their winter encampments, whence they will not depart until the grass on the plains will furnish forage for their ponies, and the early immigration tempt them to renewed plunder and outrage

I beg leave, respectfully, to suggest that for the successful prosecution of this undertaking, it is highly important that authority be granted to call on district commanders for such additional troops as in my opinion can be safely spared from the several posts during the time necessary to accomplish the purpose named. Without such authority any expedition is likely to prove, if not abortive, at least ineffectual. With it I entertain the confident opinion that an effective blow can be struck in time to prevent the renewed outrages which well may be anticipated during the coming summer. In the meantime I deem this an appropriate occasion, respectfully, to offer a few suggestions relative to the protection of the great overland mail route, and set forth for the information of the department the opinions with which some experience and much thought and examination have impressed me. Premising that no permanent peace with the Indian tribes of the plains can reasonably be hoped for until they shall have been severely chastised for past offences and made to feel the strong arm of the military power of the Government, I remark that it is equally apparent to the most casual observer that, unless some other and more effective measures be devised, the great overland mail will be liable, if not to frequent stoppage, at least to continued and oft-recurring depredations. The project of a great overland mail across the continent may now at least be considered no longer an experiment but an established fact, and its importance to the country at large need hardly be commented on, as it cannot indeed be overestimated, if its safety and permanence can be assured. The best and most practicable, if not the only possible, method of accomplishing this so much to be desired consummation would, in my opinion, be to place at each stage station between Virginia City, in Nevada, and Kiowa Station, on the Little Blue, in Nebraska Territory, a detachment of well mounted cavalry to accompany each mail coach, with a permanent company or regimental headquarters every 100 or 200 miles. These stations are located at an average distance of twelve miles, [and] the entire distance to be thus traversed is 1,650 miles, being from the western line of settlements in Nebraska to the eastern border of the cities of the Pacific slope. Thus stationed, a detachment of five well armed and mounted soldiers could with ease accompany each coach from station to station, the horses and men being relieved, provided for, stabled, &c., at each station. The service would be exceedingly light and easy of accomplishment and would afford the most efficient protection to the mails, treasure, and passengers, as well against white as against Indian desperadoes. For all ordinary cases this guard would be ample, but in the event of threatened difficulties along any part of the line a sufficient force could readily be concentrated at almost any given point. Long experience and careful investigation have convinced me that this, or some other nearly analogous plan, is the most economical and practicable, as well as effectual, method that can be devised for the perfect security of the overland mails. The necessary stables for horses and quarters for the men could be erected by the soldiers themselves at a very trifling cost to the Government. These stations between the points named number 130, requiring for the actual patrol proposed but 1,300 men. Two regiments of cavalry therefore would be amply sufficient to accomplish the entire work, affording absolute security to the mails and, incidentally, to the immigration, while in point of economy they would require a tar less expenditure of money on the part of Government than is now entailed by the system of garrisoned posts at remote distances from each other. The importance of such security to the overland route in the opening up of a certain, speedy, and safe mode of shipment of treasure from the western to the eastern borders of the continent must be as apparent to the department as it can be to me. In time of profound peace it would furnish the people a most wholesome check against exorbitant rates of freight and insurance by sea, but in case of war with any maritime power it would be not merely invaluable but essential to the entire country.

I have the honor to remain, general, very respectfully, your obedient servant,

P. EDW. CONNOR,

Brigadier-General, U.S. Army, Comdg. Dist. of Utah.

Maj. Gen. H. W. HALLECK,

Chief of Staff, U.S. Army, Washington, D.C.

SOURCE: *OR*, SERIES 1, VOLUME 41, PART 1, PAGES 908–910

OR-367

SAN FRANCISCO, CAL., *December 10, 1864.*

Hon. EDWIN M. STANTON,

Secretary of War:

I have to report in answer to your telegram that I have not, and have not had the slightest intention to order, a draft in Oregon or in any part of my command, nor have I indicated any such purpose to any one. Under the special authority you have given me in connection with the Governors of Oregon, California, Nevada, Idaho, and Utah, and the State bounties given by California and Oregon, I hope to raise sufficient force without drafting, which in any case I would not think of doing without your knowledge and orders.

IRVIN McDOWELL,
Major-General, Commanding.

SOURCE: *OR*, SERIES 1, VOLUME 50, PART 2, PAGE 1093

OR-368

HEADQUARTERS DEPARTMENT OF THE PACIFIC,
San Francisco, December 17, 1864.

ADJUTANT-GENERAL OF THE ARMY,
Washington City, D.C.:

SIR: In forwarding the application of Brigadier-General Connor of October 14 for a leave of absence for sixty days, I am constrained to notice the remark of the general "that the present quiet which reigns throughout his district is due to his policy." A reference to the correspondence between him and the headquarters of this department, a copy of which was transmitted with my letter of August 17 to the Adjutant-General of the Army, will show, I think, that the general is mistaken, and that had he been allowed to pursue "his policy" this department would have been involved in war with the Mormons. General Connor bears the reputation of being an excellent soldier, and his ready acquiescence in the instructions I had to give him, checking the policy he desired to follow, shows his reputation is merited; but I think it only right and prudent that it be well understood to what the quiet his district now enjoys is due, lest by an approval of his policy trouble may come.

This application was detained to wait the return of General Connor from his trip to Colorado, where he had gone with the object of inaugurating a winter campaign against the Indians in General Curtis' department, which he was about to set on foot under some instructions he had received direct from Major-General Halleck. I do not think these instructions required General Connor to leave his district and to go and take command of forces so far away from this department, and that they do not contemplate the carrying on systematically of operations against Indians east of the Rocky Mountains by troops from this coast; that the protection to the overland route beyond the limits of this command was to be temporary, and was not, as General Halleck says, intended to transfer troops or change commands. The general has now reported his return, and states that in consequence of the severity of the storms and lack of forage for the animals of the command he had halted the two companies he expected to take with him at Fort Bridger; that he "found but few available troops in the vicinity of Denver to co-operate with his small command, even could the latter reach the scene of the difficulties, nor could he discover a very zealous disposition, even had the ability existed, to co-operate with his forces; that it was apparent to him that to attempt to transport his command across the mountains at this season of the year would result not only in much hardship to the men, but in rendering two thirds of the horses entirely unfit for service after reaching the Platte plains." As therefore there is no probability of General Connor's services being needed this winter, I approve of his having the leave asked.

I am, very respectfully, your most obedient servant,

IRVIN McDOWELL,
Major-General, Commanding Department.

SOURCE: *OR*, SERIES 1, VOLUME 50, PART 2, PAGES 1100–1101

OR-369

HEADQUARTERS DEPARTMENT OF THE PACIFIC,
San Francisco, December 17, 1864.

Brig. Gen. P. E. CONNOR, U.S. Volunteers,
Commanding District of Utah, Camp Douglas, Utah Ter.:

GENERAL: The major-general commanding has attentively considered your several communications of October 17 (by telegraph), October 30, and December 2. He directs me to say that he does not see that the instructions of Major-General Halleck to you direct require you to quit your district for the purpose you seem to have contemplated—that of inaugurating a campaign and carrying on systematically operations against the Indians east of the Rocky Mountains by troops from this coast. The subsequent telegram from General Halleck says it was not intended to transfer troops or change commands. The protection beyond the limits of the district, which you were to give the overland route, was evidently to be by such movement of forces as you might be able to detach, and was required of you for a reason no longer existing, as, since they were given, General Curtis forces have driven off the enemy, and that officer is now doubtless in a condition to look after his end of the route. Your halting your cavalry companies at Fort Bridger, instead of moving them farther east, was eminently proper. The general has approved of your order establishing rates of pay for Government employés from and after date of receipt hereof, and will be glad of your active co-operation in the economical administration of the affairs of the department. To avoid clashing of authority, anything that you may discover of the nature treated of in your order he wishes you to please bring to the immediate notice of the deputy quartermaster-general at department headquarters, by whom, under the Quartermaster-General and the department commander, such matters are regulated. The general wishes to know what, if any, progress has been made in raising the four companies of volunteers.

I have the honor to be, very respectfully, your obedient servant,

R. C. DRUM,
Assistant Adjutant-General.

SOURCE: *OR*, SERIES 1, VOLUME 50, PART 2, PAGE 1101

OR-370

HEADQUARTERS,
Fort Ruby, December 21, 1864.

Capt. M. G. LEWIS,
Assistant Adjutant-General, Camp Douglas, Utah Ter.:

SIR: It may have come to your notice that the Indians in the section of country around Austin have stolen stock—that is, such is the report. They have probably committed a few depredations of this kind, but in my opinion starvation is the cause. Mr. Doll, clerk in the office of the Indian agency at Salt Lake, with Interpreter Huntington, has been here and distributed blankets, &c., to about twenty-five Indians of all classes, this being all that it was possible to collect during the short time the above gentlemen remained, the heavy fall of snow prohibiting the Indians from coming in. In the meantime the balance of the goods are in my hands until further orders. There are Indians at all the stations between Ruby and Austin, and a great many in the vicinity of the latter place, all destitute of food and clothing. In my opinion they should be collected together near some one of the stations and provided for. The Indians in the valley might, by a little labor, be collected near this post. I have plenty of transportation to send out on the road toward Austin and down Ruby Valley. I might have collected nearly all the Indians in this vicinity if I had but had the proper notice that persons were coming to distribute goods. Something should be done for them. I believe if we make good our part of the treaty they will also do the same. I have issued flour in small quantities to those near the post and can take it to those who cannot get here if necessary. Since writing the above the western mail has arrived, bringing a copy of the Reveille of the 19th, containing an account of the stealing of some horses, &c., in Smoky Valley, pursuit by the whites, and the killing of three Indians. I can easily spare thirty men, if you should order me to station them in that vicinity.

Respectfully, your obedient servant,

GEORGE A. THURSTON,
Captain, First Infantry Nevada Volunteers, Commanding Post.

SOURCE: *OR*, SERIES 1, VOLUME 50, PART 2, PAGES 1103–1104

OR-371

WAR DEPARTMENT, ADJUTANT-GENERAL'S OFFICE,
Washington, December 23, 1864.

Maj. Gen. S. R. CURTIS,
Commanding Department of Kansas, Leavenworth, Kans.:

SIR: I have the honor to inform you that the subject of the establishment of a mail line between Fort Laramie and Julesburg, Colo. Ter., which was presented with your indorsement upon the papers under date of December 1, 1864, has been considered by the War Department, and the following views of the Chief of Staff are concurred in and approved by the Secretary of War, viz:

> It would hardly seem wise to open new mail routes requiring military protection and the establishment of military posts at a time when all the military power of the Government is required to put down the rebellion. The Salt Lake route seems to furnish all necessary mail facilities for the present.

I am, sir, &c.,

E. D. TOWNSEND.
Assistant Adjutant-General.

SOURCE: *OR*, SERIES 1, VOLUME 41, PART 4, PAGE 922

OR-372

[*Extract*]

DECEMBER 10–23, 1864.—Expedition against Indians in Central Arizona, with skirmish (15th) on Hassayampa Creek.

REPORTS.

No. 1.—Capt. Allen L. Anderson, Fifth U.S. Infantry.
No. 2.—Capt. John Thompson. First New Mexico Cavalry.

No. 1.

Report of Capt. Allen L. Anderson, Fifth U.S. Infantry.

HEADQUARTERS DISTRICT OF NORTHERN ARIZONA,
Fort Whipple, Ariz. Ter., December 28, 1864.

CAPTAIN: I have the honor to report that on the 10th instant I started from this post on an Indian scout with Capt. J. Thompson and twenty-two enlisted men of Company K, First Cavalry, New Mexico Volunteers. Messrs. Cooler, Weaver, James, Smith, and Rice, and a Utah Indian, named Dick, volunteered their services as guides and accompanied the command.

. . .

I am, very respectfully, your obedient servant,

A. L. ANDERSON,
Captain, Fifth U.S. Infantry.

ASSISTANT ADJUTANT-GENERAL,
Hdqrs. Department of New Mexico, Santa Fé, N. Mex.

No. 2.

[Editor's note: *Report No. 2 removed for lack of relevance.*]

SOURCE: *OR*, SERIES 1, VOLUME 41, PART 1, PAGES 984–987

OR-373

[*Extract*]

OPERATIONS IN LOUISIANA AND THE TRANS-MISSISSIPPI STATES AND TERRITORIES.*

JANUARY 1–JUNE 30, 1865.

PART I.

SUMMARY OF THE PRINCIPAL EVENTS.†

. . .

February 17, 1865.—The Territory of Utah and that part of Nebraska Territory lying west of the twenty-seventh degree of longitude added to the Department of the Missouri.

. . .

The District of the Plains formed, to consist of the Districts of Utah, Colorado, and Nebraska, and Brig. Gen. Patrick E. Connor, U.S. Army, assigned to its command.

. . .

March 30, 1865.—Brig. Gen. Patrick E. Connor, U.S. Army, assumes command of the District of the Plains.

. . .

* Including Arizona, Arkansas, Colorado, Indian Territory, Kansas, Missouri, Nebraska, New Mexico, and Texas, and the Department of the Northwest, embracing Dakota, Iowa, Minnesota, and Wisconsin.

† Of some of the minor conflicts noted in this Summary no circumstantial reports are on file.

SOURCE: *OR*, SERIES 1, VOLUME 48, PART 1, PAGES 1–6

OR-374

HEADQUARTERS DISTRICT OF UTAH,
Camp Douglas, Utah Ter.,
Near Great Salt Lake City, January 3, 1865.

Lieut. Col. R. C. DRUM,
Assistant Adjutant-General, San Francisco, Cal.:

COLONEL: I have the honor to acknowledge the receipt of your communication of the 16th [17th] ultimo, apprising me of the views of the department commander relative to the late orders of Major-General Halleck on the subject of protection to the Overland Mail Route. As stated in former communications, I understood the orders of General Halleck to be to render such protection as I could to the overland mail between Salt Lake City and Fort Kearny "without regard to district or department lines." Recognizing the great necessity of early action and the speedy punishment of the savages who had then recently depredated so seriously east of the Rocky Mountains, I entertained the opinion heretofore expressed that the orders contemplated the movement of a part of my troops to the scene of difficulty, if practicable or deemed advisable, but that no transfer of troops or change of command was intended. For the reasons communicated to department headquarters in my letter of December 2, last, I halted my troops at Fort Bridger, whence they were not to be removed until further orders, and am pleased to learn that that course meets the approval of the department commander. The necessity for further movement no longer exists, as General Curtis is fully able to protect the road along the Platte, and to the limits of this department. In response to your inquiry as to "what, if any, progress has been made in raising the four companies of volunteers in Utah," I have the honor to state that since the receipt of your letter I have seen Governor Doty, and he informs me that he addressed to Major-General McDowell a letter in October last, declining to raise volunteers in this Territory for reasons which commended themselves to his judgment, and which he would be pleased to give if the department commander so desires.

Very respectfully, your obedient servant,

P. EDW. CONNOR,
Brigadier-General, U.S. Volunteers, Comdg. District of Utah.

SOURCE: *OR*, SERIES 1, VOLUME 50, PART 2, PAGE 1112

OR-375

DEPARTMENT OF THE INTERIOR,
Washington, D.C., January 12, 1865.

Hon. E. M. STANTON,
Secretary of War:

SIR: I have the honor to call your attention to the necessity that exists for the removal of the Indians who inhabit the country along the valleys of the Platte and Republican Rivers, along one of which the route of the Union Pacific Railroad will pass, in order that the engineers upon that road may prosecute their labors in security, and that the work may progress without danger of interruption as heretofore from the attacks upon the parties engaged, to which they are now and have been exposed in consequence of the disaffection of various tribes along the route. I was so solicitous in relation to this subject that I did not hesitate to recommend in my last annual report that the Indian agency at the Upper Platte be abolished, and the Indians be admonished that they would no longer be permitted to remain in that portion of the country. In this connection, representations have been made to the Department that General Connor, commanding the military department, headquarters at Salt Lake City, proposes, if it meet the approbation of the War Department, to extend his lines eastwardly to the Little Blue, and along the proposed route of the Union Pacific Railroad, and gives assurance that he can and will protect it against any hostile Indian force that may attempt to interfere with parties engaged in the work upon the road, or with emigrants or citizens crossing the plains, and I respectfully suggest, if it meet the approval of the War Department, that such orders may be issued to the proper officers as will effect the object contemplated by extending adequate military protection over the entire line.

Very respectfully, your obedient servant,

J. P. USHER,
Secretary.

[Editor's note: *This document appears in the* Official Records *as an inclosure to correspondence from J. P. Usher to Lieutenant General U.S. Grant, January 12, 1865, that is not included in this volume.*]

SOURCE: *OR*, SERIES 1, VOLUME 48, PART 1, PAGES 498–499

OR-376

SALT LAKE CITY, *January 14, 1865.*
(Received 12.20 A.M. 16th.)

Hon. EDWIN M. STANTON,
Secretary of War:

It is the universal wish of loyal men in Utah that a department of the plains, including Nebraska, Colorado, Utah, and Montana, be created, under General Connor. Without it we feel it to be hopeless to maintain our communication with the East.

H. S. RUMFIELD,
General Agent Overland Mail.
J. D. DOTY,
Governor of Utah Territory.
AMOS REED,
Secretary of Utah Territory.
WILLIAM REYNOLDS,
General Superintendent of Overland Stage Line.
G. W. CARLETON,
Manager Western Union Telegraph.
JOHN TITUS,
Chief Justice of Utah.

SOURCE: *OR*, SERIES 1, VOLUME 48, PART 1, PAGE 522

OR-377

EXECUTIVE OFFICE,
Omaha, January 17, 1865. (Received 2.50 A.M. 18th.)

Hon. E. M. STANTON, *Secretary of War:*

I send herewith a copy of joint resolution passed this day by unanimous vote of legislative assembly. The case is urgent.

ALVIN SAUNDERS,
Governor of Nebraska.

[Inclosure.]

JOINT RESOLUTION AND MEMORIAL
for the creation of the Department of the Plains.

Resolved by the Council and House of Representatives of the Territory of Nebraska, That the honorable Secretary of War be, and he is hereby, respectfully requested to create at once a special department, to be designated the Department of the Plains, embracing this together with Colorado, Montana, and Utah Territories, all to be under the control of one competent officer, who shall be charged with the responsibility of protecting the overland commerce, telegraph line, and mail transportation.

Resolved, That it is the firm conviction of this body, founded on facts constantly within our observation, that without the adoption of this measure everything must be given up to the control of hostile Indians.

S. M. KIRKPATRICK,
Speaker of the House of Representatives.
O. P. MASON,
President of the Council.

SOURCE: *OR*, SERIES 1, VOLUME 48, PART 1, PAGES 568–569

OR-378

WASHINGTON, D.C., *February 1, 1865.*

Maj. Gen. JOHN POPE,
Saint Louis, Mo.:

GENERAL: I transmit herewith copy of a letter* from General Connor in regard to the defense of the Overland Mail Route, and also several papers from General Curtis on the subject. These papers and others were on their receipt forwarded to Lieutenant-General Grant, and have been returned without any instructions from him, so far as I am informed. It is therefore presumed that he deems the large cavalry force in the Department of Kansas as sufficient for present purposes without taking others from active duty in the field. It is proper to state in this connection that others report these stories of Indian hostilities as greatly exaggerated, if not merely gotten up for the purpose of speculation, and respectable authorities assert that they are encouraged by agents of the Overland Mail Company in order to cover their frequent failure to transport the mails according to contract. Be this as it may, it is highly important that the roads to New Mexico, Colorado, Utah, and Idaho should be properly protected from Indian hostilities, so that there may be no interruption in the transmission of supplies and the mails. You will transmit these papers with the necessary instructions to General Dodge, who will give the whole matter his immediate care and attention.

Very respectfully, your obedient servant,

H. W. HALLECK,
Major-General and Chief of Staff.

* Not found as inclosures.

SOURCE: *OR*, SERIES 1, VOLUME 48, PART 1, PAGE 714

OR-379

FORT LEAVENWORTH, *February 8, 1865—2.45 P.M.*

Major-General POPE,
Saint Louis, Mo.:

Dispatch received. I find that there are two separate routes to Salt Lake from Julesburg west. The telegraph route by way of Fort Laramie and the mail route by way of Cache la Poudre, Bridger's Pass, &c. Both of the routes have troops stationed along them, making two weak lines instead of one strong one. All stages go guarded from station to station, and am told that they are running regularly. General Connor's plan to station eight or ten men at each stage station will not work now, as it would only be a bait to the Indians. I think our troops should be kept at the forts and guards furnished the stages from one fort to another as strong as the case may require. We have no telegraph to Riley, and between Fort Larned and Fort Lyon the Indians are troublesome. I will move troops from Laramie route to the Bridger route, leaving a small garrison at Laramie and one or two others on telegraph line to protect it. The troops reported stationed at Riley are guarding the New Mexico route, and I cannot draw as many troops from there as I wish. If any troops could be spared from Sioux City or the Missouri River I think it would be well to have them strike across to Columbus and Fort Kearny. As soon as I get answers to my dispatches I will post you fully as to condition of matters on Platte route.

G. M. DODGE,
Major- General.

SOURCE: *OR*, SERIES 1, VOLUME 48, PART 1, PAGE 779

OR-380

FORT LEAVENWORTH, *February 9, 1865.*
(Received 2 P.M.)

Major-General POPE,
Saint Louis, Mo.:

The following dispatch has just been received from Colonel Livingston:

FORT RANKIN, NEAR JULESBURG.

Maj. Gen. G. M. DODGE:

In reply to your inquiries I would respectfully state as follows: In the early part of January last indications of large parties of Indians moving westward on Republican [River] were reported by the scouts sent to gain information of their movements. On January 7 they had crossed South Fork of Platte River twenty-three miles west of this post; camped with their families, forming a camp of about, as near as learned, 400 lodges, containing eight warriors each, many lodges being thirty robes in size. They at once commenced the work of destruction along the road west as far as Junction Station, 100 miles from here, and attacked this post. A desperate fight there repulsed them. Their forces in this fight were not less than 2,000 men, armed with breech-loading carbines and rifles. A desperate attempt on their part to burn the Overland stage station near this post was made at this time, but was frustrated by the gallantry of Capt. N. J. O'Brien, Company F, Seventh Iowa Cavalry. Every ranch and stage station from Junction Station to this place, including the station one mile east of this post, is burned, and the charred remains of every inmate who failed to escape tell of the brutality they were subjected to. I telegraphed Hon. Samuel H. Elbert, acting governor of Colorado, early in January of the state of things. The troops of Colorado have been withdrawn from Valley fifty miles west of here, I surmise, to concentrate around Denver. The telegraph line to Salt Lake and the Denver branch line are destroyed for a distance of nearly ten miles on the northern route, and in different points throughout 100 miles along the Denver road. I am hauling poles and repairing the Salt Lake line with all the expedition I can. I have secured 450 poles at Cottonwood, which I expect here Friday morning. They are marching night and day on this duty. Meantime my troops are digging holes for poles and repairing such portions of line as admit of that course. I have but 360 troops, but so long as human endurance holds out we will work night and day to get communication perfect with the west. My opinion is that the Indians engaged in this war are the Cheyennes, Ogallalla Sioux, and Brulé Sioux. They have gone northward toward Horse Creek, beyond Fort Laramie. This trail leads in that direction, but they are slow in marching, feeling audacious and indifferent to every effort from the small body of troops in this district. I saw their signals to-day, probably those of small war parties, on the North Platte. Feel assured, general, that this is no trifling Indian war. You will hear of continued murders and robberies as long as the road is so poorly protected by troops. No stages run farther west than Cottonwood. I have prevailed on agents of the stage company to move their stations close to our forts for protection. General Mitchell, commanding district, pursued these same Indians last month through fearfully cold and stormy weather, but they reached and crossed the Platte before we struck their trail and escaped us. My district extends only this far west, but I am working in Colorado and Western Sub-District of Nebraska. No spies can be used now, owing to numerous small war parties being met everywhere in this country. I predict that if more troops are not sent into this district immediately this road will be stripped of every ranch and white man on it, the military posts alone excepted. Should these Indians swing around by L'eau-qui-court River and strike the Omaha road below Kearny, where settlements are numerous, infinite mischief will result to the settlers. What we need is troops, supplies for them, and a vigorous campaign against these hostile Indians. They must be put on the defensive instead of us. No difficulty can arise in finding them. Over 2,000 stolen cattle accompany them. I will keep the lines open for communication for Leavenworth for any further information.

Respectfully,

R. R. LIVINGSTON,
Colonel First Nebraska Cavalry, Commanding Eastern Sub-District.

I have ordered one regiment to Julesburg. They will start on Monday.

G. M. DODGE,
Major-General.

SOURCE: *OR*, SERIES 1, VOLUME 48, PART 1, PAGES 793–794

OR-381

FORT LEAVENWORTH, *February 9, 1865.*
(Received 8.40 P.M.)

Maj. Gen. JOHN POPE,
Commanding Military Division of the Missouri:

District of Utah, General Connor's command, is not in this command. It should be under you. The Third Wisconsin Cavalry, scattered over this State, is ordered to Arkansas. I think it should be retained here and that portion in Arkansas brought here.

G. M. DODGE,
Major-General.

SOURCE: *OR*, SERIES 1, VOLUME 48, PART 1, PAGE 795

OR-382

HDQRS. MILITARY DIVISION OF THE MISSOURI,
Saint Louis, Mo., February 10, 1865.
(Received 5.10 P.M.)

Maj. Gen. H. W. HALLECK,
Headquarters Army, Washington, D.C.:

Following dispatch just received from General Dodge:

FORT LEAVENWORTH, *February 10, 1865.*

Maj. Gen. JOHN POPE:

Will have telegraph open to Denver and Salt Lake by Sunday. Am ready to protect Overland mail through.

G. M. DODGE,
Major-General.

JNO. POPE,
Major-General, Commanding.

SOURCE: *OR*, SERIES 1, VOLUME 48, PART 1, PAGE 806

OR-383

HEADQUARTERS,
Camp Douglas, February 10, 1865—5.40 P.M.

Col. R. C. DRUM,
Assistant Adjutant-General:

I learn by telegraph from Fort Laramie that the Indians, though driven from the road two days since, have again returned in increased force. The troops are insufficient to contend with them. The probabilities are that communication by stage and telegraph with the East will not be resumed for some time.

P. E. CONNOR,
Brigadier-General.

SOURCE: *OR*, SERIES 1, VOLUME 50, PART 2, PAGE 1131

OR-384

War Dept., Adjt. General's Office,
Washington, February 17, 1865.

General Orders,
No. 23.

The Territory of Utah and that part of Nebraska Territory west of the twenty-seventh degree of longitude are added to the Department of the Missouri.

By order of the Secretary of War:

E. D. TOWNSEND,
Assistant Adjutant-General.

Source: *OR*, Series 1, Volume 48, Part 1, page 886

OR-385

Richmond, Va., *February 18, 1865.*

General S. Cooper,
Adjutant and Inspector General, Confederate States of America:

General: The existing crisis seems to invite the expression of our opinion touching the combination of those elements of strength which remain in a measure undeveloped in our Trans-Mississippi domains. I have therefore the honor to propose: First. That prompt and energetic measures be taken to bring into the field such warriors as the civilized and semi-barbarous Indian nations, viz, the Cherokees, Creeks, Choctaws, Chickasaws, and Seminoles, may be still enabled to furnish us the complements of their effective strength, thus adding a probable contingent of between 15,000 and 20,000 warriors to our armies. Second. That measures be promptly taken to employ the Comanche Nation and other cognate tribes, viz, the Sioux, Blackfeet, Pawnees, &c., now hostile to the Federal power, as an appropriate and energetic contingent, numbering probably some 20,000 warriors, who, when stimulated by adroit emissaries, would carry terror throughout the western border as far as the Canadian frontier. Third. That measures be promptly taken to induce the Mormons (ever strong adherents to States rights doctrines) to initiate predatory warfare along the Pacific border, stimulating the trans-mountain Indians to active co-operation, thus neutralizing the military resources of those distant States known to be lukewarm in the present aggressive warfare, and thereby gaining time, which is to us an important element of defense. Fourth. That encouragement be given by prompt and efficient diplomacy to emigration from the neighboring Mexican States for enrollment as an active contingent for field service. This should embrace the valley of the Rio Grande, including New Mexico. The present condition of Mexico favors this important object, enabling us, probably, to draw largely from those disaffected political elements hostile to the present dominant power, especially if we pursue some well-considered and systematic policy on the question of the Monroe doctrine. Fifth. That measures be immediately taken to organize and take into the field one-fifth of the effective slave population of that department, changing the tenure of their service from slavery to peonage, thus protecting the slave and industrial interests and meeting the existing military necessities of the country.

The troublesome question of eventualities in the minds of many is readily met by the impending necessity of retaining a mercenary army in time of peace, which would absorb the remnants of the servile element whenever peace shall dawn upon the nation. Thus may we combine the reserve corps of those States, the slave force, the Indian force (semi-civilized and savage), the Mexicans and Mormons, in strength sufficient to retain complete military possession of that department, enabling General Smith's army to move promptly into Tennessee, and thus co-operate with the armies of the east to meet and roll back the bloody tide of fanaticism now threatening to engulf us. With such armies wielded under the inspiration of a magnanimous will, there is much reason to believe that the impending abolition crusade may be stayed, or else, indeed, that we may define and mark our boundaries of eternal hatred as high as heaven and as deep as hell, as a memorial in the annals of mankind of a grand effort by a proud and gallant people to defend their firesides and their civil liberties as they inherited them from their revolutionary fathers. The deep interest felt by me in the success of our arms constitutes my excuse for thus tendering observations on the military resources of that distant though important field, founded on a long period of military service along that extensive Western frontier, rendering me in some measure familiar with those elements of strength, as well as geographical outlines noticed in this memorandum.

I remain, general, very respectfully, your most obedient servant,

DANIEL RUGGLES,

Brigadier-General, Provisional Army, C. S.

[Indorsement.]

February 23, 1865.

As the subject-matter of this letter takes a wide range and involves questions of state, I am compelled to submit it for the consideration of the Secretary of War.

S. COOPER,

Adjutant and Inspector General.

SOURCE: *OR*, SERIES 1, VOLUME 48, PART 1, PAGES 1393–1394

OR-386

HEADQUARTERS DISTRICT OF UTAH,
Fort Bridger, Utah Ter., February 18, 1865.

SPECIAL ORDERS,
No. 9.

I. Maj. John M. O'Neill, Second Cavalry California Volunteers, at his own request, is relieved from the command of this post, which he will turn over to Capt. Albert Brown, of the same regiment. The major will proceed to Camp Douglas and report to the commanding officer of that post for duty. The quartermaster's department will furnish the necessary transportation.

* * * *

By command of Brigadier-General Connor:

O. JEWETT,
First Lieut., First Cavalry Nevada Territory, Actg. Asst. Adjt. Gen.

SOURCE: *OR*, SERIES 1, VOLUME 50, PART 2, PAGE 1137

OR-387

BRIDGER, *February 18, 1865—10.20 A.M.*

Capt. F. HAVEN,
Acting Assistant Adjutant-General:

Lieutenant-Colonel Collins, commanding Fort Laramie, promises to keep express running over broken part of line, which will be O.K. to-morrow. I leave for Camp Douglas to-morrow. Flour is safe for the present.

P. E. CONNOR,
Brigadier-General.

SOURCE: *OR*, SERIES 1, VOLUME 50, PART 2, PAGE 1136

OR-388

SAINT LOUIS, *February 24, 1865.*

Brig. Gen. P. E. CONNOR,
Salt Lake City:

The following order is sent for your information.*

* * * *

Send your reports and communications to these headquarters. What troops are in your district?

G.M. DODGE,
Major-General.

* [*Refers to* OR-384. *See also* OR-391.]

SOURCE: *OR*, SERIES 1, VOLUME 48, PART 1, PAGE 972

OR-389

HEADQUARTERS DISTRICT OF UTAH,
Camp Douglas, Utah Ter.,
Near Great Salt Lake City, February 24, 1865.

SPECIAL ORDERS,
No. 11.

The presence of troops being no longer necessary at Camp Connor, Idaho Ter., Capt. J. W. Stillman, Company C, Third Battalion California Infantry, now commanding that post, will, as soon as the roads are passable and before his present supplies are exhausted, with his company and all the public property at the post, take up the line of march to Camp Douglas, Utah Ter., and report to the commanding officer of the post for duty. The quartermaster's department will furnish the necessary transportation.

By command of Brigadier-General Connor:

M. G. LEWIS,
Assistant Adjutant-General.

[Editor's note: *This document appears in the* Official Records *as an inclosure to* OR-390.]

SOURCE: *OR*, SERIES 1, VOLUME 50, PART 2, PAGES 1145–1146

OR-390

HEADQUARTERS DISTRICT OF UTAH,
Camp Douglas, Utah Ter., near Great Salt Lake City,
February 25, 1865.

Lieut. Col. R. C. DRUM,
Assistant Adjutant-General, San Francisco, Cal.:

COLONEL: Inclosed I have the honor to forward Special Orders, No. 11, from these headquarters. There is now a thriving settlement at Camp Connor (Soda Springs), who are sufficiently numerous to protect themselves, and deeming that the troops at that post were more needed for the protection of the Overland Mail Line, I have thought it best to withdraw them. I hope my action may meet the approval of the general commanding the department.

I have the honor to remain, very respectfully, your obedient servant,

P. EDW. CONNOR,
Brigadier-General, Commanding.

[Indorsement.]

March 10, 1865.

I do not approve of General Connor's action in this case; but as he is no longer under my orders, I forbear saying anything about it. He wanted the troops, and took this way to secure them.

I. McDOWELL,
Major-General.

[Inclosure.]

[Editor's note: *See OR-389 for this inclosure.*]

SOURCE: *OR*, SERIES 1, VOLUME 50, PART 2, PAGE 1145

OR-391

HEADQUARTERS DISTRICT OF UTAH,
Camp Douglas, February 27, 1865—2 P.M.

Lieut. Col. R. C. DRUM,
Assistant Adjutant-General:

I am in receipt of the following telegram:

February 24, 1865.

Brig. Gen. P. E. CONNOR:

The following order is sent for your information:

WAR DEPARTMENT, ADJUTANT-GENERAL'S OFFICE,
Washington, D.C., February 17, 1865.

GENERAL ORDERS,
No. 23.

The Territory of Utah and that part of Nebraska west of the twenty-seventh degree of longitude are added to the Department of Missouri.

By order of the Secretary of War:

E. D. TOWNSEND,
Assistant Adjutant-General.

Send your reports and communications to these headquarters. What troops are in your district?

G. M. DODGE,
Major-General, Commanding, Saint Louis.

P. E. CONNOR,
Brigadier-General, U.S. Volunteers.

SOURCE: *OR*, SERIES 1, VOLUME 50, PART 2, PAGE 1147

OR-392

HEADQUARTERS DEPARTMENT OF THE MISSOURI,
February 27, 1865—3.45 P.M.

Brigadier-General CONNOR,
Camp Douglas, Salt Lake:

Go to Denver, leaving District of Utah in charge of a good officer. If you have any spare troops take them with you. I am moving up troops to strike the Indians before grass grows. Orders will meet you at Denver. What about the Indians on North Platte?

G. M. DODGE,
Major-General.

SOURCE: *OR*, SERIES 1, VOLUME 48, PART 1, PAGE 1001

OR-393

[*Extract*]

Organization of troops in the Military Division of the Missouri, Maj. Gen. John Pope, U.S. Army, commanding, February 28, 1865.

. . .

DISTRICT OF UTAH.
Brig. Gen. P. EDWARD CONNOR.

Fort Bridger.
Capt. ALBERT BROWN.
2d California Cavalry, Companies L and M,
1st Nevada Cavalry, Companies A and B.

Camp Connor.
3d California, Company C Capt. James W. Stillman.

Camp Douglas.
Lieut. Col. MILO GEORGE.
3d California, Companies A, B, and D,
1st Nevada Cavalry, Companies C and F.

SOURCE: *OR*, SERIES 1, VOLUME 48, PART 1, PAGE 1042

OR-394

SAN FRANCISCO, *February 28, 1865.*

COMMANDING OFFICER AT CAMP RUBY:

Your post has been attached to the District of California, headquarters Sacramento, Cal. Report to it instead of to Utah.

By order:

R. C. DRUM,
Assistant Adjutant-General.

SOURCE: *OR*, SERIES 1, VOLUME 50, PART 2, PAGE 1148

OR-395

SAN FRANCISCO, *February 28, 1865.*

Brig. Gen. P. E. CONNOR,
Salt Lake City:

Major-General McDowell has received no orders detaching you from his command. Act, however, on the telegram from General Dodge and report to him as desired.

R. C. DRUM,
Assistant Adjutant-General.

SOURCE: *OR*, SERIES 1, VOLUME 50, PART 2, PAGE 1148

OR-396

San Francisco, *March 3, 1865.*

Commanding Officer at Camp Connor:

(Via Salt Lake City.)

All troops in Territory of Idaho belong to District of Oregon, headquarters Fort Vancouver. You will in future report to those headquarters.

By order:

R. C. DRUM.
Assistant Adjutant-General.

Source: *OR*, Series 1, Volume 50, Part 2, page 1154

OR-397

Camp Douglas,
Near Salt Lake, March 3, 1865—8.55 A.M.

Major-General Dodge:

Will leave Denver by next Monday's stage if I can procure forage. Will send two cavalry companies to Fort Halleck to await further orders. I know nothing of whereabouts of Indians, but believe they have gone to head of Yellowstone to meet Crows and Blackfeet for general war in the spring.

P. E. CONNOR.

Source: *OR*, Series 1, Volume 48, Part 1, pages 1081–1082

OR-398

Headquarters District of Utah,
Camp Douglas, Utah Ter., near Great Salt Lake City, March 7, 1865.

Maj. Gen. Irvin McDowell,

Commanding Department of the Pacific:

General: The District of Utah, under my command, having been transferred from the Pacific to the Missouri Department by order of the Secretary of War, I deem this an appropriate occasion to return to you the expression of my personal regard and thanks for the uniform kindness and approbation which I have received at your hands while connected with the Department of the Pacific. On the eve of my departure for the eastern part of my new district, in pursuance of orders from Major-General Dodge, I take the liberty of respectfully asking your views, if it be not deemed unadvisable to communicate them, relative to the future of the Third Infantry Battalion California Volunteers, to the end that I may co-operate with you in the premises. I should be pleased to learn, if not inconsistent with your views, whether it is proposed to increase the battalion by recruiting, and also the disposition, if any has been made, of the recommendation of Captain Johns for promotion to the lieutenant-colonelcy of the battalion. So long connected as I have been with the Department of the Pacific and its welfare, I shall ever entertain the liveliest, interest in its future, and hope to be able at all times to render all the assistance in my power, and, consistent with orders, to promote its well-being, security, and prosperity. Permit me again, general, to renew the expressions of my appreciation for your kindness in the past and the assurances of my high regard.

Very respectfully, your obedient servant,

P. EDW. CONNOR,
Brigadier-General, U.S. Volunteers.

SOURCE: *OR*, SERIES 1, VOLUME 50, PART 2, PAGE 1155

OR-399

HEADQUARTERS MILITARY DIVISION OF THE MISSOURI,
Saint Louis, Mo., March 9, 1865.

Lieut. Gen. U. S. GRANT,
General-in-Chief, City Point, Va.:

GENERAL: Indian affairs in Kansas and on the plains are so far settled as no longer to need the presence of General Dodge at Fort Leavenworth. All troops, except one regiment in the southern part of the State, have been sent out of Kansas. The Territories of Utah, Colorado, and Nebraska have been formed into one district, called the District of the Plains, and General Connor assigned to the command. He thus commands all the forces operating against the Indians, and I think that no further difficulties of a serious character are likely again to occur on the Overland routes. The great mass of business in General Dodge's department is in Missouri. The military prisons are all here and in Alton. All the difficulties in his department are in Missouri, and he has a great quantity of detailed daily business which it is exceedingly difficult, if not impossible, for him to attend to with his headquarters at Fort Leavenworth. I respectfully recommend that they be retransferred to Saint Louis, or that authority be given me to retransfer them. I wrote to General Halleck on the subject some time since, but he replied that the headquarters Department of the Missouri had been changed to Fort Leavenworth by your desire, and that the Secretary of War, to whom he referred my letter, declined for the present to make any change. I think it will be better for the interest of the service and for the discharge of public business that General Dodge should be in Saint Louis.

I am, general, respectfully, your obedient servant,

JNO. POPE,
Major-General, Commanding.

SOURCE: *OR*, SERIES 1, VOLUME 48, PART 1, PAGE 1131

OR-400

HEADQUARTERS DISTRICT OF COLORADO,
Denver, Colo. Ter., March 20, 1865.

LAFAYETTE HEAD,
Indian Agent, Conejos, Colo. Ter.:

DEAR SIR: I send you a communication directed to Colorado and other chiefs of the Utah Indians now in the vicinity of Colorado City. I sincerely hope you will make it your special business to attend to it at once. Something should be done by the Indian Department for these Indians. I have sent to the commanding officer at Camp Fillmore a duplicate of the same communication, with instructions to have it properly interpreted to the chiefs, and desired him to confer with you on the subject before taking any steps if possible, and at all times on business of this matter. It is my intention to be friendly to these tribes, and if a war is forced upon us with them it will be their own fault. This I know can be prevented by judicious management, and you, as the agent, should exercise vigilance and sound discretion. I trust the matter in your hands and that of the commanding officer of Camp Fillmore.

Respectfully, your obedient servant,

T. MOONLIGHT,
Colonel Eleventh Kansas Cavalry, Commanding.

SOURCE: *OR*, SERIES 1, VOLUME 48, PART 1, PAGES 1224–1225

OR-401

State of California, Executive Department,
Sacramento, March 21, 1865.

Major-General McDowell:

General: Referring to our conversation had a few days since in relation to the two companies of the Second Cavalry California Volunteers now in Utah, I have to say that from information received yesterday I learn that they are still at Fort Bridger, and will not move from there until spring opens at any rate. As all the balance of the regiment is within your department, cannot some action be taken by which these two companies may be sent back? I think you suggested that you would be willing to exchange and give General Connor two companies of Nevada cavalry, if no better arrangement could be made. It is really unjust to the officers and men that they should be detached and sent out of this department, away from the headquarters of the regiment, and beyond the control of the regimental officers. Please let me know if you think anything can be done to remedy the evil.

Very respectfully,

F. F. LOW,
Governor.

Source: *OR*, Series 1, Volume 50, Part 2, page 1167

OR-402

Hdqrs. Dept. of the Missouri,
Saint Louis, Mo., March 28, 1865.

General Orders,
No. 80.

I. Brig. Gen. R. B. Mitchell, U.S. Volunteers, is hereby relieved from the command of the District of Nebraska and will assume command of the District of North Kansas, headquarters at Fort Leavenworth, Kans.

II. The Districts of Utah, Colorado, and Nebraska, are hereby merged into one command, to be known as the District of the Plains.

III. Brig. Gen. P. E. Connor, U.S. Volunteers, is assigned to the command of the District of the Plains, headquarters at Denver, Colo. Ter.

By command of Major-General Dodge:

J. W. BARNES,
Assistant Adjutant-General.

Source: *OR*, Series 1, Volume 48, Part 1, page 1285

OR-403

Headquarters Department of the Missouri,
Saint Louis, March 29, 1865.

Brig. Gen. P. E. Connor,
Denver:

Troops en route to Laramie and Julesburg, with those on the route, will give you 2,000 or over mounted men. I want this force pushed right on after the Indians. There are 400 pack-mules with them. There is also one regiment of U.S. Volunteer Infantry on the way to Kearny that can relieve considerable body of cavalry; also one or two more regiments will soon start for Leavenworth. About May 1 General Sully will leave Sioux City with a column and push west to Powder River and establish a post there. We will have to supply that column from Laramie. Allow no purchases or contracts made except first sanctioned by Colonel Potter, depot quartermaster, or myself. I have a large number of Canadian horses en route here which will be sent you. Notify me how many horses you want to mount your command. Write me fully as to Salt Lake, &c.

G. M. DODGE,
Major-General.

Source: *OR*, Series 1, Volume 48, Part 1, page 1295

OR-404

Headquarters Department of the Missouri,
Saint Louis, Mo., March 29, 1865.

Brig. Gen. P. E. Connor,
Denver City, Colo.:

General: The District of the Plains was formed so as to put under your control the entire northern Overland route and to render effective the troops along it. With the force at your disposal you can make vigorous war upon the Indians and punish them so that they will be forced to keep the peace. They should be kept away from our lines of travel and made to stand on the defensive. Sufficient infantry to hold most of the posts will be sent you from the regiments raised from Confederate prisoners in our hands for service on the plains. They are officered by our own men. Depots should be designated where we can put in one year's supply. These depots should be well fortified. An engineer from these headquarters is now out examining the posts. I think there should be depots at Fort Kearny, Cottonwood, Julesburg, Fort Laramie, Fort Halleck, Valley Station—or some point between Julesburg and Denver—Denver, Fort Lyon, and Utah. As it is, each station is a partial depot, whereas with a few depots that other posts can draw from we can put proper staff officers at them and have our stores properly taken care of and protected. The overland mail and telegraph must be protected at all hazards, and no excuse be given or allowed for stopping the mails. Order No. 41 from these headquarters prescribes manner of organizing trains, &c., and you must see that no interference with emigrant or private trains is allowed. The troops that have been lying at the different posts should, as soon as possible, be relieved and put in the field. I hear many complaints of them. Brevet Brigadier-General Ford leaves Fort Larned in a few days with 1,200 men to operate against the Indians on the Cimarron. The force at Fort Lyon will give him any aid he may require. They will also co-operate with General Carleton's troops, who are holding two routes from Fort Union, viz, one to Lyon and one to old Fort Atkinson, on the Arkansas. You are on the ground and are therefore the best judge of what will be the best use of your troops, their disposition at posts, &c. You are a stranger to me, but I have placed you in command, believing that you will bend all your energies to the common object and infuse life, discipline, and effectiveness into the forces under you, and give the Indians no rest. You will report by letter semimonthly your operations, and telegraph me at all times anything you may have of sufficient importance. Contracts or purchases made except by my order or the order of the chief quartermaster of the department meet with great trouble in being audited and paid; in fact they are unauthorized and should be made only in most urgent cases and to answer a present emergency, and when you cannot confer with Colonel Potter or myself by letter or telegraph.

I am, general, very respectfully, your obedient servant,

G. M. DODGE,
Major-General, Commanding.

SOURCE: *OR*, SERIES 1, VOLUME 48, PART 1, PAGES 1295–1296

OR-405

COTTONWOOD, *March 29, 1865.*

Colonel MOONLIGHT:

I am in command of District of the Plains, composed of Districts of Utah, Colorado, and Nebraska; headquarters at Denver. Make no movement of troops until my return.

P. E. CONNOR,
Brigadier-General.

SOURCE: *OR*, SERIES 1, VOLUME 48, PART 1, PAGE 1296

OR-406

FORT KEARNY, NEBR. TER.,
March 30, 1865.

GENERAL ORDERS,
No. 1.

In pursuance of General Orders, No. 80, Department of the Missouri, current series, the undersigned hereby assumes command of the District of the Plains, composed of the Districts of Utah, Colorado, and Nebraska, headquarters at Denver, Colo. Ter.

P. EDW. CONNOR,
Brigadier-General, U.S. Volunteers.

SOURCE: *OR*, SERIES 1, VOLUME 48, PART 1, PAGE 1300

OR-407

HEADQUARTERS DISTRICT OF THE PLAINS,
Denver, Colo. Ter., April 5, 1865.

Maj. J. W. BARNES,
Assistant Adjutant-General, Department of the Missouri:

SIR: I returned on the 3d instant from Fort Kearny and am very glad that I made the trip, as it placed me in possession of much reliable information. I regret to say that I found but very little discipline among the troops and but little regard paid to economy, or care given to public property. Although affairs are badly mixed up at present, I hope soon to have them in different shape and trust that the major-general commanding will have patience with me for a short time. I do not approve of the plans of fortifications laid out by the district commanders who have preceded me. If completed they will cost large sums of money. If this business is left with me I will guard the road as effectively and with less expensive works. I will do everything in my power to expedite the expedition north, but supplies are coming in very slowly from the river, and it will take a longer time than you probably anticipate to get it in motion. I am not well posted in regard to what has been done at the river, not yet having time to communicate with the officers in charge. I trust that supplies will be forwarded as rapidly as possible, particularly so as I am expected to supply General Sully's command. I have received Major-General Dodge's telegrams directing that neither contracts nor purchases be made without first obtaining his approval or that of the chief quartermaster of the department. In consequence of the peculiar condition of affairs in Utah, I have deemed it necessary to purchase in open market fuel, forage, and other articles required and of which we were short. I request authority to continue said system in Utah until contracts are let for the ensuing fiscal year; also to make from time to time purchases of such small articles as may be required for immediate use, I have always made economy in use of public property and careful disbursements of public funds my first duty.

I have the honor to forward, indorsed, copies of requisitions for ordnance and ordnance stores and quartermaster's stores for Utah, with the request that the same be filled in every particular. The originals were forwarded to headquarters Department of the Pacific, but for fear they may miscarry I send duplicates. The requisitions for subsistence stores for Utah have been forwarded to the Commissary-General by Major-General McDowell, commanding Department of the Pacific. I have also the honor to inclose the resignation of Maj. Presley Talbot. I required him to tender his resignation on account of his very bad conduct, I expect that I will be compelled to exact the same action from others, in order to bring the service in this district up to the proper standard, and in doing so trust I will be sustained by the major-general commanding. It is absolutely necessary that officers here be required to reflect credit and honor on the service. Failing to do so, that they may be compelled to leave it. Will forward by next mail a communication on Utah affairs. I have not received any communication, excepting telegrams, from department headquarters.

I am, sir, very respectfully, your obedient servant,

P. EDW. CONNOR,
Brigadier-General, Commanding.

SOURCE: *OR*, SERIES 1, VOLUME 48, PART 2, PAGE 36

OR-408

HEADQUARTERS DISTRICT OF THE PLAINS,
Denver, Colo. Ter., April 6, 1865.

Maj. J. W. BARNES,
Assistant Adjutant-General, Department of the Missouri:

SIR: I propose to submit, for the information of the major-general commanding, a brief resume of affairs connected with my administration of the old District of Utah. I arrived at Salt Lake City with my command in November, 1862, and found the community almost exclusively members of the Mormon Church, bitter and unrelenting in their hostility to the Government. Persons residing in Utah and not members of the church were daily annoyed with petty persecutions calculated to force them to leave the Territory. The leaders of the church, jealous of the unlimited power they exercised over a bigoted and misguided people, employed every means in their power to prevent associations between their followers and loyal citizens. The so-termed sermons delivered in their tabernacles, boweries, and ward meetings were models of obscenity and treason. It appeared as though every effort was made by the advocates of polygamy to destroy all that native modesty characteristic of a woman, and to instill into the minds of the men the most bitter and unrelenting hatred toward our Government. The church leaders at every opportunity repeated the assertion that the war was a "Kilkenny cat" affair, so far as they were concerned; that they did not care which side whipped; in either event the war would continue until North and South were completely exhausted, and then they (the Mormons) would return to Jackson County, Mo., and control the destinies of the United States. They were able to obtain credit for this assertion among the people from this fact: The most of them are foreigners, gathered from the lower classes of Europe men and women who know nothing about the American Government or its institutions. The officers and soldiers of my command were regarded as blacklegs and scoundrels, and were so designated by Brigham Young, the head of the church. The Indians were, I firmly believe, incited to acts of hostility against the mails and immigrants, for the purpose of involving us in a war, and, as we were but few in numbers, thus hoping to get rid of us. I determined to exercise the utmost caution toward the community, consistent with my duty, but at the same time was equally determined to maintain the authority of the Government at any and all hazards. During the fall of 1862 and winter and spring of 1863 my command was actively engaged against the Shoshone, Ute, and Goshute Indians; and at the battle of Bear River I captured large quantities of wheat, together with many articles which the Indians could not have obtained had they not been on friendly terms with the Mormons. I know that on one occasion, when a detachment of cavalry in pursuit of Indians entered a town south of Salt Lake, the inhabitants had a portion of the same band in their houses, and told my officers that they had passed through a canon in the mountains several days previous. On another occasion a party of fifty or more Ute Indians entered the town of Battle Creek and attacked six soldiers of my command, and continued the attack for several hours, during which time 150 able-bodied white men, claiming to be American citizens, quietly looked on the attack from their house tops, barns, sheds, and haystacks, without offering the slightest assistance. The bravery of the men and officer in charge finally compelled the Indians to retire, with a loss of several killed and wounded. I mention these instances to show the spirit animating the community. Nothing but fear and policy caused the leaders to remain quiet; but on every occasion they sneered at the authority of the Government and predicted to their followers its speedy downfall.

After whipping the Indians into subjection I turned my attention to a development of the mineral wealth of the Territory, with a view to encourage a different class of emigration, and thus eventually break up a system of religion and government at once infamous and abhorrent, to every refined mind. In my efforts to develop the mineral wealth of the Territory I was well sustained by my officers and men, who, while they desired active service, cheerfully executed my orders, and with great energy prospected the country, and succeeded in discovering rich gold and silver bearing rock. It is now a settled fact that the mines of Utah are equal to any west of the Missouri River, and only await, the advent of capital to develop them. About the same time that I commenced this system of prospecting I caused a daily newspaper to be instituted at my own expense, which has been and is now in successful operation, and doing much toward redeeming Utah from the "one-man power" the Mormon Church. Last summer I sent an expedition from Salt Lake City for the purpose of opening a wagon-road communication between that place and the head of navigation of the Colorado River. The expedition was entirely successful, and now goods are shipped by that route. The power of the Mormon Church has been greatly exaggerated abroad. While I have every reason to know that the leaders of it are disloyal and traitors at heart, I have no fear of their taking any steps to produce difficulties between them and the troops. They content themselves with gasconade and such petty annoyances as they may be able to inflict upon the Government, in refusing to furnish from their abundance, supplies, &c. They daily violate the acts of Congress in the practice of polygamy, in the passage of laws violating the organic act and of others wholly opposed to the spirit of our institutions. The secret of the power of these leaders lies in this one word isolation. So long as they were able to keep their people from association with the outside world they were safe. To this end they employed every means possible to force Federal officers (not Mormons) out of the Territory, and they succeeded well until the advent of the troops in 1862. The condition of affairs to-day is far different from that of three years ago. The presence of troops giving protection to those not belonging to the church; the establishment of a free press; the discovery of extensive mines, and the subjection of the Indians have already gathered quite a large population of loyal men, who form the nucleus around which gather all the elements opposed to this infamous evil of our age, clothed with the name of religion. Three years ago there were not 100 Gentiles, aside from the troops, in the Territory. Now there must be not less than 1,500, with the number constantly increasing. A town (Stockton) has been established in the center of the Rush Valley mining district, thirty-eight miles from Salt Lake, by those not members of the church, which is rapidly gaining all the elements of permanency. It is a source of much pride to me that all these changes are in progress for the better, and to know that notwithstanding I had to encounter all the opposition of the Mormon Church, my policy has proved successful, and that but a few years will elapse before Utah will be redeemed from her infamy and degradation and contribute a loyal and healthy support to our common country, instead of being, as she now is, a foul and filthy ulcer upon the body politic. I do not apprehend any trouble with Indians in that Territory. They have been thoroughly whipped and taught the consequences of molesting the mail coaches and emigrant trains. The troops now serving in that Territory, consisting of California and Nevada regiments, are in hue condition, well disciplined veteran soldiers, an honor and credit to the service, and in charge of capable and experienced officers. Public property is carefully used and no extravagance permitted. The public funds are disbursed with the utmost economy consistent with the public service.

Very respectfully, your obedient servant,

P. EDW. CONNOR,
Brigadier-General, Commanding.

[First indorsement.]

HEADQUARTERS DEPARTMENT OF THE MISSOURI,
Saint Louis, April 15, 1865.

Respectfully forwarded to Capt. Joseph McC. Bell, assistant adjutant-general, Military Division of the Missouri, for the information of the major-general commanding Military Division of the Missouri.

G. M. DODGE,
Major-General, Commanding.

[Second indorsement.]

HDQRS. MILITARY DIVISION OF THE MISSOURI,
Saint Louis, April 28, 1865.

This interesting and valuable report of General Connor, concerning affairs in Utah, is respectfully forwarded for the information of the Secretary of War. It throws great light upon the condition of the Morman [Mormon] settlements and the objects of the rulers in Utah, which will prove very useful in the consideration of measures relating to the future status of that Territory.

JNO. POPE,
Major-General, Commanding.

[Editor's note: *This document is referenced in OR-416.*]

SOURCE: *OR*, SERIES 1, VOLUME 50, PART 2, PAGES 1184–1186

OR-409

[*Extract*]

HEADQUARTERS DISTRICT OF OREGON,
Fort Vancouver, Wash. Ter., April 7, 1865.

Col. R. C. DRUM,
Assistant Adjutant-General, San Francisco, Cal.:

SIR: I have delayed writing as regards the necessity of additional cavalry and the proposed uses of the troops in this district, on account of succeeding unexpectedly to the command of the district. Some days after doing so were necessary to inform myself as to the dispositions made and proposed by the former commander, who, during his short stay after turning over the command, was very kind in his efforts to impart all desired information. I will remark here that recruiting for the cavalry is progressing rather better in the last weeks than at first.

. . .

For Fort Boisé, Idaho Ter., two companies of infantry and three of cavalry. Its isolated position—500 miles from this place and about the same from Camp Douglas, in the midst of a population, a large proportion of which is not of doubtful proclivities or antecedents—of itself makes this force necessary. But this necessity, at least for some years, will be more urgent on account of the presence of thieving bands of Indians infesting all the routes leading into the extensive and rich mineral districts of which it is the center, and the protection of which within a large circuit must depend upon it.

. . .

There should also be sufficient cavalry to patrol the mail or stage route, as well as the emigrant route leading through Camas Prairie from Salt Lake City.

. . .

Very respectfully, your obedient servant,

R. F. MAURY,
Colonel First Oregon Cavalry, Commanding District.

SOURCE: *OR*, SERIES 1, VOLUME 50, PART 2, PAGES 1187–1190

OR-410

HEADQUARTERS MILITARY DIVISION OF THE MISSOURI,
Saint Louis, Mo., April 7, 1865. (Received 6.45 P.M.)

Hon. E. M. STANTON,
Secretary of War:

The Congressional committee appointed to examine into Indian matters have applied to me for an officer experienced in service in Indian country to go with them to Indian country, New Mexico, and Utah to direct their attention in the investigation to the points which need reform, and the manner in finding out what is sought by the inquiry. It is exceedingly desirable, in view of the unsatisfactory condition of Indians and the hostility of Indians to War Department officials, that such an officer be sent with the committee to see that the facts are fully brought out. Otherwise, as there are certain to be many Indian agents and superintendents along, the military will be placed in very unfavorable and false positions. I wish to send General McCook, who has served long in the Indian country and knows all about these matters. His services at Helena are not important, as Reynolds has taken away a large part of his force. Can I send him?

JNO. POPE,
Major-General.

SOURCE: *OR*, SERIES 1, VOLUME 48, PART 2, PAGE 44

OR-411

HDQRS. DISTRICT OF THE PLAINS,
Denver, Colo. Ter., April 8, 1865.

GENERAL ORDERS,
No. 4.

The District of the Plains is hereby divided into the following-named sub-districts:

I. The Territory of Colorado, excepting the post of Julesburg and Fort Halleck, Dak. Ter., will be known as the South Sub-District of the Plains, headquarters at Denver, Colo. Ter. Bvt. Brig. Gen. Guy V. Henry is assigned to the command. The Territory of Nebraska will be known as the East Sub-District of the Plains, headquarters at Fort Kearny, Nebr. Ter. Col. R. R. Livingston, First Nebraska Cavalry, is assigned to the command. All that portion of Dakota Territory, excepting Fort Halleck, lying west of the twenty-seventh degree of longitude, and formerly included in the District of Nebraska, and the post at Julesburg, Colo. Ter., will be known as the North Sub-District of the Plains, headquarters at Fort Laramie, Dak. Ter. Col. Thomas Moonlight, Eleventh Kansas Cavalry, is assigned to the command. The Territory of Utah will be known as the West Sub-District of the Plains, headquarters at Camp Douglas, Utah. Lieut. Col. Milo George, First Battalion Nevada Cavalry, is assigned to the command.

* * * *

By command of Brigadier-General Connor:

GEO. F. PRICE,
Acting Assistant Adjutant-General.

SOURCE: *OR*, SERIES 1, VOLUME 48, PART 2, PAGES 54–55

OR-412

Headquarters Department of the Missouri,
April 10, 1865.

Hon. Thomas C. Fletcher,
Governor of Missouri, Jefferson City, Mo.:

In compliance with instructions from the Secretary of War a salute of 200 guns will be fired at every post and arsenal in this department at meridian on the day of the receipt of this order in commemoration of the surrender of General Lee and the Army of Northern Virginia to Lieutenant-General Grant and the army under his command.

By order of Major-General Dodge:

J. W. BARNES,
Assistant Adjutant-General.

(Copy to commanding officers District of Central Missouri, Warrensburg; Southwestern Missouri, Springfield; District of Rolla, Rolla; District of South Kansas, Paola; District of North Kansas, Fort Leavenworth; District of Upper Arkansas, Fort Riley; District of the Plains, Denver; Alton; Franklin; Saint Louis Arsenal. Governors of Missouri, Jefferson City; Kansas, Topeka; Utah, Salt Lake City; Nebraska, Omaha; Colorado, Denver; Illinois, Springfield; and Maj. George C. Tichenor, Des Moines, Iowa.)

Source: *OR*, Series 1, Volume 48, Part 2, page 65

OR-413

Headquarters District of the Plains,
Denver, Colo. Ter., April 14, 1865.

Capt. Albert Brown,
Second California Cav., Comdg. Expedition, Fort Bridger, Utah:

Sir: A train numbering thirty wagons will leave this place for Fort Halleck on the 16th or 17th instant. Upon the arrival of this train at Halleck it will load with grain for your expedition and travel on the Overland Mail road to Fort Bridger, or until it meets you, leaving 3,000 pounds of grain at every station where it remains over night. This grain will be subject to your order. When the train meets your expedition you will transfer your stores and supplies to it and it will return with you to Halleck.

You will send back to Camp Douglas the teams you may have brought with you from Bridger. There are thirty kegs of powder on this train, invoiced respectively to Lieut. Col. Milo George, commanding officer Camp Douglas, and to Maj. Noyes Baldwin, commanding officer Fort Bridger. You will see that the powder is properly transferred to the train you send back to Camp Douglas. You will bring with you all the clothing, camp and garrison equipage, quartermaster's stores, ordnance, and ordnance stores belonging to Companies L and M, Second California Cavalry. In the event of your starting from Bridger before the train from Halleck arrives, the commanding officer of Fort Bridger will furnish you with sufficient transportation to accomplish this object. You will also bring with you from Bridger the little howitzer and the pack-saddles, instead of the howitzer mounted upon four wheels. During your march from Bridger to Halleck you will report triweekly by letter to these headquarters. Copies of this communication are furnished to Capt. C. L. Gorton, assistant quartermaster, Denver, Colo. Ter.; commanding officers Fort Halleck, Fort Bridger, and Camp Douglas, for their information and guidance.

Very respectfully, your obedient servant,

GEO. F. PRICE,
Acting Assistant Adjutant-General.

SOURCE: *OR*, SERIES 1, VOLUME 48, PART 2, PAGES 101–102

OR-414

HEADQUARTERS DEPARTMENT OF THE PACIFIC,
San Francisco, April 15, 1865.

Brig. Gen. P. E. CONNOR,
Comdg. District of Utah, &c., Hdqrs. Denver City, Colo. Ter.:

GENERAL: I thank you for the friendly expression in your letter of March 7 and the assurances of your desire to co-operate with me in the discharge of your duties under your new commander. It was not intended by the Governor of California and myself to continue the Third California Volunteer Infantry in service beyond the three years of their engagement. I understand that the Governor has commissioned Captain Johns as lieutenant colonel of the battalion.

Wishing you much success, I am, general, yours, truly and sincerely,

IRVIN McDOWELL,
Major-General, Commanding Department.

SOURCE: *OR*, SERIES 1, VOLUME 50, PART 2, PAGE 1196

OR-415

HDQRS. DISTRICT OF THE PLAINS,
Denver, Colo. Ter., April 20, 1865,

GENERAL ORDERS,
No. 7.

The following officers are announced as on the staff of the general commanding the district: Capt. M. G. Lewis, assistant adjutant-general, U.S. Volunteers, assistant adjutant-general; First Lieut. Oscar Jewett, First Battalion Nevada Cavalry, aide-de-camp; Maj. George Armstrong, First Nebraska Veteran Cavalry, chief of cavalry; Maj. J. H. Peabody, surgeon, U.S. Volunteers, medical director; Capt. Parmenas T. Turnley, assistant quartermaster, U.S. Army, chief quartermaster; Capt. William R. Irwin, commissary of subsistence, U.S. Volunteers, chief commissary; Capt. George F. Price, Second California Cavalry, district inspector; Capt. E. B. Zabriskie, First Battalion Nevada Cavalry, judge-advocate; Capt. John C. Anderson, Veteran Battalion First Colorado Cavalry, assistant commissary of musters at Denver, Colo. Ter.; Capt. John A. Wilcox, First [Fourth] U.S. Cavalry, assistant commissary of musters at Fort Kearny, Nebr. Ter.; First Lieut. S. E. Jocelyn, Third Battalion California Infantry, assistant commissary of musters at Camp Douglas, Utah; First Lieut. Charles C. Hawley, Veteran Battalion First Colorado Cavalry, acting ordnance officer for the South and West Sub-Districts of the Plains, station at Denver, Colo. Ter.; First Lieut. William H. Northrop, Seventh Iowa Calvary acting ordnance officer for the North and East Sub-Districts of the Plains, station at Fort Kearny, Nebr. Ter. They will be obeyed and respected accordingly.

By command of Brigadier-General Connor:

GEO. F. PRICE,
Acting Assistant Adjutant-General,

SOURCE: *OR*, SERIES 1, VOLUME 48, PART 2, PAGE 148

OR-416

HEADQUARTERS DEPARTMENT OF THE MISSOURI,
Saint Louis, April 24, 1865—4.10 P.M.

Brig. Gen. P. E. CONNOR,
Denver:

How are you progressing with Indian expedition? Have you staff officers? Keep Colonel Potter and Captain Murfey at Leavenworth posted well ahead in what you may need. Also let me know and keep me posted. Letter about Utah received all right.* I furnished the escort for wagon road party up Niobrara.

G. M. DODGE,
Major-General.

* [*Refers to OR-408.*]

SOURCE: *OR*, SERIES 1, VOLUME 48, PART 2, PAGE 186

OR-417

GREAT SALT LAKE CITY, UTAH TER., *April 26, 1865.*

General CONNOR:

DEAR SIR: Aware of the arduous duties you have to perform, still I trust a few lines from me will not prove an intrusion. As I intend starting for the Eastern States on the 1st of May, I could not in justice to my own feelings leave Utah without expressing my heartfelt thanks and gratitude to you for the protection you have afforded not only to myself, but to our church in general, together with the many acts of kindness you have rendered us, and in the behalf of a grateful people permit me to say our prayers shall ever be offered for your welfare before the throne of grace, and we shall ever hail with delight the announcement of your advancement to honor and trust, which we believe you so justly merit. As a people we have our religious peculiarities of belief, differing, however, in reality, not to any greater extent than the various religious sects differ from each other. But our religion teaches us loyalty to our Government, not mere lip service, but to render every assistance for its support that may be required; and we trust that the dark stigma which has been attached to the name of the Latter-Day Saints by the actions of men who, fired with ambitious views of political power, lustful and covetous desires, have basely striven to cloak their iniquitous proceedings under a mask of religion, will ere long pass away, and the Latter-Day Saints be acknowledged in the ranks of the moral, virtuous, and loyal. To this end we are laboring, and I am thankful to God that I have been instrumental in his hands of bringing many in Utah to a knowledge of the duties they owe to God, their country, and their fellow-men. I deeply deplore your absence from Utah, as affairs now present a very different aspect than during your administration in person. Our church is prosperous. I leave behind me a good organization with a competent president, and am expecting missionaries from the East this spring to prosecute the work with renewed vigor; but the fear that was gradually leaving the people has since your departure returned, and they are afraid of being placed in greater bondage than ever. Heavy threats are made by Brigham and his colleagues against those who dare to differ from him in sentiment. Dark deeds are contemplated and enacted. At the last conference Brigham instituted a military law of his own, and commanded the bishops to put it in force, viz, none of his people to be allowed in the street after 10 P.M.; also organized a strong police force in every ward, subject to his instructions, to patrol night and day, and the people are under greater surveillance than ever. I would mention the attempt that has been made to assassinate Mr. Maloney, but I understand he has written you on the subject. I cannot, however, help indulging the hope that Utah will be favored by your presence again at some period not far distant. You will pardon me, but I cannot help entertaining the impression that you are destined to shape the destiny of this Utah, mold and fashion it from its present loathsome and repulsive appearance into something more favorable and delightsome. The material is here, I am satisfied, to make a virtuous and loyal people, if their slavish chains were struck off and their corrupt leaders dealt with as they justly merit, and nothing would afford myself and friends greater satisfaction, now that peace is about to be restored to our glorious country, than to see Utah, freed from her corruption, enrolled as a State.

Once more thanking you for your kindness, allow me to remain, very respectfully,

R. H. ATWOOD.

[Indorsement.]

Atwood is a missionary of a branch of the Mormon Church called Josephites, of whom young Joseph Smith is the leader. They are anti-polygamists and loyal.

CONNOR.

SOURCE: *OR*, SERIES 1, VOLUME 48, PART 2, PAGES 219–220

OR-418

HEADQUARTERS DISTRICT OF THE PLAINS,
Denver, Colo. Ter., April 28, 1865.

Lieut. Col. WILLIAM M. JOHNS,
Third Battalion California Infantry, Camp Douglas, Utah:

COLONEL: I deem it necessary and important in a military point of view, as well as for the benefit of the Pacific States, that a better and nearer road than the present one should be made between Denver and Salt Lake; and having assurance that such a road can be made over the route by Uintah Valley and Middle Park, saving in distance 200 miles, and passing over a country fertile and well timbered, and which by building the road will be open to settlement and cultivation, and also shortening the time of transmission of the overland mail between the points named two days, over a route not subject to Indian attacks, and making a less distance to protect in case of necessity, and taking all the advantages to be gained into consideration, I had determined to build a military road; but finding that the Overland Stage Company has a charter from the Territories of Colorado and Utah for a road over the proposed route, and desiring to have the mail route changed before next autumn, you will cause the men of your command to perform such work on the road, and on such route as Bela M. Hughes, the agent of the company, may direct. Mr. Hughes will pay the men of your command a fair compensation for such labor as they may perform. I would enjoin upon you to use all possible exertion and speed in the performance of the work assigned you, and on your arrival in this city report to Bvt. Brig. Gen. Guy V. Henry, commanding South Sub-District of the Plains, for duty.

Very respectfully, your obedient servant,

P. EDW. CONNOR,
Brigadier-General.

SOURCE: *OR*, SERIES 1, VOLUME 48, PART 2, PAGES 238–239

OR-419

[*Extract*]

Organization of troops in the Military Division of the Missouri, Maj. Gen. John Pope, U.S. Army, commanding, April 30, 1865.

DISTRICT OF THE PLAINS.
Brig. Gen. P. EDWARD CONNOR.

. . .

West Sub-District.
Lieut. Col. MILO GEORGE.

Fort Bridger, Utah Ter.
Maj. NOTES BALDWIN.
2d California Cavalry, Company L, Capt. Albert Brown,
2d California Cavalry, Company M, Lieut. George D. Conrad,
1st Battalion Nevada Cavalry, Company A, Lieut. James H. Stewart,
1st Battalion Nevada Cavalry, Company B, Capt. Joseph H. Mathewson.

Camp Connor, Utah Ter.
3d California, Company C, Capt. James W. Stillman.

Camp Douglas, Utah Ter.
Lieut. Col. WILLIAM M. JOHNS.
3d California, Company A, Lieut. Charles Billig,
3d California, Company B, Capt. Joseph C. Morrill,
3d California, Company D, Capt. Willard Kittredge,
1st Battalion Nevada Cavalry, Company C, Capt. John H. Dalton,
1st Battalion Nevada Cavalry, Company F, Capt. Joseph W. Calder.

SOURCE: *OR*, SERIES 1, VOLUME 48, PART 2, PAGES 274–275

OR-420

HEADQUARTERS WEST SUB-DISTRICT OF THE PLAINS,
Camp Douglas, Utah Ter., May 4, 1865.

Capt. GEORGE F. PRICE,
Actg. Asst. Adjt. Gen., District of the Plains, Denver City, Colo. Ter.:

CAPTAIN: I have the honor to represent the following facts, which are respectfully submitted for the consideration and action of the general commanding: It has come to my knowledge from various trustworthy sources that a system of espionage and insolent interference with the affairs of individuals not belonging to the Mormon Church has been organized in Great Salt Lake City, under the auspices and by dictation of Brigham Young and others of the church authorities. I think its origin may be safely ascribed to the parties named, as they have very recently, at different times and places, in the presence of respectable witnesses, fully indorsed and recommended the unlawful proceedings that have swiftly and significantly followed such authorization. The footsteps of Gentiles, even the most respectable, are persistently dogged about the streets after night-fall by parties evidently set to watch them, and recently this annoyance has become so impertinent, and there has been shown such a disposition to violence on the part of these spies, that citizens, considering their lives in danger, have called upon me for protection, which, if found necessary, I shall give unless otherwise directed by the general commanding. On the night of the 1st instant several persons, walking quietly on the streets in company with ladies, were stopped and insolently questioned as to their business by men who when asked by what authority they acted answered "that they came to this country first and intended to do about as they pleased."

In one case a soldier was suddenly assaulted by three men and beaten with a pistol, or other weapon, and two pistols which he carried, one belonging to the Government, taken from him and not since returned. I am persuaded from representations made to me by citizens that there exists a systematic determination to harass and proscribe Gentile residents of the city, which, if persisted in, may make necessary the employment of military force for the maintenance of public order and to guarantee the personal security of those who may have become obnoxious to the church dignitaries and the objects of dangerous persecution. In view of the foregoing facts I most respectfully urge upon the general commanding the propriety of keeping all the troops now stationed here in the immediate vicinity of Salt Lake City, as I think myself justified in believing that their removal would lead to serious results and make the residence among the Mormons of citizens not professing their creed exceedingly difficult, not to say dangerous. I have further to represent that I am in possession of information which gives me some uneasiness with regard to the safety of the Government flour train in the neighborhood of Rocky Ridge. Hostile Indians are reported to be in the vicinity, and the fear of them is said to prevent the repair of the telegraph line, which is down near that point. I have directed Major Baldwin, at Fort Bridger, to make diligent inquiries into the truth of the statement, and, if any danger is to be apprehended, to order a company of cavalry there for its protection, which, although beyond my jurisdiction, I trust, if found necessary, will meet with the approval of the general commanding. I deem it my duty to call attention to certain deficiencies found to exist in the quartermaster's department at this post. They are approximately as follows, to wit: 827,000 pounds of hay, 60,000 pounds of carrots, 18,000 pounds of charcoal, 20,000 pounds of bituminous coal, and 650 cords of wood. It seems to me that these deficiencies are all of extraordinary dimensions, and without attempting to account for them, the way out of the difficulty does not to me seem quite clear.

I have the honor to be, very respectfully, your obedient servant,

MILO GEORGE,

Lieutenant-Colonel First Battalion Nevada Cavalry, Commanding.

[Editor's note: *This document is referenced in* OR-428.]

SOURCE: *OR*, SERIES 1, VOLUME 48, PART 2, PAGES 315–316

OR-421

WASHINGTON, *May 4, 1865.*

General P. E. CONNOR,

Denver, Colo. Ter.:

A copy of your report of April 6, 1865, has been forwarded to the lieutenant-general commanding, and he desires me to express his appreciation of your efforts. It is not believed that an institution like Mormonism can exist permanently in force and close communication with the civilized world. Our efforts should therefore aim to make such communication safe by thorough protection of Gentiles against Mormons, whether as transient visitors or permanent settlers, and trust mainly to the ordinary laws which govern civilization for the gradual removal of what is believed to be in opposition to those laws and which can derive vitality only from persecution.

C. B. COMSTOCK,

Lieutenant-Colonel, Aide-de-Camp, and Brevet Brigadier-General.

[Editor's note: *This document is referenced in* OR-428.]

SOURCE: *OR*, SERIES 1, VOLUME 50, PART 2, PAGE 1221

OR-422

HEADQUARTERS DISTRICT OF THE PLAINS,
Julesburg, Colo. Ter., May 18, 1865.

Brig. Gen. P. E. CONNOR:
(Care of General Dodge, Saint Louis, Mo.)

Repaired tents; sent to Denver for more. Office work, excepting return for April and papers requiring your action, completed to date. Moonlight reports no Indians nearer than Big Horn and Powder River. Quartermaster of Sixteenth Kansas stopped train bound here; took 80,000 pounds of corn. Have asked his authority. No answer yet. Flour at Rocky Ridge all right. Mormons very insolent; Brigham preaching violence. George reports large deficiencies at Douglas in quartermaster's department; unable to account for them. Sub-districts telegraph me men whose terms expire before last of May; do not understand. No information in this office. Cavalry whose term expires before 1st of October be reported soon as possible. Road quiet. Everything right in district.

GEO. F. PRICE,
Acting Assistant Adjutant-General.

SOURCE: *OR*, SERIES 1, VOLUME 48, PART 2, PAGES 500–501

OR-423

JULESBURG, COLO. TER., *May 20, 1865.*

Brig. Gen. P. E. CONNOR,
Atchison, Kans.:

Corn taken from trains on road as follows: Lieutenant Smith, Alkali, 50 sacks; Captain Cremer, Beauvais, 24 sacks; Colonel Walker, Alkali, 80,000 pounds. Colonel Walker says he had authority from you. No authority given in other cases. Colonel Moonlight reports no Indians nearer than Big Horn and Powder Rivers. He captured Two Face and two of his band. They had Mrs. Eubanks and child. She was captured last August on Little Blue by Cheyennes. Flour at Rocky Bridge all right. No Indian troubles other than reported to you yesterday by Colonel Livingston. No tents to be had in Denver. Have four hospital tents up; getting along best I can. Office work, excepting returns for April and papers requiring your action, completed to date. Captain Turnley passed here nearly a week ago. Colonel George reports large deficiencies in quartermaster's department at Douglas. Mormons insolent; Brigham preaching violence. Thirty-two men in district terms of service expire before May 31, all at Douglas. Judge from reports already in that 600 cavalrymen terms expire before October 1. General Grant has stopped for present order for mustering them out. Colfax and party expected on road soon. General Dodge directs every facility be afforded them. Lewis and Zabriskie here; former sick. No news from Brown. This is a horrible place for office business. I am almost worked down. Glad you are coming back.

GEO. F. PRICE,
Acting Assistant Adjutant-General.

SOURCE: *OR*, SERIES 1, VOLUME 48, PART 2, PAGE 524

OR-424

HEADQUARTERS DEPARTMENT OF THE MISSOURI,
Saint Louis, Mo., May 22, 1865.

Major-General POPE:

General Connor reports that 500 Indians attacked three crossings on Sweetwater and tore down telegraph wire. He says the Indians are coming down from the north in large bodies, and threaten the line all the way to Salt Lake, and that he will need considerable more cavalry. I think we better get a few regiments at Fort Leavenworth, besides those here. If I have to throw in more troops on the South Pass line it will take some three regiments more.

G. M. DODGE,
Major-General.

SOURCE: *OR*, SERIES 1, VOLUME 48, PART 2, PAGE 544

OR-425

Leavenworth, *May 25, 1865.*
(Received 9.30 a.m. 26th.)

Major-General Pope:

General Connor telegraphs that Indians attacked stage station on Green River, west of Bridger's Pass, and carried off their stock. He will have to garrison every station to Salt Lake, and is now doing so. Please have that brigade sent direct to Fort Leavenworth. This is the first time the Indians west of the mountains have molested us. They, it appears, are in the combination. Have heretofore been at peace. I don't like the attitude of the Mormons. I can see their hand in the move.

G. M. DODGE,
Major-General.

Source: *OR*, Series 1, Volume 48, Part 2, page 596

OR-426

Headquarters Military Division of the Missouri,
May 26, 1865—4.12 p.m.

General Dodge,
Fort Leavenworth:

The brigade of Michigan cavalry en route from Washington will go to you direct. The brigade now here is being rapidly mounted, orders to that effect having come from Washington. They also will be sent by regiments as fast as mounted. You can send what are necessary to Utah. With 5,000 good cavalry in addition to what you have the Indians ought to be put down. It will be necessary to make rapid cavalry expeditions against them. I hope in the course of a week to have these 5,000 additional cavalry at Leavenworth.

JNO. POPE,
Major-General.

Source: *OR*, Series 1, Volume 48, Part 2, page 613

OR-427

[*Extract*]

BRIGADE HEADQUARTERS, DISTRICT OF CALIFORNIA,
Sacramento, May 27, 1865.

Col. R. C. DRUM,
Asst. Adjt. Gen., Hdqrs. Dept. of the Pacific, San Francisco:

COLONEL: I have a telegram from Lieutenant-Colonel McDermit, dated yesterday, at Fort Churchill, asking for two additional companies of cavalry. He says, "Captain Wells had a fight with 500 Indians, who are strongly fortified. He failed to rout them;"

. . .

I am under the impression that most of the Indians who have been committing depredations beyond Honey Lake have joined the hostile bands in Humboldt, Nev. Ter. The Indian disturbances both north and south of Fort Churchill require that a full company of cavalry be permanently stationed at that post, and if the disposition of the troops will permit it, I would recommend that a company from Camp Union be sent over there. We want the services of those two companies of the Second Cavalry now serving beyond Salt Lake very much. If by any possibility those companies could be put on the march in this direction, over the Humboldt route, they would not only protect the emigrants coming over during the summer, but increase our force in Nevada, and enable us to punish those Indians so effectively that no more disturbances would take place in that State. Another consideration is, that those two companies, now so remote from their regiment, must of necessity be marched back to this State before being mustered out of service.

. . .

Very respectfully, your obedient servant,

G. WRIGHT,
Brigadier-General, Commanding.

SOURCE: *OR*, SERIES 1, VOLUME 50, PART 2, PAGES 1243–1244

OR-428

HEADQUARTERS DISTRICT OF THE PLAINS,
Julesburg, Colo. Ter., May 28, 1865.

Maj. Gen. G. M. DODGE,
Commanding Department of the Missouri, Saint Louis, Mo.:

GENERAL: I have the honor to inclose communication received from Utah Territory since my return for your information.* Brigham's power is evidently on the wane, the scepter is leaving his hands, and he is becoming desperate. I will attend to him as soon as matters are arranged with the Indians. The only difficulty I apprehend from his present conduct is that it may retard immigration and perhaps drive some of the timid Gentiles from the Territory. I have a peculiar way of managing him, and if you will trust to my judgment all will be well. I will send a part of the Sixth Infantry over as soon as they arrive. I am in receipt of a letter from Major-General Sully; he informs me he will not start until the 10th of June. I can start on the 1st of July and be at Powder River before him. I cannot start sooner, want of supplies and the condition of the animals preventing. We are entirely out of corn, except small quantity at Kearny. The stock at Laramie is suffering, the grass being poor in that vicinity as yet. Indians almost daily attack the line between Kearny and the South Pass, and are invariably repulsed with loss, but are enabled to escape pursuit in consequence of the condition of our animals.

I remain, general, very respectfully, your obedient servant,

P. EDW. CONNOR,
Brigadier-General, Commanding.

P. S.—I have the honor to inclose copy of a communication just received from the Headquarters of the Army.†

* [*Refers to* OR-420.]
† [*Refers to* OR-421.]

[Editor's note: *This document is referenced in* OR-431 *and* OR-436.]

SOURCE: *OR*, SERIES 1, VOLUME 48, PART 2, PAGE 646

OR-429

HEADQUARTERS DISTRICT OF THE PLAINS,
Julesburg, Colo. Ter., May 28, 1865.

Maj. J. W. BARNES,
Asst. Adjt. Gen., Saint Louis, Mo., Dept. of the Missouri:

SIR: I respectfully solicit that the general commanding the department request Major-General McDowell, commanding Department of the Pacific, to order the officers of Squadrons L and M, Second California Cavalry (now in California), to report to these headquarters for duty. The squadrons have been under my command for three years, and are now en route for Fort Laramie. They have 100 men in each—nearly all veterans. Squadron M has only one officer with it. He has recently been promoted to a captaincy in same regiment, and I expect he will be ordered to his squadron shortly. Captain Price is on duty at these headquarters as district inspector and acting assistant adjutant-general. First Lieut. Frederick Weed is at Camp Union, Cal., on detached service. The squadron has no second lieutenant. The captain and first lieutenant of L Squadron are with it. The second lieutenant is attached to a squadron at Camp Union, Cal. The Second California Cavalry is a veteran regiment; has over 1,200 men in it. The squadrons belonging to it, and now in my district, will take part in the coming campaign and I desire to have all the officers belonging to them with me, particularly as none of them are on staff duty, and there is not an abundant supply of line officers in the district. Maj. John M. O'Neill, Second California Cavalry, is at Camp Douglas, Utah, He can be ordered to California, as I have no use for him in this district.

Very respectfully, your obedient servant,

P. EDW. CONNOR,
Brigadier-General.

SOURCE: *OR*, SERIES 1, VOLUME 48, PART 2, PAGES 646–647

OR-430

Fort Leavenworth, *May 29, 1865.*

Brig. Gen. P. E. Connor,
Julesburg:

Can all troops west of the Rocky Mountains be supplied with forage during the summer and winter from purchase in Utah?

G. M. DODGE,
Major-General.

Source: *OR*, Series 1, Volume 48, Part 2, page 670

OR-431

Julesburg, Colo. Ter., *May 29, 1865.*

Maj. Gen. G. M. Dodge:

Troops west of Rocky Mountains can be supplied with forage there during summer and winter. I require two more regiments of infantry and four more of cavalry. They should be sent immediately, with ample supplies and transportation, and well mounted. I have no doubt about tampering with Indians west. What shall I do about Captain Turnley? Indians destroyed several miles of wire west of Laramie to-day. Wrote you to-day in reference to Utah affairs.*

P. EDW. CONNOR,
Brigadier-General.

* [*Refers to* OR-*428.*]

Source: *OR*, Series 1, Volume 48, Part 2, page 670

OR-432

MAY 26–JUNE 9, 1865.—Operations against Indians on the Overland Stage Road on the Platte and Sweetwater Rivers, with skirmishes (May 27) at Saint Mary's Station, (May 26, 28, and June 1) at Sweetwater Station, (June 3) at Platte Bridge, Dak. Ter., and (June 8) at Sage Creek, Colo. Ter.

REPORTS

No. 1. Lieut. Henry C. Bretney, Eleventh Ohio Cavalry.
No. 2. Lieut. James A. Brown, Eleventh Ohio Cavalry.
No. 3. First Sergt. Samuel B. White, Eleventh Ohio Cavalry.

No. 1.

Report of Lieut. Henry C. Bretney, Eleventh Ohio Cavalry.

PLATTE BRIDGE, DAK. TER., *June —, 1865.*

SIR: I have the honor to report that on May 26 three Indians made first attempt to take herd at Sweetwater Station, but were repulsed by garrison, the Indians having 1 killed and wounded, 1 pony crippled, without any loss to our side. On Sunday, May 28, they made another attempt at herd in force estimated at twenty-five or thirty, and succeeded in getting 4 horses and 2 mules. Stampede was owing to the two mules, which were very wild and led the horses off. Indians lost one wounded. On Thursday, June 1, they made an attempt on remainder of herd, but were repulsed; and on same day cut the telegraph wire about 1,000 yards from quarters, east, carrying off about 100 yards wire. On the 27th of May about 150 Indians attacked Saint Mary's Station, and in short time succeeded in setting fire to buildings. The garrison, consisting of five men, retreated to an old well outside of quarters, where they remained until the night of the 28th, when they escaped to South Pass. The operator, Private Chavil St. Clair, took precaution enough to secure a relay sounder and a coil of fine wire, and was thus enabled to communicate with Fort Bridger. Garrison lost everything but their firearms and the clothes on their backs. Their horse equipments burnt. There were but two horses at the station; one of these the Indians got, and the other was shot to prevent its falling into their hands, Indians cut out about 400 yards of wire and burned the poles. When Indians left they moved to the south, passing up the valley of Sage Creek. The garrison did as well as it could under the circumstances, and when Indians came within proper distance fired on them briskly. Several Indians are known to have been wounded. None of the garrison injured.

H. C. BRETNEY,
First Lieut., Comdg. Company G, Eleventh Ohio Vol. Cav.

Col. T. MOONLIGHT,
Commanding North Sub-District of the Plains, Dak. Ter.

No. 2

[Editor's note: *See* OR-*441 for this report.*]

No. 3

[Editor's note: *See* OR-*440 for this report.*]

SOURCE: *OR*, SERIES 1, VOLUME 48, PART 1, PAGE 294

OR-433

HEADQUARTERS DEPARTMENT OF THE PACIFIC.
San Francisco, June 2, 1865.

His Excellency JAMES D. DOTY,
Governor of Utah, Great Salt Lake City, Utah Ter.:

SIR: I have the honor to acknowledge the receipt of your letter of the 19th ultimo and its inclosures of the same date from Mr. Coburn on the subject of affording military protection to the route from Great Salt Lake City to Walla Walla via Boisé City, &c. I inclose herewith a copy of my General Orders, No. 36,* of this year, directing a post to be established near Camas Prairie for the purpose of affording protection on the route to which you refer. I fear I have not a sufficient force disposable to establish any other posts in that quarter, but I will direct the commanding officer of the Sub-District of Boisé to send parties on the road and afford it all the protection his means will allow.

I have the honor to be, very respectfully, your most obedient servant,

IRVIN McDOWELL,
Major-General, Commanding.

*[*Refers to Drum's General Order No. 36, May 6* [*9*]*, 1865.* OR, *Series 1, Volume 50, Part 2, page 1224.*]

SOURCE: *OR*, SERIES 1, VOLUME 50, PART 2, PAGE 1255

OR-434

Fort Leavenworth, *June 4, 1865.*

Maj. Gen. John Pope:

General Connor telegraphs that Indians attack some station on telegraph line daily. That he needs two more regiments of infantry and five of cavalry. Part of cavalry are now on road. Rest will be in few days. That his stock is poor. That he has no doubt Mormons are connected with depredations west of mountains. That he can supply troops west of Rocky Mountains with forage from Utah. If you can get two regiments of infantry who have over one year to serve it better be done, and have them shipped direct to Fort Leavenworth. The trouble now mostly west of Laramie. If Captain Coryell can send me 500 more horses I would like them. Approval of Colonel Potter's estimates arrived to-day.

G. M. DODGE,
Major-General.

(Transmitted by Pope to Grant June 5.)

Source: *OR*, Series 1, Volume 48, Part 2, page 773

OR-435

Fort Leavenworth, Kans., *June 8, 1865.*

Major-General Pope:

I desire orders to make the contracts immediately for forage and fuel in Utah. General Connor says it must be done immediately or we shall fail in getting them.

G. M. DODGE,
Major-General.

Source: *OR*, Series 1, Volume 48, Part 2, page 821

OR-436

HEADQUARTERS DEPARTMENT OF THE MISSOURI,
Fort Leavenworth, June 8, 1865.

Maj. Gen. JOHN POPE,
Commanding Military Division of the Missouri:

GENERAL: I have the honor to forward the following communication of General Connor, in relation to Mormon affairs.* I have no doubt that the Mormons are engaged in the Indian troubles indirectly. I approve the course General Connor pursues, viz, protect Gentiles and Anti-Polygamists, and aid them in every way consistent with his duties, invite immigration of that class of people, develop the mineral resources, root out gradually but surely that blotch on our continent; but at the same time avert any direct conflict. As soon as the troubles on the plains are settled, which I believe will be done this summer. General Connor will go to Utah. I shall send another regiment of infantry there as soon as possible. Under the judicious policy so far pursued there the power of the Mormon church is waning; they see it, and no doubt will make extraordinary efforts to avert it.

Very respectfully, your obedient servant,

G. M. DODGE,
Major-General.

* [*Refers to* OR-428.]

SOURCE: *OR*, SERIES 1, VOLUME 48, PART 2, PAGE 822

OR-437

FORT LEAVENWORTH, *June 8, 1865.*

Brig. Gen. P. E. CONNOR,
Julesburg:

Have your proper staff departments in Utah make their contracts for forage and fuel in such manner as the best interest of the Government will be served.

G. M. DODGE,
Major-General.

SOURCE: *OR*, SERIES 1, VOLUME 48, PART 2, PAGE 824

OR-438

HEADQUARTERS DISTRICT OF THE PLAINS,
Julesburg, Colo. Ter., June 10, 1865.

Maj. Gen. G. M. DODGE,
Saint Louis:

I am doing everything possible to hurry up the expedition. There is not a horse at Laramie for the service. No grass there. Not a pound of corn has arrived for Laramie. I am crossing the Sixteenth Kansas over the Platte at this point in a rickety scow. The Sixth U.S. Infantry is 100 miles east of here yet. The troops for the protection of the road are distributed, and matters in that respect working well. I had to keep the Sixteenth Kansas up to this time in the vicinity of Cottonwood in order to get something to eat for their horses. My two California companies have arrived at Laramie; horses in good order. I will start north with them and Sixteenth Kansas as soon as some corn arrives, which I am expecting daily. Will you send the force as I requested to east base of Black Hills? Could you not send me two regiments of infantry and two of cavalry who have more than one year to serve to send to Utah? Send one year's clothing to Laramie for Sixteenth Kansas. I may leave them at Powder River. It has nearly two years to serve, and men are almost naked.

P. EDW. CONNOR,
Brigadier-General.

SOURCE: *OR*, SERIES 1, VOLUME 48, PART 2, PAGE 849

OR-439

HEADQUARTERS DEPARTMENT OF THE MISSOURI,
Fort Leavenworth, June 13, 1865.

Brig. Gen. P. E. CONNOR,
Commanding District of the Plains:

GENERAL: The reports made to me by my staff officer show that the following estimates for commissary stores have been made by your officers, viz: Fort Laramie, rations for 2,000 men for one year; Fort Kearny, rations for 2,500 men for one year; Cottonwood, rations for 1,200 men for one year; Denver City, rations for 2,000 men for one year; Julesburg, rations for 1,500 men for one year; Fort Halleck, rations for 250 men for one year; Collins, rations for 500 men for one year; Junction, rations for

500 men for one year; Fort Lyon, rations for 1,500 men for one year; Utah, rations for 3,500 men for one year; Fort Bridger, rations for 500 men for one year; Powder River, rations for 900 men for one year; Fort Garland, rations for 230 men for one year. And the following is the estimate for quartermaster's stores and camp and garrison equipage, &c., viz: Cottonwood, one year, 1,175 cavalry and 800 infantry; Fort Garland, one year, 100 cavalry; Salt Lake, one year, 300 cavalry and 2,000 infantry; Fort Laramie, one year, 1,000 cavalry and 1,000 infantry; Fort Kearny, one year, 1,250 cavalry and 500 infantry; Denver City, one year, 1,500 cavalry and 1,000 infantry; Fort Columbus, one year, 100 cavalry; Third U.S. Volunteers, six months' supply, 900 infantry; Sixteenth Kansas Volunteers, one year, 1,000 cavalry. These are made not only to supply the depots, but the posts dependent on them. Should you deem an increase necessary telegraph me the amount. Quartermaster's stores have been forwarded to Powder River, to what extent I am unable to say. Nearly all the stores are on the road. An estimate for 500,000 bushels of corn for your command has been made, and will be forwarded and distributed as you recommended when here.

I am, very respectfully, your obedient servant,

G. M. DODGE,
Major-General, Commanding.

SOURCE: *OR*, SERIES 1, VOLUME 48, PART 2, PAGES 874–875

OR-440

No. 3.

Report of First Sergt. Samuel B. White, Eleventh Ohio Cavalry.

PLATTE BRIDGE, DAK. TER., *June 13, 1865.*

SIR: I have the honor to report that on June 3 six Indians appeared on bank of Platte River opposite quarters, whose object appeared to be to draw men from this post. As soon as the alarm was given I dispatched a messenger to Lieutenant-Colonel Plumb, of the Eleventh Kansas Cavalry, and ordered men to fire on Indians, which resulted in two of their horses being crippled. These shots were fired from 12-pounder mountain howitzer, which drove Indians over bluffs. On Colonel Plumb's arrival I sent corporal and ten men to bluffs on north side of Platte to watch movements of Indians until the command of Colonel Plumb arrived. Also one sergeant and ten men afoot in their rear to prevent their being cut off by superior forces. The mounted men saw one Indian going toward telegraph line, with the intention of cutting it.

They pursued him and crippled his horse. About 2 o'clock Colonel Plumb's detachment arrived. I then sent the mounted squad of corporal and ten men with him to pursue Indians. They returned about 8.30 o'clock and reported one man of this command killed, whose body was recovered and brought in to the post. Lieutenant Bretney and ten mounted men were absent, having started for Saint Mary's May 31. He returned to this post June 5, 1865.

Very respectfully,

S. B. WHITE,
First Sergeant, Commanding Post.

Col. T. MOONLIGHT,
Comdg. North Sub-District of the Plains, Fort Laramie, Dak. Ter.

[Editor's note: *This document is included as an inclosure to an Expedition Report covering May 26–June 9, 1865. See OR-432.*]

SOURCE: *OR*, SERIES 1, VOLUME 48, PART 1, PAGE 296

OR-441

No. 2.

Report of Lieut. James A. Brown, Eleventh Ohio Cavalry.

FORT HALLECK, DAK. TER., *June 14, 1865.*

SIR: In compliance with Special Orders, No. 7, dated headquarters Fort Halleck, Dak. Ter., June 2, 1865, I left this post with a command of thirty-one men of Company K, Eleventh Ohio Volunteer Cavalry, for the purpose of reopening the mail route between this place and Fort Bridger, Utah Ter. I arrived at the crossing of the North Platte River the same evening and camped for the night. Next morning we crossed and started westward, accompanied by Captain Lewis, of General Connor's staff, and Mr. R. I. Spotswood, division agent on the Overland Stage Line. I found Sage Creek Station deserted. Four miles beyond I found two dead emigrants lying near the road, one of them being scalped. The next two stations, Pine Grove and Bridger's Pass, I also found deserted. At the fourth station, Sulphur Spring, I found the stock tenders and drivers from the above-named stations concentrated with the stock belonging to Sage Creek and Pine Grove Stations. I also learned that the stock at Bridger's Pass Station had been driven off by the Indians. Having ascertained that the depredations extended no farther west, I remained at Sulphur Spring Station until 4 P.M. next day, then detaching three men I sent them to Waskie (next station west), and leaving five men for the protection of Sulphur Spring Station, I started for this post, accompanied by Messrs. Spotswood and Stewart, division agents on the Overland Stage Line, two coaches and stock for the line, camping that night at Bridger's Pass Station. Next morning I left, leaving a corporal and four men at the station from thence to Pine Grove Station, leaving five men there; came on to the Sage Creek Station, left a corporal and four men there; from thence to the North Platte Crossing and camped for the night. Having succeeded in establishing a tri-weekly mail between the North Platte and Sulphur Spring Station, I came to this post with the balance of my command. At daylight the morning of the 8th instant the detachment at Sage Creek Station was attacked by about 100 Indians. After one hour's severe fighting they were compelled to evacuate, in consequence of a deficiency in ammunition. The men were all well mounted and accompanied by two citizens, names unknown. The moment they left the station they were completely surrounded. There ensued a desperate fight; the detachment retreated toward Pine Grove Station. The Indians followed them for eight miles, killing George Bodine and Perry Stewart, wounding and capturing Orlando Ducket, wounding Corpl. W. H. Caldwell and Private William Wilson, all of Company K, Eleventh Ohio Volunteer Cavalry. The two citizens were also missing. Corporal Caldwell and Private Wilson escaped to Pine Grove Station. They and the detachment then retreated to Sulphur Spring Station, taking the detachment at Bridger's Pass with them. Next morning they started back, commanded by Sergeant McFaddin, who was up the road on escort duty with ten men of Company K, Eleventh Ohio Volunteer Cavalry. They found the bodies of Perry Stewart and George Bodine lying in the road horribly mutilated, the latter scalped. They also found one citizen. The other citizen and Private Ducket, of Company K, could not be found. My opinion is they were burned in Sage Creek Station, which was found burnt by the command on their return. Ten of the men have returned to this post; the balance are doing all they can to keep open the road, but the force is inadequate to cope with the number of Indians now committing depredations on the Overland Stage Line between the North Platte Crossing and Sulphur Spring Station.

I am, sir, very respectfully, your obedient servant,

J. A. BROWN,
First Lieut. Company K, Eleventh Ohio Vol. Cav., Comdg. Detach.

Capt. J. L. HUMFREVILLE,
Eleventh Ohio Vol. Cav., Comdg. Fort Halleck, Dak. Ter.

[Editor's note: *This document is included as an inclosure to an Expedition Report covering May 26–June 9, 1865. See* OR*-432.*]

SOURCE: *OR*, SERIES 1, VOLUME 48, PART 1, PAGES 295–296

OR-442

JULESBURG, *June 15, 1865.*
(Received 9.50 P.M.)

Major-General DODGE:

I ordered the Indians who surrendered at Laramie to be sent to Kearny. Colonel Moonlight sent them without first dismounting them, under charge of two companies of Seventh Iowa Cavalry. They revolted sixty miles this side of Laramie, killing Captain Fouts, who was in command, and four soldiers, and wounding seven; also killed four of their own chiefs who refused to join them; fifteen Indians were killed. Indians fled north with their ponies, women, and children, leaving all their camp equipage. Troops are in pursuit. Mail stages have stopped west of Camp Collins. Everything appears to work unfavorably owing to failure of corn contractors and incompetency of some of my subordinates. I will overcome all obstacles, however, in a short time. Have you sent me any cavalry yet? J. D. Doty, Governor of Utah, was buried at Camp Douglas Cemetery this morning. Died of heart disease.

P. E. CONNOR,
Brigadier-General.

SOURCE: *OR*, SERIES 1, VOLUME 48, PART 2, PAGE 895

OR-443

HEADQUARTERS MILITARY DIVISION OF THE MISSOURI,
Saint Louis, Mo., June 16, 1865.

Lieut. Gen. U. S. GRANT,
Washington:

I earnestly request that General Dodge may not be removed from this command, at least not until the autumn. He is thoroughly acquainted with Indian affairs on the plains, has organized the various expeditions now moving in several directions against the Indians, and is so thoroughly posted on all matters relating to the troubles on the plains and in Utah that his removal, for the present, would be likely to throw things into confusion and be very injurious to the public interests.

JNO. POPE,
Major-General, Commanding.

SOURCE: *OR*, SERIES 1, VOLUME 48, PART 2, PAGES 904–905

OR-444

JUNE 17–19, 1865.—Expedition from Denver, Colo. Ter., to Fort Halleck, Dak. Ter.

Report of Col. Carroll H. Potter, Sixth U.S. Volunteer Infantry.

FORT HALLECK, DAK. TER., *June 19, 1865.*

I have the honor to report that, in compliance with General Connor's telegraphic instructions, I started from Denver on the 17th instant; arrived at Fort Collins at 8 P.M. same date. Ordered Captain Wilson, with one company of First Colorado Cavalry, to proceed at once and establish a patrol and guard, commencing at Big Laramie and to extend along the Overland Stage line as far as his company would reach, leaving eight men and one non-commissioned officer at each station. This will guard the road to this post, which I think is absolutely necessary, as Indians have been seen in the last two days between here and Rock Creek, nineteen miles south from here, on the Denver road. Captain Humfreville, commanding Fort Halleck, has just returned from Sulphur Springs with a part of his company, where he has been on a scout. He found the Indians near that place in large numbers and all the stage stock driven off by them between Halleck and Duck Lake, a distance of 100 miles. While he was at Sulphur Springs the Indians made a dash at the station and succeeded in driving off forty-seven animals belonging to the stage company. Captain Humfreville followed them with his command until it was dark, when he gave up the chase. He reached this place on last evening, bringing through one coach drawn by cavalry horses. He also brought the [mail from the] west. The eastern mails are being forwarded as fast as possible from Denver. I am now awaiting Lieutenant Colonel Plumb's arrival. I will start with all the available troops at my command and open the road through as far as there seems to be any danger, leaving such guards as may be necessary to make the mail route safe. From what I have seen and can learn from Captain Humfreville and other officers stationed in this part of the sub-district, there is not now, and will not be with the troops ordered here with Lieutenant-Colonel Plumb, a sufficient force to guard the road and make it perfectly safe for the mail and general travel. I am doing everything in my power with the force at my command to protect both public and private property and have the mail run regularly through to Salt Lake.

Respectfully, your obedient servant,

C. H. POTTER,

Colonel Sixth U.S. Volunteers, Comdg. South Sub -District.

Capt. GEORGE F. PRICE,

Acting Assistant Adjutant-General.

SOURCE: *OR*, SERIES 1, VOLUME 48, PART 1, PAGE 328

OR-445

Headquarters District of the Plains,
Julesburg, Colo. Ter., June 20, 1865.

Maj. Gen. G. M. Dodge,
Commanding Dept. of the Missouri, Saint Louis, Mo.:

Sir: I have the honor to acknowledge the receipt of two letters from you dated loth instant. The instructions contained therein will be carried out. I am forwarding troops and supplies to Laramie as rapidly as possible after arriving at this point. The Sixteenth Kansas Cavalry has gone forward to Laramie. Four companies of the Sixth U.S. Volunteers will start from here for Laramie to-morrow. I am only delayed now for want of subsistence stores. I have not to exceed twenty days' rations on hand, including this point and Laramie, but I am daily expecting supplies to arrive. The Indians are becoming very bold, and lately have been successful in everything they have undertaken; but I confidently hope, with the assistance you are giving me, to accomplish what is desired to be accomplished this summer. It was impossible for me to start out prior to this date. The stock I had was very inferior, and there was not enough of transportation for the absolute wants of an expedition. An expedition started under such circumstances would have resulted in a complete failure and the Indians would have played around and laughed at me. Colonel Moonlight has been unfortunate in his dealings with Indians since assuming command of North Sub-District. I have relieved him, and will further investigate his conduct. I am glad that a regiment is going out on Republican Fork. I was just on the point of telegraphing (when your letters were received) asking you to send one of the regiments coming to me to that place. I will place Brevet Brigadier-General Heath in command of the East Sub-District, as Colonel Livingston will soon be mustered out. He will be instructed to co-operate with troops sent to Republican Fork and south of his sub-district. A portion of Colonel Cole's command arrived at Omaha on Sunday. I hope the remaining portion will arrive speedily, as every hour is precious. He should arrive at Black Hills as soon as I do, but I fear will not. The horses lost by Colonel Moonlight day before yesterday were California horses, belonging to the California companies recently from Utah. They were the best horses I had for the present service.

Very respectfully, your obedient servant,

P. EDW. CONNOR,
Brigadier-General, Commanding.

Source: *OR*, Series 1, Volume 48, Part 2, pages 950–951

OR-446

HEADQUARTERS DEPARTMENT OF THE MISSOURI,
Saint Louis, Mo., June 22, 1865.

Hon. JAMES HARLAN,
Secretary of the Interior, Washington, D.C.:

MY DEAR SIR: Copies of Senator Doolittle's and Commissioner Dole's letters to you of dates May 31 and June 12 have been furnished me. My acquaintance with you leads me to believe that you are endeavoring to get at the real facts of our Indian difficulties and the best methods for putting an end to them. So far as Senator Doolittle's letter refers to "some general getting up an Indian war on his own hook," and for his own purpose, I shall indulge no reply. You know me, and if it was intended any way to apply to me I leave you to judge of how much credence should be attached to it. My sincere desire is to terminate these Indian troubles, and I have no hesitation in saying that if I am allowed to carry out the policy now being pursued toward them I will have peace with them before another emigration crosses the plains. When I assumed command of the former Department of Kansas I found all the important Indian tribes on the plains in open hostility against us. Whether it was the fault of the white man or the Indian, the fact was patent. They were holding the entire Overland Route from Julesburg to Junction Station, had destroyed the telegraph lines, captured trains, burned ranches, and murdered men, women, and children indiscriminately. I soon stopped these proceedings; opened our broken lines of communication; repaired, so far as possible, the injury done; pushed troops out there, and then tried to effect a settlement with the Indians. On the southern route I found a similar state of affairs existing. The Indians were on the warpath, and I at once started expeditions after them, learning of which Colonel Leavenworth, Indian agent, informed me that he could make peace with them; that we were at fault, &c. I stopped my expeditions on the southern route to give him an opportunity to accomplish this object. He started for their camps; they robbed him, stole his mules, and he hardly escaped with his scalp, and on his return stated that it was useless to attempt to make peace with them. I then, in accordance with the orders of the Secretary of War, started for the Indians again, and had just got my forces under way when the committee, of which Senator Doolittle is a member, reached Fort Larned, and after an interview with Colonel Leavenworth gave orders for the expeditionary movements to stop. The grounds for this action the Senator gives in his letter. I was then aware that the Indians were moving north to attack that line, and was moving two columns in concert with General Ford to intercept and punish them; and I at that time telegraphed that the tribes spoken of by Senator Doolittle were on their way north to attack our trains. They had then driven out all traders, made a treaty with the southern Indians and Texans, and sent me word that they wanted no peace.

Within ten days from the time Senator Doolittle and his party left Fort Larned, and before I had time to countermand their orders and get my troops disposed, the Indians attacked the posts and trains all along the line, running off stock, capturing trains, &c., murdering men, and showing conclusively that they were determined on war at all hazards. Our overtures to them, as well as those of the agents sent out by General Carleton, were treated with disdain. From Fort Laramie I sent word to the Sioux, Cheyennes, &c., that if they wanted peace to come in and stop their hostilities. A few of each tribe responded by coming in; the rest refused, and indicated their purposes and feelings by attacking the posts west of Fort Laramie, and on Laramie Plains, murdering, stealing, &c. I undertook to remove the friendly Indians from Fort Laramie to Fort Kearny, in order to get them away from the troubles. When about sixty miles east of Fort Laramie they attacked their guard, killed a captain and four privates, turned upon five of their chiefs who were disposed to be friendly, killed them, and then escaped, leaving their camps, &c., in our hands, so that now we have every Indian tribe capable of mischief, from the British Possessions on the north to the Red River on the south, at war with us, while the whites are backing them up, and, in my opinion, the Mormons are encouraging them. These facts, it appears to me, are a sufficient answer to the letters of Senator Doolittle and Commissioner Dole. That these Indians have been greatly wronged I have no doubt, and I am certain that the agents who have been connected with them are as much to blame as any one else. So far as the Chivington massacre was concerned, it occurred before I assumed command. I condemned it, and I have issued orders that no such acts will be tolerated or allowed; that the Indians on the warpath must be fought wherever and whenever found, but no outrages or barbarities must be committed. I am convinced that the only way to effectually settle these troubles is for us to move our columns directly into their country, punish them when we find them, show them our power, and at the same time give them to know that we are ready to make peace with them—not, however, by paying them for murdering our people and plundering our trains and posts, but by informing them that if they will refrain from further hostilities they shall not be molested; that neither agents nor citizens shall be allowed to go among them to swindle them; that we will protect them in their rights; that we will enforce compliance with our part of the treaty, and will require them to do the same on their part. Let them ask for peace. We should keep citizens out of their country. The class of men sent among them as agents, &c., go there for no good purpose. They take positions for the sole purpose of making money out of the Indians by swindling them, and so long as they can do this they shield them in their crimes.

Colonel Leavenworth, who stands up so boldly for the Southern Indians, was dismissed from the U.S. service. He "blows hot and cold" with singular grace. To my officers he talks war to the knife, to Senator Doolittle and others he talks peace. Indeed, he is all things to all men. When officers of the Army deal with these Indians, if they mistreat them, we have a certain remedy for their cases. They can be dismissed and disgraced, while Indian agents can only be displaced by others perhaps no better. Now, I am confident we can settle these Indian difficulties in the manner I have indicated. The Indians say to me that when they treat they want to treat with an officer of the Army (a brave), in all of whom they seem to have confidence, while they despise and suspect civilian agents and citizens, by whom they say they have been deceived and swindled so much that they put no trust in their words. I have given orders to the commanders of each of my columns that when they have met and whipped these Indians, or even before, if they have an opportunity, to arrange, if possible, an informal treaty with them for a cessation of hostilities, and whatever they agree to do, to live to strictly, allowing no one, either citizen or soldier, to break it. I shall myself go out on the plains in a few weeks and try to get an interview with the chiefs, and if possible effect an amicable settlement of affairs; but I am utterly opposed to making any treaty that pays them for the outrages they have committed, or that hires them to keep the peace. Such treaties last just as long as they think for their benefit, and no longer. As soon as the sugar, coffee, powder, lead, &c., that we give them is gone, they make war to get us to give them more. We must first punish them until we make them fear us and respect our power, and then we must ourselves live strictly up to the treaties made. No one desires more than I do to effect a permanent peace with these Indians, and such is the desire of every officer under me, all of whom agree in the method suggested for bringing it about.

Very many of these officers on the plains have been there for years, and are well acquainted with these Indians and their character, and my own opinions in this matter are founded not alone from my experience and observations since I have commanded here, but also with intercourse with them on the plains during a number of years prior to the war, in which time I met and had dealings with nearly every tribe east of the Rocky Mountains. Until hostilities cease I trust you will keep all agents, citizens, and traders away from them. When peace is made with them, if civilian agents and citizens are sent among them, send those who you know to be of undoubted integrity. I know you desire to do so, and from the appointments you have already made I believe you will be successful. My plan, however, would be to keep these Indians under the care of officers of the Army, stationed in their country; that what is given them be given by these officers, and that all citizens, agents, and traders should while among them be subject to their (the officers) supervision and police regulations. In this way I have no doubt these Indians can be kept in their own country, their outrages stopped, and our overland routes kept safe. Now, not a train or coach of [any] kind can cross the plains in safety without being guarded, and I have over 3,000 miles of route to protect and guard. The statement that the Sand Creek affair was the first Indian aggression is a mistake. For months prior to that affair the Indians had been attacking our trains, posts, and ranches; had robbed the emigrants and murdered any party they considered too weak to defend themselves.

The theory that we cannot punish these Indians effectually, and that we must make or accept any kind of a peace in order to hold our overland routes, is not sustained by the facts, is singularly erroneous, and I cannot agree in it by any means. I have now seven different columns of troops penetrating their country in all directions, while at the same time I am holding the overland routes. This display of force alone will alarm and terrify them; will show them that we are in earnest, have the power, and intend at all hazards to make them behave themselves. After we have taught them this they will sue for peace; then if the Government sees fit to indemnify them for any wrongs inflicted upon them, they will not charge it to our fears or inability to cope with them. The cost of carrying on this war with them is, to be sure, considerable, but the question arises, had we not better bear this cost now while the preparations are made and the force on hand ready to be thrown in such strength into their country as to make quick, effective, and final work of it than to suffer a continuance of their outrages for a long time and finally have to do the work at greater expense of blood and treasure? I have written you this frankly and truly, knowing that you want to get at the facts and do that which is for the best, and I am convinced that when you fully understand these matters you will agree with me. I shall be glad at any and all times to furnish you any information in my possession that you may desire, and I assure you I shall bend all my energies to the accomplishment of the great object in view and so much desired—a lasting and just peace with these Indians.

I have the honor to be, very respectfully, your obedient servant,

G. M. DODGE,
Major-General, Commanding,

Source: *OR*, Series 1, Volume 48, Part 2, pages 971–974

OR-447

[*Extract*]

War Dept., Adjt. General's Office,
Washington, June 27, 1865.

General Orders,
No. 118.

The President directs that the United States be divided into military divisions and sub-divided into military departments as follows:

DEPARTMENTS.

. . .

18. The Department of California, Maj. Gen. Irvin McDowell to command, to

embrace the States of California and Nevada and Territories of Utah, New Mexico, and Colorado; headquarters at San Francisco.

DIVISIONS.

. . .

All officers hereby assigned will proceed, on receipt of this order, to take command of their respective departments or military divisions. All officers relieved by this order will, on being relieved by the proper officer, report by letter to the Adjutant-General for orders.

By order of the President of the United States:

E. D. TOWNSEND,
Assistant Adjutant-General.

[Editor's note: *This General Order appears five times in five separate volumes of Series 1 of the Official Record. Four times the complete order appears: (1) Volume 46, Part 3, Section 2, pages 1298–1299; (2) Volume 47, Part 3, pages 667–668; (3) Volume 48, Part 2, pages 1003–1004; and (4) Volume 49, Part 2, pages 1039–1041. The fifth instance (Volume 50, Part 2, page 1268) is an excerpt of the order; paragraph 18 is not included.*]

SOURCE: *OR*, SERIES 1, VOLUME 46, PART 3, SECTION 2, PAGES 1298–1299

OR-448

ADJUTANT-GENERAL'S OFFICE,
Washington, June 27, 1865.

Maj. Gen. IRVIN MCDOWELL,
San Francisco, Cal.:

You are assigned to command the Department of California, embracing the States of California and Nevada and Territories of Utah, New Mexico, and Colorado, headquarters San Francisco. Major-General Halleck is to command the Division of the Pacific, embracing Department of Columbia and California, and Brig. Gen. George Wright to command the Department of the Columbia. Acknowledge receipt.

By order of the Secretary of War:

E. D. TOWNSEND,
Assistant Adjutant-General.

SOURCE: *OR*, SERIES 1, VOLUME 50, PART 2, PAGE 1267

OR-449

Camp Mitchell, *June 29, 1865.*

Maj. Gen. G. M. Dodge,

Department of the Missouri, Saint Louis, Mo.:

I will not require troops to replace the Third United States. The Sixth will be sufficient for this side of the mountains after my campaign, I am taking four companies of the Sixth with me to guard trains and depots between Laramie and Powder River. Will not require them for that duty after campaign. The Third will not re-enlist. The three infantry regiments and Tibbits' brigade will, I suppose, have to do for Utah. How many men in Tibbits' brigade? General Heath telegraphs me that he is much embarrassed by Colonel Cole's conduct. Will you please telegraph to Washington to have Heath assigned, if not already so?

P. EDW. CONNOR,
Brigadier-General.

Source: *OR*, Series 1, Volume 48, Part 2, page 1029

OR-450

Headquarters District of the Plains,
Fort Laramie, Dak. Ter., July 6, 1865,

Maj. Gen. G. M. Dodge,

Department of the Missouri, Saint Louis, Mo.:

I can relieve Eleventh Kansas when Stagg's brigade arrives. Colonel Moonlight is on way to Kearny, suspended from command. I have ordered him mustered out. His administration here was a series of blunders. Colonel Cole passed Columbus yesterday; is getting along finely. He will probably meet surveyors. Colonel Kidd's regiment (Sixth Michigan) arrived at Kearny yesterday. Have ordered him here. Stagg is two days east of Kearny. Cannot possibly move without rations. Have sent an officer to hurry them up. Have also ordered rations from Kearny and Cottonwood and all subsistence trains bound for Denver and Julesburg to this post. I may be able to get away in ten days. The mail stages west of Denver have again been stopped by Indians. I leave for Camp Collins in the morning to see about it. I have six companies of cavalry at Collins and Halleck, and Utah troops are guarding line on Bitter Creek. Will start the stages again immediately.

P. EDW. CONNOR,
Brigadier-General.

SOURCE: *OR*, SERIES 1, VOLUME 48, PART 2, PAGE 1059

OR-451

FORT LARAMIE, DAK. TER., *July 8, 1865.*

Maj. Gen. G. M. DODGE,
Department of the Missouri, Saint Louis, Mo.:

General Connor left yesterday morning for Collins to arrange mail escorts west of that place. Only require subsistence stores to place left and center columns in the field. Everything quiet on mail and telegraph road. Line working through to Salt Lake. Bridging of Loup Fork and Platte River great public benefit. No field officer to send to Omaha. If deemed advisable by you, the general would be pleased to have one sent. First Battalion Nebraska Cavalry and First Nebraska Cavalry are about to be consolidated at Kearny. Colonel Livingston one of the very best and most valuable officers in the district, will have to go out unless something is done. Can not something be done in his case? Lieutenant-Colonel Baumer, who will be retained, has habits which unfit him for the service, and he is recommended mustered out by examining board under the provisions of War Department Order 86.

Respectfully,

GEO. F. PRICE,
Captain and Acting Assistant Adjutant-General.
(In absence of general commanding.)

SOURCE: *OR*, SERIES 1, VOLUME 48, PART 2, PAGE 1066

OR-452

[*Extract*]

JUNE 20–OCTOBER 7, 1865. — The Powder River Indian Expedition.

SUMMARY OF THE PRINCIPAL EVENTS

July 26, 1865.—Skirmish at Platte Bridge, Dak. Ter.
Aug. 1, 1865.—Affairs at Big Laramie and Little Laramie, Dak. Ter.
13, 1865.—Skirmish near Powder River, Dak. Ter.
16, 1865.—Skirmish at Powder River, Dak. Ter.
28, 1865.—Action at Tongue River, Dak. Ter.
Sept. 1, 1865.—Skirmish at Powder River, Mont. Ter.
2, 1865.—Skirmish at Powder River, Mont. Ter.
4, 1865.—Skirmish at Powder River, Mont. Ter.
5, 1865.—Engagement at Powder River, Mont. Ter.
7, 1865.—Skirmish at Powder River, Mont. Ter.
8, 1865.—Engagement at Powder River, Mont. Ter.

REPORTS.

No. 1.—Maj. Gen. Grenville M. Dodge, U.S. Army, commanding Department of the Missouri, and U.S. Forces Kansas and the Territories, including operations December 9, 1864–November 1, 1865.

. . .

No. 1.

Reports of Maj. Gen. Grenville M. Dodge, U.S. Army, commanding Department of the Missouri, and U.S. Forces Kansas and the Territories, including operations December 9, 1864–November 1, 1865.

HEADQUARTERS DEPARTMENT OF THE MISSOURI,
Saint Louis, Mo., July 18, 1865.

CAPTAIN: I have the honor to make report of operations in the Department of the Missouri from December 9, 1864, to the present date:

In compliance with General Orders, No. 294. War Department, series 1864, I assumed command of the Department of the Missouri December 9, 1864. The department then consisted of the State of Missouri, and had just begun to recover from the effects of Price's raid. The cavalry was mostly dismounted and the troops generally in bad discipline and condition.

. . .

I reorganized the provost-marshal's department under more perfect system and limited powers, and discharged all citizens connected with that bureau, replacing them with officers and enlisted men.

Col. J. H. Baker, the efficient chief of this department, performed his duties with signal ability, and under his able supervision his bureau became an important and indispensable auxiliary in the administration of the most difficult affairs of the department. All persons arrested were speedily and thoroughly examined and tried or released. These reforms produced an excellent effect throughout the Slate. General Orders, No. 11, War Department, current series, merged the Department of Kansas into the Department of the Missouri. On the receipt of this order I repaired to Fort Leavenworth. I found that the Indians after the Chivington affair had combined and moved north; had struck the Platte Valley and held the overland route from Julesburg Junction Station; had captured trains, demolished ranches, murdered men, women, and children; destroyed fifty miles of telegraph lines, &c. immediately ordered the troops on that line to concentrate and move against these Indians. After several severe engagements the line was retaken, the Indians moving north byway of Pole Creek and Mud Springs, where they met the troops from Fort Laramie, and two or three severe engagements ensued, the Indians still making north to the Black Hills. The telegraph line was immediately rebuilt, the overland mail stages resumed their trips, and although the line has been attacked several times since, we have succeeded in holding it open and have kept up communications. It was my desire to make a campaign against these Indians before spring, but the force on the line was entirely inadequate to the purpose.

. . .

My plan in this being disarranged, I placed the troops on our communications and commenced preparations for spring and summer campaigns. Finding every tribe of Indians of any importance from the British Possessions on the north to the Red River on the south engaged in open hostilities, I submitted my plans for operations against them, which was to strike them all at once by moving in seven columns, as follows, to wit: One to move up the Loup Pork, thence to the east base of the Black Hills; a second to move from Fort Laramie directly north to Powder River, and strike the Indians wherever found. Both of these columns were to be placed under Brig. Gen. P. E. Connor, who, on the assignment of Utah to this department, had been placed in command of the District of the Plains, embracing the Territories of Nebraska, Colorado, and Utah.

Two columns under Brig. Gen. R. B. Mitchell, commanding the District of Kansas, were to move, one up the Republican Fork of Kansas River to its source, the other up Smoky Hill Fork, crossing to the Arkansas River, and from thence to Denver.

. . .

The supplies went forward slowly; trains loitered on their way, waiting for grass, and in many eases requisitions for stores did not arrive until late, the staff officers not appearing to have appreciated the necessity for early action, careful estimates, and timely requisitions. Many of them had just been assigned to duty on the plains, and did not on the instant grasp the important and difficult nature of their duties, or comprehend the fact that it took months to transport supplies from Fort Leavenworth to Laramie, Denver, and Utah. However, these difficulties have all been overcome, and now supplies are going forward; troops are en route and have arrived. Four of the columns are on the march and the rest will be started during this month. Few posts have been established on the northern route, and now the line from Fort Leavenworth to Kearny, from Omaha to Kearny, from Kearny to Denver and Salt Lake, via Bridger's Pass, and the line from Julesburg, via Fort Laramie and South Pass to Salt Lake, and thence vest to the western line of Utah, are well protected. Every stage station has its detachment, every train and coach goes guarded, and new life, activity, and discipline has been infused into the troops. The Indians are being put on the defensive, and are now invariably beaten and in most cases severely chastised in their attacks.

General Connor has thus far exhibited marked ability, and has assisted materially in bringing about these results, although in some of his subordinates he has not been very ably assisted, and has had many difficulties to contend with. The friendly Indians at Fort Laramie, in an attempt to move them to Fort Kearny to get them away from the scenes of Indian troubles, revolted, turned upon their guard, killed a captain and four men, and then escaped. Colonel Moonlight, who was sent after them, allowed his camp to be surprised and his stock captured. I have ordered him mustered out of the service. Everything, I think, now argues a settlement of these Indian difficulties this summer. They (the Indians) are beginning to realize and appreciate the power of the Government and to fear it. Their universal success for the year past had emboldened and encouraged them until they had become to believe, that we could not subdue them. These false notions must be whipped out of them, and any peace made with them before they are thoroughly convinced that we are the masters, and not they, would prove disastrous to us, would not last six months, and would only encourage them to renewed hostilities when we, perhaps, would not be so well prepared to meet them as now.

. . .

The wooden pontoons ordered to me will not last longer than another year, and outside of purely military reasons that recommend this permanent bridging, the amount of trade and travel flowing west of Colorado, Utah, Dakota, Idaho, and Montana, and the inability of the people living near the crossings of the Platte and Loup Fork to put in these bridges, and the impossibility during a large portion of the year to keep ferries on these streams, would justify the expenditure of a sum sufficient to do this bridging in the incalculable benefits that would accrue to the Government in the development of these Territories.

I would also earnestly recommend the bridging by the Government of the South Platte at or near Julesburg. High water, treacherous fords, &c., are the cause of great delay and loss to Government every year. Especially has this been the case this year, and the amount of trade and travel flowing south from Idaho, Montana, and Western Dakota and crossing at this place is increasing and will in another year be immense. The same reasons for bridging the Platte at Fort Kearny urge the bridging of the South Platte at Julesburg. When Utah was added to my command (February 17, 1865) I approved the course pursued in that Territory by General Connor, viz., avoiding any direct collision with the Mormons, but in all ways possible inviting emigration thither by protecting the rights of the so called Gentiles, sustaining and supporting the Government officials sent there, and by keeping a respectable force there, which could be used against the Indians and in protecting mining operations, opening military roads, &c. Thus, by opening that Territory, inviting an enlightened emigration there, and encouraging a public sentiment calculated to soon root out that curse to our land—polygamy. In other reports I have more fully detailed my views and action in these matters, which have been approved by Government.

. . .

I have the honor to be, very respectfully, your obedient servant,

G. M. DODGE,
Major-General, Commanding.

Capt. JOSEPH McC. BELL,
Assistant Adjutant-General, Military Division of the Missouri.

[Editor's note: *This document is the cover correspondence for the Powder River Indian Expedition Report, which covers June 20–October 7, 1865. See* OR, *Series 1, Volume 48, Part 1, pages 329–389, for the complete report.*]

SOURCE: *OR*, SERIES 1, VOLUME 48, PART 1, PAGES 329–335

OR-453

FORT LARAMIE, DAK. TER., *July 21, 1865.*

Maj. Gen. G. M. DODGE,
Department of the Missouri, Fort Leavenworth:

I regret that Utah is taken out of my command. I pity those poor fellows who, relying upon my promise of protection, have declared their independence of Brigham. I am glad you are coming here. I have some troops in this district that are not worth their salt. The Eleventh Kansas is still mutinous, but I cannot punish them because they are scattered and I cannot dispense with their services at present. There are two companies of Eleventh Kansas who have two years to serve. Shall I send them down with regiment? I will leave nothing undone to expedite movement of columns.

P. EDW. CONNOR,
Brigadier-General.

SOURCE: *OR*, SERIES 1, VOLUME 48, PART 2, PAGE 1113

OR-454

HEADQUARTERS DEPARTMENT OF THE MISSOURI
July 21, 1865—5.40 P.M.

Brig. Gen. P. E. CONNOR,
Fort Laramie:

Get your columns off as soon as possible. We have got these Indian matters now in our hands, and we must settle them. I will come to Laramie during August or September, and I hope you will catch them before that. All the troops are giving me great trouble. Infantry at Fort Leavenworth mutinied; cavalry (some of it) the same; but are now on march under new reorganization of commands. All Territories west of Missouri River and east of Rocky Mountains are in my command. Utah goes to Department of Pacific, so that Dakota and Montana are added to us. Would not send any troops to Utah only those necessary to protect overland route. If they will not take stores to Powder River you will have to force them to do it. There are plenty of stores on road, but when they will arrive it is impossible for me to even predict. I have done all in my power to forward them. They started in time to reach their destination long ago. Mowing machines are en route. All troops going to plains have one and two years yet to serve. Seventh Kansas Cavalry are en route by boat to Omaha. Tibbits' brigade of cavalry between Fort Leavenworth and Kearny. Stagg's must be on the ground before this.

G. M. DODGE,
Major-General.

SOURCE: *OR*, SERIES 1, VOLUME 48, PART 2, PAGES 1112–1113

OR-455

HEADQUARTERS DEPARTMENT OF THE MISSOURI,
Saint Louis, Mo., July 26, 1865.

Lieut. Gen. U. S. GRANT,
General-in-Chief U.S. Army, Washington, D.C.:

GENERAL: The Territory of Utah having been taken from this department and attached to that of California, it is proper that I should suggest to you that the condition of affairs in that Territory needs immediate attention. The relations between the Mormons and other citizens of the United States not belonging to the Mormon Church are critical, and unless attended to at once are likely to break out in very serious disturbance, which will be difficult to subdue. The Mormons in all difficulties with other citizens of the United States at once resort to the Indians, and stir up hostilities to break up mail routes and obstruct or put an end to emigration. There is little doubt that they are now engaged in this manner, and it will be wise to invite the immediate attention of the proper department commander to the subject. The fact is, that for a time some military officer with troops at his command should be governor of Utah.

I am, general, respectfully, your obedient servant,

JNO. POPE,
Major-General, Commanding.

SOURCE: *OR*, SERIES 1, VOLUME 48, PART 2, PAGE 1123

OR-456

HDQRS. DEPARTMENT OF THE MISSOURI,
Saint Louis, Mo., July 27, 1865.

GENERAL ORDERS,
No. 4.

In compliance with orders from Washington, the Department of the Missouri is extended to embrace the Territories of Utah and Colorado.

By command of Major-General Pope:

JOS. McC. BELL,
Assistant Adjutant-General.

SOURCE: *OR*, SERIES 1, VOLUME 48, PART 2, PAGE 1126

OR-457

FORT LEAVENWORTH, *July 28, 1865.*

Brig. Gen. P. E. CONNOR,
Fort Laramie:

Utah has again been ordered to my command. Go on with it as heretofore. Have you made estimate for all the stores you will need for the year? Refer to my letter of June 13, and answer by telegraph if you need any more, how many, and at what point. Stores referred to in that letter are en route. Have you sent in any estimates under that order?

G. M. DODGE,
Major-General.

SOURCE: *OR*, SERIES 1, VOLUME 48, PART 2, PAGES 1128–129

OR-458

FORT LARAMIE, DAK. TER., *July 28, 1865.*

Maj. Gen. G. M. DODGE,
Department of the Missouri, Fort Leavenworth:

I am rejoiced. I will require in Utah, in addition to amount stated in your letter of June 13, clothing for 2,500 cavalry and 500 infantry (see my telegrams of June 22 and 27), and subsistence stores for 2,000 men. Have the infantry regiments started? What regiments of cavalry have started this month, or are to start this month?

P. EDW. CONNOR,
Brigadier-General.

SOURCE: *OR*, SERIES 1, VOLUME 48, PART 2, PAGE 1129

OR-459

FORT LEAVENWORTH, *July 28, 1865.*

Brig. Gen. P. E. CONNOR,
Fort Laramie:

Subsistence stores and quartermaster's stores for 5,000 men have been ordered and mostly gone forward to Salt Lake. The infantry regiment that goes to you is off. The brigade of infantry has been gone eight days. Roads are almost impassable from here to Kearny, and they will be slow in getting through. The infantry that goes to Salt Lake I think should be the U.S. Volunteers, as I am satisfied that Government will muster out of service the veteran volunteers that are now going on the plains as soon as Indian troubles are over.

G. M. DODGE,
Major-General.

SOURCE: *OR*, SERIES 1, VOLUME 48, PART 2, PAGE 1129

OR-460

FORT LARAMIE, DAK. TER., *July 28, 1865.*

Maj. Gen. G. M. DODGE,
Department of the Missouri, Fort Leavenworth:

If clothing for 5,000 men has gone to Utah it is all I will require. The term of service of Third U.S. Volunteers expires this fall. Is it worth while to send them to Utah? Will they be retained? Are Tibbits' and the infantry brigades veterans?

P. EDW. CONNOR,
Brigadier-General.

SOURCE: *OR*, SERIES 1, VOLUME 48, PART 2, PAGE 1129

OR-461

[*Extract*]

[Appendix L]

WASHINGTON, D.C., *July 29, 1865*

Maj. Gen. JOHN POPE,
Saint Louis:

The Quartermaster and Commissary Generals report requisitions of such magnitude coming from Leavenworth as to alarm them. Look into them, and stop all unnecessary expenditures, and reduce necessary orders to actual requirements. Returns show a cavalry force in Department of Missouri which it would seem might be materially reduced. Look into this matter.

U. S. GRANT
Lieutenant-General.

[Appendix M]

Approximate amount of stores on the plains.

NORTHERN ROUTE.

Station.	Number of men.	From—	To—	Remarks.
Salt Lake	2,500	1865. July 1	1866. July 1	Small rations sent 4,000 men. Requisitions and estimates called for full rations for 5,000 men, but were reduced to 2,500 August 2.
Fort Bridger	500	July 1	July 1	—
Fort Laramie	1,050	July 1	July 1	Requisitions called for 2,500 men, but were reduced to 1,000.
Powder River	500	July 1	July 1	Stores for Powder River were shipped to Laramie. Requisitions called for supplies for 1,000 men, but were reduced to 500 in August.

. . .

[Editor's note: *This document is part of the Powder River Indian Expedition Report, which covers June 20–October 7, 1865. See* OR, *Series 1, Volume 48, Part 1, pages 329–389, for the complete report. See* OR-452 *for the cover correspondence.*]

SOURCE: *OR*, SERIES 1, VOLUME 48, PART 1, PAGE 365

OR-462

[Appendix N.]

FORT LEAVENWORTH, *July 29, 1865.*

Brig. Gen. P. E. CONNOR,
Fort Laramie:

Major Mackey, of Fort Laramie, estimates for subsistence stores for Fort Laramie for 3,000 soldiers, 250 citizens, 400 Indians, 100 officers, &c., nearly doubling the estimates heretofore sent and reported to you in my letter of June 13. Estimates therein stated called for stores for 2,000 men for Laramie and 900 for Powder River for one year. This appears to me sufficient. My letter of June 13 shows that estimates have been received for 17,000 men; 1,500 have been added to that for Utah. Is this not stores enough, and more than we shall need for the ensuing year? If some posts are short, others must have a surplus, which can be transferred as they are needed. This winter our force will necessarily be reduced, and we do not want to pile up stores that cannot be used. The estimate up to June 13 and from Salt Lake makes 18,000,000 pounds for subsistence stores alone. This is as much as we can get transportation for, and is 8,000,000 more than is contracted for, and in addition thereto are quartermaster's and ordnance stores that are en route.

G. M. DODGE,
Major-General.

[Editor's note: *This document is part of the Powder River Indian Expedition Report which covers June 20–October 7, 1865. See* OR, *Series 1, Volume 48, Part 1, pages 329–389, for the complete report. See* OR*-452 for the cover correspondence.*]

SOURCE: *OR*, SERIES 1, VOLUME 48, PART 1, PAGE 365

OR-463

FORT LARAMIE, DAK. TER., *July 29, 1865.*

Maj. Gen. G. M. DODGE,
Department of the Missouri, Fort Leavenworth:

I will not require the stores estimated for by Major Mackey. The stores mentioned in your letter of June 13, and those subsequently sent to Utah, will be ample. I leave to-morrow. Will be on telegraph line for few days.

P. EDW. CONNOR,
Brigadier-General.

SOURCE: *OR*, SERIES 1, VOLUME 48, PART 2, PAGE 1133

OR-464

FORT LEAVENWORTH, *July 31, 1865.*

Maj. Gen. JOHN POPE,
Saint Louis, Mo.:

All returns of troops in this command are in Saint Louis; none here. I telegraphed Captain Bell to send me copy outside of Utah. I am sending supplies on plains for northern route for 12,000 men for one year from 1st of May; on southern route six months for 7,000 men. I do not see how I can reduce the force on the plains before fall. Several regiments go out of service then. With the Indians all hostile, over miles of overland route and every stage and train to be guarded, it takes a large force. We are putting supplies into Utah for 4,500 men. General Connor calls for supplies for 5,000 men, but I have reduced it to 4,000, and I understand this meets the approval of Government. When I spoke to you about it you approved it. We have got to put more troops in Utah this winter or we will have trouble. Last spring I could do nothing for want of supplies on the plains, and I think we should now provide sufficient for every contingency. If so directed I can reduce the supplies in Utah to 2,500 men. These men, you are aware, have to come from the 12,000 I put supplies east of the mountains for. I have concluded upon settling the matter on the southern route and withdrawing most of the troops, and therefore have only provided supplies for six months for them from May 1. No requisitions go to Washington that I know of. The depot quartermaster and commissary send their requisitions to Colonels Haines and Myers. The stores for northern route have mostly gone forward. I cut down many of these requisitions one-third, and have telegraphed about it. But when officers on the plains send in requisitions the officers here fill them. Commissary supplies, except for Utah, have gone forward for northern route. If you say I shall reduce Utah to supplies for 2,500 men, telegraph me, as the stores have not yet left.

G. M. DODGE,
Major-General.

[Editor's note: *This document is part of the Powder River Indian Expedition Report, which covers June 20–October 7, 1865. See* OR, *Series 1, Volume 48, Part 1, pages 329–389, for the complete report. See* OR-452 *for the cover correspondence.*]

SOURCE: *OR*, SERIES 1, VOLUME 48, PART 1, PAGE 351

OR-465

FORT LEAVENWORTH, *July 31, 1865.*

Brig. Gen. P. E. CONNOR,
Fort Laramie:

You will see from General Pope's dispatch that Government thinks we are making too much cost. Your estimates are very large. You ask for supplies for 17,000 men. We will not be able to keep over half that number on the plains this winter. All supplies have gone forward except for Utah. Supplies for 2,500 men are waiting to go there. Do you not think that we had better let Utah rest on supplies for 2,500 men? That is as many as you will be able to get there this winter.

G. M. DODGE,
Major-General.

[Editor's note: *This document is part of the Powder River Indian Expedition Report, which covers June 20–October 7, 1865. See* OR, *Series 1, Volume 48, Part 1, pages 329–389, for the complete report. See* OR-452 *for the cover correspondence.*]

SOURCE: *OR*, SERIES 1, VOLUME 48, PART 1, PAGE 366

OR-466

SAINT LOUIS, MO., *August 1, 1865.*

Major-General DODGE:

Supplies for 2,500 men in Utah will be sufficient.

JNO. POPE,
Major-General.

[Editor's note: *This document is part of the Powder River Indian Expedition Report, which covers June 20–October 7, 1865. See* OR, *Series 1, Volume 48, Part 1, pages 329–389, for the complete report.*

See OR-*452 for the cover correspondence. It should also be noted that the editors of the* War of the Rebellion *included this expedition document again in Series 1, Volume 48, Part 2, page 1155.*]

SOURCE: *OR*, SERIES 1, VOLUME 48, PART 1, PAGE 351

OR-467

[*Extract*]

HEADQUARTERS DEPARTMENT OF THE MISSOURI,
Saint Louis, Mo., August 1, 1865.

Col. R. M. SAWYER,
Asst. Adjt. Gen., Mil. Div. of the Mississippi, Saint Louis, Mo.:

COLONEL: I have the honor to acknowledge the receipt of your note of yesterday inclosing copy of dispatch from the General-in-Chief to Major-General Sherman in relation to the forces in the department and the requisitions made for the supplies at Fort Leavenworth.

. . .

In relation to reduction of forces on the plains I present the following statement and suggestions: All the tribes of Indians east of the mountains, and many west, are in open hostility. They attack the mail coaches, emigrant trains, and small posts continually. The United States is required to protect the great overland routes passing in several directions through this great Indian region. Protection is thus required along 3,500 miles of road, nearly all of which lies in an uninhabited country, and yet over which are daily passing the U.S. mails to the Territories and the Pacific, crowds of emigrants, and great trains of supplies for the mining regions, as well as individuals and small parties of travelers. The threatened difficulties with the Mormons in Utah also demand attention, and the civil officers appointed for that Territory by the Government, as well as the citizens of the United States now there and going there, absolutely need military protection to enable them to remain in the Territory at all. This condition of affairs certainly demands a considerable military force, if the Government means to assure security of life and of property to emigrants across the plains and to settlers in the newly opened Territories. The Indian question is the most difficult, and I confess I do not see how it is to be solved without an entire change of the Indian policy which has hitherto been and must, under the laws, now be pursued. The development of the rich mining regions in the Territories of itself has attracted great throngs of emigrants, and their number has been tenfold increased by the necessary results of the late civil war. Thousands of families who have been disloyal or have been sympathizers with the South have, since the conclusion of the war, found it difficult, if not impossible, to continue to live at their homes, and have left the States of Missouri, Arkansas, Southern Illinois, Kentucky, and no doubt other Southern States, to make their permanent homes in the new Territories. Many thousands of men who have been discharged from the Army are also seeking the mining regions. A surprising emigration has been going forward ever since the opening of spring and seems still to flow on without cessation. Not alone, or even generally, are the great overland routes pursued by these great throngs of emigrants. Every route supposed to be practicable is explored by them. They make highways in every direction across the great plains and drive off or destroy the game. No part of that great region, however inaccessible, escapes the prying eye of the gold seeker, and no route which promises discoveries of value or in any manner shortens his routes of travel is neglected. Of course, neither the movements nor the conduct of these parties can be controlled. No man except themselves can say what wrongs they do to the Indians by robbing, by violence, or by dispossessing them of districts of country which they have occupied unmolested for centuries, yet the United States Government is held responsible if any danger is incurred by them or any loss of life or property sustained anywhere in the vast and remote region they are traversing. What the white man does to the Indian is never known. It is only what the Indian does to the white man (nine times out of ten in the way of retaliation) which reaches the public.

The Indian, in truth, has no longer a country. His lands are everywhere pervaded by white men; his means of subsistence destroyed and the homes of his tribe violently taken from him; himself and his family reduced to starvation, or to the necessity of warring to the death upon the white man, whose inevitable and destructive progress threatens the total extermination of his race. Such is to-day the condition of affairs on the great plains and in the ranges of the Rocky Mountains. The Indians, driven to desperation and threatened with starvation, have everywhere commenced hostilities against the whites, and are carrying them on with a fury and courage unknown to their history hitherto. There is not a tribe of Indians on the great plains or in the mountain regions east of Nevada and Idaho of any consideration which is not now warring on the whites. Until lately the U.S. troops, small in number and utterly incapable on that account of affording security to the whites or protection to the Indians, have been strictly on the defensive. Lately large re-enforcements have been sent to the plains, and several expeditions have been organized which are now moving against the Indians in the hope to restore peace, but in my judgment with little prospect of doing so, except by violent extermination of the Indians, unless a totally different policy toward them is adopted. The commanding officers of these expeditions, as also the commanders of military posts on the frontier, have orders to make peace with the Indians if possible, and at the earliest moment that any peace which even promises to be lasting can be made. The difficulty lies in the fact that we can promise the Indian under our present system nothing that he will ask with any hope that we can fulfill our promise. The first demand of the Indian is that the white man shall not come into his country, shall not kill or drive off the game upon which his subsistence depends, and shall not dispossess him of his lands. How can we promise this, with any purpose of fulfilling the obligation, unless we prohibit emigration and settlement west or south of the Missouri River? So far from being prepared to make such engagements with the Indian, the Government is every day stimulating emigration and its resulting wrong to the Indian, giving escorts to all parties of emigrants or travelers who desire to cross the plains, making appropriations for wagon roads in many directions through the Indian country, and sending out engineers to explore the country and bands of laborers to construct the roads, guarded by bodies of soldiers. Where under such circumstances is the Indian to go, and what is to become of him? What hope of peace have we when by these proceedings we constantly are forcing the Indian to war? I do not know of any district of country west of the Mississippi where the Indian can be located and protected by the Government, and at the same time support themselves, as is their custom. I explained all these difficulties very fully in the conference which was had between the Secretaries of War and the Interior, General Grant and myself.

It is idle to talk of making treaties of peace with the Indians when not even an unmolested home in the great region which they claim can be promised them with any sort of certainty that such a promise can be fulfilled. The very soldiers placed to protect the limited district which the Government could alone protect against the incursion of white men would render it impossible for the Indian to maintain himself in the only manner known to him. It is useless to think of the Government undertaking to subsist large bodies of Indians in remote and inaccessible districts. Whatever may be the abstract wrong or right of the question, all history shows that the result in this country must inevitably be the dispossession of the Indian of all his lands and their occupation by civilized men. The only practical question to be considered is, how this inevitable process can be accomplished with the least inhumanity and the greatest moral and physical benefit to the Indian. We are surely not now pursuing such a course, nor are the means used becoming to a humane and Christian people. My duties as a military commander require me to protect the emigration, the mails, and the settlements against hostile acts of the Indians. I have no power under the laws of the United States to do this except by force. This necessity demands a large military force on the plains, which will have to be increased as the Indians are more and more driven to desperation, and less and less able to protect the game, which is their only means of life. The end is sure and dreadful to contemplate. Meantime, there is, so far as my power goes, nothing to be done except what is being done, and if this condition of affairs demands considerable military force and heavy expenditures they must either be accepted by the Government or the troops must be withdrawn and the plains again given up to the Indians. It would probably not be difficult to make such a peace now with the Indians as has been the custom in times past, but useless to do so unless we can at the same time remove the causes of certain and speedy renewal of war, when by withdrawing our forces we will be far less prepared for it than now. These treaties perhaps answered the purpose (though I think they were always unwise and wrong) so long as the Indians continued to occupy the greater portion of their country and the war only involved small encroachments by whites on its borders. Hitherto the process of dispossessing the Indian of his lands, although equally certain, was far slower and far less alarming. To-day we are at one grasp seizing the whole region of country occupied by the Indians and plunging them without warning into suffering and starvation. Treaties such as we have made with them in times past will no longer answer the purpose. I have presented my views on this subject and suggested what seems to me the proper course to be pursued so fully and so often to the War Department, and have so frequently urged the matter upon the attention of the Government, that it seems unnecessary and hardly consistent with official propriety that I should reiterate them in this manner. I only do so now because the telegram from the General-in-Chief, which you inclose to me, seems to indicate dissatisfaction that so many troops are employed in the Indian country. Either a large force must for a time be kept there, or we must furnish insufficient protection to our citizens in that region.

It is hoped that during the present season the expeditious now marching against the Indians will be able to inflict such damage upon them that they will prefer to undergo much wrong and suffering rather than again break out in hostilities. This is a cruel process, but the only one which under the present system seems to be in my power. I will withdraw and muster out of service all the troops I possibly can from day to day, and by the close of this season I will endeavor to reduce to much less force the troops serving on the plains. It is proper for the Government, however, to realize that owing to the changed condition of affairs on the plains, arising from the rapid development of the mining regions and the great emigration to and rapid settlement of the new Territories, a much larger force will for a long time be required in that region than we have heretofore considered necessary. The remote stations of these troops and the necessity of hauling in wagons from the Missouri River all supplies needed for them, renders the protection required and demanded by the mail service, the emigration, and the remote settlements an expensive undertaking, the propriety of which must be determined by the Government itself. The military commander ordered to furnish such protection has only to carry out his orders in the best and most economical manner. I trust I have no purpose except to perform my duty in this matter and in this manner. I have assigned Major-General Dodge, a well known and most efficient and careful officer, to the command of all operations in the Indian country west and south of the Missouri River, with orders to reduce forces and expenditures as rapidly as it is possible to do so. His subordinate commanders are men entirely familiar with Indians and Indian country.

In conclusion, I desire, if it be consistent with the public interests, to be informed upon two questions, in order that I may act with more full understanding of the purposes of the Government: First. Is it designed that such military pressure be kept upon the Indians that small parties of adventurers prospecting the plains and mountains in every direction, and in the most remote and uninhabited regions of the country, will be unmolested by Indians, whatever such parties may do or wherever they may go? I need not say that protection of so general and universal a character will require a large military force, which will be mainly needed to protect the Indians, by watching these white men and preventing them from committing acts for which the Indians will assuredly retaliate. Is the commander of this department responsible for hostile acts of Indians against such parties? Second. In case treaties of peace, such as have been usual, are made with the Indians by the proper officers of the Indian Department, and the troops withdrawn from the Indian country in accordance with such treaty, is the army commander to be held responsible if the Indians violate the treaty and renew the war? In short, is the army to be made responsible for every murder or outrage committed on the great plains by Indians or white men, who are officially at peace according to the records in the office of the Commissioner of Indian Affairs? When there is divided action, as is the case now in the management of Indian affairs, there should be divided responsibility. Army commanders are very willing to be held responsible for military operations under their immediate command, but they are not willing and ought not to be held responsible for breaches of treaties made by other departments of the Government which they did not approve, yet to terms of which they are obliged to conform. If these questions which are respectfully asked can be answered without official impropriety the question of troops needed in the Indian country and attendant expenses can be easily settled.

I am, colonel, respectfully, your obedient servant,

JNO. POPE,
Major-General, Commanding.

[Editor's note: *This document is referenced in* OR-472 *and* OR-488*.*]

SOURCE: *OR*, SERIES 1, VOLUME 48, PART 2, PAGES 1149–1153

OR-468

HEADQUARTERS DEPARTMENT OF THE MISSOURI,
Saint Louis, Mo., August 1, 1865.

Maj. Gen. G. M. DODGE,
Commanding U.S. Forces in Field in Kansas, Colorado, Nebraska, and Utah:

GENERAL: I have telegraphed you several times in regard to a reduction of forces and expenditures in your command, and rely upon your reducing both as rapidly as possible. I desire in this communication to ask your attention to my views on the subject of military operations and future military dispositions on the plains, and to request that you will conform to them as far as practicable. The military expeditions now marching against the Indians cannot and should not be arrested until the campaign is terminated, which I confidently expect will be the case as early as October 1. Whatever be the results of these expeditions, I wish you on their completion to return at once to a simple arrangement for the defense of the overland routes to Santa Fé and to California, so far as those routes be within the territory under your jurisdiction. Of course you will be able by this means to muster out of service a force in the aggregate equal to the whole forces composing the several expeditions now in progress. I myself consider five regiments of infantry and two regiments of cavalry (the former filled up to 900, the latter to 1,200 men each) sufficient for the purpose and for whatever military aid may be needed in Utah. You should select the most important points along the overland routes for permanent stations for the troops assigned to the protection of the routes, choosing points as nearly as circumstances will allow so as to divide the line to be protected into nearly equal intervals. These posts should be as numerous as the force designated will admit of, care being taken that no post is left without a garrison strong enough to defend it and furnish some help to other posts or to trains when needed. Each of these posts should be stockaded if possible, so as to include enough space to shelter all the stock of the garrison and of the mail station and any stock belonging to parties who may be obliged to take refuge at the post. In places where proper timber for stockades cannot be had, good field intrenchments should be thrown up. Each post should be supplied with two small pieces of artillery. Commanding officers for the posts should be selected with great care and frequent inspections of the condition of the garrisons and of the posts should be made by an officer of your own staff. By the middle of September it is hoped that you will have selected the positions for these posts, which should be immediately protected by carefully constructed stockades or field intrenchments. This precaution is essential, whether the military operations of this season terminate in peace with the Indians or not. I desire, therefore, that you will reduce the forces under your command to this number, viz, five regiments of infantry or their equivalent in force, say 4,500 men, and two regiments of cavalry (2,400 men) as soon as the expeditions now in progress have returned.

This force, as it seems to me, will be quite sufficient for the simple protection of the routes in question, and their reduction to this number is most necessary by the manifest anxiety of the Government to reduce the army to its lowest limit. I have informed you several times of the telegrams and orders received on this subject, and I trust you understand that it is essential that we should conform to them. Neither you nor I are responsible for results. I wish you to dismiss or return to their regiments every orderly or clerk not absolutely needed for official business; and also all employés in the public service not so needed. You will have to give your personal attention to this matter, or designate some entirely careful and reliable officer to attend to it. I may mention to you as showing how much personal care should be given to these matters, that when I took possession of department headquarters here when you left, I found more than twice as many clerks and five times as many orderlies as were in any manner needed. Of course it is the duty of an adjutant-general to regulate these matters, but they don't always do it. I have no doubt you will find at Fort Leavenworth as also at other posts and stations, very many men whose services are not required. Soldiers should be returned to their regiments and citizens discharged. I trust, general, you will give your earliest attention to these matters. In your progress to Laramie, please order into Leavenworth all troops not absolutely needed along the line, notifying me by telegraph. It is desirable to get rid of as many cavalry regiments as possible as they are the most expensive troops on the frontier. Please regulate your requisitions in view of the reduction of force herein suggested, and send forward no supplies except what are needed for the reduced force. The troops on the expeditions will only need to be supplied until the season is over. Select from your whole force the regiments of infantry and cavalry here designated, choosing of course the best troops and those having the longest periods to serve. The whole force retained, infantry and cavalry, should not in my judgment exceed 6,900 men. I wish you also to select from the column under Colonel Cole a regiment of infantry 600 strong to report to General Sully at Fort Randall, Fort Sully, or Fort Rice, as may be most convenient, by October 15, to relieve the troops now at those posts whose terms of service will expire in the autumn. At the conclusion of his operations Colonel Cole will be nearest to the line of posts on the Missouri River and can easily supply the force necessary. Three hundred men (with the colonel of the regiment) are needed at Rice; 200 probably at Sully, and 100 at Randall. General Sully should be notified by telegraph in time via Sioux City when these troops are detached by Colonel Cole and when they may be expected on the Missouri River.

I am, general, respectfully, your obedient servant,

JNO. POPE,
Major-General, Commanding.

[Editor's note: *This document is referenced in* OR-472.]

SOURCE: *OR*, SERIES 1, VOLUME 48, PART 2, PAGES 1154–1155

OR-469

SAINT LOUIS, MO., *August 1, 1865.*

Major-General DODGE:

Supplies for 2,500 men in Utah will be sufficient.

JNO. POPE,
Major-General.

SOURCE: *OR*, SERIES 1, VOLUME 48, PART 2, PAGE 1155

OR-470

HDQRS. U.S. FORCES, KANSAS AND THE TERRITORIES,
Fort Leavenworth, August 2, 1865.

Gen. JOHN POPE,
Commanding department of the Missouri, Saint Louis, Mo.:

GENERAL: I am in receipt of your dispatch of the 31st ultimo in regard to mustering out troops, reducing expenses, &c. I do not understand fully what the meaning or intention is, but suppose that Government thinks that we are incurring unnecessary expense and using more troops than are needed. These troops have just been sent me from the East, transported thousands of miles at large expense, to operate against the Indians. I have just got them well on their way into the Indian country, and now it is asked that they be mustered out. If it is the intention of Government to muster these men out, it would have been far better to have done it before we made our arrangements to fight the Indians and thereby have saved the immense expense of transportation and the derangement of plans. It seems that Government does not appreciate the magnitude of the difficulties on the plains that we have had to overcome, and with which we have to contend. First. Last spring we did not have a serviceable horse on the plains. Every man there had to be remounted. Second. We were almost entirely out of stores of all kinds. Third. The troops called for were sent in June, dismounted, dissatisfied, and mutinous. The press throughout the West encouraged them, and the State authorities protested openly against their going on the plains. The result is that about one-fourth have deserted, so that of the troops sent me from the East I have not got more than three-fourths for service. The force may look large on paper, but it is very small in the field when you contemplate the ground it has to cover and the work it has to do. Now that I have got the troops well under way, got subsistence stores en route to feed them, and am just getting matters where we may hope for decisive results as the fruit of our efforts, and the orders come to muster out. The troops on the plains have heard of these orders and disaffection increases. Two regiments mutinied openly, absolutely refusing to go out to fight. In all my experience in the army I have never labored more earnestly or worked so hard as I have to bring about a successful issue with these Indians, and I assure you it seems a most thankless job. I desire that the Government may understand that it has either got to abandon the country west entirely to the Indians or meet the war issue presented. If the latter, I submit if it is not better to use the force and means in readiness, and make quick work of it, than to weaken our force and drag along from year to year at a largely increased cost of blood and treasure. There are about 15,000 warriors in open hostility against us on the north, and about 10,000 on the south. Against these I have had to organize columns that were each strong enough to take care of themselves offensively, while at the same time I have had to hold troops enough to guard 3,500 miles of overland route. Every coach (daily) and every train must be guarded, even a day's delay bringing complaint that we are not protecting the mail lines. I submit if under these circumstances Government will not think more troops should be on the plains instead of less. I believe I appreciate as fully as any one can the importance of speedily settling our Indian troubles, of reducing expenses, and of bringing everything to a peace basis, and in all of my operations I have refused to buy a horse, mule, or wagon. I have wasted weeks to pick them up wherever I could find them, and have been delayed greatly thereby. I have turned out my own soldiers to build bridges washed away by the floods, to put up our own hay, to build shelters for our stock, and have in every way I could possibly think of endeavored to avoid and reduce expenses.

General Grant will, I am satisfied, give me credit for never calling upon Government for troops or of urging any expense except what was actually necessary since I have been in the service, and I most certainly do not propose to commence a career of profligacy now. The moment I think it safe to let a regiment go I shall muster it out; or if Government considers the force too large or the expenses too great, let it designate who shall be discharged and how expenses shall be cut down. The requisitions that have come in from the plains have appeared enormous, and I have cut them down as much as I dared to do. The officers of the quartermaster's and commissary departments on the plains should know what is required, and they complain that I am crippling them. Government does not take into consideration that never before have we had so extensive a war on the plains. Never before have we had one-half or one-third the country that we now have to protect. Never before have the Indians been allowed for eighteen months to have their own way to murder, rob, and plunder indiscriminately and successfully, without check or hindrance (until within the last three months), and never before have there been so large and such a perfect combination of hostile Indians on the plains, so well armed and supplied as now. They seem confident of success, fight well, and believe to-day that one Indian is equal to five white soldiers. It takes almost man to man to whip them, and will until the conceit is taken out of them by severe chastisement. If we cannot conquer them this summer and fall we must this winter; that is, I hold that now we have got after them we should not stop summer, fall, or winter until they are glad to sue for peace and behave themselves. I am confident we can strike some of them now, and in the winter I know I can catch them all. They are now on the warpath and are not making any provisions for winter; are not hunting, planting, laying in meat, or in any way providing for the future as they usually do. The consequence will be that we will in the fall and winter have them at great disadvantage. I am in hopes, however, that the matter will be settled before winter. Be that so or not, I have made provisions for carrying on the campaign in winter. In all these matters I supposed I was carrying out the instructions and the intentions of Government. I certainly have concealed nothing, but have endeavored to fully inform and press upon the attention of Government the magnitude of these operations and difficulties attending them. I have often fully presented my views and plans in this matter, but if Government now differs with me it has only to indicate its policy and wishes for me to carry them out to the best of my ability. The amount of trade and traffic seeking its way across the plains is doubling every year. This year it is immense, 5,000 teams per month having crossed. The development of the mines indicates its rapid increase yearly. My understanding is that this travel must be protected at all hazards, as thus far this year it has been. I inclose herewith copy of my statement showing the amount of supplies that has been or will be sent to the plains, which is much smaller than the amount called for by officers commanding on the plains. I leave here to-morrow for Fort Laramie to give my personal attention and supervision to affairs, and will be on the ground where I can have personal knowledge of all matters there. I shall leave no stone unturned to bring matters to an issue and the war to a successful end. All I ask is that Government be patient with us, not ask us to do too much in too short a time. Let it consider as it should that operating 15,000 troops on the plains requires more labor and care than to operate 100,000 where there is water and railroad communication and a settled country, &c.

I am, general, very respectfully, your obedient servant,

G. M. DODGE,
Major-General,

Appendix.

Amount of subsistence stores to be supplied to depots on the plains for use of troops at the depots and at posts dependent thereon, including officers, soldiers, citizens, employés, and Indians.

Fort Laramie, for 1,500 men for one year; Powder River, for 500 men for one year; Cottonwood, for 1,500 men for one year; Julesburg, for 1,500 men for one year; Fort

Halleck, for 250 men for one year; Collins, for 500 men for one year; Junction, for 500 men for one year; Utah, for 2,500 men for one year; Denver, for 2,000 men for one year; Fort Bridger, for 500 men for one year; Fort Garland, for 230 men for one year; Fort Lyon, for 1,500 men for one year; Fort Riley, for 4,000 men for six months; Fort Larned, for 2,500 men for six months. Quartermaster's and ordnance stores for a like number of troops have also been estimated for, and all the stores are now en route. As operations progress some posts will be deficient, others will have a surplus, and necessary arrangements have been made to transfer from one to the other as occasion may require. The troops to occupy Utah will have to be taken from those now east of the mountains. The provisions in Salt Lake were put there in anticipation of any trouble that may arise in that part of the country. The requisitions for Utah called for supplies for 5,500 men, but were cut down to 2,500. Supplies for these troops had also to be provided east of the mountains. We will no doubt at the end of the year have some surplus on hand, but not much. I only send rations to Forts Riley and Larned for six months, as I intend to draw in those troops in the fall, and consider that we will have rations enough to feed what will be left during the year.

G. M. DODGE,
Major-General.

SOURCE: *OR*, SERIES 1, VOLUME 48, PART 2, PAGES 1156–1159

OR-471

HDQRS. DEPARTMENT OF THE MISSOURI,
Saint Louis, Mo., August 3, 1865.

GENERAL ORDERS,
No. 7.

In accordance with recent orders from the War Department the Department of the Missouri will hereafter embrace the following States and Territories, viz: The States of Wisconsin, Minnesota, Iowa, Kansas, and Missouri, and the Territories of Dakota, Montana, Nebraska, Utah, and Colorado; headquarters at Saint Louis, Mo.

By command of Major-General Pope:

JOS. McC. BELL,
Assistant Adjutant-General.

SOURCE: *OR*, SERIES 1, VOLUME 48, PART 2, PAGE 1160

OR-472

HEADQUARTERS DEPARTMENT OF THE MISSOURI,
Saint Louis, Mo., August 3, 1865.

Col. R. M. SAWYER,
Assistant Adjutant-General, Saint Louis:

COLONEL: I have the honor to acknowledge the receipt of your note of the 31st ultimo, covering a telegram from the General-in-Chief to Major-General Sherman in relation to reduction of forces and expenditures in this department. The instructions contained in these communications I have ordered General Dodge, commanding on the plains, to execute without delay. I transmit inclosed copy of instructions to that officer for reducing everything to the minimum; also, a full statement of the condition of Indian affairs, and the difficulties which surround their settlement.* As you are aware, I have been but recently placed in command of this department, and have not yet had time to fully acquaint myself with its detail. The inclosed letter of instructions to Major-General Dodge will bring the military forces and expenditures to what seems to me the lowest possible limit for the present, in view of affording anything like adequate protection to the overland routes to the Pacific and to New Mexico, and the proper restraint upon the Mormons in Utah. I will leave nothing in my power undone to effect every possible reduction both of troops and expenses. I have the honor to request that copies of this letter and the inclosed communications be forwarded to the General-in-Chief.

I am, colonel, respectfully, your obedient servant,

JNO. POPE,
Major-General, Commanding.

* [*Refers to* OR-467 *and* OR-468.]

SOURCE: *OR*, SERIES 1, VOLUME 48, PART 2, PAGE 1161

OR-473

Headquarters Department of the Missouri,
Saint Louis, August 5, 1865.

Col. R. M. Sawyer,
Asst. Adjt. Gen., Military Division of the Mississippi:

Colonel: I have the honor to report that the volunteer organizations sent to the plains from the East and from the Army of the Tennessee are in such a state of insubordination, and many of their officers are so much in sympathy with them, that they are next to useless for any service, and have by their example infected the other troops now there to the extent of making them nearly inefficient. Of course they all have one cause of complaint, in which their officers fully sympathize with them, viz: "That with the end of the rebellion their terms of service expired, and that they are entitled to be discharged from the service." Whether wrong or right, they are so fully possessed of this feeling as to be nearly useless. I am compelled to keep some of them for the present, until the Indian expeditions return, about October 1, when the whole force in Kansas, Nebraska, Colorado, Utah, Montana, and that portion of Dakota lying west and south of the Missouri River will be reduced to an aggregate of five infantry and two cavalry regiments, as I have already informed you. The only troops in good discipline are the regiments of U.S. Volunteers which must be retained so long as possible. I submit these facts for consideration at this time because I am satisfied that when the time comes to muster out all the troops in that region, except the small force above designated, it will be impossible to select out of the whole force seven regiments which will not be still more dissatisfied than they are now at being retained, and which will not accordingly be more insubordinate and less efficient than they now are. It will be judicious, indeed necessary, by the time specified for this reduction (say October 1) to have sufficient reliable force for the service indicated, so that all volunteer organizations now on the plains can be mustered out. The regiments of U.S. Volunteers in the department have only a short time to serve, and such reorganization of the army should, if possible, be effected as will furnish the regiments needed mostly enlisted since the termination of the war. I submit these views thus early because I think the situation demands immediate attention. The few regiments needed in this department cannot, in my opinion, be kept together after all the rest have been discharged. Already proceedings of courts-martial, sentencing several privates and non-commissioned officers of the troops to death for mutinying, &c., have reached me, and reports of officers who have come in from Utah and New Mexico, along the overland routes, represent the spirit among the troops guarding those routes as even worse than I have stated.

I am, colonel, respectfully, your obedient servant,

JNO. POPE,
Major-General, Commanding.

SOURCE: *OR*, SERIES 1, VOLUME 48, PART 2, PAGES 1165–1166

OR-474

HEADQUARTERS U.S. FORCES, KANSAS AND THE TERRITORIES,
Fort Leavenworth, August 5, 1865.

GENERAL ORDERS,
No. 3.

I. By direction of Maj. Gen. John Pope, commanding the Department of the Missouri, the limits of this command are hereby extended to include the Territory of Utah.

II. The Territory will be embraced in the District of the Plains. All troops serving therein will report to Brig. Gen. P. E. Connor, commanding.

By order of Maj. Gen. G. M. Dodge:

GEO. C. TICHENOR,
Major and Aide-de-Camp

SOURCE: *OR*, SERIES 1, VOLUME 48, PART 2, PAGE 1166

OR-475

FORT LEAVENWORTH, KANS., *August 6, 1865.*

Hon. E. M. STANTON,
Secretary of War:

The results of my inquiries and observations are that the Indian expeditions have been preparing since April; that all the men and nearly all the materials have gone forward. About 22,000 men, two-thirds mounted, are supplied with ample trains and equipage. Quartermaster's and other stores, with 7,000,000 rations and 640,000 bushels of corn, have been forwarded, and are being distributed among the depots on the routes from this place to Denver and Salt Lake, and to New Mexico. Seven columns of troops, each about 3,000 strong, are to move in various directions over the plains. I estimate the cost of the quartermaster's stores and rations when delivered at the several depots at $5,250,000. The corn costs $4,250,000 more—say $10,000,000 in all for supplies when delivered at the depots, exclusive of the outfit of the troops, wagons, animals, clothing, and stores taken with the troops in their own trains. The great supplies have gone forward in contractors' trains. General Dodge is on a steamer between this and Omaha. The work is done; the troops are launched beyond recall. The expenditures for sending forward stores will not be again incurred, for they have enough to last a year if the troops are judiciously moved. With reference to the depots, in October the force will be reduced, by expiration of enlistment, to 14,000 men, with which it is proposed to make a winter campaign, should that be necessary, and for this the preparations are made, and all stores asked for by the commanding officer have been supplied. It remains to wait for results commensurate with the expense of the preparations and the further daily expense of pay of so large a force. I shall remain here only a few days and then return to Washington.

M. C. MEIGS,
Brevet Major-General and Quartermaster-General.

SOURCE: *OR*, SERIES 1, VOLUME 48, PART 2, PAGE 1167

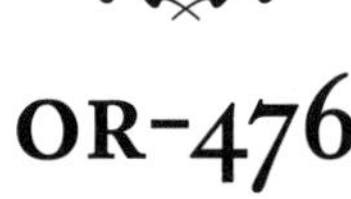

OR-476

FORT LARAMIE, DAK. TER., *August 11, 1865.*

Maj. Gen. G. M. DODGE,
Omaha, Nebr. Ter.:

Have heard from Sixth West Virginia and Twenty-first New York. Former ordered here; latter ordered on mail road between Collins and Sulphur Springs. Also hear of three infantry regiments below Kearny. Men rapidly deserting; regiments will be mere skeletons upon arrival at Kearny. Men of Sixth U.S. Volunteers are also deserting. If troops sent out act this way with us will not have force enough on plains this fall unless additional and reliable regiments are forwarded. A half-way exhibition of power toward hostile Indians will only be productive of evil. Troops sent to Utah should have not less than two years to serve. Am sending Sixth United States and Eleventh Ohio there; both only member 1,400 men. There should be not less [than] 4,000 in Utah to protect the development of the silver mines, the surest and safest method of crushing polygamy and the one-man power now crushing that country. Will you please extend your visit to Laramie.

GEO. F. PRICE,
Captain and Acting Assistant-Adjutant-General.
(In absence of general commanding.)

SOURCE: *OR*, SERIES 1, VOLUME 48, PART 2, PAGE 1178

OR-477

Council Bluffs, Iowa, *August [12], 1865.*

Capt. George F. Price,

Acting Assistant Adjutant-General, Fort Laramie:

Send no troops to Utah until I get up there. War Department has stopped the brigade of infantry en route, and I shall have to get another regiment of infantry from Fort Riley. I leave here Saturday night for Kearny.

G. M. DODGE,
Major-General.

Source: *OR*, Series 1, Volume 48, Part 2, page 1179

OR-478

Fort Laramie, Dak. Ter., *August 12, 1865.*

Maj. Gen. G. M. Dodge,

Omaha or Kearny:

I consider it proper for me to state that the companies of Sixth Volunteers are now concentrating at Middle Park, Colo. Ter., preparatory to march for Utah, over new road via Uinta Valley. It was not proposed to send Eleventh Ohio Cavalry until October, and then over telegraph road. Tour dispatch of to-day, "not to send troops to Utah until you arrive here," raises the question in my mind whether you would desire me, knowing these facts, to countermand order concentrating Sixth U.S. Volunteers. We cannot afford to lose much time in getting infantry en route for Utah. The regiment can concentrate at Middle Park, get ready, and await orders to go on or return, as may be decided. Nearly all the companies are on road for that point and would experience difficulty in countermanding order now, besides creating expense and some confusion. I desire to do right, execute your orders and wishes, in the absence of General Connor, promptly and correctly, and thus honor the confidence reposed in me by my general. This is my excuse for this telegram to you.

GEO. F. PRICE,
Captain and Acting Assistant Adjutant-General.
(In absence of General Connor.)

Source: *OR*, Series 1, Volume 48, Part 2, page 1180

OR-479

Fort Kearny, Nebr. Ter., *August 15, 1865.*

Capt. George F. Price,

Acting Assistant Adjutant-General, Fort Laramie:

(For General Connor.)

General: As I stated, General Pope has sent me positive orders to reduce the troops on the plains, as soon as your expedition is over, to 4,000 men, placing them at the prominent posts on overland route. This, he says, is to be done regardless of the success or failure of your Indian expedition. The War Department ordered the brigade of infantry en route to be sent back from Kearny and mustered out. I have ordered the Fifth United States, about 800 strong, from Fort Riley to you. This, with the Sixth United States and what California infantry you have, is all the infantry we will have this winter to carry out these orders. I see no way of sending more infantry to Utah, and have stopped movement of troops there. If we should get any more allowed us we will have to send cavalry through late in the fall. Powder River I consider of great importance, and you better take the infantry you want for that post out of the Sixth U.S. Volunteers. That portion of the Fifth U.S. Volunteers with Colonel Sawyer's wagon party is ordered to report to you when he discharges them. They must be up in that country some place. You will be the best judge of how much you can take then, and supply other posts. I have represented to the Government in what condition it will place the plains to reduce the force so much if we get no peace. But our orders are positive, and we must now lay our plans for that force on the plains this winter. If you succeed with your expedition it will be all right. Government has assured me that they would not decrease the force now on the plains until expeditions were over, but expect we can begin to do it by middle of October.

* * * *

G. M. DODGE,

Major-General.

[Editor's note: *This document is part of the Powder River Indian Expedition Report, which covers June 20–October 7, 1865. See* OR, *Series 1, Volume 48, Part 1, pages 329–389, for the complete report. See* OR-452 *for the cover correspondence.*]

Source: *OR*, Series 1, Volume 48, Part 1, page 354

OR-480

HEADQUARTERS DEPARTMENT OF THE MISSOURI,
Saint Louis, Mo., August 15, 1865.

Maj. Gen. W. T. SHERMAN,
Commanding Military Division of the Mississippi:

GENERAL: I have the honor to invite your attention to a condition of things among the troops serving in this department which needs attention, and, as it seems to me, should be remedied as soon as practicable. Nearly all of the volunteer regiments serving in this department are dissatisfied, not to say insubordinate and mutinous, from the fact that they believe their terms of service to have expired with the conclusion of the war, and that unjust discrimination has been shown in retaining them for service on the plains, whilst so many other regiments, enlisted under the same circumstances and with the same conditions, have been mustered out of service. Whether right or wrong, they are so possessed with this belief, and their officers so heartily sympathize with them in it, that they are nearly altogether inefficient, and are deserting so rapidly as to threaten disintegration of the organized forces in this department. Matters will undoubtedly be much worse when the reduction I have ordered is made, which will leave only five infantry and two cavalry regiments on duty west of Fort Leavenworth. It is essential that early steps be taken to furnish this department with the five infantry and two cavalry regiments needed for the protection of the overland routes to New Mexico and Utah. These regiments should either be regiments of the regular Army or volunteer regiments enlisted since the conclusion of the war. It might be possible to organize out of the regiments now on duty in the department the number of regiments above designated, but men must be taken for the purpose from the whole number on duty by their own consent. It would be necessary to authorize five infantry and two cavalry regiments to be organized in the department, the officers to be appointed by the President—it is hoped generally on the recommendation of the military commander of the division or department. In this way proper and suitable officers could be selected for the particular service to be done. Whatever may be determined on in the matter, some speedy steps should be taken, in view of the condition of feeling which now obtains. The only reliable troops we have are the U.S. Volunteer regiments, enlisted from rebel deserters and refugees, and even they cannot altogether escape the contagious feeling prevailing among the other regiments. I have the honor, therefore, to invite your attention to the subject in time to prevent embarrassment and trouble. By October 15 the force in the department will be reduced to five infantry and two cavalry regiments, unless I am otherwise instructed. Your attention is asked to my letter of instructions on this subject to General Dodge, dated August 1, a copy of which was furnished for your information during your absence from the city.

I am, general, very respectfully, your obedient servant,

JNO. POPE,
Major-General, Commanding.

SOURCE: *OR*, SERIES 1, VOLUME 48, PART 2, PAGES 1183–1184

OR-481

FORT LARAMIE, DAK. TER., *August 15, 1865.*

Maj. Gen. G. M. DODGE,
Kearny:

I have suspended the marching orders of Sixth U.S. Volunteers until you arrive here. There are only 100 infantry and 430 cavalry in Utah. Will lose half of the infantry by expiration of term of service before Christmas. Balance of infantry has about two years to serve. The cavalry has one year from September next to serve. Not enough troops there to protect the posts in the districts, and what few we have are scattered on mail line east as far as Washakie Station, just the other side of the Rocky Mountains. In case of any Indian troubles in Utah could do absolutely nothing, and no assistance would be rendered us by that archtraitor and violator of Congressional laws, Brigham Young. Utah is rich in mineral wealth, and the only chance to develop that wealth is in having a force sufficient to protect miners who may engage in developing it. The Mormons will never do it. On the contrary, they will do everything they can to prevent it. When the news went to Utah that that sin-ridden Territory was cut off from your command and taken from under the direct influence of General Connor, there went up a great cry of rejoicing from the polygamy traitors. They indulged in all manner of threats, and warned gentiles to leave; that they could not hunt for gold and silver any longer. The Government will make money; reap a thousandfold if now it will by furnishing troops to protect loyal men who propose to open the wealth of that country, and prove it to be, as it is, as rich as any other west of the Missouri River. You will be able to judge whether force on plains can be reduced any. I repeat, and but give the experience of every military man who has served on the frontier and understands the Indian character, that a half-way exhibition of power will only result in evil deplorable evil. These Indians have repeatedly declared that they do not want peace. We should fight them like the fiends they are until they come begging on their hands and knees for mercy. When they do this then we can afford to make peace. They are now proud and insolent. Have been able until lately to dash down on road and destroy everything. They should not only see the power of the Government, but also feel it. If peace is made with them before they are punished it will not last six months; scarcely longer than the time it will take to deliver the presents. That which may appear to be a cruel policy East is really humanity to the Indians, to say nothing of the outrages committed by them upon our women and children. It will be hazardous to weaken our force on the mail and telegraph line. In many places have not sufficient now for want of troops. We can hardly obtain men to do the necessary camp and post duties, so great is the demand for escort and scouting duty. The stage company has finally agreed to place the stock on road between Collins and Sulphur Springs. That could have been done three weeks ago if they had not been scared almost to death about the loss of a few broken-down horses and mules. The general does not yet know that infantry brigade has been ordered back. He should have another infantry regiment for this district and Powder River. One thousand infantry and one regiment of cavalry should be sent to Utah. When you arrive can talk with you fully on these subjects, telling you exactly what General Connor's ideas and plans are. The mail road and telegraph line all quiet. Our cavalry overtook Indians who committed depredations at Big Laramie several days ago, whipped them badly, and is still after them. Quartermaster and commissary stores are arriving at the different depots, and all work pertaining to winter is being pushed as rapidly as it can be under the circumstances.

GEO. F. PRICE,
Captain and Acting Assistant Adjutant-General.
(In absence of general commanding.)

[Editor's note: *This document appears in the* Official Records *as an inclosure to OR-482.*]

SOURCE: *OR*, SERIES 1, VOLUME 48, PART 2, PAGES 1187–1188

OR-482

HDQRS. U.S. FORCES, KANSAS AND THE TERRITORIES,
August 16, 1865.

Maj. Gen. JOHN POPE,
Commanding Department of the Missouri, Saint Louis:

GENERAL: I inclose herewith long dispatch forwarded from General Connor by his acting assistant adjutant general from Fort Laramie. On receiving your instructions I telegraphed General Connor what I should do, and this is a partial response to the telegram. So far matters look well. This depot is in excellent condition, troops in good discipline, but the detachments scattered along the road guarding the overland coaches are not in good discipline. I suppose it is almost impossible to keep up good discipline where troops are so scattered, many of the detachments necessarily under non-commissioned officers. The stage company will not run a coach unless we guard it over every mile. The moment they lose any stock they draw off coaches and we run them, so that the mail has never been stopped, vide the case from Camp Collins to Halleck, which I have now got to running again, and troops enough to keep the route secure. Reports from troops moving up the Republican and Smoky Hill show no Indians in that country, so that they are all north or south of our two overland routes. This guarding stages is terrible on stock.

I am, general, very respectfully, your obedient servant,

G. M. DODGE,
Major-General, Commanding.

[Inclosure.]

[Editor's note: *See* OR-481 *for this inclosure.*]

SOURCE: *OR*, SERIES 1, VOLUME 48, PART 2, PAGE 1187

OR-483

FORT KEARNY, *August 16, 1865.*

Major-General POPE,
Saint Louis, Mo.:

I have received dispatches from General Connor, who arrived on Powder River, 160 miles north of Fort Laramie, on the 11th instant. Says it is an important place and the winter quarters of the Indians. He made an excellent road to it. Plenty of wood, water, bunch grass, and buffalo, but no hay. Has established the post. Has met no Indians, but saw plenty of heavy trails about one week old making toward line of march of center column. At Powder River he leaves his base—trains take stores to last until October—and pushes right north to Panther Mountain, following trail of Indians. His entire command, he says, is in excellent condition. He also sends long dispatches on the reduction of troops, Utah matters, &c., which I will send you by mail; too long to telegraph.

G. M. DODGE,
Major-General.

SOURCE: *OR*, SERIES 1, VOLUME 48, PART 2, PAGES 1188–1189

OR-484

FORT LARAMIE, DAK. TER., *August 21, 1865.*

Maj. Gen. G. M. DODGE,

Alkali or Julesburg:

Durkee, of Wisconsin, has been appointed Governor of Utah. Mormons tried to murder Rev. Norman McLeod, Christian minister now preaching in Salt Lake City, but failed in the attempt. They are growing very insolent because of the small number of soldiers now there and are daily becoming worse. The Indians in Southern and Western Utah are also committing depredations, instigated thereto by Mormon leaders; they are doubtless attempting the same policy which they tried there three years ago, thinking in the absence of troops there will be a fair chance to succeed. That policy is to force every man, woman, and child, not a Mormon, to leave the Territory. The commanding officer of that district earnestly asks for more troops. The gold and silver interests will be seriously jeopardized and gentile life very unsafe this winter if additional force is not sent there. I am thus earnest in pressing this subject upon your attention because I have served in that Territory nearly three years and traveled all over it, and know that this condition of affairs will grow worse, if preventive measures are not adopted. Stage company from Salt Lake City to Virginia City, Idaho, are also earnestly asking for military escorts to protect mails and treasure in transit from marauding copperhead guerrillas, who have fled from east of the Missouri River and are now following their old vocations on that mail road. We have not the troops to give them; Colonel George has not men enough to perform garrison duty. Bela M. Hughes, agent Overland Stage Line, says will not be able to open new road to Denver via Uinta Valley this season, and idea of transferring stage stock to that route this fall is abandoned. This seriously annoys plans heretofore made by us. The steamer Brother Jonathan was wrecked off Crescent City, Cal., July 31 [30], and Brig. Gen. George Wright, U.S. Volunteers and colonel Ninth Infantry, was drowned. He was en route for his new command—the Department of Columbia. He formerly commanded the Department of the Pacific.

GEO. F. PRICE,

Captain and Acting Assistant Adjutant-General.

(In absence of general commanding.)

SOURCE: *OR*, SERIES 1, VOLUME 48, PART 2, PAGES 1199–1200

OR-485

HDQRS. DEPARTMENT OF THE MISSOURI,
Saint Louis, Mo., August 22, 1865

GENERAL ORDERS,
No. 20.

The District of the Plains is hereby abolished, and the following districts established:

. . .

VI. The District of Nebraska—to include the Territories of Nebraska and Montana, and that portion of Dakota lying west of the western boundary of the first-named Territory; headquarters at Laramie. Brig. and Bvt. Maj. Gen. F. Wheaton, U.S. Volunteers, to command.

VII. The District of Colorado—to include the Territory of Colorado, except that portion of the valley of the Upper Arkansas included in the District of Kansas; headquarters at Denver City. Brig. and Bvt. Maj. Gen. E. Upton, U.S. Volunteers, to command.

VIII. The District of Utah—to include the Territory of Utah; headquarters at Salt Lake City. Brig. Gen. P. E. Connor to command.

IX. District of Dakota—to include the counties of Buncombe, Sioux, Plymouth, Osceola, Inson, Emmet, Kossuth, Winnebago, Worth, Mitchell, Howard, Winneshiek, Woodbury, and Allamakee, in Iowa, and the Territory of Dakota, except that portion of the Territory included in the Districts of Minnesota and Nebraska; headquarters at Sioux City. Brig. and Bvt. Maj. Gen. A. Sully, U.S. Volunteers, to command.

The forces to be assigned to these several districts will be communicated to the commanders in letters of instructions.

The officers designated to command the foregoing districts will proceed without delay to their respective headquarters and enter upon the discharge of their duties.

By command of Major-General Pope:

JOS. McC. BELL,
Assistant Adjutant-General.

[Editor's note: *This document is referenced in OR-487.*]

SOURCE: *OR*, SERIES 1, VOLUME 48, PART 2, PAGE 1201

OR-486

HEADQUARTERS DEPARTMENT OF THE MISSOURI,
Saint Louis, August 23, 1865.

Brevet Major-General WHEATON,
Commanding District of Nebraska:

GENERAL: The assistant adjutant-general will hand you the order assigning you to the command of the District of Nebraska. You will please proceed without delay to your command and enter upon the performance of your duties. The permanent military posts in your district are Fort Kearny, Cottonwood, Julesburg, Fort Laramie, and Platte Bridge. In my opinion each of these posts should this winter be garrisoned by three infantry and two cavalry companies, and you had best make immediate arrangements for the necessary supplies for them. There have been sent to the plains by my predecessor in command of this department a large quantity of supplies of every kind, greatly in excess of the wants of the forces you will have in your district. After delivering at each post its supplies for one year you will please have all the surplus collected at some suitable and convenient post and safely stored and protected from the weather. It will not be possible probably this winter to get these supplies back to the depot at Fort Leavenworth, but they can be protected carefully, and the larger part of them will be on hand and fit for issue next season. Please give your special attention to storing and protecting these supplies and all other public property not designed for daily use at the posts. It is possible that you may find it judicious to establish some intermediate small posts in addition to those mentioned; but I think not. In relation to escorts for mail coaches, you must exercise your discretion. It is not, in my opinion, possible to furnish cavalry escorts during the winter without enormous expense and great destruction of horses, but if it be absolutely necessary you might send infantry in wagons from one post to another with the coaches. You should be careful, however, never to send less than thirty men, under a commissioned officer. The details of such matters I must leave to yourself. West of Platte Bridge it may be desirable to establish a post in the valley of the Sweetwater, perhaps at the highest point on that stream, where timber and grass can be found. Of this you can judge when you have looked over the ground. It is proper to inform you that General Connor is now north of Laramie, in command of several columns moving against the Sioux in the direction of the Yellowstone. He has orders to establish a post on or near Powder River, about 125 miles north of Fort Laramie. If established, this post will also be in your command and will be supplied from Laramie. All the Sioux tribes, as also the Cheyennes, are now hostile, but General Sully, with considerable force, is north of them on the Missouri, whilst General Connor is moving up in five columns from various points on the Platte. At last accounts he was on Powder River, moving toward Panther Mountain. It is hoped that before you reach Laramie the hostilities with these Indians will have been settled.

In any event, however, it is the purpose to return to a purely defensive arrangement for the security of the overland routes to Salt Lake. For your district I have decided that one cavalry and two infantry regiments will be sufficient force. I suggest (though without binding you further than as a suggestion) the following distribution of these forces: Fort Kearny, Cottonwood, Julesburg, Laramie, and Platte Bridge should be garrisoned by three infantry and two cavalry companies. If the Powder River post is established, it should be garrisoned by four infantry companies this winter, to which a cavalry company can be added in the spring. If you decide to establish a post on Sweetwater, you will have left to garrison it one infantry and one cavalry company. These dispositions are merely suggested to you as my general impression of the necessities of the situation in your district; to be changed or modified as you may find judicious after looking over the ground. The force I have designated for your district I consider sufficient, and I desire especially, general, to impress upon you the absolute necessity of the strictest economy in your expenditures. It is essential that you return without delay to a peace basis, and to the economical arrangements which obtained before the rebellion. As soon as you have selected the cavalry regiment and two infantry regiments for your district you will please at once relieve all other troops and send them to Fort Leavenworth for muster out of service.

Staff officers of various departments seem to me to abound on the plains, and all such as are not absolutely needed must be ordered to Leavenworth to report by letter to these headquarters. Reduce troops and expenditures to the standard herein indicated without delay. It is expected that by the 15th of October your district will be in all respects organized, and the troops reduced to the force herein designated. Report by letter to Major-General Dodge, who has general command west and south of the Missouri River, and send all reports direct to him. He is now on the plains, but will probably be on his return to Leavenworth before you reach Kearny. General Connor, with the troops operating north of the Platte, will probably come in to Laramie. He is ordered to comply with your requisition for troops, and to send all you do not want to Fort Leavenworth immediately for muster out. You will, however, find troops enough ahead along the Overland Route from Omaha to Laramie to furnish the force designated for your district. My belief is that the best disciplined and most trustworthy troops to be retained for the winter are the regiments of U.S. volunteers which you will find along the route. There is so much dissatisfaction and insubordination in the volunteer regiments now serving in your district, arising from the belief that as the war is ended they are entitled to discharge from the service, that they are not efficient, and will be less so every day. Make your selection of regiments, however, as best suits you, being careful only to select those having until next spring or summer to serve. As soon as you have posted your troops, relieve and send to Fort Leavenworth all others without delay. I leave you, general, to carry out these instructions, having full confidence that you will do so vigorously and promptly.

I am, general, respectfully, your obedient servant,

JNO. POPE,
Major-General, Commanding.

SOURCE: *OR*, SERIES 1, VOLUME 48, PART 2, PAGES 1206–1208

OR-487

HEADQUARTERS DEPARTMENT OF MISSOURI,
Saint Louis, Mo., August 24, 1865.

Brig. Gen. P. E. CONNOR,
Commanding District of Utah:

GENERAL: You will receive herewith the order assigning you to the command of the District of Utah and breaking up the District of the Plains.* You will please proceed to your command at the earliest practicable moment and enter upon the performance of your duties. One regiment of infantry and one of cavalry are assigned to your district, and no more troops must be kept there under any circumstances. I desire also to say to you that hereafter it is expected, and will be required of all officers serving in this department, that they do not interfere with officers of the disbursing departments within their districts, except so far as they are required by regulations to overlook them in the performance of their duties. All contracts and payments on contracts must be made hereafter by officers of the proper department according to law and regulations, and no account for any expenditure in violation of either will be admitted or paid, and if paid by any commanding officer's order the amount will be charged to him at the Treasury. It is impossible for any officer who attends promptly to his own duties to be able also to attend to the duties of his subordinates. I make these remarks because there has been much complaint of you in this direction, and many accounts of an extraordinary character made by you have been reported to me as paid by your orders. I do not mean to say that these expenses were not necessary, but hereafter I am very sure that with proper management the necessity will not again arise, and I desire you always to take such precautions in advance that nothing will be needed in your command which cannot be had in the usual and legal way. Your familiarity with the country and the circumstances of your command render any instructions from me unnecessary. I desire you to make such arrangements for the protection of the overland routes in Utah as you consider necessary and are capable of making with the force assigned to your command. All troops, except the regiment of infantry and the regiment of cavalry designated as the force of your district, will be put in march for Fort Leavenworth, or other proper points for muster out, without the least delay. If General Wheaton calls upon you for any of this surplus force, you will detach it to report to him. You will report by letter to Major-General Dodge, who has general command west and south of the Missouri River, and send your official reports to him.

I am, general, respectfully, your obedient servant.

JNO. POPE,
Major-General, Commanding.

* [*Refers to OR-485.*].

SOURCE: *OR*, SERIES 1, VOLUME 48, PART 2, PAGE 1209

OR-488

HEADQUARTERS DEPARTMENT OF THE MISSOURI,
Saint Louis, Mo., August 25, 1865.

Maj. Gen. W. T. SHERMAN,
Comdg. Military Division of the Mississippi, Saint Louis, Mo.:

GENERAL: I inclose herewith the order* establishing districts in this department, concerning which I have already conferred [*sic*] verbally with you. I also send the detailed instructions given to each district commander. In answer, therefore, to inquiries of the General-in-Chief and War Department, it will be ascertained by summing up the forces specially assigned in these instructions to each district, that the entire force to be retained in this department amounts to seven regiments and one battalion of infantry and four regiments of cavalry, an aggregate force, when the regiments are full, of 5,600 infantry and 4,800 cavalry. About two-thirds of this force are all that [can] be relied on as effective. These regiments will be distributed as follows: Minnesota, one infantry regiment and six companies of cavalry; in Northern Iowa and that portion of Dakota Territory lying along and east of Missouri River, one infantry regiment and six companies of cavalry; in Kansas, to include the Upper Arkansas River as far as to include Fort Lyon, one regiment and one battalion of infantry and seven companies of cavalry; in Colorado Territory, one infantry regiment and five companies of cavalry; in Nebraska and Montana and that portion of Dakota Territory west and south of the Missouri River, two regiments of infantry and one of cavalry; in Utah, one regiment of infantry and one of cavalry. This is the least force, in my opinion, which can perform the service required. West of Fort Leavenworth there are 3,500 miles of overland routes to California and New

Mexico to protect. The whole distance traversed is through the Indian country, and the overland routes are new and will for some time be infested by wandering parties of lawless white men, lately bushwhackers and deserters from the army, and men from the disbanded rebel armies. These men prowl through that whole region of country and are more dangerous to travelers than the Indians themselves. All outrages committed by them are, however, charged upon Indians, and it requires great vigilance to prevent retaliation from being practiced upon Indians guiltless of offense. A much larger force is required on the plains than has heretofore been considered necessary, arising from the state of facts set forth in my communication of August 1 to Col. R. M. Sawyer, assistant adjutant-general. Military Division of the Mississippi, an extract from which is submitted.†

By the 15th of October at latest the whole force of this department will be reduced to the number above stated, and expenditures brought down to that scale. I need not say that the accumulation of supplies on the plains and the large requisitions sent on were made before I came into command of this department. My whole attention has been given since I assumed command to reduce everything to the lowest point which actual necessity demands. As there seems to be great anxiety and some misapprehension in Washington concerning the condition of troops in this department, I have the honor to request that copies of this letter be furnished to the General-in-Chief and Secretary of War.

I am, general, very respectfully, your obedient servant,

JNO. POPE,
Major-General, Commanding.

* [*Refers to* OR-*485*.]

† The extract (omitted) begins with "The Indian question is the most difficult," and ends with "expenses can be easily settled." [*See* OR-*467*.]

SOURCE: *OR*, SERIES 1, VOLUME 48, PART 2, PAGES 1210–1211

OR-489

FORT LARAMIE, *August 29, 1865.*

Maj. Gen. JOHN POPE,
Saint Louis, Mo.:

Your dispatch about troops, commanders, &c., received. By your last dispatch you assign to General Connor's old district 3,200 infantry and 3,000 cavalry. On the 1st of November there will be only 1,500 infantry in the command. This includes

Fifth U.S. Volunteers, on march from Fort Riley. Do you want me to make up the number from cavalry? I have already ordered in, in accordance with your instructions of August 1 (including those whose term of service expires between now and November 1) enough to reduce the force in Nebraska, Colorado, and Utah to the number you designate in to-day's dispatch, and in that force to be retained I do not count troops with General Connor. In Utah we have only 400 men. There are four companies with General Connor that will make it 600 when they return. To make up the balance I shall have to send cavalry. In counting the troops I take every man belonging to the regiments that are present in my command, those left in New York, Washington, and East I don't suppose we will ever see. I learn from regimental commanders that they have unofficially learned that most of them have been mustered out. Please answer about infantry. The regiments that we will have are the Fifth and Sixth U.S. Volunteers and 280 men of Veteran Battalion Third California Infantry.

G. M. DODGE,
Major-General.

[Editor's note: *This document is part of the Powder River Indian Expedition Report, which covers June 20–October 7, 1865. See* OR, *Series 1, Volume 48, Part 1, pages 329–389, for the complete report. See* OR-452 *for the cover correspondence.*]

SOURCE: *OR*, SERIES 1, VOLUME 48, PART 1, PAGE 355

OR-490

FORT LARAMIE, *August 29, 1865.*

Major-General POPE, *Saint Louis, Mo.:*

Following received from General Connor:

HEADQUARTERS POWDER RIVER EXPEDITION,
Near Fort Connor, August 20, 1865.

Maj. Gen. G. M. DODGE:

I have the honor to acknowledge the receipt of two telegrams of 11th instant from Maj. Gen. John Pope in reference to instructions to column commanders and contracts in Utah. The general's and your own instructions will he implicitly obeyed. I hope on mv return to give such explanations as will be deemed satisfactory.

P. E. CONNOR,
Brigadier-General, Commanding.

G. M. DODGE,
Major-General.

[Editor's note: *This document is part of the Powder River Indian Expedition Report, which covers June 20–October 7, 1865. See* OR, *Series 1, Volume 48, Part 1, pages 329–389, for the complete report. See* OR-*452 for the cover correspondence.*]

SOURCE: *OR*, SERIES 1, VOLUME 48, PART 1, PAGES 356–357

OR-491

FORT LARAMIE, *August 29, 1865.*

Maj. Gen. JOHN POPE,
Saint Louis, Mo.:

Following dispatch from Salt Lake forwarded:

SALT LAKE, *August 25, 1865.*

The Salt Lake Telegraph comes out this morning defying Government. Says polygamy must live and die with Mormonism, and if interfered with will be washed out with blood.

MILO GEORGE,
Lieutenant-Colonel, Commanding.

G. M. DODGE,
Major-General.

SOURCE: *OR*, SERIES 1, VOLUME 48, PART 2, PAGE 1220

OR-492

HEADQUARTERS U.S. FORCES,
Fort Laramie, Dak. Ter., August 31, 1865.

Maj. Gen. JOHN POPE,
Saint Louis, Mo.:

I consider the Indian matters here of so much importance, and knowing no one can judge of them so well as when he is on the ground that I desire to make one proposition to the Government. If the Government will allow me to keep General Connor in the field with not to exceed 2,000 men of his present force, leaving the forces you have designated to garrison posts on the plains, I will settle these Indian difficulties before spring satisfactorily to the Government, and bring about a peace that will be lasting. I may do it in a month or two, or it may take longer. The additional expense to the Government will be the pay of that number of troops for the time detained. All the stores, forage, &c., to support them are here and en route. As soon as we settle with them we can send these troops in and take 2,000 more from our posts in addition and muster them out. General Connor left Powder River with sixty days' supplies, and I am satisfied if we will allow him time he will settle the matter before he returns. Should he come back by our orders without settling the matter, the entire Indian tribes will be down on our lines, and we will have our hands full, and more too. The forces for Utah I will soon have on the road, and when Connor gets back he can go right there.

G. M. DODGE,
Major-General.

SOURCE: *OR*, SERIES 1, VOLUME 48, PART 2, PAGES 1220–1221

OR-493

HDQRS. U.S. FORCES, KANSAS AND THE TERRITORIES,
Fort Laramie, Dak. Ter., September 1, 1865.

Capt. GEORGE F. PRICE,
Acting Assistant Adjutant-General, District of the Plains:

CAPTAIN: The garrison for Utah I have concluded to designate as follows: Three Michigan regiments, after being consolidated, say, 1,000 men; Second Battalion Nevada Cavalry,* 314 men; Second Battalion California Cavalry (now with General Connor), 183 men; First Battalion Veteran California Infantry, 250 men; three companies Sixth U.S. Volunteers, 275 men. These troops will be sent forward to Utah as fast as circumstances will permit. The three Michigan cavalry regiments, after my return from Powder River, and the Twenty-first New York Cavalry, had better be distributed from Camp Collins west, so as to cause no delay in movements of the consolidated Michigan regiments when the order arrives.

Very respectfully, your obedient servant,

G. M. DODGE,
Major-General, Commanding.

* [Editor's note: *Dyer's* Compendium *(1:176) lists only one cavalry battalion from Nevada.*]

SOURCE: *OR*, SERIES 1, VOLUME 48, PART 2, PAGE 1222

OR-494

SAINT LOUIS, MO., *September 2, 1865.*

Major-General DODGE:

I have rearranged districts west of Leavenworth. Elliott in command of Kansas, Upton of Colorado, Wheaton of Nebraska, including that portion of Dakota west of Nebraska, headquarters at Fort Laramie, and Connor of Utah. As soon as Connor returns from his expedition send him to Utah. Whole force in Utah, one infantry and one cavalry regiment. No more force than this must be sent to Utah under any circumstances. To Wheaton I have designated two regiments of infantry and one of cavalry; to Upton one regiment of infantry and five companies of cavalry; to Elliott one regiment of infantry and seven companies of cavalry. These forces are to be selected by the district commander from the troops in his district or those with Connor and Sanborn; every other man to be sent back to Leavenworth for muster out immediately. These officers are ordered to go to their districts and report by letter to you for duty. Each of them is furnished with detailed letter of instructions from me designating posts to be occupied in each district, and its garrison. I send copies of these instructions to your headquarters at Leavenworth, and have ordered each district commander who may see you on his way out to show his copy to you. Should enforce these instructions without delay. The pressure upon me about expenses on the plains is tremendous. Whether reasonable or not, the demands of the Government must be complied with. See that corn for the winter is safely stored for two companies of cavalry at Kearny, Julesburg, Cottonwood, Laramie, and Platte Bridge. There will be two companies of cavalry, and no more, at each of these posts, and corn must be saved in store for them from supplies now on the plains. I send Connor's instructions to Laramie, to be forwarded to him in Utah in case he has left. He must positively not interfere again in contracts or disbursements with the proper staff officers unless they violate law. Whatever the result of Connor's expedition, come down at once and energetically to the standard here laid down, and hurry back all other troops to Leavenworth for muster out. I have ordered all Sanborn's force, except 500 men, to go back to Leavenworth at once for discharge. Commissioners will meet Indians on Arkansas at time specified.

JNO. POPE,
Major-General.

[Editor's note: *This document is part of the Powder River Indian Expedition Report, which covers June 20–October 7, 1865. See* OR, *Series 1, Volume 48, Part 1, pages 329–389, for the complete report. See* OR-*452 for the cover correspondence.*]

SOURCE: *OR*, SERIES 1, VOLUME 48, PART 1, PAGES 355–356

OR-495

DEPOT QUARTERMASTER'S OFFICE,
Fort Leavenworth, Kans., September 15, 1865.

Bvt. Maj. Gen. M. C. MEIGS,
Quartermaster-General U.S. Army:

General: I have the honor to present herewith my annual report for the year ending on the 30th day of June, 1865.

. . .

GENERAL REMARKS.

Upon my arrival here I found a state of affairs existing of which I had no previous conception. Major-General Curtis was in command, with Capt. M. H. Insley as chief quartermaster of the department, who was also the depot quartermaster at Fort Scott. For some reason all the certified accounts of the department were being paid by Captain Hodges, the depot quartermaster, instead of the chief quartermaster, to whom such payments properly belonged. Stories of immense frauds were rife, and it was with the utmost care that any fixed data could be found to determine the status of a large number of vouchers afloat and settle upon the mode and manner of payment. Great complaints had been made that certain parties and districts had been deprived of their fair proportion of the funds sent out for the purpose of settling the indebtedness. I adopted the rule of paying a certain percentage to all claimants, until each specified amount furnished was exhausted. This plan seemed to work equal justice to all the parties interested, and soon, by the timely remittances from Washington, the greater part of this floating indebtedness was liquidated. Many of these vouchers were informal and issued by officers temporarily placed on duty as acting assistant quartermasters, and a just and fair discrimination has been exercised, to the best of my ability, to pay none but legitimate expenditures. The disbursements have been large, as will be seen by the statements.

The matter of transportation has been a subject of much study on my part, as all the supplies for the vast region of country from Utah, on the northern route, and Santa Fé, on the southern route, with all intermediate posts, have to be supplied from this depot.

From all the information I have been able to collect, from observation and other sources, I am compelled to say that I think the system of contracting freight is erroneous; that the delays, damages, &c., arising from the careless mode of shipment and want of proper care will be in a great measure avoided by using nothing but Government trains. It is not a sufficient compensation to the Government that the contractor is obliged to pay for the articles lost or damaged in transit, for it often happens that the articles most needed for immediate service are wanting. In scarcely any instance have any articles been missing from our own trains. Time, also being an important element in the shipment of supplies, is saved by the greater rapidity of the Government trains. The contractors are only bound to get all the stores through by a certain date in the fall. No contract should be made unless it has an ample though fixed time for the delivery, dating from the day of shipment. The large accumulation of stock at this depot, teams and wagons, will enable us to send forward, at all times, stores as they may be needed. From the above and many other reasons not necessary now to relate, I am decidedly in favor of the Government doing its own transportation, except in special cases. At such times the depot quartermaster can always hire trains at special rates, not exceeding the present contract rates.

From present appearances the great point of departure for trains another season will be Fort Riley, or that vicinity. The Union Pacific Railroad will be completed to that point, I am assured, by May next. It will be much cheaper for the department to pay transportation direct to Fort Riley, and send across from that point to Kearny, than to ship from Leavenworth. If good progress is made in the railroad from Omaha west, that will be the route for all goods destined for the northern line of posts, via Julesburg and Halleck, while the goods for Denver, Salt Lake, and Santa Fé should go via Riley; those destined for Denver and Utah via the Butterfield route, and those for Santa Fé by the old Santa Fé trail.

The depot of Fort Leavenworth will always be of great importance as the base of distribution for the supplies for all Western posts. From time to time extensive warehouses have been erected, which, although now crowded to their utmost capacity, by the large overstock on hand, and the accumulation from the breaking up of other posts, will, under all ordinary circumstances, be sufficient for the department. At present we are obliged to put up temporary sheds for the extra store-room needed.

Water-works have been ordered for the supply of the post and depot, and will be erected during the winter. A large amount of timber on that part of the Government reserve east of the Missouri River will be made available for use as soon as the steam mills now ordered are put into operation. The improved farms have yielded well this year, and will be a source of profit to the department.

I cannot too strongly urge upon the department the necessity for watching with the utmost care and preventing by timely remonstrance all attempts on the part of scheming politicians to get the reserved lands into market for the purpose of speculation. No one not perfectly well acquainted can estimate its value. I need not extend this report, as the merits and extent of operations at Fort Leavenworth are too well known to need comment.

Respectfully submitted.

J. A. POTTER,
Colonel and Quartermaster.

[Editor's note: *This document appears in the* Official Records *as an inclosure to correspondence from Brevet Major-General M. C. Meigs to the Hon. Edwin M. Stanton, Secretary of War, November 8, 1865, that is not included in this volume.*]

SOURCE: *OR*, SERIES 3, VOLUME 5, PAGES 464–465

OR-496

HDQRS. DEPARTMENT OF THE MISSOURI,
Saint Louis, Mo., September 19, 1865.

GENERAL ORDERS,
No. 27.

In accordance with the terms of General Orders, No. 251, 1864 War Department, Adjutant-General's Office, the Districts of Kansas, Nebraska, Dakota, Colorado, Utah, and Minnesota being composed of mixed troops, each equivalent to a brigade, are hereby designated as separate brigades.

By command of Major-General Pope:

JOS. McC. BELL,
Assistant Adjutant-General.

SOURCE: *OR*, SERIES 1, VOLUME 48, PART 2, PAGES 1234–1235

OR-497

No. 52

QUARTERMASTER-GENERAL'S OFFICE, EIGHTH DIVISION,
Washington, D.C., October 10, 1865.

Bvt. Maj. Gen. M. C. MEIGS,
Quartermaster-General U.S. Army, Washington, D.C.:

GENERAL: In consequence of my continued absence on inspection duty your circular of the 24th of July, 1865, requiring from the chief of each division a full report of the operations of his division during the fiscal year ending June 30, 1865, was not brought to my notice until yesterday, but I hope to be able to furnish all the important data in time to be embodied in your annual report to the Honorable Secretary of War.

. . .

Col. J. D. Cruttenden, inspector, Quartermaster's Department, was directed on the 17th of September, 1864, to proceed to Devall's Bluff, Ark., and enter upon a series of inspections in the Departments of Arkansas, Missouri, Kentucky, Tennessee, Kansas, and Colorado.

He was continuously employed upon such duties until August 30, 1865, when he was granted a leave of absence by the War Department for fifteen days.

On the 20th of September, 1865, he was directed to proceed upon another tour of inspections comprising the District of the Plains and Utah.

The total number of reports received from him during the fiscal year is fifteen, and since the close of said year seven; total, twenty-two.

. . .

[Editor's note: *This document appears in the* Official Records *as an inclosure to correspondence from Brevet Major-General M. C. Meigs to the Hon. Edwin M. Stanton, Secretary of War, November 8, 1865, that is not included in this volume.*]

SOURCE: *OR*, SERIES 3, VOLUME 5, PAGES 324–326

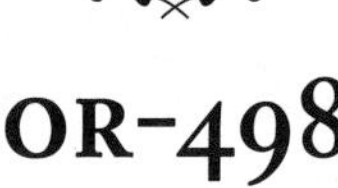

OR-498

SAINT LOUIS, MO., *October 16, 1865.*
(Received 8 P.M.)

Lieut. Gen. U. S. GRANT:

It is too late in the season to get troops out farther than Fort Kearny. Two regiments colored troops can be used this winter west of Leavenworth to replace two regiments white troops. Two more could probably be used for the same purpose in New Mexico. They could be sent in the winter via Texas. In the spring all troops needed in Minnesota, on the Upper Missouri, the Platte, and in Utah and New Mexico might be colored troops. Two regiments (colored) can be used west of Leavenworth this winter.

JNO. POPE,
Major-General.

SOURCE: *OR*, SERIES 1, VOLUME 48, PART 2, PAGES 1240–1241

OR-499

[*Extract*]

HDQRS. U.S. FORCES KANSAS AND THE TERRITORIES,
Fort Leavenworth, November 1, 1865.

COLONEL: I have the honor to submit the following report of operations in this command from the date of my assignment to the present date:

I arrived here and assumed command July 20, 1865, and in a few days thereafter started on the plains to make a personal inspection and examination of all troops, posts, routes, &c., within my command; to direct and supervise on the ground such changes and dispositions as wore deemed necessary, and to give my personal attention to matters generally. I proceeded from here to Omaha, from there to Fort Kearny, thence up the Platte, taking all intermediate posts and stations en route to Fort Laramie; thence to Powder River; thence to Denver, via base of the mountains; thence to the Middle Park, and returned along the Smoky Hill Fork of the Kansas River and via Forts Ellsworth and Riley, reaching here on the 18th ultimo, having traveled with escort and train over 2,000 miles. I deem it proper to embody the following subject-matter in my report: First, the operations of troops during the present year; second, the overland routes and the matter and method of protecting them; third, the character of the country, the means for and difficulty of supplying the troops in it; fourth, the policy now being pursued toward the Indians, and wherein in my opinion it should be different. I deem it proper to recur to the fact that when the Department of Kansas was merged into the Department of the Missouri in February last, I repaired to Fort Leavenworth and opened the Platte and Arkansas overland routes, which I found obstructed by the Indians. I found then, and so reported, that a general campaign against the Indians who were hostile would have to be made, and to that end troops [were] obtained and supplies sent to all posts on the plains. These facts, with my plan for operations, I submitted to the major-general commanding the Military Division of the Missouri, by whom I was instructed to make preparations accordingly. I was notified of the number of troops that would be sent me, and thereupon based my estimate for supplies and my instructions to district commanders. Supplies were ordered sent to the District of the Plains, which included Nebraska, Utah, and Colorado, for 12,000 men for one year for operations east of Rocky Mountains, and to the District of Upper Arkansas, including the southern overland route, for 7,000 men for six months. I also received instructions to place supplies in Utah for 3,000 men, but for reasons which will hereafter appear supplies for only 2,500 men were sent there. The contract for transporting the supplies was made by the Quartermaster's Department at

Washington and not closed until the 1st of May. The contractors were given from that time until the 1st of December to complete their contract, no time being specified for the delivery of any Supplies at designated points earlier than the limit named. This alone was almost fatal to my operations north of Fort Laramie, as after the troops arrived there they were detained from four to six weeks, for supplies that had been sent from here and been on the road from two to three months, and we had finally to haul supplies for General Connor's columns by Government trains from Fort Kearny and Cottonwood before they could move.

In forming my plans for the campaign my understanding was that the hostile Indians were to be punished at all hazards, and this I intended to do, knowing if I was allowed to press the campaign according to my plans that before another spring a satisfactory and durable peace could be obtained. My general plan of operations was marked out as follows, viz: General P. E. Connor, commanding District of the Plains, was to move against the northern Indians in three columns; General J. B. Sanborn, commanding District of Upper Arkansas, to move with three columns against the southern Indians, and two separate columns, small and light, were to move, respectively, up the Republican and Smoky Hill Forks of the Kansas River, and keep the country between the Platte and Arkansas Rivers free from Indians, and aid in keeping the great overland routes unobstructed. In addition to these dispositions troops had to be kept posted on the Platte stage and telegraph lines from Fort Kearny, via both Denver and Fort Laramie to Salt Lake City and along the Arkansas route to New Mexico. General Connor's columns were to be about 1,500 men strong each, but the non-arrival of troops reduced the number to an aggregate of 2,500, and to obtain which I had to strip the Platte route. He (Connor) moved with his force as follows, viz: One column, under Colonel Cole, Second Missouri Light Artillery, going up Loup Fork along east base of the Black Hills, crossing the Little Missouri at or near Bear Butte; thence across to near the forks of Little and Big Powder Rivers; thence to point of junction, some fifty miles from the Yellowstone, on Tongue River. One column, under Lieutenant-Colonel Walker, Sixteenth Kansas Cavalry, to move from Fort Laramie directly north along the west base of the Black Hills, crossing at head of the Little Missouri, and thence across Powder River to point of junction named. The third column, under General Connor in person, with supplies for three columns for use after effecting the junction, moved up the North Platte to its most northerly bend; thence due north to Powder River, and after establishing the post of Fort Connor, some 180 miles northwest of Laramie, moved along east base of the Big Horn Mountains to the point of junction on Tongue River. Instructions to General Connor and other district commanders are hereto appended, marked A. After a portion of these columns had moved and were all in the field I received the dispatches and instructions from Major-General Pope, which, together with my answers thereto and action thereon, arc hereto appended, marked B.

The troops ordered hither to take the place of troops taken by General Connor, after having been transported from Washington and elsewhere at great distance, and then marched to Fort Kearny, Julesburg, Fort Laramie, &c., were ordered mustered out of the service without any benefit whatever being received from them, and also after we had been at the expense of equipping them fully, and also transporting supplies to the plains for their use. By this means the number of men for use on the north were reduced from the number calculated upon, say 12,000 men, to less than 6,000, and many of them were mutinous, dissatisfied, and inefficient. It must be borne in mind that I had about 2,600 miles of overland mail and telegraph line to protect in addition to carrying on the campaign. I think that under all the circumstances General Connor accomplished all that could possibly be expected, as will be seen by his report of operations. Despite all obstacles he succeeded in chastising one tribe of Indians a manner seldom before equaled and never excelled. He also punished two other tribes quite severely, and has, I think, thoroughly explored the idea so commonly advanced, viz, that the Plains Indians on the warpath cannot be over-taken and whipped in battle. Could General Connor have moved in June, or even by July 1, I have no doubt he would have succeeded in inflicting thorough and effectual chastisement upon all the tribes in hostility on the north, and have carried out my instructions in the matter fully and completely. Copies of telegrams in relation to his campaign received and sent by me after he had moved I append hereto, marked C. For a full report of General Connor's operations, fights, &c., I respectfully refer you to his report and to the reports of his column commanders, Colonel Cole and Lieutenant-Colonel Walker, which are forwarded herewith.* Colonel Cole is entitled to great credit for the manner in which he met and overcame the many obstacles he had to contend with. Having been misled by his guides, who seem to have been entirely ignorant of the country he was in, and by the report of his scouting party sent to find General Connor, he concluded that there was a misunderstanding as to the point of junction designated, although he was then, in fact, within sixty miles of General Connor's column, and therefore moved on down Powder River, intending to go to the Yellowstone; thence up that stream, and from thence up Tongue River until he found the place of junction or struck General Connor's trail; but the severe snow-storm that killed so many of his animals and the appearance of Indians induced him to move south, take the trail of the Indians, and pursue them as far as possible, by doing which he succeeded in getting three fights, in which he chastised the Indians very severely, killing large numbers of them. An officer attached to my headquarters, who accompanied Colonel Cole as engineer, states that he saw over 200 dead Indians that were killed in these fights.

The failure on the part of General Connor's column commanders to join him at the point designated no doubt prevented him from carrying out his plans fully and successfully. Lieutenant-Colonel Walker, it seems, made no effort whatever to communicate with General Connor or ascertain his position. General Connor returned to Fort Connor, intending to reorganize an expedition from Colonels Cole's and Walker's commands and complete his campaign; but for reasons that appear in his report this was not done, and he (Connor) proceeded to Utah, in compliance with orders from Major-General Pope. Aside from the engagements detailed in the reports of General Connor and Colonels Cole and Walker, a number of fights of more or less importance were had with the Indians by my troops during the past season, in most of which the savages were chastised, in attacks upon trains, post detachments, &c. Deports of these have from time to time been made by telegraph to department headquarters. Copies of some of these telegrams are hereto appended, marked D. During General Connor's absence on his expedition the Indians deserted the overland routes and followed him to protect their families and villages. I therefore conclude that the most effectual way to protect these routes while these Indians are hostile would be to keep a movable force in the heart of their country ready to strike them at all times . . .

In July last a portion of the Third California Veteran Infantry, under Lieutenant-Colonel Johns, left Salt Lake to accompany the Overland Stage Company in opening the new route from Salt Lake, via the Uintah Valley, White River, Middle Park, and Berthoud (or Boulder) Pass, to Central City and Denver. This force reports the route practicable. They met no Indians except the Utes, who were friendly, and found no obstacles that could not be easily overcome, except the Berthoud (or Boulder) Pass, which will require considerable work before it can be used as a stage or emigrant route. This route, it is said, would save 200 miles in distance over any other route between Denver and Salt Lake. With reference to the overland routes I shall speak fully, and, I trust, clearly. The country over which they pass is, however, so marked and peculiar that they are all in many particulars much alike. After passing a belt of country about 150 miles in width that borders on the Missouri River, we strike the plains, some 400 or 500 miles in width, extending from thence to the base of the mountains with the exception of occasional spots—small, indeed, compared with this immense extent. These plains are not susceptible of cultivation or settlement. This great belt of barren country extends from the Missouri River on the north to the Canadian on the south, being the extent of any travels upon it. The valleys as a general thing are covered with grass often luxuriant and suitable for hay. The uplands generally have a straggling growth of buffalo grass, but are often, for miles, entirely destitute of vegetation, except occasionally the prickly pear, cactus, or sage bush. No part of this great area is susceptible of raising grain or vegetables except on a few streams, and then by irrigation; nor does it, as yet discovered, possess any mineral resources. It is almost entirely destitute of wood, and running water cannot be depended upon except along the great streams that rise in the Rocky Mountains, flow east, and empty into the Missouri or Mississippi or the streams rising in the Black Hills, Big Horn, and Powder River Mountains, and which flow north, emptying in the Yellowstone. Up the great valleys and even over the higher tables are the best natural roads in the world, and nature has so constructed them that through this great belt there are four great water-courses traversing it at right angles at distances from each other of from 100 to 200 miles. Commencing, then, on the north the first overland route is known as the Niobrara, up which stream the road runs to its source, and up to this time crosses to the Platte, terminating at Fort Laramie. Colonel Sawyer's wagon party endeavored this season to find a road on this route through directly to Montana, via Powder River and north of Little Horn River, but the obstacles met with determined them to abandon it, and they struck south and took the road made and explored by General Connor from Fort Laramie to base of Big Horn Mountains; thence to Three Forks of the Missouri and thence to Virginia City. This from the Platte is a line natural road, and, with the exception of running water for 100 miles from the Platte to Powder River, is abundantly supplied with clear running water, grass, wood, and game. This road is marked *aa* on map.

The road heretofore used to Montana was up North Platte via South Pass, thence up Snake River, &c. The new road, on which Fort Connor is situated, saves in distance some 350 miles, making the distance now only about 450 miles from Fort Laramie to Three Forks of the Missouri. The military operations this summer have opened this road, and as soon as our Indian troubles in that region are over it wall he the great overland route from the States to Montana. All travel concentrating from the different routes east of Fort Laramie will take that road from this converging point. This road, I believe, has an appropriation from Congress which when expended upon it, will make it equal to any route over the plains and across the mountains. The second route is known as the Platte route. Starting at different points on the Missouri River, such as Omaha, Plattsmouth, Nebraska City, Atchison, Saint Joseph, Leavenworth, Kansas City, &c., the roads all converge at or near Fort Kearny, and following the Valley of the Platte to its forks, either leads up the North Platte via Fort Laramie, South Pass, and Salt Lake, or up Lodge Pole, through Cheyenne and Bridger's Pass to Salt Lake, or continuing up South Platte go to Denver, or diverge and pass up the Cache la Poudre to Laramie Plains; thence through Bridger's Pass to Salt Lake. On this route at all times (and for the past eleven years to my knowledge) an abundance of grass, water, and wood for all practicable purposes has abounded. It has the best passes through the mountains, and it is by far the best natural road from the Missouri River to the Pacific Coast. The telegraph, mail, and express lines are on this route, and most of the emigration passes over it. From March 1 to August 10 of this year there passed Fort Kearny on this route going west 9,380 teams and 11,885 persons, which conveys some idea of the vast amount of trade, travel, and capital that is showing to the great mineral regions of Colorado, Utah, Montana, and Idaho. In going via this route west from Denver choice can be taken of the new route through Berthoud Pass and via White River and Uintah Valley, surveyed and explored the past summer by Lieutenant-Colonel Johns and party, and which is now being opened.

. . .

On the Arkansas River route Fort Riley and Fort Lyon are fine military posts. The intermediate posts are, however, poorly built, and are really unlit for troops to occupy, and lack proper protection for stores. It has been expected that most of these posts would be abandoned, hence no more expense than was actually and unavoidably necessary has been incurred in fitting them up. On the new route to Montana I recommend that posts be established at or near where the road crosses the Tongue and Big Horn Rivers. On the Smoky Hill route there are only five companies stationed, which, owing to troops being stationed along the routes north and south, is sufficient protection. Over these several routes must pass all, not only supplies for the mighty empire springing up in the mining regions of Colorado, Arizona, Utah, Montana, New Mexico, and Idaho, but also the great trade and emigrant travel to California and Oregon. As I have before stated, the country east of the Rocky Mountain range and west of the narrow fertile belt that borders the Missouri is not susceptible of cultivation or settlement—an occasional few acres only along the streams can be irrigated and made to produce crops. It therefore follows that, from the States must henceforth be sent across the plains, not only bread-stuffs to feed, and articles of manufacture to supply the hundreds of thousands now there, but also a population rapidly increasing by an immense yearly emigration which is forming a mighty empire now nearly in its infancy, an empire rich in mineral resources, and destined, with its wealth of precious metals, to form the future basis of our financial system, and even now, to a great extent, is furnishing the means to sustain the credit of the country. In view of these facts I cannot but consider it the duty of Government to promptly adopt such measures as will effectually protect these overland routes and render them at all times safe and secure. To do this the Indians of the plains, who for the past eighteen months have in deadly hostility beset these routes, and who persist in their hostility, must be so severely chastised as to make them beg for peace, repent their hostility, and in future deter them from a repetition of the outrages, in the commission of which they have for so long been engaged. This must be done or the Indians entirely removed from the country. In no other way can the end sought be accomplished. The cost of doing this would, I know, be great, but if it is necessary and unavoidable Government should not shrink from it, and now that we have the matter in hand, whilst it would cost us thousands to complete it effectually, it would, if deferred to the future, cost hundreds of thousands. I believe that with the force we had at our disposal, if we had been allowed to retain and use it, have held it in the country and pushed the campaign fall, winter, and spring, before another season every hostile tribe would have been effectually and justly punished, and made to feel our power and dread our anger forever after. . .

. . .

I take great pleasure in calling the attention of Government to the valuable services of Brig. Gen. P. E. Connor, whose promotion I heartily and earnestly recommend. This I do after careful observation and personal inspection of his past labors in organizing his district, establishing his posts and depots, and the successful management of his expedition, all under the most embarrassing circumstances and overwhelming difficulties. He has successfully protected the routes under his charge, and has kept up regular mail and telegraph communication, often by using his troops to carry the mail and rebuild the telegraph lines when interrupted by Indians and the stage and telegraph companies refused to do so; in fact he has throughout exhibited an energy, capacity, and fidelity to duty rarely excelled. I forward herewith maps of the country over which my command extends, showing the overland routes, posts, &c., and the routes taken by the different expeditionary columns during the past season.† I have, at the risk of making this report too voluminous, endeavored fully and plainly to embody and discuss all legitimate subjects of interest, believing it my duty to present these matters in their true light.

All of which is respectfully submitted.

I am, colonel, very respectfully, your obedient servant,

G. M. DODGE,
Major-General, Commanding.

Bvt. Lieut. Col. Jos. McC. Bell,
Asst. Adjt. Gen., Department of the Missouri, Saint Louis, Mo.

* Connor's and Walker's reports not found. [*For Cole's September 25, 1865 report see* OR, *Series 1, Volume 48, Part 1, pages 380–383.*]

† Maps not found.

[Editor's note: *This document is part of the Powder River Indian Expedition Report, which covers June 20–October 7, 1865. See* OR, *Series 1, Volume 48, Part 1, pages 329–389, for the complete report. See OR-452 for the cover correspondence.*]

Source: *OR*, Series 1, Volume 48, Part 1, pages 335–348

OR-500

[*Extract*]

Quartermaster-General's Office,
Washington, November 8, 1865.

Hon. Edwin M. Stanton,
Secretary of War:

Sir: I have the honor to submit the annual report of operations of the Quartermaster's Department during the fiscal year ending 30th of June, 1865:

. . .

Transportation Over the Plains.

The troops operating on the great Western plains and in the mountain regions of New Mexico, Colorado, Utah, and Idaho are supplied principally by the trains of the Quartermaster's Department from depots established on the great routes of overland travel, to which depots supplies are conveyed by contract. The contractors are the freighters or merchants of the overland trade. This department has not statistics to show the extent of this traffic, but it has of late years increased with the development of the mines of the central region of the continent until it has become a most important interest. Travelers by the stage from Denver to Fort Leavenworth, a distance of 683 miles, in the month of July, 1865, were never out of sight of wagon trains, belonging either to emigrants or to the merchants who transport supplies for the War Department, for the Indian Department, and for the mines and settlers of the central Territories.

Cost of transportation of a pound of corn, hay, clothing, subsistence, lumber, or any other necessary from Fort Leavenworth to—

Fort Riley	$0.0246
Fort Union, the depot for New Mexico	.1435
Santa Fé, N. Mex.	.1685
Fort Kearny	.0644
Fort Laramie	.1410
Denver City, Colo	.1543
Salt Lake City, Utah	.2784

The cost of a bushel of corn purchased at Fort Leavenworth and delivered at each of these points is as follows:

Fort Riley	$2.79
Fort Union	9.44
Santa Fé	10.84
Fort Kearny	5.03
Fort Laramie	9.26
Denver City	10.05
Salt Lake City	17.00

To this last point none is now sent.

The expenses of this department will be reduced by the advance of the Pacific railroads, two of which are rapidly moving westward, one from Leavenworth toward Fort Riley and the other from Omaha toward Fort Kearny.

The present general mode of transport is by heavy wagons, each drawn by ten oxen. The loads of these wagons average 5,500 pounds each. Lighter freight and passengers are carried by express in lighter wagons, drawn by mules, which animals are almost exclusively used in the winter when the grass is covered with snow.

The heavy trains in dry weather move readily over the prairie roads, which outside the limits of the settlements follow the best routes, and can make wide detours to avoid sloughs or wet places in the prairies. The progress of settlement injures these roads. No laws appear to exist reserving the road bed on these great overland routes to the public. The lines of survey of the public lands cross the trail at all angles, and each farmer is at liberty to fence in his tract according to the unyielding lines of his rectangular boundaries.

These overland trails, now well-beaten wagon tracks, were originally located upon the high and dry swells of the prairie, the most desirable land for agricultural purposes. They followed the best routes and sought the easiest crossings of the streams, low grounds, and swamps. Near Leavenworth the progress of inclosure is driving them into the wet grounds, and greatly increases the difficulties of travel.

It is much to be desired that in all future land sales the great and long-established trails, the highways across the continent, should be reserved from sale and be devoted forever as public highways. A certain width on each side of them should be marked out by actual survey and reserved for this purpose. Wagon roads across the continent will always be needed, even when the railroads are completed.

The following is an estimate of the cost of transportation of military stores westward across the plains by contract during the fiscal year ending June 30, 1865:

I. Northern and western route:		
To Utah and posts on that route		$1,524, 119.00
II. Southwestern route:		
To Fort Union, N. Mex., and posts on that route	$1,301,400	
Posts in the interior of New Mexico	138,178	
		1,439,578.00

Cost of the transportation of grain on above routes, where the grain was delivered by contractors and the transportation entered into the price paid, same year—

1. Utah route	$2,526,727,68	
2. New Mexico route	697,101.69	
		3,223,829.37

Cost of transportation of military stores across the plains same year by Government trains—

1. Utah route	$34,600	
2. New Mexico route	166,730	
		201,330.00
Total by contract and Government trains		6,388,856.37

This expenditure would be reduced by the opening of railroads by a sum which would aid materially in paying interest upon the cost of their construction.

The present season has been a very wet one upon the plains. In wet weather the heavy wagons are generally compelled to go into camp and wait patiently till dry weather makes the roads practicable. Any effort to move exhausts the animals and destroys the wagons, while the progress of such a train would not average in bad weather over many portions of the roads one mile a day. Trains from Fort Leavenworth to Denver City have this year occupied from forty-five to seventy-four days in the march.

. . .

I transmit herewith reports of officers, with many tables, giving in detail information of value in relation to the operations of the department. To these I respectfully call your attention.

All of which is respectfully submitted.

M. C. MEIGS,
Brevet Major-General, U.S. Army, Quartermaster-General.

SOURCE: *OR*, SERIES 3, VOLUME 5, PAGES 212–249

OR-501

[*Extract*]

WAR DEPARTMENT,
Washington City, November 22, 1865.

MR. PRESIDENT:

The military appropriations by the last Congress amounted to the sum of $516,240,131.70. The military estimates for the next fiscal year, after careful revision, amount to $33,814,461.83. The national military force on May 1, 1865, numbered 1,000,516 men. It is proposed to reduce the military establishment to 50,000 troops, and over 800,000 have already been mustered out of service. What has occasioned this reduction of force and expenditure in the War Department it is the purpose of this report to explain.

. . .

But now the approaching session of Congress will find the authority of the Federal Government effectually and peacefully exercised over the whole territory of the United States. All the armies heretofore arrayed against the National Government have laid down their arms and surrendered as prisoners of war. Every hostile banner has been hauled down; the so-called Confederate Government is overthrown; its President is a prisoner in close custody, awaiting trial; while its Vice-President and three of its chief executive officers have been recently enlarged from prison by your clemency. All the ordinances, laws, and organizations created or existing under or by virtue of the so-called Confederate Government have been swept away, and by your sanction the people of the insurgent States have organized, or are busily engaged in organizing, State governments in subordination to the Federal authority. In harmony with this new condition of affairs the military force of the Federal Government has been reduced, large armies disbanded, and nearly a million of brave men, lately soldiers in arms, paid and honorably mustered out of service, have gone from camps, garrisons, and posts to their homes, and most of them are engaged already in the peaceful pursuits of civil life.

Among the causes which under Divine Providence have brought about these wonderful results, successful military operations stand first in order.

. . .

The present military organization comprehends nineteen departments, embraced in five military divisions, as follows:

. . .

7. The Department of the Missouri, Maj. Gen. John Pope to command, to embrace the States of Minnesota, Iowa, Missouri, and Kansas, and the Territories of Colorado, Utah, Nebraska, Dakota, New Mexico, and Montana. Headquarters at Saint Louis.

. . .

Indian hostilities upon the plains and the overland routes to the Pacific Coast have given much annoyance, required the employment of many troops, and occasioned great expense to the military department. Several Indian councils have been held during the past season and large military expeditious sent out against hostile tribes and bands. What has been accomplished by treaty or by fighting will doubtless be exhibited in the official reports of the Indian campaigns, which have not yet reached the Department.

Disbanding the troops reduces at once the amount to be expended in some items of appropriation, but in others requires larger immediate expenditures. Upon their discharge the soldiers became entitled to all the installments of bounty which would have fallen due at later periods, and in many cases exceeding a year's pay. The transportation of large armies from the field in Southern States to their remote homes in the West, or in Eastern and Northern States, made extraordinary drafts on the Quartermaster's Department beyond what would be required for armies marching or encamped. The vast amount of live-stock on hand requires forage until sales can be made. These are effected with the utmost diligence; but still this large item of expenditure continues through a large part of the fiscal year. The financial effects, therefore, of the reduction of the Army and retrenchment of expenditures can only operate to any great extent on the next fiscal year.

. . .

Adjutant-General's Report.

. . .

From the report of the Adjutant-General it will be seen that the recruiting service of the Regular Army is progressing favorably, the number of recruits enlisted for all arms from October 31, 1864, to October 1, 1865, having been 19,555. The regiments comprising it have been distributed to stations, and their ranks are rapidly filling up, thus enabling the Department to relieve regiments of volunteer troops. The present authorized strength of the regular regiments is 1,570 officers and 41,819 enlisted men. This estimate is made on the basis of 42 privates to a company, the number now allowed by law at all except frontier posts. It is recommended in the report that the maximum standard be fixed at 100 enlisted men to a company.

. . .

The arrangements for the care of discharged troops being completed, orders to muster out and discharge the forces from service were issued as follows:

April 29.—All recruits, drafted men, substitutes, and volunteers remaining at the several State depots.

May 4.—All patients in hospitals, except veteran volunteers and veterans of the First Army Corps (Hancock's).

May 8.—All troops of the cavalry arm whose terms of service would expire prior to October 1.

May 9.—All officers and enlisted men whose terms would expire prior to May 31, inclusive.

. . .

May 29.—All organizations of white troops whose terms of service would expire prior to September 30, inclusive, in armies and departments, except Departments of the East, New Mexico, Pacific, and Northern.

June 2.—All surplus light artillery; that only absolutely required by the necessities of the service in the respective armies and departments to be retained.

June 5.—All dismounted cavalry, all infantry in the Northern Department and Department of the East, and all cavalry in the Department of the East.

. . .

5. The faith of the people in the national success, as manifested by their support of the Government credit, also contributed much to the auspicious result. While thousands upon thousands of brave men filled the ranks of the Army, millions of money were required for the Treasury. These were furnished by the people, who advanced their money on Government securities and freely staked their fortunes for the national defense.

Looking to the causes that have accomplished the national deliverance, there seems no room henceforth to doubt the stability of the Federal Union. These causes are permanent, and must always have an active existence. The majesty of national power has been exhibited in the courage and faith of our citizens, and the ignominy of rebellion is witnessed by the hopeless end of the great rebellion.

EDWIN M. STANTON,
Secretary of War.

SOURCE: *OR*, SERIES 3, VOLUME 5, PAGES 494–535

OR-502

[*Extract*]

HEADQUARTERS DEPARTMENT OF CALIFORNIA,
San Francisco, Cal., December 6, 1865.

Lieut. Col. ROBERT N. SCOTT,
Asst. Adjt. Gen., Mil. Div. of the Pacific, San Francisco, Cal.:

SIR: In answer to your letter of yesterday I have to report that, in compliance with General Orders, No. 10, from division headquarters, "to immediately muster out of service such volunteers as could be dispensed with from my command," the following corps were ordered to be mustered out, to wit: The Sixth California Volunteer Infantry, the Eighth California Infantry, six companies of the Fourth California Volunteer Infantry; the three companies of Nevada infantry, the two companies of Nevada cavalry, serving in the department; the battalion of four companies Native California Cavalry. Of these the field and staff and seven companies of the Sixth Regiment have been mustered out (October 25 and 31). Two of the companies of the Sixth were at Summit Lake, beyond the Sierra Nevada, on the road to Idaho. A small company of the Ninth U.S. Infantry (regulars) is on the march to relieve them, and when last heard from was beyond the Sierra. The lateness of the season and the heavy storms will, I fear, obstruct the road and retard the line of march of the companies of the Sixth, and make it impossible to give a date for their arrival and muster out. Another of the companies of the Sixth Regiment was at Camp Lincoln, near the Indian reservation on Smith River; a company of the Ninth has gone up to relieve it, but the storms were so heavy that the steamer could not bring the volunteers back. They are expected by the next steamer. The field and staff and all the companies of the Eighth Regiment mustered out October 24, except four of the officers on a court-martial. These were mustered out November 7. Five of the companies of the Fourth Regiment mustered out November 30. The other company ordered to be mustered out was serving in Oregon, and has not yet arrived under the orders given at division headquarters.

The company of Nevada infantry serving at Fort Ruby, on the overland route, will be mustered out as soon as the company of the Ninth (regular) Infantry, now on the march, arrives to relieve it. When last heard from this company was one day's march beyond Fort Churchill. The company of Nevada infantry at Fort Churchill will be mustered out as soon as the company of cavalry ordered there from northern Nevada arrives. The company of Nevada infantry at Fort Independence, Owen's River Valley, will be mustered out of service as soon as relieved by the company of California volunteer cavalry, now en route. As in the case of companies at Summit Lake, this post lies beyond the Sierra Nevada, which is now covered with snow. The relieving company has been obliged to march to the south through Walker's Pass, instead of direct across the mountain. It has, however, arrived by this time, and the company of Nevada infantry will soon be on the march to Fort Churchill to be mustered out, which will be toward the end of the month. The battalion of Native California Cavalry was serving in southern Arizona and will not be able to reach its place of muster-out for sometime, as it has to make a march of over 500 miles, much of it over a desert.

In addition to these corps, a detachment at Fort Churchill belonging to the Nevada cavalry serving in Utah, and detachments at the Presidio belonging to the Second California Volunteer Infantry, and Native California Volunteer Cavalry in Arizona have been mustered out. As I do not consider that they can be "dispensed with" I have not given orders for the muster-out of the Second California Volunteer Cavalry, for there is no regular cavalry in the department that could be sent to relieve it, and it is stationed in California and Nevada at points that require protection, and some of it engaged in active hostilities against the Indians. Nor have I given orders for the muster out of the volunteer regiments and companies, serving in Arizona; for the reason that they are now occupied in a vigorous campaign against the Apaches, for which large and expensive preparations have been made, and to carry on which the two battalions of the Fourteenth, even when they reach that far-off country, will be wholly inadequate. The First Battalion, recently arrived, will proceed there as soon as practicable; moving two companies at a time, which, on account of the scarcity of water on the desert, is the largest number that can march with comfort. There remains in the District of Humboldt, at Hoopa Valley and at the Indian reservation at Round Valley, two companies of the Second and one company of the Fourth California Volunteer Infantry. A long and expensive Indian war was waged in that section, which required from two to three regiments. A large number of the hostile Indians were made prisoners and sent to the Round Valley Reservation, and others have been located on the Hoopa Valley Reservation; I do not think it prudent at this time to withdraw the volunteer companies from those reservations.

. . .

I have the honor to be, very respectfully, your most obedient servant,

IRVIN McDOWELL,
Major-General, Commanding Department.

SOURCE: *OR*, SERIES 1, VOLUME 50, PART 2, PAGES 1288–1290

OR-503

[*Extract*]

HEADQUARTERS MILITARY DIVISION OF THE PACIFIC,
San Francisco, Cal., December 8, 1865.

Lieutenant-General GRANT,
Commanding Armies of the United States, Washington, D.C.:

GENERAL: In compliance with your directions, I inclose herewith maps of the Departments of California and the Columbia, on which are marked the several posts at present occupied by troops of this military division. The following remarks are submitted by way of explanation:

. . .

INDIAN FRONTIER.

In regard to the protection of the Indian frontier on the east, the policy should be to keep the troops in advance, retain them in rear of the white settlements, and to make the posts as temporary and cheap as possible. These should be maintained as depots of supplies for expeditions against the Indians and the temporary camps which may be established in their country. As these camps will be continually changing, they should be of the most temporary character. Tents and huts constructed by the troops will usually be sufficient.

. . .

NEVADA.

Fort Ruby will serve as a center of operations for the protection of the overland mail and emigrant roads to Salt Lake and the settlements on Humboldt River beyond Dun Glen. An inspecting officer has been sent to examine its condition, and will probably report in a few days. Fort Churchill is simply a depot. Some of the temporary camps near the boundary (northern) of the State must depend on it for supplies.

. . .

TROOPS.

I must again urge upon you the necessity of sending a cavalry force to this division. We have now no mounted troops in Washington, Oregon, Idaho, and Nevada, and in California and Arizona only the California volunteers, who regard their term of enlistment as having expired and wish, to be mustered out. These troops are made up of most excellent material, but men who regard themselves as unjustly retained in service will not be very efficient in the field. You will bear in mind that when your orders for mustering out the volunteers are completely carried out, the only forces in this entire division will be the Second Artillery and Ninth and Fourteenth Infantry. The Ninth is only a small regiment. The artillery will be required to garrison the forts on the coast, and the Ninth Infantry in the interior of California and Nevada.

. . .

Very respectfully, your obedient servant,

H. W. HALLECK,
Major-General, Commanding.

SOURCE: *OR*, SERIES 1, VOLUME 50, PART 2, PAGES 1290–1293

OR-504

[*Extract*]

WAR DEPARTMENT,
Washington City, November 14, 1866.

MR. PRESIDENT:

Disbandment of the volunteer forces in service at the time the rebel armies surrendered; collecting the arms, ordnance, and military stores scattered over the vast theater of war; the sale and disposition of unserviceable material; storing in arsenals, magazines, and depots that which might be used; settling and adjusting war claims; recruiting and organizing the Regular Army under the recent act; the establishment of posts and garrisons on the frontier and in the Indian country; testing the various improvements of breech-loading small-arms, and supplying them to the Army; practical experiments to determine the destructive power of projectiles and the comparative resisting qualities of materials; completing seaboard defenses and providing them with armaments; planning and carrying on harbor and river improvements—these, with the administration of the laws relating to refugees, freedmen, and abandoned lands, have constituted the chief operations of the War Department during the past year.

The entire number of volunteer troops to be mustered out was, on May 1, 1865, 1,034,064, and my last annual report recounted the operation of disbanding this force until November 15, 1865, when 800,963 troops had been transported, mustered out, and paid. The work was actively continued after that date, and on January 20, 1866, 918,722 volunteers had been mustered out; February 15, 952,452; March 10, 967,887; May 1, 986,782; June 30, 1,010,670; November 1, 1,023,021—leaving in service 11,043 volunteers, white and colored. The aggregate reduction of the colored troops during the year has been 75,024, and at this date one regiment of artillery and thirteen of infantry, numbering about 10,000 officers and enlisted men, remain in the service. Commenced in May, 1865, the work of discharging and returning to their homes 1,034,064 volunteers would have been completed within three months but for the necessity of retaining in service part of that force. Past experience shows that, should any national emergency require a larger force than is provided by the peace establishment, armies could be swiftly organized to at least the full strength of a million of men.

. . .

The present organization of military departments and divisions is as follows:

. . .

The Department of the Platte, Brig, and Bvt. Maj. Gen. Philip St. George Cooke to command, to embrace the State of Iowa, the Territories of Nebraska and Utah, so much of Dakota as lies west of the one hundred and fourth meridian, and so much of Montana as lies contiguous to the new road from Fort Laramie to Virginia City, Mont. Headquarters at Omaha.

. . .

The permanent defenses of the country have been strengthened. Their efficiency has already been much increased by substituting cannon of larger caliber and improved model for lighter guns, and wrought-iron for wooden gun carriages. This work is still in progress, and will be continued. Diligent and careful efforts, based upon the designs and recommendations of competent boards of engineers, have been made to adapt old works, as well as those in process of construction, to more powerful armaments. Construction has been suspended upon some works in order to await the completion of important experiments having in view the extensive use of iron shields or armor for the protection of guns and gunners. The results already attained give the promise of a practical and highly beneficial application of the knowledge obtained by these trials.

. . .

In conclusion it gives me pleasure to again express my obligations to the chiefs of bureaus and their subordinates, who, in reducing the War Department to a peace establishment, have evinced the same diligence, ability, and fidelity to the interests of the Government that distinguished them during the labors, anxiety, and vicissitudes of the war, and contributed so much to its successful termination.

EDWIN M. STANTON,
Secretary of War.

SOURCE: *OR*, SERIES 3, VOLUME 5, PAGES 1031–1045

CHAPTER 5

Additional Records from Utah Territory

THIS CHAPTER CONTAINS ADDITIONAL WARTIME RECORDS CREATED in or involving Utah Territory. None of these records were published in the *Official Records* or the *Supplement to the Official Records* (see appendix C). They have been collected from a variety of sources (which are listed at the end of each record) and are listed chronologically. Original spelling and punctuation has been retained. See chapter 3 for additional details regarding these records.

UT-1

RECORD OF EVENTS, POST RETURN OF CAMP FLOYD FOR JANUARY 1861
FEBRUARY 14, 1861

The name of the post was changed to "Fort Crittenden" on the 6th February, see G[eneral]. O[rders]. No 3 from the Department of Utah dated Febr 6th 1861.

C. F. SMITH
Lieut. Col. 10th Infantry
& Bvt. Col. U.S.A.
Commanding the Post.

HEAD QUARTERS, FORT CRITTENDEN, U.T.
February 14th 1861

[Editor's note: *We were unable to locate a copy of General Orders No. 3, dated February 6, 1861, that renamed Camp Floyd as Fort Crittenden. This January 1861 report was completed and signed on February 14, 1861.*]

SOURCE: "POST RETURN OF CAMP FLOYD, U.T. . . . FOR THE MONTH OF JANUARY 1861," RETURNS FROM U.S. MILITARY POSTS 1800–1916, NATIONAL ARCHIVES, RG94, M617, ROLL 268

UT-2

[*Extract*]

Record of Events, Post Return of Fort Crittenden for April 1861
May 12, 1861

Regiments.	Letters of Companies.	Number of Companies.	Present.							
			Commissioned Officers.			Enlisted Men.				
			For duty.	In arrest, or suspension.	Total.	For duty.	On extra or daily duty.	Sick.	In arrest, or confinement.	Total.
Regular Garrison.										
General Staff.			1	–	1	2	–	–	–	2
10th Infantry.	"E" and "J"	2	3		3	78	12	2	1	93
2d Dragoons.	Field and Staff and Cos "B" "E" and "H"	3	3	1	4	142	18	12	3	175
4th Artillery.	"A" "B" and "C"	3	9		9	151	24	2	9	186
	Total	8	16	1	17	373	54	16	13	456
Attached.										
Ordnance Depart			–	–	–	2	–	–	–	2
Casually at Post.										
2d Dragoons.	Field Staff and Band		2	–	2	18	–	2	–	20
10th Infantry.	"A"		–	–	–	1	–	–	–	1
5th Infantry.	"A"		–	–	–	–	–	–	–	–
	Total.		2	–	2	19	–	2	–	21

Regiments.	Letters of Companies.	Number of Companies.	Absent.											
			How.								Where.			
			Commissioned Officers.					Enlisted men.			Within the Dept. (See note 2.)		Without the Dept. (See note 2.)	
			On detached service.	With leave.	Without leave.	Sick.	Total.	On detached service.	In arrest, or confinement.	Total.	Commissioned Officers.	Enlisted men.	Commissioned Officers.	Enlisted men.
Regular Garrison.														
General Staff.			–	–	–	–	–	–	–	–	–	–	–	–
10th Infantry.	"E" and "J"	2	2	1	–	–	3	9	–	9	–	8	3	1
2d Dragoons.	Field and Staff and Cos "B" "E" and "H"	3	3	1	1	1	6	4	2	6	1	–	5	6
4th Artillery.	"A" "B" and "C"	3	3	–	–	–	3	11	1	12	–	10	3	2
	Total	8	8	2	1	1	12	24	3	27	1	18	11	9
Attached														
Ordnance Depart			–	–	–	–	–	–	–	–	–	–	–	–
Casually at Post.														
2d Dragoons.	Field Staff and Band		–	–	–	–	–	–	–	–	–	–	–	–
10th Infantry.	"A"		–	–	–	–	–	–	–	–	–	–	–	–
5th Infantry.	"A"		–	–	–	–	–	–	–	–	–	–	–	–
	Total		–	–	–	–	–	–	–	–	–	–	–	–

[Editor's note: *Each monthly post return includes tabular strength reporting information. The tables above have been included to show the size of Colonel Philip St. George Cooke's Utah forces as the Civil War began.*]

Source: "Post Return of Camp Floyd, U.T. . . . for the month of April 1861," Returns from U.S. Military Posts 1800–1916, National Archives, RG94, M617, Roll 268

UT-3

Colonel Philip St. George Cooke to Colonel Lorenzo Thomas
May 26, 1861

H^D^ Q^RS^ Dept. of Utah
Fort Crittenden, *May 26/61*

Sir,

I have just observed in several newspapers that I have been appointed a Brigadier General of Virginia Volunteers; After above 30 years pretty zealous service under the Stars and Stripes,—I once captured the "Army" of a Southern State—this announcement is a surprise, in fact, I think it a mistake, for the name of a Virginia gentleman which is very similar to mine in print: be this as it may, I feel called upon to remove the false impression likely to result from this publication.

I therefore write to make known that I am faithful to my oath: I have long considered the sovereignty and independence of States, a vain and foolish political cry; it has proved a wicked one. I love my Country. I owe her a great debt: my sense of duty would forbid me now, even to retire to private life, it would be to forsake her Standard in her hour of peril.

Very respectfully

P S[T] GEO COOKE
Colonel 2d dragoons

Col. L. Thomas
Adjt. Genl. U.S. Army
Washington City.

[Editor's note: *The following file notation accompanies this correspondence: "Rec[d]. (AGO) June 7/61. Writes to correct the false impression likely to be produced by the publication of his name, in connection with an appt. of brigadier General, of V*[*irgini*]*a Vol's." A small undated and uncited newspaper clipping follows Colonel Cooke's letter, the text of which is included below.*]

Army Appointments.—So far as we have been able to find out, the following army appointments have been made:

Aids to the Governor of Virginia.—J. F. Lay, with rank of Colonel of Cavalry by Brevet; John Echols, with rank of Colonel of Cavalry by Brevet; S. Bassett French, with rank of Lieutenant Colonel of Cavalry.

Robert E. Lee, Major General Commanding Military and Naval forces of Virginia.

Joseph E. Johnston, Major General of Volunteers.

P. St. George Cooke, Brigade General of Volunteers.*

John B. Magruder, Colonel of Volunteers.

Henry Heth, Lieut. Colonel of Volunteers.

R. S. Ewell, Lieut. Colonel of Volunteers.
J. R. Crenshaw, Major of Volunteers.—[Richmond Whig.]

* [Editor's note: *Actually, Philip St. George Cocke, a Confederate brigadier general, West Point Class of 1832, Cullum #667. Philip St. George Cooke was West Point Class of 1827, Cullum #492.*]

Source: "Received by the Office of the Adjutant General (Main Series), 1861–1870," National Archives, RG94, M619, Roll 11

UT-4

Record of Events, Post Return of Fort Bridger for May 1861
June 1, 1861

Company "I" 10th Inft., Capt Gove, arrived at this post May 28 1861. Pursuant to S[pecial] O[rders] 25 & 26 Hd. Q[uarter]s: Dept. of Utah dated Fort Crittenden UT. May 14/1861. Captain Jesse A Gove assumed command of the post May 29, 1861.

JESSE A. GOVE
Captain, Inf.
Commanding the Post.

Fort Bridger, U.T.

June 1st 1861

Source: "Post Return of Fort Bridger, U.T. . . . for the month of May 1861," Returns from U.S. Military Posts 1800–1916, National Archives, RG94, M617, Roll 146

UT-5

Colonel Philip St. George Cooke to the Assistant Adjutant General
June 10, 1861

Fort Crittenden U.T.
June 10" 1861

Sir:

I probably cannot form a conception of the magnitude and the absorbing nature of the labours of the Lieut General, and fear being considered importunate in recurring to the subject of my letter of the 25th February last: but I consider the matter of the cavalry Instruction of much importance.

My manuscript of a new system of tactics ~~which~~ is in the War Department; it could be printed and published in a very short time, and in my absence. A great merit claimed for it, is that its simplicity will give a much prompter efficiency to newly raised Cavalry. Old officers will find enough resemblance to the old system—its chief complications, the results of two ranks, being left out,—to make it easy and natural in a week.

I am partly induced to renew the subject in consideration of the promptitude and facility of legislation now to be expected (the Lieut General recommending): my system would be favored by a partial reorganization: (a bill will be found with the M. S.). The chief change, however, is the addition of a lieutenant to each company:—the company becoming the unit of manoeuvre, as well as of administration and discipline, and practically, the squadron,—as it is named in the bill.

Very respectfully
Your obedient servant

P St GEO COOKE
Colonel 2d Dragoons

To the Asst. Adjt. General
Army Head Quarters
Washington City

[Editor's note: *The following War Department file notation accompanies this correspondence: "Fort Crittenden Utah June 10/61. P S G Cooke, Col. 2 Drgs. Relative to Cavalry Tactics." The text below is also annotated on the file. Colonel Cooke's appeal on behalf of his book was successful. Entitled* Cavalry Tactics, or Regulations for the Instruction, Formations, and Movements of the Cavalry of the Army and Volunteers of the United States, *his book was published in 1861 by the Government Printing Office, Washington, D.C. Cooke authored a companion volume,* Handy Book for United States Cavalry, *published in 1863 by J. B. Lippincott & Company.*]

Head Quarters Army,
July 8, 1861.

Respectfully forwarded to the Adjt. Genl.

E. D. TOWNSEND
A. A. Genl.

Source: "Letters Received by the Office of the Adjutant General (Main Series); 1861–1870," National Archives, rg94, M619, Roll 12

UT-6

Major F. E. Hunt, Capt. R. E. Clary, and J. B. Porter to Simon Cameron, Secretary of War June 15, 1861

We, the undersigned, believing that forbearance may cease to be a virtue, and may under present circumstances become a crime; or in other words, that duty to our country in its present distracted state requires every good citizen to expose treason & rebellion and the aiders & abettors of traitors & rebels–even to the slightest circumstances–will state, for the information of the Secretary of War, and through him for the information of the President of the United States (if the Secretary of War considers it of sufficient importance): that the Governor of this Territory, A. Cumming, has openly declared himself a secessionist; approved of the course of that arch traitor, David E. Twiggs, in surrendering the troops & supplies in Texas; and when leaving this Territory, still holding the commission & drawing the pay of Governor from the United States, did give, as we have heard & believe, as a toast at Fort Bridger: "Success to the Southern Confederacy." That Wooton, the Secretary of the Territory declares himself openly a secessionist. That Crosby, the only Judge remaining ~~remaining~~ in Utah, says it is hard to decide which is the Government of the United States, the North or South, and that while he is in the city of the Saints he declares himself a secessionist, but when at Fort Crittenden among loyal officers he declares himself a Union man. That Col. Cooke, commanding the Department, has two sons in law & one son who have resigned, or contemplate resigning, to join the rebel forces. That he himself has stated that if Virginia, his native State, went out of the Union he would not resign, but would not raise his hand against her; but that if Missouri, his adopted State went out, ~~of the Union~~ he would resign & join her; that when Capt. F. Gardner resigned & left his command without having permission to leave from the proper authority, Col. Cooke sent one of the hottest secessionists in the camp to Fort Bridger to make an inspection of the post & report thereon; that upon the return of this officer, Lt. Robertson (now Capt. Robertson, 2nd Drgs.), Lt. Armistead, another secessionist at Fort Bridger, ~~at Fort Bridger~~ forwarded his unconditional resignation; that upon this Lieut. Robertson informed Lt. Armistead by "Pony Express" he should have asked for a leave of absence; that upon tender of said unconditional resignation & Lt. Armisteads after application for leave, Col. Cooke gave Lt. Armistead thirty days leave of absence to prevent the State of Virginia being disgraced by the desertion of one of her sons. That Lt. Robertson, then Ast. Adjt. Genl., informed Col. Cooke that he could not keep Lt. Armistead; that he would go when he was ready, the same as he, Lt. Robertson would do; that he would resign & join Virginia if she went out of the Union; that neither Col. Cooke nor any other power could stop him from going when he was ready to go. That in the latter part of February last Lt. Goode, of the 4th Artillery, gave at Camp Floyd as a toast: "The assassination of Lincoln & Hamlin before the 4th of March"; which toast was drank by Lts. Sanders & Merritt, of the 2nd Drgs. & that Lt. Gordon, of same regiment, declared at the time he would drink ~~it~~, but that he did not want to drink then. Mr. W. Dyer, a citizen, of the firm of Dyer & Bro. former Sutlers of the 7th Infantry, drank the toast. That Capt. Gibbon, of the 4th Artillery, has declared if his State North Carolina went out of the Union he would go with her, and scoffed at the idea of an officer remaining loyal to the Union if his State seceded. That whilst Lt. Robertson was Act. Asst. Adjt. Genl. the band of the 2nd Drags. for months past played almost daily the tune called "Dixie," which is believed by many of the loyal officers of this post to be the national air of the secessionists; that on Washington's birthday this was the only tune they played. That upon Lt. Green's becoming Act. Asst. Genl. he gave orders to the band not to play Dixie except by direction of the Col. Comdg. the Dept.; & that on the 14th June, during the absence of Col. Cooke & Lt. Green the band played Dixie at the request of someone at Capt. Gibbon's, believed to be Capt. Gibbon himself, communicated through Capt. Gibbon's little daughter to the band. That upon the reading of the "pony dispatches at Fort Crittenden announcing the fall of Fort Sumpter, Lt. Gordon waved his hands over his head in token of joy. That Lt. Saunders has declared his intention repeatedly to resign & join the Southern Confederacy, & tried to borrow funds of his brother officers for that purpose, but failed; and we believe the sole reason why he has not resigned is not having the wherewith to get away. This communication is not sent through the ordinary channel, the reason for which will be obvious to the proper authorities.

Signed by MAJOR F. E. HUNT,
CAPT. R. E. CLARY, AND
J. B. PORTER,
Surgeon U.S.A.

FORT CRITTENDEN, U.T.
June 15, 1861.

ADDITION

The foregoing was fully concurred in, except in relation to Col. Cooke, whose sentiments in regard to secession are unknown to the subscriber. There can be little doubt about the other persons named. Capt. Gibbon did have the obnoxious "Dixie" played by the band on the 14th instant, much to the annoyance of loyal officers at Fort Crittenden.

(Signed) J. B. PORTER,
Surgeon U.S.A.

The above addition may vary a word or two from the original, but there is no change of meaning.

J. B. PORTER, *Surgeon U.S.A.*

[Editor's note: *This is a copy of a letter sent by F. E. Hunt, R. E. Clary, and J. B. Porter to the Secretary of War on June 15, 1861. Clary is identified here as a captain, though elsewhere in this correspondence his rank is listed as major. National Archives Records Group 94, Microform 619, Roll 65, contains additional correspondence regarding charges and counter-charges from and to Hunt, Clary, and Porter regarding the loyalty of Colonel Philip St. George Cooke and other army officers stationed in Utah. Only selected documents from that correspondence have been included here. See* UT-7, UT-8, UT-9, UT-10, *and* UT-11.]

SOURCE: "LETTERS RECEIVED BY THE OFFICE OF THE ADJUTANT GENERAL (MAIN SERIES); 1861–1870," NATIONAL ARCHIVES, RG94, M619, ROLL 65

UT-7

COLONEL PHILIP ST. GEORGE COOKE TO BREVET BRIGADIER GENERAL LORENZO THOMAS JUNE 17, 1861

HEAD QUARTERS DEPMT. OF UTAH
Fort Crittenden *June 17" 1861*

SIR,

It will appear from the enclosures marked A. & B. that I brought to the light of day a copy of a secret report to the War Department; the signers would unmistakably appear to have used their association with gentlemen to note their most unguarded expressions of confiding social intercourse, for the information of the Department; but as it is believed not to have established a lion's mouth I take the course, which it would have been my duty to take, if these officers had obeyed the orders of the President of the United States—as they had so lately sworn to do—constrained in par: 441 of the Army regulations:—that is, I have ordered copies for the information of those affected: I have enabled the department.—as I have not the slightest doubt it would desire, and have required—to hear both sides a very essential, and a very American maxim of justice.

Dr. Porter excepts the part, affecting me—disclaims a knowledge of my "sentiments in regard to Secession": This is singular, since he is the only officer at the Station who has made me frequent visits, in which we have had long, and on my part, wholly unreserved conversations about such affairs; and to him only, I read my letter of May 26 to the Adjutant General denouncing State right Theories (and informing him that I remained "faithful to my oath"). The other signers, known to be my enemies,—I have for months barely spoken to when must; they have reported without qualification or reservation that I have stated "that if Virginia my native state, went out of the Union I would not resign, but would not raise my hand against her: but that if Missouri, my adopted state went out—I would resign and join her". I was tempted to apply a test of the reliability and character of the scout report,-by addressing them a note; ~~Enclosed marked I:—and~~ their answers are enclosed—marked C & D. substantially or expressly disclaiming any personal knowledge of it; Thus it stands,—confessedly in an important print—a compilation of Camp rumors! The charge made in the above quotation is essentially false;—as is also,—as far as my knowledge extends, — the Parthian attack upon an absent officer, Capt Robertson; they omit the only important part of the Fort Bridger Transactions; viz:—that so soon as I heard of Capt. Gardner's act,—without waiting for official information,—or even positive certainty, I reported it by express with the view, and in time, to allow of his being arrested at St. Josephs or St. Louis. (I also enclose marked E—a letter from Capt. Clary—on which comment is very unnecessary.)

I had taken occasion in the last month or two, by conversations with Capt. Gibbon, [*illegible*]: Gordon & Sanders, to assure myself of their actual loyalty to the government. It would appear that the signers of the report, neglected their duty, in not reporting the scene of the seditious tract, charged to have occurred last February: and most of the allegations are of old date; How important to the Government the information as to Govr. Cumming, after he had gone to Georgia!—or as to Mr. Secretary Wootten, after he had in a published resignation announced his disloyalty to the government. How they are full of zeal and so freely bandy about that pleasant epithet of "Traitor." They would have the world believe that this was a new West Point,—an American Gibraltar of safety and freedom endangered, with Arnolds, plenty as Richmonds in Bosworth field.

That they have chosen this period, when all but one of the officers affected are generally believed to have maturely determined to remain true soldiers to the government, for this officious display of indignant virtues,—and that now many promotions by selection are to be made in the increased Army, is one of these coincidences that now and then occur in human affairs, to the admiration of the curious, and the bewilderment of the charitable;—for, if they may be supposed to be slightly inimical to those involved in this charges–secretly sent by pony express,—so they may also be supposed to be sensible of this running some risk of doing them the slight injury, of blasting their professional prospects.

Mere hatred of the South becomes now,—especially in these non-combattants—a zealous patriotism, which they exalt as worthy of great applause. Instead of sympathizing with the unhappiness of my family disunion—one of the greatest miseries of the times.—and the patriotic fidelity of many so sorely tried as to be impelled to battle against their own blood—a generosity with which I credit the unscheming mass of my fellow country men of the West and North,—they [*illegible*] and impute it as a crime! The Department, I doubt not, knew better than they—or even than I do, of the acts of my far distant, long absent, unhappy sons;—but gloating in my misfortune, they did not stop to observe the malice betrayed: But I dismiss the subject with loathing:

I have trust that the administration can well discriminate between timely, open, <u>true</u> denunciations of treachery—which I would applaud—and the hardy zeal of hearsay informers of the Titus Oates class.

Very respectfully

P. ST. GEO. COOKE
Col. 2d Dragoons–Commanding

Brevet Brig. Genl. L. Thomas
Adjutant General U.S. Army
Washington City.

P.S. I have received communication on this subject from Officers, who urge that they should be sent by Pony Express; and I have concluded to do so,—and put all in this enclosure.

Source: "Letters Received by the Office of the Adjutant General (Main Series); 1861–1870," National Archives, RG94, M619, Roll 65

UT-8

Captain John Gibbon to Brevet Brigadier General Lorenzo Thomas June 18, 1861

Fort Crittenden, U.T. *June 18th 61*

Bvt. Brig. Genl. L. Thomas
Adjt. Genl. U.S.A.
Washington, D.C.

Genl:

Three officers at this post, Maj. Hunt Capt. Clary and Surg. Porter, for some reason best known to themselves, have treacherously and clandestinely attacked the reputation of certain officers here by writing a letter to the Secty. of War and dispatching it by the last poney express before any one interested in this contemptable effort at defamation knew any thing of the intention of their traducers. After their wrong was perpetrated I was, on demanding it, furnished with a copy of that part of their communication referring to myself.

At the risk of appearing to attach too much importance to a matter which, under ordinary circumstances, would appear too childish and absurd to notice I beg leave to submit to the President and the Genl-in-chief a statement which I feel satisfied Genl. Scott, from his knowledge of my character, will know I would not make unless strictly true.

The statement that I ever positively asserted it as my principle that if No. Ca. seceded I would resign is false, and any general remarks I may have made on the subject months ago when the unfortunate difficulties which now afflict our country commenced will not bear any such construction, even if my course since the state seceded did not give it the lie. Of course I cannot pretend to recollect ever[y] idle word I may have uttered under the supposition I was speaking among friends and honorable men, but this I can honestly assert that the scoff attributed to me was never uttered, and it is notorious among the gentlemen who really know my sentiments on the subject that they are and have been for months directly the reverse of what is stated in Maj. Hunt's letter, and that I have not only repeatedly asserted that my first duty was due to the U. States government, but that I have frequently urged upon others entertaining a different idea my own views, citing as the examples I was willing to follow, the Genl-in-chief and Maj. Robt. Anderson. Entertaining such views and being loyal to the Government and my original oath, which I regard as binding now as it ever was, my arrangement on reading this infamous libel may be immagined.

That I requested the tune of "Dixie" played is the only true statement in the extract, but it was one without the slightest regard to any political associations which might be attached to the air nor am I now satisfied that the air has the political significance given to it by Maj. Hunt. When calling for it I attached no such significance to it, and did not really know Lt. Green has prohibited it, although I had heard what I took to be a joking allusion to the prohibition. Maj. Hunt's inference of my disloyalty is as false as his other charge, and comes with a bad grace from one whose son was the first person to import the music of the air into this territory.

To show with what reckless disregard to truth statements are made in that letter I need only call attention to the fact that, instead of "Dixie" being the "only" tune played on the 22? of febry. Col. Smith's order for the celebration dericted Washington's march to be played. It was played as was also "Hail Columbia" The only inference to be drawn from that remarkable letter is that no moderate sentiment can be tolerated, but that every officer in order to get the credit of being true to the Government must be as bigoted as those who signed it and advocate the indiscriminate slaughter of men, women and children by servile insurrection.

I do not hesitate to say that I cannot endorse such inhuman doctrine, and although I should scorn to attempt to place myself right with the three individuals who have acted such an unworthy part in this transaction, I deem it due to myself and the Govt. to which I have sworn true and faithful allegiance to stigmatize the tenor and hearing of that letter, as I have stigmatized it here, as grossly false & libellous and to state, in spite of Maj. Hunt's assertion, that notwithstanding the secession of No. Ca. I remain true to my allegiance, and ready to abide by the terms of my oath, to defend the U. States against all her enemies or opposed whatsoever.

I have particularized Maj. Hunt in this communication because he is the acknowledged writer of the letter, the other two signed being used as his tools.

I am sir
Very Respectfully
Your obt. Servt.

JOHN GIBBON
Capt. 4th Arty.

[Editor's note: *On the reverse of this letter is written "Replying to charges of treason from Maj. Hunt, Capt. Clary, and Surg. Porter." The following indorsement also appears in the handwriting of Colonel Cooke.*]

HD QRS DEPT. UTAH
Fort Crittenden, *June 19/61*

Respectfully forwarded;—I have already addressed my belief of the loyalty of Capt. Gibbon.

P. ST. GEO. COOKE
Col. 2 Dragoons, Comd'g.

SOURCE: "LETTERS RECEIVED BY THE OFFICE OF THE ADJUTANT GENERAL (MAIN SERIES); 1861–1870," NATIONAL ARCHIVES, RG94, M619, ROLL 65

UT-9

F. E. Hunt, J. B. Porter, and R. E. Clary to Simon Cameron, Secretary of War
June 19, 1861

Fort Crittenden U.T.
June 19th 1861

Sir,

On the 15th of June we made a communication to you, which the Colonel Comdg this Mil. Dept has called for & of which we have forwarded him a copy. Since then some of the statements have been denied, & pronounced false & an infamous libel, by one or more officers concerned. We simply wish to advise you that by Pony express which will leave here on Sunday next we will forward affidavits tending to show the entire truth of every allegation made by us against the different officers concerned.

We are very Respectfully
Your obt. Servts

F. E. HUNT
Paymaster U. S. Army
J. B. PORTER
Surgeon U.S.A.
R. E. CLARY
Major QM

Through the Adjutant-General's Office of the War Department.
Hon. S. Cameron
Secretary of War
Washington City, D.C.

[Editor's note: *The comments below were written on a separate sheet that was sent to the Adjutant General's Office. An annotation notes that this correspondence was received in Washington, D.C., "(AGO) July 5/61."*]

Fort Crittenden U.T.
June 19th 1861

F. E. Hunt Paymaster U.S. Army
J. B Porter Surg. U.S. Army
R. E. Clary Major QM

Stating that affidavits will be furnished to support certain allegations heretofore made. Head Qrs. Department of Utah Fort Crittenden U.T. June 21 '61. Once more these officers are admonished to obey par 441 Army regulations.

This communication is returned in order that it may be corrected accordingly.

By order of Col. P. S^t^. Geo. Cooke

JOHN GREEN
Actg. Asst. Adjt. Genl.

Head Qrs. Department of Utah
Fort Crittenden U.T. *June 23 "61.*

This communication received back with the addition "Through the Adj^t^. General's Office, &c."

It indicates that the depositions will be sent direct; but if so, after this second admonition of their duty under regulations, it would seem an act of defiance of Mil^ry^ authority.

If depositions have been taken, it has been done ex-parte and secretly [*illegible*]. In keeping with this extraordinary affair,—which has shocked the moral sense of this command,—it appears that Major Clary, now undertakes to prove every allegation he has made; whereas, 4 days ago I forwarded, by Pony Express, two communications of his emphatically retracting some of the most important of them.

Respectfully forwarded

P. S^T^. GEO. COOKE
Col. 2[d] Drag[oons].
C[om]m[andin]g.

Source: "Letters Received by the Office of the Adjutant General (Main Series); 1861–1870," National Archives, RG94, M619, Roll 65

UT-10

First Lieutenant Wesley Merritt to Brevet Brigadier General Lorenzo Thomas June 19, 1861

Fort Crittenden, *June 19th 1861.*

General:

I have in my posession a copy of a letter written by Major F. E. Hunt and signed by Major Clary and Dr Porter, which letter was forwarded to the War Department by Express. My name is mentioned in a connection and under a charge which is calculated to do me great injustice. The writer assumes that there is an apparant necessity to "expose treason and rebellion and the aiders and abettors of traitors and rebels" and I am arraigned, together with other gentlemen, under this general charge as having "drank a secession toast." The attempt to identify me with "traitors and rebels" would be a dastardly outrage were it not ridiculous and the insinuation that I entertain disloyal sentiments towards the government, is basely calumnious and needs no denial with anyone who has heard me express my political views. In fact many gentlemen have told me of their surprise that my name should have been mentioned even in so wholesale an attack on the characters of officers while my political opinions have been so freely expressed in favor of the Union and the policy of the present administration.

The writer of the letter knows or has had ample opportunity for becoming convinced that any innuendo derogatory to my loyalty is false. If he has made the statement against me ignorantly, he has exhibited a disposition for the ruthless and promiscuous destruction of reputation which is in harmony with his act in sending away his letter hurriedly and secretly doubtless with the object of poisoning the minds of the authorities at Washington against those whose names are mentioned, without allowing the assailed to give a counteracting antidote. If on the other hand he knows my political sentiments—my unflinching fidelity to the Union and devotion to my country, as I am convinced is the case, it is not necessary for me to furnish any epithet for his conduct in making the charge he has.

I would not consider it necessary to make any refutation of the statement of Major Hunt were it not that my name is mentioned under the exordium of his letter which conveys the idea that all persons then mentioned are disaffected. The specific charge against me—that I "drank a secession toast" is according to Maj. Hunt's own declaration, unworthy of consideration. At an entertainment given by Messrs. Livingston

Bell & Co., sutlers at this post, at which almost all the officers of the post were present several toasts were given and drank. I have no definite recollection of the one alluded to as secession yet admitting I did drink it as charged, Major Hunt has stultified himself in attempting to make this an evidence of disloyalty, by remarking to Lieut. C. H. Morgan of the 4th Arty. immediately afterwards that no importance could be attached to such an action, as those who drank the toast were more or less under the influence of liquor and that nothing should be said about it.

So as evidence that the communication of Major Hunt was ill advised and undigested by parties engaged in it, Major Clary as an act of justice to myself and others disavows a personal knowledge of its contents. Again Dr. Porter knows if he has any personal cognizance of the matter at all that my opinions are directly the reverse of those attributed to me, for in the only conversation I ever had with him on political or other subjects, I expressed my loyalty in unmistakable terms and warmly applaud in the policy and past action of the administration.

I will not say what were the motives that actuated this assassin-like attack on the character of officers by Major Hunt—I will not say that he was incited by personal animosity against some of those named, nor that he was anxious to manufacture cheaply a paltry reputation for patriotism for the secessionist of course which he could gain in no other way: but I will say that his insinuations as to my patriotism are without a shadow of foundation in truth, as is abundantly shown by my antecedents, interests, and nativity.

Very Respectfully,

WESLEY MERRITT
1st Lt U.S. 2nd Drag[oon]s.

To Bvt. Brig. Gen. L. Thomas
Adjt. Genl.
Washington, D.C.

[Editor's note: *The following comments were included with the above correspondence when it was sent to the Adjutant Generals Office, War Department, Washington, D.C.*]

H^D^qr. Ft. Crittenden, U.T.
June 19, 1861

Respectfully forwarded to the H^d^qrs, Dep't of Utah.

F. E. HUNT
Arty Actg Comdg

H[D] Q[R] DEP[ARTMENT] UTAH
Ft. Crittenden *June 19/61*

Respectfully forwarded.

I never doubted the loyalty of Lieut. Merritt; never heard it questioned;—his letter is interesting.

P. ST. GEO. COOKE
Col. 2 Dr[a]g[oon]s
C[o]m[mandin]g

SOURCE: "LETTERS RECEIVED BY THE OFFICE OF THE ADJUTANT GENERAL (MAIN SERIES); 1861–1870," NATIONAL ARCHIVES, RG94, M619, ROLL 65

UT-11

MAJOR R. E. CLARY TO FIRST LIEUTENANT JOHN GREEN
JUNE 19, 1861

FORT CRITTENDEN U.T.
June 19th 1861

SIR:

In reply to yours of the 18th instant—I have to state for the information of the Colonel Commanding the Department—that he is not to understand me to assert, from the paper signed by me that I have heard him say—"that if Virginia, his native state went out of the Union, he would not resign, but would not raise his hand against her; but that if Missouri, his adopted state went out, he would resign and join her["].

Very Respectfully,
Your Obedient Servant

(Signed) R. E. CLARY
Q. M.

LIEUT JOHN GREEN
Actg. Asst. Adjt. Genl
Fort Crittenden U.T.

Head Qrs. Department of Utah
Fort Crittenden U.T. *June 19th 1861.*

Official:

JOHN GREEN
Actg. Asst. Adj^{t}. Genl

Source: "Letters Received by the Office of the Adjutant General (Main Series); 1861–1870," National Archives, RG94, M619, Roll 65

UT-12

Colonel Philip St. George Cooke to the Adjutant General July 27, 1861

Headquarters: Dept of Utah
Fort Crittenden, *July 27, '61*

Sir,

I march, this morning, with the garrison of Fort Crittenden, for Fort Leavenworth; the garrison of Fort Bridger, might join me, when I leave.

Very Respectfully
Your Servt

P. S^{T}. GEO COOKE
Col. 2d Drag[oon]s
Comd'g.

The Adjutant General
U.S. Army,
Washington City, D.C.

[Editor's note: *The file notation accompanying this correspondence states: "Utah, Department of Ft. Crittenden, U.T. July 27, 1861. Col. P. St. Geo: Cooke, 2d. Dragoons. Reports the evacuation of this post and Fort Bridger, U.T. Recd. Rec. (Aug. 12, 1861).*"]

Source: "Letters Received by the Office of the Adjutant General (Main Series); 1861–1870," National Archives, RG94, M619, Roll 65

UT-13

General Orders No. 13, Headquarters, Department of Utah August 5, 1861

Hd Qrs Department of Utah
Camp near Fort Bridger U.T. *Aug. 5/61.*

General Orders
No. 13

I . . Fort Bridger is retained until further Orders, and will be garrisoned by United States Troops 1" Lieut. Joseph C. Clark Junr. 4" Artillery, is detached to command it, and take charge of public property left by orders from the War Department, to be left in this Military Department he will give the usual receipts.

Ordnance Sergeant Boger is also assigned to duty at Fort Bridger: The following men of "A." and "C." Companies 4" Artillery, will remain as the garrison of Fort Bridger, viz: Sergeant W^m. H. Miller, Corporal J. A. Baker, and Privates Battron, Greely, Kearns, Openlander, McCaffrey, Odgers, and Engel of "B." Company 10" Infantry. The permanent Commanders of these Companies will furnish Lieut Clark with their complete descriptions; and will also invoice to him their Arms and Equipments.

Lieut: Morgan A[ssistant].Q[uarter].M[aster]. and A[ssistant].C[hief of].S[taff]. will turn over to Lieut Clark, such amount of funds in these Departments, as shall seem necessary and be approved.

II . . 1" Lieut: John Green 2d Dragoons will take Command of Company "B." 10" Infantry receipting for its property; this in consequence of the absence of any available officer of that Regiment.

III . . On Surgeons Certificate that the health of Military Storekeeper S. H. Montgomery incapacitates him for the duty which would have been required of him at Fort Bridger, he will accompany the march of the troops.

By order of Colonel P. S^t. George Cooke.

Signed W. MERRITT
Actg. Asst. Adjt. Genl.

Head Qrs: Department of Utah
Camp nr. Fort Bridger U.T.
Aug. 6" 1861. Official

W. MERRITT
Actg. Asst: Adjt. Genl.

Source: "Letters Received by the Office of the Adjutant General (Main Series); 1861–1870," National Archives, RG94, M619, Roll 65

UT-14

Colonel Philip St. George Cooke
to Utah Governor Francis M. Wooten
August 6, 1861

Head Qrs: Department of Utah
Fort Bridger U.T. *August 1861*

Governor F. M. Wootten,
Great Salt Lake City, U.T.
Sir,

I desire to give notice to the Territorial Executive,—and the public as well,—that the United States retains its property, in Fort Bridger, its reservations and all its appurtenances, and possession also:—it will be represented by an Ordinance Sergeant and perhaps a small garrison, until the expected arrival of other troops. The government also retains its exclusive right until the usual Official Notice, in all the reservations of this territory.

I am very respectfully
Your obedt. Servt

(Sig'd:) P. S^{T}. GEORGE COOKE
Colonel 2 Dragoons
Commanding.

Head Qrs: Department of Utah
Camp nr Fort Bridger U.T. *Aug: 6" 1861*
Official

W. MERRITT
Actg: Asst: Adjt Genl.

Source: "Letters Received by the Office of the Adjutant General (Main Series); 1861–1870," National Archives, RG94, M619, Roll 65

UT-15

COLONEL PHILIP ST. GEORGE COOKE TO
BREVET BRIGADIER GENERAL LORENZO THOMAS
AUGUST 6, 1861

BVT. BRIG. GENL. L. THOMAS
Adjutant General U.S.A.
Washington City, D.C.

HEAD QTRS. DEPARTMENT OF UTAH
Fort Bridger U.T. *Aug. 6" 1861*

SIR:

I telegraphed you yesterday morning, that the sales of all property had been made, about two weeks before the receipt of your dispatch of 27th July.

I arrived here in command of the garrison of Fort Crittenden yesterday. But one contract mule train of 14 wagons, loaded with clothing and arms has gone on: A government train of ox wagons—with beef cattle—and the bulk of the property in a contract train is behind. I shall break up the first, leaving the clothing and beef cattle here: and must break the contracts for the others, and one made here, as far as clothing is concerned; sending on the arms;—as a precaution against contingent events in this territory,—and because they were not ordered to be stopped,—and because they probably will not be needed here. I leave also here the supply of medicines & medical stores pertaining to this post—which had been packed as well worth transportation.

The government ox train left Fort Crittenden July 23rd, and is yet some days back; a company of infantry were escorting it, and on the report of a man yesterday that they had been attacked or threatened both by Indians and whites, I sent an officer and twelve Dragoons to protect and hasten their coming;—there was gross negligence in Major Clary in preparing and outfitting it.

The dirt buildings of Fort Crittenden, without occupants would go to ruin in a few months, and would have been broken up in two days by the inhabitants. The material was sold.

There are good pine log quarters here; and I had determined to leave an Ordnance Sergeant in charge: now the clothing will be stored here, and many beef cattle will be left, in obedience to the instructions: Major Clary, Quartermaster, received a dispatch—of same date from the Q[uarte]r: M[aste]r: General—to leave Mil. Store Keeper Montgomery in charge of the clothing and equipage; I enclose a statement of the Senior Medical Officer showing his unfitness; General Orders No 13.,—enclosed—will show my action: the terms of service of these men, will expire within sixty days:—Lieut. Clark can remain in charge, 50 days,—probably until the arrival of troops,—and still by stage join his company by the time of its arrival at Fort Leavenworth.

I have appointed a board to report their opinion of an equitable compensation to the contractors, for their services so far, and loss, if any, by terminating their contracts; it will be reported for the information of the proper department.

I also enclose a copy of a letter to the acting Governor of the Territory, which I requested him to publish.

I am, Sir, Respectfully
Your obd[t]. Servant

P S[T] GEO COOKE
Colonel 2" Dragoons
Commanding

[Editor's note: *The following file notations are included with this correspondence: "Reports his arrival at Fort Bridger, with the garrison of Fort Crittenden, also his action in relation to clothing, Medical Stores, &c., to be left at Fort Bridger. Recd. (AGO) August 23/61."*]

Source: "Letters Received by the Office of the Adjutant General (Main Series); 1861–1870," National Archives, RG94, M619, Roll 65

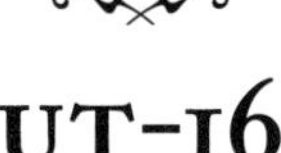

UT-16

Colonel Philip St. George Cooke to Brevet Brigadier General Lorenzo Thomas August 9, 1861

Bvt. Brgr: Genl. L. Thomas
Adjutant Genl. U. S. Army.
Washington City, D.C.

Head Quarters Department of Utah
Fort Bridger *August 9" 1861.*

Sir,

I march this morning with the ten companies of Infantry Artillery and Dragoons, which occupied this Military Department: I enclose a field return.

I leave here—in obedience to the instructions from your office of July 27"—about 5000 rations, and about 230 beef cattle

In charge of the post,—of these stores,—and of a very large amount of clothing and equipage left by order of the Quartermaster General:— as follows:

1. Lieut Clark 4" Artillery

1. Ordnance Sergeant—Boger—

1. Hospital Steward—Banks.

9. Non-commss[d]. Officers & privates, 4" Artillery,—their time expiring in about 60 days.

1. Chief Herder and 4 assistants.

A large government train, with beef cattle for draft, loaded chiefly with clothing, was broken up yesterday:—these changes have detained one here a day or two,—which would have been lost by high waters.

I am, very respectfully,
Your obedt. Servt:

P S[T] GEO COOKE
Colonel 2d Dragoons.
Commanding

[Editor's note: *The following file notation accompanies this correspondence: "Fort Bridger, U.T. August 9, 1861. Utah, Department of. Col. P. St. Geo. Cooke, 2d. Dragoons. Com'd'g. Will march this day with the troops, which occupied this Military Department, (one enclosure). Recd. (AGO) Aug: 23/61."*]

Source: "Letters Received by the Office of the Adjutant General (Main Series); 1861–1870," National Archives, RG94, M619, Roll 65

UT-17

Brevet Major James H. Carleton to Brigadier General Lorenzo Thomas August 15, 1861

Head Quarters, California Volunteers,
Raised for the protection of the Overland Mail Route.
San Francisco, Cal. *Aug 15, 1861.*

General:

I beg respectfully to request through you, of the Secretary of the Interior, that so much of a valley on the Overland Mail Route, known as Ruby Valley, as may be required for military purposes, be reserved from sale, and set apart as a Military Reserve. This valley is said to abound in grass and timber. It is 245 miles from Fort Churchill and 256 from Salt Lake City:—nearly midway between the two points; a very important site for a military post, and particularly for a depot in going eastward next after Fort Churchill. As soon as it is well known that troops are to be upon the Overland Mail Route, the best points in Ruby Valley will doubtless be "squatted" upon by Mormons and others; so that, to save trouble, it should be well to have as much of that valley reserved for military purposes as may be necessary.

Very respectfully,
Your obt. Servant,

JAMES H. CARLETON
Brevet major, U.S. Army
Comd. Cal. Volunteers.

BRIG. GEN. LORENZO THOMAS.
Adjutant General, U.S.A.
Washington, D.C.
THROUGH COMD. GENERAL OF THE DEPARTMENT OF THE PACIFIC.

[Editor's note: *The following indorsement was written on the back of the above correspondence.*]

HD QRS DEPT PACIFIC
San Francisco, *Augt 16/61*

I would respectfully and earnestly recommend that this application may be granted.

E. V. SUMNER
Brig Gen USA Comg

SOURCE: "LETTERS RECEIVED BY THE OFFICE OF THE ADJUTANT GENERAL (MAIN SERIES); 1861–1870," NATIONAL ARCHIVES, RG94, M619, ROLL 12

UT-18

Colonel Philip St. George Cooke to the Adjutant General, U.S. Army August 30, 1861

Hd. Qrs: Utah Forces
Camp near Fort Laramie *Aug. 30 1861*

To the Adjutant General
U.S. Army. Washington City.
Sir,

I received this morning a communication from the Governor of Colorado Territory, of which I enclose a copy.

I can attach little importance to its extravagant generalities; it is incredible that rebel forces should be sent five or six hundred miles through Wilderness, and also a populous territory, to attack that unimportant territory of poor miners; and if they are in want of a "prospective supply of food," it would be aggravated by consumers from this quarter: The pursuit of my orders,—and march to Fort Leavenworth,—penetrating the advance guard of 8000 indians and restoring their "Communications with the States," will be as much as can be expected of my 500 men.

There are about 2600 Stand of Arms Muskets, rifles, and Carbines,—with accoutrements,—in the trains from Utah, expected in a few days; I shall order them left here, at the requisition of the Governor; but there is no ammunition.

Very respectfully
Your obedt: Servt:

P S^T GEO COOKE
Colonel 2d Dragoons
Commanding

[Editor's note: *The Colorado governor's letter is not included. See UT-21 for the response of the War Department's Office of the Adjutant General. The file entry for this correspondence states: "Encloses copy of letter of the Governor of Colorado Territory arguing the necessity of military protection in that Territory."*]

Source: "Letters Received by the Office of the Adjutant General (Main Series); 1861–1870," National Archives, RG94, M619, Roll 12

UT-19

Record of Events, Post Return of Fort Bridger for August 1861
[Undated] September 1861

Companies H. B. & E. 2d. Drag[oon]s. A. C. & B 4th Art[iller]y. Col. Cooke Commanding arrived at this Post from Ft. Crittenden U.T. Aug. 4th, 1861.

Company E. 10. Inf[an]t[r]y arrived from Ft. Crittenden U.T. Aug. 7, 1861

Companies H. B. & E. 2d. Drag[oon]s. A. C. & B. 4th In[fan]t[r]y & I. G. B. and E. 10th Inf[an[t[r]y. Col. Cooke commanding march for Fort Leavenworth K[ansas] Aug. 9, 1861.

J. C. CLARK
1st Lt. 4th In[fan]t[r]y.
Commanding the Post.

[Editor's note: *While this August 1861 report is undated, it is presumed to have been signed during September 1861 in order to comply with both regulation and custom.*]

Source: "Post Return of Fort Bridger, U.T. . . . for the month of August 1861," Returns from U.S. Military Posts 1800–1916, National Archives, RG94, M617, Roll 146

UT-20

First Lieutenant J. C. Clark to Brigadier General Lorenzo Thomas
September 12, 1861

Fort Bridger U.T.
Sept. 12, 1861

Gen.

I have the honor to communicate that I have received the following from Col. Carleton, Commanding Cal. Volunteers, viz. "I fear the commands destines for service on the Overland Mail Route, will not get off from this city (San Francisco) before the 20th inst. (Sept) at the earliest.

"It is <u>possible</u> from the amplication of affairs that the command may not leave this winter. So, even though it go by the 20th, I could hardly hope to get even a small portion of it as far as Fort Crittenden before the snows set in."

As it appears probable from this communication, that no volunteers from California will reach this Post this winter, I respectfully recommend that a detachment of troops be ordered here from Ft. Laramie or from some other point. Of the troops left here under my command, to guard the public property until the arrival of the volunteers, only the Ord. Sergeant, Hospl. Steward and one private will be left after Oct. 4th. There are about 800 boxes and bales of clothing, equipage & Hospl. Stores and 200 head of Beef Cattle at the Post. There is a large band of thieves in the hills between this Post and Salt Lake City; a few nights since a portion of them stampeded the Government Cattle, and succeeded in the confusion in driving off 17 head of them, and knowing that the garrison is too small to send a party against them, they express I understand a determination to seize the entire herd. The measures I have taken may prevent their succeeding should they attempt it, but I consider that the other property here will be unsafe without the presence of additional troops.

I am respectfully
Your Obt Servant

J. C. CLARK
1st Lt. 4th Art.
Commandg.

BRIG. GEN. L. THOMAS
Adjt. Gen. U.S.A.
Washington, D.C.

[Editor's note: *The following file notation accompanies this correspondence: "Ft. Bridger, U.T. Sept. 12, 1861. J. C. Clark, 1st Lieut: 4th Artillery. In consequence of a letter received from Col. Carleton, commanding California Volunteers, he recommends that a detachment of troops be sent to this post from Fort Laramie or some other post, for the protection of the public property. Rec^{d}. (AGO) Sept. 26/61. Respectfully forwarded to the Head Quarters of the Army. By order of A. Baird A.A.G., A.G.O. Sep 27/61."*]

SOURCE: "LETTERS RECEIVED BY THE OFFICE OF THE ADJUTANT GENERAL (MAIN SERIES); 1861–1870," NATIONAL ARCHIVES, RG94, M619, ROLL 13

UT-21

E. D. Townsend, Assistant Adjutant General, War Department
September 23, 1861

Head Quarters Army,
Sept. 23/61

The General-in-chief supposes that Col. Cooke could not possibly do otherwise than to decline diverting the troops of his command in the manner proposed by the Governor of Colorado. The question of placing the 2600 stand of arms en route from Utah at the disposal of the Governor is respectfully submitted to the Secretary of War.

By command:

E. D. TOWNSEND
A[*ssistant*] *A*[*djutant*] *Gen*[*eral*]

[Editor's note: *This comment was recorded on the back of* UT-18.]

Source: "Letters Received by the Office of the Adjutant General (Main Series); 1861–1870," National Archives, RG94, M619, Roll 12

UT-22

Brigham Young to J. H. Wade
October 18, 1861

Great Salt Lake City, U.T., *Oct. 18, 1861.*

Hon. J. H. Wade,
President of the Pacific Telegraph Company, Cleveland, Ohio:

Sir:—Permit me to congratulate you upon the completion of the Overland Telegraph Line west to this city, to commend the energy displayed by yourself and associates in the rapid and successful prosecution of a work so beneficial, and to express the wish that its use may ever tend to promote the true interests of the dwellers upon both the Atlantic and Pacific slopes of our continent.

Utah has not seceded, but is firm for the Constitution and laws of our once happy country, and is warmly interested in such useful enterprises as the one so far completed.

BRIGHAM YOUNG.

Source: "The Completion of the Telegraph," *Deseret News*, October 23, 1861, 5

UT-23

Acting Governor Frank Fuller to President Abraham Lincoln October 18, 1861

G. S. L. City, *Oct. 18, 1861.*

To the President of the United States:

Utah, whose citizens strenuously resist all imputations of disloyalty, congratulates the President upon the completion of an enterprise which spans a continent, unites two oceans, and connects with nerve of iron, the remote extremeties of the body politic, with the great governmental heart. May the whole system speedily thrill with the quickened pulsations of that heart, as the parricide hand is palsied, treason is punished, and the entire sisterhood of States joins hands in glad reunion around the National fireside.

FRANK FULLER,
Acting Governor of Utah Territory.

Source: "The Completion of the Telegraph," *Deseret News*, October 23, 1861, 5

UT-24

J. H. Wade to Brigham Young
October 19, 1861

Cleveland, *Oct. 19th, 1861.*

Hon. Brigham Young, Prest.,
Great Salt Lake City:

Sir:—I have the honor to acknowledge the receipt of your message of last evening, which was every way gratifying, not only in the announcement of the completion of the Pacific Telegraph to your enterprising and prosperous city, but that yours, the first message to pass over the line, should express so unmistakably the patriotism and union-loving sentiments of yourself and people.

I join with you in the hope that this enterprise may tend to promote the welfare and happiness of all concerned, and that the annihilation of time in our means of communication may also tend to annihilate prejudice, cultivate brotherly love, facilitate commerce and strengthen the bonds of our once and again to be happy union.

With just consideration for your high position and due respect for you personally,
I remain your obedient servant,

J. H. WADE.
Prest. Pac. Tel. Co.

Source: "The Completion of the Telegraph," *Deseret News*, October 23, 1861, 5

UT-25

President Abraham Lincoln to Acting Governor Frank Fuller
October 20, 1861

Washington, D.C., *Oct. 20th, '61.*

Hon. Frank Fuller, Acting Gov. of Utah:

Sir—The completion of the telegraph to Great Salt Lake City, is auspicious of the stability and union of the Republic. The Government reciprocates your congratulations.

ABRAHAM LINCOLN

Source: "The Completion of the Telegraph," *Deseret News*, October 23, 1861, 5

UT-26

Colonel Philip St. George Cooke to the Secretary of War
October 28, 1861

Washington *Oct. 28th '61*

The Hon:

Secretary of War:

On my arrival in the city with my command from Utah, it was divided, & I was (kindly) directed to await orders a few days,—with an intimation of promotion.

I have waited eight days inactive;—I feel that I could be doing important Service to the Nation, at a time when it needs the best services of all.

Arriving, I find even my old subalterns generals; without being old, I am one the senior Colonels of the Army; I never made a Military failure but have received high praise in the reports of Secretaries of War, and in General orders.

Whilst engaged in my new system of tactics—which has been adopted, I visited the Seat of War in Italy—1859—purely for military observation:

I find vacancies in the regular Army of Major General and Brig^r^. Generals: so many of my old friends—in high army positions here—assert my claims good for the former that I am induced (and advised) to make it myself.

I have the honor,

to be Your Ob^t^ Servant

P. S^T^ GEO COOKE

Colonel 2d Cavalry

U.S.A.

[Editor's note: *The following file notation, from Major General George B. McClellan, accompanies this correspondence.*]

Col Cooke has run as much, or more, hard time as any officer of his rank in the Army. He is an excellent officer & eminently deserving of advancement.

Respectfully,

GEO B McCLELLAN

Maj Gnl Vols

Source: "Letters Received by the Office of the Adjutant General (Main Series); 1861–1870," National Archives, RG94, M619, Roll 250

UT-27

Lieutenant-General Daniel H. Wells to Brigham Young
March 21, 1862

G S L City, *March 21 1862*

To His Excellency
Brigham Young ~~Gov-elect~~
Gov. of the State of Deseret

Dear Sir—I hereby tender unto you my resignation of the office of Lieutenant General of the which I hold in the Nauvoo Legion and Militia of the State of Deseret Permit me on this occasion to express my grateful acknowledgements to you sir for the many favors and through you to the Legion for the courtesies and forbearances which I have so universally received been extended to me in all of my official intercourse in this connection & of in the remembrance of which will ever be kindly cherished by [*illegible*]

Your most obedient friend
and Bro in the Gospel of Christ,

DANIEL H WELLS
Lieut. Gen N.L.
Comdg.

[Editor's note: *In this and other Utah records, the abbreviation "N.L." refers to "Nauvoo Legion," the common name for the Utah militia.*]

Source: "Utah, Territorial Militia Records, 1849–1877," No. 0692–0701 (March–April 1862), Series 2210, Utah State Archives, Salt Lake City

UT-28

Frank Fuller et al. to Edwin M. Stanton, Secretary of War
April 11, 1862

Great Salt Lake City,
April 11, 1862.

The Indians in Utah are robbing the Overland Mail Company of their horses and provisions, and destroying their stations, and declare the paper wagons shall be stopped within two months. They are killing the cattle of the inhabitants and demanding provisions of them and of the superintendent, in an insolent and threatening manner, and 2,000 Shoshones are now entering the northern settlements, demanding food and clothing. An imperative necessity demands immediate military protection for the mail company and settlers.

We ask that the superintendent of Indian affairs, James Duane Doty, be authorized by the Secretary of War to raise and put in service immediately, under his command, at the expense of the general government, a regiment of mounted rangers from inhabitants of the Territory, with officers appointed by him, each man to furnish his own horse, clothing, arms and equipments, to serve three months, or longer if required, or until troops of the United States can reach the Territory, and that he be authorized to procure the necessary subsistence.

FRANK FULLER,
Acting Governor of Utah.
I. F. KINNEY,
Chief Justice Supreme Court, Territory of Utah.
LEONARD R. FOX,
Surrey or Central, Utah.
FREDERICK COOK,
Assistant Treasurer Overland Mail Company.
H. S. R. ROWE,
Superintendent Overland Mail Company.
E. R. PURPLE,
Agent Overland Mail Company.
JOSEPH HOLLADY,
Agent Eastern Division Overland Mail Company.
W. B. HIBBAD,
Assistant Superintendent Pacific Telegraph Company.

HON. EDWIN M. STANTON,
Secretary of War, Washington.

[Editor's note: *"I. F. Kinney" should be "J[ohn] F. Kinney."*]

SOURCE: *REPORT OF THE COMMISSIONER OF INDIAN AFFAIRS FOR THE YEAR 1862* (WASHINGTON, D.C.: GOVERNMENT PRINTING OFFICE, 1862), 212

UT-29

Brigham Young to John M. Bernhisel
April 14, 1862

G.S.L. City, *April 14, 1862.*

Hon. John M. Bernhisel,
Washington City, D.C.,

I am informed that a telegram has been forwarded from here over the signatures of Frank Fuller, J. F. Kinney, and six others not one of whom is a permanent resident in this Territory, to the Secretary of War, asking him to authorize James D. Doty, Superintendent of Indian Affairs, to raise and officer a regiment here for three months, or until U.S. troops can reach here, under the general allegations that the property of the Overland Mail Company and the settlers are in danger from the Indians. So far as I know, the Indians in Utah are unusually quiet; and instead of 2000 hostile Shoshonees coming into our northern settlements, Washekeeh, their Chief, has wintered in this City and near it, perfectly friendly, and is about to go to his band. Besides, the militia of Utah are ready and able, as they ever have been, to take care of all the Indians within our borders, and are able and willing to protect the mail line, if called upon so to do. The statements of the aforesaid telegram are without foundation in truth, so far as we know.

BRIGHAM YOUNG.

Source: "Utah, Territorial Militia Records, 1849–1877," Series 2210, Box 1, Folder 47 (March–April 1862), Utah State Archives, Salt Lake City

UT-30

Lieutenant General Daniel H. Wells to Colonel Robert T. Burton and Detachment April 24, 1862

G. S. L. City, *April 24, 1862.*

INSTRUCTIONS.

Col. Robert T. Burton and the detachment to guard the mail stage under you:

You are detailed for this special service, and will proceed from this place in company with Captain Hooper, General C. W. West, Judge Kinney, and probably other passengers in the mail coach for the Eastern States, as a guard to protect them against the depredations of Indians, who are said to be hostile; and continue in their company on the route as far as it may be deemed necessary by yourself and Captain Hooper for their safety. In traveling, the stage must correspond to your time, as it cannot be expected that without change of animals your detachment can keep pace with the stage, especially where the roads are good. You will obtain grain for your animals, and some provisions for your command at the mail stations, for which you will give a receipt to be paid in kind, keeping a copy of each receipt, and advising President Young by telegraph, so that we can forward the amounts by the teams going to the States, which are expected to start in a few days. In traveling be cautious, and vigilant, and keep together and allow no straggling from camp, either night or day. There must not be any drinking of spirituous liquors, neither swearing, or abusive language of any kind, and treat everybody with courtesy, and prove there is no necessity of trouble with the Indians, when white men act with propriety.

If you can get to speak with Indians, treat them kindly, showing them you are their friends; and so far as you are able, investigate the cause and origin of the present difficulties.

You had better have one or two friendly Indians to accompany you, through whose agency you may be able to communicate with others, and thus become apprised of their intentions.

When you meet the troops from the East said to be on their way, you can return, but you will remain in the vicinity of the threatened difficulties until relieved, or so long as it may be necessary.

* * * *

Keep a journal of every day's proceedings, and a strict account of every business transaction, as well of the causes leading to the disturbances, if obtainable.

Send by telegraph to President Young from every station giving us in short the current news, and prospects of Indians, state of the roads, weather, and other matters of interest.

When you arrive at or near the scene of disaster, feel your way before you, proceed so that you may not be surprised by a concealed or sudden movement of the Indians, or other evil-disposed persons.

May God bless, prosper and preserve you all.

DANIEL H. WELLS,
Lieut.-General Commanding N. L. Militia of Utah Territory.

Source: Edward W. Tullidge, *The History of Salt Lake City and Its Founders* (Salt Lake City: privately published, 1886), 253

UT-31

Acting Governor Frank Fuller to General Daniel H. Wells
April 25, 1862

Executive Dept. Utah,
Great Salt Lake City,
April 25, 1862.

Gen. Daniel H. Wells,
Commanding Militia of Utah Territory.

Sir,

A call has been made upon the Executive of Utah Territory by the Superintendent of the Overland mail Company Maj J. E. Eaton for military protection of mails, passengers and the property of the mail Company from the depredations of hostile Indians.

It is represented that the stock of the Overland Mail Company along the line east of this city, has been forcibly stolen, stations robbed, passengers attacked and mail destroyed.

I therefore require you immediately to dispatch, for purposes of protection and defence of the United States mails and the property of the mail carriers, as well as the persons of passengers and all others connected with the line of the Overland Mail Company, east of Great Salt Lake City—twenty mounted men duly officered and properly armed and equipped, carrying sufficient ammunition for thirty days service in the field, and furnished with the necessary commissary stores and forage, with proper means of transportation for the same.

The officer commanding this expedition will use his discretion as to the movements of his command, as well as the term of service necessary to ensure the safety and security of the mails and all persons and property connected therewith, and will communicate freely by telegraph when necessary, with the General commanding the Militia of the Territory, and the commander-in-chief.

FRANK FULLER
Ac'[tin]g Governor and
Commander-in-Chief.

[Editor's note: *"April 25 1862 Governor Fuller Requisition for 20 Mounted Men to guard Mails &c" is written on the reverse of the last page.*]

Source: "Utah, Territorial Militia Records, 1849–1877," No. 1502–1516 (1858–1865), Series 2210, Utah State Archives, Salt Lake City

UT-32

Special Orders No. 2, Headquarters Nauvoo Legion April 25, 1862

Headquarters Nauvoo Legion,
G. S. L. City, *April 25th, 1862.*

Special Orders,
No. 2.

1st. In compliance with the requisition this day made by His Excellency Frank Fuller, Acting-Governor Utah Territory, Col. R. T. Burton will forthwith detail twenty men, properly armed and equipped, and mounted on good and efficient animals, provided with thirty days' rations and grain for animals, and wagons sufficient to carry grain, rations and bedding, and proceed East on the overland mail route, guarding mails, passengers, and property pertaining thereto.

2d. It is expected that to have the protection of the escort, the mail coaches will travel with it, as it cannot be expected that without change of animals it can keep pace with the mail coaches, especially when the roads are good.

3d. Colonel Burton will immediately offer his services to said Mail Company, and then proceed upon his journey, and remain on the line until relieved by the troops said to be coming up from the East, or so long as it may be necessary to quiet the Indians, who are said to be hostile, and the road considered safe from their depredations.

God bless and prosper you all.

DANIEL H. WELLS,
Lieut.-General Commanding N. L. Militia Utah Territory

Source: Edward W. Tullidge, *The History of Salt Lake City and Its Founders* (Salt Lake City: privately published, 1886), 254

UT-33

Joseph Holladay to Unspecified Recipient
April 25, 1862

Great Salt Lake City, U.T.
April 25th 1862

Station Keepers between Great Salt Lake City and Sweetwater Bridge Stations will supply Capt. R. T. Burton with any supplies or provisions that they may have to spare, taking his receipts for same and forwarding them to Salt Lake City.

JOSEPH HOLLADAY
Agt.

Source: "Utah, Territorial Militia Records, 1849–1877," No. 0692–0701 (March–April 1862), Series 2210, Utah State Archives, Salt Lake City

UT-34

Abraham Lincoln to Edwin M. Stanton
April 26, 1862

April 26, 1862

Edwin M. Stanton,
Sec. of War please make an order carefully in accordance with the within.

A. LINCOLN

[Editor's note: *The following note appears in* The Collected Works of Abraham Lincoln: "*Lincoln's endorsement is written on a letter from Milton S. Latham, April 26, 1862, requesting that authority be given 'to Brigham Young in Salt Lake City to raise, arm & equip one hundred men for ninety days service to be used in protecting the property of the Telegraph & overland mail companies' against hostile Indians until 'our own troops can reach the point where they are so much needed.' Adjutant General Lorenzo Thomas issued the authorization to Brigham Young on April 28, 1862 (OR, III, II, 27).*"]

Source: Roy Basler, ed., *The Collected Works of Abraham Lincoln*, 10 vols. (New Brunswick, N.J.: Rutgers University Press, 1953), 5:200

UT-35

Brigham Young to Lieutenant General Daniel H. Wells
April 28, 1862

Territory of Utah,
Great Salt Lake City, *9 p.m., April 28, 1862.*

Lieut. General Daniel H. Wells,
Commanding the Militia,
Sir:—

In accordance with "express direction of the President of the United States," telegraphically communicated at even date from the War Department by L. Thomas, Adj't Gen'l U.S. Army, authorizing me "to raise, arm, and equip one Company of Cavalry for ninety days service," I hereby request you to forthwith muster said company into the service of the United States, officered, organized, &c., as per the aforesaid "express direction of the President" to me through the War Department, and started at once for the destination and service required in the aforenamed telegram. You will make full and complete returns to me of all your proceedings herein.

BRIGHAM YOUNG.

[Editor's note: *A handwritten note on the reverse states: "April 28 1862 Special Order from Ex. Gov Young to Lieut Genl D H Wells to raise one company of volunteers."*]

Source: "Utah, Territorial Militia Records, 1849–1877," Series 2210, Box 1, Folder 47 (March–April 1862), Utah State Archives, Salt Lake City

UT-36

Daniel H. Wells to Major Lot Smith
April 28, 1862

April 28, 1862.

Major Lott Smith,
Dear Brother:

Col Burton with a detachment of twenty men had gone East to protect the overland mail Route from threatened Indian depredations, Col. Hooper and C. West have gone in their own conveyance, under their protection owing to the Mail Co. refusing to take any more passengers or Mails until the route is protected. Col Burton is directed to feel his way not run recklessly into danger, but if he should need any more force, to send by telegraph and it would be forwarded.

You will therefore please look around you and find about twenty men who can go at short notice. Please to show this note to Col. Merril or in case of his absence show them to his adjutant and inform him to furnish 10 mounted men from his command with one baggage wagon and four animals to be in [*illegible*]. I think that some of the boys up there would like to go out if you went, and so I make this request of Col. Merril & moreover it is presumed that suitable animals are rather more plenty with you than with us. Please to lose no time in making those arrangements up there and then repair to this city to complete the arrangement other details amounting to fifty men in all will be made for a like purpose from the other two Battalions. Do me the honor when you come down to stop with me,

As ever your Brother,

DANIEL H. WELLS

9 o'clock P.M., by a telegram just received President Young is authorizing us to raise a full company of cavalry consisting of nearly one hundred Men for the purpose of protecting the Mails you will therefor get twenty men from Col. Merril's command and two wagons and teams instead of our team and report yourself in the city ready for duty to [*illegible*] training or as much sooner as possible the service is to last 90 days or until relieved by U.S. troops somewhere about Devil's Gate.

D. H. WELLS

Source: "Utah, Territorial Militia Records, 1849–1877," Series 2210, Box 1, Folder 47 (March–April 1862), Utah State Archives, Salt Lake City

UT-37

Daniel H. Wells to Colonel A. L. Fullmer
April 28, 1862

GSL City, *April 28 1862*

Col A L Fullmer

Dear Brother We are raising a company of cavalry upon the requisition of President Young authorsed by the Presid of the U.S. to perform guard service for the telegraph and overland Mail ~~as~~ companies The service will be for ninety days unless sooner relieved by U.S. Troops supposed to be already on their way It is supposable that many in your command be possessed of Animals equipments supplies &c necessary for this expedition Please therefore to look ~~whom~~ around tomorrow and see what you can do to aid us in raising this as it is desirable to start Wednesday morning and oblige|

Your Brethren in the gospel

D H W

Copied G.S.

Source: "Utah, Territorial Militia Records, 1849–1877," Series 2210, Box 1, Folder 47 (March–April 1862), Utah State Archives, Salt Lake City

UT-38

Special Orders No. 3, Headquarters Nauvoo Legion
April 28, 1862

Headquarters Nauvoo Legion,
Great Salt Lake City, *April 28th, 1862.*

Special Orders,
No. 3.

1st. Pursuant to instructions received this day from ex-Governor Brigham Young, and in compliance with a requisition from the President of the United States, Major Lot Smith of the Battalion of Life Guards is hereby directed to enlist by voluntary enrollment for the term of ninety days a company of mounted men, to be composed as follows, to-wit: One captain, one first lieutenant, one second lieutenant, one quartermaster sergeant, one first sergeant, four sergeants, eight corporals, two musicians, two farriers, one saddler, one wagoner, and seventy-two privates. Major Smith is hereby assigned to the command of the company with rank of captain, and on mustering the men into service, will administer the proper oath agreeably to instructions herewith accompanying.

2d. The object of this expedition, to which this company is assigned, as instructed and authorized by the President, is the protection of the property of the Overland Mail and Telegraph Companies, at or about Independence Rock, and the adjoining country. Captain Smith will, therefore, as soon as his company is completed proceed at once to the above named vicinity, and patrol the road so as to render all necessary aid as contemplated by the instructions. It is not anticipated that the company, or any portion of it will camp so near any of the mail stations, as to give trouble or inconvenience; but sufficiently adjacent to render prompt and ready aid when required. Captain Smith is enjoined to preserve strict sobriety in his camp and prevent the use of all profane language or disorderly conduct of any kind. No apprehension is entertained by the General commanding, but that the best and most praiseworthy deportment will characterize the expedition, the officers and men having been selected with care, and with a view to their ability to render good and efficient service.

3d. Judging from advices received from the President of the United States, troops may soon be expected on the road to relieve the company now ordered out; the commander of the detachment will receive the necessary instructions in proper time, and will remain on duty with his command until so instructed.

4th. It is desirable to cultivate as far as practicable friendly and peaceful relations with the Indians.

5th. The service to be expected from the horses and mules on the expedition will be a sufficient argument in favor of great care in marching and feeding, as well as vigilant guarding and precaution against surprises. The greatest economy must be used with ammunition; none should be heedlessly wasted.

DANIEL H. WELLS.

Lieut-General Commanding Nauvoo Legion, Militia of Utah Territory.

Source: Edward W. Tullidge, *The History of Salt Lake City and Its Founders* (Salt Lake City: privately published, 1886), 255–256

UT-39

Daniel H. Wells to Unspecified Recipient
April 28, 1862

GSL City, *April 28 1862*

Dear Bro, you will forthwith raise 30 thirty Men of your command for service guarding the overland Mail & telegram on a requisition of President Young made by the President of the U.S. The service is for 90 days or until relieved by U.S. soldiers and will be paid as other forces of the Government you will also furnish one wagon and team with four animals for each ten and report yourself in this city tomorrow evening ready for service to be organized as then directed bring good rifles yaugers or double barreled shot guns and pistols when you have them and ammunition for 100 rounds to each Man also bedding for the Men and rations for all you can ~~to be apportioned &~~ not exceeding 90 days.

Source: "Utah, Territorial Militia Records, 1849–1877," Series 2210, Box 1, Folder 47 (March–April 1862), Utah State Archives, Salt Lake City

UT-40

Daniel H. Wells to Orrin Porter Rockwell
April 28, 1862

GSL City, *April 28 62.*

Mr O. P. Rockwell:

Dear Bro

Availing myself of your kind offer of Animals I ~~have can~~ send to you ~~this~~ to night wishing you to have so many as you can spare fit for services in the city tomorrow Evening or as much sooner as possible. The fact is we want to start a company East by day after tomorrow and can get Men much easier than animals another full Company is to be got up upon the requisition of President Young which will be further explained to you hereafter

D. H. WELLS

Source: "Utah, Territorial Militia Records, 1849–1877," Series 2210, Box 1, Folder 47 (March–April 1862), Utah State Archives, Salt Lake City

UT-41

DANIEL H. WELLS TO BISHOP STEWART BRITTON CRAFT
APRIL 28, 1862

GSL CITY, *April 28, 1862.*

BISHOP STEWART BRITTON CRAFT
DEAR BROTH.

You will see the orders to Bro Rawlings please assist him all you can to fit up and set his Men in readiness so ~~that~~ they may be here tomorrow Evening without fail.

Always your Brother in the gospel,

D. H. WELLS

SOURCE: "UTAH, TERRITORIAL MILITIA RECORDS, 1849–1877," SERIES 2210, BOX 1, FOLDER 47 (MARCH–APRIL 1862), UTAH STATE ARCHIVES, SALT LAKE CITY

UT-42

DANIEL H. WELLS TO COLONEL D. I. ROSS
APRIL 28, 1862

G. S. L. CITY, *April 28 1862*

COL. D. I. ROSS,

We are receiving enlistments for 90 days service under the requisition of President Brigham Young who is authorsided [authorized] by the President of the U.S. to raise arm and equip one company of cavalry to guard the telegraph and overland Mail companies. We would be pleased to accept some Men from your command who could immediately fit themselves out and be on hand tomorrow evening Please therefore to go about tomorrow and see what you can do in aiding us in raising and fitting out this company and oblige your Brother as ever.

D H W
Copied BBC

SOURCE: "UTAH, TERRITORIAL MILITIA RECORDS, 1849–1877," NO. 0692–0701 (MARCH–APRIL 1862), SERIES 2210, UTAH STATE ARCHIVES, SALT LAKE CITY

UT-43

Lot Smith Cavalry Company Oath of Office
April 30, 1862

I, John F Kinney, Chief Justice of the Supreme Court of the United States for the Territory of Utah Do Hereby Certify, That in pursuance of the following Order from the War Department, I mustered into the Service of the United States for the period of ninety days, unless sooner discharged, the officer's whose names appear to this Certificate, by administering the usual oath, and the oath provided by the Act of Congress of August 6th 1861.

Washington, *April 28, 1862*

Mr Brigham Young,
Great Salt Lake City.

By express direction of the President of the U.S. you are hereby authorized to raise, arm, and equip one Company of Cavalry for ninety (90) days service.

This Company will be organized as follows: one Captain, one First Lieut. One Second Lieutenant, one First Sergeant, one Quarter master Sergeant, Four (4) Sergeants, and Eight (8) Corporals. Two (2) Musicians, Two (2) Farriers, one Saddler, one Wagoner, and from fifty six (56) to seventy-two (72) privates. The Company will be employed to protect the property of the Telegraph and Overland Mail Companies in or about Independence Rock where depredations have been committed and will be continued in service only, until the U.S. troops can reach the point where they are so much needed. It may therefore be disbanded previous to the expiration of ninety (90) days.

It will not be employed for any offensive operations other than may grow out of the duty hereinbefore assigned to it.

The officers of the Company will be mustered into the U.S. Service by any civil officer of the U.S. at Salt Lake City competent to administer an oath. The men will then be enlisted by the Company officers. The men employed in the service above named will be entitled to receive no other than the allowance authorized by law to soldiers the service of the U.S. Until the proper staff officers for subsisting these men arrive you will please furnish subsistence for them your self, keeping an accurate account thereof for future settlement with U.S. Government.

By order of the Sec'y of War

L. THOMAS

Adj' Genl

to wit:

Lott Smith,	Captain
Joseph S. Rawlings,	First Lieut
J. Q. Knowlton,	Second Lieut.
Richd H. Atwood	First Sergt
James M. Barlow	Quartermaster Sergeant.
Samuel H.W. Riter,	Sergeant.
John P. Weemer,	d[itt]$_{o}$
Howard Spencer,	d$_{o}$
Moses Thurston,	d$_{o}$
Seymour B. Young,	Corporal
William A. Bringhurst	d$_{o}$
John Hoagland	d$_{o}$
John Neff	d$_{o}$
Newton Myrick	d$_{o}$
Andrew Bigler	d$_{o}$
Joseph H. Felt	d$_{o}$
Hiram B. Clemons	d$_{o}$
Ira N. Hinkley	Farrier
John Helm	d$_{o}$
Charles Evans	Bugler
Josiah Eardley	d$_{o}$
Francis Platt	Saddler
Solomon Hale	Wagoner

Sworn by me this 30th day of April A.D. 1862, at Great Salt Lake City.

JOHN F. KINNEY
Chief Justice
Supr[eme] Court Ter Utah

[Editor's note: *"Oath of Office by Hon. J. F. Kinney 1862" is written on the reverse. See Editor's Note for UT-44.*]

Source: "Utah, Territorial Militia Records, 1849–1877," No. 1502–1516 (1858–1865), Series 2210, Utah State Archives, Salt Lake City

UT-44

Privates and Teamsters Certificate of Oath (Captain Smith's Company) April 30, 1862

I hereby Certify that on the 30th day of April AD. 1862, in obedience to orders of 28th April 1862 from Lieutenant General Daniel H. Wells, commanding the Militia of Utah Territory, I mustered into the service of the United States by enlistment and administering the necessary oath to each of the following named persons to serve as Privates in a company of Cavalry raised by Hon. Brigham Young, under express directions of the President of the United States, for the protection of the property of the Overland Telegraph and Mail Companies, for the term of ninety days unless sooner disbanded, to wit:

Leander Lemmon
Hiram B. North
Wm H. Rhoades
Joseph Terry
Wm Terry
Moses W. Gibson
Edward A. Noble
Peter Carney
Donald McNicol
Landon Rich
Wm W. Lutz
Alley S. Rose
Bateman H. Williams
Lewis A. Huffaker
Joseph Goddard
Edward F. M. Guest
Francis Prince
Isaac Atkinson
James Larkins
Samuel R. Bennion
Jno R. Bennion
Lars Jensen
Hugh D. Park
Ephraim H. Williams
Reuben P Miller
George Cotterel
Parley P. Draper
Jno H. Walker
Richard Howe
Evert Covert
Jno H. Standiferd
Thomas Henry Harris
Wm Grant
Adelbert Rice
James H. Steed
Wm C. Allen
Daniel C. Lill
Edwin Brown
James Imlay
Harvey C. Hullinger
Harlon E. Simmons
James Greene
Moroni W. Alexander
James H. Cragun
James H. Wells
Joseph J. Taylor

Thomas J. Lutz
John Cahoon
Thomas Caldwell
Powel Johnson
Edwin Merrill
E. M. Wiler
Charles Crisman Jr.
James Sharp
Lewis L. Polmanteer
Joseph Fisher,

Jesse J. Cherry
Alberto Davis
Wm Longstrough
John Arrowsmith
William Lynch
Hiram Kimball Jr.
Theo J. Calkin
Lewis D. Osborn,
Benj. Neff
William Bess,

Emmerson Shurtleff
Sam Hill
Charles C. Burnham
Francis R. Cantwell
James Hickson
John Gibson

Teamsters
Geo. W. Davidson
Henry L. Dolton,
Mark Murphy,
Henry N. Bird,

Elijah H. Maxfield,
Lachoneus Barnard,
Alfred Randall,
William H. Walton,

Thurston Larsen,
Wyllys D. Fuller,
Wm Bagley

LOT SMITH, Capt.

[Editor's note: *"(Copy)" is written at the top of the first page. On the left side of the second page is written: "Privates & Teamsters Certificate of Oath Capt Smith's Co." It should be noted that the original muster in and muster out rosters for the Lot Smith Utah Cavalry Company are no longer on file at the National Archives in Washington, D.C. It is unknown when they were lost or removed. A typewritten* Muster-Out Roll of Captain Lott Smith's Company of Mounted Volunteers, August 14, 1862, *"taken from the original at Washington D. C." was made by Margaret Fisher in the 1920s and is available at the Utah State Archives (MSS A 5238). Numerous spelling discrepancies exist between the "Oath of Office" (UT-43), this Certificate of Oath, the typed muster-out roster, and other relevant nineteenth-century records. See Alford,* Civil War Saints, *Appendices E and F.*]

SOURCE: "UTAH, TERRITORIAL MILITIA RECORDS, 1849–1877,"
SERIES 2210, BOX 1, FOLDER 47 (MARCH–APRIL 1862),
UTAH STATE ARCHIVES, SALT LAKE CITY

UT-45

Brigham Young to Captain Lot Smith and Company
April 30, 1862

G.S.L. City, *April 30, 1862.*

Captain Lot Smith
and Company,
Brethren:—

As already advised, you have been mustered into the service of the United States for ninety days, under authority from President Lincoln to me through the War Department, to be employed in protecting "the property of the Telegraph and Overland Mail companies in or about Independence Rock."

In this movement I trust you will readily recognize the hand of Providence in our behalf, and place a secondary consideration upon the compensation you are entitled to, realizing that you are not laboring merely for pay or money but chiefly for your own good. Let not a thought of pay swerve you from that high moral tone derivable only from an upright performance of all duties. This is the time to permanently establish the influence God has given us, wherefore I feel to strongly impress it upon you to be kind, forbearing, and righteous in all your acts and sayings in public and private, in going, tarrying, and returning, that we may greet you with pleasure as those who have faithfully performed a work worthy of great praise.

The Officers are enjoined to conduct themselves with all due courtesy and kindness toward the men, and the men to yield prompt and strict obedience to the commands and requirements of the Officers, and all to conduct themselves with that propriety, toward each other and those you may meet, that becometh gentlemen; thus you may again prove that noble hearted American citizens can don arms in the defense of right and justice, without descending one hair's breadth below the high standard of American manhood.

Let there be no card playing, dicing, gambling, drinking intoxicating liquors, or swearing indulged in by any one of the Company; and if cards or dice or any thing of the kind are found with the Company, let the Captain at once see that they are destroyed.

Do not be in the Stations; but, when a portion or the whole of the command is camping in the neighborhood of a Station, be sufficiently near to be able to promptly extend any requisite protection.

Ever be kind to your animals and give them the best care in traveling, grazing, feeding, &c, your judgment and the circumstances will permit; and be ever on the alert that they neither stray nor are stolen from you, having both day and night guard mounted on good animals, and the night guard amply strong.

Wherever the command or a portion of it tarries at one place, or a time, reasonably contiguous to poles or timber, I recommend that they improve their leisure time in building good corrals for their own use, the use and accommodation of the Mail Company, and of our own immigration when convenient for them.

A liberal use of molasses will be more healthy than too freely partaking of salt meat, which should, whenever practicable, be dispensed with for fresh meat. We will endeavor to keep you timely supplied with every thing requisite for your health, comfort, and efficiency.

You will be your own sappers and miners, for which purpose you have picks, spades, shovels, axes, &c, and it is expected that you will improve the road as you pass along, so much so as practicable diligence in reaching your destination will warrant, not only for your own convenience but more particularly for the accommodation of the Mail Company and general travel. Further, mindful that a day lost in idleness is beyond recover, wherever the command or a detachment remain a sufficient time, it is recommend that they make such improvements, within their time and ability, as will most conduce to the convenience and comfort of the Mail and Telegraph Companies and the public at large.

Wherever the Command reaches its required destination, [whether] at Independence Rock or elsewhere, they should immediately build a good storehouse, in readiness for the supplies which will soon be forwarded. Rock should be picked up, mud made, and ovens constructed at once, and the proper persons be selected for bakers, that you may have palatable and healthy bread instead of that rendered unwholesome by the use of saleratus.

Morning and evening of each day let prayer be publicly offered in the Command and in all detachments thereof, that you may constantly enjoy the guidance and protecting care of Israels God and be blest in the performance of every duty devolved upon you, for which you have also the faith and prayers of,

Your Fellow Laborer
and Brother in the Gospel,

BRIGHAM YOUNG

Source: Brigham Young to Lot Smith, April 30, 1862, "Brigham Young office files: General Correspondence, Incoming, 1840–1877," MS 1234 1, Church History Library, Salt Lake City, Utah

UT-46

"Requisition for Troops," *Deseret* [*Weekly*] *News* April 30, 1862

On Monday evening, the 28th instant, Governor Young received a telegraphic dispatch from the War Department, authorizing him to raise, arm and equip a company of cavalry for ninety days' service, to protect the property of the telegraph and overland mail companies between Forts Bridger and Laramie, and to continue in service until the United States troops shall reach the point where their services are needed.

The required company was raised and organized yesterday, consisting of one captain, two lieutenants, one first sergeant, one quarter master sergeant, four sergeants, eight corporals, two musicians, two farriers, one saddler, one wagoner, and seventy-two privates, and will start to-day to perform the service, under command of Capt. Lot Smith. The names of the other officers we have not learned.

The company will not, according to the specifications of the order, be required to perform any other service than that required for the protection of the mail and telegraph, which may not be expected to be very arduous; but the life of a soldier on the plains cannot be very desirable, whether there be much or little to be done.

The requisition came unexpectedly, but was responded to with that alacrity that has ever characterized Governor Young and the citizens of Deseret when their services have been required by the Government, either to fight the battles of their country or to protect its citizens.

Source: "Requisition for Troops," *Deseret News*, April 30, 1862

UT-47

Captain Lot Smith U.S. Volunteers Journal May 1–20, 1862

May 1st Company left Salt L. City, proceeded to the mouth of Parleys Kanyon, finding that road impassible for water the whole road being washed away camped.

2nd

Crossed over to Emigration Kanyon, received an address and instructions from President B. Young also from General D. H. Wells, one mile up the Kanyon delayed mending road, camped for noon at Big Spring, roads very bad, at crossings of the stream had to dismount all the men and put on drag ropes arrived at the other side of the little mountain, and camped, had to make a new dug way for 100 yards 5 miles up the Kanyon.

3rd

Took Lambs Kanyon roads bad mended dug ways camped there

4th

Passed over the Summit snow very deep had to put on Men with drag ropes to the wagons, on the other side had to dismount the Cavalry and pack the Baggage

5th

Started packing Baggage, took Silver Creek roads were so bad, the whole Kanyon impassable for water, went along the sides of the mountains put in about 20 men[?] to each Waggon with ropes to prevbent upsetting baralled[?] in this way for about 6 Miles camped for night at the head of the Kanyon good feed.

6th

Crossed the Weber repaired the Bridge, made a new bridge at Chalk Creek camped there.

7th

Took the mountain side arrived at the Telegraph station mouth of Echo water too high to ford built a new bridge (one horse belonging to Bro Sell drowned / followed up the Kanyon built another new bridge and camped.

8th

Could not go up the Kanyon further took the side of the mountain camped a little beyond Cache Cave

9th

Arrived at Yellow Creek the whole bottom flooded, built a foot bridge unloaded the wagons, carried over the baggage men working in the water 4 Hours drove over the empty wagons reloaded, one horse got mired and broke his leg striving to extricate himself (belonging to Bishop Smith)

10th

Pleasant Journey camped on Muddy

11th

Made Fort Bridger camped one mile beyond the Fort, on our arrival within ¼ of a mile the Fort were met by one of the Mail Co. Mr Hugh ONeil who informed us we were just in time that the Indians had attacked a Mail carriage 4 Miles below Bridger Camp. Smith detailed Lieut. Rawlings and 16 Men to proceed there with all possible dispatch. After riding some 15 or 16 Miles they returned found no trace or track of Indians. The truth[?] is the Mail carriage started from Bridger, the men saw an Indian Squaw, fired on her turned their horses around and fled back to the Fort.

12.

Left Bridger nothing extra camped at Blacks Fork same night

13th

Crossed over to Hams Fork borrowed 1000 lbs of Flour from Mr. Granger at the Station to be repaid by the supply trains on their arrival camped at the bad crossing took out the baggage packed over.

14

Arrived at Green River ferry at Lewis Robison crossed over travelled 6 Miles camped.

15

Did not travel sent back 1 Waggon and 6 Men for 800 lbs Bacon and 800 lbs Flour at Hams Fork belonging to Mr. Robison

16

Snow on the ground Waggon came up with provisions from Ham's Fork travelled on camped on Big Sandy very cold.

17

Cold and stormy snow on Ground, camped for noon on Dry Sandy took 9 Sacks Barley 2 oats from Mail Station to be reported to the company the first opportunity camped for night in sight of the Pacific Springs

18

Mail Station at Pacific Springs deserted passed through a deep snow bank 6 or 7 feet took the Semmole cut off very cold.

19.

Met a Company of Imigrants 40 or 45 in number from Denver en route to Salmon River camped on Sweet Water.

20

Came to the Mail Station at 3 Crossings mail matter burst open and strewn[?] around Split Rock Station not burned but deserted camped on Sweet Water 3 imigrants from Denver with a Handcart camped about one mile from us. W. S. Gadble arrived in Camp 11 P.M.

R. H. ATTWOOD
O[rdnance] Serg[eant]

LOT SMITH
Captain

[Editor's note: *A bracket has been drawn on the right edge of several entries with an annotation, written in a different hand, as follows: 7th "Entered", 13th "chgd"* [*charged*], *15 "entered", and 17 "May 21/62 sent out by HW Miller ropes*[*?*] *his rect"* [*receipt*].]

Source: "Utah, Territorial Militia Records, 1849–1877," No. 1502–1516 (1858–1865), Series 2210, Utah State Archives, Salt Lake City

UT-48

Brigham Young to Adjutant General Lorenzo Thomas
May 1, 1862

Great Salt Lake City, *May 1, 1862*

Adj'T Genl. L. Thomas
U.S. Army, Washington City, D.C.

Immediately on the receipt of your telegram of the 28th ult. at 8–30 P.M., I requested Gen'l Daniel H. Wells to proceed at once to raise a company of Cavalry to be mustered into the service of the United States for ninety days, as per your aforesaid telegram. Gen'l Wells forthwith issued the requisite orders, and yesterday the Captain and other officers were sworn by Chief Justice J.F. Kinney, the enrolling and swearing the privates attended to, and the command moved into camp adjacent to this city. To day the Company seventy two (72) privates, officered as directed, and ten (10) baggage and supply wagons, with one assistant teamster deemed necessary, took up their line of march for the neighborhood of Independence Rock.

BRIGHAM YOUNG.

[Editor's note: *A handwritten note at the top of this telegram states: "Brigham Young's telegram to War Department."*]

Source: "Utah, Territorial Militia Records, 1849–1877," Series 2210, Box 1, Folder 48 (May–June 1862), Utah State Archives, Salt Lake City

UT-49

Lewis Robinson to Daniel H. Wells
May 1, 1862

May 1st 1862, 20 Miles up Echo
3 o'clock P.M.

D. H. Wells Esq.

Dear Brother, we are all well. We have been two days on this creek Swiming at every crossing of the streeem, we are leaving one Waggon hear & all the Oats, we Shall train from the Stations till we git to Fort Bridger The company left 20 bushels of Oats at Wm Kimballs & drew the same amount of me at Webber Please instruct your teamster to git the 20 bushels at Kimballs & 30 at Wm. Smiths, Chalk Creek. The traveling is offule [awful] Snow Deep Watters high, & where ever the snow is gone their is no bottom to the mud. We shall try to get to cash cave to night if Possible

As Ever your Brothe[r],

LEWIS ROBI[NS]ON.

You can form no idea of the travelity, & but little of the snow & watte [water]

L R

[Editor's note: *The signature on this handwritten letter appears as "Robion," but an explanatory note on the reverse side records the author's name as "Lewis Robinson." See UT-51.*]

Source: "Utah, Territorial Militia Records, 1849–1877," Series 2210, Box 1, Folder 48 (May–June 1862), Utah State Archives, Salt Lake City

UT-50

Ben Holladay to Governor Brigham Young May 2, 1862

New York, *May 2, 1862*

To Gov. Brigham Young,

Many thanks for your prompt response to President Lincoln's request. As soon as the boys can give protection the mails shall be resumed. I leave for your city Sunday next.

BEN HOLLADAY.

Source: "Utah, Territorial Militia Records, 1849–1877," Series 2210, Box 1, Folder 48 (May–June 1862), Utah State Archives, Salt Lake City

UT-51

J. S. M. Barlow to General Daniel H. Wells
May 5, 1862

Strawberry Ranch
Parleys Park, *5 May 1862.*

General D. H. Wells,

Sir, The roads being unusually bad in consequence of which we have had considerable delay and of necessity having to feed out liberally to our, animals, we have availed ourselves by taking 25 Bushels of Oats left by Col Burton at this station ~~which were left~~ who drew them from Louis Robinson on Weber where we expect to draw 75 Bushels if on hand as stated. No particular accidents have occurred. The health of the Company is good except slight colds in some few cases. A number of men are considerably anxious in relation to more bedding and Boots and really in need of them. No animals missing. Mr. Robinson wishes the grain to be returned to him at Green River.

I am Sir Yours respectfully,

J S M BARLOW QTR.

[Editor's note: *James Madison Barlow served as a Quartermaster Sergeant for the Lot Smith Utah Cavalry Company. "Mr. Robinson" is presumably Lewis Robinson; see UT-49.*]

Source: "Utah, Territorial Militia Records, 1849–1877," Series 2210, Box 1, Folder 48 (May–June 1862), Utah State Archives, Salt Lake City

UT-52

"Departure of the Company for the Protection of the Mail and Telegraph Lines," *Deseret [Weekly] News*
May 7, 1862

The company raised by Governor Young on the requisition of the President, through the War Department, for the protection of the property of the Overland Mail and Telegraph Companies, did not get off till Thursday afternoon, as there was some little delay in getting all things ready for the expedition, more than was anticipated: but there was nothing lacking for the performance of the service when the company marched.

The officers of the company were as follows:—Capt. Lot Smith; 1st Lieut. J.S. Rawlins; 2d Lieut. J.Q. Knowlton; Orderly Sergeant R.H. Attwood; Quartermaster

Sergeant J. M. Barlow; Sergeants S. H. W. Riter, John P. Weimer, H. O. Spencer, Moses Thurston; Corporals Seymour B. Young, Newton Myrick, Wm. A. Bringhurst, John Hoagland, Jos. H. Felt, Jno. Neff, Andrew Bigler, Hyrum B. Clemons; Farriers, Ira N. Hin[c]kley, John Helm; Saddler, Francis Platt; Wagoner, Solomon Hale; Musicians, Josiah Eardley, Charles Evans.

The company was provided with ten baggage wagons and took with them rations for thirty days. On Monday three or four other heavy mule wagons followed, with rations for thirty days more. The balance that will be required will probably be taken out by the trains going to the Missouri river, which are expected to start in about ten days.

Source: "Departure of the Company for the Protection of the Mail and Telegraph Lines," *Deseret News*, May 7, 1862

UT-53

S. Downs, J. Moarley, T. Gooddell, J. Warner and Others to Unspecified Recipient May 10, 1862

Plante Station, *May 10, 1862.*

To all whom it may Concern.

There has been depredations committed on the Mail road by either Indians or Mormons, or both together. Some of the stations have been pillaged, and the stock driven off. we therefore deemed it necessary to inform all emigrants on this road of the facts and warn them to be careful of their stock. We are about 25 men in number and are now in camp at a station about 5 miles below the station at the junction of this road with the mail road. we shall probably stay there about a week. from date in order to collect a larger company. to go through to Salmon River: all persons wishing to join us, will find at the above name places. feed is better there than here and stock more secure.

(Signed in one hand)
S. DOWNS
J. MOARLEY
T. GOODDELL
J. WARNER
& OTHERS.

Source: "Utah, Territorial Militia Records, 1849–1877," Series 2210, Box 1, Folder 48 (May–June 1862), Utah State Archives, Salt Lake City

UT-54

John D. Gibson to Lieutenant General Daniel H. Wells
May 11, 1862

Fort Bridger, *May 11th, 1862*

Lieut. Gen Wells,

Dear Sir, We Arrived hear today Before arriving to this place a man came out and met us saying that we had just came in time to Save the fort. The mail had left here for the East and had got about six miles when seven Indians came out of the brush in to the road The men in the coach fired at them and then Turned and came as hard as they could to the Fort. Telling a great story of about the indians Capt Smith orde[re]d seventeen of us to go in pursuit of them. We went but did not see Any thing of them. We have had some bad Luck since we left we have lost two horses: The wauter is high and the roads is bad we ~~have to~~ have built six bridges And made a great deal of road. we are all well and are getting along first rate I would like to hear from you all very mutch. give my respects To all of the Family. ~~your obedt svt~~
your Brother in the church

JOHN. D. GIBSON

Source: "Utah, Territorial Militia Records, 1849–1877," Series 2210, Box 1, Folder 48 (May–June 1862), Utah State Archives, Salt Lake City

UT-55

Brigham Young to Lot Smith
May 14, 1862

All well at home. Make as good time for your destination as possible. If all is peaceable~~, let Burtons company return~~ ~~when you meet Burtons~~ ~~when you get to Burtons Company let them return home~~ ~~If all is peaceable,~~ when you meet with Burtons Company let them return home immediately. ~~Provisions & clothing are on~~ Supplies are being sent by the ox teams This morning a Company of cavalry left Laramie for Sweetwater.

B. YOUNG.
May 14/62

[Editor's note: *An explanatory annotation at the top of the handwritten telegraph message states: "Telegram to Capt. Lott Smith—May 14, 1862 in the evening on his arrival at Green River."*]

Source: "Utah, Territorial Militia Records, 1849–1877,"
Series 2210, Box 1, Folder 48 (May–June 1862),
Utah State Archives, Salt Lake City

UT-56

"Captain Smith's Command," *Deseret* [*Weekly*] *News*
May 14, 1862

The company of volunteers for the protection of the Overland Mail under Capt. Smith, arrived at Fort Bridger on Sunday morning last, all safe, and will soon reach the most eastern point on the route indicated in the order requiring the service. The most timid can now pass that way with much safety. If there be any "hostile Indians" found at the "Seat of War," they will soon migrate.

Source: "Captain Smith's Command," *Deseret News*, May 14, 1862

UT-57

Telegram from Colonel Robert T. Burton to Governor Fuller
May 16, 1862

Deer Creek. *May 16. 1862.*

Governor Fuller:

My detachment arrived here yesterday at 3 p.m. Encountering no difficulty, save that caused by snow and mud, etc. We have seen no Indians on the route; found all the mail stations from Green River to this point deserted, all stock having been stolen or removed and other property abandoned to the mercy of Indians or white men.

We found at the Ice Springs Station, which had been robbed on the night of the 27th, a large lock mail—twenty-six sacks, a great portion of which had been cut open and scattered over the prairie. Letters had been opened and pillaged, showing conclusively that some renegade whites were connected with the Indians in the robbery. The mail matter after being carefully collected and placed in the sacks, I have conveyed to this point, also ten other sacks of lock mail, from the Three Crossings:

all of which will be turned over to the mail agent at Lapareil. Twenty miles from this we will meet men from the East for this purpose. The United States troops from the East will be in this vicinity tomorrow: and unless otherwise directed by yourself, or Gen. Wells, I will return immediately halting on the Sweet Water to investigate still farther into the causes of the difficulty, as I have not been able to learn who or what Indians positively have been engaged in the matter but suppose it to be a band of about thirty renegade Snake and Bannocks from the North. Some of the party spoke English plainly, and one the German language.

Hon. W. H. Hooper and Mr. C. W. West, will take passage in the coach that comes for the mail.

ROBERT T. BURTON.
Commanding.

Source: "Latest from the Plains," *Deseret News*, May 21, 1862

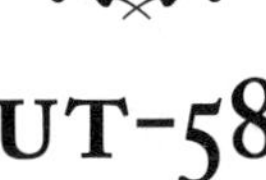

UT-58

"Returning," *Deseret* [*Weekly*] *News*
May 21, 1862

The troops under command of Col. Burton, after escorting Senator Hooper and Bishop West through the hostile country, received orders to return home, and were yesterday at Independence Rock on their way westward.

Capt. Smith and his command will probably meet the U.S. troops from Laramie in a day or two. The Eastern troops are expected to come no further west than Sweetwater.

Source: "Returning," *Deseret News*, May 21, 1862

UT-59

Capt. Lot Smith U.S. Volunteers Journal
May 22–July 14, 1862

May 22' 1862.

Moved the Command 5 Miles up the River and Camped

23

Captain Smith and 25 Men, marched to Sweetwater Bridge Hoisted U.S. Flag at the Station. Here we found the California Mail scattered all around. Turned out for Troop Drill in the afternoon.

24

Company paraded mounted for Inspection and Drill.

25.

U.S. Troops reported within 6 Miles Captn. Smith and Escort went to meet them false report proved to be a large Company of Emigrants.

26.

Company left Sweetwater Bridge, 1 Serj^{t}. and 10, Privates detailed to remain and guard the Station command camped at Devils Gate.

27.

Sent teams for Wood Poles &c. for Building Surveyed and marked out place for Corral Houses &c.

28.

Commenced Building Corral.

29.

Rec.^{d} orders from General Craig to march to Hams Fork, Indians having stolen Mail Animals from that Station. Detailed 50 Men to accompany Capt. Smith en route for foregoing place, the commander of the Company under Command of Lieu$^{t.}$ Rawlings to remain at Devils Gate. The Corral and 1 House for Storage was completed at this place by L^{t}. Rawlings Command

30

Captn Smith and Head Quarters of Company marched this morning en route for Hams Fork camped for night at Bitter Cottonwood Creek.

31

Continued the March found the Telegraph line broke in two places on the Sweetwater swam the River and repaired it camped at the Ice Springs here we found Mail Sacks torn open and mail matter scattered all around.

June 1st

Marched to Antelope Creek and Camped.

2

Marched to South Pass and Camped.

3

Marched to Dry Sandy met Serj.^{t} Thurston and Detach^{t} with Supplies Camped.

4.

Met M^{r}. Bromley with Animals to restock the Mail Line passed Captn Murdock and train Capt. Smith and Escort went to Green River for supplies, 1 Serj. and 10 Privates left as Guard at Green River.

5 & 6.

Encamp^{d} Drill and Inspection of Arms.

7th

Captain Smith arrived with supplies marched to Pacific Springs and camped.

8th

Serj.^{t} Attwood went to Mail Station for Letters Genl Craig arrived there had a pleasant interview.

9th

Capt. Smith Lieu^{t} Knowlton and Serjeant Attwood waited upon Genl Craig. The General gave written instruction to Captain Smith placing the whole of Nebraska Territory under martial law &c. &c. met Horns C^{o}_rec^{d} Letter from M^{r}. Holliday stating Mail Animals had been stolen from Big Sandy Station this was late in the afternoon and the notification did not arrive until 3 days after the occurrence, nevertheless the Captain started in pursuit with command Travelled 30 Miles that evening and Camped.

10th

Marched at day light arrived at Big Sandy Struck the Indian Trail Travelled about 20 Miles across towards Wind River Mountains camped for noon sent back the Waggons dismounted 5 of the Men and packed their animals followed the trail travelled about 75 Miles that day.

11th

Still following the Trail Travelled about 50 Miles and camped for noon at the three Forks of Green River, from signs of trail found it useless to pursue farther, Indians too much start, killed two Bears and camped.

12

Marched down the River struck the Lander Road and Camped.

13.

En Route to Pacific Spring's crossed the Sandy's and camped 40 miles from the Spring's

14.

Snow storm all morning, cleared up at noon took up the line of march encountered a terrific storm reached Pacific Spring's 6 P.M.

15

Snow storm all day. Lieu^{t} Knowltons Horse chilled to death

16

Snow storm continued

17th

Moved Camp 2 Miles.

18th 19

Encamped. Troop Drill both days

20th

Moved Camp 3 Miles.

21.

U. States regulars under command of Lieu^{t} Wilcox came up reported to Captn Smith and marched back en route for Laramie.

22. 23. 24

Encamped. Troop Drill.

25th

Other Volunteers under command of the Lieu^{t} Col Collins arrived.

26th

Capt. Smith and Escort paid a visit to Col Collins

27.

Recd orders from General Craig to march for Fort Bridger and there establish Head Quarters. The Company under Captain Smith to guard the Line from Green River to Great Salt Lake City

28.

Marched and camped on Dry Sandy.

29.

Marched to Big Sandy and camped.

30.

Marched to Green River and camped

July 1st

Crossed Green River and camped leaving 1 Serj^{t}. and 10 Privates.

2

Marched on. Horses stampeded at noon camped on Hams Fork

July 3rd

Marched on Captured Manhart (torn page) convict on the Hills camped two miles this side (torn page) Bridger.

4.

At day break celebrated the 4th trumpets sounding salute and firing by the command, broke Camp marched through and camped 2 miles from Fort Bridger. Rec^{d}. telegram from Col Collins requesting Captain Smith to apprehend if possible 5 Deserters from his command supposed to have started for Salmon River. Lieu^{t}. Knowlton and 10 Men detailed for this duty with orders to proceed to the Lander Road and intercept them if possible.

5th

Corporal Myrick and 10 Men detailed as an escort to proceed with Judge Carter, en route for Denver as a protection for himself and family until he overtook his train. This detachment travelled about 150 Miles on the Denver Route apprehended two thieves and recovered 8 Mail mules, the thieves were handed over to Judge Carter to be taken to Denver, and the Animals restored to the Mail Co.

6. 7. 8.

Inspection of Arms and Troop Drill each day on the 8th. Recd. orders from Col Collins to furnish an Escort for Judges Waite and Drake from Fort Bridger to S.L. City. Serjt. Attwood and 8 Men detailed for this Service also to escort in 2 prisoners Manhart & Angles the former captured by the Command, the latter handed over by Judge Carter. (torn page) arrived in Salt Lake City on the 11th. (torn page) returned to Fort Bridger arrived there.

10th. 11th. 12th. 13th. 14th.

The remainder of the journal can not be completed until I receive the Reports of Detachments.

R H ATTWOOD

[Editor's note: *A typewritten note taped to each page reads: "Journal of R. H. Attwood, 1st Sgt. Capt. Lott Smith's Co. Cavalry Civil War May 22, 1862 through July 14, 1862."*]

Source: "Utah, Territorial Militia Records, 1849–1877," Series 2210, Box 1, Folder 48 (May–June 1862), Utah State Archives, Salt Lake City

UT-60

"Col. Burton's Command," *Deseret* [*Weekly*] *News* May 28, 1862

We expect Col. Burton and the company that was sent out as escort to Senator Hooper will arrive in the city on Saturday. We have heard of no casualties.

Source: "Colonel Burton's Command," *Deseret News*, May 28, 1862

UT-61

"The Mails," *Deseret* [*Weekly*] *News* May 28, 1862

We are not informed of the day on which the daily mail will again leave this city for the States, east and west, but presume that before another issue of the *News*, the overland Daily Mail Company will be again in the discharge of its public obligations.

We understand that Col. Burton was to arrive at Bridger last evening with several sacks of back mail matter, found at the Sweetwater. In all probability the company's stage will bring that mail into the city and have it here for delivery on Saturday.

SOURCE: "THE MAILS," *DESERET NEWS*, MAY 28, 1862

UT-62

COLONEL ROBERT T. BURTON'S REPORT OF MARCH ALONG LINE OF OVERLAND MAIL JUNE 3, 1862

GREAT SALT LAKE CITY, *June 3rd 1862.*

GENERAL:

I have the honor to report the result of the expedition ordered out for the protection of the Eastern Mail and Telegraph line, agreeable to your special orders No. 2 April 25th 1862.

With a detachment of Twenty mounted men of the First Cavalry, Nauvoo Legion (Militia of Utah) an interpreter and guide; Four Baggage Waggons rations for twenty days etc. I left this City on the morning of the 26th of April—The first part of the March was over Snow from four to five feet in depth, commencing at a point two miles west of the summit of the Wasatch mountains until the Road enters Silver Creek Kanyon, a distance of twelve or Fifteen miles. It was thawing at the time and was insufficient to bear the weight of the men, consequently we had a severe task to take through our animals and wagons. From this point until we reached Ft Bridger, we encountered heavy snow drifts, overflowing streams and very deep mud. The narrative of a single day's march is the history of the whole–at least for the first nine days. We were compelled to cut through deep drifts of snow with spade and shovel; to extract mules and wagons therefrom with ropes dragging the latter up steep hills and through overflooded streams and sometimes through almost fathomless mud; the men were necessarily much–exposed, were wet from morning until night and compelled to sleep in the snow or mud.—Arrived at Ft. Bridger May 4th Found Considerable excitement in consequence of the arrival of some men who had been wounded near Split Rock Station on the Sweet Water, and also from rumors that there were Fifteen hundred Indian warriors near the head of this stream, & from various other reports—Left this point—May 3rd and arrived at Green River on the morning of the 7th. Here some traces of Indians were discovered and my Interpreter Mr. Terry, an experienced guide—supposed these signs to be some two weeks old, and that the party numbered twenty or twenty five, what tribe he could not tell. Their trail seemed to take a direction towards Bitter Creek leaving the mail rout entirely—The road from that point to Pacific Springs passible-mail stations deserted, no further signs of Indians arrived at the Upper Crossing of the Sweet water on the evening of the 9th The stream very high—and the snow very deep from this point to the East foot of Rocky Ridges where we arrived on the 11th and found at this place the Keeper of the Ice Spring—Station and some passengers who had been endeavoring to go east by mail Coach; I learned from them the robbery of that station on the night of the 27th of April, and determined to make a forced March and reach there if possible that evening, which I succeeded in doing, and found mail sacks cut open—letters scattered in every direction, some of them torn open—money drafts & other valuables extracted—All the mail matter here was carefully collected by my order & put into sacks & disposed of as before reported to his Excellency—F. Fuller acting Gvr of Utah Territory—The following is in substance the statement made to me by Robert Kefernick keeper of the above named station at Ice Spring—A party of about twenty five persons supposed to be Indians came about 10 o'clock at night and commenced an attack on the Station by trying to break the locks on the gates—failing in this, they then cut out some logs in the West end of the Stables, Succeeding in entering the Stable they built a fire. took out the animals, cut the harness and took what parts of it they wanted. then handled the mail matter which was stacked up in the east end of the stable—cut open the sacks, took out the letters—tore them open and strewed them about the premises, They also took the Trunks and Blankets belonging to the passengers before refered to. There were seven men in the Station who had Six Guns and several Revolvers, but not a shot was fired. The Indians remained there all night and until the sun was two hours high next morning—As soon as the Indians left, the seven men fled to the Rocky Ridge Station, a distance of twenty two miles.

May 12th we left Ice Spring Station taking all the locked mail with me (twenty six sacks) and arrived at the Three Crossings station at 10 A.M.—Found there Ten sacks locked mail exposed to Indians or white men—this I also took along as by Telegraph reported.

At 2 o'clock the same day we passed the two mail Coaches that ~~were~~ had been attacked & robed near the Split Rock Station on the 2nd of April. Found there evidence of the mail ~~brought~~ contained by those two Coaches having been burned by the marauders—two. Trunks were lying near cut open and robbed of their contents, the remains of several sets of Stamps were also found near the places—the sides of the Coaches pierced by several bullets—some of them apparently at long range—Coaches robbed of their canvass tops &—two small arrows & one bow were found nearby—guide could not tell to what Tribe they belonged—Camped at Plaunts Station, which we found deserted—Stable and part of corral burned. From Battese, Lonsham and other mountaineers I learned that a party of some twenty five or thirty Indians, supposed to be Snakes and Bannacks, had taken the stock from this Station,—that when the place was attacked, there were twelve or fourteen men in the Fort armed with Guns and Revolvers, and had port holes through the sides of the House, but for some reason the robing party were quietly permitted to take the stock without any resistance: they also reported that some of the party spoke English and French fluently and others the German language.

13th passed a company of Emigrants from Denver camped at Wheeler & Merchants station near "Devils Gate," also met another company the same day—travelling west. 14th Arrived at Platte Bridge—found collected at this place Mr. Plaunt and several other Mountaineers and Indian traders—All seemed somewhat excited about Indian difficulties~~—Naturally has a limited supply of Flour & Beef~~ 13th Storming all day, in consequence of which I halted my detachment at Platte Station 14 miles below the Bridge, pushing forward with two or three men to Deer Creek to obtain Communication with the mail agent relative to the locked mail before refered to. said agent meeting me at La Preel 20 miles East of Deer Creek at which point he received the U.S. mail—

From G.S.L. City to this point I had the pleasure of extending to Hon. W. H. Hooper and C. W. West Esq. such assistance and protection as my detachment afforded—From this place as you are already advised I had instructions to return, collecting such information as I could on my march relative to the difficulties on the mail line.

Accordingly on the 18th of May I commenced my return, arriving at Sweet Water Bridge on the 20th Found at this Station a large quantity of locked mail which has been Cashed by the mail employees and partly uncovered. Supposed to be done by some Denver Emigrants on their way to Salmon River. From the exposed situation of this mail, it being very much injured by the storms of Snow and rain. I directed it to be placed under shelter in one of the buildings and arrised the Executive and yourself of the same. Total amt. of locked mail at this station 45 Sacks—35 for California and 10 Sacks for Utah. The latter we brought along by instructions from Govr. Fuller,

The Station of Messrs Wheeler & Merchant mentioned before had been burned since we passed it on the 13th on our downward march—Reported by my informant Tim Goodall a Mountaineer to have been done by a Company of Emigrants from Pikes Peak—I met Capt. Smiths command, Utah Volunteers, at Plaunts Station on the 21st—men in excellent health and Spirits—

On the 27th immediately after crossing Hams Fork, I learned from some mountaineers who were camped near, that some Indians had visited one of their camps three or four miles above during the night previous and had driven off some thirty five head of stock. My detachment being under march and animals being too much jaded for pursuit, I let ~~my~~ the baggage waggons and most of my command continue on, taking with me five men and proceeded up Hams Fork to the Camp before mentioned, and learned from the Mountaineers that they had followed the trail of the Stolen Stock up the River some ten miles and found where they had crossed & saw four Indians driving the animals, but could not cross to them—They did not know to what Tribe they belonged, but supposed them to be Crows, They also reported to me of having a difficulty with the Bannacks some time previous, and had Killed two or three of them, but did not know of the Indians following them~~—Met several Ox and Mule trains between Ft. Bridger and the Weber, all getting along quietly and in good order.~~

It might not be amiss here to state, that at almost all the stations between Ft. Bridger and Deer Creek there is more or less mail matter laying in and about the stations, principally paper mail for California and Oregon.

Accompanying this report you will find a Notice, found posted up on the Road near Plaunts Trading Post, signed by "Tim Goodall & others, also Goodall's statement denying any knowledge of the same~~, with a journal of each days proceedings during my expedition~~.

I would do injustice to the officers and men of my detachment, were I to close this report without bringing to your favorable notice, the cheerfulness and patience with which they endured the fatigues & hardships of the ~~trip~~ ~~Quest~~ expedition which I assure you were of no ordinary character.

I am very respectfully your obdt. Servant

R. T. BURTON
Commanding Detachment

DANIEL H. WELLS
Lieut Genl. Commanding
N.L. Militia
Utah Territory
(added in one sent to Gov Fuller)

The foregoing is a true copy of original in file in this office.

H B CLAWSON
Asst. Adjt. General Militia UT
Adjt Gen's office
Militia UT

SOURCE: "UTAH, TERRITORIAL MILITIA RECORDS, 1849–1877," SERIES 2210, BOX 1, FOLDER 48 (MAY–JUNE 1862), UTAH STATE ARCHIVES, SALT LAKE CITY

UT-63

"The Mails," *Deseret [Weekly] News*
June 4, 1862

Ten sacks of mail matter were brought into the city on Friday evening. Col. Burton brought them on from the Sweetwater Station to Fort Bridger, whence it came by the mail contractor's stage to the city. The latest date from New York was to the 12th of April. When another mail will arrive from or leave for the east is to us unknown, and, as far as we can learn, everybody else is enveloped in the same darkness. This may be all proper but we do not believe it, and we shall take proper measures to represent such conduct where it should be known.

Source: "The Mails," *Deseret News*, June 4, 1862

UT-64

"Return from the Road," *Deseret [Weekly] News*
June 4, 1862

Col. R. T. Burton and his command returned to the city on Saturday evening, in excellent health, but considerably fatigued with their travels. On arrival in the city, they reported to Gen. Wells, and repaired to the Executive Office, where they were disbanded. A juvenile singing class greeted the company with "Home Again," which sounded well in the still calm evening, and was courteously acknowledged to the youngsters by the applause of the company.

We have seen several of the company who impart information not over favorable to some persons on the eastern road, but we think it proper to defer what we have to say till we see the report of Col. Burton. Our former apprehensions of white Indians being mixed up in the plundering of mails were not without too much foundation, and we change in nothing our before-expressed opinion on the conduct of those who have left us without mail facilities during this, to us, most important season of the year. We hope that a proper investigation will be had into all these affairs; but of this we shall have more to say before long.

Source: "Return from the Road," *Deseret News*, June 4, 1862

UT-65

"The Companies for the Missouri River," *Deseret* [*Weekly*] *News*
June 4, 1862

The companies with teams for the Missouri have been often heard from since their departure and were getting along quite well considering the high waters and bad roads, which, as anticipated, had impeded their progress. Those difficulties, however, had, to latest dates from the several trains, been, by diligence and perseverance, overcome with but little loss or damage–a few wagons up-set and broken, with some little loss of provisions and other articles comprising their casualties.

Col. Burton and company, returning from the "seceded" or "infested" section of the eastern road, through which he escorted Mr. Hooper and those accompanying him, met Capt. Murdock and company at Fort Bridger, which place they left on the morning of May 28th, expecting to camp that night on Muddy, twenty miles distant. Captain Duncan's train, with Captain Horn's close in the rear, was met that forenoon a few miles this side of Fort Bridger. Captain Harmon left Bear river on the morning of the 29th, and the companies in charge of Captains Haight and Miller, respectively, were met on that day near each other about fifteen miles up Echo, all well and progressing finely.

Source: "The Companies for the Missouri River," *Deseret News*, June 4, 1862

UT-66

Lot Smith to Brigham Young
June 16, 1862

Pacific Springs
June 16th 1862.

President B. Young
D[ear] Sir,

I am happy to inform you the Company are all well some few exceptions of cold and slight fever, the Brethren who have suffered are now fast recovering.

On Monday 8th Inst. I had an interview with Br. General Craig who arrived by

Stage at the Pacific Springs Station, he expressed himself much pleased with the promptness of our people in attending to the call of the General Government also the exertions we had made to overcome the obstacles on the Road, spoke in high terms of our people generally, informed me that he had telegraphed President Lincoln to that effect and intended writing to him more fully by Mail, was much pleased with the Corral and Houses we were building at Devils Gate wished us to leave a Guard there, and desired us to contribute as much as possible to our own comfort, and render all the assistance possible to the Mormon Emigration.

I rec^d. written instructions to the effect that he had placed the whole of Nebraska Territory under Martial Law. Utah he remarked was perfectly quiet and loyal and always had been for anything he knew to the contrary. He alluded to the pleasant time he had spent in Salt Lake City in 1849 at the Dinner &c on the 24th of July, gave me full power to act according to my discretion for the benefit of the public good.

On the whole I consider him a Gentleman and about one of the best specimens of the tribe he belongs to.

He also remarked we were the most efficient troops he had for the present Service, and thought as we had broke into our summers work of requesting President Lincoln to engage our Services for. 3 Months longer. He allotted us as our portion of the Route from the 1st crossing of Sweet Water to Green River, considering it would be more to our advantage to be near home.

I should have written to you immediately after my interview with the General, but on our return to Camp, we were notified that 4 Animals had been stolen from Big Sandy Station through neglect on part of the Mail Company we did not learn this until 3 days after it ocurred we however took 20 Men and 4 Pack Animals started in pursuit and tracked them to a North Bend of Green River near the Wind River Mountains travelling 150 Miles in two days, the Indians had there crossed. I swam the River with 3 Men, but a number of the Men being unable to swim and believing it to be impossible to cross over the Pack Animals and also the command without very considerable risk of life. I did not pursue any further.

Had they promptly notified me we could easily have overtaken them before they arrived at the River.

I have sent for Lieut. Rawling's Detachment to join me here leaving 1 Serj^t. and 15 Men at Devils Gate to guard that Station and any Storage that may be left there Since my return I have been informed all of Louis Robison's Stock had been taken from Green River I warned him as I passed by to be more careful as he usually let them range 5 or 6. Miles away without army Guard. I had detailed Serj^t Riter and 12 Men to remain near that Station but two days before Louis Stock was taken Ben Halliday passed through and requested them to move back to Big Sandy consequently there was none of my command near enough to follow.

I intend as soon as Rawling's Detachment arrives to take about 40 Men and Pack

Animals and make a Trip into Wind River Valley, where I believe the Stock stolen is concealed; as the Mail is however now running, I should be glad to receive some instructions from you as to any course you may deem it wisdom for me to pursue.

4 3 ox ~~Teams~~ trains Murdock, Duncans and Harmon & Horn have passed this place. Should any thing special occur we will write immediately.

The boys all wish to be kindly remembered to you and all the Saints.

I am happy to state that the Brethren have all conducted themselves as men of God since they have been under my command.

Our animals are most of them improving. We have had 2 ways and nights 14th & 15th Inst. snowstorm and heavy winds, one horse chilled to death.

With kind love
I remain
Yours affectly in the Gospel

LOT SMITH.

P.S. I omitted to mention there was no guard or watch kept over the animals at Big Sandy

[Editor's note: *"June 16, Rcvd June 26,/62. From Cap. Lot Smith" is written on the reverse of the last page.*]

Source: Lot Smith to Brigham Young, June 16, 1862, "Brigham Young office files: General Correspondence, Incoming, 1840–1877," MS 1234 1, Church History Library, Salt Lake City, Utah

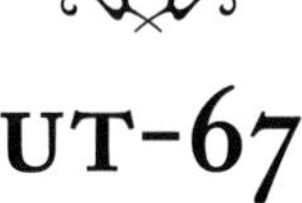

UT-67

Lot Smith to Brigham Young
June 27, 1862

Pacific Springs, *June 27th, '62.*

President Young:

D[ear] Sir,

I have just received orders from General Craig through Colonel Collins to march my command to Fort Bridger to guard the Line from Green River to Salt Lake City and start from here tomorrow morning.

Lieut. Rawlings and command arrived here yesterday; owing to neglect of the

Mail, my orders to Lieu[t]. Rawlings did not reach him until eight days after they were due consequently there has been no detail left at Devils Gate.

There has been built by the command at the former place a Log House 20 f[t]. by 16 with Bake Houses & detached also a commodious corral. Lieu[t]. Rawlings has left the above in charge of Major O'Farral, Ohio V[olunteers]. but occupied by Mess[rs]. Merchant and Wheeler Traders who formerly owned the Station that was destroyed there. The property is subject to our order at any time. The command also made a good and substantial Bridge on Sweetwater, three of our trains crossed over; the Mail bridge would have been $200 per waggon, this bridge is free, and also in charge of Major O'Farral. Several Imigration Companies crossed during the time the command was there free. One Company presented us with a good waggon, which Lieu[t]. Rawlings handed over to Captain Harmon.

I have had frequent interviews with Col Collins & officers, they have behaved very gentlemanly, and expressed themselves much pleased with our exertions and seemed disposed to render us every assistance to contribute to our comfort.

Col Collins is decidedly against killing Indians indiscriminately and will not take any general measures, save on the defensive, until he can ascertains satisfactorily by whom the depredations have been committed, and not then resort to killing until he is satisfied that peaceable measures have failed.

Col Collins & officers all allow that we are best suited to guard this road both men and Horses, they are anxious to return and if they have any influence I imagine they will try to get recalled and recommend to Utah to furnish the necessary Guard. The Colonel has just left our Camp he has sent for Washkee Chief of the Snakes with a view to make treaty or obtain information

No sickness at all in Camp at present. We are attached to Col Collins Regiment General Craig's division, and furnish our Muster Descriptive and other Returns to that Command, should General Wells require duplicates we will forward them.

I am

Sir,

Yours respectfully,

LOT SMITH.

[Editor's note: *A handwritten note on the last page states: "June 27, Rcvd Jul 5,/62. From Lot Smith, about & his command at date. Report"*]

SOURCE: "UTAH, TERRITORIAL MILITIA RECORDS, 1849–1877," SERIES 2210, BOX 1, FOLDER 48 (MAY–JUNE 1862), UTAH STATE ARCHIVES, SALT LAKE CITY

UT-68

"Chasing Indians and Killing Grizzlies," *Deseret [Weekly] News*
July 9, 1862

We have been favored with the perusal of a letter from a young man in Major Smith's command, written at the South Pass, a few days since, in which he gave a very graphic account of a bear chase, of which he was an 'eye witness,' illustrative of the daring of the 'Mountain boys' who are serving on the Overland route.

A few weeks since, the Indians stole four or five mules from Big Sandy station, and Major Smith, with Lieut. Knowlton and twenty men, getting on the trail of the red-skins, who took a northern direction towards the Wind River mountains, followed them about one hundred and fifty miles to where they had crossed a branch of Green river, which was so high that it could not be crossed excepting by shimming, which the Major thought not prudent to undertake, as some of big men were not proficient in the art. The pursuit of the native thieves was therefore abandoned and the company moved down the river on their return to camp.

They had not proceeded far before a bear was discovered on the opposite side of the stream, and Major Smith, Lieut. Knowlton and Sergt. H. O. Spencer resolved to swim their horses over and give 'grizzly' a chase, which they did, and, on reaching the shore, they found two bears instead of one. The beasts moved off up the bluff at a rapid rate, and the Major and his comrades immediately gave chase. The grizzlies made good time, but the horses gradually gained on them till they came within short range, when the riders opened fire which caused the 'varmints' to change tactics, face and charge occasionally upon their pursuers, producing a lively and interesting scene. After some maneuvering of that kind, the bears tried their mettle in a downhill movement towards the river, receiving a shot now and then, making them each time more fierce as they turned to charge upon the sportsmen, who, in turn, became the pursued. The sport was continued in that way back to the river, where the smaller of the two was killed, and the other put off, endeavoring to effect an escape, pursued by Knowlton and Spencer, who, after following a long distance, succeeded in taking their game not far from the river to which they managed to haul it, although extremely large, and after attaching a large bundle of brush, rolled it into the water, hoping that it would ultimately float to the left bank, where they could get it, after swimming back to the company.

To get the first bear across the river, a different course was taken. All the ropes in the company were tied together and then one of the men attaching one end of it to his body, swam across the stream, when the rope was tied around the neck of the horse some distance from the end and then fastened, to the bear, after which the Major mounted and plunged into the river. The men pulling heavily upon the rope, towed the horse and bear into the swift current, when the horse rolled over, feet upwards, and the Major swam ashore. The boys were not long in hauling the horse and bear out on dry land, but not till the horse had been nearly drowned, his head having been under water most of the time while being towed over.

All things were soon arranged, and the march back to camp resumed. Next day as they were proceeding down the river, the big bear, which Knowlton and Spencer had killed and rolled into the river, was found stranded as expected, and recovered.

After an absence of five days the party arrived back to their camp, having rode about three hundred miles, with the loss of one animal which died from fatigue.

Source: "Chasing Indians and Killing Grizzlies," *Deseret News*, July 9, 1862, 4

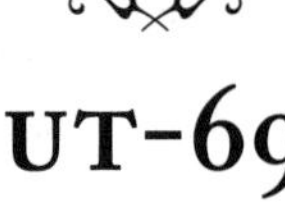

UT-69

Lot Smith to Brigham Young
July 13, 1862

Fort Bridger *July 13th, 1862.*

Prest Brigham Young

Dear Sir

I telegraphed you this morning that Lieut. Knowlton and party had returned and I thought I would give you a short detail of there trip they traveled 80 miles on the Sublet road and came to bear river and down bear river 25 miles to Smiths fork hereing nothing of the deserters on this road they made up there minds to go across the country to the Landers Road distance about 80 miles but in the evening they got into conversation with a French trader who told than that Washakee was encamped about 40 miles from there on bear lake and as Col. Collins was very desired to see him and as they were intrusted with a Letter to him by the Indian Agent at this place they concluded to go and see him and let the diserters go and therefore they started the next morning to hunt for him leaving Sergent Boger who is the ordinance sergt of Ft Bridger he was very desirous to go with them he was in a great hury to get off and said he could have got 50 men ready to march sooner than the boys got ready to go [the boys were only ½ hour getting started] he was out fited with one blanket for bedding and said it was all he wanted the rest of his outfit consisted of about ½ gal of Lighting whiskey well taken before shaken I told the boys to ware him out in some way which they done with interest freezing him nights and traveling him to death in the day time so that when they got to Smiths fork he was glad to stop and stay there untill the boys returned they traveled down bear 20 miles to Thomass fork of Bear river which they had to swim getting every thing well soaked after stopping here long enough to dry there Blankets & Provisions they traveled down 20 miles further they were were sudinly charged upon by a war party of about 30 Snakes who took them to be Chiennes [Cheyennes] but when they found out who they were they manifested great friendship and envited the boys to there camp which was about 5 miles further down the river, the next morning they hired 3 Indians to ferry them across hear River they took one of three lodges and spread it out double filling the center with about 9[?] arm loads of dry willows then putting three things on the top with all who were afraid to attempt swiming the river they drew the sides of the lodge up all around the Indians swam there horses across towing they boat behind them they crossed ~~about~~ without any difaculty and traveled up bear river two days before they got to Washakees camp they crossed several large mountain streams the most of which they had to swim they came to one large mountain stream about the size of Big Cottenwood which they could not cross they turned up the stream to hunt for a ford and about ¾ of a mile from the Lake they came to the head of the stream where it came out of the mountain in a body they passed one Indian camp where they all took to the mountains on there approach but when they got close enough to call them they came down and told them where Washakee was camped. They found Baptest Kawet at the camp who was a good interpeter they read the letter they had to him and he {Washakee} told them that he could not tell them untill the next morning what he would do they staid at his camp all the next day to rest there horses. Washakee told them that Big [?]Utah told him that you said for him not to go out on the road and he would not go the boys started home the next day Washakee sending an Indian with them to ferry them across bear river with a Lodge the boys got out of Provisions and had to live some of the time on frogs and boiled flour as a grazing country the Bear River & Bear Lake Country is the best they say that they ever saw but in most part wood & timber is scare around the Lake timber is very handy, inclosed you will find Col Collins Telegram in answer to mine, concerning the trip

There is some of the Indian goods that was sent along that I don't suppose we will see any Indians to trade with and some of the boys want to buy some of that scarlet for saddle Blankets is it for sale if so what is the price. Willis Fuller was not very well and wished to go in with your teams and said he would return soon. The boys all well and feeling well. I remain Respectfuly your Bro in the gospel

LOT SMITH

[Editor's note: *"Jul 13, Rcvd Jul 20/62. From Cap. Lot Smith. Telegraphed about* [*illegible*], *Jul 21,/62." is written on the reverse of the last page.*]

Source: Lot Smith to Brigham Young, July 13, 1862, "Brigham Young office files: General Correspondence, Incoming, 1840–1877," ms 1234 1, Church History Library, Salt Lake City, Utah

UT-70

"Arrived," *Deseret* [*Weekly*] *News* July 16, 1862

On Friday evening last Associate Justices Waite and Drake arrived in this city, having been, as we are informed, about two months in crossing the plains. From Fort Bridger they were furnished with an escort of eight or ten men from Captain Smith's command, under Lieut. Attwood. Judge Waite is accompanied by his family—a very sensible arrangement. He made a short but very agreeable visit at our sanctum yesterday. It is understood that Judge Drake (although considerably advanced in age) has never taken to himself a wife, and is emphatically an "old bachelor." He may be "learned in," and a good judge of the "law" nevertheless.

Source: "Arrived," *Deseret News*, July 16, 1862

UT-71

"The Celebration of the Fourth of July near Fort Bridger, by Capt. Lot Smith's Command," *Deseret* [*Weekly*] *News* July 23, 1862

Editor *Deseret News*:—We were made aware that the glorious Fourth had dawned upon our camp by the firing of muskets and revolvers incessantly for about half an hour, when we were saluted by the enlivening strains of our National airs, Hail Columbia, Star Spangled Banner, Yankee Doodle, etc., performed with excellent spirit by our two brass buglers, Charles Evans and Josiah Eardley. At eight o'clock we took up our line of march under Capt. Smith and Lieuts. Rollins and

Knowlton, for the Fort, with our brave mountain flag waving in our front, borne by Joseph J. Taylor, color bearer. The Sergeant in charge of the Fort raised the stars and stripes upon their lofty liberty pole to greet us on our approach. We marched directly through the place and encamped about half a mile east of it. Here our flag-staff was made fast to the top of one of the wagons and again our "Grizzly Bear" waved his paws over a band of honest hearts, on the anniversary of our glorious independence.

At three o'clock, we partook of a sumptuous dinner, consisting of excellent bread, fresh beef and coffee. At sunset the flag was lowered, and the ceremonies of the day were at an end in camp, with some of us at least, for we were started out to hunt for some deserters from Col. Collins' command, whom we pursued all night but did not find.

Yours in haste,

SOLDIER BOYS.

Source: "The Celebration of the fourth of July near Fort Bridger, by Capt. Lot Smith's Command," *Deseret News*, July 23, 1862

UT-72

R. H. Attwood Telegram to Brigham Young
July 26, 1862

Bridger [*July*] *26* [*1862*]

On Sunday last Capt Smith With 50 men and pack animals started in pursuit of Indians Supposed to be One Hundred fifty (150) animals having been stolen 6 miles from this station from the mountaine[e]rs. The command has not returned

I will report as soon as they do also when he start for the city we cannot be at Home by the Expiration of our Term

R H ATWOOD

[Editor's note: *Writing at the bottom of page 2 states: "Telegram, July 26, Recd 26/62. From R. H. Attwood."*]

Source: "Brigham Young office files: General Correspondence, Incoming, 1840–1877," MS 1234 1, Church History Library, Salt Lake City, Utah

UT-73

Lot Smith to Brigham Young
[Summer] 1862

[Fort] Bridger [*1862*]

Brigham Young
The quarter master reports only about three days. Rations of flour in camp most of our Hard Bread damaged at Green [River.] High water before we could get to the ferry no sugar or Coffee.

LOT SMITH

[Editor's note: *This correspondence is undated. Based on where it was filed in the Utah Territorial Militia Records, it is presumed to have been sent during July or August 1862.*]

Source: "Utah, Territorial Militia Records, 1849–1877," Series 2210, Box 1, Folder 49 (July–December 1862), Utah State Archives, Salt Lake City

UT-74

R. H. Attwood Telegram to Brigham Young
August 2, 1862

Weber *Aug. 2d*
Recd Aug. 2 / 62

Brigham Young
Lieut Rawlins & Command passed at five oclock this Evening Expect to be in the City five P.M. tomorrow

R H ATTWOOD
Orderly Sgt

Source: "Brigham Young office files: General Correspondence, Incoming, 1840–1877," MS 1234 1, Church History Library, Salt Lake City, Utah

UT-75

"The Expedition After Indians," *Deseret [Weekly] News*
August 13, 1862

Notwithstanding the general high opinion entertained of Captain Lott Smith as a cautious officer and a brave man, a feeling of intense anxiety was creeping over the community for his safety and that of the volunteers under his command, ever since the tidings of his expedition northward was learned from the lips of those who had to return from inability to continue the pursuit. It was, therefore, with sincere gratification and thankfulness that we heard of the arrival of a messenger to Governor Young on Friday night reporting the safety of the command and their arrival at the Weber that evening, and since we have listened to the narrative of the pursuit, the labors performed and the privations endured, we feel the more grateful to our heavenly Father for the preservation of the lives of our Mountain boys.

Up to the present time, we have not seen Capt. Smith and know nothing of the report he may intend to make to his General; but we presume it will not be deemed intrusive on our part to furnish our readers a sketch of the expedition that has caused so much interest, such as we have gleaned from several of the parties who have returned to the city.

From a variety of circumstances there had been a strong suspicion that much of the depredations committed on the Eastern Mail Route, by others than whites, was done by the northern Indians, or a strolling portion of renegades from that quarter; but till the aggression we are about to notice, the evidence was anything but conclusive against them; now, there seems to us, but little room for doubting their being a roving band of thieving desperadoes, that need close watching and proper attention.

From the information we have gathered, it appears that a band of Indians visited the ranch of "Jack" Robinson—one of the oldest mountaineers of the Wasatch Range, about 6 miles from Bridger, on the night of the 19th July, and ran off upwards of 200 head of horses and mules of which number 30 returned in the morning. Capt. Smith, being in the vicinity of Bridger, was notified next day of the theft and in an hour and a half from the first sounding of the bugle, gathering in the scattered Volunteers, sixty-two men were in the saddle, with provisions for a few days, on twelve pack animals.

The following is a list of the names of the expedition:

Captain: Lott Smith.

Lieutenants: Jos. Rollins, J. Q. Knowlton.

Wagon Master: Sol. Hale.

Sergeants: S. H. W. Ritter, Howard Spencer.

Corporals: S. B. Young, W. Bringhurst, N. Myrick, A. Bigler, H. B. Clemons.

Privates: Joseph Goddard, L. A. Huffaker, J. Cherry, L. Rich, Thos. Harris, Wood Alexander, E. M. Shirtliff, James Sharp, Thos. Caldwell, Theodore Calkins, John Cahoon, Mark Murphy, Joseph Fisher, A. Randall, Henry Bird, Wm. Longstroth, Wm. Lutz, Wm. Grant, H. Kimball, P. Corn-y, E. A. Noble, Isaac Atchison, H. E. Simmons, Donald McNichol, Lewis Osborn, Mahlon Weiler, Joseph Taylor, C. Crisman, Wm. C. Allen, Joseph Terry, Chas. Burnham, Geo. Cotterell, A. S. Rose, L. Barnard, R. Hereford, J.M. Hixon, Wm. Rhodes, H. Parks, J. Wells, Laiz, Jenson, James Carrigan, E. Brown, J. Arrowsmith, F. Cantwell, M. Gibson, John R. Bennion, Saml. Bennion, J. Larkin, James Green, James Imlay, F. Prince.

The tracks of the stolen animals indicated that the Indians had taken a northwesterly course which the pursuers followed for eight days—going as far as the head of Snake River Valley, near the Three Tetons, about 135 miles northeast of Fort Hall.

Their first ride in the afternoon was 35 miles to the Muddy, through which the company had to drag their animals with ropes; submerging the packs, provisions and clothing. The Indians in their hasty flight abandoned there two ponies and three of the stolen colts.

Second Day:—The company started at daylight, passed an abandoned mule, traveled 15 miles and breakfasted at a branch stream of a small spring. Three miles farther, they crossed Ham's Fork, where, from the tracks of the animals at the crossing, the Indians appeared to have had great difficulty to keep together their booty: three more colts had been abandoned. The company swam their animals over the Fork and travelled 17 miles before dinner. After resting their animals a couple of hours, they resumed their travel and made 35 miles, arriving at Fontenelle—a fork of Green River, 5 miles from Sublette's cut off.

Third Day.—Started at daylight and rode 18 miles before breakfast, traveled 25 miles farther, stopped to take dinner and rest the animals on the Big Island of Green River—5 miles below the Lander road. During this ride they found the first camping place of the thieves since they had left Bridger. The Indians having traveled so fast, suggested the necessity of preparations for a longer expedition than was contemplated at starting, accordingly Capt. Smith and Lieut. Knowlton rode ahead to a camp of emigrants, on the Lander road, to obtain provisions, but were unsuccessful. The expedition afterwards came up and continued on 15 miles before camping for the night. In conversing with the emigrants, it was ascertained that, on the Thursday previous, the Indians had stolen four animals from an emigrant train to Salmon River. Seven of the emigrants followed them and had a fight, resulting in one of the whites being killed and three wounded. Nothing was recovered. On the night preceding the arrival of the expedition, some Indians attacked an emigrant train, wounding one man, stealing a horse and some cattle.

Fourth Day.—the expedition rested their animals in the morning, during which Lieut. Knowlton, Seymour Young and Solomon Hale returned to the Lander road, and tried to purchase provisions from a train of eighty wagons, but could obtain none. The immigrants refused to furnish anything, though the boys were willing to pay them any price. In fact, the style of the immigrants was everything but complimentary, underlying which was something like the suspicion that the expedition was possibly connected with the Indians who had attacked the immigrants already noticed.

Started at noon, traveled 35 miles, and camped on a small stream near the base of the Green River Mountains. On the way, came upon a camp that had been suddenly abandoned by the Indians, in which was found a good deal of fat beef, the remnants of five oxen; but having been apparently two days exposed was unfit for use. The Indians had evidently been surprised, as there were evidences of a very sudden departure and indications of a fight. Among other things, an immigrant's cap was lying on the ground perforated by a bullet.

Fifth Day.—Started at daylight, and traveled 21 miles, crossing the north fork of Green River. Rested two hours, and found a mare abandoned. Five miles further, struck the south fork of Lewis' Fork, commonly called Snake River, but among the Indians Shoshone River. Crossed over to the north side, and traveled 30 miles down it—a fearful road. The trail taken by the Indians here was over land slides, rocks and loose stones: some places a thousand feet above the river, where one misstep would have sent horse and rider precipitately into the stream. On this trail, the company found evidences of other thefts, as the tracks of large American horses, mules and cattle were very clear; justifying the conclusion that the original band pursued from Bridger had gathered strength in numbers during their flight. By taking such a direct northern route, the red skins probably intended to mislead the pursuers into the belief that the Crow Indians had been the aggressors. But for this, the Indians would certainly have preferred another trail to that so dangerous passed over that day. The expedition crossed the middle fork of Shoshone River, and camped all night. From the freshness of the track, and the remnants of a sage hen, the Indians seemed here to have been not more than six hours ahead of the expedition. A white horse abandoned was found here.

Sixth Day.—The animals getting badly used up, Lieut. Rawlings and the following persons were sent back to Bridger with the worst animals:—Corporal N. Myrick, Privates Wm. C. Allen, J. Terry, C. Burnham, G. Cotterell, A. S. Rose, J. M. Hixon, H. Parks, Wm. Rhodes, L. Jenson, J. Carrigan, E. Brown, J. Arrowsmith, F. Cantwell, J. Green, J. Imlay, F. Prince, L. A. Huffaker.

The company then traveled 10 miles through a similar kanyon, thickly wooded, and 8 miles further camped on the north fork of Lewis' Fork: found two colts abandoned. Traveled 5 miles further, crossed a small stream, and found two mules and one colt abandoned. These mules had belonged to some other party—not of the Bridger stock. The expedition then came up to a grass valley of some extent, where the Indians had spread out the animals to mislead them from the track, and which caused a delay of some hours before the trail could be found. Traveled 5 miles, and crossed the north fork of Lewis' Fork, about 10 miles below the Three Tetons.

The expedition had much difficulty in crossing this fork of the river, the water being divided into three branches. The first branch, about a hundred feet wide, was not so deep as to cause much difficulty; but the second was deep and the current swift. Traveling about 300 yards, up a gravelly sand bar, the second branch of the river was forded, in which one man was nearly drowned. Capt. Smith had led the way, and a portion of the command had got through the third stream to the opposite bank, when Donald McNichol's horse became unmanageable, and, refusing to breast the current, kept down the stream about 50 yards. McNichol was trying to drive his horse from the shallow water, when suddenly it fell into deep water and almost instantly disappeared. McNichol, following after, probably in expectation of aiding his horse, seemed to immediately be carried away by the swift current beyond all human aid. The captain and Sergeant Spencer ran down the bank of the stream to his assistance, but the current was so rapid that he was carried away quicker than their utmost speed. McNichol was the best swimmer in the company; but having his clothes, boots and pistol on his person, he was unable to battle with the water element. He made no call for assistance, and appeared to want none, possibly thought he could still deliver himself till at last, after being carried away about 300 yards, he was engulphed in the surging water, and disappeared forever from the view of his sorrowing comrades. The remainder of the company got over in safety, and pitched their camp for the night—a sorrowful, hungry band of brave men, with only 8 lbs. of flour left for the future subsistence of forty-two men.

Seventh Day.—Started again on the Indian track in a westerly direction, over a mountain steep and heavily timbered. Found on a tree, the name of J. M. Crist, July 11th, 1832, on a second tree, the same name, in 1833, and, on a third tree, two B's, one inverted, and Joy, with other signs of white men having past over that trail "just thirty years ago." The expedition traveled 20 miles through this densely wooded country and stopped three hours to rest their animals, being now relieved from the labors of cooking, their last meal having disappeared with the former evening's setting sun. Found here Lieut. Knowlton's mare that had been stolen from Bridger; also two mares belonging to Robinson, terribly jaded and a mass of sores from the punishment received in the flight and from over heating. Traveled 8 miles further and killed a small bear, rather poor in flesh; but, under such circumstances, economy suggested him for two repasts. A splendid mare belonging to Robinson, was here found standing in the woods with two knife cuts and a bullet hole in her body.

The Indians at this place could not be far in advance of the expedition; but there were not six horses fit to travel another day at the rate of pursuit; and being entirely out of provisions, it was concluded that, unless the Indian's trail should take a direction in which the expedition might hope to find means of subsistence, the pursuit would have to be abandoned. Mr. Hereford, who was personally the most directly interested in the recovery of the stock stolen from Bridger, expressed his entire satisfaction to Capt. Smith and the company that every thing had already been done that was possible. The Indians having taken a direct northerly course near the base of the Snake river mountains, to avoid the high waters, the expedition, after eight miles further travel, abandoned the pursuit entirely.

Eighth Day.—Traveled about 15 miles to the south fork of Snake river. Got some quaking asp logs, made a raft, and Capt. Smith, H. Spencer, A. Bigler, S. Young, P. Corney, J. Sharp and T. Caldwell, with the baggage of their mess, attempted to cross over. On reaching near the opposite bank, the boys got into the water in hopes of swimming the raft ashore and fixing it with ropes for the ferrying of the rest of the company; but the current was so powerful that the raft was swept out of their hands. The captain, seeing Caldwell still on it and being carried away, plunged after it and got on the raft with him, and the two were carried down the stream about a mile and landed upon an island in the middle of the water. The captain and Caldwell made another raft, and with the assistance of ropes which Wm. Longstroth had swam with from the shore on which the company was left, the boys drew them ashore, with the loss of two saddles, cooking utensils, and a good deal of clothing. Bigler and Corney, suffering intensely from mosquitoes, determined to risk everything to regain the opposite shore. One of them entirely nude, and the other with only a very partial covering to his body, made their way through brush, wood and brambles for about a mile up stream, where, finding a dry log, rolled it into the water, and, clinging to it, were carried by the stream to the other side. Spencer, Young and Sharp were left on the opposite bank all night, with their garments only to serve them as protection from the myriads of mosquitoes that literally covered them as a new suit. After the fashion of other lonely exiles, they exercised their ingenuity in weaving willows into coverings, but with them all it failed to save the draining of their blood.

Ninth Day.—The company despairing of passing over their animals and baggage, after the rough experience of the preceding day, made signal to the three to recross, and taking the same route through the words and down the stream as their comrades the preceding evening, they reached the shore in safety. Being again altogether, part of the expedition went south, and part north in search of a crossing. In the afternoon they were re-united and travelled twelve miles north-west to the north fork of Snake river, through a terrible hail-storm, which lasted an hour and a half. Killed a swan, badger and porcupine during the day, which served three excellent repasts. Very little was wasted.

Tenth Day.—Traveled a few miles and crossed again two branches of Lewis Fork, swimming the animals, their owners following after, and holding on by the *queue*. Four of the boys who could not swim were placed on a raft, and the captain taking the rope in his teeth, plunged into the river to guide them across. Two other boys swam from the opposite bank with another rope to the captain, and in this manner the connection was formed for drawing the raft ashore; but the captain, from his exertions, becoming weak, and the current strong, the raft was carried away from him several hundred yards down the stream. Seeing the raft under water, and the four boys in danger, James Wells plunged into the water after them with a larriat, to which those on the shore kept adding other larriats till he reached the raft. After considerable labor, the praiseworthy exertions of Wells were crowned with success, and the four boys were brought ashore. All got safely over, but Crisman's horse getting entangled was drowned, taking down stream with him the saddle, pistol and clothing. Game being very scarce, the boys weak and hungry, the captain ordered Mr. Clemon's horse, which was in the best condition, to be shot and cooked for the company. The expedition rested the remainder of the day, while Captain Smith, Lieut. Knowlton, Mr. Hereford and a few others went exploring for a crossing, but returned without success.

Eleventh Day.—Returned on the trail, and recrossed the same streams by rafts, and reached the south bank of the north fork, where they had camped two nights before. The remnants of the horse still held out, and the boys worked vigorously hauling logs some three or four miles in order to construct a raft.

Twelfth Day.—Mr. Hereford superintended the construction of a substantial raft, and crossed over the men and baggage in safety. The stream being deep, the animals swam over without difficulty. Traveled over a very swampy, marshy ground, that had to be bridged over with willows for nearly a mile, the men having to carry the baggage to free the animals. Forded another stream, and got on to high ground. After resting a few hours, resumed travel; made 15 miles, and reached the outlet of Market Lake. Lieut. Knowlton tried to ford it, but had to swim, and returned again in the same manner after dark. Here the last of the horseflesh was consumed, and the company left entirely without sustenance.

Thirteenth Day.—Swam across the outlet, repacked the animals, traveled 12 miles, and camped to allow the animals to graze—no breakfast to cook. Capt. Smith and Seymour Young went in advance of the company, and after a 30 miles ride, came up with an emigrant train camped for dinner. After a good deal of solicitation they furnished a hundred of flour, some bacon and tobacco, for which they charged and were paid high prices. The Captain gave up his horse and stayed with the train, while Young packed back to the company the provisions, which were received with gladness, and soon the kitchen battery was in operation. The company and the immigrants camped together that night. It is due to notice here that when the immigrants saw the company, and believed their real position, they were kind enough, and probably sorry for their former unbelief.

Fourteenth Day.—Traveled 15 miles and crossed the Snake River ferry, owned by Jacob Meeks. Found plenty of provisions for sale, and replenished their larder. Here ended the troubles of the expedition. From that time, to arrival in this city on last Saturday afternoon, the citizens on their route showed them every kindness and ministered to their wants.

We have given more space to this narrative of the expedition than we could well spare and have written it in the midst of a variety of other business; but we need make no apology for this. We must add that it has given us particular pleasure in our int4ercourse with the boys to hear them speak unqualifiedly in praise of Capt. Smith. They are sincerely and affectionately attached to him, and never expect to find a better leader. Of Lieut. Knowlton, they likewise speak in terms of praise, and we must add that we have not heard the first whisper of an unpleasant word breathed against a single member of the expedition; we conclude, therefore, they all did their duty and nobly comported themselves in the time of trial.

Not having had the advantages of a personal experience in the travels of the expedition, we fear that our sketch is very imperfect; what is of it, however, can be relied on. We are glad that it was no worse, and that the sacrifice of human life was limited to the loss of one young man, who had earned the confidence of his comrades by his constant readiness to do his duty. What the result will be, we are unable to conjecture; but the fact that the Indians made such a desperate ride to save themselves, abandoning in the flight between thirty and forty of the animals, would lead to the conclusion that they had the conviction that "somebody" was after them. We are satisfied that the lesson will not be lost upon them, and feel as satisfied if the same determination to handle them had been manifested at the first attack on the mail line, we should not have been called upon to record the incidents of this expedition.

The Volunteers will be mustered out of service to-morrow.

Source: "Expedition After Indians," *Deseret News*, August 13, 1862

UT-76

James Duane Doty to W. P. Dole
August 13, 1862

Utah Superintendency Indian Affairs,
Great Salt Lake City, *August 13, 1862.*

Sir: On the 6th of March last I deemed it my duty to advise your department, as also the Secretary of War, of the threatened attacks by the Shoshones upon the emigrant trains passing through the mountains the then coming season, and to suggest the occupation by a regiment of troops of some point in the vicinity of Fort Hall, on Shoshone river, near the point of intersection of the northern California road with the roads to Oregon, and from this city to Salmon river gold mines.

Subsequently, as additional information was received from friendly Indians that it was the intention to assemble a large force, estimated by them at two thousand, sufficient to overpower any train, I ventured again to call the attention of the government to the threats and conduct of these Indians, and the prospect that many emigrants would lose their lives or be fobbed of their property if military protection was not given at that point, and asked of the Secretary of War a portion of the

$25,000 appropriation for the defence of emigrants, to provide for their protection at the place threatened.

The subject was renewed in my letters of April 11, with the further information that they would certainly commence their depredations upon the overland mail line east of this city.

All the officers of the United States then here, and the officers of the overland mail and telegraph companies united in a telegram to the Secretary of War, a copy of which is enclosed herewith, conveying to him the same intelligence, which they deemed altogether reliable, and urging that troops be raised here for temporary service, and until the troops of the United States could reach this country. No notice appears to have been taken of these representations, certainly no favorable response was given, and it is supposed, from the published letter of Brigham Young, also herewith enclosed, and from other information, our efforts to protect the lives and property of our citizens and the overland trail and telegraph lines have been counteracted by his, or some other invisible influence, and that our exertions have resulted only in increasing his power in this country and not that of the United States. The President having conferred upon him the authority to raise troops and withheld it from the officers of the United States.

The events which have occurred since our communications were made confirm the correctness of our information, and prove that the assertion of Brigham Young was not reliable, that "the statements of the aforesaid telegram are without foundation in truth," as lie believed.

Before the emigration appeared on the road the Shoshones, in connexion with the Dacotahs and Cheyennes, robbed the overland company of their stock upon more than three hundred miles of the road west of Fort Laramie, killed several of their drivers and employés, and effectually stopped the mail.

Early in June, Smith, Kinkaid, and others, forming a small party, on their way from California to the States, were attacked by the Eastern Bannacks, who hunt with the Shoshones between Raft river, near Fort Hall, and Bear river, and all but Smith and another were murdered, and the entire party robbed. Smith was shot in the back, with an arrow, but succeeded in reaching the settlement on Bear river, with the arrow yet in him.

In that month three emigrant trains were waylaid by the Shoshones near Soda springs, and the people robbed and killed. During the month of July I am informed of several trains being attacked and robbed and many people

A man returned from Salmon river informed me that at the crossing of the Salt Lake and California roads he saw two wagons standing in the road, and the dead bodies of three white men lying beside them.

There is no doubt that there have been many murders committed there of which no account has been given. The robbery of two hundred head of stock last month, owned by Jack Robinson and other settlers, took place near Fort Bridger, and within six miles of the camp of the forces put into service by Brigham Young.

I also transmit herewith a statement of the chief "Little Soldier," of the danger of a proposed general rising of the Shoshones and Utahs, made to the interpreter, and yesterday I received information that the Indians in Tavilla and Kush valleys declared their intention to commence robbing on the western road.

They have stolen many horses and cattle of late from the settlement, and they enter the houses of formers and in an insolent manner demand food, and that meals shall be cooked for them.

A regiment of California volunteers, under the command of Colonel Conner, are said to be at Fort Churchill, in Nevada, six hundred miles west of this, on their way to this city, but unless their march is hastened they will not reach here until winter.

A telegraph order from the Secretary of War to increase their speed would soon bring them upon that part of the road which is threatened by these Utah Indians.

It is stated that General Craig is five hundred miles east of this city, and that he has no order to advance his troops into this Territory nor into the Washington Territory.

I am, very respectfully, your obedient servant,

JAMES DUANE DOTY.

Hon. W. P. Dole,
Commissioner of Indian Affairs.

Source: *Report of the Commissioner of Indian Affairs for the Year 1862* (Washington, D.C.: Government Printing Office, 1862), 210–212

UT-77

Ben Holladay to M. P. Blair
August 26, 1862

Salt Lake, *August 26, 1862.*

Sir: A general war with nearly all the tribes of Indians east of the Missouri river is close at bond. I am expecting daily an interruption on my line, and nothing but prompt and decisive action on the part of government will prevent it. The lines should be protected by soldiers at intervals of one hundred miles. General Paige's force is too small. I think it my duty to give government this information through you. Colonel Conner's forces are four hundred miles west, travelling slowly.

I leave for home in the morning. Hope to see you by September 10.

BEN. HOLLADAY.

Hon. M. P. Blair.

Source: *Report of the Commissioner of Indian Affairs for the Year 1862* (Washington, D.C.: Government Printing Office, 1862), 214

UT-78

"The March of Colonel Connor's Command to and through Salt Lake City," *Deseret* [*Weekly*] *News* October 18, 1862

A few weeks since, we published a communication, from the correspondent of the *Bulletin* [S. F.] accompanying Col. Connor's command, written at Ruby, on the day the command left there for Salt Lake. The following giving the details of the march from Fort Crittenden to and through the city, may be equally interesting to those not fully advised in the premises.

Jordan Springs, U.T.
Saturday, October 18, 1862.

The Salt Lake Expedition, numbering 750 men, is within 25 miles of the City of the Saints, having marched 20 miles north of Fort Crittenden to-day. From the slope on which our camp is pitched we can discern the white specks which constitute the residences of the modern apostles; but at present we are more interested in the designs and doings of said apostles than in the general appearance of their habitations. I closed yesterday's letter [see *Bulletin* of 30th October] by mentioning a camp rumor, to the effect that the Mormons would prevent a nearer approach of our troops to the city than Fort Crittenden, and that the banks of the narrow stream called Jordan, which empties the waters of Lake Utah into Great Salt Lake, would form the field of battle. At the time it caused no further thought than as the starting-point of rambling conversations respecting Mormondom and the mission which the command has been detailed to execute—both subjects upon which we have but little information. However, at the present writing—sundown—reliable advices received tend to establish the probable truthfulness of the report. When information reached the city, as it did last night, that Col. Connor would not purchase the buildings erected by Johnson's command in 1858 at what was then Camp Floyd, now Fort Crittenden, and that he designed to occupy some locality within striking distance of the heart of Mormondom, the most intense excitement is said to have prevailed. The leaders are represented to be in conclave, meditating upon the question and striving to arrive at a determination, while the people were in a high state of expectancy as to what the leaders would do, what the troops would do, and what they themselves would be called upon to do. The Chief of the Danites—better known perhaps as the Destroying Angels, whose duty it is, if report be true, to place parties odious to the leaders where they never can tell tales—is represented as riding through the streets offering to bet $500 that we would not and should not cross the river Jordan, the bet being untaken. Furthermore, not simple camp rumor, but reliable parties assert that Brigham Young would, when we near Jordan, have us met by Commissioners empowered to inform us that the Mormons objected to our close proximity to their city and would forcibly resist an attempt on our part to cross that stream.

How much truth there may be in these advices, or how much the real state of affairs in Salt Lake is exaggerated I know not. As a faithful correspondent it is only my province to inform you of the exact condition and operations of this command but further than that I cannot go, and, of course, will not be held responsible for the correctness or incorrectness of the rumors which reach the command. Be they, however, true or untrue, and be the opinion entertained by our Colonel what it may, certain it is that he is moving with the utmost prudence, that 30 rounds of ammunition have just been issued to each man, that the two 6-pounders are abundantly furnished with destructive missiles and the 12-pound mountain howitzer amply supplied with shells, that the camp is so pitched upon an open plain that no force can get to it, without a fair fight; in short, that every preparation for war that can be made is made, and equally certain is it that on to-morrow we will cross the river Jordan if it lies within our power.

Col. Connor sent word to-day to the aforementioned chief of the Danites that he would "cross the river Jordan if hell yawned below him;" and the battlefields of Mexico testify that the Colonel has a habit of keeping his word.

Thus you see that whether we are to have a fight or not rests entirely with the Mormon rulers. And if it be true that United States troops, when ordered by Government to occupy United States territory, are to be forcibly prevented, by those who live upon United States lands, from executing that order—if this principle is to constitute the national policy, then the nation has ceased to be a live nation, and the sooner it recognizes the Southern Confederacy the better. But if our troops are to march on United States territory wherever Government sends them, then those who resist their march, because of polygamy, are as really traitors as those who resist because of slavery, and are to be dealt with as such. This command, from the highest to the lowest, is disposed to treat the Mormons with true courtesy and the strictest justice, so long as they remain friendly to the Government; but the moment they become traitors the river Jordan will be as acceptable to us as the river Potomac, for we shall be fighting for the same precise principle—the flag and national existence—as are our Eastern brethren; and even should annihilation be our fate, of which we have no fears, the belief that our countrymen would think of our grave as they do of those in Virginia, and that the Union men of California, our old friends, would swarm forth by the thousand to avenge us—such a hope and belief would nerve us for death.

Nevertheless, unless he fails to exercise the statesmanship universally accorded to him, Brigham Young cannot but forsee the results which would flow from a war of his beginning. Admitting him to have an army of 8,000 well-drilled and effective men, or, for that matter, one of 50,000—and admitting him to be able to capture our force and all the forces which California could send hither, yet, in the course of one, or two or three years, the Government could flood his valley with regiments, and sweep it with a gulf stream of bayonets. That he is prepared to initiate a movement which cannot fail to bring upon his people the full power of the nation, I do not believe; and yet there may be hot-heads over whom he has but partial control. A small spark can ignite the powder of a vast magazine.

Having given you the prevalent opinion of the camp, there should also be given what probably may turn out to be the cause why some, if not most, of the rumors current in Salt Lake were set afloat. When Floyd, after expending $5,000,000 in the erection of quarters in Camp Floyd, ordered the disgraceful and outrageous sale of the same, the buildings were bought for a mere song by private parties. On several occasions, in fact during the whole march, Col. Connor has been solicited by the agents of owners to re-purchase them. He did not see fit to do so; but it was expected that the smallness of the command and the avowal that the Mormons would not permit him to locate nearer the city, taken in connection with the fact that his arrival so late in the season would prevent him from erecting winter quarters, it was expected, I say, that these and other prudential reasons would induce him to effect the purchase of Fort Crittenden; and it is more than probable that his refusal of the offers was regarded as a financial manouvre by which to secure the property at low figures. Hence the idea that we really would not winter at that point has never been realized by them; and so thoroughly has the belief that we would winter there pervaded the Mormon people, that when we march beyond it, they—unable to understand the object of the expedition and fearful that the real, and to them a hostile, design is hidden under the avowed one—have their fears a thousand fold quickened, and imagine an attack upon the city possible. In addition, it appears that the Chief of the Danites is the principal owner of the buildings, and decidedly anxious to sell, and that the agents have from time to time assured him of the certainty of his prospects. Up to the hour that Col. Connors decision was unknown at Fort Crittenden, the city is reported to have been perfectly quiet; but in about the time that it would take to telegraph his refusal to Salt Lake, the excitement is said to have begun. There can, therefore, be little doubt that the already aroused suspicions of the Mormons have been worked upon by parties interested in the sale of the property, and who, failing to persuade Col. Connor into buying, now seek to frighten him therein by threats of forcible resistance, and mayhap a display of military power. In this they will most signally fail, for I must say that he is a blessed hard man to scare. At the same time, if it is the settled Mormon policy to resist the Federal government, and if the people have been toned up to the Union pitch, a few leaders actuated by selfish motives, can easily initiate its execution. A courier will arrive late to-night with authentic intelligence, which I will endeavor to obtain.

I make my evening bow with the following scraps for your lady readers; As we came into camp, a middle-aged lady, dressed in home-spun, a yellow sun-bonnet, nature's stockings, and NO hoops, was espied sitting near the spring busily engaged in sock knitting. Scarcely any power extant could have restrained the embodied and hooped female curiosity of the regiment from paying a scouting visit. We learn that the visitee was married in the States; that her husband became a convert to Mormonism and moved hither; that against the solicitations of her friends she clung to his fortunes; that in the course of time he proposed to take a second wife, whereupon she "reared, kicked, plunged," but finally consented; that he also took a third wife, who was divorced from a former husband for that purpose, and that by her he had a daughter, whom the first wife raised; that said daughter grew into maturity; finally, that he made said mature daughter his fourth wife, and has by her a child one year old. Whether he will also marry his third wife's granddaughter has not yet transpired; but if he should, and his third wife's granddaughter should have a daughter, what relation will that daughter be to each wife, and the whole concern? The first wife lives in a house by herself and takes care of all the children that are born unto her liege lord. She says that she is perfectly contented; keeps her house thoroughly clean; is thrifty and frugal; is a simple-hearted, frank, and child-like mother, and a devoted lover of her husband.

SALT LAKE CITY, *October 20, 1862.*

When Sunday's *reveille* awoke the command, it awoke expectant of battle ere another one should roll out upon the grey day-break. Blankets never were got from under and compactly strapped in knapsacks more promptly; cooks never prepared steaming breakfast with greater alacrity, and upon the principle that the aggregate stomach of a regiment has a great deal to do with the aggregate prowess of a regiment, they never prepared a more bountiful repast. Upon the same principle, no breakfast during the whole march was ever stowed away in a more cool, nonchalant, jovial manner. The routine of months was dissipated, and, doubtless, each man's curiosity to know how he would personally stand fire, and the more general question—which side would whip—made everybody happy. The first scene which met my eyes was Col. Connor seated upon a log, calmly engaged in loading his revolvers and playing with his toddling child. In some directions were heard the popping of muskets and the thud of ramrods, as the men made sure of their pieces, while in others could be seen individuals seated on the ground, vigorously burnishing up their already glittering muskets and brasses—determined no doubt to die according to regulations, if die they must. No difference what thoughts raged within each breast, the exterior seemed quiet and determined.

An incident at the hospital will serve as a criterion of the general *animus.* Five men were sick in the hospital and 30 sick in quarters. At sick call, Surgeon Reid, who had been arranging his abominable knives, saws and probes, said that this was a day when every man able to carry a musket should do so, and one that would determine who were loafers and who were soldiers. 28 out of the 41, many of whom were really unfit for service, shouldered their pieces, and the remainder did not, only because they could not.

A strong force of cavalry preceded the staff and the command moved forward in so compact a body, and with such a steady springing step that Gen Wright's heart would have rejoiced at the sight. The fact that the carriages formed behind the staff as usual was an imitation to the men that a light was improbable, and word presently passed that a courier had arrived with information that no resistance would be made at the bridge. Before it did so, however, as the Colonel passed the artillery, he put several questions to Lieut. Hunneyman, commanding, respecting the quantity and kind of ammunition in the caissons, and also the numbers of the ammunition wagons. When through, the Lieutenant, who has seen service, said: Colonel, if you expect an attack to-day, I will overhaul those wagons and take more cannister," with the same air that one calls for fried oysters in a restaurant. The reply was, "Not to-day; but to-morrow do so" There were other incidents of the same kind, but I did not happen to see them.

After a speedy march of 15 miles—during which not one of the usual stragglers fell back from his position—we crossed the Jordan at 2 P.M. and found not a solitary individual upon the eastern shore. It was a magnificent place for a fight, too, with a good-sized bluff upon the western side from which splendid execution could have been done; but all were glad that no necessity existed therefor, as we heartily desire to avoid difficulty with the loyal citizens.

While camped for the night, it was definitely ascertained that although there had been some excitement in the laity, yet it was far from general, and was instigated by parties interested in selling the Fort Crittenden buildings. Furthermore, that the mass of the people were glad of our near location, as it would bring many a dollar into the city circulation. Bishop Heber Kimball, who, I am told, ranks next to President Young, is reported to have spoken thus in his sermon at the temple: "Letters have been written to Col. Connor's command, to California and the East, that we are opposed to the coming of the troops; that we are disloyal to the Government and sympathizers with Secessionists. It is all a d—d lie." This certainly was a gratifying assurance, though not mildly expressed.

This morning, Monday, we resumed the line of march, thoroughly ignorant of the spot that would next receive our tents, but decidedly hopeful that it would receive them permanently. That it was to be near the city we knew; that the leading Mormons objected to its proximity because of the danger of difficulties between the soldiers and citizens, we knew; that in 1858 they had resisted the now traitor Johnson's 10,000 men, and after compelling him to winter in the mountains, had, late in the Spring forced him into a treaty, by which he bound himself not to locate within 40 miles of Salt Lake, we knew; that they were far stronger and better armed now than they then were, we knew; and that more than one of their leading men—among them a Bishop—had offered to bet that we would not come within twenty miles of the Temple, we also knew. A large and influential party was avowedly opposed to any near approach, and, in view of the advices received by our commander—which were from reliable sources—the precise *animus* of the people and the treatment that would meet us, we did not know. That, should they see fit, it was in their power to vastly outnumber and in all probability annihilate us, was more than possible, and that we were 600 miles of sand and drought from reinforcements, was certain. All these certainties and uncertainties conspired to create the same excitement that passengers in olden days felt when two Mississippi steamers lapped guards, burned tar, and carried the engineer as a weight on the safety valve. We had generally supposed, and the people had universally supposed, that the command would pass around the city, or at the most but through the outer suburbs, which course, under all the circumstances, was considered decidedly bold, and upon the whole not as conciliatory a policy as had been adopted by Gen. Johnson's thousands.

Accordingly, when some two miles out a halt was sounded and the column formed as follows: Advance guard of cavalry; Colonel Connor and staff; Cavalry brass band; Cos. A and M of 2d Cavalry, C. V.; Light Battery; Infantry field Band; 3d Infantry Battalion; Staff, Company Quartermasters and Commissary wagons; Rear-guard of Infantry. You may imagine our surprise—strive to imagine the astonishment of the people, and the more than astonishment of the betting Bishop—as the column marched slowly and steadily into the street which receives the overland stage, up it between the fine trees, the sidewalks filled with many women and countless children, the comfortable residences, to Emigration Square, the theatre and other notable landmarks were passed, when, about the centre of the city, I should think, it filed right through a principal thoroughfare to Gov. Harding's mansion—on which, and on which alone, waved the same blessed stars and stripes that were woven in the loom of '76. Every crossing was occupied by spectators, and windows, doors and roofs had their gazers. Not a cheer nor a jeer greeted us. One little boy, running along close to the staff, said—"You are coming, are you?"—to which it was replied that we thought we were. A carriage, containing three ladies, who sang *John Brown* as they drove by, were heartily saluted. But the leading greeting was extended by Gov. Harding, Judges Waite and Drake, and Dr.—, who met us some distance out. Save these three instances, there were none of those manifestations of loyalty that any other city in a loyal territory would have made.

The side-walk by the mansion was thoroughly packed with Mormons, curious to know what would be the next feature. It was this: The battalion was formed in two lines, behind them the cavalry with the battery resting upon their right, in front of the Governor's residence.

After giving the Governor the salute due his rank, he was introduced by Col. Connor to the command, and, standing in his buggy, spoke precisely thus:

Here followed the speech as published in the NEWS, NO. 17.

At the conclusion of the speech, Colonel Connor called for three cheers for our Country and Flag, and three more for Gov. Harding, all of which would have drawn forth the admiration of your Fire Department. Thereupon the march through the city was resumed—the bands continuing their flood of music; and a tramp of 2 1/2 miles east brought us to the slope between Emigration and Red Bute kanyons, where a permanent post will probably be established.

I have very astutely discovered that we could have reached the spot by a much shorter road, and that we marched over 6 miles for the purpose of passing through the well-built metropolis of the modern Saints. There was no reason why we should not do it that is recognized by the United States Government, and I for one was curious to see rosy cheeks and sparkling eyes.

And so ended the long tramp from your good State, and the attempts to frighten Col. Connor into the purchase of Fort Crittenden.

Source: "The March of Colonel Connor's Command To and Through Salt Lake City," *Deseret News*, November 12, 1862, 5

UT-79

Post Order No. 1, Headquarters, Camp Douglas October 26, 1862

Head-Quarters, Camp Douglas,
Oct. 26, 1862.

Post Order,
No. 1.

The following is declared to constitute the military reserve pertaining to this post. Commencing at a post due north, one mile distant from the garrison flag staff, and running thence west one mile; thence south two miles; thence east two miles; thence north two miles, and thence west one mile to the place of beginning, containing twenty five hundred and sixty acres more or less.

By order of

P. EDWD. CONNOR,
Col. Commanding Post.

Source: "Camp Douglas," *Deseret News*, January 7, 1863, 8

UT-80

[*Extract*]

Post Return of Camp Douglas for October 1862
October 31, 1862

Remarks

This Post was established Oct. 26 "62 by Colonel P. Edw Connor Comdg Dist of Utah per Dist Order No 14 dated October 26, 1862. It is situated East of Salt Lake City 7 miles, at which place there is a P.O. and Telegraph office, with good facilities for communication with East and West & city.

Regiments.	Letters of Companies.	Number of Companies.	Present.								Absent.					
			Commissioned Officers.			Enlisted Men.					How.				Where.	
											Commissioned Officers.		Enlisted Men.		Within the Dept. (See note 2.)	
			For duty.	Sick.	Totals	For duty.	On extra, or daily duty.	Sick.	In arrest, or confinement.	Total.	On detached service.	Total.	On detached service.	Total.	Commissioned Officers.	Enlisted Men.
3d Infty C.V.	Field Staff	–	3	–	3	–	–	–	–	–	3	3	–	–	3	–
	"C"	1	–	–	–	–	–	–	–	–	–	–	–	–	–	–
	"E"	1	2	1	3	64	14	1	–	79	–	–	1	1	–	1
	"F"	1	–	–	–	–	–	–	–	–	–	–	–	–	–	–
	"G"	1	2	–	2	61	14	4	3	82	1	1	–	–	1	–
	"H"	1	3	–	3	26	34	3	–	63	–	–	–	–	–	–
	"I"	1	2	–	2	60	21	5	–	86	1	1	2	2	1	2
	"K"	1	1	1	2	56	13	3	–	72	1	1	3	3	1	3
Totals		7	13	2	15	267	96	16	3	382	6	6	6	6	6	10
Attached 3d Infty C.V.	E G & K		3	–	3	6	–	–	–	6	–	–	–	–	–	–
Casually at Post 3d [illegible]			1	–	1	–	–	–	–	–	–	–	–	–	–	–
2d Cav. Cal. Vol.	L		3	–	3	4	–	–	–	4	–	–	–	–	–	–
Totals			7	–	7	10	–	–	–	10	–	–	–	–	–	–

Regiments.	Letters of Companies.	Number of Companies.	Present and Absent.													Aggregate.	Aggregate Last Monthly Return.
			Commissioned Officers.					Enlisted Men.									
			Regimental Field Officers.	Regimental Field Staff.	Captains.	Subalterns.	Total Commissioned.	Non-commissioned Staff of Regts.	Hospital Stewards.	Sergeants.	Corporals.	Musicians.	Privates.	Wagoneers.	Total Enlisted.		
	Field Staff.	–	3	3	–	–	6	3	1	–	–	–	–	–	4	10	10
	"C"	1	–	–	–	–	–	–	–	–	–	–	–	–	–	–	77
	"E"	1	–	–	1	2	3	–	–	5	8	2	64	1	80	83	82
3d Infty. C.V.	"F"	1	–	–	–	–	–	–	–		–	–	–	–	–	–	88
	"G"	1	–	–	1	2	3	–	–	5	8	2	66	1	82	85	90
	"H"	1	–	–	1	2	3	–	–	5	8	2	47	1	63	66	68
	"I"	1	–	–	1	2	3	–	–	5	8	2	72	1	88	91	94
	"K"	1	–	–	1	2	3	–	–	5	8	1	60	1	75	78	82
Total		7	1	1	5	10	17	3	1	25	40	9	309	5	392	413	591
Attached 3d Infty C.V.	E, G, & K		–	–	–	3	3	–	–	–	–	–	6	–	6	9	17
Casually at Post 3rd [illegible]			–	–	1	–	1	–	–	–	–	–	–	–	–	1	–
2d Cav. Cal. Vol.	L		1	1	1	–	3	–	–	–	–	–	4	–	4	4	–
Totals			1	1	2	3	7	–	–	–	–	–	10	–	10	14	17

Record of Events

The Hd Qrs. and Cos E. G. H. I. & K. 3d Inft C. V. left Fort Ruby: N.T. October 2d, 1862. En Route for Salt Lake City U.T. and advanced via: "Mountain Springs" "Butte", "Egan Station," "Shell Creek," "Blind Springs," "Antelope Springs," "Deep Creek," "Canon Station," "Willow Springs," Fish Springs," "Dug Way," "Indian Springs," Government Meadows," "Rush Valley," Camp Crittenden," "Jordan Springs," Jordan Bridge," and Through Salt Lake City to this place where they arrived in the evening of the 20th of October distance marched _ miles.

P. EDW. CONNOR

Col. 3d Infty Vol.

Camp Douglas U.T.

October 31st 1862.

[Editor's note: *The strength tables above list Colonel Patrick E. Connor's reported strength soon after arriving at Great Salt Lake City, Utah Territory, and establishing Camp Douglas. A space left between the last two words ("marched" and "miles") for a mileage figure was not added in the Record of Events text before this Post Return was submitted. Some of the rows and columns do not total correctly—reflecting errors in the original report.*]

SOURCE: "POST RETURN OF CAMP DOUGLAS, U.T. . . . FOR THE MONTH OF OCTOBER 1862," RETURNS FROM U.S. MILITARY POSTS 1800–1916, NATIONAL ARCHIVES, RG94, M617, ROLL 324

UT-81

"EXPEDITION FOR THE RECOVERY OF A CAPTIVE," *DESERET* [*WEEKLY*] *NEWS* NOVEMBER 26, 1862

On last Thursday evening, a detachment of some sixty men belonging to the 2d cavalry Cal. Volunteers, under Major McGarry, left Camp Douglas, by order of Col. Connor, for Cache Valley, the object of the expedition being, as understood, the recovery of a white boy, held as a captive by an Indian, belonging to a band of Shoshones, now encamped, a reported, on the north side of Bear River, not far from Franklin. How long the boy has been a captive, who his parents were, and where and when he was taken by the Indians, we know not; but have been informed that the Indian who now has him in possession, was not his captor; but that he was obtained by purchase or otherwise, from another band, together with a sister, younger than he; that after it became known to the people in Cache county, that the band of Indians who frequently roam through that part of the Territory had two white children in their possession, efforts were made to get them by fair means, if possible; that the little girl, who was sickly, was obtained from the Indian who claimed her, by some person who succeeded in persuading him to part with her, for a pecuniary consideration; but nothing would induce the owner of the boy to give him up to the whites. The little girl subsequently died, and the boy is yet with the Indians, who are said to think highly of him, and value him at twenty ponies.

The little fellow is represented as being a very active, sprightly lad, about ten years of age, and can speak the Shoshone dialect as well as the English language quite fluently. He is said to remember the massacre of his father and mother by the Indians, somewhere on the plains, who took him, a younger brother and two sisters captives. He says his brother cried a good deal, and that the Indians took him off with them one day, after which, he never saw him again, and does not know what became of him—neither does he know whether the other sister is dead or alive.

The circumstances which led to the expedition to which reference is made, as understood, are in substance as follows:

Some weeks since, a man from Oregon, whose name has not transpired, claiming to be the boy's uncle, while at Smithfield, saw the lad and conversed with him, and, altho' the Indians were about, had a very good opportunity to take and bring him away, which for some cause, he thought proper not to do, but subsequently made some threats of what he would do, in the event that he could not obtain the custody of the boy, and then came to Salt Lake City and succeeded in getting the detachment of troops sent out to take him from the Indians by force. The result of the expedition will shortly be made known. It is hoped that it will be favorable, but fears are entertained that it will not, and that the life of the boy will be imperiled thereby.

Source: "Expedition for the Recovery of a Captive,"
Deseret News, November 26, 1862, 4

UT-82

Record of Events, Post Return of Camp Douglas for November 1862
November 27[?], 1862

Major McGarry accompanied by Capt. S. P. Smith and Lt. Conrad and a detachment of Sixty men of the 2nd C[avalry] D[ragoo]n[s] ordered to proceed to Cache Valley, to recapture from the Indians an Emigrant Boy. who had been a Captive among them three years and also, to ascertain as to the whereabouts of stock stolen from Emigrants, left the Post on the 20th inst[ant], and returned on the 26[?]th having Engaged the Indians, in which Engagement three Indians were killed and one wounded. when the Indians surrendered and delivered up the Boy who was brought back to this Post. and is now with his relations. No stock was found with the Indians belonging to Emigrants.

P. EDW. CONNOR
Col. 3rd Inf[an]t[r]y C[omman]d[in]g

Camp Douglas, U.T.

November 27[?], 1862

[Editor's note: *The second number of the day of the month is difficult to read but is presumed to be a "7."*]

Source: "Post Return of Camp Douglas, U.T. . . . for the month of November 1862," Returns from U.S. Military Posts 1800–1916, National Archives, RG94, M617, Roll 324

UT-83

ORDER NO. 72, HEADQUARTERS, CAMP DOUGLAS
DECEMBER 23, 1862

[HEAD-QUARTERS, CAMP DOUGLAS,]
Dec. 23, 1862.

ORDER NO. 72.
ADDITIONAL,

The military reserve pertaining to this post, is extended as follows: Commencing at the north-east corner of the present reserve, and running thence east two miles; thence south four miles; thence west four miles; thence north two miles to the south-west corner of the present reserve, containing, including the original reserve, ten thousand two hundred and forty acres more or less.

By order of

P. EDWD. CONNOR,
Col. Commanding Post.

H. L. USTICK, 1ST LIEUT, AND ADJUTANT.

[Editor's note: *H. L. Ustick should be W[illiam]. L. Ustick.*]

SOURCE: "CAMP DOUGLAS," DESERET NEWS, JANUARY 7, 1863, 8

UT-84

QUARTER MASTER GENERAL'S OFFICE TO HON. E. M. STANTON
JANUARY 21, 1863

QUARTER MASTER GENERAL'S OFFICE
Washington City, *Jan 21st 1863.*

HON. E. M. STANTON
Secretary of War

SIR—In reference to the communication of the Hon John M. Bernhisel, enclosing accounts of Brigham Young and others, for services and supplies furnished in connection with a company of Utah Militia cavalry, authorized by the President of the United States, to protect the property of the Telegraph and Overland Mail Companies, I have the honor to report, so far as the claims appear to relate to the Q. Master's Department:—

1st Pay Roll of Company and eleven teamsters, $13,834.60. The pay of the teamsters at $25 per month is reasonable. Wheather or not the amount charged in some cases for subsistence of these teamsters, furnished by themselves, is connect, cannot be decided, as the account does not state the member of days they so subsisted themselves, or the price charged per ration.

2nd Account for the use of ten wagons and teams hauling baggage and supplies of the company. $5911.75. Teams of four animals are charged at $5. per day each, and teams of six animals at $6.75 each. This charge would be reasonable, if the pay of the teamsters was included; but as a separate charge against the United States is made for their services as above, $4 per day for the use of wagon and team of four animals, and $5.75 for the use of wagon and team of six animals, would be a fair allowance to make.

3rd Account for Camp Equipage, and Thompsonian, Patent, and House medecines: Stationery Tobacco &c. &c, $1654.85. Of the items set forth in this account, the following pertain to the Q. Master's Department viz: Camp Kettles, Canteens, shovels, and spades; Liniment, ammonia, British oil, Castile soap, and opodeldoc, if used for House medecine; nails, screws, axes, gimlets, Ink, Envelopes, writing Paper, Lead pencils, memorandum books, Hand saw, axe-helves, Files, Augurs, Pick-axes, Sibley tents, Rasps, Buckskins, and Hatchets. The prices appear to be reasonable, for the country in which they were furnished, except in the following cases: Camp Kettles should not average more than $2 each: Shovels $2.40, Spades $2.20, Buckskins $2.00 Mess Pans 75¢. But before the account is paid, the property should be accounted for, and such of it as may not have been properly expended in the public service, turned over to the U.S Military Authority in Utah.

4th Account for supplies and transportation $11,583.58. Of this account the items of corn, oats, and transportation, pertain to the Q Masters Department. The price charged for corn and oats, $2.24 per bushel for the former, and $1.00 per bushel for the latter, is reasonable, but the property should be accounted for before payment is made. The rate charged for transportation, $2 per 100 lbs. per 100 miles, is very high. The contract rate on the plains this year is $1.20 but the contract covers several months, and probably better routes than this. The circumstances under which this service was performed, would justify an increase of the contract rates, and $1.50 per 100 lbs. per 100 miles, would be a fair rate to allow. The account however should show the kind of stories, and from and to what points they were transported.

5th Account for Horse shows and nails, and Blacksmith work furnished, $252.83. As this account fails to set out the number or quantity of shoes and nails furnished, or the price thereof, or the nature and extend of the work done, no opinion can be formed as to the correctness of the sum charged.

6th Account for medecine, curry Combs, Butter &c. $28.15 none of these items pertain to the Q. Master's Department, except the Liniment, which does if used as

Horse medicine. The charge for Liniment in this account, is $1.00 per bottle, double the price charged in the third account. Fifty cents per bottle is enough to allow.

7th Account for 7 Pack saddles $7.50: damage to 8 Pack Saddles $25, and use of one mule on detached service, $25. The first item is reasonable, but the Pack Saddles should be turned over to the Government, or otherwise satisfactorily accounted for: the second item requires explanation, and the third should show by whom, under what circumstances, and for what period the mule was used.

8th Accounts for 5 lbs. Horse shoe nails a $1.00: Blacksmith work $9: use of shop, tools, and coal $5. The first item is too high: 50 c per lb. would be a fair price. The other items require explanation, as to the nature and extent of the work done, the number of days the shop was used, and the quantity of Coal expended.

9th Account for Saddlery findings &c $85.40. As the men of the Company charge 40 ct per day for the use and risk of horse and equipments, the latter should be kept in repair at their own expense. The item of Saddlery however pertains to the Ordnance Department. It is noticed that there is a charge in this account for "use of horse furnished for Saddler $10," while in the Pay roll of the Company, the Saddler charged 40¢ per day, for the use and risk of his own horse.

10th Account for forage across Green River between May 14th and July 15th 1862. $341.20 wagons are charged at $3.00 each, horses and riders 50c. The rates appear to be high but The Qr Master General is not prepared to say that they are excessive. The claimant however should be requested to make affidavit, or show by other satisfactory evidence that the service is not charged at higher rates than is customary and legal.

11th Accounts for horses lost, stolen, used up, and killed for food $1,475.00. If the owners did not agree to incure the risk to which their horses would be exposed in this service, the claim must be adjusted by the Head Auditor under Section 2 & 3, Chap 129, Act of March 3d 1849

[Editor's note: *The 10th and 11th sections are written in a different hand than the rest. Additional pages are possibly missing, and there is no closing or signature.*]

Source: "Utah, Territorial Militia Records, 1849–1877," No. 1502–1516 (1858–1865), Series 2210, Utah State Archives, Salt Lake City

UT-85

Lieutenant-General Daniel H. Wells to
Governor Stephen S. Harding
January 26, 1863

~~Head~~ Adjutants Gen.
Office, G S L City, *Jan 26 1863*

To His Excellency Stephen S Harding Gov. U.T.,

Sir your Order No (1) one of the 20th inst requiring Duplicate returns ~~of the~~ before the 1st Proximo ~~in~~ of ~~relation to~~ the ordnance, ordnance belonging to this territory Stores, Calibers, where stored, &c is duly received Strictly speaking there are no ~~ordnance~~ arms or munitions of arms belonging to this Territory. In 1851 Judge Perry E. Brochus for his protection accross the plains was furnished by the department one bronze 12 pounder Mountain Howitzer which it is understood was charged up to ~~Utah~~ the Territory on account of his quota of Public arms. If this piece can be said to belong to the Territory it is the only ordnance and ordnance Stores of every description that I have any knowledge of coming within the province of your Excellency's enquiry and it is in good condition and stored in the Arsenal in this City.

I have the honor to remain very respectfully,

D H WELLS
Lieut. Gen.
Comd'g N.L. & Militia U.T.

Source: "Utah, Territorial Militia Records, 1849–1877," Series 2210, Box 1, Folder 47 (March–April 1862), Utah State Archives, Salt Lake City

UT-86

"Expedition for the Arrest of Indian Chiefs,"
Deseret [Weekly] News
January 28, 1863

On the affidavit of William Bevins, a miner, made before his honor Chief Justice Kinney, on the 19th instant, a warrant was issued and placed in the hands of Marshal Isaac L. Gibbs, for the arrest of Bear-hunter, Sandpitch and Sagwitch, chiefs of a band of several hundred warriors of Snake Indians, now inhabiting Cache Valley.

Bevins is understood to have stated in his affidavit that, on the 8th instant, while on his way from the Grasshopper Gold Mines, in Dacotah Territory, to this city, he and seven other men of his party were attacked by the Indians referred to, in Cache county; that one of said party, John Henry Smith, was killed by said Indians, and that Bevins and the others lost gold dust, animals and other property, to the amount of about two thousand dollars. He further represents that another party of about ten men from the mines, en route for this city, had been murdered by the Indians only three days preceding the attack in which he was a sufferer as narrated.

Anticipating, from representations of Bevins and others, that no legal process could be served upon the chiefs named, without a military force to sustain the officer of the law, the Marshal, by direction of Judge Kinney, made representations to Col. Connor, commanding the California Volunteers in this vicinity, which resulted in the march of a company of infantry northward on Thursday afternoon, under command of Capt. Hoyt.

On Sunday evening, about sundown, four companies of cavalry marched through the city, under the direct command of Col. Connor, Marshal Gibbs accompanying, for the same place, with the expectation, no doubt, of surprising the Indians, who would be looking for the infantry only.

We understand the expedition has taken forty days' rations, but counting on returning within ten days: of course, none can tell when starting on such an expedition when and how they may return, and prudence is a very essential element in generalship while among Indians and deep snows.

Of the present condition and number of the Indians and their locality we have heard various reports; the commander of the troops, however, we anticipate, marches with the expectation that he will come up with the red skins about eighty or ninety miles from here on Bear River, and that with ordinary good luck the volunteers will "wipe them out," if the chiefs named in the writ do not deliver themselves up.

The Indians are said to have seventy-five lodges—six hundred warriors under Sandpitch, about 125 miles from here, and forty other lodges and one hundred and seventy warriors on Bear River, the whole ready for a fight, with "breastwork and rifle pits," awaiting the arrival of the volunteers. This all may be so; and again it may not be so. However, Col. Connor is well posted, and well supplied with guides, infantry, cavalry, howitzers and shell to meet mountain or scientific warfare.

We stated in previous issues of the NEWS that the Indians were determined to be revenged for their comrades who were killed in the other expeditions, and the recent facts confirm our past statements. Parties who arrived in this city from the Indian country while the troops were marching through make the same statements. The Indian has ever been a difficult subject to handle with nicety and justice. We believe in treating him like a human being as long as we can, never expecting from him more than from white men, and often expecting much less. When he is determined on robbery and murder he needs looking after, and when chastised must be handled effectively; but we think, in dealing with him, Crockett's a sure maxim--"first know you are right, then go-a-head." The present warlike attitude of the Indians may be without cause; but they aver that they have been the injured and provoked party. However, as we may expect better information shortly, on the return of the Volunteers, we shall defer further remarks.

In this connection it may be stated that we have heard of charges ag[a]inst parties trading with the Indians, purchasing from them emigrant plunder, and in return supplying them with "munitions of war." We expect that unprincipled persons are to be found on every frontier who would purchase from Dick, Tom or Harry, if they could only "get a bargain" without regard to the color—white, red or black, of the seller. There is no apology for such illegal traffic, and if our information is correct, the present expedition north is likely to seek some light on this subject. We wish this community rid of all such parties, and if Col. Connor be successful in reaching that bastard class of humans who play with the lives of the peaceable and law-abiding citizens in this way, we shall be pleased to acknowledge our obligations.

SOURCE: "EXPEDITION FOR THE ARREST OF INDIAN CHIEFS," *DESERET NEWS*, JANUARY 28, 1863, 4

UT-87

RECORD OF EVENTS, POST RETURN OF CAMP DOUGLAS FOR JANUARY 1863 JANUARY 31, 1863

Capt' Hoyt & 2d. Lieut Honeyman and 2d Lieut Ingham with 78 Enlisted men of 3rd Infy C. V. and 10 of 2d Cav C. V. left the Post on 22d Jany 1863 per order of Col' Connor on a Scout against Indians. On the 24th Jany' Col Connor Majs M[c]Garry, Gallagher, Surgeon Reid, Captains M[c]Lean, Price and Lieut's Chase, Berry, Quinn Clark and Conrad accompanied by four Citizens as Guides and Interpreters with 233 Enlisted Men of the 2d Cav C. V. left the Post to Join the former detachment. On the Morning of the 29th Jany' arrived on Bear River 12 Miles from Franklin W. T. and gave battle to the Indians about Three hundred strong—the battle lasted four hours and was fought with desperate Courage on both sides—our loss was 15 killed and 4 officers and 38 men wounded Captain M[c]Lean and Lieut' Chase 2d Cav C. V. supposed fatally. Captured 175 Horses, large quantity arms, destroyed large amount of provisions and burned their lodges and killed 224 Indians.

GEO. S. EVANS

[Editor's note: *The bottom of page 1, immediately after George S. Evans's signature, of this Post Return has been torn off so the report is undated. The following circumstantial evidence leads to an assumption that this report was completed and signed on January 31, 1863: (a) Camp Douglas almost always completed Post Return reports on the last day of the month, and (b) the upper right corner of this page notes that the report was received on February 14, 1863.*]

Source: "Post Return of Camp Douglas, U.T. . . . for the month of January 1863," Returns from U.S. Military Posts 1800–1916, National Archives, RG94, M617, Roll 324

UT-88

Brigadier General G. Wright to Brigadier General L. Thomas February 2, 1863

[Telegram.]

Sacramento, Cal. *February 2, 1863.*

Brig. Gen. L. Thomas,
Adjutant-General:

Colonel Connor had a severe battle with Indians on Bear River, Utah. Enemy routed and camp destroyed. Our loss fifteen killed and four wounded.

G. WRIGHT,
Brigadier-General.

Source: U.S. Senate, 50th Congress, 2d Session, Ex. Doc. No. 70, "Letter from the Secretary of War . . . relative to the raising volunteer troops to guard overland and other mails from 1861 to 1866" (Washington, D.C.: Government Printing Office, 1889), 137

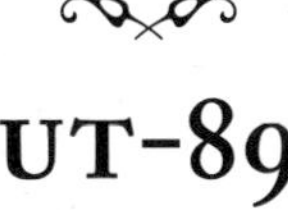

UT-89

"The Fight with the Indians," *Deseret* [*Weekly*] *News* February 4, 1863

Col. Connor and the Volunteers who went north last week to look after the Indians on Bear River have, in a very short space of time, done a larger amount of Indian killing than ever fell to the lot of any single expedition of which we have any knowledge. General Harney obtained a world wide reputation for a much less piece of work—possibly the California influence with the War Department will see that the Colonel receives that Brigadier's Commission of which all around him seem to think him so deserving. Leaving aside, however, the rewards that await the victors, we shall proceed to the details of the Expedition as far as we have been able to learn them up to the moment of going to press.

We noticed in our last issue the departure of the infantry under Capt. Hoyt, on Thursday the 22d, and the departure of the cavalry, with Col. Connor and staff, on the Sunday evening following. The cavalry's first night's march was continued up to Brigham's city, where they rested all day on Monday, and left at night for Cache Valley, arriving at Mendon early on Tuesday, where they came up with the infantry. The cavalry rested there that day and the infantry moved for Franklin—and northward for Bear River. The cavalry left on Wednesday morning at 4 o'clock, went to Summit and rested there till nine P.M. and then entered upon the last night's march. Before daylight on Thursday, the cavalry pissed the infantry and got first to the river, about 15 miles north of Franklin.

Two companies of the cavalry immediately crossed to the north side of the river, and had hardly got orders before the Indians showed fight—in the first fire, shooting one of the cavalry through the head. The Indians had selected for their position of defence, a deep ravine, about a quarter of a mile from the river, where they could not easily be reached in front.

Not having a special reporter on the field, we are unable to give in graphic detail the fight, but have been informed that it was a hard contested battle that lasted between three and four hours. The first charges of the Volunteers were very disastrous to them, as the Indians had every advantage, and could pick them off as they advanced. After the first repulses, the order was given to some of the troops to take position on an eminence that enabled the minnie rifles to enfilade the ravine. Gradually the Volunteers got upon the red skins and drove them to the mouth of the ravine, where a portion of the cavalry met the retreating Indians and played dreadful havoc with them. In one pile forty-eight bodies were counted, and a great many more were killed in attempting to get into the river and after they reached it. We have no official data from which to give figures, but it is stated with the greatest confidence that from 250 to 300 Indians were killed and wounded. Only about fifteen of the warriors are supposed to have escaped. Several squaws were killed and the rest left to take care of themselves as best they could.

The following is the list of the killed and wounded of the Volunteers:—

2d Cavalry, Co. A—Killed: Privates James W. Baldwin and George German. Wounded: Privates John W. Wall, John Welsh, Wm H. Lake and James S. Montgomery.

Co. H—Killed: Privates Charles Hollowell and John K. Briggs. Wounded: Sergt. Jas. Cantillon, Corp. Philip Schaub, Corp Patrick Frauley; Privates Michael O'Brien,

H. L. Fisher, Bartele C. Hutchinson, John Franklin, Frank Farley, Harvey Smith, Hugh Connor, Geo. B. Wing and Thos. Bradley.

Co. K—Killed: Bugler Christian Smith; Privates Shelbourne C. Reed, Adolphus Rowe, Lewis Anderson and Henry W. Trempf. Wounded: Wm. Slocum, Nathaniel Kinsley, Albert N. Parker, Benj. Landis, John Lee, John Daley, Morris Illig, Walker B. Welten, Silas C. Bush, Alonzo P. V. McCoy.

Co. M—Killed: Privates George C. Cox, George W. Hoton, Asa F. Howard and Wm. Davis. Wounded: Sergt. Anthony Stevens, Corp. Leander W. Hughes, Joshua Legget, Thaddeus Barcafar, Wm. H Hood and—Hughes.

3d Infantry, Co. K—Killed: Privates John E Baker and Sam'. J Thomas. Wounded, Sergts A. J. Austin, E. C. Hoy; Privates W. T. B. Walker and J. Hensley.

About a dozen more of the Volunteers had their feet severely frost-bitten.

Capt. Daniel McLean was first wounded in the right hand and then afterwards shot through the left thigh. Lieut. Darwin Chase is reported very seriously wounded and not likely to recover. Major Gallagher received a flesh wound in the right arm. Capt. Berry was shot through the right shoulder.

From every statement that we have heard from those who were on the field, we conclude that the Volunteers must have met the Indians with a bravery seldom equalled by regulars. Instances of individual daring are so numerous, that it would be invidious to give the names of only the few that may have reached our ears; we, therefore, leave their mention for the official report. The wounded now in Camp bear on their persons the evidences of close work. The greater portion of the wounded are shot through the lungs, and only two cases of wounds in the lower extremities.

We are glad to learn that the citizens of the settlements through which the wounded returned, contributed in every way they could to their comfort. The wounded were immediately cared for by Surgeon Reed, who was unceasing in his labor and care for them, from the first hour of the battle till they reached Camp Douglas between Monday night and Tuesday morning. Dr. Williamson, attached to the command, accompanied by Dr. Steel of Nevada Territory, present here, went North on Sunday morning as far as Ogden, and met there the wounded, and have since been in constant attendance upon them with Dr. Reed.

Col. Connor was expected at Camp Douglas during the past night, but we had not learned of his arrival up to going to press.

Source: "The Fight with the Indians,"
Deseret News, February 4, 1863, 5

UT-90

"The Order of the Day," *Deseret* [*Weekly*] *News*
February 6, 1863

At Dress Parade on Sunday afternoon the following complimentary order was read to the troops:—

Headquarters District Utah,
Camp Douglas, U.T., *Feb 6th, 1863.*

The Colonel commanding, has the pleasure of congratulating the troops of this post upon the brilliant victory achieved at the battle of Bear River, Washington Territory.

After a rapid march, of four nights in intensely cold weather, through deep snow and drifts which you endured without murmur or complaint, even when some of your number were frozen with cold and faint with hunger and fatigue, you met our enemy, who have heretofore on two occasions, defied and defeated Regular Troops, and who have, for the last fifteen years, been the terror of the emigrants, men, women, children, and citizens, of these valleys—murdering and robbing them without fear of punishment.

At daylight on the 29th of January, 1863 you encountered the enemy greatly your superior in numbers, and in a desperate battle, continued with unflinching courage for over four hours, you completely cut him to pieces, captured his property and arms, destroyed his stronghold, and burned his lodges.

The long list of killed and wounded is the most fitting eulogy on your courage and bravery.

The Colonel commanding returns you his thanks—the gallant officers and men who were engaged in this battle, without invidious distinction, merit the highest praise—your uncomplaining endurance and unexampled conduct on the field, as well as your thoughtful care and kindness for the wounded, is worthy of emulation.

While we rejoice at the brilliant victory you have achieved over your savage foe, it is meet that we do honor to the memory of our brave comrades, the heroic men who fell fighting to maintain the supremacy of our arms—we deeply mourn their death and acknowledge their valor.

While the people of California will regret their loss, they will do honor to every officer and soldier who have by their heroism added new laurels to the fair escutcheons of the State.

By order of Colonel Connor.

(Signed) WM. L. USTICK,
1st Lieut, 3d Infantry, C. V.,
A.A.A. Gen.

Source: "The Order of the Day," *Deseret News*, February 11, 1863, 5

UT-91

"Sale of the Spoils," *Deseret* [*Weekly*] *News*
February 11, 1863

The arms, mules, horses, ponies and other property taken from the Indians at the recent battle of Bear River, will be sold as per announcement, at public auction at Camp Douglas, on Thursday the 12th inst (tomorrow)—the sale to commence at 10 o'clock in the fore-noon.

Many of the animals taken, had been stolen from citizens of this Territory, by those thieving red men, some of which, as we have been informed, were claimed by their owners, as the command passed through the northern settlements, returning from the battle-field, and when satisfactory proof was made, they were restored to the claimants. Since the return, of the expedition to Camp Douglas with the captured animals, several other claims have been made, to adjudicate which, as reported, a commission has been appointed by the Colonel commanding. The officers designated for that purpose, entered upon the duty yesterday, and will continue to hear or receive evidence in such cases till the time of sale, a course which cannot fail to give satisfaction to all concerned, as justice no doubt will be done in the premises.

Source: "Sale of the Spoils," *Deseret News*, February 11, 1863, 4

UT-92

[*Extract*]

"The Battle of Bear River," *Deseret* [*Weekly*] *News*
February 11, 1863

In the last issue of the News, and the one preceding that, we noticed, as far as we had information, "The expedition for the arrest of Indian Chiefs," and "The fight with the Indians." The Volunteers have now returned to their Quarters on the bench, east of the city, and through them we learn the facts in detail of the expedition, and of a hard fought battle, which, though in a locality outside of our Territorial limits, will not be the less felt in its results by our citizens. As we have been freely furnished with what information we have requested, we give it as freely to our readers at home and abroad.

THE EXPEDITION.

At the time we noticed the departure of the Infantry under Capt. Hoyt; and of the Cavalry under Major McGarry. We now learn that the former had 69 men of Company "K" 3rd Infantry, and the latter had 220 men of Companies "A" "H" "M" and "K" 2nd Cavalry. These, together with 12 mounted men as an escort to the baggage train, and Col. Connor, Major McGarry, Major Gallagher and Lieut. Berry, constituted the entire fighting force that went North. Guides and others attached to the company are, of course, not counted. Five or six irregulars, among them "Dutch Joe," a gentleman with whom we have no acquaintance, went in and had a free fight by way of wiping off all scores with the Indians; so altogether, the force exceeded a little over 300 men.

The judiciary, probably, regard the marching of the expedition as an aid to the U.S. Marshal, in serving writs for the apprehension of several chiefs; but it is quite as probable that the movement was but a part of the campaign upon which Col. Connor and the Volunteers have entered to clear the north and central routes to California of the marauding, thieving Indians, whose murderous hostilities we were so frequently called upon to record last summer. Two previous expeditions under Major McGarry were but the prelude to that which we have now to record, and as far as we can learn, conjecture leads to the conclusion that the end of expeditions has not yet come, and that the colonel will either make an end of Po-co-tello and San Pitch, with their bands, this summer, or drive them far enough from the northern route to render it safe for the emigrants.

THE ARRIVAL AT BEAR RIVER.

On reaching Bear river, though it was yet early daylight, by the aid of his field glass, the Colonel could plainly discover the position of the Indians on the north side of the river. The cavalry dismounted, loaded arms, remounted, and Major McGarry had orders to lead across the river and if possible surround the Indians. Companies "K" and "M," Lieut. Chase and Capt. Price, first reached the banks on the north side, after considerable difficulty from the ice in the bottom of the river and from the masses of ice that were carried along with the current: companies "H" and "A," Capt. McLean and Lieut. Quinn, followed close behind them. The first companies galloped up to the base of a range of hills to the east and formed in line of battle; but before all the men had dismounted, the Indians sent a shower of lead among them, wounding one of the volunteers. The first companies were deployed at skirmishers, and ordered along the front of the ravine. The two other companies were up immediately after, and dismounting were ordered forward in the same manner.

THE POSITION OF THE INDIANS.

The Indians had excellent winter quarters in a deep ravine, about three-fourths of a mile long, running almost directly due north from Bear River into the mountains that formed their protection on the left. The banks of the ravine east and west were almost perpendicular, with only three places of difficult approach, which the Indians had made for their own convenience and for the annoyance of any approaching enemy. Anticipating an attack, they had cut steps in the east side of the banks of the ravine, from which they could conveniently fire without exposure, and descend again for perfect security. Besides these natural advantages in the ravine, on each side there were rising benches about ten feet apart, which also gave the Indians the advantage over their exposed enemy, who had to discover suddenly that ready rifles awaited their approach.

In the ravine, the wick-i-ups were planted among the willows, which partly concealed them, and the lower portions were embanked outside with rock and earth. With considerable ingenuity, they had interwoven the willows to the east of their wick-i-ups, with loop holes through which they could fire without exposure. They had also forked sticks set in the ground to serve as rests for their rifles, and with these, no doubt considered themselves safe enough against any force likely to be brought against them.

THE FIGHT.

As the troops formed in line of battle, the Indians seemed to look upon the coming struggle with particularly good humor. While one of the chiefs rode up and down the front of the ravine, brandishing his spear in the face of the volunteers, the warriors in front sung out: "Fours right, fours left; come on, you California sons of b—hs!" On such a polite invitation the word was given to "advance," and gradually as the volunteers neared the ravine the Indians retired over the benches, awaited calmly their approach, and sent at them a murderous fire that was sensibly felt everywhere. A large number of men fell dead, several fell mortally wounded and others threw themselves to the ground to abide their time and to adopt another style of fighting. The word was passed along the line for the men not to waste their ammunition, and to protect themselves as much as possible. In the advance of company "K," Lieut. Chase was first wounded in the wrist and in a moment or two received his mortal wound, but kept his saddle for about twenty minutes longer, urging on his men in the fight. Capt. McLean in the advance with Co. "M" was wounded in the right hand, but kept on towards the ravine with revolver in his left hand till he received a dangerous wound in the left thigh, which has caused him much suffering and threatens his life.

The Colonel seeing the advantageous position of the Indians, resorted to strategy, and sent Major McGarry with a small detachment of dismounted cavalry to cross the north end of the ravine, to flank the Indians on the left and take them in the rear. The infantry hearing the firing, while yet distant from the scene of action, hastened up and attempted to cross the river but it was too deep for footmen, and they had to fall back. Col. Connor sent over to them the cavalry horses with which they crossed, and wet and freezing they entered the fight. Capt. Hoyt was ordered to support Major McGarry in the flanking movement, and with his company succeeded in scrambling up the hill—skirmishing as they went, till they finally reached the west side, where, with the troops north and east they kept up an enfilading fire on the Indians that ultimately drove them down into the central and lower portions of the ravine. The Indians in the opening of the fight had the best of it and the volunteers "fell like the leaves in autumn;" but the tide of fortune changed, and savage ferocity was outmatched by generalship, brave men and good rifles.

As the work of death progressed, and the result was now clearly seen, the lower portion of the ravine became the object of interest. Capt. Price with a detatchment of men from companies "K" and "M" were doing fearful execution. In the space of five minutes, eight of his men had fallen in death or were mortally wounded; but others taking their places, the contest was kept up, and at the close of the struggle, forty-eight Indians were lying together in a heap, which showed how bravely they had fought for life. Lieut. Quinn with a small detatchment had entered the ravine from the east, and did in the language of report "excellent execution," while Lieut. Clark, with another detatchment, commanded the mouth of the ravine, and did also "his duty" as the Indians were driven towards the river.

By this time the fight had lasted nearly four hours, many of the men with feet so badly frozen that they could scarcely walk, and others with fingers so frozen that they could not tell they had a cartridge in their hands unless they looked for it there.

The Indians, bravely as they fought could not withstand the indomitable will and bravery of the troops, and presently the detatchments stationed at the mouth of the ravine detected the Indians breaking. A wild yell from the troops announced this fact to the Colonel, and in an instant he had Lieuts. Berry, Quinn, and Conrad with a detatchment of mounted cavalry charging furiously down the river, and cut off the Indian retreat at that point. The Indians being thus encircled and brought to bay, an almost hand to hand conflict ensued all along the river bank. Col. Connor and Major Gallagher then galloped down among the troops, and another severe fight took place. In a few seconds Lieut. Quinn had his horse shot from under him, and Lieut. Berry was badly wounded in the right shoulder, and here also a number of the men fell. A few minutes after Lieut. Berry fell, Major Gallagher received a painful wound in the left arm, the ball passing through it entering his side, while one of the men close by Col. Connor was shot from his horse. Soon the Indians were completely broken and in full retreat; but very few of them escaped.

THE RESULTS OF THE BATTLE.

We have learned nothing more definite with regard to the number of Indians killed than what we stated last week. From two hundred and fifty to three hundred were undoubtedly killed in the fight or in the river in the attempt to escape. The Chiefs Bear-Hunter, Sag-witch and Lehi were among the slain. A thousand bushels of wheat and a large amount of beef and provisions, together with an abundant supply of powder, lead, bullets and caps were found in the encampment. There were numerous evidences of emigrant plunder, such as modern cooking utensils, looking glasses, combs, brushes, fine rifles and pistols, and such things as the Indians were likely to consider worthy of preservation, when they had attacked and robbed the emigrants. Wagon covers, with the names of their unfortunate owners, were also lying around and patching up their wick-i-ups. What the command thought worth bringing to camp they took, and destroyed the balance, leaving enough only for the preservation of the squaws and papooses. Among the trophies of war were 175 ponies that the Indians had tied up to the willows during the fight.

On the side of the volunteers, the following is a carefully prepared

LIST OF KILLED AVD WOUNDED IN THE BATTLE,
AND CASUALTIES ON THE EXPEDITION.

2d Cavalry, Co. "A."

Killed: Privates James W. Baldwin and George German.

Mortally wounded: Private John W. Wall.

Badly wounded: Privates James S. Montgomery, John Welsh and Wm. H. Lake.

Slightly wounded: Wm Jay.

Feet frozen badly: Corporal Adolphus Spraggle and Private John D. Marker.

Feet frozen slightly: Bugler I Kearney; Privates Samuel L'hommedieu, R. McNulty and G. Swan.

Co. "M"

Killed: Wagoner Asa F. Howard; Privates George C. Cox and George C. Hoton.

Seriously wounded: Sergeant Anthony Stevens; Corporal L. W. Hughes; Privates W. H. Hood, L. D. Hughes, J. Legget, E. C. Chase, T. Barcafar and Wm. Davis.

Slightly wounded: Sergeant Lorin Robbins; Privates R. Miller, M. Forbes and P. Hunbert; Bugler A. Hoffner.

Feet frozen: Sergeant John Cullen; Corporals. A. P. Hewett and Wm. Steel; Privates W. W. Collins, James Dyer and John McGonagle.

Hand frozen: Private A. J. Case.

Co. "H"

Killed: Privates John K. Briggs, Charles L. Hollowell.

Seriously wounded: Capt. Daniel McLean; Sergt. James Cantellon; Corpls. Phillip Schaub, Patrick Frauley; Privates Michael O' Brine, H. L. Fisher, John Franklin, Hou Connor, Joseph Clows, Thompson Ridge, James Logan.

Slightly wounded: Privates Barbele, C. Hutchinson, Frank Farley.

Co. "K"

Killed: Privates Lewis Anderson, Chrisian Smith, Shelbourne C. Reed, Adolphus Rowe and Henry W. Trempf.

Seriously wounded: Lieut. Darwin. Chase, Private Wm. Slocum

Badly wounded: Privates Albert N. Parker, John S. Lee, Waker B. Welton, Nathaniel Kensley.

Slightly wounded: Sergt Sylvanius S. Longley, Corpl. Benjamin Laudis; Privates Patrick H. Kelly, Hugene J. Brady, Silas C. Bush, John Daley, Robert Hargrave, Morris Illig, Alonzo A.P.V. McCoy.

Frozen feet: Sergt. Wm. L. Beach; Corpls. Wm. L. White and James R. Hunt; Privates Siradge Ansley, Matthew A'mone, David Briston, Fred. W. Becker, Nathaniel Chapman, Samuel Caldwell, Joseph Chapman, John G. Hertle, Charles B. Horse, Joseph Hill, George Johnston, Jefferson Lincoln, Arthur Mitchell, James McKown, Alonzo R. Palmer, Charles Wilson.

3rd Infantry, Co. "K."

Killed: Privates John E. Barker, Samuel W. Thomas.

Seriously wounded: Sergt. A. J. Austin, E. C. Hoyt; Privates John Hensley, Thomas B. Walker

Feet frozen: Sergts. C. J. Herron, C. F. Williams, Corpls. William Bennett, John Lattman, John Wingate; Privates: Joseph German, James Urquhart, William S. John, Algeray Ramsdell, James Epperson, A. J. F. Randell, William Farnham, John Baurland, Giles Ficknor, Alfred Peusho, B. B. Bigelow, J. Anderson, F. Bouralso, F. Brouch, A. L. Bailey, William Carleton, D. Donahue, C. H. Godbold, J. Heywood, C. Heath, J. Mauning, William Way.

Recapitulation.

Co.	REG'T.	KIL'D.	WOUN'D.	FEET FROZEN.	TOTAL.
"A"	2d cav.	2	5	7	14
"H"	"	2	11	16	29
"K"	"	5	14	21	40
"M"	"	3	15	8	26
"K"	3 inf'y.	2	4	27	33
	—	—	—	—	
	14	49	79	142	

DIED SINCE THE BATTLE.

Private Wm. Davis, Co. "M" 2nd Cavalry, Feb. 2, at Ogden.
Lieut. Darwin Chase, Co "K" 2nd Cavalry. Feb. 4, at Farmington.
Sergt. Jas. Cantillon, Co. "H" 2nd Cavalry, Feb. 5, at Camp Douglas.
Private Wm. Slocum, Co. "K" 2nd Cavalry, Feb. 5, at Camp Douglas.
Sergt. A. Stevens, Co, "M" 2nd Cavalry, Feb. 6, at Camp Douglas.
Private M. O'Brian, Co. "H" 2nd Cavalry, Feb, 6, at Camp Douglas.

Corp. P. Frawley, Co. "H" 2nd Cavalry, Feb. 8, at Camp Douglas.
Private W. Wall, Co. "A" 2nd Cavalry, Feb. 8, at Camp Douglas.

THE RETURN TO CAMP DOUGLAS.

The moment the battle was over, the first attention was given to the wounded, and before the sun had set in the west, and closed to them that memorable day. Col. Connor had them all transported to the south side of the river, where Dr. Reed rendered them every surgical aid, and as well as possible dressed their wounds to prepare them for the return journey to Camp. The living gathered up the dead and placed them in the baggage wagons, and then the command all re-crossed the river and bivouacked in the snow for the night. Next morning, the wounded were started homewards on sleighs, in which they traveled as far as Farmington, where they were changed into carriages and wagons, and continued their journey till they arrived at Camp during the night of the 2nd instant. On the evening of the 4th, Col. Connor and the survivors of his command returned to their quarters, and so far ended their expedition.

On Thursday, the 5th, fifteen of the dead were interred with military honors by the entire command, which attracted a large concourse of spectators from the city.

FUNERAL OF LIEUT. DARWIN CHASE.

The funeral of Lieut. Chase took place on Friday, under the auspices of members of the Masonic fraternity. There being no lodge in this vicinity, the brethren of the mystic tie attached to the command, together with a few from the city, met, and, with the usual public formalities, consigned "dust to dust."

The deceased was a Royal Arch Mason, but the small number at Masons of that grade in attendance rendered the adoption of the Master Masons' burial service necessary. Sir Knight, Hon. Frank Fuller, Secretary of the Territory, officiated as W. M., and Col. Evans of the cavalry, as Marshal; His Honor Chief-Justice Kinney, and U.S. Marshal Gibbs walked in the Masonic procession. The services at the grave were of a highly impressive character, and were witnessed by nearly the whole command, together with numerous citizens. At the close of the solemnities the fraternity changed their position, while a dirge was being performed by the band, and gave place to a detail of forty-eight soldiers, who fired three volleys over the grave. The procession then returned to camp in reversed order.

Three others of the dead were interred on Saturday and two more on Sunday, with the same military honors.

. . .

We have so far extended this article that we must now only add that while the commanding officer compliments his officers and men for their bravery, they are as loud in their praises of the colonel for his coolness and bravery in the field.

[Editor's note: *UT-90, the February 6, 1863, Order of the Day, also appeared within this newspaper article.*]

Source: "The Battle of Bear River,"
Deseret News, February 11, 1863, 4–5

UT-93

Record of Events, Post Return of Camp Douglas for February 1863
February 28, 1863

On 4th Inst Col Connor accompanied by Major M^c^Garry 2d Cav C. V. Major Gallagher and Surgeon Reid 3d Infy C. V. Capt. Hoyt 3d Infy C. V. Captain Price Lieuts Clark. Quinn & Conrad 2d Cav C. V. Lieut. Honeyman with two Howitzers & Lieut Ingham 3d Infy C. V. Detachments of Co "K" 3d Infy C. V. and A, H, K & M 2d Cav C. V. numbering 172 men bringing with them the dead bodies of 1st Lieut Darwin Chase 2d Cav C. V. 13 Enlisted men 2d Cav C. V. 2 of Co K 3d Infy C. V. Capt M^c^Lean & Berry 2 Cav C. V. 49 Enlisted men wounded and 79 badly frost bitten in the feet & hands. Feby 6th 1863 Sergt. J. Cantillon Co H 2d Cav died from effects of wounds received in the Battle of Bear River W. T. Jany 29, 63 Feby 7th Pvt W^m^. Slocum Co "K" and M O'Brien Co "H" 2d Cav died of same cause, Feby 8th Corpl P Frawley & Pvt Wm Wall of Co "A" 2d Cav C. V. died of same cause

P. EDW CONNOR
Col. 3rd Infy C. V.

Camp Douglas, U.T.
February 28th, 1863.

Source: "Post Return of Camp Douglas, U.T. . . . for the month of February 1863," Returns from U.S. Military Posts 1800–1916, National Archives, RG94, M617, Roll 324

UT-94

Colonel P. Edward Connor and U.S. Army Officers Stationed at Camp Douglas to President Abraham Lincoln
March 8, 1863

Headquarters, Column for Utah, Camp Douglas,
Utah Territory, near Salt Lake City, *March 8, 1863.*

To His Excellency Abraham Lincoln, President of the United States:—

It is an unusual proceeding for officers of the army to join in representing to the Government their knowledge of facts and opinion of proceedings, having reference to civil authority, or to the actions of the people for expressing their displeasure at the conduct of their officers.

The condition of affairs in the Territory of Utah, however, and the result of this condition of affairs, which culminated in a mass meeting in Salt Lake City on the 3d inst., in our opinion demands from us a respectful statement to your Excellency of the matter having allusion to ourselves, simply as an act of duty we owe to our Government.

We do not propose to inquire into recommendations affecting the laws of the Territory, made by the Governor and Associate Judges of the Supreme Court of Utah. The Government must know, as regards the justice or injustice of the proposed amendments to existing laws, made by the officers above named.

But when the community residing in Salt Lake City solemnly declare in their petition to your Excellency, that Governor Harding, and Judges Waite and Drake are studiously endeavoring to create mischief and stir up strife between the people of the Territory and the troops now at Camp Douglas (situated within the limits of Salt Lake City), they simply assert a base and unqualified falsehood.

On the contrary, it has been the aim of these gentlemen to preserve friendly relations between the people of Utah and the troops, who have also labored to the same end, now stations at Camp Douglas.

And further; during a period of nearly five months, we know that (Governor Harding, and Judges Drake and Waite have attended to the duties of their offices, honored their appointments, regarded the rights of all, attended to their own affairs, and have not disturbed or interfered with the affairs of others, outside of their legitimate duty to the Government; and in all their conduct, His Excellency Governor Harding, and Judges Drake and Waite, have, during our acquaintance with them, demeaned themselves as honorable citizens, and officers worthy of commendation by your Excellency, our Government, and all good men.

And we further represent to your Excellency that these officers have been true and faithful to the Government, and fearless in the discharge of their duties to all they have, on all proper occasions, spoken plainly to the people of their duty. They have not been subservient to any person or persons, and they stand proudly preeminent as in contrast with other officers who have represented in the past, and who do now represent, the Federal Government in this Territory.

Our respectful opinion is, that there is no good and true cause for the removal of His Excellency Governor Harding, and Judges Drake and Waite, from the offices they now hold.

With much respect, we have the honor to remain your Excellency's obedient servants,—

P. Edward Connor, Colonel 3d Infantry, California Volunteers, commanding District of Utah; Geo. S. Evans, Colonel 2d Cavalry, Cal. Vol.; P. A. Gallagher, Major 3d Infantry, C. V.; J. M. Williamson, Surgeon, 2d Cavalry, C. V.; Robert K. Reid, Surgeon 3d Infantry, C. V.; George Wallace, Capt. and Asst. Q. M. U.S.A.; Thomas B. (lately, 1st Lieut, and Reg. Q. M.; William L. Ustick, 1st Lieut, and Adjt. 3d Infantry, and A. A. A. G.; T. S. Harris, 1st Lieut, and Adjt 2d Cavalry, C. V.; Henry R. Miller, 2d Lieut, and Reg. C. S., 2d Cavalry, C. V.; F. A. Peel, 2d Lieut, and Reg. Q. M. 2d Cavalry, C. V.; Charles Tupper, Captain 3d Infantry, C. V.; John B. Urmy, Captain 3d Infantry, C. V.; Samuel N. Hoyt, Captain 3d Infantry, C. V.; David Black, Captain 3d Infantry, C. V.; S. P. Smith, Captain 2d Cavalry, C. V. Daniel McLane, Captain 2d Cavalry, C. V.; George F. Price, Captain 2d Cavalry, C. V.; David J. Berry, Captain 2d Cavalry, C. V.; Josiah Hosmer, 1st Lieut. 3d Infantry, C. V.; James W. Stillman, 1st Lieut. 3d Infantry, C. V.; Lysander Washburn, 2d Lieut. 3d Infantry, C. V.; Michael McDermott, 1st Lieut. 3d Infantry, C. V.; John Quinn, 1st Lieut 2d Cavalry, C. V.; Cyrus D. Clark, 1st Lieut. 2d Cavalry, C. V.; Francis Honeyman, 2d Lieut. 3d Infantry, C. V.; S. E. Joelyn, 2d Lieut. 3d Infantry, C. V.; James Finnerty, 2d Lieut. 3d Infantry, C. V.; Edward Ingham, 2d Lieut. 3d Infantry, C. V.; Anthony Ether, 2d Lieut 2d Cavalry, C. V.; J. Bradley, 2d Lieut. 2d Cavalry, C. V.; Geo. D. Conrad, 2d Lieut 2d Cavalry, C. V.

Source: C. V. Waite, *The Mormon Prophet and His Harem; or, an Authentic History of Brigham Young, His Numerous Wives and Children* (Chicago: J. S. Goodman and Company, 1868), 105

UT-95

"Promotion," *Deseret* [*Weekly*] *News*
March 29, 1863

Late on Sunday evening the following dispatch was received at Camp Douglas:

Washington, D.C.,
March 29th, 1863.

To Brigadier Gen. P. Edw. Connor:

I congratulate you, and your command on the heroic conduct and brilliant victory on Bear River.

You are this day appointed a Brigadier General.

(Signed)
H. W. HALLECK.
Gen.-in-Chief.

A salute of eleven guns was fired between ten and eleven o'clock that night which, together with the music and personal congratulations at the Commander's Headquarters, finished up the late hours of Sunday evening very joyously.

From all we learn of the new Brigadier General, we are satisfied that he is a brave soldier who will yet honor the appointment. His friends are sanguine of higher promotion awaiting him, when he reaches the field of his ambition. We congratulate him upon his promotion and wish him all the good fortune that an honorable soldier can desire; and if he keeps clear of politicians and wire-workers, we have no doubt that his own "back bone" will carry him where the country can appreciate him.

Source: "Promotion," *Deseret News*, April 1, 1863, 1

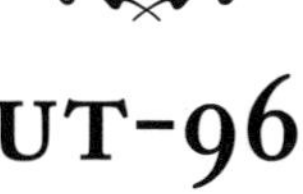

UT-96

"The Indian Affairs," *Deseret* [*Weekly*] *News*
April 1, 1863

We are pleased to learn that the Overland Mail Company feels perfectly satisfied that the Indians, who threatened last week to interrupt the communication between this and Carson, are now unable to make any successful demonstration of hostility. Since our issue we have seen several gentlemen from the west, who report "no Indians to be seen," and the public business over that route goes on uninterruptedly.

A detachment of fifty men, 2d Cavalry, C. V., have gone by the Humboldt to Ruby, and to Deep creek, if required. Another detachment of twenty-five men were sent over the mail route, and a third detachment of twenty-five men were sent by Skull valley, in the hopes of coming up with the Indians somewhere.

Willow Station was attacked for several hours by about a dozen Indians, on Thursday last; but were successfully kept off by a few men. Boyd's station was afterwards attacked; three horses taken and some hay burned. It was currently reported that Dr. Anderson, of this city, with Supt. Gooding, had fallen into the hands of the red skins at that station, but we have seen both gentlemen since that time in the city.

SOURCE: "THE INDIAN AFFAIRS," *DESERET NEWS*, APRIL 1, 1863, 1

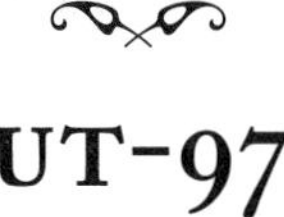

UT-97

"A SOLDIER'S COMPLAINT," *DESERET [WEEKLY] NEWS* APRIL 7, 1863

FORT BRIDGER,
April 7th, 1863.

EDITOR DESERET NEWS:

Having nothing else to do to-day, I thought that I would write you a note that would give you and the public some idea of the hardships and privations which attend a soldier's life.

We left Camp Douglas on the 4th of Dec. last, and after marching four days, arrived at this post, on the 8th, a distance of 115 miles—an average of about 29 miles per day—on foot. On our arrival we found the buildings, with the exception of the guard house, in a dilapidated condition. The weather was cold and we found no wood here, with the exception of a few cords that the post swindler had previously bought of government for the small sum of twenty-five cents per cord, which he readily offered to sell to our gallant commander for the sum of eight dollars per cord, but as green backs were not very plenty and 40 per cent, below par, very little wood could be bought—and the result was that we had to travel from twelve to fifteen miles through snow, from one to two feet deep, to get wood to prevent us from freezing to death. Whilst performing this duty, if such it can be called, some of the men got their feet so badly frost-bitten as to disable them for several months.

I will now try to give a description of our living. Shortly after our arrival here, our supplies of provisions gave out, with the exception of flour, meat, sugar and coffee. The meat consisted in part of a lot of old government bacon that was condemned in Mexico in 1848, and then sent out here in 1857, under the gallant General Johnston, who figured things so close, that he only swindled government out of one million of dollars by the operation, as many others would do if they were smart enough, judging from what little they do now, or from what little smartness they have exhibited. We get a little beef three days in a week, but instead of its being a number one article as government intended it to be, it consists of the remains of Russell's and Waddell's old bull teams that came out here in 1857–8.

J. H. S.,
Co. I., 3d Infantry, C. V.

Source: "A Soldier's complaint," *Deseret News*, April 22, 1863, 5

UT-98

"The Indian Attack at Battle Creek," *Deseret* [*Weekly*] *News*
April 14, 1863

Pleasant Grove,
April 14th, 1863.

Editor News:

On Sunday morning last, the 12th inst., a small party of soldiers from Camp Douglas, with one baggage wagon, came into our place and camped on the premises of Mr. John Green. Not far in the rear of this party, two Indians were seen following, who would not enter the town, but took to the left towards the mountains. The day passed off quiet, and the fact that soldiers were present, or Indians near, was not thought of till near sundown, when a party of Indian warriors, report says, forty-two in number, was seen coming from the mountains in great haste. The soldiers were the first who noticed the movement, and took immediate steps to be ready for contingencies. The family of Mr. Green was notified to vacate forthwith, which was immediately complied with, notwithstanding Mrs. Green was confined to her bed, having a child but eight or nine days old, and the soldiers took possession, placed their cannon in position and brought in their ammunition and other articles of value, as far as time would permit, which from the first notice of the approaching enemy, did not exceed ten minutes until the house was besieged. Our citizens, (except a few who saw the Indians approaching) remained ignorant of what was going on, until they were suddenly aroused by the discharge of a cannon and subsequent bursting of a shell, which passed over a portion of the town, bursting a short distance beyond its limits on the west. The excitement which followed on hearing the first gun, coupled with the report that a fight was going on between the soldiers and Indians was intense, families fleeing from the vicinity where the fight was progressing to parts more remote. An incessant fire of small arms was kept up from the commencement until some time after dark, say one hour and a half, and was, as the result shows, conducted on the most scientific and approved plan of modern warfare, no one having been killed or wounded on either side.

A visit to the scene of action by some of our citizens as soon as they deemed it prudent to venture, found the party, nine in number, forted up in the house, in safe, though not very comfortable quarters, which position they seemed quite reluctant to vacate, until fully assured that all was right outside.

On learning that reinforcements were looked for, an express was sent out to meet them, which returned before morning, with a force strong enough to insure safety. Another detachment has since arrived, so that the party is now considered sufficiently strong for any contingency.

Another fight may soon be expected, if the Indians do not retreat into parts inaccessible.

RESULT OF THE BATTLE.

Of the twelve horses and mules belonging to the party, five were killed; two by the soldiers and three by the Indians; one skedaddled, and six were taken by the Indians. The wagon was plundered of everything portable. Damage to Mr. Green's house and contents is estimated at about one hundred dollars.

M.

[Editor's note: *The identity of M. is unknown.*]

Source: "The Indian Attack at Battle Creek," *Deseret News*, April 22, 1863, 5

UT-99

"Expedition After Indians," *Deseret* [*Weekly*] *News* April 15, 1863

Col. Evans, as reported, left Camp Douglas on Sunday evening last, with a detachment of about eighty men—cavalry—to hunt up some Indians, said to have congregated somewhere in the mountains east of Utah lake, in consequence of the attack on the small band near Fort Cedar, by the detachment of soldiers under Lieut Ether, and the subsequent attack on a smaller number of the natives near Payson.

We are informed by a gentleman from Lower California, who came in with Woodmansee's train, that Col. Evans arrived at Pleasant Grove a little before daylight on Monday morning, and that, on Sunday evening, a lieutenant, with a squad of five or six men, who had preceded Col. Evans with one or two baggage wagons, was attacked by a band of red skins at or near that place, where they had encamped for the night, and that a skirmish ensued, resulting favorably to the attacking party.

The soldiers had a howitzer with them, as stated by our informant, which they fired twice at the Indians from a house in which they took refuge. The first time they fired a shell, and then they treated the assailants to a charge of canister, which, however, in consequence of the wrong direction given to it, killed four Government mules in the corral into which they had been turned for the night. The mistake might not, however, have been so very unlucky after all, as the Indians captured the balance of the mules, some six or eight, and put off after an hour's fight, in which none of the soldiers were hurt; but how many Indians were killed and wounded was not known.

If Col. Evans can find the main body of the warriors said to have gathered for a fight, to which, no doubt, the party belonged who made the attack at Pleasant Grove, he will be very apt to chastize them severely.

The policy, however, of provoking a collision in the first instance, with Indian bands heretofore peaceable and friendly, is seriously questioned by many thinking men who have witnessed the horrors of Indian wars.

Source: "Expedition after Indians," *Deseret News*, April 15, 1863, 8

UT-100

"The Battle of Spanish Fork," *Deseret* [*Weekly*] *News*
April 16, 1863

Spanish Fork,
April 16th, 1863.

Editor News:

Night before last, or rather early yesterday morning, the troops—two companies or more, with a howitzer—marched into Spanish Fork kanyon and came upon a body of Indians between the two bridges, one mile above the mouth of the kanyon, on the south side of the river—evidently unexpectedly, as the position for retreat was illy taken, and as it was raining heavily; it was, probably, a perfect surprise. How long or fierce the battle was we have not learned, but appearances indicate something of a struggle, and that a portion of the more active and ready of the Indians succeeded in getting up the kanyon whilst the others took up a ravine that led to a side kanyon. There they were exposed, and certainly three were killed and two wounded—perhaps more. The soldiers had three wounded; Lieut. Peel mortally, who died at Springville last night. They reported that from ten to twenty were killed and many wounded. I think the main body of Indians were some miles up the kanyon.

LATER.—From the best information gained, there were four Indians killed and two wounded.

Respectfully,

A. K. THURBER.

P. S.—17th: a heavy rain, and snow last night.

A. K. T.

SOURCE: "THE BATTLE OF SPANISH FORK," *DESERET NEWS*, APRIL 22, 1863, 5

UT-101

"MOVEMENT OF TROOPS," *DESERET [WEEKLY] NEWS*
MAY 6, 1863

Yesterday afternoon Company H., 3rd Infantry, C. V., Capt. Black left Camp Douglas to establish a post at or near Soda Springs as we announced last week, and company E., of the same regiment, left for the West to establish a post at Reese River, Overland Mail Route, as we are credibly informed. Capt. Black took with him about thirty baggage wagons, one third of which were ox teams. We understand a company of cavalry will follow shortly, which will return as soon as the post shall have been located.

About one hundred of the scapegraces who have been hanging about Camp Douglas all the winter, went north with Capt. Black's command, and about the same number went west with company E. Thus far all right, and we hope the balance of the Camp followers will soon imitate their example.

SOURCE: "MOVEMENT OF TROOPS," *DESERET NEWS*, MAY 6, 1863, 5

UT-102

"INDIAN OUTRAGE IN BOX ELDER COUNTY," *DESERET [WEEKLY] NEWS*
MAY 13, 1863

On the afternoon of Friday last, the 18th inst., as reported by Mr. Burt, of Brigham city, six or eight Indians of Sagwitch's band, as supposed, made their appearance in Box Elder kanyon or valley about four miles from Brigham city at a herd-house, and made inquiry of a boy who was there alone relative to the whereabouts of the soldiers. The boy replied that he did not know, but supposed that they were in Salt Lake City, for he had not heard that any portion of Gen. Connor's command was moving northward. The savages told the boy that he was a liar, and designated the place where the soldiers encamped the night before. They then took the lad's hat and two horses that were near by and went to the herd some distance away, where they got eight or nine more, which they succeeded in driving off, making ten or eleven in all.

They made a strong effort to drive away the entire herd of cattle grazing in the kanyon, but were prevented by the timely interference of some eight or ten Danish men, who were making a farm in the valley not far distant from the herd. The men were unarmed but on seeing the movements of the freebooters immediately took measures to defeat their object, which, after a severe struggle with the red men, they succeeded in accomplishing.

On being convinced that they could not get the cattle the Indians fled with the horses, and in their flight came upon a man by the name of Thorp who was burning coal in a small side kanyon, whom they killed with arrows, the party having no guns. The body of the murdered man was found next day considerably mutilated. A wife and five or six children mourn his loss. He came into the Territory last fall, as reported, was not wealthy, and his family were entirely dependent upon his labor for support. We understand that the facts were immediately communicated to Gen. Connor, who left Brigham city on his way north before the particulars in relation to the raid became fully known.

Source: "Indian Outrage in Box Elder county," *Deseret News*, May 13, 1863, 4

UT-103

"Military Expedition," *Deseret* [*Weekly*] *News*
May 13, 1863

On Wednesday last Gen. Connor left Camp Douglas with a company of cavalry for Soda Springs, Idaho Territory, for the purpose of selecting a site for the new military post in that vicinity, and, as understood, to look after Pocotello and his braves for the purpose of ascertaining the truth of the report relative to his wanting to fight the C. V.'s. It is our opinion that the chief will skedaddle with his band when he shall have ascertained that the General desires to make his acquaintance, but perhaps he will make fight should opportunity present.

The infantry company which marched on Tuesday was overtaken before reaching Brigham city, where the command camped on Friday and remained till Saturday, when it moved on towards Bear river. Several civilians accompanied the expedition—Judge Waite of the number, and the presumption is that he does not intend to hold any court whatever in his district, and perhaps intends to take up his abode in Gen. Pope's military district.

Source: "Military Expedition," *Deseret News*, May 13, 1863, 4

UT-104

"Another Fight with Indians," *Deseret [Weekly] News* May 13, 1863

According to report, Capt. Smith, 2d cavalry, C. V., who marched with his company from Camp Douglas soon after the late Indian attacks on the Western Mail route in the vicinity of Shell creek, for that point, by order of Gen. Connor, taking the Northern route via the Humboldt, had a fight with Indians on the 4th of May, fifty miles south of Shell creek, in which twenty-nine Aborigines were killed. In another conflict on the 6th, twenty-three others were killed and considerable stock captured. In the two fights only one soldier was wounded.

It has not been stated what Indians they were, nor whether they were those who committed the depredations along the Overland route or not, but the presumption is that they were. It has been rumored, however, that the Indian mode of retaliation has been adopted by the volunteers—that is, when an Indian or band of Indians commits a depredation, punishment is to be inflicted upon the first red men found, whether innocent or guilty, friendly or belligerently inclined to the whites, the same as red men are wont, for when some scapegrace infringes upon their rights or wantonly kills some of their number, they take as much property or shed the blood of as many whites as will pay the debt or make atonement for the offense according to their code, oftener slaying those who never did them an injury than those who have, because they can be more readily found. It has been stated also that orders have been given to shoot all Indians wherever seen in this military district, whether friends or enemies, without distinction. We do not believe the report, for we cannot think that any gentleman wearing lace can be thus void of humanity.

Source: "Another Fight with Indians,"
Deseret News, May 13, 1863, 4

UT-105

"Indian War in Idaho," *Deseret [Weekly] News*
May 13, 1863

[*Extract*]

A messenger arrived here on Thursday last from Bannock City, Idaho Territory, with a request or petition from the whites in that place, to Gen. Connor, soliciting aid in suppressing an Indian war, which has recently broke out in that region, somewhat threatening in its aspects, and as per statement, had resulted in the shedding of some considerable blood before the messenger left. He came through in great haste, having been only about five days in making the trip from Bannock City. He met Gen. Connor at Kay's Creek, or in that vicinity, on his way to Soda Springs, to select the site for the new military post and city, to be established at or near that place, and delivered the message, after which he came on to the city. We have not been advised whether the General will respond to the call or not, but the presumption is that he will not, although all the troops at Camp Douglas might be sent on that service as well as not, so far as their presence is necessary to the protection of the Overland Mail and Continental Telegraph Line, for their being stationed in Great Salt Lake Valley is no guarentee whatever against Indian attacks on the stations either east or west. They afford no protection to the mail stages and passengers when travelling over the road, and so far as respects those institutions, they might just as well be stationed at Bannock City or on the Potomac as in Great Salt Lake, where hostile Indians have never come since the settlement of these Valleys by the whites. The various bands inhabiting the surrounding country know full well that the people here are always prepared to give them an unwelcome reception, should they make any hostile demonstrations in this valley. They have not forgotten the battle-fields of Utah and Tooele Counties, on which the citizens of Great Salt Lake punished them so severely for their murderous and thieving deeds, since which they have kept at a respectful distance when thus inclined, excepting the little stealing they did for the benefit of Buchanan's invading army, when stationed at Fort Bridger, in the spring of 1858, and to which they were incited, if reports were true, by men now numbered with the dead, and who, if strict justice had been meted out to them, would never have perished on a battle-field nor died a natural death. . . .

Source: "Indian War in Idaho," *Deseret News*, May 13, 1863, 4

UT-106

Lieutenant Anthony Ethier to Editor, *Deseret* [*Weekly*] *News*
July 8, 1863

Mr Editor

In one of the articles of your last issue, entitled "Peace with Little Soldier" some person with more malice than knowledge undertakes to give an account of the difficulties finally resulting in the various treaties lately made with Indians, and specially in that made with the Chief called "Little Soldier";—and calling on his imagination for his facts, he states that the said Chief and his Band were wantonly attacked by me last winter near Cedar Fort being peaceable Indians.

Truth compels me to say that the Indians, amounting to over one hundred warriors (as stated by "Little Soldier," corroborated by our own eyesight) had taken their position, more than an hour before we got there, and on our arrival were riding the "war circle," and challenging us to the fight.

Notwithstanding this, obeying instructions from District Head Quarters, I did not allow an attack, until we were first fired on by the Indians. I was quite as well aware, as is the writer of that article, that I had in rear, in the population of Cedar Fort an enemy, much meaner, more *false*, *treacherous* and *cowardly*, than any Indians west of the Rocky Mountains.

It is high time that these constant misrepresentations be stopped, the *venomous liars* who utter them seem to gather strength by impunity; but their malignity can be no longer tolerated and they will do well to take warning in time, of course, it is very thoroughly, and universally understood by all sensible men here and elsewhere, that it is not the policy of the Leaders in this community to have peace made with the Indians;—but henceforth, in the expression of such sentiments, they will do well to remember the proverb, that "a still tongue makes a wise head"

ANTHONY ETHIER
2d Lieut 2d Cav, Cal Vols
then in charge of Detachment
Camp Douglas U.T.
July 2d 1863

To Editor Deseret News.

Source: "To Editor *Deseret News*," *Deseret News*, July 8, 1863, 2

UT-107

James Duane Doty to W. P. Dole, Superintendency of Indian Affairs July 18, 1863

No. 237.

Superintendency of Indian Affairs,
Utah Territory, Great Salt Lake City, *July 18, 1863.*

Sir: On the 7th of this month General Conner and myself made a treaty of peace with Little Soldier and his band of Weber Utes, who had assembled at a point in the vicinity of this city indicated by us for their camp, about twenty miles distant.

We found with him individuals of several other bands, who attended our meeting to ascertain, it is presumed, if we were sincere in accepting Little Soldiers proposals for peace; and if so, to let us know that the disposition of other bands was favorable to peace. All who were present participated in the presents of provisions and goods which I made to Little Soldier, and which were distributed by him, and promised to cease all further depredations, and faithfully to maintain peace and friendship with all white men.

The other bands of Utahs, to whom messengers had been sent, proposed to meet us at Spanish fork at an early day, to be appointed for the purpose of making peace. The 14th instant being the time selected by General Conner, we met there on that day all of the principal men of those bands excepting two, who sent word by others that they would abide by whatever terms were agreed upon.

It was agreed that hostilities should cease immediately; that the past should be forgotten; that the Utahs should give up any stolen horses they had in their possession; that no further depredations should be committed by them; that they would remain peaceable and quiet in future; and if any of their people should hereafter murder white men or steal their horses, they would make every exertion to arrest the offenders, and deliver them up for punishment.

We promised them liberal presents of provisions and clothing, and that these presents would be continued to them by the government as long as they kept their word, but no longer. We assured them that if any act of aggression upon the whites was committed by them, the soldiers would immediately enter their country and pursue the culprits until redress was obtained, to which they assented. We also assured them that if any injury was done to them by white men, the offenders should be punished if they made complaint, and gave the proper information to General Conner, or to the superintendent.

They appeared to be very anxious for peace and to have their friendly relations with the government restored, and I feel confident the troubles with the Utah nation (in this Territory) are now terminated. The large presents which I have made them this spring, and on this occasion, have undoubtedly contributed to this result, but I think the government is mainly indebted for it to the able commanding officer of this military department, General Conner, and the efficiency and bravery of the officers and soldiers under his command.

These treaties were made orally and not reduced to writing, being without instructions from the department, and our only purpose being to obtain peace with these Indians, and to stop further hostilities on their part, for the present at least.

They appeared to be very thankful for the food and clothing which I gave them, and I promised them when the goods arrived, which are now on the way, further presents would be made them if they remained good. This I consider the best application of the funds under my control for the general service which could be made for the benefit of the Indians, the security of emigrants, and of the telegraph and overland mail lines, and the interests of the government.

When they are again assembled to receive presents, provisions, and goods, I think a treaty may be effected with them upon such terms as the department may desire.

I can but repeat the recommendation which I have heretofore made, that the Utah bands ought to be collected on the Uintah reservation, and provision made for them as herdsmen. General Conner informs me that some of the troops under his command can be employed (peace being now established with the Shoshonees) in settling and protecting them there, and in aiding them in erecting their houses, and making other improvements for permanent homes. In this manner government may soon obtain perfect control over this nation, and with a less expenditure of money than is now required to maintain the very unsatisfactory and imperfect relations existing at present.

Very respectfully, your obedient servant,

JAMES DUANE DOTY,
Superintendent.

Hon. W. P. Dole,
Commissioner of Indian Affairs.

Source: *Report of the Commissioner of Indian Affairs for the Year 1863* (Washington, D.C.: Government Printing Office, 1864), 393–394

UT-108

General Orders No. 33, Headquarters, District of Utah, October 27, 1863

Head Quarters, Dist. of Utah,
Great Salt Lake City, U.T.,
October 27th, 1863.

General Orders.
No. 33.

1. A Court of Inquiry convened at the request of 2d Lieut. Anthony Ethier, 2d Cav. C. V., to investigate a charge of having enticed from her home a young female, resident of Great Salt Lake City, having fully and honorably acquitted him of the charge, the proceedings of the court are approved, and Lieut. Ethier is Honorably acquitted of the charge.

2. The Court of Inquiry convened at the request of 1st. Sergeant John M. McFadden, of Co., A, 3d Inf., C. V., to investigate charges preferred against him, having acquitted him of all the said charges, except that of using disrespectful language to his superior officer, and recommended his restoration to duty after reprimand in general orders. The General commanding the District, takes occasion to reprehend in the severest manner the language used by Sergeant McFadden to his commanding officer, as unbecoming a soldier, and meriting the deepest censure. The District Commander regards with disapprobation such conduct on the part of any officer, non-commissioned officer or soldier, but in view of the general good conduct and soldierly bearing of Sergeant McFadden, proven on the trial, indulges the hope that this public reprimand will effectually prevent its repetition without the infliction of further punishment. Respect to superiors, both in demeanor and language, is one of the first duties of the soldier, and if not for the attendant circumstances, and the recommendation of the Court, its infraction in this case, would meet with the highest punishment known to the law. Sergeant McFadden is hereby strongly reprimanded for this breach of discipline and good conduct, and, in accordance with the recommendation of the Court, will be returned to duty with his company with his former tank as Sergeant.

3. In its opinion, the Court, referring to the disobedience of orders by the accused, says, "In this whole matter the Court can glean no evidence of insubordination on the part of the accused, who finds his full justification in the orders of Lieut. Col. Moore. As a soldier, he found himself in the anomalous position of being the subject of conflicting orders from his superiors, and he chose to obey the superior

in rank. So far therefore, as the accused is concerned, the Court is of the opinion, that he was *guiltless* and *fully justified* in his course; and this Court cannot consent that commissioned officers shall fight their battles or settle questions of rank or authority at the expense of private soldiers or non-commissioned officers, and to the detriment of the service."

Referring to the first part of the foregoing paragraph the General Comd'g has to say that he does not concur in the opinion expressed that the accused was "guiltless and finds tall justification in the ciders of Lieut. Col. Moore." The evidence discloses the fact that the last order emanated from his company commander—and the rule is strict and without exception, that the last order must be obeyed. If wrong, the responsibility lies with him who gives it, not with him who executes.

The Court, therefore, erred and the accused was neither guiltless nor justified, although under the circumstances, the General Comd'g concurring the Court, does not deem necessary or advisable the infliction of further punishment for this disobedience of orders; but desires to impress upon all Office is and soldiers, the necessity and property of always obeying the last order when emanating from a superior officer on duty with the command to which he is attached.

Officers or soldiers cannot of course, control the action of officers or soldiers of other departments, districts or posts, unless by superior orders, or when acting contrary to law and regulations.

The concluding remarks of the Court in the above quoted paragraph from its opinion, are eminently correct and proper, and meet with the full concurrence of the Commanding General. The conduct animadverted upon is highly reprehensible and detrimental to the service, and can in no case meet the approval of the Commanding General.

4. The Court of Inquiry of which Maj. Edward McGarry, 2d Cav., C. V., is President, is hereby dissolved.

By command of Brig Gen Connor.

JAMES FINNERTY,
Lieut, and Aid-de-Camp, A.A.A. Gen.

SOURCE: "GENERAL ORDERS NO. 33,"
UNION VEDETTE, NOVEMBER 27, 1863, 4

UT-109

Circular, Headquarters, District of Utah
November 14, 1863

Head Quarters, District of Utah
Great Salt Lake City, U.T., *November 14th, 1863*

Circular:

The General commanding the District has the strongest evidence that the mountains and cañons in the Territory of Utah abound in rich veins of gold, silver, copper and other minerals, and for the purpose of opening up the country to a now, handy, and industrious population, deems it important that prospecting for minerals should not only be untrammelled and unrestricted, but fostered by every proper means. In order that such discoveries may be early and reliably made, the General announces that miners and prospecting parties will receive the fullest protection from the military forces in this District, in the pursuit of their avocations; provided, always, that private rights are not infringed upon. The mountains and their now hidden mineral wealth, are the sole property of the Nation, whose beneficent policy has ever been to extend the broadest privileges to her citizens, and, with open hand, invite all to seek, prospect and possess the wonderful riches of her wide spread domain.

To the end then that this policy may be fully carried out in Utah, the General commanding assures the industrious and enterprising who may come hither, of efficient protection, accorded as it is by the laws and policy of the nation, and enforced, when necessary; by the military arm of the Government.

The General, in thus setting forth the spirit of our fierce institutions for the information of commanders of posts within the District, also directs that every proper facility be extended to miners and others in developing the country; and that soldiers of the several posts be allowed to prospect for mines, when such course shall not interfere with the due and proper performance of their military duties.

Commanders of posts, companies and detachments within the District, are enjoined to execute to the fullest extent the spirit and letter of this circular communication, and report, from time to time, to these Head-quarters tire progress made in the development of the Territory in the vicinity of their respective posts or stations.

By command of Brig. Gen. Connor.

CHAS. H. HEPMSTEAD,
Capt. C. S. and A. A. A. Gen'l.

[Editor's note: *This circular was issued by Charles H. Hempstead (not Hepmstead). See "The Union Vedette,"* Pioneer *59, no. 3 (2012), 16–17, for additional information about Hempstead, who served as the first editor of Camp Douglas's first newspaper, the* Union Vedette.]

Source: "Important Circular from General Connor,"
Union Vedette, November 20, 1863, 3

UT-110

Orders No. 51, Headquarters, Camp Douglas, Utah Territory
November 18, 1863

Head Quarters, Camp Douglas, U.T.,
November 18th, 1863.

Orders,
No. 51.

Owners of stock which is now running loose on this Government Reserve, are hereby ordered to have the same kept up, or corralled. All stock found running at large, after this date, will be shot.

By Order Col. Pollock,

WM L. USTICK,
1st Lieut. And Adjt 3rd Inf'y, Post. Adj't.

Source: "Important to Stock Owners,"
Union Vedette, November 20, 1863, 3

UT-111

"New Arrivals," [*Weekly*] *Union Vedette*
November 27, 1863

New Arrivals.—We are pleased to announce the safe arrival, on Saturday last, of companies A and B, 1st Cavalry, Nevada Territory Volunteers, at Camp Douglas, after a long though successful march from Fort Churchill, via Ruby Valley and the Humboldt. The detachment was under the command of Capt. N. Baldwin, of Co. B.

The following other officers are attached to the command: Capt. E. B. Zabriskie. 1st. Lieut. A. B. Wells, and 2d. Lieut. J. H. Stewart, of Co. A, and 1st. Lieut. J. H. Matthewson, of Co. B.

Source: "Important to Stock Owners," *Union Vedette*, November 27, 1863, 3

UT-112

General Order No. 1, Headquarters, District of Utah January 13, 1864

Head Quarters, District of Utah,
Great Salt Lake City,
Jan. 13th, 1864.

General Order,
No. 1.

I. In pursuance of General Orders No. 48, Department of the Pacific, Dec. 26th, 1863, First Lieut. Stephen E. Jocelyn, 3rd Inf'y, C. V., is hereby appointed Assistant Commissary of Musters for this District.

II. Lieut. Jocelyn will immediately report by letter to Col. Washington Seawell, U.S.A., Commissary of Musters at Department Head Quarters for instructions.

By command of Brig. Gen. Connor.

M. G. LEWIS, *Ass't Adj't Gen.*

Source: "General Order No. 1," *Daily Vedette*, January 19, 1864, 2

UT-113

Special Order No. 9, Headquarters, District of Utah
January 20, 1864

Head Quarters, Dist. of Utah,
Great Salt Lake City, U. Ter.
January 20th, 1864.

Special Orders,
No. 9.

I. The General Commanding the District; deems the Anniversary of the signal victory at Bear River, of a portion of the California Volunteers, over a wily, well armed and numerous savage foe, as an appropriate and fitting time for an act of clemency towards those soldiers who have infringed upon good order and Military Discipline, and rendered themselves amenable to the stern rigor of Military law. In remembrance of the soldierly qualities of those heroic men who fell in bloody battle one year ago, and on the occasion of Consecrating their burial place, he desires to make the day with an act of clemency which he feels will not be construed into a relaxation of that discipline as necessary to the life as it is to the efficiency of the Army.

Believing that this order will not be misconstrued in spirit or intent by the recipients of its benefits, but hoping rather, that it will inspire them with a determined effort in the future to maintain soldierly bearing, good order, correct deportment, and all the qualities which are at once the pride and pleasure of the true soldier; it is announced that all enlisted men confined in the guard house at Camp Douglas, upon any charge whatever, save and except alone that of desertion, shall and hereby do receive a full and complete pardon for offences committed.

II. It is therefore ordered, that in pursuance of the pardon herein set forth, that all enlisted men confined in the Guard House, except those charged with desertion, be released and returned to duty in their respective Companies.

By Command of

BRIG. GEN. CONNOR

M. G. Lewis,
Asst. Adjt. Gen.

Source: "Special Orders No. 9,"
Daily Union Vedette, January 30, 1864, 2

UT-114

Post Order No. 3, Headquarters, Camp Douglas, Utah Territory
January 26, 1864

Head-Quarters, Camp Douglas, U.T.
January 26th, 1864.

Post Order,
No. 3.

The following Programme having been submitted by the Committee of Arrangements for the celebration of the Battle of Bear River on the 23th day of January, 1864 is hereby approved, and will be observed as the Order of Exercises on that day;

By order of Col. Robert Pollock,

J. C. MORRILL,
1st Lieut, and Adj., 3d Inft, C. V.,
Post-Adjutant.

ORDER OF EXERCISES.

For the celebration of the Battle of Bear River, Jan. 29th, 1864.

The troops will assemble at 11 o'clock. A.M., for Review by Brig-Gen., P. Ed. Connor, Commanding District of Utah. After which the following will be observed:

ORDER IN COLUMN.

Brig-Gen. P. Ed. Connor, (Com'ding District,) and General Staff.
Band and Field Music.
Orator of the Day.
Governor of the Territory.
Judges of the Supreme Court, and other U.S. Officials.
Invited Guests.
U.S. Officers casually at Post.
Col. Robert Pollock, 3d Inft., C. V., (Comd'g. Post.) with Regimental Staff.
Company A, 3d Infantry, C. V.
Company G, 3d Infantry. C. V.
Company F, 3d Infantry. C. V.
Company C, 3d Infantry, C. V.
Company K, 3d Infantry, C. V.
Company D, 3d Infantry, C. V.
Detachment of Artillery.
Lt-Col Wm. L. Jones, (Comd'g. 2d Cav.,) C. V., with Regimental Staff.

Company L, 2d Cavalry, C. V.
Company A, 2d Cavalry, C. V.
Company H, 2d Cavalry, C. V.
Company K, 2d Cavalry, C. V.
Company D, 1st Cavalry, Nev. Ter'y V.
Company A, 1st Cavalry, Nov. Ter'y V.
Citizens in Carriages.
Citizens Mounted.
Citizens on Foot.

ORDER OF EXERCISES AT THE CEMETERY.
Prayer.
Report of Treasurer of Monument Fund.
Oration—Capt. Chas. H. Hempstead, Commissary of Subsistence.
Music by the Band.

The Column will reform after the Exercises are ended, and return to Camp in the order enumerated above.

SOURCE: "PROGRAMME OF CELEBRATION TO-DAY," *DAILY UNION VEDETTE*, JANUARY 29, 1864, 2

UT-115

FIRST LIEUTENANT G. D. CONRAD TO LIEUTENANT T. S. HARRIS
JANUARY 29, 1864

FORT BRIDGER, *Jan. 29th, 9 A.M.*

LIEUT. T. S. HARRIS, ADJ'T. 2D CAV. C. V.:

Company M, sends greetings on the morning of the Anniversary of the great Battle of Bear River, and joins you in paying homage to the memory of the brave men of the gallant Third.

(Signed:)

G. D. CONRAD,
1st Lieut. Co. M, 2d Cav, C. V. Comd'g.

SOURCE: "FROM COMPANY M, 2D CAVALRY, C. V.," *DAILY UNION VEDETTE*, JANUARY 30, 1864, 3

UT-116

Circular, Headquarters, District of Utah
January 29, 1864

Head Quarters, Dis't of Utah,
Great Salt Lake City,
Jan. 29th, 1864.

Circular:

The General commanding addresses himself with confidence to the patriotism of the troops in the District; and on this the anniversary of the heroic struggle of your comrades on the battlefield of Bear River, calls upon all for a renewed evidence of the self-sacrificing spirit which has characterized your past conduct in the service of your Country. There is no higher exhibition of patient bravery and true loyalty, than when the soldier voluntarily steps forward, foregoing the joys and comforts of home and friends, and enrolls his name for service whenever and wherever his country's needs demand.

There is a peculiar fitness in the citizen soldier taking the place his country may assign him in her hour of peril. Though remote from the great heart of the present National struggle, the General, Commanding, appeals to the loyalty and patriotism of the troops within his command, satisfied that the most heroic sacrifices will be made in the future, as they have been in the past, in the cause of Truth, Liberty and Humanity, to the end that an enduring peace, based on the overthrow of rebellion and a reinstatement of an undissevered and indissoluble Union may be secured throughout all coming time. Your country rent, distracted, yet triumphant on so many battle fields, and strong in the conviction of right and truth, needs your services yet a little longer, and your General, in pursuance of the call of the Nation, addressed to all her sons, is confident that you will make full proof of your devotion and oft repeated utterances of patriotism.

Let the beauty and sublimity of your heroism and love of country be attested by bringing anew your sacrifice to the altar of the Constitution and the Union. In making this appeal to the brave hearts of her noble sons, the Government has not been forgetful of their wants, and deals out her bounties with a generosity which enables the soldier to meet the obligations of home and kindred while in the discharge of duty to his country; not as a reward, for that, to the true man, can only be found in the consciousness of having performed his duty, and in the grateful remembrance of posterity—but in outer that the claims and wants of those independent upon his stout arm for the material comforts of life, may not conflict with the high duties he owes to his native or adopted land.

While the General looks back with pride upon the heroic, behavior of his command in every trial, it would fill his heart with renewed pleasure and gratitude to know that every one of California's brave sons serving with; him, has responded to the call now, made and enlisted as a Veteran to the end of the war.

In order that the enlisted men of this command may have an opportunity to re-enlist before the first of. March, the time to which Veteran enlistments are limited, the commanders of regiments in this District will at once appoint a recruiting officer for the irrespective commands.

By command of Brig. Gen. Connor.

M. G. LEWIS,
Ass't Adj't Gen.

SOURCE: "CIRCULAR," *DAILY UNION VEDETTE*, JANUARY 30, 1864, 3

UT-117

GEORGE WRIGHT TO EDITOR, *SAN FRANCISCO ALTA* NEWSPAPER
FEBRUARY 15, 1864

HEAD QUARTERS DEPARTMENTS OF THE PACIFIC,
Sacramento, *Feb 15, 1864.*

SIR: In the date in the Assembly, a few days since I observe that my name, as well as that of my Adjutant-General Col. Drum has been mentioned in connection with the resolution then under consideration. I have served nearly twelve years on this coast a portion of the time in command of the District and Department of Oregon, and for the past two and a half years in command of the Department of the Pacific and this is the first time that my loyalty or devotion to the Union has ever been called in question. My Department is of vast dimensions, extending from the British Possessions on the north to the borders of the Republic of Mexico on the south and from the Pacific Ocean on the west to the Rocky Mountains. Including the giant State of California and Oregon with Territories of Washington, Idaho, Nevada, Utah, and a portion of Arizona—a million of square miles, with about sixty military stations some of them more than two thousand miles apart. To those unacquainted with the routine of military duties it is difficult to impress the fact that it requires the most untiring valor and watchfulness to keep all these posts supplied and to distribute five thousand troops over such an extent of country so as to afford protection to remote settlers against hostile Indians and at the same time to be prepared to meet foes from without or traitors within. I certainly feel gratified that all my acts, since I assumed command of this Department, have received the most unqualified approval of my Government. Identified as I am with the people of this coast I have labored most assiduously to preserve peace and quiet; and I point with pride to the present condition of affairs in the Department. I have not attempted to please all; but, guided by what I believe to be the best interests of the country, I have pursued a course which thus far, I have seen no reason to regret.

As for Col. Drum and the other officers of my staff their loyalty is too well established to be injured by fault finding politicians. As for myself, I shall never stop to defend my loyalty. I am not to be read out of the Unions ranks. I have served long, in peace and war; I have fought and bled under the old flag and if I could harbor a thought save for the honor of that flag, and the prosecution of this war until the rebellion is entirely crushed the very green mountains of my native State would rise up in judgment against me.

With great respect, your most obed't serv't,

GEORGE WRIGHT.

Source: "Loyalty of General Wright," *Daily Union Vedette*, February 27, 1864, 2

UT-118

Post Orders No. 7, Headquarters, Camp Douglas, Utah Territory February 20, 1864

Head Quarters, Camp Douglas, U T
February 20th, 1864.

Post Orders,
No. 7.

The following Daily Calls will be observed at this Post, until further orders:

Reveille, daylight.
Stable Call, immediately after Reveille.
Drill Call. 6 1–2 o'clock, A.M.
Recall from Drill, 7 1–2 o'clock, A.M.
Breakfast Call, 8 o'clock, A.M.
Sick Call, 8 1–2 o'clock, A.M.
Fatigue Call, 9 o'clock, A.M.
Guard-Mount, 9 o'clock, A.M.
Orderly Call, 11 1–2 o'clock, A.M.
Recall from Fatigue, 11 o'clock 45 min., A.M.
Dinner Call, 12 o'clock [P.]M.

Fatigue Call, 12 o'clock 45 min. P.M.
Drill Call, (Battalion) Infy., 2 o'clock, P.M.
Recall from Drill. Infy., 3 o'clock, P.M.
Drill Call. (Battalion) Cav., 3 o'clock, P.M.
Recall from Drill. Cav., 1 o'clock P.M.
Recall from fatigue, 1 1–4 o'clock, P.M.
Stable Call, 4 1–4 o'clock, P.M.
Retreat, Sunset.
Tattoo, 8 1–2 o'clock, P.M.
Taps, 9 o'clock, P.M.
Company Inspection, (Sun.) 9 o'clock, P.M.
Dress Parade, (Sundays) 1 1–2 o'clock, P.M.
Guard-Mount, Sundays, immediately after Company Inspection

By order of Col Pollock.

J. C. MORRILL,
1st Lieut. and Adjt., 3d Infy., C. V.,
Post Adjutant.

SOURCE: "NEW DAILY CALLS,"
DAILY UNION VEDETTE, FEBRUARY 24, 1864, 2

UT-119

CIRCULAR, HEADQUARTERS, DISTRICT OF UTAH MARCH 1, 1864

HEAD-QUARTERS, DISTRICT OF UTAH,
Camp Douglas, U.T., *March 1st, 1864.*

CIRCULAR:

The undersigned has received numerous letters of complaint and inquiry from parties within and without the District, the former alleging that certain residents of Utah Territory indulge in threats and menaces against miners and others desirous of prospecting for precious metals, and the latter asking what, if any, protection will be accorded to those coming hither to develop the mineral resources of the country.

Without giving undue importance to the thoughtless or reckless words of misguided, prejudiced, or bad-hearted men who may be guilty of such threats as those referred to, and indulging the hope that they are but individual expressions rather than menaces, issued by any presumed or presumptuous authority whatsoever, the undersigned takes occasion to repeat that no loyal citizen will gainsay, that this Territory is the public property of the Nation, whose wish it is, that it be developed at the earliest possible day, in all its rich resources, mineral as well as agricultural, pastoral and mechanical. To this end, citizens of the United States, and all desirous of becoming such, are freely invited by public law and national policy, to come hither to enrich themselves and advance the general welfare from out the public store, which a bountiful Providence has scattered through these richly laden mountains and fertile plains. The mines are thrown open to the hardy and industrious, and it is announced that they will receive the amplest protection in life, property and rights, against aggression from whatsoever source, Indian or white.

The undersigned has abundant reason to know that the mountains of Utah, north, south, east and west, are prolific of mineral wealth. Gold, silver, iron, copper, lead and coal, are found in almost every direction, in quantities which promise the richest results to the adventurous explorer and the industrious miner.

In giving assurance of entire protection to all who may come hither to prospect for mines, the under signed wishes at this time most earnestly, and yet firmly, to warn all, whether permanent residents or not of the Territory, that should violence be offered, or attempted to be offered to miners in the pursuit of their lawful occupation, the offender or offenders, one or many, will be tried as public enemies, and punished to the utmost extent of martial law.

The undersigned does not wish to indulge in useless threats, but desires most fully and explicitly to apprise all of their rights, and warn misguided men of the inevitable result, should they seek to obstruct citizens in those rights, or throw obstacles in the way of the development of the public domain. While miners will be thus protected, they must understand, that no interference with the vested rights of the people of the Territory will be tolerated, and they are expected to conform in all things to the laws of the land which recognize in their fullest extent the claims of the *bona fide* settler on public lands.

While the troops have been sent to this district to protect from a savage foe the homes and premises of the settlers, and the public interests of the nation, they are also here to preserve the public peace, secure to all the inestimable blessings of liberty, and preserve, intact, the honor, dignity and rights of the citizen, vested by a free Constitution, and which belong to the humblest equally with the highest in the land. This, their mission, it is the duty of the undersigned to see fulfilled by kindly and warning words, if possible, but if not, still to be enforced at every hazard and at any cost. He cannot permit the public peace and the welfare of all, to be jeoparded by the foolish threats or wicked actions of a few,

P. EDW. CONNOR,
Brig. Gen., U.S. Vols.,
Comd'g Dist.

[Editor's note: *This circular was published in several March 1864 issues of the* Daily Union Vedette.]

Source: "Circular," *Daily Union Vedette*, March 2, 1864, 2

UT-120

"Indian Visitors to Camp Douglas," *Daily Union Vedette*
March 3, 1864

Indian Visitors to Camp Douglas—Within the last few days several bands of Ute Indians have visited Camp Dauglas [*sic*] headed by the Chiefs Tobby, Little Soldier, and other noted braves. They came on a friendly visit to thank General Connor for his kindnesses to them and their tribes, and renew their pledges of peace and good will. They are hearty and profuse in their expressions of desire to maintain their present friendly relations with the soldiers, and we are confident will not easily be tempted again into acts of hostility. The commanding General distributed among them small presents of food for their immediate necessities, as evidence of his kindly disposition to the red-men so long as they behave themselves. The swarthy chieftains with their retinue departed highly pleased with their visit and the reception accorded to them. They are beginning to appreciate that it is better for them to have the soldiers for friends than to make them their enemies.

Source: "Indian Visitors to Camp Douglas,"
Daily Union Vedette, March 3, 1864, 2

UT-121

"Confirmation of General Connor by the Senate,"
Daily Union Vedette
April 4, 1864

By reference to the general telegraphic news, it will be seen that the Senate in Executive session has confirmed the President's appointment of Col. P. Edw. Connor, 3d Inft., C. V., as Brigadier General U. S. volunteers, to date from March 30th. 1863. His numerous friends in this city and throughout the Territory, as well as the entire command at Camp Douglas, will be rejoiced at this news; and all who know General Connor must agree that both the appointment and confirmation have been fully deserved, and will be honored in the person of the appointee.

Source: "Confirmation of General Connor by the Senate,"
Daily Union Vedette, April 4, 1864, 2

UT-122

"Interment of the Remains of the Slain Soldiers,"
Daily Union Vedette
April 9, 1864

The remains of the soldiers of the command at Camp Douglas, who were killed last summer by Indians while guarding the Overland Mail route, were solemnly interred in the Camp Cemetery, on yesterday, with appropriate military honors. The entire command, officers and men, were paraded in honor of the memory of these gallant men, who died in the discharge of their duty; and by special permission of Colonel Pollock, commanding the Post, the Lodge of Good Templars in Camp, (Garrison Lodge, No. 65) was allowed to attend the remains of their brethren, without arms, and wearing their regalia.

The occasion and the manner of its celebration, were alike honorable to the officers, creditable to the soldiers, and indicative of the high estimation in which the memory of these unflinching soldiers is held by both.

Source: "Interment of the Remains of the Slain Soldiers," *Daily Union Vedette*, April 9, 1864, 2

UT-123

"A Familiar Epistle to Brother Brigham," *Daily Union Vedette*
April 12, 1864

A Familiar Epistle to Bro. Brigham.

"The boys can go up in Parley's Canon some fine morning, and clean out the troops before breakfast. The troops are no better than the members of Congress."—*Brigham Young in the Tabernacle, April 8th, 1864.*

Now don't, Brother Brigham! For undoubtedly somebody would get hurt, and perchance go to Hades across lots! I am sure we have done nothing to draw down such terrible vengeance on our heads,—and that on an empty stomach, too, before breakfast! On the contrary, have we not brought peace and prosperity to the people of Utah, and don't we intend that they shall not only be happy, but free? aye free, do you understand the word? Free, as God and the laws of our Country intend they shall be. Free to worship God according as their consciences may dictate, without fear of persecution and being stripped of the hard earnings of years of toil and privation. Free to pay tithing, if they can afford it, and think they can spare it from their wives and little ones. Free to ask you, Bro. Brigham, some day not far distant, where is all the tithing we have paid, for so many years? where the sweat of our brow? where that which, for the sake of our religion, we paid into your hands as the almoner of Jehovah, and in doing so deprived ourselves and those dependent on us, of the comforts, aye, even necessaries of life? True we see about as much as we pay you in six months, expended on the Temple. But good Bro. Brigham don't spend your precious breath in such outpourings of wrath as forms my text, but give us an account of your stewardship, and show us for once, just once—the debit and credit side of that big Ledger? And then, if I am not impertinent, let us see the account with the Bank of England, and kindled institutions in other parts of the world. And finally, free to go and come when and where they please, and follow such occupation as they deem most suited to their health and tastes, without fear of being cut off (above the shoulders). Now notwithstanding all that has been done, and is intended to be done for your people, you threaten us with your Priestly vengeance. Fy! for shame on you, for an ingrate. What! smite the faithful servants of your country, who have done and intend yet to do so much for the disenthralment of the people of Utah! And now, as I intend to leave you for the present, let me whisper in your ear—let the troops alone;—even in your most passionate moments. They are doing you no harm; on the contrary, you know they are enriching you; and let me tell you a secret!—don't whisper it to any body for your life!—if a drop of our blood—I say us—because I am one of the "rag tag and bobtail," as one of your Bishops calls us—and by the bye, how ungrateful of him! Are we not instrumental in bringing purchasers to his door who pay him $15 a hundred for his flour, instead of the $3 in store pay he received previous to our arrival? But let me go on with my whisper. Shed but one drop of the loyal blood of this command, and all the tears of the recording Angel, will not suffice to wipe away the stain; nor will there remain a spot on this fair Continent of ours, in which you can hide your head from the wrath of the avenging hand. Excuse me brother Brigham, I fear I am getting in a passion; but between you and me, when I look back—but no matter—we will chat upon the past at another time. And now, let me give you a bit of advice. Do all you can to keep us near you—for I have had a dream which portends you no good. In that dream (which was not all a dream) I saw you, as plain as day, running for dear life up the bench toward this Camp, pursued by hundreds of people, crying vengeance! vengeance! on our betrayer and false Steward! While with every fleeing step, you cried "soldiers, country men—save me, save me!"—and sure enough, like true soldiers and Christian men, we did save you, notwithstanding all the past, and we got you safely housed in the magazine; and those guns of ours (that you threaten to make into wagon tires) drawn up loaded to the muzzle, with grape and canister, for your protection, shielded you from as cruel a mob as that you and yours are seeking to rouse against those who desire to protect both you and them, under the Constitution and laws. But, it was only a dream, and when I awoke I found that my sleeping thoughts but mirrored what is even now passing through the waking minds of many and many a thoughtful man.

Make the application if you list, brother Brigham, but keep your temper, and don't let an unruly tongue get the better of judgment—if you can help it. Place yourself not beyond the pale of forgiveness and protection when the evil time cometh, and "the days draw near when thou shalt say, I have no pleasure in them." Affectionately, yours, etc.

CUIDADO.

[Editor's note: *The identity of Cuidado is unknown.*]

SOURCE: "A FAMILIAR EPISTLE TO BROTHER BRIGHAM," *DAILY UNION VEDETTE*, APRIL 12, 1864, 2

UT-124

GENERAL ORDERS NO. 7, HEADQUARTERS, CAMP RELIEF, UTAH TERRITORY APRIL 18, 1864

HEAD-QUARTERS, 2D CAV., C. V.,
Camp Relief, U.T., *April, 18, 1864.*

GENERAL ORDERS,
No. 7. EXTRACT.

I. The resignation of 1st Lieut. and Adjt., Thomas S. Harris, of this regiment, having been accepted, to take effect on the 20th inst., 2d Lieut. Frederick Weed, of Co. M, 2d Cav., C. V., is hereby appointed Regimental Adjutant, to fill the vacancy *vice* Harris, to date from April 20th, 1861.

* * * *

IV. The Colonel commanding, takes this occasion to express his regret for the necessity which actuated the resignation, and the consequent loss to the regiment of 1st Lieut. Thos. S. Harris, who has so long and faithfully filled the responsible position of Adjutant of the 2d Cavalry, California Volunteers, discharging his duties to his regiment and country, with honor and fidelity; and he hereby acknowledges the valuable services of Lieut. Harris, in faithfully keeping the records of the regiment during the time the regimental Commander (nearly eight months) was not permitted to assume command, and which had accumulated in the Adjutant's office, only awaiting the arrival of the Commanding officer to complete the same by signing and transmitting to the proper authorities.

WM. JONES,
Lieut-Col., 2d Cav., C. V., Commanding regiment.

SOURCE: "GENERAL ORDERS NO. 7," *DAILY UNION VEDETTE*, APRIL 22, 1864, 2

UT-125

"How Salt Lake City Is Commanded," *Daily Union Vedette*
April 19, 1864

How Salt Lake City is Commanded—A correspondent of an Eastern paper who has lately visited Salt-Lake City, thus speaks of the chief city of the Mormons:

The Mecca of the Mormons occupies one-fourth of the bottom of a huge saucer, the remaining three-fourths being at present partly arable land and partly desert. The Wasatch Mountains form the sides of a saucer, and, with portions of another range, encircle the city, shutting it in from the outer world with a wall too high for even the odor of its sanctity to escape over the mountain tops. Approaching from the west, you cross the Jordan, have the Great Salt Lake to your left and the city spread out in quadrilaterals before you, more like a huge map than an actual city. High up, and away to the right, occupying what is geologically termed "a bench," is Camp Douglas, the big guns of which frown down upon the city, three miles off, to remind Brigham Young that though he is "boss" of the saints, Uncle Sam is the bigger boss of both saints and sinners.

Source: "How Salt Lake City Is Commanded,"
Daily Union Vedette, April 19, 1864, 1

UT-126

Circular, Headquarters, District of Utah
April 21, 1864

Head-Quarters, District of Utah,
Camp Douglas, U.T.,
April 21st, 1864.

Circular:

The General commanding the District, desires most fully and explicitly to caution the soldiers under his command as to their course and bearing towards the people of Utah. He has seen with just pride that officers and men, during our sojourn here, have manifested a proper spirit, such as becomes soldiers of the Nation, and have refrained, in general, from retaliatory measures or conduct under provocation.

But the General is apprised that it is the object of the teachings of many of the leaders of the people to wean them from their love of country, and instill in their hearts bitterness and hatred towards the soldiers as the representatives of the Government. Bad men have sought and still seek to educate the mass of their followers in constant lessons of antagonism towards Government, and lead them to the very verge of open-handed treason by covert sneers or bold denunciations. That these efforts thus far have not been followed by their legitimate, if not intended results, redounds to the credit of the people, aided by the straightforward bearing of the soldiers of this command. It is, however, especially enjoined upon soldiers, officers and men, that they refrain on all occasions from interference in any shape with the rights of person, property or liberty of the inhabitants of Utah, as well because of their duty to the Government, Constitution and Laws of the land, as because of justice to a whole people, some of whom indeed may be misled by evil disposed persons in their midst.

It is ever to be remembered, and cannot too fully be impressed on your minds, that the military forces were sent to this District to protect and foster your every interest under the broad panoply of our free institutions.

Relying on the Intelligence of the mass of the people, to counteract the evil influences and unpatriotic counsels of evil disposed and ambitious men, anxious to retain their hold on power and place, the soldiers of this command are directed to abstain from retaliating in kind, for the real or fancied injuries received at the hands of some of the people. It is hardly deemed necessary to repeat to you, that with the private relations, domestic practices, methods of belief or religion, you have naught to do, in your capacity as soldiers of the nation. However contrary these may seem to us, whoso history, habits, education and daily walk, have instilled totally different and repugnant ideas, it is not our province to reform by violent measures, but, to protect all, so long as they violate not the Constitution and laws of the country, in manner subject to military laws.

No officer or soldier of this command, will, therefore, assume to right real or imagined wrongs among or by the civil inhabitants; but, in all such cases, will report the facts to these Head-Quarters, for such action as may be deemed necessary or proper. Interference with civil authorities or persons by subordinates, will not be countenanced, and is expressly prohibited, except in those special cases heretofore explained and set forth in general and special orders from these Head-Quarters, relative to treasonable language and violations of the regulations of Military Reservations.

Fully alive to the rights and interests committed to his care, your General will ever take the proper measures to protect the one and advance the other; but, he desires you to understand, that the residents of Utah, are entitled to, and should receive, the same protection and courtesies, which the American soldier ever extends to the citizens of our common country.

By command of

BRIG. GEN. CONNOR.

M. G. Lewis, A.A.G., U.S.V.

[Editor's note: *This circular appeared in several additional issues of the* Daily Union Vedette *through the end of April 1864.*]

Source: "Circular," *Daily Union Vedette*, April 23, 1864, 2

UT-127

Record of Events
May 20, 1864

Camp Douglas U.T.
May 20th 1864

Head Quarters 1st Cav. Nivada Ter'y Vols established at this Post pursuant to Spl Orders No 45, H[d] Qts Dist Utah May 11th 1864.

ROB[T] POLLOCK
Col 3d Infty C. V.

Source: "Post Return of U.S. Volunteers stationed at Camp Douglas, U.T. . . . for the month of May 1864," Returns from U.S. Military Posts 1800–1916, National Archives, RG94, M617, Roll 324

UT-128

Captain George F. Price to Captain M. G. Lewis
May 25, 1864

Salt Lake and Fort Mojave W. R. Expedition,
Camp No. 16, Mountain Meadow, U.T.,
May 25th, 1864.

Captain:—It may be interesting to the General commanding the District of Utah, to know that on yesterday and to-day I caused a monument to be erected beside the grave containing the bones of the victims of the Mountain Meadow massacre of September, 1837. Upon my arrival here on yesterday I found the monument which was erected several years ago by an army officer, torn down—the cross taken away, and the stones forming the monument, scattered around the springs. Near the remains of this monument is the grave, giving evidence of much decay—both grave and monument having been defaced by impious hands, I immediately determined to repair the grave and rebuild the monument. Yesterday afternoon I had erected a substantial monument of stone of the following size and dimensions, viz: Twelve feet square at base, and four feet high, compactly filled in with loose stone and earth. From the centre of: this square, rises a pyramidal column seven feet high, of stone, compactly laid. We planted in the centre of it a substantial cedar pole, on which is fastened a small cross, manufactured from one of our packing boxes. This cross reaches three feet above the apex of the pyramid—making the height of monument fourteen feet. On the side of the cross facing to the East, so that the rising sunlight of God may each day cast its rays of beauty upon it, are these words:

"Vengeance is mine, I will repay saith the Lord"

Below those words and on the arm of the cross, are these words:

"Mountain Meadow massacre, September 1857"

On the opposite side are these words:

"Erected by officers and men of Company M,
2d California Cavalry, May 24th and 25th, 1864"

The monument, rudely but substantially erected, appears well from the road, and will stand for years, if no impious hand destroy it. The grave has also been neatly repaired, filling it with earth and rounding it on the surface—covering the whole with a layer of stones. Myself, Lieut. Conrad, and every soldier of my command, consider that the fatigues and hardships of a twelve hundred mile march to Mojave and back to Camp Douglas, are cancelled in the privilege of erecting at this place beside the remains of the murdered innocent, who were betrayed and massacred in cold blood by white fiends and their Indian allies—a monument at once expressive of our honor at the act—our respect for the memory of the murdered dead, and our sympathy for their fate. I cannot refrain at this time, from entering my protest as a soldier and as an American, at the delay of a powerful Government in at least attempting to bring the leaders of this infamous crime to justice and holding them up for the execration of the entire Christian world. The Mountain Meadows are 302 1-2 miles from Camp Douglas.

Very resp't, your obd't servant.

GEO. F. PRICE, *Capt. 2d Cal. Cav.,*
Commanding expedition.

To Captain M. G. Lewis, A. A. G.,
District of Utah, Salt Lake City, U.T.

Source: Untitled, *Daily Union Vedette*, June 8, 1864, 2

UT-129

"Indian Policy in Utah—Restoration of Stolen Stock,"
Daily Union Vedette
June 27, 1864

In a letter (before us) from the Commanding Officer at Fort Bridger, we have a most striking illustration of the good effects of the policy heretofore pursued by the military authorities in reference to the Indians of this and adjacent Territories. So long as they degenerate savages were blindly led by the people and the authorities, and their every demand, no matter how outrageous, immediately complied with, they were haughty, impertinent and overbearing, and wantonly committed all sort of outrages on defenseless emigrants and timid settlers. The advent of the military, however, inaugurated a new system. For their repeated outrages and butcheries, the Commander of the District instituted at once the most summary methods of punishment. The battle of Bear River in January of last year, was a crushing blow to the war-like Snakes under Pocatello, Bear Hunter, Sagwitch, and other chiefs whose depredations were each year becoming more and more audacious and cruel. So, too, in other parts of the Territory the prompt distribution of troops north and south of the Overland Mail Line, and their activity in punishing bad Indians, impressed the savages with the power of the military arm, and with the utter feebleness of their attempt to cope with the soldiers. Then having enforced submission and extorted treaties form the several bands of warlike savages the milder and more congenial policy of treating them kindly and administering to their wants was adopted. Thus have the ruthless and marauding bands of Shoshones, Utes, Goshutes, etc. been taught that it is better to have the Government for their friends than for their enemy and that "honesty is the best policy." A wise union of punishment and kindness has worked a great change in Indian affairs in Utah, and we are now reaping its benefits.

The foregoing remarks were induced and find ample vindication in the letter above referred to. Major Gallagher, commanding Fort Bridger, reports that a few days since one of Washakee's Indians brought to the Post and delivered up no less than 19 horses, which had been stolen in the Wind River Mountains from the miners in that region by a band of Snakes Indians. The Indian, Wo au-gant came upon four lodges of the Snakes in Wind River Mountains, and when informed by them that they had stolen 23 horses from the miners near Beaver Head, he told them that a treaty had been made with Gen. Connor last summer, and that their act were violative of that treaty. Thereupon, they delivered up to Wo au-gant 20 horses (three having previously escaped) and requested him to take them to Fort Bridger in pursuance of the treaty. One of the horses was retained by Washakee's Indians, temporarily, and the balance sent in as above set forth.

We regard this act of a wandering band of Snakes, who until they had not heard of the treaty, as one of the most remarkable cases on record. It shows how thorough was the punishment administered last Spring and Summer, and how wholesome is the effect of the policy pursued. Washakee has long been the friend of the white man, and we are glad to see that the wandering bands of his once great tribe, and first returning to their allegiance to him, and manifest a disposition to be obedient to his peaceful and wise counsels. It will be remembered that in the treaty made by Gen. Connor with the formerly hostile Snakes last Spring at Fort Bridger, it was stipulated that the tribe should recognize Washakee as their Chief. It is evident that Indians have a good deal of human nature in their composition and that prompt and speedy punishment for crime, with kindness while they remain peaceful, is the proper and only policy to be pursued towards them.

We are requested to notify those interested, that the horses delivered up by these Indians, will be kept at Bridger until the rightful owners can prove property, when they will be restored.

Source: "Indian Policy in Utah—Restoration of Stolen Stock," *Daily Union Vedette*, June 27, 1864, 2

UT-130

"Whereabouts of the Companies of the Command in Utah,"
Daily Union Vedette
June 30, 1864

Whereabouts of the Companies in the Command in Utah.—As an item of interest to the relatives and friends of officers and enlisted men in this command, we publish the present whereabouts of the different companies of the 3d Infantry and 2d Cavalry, C. V.

Companies A, C, D; G, K and F, 3d Infantry. C. V., are at Camp Douglas;—Company I, at Fort Bridger;—Companies B and E at Fort Ruby, Nevada Territory, and Company H, at Camp Connor, Idaho Territory.

Companies A and M, 2d Cavalry, C. V., are on expeditions south—the latter as far as Fort Mojave, and both these Companies are soon expected back. Company K, is encamped at the crossing of Raft river on Sublette's cut-off, north. Company H, is at Camp Conness, and Company L, is now encamped at the base of the Oquirrh Mountains, west.

Company A, 1st Cavalry, Nevada Territory Volunteers, is at Camp Conness, U.T., and Company B, of the same regiment, in the Uintah valley, east from here.

Source: "Whereabouts of the Companies of the Command in Utah," *Daily Union Vedette*, June 30, 1864, 2

UT-131

Special Order No. 53, Headquarters District of Utah July 9, 1864

Head-Quarters District of Utah,
Camp Douglas, Utah Territory,
Near Great Salt Lake City,
July 9th, 1864

Special Order,
No. 53.

1st. Capt. Chas. H. Hempstead, Commissary of Subsistence U.S. Vol's, is hereby appointed Provost Marshal of Great Salt Lake City, U.T., and will immediately enter upon the duties of his office. He will be obeyed and respected accordingly.

2d. Company L. 2d Cav. C. V., Capt. Albert Brown, is hereby detailed as Provost Guard, and will immediately report to Capt. Chas. H. Hempstead, Provost Marshal, Great Salt Lake City, for duty.

3d. The Quartermaster's Department will furnish the necessary quarters, offices, etc.

By Command of

BRIG. GEN. CONNOR.

Chas. H. Hempstead,
Capt. C.S. U.S. Vol's, and A.A.A. Gen'l.

Source: "Special Order, No. 53," *Daily Union Vedette*, July 11, 1864, 2

UT-132

"Company L, Second Cavalry, C. V.," *Daily Union Vedette*
July 11, 1864

Company L. Second Cavalry. C. V.—This Company, Captain A. Brown, commanding, arrived in town on yesterday, at 1 1–2 o'clock, p.m. and went immediately into quarters in the building next to the State House, opposite the Tabernacle on South Temple street. They come detailed as a Provost Guard for Salt Lake City, pursuant to orders of Gen. Connor, commanding District, published in another column.

Source: "Company L, Second Cavalry, C. V.,"
Daily Union Vedette, July 11, 1864, 2

UT-133

Captain A. Smith Lybe to Colonel George, *Daily Union Vedette*
July 17, 1864

Three Crossings, *July 17* [*1864*].

Col. George, *Camp Douglas.*
Sir:—At your suggestion I left for Sweetwater Station, on Wednesday evening last, at 5 p.m., to repair, if possible, the line. Twelve miles west of Sweetwater, I found 1200 to 1300 yards of line down. Indians, some 50 in number, had camped the night before where they cut the line, frames of their lodges still standing. I had not wire enough at Sweetwater to fix it. Tuesday, 4 p.m., telegraphed to Platte Bridge for wire, which arrived yesterday, at 8 a.m., by freight train; by 5 p.m. yesterday wire was up—returned this p.m. Absent only one week, I thought I noticed a disposition on the part of Captain Matthison to say he thought there was no Indians near here—wish he could have been here to see the fact as they transpired only 48 hours after passing. You will observe Col. that the trip down, 40 miles, was made in about 12 hours—received 4 copies of the Vedette by mail brought up.

A. SMITH LYBE,
Captain Commanding.

Source: Untitled, *Daily Union Vedette*, July 19, 1864, 2

UT-134

Colonel Patrick Edward Connor to
Lieutenant Colonel R. C. Drum
July 21, 1864

Headquarters District of Utah,
Camp Douglas, Utah Territory,
Near Great Salt Lake City, *July 21st, 1864.*

Colonel:

Having had occasion recently to communicate with you by telegraph on the subject of the difficulties which have considerably excited the Mormon community for the past ten days, it is perhaps proper that I should report more fully by letter relative to the real causes which have rendered collision possible.

As set forth in former communications, my policy in this Territory has been to invite hither a large Gentile and loyal population, sufficient by peaceful means and through the ballot-box to overwhelm the Mormons by mere force of numbers, and thus wrest from the Church—disloyal and traitorous to the core—the absolute and tyrannical control of temporal and civil affairs, or at least a population numerous enough to put a check on the Mormon authorities, and give countenance to those who are striving to loosen the bonds with which they have been so long oppressed. With this view, I have bent every energy and means of which I was possessed, both personal and official, towards the discovery and development of the mining resources of the Territory, using without stint the soldiers of my command, whenever and wherever it could be done without detriment to the public service. These exertions have, in a remarkably short period, been productive of the happiest results and more than commensurate with my anticipations. Mines of undoubted richness have been discovered, their fame is spreading east and west, voyageurs for other mining countries have been induced by the discoveries already made to tarry here, and the number of miners of the Territory steadily and rapidly increasing. With them, and to supply their wants, merchants and traders are flocking into Great Salt Lake City, which by its activity, increased number of Gentile stores and workshops, and the appearance of its thronged and busy streets, presents a most remarkable contrast to the Salt take of one year ago. Despite the counsel, threats, and obstacles of the Church, the movement is going on with giant strides.

This policy on my part, if not at first understood, is now fully appreciated in its startling effect, by Brigham Young and his coterie. His every efforts, covert and open, having proved unequal to the task of checking the transformation so rapidly going on in what he regards as his own exclusive domain, he and his Apostles have grown desperate. No stone is left unturned by them to rouse the people to resistance against the policy, even if it should provoke hostility against a government he hates and daily reviles. It is unquestionably his desire to provoke me into some act savoring of persecution, or by the dextrous use of which he can induce his deluded followers into an outbreak, which would deter miners and others coming to the Territory. Hence he and his chief men make their tabernacles and places of worship resound each Sabbath with the most outrageous abuse of all that pertains to the Government and the Union—hence do their prayers ascend loudly from the housetops for a continuance of the war till the hated Union shall be sunk—hence the persistent attempt to depreciate the national currency and institute a gold basis in preference to Lincoln skins, as treasury notes are denominated in Sabbath day harangues.

Hence it was that the establishment of a provost guard in the city was made the pretext for rousing the Mormon people to excitement and armed assembling, by the most ridiculous stories of persecution and outrage on their rights, while the fanatical spirit of the people, and the inborn hatred of our institutions and Government were effectually appealed to, to promote discord and provoke trouble. I am fully satisfied that nothing but the firmness and determination with which their demonstrations were met, at every point, prevented a collision, and the least appearance of vacillation on my part would surely have precipitated a conflict. I feel that it is not presumptuous in me to say that in view of what has already been accomplished in Utah, that the work marked out can and will be effectually and thoroughly consummated if the policy indicated be pursued and I am sustained in my measures at department headquarters. I am fully impressed with the opinion that peace is essential to the solving of the problem, but at the same time conscious that peace can only be maintained by the presence of force and a fixed determination to crush out at once any interference with the rights of the Government by persons of high or low degree. While the exercise of prudence in inaugurating measures is essential to success, it should not be forgotten that the display of power and the exhibition of reliance on oneself have the most salutary restraining effect on men of weak minds and criminal intent. Deeply as Brigham Young hates our Government, malignant and traitorous as are his designs against it, inimical as he is against the policy here progressing of opening the mines to a Gentile populace, and desperate as he is in his fast-waning fortunes, he will pause ere he inaugurates a strife, so long as the military forces in the Territory are sufficiently numerous to hold him and his deluded followers in check. The situation of affairs in Utah is clear to my own mind, and, without presumption, I have no fear for the result, if sustained by the department commander as indicated in this and former communications. Desirous as I am of conforming strictly to the wishes and judgment of the Major-General commanding the department, and having thus fully set forth my views and the facts bearing on the case, I beg leave respectfully to ask from the department commander an expression of opinion as to the policy of the course pursued, and such suggestions or instructions as he may deem proper, as a guide in the future.

Very respectfully, your obedient servant,

P. EDW. CONNOR.
Brig.-Genl. U.S. Vol., Commanding District.

LIEUT-COL. R. C. DRUM,
Asst. Adjt.-Genl. U.S.A., San Francisco, Cal.

SOURCE: EDWARD W. TULLIDGE, *THE HISTORY OF SALT LAKE CITY AND ITS FOUNDERS* (SALT LAKE CITY: PRIVATELY PUBLISHED, 1886), 328–330

UT-135

"ARRIVAL," *DAILY UNION VEDETTE*
JULY 26, 1864

ARRIVAL.—Major Edw. McGarry, 2d Cav., C. V., arrived on Saturday morning from San Francisco, California, and will probably be for some time permanently stationed at Camp Douglas, U.T. It will be remembered that Major McGarry has been for some time past on duty to the East, whether he conducted the pirate Ridgely Greathouse, whom he there delivered over to the proper military authorities.

SOURCE: "ARRIVAL," *DAILY UNION VEDETTE*, JULY 26, 1864, 2

UT-136

"BY PACIFIC TELEGRAPH," *DAILY UNION VEDETTE*
JULY 26, 1864

FORT BRIDGER, *July 26th.*

The Indians on Green River yesterday evening stopped a large freight train, and robbed it of everything they could take away. They also stopped the stage coach, but did not molest anything on it.

HAM'S FORK, *July 26th.*

About 250 Sioux Indians were at the mail station, on Green River, yesterday P.M. They took all the provisions they could find; but had killed no person up to the time the coach left.

SOURCE: "BY PACIFIC TELEGRAPH," *DAILY UNION VEDETTE*, JULY 27, 1864, 2

UT-137

"The Indian Troubles East," *Daily Union Vedette*
July 27, 1864

In another column will be found special and private dispatches conveying the latest news from the East relative to Indian troubles. From the stage passengers who arrived yesterday at Bridger, we learn that 275 were at the crossing of Green River, well armed and mounted. They had surrounded several trains and were helping themselves promiscuously to everything they wanted. Citizens were in great fear. The Indians had crossed Green River and robbed the Mail Station of provisions.

The Indians seemed to be bent on plunder to satisfy their immediate wants, and as yet have not destroyed property or attacked emigrants. It is surmised that they are a war party on the hunt for the Snakes, and it may be that they will not seriously interfere with the stages or the emigration.

One hundred mounted men, under Capt. Baldwin, 1st Nevada Cavalry, with a mountain howitzer, have been sent out from Bridger to punish the marauders—should the reports be true, and to protect the road. We feel authorized to promise that the emigrant, stage and telegraph roads in the District of Utah will be speedily cleared of marauders and amply protected from molestation.

Source: "The Indian Troubles East," *Daily Union Vedette*, July 27, 1864, 2

UT-138

Record of Events, Post Return of U.S. Volunteers
Stationed at Camp Douglas
July 31, 1864

Head Quarters 1st Cav N[evada].T[erritory].V[olunteers]. transfered to Fort Bridger Utah Territory per Sp[ecia]l Orders No 58, July 26th 1864 H$^{d.}$ Qrs. Dist Utah.

ROBT. POLLOCK
Col. 3d. Inf Cal. Vols.

Camp Douglas U.T.

July 31st 1864

Source: "Post Return of U.S. Volunteers stationed at Camp Douglas, U.T. . . . for the month of May 1864," Returns from U.S. Military Posts 1800–1916, National Archives, RG94, M617, Roll 324

UT-139

MAJOR GENERAL IRVIN MCDOWELL TO GOVERNOR J. DUANE DOTY
OCTOBER 3, 1864

HEAD QUARTERS DEPARTMENT OF PACIFIC,
San Francisco, *October 3rd 1864.*

HIS EXCELLENCY J. DUANE DOTY ESQ[R]
Governor of Utah,
Great Salt Lake City

SIR:

I telegraphed for, and have received authority to raise, to the extent, the circumstances of the service may require, certain forces in the several States and Territories in this Department.

The Governor's of California and Oregon joined with me in the application for the quotas arbitrarily established for their respective States.– but you were too far off to be consulted, at the time, and I therefore asked, in advance of doing so, for authority to raise, not to exceed four companies from Utah in case they should be necessary. I have supposed it might become expedient, and that it might be possible to raise that number in addition to the recruits the forces now there might be able to make in the Territory among its loyal inhabitants.

Under the authority therefore given to that effect from the War Department, I have the honor to request you will, in connection with the Provost Marshal Generals Department raise by voluntary enlistment for the service of the United States four companies of Infantry, to be mustered into service at Great Salt Lake City, or such other points as may be determined upon and shall be most convenient.

As the U.S. forces in Utah are simply for the protection of the Overland communications; and maintaining the authority of the United States, and have no special reference to the Mormons, I have supposed the raising of these companies if it is practicable to do so—would meet with no opposition from that community.

Will you please write one fully on this question,

If the companies can be raised I need hardly say it is of great importance that the Officers to command them and the Battalion should be men not only of character, and education, and judgment but of unquestionable loyalty to the United States.

The Acting Assistant Provost Marshall General, Brig[r] General Mason will confer with you concerning the details of this duty, and Brigadier General Connor, Commanding District of Utah will aid you in every way within his power, to get these companies into the service at the earliest day practicable, so as to meet in part the deficiencies arising from the muster out of the principal part of the forces under his command.

I have the honor to be
Very Respectfully
Your obd[t] Serv[t]

IRVIN McDOWELL
Major General
Comm[dg] Department

Source: "Utah, Territorial Militia Records, 1849–1877," No. 1502–1516 (1858–1865), Series 2210, Utah State Archives, Salt Lake City

UT-140

Captain John Green to Governor J. Duane Doty October 10, 1864

Head Quarters Superintendent Volunteer Recruiting Service,
San Francisco, Cal., *October 10rd 1864.*

His Excellency J. Duane Doty Esqr.
Governor of Utah

Sir:

Genl Mason, Supt. V.R. Service for Cal'a & Nevada Tery., directs me to say to you, that he has received a Copy of a letter from Maj. Genl. McDowell to yourself accompanied with a request that he would communicate with you, on the subject of raising Troops in Utah.

He directs me to enclose to you the order and instructions on the subject as requested by Genl. McDowell. He thinks that the troops should rendezvous at Camp Douglas, as great expense can be saved in subsistence. He thinks it would be well to recommend a suitable citizen for the appointment of Provost Marshal of the District of Utah, to be stationed, at Salt Lake City, who will be Ex-Officio, a mustering officer.

Enclosed you will find blank-forms for making contracts if you find it necessary to subsist or rendezvous any men away from Camp Douglas.

The form marked 1 in red ink is used for the rent of rendezvous. Form marked 2 in red ink is used for subsistence. The five copies of all contracts should be approved by the Supt. Vol. Rec[rui]t[in]g S[er]rv[i]ce and by him forwarded to the proper offices of the War Department. Form marked 3 in red ink is used as a form of General Voucher. The other blanks enclosed are fully explained by the notes at the bottom of each.

I am Governor
Very Respectfully
Your obdt Sr't

JNO GREEN
Capt & A.A.G.

SOURCE: "UTAH, TERRITORIAL MILITIA RECORDS, 1849–1877," No. 1502–1516 (1858–1865), SERIES 2210, UTAH STATE ARCHIVES, SALT LAKE CITY

UT-141

GOVERNOR J. DUANE DOTY TO BRIGADIER GENERAL MASON
OCTOBER 21, 1864

EXECUTIVE OFFICE, UTAH TERRITORY
Great Salt Lake City, *October 21, 1864*

BRIGADIER GENERAL MASON
Asst. Provost Marshal General
San Francisco.

SIR. I have the honor to acknowledge the receipt of your Letter dated October 10, '64 together with the forms required for enlistments in the Volunteer Service of the United States. Allow me to refer to a copy of the answer to Major Genl. McDowells request herewith enclosed, in reply to your communication, and to assure you that

I am, very respectfully, your obdt svt.

JAMES DUANE DOTY
Governor U.T.

[Editor's note: *This is a copy of the response answering Captain John Green's October 10, 1864, letter and is written on the reverse of the last page of Green's letter. See* UT-*140. "Capt. Jno. Green for Brigadier Genl. Mason, Oct. 10, '64. Ans Oct 21, '64" is written underneath.*]

SOURCE: "UTAH, TERRITORIAL MILITIA RECORDS, 1849–1877," No. 1502–1516 (1858–1865), SERIES 2210, UTAH STATE ARCHIVES, SALT LAKE CITY

UT-142

"Camp No. 6, Platte Expedition," *Daily Union Vedette*
November 12, 1864

Camp No. 6, Platte Expedition.
Fort Bridger, *Nov. 12th, '64.*

THE PLATTE EXPEDITION

arrived here yesterday afternoon after a pleasant march of six days. We say pleasant march—simply, because the weather proved so much better than we expected. Our first night out was disagreebly cold and stormy. The Storm King favored us with sundry tokens of his affection, and everything indicated a "rough starter;"—however, the next night found us at Kimball's, with a fair sky but a keen cool atmosphere, which, before daylight caused blankets to increase more rapidly in value than gold in the New York market. Everything has worked beautifully thus far—men contented and comfortable, taking the march as it comes without a word of complaint, and acting as gaily as though going on a pic-nic in the month of June. The stock has been plentifully supplied with forage to this point—not from the trail stations—but by purchase from private parties.

OUR SOLDIER VOTE

[*illegible*] at Weber station on the 8th inst., is a source of much pride to all of us. One hundred and thirty-eight votes were given for Lincoln and Johnson—not one for McClellan and Pendleton. Sixty other men would have voted for Lincoln had their names been on the Adjutant General's roster. It is a fact worthy of mention, that Companies L and M, 2d Cavalry. C. V., have never yet had to record a Copperhead vote in their ranks. We were pained to know that five soldiers at Camp Douglas voted for McClellan. We would like for those five men to explain to the readers of the Vedette how they reconcile those votes with the uniform they wear? How they can reconcile their vote for the treason party with their act in entering the Union army, and holding their lives in their hands for the avowed object of preserving the nation from treason?

FORT BRIDGER

is the same genial pleasant Post as ever. We always liked Bridger, and upon arrival here yesterday felt perfectly at home, wandering around greeting old friends and making, we trust, the acquaintance of new ones. Bridger is garrisoned by two Companies of the 1st Nevada, Cav., under command of Major O'Neill, 2d Cavalry, C. V. The soldiers' vote here on the 8th inst., was: For Lincoln 102; McClellan 7;—and again, we have the same questions to ask those seven voters as have already been asked the five voters at Camp Douglas.

OTHER ITEMS

No mail eastward bound, has passed Green River for ten days;—cause, deep snows. Several trains are stormed in on Rock Creek—two trains, we understand, are loaded with Government supplies. Stage passengers report an average of two feet of snow along the road below Halleck. We do not know how long we will remain here; but, a few days will determine our future movements. If they be Kearney—ward, we will propell; and like John Brown, of sacred memory, our souls will march on, if we do not. If, however, soul and body arrives safely at Kearney, please join us in singing that familiar Hymn. "Johnny why did you go for a Soldier?"

PLATTE.

[Editor's note: *The identity of Platte is unknown.*]

Source: "Camp No. 6, Platte Expedition," *Daily Union Vedette*, November 17, 1864, 2

UT-143

Brigadier General Patrick Edward Connor to E. D. Townsend December 1, 1864

Salt Lake, *Dec. 1, 1864.*

E. D. Townsend
AAG

I received the Indian Pocolello on the fifth (5th) ult

P. EDWARD CONNOR
Brig. Gen.

[Editor's note: *The Indian referenced is almost certainly the Shoshone chief Pocatello, the namesake of Pocatello, Idaho.*]

Source: "Letters Received by the Office of the Adjutant General (Main Series); 1861–1870," National Archives, RG94, M619, Roll 250

UT-144

Letter to the Editor, *Daily Union Vedette*
February 1, 1865

Fort Bridger, U.T.
February 1st, 1865.

Editors Vedette:—I seat myself to let you know how we, (the Enlisted men) at Fort Bridger, celebrated the memorable 29th of January, the anniversary of our victory over the Indians at Bear River. W. T., Jan. 29th, 1863. As the 29th came on Sunday this year, we had to postpone the festivities until Monday evening, when we had one of the finest Balls ever given at Fort Bridger. The room was decorated with evergreens, transparencies, sabres and carbines; while last, but not least amongst the decorations, were about twenty ladies, which made it one of the most agreeable parties ever given at Fort Bridger. The getting up of the supper was conducted by Serg. Farley of Company M, 2nd Cav. C. V., and it was indeed a feast. For you know that Mr. Stultz of the Camp Douglas Bakery can't be beat in his line. There were but forty-seven tickets sold, owing to the limited size of our hall. They tripped the "light fantastic" until half past four, when we all dispersed highly pleased with the arrangements—only regreting that we did not have it to do over. By giving this a place in your columns you will oblige

ONE OF YOUR SUBSCRIBERS.

Source: "Letter to the Editor,"
Daily Union Vedette, February 8, 1865, 2

UT-145

"The Loyalty of Utah," *Daily Union Vedette*
February 13, 1865

The Indians are threatening the Overland route and the telegraph line with serious disaster. They are now this side of Fort Laramie, and reported six thousand strong. This community looks to the troops in this District for protection, should the Indians extend their depredations into Utah; and yet the cavalry squadrons stationed at this camp and Fort Bridger, have not a horse fit for service. The Quartermasters have not a mule able to work to Green River.

Mormon leaders refuse to sell forage to the Government. They forbid the people to do it. And what little grain we do obtain is by strategy. The most precious months of spring and early summer must be employed in recruiting half-starved animals. In the meantime officers and men must travel after Indians on foot—if they travel after them at all.

If the General commanding this District were to do as all other Generals in command do when they require forage—seize it and allow a fair price for it—we have no doubt that these leaders would raise the old cry of persecution.

SOURCE: "THE LOYALTY OF UTAH,"
DAILY UNION VEDETTE, FEBRUARY 13, 1865, 2

UT-146

"CHIEF MEDICAL OFFICER'S REPORT," *DAILY UNION VEDETTE*
FEBRUARY 15, 1865

We publish below the annual report of the Chief Medical Officer of the District of Utah, which will interest our readers:

Camp Douglas, Utah Territory, is situated within the limits and two miles from the centre of the City of the Great Salt Lake, on a plateau near the base of the Wasatch Mountains.

The location commands the entire city.

Latitude ....40° 46' North.
Longitude ......112° 06' West.
Altitude..............4.500 Feet.

The reservation is four miles square, embracing an area of over 10,000 acres. The soil is light, sandy and porous, with irrigation, will produce all the fruits and cereals of the temperate zone.

The climate is variable and inconstant. In winter the changes are frequent and very great. At night, frost and snow; in morning, ice and extreme cold, and slush and mud at mid-day.

The alternation of snow and thaw is remarkable, and it is often difficult to tell which will triumph. The summers are hot, dry and without rain. The vegetation is burned up with the intense heat, while terrible winds and clouds of dust render the atmosphere almost intolerable.

The monthly mean of Thermometer and Hygrometer registered at this Post, for the quarter commencing Jan. 1, 1863, and ending March 31, 1853, is as follows:

	Ther.	Hyg.	Fair days.	Cloudy days.	Rain & snow.
Jan........	28° 25'	26° 60'	11⅔	19⅔	2
Feb'y....	30° 02'	26° 61'	14	14	3
Mch......	41° 00'	37° 00'	28⅓	2⅔	3

According to observations made in the City of Great Salt Lake during the year 1860, the whole amount of rain was only 12 1-2 inches. The number of fair days, 240; stormy, 30; cloudy and foggy, 95.

The inhabitants of this great central basin of the continent are as peculiar as the country in which they dwell, or the religious faith they profess.

The mass are English, Welsh, Danes and Norwegians. Their chiefs—apostles and prophets—Americans. Their government a theocracy. Their creed, a fungous growth of the present century. It repudiates the celibacy of the Roman Church, and embraces the voluptuous impositions of the Mahommedan. It degrades woman by a legalized system of debauchery and prostitution.

It sanctifies falsehood. It teaches that to commit theft and robbery for the benefit of the church, is a duty. It preaches shedding of blood and human sacrifices for the remission of sin.

The entire system is repulsive to every educated and enlightened mind, and abhorrent to the civilization of the age.

It is a foul blot on the Republic, and a disgrace to the government which tolerates it.

The diseases of the country exhibit no peculiarity. Intermittent, Remittent and Typhoid fevers are known under the generic name of "Mountain fever." It is characterized by intense head-ache, mental confusion, epigastric oppression, vomiting and purging, absence of vigor, and great prostration. If not efficiently treated the prognosis is unfavorable. Catarrhs and Bronchitis, Pleuritis and Pneumonia, follow exposure and are persistent and troublesome.

Opthalmic diseases, arising from an alkaline soil, acrid dust, and a dazzling sun, are as frequent as in Egypt. Rheumatism and Neuralgia are severe and troublesome. Erysipelas is endemic, and an almost invariably attendant on severe wounds.

Rubeola and Variola have, as usual, proved exceedingly fatal among the aborigines—not extended much among the white settlers.

Diptheria has recently made its appearance. Goitze and cretinism are unknown, although the altitude is great, and the water used flows from mountains covered with perpetual snow

Employment of the troops, erecting shelter from the weather, building good quarters for officers and men, drilling, scouting, protection of Overland mail and telegraph, killing Indians, and marrying Mormon women.

The habits of the soldiers are excellent, moral and temperate, more than one-half are members of the "Sons of Temperance," or of the Order known as "Good Templars."

Cleanliness, facilities for bathing are superior—unsurpassed in any country—hot, warm and sulpher springs exist near the city and are enjoyed by all.

Food of good quality, and quantity ample. Though at Ruby and Bridger the men suffered for want of vegetables, they had to be supplied from this post, a distance of 300 and 120 miles.

Water, excellent, clear and cold, flowing from the Wasatch Mountains and diverted on the east and west sides of the camp.

This command has fought only one battle of any consequence, that of Bear River, Washington Territory, January 29, 1863.

Company K, 3d Infantry, and A, H, K and M, 2d Cavalry, numbering 203 men were engaged. Of these, fourteen were killed, fifty-three wounded and seventy-nine frost bitten. Of the killed, two were shot through the head, seven through the heart, and five through the chest: Of the fifty-three wounded, twelve were shot through chest, six through head and neck, eleven through hand and arms, five through thigh and leg, seven in side and groin, two in eye, ten in shoulder.

No capital operation has been required; all the arms and legs have been saved. The partial amputation of two feet, a couple of fingers and a dozen toes, the sum total.

One officer and seven men have since died, all shot through lungs. The balance have nearly all recovered.

Two officers and probably twenty men will demand to be discharged.

Source: "Chief Medical Officer's Report," *Daily Union Vedette*, February 15, 1865, 2

UT-147

General Orders No. 1, Headquarters District of Utah February 27, 1865

Head-Quarters District of Utah,
Camp Douglas, U.T.
(Near Great Salt Lake City.)
February 27, 1865.

General Orders,
No. 1.

The following Telegram and General Orders are published for the information of all concerned:

St. Louis, *Feb. 24th, 1865.*

Brigadier General P. E. Connor.

The following order is sent for your information:

War Department, Adj. Gen's Office,
Washington, *Feb. 17th, 1865.*

General Orders,
No. 23

The Territory of Utah and that part of Nebraska Territory west of the twenty-seventh (27th) degree of longitude, are added to the Department of Missouri.

By order of the Secretary of War.

(Signed) E. D. TOWNSEND,
Asst. Adj. General.

Send your reports and communications to these Head-quarters. What troops are in your District?

G. M. DODGE,
Maj Gen. Commanding.

Head-quarters, Dept. of Pacific
San Francisco, Cali.
February 14th, 1865.

General Orders,
No. 6

All discharges and re-enlistments since September 6th, 1864, (date of circular No. 72, War Department A.G.O. 1864) made under General Orders No. 191, War Department, 1863, and General Orders No. 305, War Department, 1863, are null and void; and in all such cases the men discharged and re-enlisted will continue to be borne on their company muster-rolls under their first enlistments for three years or until they come within the limits prescribed by General Orders No. 235, War Department, A.G.O., 1864.

By command of
Maj. Gen. McDowell

F. HAVEN,
A. A. A. General.

II. All reports and communications from Posts in the Territory of Utah to Department Head-Quarters, will in future be directed to Head Qrs Dep't of Missouri, St. Louis, Mo. Fort Ruby, Nevada, not being in this District, the Commanding Officer of that Post will in future send his reports to Head-Quarters Department of the Pacific.

III. All re-enlistments of men subsequent to September, 1864, who had more than sixty days to serve, are illegal. The men thus enlisted will be borne on the next muster-rolls, as in the original enlistment, and the proper remarks set opposite their names.

By Command of
Brig. Gen. Connor.

M. G. LEWIS,
Ass't Adj't General.

[Editor's note: *These orders and telegram are included in a single Camp Douglas General Order and were printed in a single newspaper article in the* Daily Union Vedette.]

Source: General Orders No. 1,
Daily Union Vedette, February 28, 1865, 2

UT-148

General Order No. 1, Headquarters, Denver
March 30, 1865

Head-Quarters, Denver,
March 30th [1865]

General Order,
No. 1.

In pursuance of General Order No. 80 Department of the Missouri, current series, the undersigned hereby assumes command of the District of the Plains, composed of the Districts of Utah, Colorado and Nebraska. Head-quarters at Denver.

P. E. CONNOR,
Brig. Gen'l, U.S.A.

Source: "General Order, No. 1,"
Daily Union Vedette, April 3, 1865, 2

UT-149

Schuyler Colfax to Edwin M. Stanton
June 14, 1865

Salt Lake, *June 14 1865*

Hon. E. M. Stanton,
Secy of War.

Utah's best Governor Doty, died last night. Family, poor—Mrs. Doty's only son Capt. Charles Doty is Commissary Subsistence St. Louis. She would be grateful if he could be ordered here even if temporarily and transportation furnished—Answer, please.

(Signed) SCHUYLER COLFAX.

[Editor's note: *Schuyler Colfax was speaker of the U.S. House of Representatives; Edwin M. Stanton was the secretary of war. On the reverse of this letter is written "Announces death of Gov. Doty of Utah, and asks that his son* Capt Charles Doty *Com*[*missary*] *Subs*[*istence*] *St. Louis be orderrded* [*sic*] *here even if temporarily & transportation furnished." The following indorsements were included with this correspondence at the Adjutant Generals Office, War Department, Washington, D.C.*]

The Adjutant General will grant leave of absence to Capt. Doty with transportation to Salt Lake City.

By order of Sec. of War,

(Sgn). WM. G. MOORE,
A.A.G.

W[ar] D[epartment]
Recd. Adjt. Gens. Office, 1.50 P.M. June 19th 65

Capt. Doty telegraphed at St. Louis, Mo., that 2 months leave of absence with transportation to Salt Lake City had been granted him. Telegram sent 3 P.M. June 19, '65

[*illegible*] WILLIAMS
Asst Adjt General

Source: "Letters Received by the Office of the Adjutant General (Main Series); 1861–1870," National Archives, RG94, M619, Catalog ID 300368

UT-150

"Correspondence," *Daily Union Vedette*
July 15, 1865

Hobble Creek Cañon, U.T.,
July 15, 1865.

Dear Vedette:—It may appear almost an unpardonable offence in the eyes of some that no communication from the "Gallant Third" has appeared in the *Vedette* since Co's "A" and "B" left camp Douglas.

Our excuse is not an unwillingness to correspond with our friends there. The piles of letters sent through the Adjutant's office here prove the contrary of that assertion, should any one be base enough to insinuate that as the reason for our non-communication to you. The girls we left behind us demand some attention, and have the first claim upon our spare time; our friends of the masculine persuasion come next; then we have our friends and relatives at a distance, who expect their correspondence to be sustained; and finally "that road" [*illegible*] so much of our physical energies that when we return to camp after a days experience thereon, we seldom have the will to prepare such a letter as we deem worthy of place in "Our Vedette." However, we are here, at camp No. 12, Hobble Creek Cañon, above 27 miles from Springville. This town enjoys the honor of being the only place in Utah Territory, except Camp Douglas and Great Salt Lake City, which possesses a printing press and publishing office. Here the *Farmer's Oracle* had its birth, still exists and enjoys a limited circulation—much less than it deserves. It is issued monthly, and, as its name intimates is a magazine devoted to the agricultural interests of Utah. We entered this cañon on the 10th of June, and having only traveled the distance above named since that day, this will give you, taking into consideration our known energy and perseverance, some idea of the difficulties we have had to overcome, the ugliness of the work we had, and the many obstacles we had met with. These would have deterred almost any other corps than ourselves from attempting the almost Herculean task of making a road through this cañon. As far as we have come, we have made a road of which we are proud—one over which any amount of traffic may travel with safety, without any fear of an upset on the one hand, or Indians or any other kind of varmint on the other.

Our route led us through the towns of Gorchen [Goshen], Payson, Pondtown, Spanish Fork and Springville, the loyalty of whose inhabitants, their hospitality and kindly [*illegible*]ing towards us, may be judged by the fact that everything in the shape of produce was, when we proposed purchasing, in "obedience to counsel," raised in price from 40 to 1.50 per cent, instead of display of that loyalty and patriotism of which so much has been said latterly by oracles of the church. We were looked upon with suspicion and distrust, and the inhabitants generally seemed pretty much in the predicament of Gov. Harding, "not knowing what for or why we came; whether we were going or who sent for us!"

Our "Fourth" passed off quietly; it was literally a day of rest. We cannot boast of either hearing the Declaration of Independence read, an oration delivered, enjoying the pleasures of the dance, or joining with the Mormon population in celebrating that day, like some in our "rear," who are "waiting on us while we open the road," and whose only employment seem to be carrying "that express bag" once in a while to Camp Douglas. We think did they take a turn on the road they would care little for getting up displays of patriotism with a people, whom, when they know as well as we do, will think with us, that all their expressions of loyalty and patriotism have no more substance in them than the smoke which ascends from our camp fires.

This evening the attention of all hands, and the cooks, was called to a strange visitor on the mountain top to the north of our camp. Various surmises were made as to what the animal was. Some thought it was an Indian, others a lion, some a stray Nevadian, others, more correctly, judged it a bear. Instantly a dozen muskets were loaded, and the owners, with a goodly supply of ammunition, took their way through brush and timber to where the animal was last seen. Not liking the looks of our camp, or smelling danger to his life and liberty. Brain, for such it was, had taken advantage of the time occupied by his pursuers in gaining the summit of the hill, had "changed his base," made good his retreat, and could not be traced. Some of the most adventurous of the Veteran Company are gone on a "bear hunt," and most probably bear meat will be amongst the other luxuries on the mess tables of Co. "A" next week. Co. "A" are in messes of ten or twelve men each, and some little rivalry exists as to which mess is entitled to the honor of having the best supplied table; it is, however, generally conceded that messes Nos. one and two are the "Delmonico's" of the crowd.

Lieut. Heitz and a detachment of four men left us on the 6th inst. to prospect the road to Green River, they went through Strawberry Valley via Major Baldwin's road, crossed Currant River, Red Creek and Dutchene [Duschene] River, which, they followed for 15 miles, and then struck across to Uinta Valley until they came to the South Fork of the Uinta River, still following the Baldwin road, they reach the end of Uinta Valley; here the Baldwin trail ceased, they struck across the country about 27 miles until they reach Green River; they calculate that after reaching Strawberry Valley, not more than 20 days work will be required to enable this command to reach Green River. They arrived here on the 13th inst, having returned by a different route. Their unanimous opinion is that the Baldwin road is the only practicable one to be worked through this year.

Our muskets are much admired by "this people," who seem very anxious to procure some of them. They told us they thought they would be very useful in catching trout; when this adaption was first named, we were somewhat puzzled to "see the point," and were somewhat amused to discover they thought the bayonet was a spear! and that they could at the same time with a Minnie musket fire at, and spear a trout.

Some few of the people converse freely and speak of "the new religion" that has sprung up in Salt Lake City. Shades of the Pilgrim fathers! Spirits of the Beechers! think of this: the faith professed by Oliver Cromwell, and whose adherents were the main works in the overthrow of the Stuart Dynasty; being called a new religion; having Great Salt Lake City as the place of its birth; and the Rev. Norman McLeod as its founder. Verily, the Common School system needs an extension in this territory, the Schoolmaster is abroad: when, in this, the enlightened nineteenth century, statements like this one are made in all sincerity.

If this hastily written paper is deemed worthy of insertion, I will soon after leaving this *Horrible* Creek Cañon, as some of the facetious comrades express it, send a few more items from Strawberry Valley, which is, I believe, to be our next camp.

PLOY.

[Editor's note: *The identity of Ploy is unknown.*]

SOURCE: "CORRESPONDENCE,"
DAILY UNION VEDETTE, JULY 20, 1865, 2

UT-151

SPECIAL ORDER NO. 28, DISTRICT OF THE PLAINS
JULY 23, 1865

HEAD-Q'RS, W. S. DIST. OF THE PLAINS,
Camp Douglas, U.T.
July 23d, 1865.

SPECIA[L] ORDER,
NO. 28.

I. In complians with instructions from Head-Quarters, District of the Plains, Capt. J. H. Mathewson, with Co. "B," from Bridger and sixty (60) men of Co. "C," 1st Batl. Nev Cav. from this Post, will immediately take up the line of march from Waskie Station on the O[verland]. Stage route, where he will establish his Head-Quarters, with a detachment of thirty (30) men of his command, having made the following distribution of his force along the line, viz;

Lt. D. R. Firman with thirty (30) men at Green River, which place is designate as the supply depot. Five (5) men at each of the following named Stations, under the command of a competent non-commissioned officer—Rock Springs, Salt Wells, Rock Point, Black Buttes and Big Pond.

Lieut. J. H. Stewart with fifteen (15) men at Lie[*illegible*] and a similar number at each of the following named Stations, to wit: Dug Springs and Duck Lake.

II. Capt. Mathewson will patrol the road with the force under his command and make such distribution thereof as will ensure the regular transportation of the mails and protect the line against the depredations of hostile Indians, making his proper returns and reports to these Head Quarters.

III. Lieut. F. M. Shoemaker, 3d Inft. Batt. C. Vols. will accompany the expedition as A. C. S. and A. A. Q. M. remaining at the supply depot except when making necessary issues to detachments along the line.

The Quarter-master's Department will furnish the transportation necessary to carry this order into effect.

By com'd of Lt. Col. Milo George,

S. E. JOCELYN
A. A. A. General.

SOURCE: "OFFICIAL ORDERS," *DAILY UNION VEDETTE*, JULY 28, 1865, 2

UT-152

"GOLD MINED ON THE NEW ROAD TO DENVER," *DAILY UNION VEDETTE* JULY 25, 1865

HOBBLE CREEK CAÑON
July 25, 1865.

DEAR VEDETTE.—We left "our girls behind us," therefore we have no extenuating apologies to offer for not communicating, occasionally, to your valuable paper, relative to the past, present and future of this expedition.

The "Third" are making rapid progress with the road considering the obstacles they have had to contend with It is a stupendeous piece of work and reflects great credit on the soldiers who daily toil for its completion.

Lieut. Whitney, with a small party, made a tour of observation for ten days in the direction of our destination. They found gold in small quantities and brought some (from appearances) good paying rock into camp. They report that the mountains around where they found gold were literally covered with quartz boulders and ledges—wood and water in abundance. Also, plenty of deer, elk, antelope, grizzly, beaver and porcupine. We do not know the exact attitude of our present encampment, but the air is very light, and it rains, snows, or hails seven eighths of the time. Col Johns' command crossed Strawberry Peak to day.

Your correspondent seems to lay considerable stress on our co-operating with the Mormons, and celebrating the Glorious Fourth in a manner becoming good and loyal citizens—thinks that we might have been otherwise engaged to better advantage. We don't see the point. We know nothing about road-building—(if we did, the pay wouldn't justify us). Still we may "take a turn on the road," by way of maintaining our reputation as "guerrillas." Well, we had a gay time.

As to that object which was seen on the mountain, that caused so much excitement, and so many conjectures as to whether it was a Lion, Indian, Bear or stray Nevadian. Your humble correspondent thinks that they showed admirable discretion in going in pursuit (a dozen or more) armed *cap a pie*, for had it proved a stray Nevadian, with hostile intent, their force would not have been more than adequate to have effected his capture.

In our next, which will probably be from Strawberry Valley, we will give a correct description of the country, etc, etc.

MC.

[Editor's note: *The identity of MC is unknown.*]

Source: "Gold Mined on the New Road to Denver,"
Daily Union Vedette, August 2, 1865, 2

UT-153

"From the Uinta Valley and Middle Park Exploring Expedition,"
Daily Union Vedette
August 14, 1865

Camp No. 26, Green River, U.T.,
August 14, 1865.

Editor Vedette:—My last letter was sent from Red Creek, U.T., on the 30th ult. Col. Johns and party returned from their exploring expedition the following day, broke up camp, and we proceeded towards Duchien [Duschene] River on the 1st inst., arriving thither on the 2d inst. The country between Red Creek and Duchien [Duschene] River is considerable of a sagebrush one, though here and there are spots of tillable land, with abundance of timber, and in my opinion, water could be obtained with little trouble. Rabbits and hares were frequently seen, but too small to become the prize of our sportsmen. Signs of antelope and bear were also visible, and one or more of the latter genus has been prowling around our camp nightly since our arrival hither. To sum up the nature of the soil and the general appearance of the country since we entered Strawberry Valley, I can only reiterate what I said in my former letter: that when the road is finished and the O.S. Co have their stages running, and their stations built, and one year's emigration has passed through, we who have seen it as it is, and may have to pass through it again, will scarcely be able to recognize it as the same. Its suitability for fruit raising is evinced by the large size of the wild fruits found here is such abundance and the veriest greenhorn, in a knowledge of the nature of land, cannot but see that almost every description of grain can be raised here, while the mountain sides furnish abundance of grazing land.

We left Camp No. 20 on the 5th inst., camping that evening at Falls Fork, a tributary of the Duchien [Duschene]; on the 6th, we camped of the South Fork of the Duchien [Duschene]; and on the 7th, arrived at the Uinta River. The next day, after traveling some fifteen miles of table land, sandy and destitute of almost any sign of vegetation, we reached Uinta Valley: arriving in sight of this place, we were grievously disappointed. Judging from the notoriety given to it in connection with our excursion, we had supposed it would be one of the most fertile spots in Utah; imagine our feelings when upon viewing it from a distance, which the poet says, "lends enchantment to the view," we unanimously decided that we had not seen a spot in Utah so barren, so sterile, nor so unpromising as the said Valley. We thought of that promised picnic excursion on the Fourth of July last and opined that could the promoter have seen Uinta, he would agree with us in saying that there was more verdancy in his proposition than in the whole of Uinta. We traversed the valley by the river, until we reached the North Fork of it on the 10th inst; we left that camp early on the morning of the 11th and arrived at Camp No. 26 on the banks of Green River, between one and two o'clock on the afternoon of the same day. Our camp is a little above the junction of Green and Uinta rivers; at the new crossing, the river is about 430 feet wide. From the North Fork of the Uinta to this crossing at Green River, and so far as eye can see and judge on the opposite banks, there is abundance of feed for any amount of stock, with plenty of wood and water, considerable game, and considerable prizes have rewarded the efforts of the followers of the piscatorial art; trout, sturgeon, pike and other varieties of fish too numerous to mention have been caught since our arrival here; several of the latter species weighing from ten to eighteen pounds each. These with mild fruit pies and puddings, make a very agreeable change from "pork and beans."

Every available hand is at work on the ferry-boat under the superintendance of our "Dusky" wheelwright; our "Odd" blacksmith, and his "Stern" helper are also busy in their department; and we expect to leave the other side of the river on the

18th inst; so you may judge the determination we have to go forward animates one and every mind.

In my letter to you of the 15th ult., I named about 130 miles as the distance from our 4th of July Camp, and twenty days as the time which would be required to reach it from Strawberry Valley. On reckoning up the distance traveled since that day, I find it to be 123 miles and that eighteen days have elapsed since we entered Strawberry Valley. I have no positive criterion to judge of the time it will occupy for us to reach Denver; but the end of September appears to be the latest time that any one wishes to be on the road. The health of the command is good, and excepting the small matter of clothing, we all look and feel better than we were when we left camp Douglas.

PLOY.

Source: "From the Uinta Valley and Middle Park Exploring Expedition," *Daily Union Vedette*, September 9, 1865, 2

UT-154

Sixth Infantry U.S. Volunteers at Fort Bridger to Camp Douglas
October 2, 1865

A telegram received from Fort Bridger on Saturday evening, announces that three companies of the Sixth Infantry, U. S. Vols., under command of Lieut. Col. Smith, are en route to Camp Douglas. They encamped at Green River Station Thursday night last. The same telegram, reports everything quiet on the line in that vicinity.

Source: Untitled, *Daily Union Vedette*, October 2, 1865, 3

UT-155

JOHN CRADLEBAUGH TO COLONEL R. C. DRUM
JANUARY 24, 1866

GENERAL HEADQUARTERS, STATE OF NEVADA,
ADJUTANT-GENERAL'S OFFICE,
Carson City, *January 24, 1866.*

GENERAL: I have the honor to transmit herewith copy of a resolution lately passed by the Nevada legislature.

The resolution, no doubt, was called out by complaints from volunteers of Company B, Infantry, mustered out of the service at Fort Ruby, in this State, on the 15th of December last.

They complain that after being mustered out it was impossible to procure provisions at the fort or within very long distance therefrom and of having suffered on that account. They also complain that the amount received for commutation of rations was wholly inadequate to bring them to their homes.

The justice of their complaints can only be appreciated by those who are acquainted with the high prices and scarcity of provisions on that part of the route from Fort Ruby into Austin and to this place. It is, doubtless, in view of this fact and the probability that the remainder of our volunteers, now numbering something over three hundred, who are in the vicinity of Salt Lake, will soon be discharged, and to provide against like complaint on their part, that the resolution was adopted.

In calling your attention to this matter, in view of the difficulties with the Indians of the Humboldt during the past year and their continued unfriendly and hostile disposition, I would most respectfully suggest that I believe much good could be accomplished by our volunteers being brought back *en force* and making an early campaign through the upper Humboldt country.

The bands of Indians in that section that have been committing depredations are not large. It occurs to me that if one company should march down the Humboldt River, another north of it, and the other south they would make an effective campaign that would subjugate the Indians to such an extent that we would have but little trouble with them during the balance of the year, and there certainly could be no great additional expense in having them brought back in this way.

I am, sir, very respectfully, your obedient servant,

JOHN CRADLEBAUGH,
Adjutant-General.

COL. R. C. DRUM,
Assistant Adjutant-General, Department of California.

CONCURRENT RESOLUTION relative to transportation of troops.

Resolved by the senate (the assembly concurring), That the adjutant-general of the State be requested to communicate with the major-general commanding Department of the Pacific, asking that the Nevada volunteers now at Camp Douglas, Utah, when discharged, or before being mustered out of service, be furnished with transportation by the Federal Government from the present post to the place of their recruiting.

J. S. CROSMAN,
President of the Senate.
GEO. R. AMMOND,
Secretary of the Senate.
JAS. A. BANKS,
Speaker of the Assembly.
N. E. ALLEN,
Clerk of the Assembly.

Senate concurrent resolution No. 24, introduced in the Senate January 11th, 1866. Passed the senate January 13th, 1866.

GEO. R. AMMOND,
Secretary of the Senate.

Passed the assembly January 22nd, 1866.

N. E. ALLEN,
Clerk of the Assembly.

SOURCE: U.S. SENATE, 50TH CONGRESS, 2D SESSION, EX. DOC. NO. 70, "LETTER FROM THE SECRETARY OF WAR . . . RELATIVE TO THE RAISING VOLUNTEER TROOPS TO GUARD OVERLAND AND OTHER MAILS FROM 1861 TO 1866" (WASHINGTON, D.C.: GOVERNMENT PRINTING OFFICE, 1889), 308

Appendices

APPENDIX A

Glossary and Abbreviations

This glossary defines nineteenth-century terms and abbreviations that appear in chapters 4 and 5. Terms are defined, as far as possible, as they were understood and used during the Civil War. The definitions in this appendix were assembled from a variety of sources. Source information, shown in brackets, refers to the Sources List found below. For example, "[1860]" is the *Dictionary of the English Language* published in Boston in 1860. Each term also includes an example record where that word, phrase, or abbreviation is used within this volume.

Source List and Abbreviations

1860 Joseph E. Worcester, *Dictionary of the English Language* (Boston, Mass.: Hickling, Swan, and Brewer, 1860).

AHD *American Heritage Dictionary,* http://ahdictionary.com.

BCC Bruce C. Cooper, *Riding the Transcontinental Rails: Overland Travel on the Pacific Railroad* (Philadelphia, Penn.: Polyglot Press, 2004).

CED *Collins English Dictionary—Complete & Unabridged 10th Edition,* http://dictionary.reference.com.

CWAT James Morgan, "Mounted But Not Mounted: The Confusing Terminology of Artillery," *Civil War Artillery Terminology,* http://www.civilwarhome.com/artilleryterms.html.

CWD Mark May Boatner III, *The Civil War Dictionary* (New York: David McKay, 1959).

CWT "Glossary of Civil War Terms," *Civil War Trust,* http://www.civilwar.org/education/history/glossary/glossary.html.

DCU *Dictionary.com Unabridged,* http://dictionary.reference.com.

EBO "Washakie (Shoshoni chief)," *Encyclopedia Britannica Online,* http://www.britannica.com/EBchecked/topic/423523/Titus-Oates.

FAW Louis A. Garavaglia, *Firearms of the American West, 1803–1865* (Albuquerque: University of New Mexico Press, 1984).

HHB Hubert Howe Bancroft, *History of Oregon, Volume II, 1848–1888* (San Francisco: The History Company, 1888).

HVW Victor E. Harlow, *Harlow's Oklahoma History* (Oklahoma City: Harlow Publishing, 1961).

JDW John D. Wright, *The Language of the Civil War* (Westwood, Conn.: Greenwood Publishing Group, 2001).

LOA Kathy Weiser, ed., "Old West Legends: Adventures in the American West," *Legends of America: Old West Legends*, http://www.legendsofamerica.com.

MMD *MacMillan Dictionary*, http://www.macmillandictionary.com.

MWD *Merriam-Webster Dictionary,* http://www.merriam-webster.com.

SHO Robert H. Lowie, *The Northern Shoshone,* Anthropological Papers of the American Museum of Natural History. Vol. 2, part 2. New York, 1909.

TITP "Bowery," *This is the Place Heritage Park,* http://www.thisistheplace.org/heritage_village/buildings/bowery.html.

UDN *Utah Digital Newspapers,* http://digitalnewspapers.org.

&C. Abbreviation for "etc." [1860, "et cætera"]. *Example: OR-12.*

A.A.A. GEN. (A.A.A.G.) Abbreviation for "acting assistant adjutant general." *Examples: UT-90, UT-94.*

ABETTOR "One who abets, or gives aid or encouragement in an unlawful or criminal act; an accessory; an accomplice" [1860]. *Example: UT-6.*

ACCOUTERMENTS "Pouches, belts, &c., of a soldier; military dress and arms; equipments" [1860]. "Items of equipment, other than weapons and clothing, carried by a soldier (e.g., cartridge box, canteen)" [CWD]. *Example: OR-48.*

ADJT. GEN. Abbreviation for "adjutant general." *Example: OR-26.*

ADJUTANT "A military officer, whose duty it is to assist the commandant or major of a regiment" [1860]. "A military staff officer who helps a commanding officer" [AHD]. *Example: OR-17.*

ADJUTANT GENERAL "A staff officer, who assists a general with his counsel and personal service" [1860]. "The chief administrative officer of a major military unit (as a division or corps)" [MWD]. *Example: OR-55.*

ADJUTANT-GENERAL UNITED STATES "The chief administrative officer of the Army" [DCU]. *Example: OR-35.*

AFORENAMED "Named before" [1860]. *Example: UT-35.*

AFRIC'S SONS A reference to slaves. *Example: OR-273.*

AGO (A.G.O.) Abbreviation for "Office of the Adjutant General." *Example: UT-147.*

AGT. Abbreviation for "agent." *Example: UT-33.*

AIDE-DE-CAMP "A military officer appointed to attend a general officer, to receive and carry his orders" [1860]. "Officer on the personal staff of a general, admiral, or other high-ranking commander who acts as a confidential secretary" [MWD]. *Example: OR-334.*

AIDER "One who aids or promotes the commission of a crime; an accessory before or at the fact; a principal in the second degree; an abettor" [1860]. *Example: UT-6.*

ALA. Abbreviation for "Alabama." *Example: OR-4.*

ANON "In a short time; quickly; soon" [1860]. *Example: OR-127.*

APAREJOS "A packsaddle of stuffed leather or canvas" [MWD]. *Example: OR-280.*

APPURTENANCE "That which appertains; something belonging; an adjunct" [1860]. *Example: UT-14.*

ARAPAHOES "A member of a North American Indian people living chiefly on the Great Plains, especially in Wyoming" [MWD]. *Example: OR-211.*

ARIZ. Abbreviation for "Arizona." *Example: OR-1.*

ARTILLERY "Gunnery; large ordnance, as cannon, howitzers, mortars, rockets, and engines of war of all kinds, with their carriages, ammunition, and apparatus" [1860]. See "cannon." *Example: OR-2.*

ARTY. Abbreviation for "artillery." *Example: UT-8.*

BATTALION "A division of the infantry in an army, variable in number, from 500 to 1000 men" [1860]. "A ground force unit composed of a headquarters and two or more companies or similar units" [DCU]. *Example: OR-5.*

BATTERY "The frame, mound, or parapet on which cannon or mortars are mounted" [1860]. "A tactical unit of artillery, usually consisting of six guns together with the artillerymen, equipment, etc., required to operate them" [DCU]. *Example: OR-29.*

BOWERY "A place of shelter" [1860]. "The bowery was generally the first structure built in a settlement until more permanent buildings could be constructed. [The

Salt Lake bowery] served as a gathering place for new arrivals, religious and social events, as well as a venue for theatrical productions. The original bowery in Salt Lake City was built in a single day July 31, 1847. The 40' × 28' structure was built of wood posts, with a hardened dirt floor, and a roof of thatched brush and willows" [TITP]. *Example: OR-273.*

BREVET "A commission or warrant without seal, giving a title and rank in the army above that for which pay is received. . . . A brevet lieutenant-colonel, who is a lieutenant-colonel in rank, but without the pay of a lieutenant-colonel" [1860]. *Example: OR-5.*

BRIG. GEN. Abbreviation for "brigadier general." *Example: OR-17.*

BRIGADE "A division of troops. A brigade of horse generally consists of eight or ten squadrons; a brigade of foot, of four, five, or six battalions" [1860]. "Brigades were made up of two or more regiments and two or more brigades comprised a division" [CWD]. *Example: OR-25.*

BRIGADIER / BRIGADIER GENERAL "A general officer who commands a brigade" [1860]. A general officer senior to a colonel and subordinate to a major general. *Examples: OR-13, OR-25.*

BURLESQUE "Tending to excite laughter by contrast between the subject and the manner of treating it; comic; sportive; jocular" [1860]. *Example: OR-271.*

BVT. Abbreviation for "brevet." *Example: OR-254.*

CAISSON "A chest filled with bombs and gunpowder . . . a covered ammunition wagon" [1860]. "A horse-drawn two-wheeled vehicle formerly used for carrying ammunition" [AHD]. *Example: OR-170.*

CAL. / CALI. Abbreviation for "California." *Examples: OR-13, UT-147.*

CAMAS "Plants of the lily family chiefly of the western United States with edible bulbs" [MWD]. *Example: OR-241.*

CAMP "The ground on which an army pitches its tents" [1860]. "A place where an army or other group of persons or an individual is lodged in a tent or tents or other temporary means of shelter" [DCU]. *Example: OR-4.*

CANNON "A military engine for projecting balls, &c., by gunpowder; a great gun" [1860]. "'Cannon' is the best generic term for all firearms larger than small arms. Strictly speaking, it is a metal tube; put on a mount, it becomes 'artillery'" [CWD]. *Example: OR-126.*

CAÑON An alternate spelling of "canyon." *Example: OR-1.*

CANTONMENTS "A portion of a town or village assigned to a body of troops" [1860]. "A group of temporary buildings for housing troops" [AHD]. *Example: OR-93.*

CAP A PIE "From head to foot" [1860]. *Example: UT-152.*

CAPTAIN "The commander of a ship, of a troop of horse, or of a company of infantry or artillery" [1860]. "An officer ranking in most armies above a first lieutenant and below a major" [DCU]. *Example: OR-16.*

CAVALRY "A body of troops, or soldiers, that serve on horseback" [1860]. *Example: OR-7.*

CHEYENNES "A member of an American Indian people formerly living between the Missouri and Arkansas rivers but now on reservations in Montana and Oklahoma" [MWD]. *Example: OR-64.*

CIRCULAR "A letter, generally printed, of which a copy is sent to several persons" [1860]. "A letter, advertisement, notice, or statement for circulation among the general public" [DCU]. A type of military correspondence often used to disseminate policies and announcements. *Example: OR-42.*

COADJUTOR "One who is appointed to assist a bishop, or other prelate" [1860]. "A coworker; assistant" [AHD]. *Example: OR-311.*

COL. Abbreviation for "colonel." *Example: OR-1.*

COLO. Abbreviation for "Colorado." *Example: OR-29.*

COLONEL "The chief commander of a regiment, ranking next below a brigadier-general" [1860]. *Example: OR-4.*

COLUMN "A body of troops in deep files and narrow front, so disposed as to move in regular succession" [1860]. "A narrow formation in which individuals or units follow one behind the other" [CED]. *Example: OR-11.*

COMANCHES "A member of an American Indian people of the southwestern U.S. The Comanche were among the first to acquire horses (from the Spanish) and resisted white settlers fiercely" [MWD]. *Example: OR-286.*

COMDG. Abbreviation for "commanding." *Example: OR-56.*

COMMISSARIAT "The whole body of officers attending an army under the commissary-general, and constituting the department charged with the supply of provision, ammunition, &c" [1860]. "The organized method or manner by which food, equipment, transport, etc., is delivered to armies" [DCU]. *Example: OR-35.*

COMMODIOUS "Adapted to some use or design; convenient; suitable; useful" [1860]. *Example: UT-67.*

COMPANY "A subdivision of a regiment or of a battalion" [1860]. "In the Union Army an infantry company had a maximum authorized strength of 101 officers and men, and a minimum strength of 83. The company was allowed to recruit a minimum of 64 or a maximum of 82 privates. Other company positions were fixed as follows: one captain, one first lieutenant, one second lieutenant, one first sergeant, four sergeants, eight corporals, two musicians, and one wagoner. Company officers were elected in most volunteer units" [CWD]. *Example: OR-7.*

COPPERHEADISM "Those Northern Democrats who opposed the Union's war policy and favored a negotiated peace. Lincoln assumed strong executive powers in suppressing them, including arrests, suppression of the press, suspension of *habeas corpus*, and censorship" [CWD]. *Example: OR-342.*

CORPL. Abbreviation for "corporal." *Example: OR-441.*

CORPORAL "A non-commissioned officer in a battalion of infantry immediately under the sergeant" [1860]. *Example: OR-54.*

CORPS "A body of forces or troops; applied to a regiment or to any division of an army" [1860]. "Corps were composed of two or more divisions. Standard organization on the Union side was 45 infantry regiments and nine batteries of light artillery. There were about five regiments to a brigade, about three brigades to a division, and about three divisions in a corps. The South did not adopt the corps organization until 6 November 1862" [CWD]. *Example: OR-23.*

COUNTERMAND "A change or repeal of a formal command" [1860]. *Example: OR-446.*

COURIER "A messenger, especially one on urgent or official business" [AHD]. *Example: OR-214.*

COVER "Shelter, protection" [1860]. "To protect (a soldier, force, or military duty assignment) during an expected period of ground combat by taking a position from which any hostile troops can be fired upon" [DCU]. *Example: OR-132.*

C.V. Abbreviation for "California Volunteers." *Example: UT-78.*

DAK. Abbreviation for "Dakota." *Example: OR-411.*

DANITES "A member of a secret association of Mormons held to have been pledged to use violent means to destroy their enemies" [MWD]. A vigilante group, the Danites began in 1838 during the Missouri Mormon War. *Example: OR-15.*

DEPARTMENT "The basic and best-known territorial subdivisions of the Union forces . . . they generally gave their names to the field army operating within its boundaries and under the same commander" [CWD]. *Example: OR-1.*

DEPREDATIONS "Robbery; pillage; plunder" [1860]. *Example: OR-40.*

DEPT. Abbreviation for "department." *Example: OR-26.*

DETACHMENT "A body of troops sent out from the main army" [1860]. *Example: OR-27.*

DISENTHRALMENT "To release from thraldom; to set free" [1860]. See "Thraldom." *Example: UT-123.*

DISPATCHES "A communication, or message, on public business, sent with expedition, and often by a special messenger" [1860]. "An official communication or report, sent in haste" [CED]. *Example: OR-23.*

DISTRICT "A portion of territory, as of a state, county, city, or town, defined by law within which a certain jurisdiction or authority may be exercised" [1860]. During the Civil War, districts were subdivisions of a military department. *Example: OR-1.*

DITTO "As said or as aforesaid" [1860]. "Used in accounts and lists to indicate that an item is repeated" [MWD]. *Example: OR-2.*

DIVISION "A portion of an army commanded by a general officer, and comprising cavalry, infantry, and artillery" [1860]. "Divisions were formed of two or more brigades" [CWD]. *Example: OR-48.*

DIVISION AGENT "The person in charge of 250 miles of road on the Overland Route, also called Superintendent. They were in charge of purchasing animals and equipment, maintaining the stations, and hiring station keepers, conductors, hostlers, drivers and blacksmiths" [LOA]. *Example: OR-441.*

DO. Abbreviation for "ditto." *Example: OR-2.*

DRAGOON "An appellation given to horsemen, perhaps for their rapidity and fierceness" [1860]. *Example: OR-2.*

EMPLOYÉS An alternate spelling of "employees." *Example: OR-8.*

ENGAGEMENT "Fight; conflict; battle" [1860]. *Example: OR-1.*

EQUIPAGE "Furniture, apparatus, or equipments used in war, particularly by land forces" [1860]. *Example: OR-22.*

EQUIPMENTS "The act of equipping or fitting out" [1860]. "Equipment" was considered singular; the plural was "equipments." *Example: OR-23.*

Escutcheon "A shield of a family on which coats of arms are emblazoned; the ensigns armorial" [1860]. *Example: UT-90.*

Esq. Abbreviation for "esquire." "By courtesy, a title extended indefinitely to men of the liberal professions and pursuits" [1860]. *Example: OR-34.*

Expedition "A military, naval, or other important enterprise" [1860]. "An excursion, journey, or voyage made for some specific purpose, as of war or exploration" [DCU]. *Example: OR-1.*

Express "A messenger sent on purpose; a regular and speedy conveyance for messages, packages, &c" [1860]. "A system for sending merchandise, mail, money, etc., rapidly" [CED]. *Example: OR-15.*

Express messenger See "courier." *Example: OR-37.*

Faro "A game of hazard with cards" [1860]. *Example: OR-32.*

Farrier "A shoer of horses; a horse-doctor" [1860]. "A blacksmith" [DCU]. *Example: OR-54.*

Fiat "Used as a noun to denote a peremptory decree or order" [1860]. "Authorization or sanction" [AHD]. *Example: OR-41.*

Flanking "To attack, as a body of troops, on the side, or to dispose troops so as to attack them" [1860]. *Example: OR-132.*

Forage "The hay, straw, and oats brought by the troops into the camp, for the sustenance of the horses of an army during the campaign" [1860]. *Example: OR-46.*

Force "A body of troops equipped for war" [1860]. *Example: OR-3.*

Fort "A small fortified place or post, environed on all sides" [1860]. "A fortified place, esp. a permanent post" [AHD]. *Example: OR-1.*

Fy "A word of blame: for shame" [1860]. *Example: UT-123.*

Gammon "Imposition; humbug; hoax; cheat" [1860]. "Misleading or nonsensical talk; blather" [AHD]. *Example: OR-94.*

Gasconade "A boast; bravado; brag; vaunt" [1860]. *Example: OR-408.*

General "The chief commander of an army" [1860]. An officer rank senior to colonels. "In the Union Army 1,978 generals were appointed during and immediately after the war. Of this number, 1,700 held only the brevet rank of general. . . . With the exclusion of Grant, who was a Lt. Gen., only two grades of general officer existed in the Union Army: Major General (two stars) and Brigadier General (one star). . . . There were 427 *bona fide* Confederate generals . . ." [CWD]. *Example: OR-7.*

General orders "A set of permanent orders from a headquarters establishing policy for a command or announcing official acts" [dcu]. *Example: or-1.*

Genl. An abbreviation for "general." *Example: ut-7.*

Godspeed "An expression of good wishes to a person starting a journey" [mwd]. *Example: or-158.*

GSL An abbreviation for "Great Salt Lake (City)." *Example: ut-37.*

Gunner "One who shoots; a cannoneer" [1860]. *Example: or-190.*

Halloing "A loud and vehement cry" [1860]. "A shout of exultation" [dcu]. *Example: or-111.*

Hdqrs. / Hd Qrs Abbreviations for "headquarters." *Example: or-4 and ut-3.*

Headquarters "A place from which a commander performs the functions of command" [wmd]. "The place . . . from which orders are issued" [1860]. *Example: or-5.*

Hierophant "One who expounds mysteries or sacred things; a priest" [1860]. *Example: or-15.*

Howitzer "A short piece of ordnance, either of brass, iron, or other metal, of much larger caliber than a cannon of the same weight" [1860]. "A cannon that delivers shells at a high trajectory" [ahd]. *Example: or-48.*

Impolicy "Want of policy; state of being impolitic; imprudence; indiscretion; want of forecast" [1860]. *Example: or-227.*

Indian Territory Originally the entirety of the western portion of Louisiana Purchase, the Indian Territory initially included the present states of Oklahoma, Kansas, Nebraska, Colorado, Wyoming, Montana, and North and South Dakota. However, as new western territories were created throughout the latter half of the nineteenth century, the Indian Territory saw its boundaries slowly diminish until they reached the modern-day boundaries of the state of Oklahoma. [hvw] *Example: or-292.*

Infantry "The soldiers of an army who serve on foot" [1860]. *Example: or-1.*

Infty. / Inft / Inf'y Abbreviations for "infantry." *Examples: or-87, ut-4, ut-110.*

Inimical "Unfriendly; hostile; unkind; adverse; hurtful; pernicious" [1860]. *Example: or-139.*

Inst. Abbreviation for "instant." *Example: ut-20.*

INSTANT "Current; present; now passing; the present or current month" [1860]. See "ultimo" and "proximo." *Example: OR-15.*

INTRENCH "To cut off, as a part of what belongs to another; to trespass upon; to invade; to encroach; to trench." Also, "to make secure against the attack of an enemy by digging a ditch or trench, &c." [1860]. *Example: OR-87.*

JEOPARDED "To hazard; to put in jeopardy or danger; to imperil; to peril; to endanger" [1860]. *Example: OR-276.*

JNO. Abbreviation for "John." *Example: OR-19.*

JOSEPHITES Members or followers of the Reorganized Church of Jesus Christ of Latter Day Saints (today known as the Community of Christ), a restorationist church that claims Joseph Smith Jr. restored the Church of Christ on April 6, 1830; reorganized April 6, 1860, at Amboy, Illinois. Joseph Smith III presided over this church during the Civil War. *Example: OR-417.*

JUNR. Abbreviation for "junior." *Example: UT-13.*

KANYON An alternate nineteenth-century spelling of "canyon." *Example: UT-47.*

KILKENNY CAT AFFAIR "A rough and tumble fight or argument" [JDW]. *Example: OR-408.*

KIOWA "A member of an American Indian people of the southern plains of the US, now living mainly in Oklahoma" [MWD]. *Example: OR-245.*

KNAPSACK "A bag or sack in which a soldier or a foot-traveler carries his provisions and necessaries on his back" [1860]. *Example: OR-67.*

LARIAT "A long cord or strip of leather, with a noose at one end, used for catching wild horses and cattle" [1860]. *Example: OR-190.*

LATTER-DAY SAINTS See "Mormons." *Example: OR-417.*

LIEUT. Abbreviation for "lieutenant." *Example: OR-28.*

LIEUT. COL. Abbreviation for "lieutenant colonel." *Example: OR-27.*

LIEUTENANT "An officer next in rank below a captain; the second commissioned officer of a company" [1860]. *Example: OR-8.*

LIEUTENANT COLONEL "An officer next in rank below a colonel; the second commissioned officer of a regiment" [1860]. *Example: OR-45.*

LIEUTENANT GENERAL "An officer next in rank below a General" [1860]. *Example: UT-27.*

LIEUT. GEN. Abbreviation for "lieutenant general." *Example: OR-12.*

LIGHT ARTILLERY "In artillery, 'light' is not the opposite of 'heavy' . . . 'light artillery' is almost universally used as a synonym for 'field artillery.' Historically and technically, the term is more limited and means only 'horse artillery'" [CWAT]. *Example: OR-61.*

LIGHT BATTERY "A battery of light artillery" [MWD]. *Example: OR-50.*

MAHOMMEDAN "A follower of Mohammed" [1860]; a Muslim. *Example: UT-146.*

MAJ. Abbreviation for "major." *Example: OR-15.*

MAJOR "A filed officer, next in rank above a captain and below a lieutenant-colonel" [1860]. *Example: OR-7.*

MESSRS (MESSIEURS) "Sirs; gentlemen; plural of *Mr.*; abbreviated to *Messrs.*" [1860]. *Example: OR-39.*

MILITARY OPERATIONS "The act of carrying out preconcerted measures by regular movements" [1860]. "A campaign, mission, maneuver, or action" [DCU]. *Example: OR-8.*

MILITIA "An army composed of ordinary citizens rather than professional soldiers" [AHD]. *Example: OR-4.*

MONTE BANK "A card game in which players select any two of four cards turned face up in a layout and bet that one of them will be matched before the other as cards are dealt one at a time from the pack" [MWD]. *Example: OR-32.*

MORMONS "A member of the Church of Jesus Christ of Latter-day Saints, a religion founded in New York in 1830 by Joseph Smith, Jr." [MWD]. The church was headquartered between 1830 and 1846 in New York, Ohio, Illinois, Missouri, Illinois, and Nebraska Territory; the first Mormons arrived July 1847 in Utah. Brigham Young presided over this church during the Civil War. *Example: OR-7.*

MUSTER "To assemble under arms for review, parade, exercise, and inspection" [1860]. *Example: OR-5.*

NAUVOO LEGION Territorial militia of Utah. Initially mustered in Nauvoo, Illinois, as a state-authorized city militia. *Example: UT-27.*

NAVAJOES "A member of an American Indian people of New Mexico and Arizona" [MWD]. *Example: OR-228.*

NEBR. Abbreviation for "Nebraska." *Example: OR-9.*

NEV. Abbreviation for "Nevada." *Example: OR-1.*

N.L. Abbreviation for "Nauvoo Legion." *Example: UT-27.*

N. Mex. Abbreviation for "New Mexico." *Example: OR-32.*

Obdt. / Obedt. / Obt. Abbreviation for "obedient." *Examples: UT-62, UT-14, UT-8.*

Operations See "military operations." *Example: OR-1.*

Orders "Mandate; precept; command; injunction" [1860]. "A command or notice issued by a military organization or a military commander to troops, sailors, etc." [DCU]. *Example: OR-5.*

Ordnance "Canon; a term applied to all sorts of great guns used in war, as cannons, mortars, howitzers, carronades, &c" [1860]. *Example: OR-48.*

Oreg. Abbreviation for "Oregon." *Example: OR-105.*

Outpost "A post or station without the limits of the camp, or at a distance from the army" [1860]. "A station established at a distance from the main body of an army to protect it from surprise attack; perimeter guard" [DCU]. *Example: OR-21.*

Overland Trail "Any of various routes traveled by settlers from the Missouri River to Oregon and California beginning in the 1840s" [DCU]. *Example: UT-76.*

Overslaugh "To pass over; to omit" [1860]. "To pass over or disregard (a person) by giving a promotion, position, etc., to another instead" [DCU]. *Example: OR-32.*

Papoose "A word used by the North American Indians for a child" [1860]. *Example: UT-92.*

Paymaster "An officer entrusted with the payment of a regiment" [1860]. *Example: OR-91.*

Pecuniary "Of or pertaining to money; monetary" [1860]. *Example: OR-308.*

Perfidious "Breaking or violating good faith; treacherous; unfaithful" [1860]. *Example: OR-190.*

Polygamic "Plurality of wives or husbands; the state or the custom of having more than one wife or husband at the same time" [1860]. *Example: OR-308.*

Post "A military station; a place where a soldier or a number of troops are stationed" [1860]. *Example: OR-1.*

Powder "A combination of nitre, sulphur, and charcoal granulated; gunpowder" [1860]. *Example: OR-33.*

PRACTICABLE "(1) That may be done, practised, or accomplished; performable; feasible; possible. (2) *(Mil.)* Noting a breach which is easy to be entered or ascended by assailants" [1860]. *Example: OR-5.*

PRIMA FACIE "On the first view or appearance; at first sight" [1860]. *Example: OR-190.*

PRIVATE "A common soldier" [1860]. The lowest ranking enlisted rank in the Army. *Example: OR-54.*

PROVOST-MARSHAL "An officer whose duties are to take steps for the prosecution of crime and offences against the military discipline, to seize and secure deserters, to punish marauders, &c" [1860]. *Example: OR-115.*

PROXIMO "Next, or next month" [1860]. See "Instant," and "Ultimo." *Example: OR-55.*

PURSUANCE "The act of pursuing or following out" [1860]. "A carrying out or putting into effect" [AHD]. *Example: OR-56.*

QUARTERMASTER "An officer whose business is to look after the quarters of the soldiers, and to attend to their clothing, bread, ammunition, &c" [1860]. *Example: OR-8.*

QUARTERS "Stations in which soldiers and officers are lodged" [1860]. "The buildings, houses, barracks, or rooms occupied by military personnel or their families" [DCU]. *Example: OR-22.*

RECONNOITERING "To view, survey, or examine, particularly for military purposes" [1860]. *Example: OR-111.*

RECUSANCY "The tenets or the practice of a recusant [one who refuses to acknowledge some principle or party]; nonconformity" [1860]. *Example: OR-15.*

REGIMENT "A body of troops commanded by a colonel, consisting usually of from 800 to 1000 or 1200 men, divided into companies, each of which is commanded by a captain" [1860]. "The basic unit of Civil War soldiers, usually made up of 1,000 to 1,500 men. Regiments were usually designated by state and number (as in 20th Maine). 1 company = 50 to 100 men, 10 companies = 1 regiment, about 4 regiments = 1 brigade, 2 to 5 brigades = 1 division, 2 or more divisions = 1 corps, 1 or more corps = 1 army" [CWT]. *Example: OR-5.*

REQUISITION "Application for a thing to be done by virtue of some right" [1860]. "A formal request for something that is needed" [AHD]. *Example: OR-17.*

Reveille "The beat of drums at the break of day, for awaking the soldiers, and putting a stop to the challenging sentries" [1860]. "A signal, as of a drum or bugle, sounded early in the morning to awaken military personnel and to alert them to assembly" [DCU]. *Example: OR-306.*

Richd. Abbreviation for "Richard." *Example: OR-59.*

Sabre "A kind of sword, with a broad, heavy blade, falcated [hooked] or crooked towards the point; a dragoon's sword" [1860]. *Example: UT-144.*

Saddler "One whose trade it is to make saddles; a saddle-maker" [1860]. *Example: OR-54.*

Saleratus "A salt intermediate in composition between a carbonate and a bicarbonate of potash, prepared from pearlash [purified potash] by exposing it to carbonic acid gas; much used in making bread, to neutralize acetic acid, or tartaric acid, and thus render the bread light by the escape of the carbonic acid gas" [1860]. *Example: UT-45.*

Scapegrace "A vile or worthless fellow; a knave" [1860]. *Example: UT-101.*

Scout "A person employed to observe the movements, and gain intelligence of the numbers of an enemy; a spy" [1860]. *Example: OR-66.*

Seceders "One who secedes . . . to withdraw from union or fellowship in society" [1860]. *Example: OR-16.*

Secesh A slang term for anyone who supported the Confederate States of America or secession from the United States [MWD]. *Example: OR-338.*

Secession "Act of seceding or withdrawing; separation" [1860]. "The withdrawal from the Union of 11 Southern states in the period 1860–1861, which brought on the Civil War" [DCU]. *Example: OR-3.*

Secretary of War A presidential cabinet member; head of the War Department. *Example: OR-3.*

Sergeant "A non-commissioned officer, of the second rank, in a company or troop" [1860]. *Example: OR-54.*

Shoshone "The Shoshone, or Snakes, constitute the northernmost division of the Shoshonean family [of Native Americans]. They occupied western Wyoming and Montana, central and southern Idaho, northern Utah and Nevada, and all but the westernmost part of Oregon. . . . In Utah, most of the settlements were north of [the] Great Salt Lake." [SHO]. *Example: OR-98.*

SKELETON COMPANY "Just enough workers to keep a service or office operating" [MMD]. *Example: OR-66.*

SKIRMISH "A loose, desultory kind of engagement in presence of two armies, between small detachments sent out for the purpose either of drawing on a battle, or by concealing by their fire the movements of the troops in the rear; a slight fight in war" [1860]. *Example: OR-1.*

SNAKE (INDIANS) "Snake Indians is a collective name given to the Northern Paiute, Bannock and Shoshone Native Americans" [HHB]. See "Shoshone." *Example: OR-8.*

SOLECISM "An offence against the rules of grammar by the use of words in a wrong construction; any unfitness, incongruity, or impropriety" [1860]. *Example: OR-311.*

SPECIAL ORDERS "A set of instructions from a headquarters affecting the activity or status of an individual or group of individuals" [DCU]. *Example: OR-5.*

SQUAW "A wife or a woman; so used among some tribes of North American Indians" [1860]. *Example: OR-106.*

STATION "A place calculated for the rendezvous of troops, or for the distribution of them; also a spot well calculated for offensive or defensive measures" [1860]. *Example: OR-22.*

STOCKADE "A line of stakes or posts fixed in the ground as a barrier to the advance or approach of an enemy; a pen or enclosure for cattle" [1860]. *Example: OR-468.*

SUBSERVIENCY [also SUBSERVE] "State of being subservient . . . acting in a subordinate capacity; subordinate" [1860]. *Examples: OR-19, OR-308.*

SUBSISTENCE "The state of being subsistent; means of support; livelihood" [1860]. *Example: OR-10.*

SUPERFLUOUS "Abounding to excess; copious or plentiful beyond need or use" [1860]. *Example: OR-139.*

SUPERINTENDENCY "The act of super-intending; oversight; superior care; direction; inspection" [1860]. *Example: OR-266.*

SURGEON-GENERAL "The chief of medical services in one of the armed forces" [DCU]. *Example: OR-254.*

SURPLUSAGE "Overplus; surplus . . . A superfluous and useless statement of matter wholly foreign an impertinent to the cause: a greater disbursement than the charges of the accountant amount to" [1860]. *Example: OR-168.*

SUTLER "A person who follows an army as a seller of provisions and liquors" [1860]. *Example: OR-22.*

SWARTHY "Dark of complexion; black; dusky; tawny" [1860]. *Example: UT-120.*

TENDER "An offer; a proposal for acceptance" [1860]. "A formal offer" [AHD]. *Example: OR-227.*

TER. Abbreviation for "territory." *Example: OR-1.*

TERRITORY "A large district of country belonging to the United States, not forming a part of any individual state, and having a temporary government" [1860]. *Example: OR-1.*

THRALDOM "The state of a thrall or slave; subjection; bondage; slavery" [1860]. *Example: OR-214.*

"TITUS OATES CLASS" A "renegade Anglican priest who fabricated the Popish Plot of 1678. Oates's allegations that Roman Catholics were plotting to seize power caused a reign of terror in London and strengthened the anti-Catholic Whig Party" [EBO]. *Example: UT-7.*

TRADUCER "One who traduces; a calumniator; a slanderer" [1860]. *Example: UT-8.*

TURNPIKE "A gate on a road to obstruct passengers, in order to take a toll; originally consisting of crossbars armed with pikes, and turning on a post or pin" [1860]. *Example: OR-39.*

ULT. Abbreviation for "Ultimo." *Example: UT-48.*

ULTIMO "In or of the last month" [1860]. See "Instant," and "Proximo." *Example: OR-4.*

UNBOSOMED "To have revealed in confidence; to divulge; to open; to disclose" [1860]. *Example: OR-333.*

UNDISSEVERED "Not dissevered." Dissevered is "To part in two; to break; to divide; to sunder; to separate; to sever" [1860]. *Example: UT-116.*

UNION PACIFIC RAILROAD "The Pacific Railroad Act of 1862 designated the Union Pacific Railroad Company to build west from Council Bluffs, Iowa, and Omaha through Nebraska, Wyoming, and into Utah." [BCC]. *Example: OR-375.*

U.S.V. Abbreviation for "United States Volunteers." *Example: UT-126.*

U.T. Abbreviation for "Utah Territory." *Example: UT-1.*

UTAH TERRITORY A federally administered territory created September 9, 1850. See Appendix E. *Example: OR-10.*

UTES "A member of an American Indian people living chiefly in Colorado and Utah" [MWD]. *Example: OR-207.*

VEDETTE "A mounted sentry, stationed at an outpost or elevated point, to observe the enemy" [1860]. The *Union Vedette* was a post newspaper that was published at Camp Douglas, Utah Territory, during the Civil War, beginning November 20, 1863. [UDN]. *Example: OR-98, UT-108.*

VICISSITUDES "Regular change; alternate or reciprocal succession; return of the same things in the same succession" [1860]. *Example: OR-504.*

VIDE "Used to refer to something, as a note or remark" [1860]. *Example: OR-482.*

VIOLATIVE "Tending to, or causing, violation; infringing" [1860]. *Example: UT-129.*

VIZ "[A contraction of videlicet.] To wit; namely; that is. . . . the adverb *namely* is, in reading, commonly used instead of it" [1860]. *Example: OR-28.*

VOLS. Abbreviation for "Volunteers." *Example: OR-56.*

WAGONER (WAGONEER) "One who drives a wagon" [1860]. *Examples: OR-54, UT-80.*

WAGONMASTER "An officer in charge of a baggage-train" [1860]. *Example: OR-256.*

YAUGER "One of the light infantry armed with rifles; written also jager" [1860]. Nickname for a U.S. Army model 1841 rifle; also known as the Mississippi rifle. Yauger, sometimes spelled Yaeger, is possibly a corruption of "Jäger" (German for "hunter"). [FAW]. *Example: UT-39.*

YOUR OBEDIENT SERVANT "A formula used to end a letter" [MWD]. A popular correspondence salutation. *Example: OR-7.*

APPENDIX B

Chronological Records List

RECORDS FROM CHAPTERS 4 (OR-#) AND 5 (UT-#) ARE LISTED CHRONOLOGICALLY below. Records that are associated with more than one date or a date range are marked with an asterisk (*). For example, OR-28 is dated September 10, 1861, but as noted in a header line, it is a report of an attack on an emigrant train that occurred on August 8–9, 1861.

1861

January 1
OR-1*
OR-2*

February 14
UT-1

May 1
OR-3

May 6
OR-4

May 12
UT-2

May 17
OR-5

May 26
UT-3

May 30
OR-6

June 1
UT-4

June 3
OR-7

June 10
UT-5

June 14
OR-8

June 15
UT-6

June 17
UT-7

June 18
UT-8

June 19
UT-9
UT-10
UT-11

June 24
OR-9

June 27
OR-10

July 1
OR-11*

July 16
OR-12

July 24
OR-13
OR-14

July 27
UT-12

July 31
OR-15

August 5
OR-16
UT-13

August 6
OR-17
UT-14
UT-15

August 9
OR-18
UT-16

August 10
OR-19
OR-20

August 13
OR-21

August 15
UT-17

August 25
OR-22

August 26
OR-23

August 27
OR-24

August 30
UT-18

September [undated]
UT-19

September 2
OR-25

September 7
OR-26

September 10
OR-27*
OR-28*

September 12
UT-20

September 13
OR-29*

September 14
OR-30

September 16
OR-31

September 23
UT-21

September 27
OR-32

October 3
OR-33

October 5
OR-34

October 11
OR-35

October 18
UT-22
UT-23

October 19
OR-36
UT-24

October 20
UT-25

October 23
OR-37

October 28
UT-26

October 30
OR-38

November 10
OR-39

November 20
OR-40

November 22
OR-41

November 26
OR-42

December 16
OR-43

December 20
OR-44*

December 23
OR-45
OR-46

1862

January 16
OR-47

February 25
OR-48*

March 21
UT-27

March 26
OR-49

March 27
OR-50

April 10
OR-51*

April 11
UT-28

April 14
UT-29

April 24
OR-52*
UT-30

April 25
UT-31
UT-32
UT-33

April 26
UT-34

April 27
OR-53

April 28
OR-54
UT-35
UT-36
UT-37
UT-38
UT-39
UT-40
UT-41
UT-42

April 29
OR-55

April 30
UT-43
UT-44
UT-45
UT-46

May 1
UT-47
UT-48
UT-49

May 2
UT-50

May 3
OR-56

May 5
UT-51

May 7
UT-52

May 10
UT-53

May 11
UT-54

May 13
OR-57

May 14
UT-55
UT-56

May 16
UT-57

May 21
UT-58

May 22
UT-59

May 28
UT-60
UT-61

May 30
OR-58

June 3
UT-62

June 4
UT-63
UT-64
UT-65

June 6
OR-59

June 12
OR-60

June 16
UT-66

June 21
OR-61

June 26
OR-62

June 27
UT-67

June 28
OR-63

July 1
OR-64

July 5
OR-65

July 9
UT-68

July 11
OR-66

July 12
OR-67

July 13
UT-69

July 16
UT-70

July 23
UT-71

July 25
OR-68

July 26
UT-72

Summer [undated]
UT-73

August 2
UT-74

August 3
OR-69

August 6
OR-70

August 11
OR-71

August 13
UT-75
UT-76

August 14
OR-72

August 15
OR-73
OR-74

August 19
OR-75
OR-76

August 20
OR-77

August 21
OR-78

August 23
OR-79

August 24
OR-80

August 25
OR-81

August 26
UT-77

August 27
OR-82

August 30
OR-83

September 1
OR-84

September 2
OR-85

September 11
OR-86

September 14
OR-87

September 15
OR-88

September 17
OR-89

September 22
OR-90

September 24
OR-91

September 29
OR-92

October 1
OR-93

October 3
OR-94

October 4
OR-95

October 14
OR-96

October 17
OR-97

October 18
OR-98
UT-78

October 20
OR-100
OR-99

October 23
OR-101

October 24
OR-102

October 25
OR-103

October 26
OR-104
UT-79

October 30
OR-105*

October 31
OR-106
UT-80

November 6
OR-107*

November 9
OR-108

November 18
OR-109*

November 20
OR-110

November 26
UT-81

November 27[?]
UT-82

November 28
OR-111

December 2
OR-112
OR-113*

December 6
OR-114
OR-115

December 9
OR-116
OR-117

December 11
OR-118

December 12
OR-119
OR-120
OR-121

December 13
OR-122

December 15
OR-123*
OR-124

December 16
OR-125

December 20
OR-126

December 23
OR-127
UT-83

December 29
OR-128

December 31
OR-129

1863

January 3
OR-130

January 21
UT-84

January 26
UT-85

January 28
UT-86

January 31
OR-131*
UT-87

February 2
UT-88

February 4
UT-89

February 6
OR-132
UT-90

February 10
OR-133

February 11
OR-134
UT-91
UT-92

February 16
OR-135
OR-136

February 19
OR-137
OR-138
OR-139

February 20
OR-140*
OR-141

February 26
OR-142

February 28
OR-143
UT-93

March 3
OR-144
OR-145

March 5
OR-146

March 6
OR-147

March 7
OR-148

March 8
OR-149
UT-94

March 9
OR-150

March 10
OR-151
OR-152

March 11
OR-153
OR-154

March 12
OR-155

March 14
OR-156
OR-157

March 15
OR-158

March 19
OR-159

March 20
OR-160

March 23
OR-161
OR-162

March 24
OR-163

March 29
OR-164
OR-165
OR-166
UT-95

March 30
OR-167
OR-168

March 31
OR-169
OR-170

April 1
OR-171
UT-96

April 2
OR-172
OR-173

April 3
OR-174

April 6
OR-175*
OR-176*

April 7
UT-97

April 8
OR-177

April 9
OR-178*

April 13
OR-179
OR-180

April 14
OR-181
UT-98

April 15
OR-182
UT-99

April 16
OR-183
UT-100

April 20
OR-184

April 22
OR-185
OR-186

April 28
OR-187

April 30
OR-188

May 2
OR-189

May 4
OR-190*

May 6
OR-191
UT-101

May 9
OR-192

May 11
OR-193
OR-194
OR-195

May 13
UT-102
UT-103
UT-104
UT-105

May 20
OR-196

May 22
OR-197

May 25
OR-198

May 29
OR-199

May 31
OR-200

June 2
OR-201*
OR-202

June 7
OR-203

June 9
OR-204

June 10
OR-205

June 11
OR-206
OR-207

June 12
OR-208
OR-209

June 14
OR-210

June 18
OR-211

June 19
OR-212

June 22
OR-213*

June 24
OR-214

June 25
OR-215

June 26
OR-216

June 27
OR-217

June 28
OR-218*
OR-219

June 29
OR-220

June 30
OR-221
OR-222
OR-223

July 8
UT-106

July 10
OR-224
OR-225

July 11
OR-226

July 18
OR-227
UT-107

July 24
OR-228

July 30
OR-229

July 31
OR-230
OR-231
OR-232

August 4
OR-233

August 9
OR-234

August 15
OR-235

August 18
OR-236
OR-237

August 19
OR-238

August 20
OR-239
OR-240

August 23
OR-241

August 24
OR-242

September 5
OR-243

September 10
OR-244

September 12
OR-245

September 17
OR-246

September 21
OR-247

September 22
OR-248

September 23
OR-249

September 27
OR-250

September 28
OR-251

September 29
OR-252
OR-253

October [undated]
OR-254

October 2
OR-255

October 3
OR-256

October 5
OR-257

October 6
OR-258*

October 19
OR-259

October 26
OR-260

October 27
OR-261
UT-108

October 30
OR-262

November 6
OR-263

November 9
OR-264

November 10
OR-265

November 14
UT-109

November 18
UT-110

November 20
OR-266

November 27
UT-111

December 27
OR-267

December 31
OR-268

1864

January 4
OR-269

January 13
UT-112

January 20
UT-113

January 26
UT-114

January 29
UT-115
UT-116

February 3
OR-270

February 5
OR-271

February 10
OR-272

February 15
OR-273
UT-117

February 20
UT-118

February 23
OR-274

February 25
OR-275

March 1
OR-276
UT-119

March 3
OR-277
UT-120

March 4
OR-278

March 5
OR-279

March 6
OR-280

March 12
OR-281

March 18
OR-282

March 30
OR-283

April 2
OR-284

April 4
UT-121

April 9
OR-285
OR-286
UT-122

April 11
OR-287

April 12
UT-123

April 13
OR-288
OR-289

April 14
OR-290

April 18
UT-124

April 19
UT-125

April 21
UT-126

April 23
OR-291

April 25
OR-292

April 30
OR-293
OR-294

May 2
OR-295
OR-296

May 9
OR-297

May 11
OR-298

May 13
OR-299

May 15
OR-300

May 20
UT-127

May 24
OR-301*

May 25
UT-128

May 31
OR-302
UT-122

June 7
OR-303
OR-304

June 20
OR-305

June 22
OR-306*

June 27
UT-129

June 30
OR-307
UT-130

July 1
OR-308

July 2
OR-309

July 3
OR-310

July 9
OR-311
UT-131

July 11
UT-132

July 12
OR-312

July 13
OR-313

July 15
OR-314
OR-315

July 16
OR-316
OR-317
OR-318

July 17
UT-133

July 19
OR-319
OR-320

July 20
OR-321

July 21
UT-134

July 24
OR-322

July 26
OR-323
UT-135
UT-136

July 27
OR-324
UT-137

July 28
OR-325

July 31
UT-138

August 1
OR-326

August 5
OR-327
OR-328

August 8
OR-329

August 9
OR-330

August 15
OR-331

August 17
OR-332

August 20
OR-333

August 27
OR-334
OR-335

August 30
OR-336

August 31
OR-337
OR-338

September 1
OR-339

September 6
OR-340

September 15
OR-341

September 17
OR-342*
OR-343*

September 19
OR-344

September 21
OR-345
OR-346

September 26
OR-347
OR-348

September 27
OR-349

September 29
OR-350

October 1
OR-351

October 3
OR-352
OR-353
UT-139

October 10
OR-354
UT-140

October 11
OR-355

October 14
OR-356
OR-357

October 15
OR-358

October 16
OR-359

October 17
OR-360
OR-361

October 18
OR-362

October 21
UT-141

October 26
OR-363*

October 30
OR-364*

November 1
OR-365*

November 12
UT-142

November 21
OR-366*

December 1
UT-143

December 10
OR-367

December 17
OR-368
OR-369

December 21
OR-370

December 23
OR-371*

December 28
OR-372*

1865

January 1
OR-373*

January 3
OR-374

January 12
OR-375

January 14
OR-376

January 17
OR-377

February 1
OR-378
UT-144

February 8
OR-379

February 9
OR-380
OR-381

February 10
OR-382*
OR-383

February 13
UT-145

February 15
UT-146

February 17
OR-384

February 18
OR-385
OR-386
OR-387

February 24
OR-388
OR-389

February 25
OR-390*

February 27
OR-391*
OR-392
UT-147*

February 28
OR-393
OR-394
OR-395

March 3
OR-396
OR-397

March 7
OR-398

March 9
OR-399

March 20
OR-400

March 21
OR-401

March 28
OR-402

March 29
OR-403
OR-404
OR-405

March 30
OR-406
UT-148

April 5
OR-407

April 6
OR-408*

April 7
OR-409
OR-410

April 8
OR-411

April 10
OR-412

April 14
OR-413

April 15
OR-414

April 20
OR-415

April 24
OR-416

April 26
OR-417

April 28
OR-418

April 30
OR-419

May 4
OR-420
OR-421

May 18
OR-422

May 20
OR-423

May 22
OR-424

May 25
OR-425

May 26
OR-426

May 27
OR-427

May 28
OR-428
OR-429

May 29
OR-430
OR-431

June [undated]
OR-432*

June 2
OR-433

June 4
OR-434

June 8
OR-435
OR-436
OR-437

June 10
OR-438

June 13
OR-439
OR-440*

June 14
OR-441*
UT-149*

June 15
OR-442

June 16
OR-443

June 19
OR-444*

June 20
OR-445

June 22
OR-446

June 27
OR-447
OR-448

June 29
OR-449

July 6
OR-450

July 8
OR-451

July 15
UT-150

July 18
OR-452*

July 21
OR-453
OR-454

July 23
UT-151

July 25
UT-152

July 26
OR-455

July 27
OR-456

July 28
OR-457
OR-458
OR-459
OR-460

July 29
OR-461*
OR-462*
OR-463

July 31
OR-464*
OR-465*

August 1
OR-466*
OR-467
OR-468
OR-469

August 2
OR-470

August 3
OR-471
OR-472

August 5
OR-473
OR-474

August 6
OR-475

August 11
OR-476

August 12
OR-477
OR-478

August 14
UT-153

August 15
OR-479*
OR-480
OR-481

August 16
OR-482
OR-483

August 21
OR-484

August 22
OR-485

August 23
OR-486

August 24
OR-487

August 25
OR-488

August 29
OR-489*
OR-490*
OR-491*

August 31
OR-492

September 1
OR-493

September 2
OR-494*

September 15
OR-495*

September 19
OR-496

October 2
UT-154

October 10
OR-497

October 16
OR-498

November 1
OR-499

November 8
OR-500*

November 22
OR-501*

December 6
OR-502

December 8
OR-503

1866

January 24
UT-155*

November 14
OR-504

TABLE B.1. UTAH TERRITORY RECORDS BY MONTH

Month/Year	*Chapter 4 (OR-#)*	*Chapter 5 (UT-#)*	*Totals*
1861	**46**	**26**	**72**
January 1861	2	–	2
February 1861	–	1	1
May 1861	4	2	6
June 1861	4	8	12
July 1861	5	1	6
August 1861	9	6	15
September 1861	8	3	11
October 1861	6	5	11
November 1861	4	–	4
December 1861	4	–	4
1862	**83**	**57**	**140**
January 1862	1	–	1
February 1862	1	–	1
March 1862	2	1	3
April 1862	5	19	24
May 1862	3	15	18
June 1862	5	6	11
July 1862	5	5	10
August 1862	15	5	20
September 1862	9	–	9
October 1862	14	3	17
November 1862	5	2	7
December 1862	18	1	19
1863	**139**	**28**	**167**
January 1863	2	4	6
February 1863	12	6	18
March 1863	27	2	29
April 1863	18	5	23
May 1863	12	5	17
June 1863	23	–	23
July 1863	9	2	11
August 1863	10	–	10
September 1863	11	–	11
October 1863	9	1	10
November 1863	4	3	7
December 1863	2	–	2

Table B.1. Utah Territory records by month (*continued*)

Month/Year	*Chapter 4 (OR-#)*	*Chapter 5 (UT-#)*	*Totals*
1864	**104**	**32**	**136**
January 1864	1	5	6
February 1864	6	2	8
March 1864	8	2	10
April 1864	11	6	17
May 1864	8	2	10
June 1864	5	2	7
July 1864	18	8	26
August 1864	13	–	13
September 1864	12	–	12
October 1864	14	3	17
November 1864	2	1	3
December 1864	6	1	7
1865	**131**	**11**	**142**
January 1865	5	–	5
February 1865	18	4	22
March 1865	11	1	12
April 1865	13	–	13
May 1865	12	–	12
June 1865	18	1	19
July 1865	16	3	19
August 1865	27	1	28
September 1865	4	–	4
October 1865	2	1	3
November 1865	3	–	3
December 1865	2	–	2
1866	**1**	**1**	**2**
January 1866	–	1	1
November 1866	1	–	1
Totals	**504**	**155**	**659**

APPENDIX C

Supplement to the Official Records

The Supplement to the Official Records of the Union and Confederate Armies, published by Broadfoot Publishing in Wilmington, North Carolina, was a significant multi-year publishing effort.[1] The result is an additional one hundred volumes of Civil War records. The *Supplement* is "divided into four parts (Reports, Records of Events, Correspondence, and Secret Service) and includes official accounts of battles, skirmishes, scouting expeditions, signal maneuvers, narratives of troop movements, correspondence, and intelligence files. Also included are a few courts-martial, courts of inquiry, and court proceedings."[2] These volumes have not been digitized. The *Supplement* includes several extended entries about Utah:

Volume 3, Serial No. 15, page 63–78
Volume 3, Serial No. 15, pages 98–101
Volume 3, Serial No. 15, pages 105–122
Volume 3, Serial No. 15, pages 214–237
Volume 7, Serial No. 7, pages 887–890
Volume 7, Serial No. 7, pages 984–989
Volume 21, Serial No. 33, pages 359–360
Volume 21, Serial No. 33, pages 368–371
Volume 21, Serial No. 33, page 380
Volume 39, Serial No. 51, page 25–27
Volume 39, Serial No. 51, page 30
Volume 50, Serial No. 62, pages 202–203
Volume 56, Serial No. 68, pages 492–493

Those records are primarily Summaries of Principal Event lists for the Second California Cavalry, Third California Infantry, Eleventh Ohio Cavalry, First Nevada Cavalry, Ninth Kansas Cavalry, and the First Oregon Cavalry. Here is a sample *Supplement* record that mentions Utah:

1. Hewett, *Supplement to the Official Records of the Union and Confederate Armies.*
2. Hewett, "Updating the Documentary History of the U.S. Civil War," 43–55.

Record of Events for Second California Cavalry

Field and Staff

. . .

January 23.—

Major Edward McGarry, with a detachment of the Second Cavalry, California Volunteers (composed of portions of Companies A, H, K and M), left Camp Douglas, Utah Territory, the evening of January 23, 1863 on an Indian scout to Bear River, Washington Territory, some 130 miles north of Salt Lake City.

January 29.—

At daylight on the morning of January 29 they arrived at the winter encampment of a band of Snake Indians who were aware of the approach of the troops and awaited them behind natural fortifications. The troops, notwithstanding they were suffering with cold—having had a long night's march in intensely cold weather, immediately gave battle, which lasted four hours, and succeeded in killing some 220 out of a number some 300 strong. One hundred seventy-three Indian ponies and a number of rifles fell into our hands.

The detachment was composed of 244 men (including officers), while but 208 participated in the fight. We lost twelve men, killed. One officer (First Lieutenant Darwin Chase, of Company K) and seven men have since died of wounds there received. Two officers were seriously wounded and thirty-seven men were wounded, some seriously.

Thirty-four men had their hands or feet severely frozen, a number of whom have since been obliged to suffer amputation.

Stationed at Camp Douglas, near Salt Lake City, Utah Territory, March–April 1863.

April 12.—

An expedition composed of detachments of Companies A, H and M, Second Cavalry, California Volunteers, comprising in the aggregate 178 men, under command of Colonel George S. Evans, Second Cavalry, Company A, left the post in accordance with verbal instructions from General [Patrick Edward] Connor, commanding District of Utah on April 12, 1863, proceeding southwards ninety miles to Spanish Fork Cañon, where a band of Utah Indians numbering some 300 had congregated, awaiting the approach of the troops.

April 15.—

On the morning of April 15 the command entered the Cañon, where a fight ensued, lasting six hours, until the enemy was driven over the tops of the mountains, rendering it impossible to pursue him with advantage. The enemy lost some thirty warriors, including the Chief Black Hawk, eighteen horses and a number of horses captured. Our loss was one lieutenant (Fernando A. Peel), killed, and two sergeants, wounded slightly.

April 17.—

The expedition returned to camp April 17, 1863.

. . .

SOURCE: *SUPPLEMENT TO THE OR*, VOLUME 3, SERIAL NO. 15, PAGE 63–65

Three *Supplement* volumes include entries that are associated with, but do not directly mention, Utah:

Volume 21, Serial No. 33, pages 369–371
Volume 21, Serial No. 33, page 573
Volume 49, Serial No. 61, page 784–785
Volume 50, Serial No. 62, pages 202–223
Volume 50, Serial No. 62, page 224
Volume 50, Serial No. 62, page 229

Here is a sample *Supplement* record associated with Utah Territory that does not explicitly mention Utah. (In June and July 1862 the Utah Cavalry Company was also serving on the Overland Trail.)

[ELEVENTH OHIO CAVALRY]

Company B (Haye's Company)

. . .

June 30, 1862.—

Last mustered. Camp Highland, South Pass, Rocky Mountains. Stationed at that point for defense of overland mail and telegraph line by order of Brigadier-General James Craig by order of Lieutenant-Colonel William O. Collins commanding.

July 11.—

Moved to Upper Sweetwater River Crossing.

July 24.—

A detachment of ten men made scout over Wind River passage of mountains in search of Indians who had stolen sixty head of horses and mules retaking forty-eight. Gone three days, distance 100 miles. By order of William O. Collins, twenty-four men were stationed at Upper Sweetwater Crossing, twenty-four at the Three Crossings and twenty-six on Deer Creek all on overland mail and telegraph line preparing for winter.

. . .

SOURCE: *SUPPLEMENTAL OFFICIAL RECORDS*, VOLUME 50, SERIAL NO. 62, PAGES 213–216

APPENDIX D

Official Records *Associated with Utah*

THIS APPENDIX CONTAINS RECORDS FROM THE *OFFICIAL RECORDS* that refer to events, people, or locations associated with Utah Territory, as well as general proclamations and orders that affected military units serving in Utah, but these records do not contain any of the Utah-related keywords used to select records for inclusion in chapter 4. Records are grouped chronologically by *OR* volume and include the page number(s). Here is a sample record from this collection that discusses Colonel Connor's progress en route to Utah:

HEADQUARTERS DEPARTMENT OF THE PACIFIC,
San Francisco, April 10, 1862.

Brig. Gen. L. THOMAS,
Adjutant-General U.S. Army, Washington, D.C.:

GENERAL: Since my communication addressed to you on the 5th instant nothing of moment has transpired.

. . .

The weather is steadily improving and the active operations have already commenced. Colonel Connor, Third Infantry California Volunteers, the officer whom I have selected to command all the troops designated for the protection of the Overland Mail Route, is making his preparations to cross the mountains as soon as the roads are practicable.

Very respectfully, your most obedient servant,

G. WRIGHT,
Brigadier-General, U.S. Army, Commanding.

SOURCE: *OR*, SERIES 1, VOLUME 50, PART 1, PAGES 995–996

Series 1, Volume 8

April 6, 1862, page 668
April 7, 1862, page 672

Series 1, Volume 9

July 10, 1862, pages 683–684

Series 1, Volume 13

April 16, 1862, page 362
July 20, 1862, pages 483–484
November 20, 1862, page 811

Series 1, Volume 22, Part 1

December 9, 1862, pages 819–820
December 31, 1862, page 893

Series 1, Volume 22, Part 2

February 28, 1863, page 131
March 7, 1863, page 146
April 4, 1863, page 198
June 18, 1863, page 325
June 23, 1863, pages 333–334
June 30, 1863, page 347
July 31, 1863, page 421
December 31, 1863, page 764

Series 1, Volume 29, Part 2

August 7, 1863, pages 14–15

Series 1, Volume 34, Part 2

January 3, 1864, page 14
January 5, 1864, pages 28–29
January 31, 1864, page 206
March 5, 1864, pages 510–511
March 20, 1864, pages 677–678

Series 1, Volume 34, Part 4

June 11, 1864, page 318
June 30, 1864, page 620

Series 1, Volume 41, Part 2

August 31, 1864, pages 981–982

Series 1, Volume 41, Part 3

September 23, 1864, page 334

Series 1, Volume 46, Part 3, Section 2

April 16, 1865, pages 788–789
April 17, 1865, page 809
June 2, 1865, page 1248

Series 1, Volume 48, Part 1

January 11, 1865, pages 486–487
January 20, 1865, pages 597–598
January 21, 1865, page 599
January 26, 1865, page 653
January 30, 1865, page 687
January 31, 1865, page 694
February 6, 1865, pages 760–761
February 7, 1865, page 770
February 8, 1865, pages 778–779
February 8, 1865, page 782
February 9, 1865, page 793
February 9, 1865, page 795
February 9, 1865, page 799
February 10, 1865, pages 807–808
February 10, 1865, page 811
February 11, 1865, page 820
February 13, 1865, page 835
February 16, 1865, page 876
February 27, 1865, pages 997–998
February 27, 1865, page 1001
March 3, 1865, page 1069
March 10, 1865, page 1143
March 13, 1865, pages 1160–1161
March 18, 1865, page 1205
March 20, 1865, page 1225
July 27, 1865, page 357
August 7, 1865, page 352
August 11, 1865, page 356

Series 1, Volume 48, Part 2

April 14, 1865, pages 100–101
April 15, 1865, page 104
April 27, 1865, page 227
April 28, 1865, page 237
May 1, 1865, page 288
May 5, 1865, page 326
May 23, 1865, page 565
May 26, 1865, pages 612–613
May 30, 1865, pages 688–690
May 31, 1865, pages 709–710
June 1, 1865, pages 724–725
June 2, 1865, pages 730–731
June 3, 1865, pages 764–765
June 6, 1865, page 799
June 19, 1865, page 933
June 21, 1865, page 961
June 24, 1865, page 988
June 26, 1865, page 998
June 26, 1865, page 998
June 29, 1865, page 1029
July 3, 1865, page 1045
July 5, 1865, pages 1051–1052
July 6, 1865, pages 1056–1058
July 6, 1865, page 1060
July 9, 1865, page 1067
July 14, 1865, page 1079
July 29, 1865, page 1132
August 12, 1865, pages 1178–1179
September 15, 1865, page 1229
October 24, 1865, page 1243
October 25, 1865, page 1244

Series 1, Volume 50, Part 1

September 16, 1861, page 620
October 9, 1861, page 652
November 5, 1861, pages 702–703
November 13, 1861, page 720
December 7, 1861, page 751
December 9, 1861, pages 753–754
December 10, 1861, page 757
December 31, 1861, page 794
January 9, 1862, pages 798–799
March 26, 1862, page 953–954
March 28, 1862, page 960
April 10, 1862, pages 995–996
April 18, 1862, pages 1011–1012
May 17, 1862, page 1079
May 19, 1862, page 1081
May 22, 1862, page 1091
May 26, 1862, page 1100
May 27, 1862, page 1104
June 30, 1862, pages 1168–1170
August 13, 1862, page 88

Series 1, Volume 50, Part 2

July 14, 1862, pages 19–20
July 18, 1862, page 26
July 19, 1862, page 31
August 1, 1862, page 46
August 5, 1862, page 53
September 15, 1862, page 120
September 15, 1862, pages 124–125
September 16, 1862, page 125
September 19, 1862, page 128
September 20, 1862, page 128
September 24, 1862, page 133
November 22, 1862, page 229
February 1, 1863, page 301
February 16, 1863, page 314
March 19, 1863, page 357
March 30, 1863, page 374
May 23, 1863, page 453
August 3, 1863, page 551
September 28, 1863, pages 630–631
July 11, 1864, page 895
February 15, 1865, page 1136

Series 1, Volume 53

April 7, 1862, page 520

Series 2, Volume 4

August 15, 1862, page 393

Series 2, Volume 8

March 5, 1865, pages 358–359

Series 3, Volume 2

April 10, 1862, page 14
June 20, 1862, page 169
July 7, 1862, pages 206–207
July 16, 1862, page 227
July 29, 1862, pages 270–273
August 7, 1862, page 315
August 11, 1862, page 348

Series 3, Volume 3

March 30, 1863, pages 106–107
April 1, 1863, page 109
November 15, 1863, pages 1037–1043

Series 3, Volume 4, Section 2

November 10, 1864, page 923
November 22, 1864, pages 941–942
December 17, 1864, page 1020
March 8, 1865, page 1238
April 6, 1865, pages 1257–1258
April 29, 1865, page 1281

Series 3, Volume 5

May 6, 1865, page 5
October 20, 1865, pages 126–127
November 3, 1865, pages 211–212
December 28, 1865, page 580

APPENDIX E

Utah's Territorial Borders

THE PROVISIONAL STATE OF DESERET PROPOSED IN 1849 BY BRIGHAM Young and Mormon leaders—but rejected by Congress—contained 265,000 square miles. "The act creating Utah Territory" was signed by President Millard Fillmore on September 9, 1850, as part of the Compromise of 1850. While not as large as the proposed 1849 boundaries, Utah Territory was enormous, with 225,000 square miles to govern. As historian William P. MacKinnon observed, "It was an entity so large that several of its initial counties were more than six hundred miles wide, or about 20 percent of the width of the United States."[1] The boundaries of the newly created territory were the forty-second parallel on the north, the thirty-seventh parallel on the south, the summits of the Rocky Mountains to the east, and the Sierra Nevada Mountains to the west.

In February 1861, during President James Buchanan's last week in office, Utah Territory was significantly reduced when a large eastern section was removed to create Colorado Territory. A few days later, a large slice of western Utah was detached to create Nevada Territory (which would be admitted to the Union, with a smaller population than Utah, shortly before the presidential election of 1864), and the northeastern corner of Utah Territory was transferred to Nebraska Territory. In July 1862 an additional slice of western Utah was transferred to Nevada Territory. More territorial nibbles continued until 1868, which resulted in Utah's distinctive shape and left it with approximately 85,000 square miles to administer. It is worth noting geographer Albert L. Fisher's comment that "geometric boundaries are used when there is ignorance of the land or the people or both. This must have been true for Utah."[2] (See the map on page 34.) Federal legislation affected Utah's borders five times prior to the end of the Civil War:

- September 9, 1850: Utah Territory created
- February 28, 1861: Colorado Territory created
- March 2, 1861: Nevada Territory created
- March 2, 1861: Land transferred to Nebraska Territory
- July 14, 1862: Nevada Territory extended

---

1. MacKinnon, "'Like Splitting a Man Up His Backbone,'" 100–124. See footnote 1 in MacKinnon's article for a list of additional articles on this subject.
2. Fisher, "Boundaries and Utah: Sense or Nonsense?" 127.

APPENDIX F

Utah's Wartime Military Geography

DURING THE CIVIL WAR, STATES AND TERRITORIES WERE ORGANIZED into military divisions, departments, and districts. Utah became a separate military department during the Utah War of 1857–1858 and was assigned to several military departments during the Civil War. Several records in this volume address those assignments; see, for example, OR-1, OR-70, OR-373, OR-399, OR-402, OR-404, OR-405, OR-406, OR-411, OR-419, and OR-485. Utah's military geographic assignments prior to 1866 were catalogued by Raphael P. Thian, Adjutant General's Office chief records clerk (1871–1911), as follows:[1]

DEPARTMENT OF UTAH

January 1, 1858.—To consist of Utah Territory. *(Formed of part of the Department of the West.—G.O. No. 12, Headquarters Army, June 30, 1857.)*

January 1, 1858.—[Commanded by] Colonel ALBERT S. JOHNSTON, Second Cavalry; headquarters in the field. *(Assigned by G.O. No. 12, Headquarters Army, June 30, 1867 [sic].[2])*

January 14, 1858.—To consist of that part of Utah Territory east of the 117th degree of west longitude. *(Western portion of Utah Territory transferred to the Department of the Pacific.—G.O. No. 2, Headquarters Army, 1858.)*

February 29, 1860.—[Commanded by] Bvt. Col. CHARLES F. SMITH, Lieutenant-Colonel Tenth Infantry. *(Assigned by G.O. No. 4, Department of Utah, 1860.)*

August 20, 1860.—[Commanded by] Col. PHILIP ST. G. COOKE, Second Dragoons. *(Assigned by G.O. No. 6, Headquarters Army, March 12, 1860.)*

---

1. Thian, *Notes*. The listing here was created from entries on pages 23–24, 74–75, 86–87, 100–101, and 157. "G.O." and "S.O." are abbreviations for General Order and Special Order, respectively.
2. 1867 should be 1857.

July 3, 1861.—Discontinued.[3] *(Part of Department of Utah east of the Rocky Mountains merged into the Western Department.—G.O. No. 40, A.G.O., 1861.)*

Department of the Pacific

April 25, 1861.—[Commanded by] Brig. Gen. Edwin V. Sumner, U.S. Army. *(Assigned by S.O. No. 86, A.G.O., March 23, 1861.)*

July 3, 1861.—To consist of the country west of the Rocky Mountains except New Mexico and so much of Utah as lies east of the 117th degree of west longitude. *(. . . G.O. No. 40, A.G.O., 1861.)*

October 20, 1861.—[Commanded by] Col. George Wright, Ninth U.S. Infantry. *(Assumed command by right of seniority; subsequently assigned by S.O. No. 309, A.G.O., November 19, 1861.)*

July 1, 1864.—[Commanded by] Maj. Gen. Irvin McDowell, U.S. Vols. *(Assigned by G.O. No. 201, A.G.O., May 21, 1864.)*

Department of the Missouri

February 3, 1865.—[Commanded by] Maj. Gen. John Pope, U.S. Vols.; headquarters at Saint Louis. Mo. *(Assigned by G.O. No. 11, A.G.O., January 30, 1865.)*

February 17, 1865.—To consist of the States of Missouri, Kansas, Wisconsin, Iowa, Minnesota, and the Territories of Utah, Nebraska, Colorado (except Fort Garland), and Dakota. *(Territory of Utah, part of which was in the Department of the Pacific, transferred to Department of the Missouri.—G.O. 23, A.G.O., 1865.)*

June 27, 1865.—Discontinued. *(G.O. No. 95, A.G.O., 1865.)*

June 27, 1865.—Merged into the Departments of California and Oregon. *(G.O. No. 118, A.G.O., 1865.)*

Thian did not record Utah's geographic reassignment on June 27, 1865, but historian Frank J. Welcher did.

3. "Colonel Cooke, agreeably to S.O., Headquarters Army, May 17, 1861, ordered the troops of the Department to commence their march eastward August 9, 1861, thus virtually discontinuing the Department of Utah." See Thian, *Notes,* 101.

Department of California

In the reorganization of the military divisions and departments of the army June 27, 1865, the Department of California was re-created to consist of the states of California and Nevada and the territories of Colorado, New Mexico, and Utah. Irvin McDowell was assigned command, with headquarters at San Francisco, but he did not assume command until July 27."[4]

Welcher also included the following details regarding Utah's wartime military geographic assignments:

Department of Utah

The Department of Utah was in existence at the beginning of the Civil War . . . Headquarters of the department, and the principal post in the department, was Camp Floyd (later Fort Crittenden), which was about forty miles southwest of Salt Lake City in Cedar Valley. Philip St. G. Cooke, who was in command of the department at the outbreak of the Civil War, was assigned command August 20, 1860.

The troops in the Department of Utah at Fort Crittenden consisted of the following: companies B, E, and H of the 2nd United States Dragoons; companies E and I of the 10th United States Infantry; and batteries A, B, and C of the 4th United States Artillery. In addition, companies B and G of the 10th United States Infantry were at Fort Bridger.

On July 27, 1861, Fort Crittenden was abandoned, and Cooke marched eastward with his command to Fort Leavenworth, Kansas. From there his troops were moved on to Washington.

On the same day that Fort Crittenden was abandoned, the Territory of Utah was attached to the Department of the Pacific as the District of Utah. It was not until August 6, 1862, however, that California Volunteers under the command of P. Edward O'Connor moved in to occupy the district. By that time the Territory of Utah had been greatly reduced in size by the creation of the Territory of Nevada and the Territory of Colorado.[5]

Department of the Pacific

The Department of California was created September 13, 1858 to include the territory west of the Rocky Mountains and south of Oregon, except that part of Utah lying east of 117 degrees west longitude and of New Mexico lying east of 110 degrees west longitude. . . . July 3, 1861, the boundary was modified, and the department then consisted of the country west of the Rocky Mountains except New Mexico and that part of Utah lying cast of 117 degrees west longitude. . . .

4. Welcher, *The Union Army,* 18.

5. Ibid, 152.

February 17, 1865, Utah Territory and that part of Nebraska west of 104 degrees west longitude were transferred to the Department of the Missouri. At that time, the western boundary of Utah Territory was along 114 degrees west longitude. . . .

COMMANDERS OF THE DEPARTMENT OF THE PACIFIC

Albert Sidney Johnston	January 15, 1861 to April 25, 1861
Edwin V. Sumner	April 25, 1861 to October 20, 1861
George Wright	October 20, 1861 to July 1, 1864
Irvin McDowell	July 1, 1864 to June 27, 1865

Note. Wright assumed command by seniority October 20, 1861, and was formally assigned November 19.[6]

District of Utah. At the outbreak of war, Philip St. George Cooke commanded the Union Department of Utah. At Fort Crittenden (formerly Camp Floyd), about forty miles south and a little west of Salt Lake City in Cedar Valley, were two companies of the 2nd United States Cavalry, two companies of the 10th United States Infantry, and two companies of the 4th United States Artillery; and at Fort Bridger, northwest of Salt Lake City, were two companies of the 10th United States Infantry.

Cooke abandoned Fort Crittenden July 27, 1861, and marched eastward with his command to Fort Leavenworth, Kansas, picking up the troops at Fort Bridger on the way. Troops from California were to occupy the territory after Cooke departed.

P. Edward Connor assumed command of the District of Utah, Department of the Pacific August 6, 1862 at Fort Churchill, Nevada Territory. He defined his command as consisting of the territories of Nevada and Utah. Connor left Fort Churchill in mid-August and then marched eastward for two weeks along the Overland Mail Route to Ruby Valley, where he established Fort Ruby. He then moved on to Salt Lake City, where he arrived about the first of October, and then established Camp Douglas, east of the city.

August 20, 1863, the District of Utah was defined as consisting of the Utah Territory; Camp Ruby, Nevada Territory; and the post of Soda Springs, Idaho Territory.

February 17, 1865, Utah Territory and that part of Nebraska west of 104 degrees west longitude were transferred to the Department of the Missouri.

The principal posts in the District of Utah were Camp Douglas and Fort Bridger in Utah Territory; Fort Ruby and Fort Churchill in Nevada Territory; and Camp Connor in Idaho Territory.

The troops that served in the District of Utah consisted of the 3rd California Infantry, five companies of the 2nd California Cavalry, and the 1st Nevada Cavalry.

P. Edward Connor was in command of the district from August 6, 1862 to February 17, 1865.[7]

---

6. Ibid, 138. Note in the original.
7. Ibid, 143.

Department of the Missouri
September 19, 1862–May [sic] 27, 1865[8]

February 17, 1865, the Utah Territory and that part of the Nebraska Territory lying west of the 104th degree west longitude were added to the Department of the Missouri, which then consisted of the states of Missouri and Kansas; Alton, Illinois; Colorado Territory, except Fort Garland; Utah Territory; Nebraska Territory; all of present-day Wyoming, except a small area in the western part; and all of Dakota Territory west of the 104th degree west longitude. Part of Utah was taken from the Department of the Pacific . . .

COMMANDERS OF THE DEPARTMENT OF THE MISSOURI

. . .

Grenville M. Dodge .... December 9, 1864 to July 21, 1865
John Pope .... July 21, 1865 to August 20, 1866

. . .

District of Utah. . . . The Utah Territory was added to the Department of the Missouri February 17, 1865, and was merged into the District of the Plains on March 28 . . .

District of the Plains. The District of the Plains was formed March 28, 1865 from the District of Utah, District of Colorado, and District of Nebraska, and it was organized to aid in the protection of overland commerce, the telegraph line, and mail transportation. P. Edward Connor was assigned command, with headquarters at Denver, Colorado Territory. Headquarters was moved to Julesburg, Colorado Territory May 1, 1865. . . .

West Sub-district of the Plains. This sub-district consisted of Utah Territory. Milo George was assigned command, with headquarters at Camp Douglas. The principal posts in the district were Fort Bridger, Camp Douglas, and Camp Connor.[9]

---

8. Should be June 27, 1865.
9. Welcher, *The Union Army,* 92, 100–101, 105.

APPENDIX G

Military Units Serving in Utah Territory 1861–1865

During the Civil War, the following military units were assigned duty in Utah Territory or on the Overland Trail (between Fort Laramie, Nebraska Territory, and Fort Bridger, Utah Territory). Regimental histories for these units are available in Frederick H. Dyer's *A Compendium of the War of the Rebellion, Volume 3* (Des Moines, Iowa: The Dyer Publishing Company, 1908).

Service in Utah Territory

California Volunteers

1st Regiment Infantry
2nd Regiment Cavalry
3rd Regiment Infantry

Michigan Volunteers

1st Regiment Cavalry

Nevada Volunteers

1st Battalion Cavalry

United States Volunteers

5th Regiment Infantry
6th Regiment Infantry

Service on the Overland Trail (between Fort Laramie and Fort Bridger)

Kansas Volunteers

9th Regiment Cavalry
11th Regiment Cavalry

Missouri Volunteers

12th Regiment Cavalry

Nebraska Volunteers

1st Regiment Cavalry
1st Battalion Cavalry

Ohio Volunteers

1st Independent Battalion Cavalry
11th Regiment Cavalry

United States Regular Army

2nd Regiment Infantry
10th Regiment Infantry

APPENDIX H

Records Listed by Senders and Receivers

THE PURPOSE OF THIS APPENDIX IS TO MAKE RECORDS ORIGINATED and received by the same person easier to locate. Records for an individual are listed numerically in this order:

- SENDER records: Chapter 4 (OR-#) followed by Chapter 5 (UT-#) records
- RECEIVER records: Chapter 4 (OR-#) followed by Chapter 5 (UT-#) records

First and middle names have been added when known. For example, William P. Dole, U.S. commissioner of Indian Affairs, appears in chapter 5 as W. P. Dole, but as William P. Dole in this appendix. When records do not identify the name of a sender or receiver but instead identify only an office, position, or rank, we have added the individual's name when it is known. For example, record OR-14 (dated July 24, 1861) lists the recipient as the "Governor of California," not as John G. Downey. Records of this nature are cross-listed, such as:

Downey, John G. (Governor of California). *SENDER:* OR-25; *RECEIVER:* OR-14.
and
Governor of California (1861, see Downey, John G.).

This appendix also includes record numbers for circulars, general orders, special orders, orders, post returns, organization of troops, reports, and newspapers, as well as pseudonyms, such as "Cuidado" (UT-123) and "Ploy" (UT-150). Endorsements and inclosures are included as well—making it possible for the same individual to be both a sender and a receiver for the same record number if they endorsed correspondence they received. (See Cooper, S., OR-385, for example.) A few additional records with no known sender or receiver are not included in this appendix.

Acting Assistant Adjutant-General, Hdqrs. District of Oregon, Fort Vancouver, Wash. Ter. (see Hopkins, John W.).
Allen, A. *Sender:* OR-224.
Allen, N. E. *Sender:* UT-155.
Alvord, Benjamin. *Sender:* OR-96, 102, 133, 147, 157, 192, 199, 237, 258, 272, 275, 277, 302; *Receiver:* OR-105, 205, 242, 295.
Ammond, George R. *Sender:* UT-155.
Anderson, Allen L. *Sender:* OR-372.
Arny, William Frederick Milton. *Sender:* OR-122.
Ashley, D. R. *Sender:* OR-342.
Assistant Adjutant-General, Department of New Mexico. *Receiver:* OR-228, 372.
Attwood (Atwood), Richard H. *Sender:* OR-417, UT-47, 59, 72, 74.
Ayers, Z. G. *Sender:* OR-30.
Babbitt, Edwin Burr. *Sender:* OR-78, 131, 135.
Baker, Eugene M. *Sender:* OR-27.
Baldwin, Noyes. *Receiver:* OR-298.
Banks, James A. *Sender:* UT-155.
Barlow, J. S. M. *Sender:* UT-51.
Barnes, J. W. *Sender:* OR-402, 412; *Receiver:* OR-407, 408, 429.
Barse, W. H. *Sender:* OR-42.
Bell, Joseph McC. *Sender:* OR-456, 471, 485, 496; *Receiver:* OR-452, 499.
Bennett, Clarence E. *Sender:* OR-17.
Bernhisel, John M. *Receiver:* UT-29.
Berry, David J. *Receiver:* OR-299.
Blair, Montgomery P. *Receiver:* OR-98, UT-77.
Blake, George A. H. *Sender:* OR-26, 28; *Receiver:* OR-27.
Blunt, James G. *Receiver:* OR-62, 64, 66, 83.
Bretney, Henry C. *Sender:* OR-432.
Brooks, J. W. *Sender:* OR-24.
Brown, Albert. *Sender:* OR-94; *Receiver:* OR-413.
Brown, James A. *Sender:* OR-441.
Brown, Richard. *Sender:* OR-342.
Buell, D. C. *Receiver:* OR-15, 19, 21.
Burton, Robert T. *Sender:* UT-57, 62; *Receiver:* UT-30.
Caldwell, J. H. *Receiver:* OR-157.
Cameron, Simon. *Sender:* OR-11, 14; *Receiver:* OR-3, 9, 23, 24, 32, UT-6, 9, 26.
Canby, E. R. S. *Receiver:* OR-37.
Carleton, G. W. *Sender:* OR-376.
Carleton, James H. *Sender:* OR-15, 46, 98, UT-17; *Receiver:* OR-16, 17, 22.
Carson, C. *Sender:* OR-228.
Chambers, Rowland. *Receiver:* OR-157.
Charlot, C. S. *Receiver:* OR-363.
Chivington, John Milton. *Sender:* OR-245, 356, 363; *Receiver:* OR-224.
Circular. OR-276, UT-109, 116, 119, 126.
Clark, Joseph C. *Sender:* OR-22; UT-19, 20.
Clary, R. E. *Sender:* UT-6, 9, 11; *Receiver:* UT-9.
Clawson, Hiram B. *Receiver:* UT-62.
Clemens, O. *Receiver:* OR-172.
Colfax, Schuyler. *Sender:* UT-149.
Commanding Officer at Camp Connor (see Stillman, James W.).
Commanding Officer at Camp Ruby (see Thurston, George A.).
Comstock, C. B. *Sender:* OR-421.
Connor, Patrick Edward. *Sender:* OR-67, 69, 71, 74, 78, 85–87, 91–93, 97, 99, 104, 107, 108, 110, 112, 126, 132, 139, 142, 144, 146, 149, 150, 152, 155, 158, 162, 166, 178–180, 183, 186, 187,

200–203, 205, 207, 209, 213, 214, 219, 220, 227, 231, 246, 250, 260, 261, 273, 274, 276, 283, 300, 308, 309, 311–314, 318, 322, 328, 339, 357, 360, 361, 363, 364, 366, 374, 383, 387, 390, 391, 397, 398, 405–408, 417, 418, 428, 429, 431, 438, 442, 445, 449, 450, 453, 458, 460, 463, 490; UT-79, 80, 82, 83, 93, 94, 113, 119, 126, 131, 134, 143, 147, 148; *RECEIVER:* OR-73, 75, 76, 106, 121, 125, 154, 159, 163, 164, 171, 191, 192, 226, 232, 238, 241, 271, 281, 315, 317, 320, 321, 324, 327, 330, 342, 348, 353, 359, 362, 364, 369, 388, 391, 392, 395, 403, 404, 414, 416, 417, 421–423, 430, 437, 439, 454, 457, 459, 462, 465, 487, UT-95, 147.

Conrad, George D. *SENDER:* UT-115.

Cook, Frederick. *SENDER:* UT-28.

Cooke, Philip St. George. *SENDER:* UT-3, 5, 7–10, 12, 14–16, 18, 26.

Cooper, S. *SENDER:* OR-385; *RECEIVER:* OR-385.

Corning, Erastus. *SENDER:* OR-3.

Cradlebaugh, John. *SENDER:* UT-155.

Craft, Stewart Britton. *RECEIVER:* UT-41.

Craig, James. *SENDER:* OR-62, 64, 66, 79, 81, 83; *RECEIVER:* OR-80, 82.

Crawford, Medorem. *SENDER:* OR-105.

Creighton, E. *SENDER:* OR-160.

Crossman, J. S. *SENDER:* UT-155.

Cuidado. *SENDER:* UT-123.

Curtis, S. S. *RECEIVER:* OR-334, 340.

Curtis, Samuel R. *SENDER:* OR-292, 340; *RECEIVER:* OR-277, 302, 331, 354, 371.

Daily Vedette, Daily Union Vedette (see *Vedette*).

Dave. *RECEIVER:* OR-212.

Davidson, John W. *SENDER:* OR-19, 21, 31; *RECEIVER:* OR-30.

Davis, Jefferson. *RECEIVER:* OR-4.

Denver, J. W. *SENDER:* OR-51.

Deseret News. UT-22–25, 46, 52, 56–58, 60, 61, 63–65, 68, 70, 71, 75, 78, 79, 81, 83, 86, 89–92, 95–106.

Dodge, Grenville M. *SENDER:* OR-301, 379–382, 388, 391, 392, 403, 404, 408, 416, 424, 425, 430, 434–437, 439, 446, 452, 454, 457, 459, 462, 464, 465, 470, 477, 479, 482, 483, 489–493, 499, UT-147; *RECEIVER:* OR-380, 397, 426, 428, 431, 438, 442, 445, 449–451, 453, 458, 460, 463, 466, 468, 469, 476, 478, 481, 484, 490, 494.

Dole, William P. *RECEIVER:* UT-76, 107.

Doty, James Duane. *SENDER:* OR-229, 234, 376, UT-76, 107, 141; *RECEIVER:* OR-352, 433, UT-139, 140.

Downey, John G. *SENDER:* OR-25; *RECEIVER:* OR-14.

Downs, S. *SENDER:* UT-53.

Drum, Richard C. *SENDER:* OR-59, 65, 67, 72, 73, 75, 76, 78, 89, 115, 121, 125, 137, 141, 163, 168, 170, 174, 185, 191, 196, 198, 206, 208, 226, 232, 236, 238, 240, 252, 253, 281, 290, 315–317, 319–321, 324, 325–327, 330, 336, 345, 348, 350, 353, 369, 394, 395, 396; *RECEIVER:* OR-26, 28, 31, 67, 69, 71, 78, 85–87, 93, 94, 96, 97, 99, 107, 112, 126, 132, 133, 139, 142, 144, 146, 149, 150, 152, 155, 158, 162, 166, 178, 180, 183, 186, 187, 200–203, 207, 213, 214, 219, 220, 227, 231, 237, 246, 250, 260, 261, 274, 275, 283, 300, 308, 309, 311–314, 318, 322, 328, 339, 361, 364, 374, 383, 390, 391, 409, 427, UT-134, 155.

Easton, L. C. *SENDER:* OR-247.

Eckert, T. T. *RECEIVER:* OR-160.

English, T. C. *SENDER:* OR-280.

Ethier, Anthony. *SENDER:* OR-175, UT-106.
Evans, George S. *SENDER:* OR-190, UT-87; *RECEIVER:* OR-56.
Evans, John. *SENDER:* OR-211, 364.
Field, J. *RECEIVER:* OR-157.
Finnerty, James. *SENDER:* UT-108.
Fisk, C. B. *RECEIVER:* OR-334.
Fletcher, Thomas C. *RECEIVER:* OR-412.
Ford, John S. *SENDER:* OR-267.
Fox, Leonard R. *SENDER:* UT-28.
Fuller, Frank. *SENDER:* UT-23, 28, 31; *RECEIVER:* UT-25, 57.
Fullmer, Almon L. *RECEIVER:* UT-37.
Gallagher, Patrick A. *SENDER:* OR-113, 173, 177, 189, 215, 216, 218, 305.
General Orders. OR-89, 137, 151, 284, 325, 384, 391, 402, 406, 411, 415, 447, 456, 471, 474, 485, 496, UT-13, 108, 112, 124, 147, 148.
George, Milo. *SENDER:* OR-420, 491; *RECEIVER:* UT-133.
Gibbon, John. *SENDER:* UT-8.
Gibbs, Addison C. *SENDER:* OR-337; *RECEIVER:* OR-147, 233, 248, 272.
Gibson, John D. *SENDER:* UT-54.
Gilpin, William. *SENDER:* OR-23, 37; *RECEIVER:* OR-6.
Gooddell, T. *SENDER:* UT-53.
Gove, Jesse A. *SENDER:* UT-4.
Governor of California (1861, see Downey, John G.).
Grant, Ulysses S. *SENDER:* OR-461; *RECEIVER:* OR-301, 399, 443, 455, 498, 503.
Green, John. *SENDER:* UT-9, 11, 140; *RECEIVER:* UT-11.
Greene, O. D. *SENDER:* OR-284.
Grow, Galusha A. *RECEIVER:* OR-48.
Hall, Benjamin F. *SENDER:* OR-29, 38.
Halleck, Henry W. *SENDER:* OR-114, 116, 140, 159, 164–166, 182, 197, 243, 269, 359, 362, 364, 378, 503, UT-95; *RECEIVER:* OR-51, 53, 81, 91, 179, 209, 269, 273, 337, 360, 366, 382.
Hammond, W. A. *RECEIVER:* OR-254.
Harding, Stephen S. *SENDER:* OR-136; *RECEIVER:* OR-143, 195, UT-85.
Harlan, James. *RECEIVER:* OR-446.
Harris, Thomas S. *RECEIVER:* OR-111, 113, 176, UT-115.
Haven, F. *SENDER:* UT-147; *RECEIVER:* OR-387.
Head, Lafayette. *RECEIVER:* OR-400.
Hempstead, Charles H. *SENDER:* OR-349, UT-109, 131; *RECEIVER:* OR-215, 216, 218.
Hibbad, W. B. *SENDER:* UT-28.
Holladay (Holliday), Benjamin "Ben." *SENDER:* OR-358, UT-50, 77; *RECEIVER:* OR-356.
Holladay, Joseph. *SENDER:* UT-28, 33.
Hopkins, John W. *SENDER:* OR-278, 286; *RECEIVER:* OR-235, 244, 249, 257, 280, 304, 310, 329, 343, 346.
Hovey, Alvin P. *SENDER:* OR-341.
Hughes, Bela Metcalf. *SENDER:* OR-354.
Humfreville, J. L. *RECEIVER:* OR-441.
Hunt, Franklin Eyre. *SENDER:* UT-6, 9, 10; *RECEIVER:* UT-9.
Huntington, J. W. Perit. *SENDER:* OR-295.
J. H. S. *SENDER:* UT-97.
Jewett, O. *SENDER:* OR-386.
Jocelyn, S. E. *SENDER:* UT-151.
Johns, William M. *RECEIVER:* OR-418.
Johnson, Andrew. *RECEIVER:* OR-501, 504.
Johnston, W. I. *SENDER:* OR-338.
Jones, William. *SENDER:* UT-124.

Keller, Matthew. *SENDER:* OR-19.
Kellogg, John. *SENDER:* OR-131; *RECEIVER:* OR-174.
Kennedy, Joseph C. G. *SENDER:* OR-134.
Ketchum, W. Scott. *SENDER:* OR-53.
King, Isaac. *RECEIVER:* OR-157.
Kinney, John F. *SENDER:* OR-269, UT-28, 43.
Kirkpatrick, S. M. *SENDER:* OR-377.
Lander, F. W. *SENDER:* OR-47.
Lebeau, M. *SENDER:* OR-271.
Leonard, James. *SENDER:* OR-30.
Lewis, Micajah G. *SENDER:* OR-282, 289, 291, 294, 297–299, 323, 335, 344, 355, 389, UT-112, 116, 147; *RECEIVER:* OR-256, 303, 305, 306, 370, UT-126, 128.
Lincoln, Abraham. *SENDER:* UT-25, 34; *RECEIVER:* OR-11, 25, 29, UT-23, 94.
Livingston, R. R. *SENDER:* OR-365, 380.
Low, Frederick F. *SENDER:* OR-347, 401; *RECEIVER:* OR-351.
Luffing, Pete. *SENDER:* OR-271.
Lugenbeel, Pinkney. *RECEIVER:* OR-229.
Lybe, A. Smith. *SENDER:* UT-133.
M. *SENDER:* UT-98.
Mason, John S. *RECEIVER*: UT-141.
Mason, O. P. *SENDER:* OR-331, 377.
Maull, G. W. *SENDER:* OR-338.
Maury, Reuben F. *SENDER:* OR-233, 235, 241, 242, 244, 248, 249, 257, 304, 310, 343, 346, 409; *RECEIVER:* OR-199, 286.
MC. *SENDER:* UT-152.
McAllister, Julian. *RECEIVER:* OR-59, 141.
McClellan, George B. *RECEIVER:* OR-47, UT-26.
McDermit, Charles. *RECEIVER:* OR-206, 253, 326, 345.
McDowell, Irvin. *SENDER:* OR-332, 337, 351, 352, 367, 368, 390, 414, 433, 502, UT-139, 147; *RECEIVER:* OR-338, 347, 398, 401, 448.
McGarry, Edward. *SENDER:* OR-106, 111; *RECEIVER:* OR-92, 110, 168.
McLane, Louis. *RECEIVER:* OR-43.
McLaughlin, M. A. *RECEIVER:* OR-185, 196.
McNulty, James M. *SENDER:* OR-254.
Meigs, Montgomery C. *SENDER:* OR-475, 500; *RECEIVER:* OR-247, 495, 497.
Merritt, Wesley. *SENDER:* UT-10, 13, 14.
Miller, Morz. *SENDER:* OR-342.
Mitchell, D. C. *SENDER:* OR-338.
Moarley, J. *SENDER:* UT-53.
Mogo, Charles. *SENDER:* OR-30.
Monchard, M. *SENDER:* OR-271.
Moonlight, Thomas. *SENDER:* OR-400; *RECEIVER:* OR-405, 432, 440.
Moore, Jeremiah B. *SENDER:* OR-256, 303.
Moore, S. B. *SENDER:* OR-342.
Moore, William G. *SENDER:* UT-149.
Morgan, I. W. *SENDER:* OR-342.
Morrill, Joseph C. *SENDER:* UT-114, 118.
Mr. President. (see Johnson, Andrew).
Need, William. *SENDER:* OR-32.
Nickerson, Mulf. *SENDER:* OR-342.
Nye, James W. *SENDER:* OR-88; *RECEIVER:* OR-41, 262, 287.
Officer Commanding the Troops of the United States at Fort Boise and in the Snake River Country (see Lugenbeel, Pinkney).
O'Neill, John M. *RECEIVER:* OR-208.
Oath of Office. UT-43, 44.
Orders. OR-70, 74, 77, 104, UT-83, 110.

Organization of Troops. OR-129, 223, 268, 307, 393, 419.
Paddock, A. S. *SENDER:* OR-9.
Pereau, Joseph H. *SENDER:* OR-30.
Pickering, William. *SENDER:* OR-128; *RECEIVER:* OR-124.
Pierce, Franklin. *RECEIVER:* OR-44.
Pierce, N. P. *SENDER:* OR-56.
Platte. *SENDER:* UT-142.
Pleasonton, Alfred. *SENDER:* OR-6.
Ploy. *SENDER:* UT-150, 153.
Plumly, B. Rush. *SENDER:* OR-33.
Pollock, Robert. *SENDER:* UT-127, 138.
Pope, John. *SENDER:* OR-301, 382, 399, 408, 410, 426, 443, 455, 466–469, 472, 473, 480, 486, 487, 488, 494, 498; *RECEIVER:* OR-301, 378–382, 424, 425, 434–436, 461, 464, 470, 482, 483, 489–492.
Porter, John B. *SENDER:* UT-6, 9; *RECEIVER:* UT-9.
Post Orders. UT-79, 114, 118.
Post Return. UT-1, 2, 4, 19, 80, 82, 93, 127, 138.
Potter, C. H. *SENDER:* OR-444.
Potter, J. A. *SENDER:* OR-495.
Pratt, Thomas A. *RECEIVER:* OR-45.
President of the United States (see Lincoln, Abraham).
Price, George F. *SENDER:* OR-176, 306, 411, 413, 415, 422, 423, 451, 476, 478, 481, 484, UT-128; *RECEIVER:* OR-420, 444, 477, 479, 493.
Purdy, E. Sparrow. *SENDER:* OR-263.
Purple, E. R. *SENDER:* UT-28.
Quarter Master General's Office. *SENDER:* UT-84.
R. M. C. *RECEIVER:* OR-34.
Record of Events. UT-1, 2, 4, 19, 82, 87, 93, 127, 138.
Reed, Amos. *SENDER:* OR-376.
Report. OR-28, 52, 105, 109, 113, 123, 140, 175, 176, 178, 190, 201, 213, 218, 254, 258, 306, 343, 365, 366, 372, 432, 440, 441, 444, 452, UT-28, 62, 76, 77, 107, 146.
Reynolds, William. *SENDER:* OR-376.
Robinson, Lewis. *SENDER:* UT-49.
Rockwell, Orrin Porter. *RECEIVER:* UT-40.
Rosecrans, W. S. *RECEIVER:* OR-333, 341.
Ross, D. I. *RECEIVER:* UT-42.
Rowe, H. S. R. *SENDER:* UT-28.
Ruggles, Daniel. *SENDER:* OR-385.
Rumfield, H. S. *SENDER:* OR-376.
San Francisco Alta. UT-117.
Sanderson, J. P. *SENDER:* OR-333.
Saunders, Alvin. *SENDER:* OR-377.
Sawyer, Roswell M. *RECEIVER:* OR-467, 472, 473.
Schofield, John M. *RECEIVER:* OR-197, 211, 243, 245.
Scott, Robert N. *RECEIVER:* OR-502.
Scott, Thomas A. *SENDER:* OR-29; *RECEIVER:* OR-33, 36.
Scott, Winfield. *RECEIVER:* OR-12.
Secretary of War (March 5, 1861 to January 14, 1862, see Cameron, Simon; January 20, 1862 to May 28, 1868, see Stanton, Edwin M.).
Seidenstriker, F. *SENDER:* OR-329; *RECEIVER:* OR-278.
Seward, William H. *SENDER:* OR-29, 44; *RECEIVER:* OR-38, 42, 122.
Sherman, Edwin A. *SENDER:* OR-7, 30.
Sherman, William Tecumseh. *RECEIVER:* OR-480, 488.
Smith, Charles F. *SENDER:* UT-1.
Smith, Lot (Lott). *SENDER:* UT-44, 47, 66, 67, 69, 73; *RECEIVER:* UT-36, 45, 55.
Smith, Samuel P. *RECEIVER:* OR-297.
Soldier Boys. *SENDER:* UT-71.

Soule, S. S. *SENDER:* OR-221.
Special Orders. OR-65, 72, 115, 170, 198, 236, 240, 252, 263, 282, 289–291, 294, 316, 319, 323, 335, 336, 344, 349, 350, 355, 386, 389, UT-32, 38, 113, 131, 151.
Stager, Anson. *SENDER:* OR-36; *RECEIVER:* OR-160.
Stanton, Edwin M. *SENDER:* OR-48, 80, 82, 140, 262, 501, 504; *RECEIVER:* OR-79, 358, 367, 375–377, 410, 475, 500, UT-28, 34, 84, 149.
Stearns, Abel. *SENDER:* OR-18, 20.
Steen, E. *SENDER:* OR-8.
Stillman, James W. *SENDER:* OR-70, 77; *RECEIVER:* OR-396.
Stuart, J. E. B. *SENDER:* OR-45.
Sumner, Edwin Vose. *SENDER:* UT-17; *RECEIVER:* OR-7, 13, 17–20.
Taylor, J. P. *RECEIVER:* OR-131.
Tessnant, Thomas J. *SENDER:* OR-342.
Thomas, Lorenzo. *SENDER:* OR-10, 12, 13, 48, 52, 54, 151, UT-43; *RECEIVER:* OR-8, 35, 49, 50, 55, 57, 58, 60, 61, 63, 68, 84, 90, 95, 100, 101, 103, 108, 109, 117–120, 123, 127, 130, 138, 140, 148, 153, 156, 161, 167, 169, 181, 184, 188, 190, 193, 194, 204, 210, 217, 225, 230, 239, 258, 279, 285, 293, 296, 332, 357, 368, UT-3, 7, 8, 10, 12, 15–18, 20, 48, 88.
Thompson, Meriwether Jeff. *SENDER:* OR-4.
Thornton, O. F. *SENDER:* OR-338.
Thurber, A. K. *SENDER:* UT-100.
Thurston, George A. *SENDER:* OR-342, 370; *RECEIVER:* OR-394.
Tichenor, George C. *SENDER:* OR-474.
Titus, John. *SENDER:* OR-376.
Townsend, Edward D. *SENDER:* OR-5, 29, 288, 371, 384, 391, 447, 448, UT-5, 21, 147; *RECEIVER:* OR-40, 251, 255, 259, 264–266, 270, 292, UT-5, 143.
Turner, Edmund P. *RECEIVER:* OR-267.
Turnley, Parmenas T. *SENDER:* OR-35.
Union Vedette (see *Vedette*).
Usher, John Palmer. *SENDER:* OR-375; *RECEIVER:* OR-134.
Ustick, William L. *SENDER:* UT-90, 110; *RECEIVER:* OR-173, 177, 189, 190.
Vedette. UT-108–122, 124–126, 128–133, 135–137, 142, 144–148, 150–154.
Wade, Jeptha H. *SENDER:* OR-160, UT-24; *RECEIVER:* UT-22.
Wallace, William S. *SENDER:* OR-171.
Warner, J. *SENDER:* UT-53.
Watterson, T. A. *SENDER:* OR-342.
Wells, Daniel H. *SENDER:* UT-27, 30, 32, 36–42, 85; *RECEIVER:* UT-31, 35, 49, 51, 54, 62.
Westwood, Phebe. *SENDER:* OR-212.
Wheaton, Frank. *RECEIVER:* OR-486.
White, Samuel B. *SENDER:* OR-440.
Williams. *SENDER:* UT-149.
Willis, Henry M. *SENDER:* OR-16.
Wootten, Francis M. *RECEIVER:* UT-14.
Worthington, H. G. *SENDER:* OR-342.
Wren, Thomas. *SENDER:* OR-342.
Wright, George. *SENDER:* OR-40, 41, 43, 49, 50, 55, 57, 58, 60, 61, 63, 68, 84, 90, 95, 100, 101, 103, 109, 117–120, 123, 124, 127, 130, 138, 140, 143, 148, 153, 154, 156, 161, 167, 169, 172, 181, 184, 188, 190, 193–195, 204, 210, 217, 225, 230, 239, 251, 255, 259, 264–266, 270, 279, 285, 287, 293, 296, 427, UT-88, 117; *RECEIVER:* OR-88, 114, 116, 128, 135, 136, 165, 182, 234, 288.
Wynkoop, E. W. *RECEIVER:* OR-221.
Young, Brigham. *SENDER:* UT-22, 29, 35, 45, 48, 55; *RECEIVER:* OR-54, UT-24, 27, 43, 50, 66, 67, 69, 72–74, 123.

Bibliography

War of the Rebellion Volumes

U.S. War Department, *The War of the Rebellion: A Compilation of the Official Records of the Union and Confederate Armies.* Series 1, vol. 1. Washington, D.C.: Government Printing Office, 1880.

———. Series 1, vol. 3. 1881.

———. Series 1, vol. 4. 1882.

———. Series 1, vol. 5. 1881.

———. Series 1, vol. 8. 1883.

———. Series 1, vol. 9. 1883.

———. Series 1, vol. 13. 1885.

———. Series 1, vol. 15. 1886.

———. Series 1, vol. 22, part 1. 1888.

———. Series 1, vol. 22, part 2. 1888.

———. Series 1, vol. 26, part 1. 1889.

———. Series 1, vol. 29, part 2. 1890.

———. Series 1, vol. 34, part 2. 1890.

———. Series 1, vol. 34, part 3. 1890.

———. Series 1, vol. 34, part 4. 1890.

———. Series 1, vol. 41, part 1. 1893.

———. Series 1, vol. 41, part 2. 1893.

———. Series 1, vol. 41, part 3. 1893.

———. Series 1, vol. 41, part 4. 1893.

———. Series 1, vol. 46, part 3, section 2. 1895.

———. Series 1, vol. 47, part 3. 1895.

———. Series 1, vol. 48, part 1. 1896.

———. Series 1, vol. 48, part 2. 1896.

———. Series 1, vol. 49, part 2. 1897.

———. Series 1, vol. 50, part 1. 1897.

———. Series 1, vol. 50, part 2. 1897.

———. Series 1, vol. 51, part 2. 1897.

———. Series 1, vol. 53. 1898.

———. Series 2, vol. 2, section 2. 1897.

———. Series 2, vol. 4. 1899.

———. Series 2, vol. 7, section 1. 1899.

———. Series 2, vol. 8. 1899.
———. Series 3, vol. 1. 1899.
———. Series 3, vol. 2. 1899.
———. Series 3, vol. 3. 1899.
———. Series 3, vol. 4, section 2. 1900.
———. Series 3, vol. 5. "1900.

Supplemental Official Records

Janet B. Hewett, ed. *Supplement to the Official Records of the Union and Confederate Armies.* Part 1, vol. 3, serial 7. "Reports." Wilmington, N.C.: Broadfoot Publishing Company, 1994.
———. Part 2, vol. 7, serial 15. "Record of Events." 1994.
———. Part 2, vol. 21, serial 33. "Record of Events." 1996.
———. Part 2, vol. 39, serial 51. "Record of Events." 1996.
———. Part 2, vol.49, serial 61. "Record of Events." 1996.
———. Part 2, vol. 50, serial 62. "Record of Events." 1997.
———. Part 2, vol. 56, serial 68. "Record of Events." 1997.

Official Records

A Resolution to Provide for the Printing of Official Reports of the Operations of the Armies of the United States. 38th Congress, Session 1, 13 Stat. 406 (1864).
Congressional Globe. 37th Congress, Session 2 (December 1861).
Davis, Maj. George B., et al., eds. *Atlas to Accompany the Official Records of the Union and Confederate Armies.* Washington, D.C.: Government Printing Office, 1891–1895.
Morrill Anti-Bigamy Act. 37th Congress, Session 2, ch. 126, 12 Stat. 501 (1862).
National Archives. "Letters Received by the Office of the Adjutant General (Main Series): 1861–1870." Record Group 94. Washington, D.C.
———. "Returns from U.S. Military Posts, 1800–1916." Record Group 94, Washington, D.C.
———. "Utah Territory, 1860–1873." Utah Territorial Papers. Record Group 59, Washington, D.C.
Report of the Commissioner of Indian Affairs, Accompanying the Annual Report of the Secretary of the Interior for the Year 1861. Washington, D.C.: Government Printing Office, 1862.
———. *Accompanying the Annual Report of the Secretary of the Interior for the Year 1862.* Washington, D.C.: Government Printing Office, 1863.
———. *Accompanying the Annual Report of the Secretary of the Interior for the Year 1863.* Washington, D.C.: Government Printing Office, 1864.
———. *Accompanying the Annual Report of the Secretary of the Interior for the Year 1865.* Washington, D.C.: Government Printing Office, 1865.
Sanger, George P., ed., *The Statutes at Large, Treaties and Proclamations of the United States of America from December 5, 1859 to March 3, 1863.* vol. 12. Boston, Mass.: Little, Brown and Company, 1863.

Treaties, Conventions, International Acts, Protocols and Agreements between the United States of America and Other Powers, 1776–1909, 2 vols., ed. William M. Malloy. Washington, D.C.: Government Printing Office, 1910.

Utah State Historical Society. Utah Military Files. MSS 242. Utah State Archives, Salt Lake City.

———. Utah Military Files. MSS 2210. Utah State Archives, Salt Lake City.

Manuscripts

Brigham Young Letterpress Copybook, 1844–1879. CR 1234 1. LDS Church History Library, Salt Lake City, Utah.

Brigham Young Letters. Beinecke Rare Book and Manuscript Library, Yale University, New Haven, Conn.

Brigham Young Office Files. LDS Church History Library, Salt Lake City, Utah.

Brigham Young Office Journal. LDS Church History Library, Salt Lake City, Utah.

Douglas, Stephen A. "Kansas, Utah, and the Dred Scott Decision." Address at State House, Springfield, Ill., June 12, 1857.

Frank Fuller Papers. J. Willard Marriott Library, University of Utah, Salt Lake City, Utah.

Harvey Coe Hullinger Journal. MS 1632. LDS Church History Library, Salt Lake City, Utah.

Historian's Office Journal. LDS Church History Library, Salt Lake City, Utah.

History of Brigham Young. Historian's Office History of the Church, 1839–circa 1882: January 1–December 30, 1862. CR 100 102. LDS Church History Library, Salt Lake City, Utah.

Journal History. LDS Church History Library, Salt Lake City, Utah.

Lot Smith Papers. L. Tom Perry Special Collections. Harold B. Lee Library, Brigham Young University, Provo, Utah.

Martha Cragun Cox Journal. MS 1661, LDS Church History Library, Salt Lake City, Utah.

Wilford Woodruff's Journal: 1833–1898. Typescript. vols. 5–6. Salt Lake City, Utah: Signature Books, 1983–85.

Newspapers

Boston Herald.

The Daily Vedette, Camp Douglas, Utah Territory.

Daily Union Vedette, Camp Douglas, Utah Territory.

Deseret News, Salt Lake City.

New York Times, New York City.

Richmond Whig, Richmond, Va.

Sacramento Daily Union, Sacramento, Calif.

Salt Lake Tribune, Salt Lake City, Utah.

The Union Vedette, Camp Douglas, Utah Territory.

Books

Aimone, Alan C., and Barbara A. Aimone. *A User's Guide to the Official Records of the American Civil War.* Shippensburg, Penn.: White Mane Publishing Company, Inc., 1993.

Alford, Kenneth L., ed. *Civil War Saints.* Provo, Utah: Brigham Young University Religious Studies Center and Deseret Book Company, 2012.

———. "The Utah War (1857–1858): 'A Dark Time for the Saints.'" In *The Mormon Wars*, edited by Glenn Rawson and Dennis Lyman. American Fork, Utah: Covenant Communications, 2014.

———. "Utah's Role in Protecting Emigrant Trails during the Civil War." In *Far Away in the West,* edited by Scott C. Esplin, Richard E. Bennett, Susan E. Black, and Craig K. Manscill. Provo, Utah: Brigham Young University Religious Studies Center and Deseret Book Company, 2015.

Angle, Paul M., comp., *New Letters and Papers of Lincoln.* Boston: Houghton Mifflin, 1930.

Arrington, Leonard J. *Brigham Young: American Moses.* Chicago: University of Illinois Press, 1985.

Bagley, Will. *South Pass: Gateway to a Continent.* Norman: University of Oklahoma Press, 2014.

Bancroft, Hubert Howe. *History of Oregon, Volume II, 1848–1888.* San Francisco, Calif.: The History Company, 1888.

———. *History of Utah, 1540–1886.* San Francisco, Calif.: The History Company, 1889.

Basler, Roy, ed. *The Collected Works of Abraham Lincoln,* 10 vols. New Brunswick, N.J.: Rutgers University Press, 1953.

Bennett, Richard E. "We Know No North, No South, No East, No West." In *Civil War Saints,* edited by Kenneth L. Alford, 93–105. Provo, Utah: Brigham Young University Religious Studies Center and Deseret Book, 2012.

Bigler, David L. *Forgotten Kingdom: The Mormon Theocracy in the American West, 1847–1896.* Logan: Utah State University Press, 1998.

———, and Will Bagley. *The Mormon Rebellion: America's First Civil War, 1857–1858.* Norman: University of Oklahoma Press, 2011.

Blackhawk, Ned. *Violence over the Land: Indians and Empires in the Early American West.* Cambridge, Mass.: Harvard University Press, 2006.

Boatner, Mark May, III. *The Civil War Dictionary.* New York: David McKay Company, 1959.

Bringhurst, Newell C. *Saints, Slaves, and Blacks: The Changing Place of Black People Within Mormonism.* Westport, Conn.: Greenwood Press, 1981.

Brown, Dee. *The Galvanized Yankees.* Lincoln: University of Nebraska Press, 1963.

Carter, Kate B. "Utah during Civil War Years." In *Treasures of Pioneer History.* Salt Lake City: Daughters of Utah Pioneers, 1956.

Child, Paul W., ed. *Register of Graduates and Former Cadets of the United States Military Academy, 1802–1990.* West Point, N.Y.: Association of USMA Graduates, 1990.

Collier, Fred. C., ed. *The Office Journal of President Brigham Young: 1858–1863. Book D.* Hanna, Utah: Collier's Publishing Co., 2006.

Colton, Ray C. *The Civil War in the Western Territories: Arizona, Colorado, New Mexico, and Utah.* Norman: University of Oklahoma Press, 1959.

Cooper, Bruce C. *Riding the Transcontinental Rails: Overland Travel on the Pacific Railroad.* Philadelphia, Penn.: Polyglot Press, 2004.

Culmsee, Carlton F. *Utah's Black Hawk War: Lore and Reminiscences of the Participants War.* Logan: Utah State University Press, 1973.

Dickson, Ephriam D., III. "Addendum." In *Civil War Saints*, edited by Kenneth L. Alford, 234–235. Provo, Utah: Brigham Young University Religious Studies Center and Deseret Book Company, 2012.

———. "Protecting the Home Front: The Utah Territorial Militia during the Civil War." In *Civil War Saints*, edited by Kenneth L. Alford, 143–160. Provo, Utah: Brigham Young University Religious Studies Center and Deseret Book Company, 2012.

Doctrine and Covenants. Salt Lake City: The Church of Jesus Christ of Latter-day Saints, 2013.

Dyer, Frederick H. *A Compendium of the War of the Rebellion*. 3 vols. Des Moines, Iowa: The Dyer Publishing Company, 1908.

Edrington, Thomas S., and John Taylor. *The Battle of Glorieta Pass: A Gettysburg in the West, March 26–28, 1862*. Albuquerque: University of New Mexico Press, 1998.

Eicher, David J., John H. Simon, and John Y. Eicher. *Civil War High Commands*. Palo Alto, Calif.: Stanford University Press, 2001.

Esplin, Scott C., Richard E. Bennett, Susan E. Black, and Craig K. Manscill, eds. *Far Away in the West*. Provo, Utah: Brigham Young University Religious Studies Center and Deseret Book Company, 2015.

———, and Kenneth L. Alford, eds. *Salt Lake City: The Place Which God Prepared*. Provo, Utah: Brigham Young University Religious Studies Center and Deseret Book Company, 2011.

Esshom, Frank. *Pioneers and Prominent Men of Utah*. Salt Lake City: Utah Pioneers Book Publishing Company, 1913.

Firmage Edwin B., and Richard C. Mangrum. *Zion in the Courts: A Legal History of the Church of Jesus Christ of Latter-day Saints, 1830–1900*. Urbana: University of Illinois, 1988.

Fisher, Margaret M., C. N. Lund, and Judge Nephi Jensen, eds. *Utah and the Civil War: Being the Story of the Part Played by the People of Utah in that Great Conflict, with Special Reference to the Lot Smith Expedition and the Robert T. Burton Expedition*. Salt Lake City: Deseret Book, 1929.

Fleisher, Kass. *The Bear River Massacre and the Making of History*. Albany: State University of New York, 2004.

Foote, Shelby. *The Civil War: A Narrative*, 3 vols. New York: Random House, 1958.

Frazer, Robert Walter. *Forts of the West*. Norman: University of Oklahoma Press, 1965.

Frederick, J. V. *Ben Holladay, The Stagecoach King: A Chapter in the Development of Transcontinental Transportation*. Glendale, Calif.: Arthur H. Clark, 1940.

Furniss, Norman F. *The Mormon Conflict, 1850–1859*. New Haven, Conn.: Yale University Press, 1960.

Garavaglia, Louis A., and Charles G. Worman, *Firearms of the American West, 1803–1865*. Albuquerque: University of New Mexico Press, 1984.

Grow, Matthew J., and Ronald W. Walker. *The Prophet and the Reformer: The Letters of Brigham Young and Thomas L. Kane*. New York: Oxford University Press, 2015.

Hafen, LeRoy R. "The Indian Peril. " In *The Overland Mail*. Mansfield Centre, Conn.: Quarterman Publications, 1977.

———. *Utah Expedition, 1857–1858: A Documentary Account*, 2d ed. Glendale, Calif.: Arthur H. Clark, 1983.

Harlow, Victor E. *Harlow's Oklahoma History*. Oklahoma City: Harlow Publishing, 1961.

Hart, Herbert M. *Old Forts of the Far West*. Seattle: Superior, 1965.

Hartley, William G. "Latter-day Saint Emigration during the Civil War." In *Civil War Saints*, edited by Kenneth L. Alford, 237–265. Provo, Utah: Brigham Young University Religious Studies Center and Deseret Book Company, 2012.

Horton, J. H., and S. Teverbaugh, *A History of the Eleventh Regiment, (Ohio Volunteer Infantry)*. Dayton, Ohio: W. J. Shuey, 1866.

Hubbell, John T., and James W. Geary. *Biographical Dictionary of the Union: Northern Leaders of the Civil War*. Westport, Conn.: Greenwood Press, 1995.

Hunt, Aurora. *The Army of the Pacific: Its Operations in California, Texas, Arizona, New Mexico, Utah, Nevada, Oregon, Washington, Plains Region, Mexico, Etc. 1860–1866*. Glendale, Calif.: Arthur H. Clark, 1951.

Jensen, Andrew. *Church Chronology*. Salt Lake City: Deseret News, 1899.

———. *Latter-day Saint Biographical Encyclopedia*. Salt Lake City: Andrew Jenson History Company, 1914.

Jessee, Dean C., ed. *Letters of Brigham Young to His Sons*. Salt Lake City: Deseret Book, 1974.

Johannsen, Robert W. *Stephen A. Douglas*. New York: Oxford University Press, 1973.

Jones, Robert Huhn. *Guarding the Overland Trails: The Eleventh Ohio Cavalry in the Civil War*. Spokane, Wash.: Arthur H. Clark, 2005.

Jones, Terry L. *Historical Dictionary of the Civil War, Volume 1: A–L*. New York: Roman and Littlefield, 2002.

Josephy, Alvin M., Jr. *The Civil War in the American West*. New York: Vintage Books, 1993.

Journal of Discourses, 26 vols. London: Latter-day Saints' Book Depot, 1854–1886.

Kautz, August Valentine. *The Company Clerk: Showing How and When to Make Out All the Returns, Reports, Rolls, and Other Papers, and What to Do with Them: How to Keep All the Books, Records, and Accounts Required in the Administration of a Company, Troop, or Battery in the Army of the United States*. Philadelphia: J. B. Lippincott & Co., 1864.

Kerby, Robert Lee. *The Confederate Invasion of New Mexico and Arizona, 1861–1862*. Tucson, Ariz.: Westernlore Press, 1958.

Krisman, Michael J., ed. *Register of Graduates and Former Cadets of the United States Military Academy*. Chicago, Ill.: R. R. Donnelley & Sons Company, 1980.

Long, E. B. *The Saints and the Union: Utah Territory during the Civil War*. Urbana: University of Illinois Press, 1981.

Lonn, Ella, *Desertion during the Civil War*. Gloucester, Mass.: The American Historical Association, 1966.

Lowie, Robert H. *The Northern Shoshone*. Anthropological Papers of the American Museum of Natural History. Vol. 2. Part 2. New York, 1909.

MacKinnon, William P., ed. *At Sword's Point, Part 1: A Documentary History of the Utah War to 1858*. Kingdom in the West: The Mormons and the American Frontier, vol. 10. Norman, Okla.: Arthur H. Clark, 2008.

———. *At Sword's Point, Part 2: A Documentary History of the Utah War, 1858–1859*. Kingdom in the West: The Mormons and the American Frontier, vol. 11. Norman, Okla.: Arthur H. Clark, 2016.

———. "Prelude to Civil War: The Utah War's Impact and Legacy." In *Civil War Saints*, edited by Kenneth L. Alford, 1–21. Provo, Utah: Brigham Young University Religious Studies Center and Deseret Book Company, 2012.

Madsen, Brigham D. *Glory Hunter: A Biography of Patrick Edward Connor.* Salt Lake City: University of Utah Press, 1990.

———. *The Northern Shoshoni.* Caldwell, Idaho: Caxton Printers, 1980.

———. *The Shoshoni Frontier and the Bear River Massacre.* Salt Lake City: University of Utah Press, 1985.

Masich, Andrew E. *The Civil War in Arizona: The Story of the California Volunteers, 1861–65.* Norman: University of Oklahoma Press, 2006.

Maxwell, John Gary. *The Civil War Years in Utah: The Kingdom of God and the Territory That Did Not Fight.* Norman: University of Oklahoma Press, 2016.

McGinnis, Ralph Y., and Calvin N. Smith, eds. *Abraham Lincoln and the Western Territories.* Chicago: Nelson-Hall, 1994.

Morgan, Dale L. *Shoshonean Peoples and the Overland Trails: Frontiers of the Utah Superintendency of Indian Affairs, 1849–1869,* edited by Richard L. Saunders. Logan: Utah State University Press, 2008.

———. *The State of Deseret.* Logan: Utah State University Press with Utah State Historical Society, 1987.

Murphy, Miriam B. "Territorial Governors." In *Utah History Encyclopedia*, edited by Allan Kent Powell. Salt Lake City: University of Utah Press, 1994.

Neff, Andrew Love. *History of Utah: 1847 to 1869.* Salt Lake City: The Deseret News Press, 1940.

Peterson, John A. *Utah's Black Hawk War.* Salt Lake City: University of Utah Press, 1999.

Rawson, Glenn, and Dennis Lyman, eds. *The Mormon Wars.* American Fork, Utah: Covenant Communications, 2014.

Roberts, B. H. *A Comprehensive History of the Church of Jesus Christ of Latter-day Saints,* vol. 5. Provo, Utah: Brigham Young University Press, 1965.

Roberts, Robert B. *Encyclopedia of Historic Forts: The Military, Pioneer, and Trading Posts of the United States.* New York: Macmillan, 1988.

Schindler, Harold. *Orrin Porter Rockwell: Man of God, Son of Thunder.* Salt Lake City: University of Utah Press, 1966.

Seegmiller, Janet Burton. *Be Kind to the Poor: The Life Story of Robert Taylor Burton.* N.p.: Robert Taylor Burton Family Organization, 1988.

Sifakis, Stewart. *Who Was Who in the Civil War.* New York: Facts on File Publications, 1988.

Stansbury, Howard. *An Expedition to the Valley of the Great Salt Lake of Utah, including a Description of Its Geography, Natural History, and Minerals, and an Analysis of Its Waters; with an Authentic Account of the Mormon Settlement.* Philadelphia: Lippincott, Grambo, 1852.

Stenhouse, T. B. H. *The Rocky Mountain Saints.* London: Ward, Lock, and Tyler, 1874.

Thian, Raphael P. *Notes Illustrating the Military Geography of the United States: 1813–1880*, edited by John M. Carroll. Austin: University of Texas Press, 1979.

Tucker, Spencer C., ed. *American Civil War: The Definitive Encyclopedia and Document Collection.* Denver, Colo.: ABC-CLIO, 2013.

Tullidge, Edward W. *The History of Salt Lake City: By Authority of the City Council and under the Supervision of a Committee Appointed by the Council and Author.* Salt Lake City: Star Printing Company, 1886.

Turner, John G. *Brigham Young: Pioneer Prophet.* Cambridge, Mass.: The Belknap Press of Harvard University Press, 2012.

Urbanek, Mae B. *Wyoming Place Names.* Missoula, Mont.: Mountain Press, 1988.

Van Cott, John. *Utah Place Names.* Salt Lake City: University of Utah Press, 1990.

Van Wagoner, Richard S., ed. *The Complete Discourses of Brigham Young.* Salt Lake City: The Smith-Pettit Foundation, 2009.

Varley, James F. *Brigham and the Brigadier.* Tucson, Ariz.: Westernlore Press, 1989.

Vetterli, Richard. *Mormonism, Americanism and Politics.* Salt Lake City: Ensign Publications, 1961.

Waite, C. V. *The Mormon Prophet and His Harem; or, an Authentic History of Brigham Young, His Numerous Wives and Children.* Chicago: J. S. Goodman and Company, 1868.

Ware, Eugene F. *The Indian War of 1864.* New York: St. Martin's Press, 1960.

Welcher, Frank J. *The Union Army: 1861–1865. Organization and Operations. Volume II: The Western Theater.* Bloomington: Indiana University Press, 1993.

Whitney, Orson F. *Popular History of Utah.* Salt Lake City: Deseret News, 1916.

———. *The Making of the State: A School History of Utah.* Salt Lake City: Deseret News, 1908.

Woodger, Mary Jane. "Abraham Lincoln and the Mormons." In *Civil War Saints*, edited by Kenneth L. Alford, 61–81. Provo, Utah: Brigham Young University Religious Studies Center and Deseret Book Company, 2012.

Worcester, Joseph E. *Dictionary of the English Language.* Boston: Hickling, Swan, and Brewer, 1860.

Wright, John D. *The Language of the Civil War.* Westwood, Conn.: Greenwood Publishing Group, 2001.

Wright, Marcus J. "Records of the War Between the States." In *The Civil War through the Camera, Part I*, edited by Henry W. Elson. Springfield, Mass.: Patriot Publishing Company, 1912.

Young, Otis. E. *The West of Philip St. George Cooke: 1809–1895.* Glendale, Calif.: Arthur H. Clark, 1955.

Journals and Periodicals

Barnes, John P. "The Struggle to Control the Past: Commemoration, Memory, and the Bear River Massacre of 1863." *The Public Historian* 30 (February 2008): 81–104.

Beller, Jack. "Negro Slaves in Utah." *Utah Historical Quarterly* 2, no. 4 (1929): 122–126.

"Captain Lot Smith's Company of Volunteers." *The Utah Genealogical and Historical Magazine* (January 1911): 138–139.

Carter, Kate B. *Utah during Civil War Years: Lessons for March 1956.* Salt Lake City: Daughters of Utah Pioneers (March 1956), 373–432.

Childers, Christopher. "Interpreting Popular Sovereignty: A Historiographical Essay." *Civil War History* 57, no. 1 (March 2011): 48–70.

Etulain, Richard W. "A Virginian in Utah Chooses the Union: Col. Philip St. George Cooke in 1861." *Utah Historical Quarterly* 42, no. 4 (October 1974): 381–385.

"Extract of a Letter from Hon. W. H. Hooper." William H. Hooper to George Q. Cannon, December 16, 1860. *Millennial Star* 23, no. 2 (January 12, 1861): 29–30.

Fisher, Albert L. "Boundaries and Utah: Sense or Nonsense?" *Encyclia, The Journal of the Utah Academy of Sciences, Arts, and Letters* 56 (1979): 127–133.

Hampton, H. D. "The Powder River Expedition 1865." *Montana: The Magazine of Western History* 14, no. 2 (1964): 2–15.

Hewett, Janet B. "Updating the Documentary History of the U.S. Civil War: The Supplement to the Official Records of the Union and Confederate Armies." *Journal of Government Information* 26, no. 1 (1999): 43–55.

Hubbard, George H. "Abraham Lincoln as Seen by the Mormons." *Utah Historical Quarterly* 31 (Spring 1963): 91–108.

Lythgoe, Dennis L. "Negro Slavery in Utah." *Utah Historical Quarterly* 30, no. 1 (1971): 40–54.

MacKinnon, William P. "125 Years of Conspiracy Theories: Origins of the Utah Expedition of 1857–58." *Utah Historical Quarterly* 52, no. 3 (Summer 1984): 212–230.

———. "'Like Splitting a Man Up His Backbone': The Territorial Dismemberment of Utah, 1850–1896." *Utah Historical Quarterly* 71, no. 2 (Spring 2003): 100–124.

News Department. "Journal of Indian Treaty Days." *Washington Historical Quarterly* 11, no. 1 (January 1920): 75–76.

Orton, Chad M. "'We Will Admit You as a State': William H. Hooper, Utah and the Secession Crisis." *Utah Historical Quarterly* 80, no. 3 (2012): 208–225.

Rich, Christopher B., Jr. "The True Policy for Utah: Servitude, Slavery, and 'An Act in Relation to Service.'" *Utah Historical Quarterly* 80, no. 1 (2012): 54–74.

Robinett, Paul M., and Howard V. Canan. "Military Career of James Craig." *Missouri Historical Review* 66, no. 1 (1971): 49–75.

Robrock, David P. "The Eleventh Ohio Volunteer Cavalry on the Central Plains, 1862–1866." *Arizona and the West* 25, no. 1 (Spring 1983): 23–48.

Schindler, Harold. "The Bear River Massacre: New Historical Evidence." *Utah Historical Quarterly* 67, no.4 (Fall 1999): 300–308.

Sternhell, Yael A. "The Afterlives of a Confederate Archive: Civil War Documents and the Making of Sectional Reconciliation." *Journal of American History* 102, no. 4 (March 2016): 1025–1050.

"The Union Vedette." *Pioneer* 59, no. 3 (2012): 16–17.

Young, Seymour B. "Lest We Forget: I. John Brown." *Improvement Era* 25, no. 1 (November 1921): 61–63.

———. "Lest We Forget: II. Abraham Lincoln." *Improvement Era* 25, no. 2 (December 1921): 115–119.

———. "Lest We Forget: III. Abraham Lincoln (continued)." *Improvement Era* 25, no. 3 (January 1922): 259–262.

———. "Lest We Forget: IV. The Incident of Mason and Slidell." *Improvement Era* 25, no. 4 (February 1922): 334–338.

———. "Lest We Forget: VI. What Utah Stood for in the Civil War." *Improvement Era* 25, no. 5 (March 1922): 420–423.

———. "Lest We Forget: VII. The Snake River Expedition." *Improvement Era* 25, no. 7 (May 1922): 608–614.

———. "Lest We Forget: VIII. The Snake River Expedition (Continued)," *Improvement Era* 25, no. 8 (June 1922): 722–726.

———. "Lest We Forget: IX. Captain Lot Smith." *Improvement Era* 25, no. 10 (August 1922): 900–903.

———. "Lest We Forget: X. Captain Lot Smith (Concluded)." *Improvement Era* 25, no. 11 (September 1922): 1005–1008.

Online Resources

"1860 U.S. Census, Schedule 2—Slave Inhabitants, June 13, 1860." *Ancestry.com.* http://search.ancestry.com.

"Act of Congress (1861) Organizing the Territory of Nevada." http://www.leg.state.nv.us/Division/Research/Library/Documents/HistDocs/1861Act.pdf.

"Bowery." *This Is the Place Heritage Park.* http://www.thisistheplace.org/heritage_village/buildings/bowery.html.

Collaborative International Dictionary of English v.0.48. http://onlinedictionary.datasegment.com.

Collins English Dictionary—Complete & Unabridged 10th Edition. HarperCollins Publishers. http://dictionary.reference.com.

Dawson, John W. "Governor's Message to the Legislative Assembly of Utah. December 10, 1861." https://archive.org/details/govemesslegislatooutahrich.

Dictionary.com Unabridged. Random House, Inc. http://dictionary.reference.com.

"Glossary of Civil War Terms." *Civil War Trust.* http://www.civilwar.org/education/history/glossary/glossary.html.

HeinOnline. http://www.heinonline.org/.

Legal Dictionary. *The Free Dictionary Online.* http://legal-dictionary.thefreedictionary.com.

MacMillan Dictionary Online. http://www.macmillandictionary.com.

Merriam-Webster Dictionary Online. http://www.merriam-webster.com.

Morgan, James. "Mounted But Not Mounted: The Confusing Terminology of Artillery." *Civil War Artillery Terminology.* http://www.civilwarhome.com/artilleryterms.html.

Mormon Migration Database. http://mormonmigration.lib.byu.edu.

Princeton University. *WordNet 3.0,* 2006. http://wordnet.princeton.edu.

"Transcript of Compromise of 1850." U.S. National Archives & Records Administration. http://www.ourdocuments.gov/doc.php?doc=27&page=transcript#no-2.

"Utah Digital Newspapers." http://digitalnewspapers.org.

Utah State Historical Society. "The Stephen Selwyn Harding Papers, 1862–1901." http://heritage.utah.gov/apps/history/findaids/B00029/B0029.xml.

"Washakie (Shoshoni chief)." *Encyclopedia Britannica Online.* http://www.britannica.com/EBchecked/topic/636280/Washakie.

Weiser, Kathy, ed. "Old West Legends: Adventures in the American West." *Legends of America.* http://www.legendsofamerica.com.

Index

Abbreviation "U.T." stands for Utah Territory.
Refer to Appendix H for a complete alphabetical listing of
Senders and Receivers of *Official Records* and Utah Territorial Records.

Abbot (Private), 294–95
Adobe Meadows, 157, 159
African Americans
  colored troops, 558, 575
  free colored of arms-bearing age, 213–15
  Utah census of 1860, 40, 40n24
  See also slaves/slavery
Alabama, 24, 30, 31, 63–64, 131, 214
Alexander, E. B., 140, 141
Alexander, Moroni Wood, 624, 658
Allen (Lieutenant), 248
Allen, A., 299–300
Allen, James, 21
Allen, L., 445
Allen, N. E., 757–58
Allen, William C., 624, 658–59
Alvord, Benjamin
  commander, District of Oregon, 148, 176, 298, 336–37, 347
  creation of Montana Territory, 382–83
  establishment of Fort Boisé, 275, 314–15
  expedition against Snake Indians, 212, 262, 318–20
  exploration of Three Forks area, 358–59, 371–72
  forming volunteer companies, 204, 229–30, 235
  Indian peace treaties, 282, 293
  Indian policy/actions against, 177, 363, 376–77
  protection of emigrants and miners, 269–70, 352–53, 359, 361–62, 369
  relations with Nez Perce, 181–82
  request for reinforcements, 352
Amboy, Illinois, 770
Ammond, George R., 757–58
A'mone, Matthew, 692
Anderson (Dr.), 698
Anderson (General), 89
Anderson, Allen L., 445
Anderson, J., 692
Anderson, John C., 479
Anderson, Lewis, 685, 691
Anderson, Robert, 588
Angles (prisoner), 641
annual reports
  about inclusion in the records, 65, 67
  1861 U.S. militia, 134–36
  1862 Commissioner of Indian Affairs, 609–10, 663–65
  1863 Commissioner of Indian Affairs, 707–8
  1863 Union Army annual report, 63
  1865 Chief Medical Officer, 744–46
  1865 Department of the Interior, 448
  1865 Quartermaster's Office, 555–58, 565–68
  1865 Secretary of War, 574–75
  See also Record of Events
Ansley, Siradge, 692
Antero (Ute Chief), 303
Apache Indians, 572
Apache Pass, 178
Arapaho Indians, 52n108, 285, 436
Arizona Territory
  Civil War engagements, 64
  Confederate presence/sympathies, 332

Arizona Territory *(continued)*
deployment of troops to, 84, 94, 118, 145, 148, 175, 180, 183, 230
Fort Mojave expedition, 29
Indian expeditions, 445
Indian hostilities, 304
military units, Civil War, 15n1
mines/mining, 391
mustering out the troops, 572, 574
protection of emigrant and mail roads, 564
reoccupation by U.S. troops, 344–45, 369
reorganization of military districts, 718
summary of military operations, 446
suppression of rebellion, 170–71
Arkansas
Civil War engagements, 64
deployment of Army troops, 453
emigration to escape war, 524
population, 123, 214
Quantrill raids, 421, 433
reorganization of military district, 374, 446, 477, 545, 558
secession from the Union, 25
Arkansas River, 123, 323, 325, 439, 468, 512, 549, 559–60, 564
Armistead (Lieutenant), 583–84
Armistead (Major), 118
Armstrong, George, 479
Arny, William Frederick Milton, 199
Arrowsmith, John, 625, 658–59
Ashley, D. R., 421
Atkinson [Atchison], Isaac, 624, 658
Atlas to Accompany the Official Records of the Union and Confederate Armies, 64
Atwood [Attwood], Richard H., 480–81, 623, 630, 633, 639, 641, 654–56
Au-ke-wah-kus (Ute Chief), 303
Austin, A. J., 685, 692
Austin, Nevada Territory, 421–22, 443, 757
Austine (Major), 127
Ayers, Z. G., 115

Babbitt, Edwin Burr, 147, 154, 161–62, 208, 216, 219
Backus (Captain), 141
Bagley, William, 625
Bailey, A. L., 692
Baird, A., 604
Baker, Eugene M., 110–12
Baker, J. A., 596
Baker, J. H., 512
Baker, John E., 685
Baldwin, James W., 684, 691
Baldwin, Noyes, 379, 478, 483, 485, 712, 737
Baldwin road [trail], 751
Baltimore and Ohio Railroad, 133
Banks (General), 89
Banks (hospital steward), 600
Banks, J. S., 100
Banks, James A., 758
Bannock City, 276, 280, 282, 319, 705
Bannock Indians
capture of emigrant boy, 190–93
defined/identified, 775
expeditions against, 193–94
hostilities following Army withdrawal, 43
hostilities on emigrant and mail routes, 138, 178, 636–37
peace treaties, 29, 306, 318, 329
Bannock Mines, 282, 341
Barbele (Private), 691
Barcafar, Thaddeus, 685, 691
Barker, John E., 692
Barlow, James S. Madison, 623, 633–34
Barnard, A. D., 229
Barnard, Lachoneus, 625, 658
Barnes, J. W., 466–67, 470–71, 477, 491
Barse, W. H., 128–29
Battese (mountaineer), 643–44
Battle Creek, Indian attack at, 699–701
Battle of Spanish Fork. *See* Spanish Fork Cañon Expedition
Battle of the Little Big Horn, 56–57n137
Battron (Private), 596
Baurland, John, 692
Baylor, John R., 118
Beach, Walter P., 129
Beach, William L., 692
Beall (secessionist), 97
Bear-Hunter (Snake chief), 190–91, 211, 680, 690, 730
Bear River, ferry crossing, 277, 296, 653
Bear River massacre
attack by Connor's forces, 28, 51–52, 52n107, 64n3, 78
celebrating the anniversary, 714–18, 743
Connor promotion for, 28, 52, 241–42, 697
description of, 208–12, 472, 682–94, 792
Deseret News account, 52, 681, 683–85
killed and wounded, 225, 683, 694, 746
reporting the outcome, 55, 217–19, 222, 270, 682–83, 687, 730–31
Beauregard, P. G. T., 41, 126
Beaver and Reese River Road, 376

Beaver City, 387–88, 390
Beaver County/Beaver Creek, 59n148, 152, 389, 419
Beaver Head (Beaverhead) country/mines, 208, 260, 319, 358, 382, 385, 393, 425, 730
Becker, Fred W., 692
Bell, Joseph McC., 474, 514, 516, 521, 533, 545, 557, 565
Benavides (Colonel), 346
Benicia Barracks and Arsenal, 126, 137, 146, 158, 223, 245, 298, 428
Bennett, Clarence E., 98–100, 113, 115
Bennett, William, 692
Bennion, John R., 624, 658
Bennion, Samuel R., 624, 658
Bernhisel, John M., 44, 46, 611, 677
Berry, David J., 209, 376, 380, 682, 685, 688, 690, 694, 696
Bess, William, 625
Bettis (Mrs.), 97
Bevins, William, 680–81
Bigelow, B. B., 692
Big Horn Mountains, 560, 562–63
Big Horn River, 56–57n137, 352, 486, 564
Bigler, Andrew, 623, 634, 658, 661
Big Pond Station, 752–53
Big Sandy Station, 192–93, 292, 411, 630, 639–40, 648–49, 651
Billig, Charles, 483
Bird, Henry N., 625, 658
Bitter Root Mountains, 85, 361–62
Bivan's Gulch, 358, 361
Black (Colonel), 369
Black, David, 253, 276, 299, 348, 392, 696
Black Buttes Station, 752–53
Blackfoot Creek, 278–79, 318
Blackfoot Indians, 85, 164, 455, 463
Black Hawk (Ute Chief), 303, 793
Black Hawk Indian War, 30, 58–59, 59n148
Black Hawk War of 1832, 58
Black Hills, 497, 503, 512, 560, 562
Black Mountains, 387
Blacks Fork, 629
Blair, Montgomery P., 178, 665
Blake, George A. H., 110–12
Blenker (officer), 125
Blunt, James G., 149–51, 164
Bodine, George, 500
Boger (Sergeant), 596, 600, 652
Bogert, C., 100
Boisé City, 494
Boisé Mines, 203, 282, 327, 341
Boisé River, 86, 185, 379, 396. *See also* Fort Boisé
The Book of Mormon, 36n5, 45n55
Booth, John Wilkes, 30
Boren (Judge), 98, 100
Bouralso, F., 692
Bowie (Colonel), 138
Bowman, Isabella, 33
Box Elder (Brigham City)/ Box Elder Valley, 28, 276–77, 308, 351, 702–3
Bradley, James, 264, 266–67, 279, 696
Bradley, Thomas, 685
Brady, Hugene J., 692
Brandley, Henry, 299
Bremer (Lieutenant), 430
Bretney, Henry C., 493–94, 499
Bridger, Joseph, 97
Bridger's Pass, 488
Briggs, John K., 684, 691
"Brigham Young Office Files . . . ," 626–27, 647–49, 652–54, 655–56
Brigham Young University, 11–12
Bringhurst, William A., 623, 634, 658
Briston, David, 692
Brochus, Perry E., 680
Brooks, J. W., 108–9
Brouch, F., 692
Brown (General), 89
Brown (secessionist), 96–97
Brown (Sergeant), 268
Brown, A., 175
Brown, Albert, 259, 272, 283, 284, 457, 461, 477, 483, 487, 732–33
Brown, Dee, 59
Brown, Edwin, 624, 658–59
Brown, James A., 493, 499–500
Brown, John, 23, 742
Brown, Richard, 421
Brown's Hole, 380
Buchanan, James, 22–23, 37–38, 41, 41n30, 801
Buckner, Simon B., 31
Buell, D. C., 93, 98, 102, 104
Buffalo soldiers, 558, 585
Burgess (Dr.), 420
Burgess, Henry Volney (aka Charles Hart, aka William Quantrill), 419–20
Burgher (Private), 294–95
Burnham, Charles C., 625, 658–59
Burt (Mr.), 702
Burton (Major), 127
Burton, Robert T.
  call to militia service, 26, 612–15
  capture of Joseph Morris, 26, 49

Burton, Robert T. *(continued)*
  commander, Nauvoo Legion First Cavalry Regiment, 46
  correspondence, mentions in, 617, 633, 635–36
  dealing with Morrisite insurrection, 49
  Deseret News reporting on, 636–37, 641–47
  Governor Fuller correspondence to/from, 636–37
  protection of mail routes, 46, 46n66
  report of march, 642–45
  return, 637, 641, 646–47
  serving on the Overland Trail, 615
  trial for murder of Isabella Bowman, 33
Bush, Silas C., 685, 692
Butler (General), 89
Butler (secessionist), 129
Buxton (Sergeant), 193

Cabanis (Lieutenant), 364–65
Cache Cave, 629
Cache la Poudre, 451, 563
Cache Valley Expedition
  departure for/Indian skirmish, 27, 78
  orders for/report on, 190–92, 200, 276–80, 675–76
  Stansbury Expedition (1849–51), 21
Cady (Lt. Colonel), 147
Cahoon, John, 625, 658
Calder, Joseph W., 483
Caldwell, J. H., 235
Caldwell, Samuel, 692
Caldwell, Thomas, 625, 658, 661
Caldwell, W. H., 500
California
  authorization to raise volunteers, 109
  Civil War engagements, 64
  Compromise of 1850, 21, 36, 40n25, 801
  Indian removal to reservations, 316, 333–34
  secessionist presence/sympathies, 83–84, 96–105, 114–16
  See also Department of California; Department of the Pacific
California Volunteers. *See* military units, California
Calkin, Theodore J., 625, 658
Camas Prairie, 275, 311, 318–21, 327, 384, 396, 409, 475, 494
Cameron, Simon, 80, 83, 86–88, 91–92, 107–9, 117, 122, 125, 583–84, 590
Camp Albert, 149
Camp Alvord, 410
Camp Babbitt, 257, 259, 342, 372
Campbell (Judge), 97
Camp C. F. Jackson, 75, 81
Camp Cady, 144
Camp Collins, 297, 501, 509, 543, 553
Camp Conness, 392, 732
Camp Connor
  Camp Douglas headquarters relocation, 310
  establishment of the post, 296
  mineral deposits, 340
  officers and troops assigned, 298–99, 347–48, 392, 406, 415, 424, 461–62, 483, 731
  organization of military districts, 463, 806–7
  Shoshone peace treaty, 340–41
  withdrawal of troops, 458–59
  See also Soda Springs
Camp Douglas
  area defined, 672, 677
  arrival of California Volunteers, 669–73
  arrival of Nevada Cavalry, 330, 375, 712–13, 728
  arrival of Second Cavalry, 314, 367
  arrival of Sixth Infantry, 756
  burial of J. D. Doty, 501
  communications, District of Utah, 190, 192–93, 202–3, 220–21, 256, 372, 379–80, 381, 393–94, 422, 432, 442–43, 460, 463–64, 713
  communications, Second Cavalry, 185–87, 190–92, 386–90
  communications, Third Infantry, 222–26, 229, 231–33, 236–38
  departure of the "Gallant Third," 750–52
  discharges and reenlistments, 746–48, 758
  establishing and naming, 27, 50–51, 77, 183–84, 694–96, 726, 744–46, 806
  expeditions during 1862–63, 77
  expedition to Cache Valley, 190–92, 200, 675–76
  expedition to Fort Mojave, 728–29
  headquarters, West Sub-District of the Plains, 476, 484–87, 752–53, 807
  Indian expeditions, 249–55, 264–68, 375–76, 378–80, 704, 792–93
  officers and troops assigned, 206, 298–99, 342, 347–48, 373, 392, 400, 403, 406, 431, 457, 461–62, 478–79, 483, 491, 695–96, 731–32, 736
  as *Official Record* keyword, 74, 77
  Order (No. 51), 712
  organization of military districts, 747
  Post Orders, 672, 677, 715–16, 719–20
  Post Returns, 673–76, 682–83, 694, 728, 737
  protection of mines and settlements, 360–62, 371, 720–21
  protection/opening of roads, 256–60, 276–80, 352–53, 367–68, 432–36, 447, 454, 457, 482,

705, 723
publication of *Union Vedette*, 29, 712
reinforcing the garrison, 148, 223, 244, 246, 261, 283–84, 287–91, 406–8, 415–16, 424, 426, 458
relationship with Indians, 393, 443–44, 461, 722
relationship with Mormons, 312, 315, 348–51, 353–58, 364, 393–95, 396–400, 403–6, 726–27, 734–36
Camp Fillmore, 465
Camp Fitzgerald, 93–94, 102, 104, 114–16. *See also* Los Angeles
Camp Floyd. *See* Fort Crittenden
Camp Halleck. *See* Fort (Camp) Halleck
Camp Highland, 793
Camp Latham, 132, 144, 332. *See also* Los Angeles
Camp Lincoln, 162, 571
Camp Mitchell, 509
Camp Union, 195, 246, 258, 285, 298–99, 426–27, 489, 491
Camp Wild, 141
Canby, E. R. S., 82, 89, 123, 148, 176
Cannon, George Q., 45, 58
Canosh (Ute Chief), 303
Cantillon (Cantellon), James, 684, 691, 692, 694
Cantwell, Francis R., 625, 658–59
Carleton (General), 147–48, 166, 175–76, 183, 199, 350, 468, 505
Carleton, G. W., 449
Carleton, James H. (Colonel/General), 109–10, 126–27, 132–33, 136–39, 143, 145, 147–48, 166, 175–76, 178–79, 183, 199, 308, 332, 350, 371, 468, 505, 603–4
Carleton, James H. (Major), 93–98, 102–6, 332, 600–601
Carleton, William, 692
Carney, Peter, 624
Carrigan, James, 658–59
Carson, C., 307–8
Carson City, Nevada Territory, 43, 111, 145, 154, 161, 175, 258, 280, 329–30, 386, 389, 697
Carson Valley/Carson River, 92, 111, 139, 153, 290, 304, 329
Carter (Judge), 106–7
Cascade Mountains, 352, 377
Case, A. J., 691
Cavalry Tactics . . . (Cooke), 582
Cedar City, 380, 387–88
Cedar Fort, 78, 249–51, 254, 390, 706
Cedar Mountains/Cedar Valley, 28, 78, 249–51, 254, 805–6
Cedar Mountains Expedition, 78, 254–55
Cedar Swamp, 376, 380
Chalk Creek, 629, 632
Chambers, Roland, 235
Chapman, Joseph, 692
Chapman, Nathaniel, 692
Charlot, C. S., 435
Chase, Darwin, 186–87, 209, 218, 682, 685, 688–89, 692–94, 792
Chase, E. C., 691
Cherokee Indians, 59n149, 123–24, 325, 455
Cherry, Jesse J., 625, 658
Cheyenne, Wyo., 563
Cheyenne Indians, 43, 43n44, 52n108, 150, 285, 436, 452, 486, 505, 546, 653, 664, 765
Chickasaw Indians, 455
Chivington, John Milton, 286, 299, 322–24, 431, 435, 505, 512
Choctaw Indians, 87, 455
Chouteau (Mr.), 362
Church of Christ, 770
Church of Jesus Christ of Latter-day Saints
The Book of Mormon, 36n6, 45n55
Doctrine and Covenants, 39–40, 40n23
founding and relocation to Utah, 36, 36n6
See also Mormon/Mormonism
Church History Library, 12, 626–27, 647–49, 652–56
Circulars
defined, 765
military report requirements, 557–58
promotion of mining, 711–12
protection of settlements and mining, 360–61, 366
soldier commendations, 717–18
threats against miners, 720–21
treatment of Utah residents, 726–28
voiding discharges and re-enlistments, 747–48
City of Rocks, 173, 185, 371, 375–76, 379
Civil War
collection/publication of military records, 15–16, 29, 63–66
Jefferson Davis, capture of, 31
Lincoln assassination, 58, 584
Lincoln conspirators hanged, 31
as Mormon prophecy, 39
New York draft riots, 29
Proclamation 157, 32
Reconstruction era, 29
Second Confiscation Act of 1862, 170–71
Sherman's "march to the sea," 30
surrender of Confederate forces, 30, 31, 58, 477
Utah Territory role, 35–36, 47–50, 662. *See also* secession/secessionist movement

The Civil War: A Narrative (Foote), 41n31
Civil War battles
battle count by state/territory, 63–64
Battle of Antietam, 27
Battle of Atlanta, 29
Battle of Chancellorsville, 28
Battle of Chickamauga, 29
Battle of First Manassas, 25
Battle of Fort Sumter, 25
Battle of Fredericksburg, 27
Battle of Gettysburg, 29
Battle of Nashville, 30
Battle of Palmito Ranch, 31
Battle of Second Manassas, 27
Battle of Shiloh, 26
Battle of the Crater, 29
capture of Mobile, 30
capture of New Orleans, 26
capture of Richmond and Petersburg, 30
capture of Savannah, 30
Siege of Vicksburg, 28–29
Civil War Saints (Alford, ed.), 16, 35n2
The Civil War Years in Utah (Maxwell), 35n2
Clark, Cyrus D., 186, 209, 264–68, 277–80, 696
Clark, Joseph C., 106, 596, 599–600, 603–4, 682, 690, 694
Clary, R. E., 583–94, 598
Clawson, Hiram B., 645
Clemens, O., 247
Clemons, Hiram B., 623, 634, 658
Clows, Joseph, 691
Cocke, Philip St. George, 580n
Cole, N., 53n104, 503, 509, 529, 560–62, 565
Colfax, Schuyler, 31, 487, 749
The Collected Works of Abraham Lincoln, 75, 615–16
Collins, W. W., 691
Collins, William O., 50, 152, 300, 323, 457, 640–41, 649–50, 652–53, 655, 793–94
Colorado River, 132–33, 332, 367, 386, 390–91, 472
Colorado Territory
Army withdrawal to the East, 83
authorization to raise volunteers, 163–65
Civil War engagements, 64
Confederate presence/sympathies, 123, 199, 602
created from part of Utah, 24, 37, 801
deployment of troops, 296–97, 452–53, 549–51, 557, 605
deployment of troops to Utah, 321–24
Indian expeditions, 132–33, 436–42, 535
Indian hostilities, 107, 150, 164, 299–300, 431
Indian peace treaties, 323
Indian policy, 465
male population, white/black, 214–15
mines/mining, 564
Navajo Expedition, 307–8
opening of new roads, 367
protection of emigrant and mail roads, 59, 435, 451, 502
quartermaster supplies sent, 325
raising volunteer companies, 48n76, 165, 274
reorganization of military districts, 82–83, 285–86, 446, 449–50, 464–66, 469, 476, 507–8, 512, 516, 533, 545, 554, 569, 748, 804–5, 807
request for troops, 107, 113–14
road survey/construction/repair, 482, 563
secessionist presence/sympathies, 123
statehood, 56n137, 62n164
summary of military operations, 446
supplies sent to, 325, 559, 566
See also military units, Colorado
Colorado Territory Expedition, 438–40
Columbia River, 137, 205, 277
Comanche Indians, 323, 337, 370, 455, 765
Command Lists, 72–73, 206, 298–99, 347–48, 392, 461–62, 483
Commissioner of Indian Affairs, 75, 113, 377, 527, 610, 663–64, 707–8
Community of Christ (Reorganized Church of Jesus Christ of Latter-day Saints), 770
The Company Clerk (Kautz), 72
A Compendium of the War of Rebellion (Dyer), 809
Compromise of 1850, 21, 36, 40n25, 801
Comstock (mine), Nevada Territory, 391
Comstock, C. B., 485
Confederate States of America
Army officer appointments, 580–81
Indian peace treaties, 123–24
secession of U.S. states to, 24–25
use of Indians as fighters, 455
See also secession/secessionist movement
Connor, Hou, 691
Connor, Hugh, 685
Connor, Patrick Edward
Bear River massacre, 51–52, 217–19, 222, 241–51, 270, 686–94, 697
command of District of the Plains, 446, 449, 466, 469–74, 476, 479, 483, 485–87, 536, 545, 548, 748, 807
command of District of Utah, 27, 77, 156–60, 172–74, 206–7, 298, 343–44, 347, 373, 392, 429, 461, 463–64, 554, 715–18, 720–21, 806
death and burial, 62
establishing Camp Douglas, 672–75, 694–96
Indian policy/actions against, 55n130, 185–90,

201, 286–87, 408–9, 461, 487–88, 492, 495, 501, 546–48, 552–53, 681–85, 703–5, 742
Indian treaties, 281–82, 293, 308–9, 311, 319, 337, 343, 722, 730–31
leave of absence, 432, 441–43
mentions in records, 143, 165–66, 169–71, 262, 264, 301, 373, 384, 453, 510, 512–14, 792
military service, 49n83
occupation of Fort Bridger, 196–98
operations in Colorado Territory, 438–40
ordered to Utah, 26, 27, 49–51, 145–51, 154–55
orders/instructions, 239, 271–72, 275–76, 296, 302, 317–18, 366–67, 369, 372, 375–76, 378–80, 410, 426–27, 431, 457–60, 462, 467–68, 478, 480, 503, 517–18, 551–52, 560–65, 675–77, 709–15, 732–33, 747–48
Powder River Expedition, 52n108, 512–15, 520–22, 538–39, 543, 553
promotion to brigadier general, 28, 52, 222, 697, 722
protection of emigrants and mail, 200, 256–57, 276–80, 295, 348–50, 432–36, 448, 457–60, 482, 510, 738–39, 795
raising new companies, 429–30
reinforcement of the command, 226, 230, 254–55, 259–61, 269, 283, 297–98, 321, 491–92, 496–99, 509–10
relationship/views on Mormonism, 52–58, 208–11, 220–21, 226, 231, 254–56, 264, 276–79, 283, 295, 301–6, 338–40, 351, 393–407, 412, 726–28, 734–36
relationship with Brigham Young, 57–58, 62, 202–3, 233–34, 236–38, 242–43, 259–61, 287–91, 354–56, 396–98, 405, 471–73, 490
relocation to Salt Lake City, 156–60, 171–72, 176, 179–80, 353, 364
reoccupation of Fort Crittenden, 310, 315, 666–72
Conrad (Mr.), 388–89
Conrad, George D., 186–87, 191, 209, 251–52, 386, 483, 676, 682, 690, 694, 696, 716, 729
Cook (Mr./Lieutenant), 248, 308, 411
Cook, Frederick, 609–10
Cooke, Philip St. George, 99, 113, 603
charges of disloyalty, 75, 580, 583–94
closure of Fort Crittenden, 595–600, 806
commander, Department of the Platte, 575
commander, Department of Utah, 89, 803, 805–6
departure for Fort Leavenworth, 595, 602, 804n3, 805
departure from Fort Bridger, 25, 42, 43n42, 596, 597, 599–600, 603
diverting troops to Colorado, 602, 605
false report as Confederate officer, 580
loyalty to the Union, 583–84
Mexican War service, 42n35
native of Virginia, 125, 586, 594
post-Utah service, 608
promotion to brigadier general, 125, 608
publication of cavalry tactics manual, 581–82
troop request from Colorado, 602, 605
Cooler (Mr.), 445
Cooper, S., 455–56
Cornelius (Colonel), 136–37
Corney, P., 658, 661
Corning, Erastus, 80–81
Correspondence in the *Official Records*, explained, 68–70
Coryell (Captain), 495
Cotterel (Cotterell), George, 624, 658–59
Cottonwood, U.T., 419, 452, 468–69, 497–98, 509, 532, 546–47, 554, 560
Cottonwood Creek, 638
courts-martial, 174, 209, 225, 535, 572. *See also* discipline, military
Courts of Inquiry, 709–10
Covert, Evert, 624
Cox, George C., 174, 685, 691
Cox, Martha Cragun, 60
Cradlebaugh, John, 757
Craft, Stewart Britton, 621
Cragun, James H., 624
Craig, James, 46, 49–50, 50n95, 162–63, 638–40, 647–50, 665, 793
Craigie (Mr.), 86
Crawford (Mr.), 136–37
Crawford, Medorum, 184–85, 212, 270, 313, 319, 337
Creek Indians, 455
Creighton, E., 239
Crenshaw, J. R., 581
Crisman, Charles, Jr., 625, 658, 662
Crist, J. M., 660
Crosby (Judge), 583
Crosby, Oscar (slave), 40n25
Crosman, J. S., 757–58
Crow Indians, 150, 359, 463, 645, 659
CSS *Shenandoah*, 31
Cuidado (pseudonym), 725
Cullen, John, 691
Cumming, Alfred, 23, 25, 42–43, 236, 238, 581, 586
Currey (Captain), 364–65, 370, 384, 396, 410
Curtis, N. Greene, 84
Curtis, S. S., 415, 419

Curtis, Samuel R., 107–8, 138, 273, 298, 347, 361, 374, 382, 411, 415, 419, 430, 433, 437, 441–42, 444, 447, 450, 555
Custer, George A., 56–57n137
Cutts, A. S., 131

Daily Alta California, 54
Daily Union Vedette
about inclusion in UT records, 75
"Arrival," 736
"By Pacific Telegraph," 736
"Camp No. 6, Platte Expedition," 741–42
"Chief Medical Officer's Report," 744–46
"Circular," 717–18, 720–21, 726–28
"Company L, Second Cavalry, C.V.," 733
"Confirmation of General Connor by the Senate," 722
"Correspondence" (from the Gallant Third), 750–52
correspondence, Captain Lybe to Colonel George, 733
"A Familiar Epistle to Brother Brigham," 723–25
"From Company M, 2d Cavalry, C. C.," 716
"General Orders No. 7, 725
"General Orders No. 1," 713, 746–48
"Gold Mined on the New Road to Denver," 753–54
"How Salt Lake Is Commanded," 726
"Indian Policy in Utah - Restoration of Stolen Livestock," 730–31
"The Indian Troubles East," 737
"Indian Visitor to Camp Douglas," 722
"Interment of the Remains of the Slain Soldiers," 723
"Letter to the Editor," 743
"Loyalty of General Wright," 718–19
"The Loyalty of Utah," 743–44
"New Daily Calls," 719–20
"Program of Celebration To-day," 715–16
"Salt Lake and Fort Mojave W.R. Expedition," 728–29
"Sixth Infantry U.S. Volunteers at Fort Bridger to Camp Douglas," 756
"Special Order No. 9," 714
"Special Order No. 28," 752–53
"Special Order No. 53," 732
"Uinta Valley and Middle Park Expedition," 754–56
"Whereabouts of the Companies of the Command in Utah," 731–32
See also Union Vedette
Dakota Territory
Civil War engagements, 64
emigration and trade, 513–14
Grasshopper Gold Mines, 681
Indian expeditions, 535
male population, white/black, 214–15
military units, Civil War, 15n1
organization of military district, 476, 515, 533, 545, 549, 554, 557, 569, 575, 804, 807
Overland Trail, 42
as part of Indian Territory, 769
statehood, 62n164
summary of events, 446n
Daley, John, 685, 692
Dalton, John H., 483
Danites (Destroying Angels), 95, 666–68, 766
Dave (soldier), 286
Davidson, George W., 625
Davidson, John W., 98, 102, 104–5, 114–16
Davis, Alberto, 625
Davis, George B., 64–65
Davis, Jefferson, 24, 31, 75, 81, 123, 238, 397, 417
Davis, William, 685, 691, 692
Davis County, 40n24
Dawson, John W., 25, 43–44, 44n51
"Dean Mountain Jack," 420
Deer Creek Station, 636–37, 644–45, 794
Denver, J. W., 138, 140
Department of Annapolis, 89
Department of Arkansas, 374, 446, 477, 545, 558
Department of California, 78n–79, 101, 507–8, 571–73, 805
Department of Columbia, 508, 544, 573
Department of Florida, 89
Department of New Mexico, 82, 89, 123, 178, 307–8, 350, 445
Department of Northeastern Virginia, 89
Department of the East, 89, 570
Department of the Mississippi/Military Division of the Mississippi, 31, 141, 523, 535, 540, 549–50
Department of the Missouri
about, history/role of, 807
celebrating surrender of Confederate forces, 477
commanding officers, 273, 511, 807
dispatching troops to Utah, 272
headquarters relocation, 464–65
Indian expeditions, 461, 467, 480, 487, 504–7
investigation of Order of American Knights, 413
Mormon relations, 496
officers and troops assigned, 497–98, 509–10, 557

operations in Kansas and the Territories, 559–65
organizational boundary, 78, 446, 455
personnel/disciplinary issues, 510, 514–15
Pope as commander, 804
Powder River Expedition, 511–14
reduction of forces/mustering out, 517–18, 523, 527–33
reorganization of military districts, 446, 467–69, 516, 533, 549–50, 559, 569, 804, 806
Schofield as commander, 273, 322–23
status of issues in the department, 523–27
Department of the Northwest, 446
Department of the Ohio, 89
Department of the Pacific
about, history/role of, 805–6
Civil War, disloyalty issues, 302, 417–18, 718
Civil War, raising troops for service, 182–83, 234, 247, 258–59, 344–45, 416, 428–29, 440–41
commanding officers, 804
dispatching troops to Arizona, 144–45
establishment of Fort Boisé, 203–4
Indian expeditions/peace treaties, 218–19, 222, 264, 281, 333–34, 343, 359, 411, 443
McDowell as commander, 57, 89, 804
Mormon relations, 234, 242–43, 301, 343, 364, 401–2, 412
notification of Second Confiscation Act, 170–71
occupation of Fort Bridger, 196–98
officer assignments/reassignments, 160, 241, 314, 342, 373, 400, 403–4, 416, 713
organization of troops, 206, 298–99, 347–48, 392
personnel present for duty, 89
protection of emigrants and mail roads, 136–39, 143, 150–51, 178–80, 200–201, 494, 795
protection of settlements and miners, 366, 369, 371
reoccupation of Fort Crittenden, 310, 315
reorganization of military districts, 317, 478, 491, 508, 747, 803, 805
status of affairs in Utah, 309
status of affairs in western Territories, 175–76, 262, 316–17, 329–30, 378, 544
Sumner as commander, 101, 804
troop movements in California, 195
Utah, California Volunteers arrival, 157–58, 165–66, 171, 180, 188
Utah, dispatching troops to, 43, 46, 92, 126–28, 130, 145–49, 196, 207, 226, 230, 245–46, 248, 259, 330, 337–38, 375, 407, 410
Utah, leave of absence for Connor, 429–30, 432, 441–43
Utah, raising troops in, 269, 429–30
Utah, request for troops, 101–4
Utah, Second Cavalry departure for, 244, 272, 274–75, 284–85, 293, 301
Utah, sending supplies to, 219, 350, 470
Utah, Third Infantry Regiment departure for, 153–55, 196, 223, 258–59, 271–72, 285, 293, 301
Utah, troop withdrawal/mustering out, 427–28, 758
Wright as commander, 718–19
Department of the West, 46, 79, 89, 193, 803
Department of Utah
about, history/role of, 805
Cooke as commander, 75, 803, 805
formation, 803–4
forts/units/officers assigned, 79, 89, 596–600
removal of troops to the East, 82
renamed Camp Floyd, 577
request for reinforcements, 284
See also District of Utah
Department of Virginia, 89
Department of Washington, 89
Deseret, State of
Congressional actions, 36, 58
Constitutional Convention and General Assembly, 26, 45
explanation of the name, 45n55
governor, 45, 58, 609
perceived rebellion, 60
petition for statehood, 21, 26, 36
as "shadow" government, 53, 58, 62, 628
Deseret News
about inclusion in UT records, 75
coverage of Brigham Young, 227–29
coverage of Indian attacks, 43, 51–52
coverage of secessionist politics, 38
Mormon image outside Utah, 60
publishing the first issue, 21
rejection of Utah statehood, 56
"Another Fight with Indians," 704
"Arrived," 654
"The Battle of Bear River," 687–94
"The Battle of Spanish Fork," 701–2
"Camp Douglas," 672, 677
"Captain Smith's Command," 636
"Celebration of the Fourth of July . . . ," 654–55
"Chasing Indians and Killing Grizzlies," 651–52
"Colonel Burton's Command," 641
"The Companies for the Missouri River," 647

Deseret News (continued)
"The Completion of the Telegraph," 605–7
"Departure of the Company for Protection of the Mail and Telegraph Lines," 633–34
Ethier "Letter to the Editor," 706
"Expedition After Indians," 657–63, 700–701
"Expedition for the Arrest of Indian Chiefs," 680–82
"Expedition for the Recovery of a Captive," 675–76
"The Fight with the Indians," 683–85
"The Indian Affairs," 697–98
"The Indian Attack at Battle Creek," 699–700
"Indian Outrage in Box Elder County," 702–3
"Indian War in Idaho," 705
"Latest from the Plains," 636–37
"The Mails," 641–42, 646
"The March of Colonel Connor's Command . . . ," 666–72
"Military Expedition," 703–4
"Movement of Troops," 702
"Nothing Is Talked of But Secession," 36
"The Order of the Day," 686
"Promotion," 697
"Requisition for Troops," 628
"Return from the Road," 646
"Returning," 637
"Ruin By Civil War Stares This Whole Nation in the Face," 35
"Sale of the Spoils," 687
"A Soldier's Complaint," 698–99
desert, 56, 148, 157, 167, 178, 184, 249, 321, 331–32, 349, 387–88, 390, 572, 726
desertions, 59, 83, 157, 225, 228, 232, 311, 315, 362, 530, 537, 540, 550, 562, 583, 640, 652, 655, 714. *See also* discipline, military
Devil's Gate, 48n80, 617, 638, 644, 648, 650
Dick (Utah Indian), 445
Dickey, D. R., 98–99
Dimmick (attorney), 105
Dimmitt, John, 292
discipline, military, 72, 90, 166, 180, 223, 243, 330, 470, 512–13, 542–43, 547, 709. *See also* courts-martial; desertions
disloyalty toward U.S. government
accusations against Army officers, 75, 586, 588, 592–93
Army actions against, 302, 316
Brigham Young viewed as, 397–98
emigrants viewed as, 182–83, 305–6
Mormons viewed as, 41, 52–53, 61, 165, 220, 228, 255, 260–61, 288, 338, 354, 394–95, 402, 473, 523–24, 670, 734
viewed as treasonable offense, 156
See also oath of allegiance
District of Colorado, 296–97, 299–300, 322–24, 431, 435, 465, 545, 807
District of Columbia, 63, 171, 213–15
District of Humboldt, 145–47, 154, 158, 166, 176, 258, 298, 333, 347, 369, 572. *See also* Fort Humboldt
District of Kansas, 512, 545. *See also* Kansas
District of Minnesota, 545, 557, 569, 804. *See also* Minnesota
District of Northern Arizona, 445
District of Oregon, 145, 147–48, 154, 166, 176–77, 193, 212, 229, 235, 262, 269, 275, 282, 293, 298, 314, 316, 336–37, 352–53, 358–59, 361–64, 369–70, 372, 378, 382–84, 411, 463, 474–75. *See also* Fort Vancouver
District of the Plains, 446, 464, 466–71, 476–77, 479, 482, 484, 486, 490–91, 497–99, 503, 509, 512, 536, 545, 548, 558–60, 748, 752–53, 807
District of Utah
about, history/role of, 75, 806–7
area defined, 78, 317
assigned mission, 207, 343
Bear River massacre, 185–89, 208–11, 222, 276–80
Cache Valley Expedition, 189–93
Camp Connor, closure, 458–59
Camp Douglas, establishment/condition, 171, 183–84, 223–25
Camp Douglas, removal of troops, 221, 226, 309, 315–16, 348–49, 355, 364, 400–402, 484
celebrating the Bear River anniversary, 714–18
Connor, as commander, 27, 77, 156–57, 161, 173–74, 202–3, 220–21, 357–58
Connor, leave of absence, 432
Court of Inquiry, disciplinary report, 709–10
Department of Missouri, reassignment to, 460, 463–64, 469, 746–48
District of the Plains, creation/abolishment, 471–73, 545, 548–49
Fort Mojave expedition, 386–91
forts/units/officers assigned, 206, 298–99, 347–48, 392, 461–62
Indian expeditions, 251–53, 258, 263–70, 281–82, 286–87, 375–76, 396, 461
Indian peace treaties, 302–6, 309, 340–41, 343
locations for new posts, 167–69, 198
medical officer's report, 744–46

Mormon relations, 287–91, 338–40, 353–57, 393–98, 401–7, 412, 726–28, 734–35
Mountain Meadow monument, 728–29
officer assignments/reassignments, 159–60, 372–73, 400, 403, 406, 415, 424, 431, 457, 712–13, 732
operations in Colorado Territory, 438–40, 442–43
protection of emigrant and mail roads, 199–200, 256, 367–68, 435–37, 737
protection of settlements and miners, 360–61, 366, 378–80, 422, 711–12, 720–21
raising volunteers in Utah, 259–60, 429–30, 738–40
reinforcing the command, 230, 261–62, 270–72, 282–85, 301, 330
removal of Connor as commander, 357–58
removal of troops, 426
reoccupation of Fort Crittenden, 310, 315
report to the President, 695–96
sending troops East to fight, 172
status of Indian affairs, 172–73, 254–55, 393
See also Department of Utah
"Dixie" (aka "Dixie's Land" / "I Wish I Was in Dixie"), 584, 588
Doctrine and Covenants, 39–40, 40n23, 339
Dodge, Grenville M.
commander, Department of the Missouri, 807
correspondence, mentions in, 58, 451, 462, 464–65, 487, 534, 537, 540, 547, 549
correspondence from, 381–82, 451–54, 458, 460–61, 467–68, 474, 480, 487–88, 492, 495–98, 504–7, 509–10, 517–18, 520–22, 530–33, 537–39, 542–43, 550–53, 747
correspondence to, 463, 488, 490, 492, 497, 501, 503, 514–15, 517–18, 520–23, 527–30, 538, 541–42, 544, 551–52, 554
reports, 511–14, 559–65
Dole, William P., 377, 505, 663–65, 707–8
Doll (Mr.), 443
Dolton, Henry L., 625
Donahue, D., 692
Doolittle (Senator), 504–5
Doty, Charles, 749
Doty, James Duane
appointed governor, 29, 43n45
correspondence from, 313, 316–18
correspondence to, 57, 57n139, 309, 428–29, 449
death and burial, 31, 59, 59n149, 501, 749
Indian treaties, 319, 335, 337, 340–41, 363
raising volunteers in Utah, 447, 610–11, 738–40
as Superintendent of Indian Affairs, 55, 278, 303, 663–65, 707–8
Douglas, Stephen, 23, 39
Downey, John G., 84, 92, 94, 115, 811
Downs, S., 634
Drake, Thomas I., 53–54, 226–29, 236, 238, 243, 255, 359, 370, 384, 641, 654, 671, 695–96
Draper, Parley P., 624
Dred Scott v. Sanford (1857), 22
Drum, Richard C.
communications, General Orders, 170–71, 218–19
communications, Special Orders, 150–51, 158, 195, 246, 274–75, 314, 317, 330, 373, 400, 403, 416, 427
correspondence, mentions in, 144, 718–19
correspondence from, 146, 153–54, 159–61, 198, 201, 223, 241, 244, 248, 259, 269, 272, 283–84, 310, 315, 331, 366, 410, 424, 426, 429–30, 442–43, 462–63
correspondence to, 110, 112, 115, 155, 157, 161–67, 173–75, 187, 192, 202, 211, 217, 220, 229, 231–36, 240, 242, 254–61, 280–81, 287–92, 295–96, 302–3, 324, 329, 338–41, 357–59, 381, 393, 395–99, 402–4, 418, 434–35, 447, 454, 459–60, 474–75, 489, 734–36, 757
Dry Cañon, 266–68
Ducket, Orlando, 500
Duncan (Captain), 647, 649
Dunn, Charles B. [E.], 413–14
Durkee, Charles (governor), 31, 32, 544
Dyer, Frederick H., 809
Dyer, James, 691
Dyer, W., 584

Eardley, Josiah, 623, 634, 654
East Bannock, Utah, 358–59, 361, 382, 425
Easton, L. C., 324–26
Eaton, J. E., 46, 613
Echols, John, 580
Eckert, T. T., 239
Edwards (spy), 417
Elliott (Private), 294–95
Emancipation Proclamation, 27, 28
emigrants/emigration
Indian hostilities, 43, 77, 111–12, 152, 256, 261, 473, 523, 658, 663–64, 690–91
military protection, 154, 184–85, 205, 212, 255, 270, 273–74, 290, 317, 341, 411, 475, 573, 737
raising volunteer companies, 257, 259–60, 269
relocation to avoid war, 523–24

emigrants/emigration *(continued)*
rescuing Indian captives, 190–91, 676
road survey/construction/repair, 85–86, 177, 279, 359, 362, 562–64
Emigration (Kanyon) Canyon, 628–29, 672
Engel (Private), 596
English, J. L., 84
English, T. C., 364–66
Epperson, James, 692
Ethier [Ether], Anthony, 249–52, 254, 264, 267, 696, 700, 706, 709
Evans, Charles, 623, 634, 654
Evans, George S., 144, 195, 256, 258, 264–68, 282, 682, 693, 696, 700–701, 792
Evans, John, 285–86, 323, 436
Ewell, R. S., 581

Far Away in the West (Esplin et al.), 35n2
Farley, Frank, 685, 691, 743
Farmer's Oracle (magazine), 750
Farnham, William, 692
farriers, 142, 619, 622–23, 628, 634
Felt, Joseph, 623, 634
Fergusson, D., 175, 180
Ficknor, Giles, 692
Field, J., 235
Fillmore, Millard, 801
Finnerty, James, 267, 696, 709–10
Firman, D. R., 752
Fisher (Memphis gambler), 420
Fisher, Albert, 801
Fisher, H. L., 685, 691
Fisher, Joseph, 625, 658
Fisher, Margaret M., 625n
Fisk, C. B., 415
Flake, Green (slave), 40n25
Fletcher, Thomas C., 477
Florida, 24, 31, 63, 89, 214
Floyd, John B., 91, 668
Foote, Shelby, 41n31
Forbes, M., 691
Ford (Colonel), 118
Ford (General), 504
Ford, John S., 118, 468, 504
Foreman, Hamilton, 100
Foreman, W., 100
Forney, J. H., 131
Forrest, Nathan Bedford, 31
Fort (Camp) Baker, 133, 162, 298
Fort (Camp) Collins, 297, 497, 501–2, 509–10, 533, 537, 542–43, 553
Fort (Camp) Halleck, 153, 162, 299, 323, 463, 468, 476–78, 497, 499–500, 502, 510, 532–33, 543, 556, 742
Fort (Camp) Independence, 272, 572
Fort Atkinson, 468
Fort Baker, 133
Fort Barrett, 148
Fort Benton, 85–86
Fort Boisé, 86, 177, 203–4, 212, 235, 262, 269–70, 275, 293, 308, 314–20, 337, 359, 361, 363, 365, 370, 384, 409, 423, 425, 475. *See also* Boisé River
Fort Bridger
Cooke's departure, 25, 42
correspondence, mentions in, 79, 136, 139, 143, 152, 192, 194–98, 202–3, 255, 266, 280–82, 293, 297, 304, 308, 312–13, 323, 373, 376, 379, 393
correspondence from, 106, 385, 457, 581, 596–600, 603, 635, 652, 656, 698, 716, 741, 743
facilities and stores, 106
Lot Smith Cavalry Company at, 48–49
officers and troops assigned, 206, 298–99, 347–48, 392, 461–62, 478, 483
as *Official Record* keyword, 74, 77
orders to reoccupy, 197–98
Post Returns, 581, 603
Snake Indian treaty, 281
Fort Canby, 307
Fort Cedar, 700
Fort Churchill, 46, 79, 110–12, 127, 136, 139, 143, 146, 153–61, 167, 173–75, 196, 206, 243–44, 258, 272, 283–85, 293, 298–99, 301, 316, 329–31, 334, 337–38, 375, 378, 383, 405–8, 410, 416, 422, 424, 489, 572–73, 601, 665, 712, 806. *See also* Nevada Territory
Fort Collins, 502
Fort Craig, 118
Fort Crittenden (formerly Camp Floyd), 83, 674
about the renaming, 24, 79, 577
Army reoccupation of, 127, 133, 168, 316, 348, 577–79
Army units stationed at, 79, 806
arrival of Connor's command, 666–72
Bennett stationed at, 99
closure/abandonment, 106, 174, 598, 603, 805–6
correspondence to/from, 167, 178, 246, 286, 580–82, 585, 587, 590–95
establishing the garrison, 23, 27, 37, 805
expedition to Fort Mojave, 29, 78, 386–91
headquarters relocation from Camp Douglas, 310, 315, 316
as *Official Record* keyword, 74, 77
Post Returns, 577–79
protection of mail routes, 42, 180

provisions for Indians near, 130
secessionist attempt to capture, 98–99
Fort Dalles, 359, 369–70, 378
Fort Davis, 420
Fort Defiance, 307–8
Fort Douglas. *See* Camp Douglas
Fort Fauntleroy, 117–19
Fort Fillmore, 118
Fort Garland, 123, 323
Fort Gaston, 411
Fort Hall, 85–86, 136–37, 164, 177, 184, 212, 270, 278, 282, 311, 313, 318–20, 337, 359, 375–76, 382, 425, 663–64
Fort Hoskins, 229–30, 235
Fort Humboldt, 147, 154, 166, 170. *See also* District of Humboldt
Fort Kearny, 139–40, 325, 415, 419, 432–33, 435, 437, 467–70, 476, 479, 497–98, 501, 505, 509–10, 513–14, 537–39, 541, 543, 546–47, 554, 558–63, 566, 742
Fort Klamath, 377, 378
Fort Lafayette, 128–29
Fort Lapwai, 181, 269, 275, 293, 352, 365
Fort Laramie
arrival of California Volunteers, 491
assignment to District of Nebraska, 545–46
commanding officers, 141, 457, 499
establishment of the garrison, 43n42
headquarters, North Sub-District of the Plains, 476
Indian hostilities, 492, 498, 501, 743
Indian peace treaties, 285, 505
mail service, 444
protection from Indian hostilities, 451–52, 454
protection of emigrant and mail roads, 151, 162–65, 628
protection of mines and settlements, 361–62
protection of the Overland Trail, 46, 140–41
reinforcements, 149, 150, 300, 467–68, 537–39
reorganization of military districts, 554, 575
road survey/construction, 383
supplies and animals, 490, 497, 503, 513, 519–22, 532–33, 566
transportation of supplies to, 325
troops assigned, 550–52
withdrawal of troops, 529, 539, 541–42
Fort Larned, 82, 325, 451, 468, 504–5, 533
Fort Leavenworth, 21, 22, 82, 140, 165, 178, 323, 325, 419, 437, 453, 464–67, 477, 480, 487–88, 495, 512–13, 515, 518, 523, 529, 540, 546–50, 554–56, 559, 563, 566–68, 595, 602–3, 805–6
Fort Limhi, 23
Fort Lyon, 323, 325, 451, 468, 498, 533, 549, 564
Fort McIntosh, 346
Fort Merritt, 346
Fort Miller, 316, 403
Fort Mojave Expedition, 29, 78, 367, 386–98, 728–29, 731
Fort Navajo, 133
Fort Point, 127
Fort Randall, 362, 529
Fort Rice, 529
Fort Riley, 477, 533, 538–39, 551, 556, 564, 566
Fort Ruby, 11, 171, 185–86, 189, 193–94, 206, 335, 347–48, 392, 422, 425–26, 428, 462, 572–73, 674, 731, 747, 757, 806. *See also* Ruby Valley
Fort Scott, 325, 555
Fort Sully, 529
Fort Sumter, 25, 41
Fort Tejon, 316
Fort Trinity (Eight-Mile Station), 383
Fort Union, 141, 325, 468, 566–67
Fort Vancouver, 181, 212, 314–16, 328, 409–10, 423, 425. *See also* District of Oregon
Fort Walla Walla, 85–86, 135–36, 148, 154, 184, 201, 205, 293, 314, 316, 318–19, 322, 364–65, 378, 494
Fort Wise, 82, 123–24
Fort Yamhill, 230
Fort Yuma, 132, 136, 138, 144–45, 316, 332, 391
Fourth of July, 654–55, 751, 754
Fouts (Captain), 501
Fox, Edward R., 46
Fox, Leonard R., 609–10
Franklin, John, 685, 691
Franklin, Texas, 420
Franklin, Utah Territory, 209, 280, 296, 351, 356, 358, 675, 682, 684
Frauley, Patrick, 684, 691
Frawley, P., 693–94
Freemasonry, 84, 693, 723, 745
French, S. Bassett, 580
Fuller, Frank
appeal for protection of mail routes, 46–47
becomes acting governor, 25, 44, 44n52
call for Harding resignation, 236
correspondence with Lincoln, 606, 607
as freemason, 693
orders for Burton's march, 614–15
protection from Indian predation, 609–11, 613–14
report on Burton's march, 636–37, 643–45
Fuller, Willis, 653
Fuller, Wyllys D., 625

Fullmer, Almon L., 618

Gadble, W. S., 630
Gail, W. W. Y., 100
Gaines, R., 100
Gallagher, Patrick A., 193–94, 206, 209, 211, 218, 247–48, 253–54, 263, 291–92, 294–95, 347, 385, 392, 393, 682, 685, 688, 690, 694, 696, 730
Gallatin (town), 358
Gallatin River, 361
Galvanized Yankees, 59, 91, 140–41, 518
Garland, S, 131
General Orders
  California Volunteers, formation, 223, 344–45
  Court of Inquiry disciplinary report, 709–10
  dealing with desertion and absence without leave, 231–32
  dealing with Indian affairs, 363
  Department of California, creation of, 78n
  Department of the Missouri, reorganization, 455, 460, 512, 516, 533, 536
  District of the Plains, creation/abolishment, 466–67, 469, 476, 479, 536, 545, 748
  District of Utah, 713, 725, 746–48
  enforcing Congressional act against rebellion, 170–71
  establishing Camp Connor, 296
  Fort Bridger, retained/garrisoned, 596
  inclusion in the records, 64, 68, 70–71, 769, 803n1, 811
  military divisions/departments, creation, 507–8, 557
  mustering out troops in Utah, 571
  Nevada troops ordered to Utah, 407, 410
  Oregon Cavalry, formation, 204
  protection of mail routes, 494
  Provost-marshal, authorization/duties, 368
  recognition of Bear River victory, 218–19
  renaming Camp Floyd to Fort Crittenden, 577
  reporting in compliance with, 307–8, 324–25, 511, 598–99
  wartime trade in the Territories, 368
General Orders No.
  Camp Connor (No. 1), 296
  Camp Floyd (No. 3), 577
  Camp Relief (No. 7), 725
  Department of California (No. 10), 571
  Department of New Mexico (No. 15), 307
  Department of the Missouri (No. 4), 516
  Department of the Missouri (No. 7), 533
  Department of the Missouri (No. 20), 545
  Department of the Missouri (No. 27), 557
  Department of the Missouri (No. 32), 368
  Department of the Missouri (No. 50), 368
  Department of the Missouri (No. 80), 466–67, 469, 748
  Department of the Pacific (No. 2), 363
  Department of the Pacific (No. 6), 218–19, 747
  Department of the Pacific (No. 18), 296
  Department of the Pacific (No. 34), 170–71
  Department of the Pacific (No. 36), 494
  Department of the Pacific (No. 39), 407
  Department of the Pacific (No. 40), 344
  Department of the Pacific (No. 48), 713
  Department of the Pacific (No. 126), 204
  Department of Utah (No. 1), 713, 746–48
  Department of Utah (No. 13), 596, 598–99
  Department of Utah (No. 33), 709–10
  District of the Plains (No. 1), 469, 748
  District of the Plains (No. 3), 536
  District of the Plains (No. 4), 476
  District of the Plains (No. 7), 479
  Quartermaster-General (No. 13), 324
  War Department (No. 10), 78n
  War Department (No. 11), 512
  War Department (No. 23), 455, 460, 747
  War Department (No. 58), 231–32
  War Department (No. 118), 68, 507–8
  War Department (No. 126), 223
  War Department (No. 191), 747
  War Department (No. 235), 747
  War Department (No. 251), 557
  War Department (No. 294), 511
  War Department (No. 305), 747
George, Milo, 416, 462, 476, 478, 483, 807
Georgia, 24, 29–30, 31, 63, 123, 214, 586
German, George, 684, 691
German, Joseph, 692
Gettysburg Address, 29
Gibbon, John, 584, 586–89
Gibbs, Addison C., 230–31, 311, 326–27, 352–53
Gibbs, Isaac L., 680–81
Gibbs, Marshall, 211, 681, 693
Gibson, John D., 625, 635
Gibson, Moses W., 624, 658
Giddings, Charles, 420
Gilman (Lieutenant), 153
Gilpin, William, 82–83, 117, 124
Godbold, C. H., 692
Goddard, Joseph, 624, 658
Gold Hill, Nevada Territory, 174–75, 329
Gooddell (Goodall), Tim, 634, 645
Goode (Lieutenant), 584
Gooding (Superintendent), 698

Goose Creek Mountains, 339–40
Gordon (Lieutenant), 584
Gordon (Major), 131
Goshen [Gorchen], 251, 750
Goshute Indians, 29, 254, 283, 304, 311–12, 342, 472, 730
Gould and Curry (mine), Nevada Territory, 391
Gove, Jesse A., 581
Government Springs, U.T., 78, 286–87
Governor of California. *See* Downey, John G.
Granger (Mr.), 630
Grant, Ulysses S.
  correspondence, mentions in, 450, 487, 525, 531
  correspondence to, 381–82, 448, 464, 495, 501, 516, 558, 573
  inaugurated president, 33
  Indian skirmishes, 32
  surrender at Appomattox, 30, 477
Grant, William, 624, 658
Grasshopper Gold Mines, 681
Gravelly Ford, 170, 174, 186
Greathouse, Ridgely, 736
Great Salt Lake City. *See* Salt Lake City
Greeley, Horace, 23
Greely (Private), 596
Green, James, 659
Green, John (Captain), 57n139, 739–40
Green, John (Lieutenant), 584, 588, 594–96
Green, John (Mr., family of), 699
Greene (Green), James, 624, 658
Greene, O. D., 368
Green River
  Burton's report of march, 642–43
  delay of mail, 742
  ferry crossing, 679
  Fort Bridger on, 106, 380
  Indian hostilities, 141, 149, 185, 304, 488, 736–37
  Lot Smith Cavalry Company, 630, 636, 638–40, 648–49, 658–59
  mail stations attacked/deserted, 636–37
  road survey/construction, 751
Green River Mountains, 659
Green River Station, 752–56
Greenwade, James M., 97
Grover (Colonel), 133
Grow, Galusha A., 134
Guest, Edward F. M., 624
Gunnison, John W., 22
Gunnison massacre, 22

Haight (Captain), 647
Haines (Colonel), 521
Hale, Solomon, 623, 634, 657, 659
Hall, Benjamin F., 113–14, 124–25
Halleck, Henry Wager ("Old Brains")
  Bear River massacre, 52, 52n107, 241
  commander, Department of the West, 46, 138, 172, 239–40
  garrisoning of Fort Bridger, 194–98
  Indian expeditions, 442
  promotion of Connor, 222
  protection of mail routes, 141, 256, 433–36, 447, 450–51, 454
  publication of *Official Records*, 63
  raising volunteer companies, 257–58, 416
  re-enlistment of Lot Smith Cavalry Company, 27, 163
  relieving Curtis from Department of the Missouri, 273–74
  relocation of Camp Douglas, 348–50, 353–57, 364
  reorganization of military districts, 465
  request for reinforcements, 284, 321
Hambleton, John, 100
Hamblin, Jacob, 391
Hammond, W. A., 331–32
Hams Fork, 630, 638, 640, 644–45
Hancock (Captain), 98, 103
Handy Book for United States Cavalry (Cooke), 582
Hannibal and Saint Joseph Railroad, 80–81, 108
Harding, Stephen S., 27–28, 44n52, 50, 53–56, 163, 217–18, 226–27, 236–38, 243, 271, 671, 680, 695–96, 751
Hargrave, Robert, 692
Harlan, James, 504
Harmon (Captain), 647, 649, 650
Harney, William S., 53n114, 683–84
Harold B. Lee Library, 12
Harper's Ferry, Va., 23
Harris, Thomas Henry, 624, 658
Harris, Thomas S., 70, 190–94, 253, 267, 696, 716, 725
Hart, Charles [aka Burgess] (Quantrill alias), 419
Hart, N. H., 129
Haven, F., 457
Hawley, Charles C., 479
Hayward (Mr.), 108
Head, Lafayette, 323, 465
Heath (General), 503, 509
Heath, C., 692
Helm, John, 623, 634
Hempstead, Charles H., 291–92, 294–95, 711–12, 716, 732
Henry, Guy V., 482

Hensley, John, 685, 692
Hereford, R., 658, 660–62
Herron, C. J., 692
Hertle, John G., 692
Hervey (Corporal), 294–95
Heth, Henry, 580
Hewett, A. P., 691
Heywood, J., 692
Hibbad, W. B., 609–10
Hickson, James, 625
Hill, Joseph, 692
Hill, Sam, 625
Hinkley (Hinckley), Ira N., 623, 634
The History of Salt Lake City and Its Founders (Tullidge), 75, 612–15, 618–19, 734–36
Hixon, J. M., 658–59
Hoagland, John, 623, 634
Hobart (Lieutenant), 366
Hoffman's trail, 133
Hoffner, A., 691
Holladay (Hollady), Joseph, 609–10, 615
Holladay (Holliday) Benjamin ("Ben"), 47, 632, 665
Holliday (Mr.), 430, 639
Hollowell, Charles, 684, 691
Honey Lake, 145, 378, 489
Honeyman, Francis, 209, 264–68, 681–82, 694, 696
Hood, William H., 685, 691
Hooper, William H., 38–40, 45, 45n58, 61, 612, 617, 637, 641, 644, 647
Hopkins, Guy S., 128–29
Hopkins, John W., 363, 370, 396, 423, 425
Horn (Captain), 639, 647, 649
Horse, Charles B., 692
Hosmer, Josiah, 294, 383, 696
Hoton, George W., 685, 691
Houston, Sam, 23
Hovey, Alvin P., 419–20
Howard, Asa F., 685, 691
Howard, W. A., 128
Howe, Richard, 624
Hoy, E. C., 685
Hoyt (Captain), 209–10, 681–82, 684, 688–89, 694
Hoyt, E. C., 692
Hoyt, Samuel N., 696
Hudson Bay Company, 86
Huffaker, Lewis A., 624, 658–59
Hughes (unidentified), 685
Hughes, Bela Metcalf, 430, 482, 544
Hughes, L. D., 691
Hughes, Leander W., 685, 691
Hughes, W. B., 262
Hullinger, Harvey Coe, 624
Humboldt, Kansas, 374, 378
Humboldt, Nevada Territory, 489
Humboldt Indians, 203, 240, 757
Humboldt Mountains, 384
Humboldt River, 77, 110, 138, 169, 172–73, 186–87, 192, 278, 306, 371, 573, 698, 704, 712, 757
Humboldt River massacres, 189
Humfreville, J. L., 499–500, 502
Hunbert, P., 691
Hunt, Charles L., 413
Hunt, Franklin Eyre, 583–85, 587–93
Hunt, James R., 692
Hunter (General), 139
Huntington, J. W. Perit, 370, 376–77, 443
Hutchinson, Bartele C., 685, 691
Hyde, Orson, 38

Ice Springs Station, 141, 150, 636, 638, 643
Idaho Territory
  Civil War engagements, 64
  creation of, 28
  dispatching troops to, 260, 282, 378, 703–4
  Indian expeditions, 375–76
  protection of settlements and miners, 361–62
  reducing the territory boundary, 382
  reorganization of military districts, 285–86, 337
  request for troops, 705
  territorial representation, 358–59
  See also Camp Connor; Soda Springs
Illig, Morris, 685, 692
Illinois, Civil War engagements, 64
Imlay, James, 624, 658–59
Independence Rock, 48, 48n80, 140, 142, 619, 622, 626–27, 631, 637
Indiana, Civil War engagements, 64
Indians
  actions on the Overland Trail, 42
  attack at Battle Creek, 699–701
  attack at Sweetwater Station, 28, 31, 487, 493, 638
  attacks on emigrants and mail routes, 110–12, 609–10
  Black Hawk Indian War, 30, 58–59, 59n148
  Congressional investigation of conditions, 475–76
  holding white captives, 192, 201, 675–76
  Idaho Territory uprising, 705
  Mormon influence over, 261, 265–66
  peace treaties, 29, 55, 55n130, 280–81, 302–6, 308–11, 323, 329, 335, 341, 363, 505–7, 707–8
  raid at Box Elder Valley, 28, 702–3

removal to reservations, 154, 166, 303, 316, 333–34, 370, 376–77, 411–12
Sand Creek affair, 506
skirmish at Cache Valley, 27, 680–82
skirmish at Cedar Fort, 28
skirmish at Pleasant Grove, 28
skirmish at Spanish Fork, 28, 701–2, 792–93
support of Confederate war effort, 123–24, 455
U.S. failure in dealing with, 524–27
See also individual tribes by name
Indian Territory, 31, 64, 374, 446, 769
Ingham, Edward, 682, 694, 696
Iowa, 446n, 569. *See also* military units, Iowa
Iron County, 59n148
Irwin, William R., 479
Italy, 608

J. H. S. (soldier), 698–99
J. Willard Marriott Library, 12
James (Mr.), 445
Jensen (Jenson), Lars, 624, 658–59
Jewett, Oscar, 457, 479
Jocelyn, Stephen E., 335, 479, 696, 713, 753
John, William S., 692
Johns, William M., 464, 478, 482–83, 562–63, 754
Johnson (General), 666, 670–71
Johnson (spy), 419
Johnson, Andrew, 30, 32, 568, 574, 741
Johnson, Powel, 625
Johnston, Albert Sidney, 26, 37, 101, 118, 121, 803, 806
Johnston, George, 692
Johnston, Joseph E., 30, 126, 580, 698
Johnston, W. I., 418
Jones (Sergeant), 383
Jones, Samuel, 31
Jones, William, 259, 342, 367, 372, 403
Jordan Springs, U.T., 666–69
Josephites, 480–81, 770
Julesburg, Colorado Territory, 476, 497, 504, 509, 512–14, 532, 546–47, 554, 556, 561, 807

Kane, Thomas L., 23, 132
Kane County, 59n148
Kansas
Civil War engagements, 64
Quantrill raids, 374
reorganization of military districts, 569
statehood, 24
summary of military operations, 446
See also District of Kansas; military units, Kansas
Kansas-Nebraska Act of 1854, 22, 40n25
Kansas River, 419, 437, 439, 448, 452, 503, 512, 543, 559–60, 564
Kautz, August Valentine, 72
Kawet, Baptest (interpreter), 653
Kaw Indians, 87
Kearney, I., 691
Kearns (Private), 596
Keller, Matthew, 102–3
Kellogg, John, 208, 216, 219, 248
Kelly, Patrick H., 692
Kelsey, Samuel, 97, 100
Kennedy, Joseph C. G., 213
Kensley, Nathaniel, 692
Kentucky, 64. *See also* military units, Kentucky
Ketchum, W. Scott, 96, 100, 141
Kilgore, William, 100
Kimball, Heber C., 41, 237, 670
Kimball, Hiram, Jr., 625, 658
Kimball, William, 632, 741
King, Isaac, 235
Kinkaid (Mormon man), 664
Kinney, John F.
call for Harding resignation, 236
dealing with Morrisite situation, 26, 49
as freemason, 693
guarded by Utah militia, 612
oath of office to Lot Smith Cavalry Company, 622–23, 631
plea for protection of mail routes, 46, 609–10, 611
plea for relocation of Camp Douglas, 348–50, 353–58, 364
plea to Congress for Utah statehood, 56–57
warrant to arrest Indian chiefs, 211, 680–81
Kinsley, Nathaniel, 685
Kiowa Indians, 43, 323
Kiowa Station, Nebraska Territory, 439
Kirkham, R. W., 330, 365
Kirkley, Joseph W., 64–65
Kirkpatrick, S. M., 161, 294, 450
Kittredge, Willard, 483
Klamath Indians, 377
Knowlton, J. Q., 249, 623, 633, 639–40, 651–52, 654–55, 657–60, 662–63

L. Tom Perry Special Collections, 12
Laiz (Private), 658
Lake, William H., 684, 691
Lambs (Kanyon) Canyon, 629
Lander, F. W., 133
Landis [Laudis], Benjamin, 685, 692
Larkin, James, 624, 658
Larsen, Thurston, 625

Las Vegas, 133, 388–90
Latham, Milton S., 47, 140, 615n
Lattman, John, 692
Lay, Hark (slave), 40n25
Lay, J. F., 580
LDS. *See* Church of Jesus Christ of Latter-day Saints; Mormon/Mormonism
Leavenworth (Colonel), 504–5
Lebeau, M., 351
Lee, John, 685
Lee, John D., 391
Lee, John S., 692
Lee, Robert E., 23, 30, 58, 477, 580
Legget, Joshia, 685, 691
Lehi (Snake chief), 690
Lemhi/Fort Lemhi, 352, 358–59, 365, 372
Lemmon, Leander, 624
Leonard, James, 115
Lest We Forget (Young), 75
"Letter from the Secretary of War . . ." (Government Printing Office), 683, 758
"Letters Received by the Office of the Adjutant General . . ."
  arrival of California Volunteers at Fort Bridger, 603–4
  claims of secessionist sympathies in the Army, 583–94
  Cooke departure for Fort Leavenworth, 595
  Cooke promotion to General, 608
  Cooke relocation to Fort Bridger, 596–600
  death of Governor Doty, 749
  diversion of troops Colorado Territory, 602, 605
  Indian relations, 742
  Ruby Valley as military reserve, 600–601
Lewis (Mr.), 411
Lewis, Micajah G., 192–93, 286–87, 334, 367, 373–74, 376, 379–80, 383–85, 391, 406, 415, 424, 431, 443, 458, 479, 499, 713–14, 717–18, 727–29, 748
Lewis' Fork, 659–61
Lewis' Spring, 388–89
L'hommedieu, Samuel, 691
Lill, Daniel C., 624
Lincoln, Abraham, 280
  assassination, 30, 58, 584
  authorization of Utah military unit, 47, 49, 61, 615–16, 626, 632, 648
  Battle of Atlanta, 29
  call for volunteers, 25, 108
  Dawson appointed Territorial governor, 43
  dismissal of Harding as governor, 54–55, 695–96
  election/inauguration as president, 24
  Emancipation Proclamation, 27
  Gettysburg Address, 29
  Morrill Anti-Bigamy Act, 27, 37
  postwar Reconstruction (Ten-Percent Plan), 29
  re-election/inauguration, 29–30, 56n137, 57–58, 741
  sending the Army to Utah, 355
  transcontinental telegraph, 606–7
Lincoln, Jefferson, 692
Lincoln-Douglas debates, 23
Lippitt, Francis J, 145, 147, 166, 403
Little Horn River, 563
Little Soldier (Chief), 303, 665, 706, 707, 722
Livingston, R. R., 382, 437–38, 452–53, 476, 486, 503, 510
Livingston Bell & Co., 592–93
Logan, James, 691
Long, E. B., 35, 44–45, 56, 58n144, 62
Longley, Sylvanius S., 692
Longstrough, William, 625, 658
Lonsham (mountaineer), 643–44
Loring (Colonel), 82
Los Angeles, 83–84, 96–97, 101–5, 114, 133, 145, 178–79. *See also* Camp Fitzgerald; Camp Latham
Los Angeles Star, 97
Lot Smith Cavalry Company. *See* military units, Utah; Smith, Lot (Lott)
Louisiana, 24, 31, 64, 214
Louisiana Purchase, 769
Low, Frederick F., 417, 426–28, 466
Luffing, Pete, 351
Lugenbeel, Pinkney, 262, 293, 314
Lutz, Thomas J., 625
Lutz, William W., 624, 658
Lybe, A. Smith, 733
Lynch, William, 625
Lyon (General), 89
Lythgoe, Dennis L., 40n25

M. (OR sender), 699–700
Mackey (Major), 520
Madsen, Brigham D., 52n107
Magruder, John B., 580
mail/mail service/mail roads
  beginning/end of Pony Express, 24, 25
  Big Pond Station, 752–53
  Big Sandy Station, 192–93, 292, 411, 630, 639–40, 648–49, 651
  Black Buttes Station, 752–53
  Deer Creek Station, 636–37, 644–45, 794
  Fort Trinity (Eight-Mile Station), 383

Green River Station, 636–37, 752–53, 754–56
Ice Springs Station, 141, 150, 636, 638, 643
interrupted mail service, 634, 641–42, 646
Kiowa Station, Nebraska Territory, 439
Pacific Springs Station, 193, 203, 630, 639, 643, 647–50
Platte Bridge/Platte Station, 150, 493, 498–99, 511–14, 546–47, 554, 644, 733
Plaunts Station/Trading Post, 643–45
postmaster, 99, 128, 151, 178, 397
protection, request for Army troops, 613–14
protection by California Volunteers, 49
protection by Lot Smith Cavalry Company, 47–48, 617–19, 622, 626–27, 642–45
protection by Nauvoo Legion, 46
Rock Point Station, 752–53
Rock Springs Station, 752–53
Rocky Ridge Station, 150, 484, 486, 643
Salt Wells Station, 752–53
Split Rock Station, 630, 642–43
Sweetwater Station/Bridge/Crossing, 28, 31, 487, 493, 635, 637–38, 642, 646, 650, 733, 794
Three Crossings Station, 141, 487, 636–37, 643, 733, 794
Washakie Station, 541
Willow Springs Station, 674, 698
Mallinsbery (Sergeant), 410
Maloney (Mr.), 481
Manhart (prisoner), 640–41
Mansfield (General), 89
Marker, John D., 691
martial law, 23, 53, 53n114, 221, 323, 339, 360, 639
Maryland, Civil War engagements, 63
Mason, O. P., 411, 429, 450, 738–40
Masons. *See* Freemasonry
Mastin, Thomas J., 118
Mathewson [Matthewson], James H., 483, 713, 752, 753
Maull, G. W., 417–18
Mauning, J., 692
Maury, Dabney, 31
Maury, Reuben F., 177, 269–70, 275, 293, 316, 337, 352, 363, 365, 369–70, 376–77, 409, 423
Maxfield, Elijah H., 625
MC (soldier), 753–54
McAllister, Julian, 146, 223
McCaffrey (Private), 596
McClellan, George B., 89, 119, 125–26, 133, 139, 178, 608, 741
McClellan, Robert, 128
McCord, J. E., 346
McCoy, Alonzo P. V., 685, 692
McDermit, Charles, 155, 157–58, 206, 283, 299, 329, 331, 408, 424, 489
McDermott, Michael, 696
McDowell, Irvin
commander, Department of Northeastern Virginia, 89
commander, Department of the Pacific, 57, 432, 470, 804, 806
Department of the Pacific orders issued, 400, 403, 407, 416, 427, 747
dispatching troops to Utah, 491
Indian policy/actions against, 411–12
invitation to Utah raise volunteer companies, 738–39
leave of absence for Connor, 432, 441–42
mustering out of volunteer forces, 425–26, 428, 466, 478, 571–73
protection of mail routes, 494
raising volunteer companies, 57, 57n139, 428–29, 440–41, 738–39
reorganization of military districts, 463–64, 507–8
warned of secessionist activities, 417–18
McFadden, John M., 709
McFaddin (Sergeant), 500
McGarry, Edward
Bear River massacre, 218, 682, 688–89, 694, 792
cavalry company commander, 159, 172, 241
cavalry regimental commander, 400, 406
command of Fort Ruby, 244
departure from Fort Churchill, 167, 174
duty in the East, 736
Indian expeditions, 187, 189, 209–11
member Third Infantry, 157, 160
ordered to Camp Connor, 424
ordered to Camp Douglas, 314, 402, 404–5
ordered to Camp Union, 426
president of Court of Inquiry, 710
recovery of white captives, 190, 192, 201, 675–76
report on operations, 200
McGonagle,John, 691
McKean, Theodore, 49
McKee (Captain), 123–24
McKown, James, 692
McLane, Daniel, 696
McLane, Louis, 126, 130, 137, 139, 179
McLaughlin, M. A., 259, 272
McLean, Daniel, 174, 186, 209, 682, 685, 688–89, 691, 694
McNicol, Daniel [Donald], 27, 48, 48n79, 624, 658, 660
McNulty, James M., 331–33, 691

Meadow Valley, 387
Meadow Valley, mines/mining district, 380
Meeks, Jacob, 662
Meigs, Montgomery C., 324, 537, 555–58, 565–68
Mendon, U.T., 209
Merchant & Wheeler Traders, 216, 644, 650
Merrill, Edwin, 625
Merritt, Wesley, 584, 592–94, 596–97
Mesilla, Arizona Territory, 118, 178–79
Mexican War (1846–48), 21, 36n2, 42n35, 49n83
Mexico, 456
Michigan. *See* military units, Michigan
Middle Park, 482, 538, 559, 562, 754–56
Military District of Utah. *See* District of Utah
Military Division of the Mississippi. *See* Department of the Mississippi
military units
  basic units, described, 773
  colored troops, 558, 575
  Dyer *Compendium* list, 809–10
  Territorial contributions to Civil War, 15n1
  See also U.S. Army
military units, Alabama (Confederate), Tenth Volunteers, 131
military units, California
  First Battalion Veteran Infantry, 553
  First Cavalry Volunteers, 109, 115–16, 138, 175, 180, 183, 245, 332, 369
  First Infantry Volunteers, 109, 132–33, 138, 332, 809
  Second Battalion Cavalry, 553
  Second Cavalry Volunteers, 138, 144, 146, 148–51, 154, 159, 160, 165, 172, 174, 185–87, 189–92, 195, 200, 206, 209–11, 218–19, 223, 230, 244–45, 249–54, 259, 264, 268, 272, 274, 277, 284–85, 298–99, 301–4, 314, 329, 342, 347, 356, 367, 372–73, 375–76, 386–92, 400, 415, 424, 426, 431, 434–36, 457, 461, 466, 477–79, 483, 489, 491, 553, 572, 671, 673–75, 682, 693, 696–97, 704, 716, 725, 729, 731–33, 791–92, 809
  Second Infantry Volunteers, 145, 166, 316, 403–8, 572
  Third Infantry Battalion Volunteers, 458, 464, 479, 482, 731
  Third Infantry Veteran Battalion, 551, 562
  Third Infantry Volunteers, 49n83, 77, 126, 137, 145–50, 153–60, 165–69, 171–74, 176, 179, 183–84, 187–90, 192–94, 196, 198, 201–3, 206, 209–11, 218–26, 229–31, 232–34, 238, 240–43, 246–48, 253–54, 257, 258, 263, 276, 279, 285, 291–95, 298–99, 301, 335, 347–48, 383–84, 385, 392, 406, 407, 425, 427–29, 461–62, 478, 483, 673–74, 716, 750, 753, 791, 795
  Fourth Infantry Volunteers, 137, 158, 245, 571–72
  Fifth Infantry Volunteers, 138
  Sixth Infantry Volunteers, 59, 316, 369, 571, 756
  Eighth Infantry Volunteers, 571–72
  Native Volunteer Cavalry, 571–72
military units, Colorado
  First Cavalry, 297, 322–24, 479, 502
  First Colorado Battery, 322
  Third Cavalry, 48n76
  Third Volunteers, 323
military units, Confederate
  First Kentucky Volunteers, 131
  Sixth South Carolina Volunteers, 131
  Tenth Alabama Volunteers, 131
  Eleventh Virginia Volunteers, 131
  Seventeenth Kentucky Infantry, 420
  Fifty-second Virginia Cavalry, 131
  One Hundredth North Carolina Cavalry, 131
  Missouri Volunteer Militia, 81
  Sumter Flying Artillery, 131
  See also Galvanized Yankees
military units, Iowa, Seventh Cavalry Volunteers, 438, 452, 479, 501
military units, Kansas
  Seventh Cavalry, 515
  Ninth Volunteer Cavalry, 299–300, 323, 791, 810
  Eleventh Cavalry, 465, 476, 498, 509, 514–15, 810
  Sixteenth Volunteer Cavalry, 486, 497–98, 503, 560
military units, Kentucky (Confederate)
  First Volunteers, 131
  Seventeenth Infantry, 420
military units, Michigan
  cavalry (unidentified), 488, 553
  First Cavalry Regiment Volunteers, 809
  Sixth, 509
  Eleventh Regiment Volunteers, 128
military units, Missouri
  Second Light Artillery, 560
  Twelfth Cavalry, 810
  Volunteer Militia (Confederate), 81
military units, Nebraska
  cavalry (unidentified), 273, 430
  First Battalion Cavalry, 476, 510, 810
  First Cavalry Veteran Volunteers, 437–38, 452–53, 479
  First Regiment Cavalry, 510, 810
military units, Nevada
  First Battalion Cavalry, 299, 306, 316, 337–38, 347, 373, 375–76, 407–8, 410, 416, 431, 457,

461–62, 466, 476, 479, 483–85, 571–72, 712, 716, 728, 732, 737, 741, 746, 752, 791, 806, 809
First Infantry Volunteers, 407–8, 422, 443–44, 571–72
Second Battalion Cavalry, 553
military units, New Mexico, First Cavalry Volunteers, 307–8, 445
military units, New York, Twenty-First Regiment, 537, 553
military units, North Carolina (Confederate), One Hundredth Cavalry, 131
military units, Ohio
First Independent Battalion Cavalry, 810
Second Volunteer Cavalry, 72
Sixth Cavalry, 152
Eleventh Cavalry, 50, 493–94, 498–500, 537, 538, 791, 793–94, 810
military units, Oregon
cavalry (unidentified), 136–37, 148, 154, 204
First Cavalry Volunteers, 182, 269, 275, 311, 313, 317–22, 326–28, 335–37, 352, 363, 369–70, 384, 396, 423, 425, 474–75, 791
military units, South Carolina (Confederate), Sixth Volunteers, 131
military units, U.S. (Regular Army)
Cavalry of the West, 345
First Army Corps, 570
First Cavalry, 332, 479
First Dragoons, 85–86, 96–98, 102, 104–5, 106, 110–12, 114
Second Artillery, 574
Second Cavalry, 803
Second Dragoons, 79, 578–79, 580, 584, 593, 595–96, 600, 602–3, 803
Second Infantry, 810
Third Artillery, 127, 138
Third Regular Cavalry, 140–41
Third Volunteers, 498, 509, 518
Fourth Artillery, 79, 106, 578–79, 584, 593, 596, 600, 603–4, 805–6
Fourth Cavalry Regiment, 151–52, 479
Fifth Infantry, 82, 445, 539, 578–79
Fifth Infantry Volunteers, 539, 551, 809
Sixth Cavalry, 72
Sixth Volunteer Infantry, 59, 490, 497, 502–3, 509, 537–42, 551, 553
Seventh Infantry Regiment, 82, 584
Eighth Division, 557
Ninth Infantry, 137, 192, 544, 571–72, 574, 804
Tenth Infantry, 79, 82, 99, 140, 578–79, 581, 596, 603, 803, 805–6, 810
Fourteenth Infantry, 572, 574
See also Galvanized Yankees
military units, Utah
contributions during Civil War, 15n1
Lot Smith Cavalry Company
authorization to raise volunteers, 26, 45–48, 142, 621
Brigham Young correspondence to/from, 142, 611, 616, 626–27, 631–32, 635, 647–50, 652–56
contribution to Civil War effort, 15, 61
Daniel Wells correspondence to/from, 616–21, 631–32, 633, 635
Deseret News reporting on, 628, 633–34, 636–37, 646–47, 651–52, 654–55, 657–63
Indian expeditions, 657–63
oath of office, 622–25
presence at Fort Bridger, 47–49, 629, 631–32, 635–36, 640–42, 645–47, 649, 652–61, 664
re-enlistment/mustering out, 27, 50, 50n95, 625n, 663
request for military service, 45–48, 142, 609–11, 616–20, 628
serving on the Overland Trail, 48–50, 628–30, 633–34, 635, 637–41, 647–55, 657–63, 793
Nauvoo Legion
attack on Fort Limhi outpost, 23
Battalion of Life Guards, 47
deployed in Utah War, 23
First Cavalry Regiment, 46, 642
Indian skirmishes, 32
Lot Smith service with, 47, 47n75
protection of mail routes, 26, 46–47, 609–16
readiness to fight, 53–55, 351, 399
report of Overland Mail line march, 642–45
resignation of Daniel Wells, 609
Special Orders No. 2 (UT-32), 614–15
Special Orders No. 3 (UT-38), 47, 618–19
U.S. Army, arrival in territory, 22–23, 27, 43, 43n42, 49–51, 143, 145–51, 153–56, 158–61, 165–67, 169–74, 176, 178–80, 183–83, 188
U.S. Army, withdrawal from territory, 43, 107, 238, 255, 261, 271, 290, 305, 309, 315, 355, 394, 404, 521
military units, Virginia (Confederate)
Eleventh Volunteers, 131
Fifty-Second Cavalry, 131
military units, Washington, First Infantry Volunteers, 145, 154, 166, 364–66, 409–10, 416, 425

military units, West Virginia
  Sixth Regiment, 537
  Tibbits' Cavalry Brigade, 509, 515, 518
military units, Wisconsin, Third Cavalry, 453
military units, unspecified
  artillery, 41–42, 84, 113, 132, 135, 137, 148, 209, 245, 399, 570, 575, 670
  cavalry, 43, 46, 51, 83, 92, 102–4, 118, 124, 132–33, 135–39, 141, 145, 147, 157, 166, 172–73, 184, 224–25, 234, 240, 243, 247, 256, 258, 260, 263, 271–72, 293–94, 312, 325–26, 331–32, 357, 359, 381–82, 384, 407, 416, 421–22, 438–40, 442, 450, 463, 467, 472, 485–87, 492, 495, 497–98, 512, 517, 519, 528–29, 535, 539–42, 546–51, 554, 570, 574, 580, 582, 681, 702–3, 743
  infantry, 42–43, 46, 92, 104, 116, 118, 131, 134, 136–39, 146–48, 164, 260, 269, 272, 282, 319, 337, 362, 375, 382, 399, 416, 468, 475, 492, 495–98, 515, 517–18, 528–29, 546–51, 554, 570, 575, 598–99, 681, 684, 703, 738
Miller (Bishop), 221
Miller (Captain), 647
Miller, A. B., 124
Miller, H. W., 630
Miller, Henry R., 696
Miller, Morz, 421
Miller, Reuben P., 624, 691
Miller, William H., 596
miners
  disloyalty/secessionist sympathies, 94, 97, 103, 358
  emigration/increasing population, 212, 277–78, 331, 361, 734
  Indian hostilities, 208–9, 341, 393–94, 730
  Mormon resentment toward, 351, 360–61, 541, 720–21, 735
  Nevada Territory, 391
  protection by Army troops, 355–56, 376, 379–80, 602, 711
  soldiers as, 53, 314–15, 334–35, 524, 711
mines/mining
  Arizona Territory, 391
  Bannock mines, 176, 282, 341
  Beaver City, 387
  Beaver Head mines, 208–9, 260
  Boisé Mines, 204, 282, 327, 341
  California, 94
  emigration and trade, 523, 526, 532, 564, 566
  Goose Creek Mountains, 339–40
  Grasshopper Gold Mines, 681
  impact on Indian relations, 181, 359
  Indian hostilities, 381, 385
  Meadow Valley, 380
  Nevada Territory, 329
  Oregon and Washington Territory, 85, 137, 163, 184–85, 352, 358
  Owyhee mines, 384
  protection by Army troops, 123, 136–37, 204, 301, 360, 371, 394, 514, 537, 663–64, 721
  Reese River mines, 329
  Rush Valley, 473
  solving the Mormon situation, 53, 339, 343, 394, 735
  Utah Territory, richness/value, 262, 339, 395, 472–73, 734
Minnesota, 62n164, 64, 131n, 162, 214–15, 446n, 533, 545, 558. *See also* District of Minnesota
Minor, H. C., 100
Mississippi, State of, 24, 28–29, 64, 214–15, 446
Mississippi River, 79–81, 108, 181, 390, 525, 562
Missouri
  as Civil War battleground, 80–81
  Civil War engagements, 64
  Mormon emigration, 36, 86–87
  secession from the Union, 25, 87, 108–9
  state population, 214
  troop and supply movement from, 216, 218, 324–26, 556, 633–34, 647
  See also Department of the Missouri; military units, Missouri
Missouri River
  delineating military districts, 437–38, 515, 547–49
  dispatching troops to, 46
  movement by steamboat, 121
  origin of Overland Trail, 42n33, 772
  protecting emigration and settlement, 525, 541
  protecting roads and mail routes, 151–52, 526–29, 562–63
Mitchell, Arthur, 692
Mitchell, D. C., 417–18, 453
Mitchell, R. B., 466, 512
Moarley, J., 634
Modoc Indians, 377
Mogo, Charles, 115
Monchard, M., 351
Montana Territory
  creation as Territory, 382–83, 769
  formation of District of the Plains, 449–50
  formation of volunteer companies, 434
  post construction, 564
  Powder River Expedition, 52n108
  protection of mail routes, 415
  road and bridge construction, 513–14, 563

statehood, 62n164
transfer to Department of the Missouri, 515, 533, 569
transfer to Department of the Platte, 575
transfer to District of Nebraska, 545
withdrawal of troops, 535, 549
Montgomery, Alabama, 24, 81
Montgomery, James S., 684, 691
Montgomery, S. H., 596, 598
Moonlight, Thomas, 465, 469, 476, 486, 494, 499, 501, 503, 509, 513
Moore (Captain), 161
Moore (Colonel), 709
Moore, Jeremiah B., 285, 293, 299, 310, 315, 334–35, 347, 384, 392, 407, 709–10
Moore, S. B., 421
Moore, William G., 749
Morgan (Lieutenant), 596
Morgan, C. H., 593
Morgan, I. W., 421
Mormon/Mormonism
arrival in Salt Lake Valley, 21, 36, 40n25
birthplace, Salt Lake City mentioned as, 752
in California, 83–84, 93–94, 96–103, 114–16
Civil War prophecy, 39
comparison to secessionist movement, 60–61, 61n162
Connor, views/tension regarding, 52–58, 168–69, 220–21, 287–91, 351, 354–57, 393–407, 421–22, 471–73, 541, 734–36
Danites (Destroying Angels), 95, 666–68, 766
defense of polygamy, 38, 552
defined/described, 94–96, 771
Department of the Missouri correspondence on, 496
Department of the Pacific correspondence on, 234, 242–43, 301, 343, 364, 401–2
District of Utah correspondence on, 338–40, 353–57, 393–98, 402–7
doctrine of polygamy, 22, 772
emigration from Missouri, 86–87
Indians, influence over, 55, 55n130, 261, 265–66
Josephites, 480–81, 770
in Michigan, 119–21, 128–29, 131
miner resentment toward, 351, 360–61, 541, 720–21
mining as solution to, 53, 339, 343, 394, 735
Morrisites, 24–28, 33, 49, 260, 276–77, 280
as *Official Record* keyword, 74
perceived secessionist sympathies, 97, 99, 101
perceived threats against U.S. Army, 351
presence in New Mexico Territory, 117–18
relationship with Camp Douglas, 312, 315, 348–51, 353–58, 364, 393–400, 403–6, 726–27
relationship with U.S. Army, 28, 50–55
reported as traitors/treasonous acts, 40, 49, 55, 144, 156, 173, 264, 306, 397–98, 471, 473, 541, 583, 667, 734–35
reported defiance of federal authority, 90–91, 236–40, 243
reporting in *Deseret News*, 60, 227–29
report of Brigham Young call to arms, 232–34
Salt Lake City, mentioned in connection with, 84, 87, 99, 122, 133, 140, 168, 233, 236, 239, 243, 250, 301, 340, 353–57, 396–98, 401, 406, 412, 471–73, 484, 488, 522, 544, 622, 666–72, 726, 734–36
treatment of Gentiles, 95, 217, 266, 356, 484, 485, 496, 514, 541, 544
U.S. Army settling the question of, 305, 338–40, 393–94, 405, 412
Utah War (1857–58), 38, 41
viewed as disloyal toward U.S., 41, 61, 165, 228, 255, 260–61, 288, 338, 354, 394–95, 402, 523–24, 670
See also Church of Jesus Christ of Latter-day Saints; Smith, Joseph, Jr.; Wells, Daniel H.; Young, Brigham
Mormon-Ute Treaty of 1849, 21
Mormon War, 414, 766
The Mormon Wars (Rawson and Lyman), 35n2
Morrill, Joseph C., 483, 715
Morrill Anti-Bigamy Act of 1862, 26, 27, 37, 55, 62
Morris Joseph (Morrisites), 24–28, 33, 49, 260, 276–77, 280
Mountain Meadow, 386–87, 389, 390
Mountain Meadow massacre, 23, 386, 391, 728–29
Mullan (Lieutenant), 85–86, 137
Murdock (Captain), 638, 647, 649
Murfey (Captain), 480
Murphy, Mark, 625, 658
musicians, 134–35, 142, 619, 622, 628, 634, 674
Myers (Colonel), 521
Myrick, Newton, 623, 634, 640, 658–59

National Archives
Civil War documents at, 72n1, 75
Confederate Army appointments, 580–81
"Letters Received by the Office of the Adjutant General . . . ," 581–605, 608, 742, 749
missing documents, 50n94, 625
"Post Return of Camp Douglas . . . ," 673–76, 682–83, 694

National Archives *(continued)*
"Post Return of Camp Floyd . . . ," 577–79
"Post Return of Fort Bridger . . . ," 581, 603
"Post Return of U.S. Volunteers Stationed at Camp Douglas . . . ," 728, 737
Native Americans (Native peoples), 36n8. *See also* Indians
Nauvoo, Illinois, 771
Nauvoo Legion. *See* military units, Utah
Navajo Indians, 132, 307–8
Nebraska Territory, 24, 37, 64, 78, 446, 455, 563, 639, 747, 801, 807, 809
Indian expeditions, 437–39
organization of military district, 569
placed under martial law, 648
See also military units, Nebraska
Need, William. *See* Johnson, Andrew
Neff, Benjamin, 625
Neff, John, 623, 634
Nevada Territory
admission to statehood, 56n137
authorization to raise volunteers, 257–58
Civil War engagements, 64
Confederate sympathies, 174–75, 182–83
created from part of Utah, 24, 27, 37, 801
dispatching Army troops to, 127–28
dispatching troops to Utah, 272, 285, 293, 316, 337–38, 373, 375–76, 379–80, 407–8, 422, 712–13
Indian peace treaties, 335
military units, Civil War, 15n1
protection of emigrant and mail roads, 170, 183, 258, 285, 371
protection of settlements and miners, 391
raising volunteer companies, 247, 271–72, 293, 301, 330, 369
reorganization of military districts, 507–8
secessionist sympathies, 182, 417
statehood, 37n13
See also Fort Churchill; military units, Nevada
New Mexico Territory
area of military operations defined, 78n
Army withdrawal to the East, 82, 138, 176
California Volunteers sent to, 230, 235, 245
Civil War engagements, 64
Confederate sympathies, 41, 107, 113, 117–19, 123, 170–71, 199, 332
discharge/mustering out of troops, 570
dispatch of colored troops, 558
Indian expeditions, 307–8
Indian hostilities, 124, 475–76
Indian peace treaties, 323
male population, 213–15
Mormon presence, 117–18
protection of roads and mail routes, 127–28, 178–79, 183, 382, 450–51, 534–35, 540
protection of settlements and miners, 141, 564
quartermaster supplies sent, 325, 350, 536–37, 565–68
raising volunteer companies, 145, 456
reoccupation by U.S. troops, 344–45
reorganization of military districts, 507–8, 569, 804–5
summary of military operations, 446
wartime trade restrictions removed, 368
See also Department of New Mexico; military units, New Mexico
New York, Civil War engagements, 63. *See also* military units, New York
New York Sun, 59
New York Times, 37n11, 43n45, 50, 54n126, 57, 60
Nez Percé Indians, 85, 137, 181–82, 262, 269, 293
Nickerson, Mulf. *See* Johnson, Andrew
Noble, Edward A., 624, 658
North, Hiram B., 624
North Branch, Michigan, 75, 119–20, 128–29, 131n
North Branch, Minnesota, 131n
North Carolina, 25, 63, 118, 214, 584. *See also* military units, North Carolina
Northrup, William H., 479
Nullification Crisis of 1832–33, 39n23
Nye, James W., 117, 127, 145, 174, 182, 335, 342, 371, 417

Oates, Titus, 587, 776
oath of allegiance
false accusations against Cooke, 580, 585–89
Lot Smith Cavalry Company, 622–25
secret societies, 100, 413–14
to U.S. Government, 117, 142, 156, 175, 292, 297, 305, 349
See also disloyalty toward U.S. government
O'Brian [O'Brien, O'Brine], Michael, 684, 691–94
Odgers (Private), 596
O'Farra; (Major), 650
Official Records (OR)
about the collection/publication, 63–66
accuracy/limitations, 66
authorization by Congress, 29
digitization and the selection criteria, 15–16
organization of this volume, 73–76
record types/organization, explained, 67–73
Ohio, Civil War engagements, 64. *See also* military units, Ohio

"Old Horn," 420
O'Neill, John M., 274–75, 284, 372, 431, 457, 491, 741
O'Neill, M. Hugh, 629
Openlander (Private), 596
The Order of American Knights (O.A.K.), 413–14
Orders
 about, meaning/use explained, 70–71
 Headquarters, Camp Douglas (No. 51), 712
 See also General Orders; Post Orders; Special Orders
Oregon
 attack on Fort Limhi, 23
 Civil War engagements, 64
 emigrant arrival, 396
 Indian removal to reservations, 370, 376–77, 411–12
 military units, Civil War, 15n1
 See also military units, Oregon
Organization of Troops. *See* Command Lists
Orman, Van, 190
Osborn, Lewis D., 625, 658
Otis, Elmer, 123–24
Otoe Indians, 87
Overland Mail Company, 46, 151, 168, 195–96, 202–3, 261–62, 291., 425, 609–11, 613, 697
Overland Mail Route
 agent/superintendent responsibilities, 767
 dealing with Indian hostilities, 185–86, 192, 208–9, 211, 254, 262, 309, 447, 450–51, 504, 657
 establishing military posts, 188, 198, 702, 806
 Indian expeditions, 296–97
 Indians as threat to, 51
 Nauvoo Legion march, 642–45
 opening the Southern Route, 178–79, 183
 protection by California Volunteers, 43, 49, 92, 106, 126–27, 136–37, 139–41, 145–46, 150, 154, 166, 172, 180, 200, 600–601, 603, 795
 protection by Lot Smith Cavalry Company, 617
 protection by Sub-District of Nebraska, 437–38
 raising volunteer companies for, 246–47, 258, 332, 345
 relationship with Indians, 130
 relocation of troops to, 147–49, 171
 secessionist presence, 113
Overland Telegraph Company, 43n41, 605–7, 619, 622, 624, 633
Overland Trail
 army protection, 43, 46–47, 809–10
 defined, 42n33, 567
 importance during the Civil War, 41–42
 Indian attack at Sweetwater Station, 28, 31, 487, 493, 638
 Indian attacks on, 46
 Indian stealing and pillaging, 42
 Mormons mentioned in connection with, 664
 protection by California Volunteers, 49
 See also Lot Smith Cavalry Company; Nauvoo Legion
Owen's Lake, 145, 154
Owen's River Valley, 154, 258–59, 272, 281, 285, 316, 572
Owyhee River, 185, 319, 365–66, 384, 423

Pacific Railroad Act of 1862, 776
Pacific Springs Station, 193, 203, 630, 639, 643, 647–50
Pacific Telegraph Company, 46, 59, 122, 323, 605–7, 610
Paddock, A. S., 86–88
Palmer, Alonzo R., 692
Park, Hugh D., 624
Parker, Albert N., 685, 692
Parks, H., 658–59
Parleys [Kanyon] Canyon, 628–29, 723
Parley's Park, 379, 633
Parowan Indians, 380
Patterson (General), 89
Paul (Major), 141
Pawnee Indians, 87, 455
Pawnee Ranch, 430
Payson, 700, 750
Peabody, J. H., 479
Peel, F. A., 258, 267–68, 696, 701, 793
Pegram, Benjamin R., 107
Pennington, E. A., 420
Pennsylvania, Civil War engagements, 63
Pereau, Joseph H., 114–15
Perry, Leslie J., 64–65
Peusho, Alfred, 692
Pickering, William, 200–201, 205
Pierce, Franklin, 128, 130
Pierce, N. P., 144
Pitzer (Captain), 131
Piute County/Piute Creek, 59n148, 388
Platt, Francis, 623, 634
Platte (*Official Record* sender), 741–42
Platte Bridge/Platte Station, 150, 493, 498–99, 511–14, 546–47, 554, 644, 733
Platte Valley/River, 151, 164, 184–85, 292, 447–48, 452–53, 461, 497, 500, 558–60, 563
Plaunts Station/Trading Post, 643–45
Pleasant Grove/Pleasant Valley, 28, 78, 248, 264–66, 494, 629, 699–701
Pleasonton, Alfred, 82–83

Ploy (pseudonym), 750–52, 754–56
Plumb (Colonel), 498–99, 502
Plumly B. Rush, 119
Pocatello [Pocotello, Pocolello] (Shoshone chief), 211, 278, 304, 306, 308, 321–22, 688, 703, 742
Pollock, Robert, 158, 161, 246, 298, 347, 356, 392, 712, 715, 720, 723, 728, 737
Polmanteer, Lewis L., 625
polygamy/polygamic (plural marriage)
  anti-polygamy view of, 481, 496
  as doctrine of Mormonism, 22, 38
  barbarism, as relic of, 38, 59, 117
  defined, 772
  Mormon defense of, 38, 552
  Morrill Anti-Bigamy Act, 26–27, 37, 55, 62
  "popular sovereignty" doctrine and, 40, 40n25
  press coverage, 37n11, 59
  roadblock to statehood, 45, 62
  threat of military action against, 537
  U.S. negative view of, 38, 59, 61–62, 117, 355, 471, 514
  violation of U.S. prohibitions, 220–21, 237, 291, 473
  women's role in, 668–69
Pony Express, 24, 25
Pope, John
  commander, Department of the Missouri, 461, 483, 536, 569, 804, 807
  correspondence, mentions in, 273, 539, 560, 562
  correspondence from, 488, 516, 533–34, 545–50, 557–58
  correspondence to, 382, 450–54, 487–88, 495–96, 521–22, 530–32, 542–43, 550–53
popular sovereignty, 40, 40n25
Port Neuf River, 277, 279, 317–18, 322, 375–76, 379
Porter, John B., 583–85, 587, 589–93
postmaster, 99, 128, 151, 178, 397
Post Orders, Headquarters, Camp Douglas
  Battle of Bear River commemoration, 715–16
  designating post boundary, 672
  new Daily Calls list, 719–20
Post Returns, meaning/use explained, 68, 72, 72n1. *See also* Record of Events
Potter (Mormon man), 267
Potter, C. H., 467–68, 480, 502
Potter, J. A., 555–56
Potts (Captain), 193–94
Powder River, 185
Powder River Expedition, 52n108, 467, 486, 490, 497–98, 509, 511–15, 519–20, 522n, 532, 539, 542–43, 546–47, 550–51, 553–54, 559–63
Pratt (unidentified man), 228
Pratt, Orson, 38
Pratt, Thomas A., 75, 132
President of the United States, reports/correspondence to/from
  authority to suppress rebellion, 170–71
  claims of Army secessionist sympathies, 583–89
  disbandment of volunteer forces, 574–75
  raising volunteers, 45, 87, 142, 332, 616
  removal of Army officers, 273–74
  removal of political appointees, 255
  reorganization of military districts, 507–8
  report on Army status, 1861, 90–91
  report on Army status, 1865, 568–71
  report on conditions in Utah Territory, 287–91
  secessionist repudiation of, 99
  soldiers absent without leave, 231–32
  support for use of volunteers, 90–91
  Utah request for assistance, 113–14
  See also individual presidents by name
Preston, U.T., 51
Price, George F., 209, 250–53, 266–67, 299, 373, 386–91, 479, 484, 491, 502, 538–39, 553, 682, 688, 690, 694, 696, 728–29
Prince, Francis, 624, 658–59
Principal Events, summary/extract
  Department of the Missouri, 511–14
  Department of the Pacific, 77–78
  operation in the Territories, 446
Provo, U.T., 253, 267
Provo Cañon, 266–67
Purdy, E. Sparrow, 342, 345
Purple, E. R., 609–10
Pyramid Lake, 146, 378

Quantrill, William (alias Charles Hart, aka Henry Burgess), 374, 419–21
Quarter Master General's Office, 85, 147, 557–58, 565–68, 677–79
quartermaster supplies and rations
  accounting for, 85, 325, 486, 557–58, 565–68, 599–600, 656, 677–79
  authorized for Lot Smith Cavalry Company, 142, 622, 628
  calculating troop requirements, 497–98, 518–20, 532–33, 559–60
  movement to the West, 207–8, 226, 324–26, 536–37, 542, 555–56, 569
  wagon requirements for, 161–62, 753
Quilliute Indians, 411
Quincy, Illinois, 80–81
Quinn, John, 209, 248, 253, 294, 356, 682, 688, 690, 694, 696

R. M. C., Esq., 75, 119–20, 128
Raft River, 375–76, 378–79, 384, 396, 664, 731–32
railroads
  construction of transcontinental link, 33, 181, 566–67
  Indian hostilities, 448
  Mormon emigration, 61
  Pacific Railroad Act of 1862, 776
  protection by military, 133
  quartermaster supplies sent by, 555–68
  secessionist seizure, 80–81
Rains, John, 97
Ramsdell, Algeray, 692
Randall, Alfred, 625, 658
Randell, A. J. F., 692
Rawlings, Joseph S., 621, 623, 629, 638, 649–50, 659
Reconstruction, Ten-Percent Plan, 29
Record of Events
  about inclusion in the records, explained, 72
  Camp Douglas, 673–75, 676, 682, 694, 728, 737
  Camp Floyd, 577–79
  Fort Bridger, 581, 603
  Second Cavalry, California Volunteers, 792
  See also annual reports
Red Bute (Kanyon) Canyon, 672
Red Creek, 751, 754
Reed (Dr.), 685, 693
Reed, Amos, 449
Reed, C., 685
Reed, Shelbourne C., 685, 691
Reese River, 329, 334, 341, 376, 422, 702
Reid, Robert K., 209, 211, 218, 269, 682, 694, 696
Religious Studies Center, 12
Rencher (governor), 118
Reorganized Church of Jesus Christ of Latter Day Saints (Community of Christ), 480–81, 770
Report of the Commissioner of Indian Affairs, 36n8, 609–10, 663–65, 707–8
Reports
  about inclusion in the records, explained, 71–72
  Bear River massacre, 208–12, 222
  California Volunteers move to Utah, 331–33, 502
  Fort Mojave Expedition, 386–91
  Indian expeditions, 187–89, 193–94, 249–50, 254–56, 286–87, 437–38, 445
  Indian hostilities, 111–12, 294–95, 493–94, 498–99, 609–10, 663–65
  Indian peace treaties, 707–8
  medical conditions/status of Camp Douglas, 744–46
  operations in Colorado Territory, 438–40
  operations in Kansas and the Territories, 559–65
  operations in Oregon, 336–37, 423
  Powder River Expedition, 511–14, 518–23, 539, 550–52, 554
  protection of emigrants, 184–88, 276–80
  protection of mail routes, 139–41, 200, 499–500, 543, 642–45
  recovery of captives, 192–93
  Spanish Forks Expedition, 251–53, 264–68
  troop recruitment for war service, 570–71
Republican Fork, Kansas River, 439, 503, 512
Republican Party, 38, 43, 59, 117–18
Republican River, 419, 437, 448, 452, 543, 560
Reynolds (officer), 476
Reynolds, William, 449
Rhoades, William H., 624
Rhodes, William, 658–59
Rice (Mr.), 445
Rice, Adelbert, 624
Rich, Landon, 624, 658
Richards, Franklin D., 58
Ridge, Thompson, 691
Riley (wagonmaster), 334
Ringgold (Lt. Colonel), 269
Riter, Samuel H. W., 623, 634, 648
Ritter, S. H. W., 658
Robbins, Lorin, 691
Robertson (Lieutenant/Captain), 583–84, 586
Robinson, "Jack," 657, 660, 664
Robinson, Lewis (Louis Robison), 630, 631–33, 648
Rock Creek, 300, 384, 425, 502, 742
Rock Point Station, 752–53
Rock Springs Station, 752–53
Rockwell, Orrin Porter, 51, 51n103, 620
Rocky Ridge Station, 150, 484, 486, 643
Rollins (Major), 97
Rollins, Joseph, 654, 657
Root, Elihu, 64
Rose, Alley S., 624, 658–59
Rosecrans, W. S., 125–26, 368, 413, 419
Ross, D. I., 621
Ross Fork (of the Snake River), 279, 319
Rowe (Captain), 173–74
Rowe, Adolphus, 685, 691
Rowe, H. S. R., 609–10
Rubottom (Mr.), 97
Ruby Valley, 126–27, 143, 147–48, 153–55, 157–58, 161, 165, 169–72, 174–76, 202, 244, 264, 339, 443, 600–601, 712, 806. *See also* Fort Ruby

Ruggles, Daniel, 455–56
Rumfield, H. S., 449
Rush Valley, 418, 473

Sac and Fox Indians, 87
saddlers, 142, 619, 622–23, 628, 634, 679
Sagwitch [Sagwich] (Snake Chief), 211, 278, 280, 308, 680, 690, 702, 730
Saint Joseph, Missouri, 75, 81, 113, 368, 415, 563
The Saints and the Union (Long), 35n2
Salmon Falls, 177, 204, 270, 275, 318–19, 363, 384, 396, 409
Salmon Falls massacre, 85, 326–28, 335–36, 423
Salmon River, 630, 634, 640, 644, 658, 663–64
Salt Creek, 286, 295
Salt Lake City
  arrival of Mormons, 36
  arrival of Steptoe Expedition, 22
  arrival of the Army (Utah War), 37
  arrival of the California Volunteers, 179–80, 251, 666–72, 806
  arrival of the telegraph, 25, 40n26, 43, 122, 607
  death of Brigham Young, 62
  death of Governor Doty, 59
  death of Patrick Edward Connor, 62
  Deseret News description, 726
  enlistment of Lot Smith Cavalry Company, 26, 48, 622
  establishment of Camp Douglas, 27, 50, 168, 188, 198, 243, 353, 673–75
  establishment of Camp Floyd, 23, 37
  establishment of provost guard, 398, 401, 732–33, 739
  honoring Abraham Lincoln, 58
  mail service, 151, 166, 247, 332, 447
  Mormon call to arms, 232–34
  mustering out Army troops, 428
  name change from Great Salt Lake, 32, 37n10
  negotiating end of Utah War, 23
  as *Official Record* keyword, 74, 77
  overland stage service, 264, 544
  raising volunteer companies, 429, 738
  removal of troops from Camp Douglas, 309–10, 316, 484
  road survey/construction, 386, 390–91, 472
  statehood convention, 26, 45
  tabernacle, 53, 236
  Telegraph (newspaper), 397
  tensions from Army presence, 51, 55, 55n129, 348, 412, 471, 695–96
  treatment of Gentiles, 484, 544, 734
Salt Lake City (Esplin and Alford), 35n2
Salt Lake Telegraph (newspaper), 397, 552, 643
Salt Lake Valley
  Army presence/strength, 196
  California Volunteers arrival, 43, 50
  establishment of Camp Douglas, 188, 705
  Indian hostilities, 150
  Mormon arrival, 21, 36
Salt Wells Station, 752–53
San Bernardino, California, 83–84, 93–94, 96–99, 102–5, 114–16, 316, 386–87
Sanchez, Tomas, 105, 116
Sanders (Lieutenant), 584
Sanderson, J. P., 413
Sandpitch (Snake Chief), 211, 278, 286, 304, 308, 680–81, 688
San Francisco Alta, 718–19
San Francisco *Bulletin*, 666
Sanpete County, 59n148
Saunders (Lieutenant), 584
Saunders, Alvin, 449
Sawyer, Roswell, M., 523, 534–35, 539, 550, 563
Scale, J. S., 100
Schaub, Philip, 684, 691
Schindler, Harold, 52
Schofield, John M., 273, 285, 321–22
Scott, Robert N., 64–65, 571
Scott, Thomas A., 114, 119, 122
Scott, Winfield, 82, 91, 114, 133, 588
Seale, Charles, 100
Seawell, Washington, 713
secession/secessionist movement
  allegiance to U.S., 414, 583–85, 588–89, 592–93
  beginning in South Carolina, 38
  control over mail routes, 113, 140
  Deseret News reporting on, 36, 38
  emigration of former rebels, 291–92
  Indian alliance with, 87
  invasion of New Mexico, 199
  Mormonism comparison to, 60–61, 61n162
  Morrisites and, 276
  presence in California, 83–84, 94, 96–100, 101–3, 105, 128, 132, 401, 412, 417
  presence in Michigan, 1128–29
  presence in Missouri, 80, 108–9
  presence in Nevada Territory, 155, 169, 174–75, 182–83, 421
  presence in New Mexico, 119, 123
  presence in Washington Territory, 177
  Utah and, 39–41, 605–6, 670
  See also Civil War; Confederate States of America
Second Confiscation Act of 1862, 170–71

Secrest (Lt. Colonel), 131
Secretary of War
authorization to raise volunteers, 163–65, 199, 204, 257
commemoration of Confederate surrender, 477
communications, by order of, 142, 232, 747
leave of absence for Connor, 432
ordering Indian expeditions, 504, 605
protection of roads and mail routes, 137–40, 184, 435, 444
publication of official war records, 64–65
relocation of Camp Douglas, 348–50, 353–58
reorganization of military districts, 450, 455, 460, 463–65, 508
reports to, 85–87, 113–14, 343–45, 549–50, 557–58, 608–10
request for troops in Kansas, 374
request for troops in Montana, 359, 372
request for troops in Utah, 611, 663–65
See also Cameron, Simon; Floyd, John B.; Stanton, Edwin M.
Seidenstriker, F., 363, 409–10
Sell (Brother), 629
Seminole Indians, 455
Seminole War, 49n83
Sevier County/Sevier River, 59n148, 387, 391
Seward, William H., 114, 124–25, 128, 130, 199
Sharp, James, 625, 658, 661
Sherman (Major), 84
Sherman (Mr.), 94
Sherman, Edwin A., 83–84, 114–15
Sherman, William Tecumseh, 30, 523, 534, 540, 549
Shinn (Lieutenant), 148
Shirtliff, E. M., 658
Shoemaker, F. M., 753
Shoshone Indians (Snake Indians)
defined/identified, 774–75
encampment at Snake River Ferry, 277–78
expeditions against, 317–18, 321–22, 375–76, 472
hostilities following Army withdrawal, 43
hostilities on emigrants and mail routes, 178–79, 609–11, 663–65
movement onto reservation, 708
peace treaties, 29, 293, 304, 308, 335–36, 341, 730
recovery of white captives, 190–92, 675–76
returning stolen property, 281, 385, 393
Shoshone Peoples and the Overland Trails . . . , 1849–1869 (Morgan), 11
Shoshone River. *See* Snake River
Shurtleff, Emmerson, 625
Silver Creek (Kanyon) Canyon, 629, 642
Simmons, Harlon E., 624, 658
Simpson's Park, 126, 127
Sims, Columbus, 148–51, 154–55, 157–60
Sioux City, 451, 467, 529, 545
Sioux Indians, 52n108, 85, 150, 178, 273, 285, 359, 436, 452, 455, 505, 546, 736
Skull Valley/Creek, 249, 263, 698
slaves/slavery
barbarism, as relic of, 38, 59, 117, 667
Civil War prophecy of Joseph Smith, 39, 39n23
Confederate protection/support of, 100, 456
expansion to the territories, 199
Missouri as battleground over, 81
Mormonism perceived as, 354
Mormon views on, 61, 288
newspaper reporting on, 37, 37n11
U.S. male population, 213–15
Utah slave/free colored population, 40, 40nn24–25
slave states, 81, 163, 199, 213–15
Slocum, William, 685, 692, 694
Small, H. C., 235
Smith (Mr.), 445
Smith, Charles F., 577, 803
Smith, Christian, 685
Smith, George A., 42
Smith, Harvey, 685
Smith, Joseph, Jr., 39, 39n23, 51n103, 237, 481, 770
Smith, Joseph, III, 770
Smith, Lot (Lott)
authorization to recruit cavalry company, 47–49, 617–19
Brigham Young, correspondence to, 647–50, 652–54, 656
Brigham Young, instructions from, 626–27, 635–36
cavalry company oath of office, 622–25
daily journal entries, 628–30, 637–41
Deseret News reporting on, 628, 633–34, 636, 654–55
discharge of cavalry company, 50
service with Nauvoo Legion, 47, 47n75
shot with arrow, 664
See also military units, Utah
Smith, Samuel P., 367, 378, 696
Smokey Hill Fork, Kansas River, 512, 543, 559–60, 564
Snake Indians, 775. *See also* Bannock Indians; Shoshone Indians
Snake River (aka Shoshone River)
drowning of Private McNicol, 27, 48n79

Snake River (aka Shoshone River) *(continued)*
emigrant crossing, 86, 177, 270
establishment of Fort Boisé, 203–4, 314
ferry at Fort Hall and Boisé, 86, 313, 318–19
steamboat navigability, 204
Snake River country
end of Indian difficulties, 304, 306, 318, 341, 376, 396
expedition against Indian activities, 425, 658–63
expedition against the Shoshones, 318–22, 326–28
opening of road to Montana, 563
protection of emigrant road, 137, 184–85, 205, 275, 282, 293, 337, 369, 379
protection of settlements, 378, 409–10
road agent activities, 425
Shoshone peace treaty of 1863, 306
Snake River Ferry, 277–80, 282, 662
Soda Springs
establishing a military post, 78, 296, 317, 702–5
Indian expeditions, 78, 276–80, 293
Indian hostilities, 664
Indian peace treaties, 329
posting Army troops, 282, 312–13
withdrawal of Army troops, 459
See also Camp Connor; Idaho Territory
Soldier Boys (pseudonym), 654–55
Soule, S. S., 296–97
South Carolina, 24–25, 38–39, 41, 57–60, 63, 214. *See also* military units, South Carolina
South Pass, 46, 86, 138, 177, 205, 212, 362, 382, 487, 490, 493, 513, 563, 651, 793
South Weber, U.T., 25, 33, 49
Spanish Fork Cañon Expedition, 28, 78, 251–53, 258, 264–68, 282, 302–3, 701–2, 792
Special Orders
authorization to recruit Utah volunteers, 614–15, 616, 618–19
celebrating Bear River anniversary, 714
defining the District of Utah, 317
establishment of Camp Connor, 296
expedition against Snake Indians, 275
inclusion in the records, 70–71, 775, 803n1, 811
inspection report on California Volunteers, 223–25
movement of California Volunteers, 150–51, 158, 246, 342, 403
movement of Nevada Cavalry, 330, 373, 416
protection of emigrants and miners, 375–76
protection of mail routes, 499, 642, 752–53
quartering Army in Salt Lake City, 403–4, 732
redeployment of Army from Utah, 82
relationship with Mormons, 727
removal of troops from Idaho Territory, 458–59
reorganization/removal of troops from Utah, 427
Second Cavalry, California Volunteers, 195, 274–75, 314, 367, 372–73, 400, 406, 415, 424, 426–27, 431, 457
Second Infantry, California Volunteers, 403
shooting stray cattle, 356
Third Infantry, California Volunteers, 427
Special Orders No.
Camp Connor (No. 1), 296
Department of the Pacific (No. 15), 223
Department of the Pacific (No. 80), 373
Department of the Pacific (No. 85), 246
Department of the Pacific (No. 87), 254
Department of the Pacific (No. 115), 150–51
Department of the Pacific (No. 126), 274–75
Department of the Pacific (No. 140), 158
Department of the Pacific (No. 155), 400
Department of the Pacific (No. 156), 403
Department of the Pacific (No. 189), 416
Department of the Pacific (No. 193), 314
Department of the Pacific (No. 195), 317
Department of the Pacific (No. 210), 427
Department of the Pacific (No. 220), 195
Department of the Pacific (No. 223), 330
Department of the Pacific (No. 251), 342
District of Oregon (No. 56), 275
District of Utah (No. 1), 367
District of Utah (No. 9), 457, 714
District of Utah (No. 11), 458
District of Utah (No. 32), 372
District of Utah (No. 36), 373
District of Utah (No. 40), 375–76
District of Utah (No. 53), 403–4
District of Utah (No. 59), 406
District of Utah (No. 65), 415
District of Utah (No. 69), 424
District of Utah (No. 74), 426–27
District of Utah (No. 79), 431
Fort Halleck (No. 7), 499
Headquarters of the Army (No. 86 1/2), 82
Nauvoo Legion (No. 2), 614–15, 642
Nauvoo Legion (No. 3), 47, 618–19
Spencer, Howard O., 623, 634, 651–52, 658, 660–61
Split Rock Station, 630, 642–43
Springville, 303, 701, 750
Stager, Anson, 122, 239
Standiferd (Standifird), John H., 624
Stanford (Governor), 182, 197

Stansbury, Howard, 21
Stansbury Expedition (1849–51), 21–22
Stanton, Edwin M., 27, 46–47, 50, 50n94, 52, 162–63, 222, 432, 440, 449–50, 475–77, 536, 557–58, 565, 609–11, 615, 677–79, 749. *See also* Secretary of War
Staples, John F., 299
Star of the West (steamship), 25
Stearns, Abel, 103–4, 191
Steck (Dr.), 323
Steed, James H., 624
Steel (Dr.), 685
Steel, William, 691
Steen, E., 85–86
Steinberger (Colonel), 145, 147, 154, 166, 262
Stenhouse, T. B. H., 397
Stepfield (spy), 417
Steptoe Expedition of 1854, 22
Sternhell, Yael A., 66
Stevens, Anthony, 685, 691–92
Stewart, James H., 483, 713, 753
Stewart, Perry, 500
Stillman, James W., 156, 160, 458, 461, 483, 696
Stockton, California, 29, 49, 103, 126, 146–50, 153, 158, 473
Stover (Captain), 372
Strawberry Ranch, 633
Strawberry Valley, 751–52, 754–56
Stuart, Charles, 128–29
Stuart, J. E. B., 75, 131–32
Sturgis (General), 141
Sully, A., 383, 467, 470, 490, 529, 546
Summit Lake, 571–72
Summit/Summit County, 59n148, 684
Sumner, Edwin Vose, 42–43, 83, 89, 92, 98–104, 115, 332, 601, 804, 806
Supplement to the Official Records, 17, 577, 791–94
sutlers, 106–7, 168, 202, 297, 584, 593
Swan, G., 691
Sweetwater Station/Bridge/Crossing, 28, 31, 487, 493, 635, 637–38, 642, 646, 650, 733, 794
Sweetwater Valley/Sweetwater River, 48n80, 184, 546–47

Tabby (Ute Chief), 303
Tappan, S. F., 323
Taylor ("foreigner"), 228
Taylor, J. P., 207
Taylor, John, 53
Taylor, Joseph J., 624, 655, 658
Taylor, Richard, 31
Taylor, Thomas H., 131
telegraph
  arrival at Fort Bridger, 106
  arrival in Utah, 25, 40, 40n26, 43, 60–61, 122, 188, 605–6, 607
  destruction by Indians, 43, 46, 151–52, 452, 454, 487, 493, 495, 498–99, 504, 512, 743
  protection by Army troops, 49, 59, 162, 164–65, 192–93, 290, 323, 348, 449–51, 468, 542, 560–65, 664
  protection by Burton's militia unit, 642–45
  protection by District of the Plains, 807
  protection by 11th Ohio Cavalry, 793–94
  protection by Lot Smith Cavalry Company, 140, 142, 618–19, 621–28, 633–34, 638, 664, 677–79
  protection by Nevada Cavalry, 306, 737
  repairs, 48, 512, 565
  reported Mormon attacks on, 203
  termination in California, 94
Tennessee, 25, 64
Territorial Enterprise (newspaper), 160
Terry (Judge), 115
Terry (Mr.), 462
Terry, Joseph, 624, 658–59
Terry, William, 624
Tessnant, Thomas J., 421
Texas
  Battle of Palmito Ranch, 31
  Civil War engagements, 64
  Confederate recruitment, 99
  excluded from Department of the West, 79
  procurement of cavalry horses, 103
  Quantrill presence in, 420
  secession from the Union, 24, 583
  state population, 214
  strength of Confederate forces, 118, 123, 199
  U.S. Army advance into, 175–76
Thian, Raphael P., 803
Thomas, Lorenzo
  correspondence, mentions in, 616
  correspondence, receiver, 85–86, 88, 121–22, 136–38, 143–49, 154, 165–66, 171, 175–76, 180, 182–83, 189, 196–98, 200, 203–4, 207, 219, 222, 230, 233–34, 240, 242–43, 245, 257–59, 262, 264, 270–71, 281, 285, 293, 301, 432, 580, 585–89, 592–93, 598–604, 631, 683, 795
  correspondence, sender, 91–92, 134–36, 139–42, 231–32, 622
  dispatching troops from California, 42–43
Thomas, Samuel J. [W.], 685, 692
Thompson, John, 445
Thompson, Meriwether Jeff, 75, 81

Thornton, O. F., 417–18
Three Crossings Station, 141, 487, 636–37, 643, 733, 794
Three Forks of the Missouri, 358–59, 361–62, 372, 563
Thurber, A. K., 701–2
Thurston, George A., 422, 443–44
Thurston, Moses, 623, 634
Tichenor, George C., 477, 536
Tintic Valley, 380, 387
Titus, John, 449
"Titus-Oates class," 587, 776
Tobby (Chief), 722
Tooele Valley, 254, 311, 341, 705
Totten (General), 358, 372
Townsend, Edward D., 64, 82, 329, 333, 337, 343–44, 350, 371–72, 374, 444, 455, 460, 508, 582, 605, 742, 747
Treaty of Guadalupe Hidalgo (1848). *See* Mexican War
Trempf, Henry W., 685, 691
Tripp, Jonathan, 129
Tucson, Arizona Territory, 148, 175, 178, 180
Tufts (Judge), 358–59
Tullidge, Edward, 75
Tupper, Charles, 696
Turner, Edmund P., 345–46
Turner, John G., 40
Turnley, Parmenas T., 121–22, 479, 487, 492
Twain, Mark, 44n52
Twiggs, David E., 583

Uintah reservation, 708
Uintah Valley, 313, 376, 379, 482, 562, 563, 732
Uinta Valley, 538, 544, 751, 754–56
Union Pacific Railroad, 448, 556, 776
Union Vedette
  about inclusion in UT records, 75
  first issue published, 29
  "General Orders No. 33," 709–10
  "Important Circular from General Connor," 711–12
  "Important to Stock Owners," 712
  "New Arrivals," 712–13
  See also Daily Union Vedette
United States, history timeline 1846–1870, 21–33
University of Utah, 12
Urmy, John B., 696
Urquhart, James, 692
U.S. Army
  arrival of Connor's troops, 27
  authorization to raise companies, 92
  Battle at Spanish Fork, 701–2
  Cache Valley Expedition, 27, 78, 190–92, 200, 672–75
  Cedar Mountains Expedition, 254–55
  Colorado Territory Expedition, 438–40
  commissioning of Lot Smith, 47
  discharge/mustering out, 297, 369, 425–26, 524, 529, 535, 547, 569–70, 575, 757–58
  1861 strength, 89
  end of Utah War, 23
  establishment of Camp Floyd, 23
  Ft. Crittenden to Ft. Mojave Expedition, 29, 386–90
  Fort Ruby expedition to Sierra Nevadas, 193–94
  furloughs/re-enlistment, 27, 50, 50n95, 162–64, 350, 352, 362, 509, 718, 747–48
  Indian attack at Battle Creek, 699–701
  raising new companies in Utah, 57, 57n139, 247
  raising the Lot Smith Cavalry Company, 47–48, 616–25
  reenlistment of Lot Smith Cavalry Company, 162–65
  relationship with Mormons, 28, 50–55
  removal to fight in the East, 42–43
  settling the Mormon question, 305, 338–40, 393–94, 405
  Snake Indian Expedition, 212, 311, 317–19, 321–22, 326–28, 335–36
  Soda Springs Expedition, 276–80
  Spanish Forks Expedition, 251–53, 264–68
  See also military units
U.S. Census of 1860, 40, 40n24
U.S. Congress
  anti-polygamy law, 393, 473
  authorization to raise Utah volunteers, 662
  authorization to suppress rebellion, 170–71
  beginning of the Utah War, 39
  Brigham Young views of, 723
  construction of military posts, 205
  construction of railroads, 181
  creation of Montana Territory, 382
  creation of roads and mail routes, 151, 563
  dealing with Indian affairs, 370, 377, 475–76
  military appropriations, 568
  prescribed loyalty oath, 349
  publication of official war records, 29, 63–66
  reducing Utah Territory boundary, 17, 27, 37n13, 53n114, 801
  State of Deseret, constitution introduced, 26
  State of Deseret, statehood petition, 21, 801

Utah, delegate representation, 113, 357, 364
Utah, statehood petition, 40, 45, 51, 56–58, 62, 62n164
U.S. Constitution
13th Amendment, passage/adoption, 30, 32
14th Amendment, adoption, 32
15th Amendment, adoption, 33
separation of church and state, 45
U.S. Department of State, 130
U.S. Government Printing Office, 64
U.S. Supreme Court, 22, 99, 695, 715
Usher, John Palmer, 213, 448
Ustick, William L., 247, 253, 263–68, 279, 677, 686, 696, 712
Utah and the Civil War (Fisher et al.), 35n2
Utah Cavalry Company (aka Lot Smith Cavalry Company). *See* military units, Utah
Utah militia (aka Nauvoo Legion). *See* military units, Utah
Utah State Historical Archives, 75, 609, 611, 613–18, 620–25, 628–36, 637–45, 649–50, 656, 677–80, 738–40
Utah Superintendency of Indian Affairs, 11, 22, 43n45, 55, 154, 166, 278, 303, 609–11, 663–65, 707–8
Utah Territorial Militia Records, 67, 609, 611, 613–25, 628–36, 637–41, 642–45, 649–50, 656, 679–80, 738–40
Utah Territorial Records (UT)
articles, *Deseret News*, 628, 633–34, 636–37, 641–42, 646–47, 651–52, 654–55, 657–63, 666–72, 675–76, 680–94, 697–705
articles, *Vedette*, 712–13, 722–26, 730–33, 736–37, 741–46, 750–56
Atwood, R. H., correspondence, 655–56
Barlow, J. S. M., correspondence, 633
Bernhisel, John, correspondence, 611
Blair, M. P., correspondence, 665
Burton, Robert, correspondence, 612–13, 636–37, 642–45
Cameron, Simon, correspondence, 583–85, 590–91
Carleton, James, correspondence, 600–601
Clarke, J. C., correspondence, 603–4
Clary, R. E., correspondence, 594–95
Colfax, Schuyler, correspondence, 749
Connor, P. Edward, correspondence, 695–96, 734–36, 742
Conrad, G. D., correspondence, 716
Cooke, Philip St. George, correspondence, 580–82, 585–87, 595, 597–600, 602, 608
Cradlebaugh, John, correspondence, 757–58
Craft (Bishop), correspondence, 621
Dole, W. P., correspondence, 663–65, 707–8
Doty, James, correspondence, 663–65, 707–8, 738–40
Downs, S., correspondence, 634
Drum, R. C., correspondence, 734–36, 757–58
Ethier, Anthony, correspondence, 706
Fuller, Frank, correspondence, 606, 607, 609–10, 612–14, 636–37
Fullmer, A. L., correspondence, 618
General Orders, 596, 709–10, 713, 725, 746–48
Gibbon, John, correspondence, 587–89
Gibson, John, correspondence, 635
Gooddell, Tim, correspondence, 634
Green, John, correspondence, 594–95
Harding, Stephen, correspondence, 680
Harris, T. S., correspondence, 716
Holladay, Ben, correspondence, 632, 665
Holladay, Joseph, correspondence, 615
Lewis, M. G., correspondence, 728–29
Lincoln, Abraham, correspondence, 606, 607, 615–16, 695–96
Lot Smith Cavalry Company, 622–25, 636
Mason, John, correspondence, 740
McDowell, Irvin, correspondence, 738–39
Merritt, Wesley, correspondence, 592–94
Moarley, J., correspondence, 634
Orders and Circulars, 711–12, 717–18, 720–21, 726–28
Post Orders (Camp Douglas), 672, 677, 715–16, 719–20
Post Returns (Camp Douglas), 673–75, 676, 682–83, 694, 728, 737
Post Returns (Camp Floyd), 577–80
Post Returns (Fort Bridger), 581, 603
Price, George, correspondence, 728–29
Report, march along Overland Mail route, 642–45
Robinson, Lewis, correspondence, 631–32
Rockwell, Orrin, correspondence, 620
Ross, D. I., correspondence, 621
selection criteria, 16, 75–76
Smith, Lot (Lott), correspondence, 617, 622, 626–30, 635–42, 647–50, 652–54, 656
Special Orders, 614–15, 618–19, 714, 732, 752–53
Stanton, Edwin, correspondence, 609–10, 615–16, 677–79, 749
Thomas, Lorenzo, correspondence, 580–82, 585–89, 592–95, 598–604, 608, 631, 683

Utah Territorial Records (UT) *(continued)*
Townsend, E. D., correspondence, 605, 742
Utah Cavalry Company, 622–25, 636
Wade, J. H., correspondence, 605–6, 607
Warner, J., correspondence, 634
Wells, Daniel, correspondence, 609, 613–14, 616–18, 620–21, 631–32, 633, 635, 680
Wright, George., correspondence, 683, 718–91
Young, Brigham, correspondence, 605–7, 609, 611, 616, 626–27, 631–32, 635–36, 647–50, 652–56
Utah Territory
authorization to raise volunteers, 57, 142, 257, 259–60, 269
boundary changes, 17, 34, 37, 801
Brigham Young becomes governor, 21
California Volunteers arrival, 50–51, 608
Civil War role, 35–36, 41
Compromise of 1850, 21, 36, 40n25, 801
Constitutional Convention, 44–45
Cumming appointed governor, 23
currency issues, 262, 314, 395–99, 401, 407, 735
declaration of martial law, 23, 53, 53n114, 221, 323, 339
1861 U.S. militia presence, 134–36
emigration during Civil War period, 61
history timeline 1846–1870, 21–33
Indians and Grizzly bears, 651
invitation to raise volunteer companies, 738–39
Mormon arrival, 36
as *Official Record* keyword, 74, 77
perceived secessionist sympathies, 583–84
protection of roads and mail routes, 46–48, 382, 450–51, 534–35, 540
quartermaster supplies sent, 325, 536–37, 565–68
removal/return of U.S. Army, 42–43, 46, 48–51, 82
reorganization of military districts, 446, 507–8, 569
request for army troops, 613–14
request for reinforcements, 261, 270–72
statehood, 45, 51
suppression of perceived rebellion (Utah War), 23, 37
wartime trade restrictions removed, 368
See also military units, Utah
Utah Territory Supreme Court, 23, 28, 49, 53
Utah War (1857–58)
beginning/end of the war, 23, 37
declaration of martial law, 23
Douglas view on, 39
mediation by Kane, 23
Mormon loyalty/perceived resentment, 38, 41
use of volunteer forces, 90–91
Ute Indians, 43, 165, 282–84, 286, 299–300, 302–5, 307–8, 313, 472, 562, 707, 722, 730
Mormon-Ute Treaty of 1849, 21
Ute-Pete (Ute Chief), 303

Van Dorn (Confederate), 332
Van Orman, Z., 190, 423
vedettes, 178, 777. *See also Daily Union Vedette*; *Union Vedette*
Vetterli, Robert, 42n34
Virginia
Civil War battles, 25, 27, 28, 29, 63
Confederate forces, 121, 580–81
Cooke as native, 125, 580, 583–84, 586, 594
Harper's Ferry attack, 23
male population, white/black, 214–15
secession from the Union, 25
surrender at Appomattox, 30, 477
troops present for duty, 89
See also military units, Virginia
Virginia City, Nevada Territory, 110–11, 157, 160, 175, 329, 358–59, 361–62, 382, 439, 544, 563, 575
Virgin River, 391

Wade, Jeptha H., 40, 122, 239, 605–7
wagoner (wagonneer), 142, 622–23, 628, 634, 674, 691
Waite, Charles B., 53–54, 226–29, 236, 238, 243, 255, 379, 641, 654, 671, 695–96, 704
Walker (Colonel), 486, 560–62
Walker, John H., 624
Walker, Thomas B., 692
Walker, W. T. B., 685
Wall, John W., 684, 691, 693–94
Wall, W., 693, 694
Walla Walla District. *See* Fort Walla Walla
Wallace, George, 696
Wallace, W. H., 359
Wallace, William S., 246, 249–50, 254
Waller (Major), 118
Walton, William H., 625
The War of Rebellion: A Compilation of the Official Records of the Union and Confederate Armies. See Official Records (OR)
War of Rebellion Official Records, 64
Warner, J., 634
Wasatch County/Wasatch Mountains, 59n148, 642, 657, 726, 744, 747

Washakie [Washkee] (Snake Chief), 164, 385, 650, 652–53, 730–31
Washakie Station, 541
Washburn, Lysander, 696
Washington, D.C., Civil War engagements, 63
Washington County, U.T., 59n148, 376
Washington Territory
  Civil War engagements, 64
  District of Oregon, as part of, 336–37
  emigration, road conditions and army protection, 184–85
  government communications to/from, 200–210
  military actions against the Indians, 230, 270
  military communications to/from, 365–66
  military posts, location/building, 314
  See also military units, Washington
Washoe River, 329
Watie, Stand, 31, 59n149
Watterson, T. A., 421
Wattles, David C., 129
Waugh, S. N., 300
Way, William, 692
Waymire (Lieutenant), 359
Weaver (Mr.), 445
Weed, Frederick, 267, 491, 725
Weekly Patriot (newspaper), 83–84
Weemer (Weimer), John P., 623, 634
Weiler, Mahlon, 658
Welcher, Frank J., 804–5
Wells, A. B., 713
Wells, Daniel H.
  authorization to raise volunteers, 47–48, 616, 631
  commander, Nauvoo Legion, 46
  correspondence from Barlow, 633
  correspondence from John Gibson, 635
  correspondence from Lewis Robinson, 631–32
  correspondence to Governor Harding, 680
  Indian encounters, 489
  instructions to Burton, 612–13, 637
  instructions to Lot Smith, 617, 628
  protection of mail routes, 613–14
  report on Burton's march, 642–46
  resignation from Nauvoo Legion, 609
Wells, James H., 624, 658, 662
Welsh, John, 684, 691
Welten, Walker B., 685
Welton, Waker B., 692
West, C. W., 612, 617, 637, 644
Western Union Telegraph, 449
West Virginia, 28, 62n164, 63, 125. *See also* military units, West Virginia
Westwood, Phebe, 286, 295
Wheaton, Frank, 545–46, 549, 554
Wheeler (trader). *See* Merchant & Wheeler Traders
White, Samuel B., 493, 498–99
White, William L., 692
Whiteley (Indian agent), 323
White River, 562–63
Whitney, Orson F., 42n34, 753
Wilcox (Lieutenant), 151, 153
Wilcox, John A., 479
Wiler, E. M., 625
Willamette Valley, 148, 235
Williams (Major), 350
Williams (Mrs.), 44
Williams (officer), 749
Williams, A. A. C., 373, 431
Williams, Bateman H., 624
Williams, C. F., 692
Williams, Ephraim H., 624
Williams, Hugh H., 299
Williamson, J. M., 161, 685, 696
Willis, Henry M., 96–98
Willis, J. J., 100
Willow Springs Station, 674, 698
Wilson, Charles, 692
Wilson, James H., 100
Wilson, William, 500
Wind River Mountains, 385, 639, 648–49, 651, 730, 794
Wing, George B., 685
Wingate, John, 692
Wisconsin, 446n. *See also* military units, Wisconsin
Wo-an-gant (Washakee Indian), 385
Woeber Tom [aka Utah Tom] (Snake Indian), 191
Wofford, William T., 31
women
  foreigners/emigrants, 111–12, 471–72
  Governor Dawson sexual advances, 44
  held captive by Indians, 307
  Indians resisting capture, 501
  killed/captured during Indian expeditions, 52, 52n108, 259
  killed/scalped by Indians, 209, 504, 512, 542, 686
  marriage to Army troops, 745
  molestation, Army admonishment on, 172
  role in a polygamous marriage, 669
Woodruff, Wilford, 58, 62
Wool (General), 89

Wootten, Francis M., 583, 586, 597
Worthington, H. G., 420
Wren, Thomas, 421
Wright (Colonel), 332
Wright, George
  commander, Department of the Pacific, 804, 806
  correspondence, mentions in, 139, 177–78, 332, 358, 426, 508, 544
  correspondence from, 126–30, 136–38, 141, 143–48, 149, 154–55, 165–66, 171, 175–76, 180, 182–83, 189, 196–98, 200–201, 203–4, 207, 219, 222, 226, 230, 233–35, 240, 242–43, 245, 247, 257–59, 262, 264, 270–72, 281, 285, 293, 301, 309, 316–17, 329–30, 333–34, 337–38, 343–45, 350, 364, 369, 371, 375, 378, 489, 683, 795
  correspondence to, 169–70, 194–95, 205, 216–18, 241, 257, 371–72
  letter to *San Francisco Alta*, 718–19
  Mormon and Indian relations, 55, 55n130
  organization of Department troops, 206, 298–99, 347–48, 392
  Special Orders, by order of, 150–51, 158, 170–71, 195, 218–19, 246, 274–75, 314, 317, 330, 342, 373
Wright, Marcus J., 63
Wynkoop, E. W., 296
Wyoming Territory
  arrival of Sixth U.S. Volunteer Infantry, 59
  created as territory, 37, 37n13
  establishment of Fort Laramie, 43n42
  Independence Rock, 48n80
  part of Department of Missouri, 807
  as part of Indian Territory, 769
  Powder River Expedition, 52n108
  railroads, 776
  Shoshone Indians in, 774
  statehood, 62n164

Yellow Creek, 629
Yellowstone River, 352, 359, 362, 383, 463, 546, 560–62
Young, Brigham
  army arrest of, 28, 54–55, 55n129
  arrival at Salt Lake Valley, 21
  authorization to recruit cavalry company, 26, 45, 47–48, 140, 142, 615–22, 631–33, 677
  calling out Utah militia, 233–34, 236–38, 243, 405
  charges of disloyalty and resistance, 471–72, 541, 666–67, 723, 726, 734–35
  charges of treason, 397–98
  correspondence to/from, 49, 605–7, 635–36
  correspondence to/from Lot Smith, 626–28, 647–50, 652–54, 656–57
  correspondence to/from R. H. Atwood, 655–56
  declaring the State of Deseret, 21, 26, 36, 45, 60, 801
  deploys militia, declares martial law, 23, 612–13
  Deseret News reporting on, 227–29
  governor of "state" of Deseret, 45, 58, 609
  governor of Utah Territory, 22, 45
  Greeley interview, 23
  leadership role in Utah, 94–95, 168, 202–3, 227–29, 287–91, 301, 354–55, 397
  messages on completion of telegraph, 605, 607
  as *Official Record* keyword, 74, 77
  portrayal in *Official Records*, 122, 124, 163, 243, 250, 312
  protection of emigrant and mail roads, 254–55, 261, 290, 611, 664
  recruiting Lot Smith Cavalry Company, 45–48, 616
  re-enlistment of Lot Smith Cavalry Company, 50, 162–63
  relationship with Connor, 51–53, 57–58, 58n144, 62
  relationship with Indians, 46, 261, 289
  reported Southern entreaties, 199
  resignation of Wells from Nauvoo Legion, 609
  sending first telegraph messages, 25, 40, 40n26, 43n41
  Utah War and, 23, 60
  view on Army departure from Utah, 42
  view on secession and the Civil War, 39, 39n22, 40–41, 41n30, 60–61
  withdrawal of Army from Utah, 312, 355–56, 484
Young, Seymour B., 75, 623, 634, 658–59, 661–62

Zabriskie, E. B., 479, 713